HUMAN RESOURCE MANAGEMENT
STRATEGIES & PROCESSES

HRM

$95
4035260100

HUMAN RESOURCE MANAGEMENT
STRATEGIES & PROCESSES

SIXTH EDITION

ALAN **NANKERVIS**
ROBERT **COMPTON**
MARIAN **BAIRD**

Human resource management: strategies and processes
6th Edition
Alan Nankervis
Robert Compton
Marian Baird

Publishing manager: Michael Tully
Senior publishing editor: Dorothy Chiu
Project editor: Ronald Chung
Developmental editor: Penelope Goodes
Production controller: Adele Psarras
Text designer: Rina Gargano
Cover designer: Olga Lavecchia
Editor: Craig MacKenzie
Permissions researchers: Karen Forsythe, Lisa Piemonte
Indexer: Russell Brooks
Typeset in ITC Century 9/12pt by ITC

Any URLs contained in this publication were checked for currency during the production process. Note, however, that the publisher cannot vouch for the ongoing currency of URLs.

First published in 1992 by South-Western Publishing Co. as Managing Human Resources
by Arthur W. Sherman & George W. Bohlander. Authorised adaptation of the original
edition by South-Western Publishing Co., Cincinnati, Ohio.
First edition adaptation published as Strategic Human Resource Management in 1993
Second edition published in 1995
Third edition published in 1999
Fourth edition published in 2002
Fifth edition published in 2005
This Sixth edition published in 2008

Acknowledgements
Cover Image supplied by Getty Images

For product information and technology assistance,
in Australia call 1300 790 853;
in New Zealand call 0800 449 725

For permission to use material from this text
or product, please email **aust.permissions@cengage.com**

National Library of Australia Cataloguing-in-Publication Data
Nankervis, Alan R.
Human resource management: strategies
and processes.

6th ed.
Bibliography.

Includes index.
ISBN 9780170134200 (pbk.).

1. Personnel management. I. Compton, R. L.

II. Baird, Marian. III. Title

658.3

Cengage Learning Australia
Level 7, 80 Dorcas Street
South Melbourne, Victoria Australia 3205

Cengage Learning New Zealand
Unit 4B Rosedale Office Park
331 Rosedale Road, Albany, North Shore 0632, NZ

For learning solutions, visit **cengage.com.au**

Printed in China by China Translation & Printing Services.
4 5 6 7 8 9 10 13 12 11 10 09

Brief contents

Contents

Chapter 11 **Managing occupational health and safety** **438**

Preface

In the two years since the publication of the last edition of this book, the world of work in Australia and throughout the Asian region has been transformed irrevocably due to a number of significant developments which permeate this sixth edition. Apart from the relentless pressures of globalisation and technological innovation which continuously drive changes in the nature of work, the ways in which it is organised and conducted, and the associated requisite competencies, a series of geopolitical, demographic, and industrial relations developments have ensured that work into the future will be very different from our previous expectations. The roles of human resource management professionals and industry managers are necessarily changing dramatically in response to these challenges, and are likely to remain dynamic for the foreseeable future.

Geopolitical changes in the region have included (but are not restricted to) the rise and rise of China as a global economic power; closely followed by the transformation of India as a critical information technology provider; the democratisation of Indonesia and the progressive modernisation of its economy, despite its manifold recent difficulties; Hong Kong's struggle to maintain its market position in the face of serious competition from such Chinese cities as Shanghai and Guangzhou; and Singapore's challenge to ensure its relevance, in comparison with Malaysia and Thailand. These geopolitical developments simultaneously provide both significant competition to many Australian organisations, as all economies have moved towards similar service industry sectors on an uneven playing field, and offer them major offshore business opportunities. All of these factors naturally have interesting impacts on human resource management strategies, plans and processes, which require careful consideration by those charged with these responsibilities.

The ageing of the workforces in Australia, New Zealand, Japan and Singapore, resulting in the actual or impending retirement of large numbers of 'babyboomers,' has caused labour shortages at both the professional and managerial levels, and in the trades, and presents considerable challenges for industry and HR planners. In addition, the entry of Generations X and Y into the workplace, with different expectations and priorities from their parents, provides greater opportunities and demands for human resource management professionals in terms of job design, work–life options, attraction and retention, and remuneration systems.

However, perhaps the most significant challenge for those responsible for managing human resources has been the transformation of industrial relations in Australia heralded by the federal *Workplace Relations Amendment (WorkChoices) Act 2005*. The Act reflects the present Australian government's concern to create more 'flexibility' in formal relationships between employers and their employees, in an attempt to make Australian industry more competitive, but its effect has arguably been to create an imbalance in the employment contract in favour of employers. Similar changes have also occurred in New Zealand, and in many regional countries. While many Australian employers and employer associations support the underlying principles of *WorkChoices* – including greater flexibility in employment conditions, and the decentralisation of agreement-making processes to the workplace – some have merely used these new opportunities to exploit their employees. With a federal election due in late 2007, the Australian Labor Party's attitude towards these changes is as yet unclear.

The challenges for astute employers and their human resource management professionals resulting from all these contemporary developments is to ensure that their HR strategies and processes truly reflect the long-term best interests of both their organisations and their increasingly valuable human resources. This is the essence of the concept and practice of 'strategic choice' which underpins strategic human resource management.

Alan R. Nankervis
Robert L. Compton
Marian Baird
September 2007

Acknowledgements

Many people have contributed to the production of this book in different ways, either through active involvement or more indirectly. All such contributions are greatly appreciated, but not all can be directly acknowledged. The following people, however, deserve special recognition:

Professor Samir Chatterjee, School of Management, Curtin University of Technology ('Ethics' section in Chapter 1)

Associate Professor Kevin Brown, School of Business Law, Curtin University of Technology ('Legal framework' section in Chapter 2)

Associate Professor Bradon Ellem and the research assistance of Ms Alison Page and Ms Jennifer Whelan (Chapter 3)

Jane Coffey, School of Management, Curtin University of Technology (Chapter 5, and co-author of Chapter 12)

Dr Peter Hosie, for his helpful suggestions in Chapter 8

Harry Anneveld ('Termination' section in Chapter 9)

Associate Professor John Shields, Sydney University (Chapter 10)

Lyle Potgieter and Peter Vlant, Peoplestreme.com ('HR Metrics' section and cases in Chapter 13)

Marianne Gloet and Professor Mike Berrell, RMIT University ('Knowledge management' section in Chapter 14).

Finally, our thanks to the 'slave drivers,' Dorothy Chiu and Penelope Goodes, and Mike Tully of Thomson Learning, who ensured that the book was prepared on time and to their usual high quality standards.

Authors and contributors

About the authors

ALAN NANKERVIS is the Associate Professor of Human Resource Management in the School of Management at RMIT University in Melbourne. He was formerly the Research Director and HRM Area Head in the School of Management at Curtin University of Technology in Perth, and the Deputy Director of the Sydney Graduate School of Management.

He has a Bachelor of Arts (Honours) degree from the University of Adelaide, a postgraduate Bachelor of Social Administration degree from Flinders University, and a Doctor of Business Administration (Management) degree from the University of Western Sydney. He has taught and consulted throughout Australia, and in Singapore, Malaysia, Indonesia, Thailand, the United Kingdom and China, and is the author or co-author of books on HRM in Asia, services management, and Asian management.

DR ROBERT-LEIGH (BOB) COMPTON is currently Head of the School of Business and Informatics (NSW) at the Australian Catholic University and is the immediate past Director of Academic Programs and Quality at the Sydney Graduate School of Management. Prior to this appointment Bob was MBA Director at the University of Western Sydney, Nepean and earlier was Head of the Department of Employment Relations at UWS. From 1999 he has been an Adjunct Lecturer with the Macquarie Graduate School of Management. He has also taught at UTS and has performed guest lectures at the AGSM. He has taught human resource management in Sydney, China, Hong Kong, India, Sri Lanka, Malaysia and Singapore. He has also worked for the past three years on a business education program with Karen refugees on the Thai–Burma border.

A member of the Australian Human Resources Institute since 1979, Bob has held several key positions including those of NSW Councillor and member of the Education Committee of Council. He is currently a Fellow of AHRI, a member of editorial boards with CCH Australia and Curtin University of Technology and a member of the Board of Academic Advisors with the Management Learning College in Hong Kong.

MARIAN BAIRD BEc (Hons) Grad. Dip. Ed. PhD is Associate Professor in Work and Organisational Studies at the University of Sydney. Marian is a highly recognised academic and researcher in the field of industrial relations and human resource management. Since 1997 she has held several academic positions in Work & Organisational Studies in the Faculty of Economics and Business, University of Sydney specialising in teaching human resource management, employment relations and research methods in undergraduate and postgraduate courses. More recently, Marian has also been a visiting scholar at MIT and Michigan State University.

Marian has held several major research grants from funding bodies, including the Australian Research Council and state governments, to explore critical aspects of working life and the impact of *WorkChoices* across the public and private sectors. She is the co-author of a major report on parental leave in Australia and has published extensively in national and international journals and delivered conference papers to prestigious international bodies.

Contributors

JANE COFFEY is the Associate Head – Human Resources and Lecturer – Human Resources and Industrial Relations with the School of Management, Curtin Business School at Curtin University. She manages and teaches a range of human resource management and industrial relations programs throughout Australia and Southeast Asia and has actively contributed to the last three editions of the this text.

In addition to her academic background, Jane has significant corporate professional experience, operating a highly successful human resource management consultancy business prior to joining Curtin University. She specialised in providing support and advice to the public sector and maintains a significant consultancy profile in this area with the University. She also conducts and facilitates workshops in the areas of staff attraction and retention and performance management.

JOHN SHIELDS is an Associate Professor in the Work and Organisational Studies at the University of Sydney. He teaches human resource management and specialises in research on performance and reward management, executive remuneration and corporate governance, as well as business and labour history.

In addition to delivering numerous conference papers, John has published in a range of prominent journals and recently authored a book on managing employee performance and reward.

Reviewers

Our sincere gratitude and appreciation are expressed to the following colleagues who have added inestimable value and quality to this new edition.

- Richard Ballantyne, Swinburne University

- Dr Paul Corcoran, University of the Sunshine Coast

- Ken Dundas, Southern Cross University

- Dr Amanda Gudmundsson, Queensland University of Technology

- Megan Paull, Edith Cowan University

- Terry Waters-Marsh, Central Queensland University

- Dr John Whiteoak, University of the Sunshine Coast

- Christa Wood, University of Wollongong

Resources guide

FOR THE STUDENT

As you read this text you will find a wealth of features in every chapter to enhance your study of Human Resource Management and help you understand its applications.

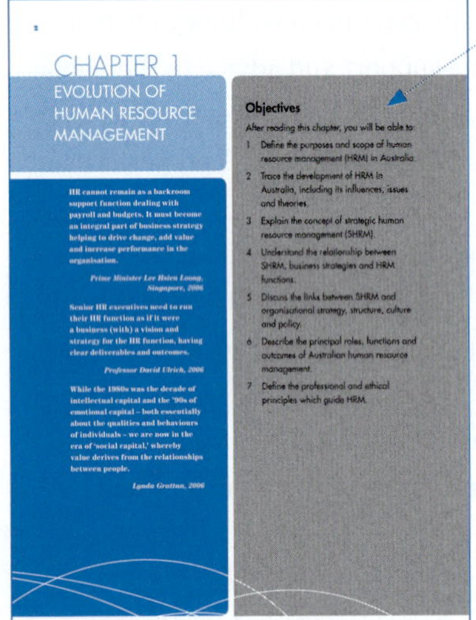

Learning objectives are listed at the start of each chapter giving you a clear sense of what the chapter will cover.

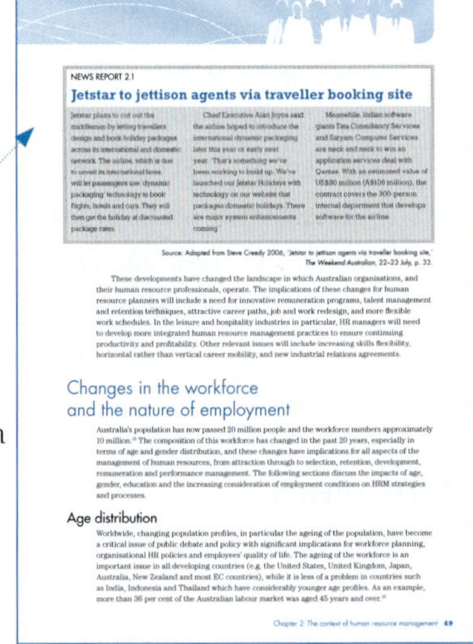

In every chapter, *News Report* boxes highlight the relevance of Human Resource Management in real-world situations.

Included with this text is a passcode that gives you a FREE four-month subscription to InfoTrac® College Edition. At the end of each chapter you will find a list of search terms called *Online reading* that you can use to help guide you through InfoTrac®. This online library will provide you with access to full-text articles from hundreds of scholarly and popular periodicals. Don't restrict yourself to the search terms provided throughout the book, think of your own search terms and expand your understanding of Human Resource Management.

Please note you will need to use American spellings for the InfoTrac® terms. For instance, 'organization' for 'organisation. In many cases it is also necessary to proceed to a subdivision in order to get focused, meaningful results. For example, for 'Financial services, international aspects', 'international aspects' should be considered as a subdivision of 'financial services'.

A full list of key terms is also available in the glossary, which can be found at the back of the book.

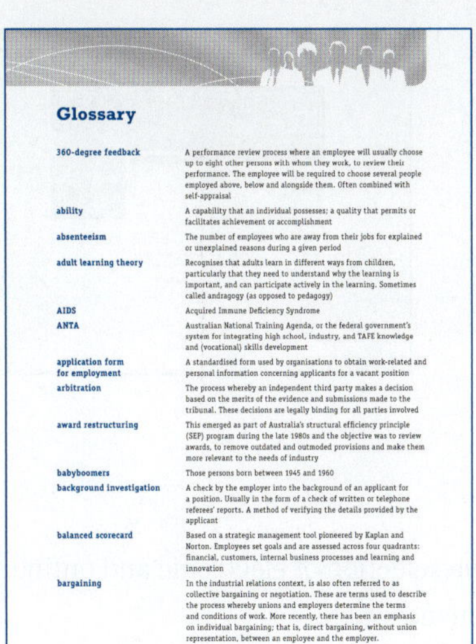

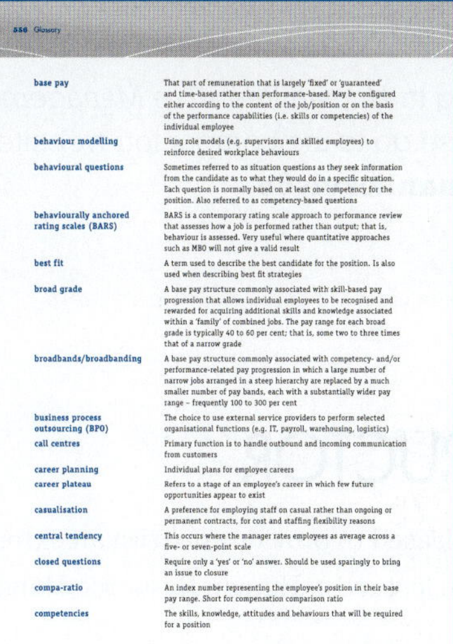

At the end of each chapter you will find several learning tools to help you to not only review the chapter and key concepts but to help you extend your learning.

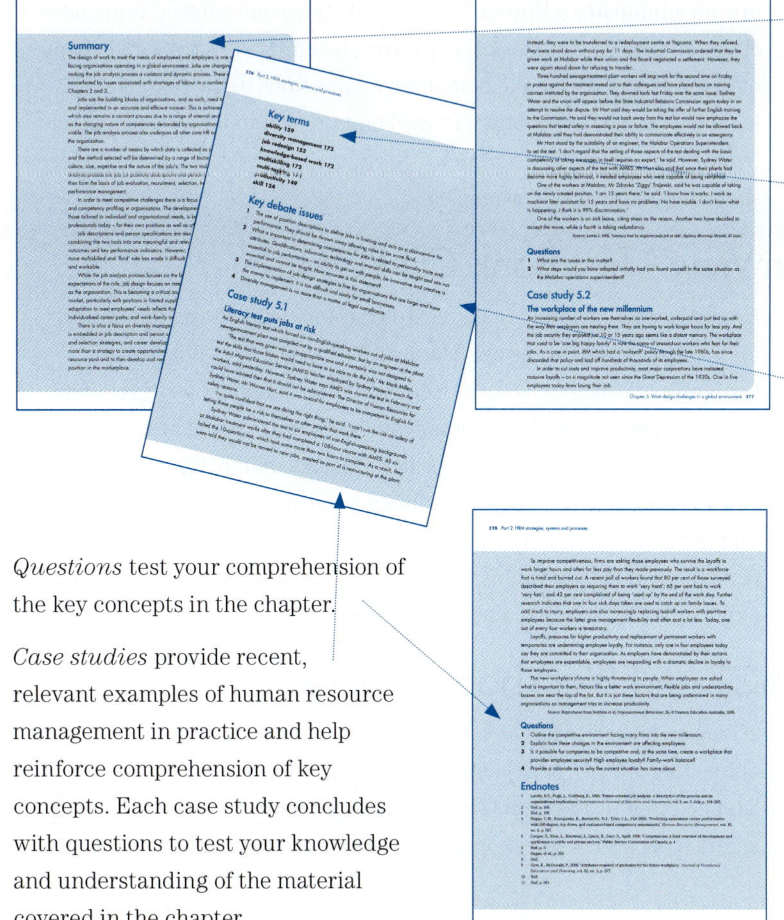

The end of chapter *Summary* lists key points from the chapter, giving you a snapshot of important concepts covered.

Key terms are listed at the end of each chapter. This will help you identify key concepts throughout the text. Definitions can be found in the glossary.

Key debate issues promote the application and critical analysis of theories and practices as well as encourage group discussion.

Questions test your comprehension of the key concepts in the chapter.

Case studies provide recent, relevant examples of human resource management in practice and help reinforce comprehension of key concepts. Each case study concludes with questions to test your knowledge and understanding of the material covered in the chapter.

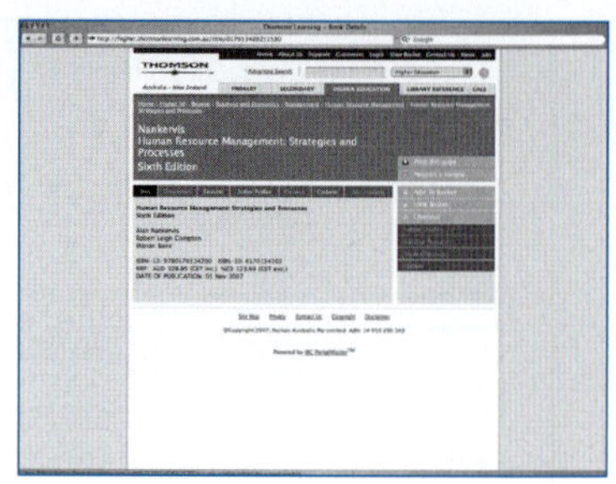

For updates and news relating to *Human Resource Management: Strategies and Processes* please go to the companion website at **www.cengage.com.au/nankervis6e**

FOR THE INSTRUCTOR

Thomson Learning is pleased to provide you with an extensive selection of electronic and online supplements to help you lecture in Human Resource Management.

Instructor's Manual and PowerPoint Presentation on CD-ROM

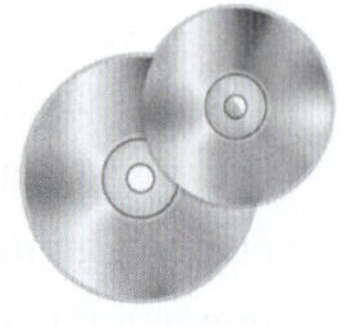

The Instructor's Manual provides you with a wealth of content to help set up and administer a Human Resource Management subject. It includes chapter purpose summaries, key terms, teaching objectives and chapter outlines as well as sample responses to questions in the text. Also included on the CD-ROM are PowerPoint presentations to accompany *Human Resource Management: Strategies and Processes*. Use these slides to reinforce key principles.

ExamView® Test Bank CD-ROM

ExamView® helps you create, customise and deliver tests in minutes for both print and online applications. The Quick Test Wizard and Online Test Wizard guide you step by step through the test-creation process. The program also allows you to see the test you are creating on the screen exactly as it will print or display online. With ExamView's complete word-processing capabilities, you can add an unlimited number of new questions to the bank, edit existing questions and build tests of up to 250 questions using up to 12 question types. You can also export the files into Blackboard or WebCT.

WebCT and Blackboard content

Thomson Learning has developed unique content that can be placed onto either *WebCT* or *Blackboard* platforms through a cartridge supplied free to adopters. This original content includes topic summaries, review questions, case projects and web links.

PART

1

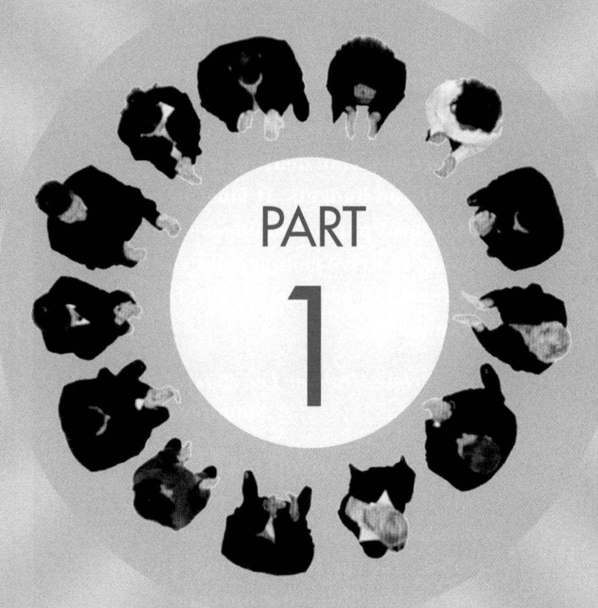

CHAPTER 1
EVOLUTION OF HUMAN RESOURCE MANAGEMENT

HR cannot remain as a backroom support function dealing with payroll and budgets. It must become an integral part of business strategy helping to drive change, add value and increase performance in the organisation.

Prime Minister Lee Hsien Loong,
Singapore, 2006

Senior HR executives need to run their HR function as if it were a business (with) a vision and strategy for the HR function, having clear deliverables and outcomes.

Professor David Ulrich, 2006

While the 1980s was the decade of intellectual capital and the '90s of emotional capital – both essentially about the qualities and behaviours of individuals – we are now in the era of 'social capital,' whereby value derives from the relationships between people.

Lynda Grattan, 2006

Objectives

After reading this chapter, you will be able to:

1 Define the purposes and scope of human resource management (HRM) in Australia.

2 Trace the development of HRM in Australia, including its influences, issues and theories.

3 Explain the concept of strategic human resource management (SHRM).

4 Understand the relationship between SHRM, business strategies and HRM functions.

5 Discuss the links between SHRM and organisational strategy, structure, culture and policy.

6 Describe the principal roles, functions and outcomes of Australian human resource management.

7 Define the professional and ethical principles which guide HRM.

Introduction

Organisations exist for a variety of purposes. Some produce goods for local or overseas consumption while others provide necessary services for profit or community benefit. In pursuit of their objectives all organisations rely on the availability and effectiveness of several kinds of resources, which can be divided into finances, technology and people. Some organisations emphasise their financial resources (banks, credit unions, stockbroking companies), others rely on the sophistication of their technology (telecommunications, manufacturing, information technology), while the growing service sector throughout the world depends heavily on the quality of its employees, its human resources.

Regardless of the particular resource emphasis in an industry, the human resource is almost always the key ingredient for organisational success. People design, operate and repair the technology, people control the financial resources, and people manage other people in all organisations. Compared with technological or financial resources, employees (the human resources) are the most unpredictable and often the largest, ongoing cost factor in any organisation, and they may also be regarded as its most valuable assets. It is therefore crucial that they are managed effectively and that their personal and work needs are satisfied, if organisational objectives are to be achieved.

A number of recent developments have begun to transform the nature of jobs and the workplaces in which they are performed. These developments include the influences of the twin forces of globalisation and technological development, as well as more gradual political, economic and social changes associated with significant amendments to industrial relations systems and processes. Globalisation has broadened the markets for Australian and regional businesses and, with the aid of enhanced information technology and telecommunications systems, has begun to demand new kinds of jobs, new forms of workplaces and increasingly, more innovative approaches to all HRM processes. McNally[1] summarises the implications of these global pressures on contemporary organisations as the need for international strategic alliances supported by managers with new mindsets; routine international staff deployment; the identification and nurturing of global talent; and increasingly sophisticated management of HRM systems. These imperatives are discussed in detail later in this chapter, and throughout the text. In particular, the changes to industrial relations processes, including increased flexibility and cooperation between employers, employees and unions, has enabled many organisations to adapt their systems to the demands of the Knowledge Era. In particular, in Australia, the introduction of the federal government's *Workplace Relations Act 1996*, and the *Workplace Relations Amendment (WorkChoices) 2005* legislation, in an attempt to 'transform the industrial relations culture from the stultifying effects of the old centralised model',[2] threaten to create a significant imbalance in the employment relationship in favour of employers. Dawson[3] suggests that the major external pressures for organisational change include such new government regulation and legislation, global markets and the 'internationalisation' of business, technological developments, and major social political changes; while internal pressures include technology, organisational restructuring, and changing employee expectations.

The implications of these changes to the theories, nature and functions of HRM are discussed later, but at this stage it is important to consider the origins and historical development of the discipline in order to understand its future role.

Early employee specialists were called personnel managers (or personnel administrators), and this term is still in use. 'Personnel management' refers to a set of functions or activities (e.g. recruitment, selection, training, salary administration, industrial relations) often performed effectively but with little relationship between the various activities, or with overall organisational objectives.

Over the past two decades, the concept of human resource management (HRM) has become the focus of professional practice. HRM assumes that all personnel activities are integrated and strategically linked to organisational objectives. This perspective views employees as 'human resources,' 'human assets,' 'intellectual capital,' or 'human capital' and that HR managers should strive to utilise them as 'critical investments' in an organisation's future: '... people are the key strategic resource, and strategy must be built on human-resource foundation'.[4]

Different perspectives of HRM emphasise either the effective management of employees through greater accountability and control, the greater involvement of employees in decision-making processes, or both of these.

Origins of, and influences on, human resource management

People management has existed in one form or another since the beginning of time. Certain HR processes, even though informal in nature, were performed whenever people came together for a common purpose. In recent decades, however, the processes of managing people have become more formalised and specialised. As a result, a growing body of knowledge about these processes has been accumulated by practitioners and scholars.

Personnel management in the United Kingdom and the United States developed earlier than in Australia in response to the earlier and more widespread adoption of mass production work processes in both countries. Power-driven equipment and improved production systems enabled products to be manufactured more cheaply. This process also created many jobs that were monotonous, unhealthy or even hazardous. The concentration of workers in factories served to focus public attention upon conditions of employment, and enabled workers to act collectively to achieve better conditions. The humanitarian, cooperative and Marxist influences of the early 1900s highlighted the potential conflicts between worker and employer interests in modern industry, situations which laid the foundations for the growth of trade unionism and industrial relations systems.

Governments in both the United Kingdom and the United States became involved in these issues and passed a series of laws to regulate the hours of work for women and children, to establish minimum wages for male labour and to protect workers from unhealthy or hazardous working conditions. Australian governments, both state and national, gradually began to follow suit from the early 1900s, though Australia and New Zealand adopted a different system based on conciliation and arbitration rather than mandated conditions (see Chapter 3).

During this period, management writers in the United States and United Kingdom began to examine the nature of work and work systems, and to develop models based upon emerging psychological and sociological research. The ways in which these theories have developed, and have been applied by both general management and specialist HR managers, reflect changing attitudes to jobs, work processes and organisational structures. The Classical school, for example, puts its emphasis on the job itself and the efficient adaptation of workers to work processes. The Behavioural school focuses on workers themselves, and the satisfaction of their needs, to achieve greater organisational productivity. Subsequent management theories (e.g. systems theory, contingency approaches) attempt to build on earlier ideas to benefit both workers and their organisations.

Contingency, Excellence and Total Quality Management (TQM) theorists have applied these ideas to particular industries and organisations, or to different economic and social situations. The relevance of these theories to HRM is twofold. First, personnel management has historically developed into human resource management by incorporating management theories and, second, a sound knowledge of these theories can assist HR managers to more effectively adapt their practices to organisational requirements and realities.

Stages in the development of HRM

Human resource management in Australia has progressed along similar lines to its United States and United Kingdom counterparts, but with differences in the stages of development, and in the relative influence of social, economic, political and industrial relations factors. The two main features of the US development of HRM are its initial emphasis on largely administrative activities, directed by senior management, and then the move to a more confident, business-oriented and professional approach in the 1980s and 1990s. Similar processes occurred in the United Kingdom, with more early emphasis on the 'welfare' roles of personnel practitioners because of the excesses of early capitalist industry, a strong humanitarian movement and developing trade unionism.

In Australia, HRM has developed through the following stages:

- *Stage one*: 1900–1940s; welfare and administration

- *Stage two*: 1940s–mid-1970s; welfare, administration, staffing and training – personnel management and industrial relations

- *Stage three*: mid-1970s–late 1990s; human resource management and strategic human resource management (SHRM)

- *Stage four*: 2000; SHRM in the new millennium

We will now describe some of the major features of each developmental stage.

Stage one: welfare and administration (1900–1940s)

Personnel functions were performed by supervisors, line managers and early specialists (e.g. recruitment officers, trainers, welfare officers) long before the establishment of a national association representing a 'profession' of personnel or human resource management. The early management theorists contributed ideas that would later be incorporated into personnel management theory and practice. Scientific management (e.g. Frederick Taylor, Frank Gilbreth, Alfred Sloan) through job design, structured reward systems and 'scientific' selection techniques helped to refine personnel management practice in the recruitment and placement of skilled employees. Behavioural science (or industrial psychology) added psychological testing and motivational systems, (e.g. Elton Mayo), while management science contributed to performance management programs.

In Australia, however, these overseas influences were of only marginal importance until the 1940s. Prior to the Second World War, personnel management functions were largely fragmented, and often conducted by line managers as part of their overall management responsibilities.

During this period, Australia had a relatively stable economy, with certain markets for its agricultural and (limited) manufacturing products, in the United Kingdom and Europe. Society was generally stable, though disrupted by the First World War and the Great Depression. Unemployment was low until the 1930s when labour became readily available for employers. Trade unions were active, largely focusing on issues of pay and working conditions. Personnel functions during this period were mainly restricted to administrative areas (e.g. wage/salary records, minor disciplinary procedures and employee welfare activities). In 1927, A.H. Martin established the Australian Institute of Industrial Psychology at Sydney University to promote the ideas of behavioural scientists and industrial psychologists in Australia.

Stage two: welfare, administration, staffing and training (1940s–mid-1970s)

This second stage marks the beginning of a specialist and more professional approach to personnel management in Australia. The Second World War had significant repercussions for both those who went overseas and those who stayed behind, and particularly for business, the economy and the labour market.

During the Second World War, not only was there a scarcity of labour for essential industries such as munitions and food, but there was also a corresponding increase in the problems and performance of existing employees. Many more women had become involved in all areas of Australian industry, to replace their husbands and brothers who were in military service. Financial, social and family pressures began to hinder the productivity and output of such employees, and they became increasingly harder to recruit. When the war ended, returning soldiers flooded the labour market, often with few work skills. Thus, employers, spurred on by government initiatives and their own postwar requirements for skilled employees in a developing economy, began to focus on the importance of a wider range of personnel functions.

Increased provision of welfare services for employees was seen by some employers, notably government departments such as the Postmaster-General, as a means of attracting and maintaining employees and ensuring their continued productivity. The Commonwealth Department of Labour and National Service established an Industrial Welfare Division in the 1940s to promote the welfare function, offering emergency training courses to equip practitioners with the necessary skills. These activities were supported by the new human relations theories that were filtering into Australia from the United States.

In addition, scientific management, the quantitative school and behavioural science contributed employee and management assessment and development techniques such as productivity measures, management planning and control mechanisms (e.g. Drucker, McGregor, Chandler), psychological testing and applications of the emerging employee motivation theories (e.g. Mazlow, Hertzberg, McGregor). Many more organisations began to employ specialists to conduct recruitment, training and welfare activities, taking these functions away from line managers.

In 1943, the first personnel officer was appointed to the St Mary's Explosives Factory in New South Wales, and in the same year a Personnel and Industrial Welfare Officers' Association was established in both Victoria and New South Wales. These state associations combined to form the national Personnel Officers' Association in 1949, renamed the Institute of Personnel Management Australia (IPMA) in 1954.[5] Subsequently, the Commonwealth Employment Service (CES) was set up to help employers obtain suitable employees, and both Sydney Technical College and Melbourne University developed personnel management courses.

Business schools with personnel management strands were established in most Australian states during the 1950s, encouraged by the development of the national professional association, IPMA, with members in Victoria, New South Wales, South Australia, Western Australia and Queensland.

This stage can be characterised by the expansion of necessary personnel functions for the postwar Australian economy (welfare, recruitment, selection, training); a gradual move from specialist to more general approaches; the adoption of overseas theories, including scientific management, behavioural science and human relations; and the emergence of professional associations and courses. The resurgence of unionism during these decades cannot, of course, be overlooked. Unions, in a buoyant economy, focused on pay and work conditions issues, forcing further expansion of personnel activities to include industrial relations considerations. The complex industrial relations structure at the national level was originally established by the *Conciliation and Arbitration Act 1904*, with similar developments at each of the state levels. They were further developed during the postwar period (see Chapter 3).

While the range of functions performed by the growing number of personnel specialists expanded greatly during this period, they were often conducted in isolation from one another and generally without any consideration of their impact on overall organisational effectiveness. Personnel management activities were largely separated from those concerned with industrial relations, and a clear professional philosophy did not exist.

Stage three: human resource management and strategic HRM (mid-1970s–late 1990s)

During the 1970s the majority of Australian organisations found themselves in turbulent business and economic environments, with severe competition from US and European organisations and emerging Asian markets. The influences of the 'Excellence' theories (e.g. Peters and Waterman) were beginning to affect the management of employees, together with increasing cost–benefit pressures (see Chapter 2).

At the same time, the professional association (the Institute of Personnel Management Australia) and training institutions (TAFE and the universities) were becoming more sophisticated in their approaches, incorporating the ideas of the 'Excellence,' leadership (e.g. Bennis and Nanus 1985; Senge 1990; Prahalad and Hamel 1990) and Total Quality Management (e.g. Deming) theories, with more recent developments such as Kaplan and Norton's 'Balanced Scorecard' (1992). During this period, the IPMA held a number of international conferences, initiated relationships with the Asia–Pacific region, developed minimum criteria for practitioner accreditation (the 1987 rule) and a journal for academic and practitioner discussion (*Human Resource Management Australia*, later retitled *Asia Pacific HRM*, and still later the *Asia Pacific Journal of Human Resources*).

Personnel management was becoming human resource management, representing a change towards the integration of personnel functions, strategically focused on overall organisational effectiveness. Significantly, the use of the term 'human resource management' was first noted in Australia in these years,[6] reflected in the formation of the Australian Human Resources Institute to replace the IPMA.[7] It has been enhanced by recent industrial relations changes, including award restructuring and enterprise agreements, increasing employment legislation, and economic realities such as declining trade with Britain and Europe and increasing opportunities in our own region. Exhibit 1.1 below illustrates the essential differences between personnel management and HRM.

Building upon previous developments, this stage represents the integration of personnel management and industrial relations and HRM into a coordinated and strategic approach to the management of an organisation's employees – 'Strategic HRM.' SHRM can be perceived as a 'macro' perspective (e.g. strategies and policies), whereas HRM represents more of a 'micro' approach (e.g. activities, functions and processes), but both are intertwined, as described later in this chapter. SHRM also provides practitioners with renewed confidence to perform their activities as an integral component of organisational success.

Exhibit 1.1 What's the difference?

	Personnel management	Human resources management
Time and planning perspective	Short term, reactive, ad hoc and marginal	Long term, proactive, strategic, integrated
Psychological contract	Compliance	Commitment

	Personnel management	**Human resources management**
Control systems	External controls	Self-control
Employee relations perspective	Pluralist, collective, low trust	Unitarist, individual, high trust
Preferred structure/system	Bureaucratic/mechanistic, centralised, formal defined roles	Organic, devolved, flexible roles
Roles	Specialised/professional	Largely integrated into line management
Evaluation criteria	Cost minimisation	Maximum utilisation (human asset accounting)

Source: Adaptation from 'Human Resource and Industrial Relations,' *Journal of Management Studies*, 24 May, p. 507. By permission of Blackwell Publishing.

Stage four: SHRM in the new millennium

While it is difficult to predict the nature of HRM in the future, there are strong indications that its theory and practice will be transformed as a consequence of globalism, new technology and associated fundamental changes in the nature of work and jobs. The external and internal pressures on all workplaces are discussed in detail throughout the text, as are the likely impacts on organisations, their employees and overall employment conditions. It is sufficient, at this stage, to suggest that earlier concepts of HRM and the roles of HR professionals will need to change significantly in order to remain relevant in the Knowledge Era.

Some contemporary observers of HRM theory and practice (e.g. Patrickson and Hartmann 2001; Weisner and Millett 2003; Bartlett and Ghoshal 2003; Zanko 2003; Lansbury et al. 2003; Losey, Meisinger and Ulrich (eds) 2006) suggest that the implications of global economic forces such as the shift to low inflation economies, widespread tariff reductions, and the current growth in multilateral and bilateral free trade agreements (e.g. Australia–Singapore, New Zealand–Singapore, Australia–New Zealand, Australia–US, APEC) demand more attention towards international HRM models. Communication and information technology changes such as the digital revolution, satellite links, cellular telephone networks and high speed fibre optic cables[8] will require the adoption of strategic international or global HRM models implemented through radical new approaches to HRM strategies, structures, organisational cultures, HRM practices, and employment relationships as a whole. As Erwee explains,

> … in the competitive process of globalisation and complexity, it is becoming critical to manage sustainable multinational organisations more effectively by using SHRM, and to link this with strategic needs in the larger organisational context. (However they)… must also work within the confines of (their) local environment as well as a range of laws, politics, culture, economies and practices between societies.[9]

These issues are discussed in considerably more detail later in this chapter, and throughout the text.

HR thought leaders such as Ulrich, Huselid, Lepak and Snell, and Collins imply that the 'new' HRM will either specialise in HRM 'value management,' 'strategic partnering' and establishing the HR 'architecture' for organisational success, or will combine such 'macro connections'[10] with the devolvement or outsourcing of traditional HR processes respectively to line managers and external HR consultants. More recently, Professor Ulrich has suggested that the survival of HRM demands that HR professionals are perceived to add value to four key stakeholders in organisations, namely:

(1) employees who want competence and commitment

(2) line managers who want to make strategy happen

(3) key customers who want to buy more products/services; and

(4) investors who want the stock price to go up.[11]

This will involve the formulation of HR strategies for the business, the workforce and the HR function itself. The theme of 'partnership' between senior managers and HRM specialists is echoed by HR professionals and by their general managers. Chris Georgiou, HR Director, AGC and Westpac Financial Services, suggests that 'to be effective, you need to partner with the business very closely and that means not necessarily just understanding the business but really participating at the business level'.[12] John Cooper, a partner at Freehills consultancy goes further, emphasising that 'HR needs to make sure it is a critical part of the decision-making processes that go with the new technology and the strategies to globalise'.[13] As the quotation from Lynda Grattan (Professor of Management Practice at London Business School) at the beginning of this chapter suggests, 'innovation is not about individuals, but about relationships'.[14] She further suggests that 'as innovation becomes the most crucial challenge facing companies, increasingly HR professionals will be called upon to facilitate strong relationships, to support the practices and processes of networks, and to develop policies and procedures … that focus on relationships between individuals rather than on individuals per se'.[15]

Perhaps the most dominant theme of the current stage in the development of SHRM is its emphasis on 'knowledge management,' 'human capital management' or 'talent management.' Some authors argue that there has been a '… shift in the locus of economic power as profound as that which occurred at the time of the Industrial Revolution. Knowledge has displaced labour, materials and money as the key input into an organisation's income-generating process',[16] and others assert that, consequently, 'managing the knowledge capital (sometimes referred to as the knowledge asset or knowledge resource) of an organisation has become one of the key activities for organisations in the 21st century'.[17]

The implications of this paradigm shift in perceptions of the employment relationship for HRM professionals are likely to be significant, in relation to human resource planning, organisational structure and culture, and strategies for job design, recruitment and selection, human resource development, performance management, remuneration and the management of employee retention. It may also signal the reinvention, or at least the transformation, of the HRM concepts, roles and functions, explained in the following sections of this chapter, towards new, dynamic models of practice.

Human resource management and strategic human resource management – evolving concepts and models

Human resource management

In essence, HRM differs from earlier personnel management models in relation to its focus, its principles and its applications. Thus, the focus of HRM today is on the effective overall management of an organisation's workforce in order to contribute to the achievement of desired objectives and goals. All HR processes (e.g. recruitment, human resource development, performance appraisal, remuneration) are seen to be integrated components of overall HRM strategies. As David Guest points out: '… HRM was born out of the failure of personnel management to manage people effectively in the pursuit of the strategic (organisational) imperative …'[18]

Exhibit 1.2 The 'Harvard' model of HRM

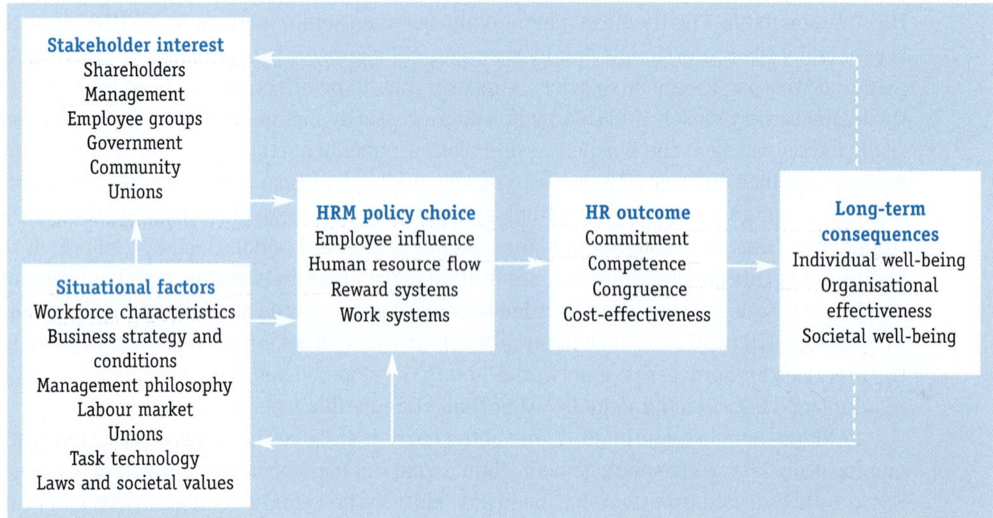

Source: Beer M., Spector B., Lawrence P., Mills D., Walton R. 1995. *Human resource management: A general manager's perspective,* New York, Free Press.

Exhibit 1.2, known as the 'Harvard' model of HRM, shows HRM as a set of broad policy 'choices' in response to the demands of organisational characteristics (e.g. stakeholders, business strategy and conditions, management philosophy, technology) within the context of the external labour market and social, economic and political conditions. 'Choices' of HRM policies encompass the nature of all traditional HR processes (e.g. work design, recruitment and selection, performance management and remuneration systems), and hopefully lead to desirable HR outcomes and long-term consequences for the organisation.

As this model indicates, the principles on which HRM theories are based are generally broader and more managerial in their emphasis than personnel management. The central principle is, of course, the effective utilisation of employees in order to enable the achievement of organisational objectives. Thus, the entire 'resource' of the employee should be tapped (i.e. physical, creative, productive and interpersonal components) in order to achieve this goal. In contemporary organisations, the emphasis may be more on the 'intellectual capital,' or 'knowledge worker,' than on manual or physical skills. These issues are discussed in more detail later in this chapter.

However, HRM theories also recognise that the human resource, unlike financial or technological 'resources,' cannot be manipulated or 'exploited,' and that it requires complex and sensitive management in order to fully realise its potential. Variations of HRM theory emphasise different aspects of management of the employment relationship, reflective of diverse national or industry environments. These are discussed later as 'soft' or 'hard' HRM, or 'unitarist' or 'pluralist' perspectives, and include such principles as merit selection, equity, ethical conduct and natural justice.

All HRM theories are, however, essentially managerialist in their emphasis on the management of the workforce and accountability to ensure the achievement of desired objectives and goals. Thus, HRM practitioners are no longer seen as employee 'advocates,' except when such activities are necessary to assist the achievement of the organisation's goals. As Lees explains:

> The central task of HRM is to regulate the management of people in pursuit of the strategic and economic imperatives, but with the added proviso that, in doing so, there must also be conformity with the institutional and cultural environment in which the organisation is embedded.[19]

The imperatives of contemporary HRM theory include such principles as efficiency, effectiveness, productivity, labour flexibility and competitive organisational advantage. Baird and McGrath-Champ[20] suggest that HRM concepts represent the strengthening of managerial prerogatives, and Patrickson and Hartmann (2001) summarise its dominant strategic emphases as 'productivity enhancement, cost minimisation, work intensification (and) to seek markets abroad'.[21]

Some other HRM observers note that recent trends in the nature of employment (such as casualisation, more flexible conditions based upon workplace agreements and a more cooperative industrial relations climate), and the various impacts of technology and globalisation, together with innovative HR practices such as rightsizing and outsourcing (discussed later in the text), present serious challenges to the future of HRM.

Applications of HRM theory differ from personnel management in their dismissal of prescriptive 'one best way' models of practice. Diverse national and industrial relations environments demand different HRM applications. Thus, an HRM theory derived from US experience will be diffused and adapted differently in the United Kingdom, Europe, Australia or New Zealand, according to their different social, political and industrial relations histories and circumstances. It may, however, apply in more 'unitarist' industrial relations environments, such as those in Singapore, Malaysia, Indonesia or Thailand.

Different theories of HRM and different principles and applications will be more (or less) relevant within the contexts of particular countries or esoteric industry environments. These issues are now discussed in more detail in relation to the 'unitarist' and 'pluralist,' and 'hard' and 'soft' perspectives of various HRM theories.

HRM – a unitarist or pluralist approach to the employment relationship?

All HRM models are based upon assumptions, values and beliefs about the nature of relationships between employers, their employees and unions, and all HR processes take place within the national, industry and industrial relations contexts which shape them. Accordingly, a single model of HRM will not be appropriate for all environments.

Considerable debate takes place over whether HRM is essentially 'unitarist' or 'pluralist' in its perception of the employment relationship. A unitarist approach, often reflected in American models of HRM and the practices of countries such as Singapore, Malaysia and Indonesia, assumes common interests between employers and employees, and attempts to encourage commitment by both inclusive (e.g. communication, consultation, rewards systems) and exclusive (e.g. discouragement of union membership, 'greenfield' sites) means.

While this perspective may prove effective in countries or industries with low rates of union membership, authoritarian management traditions or high unemployment levels, it is not appropriate in all industries or countries (see Chapter 3).

A pluralist approach, on the other hand, recognises that employers and their employees will inevitably experience conflicts of interest, which HRM will need to negotiate and resolve in order to meet organisational goals.

Given the contemporary changes in industrial relations systems and a significant decline in union membership in many countries, notably New Zealand and Australia, through individual contracts and, in Australia, Australian Workplace Agreements (AWAs), HRM approaches may be influenced by elements of both perspectives.

'Hard' or 'soft' HRM?

Depending on the assumptions about the nature of the employment relationship, different HRM models and practices have been developed to accommodate the diverse industry and workplace contexts in which they operate. Both 'hard' and 'soft' HRM approaches reflect their underlying management theories as well as different national or industry environments. Strategic human resource management as a concept incorporates both perspectives – the 'hard' management aspects of strategy formulation, human resource planning and program evaluation, and the 'soft' features of communication and consultation with employees, motivation and leadership.

'Hard' HRM has a strategic and managerial focus, emphasising the effective utilisation of human 'resources' towards broad organisational objectives and goals, whereas 'soft' HRM infers the involvement of employees through such means as consultation, empowerment, commitment and communication.

Some authors warn that 'hard' HRM, without corresponding 'soft' approaches, can result in undesirable consequences. Kaye (1999), for example, notes:

> Rather than putting people first and drawing from the external research which
> confirms that organisations do gain enduring competitive advantage through
> the way they manage people, organisations continue to seek solutions to their
> competitive challenges by downsizing, outsourcing and weakening their
> organisational culture.[22]

Obviously, both approaches have validity in particular industry and organisational contexts, and both can contribute to overall organisational goals, and consequently HRM models and practices need to be sufficiently flexible to accommodate the particular paradigms of the environments in which they operate.

Human resource management and industrial relations

An issue for subsequent discussion (Chapter 3) is that of the relationship between human resource management and industrial relations. Some writers suggest that industrial relations systems and traditions interfere with (or even prevent) the application of HRM theories. Others observe that the management of human resources includes the management of the industrial (or employee) relations systems and practices of each organisation. Yet others see industrial relations systems and practices as merely a part of the overall environment within which HRM functions.

Kelly (2003), for example, suggests that, while industrial relations has '… an *institutional* focus with most interest in trade unions, employer associations, and the state and state agencies such as the conciliation and arbitration systems', human resource management has a *managerialist* focus, which is concerned with '… the control and administration of the employment relationship'.[23] Given the gradual shift of bargaining in Australia, from centralised institutions such as the Australian Industrial Relations Commission and the various state industrial tribunals towards the enterprise level (see Chapter 3), it is not surprising that both industrial relations and HRM practitioners and academics have had to adjust their strategies and approaches.

Recent imperatives of the Australian federal government, expressed in the *WorkChoices* legislation, reflect a deliberate move to disassociate unions from enterprise bargaining, leading potentially to a significant imbalance towards employers in the employment relationship.

Professor Russell Lansbury, from Sydney University, suggests that 'while some HR managers may feel that the changes introduced by *WorkChoices* will give their companies an economic advantage, and even the capacity to be more internationally competitive, the danger is that the legislation may lead Australia down the low road, to a less skilled and less productive society'.[24]

Generically, Legge argues that HRM models pose a threat to industrial relations (IR) in several ways:

- 'Soft' HRM models appear to bypass the 'collectivist' nature of IR representation and negotiation.

- The need for unions in the employment relationship is accordingly reduced, and unions become 'marginalised.'

- If HRM really delivers on employee 'commitment,' why will organisations need to negotiate with a third party (unions)?[25]

Notwithstanding enabling industrial relations changes such as *WorkChoices*, many Australian organisations have begun to realise that if they can manage their employees in ways that satisfy both organisational goals and employee needs, there is little need for complex negotiations with industry unions. Companies such as CRA (Weipa), the Commonwealth Bank, Telstra and Goodman Fielder have focused on formulating attractive and performance-based workplace agreements, which benefit both their 'bottom line' goals and employee expectations, and thus bypass relevant industry unions. This process has been facilitated by an Australia-wide decrease in the proportion of union membership (see Chapter 3), together with favourable federal government policies since 1996.

Of necessity, the ways in which HRM and IR operate are heavily dependent on national, industry and workplace contexts. Thus, in US corporations, unions may be neutralised or excluded, as within some of our regional neighbours, while in Australia and New Zealand unions may be fully included in the formalisation of enterprise agreements, or provide active opposition to the implementation of HRM programs. This merely reinforces the need for HRM models to be sufficiently flexible to accommodate the differing requirements of the environments in which organisations operate.

Strategic human resource management

Strategic human resource management (SHRM) emphasises the need for HR plans and strategies to be formulated within the context of overall organisational strategies and objectives, and to be responsive to the changing nature of the organisation's external 'environment' (i.e. its competitors, the national and international arenas). A strong implication of SHRM theory is that HR plans and strategies should be developed on a long-term basis, taking into account likely changes in the society, industrial relations systems, economic conditions, legislation, and global and technological issues, as well as new directions in business operations. As Martin-Alcazar et al. (2005, p. 651) explain, SHRM is 'the integrated set of practices, policies and strategies through which organizations manage their human capital, that influences and is influenced by the business strategy, the organizational context and the socio-economic context'.[26]

SHRM is a model for practice, which, like all models, requires interpretation and adaptation by HR practitioners to ensure the most suitable alignment or 'fit' between HR and business strategies and plans. Exhibit 1.3 summarises the characteristics of SHRM and the roles of HR, senior and line managers.

According to Tyson, the roles of HRM practitioners become those of '... strategic integration ... culture management ... winning [employee] commitment ... investment in the employee resource ... flexible organisations ... total quality ... partnerships with trade unions ... [and] managerialism'.[27] Some authors suggest that HR management systems need to focus not on 'standardised job systems' but rather on the skills and knowledge acquired by individuals, while others argue that such systems should develop 'workplace cultures that are more self-sustaining and allow individuals to have more choice in how and when they learn, while also ensuring that agreed business priorities and expectations are met'.[28] Thus, the overall themes of SHRM – the integration of all HRM functions, adherence to broad organisational goals and responsiveness to the external environment – remain, but the ways in which this integration may be achieved will differ from organisation to organisation.

SHRM and business strategy

The term 'strategy' has its origins in the military campaigns of ancient Greece and has subsequently been adopted by many organisations as a way of describing their progress towards desired long-term objectives. 'Business strategy' is used to explain both the processes (e.g. organisational restructuring, rightsizing, multiskilling, product development) and the outcomes (e.g. market position, profitability, competitiveness) of chosen long-term directions. It can be either a conscious, planned activity or a series of events which lead to a desirable objective.

Exhibit 1.3 Characteristics of strategic HRM (SHRM)

- **A longer-term focus** – An inclusion of multiple-year strategic plans for human resource use is often considered the first step in the evolution of a strategically oriented HRM function.

- **New linkages between HRM and strategic planning** have emerged as a critical element in many models of SRHM. One-way linkages focus on the role of HRM activities in assisting strategy implementation, while a two-way linkage describes a more proactive approach where HRM exerts influence on strategy formulation as well.

- **Proposed linkages between HRM and organisational performance** – Most models of SHRM include the proposition that HRM plays a key role in the achievement of strategic goals. Since the expected outcome of company strategies is an improvement in the firm's economic value, HRM must thus directly contribute to the firm's 'bottom line' in order to be judged effective.

- **Inclusion of line managers in the HRM policy-making process** – The recognition of HRM's strategic importance may make it more of a line management responsibility, particularly in areas involving the selection and compensation of managers. A CEO of a large trucking company echoed this sentiment to us when he told us that 'HRM is too important to be left to the HRM department.'

Source: Adaptation from Martell K., Carroll S. 1995. 'How strategic is HRM?,'
Human Resource Management, Summer, 4(2), pp. 253–67. By permission of Blackwell Publishing.

'Strategy' is a neutral term, so business strategies can result in both successes and failures. As examples, many organisations have consciously chosen to extend their operations, or even to relocate, to other countries to take advantage of less expensive labour markets or to create new market opportunities (e.g. Cathay Pacific, Telstra, Dome Coffee Shops, BHP Billiton, Singapore Airlines). As a typical example of a truly global HR strategy, the international publisher Palgrave Macmillan outsources its copy-editing and proofreading operations to countries such as India, and its printing functions to China, while retaining coordination from the United Kingdom.

Other organisations have 'offshored' parts of their operations, lured by host government incentives, industry promotions or the promise of lucrative markets.

As discussed earlier, SHRM is concerned with ensuring a strategic 'alignment' or 'fit' between business and HRM strategies. It necessarily involves an evaluation of the likely impacts of both the external and internal organisational environments, the long-term goals of the organisation and the ways in which HRM strategy will enable the 'adaptation' of human resources to meet these goals. Thus, the HRM strategy of one organisation may involve more selective recruitment or the multiskilling of employees, while another may require rightsizing (or redundancy), job redesign or the elimination of manual or repetitive job functions.

Porter[29] divides all business strategies into three categories – cost leadership, product differentiation and market segments – while Storey and Sisson (1990) refine these as innovation, quality improvement and cost reduction strategies.

Exhibit 1.4 illustrates the 'alignment' between these three kinds of organisational strategies and associated HRM strategies and functions.

Some organisations may wish to pursue either 'innovation' and 'quality enhancement,' or 'quality enhancement' and 'cost reduction' strategies, and some may wish to pursue all three business strategies. In those cases, HRM specialists will need to devise strategies which incorporate comprehensive HRM approaches aligned with desired overall goals and objectives. These may involve macro-approaches, such as culture change, or substantial organisational restructuring and/or micro HR techniques, such as job redesign, selective recruitment and career management.

Exhibit 1.4 Linking HRM and strategy

Organisation strategy focus	Recommended HRM strategies
Innovation	1 Jobs that require close interaction and coordination among groups of individuals
	2 Performance appraisals that are more likely to reflect long-term and group-based achievements
	3 Jobs that allow employees to develop skills that can be used in other positions in the firm
	4 Compensation systems that emphasise internal equity rather than external or market-based equity
	5 Pay rates that tend to be low, but that allow employees to be stockholders and have more freedom to choose the mix of components that make up their pay package
	6 Broad career paths to reinforce the development of a broad range of skills
Quality improvement	1 Relatively fixed and explicit job descriptions
	2 High levels of employee participation in decisions relevant to immediate work conditions and the job itself
	3 A mix of individual and group criteria for interdependent behaviour
	4 Performance appraisal that is mostly short-term and results-orientated
	5 A relatively egalitarian treatment of employees and some guarantees of employment security
	6 Extensive and continuous training and development of employees

Some overlap b/tw QI & cost reduction.

Organisation strategy focus	Recommended HRM strategies
Cost reduction	1 Relatively fixed and explicit job descriptions that allow little room for ambiguity
	2 Narrowly designed jobs and narrowly defined career paths that encourage specialisation, expertise and efficiency
	3 Short-term, results-orientated performance appraisals
	4 Close monitoring of market pay levels for use in making compensation decisions
	5 Minimal levels of employee training and development

This table illustrates the organisation strategy and HRM policy fit of the Schuler and Jackson model, which is based on Porter's three generic strategy types of innovation, quality improvement and cost reduction.

Source: Caro Gill, 'A fitting strategy,' *hrmonthly*, November 2002, p. 30.

Research conducted by the Australian Human Resources Institute (AHRI) and the Committee for Economic Development of Australia (CEDA) has pinpointed the most crucial business success factors for Australian industry associated with HRM strategies. These are in order of importance and apply to many other countries as well:

- recruiting and retaining skilled employees
- increasing customer satisfaction
- employing and developing leaders
- sustaining a competitive advantage
- managing risk
- managing change and corporate culture
- becoming a more innovative organisation.[30]

HRM strategies (like business strategies) will need to take account of changes in both the external and internal environments of their organisations, and consequently to provide for contingencies which may arise during the planning period.

In order to be a 'strategic partner,' HRM specialists need to develop close links with all levels of management, and to form relationships which promote the 'bottom line' value of the strategic management of an organisation's employees (see Chapter 13). Partnership may involve devolving the majority of practical HR processes (e.g. job design, recruitment and selection, human resource development, performance management) to line managers, or the outsourcing of specialist activities such as payroll administration and employee benefits. Other HRM specialists will focus on the development of close relationships with senior management in order to effectively contribute to the formulation and revision of strategic plans. Exhibit 1.5 illustrates the relationships between business success factors and associated business challenges.

Several types of linkages between HR and organisational strategies have been identified as follows:

- *Accommodative*: HR strategies simply follow organisational strategies, 'accommodating' the staffing needs of already chosen business strategies.
- *Interactive*: A two-way communication process between HRM and corporate planning in which HRM contributes to, and then reacts to, overall strategies.

- *Fully integrated*: The HR specialist is intimately involved in the overall strategic process in both formal and informal interactions, a real reflection of strategic human resource management in practice.[31]

Exhibit 1.5 Business challenges and success factors matrix

	Challenges			Business success factors			
	Skills shortage	Labour supply	Short-term expectations	Harnessing technology	Legislative compliance	Budget constraints	Productivity
Recruiting and retaining skilled employees	X	X	X	X		X	
Increasing customer satisfaction	X	X	X	X		X	X
Employing and developing leaders		X	X		X		X
Sustaining a competitive advantage	X	X	X	X	X	X	X
Managing risk	X	X	X	X	X		
Managing change and corporate culture	X	X	X	X	X		
Becoming a more innovative organisation	X	X	X	X	X		

Source: Mithen J., Edwards D. 2003. *HR: Creating business solutions*, Melbourne, AHRI-CEDA, p. 18.

The ideal linkage is, of course, where HR and organisation strategies are 'fully integrated' with each other, and where the HR specialist has direct reporting and communication relationships with the highest levels of management in the organisation. Some US research suggests that the link between senior managers, HR specialists and line managers is best achieved when the practitioners adopt new roles – 'a partner in strategy execution … an administrative expert … an employee champion … [and] … a change agent'.[32]

'Case 1: The Ritz-Carlton Millenia, Singapore' illustrates the ways in which one global company has attempted to align its business and HRM imperatives. In particular, it demonstrates the integration of business goals and ethical values into all of its HRM programs, and its attempts to integrate employee and company needs.

Case 1: The Ritz-Carlton Millenia Singapore

Motto

Excellence in service delivery through talented, trained and empowered employees.

Company's Business Objectives – 'The Pyramid'

The Ritz-Carlton 'Pyramid' plays a major role in guiding our organization to systematically pursue higher performance levels. It is designed to ensure our strategies are balanced – that they don't inappropriately trade-off among the needs of our key stakeholders or long and short-term goals.

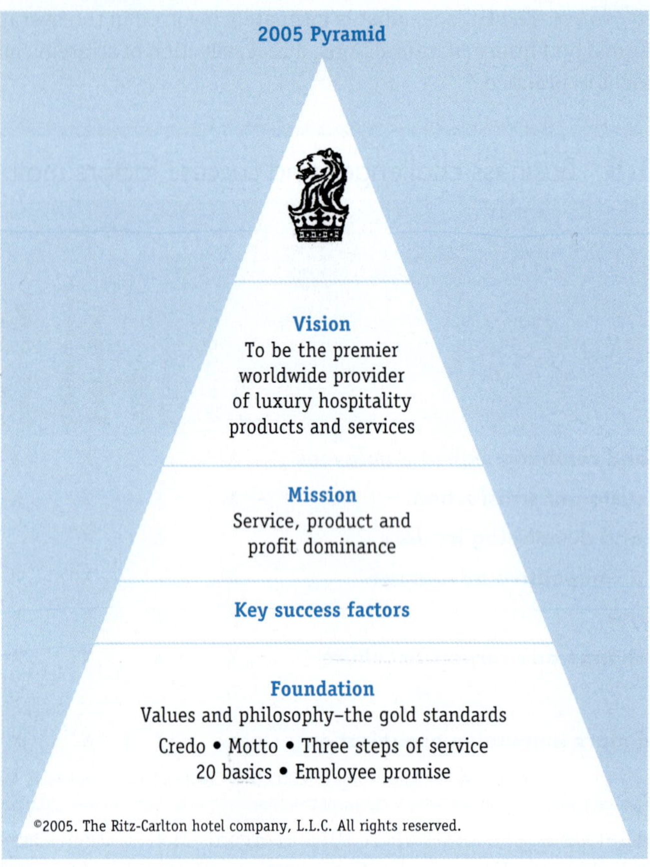

Vision

To be the premier worldwide provider of luxury hospitality products and services. The Ritz-Carlton
Millenia strives to be 'the best business hotel in the world.'

Mission

'Service, Product and Profit Dominance'

Service is exceptional delivery of The Gold Standards

Product represents superior facilities and amenities

Profit is outstanding financial results necessary to operate and grow our business

2005 Pyramid

**2005
Key success
factors**

1. The Ritz-Carlton mystique
create exceptional memories
enhance global recognition

2. Employee loyalty
fulfill the employee promise
encourage employee innovation

3. Customer loyalty
instill a sense of well-being
personalize customer relationships
eliminate defects – never lose a guest

4. Owner loyalty
maximize profitability
increase owner satisfaction

5. Revenue
maximize hotel revenue
enlarge customer base

6. Profit
maximize hotel profit
optimize Labor Management System (LMS)
maximize management fees

7. Brand
enhance the Ritz-Carlton brand

The Employee Promise

At the Ritz-Carlton, our Ladies and Gentlemen are the most important resource in our service commitment to our guests. By applying the principles of trust, honesty, respect, integrity and commitment, we nurture and maximize talent to the benefit of each individual and the company. The Ritz-Carlton fosters a work environment where diversity is valued, quality of life is enhanced, individual aspirations are fulfilled, and the Ritz-Carlton Mystique is strengthened.

Source: Adapted from material presented by the Ritz-Carlton Millenia Hotel, Singapore, for the Singapore HR Institute Awards of Excellence, 2005.

Critics of SHRM

As discussed earlier, many authors question the underlying philosophies and practical applications of HRM models. Similar concerns are raised about SHRM. Its managerial focus, strategic perspectives and the 'realities' of HR practice have been questioned by several writers (e.g. Boxall 1992, Legge 1995, Storey 1995, Guest 1997, Martin-Alcazar et al. 2005). SHRM is certainly concerned primarily with contributing to the 'bottom line' success of organisations, which may sometimes involve a neo-unitarist approach to the management of employees. On other occasions, the nature of the industrial relations system within and outside the organisation will require a guiding pluralist framework. As Tyson explains: 'All the major models of HRM suggest that the strategic activity of HRM stands in a symbiotic relationship to the organisation's stakeholders … and manages an inner context in relation to an "outer context".'[33]

SHRM may also infer a 'hard' (rather than a 'soft') HRM focus, which does not sit comfortably with some authors. However, as Legge points out, 'If HRM, in either its "hard" or "soft" guises, involves the reassertion of managerial prerogative over the labour process, the strategies of flexibility reflect and constitute a path to this, … employees as both resourceful humans … and human resources …'[34]

In other words, the essence of SHRM is to adopt a flexible but strategic perspective which accurately analyses both the internal and external environments of organisations to assure 'fit' between HR strategies and practices, and between these and business strategies.

SHRM theory assumes the capacity and commitment of senior managers and HR specialists to broad- and long-term perspectives of organisational planning. Some studies question both their managerial capacity and their commitment, despite some encouraging signs (see below). In addition, some HR practitioners appear to lack the status, self-confidence or business acumen to implement the SHRM agenda.

SHRM – research evidence

Some research (although by no means conclusive) has been conducted into the application of SHRM theory to organisational HR practice in the United States, the United Kingdom, Europe and, more recently, in Australia, New Zealand and Asia. Most studies have been relatively small and, arguably, unrepresentative of industry as a whole in these regions. Schuler, and Martell and Carroll, among others, have researched SHRM in the United States; Purcell, Storey, Legge, Tang et al., Dowling and Fisher in the United Kingdom, Australia and Asia have conducted surveys to determine whether organisations have actually converted the 'rhetoric' of SHRM into operational practice. Overall the results are not greatly encouraging.

The American studies provide most support for the practice of SHRM. Martell and Carroll, for example, reporting on a small survey, suggest that two-thirds of their sample linked HRM and strategic planning processes and that HRM 'executives' were considered by their companies as 'valuable members of the top management team'.[35] However, they also concluded that while considered important, HRM was not seen as important as other business functions (e.g. marketing and finance) in their contribution to overall organisational success. In the United Kingdom, again based upon relatively small samples of organisations, Storey (1995) found some evidence for SHRM in practice, especially in large companies.

In Australia, evidence is scant, but growing. Dowling's 1995 survey of 2 795 HR practitioners in Australia found that only 17 per cent of respondents had full HR representation at board-of-director level, although 28 per cent had partial representation. Encouragingly, 56 per cent of the sample of companies had a 'committee of senior executives that meet regularly to consider HR matters,' and more than 59 per cent were located at the corporate headquarters.[36]

Both Australian and international studies suggest that the link between SHRM theory and practice is still somewhat tenuous. The State of the Art/Practice study,[37] the Cranfield Network's International Strategic Human Resource Management project,[38] and the HRM Consulting study,[39] all concluded that, while advances have been made towards the vertical (i.e. alignment of HR and business plans) and horizontal (i.e. alignment of all HRM processes) integration of HRM within organisations, HR managers '… still have to demonstrate their credibility and the contribution they can make to the business'.[40] Roger Collins (2003), in his ongoing study conducted jointly by the Australian Graduate School of Management and CCH Australia, found that 74 per cent of his 669 respondents included HR issues (e.g. outsourcing, downsizing, succession training) in their business planning, and that they used these business plans to formulate or review their HR plans, but his overall conclusion was that 'progress has come to a halt in these areas'.[41]

More recently, a study conducted by Sheehan, Holland and De Cieri (2006) found that HR representation on organisational boards has grown from 17 per cent (1995) to 25 per cent (2005), and on senior management committees from 56 per cent to 68 per cent during the same period.[42] Their interpretation of the findings is that '… the HR function continues to accept and adjust to the role of strategic partner,' but that this development ' … involves further challenges that include the development of business breadth in the HR career base, the need for improved HR metrics and a broader commitment to attraction and retention initiatives.[43]

Research evidence so far suggests that SHRM has been constrained by factors such as the status of HR practitioners, the lack of acceptance of HRM by senior organisational managers and the limited ability of HR practitioners to exercise a more 'strategic' approach to the management of their human resource responsibilities. As some writers caution, '… many claims about strategic HRM are exaggerated and rhetorical rather than realistic and generally implemented'.[44]

SHRM – our model and this text

Some models of HRM have already been discussed. Exhibit 1.6 illustrates our notion of SHRM, derived both from consideration of the theory and from our collective practical experience in human resource management. It is used as the guiding framework for SHRM practice in several organisations and forms the 'spine' of this text.

This model incorporates the major themes of SHRM:

- There is awareness of, and responsiveness to, the characteristics of the dynamic external environments (e.g. global, national, industrial) of organisations.

- Business acumen and knowledge of the HR specialist feeds into the strategic business plan of the company.

- Human resource strategy is directly responsive to identified business requirements, which then inform specific human resource plans and policies.

- In their turn, the HR plans and policies guide the development and refinement of all HR practices and systems, which are shown as clearly integrated with each other, and with the HR strategies and plans.

- The effectiveness or outcomes of the HR processes are reflected in desired strategic organisational outcomes (e.g. performance, productivity, effectiveness, cost effectiveness, profitability) and the achievement of overall business strategies.

- The process is long term and cyclical, with sufficient flexibility to permit directional changes in human resource strategy according to changes in organisational strategies and/ or the 'dynamic' external environments.

Like all such models, ours is represented as a linear process, when in reality SHRM is multidimensional. This is due to the limitation of text-based representation rather than a constraint on the creativity of innovative HR practice.

This SHRM model is used as the overall structure of the text. Thus, this chapter has described the essential features of SHRM and its origins and will further discuss the relationships between SHRM and organisational strategy, structure, culture and policy. Chapters 2, 3 and 4 extend discussion to the nature of the environments in which HR operates, the industrial relations systems and human resource planning. The model also incorporates the influence of diversity management on overall HR plans and on the various HR processes. Links are made between HR plans and HR strategies and between HR plans and specific HR processes.

☆ Exhibit 1.6   A strategic human resource management model ☆

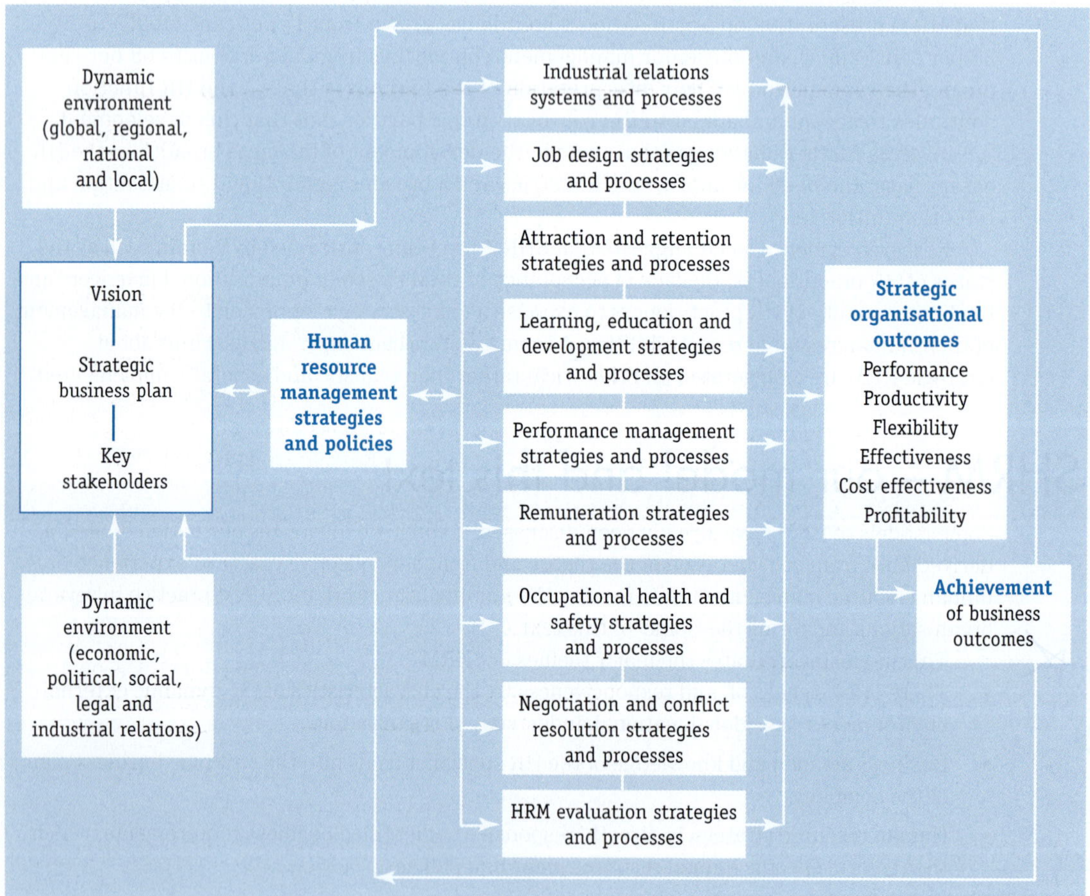

Chapters 5 to 12 explore the broad range of HR processes (e.g. job design, staffing, human resource development, performance management, remuneration systems and the management of occupational health and safety, negotiation and conflict resolution). While many of these processes will be performed by line managers in decentralised organisations, each chapter examines the specific techniques and systems used, within the context of their 'strategic' relationships with each of the other functions and with overall HR plans and strategies. The text incorporates the notion of an HR 'community,' within which both these functional and strategic operations of SHRM are encompassed and integrated.

Chapter 13 ('Evaluating human resource management') discusses the ways in which HR specialists and senior managers can assess whether HR strategies and functions have been successful in contributing to the 'bottom line' expectations of their business strategies, that is, strategic organisational outcomes and business outcomes. The final chapter then attempts to predict the likely future of HRM in Australia.

It is important to note that the concepts of HRM and SHRM do not assume a 'one best way' of implementation, and in fact the essence of SHRM is to adopt a flexible but strategic perspective which accurately analyses both the internal and external 'fit' between HR strategies and practices, and between these and business strategies. As Zanko (2003), reporting on an Asia Pacific Economic Forum (APEC)-sponsored research study, concludes, 'there was no evidence of a universalistic "one best way" of HRM being followed by economies in APEC. Each economy and its constituents have their own recipes for dealing with HRM issues'.[45] The following section discusses the emerging concept of 'Strategic International HRM,' which adds the global dimension to the SHRM model discussed above.

Strategic international human resource management

The field of international human resource management (IHRM) has been in existence for more than 20 years, particularly in the United States, and to a lesser extent in Europe and Australia (e.g. Tung 1985; Black 1999; Dowling, Welch and Schuler, 1999). Its emphasis has begun to change from a focus on the management of expatriate managers and employees in multinational organisations towards a broader and more integrated perspective which incorporates the study of strategic HRM in the global context. This is often referred to as *strategic international human resource management* (SIHRM), or *strategic global human resource management*.

This newer model recognises the growth in international operations of many kinds of organisations, not only those which can be classified as multinational corporations (e.g. IBM, BHP Billiton, Shell, Deutsche Bank, Intercontinental and Hilton hotel chains), and includes the plethora of Internet-based companies (e.g. Amazon.com) which trade online throughout the world. SIHRM is now defined as the study of three major aspects of SHRM:

- strategic HRM in multinationals (i.e. the impact of context and culture on SHRM)

- comparative HRM (i.e. comparisons of HRM theories and practices in different countries or regions)

- the management of expatriates in different countries or regions.

In essence, SIHRM is concerned with the management of global workforces, including features such as the choice and development of global leaders and global 'mindsets,' 'global employees' and 'global HRM systems'.[46] Brewster et al. (2005, p. 966) suggest that:

> the added value of the HR function in an international organization lies in its ability to manage the delicate balance between overall co-ordinated systems and sensitivity to local needs, including cultural differences, in a way that aligns with both business needs and senior management philosophy. There is a distinction between international HRM and global HRM. Traditionally, IHRM has been about managing an international workforce … higher-level organizational people … Global HRM is not simply about these staff. It concerns managing all HRM activities, wherever they are, through the application of global rule sets.[47]

Thus, it encompasses not only traditional processes of expatriation (i.e. sending home-country managers and employees to foreign locations), but also newer practices such as '… global teamwork, short-term international travel, short-term projects, international commuting, and frequent flying,[48] and even 'virtual assignments' (routine international job rotation schemes, 'commuter' projects).[49] While these kinds of jobs and work regimens require some of the same HRM activities as those in domestic operations, they also present more complex problems, including the need for more sophisticated employee skills (e.g. language, cross-cultural); additional human resource development and career plans; complicated international remuneration and performance management schemes; and a broader range of occupational health and safety issues (e.g. stress, fatigue, terrorism and security threats, deep vein thrombosis) and associated family issues such as 'intermittent spouse syndrome'.[50]

All of these aspects of SIHRM are discussed in more detail in the following chapters.

The following section explores the important relationships between organisational culture, strategy, structure and SHRM in all national or global markets.

Relationships between culture, strategy, structure and SHRM

Just as there is considerable debate about the relationship between corporate and HR strategy, there is also disagreement about the connection between HR strategies and organisational culture. Is culture effectively modified by HR strategy, or does culture drive strategy? There is, of course, no single answer to this question, rather many answers, depending on factors such as the size, nature, history and business context of the organisation.

The relationships between organisational culture and structure (its management levels, sectional arrangements and responsibilities) are similarly problematic. Are the ways in which organisations arrange themselves a significant influence on culture, or does existing culture determine the nature of such arrangements? If, for example, a company regards itself as a 'family' organisation, will it naturally divide into small semi-autonomous work groups with little formal structure? On the other hand, will the same company develop an informal, friendly culture as the result of a 'flat' structure with few management levels?

Organisational structure

A similar dilemma exists in the relationship between corporate strategy and structure.[51] Does the nature of an organisation's structure hinder or assist proposed business strategies, or do the strategies themselves determine the appropriate structure of the organisation? Current initiatives of enterprise and individual agreements, organisational reviews and the imperative for more effective and efficient production methods seem to suggest that strategies are in fact changing the nature of organisational structure. As examples of this, the drive towards improved productivity and efficiency in many organisations (strategy) has involved the removal of middle-management levels, the formation of semi-autonomous work groups and increases in management spans of control (structures).

The emergence of the 'new' (or e-commerce) economy based on information technology, and on fluid and changing notions of work and conditions of employment, is already challenging more conventional forms of organisational structure and culture, and thus provides a significant dilemma for HR strategists. This issue is discussed in detail in Chapter 2, but it is worth noting here that the management of the 'virtual workplace' will require far more complex and contingent approaches to the structuring of organisations and to the development of appropriate work cultures than have been formerly used. The establishment of structures that will both facilitate and control the performance of smaller numbers of employees who may work '… anywhere, any time … [the] car, [the] home, [the] office, even the client's office … alone, coupled, teamed … in real space or in cyberspace',[52] and then to nurture a supportive and productive culture to enable the achievement of organisational goals, is a major challenge for HRM professionals.

With respect to deliberate organisational change through restructuring, the trend away from hierarchical organisational structures towards leaner, customer-focused frameworks has been consistent in Australia over the last decade. In both HRM theory and practice, the notion of the 'flexible' firm has persisted, in order to achieve labour economies of scale, and to enable organisations to be more responsive to the demands of the internal and external environment.

One outcome of these pressures on organisations, in Australia and elsewhere, has been the development of the so-called 'flexible firm' model (see Chapter 2), which tries to combine cultural and structural change with enhanced labour flexibility, a crucial element in enhanced competitiveness and productivity. Developed at the Institute of Manpower Studies, University of Sussex (Atkinson, 1984–5), and further refined by writers such as Legge and Storey, this model suggests that productivity may be enhanced by several kinds of labour 'flexibility.' The increasing 'casualisation' of the workforce, especially in certain sectors of the Australian economy (e.g. hospitality, banking), together with increased 'contracts,' at the expense of full-time employment in many industry sectors, suggests that this model is gaining increased importance as a strategic structural solution to HRM issues, expanded more recently by the Australian federal government's *WorkChoices* legislation.

Organisational culture

What is organisational culture, and does it really influence organisational effectiveness? What role does the human resource specialist play in the development or modification of an organisation's culture towards its strategic objectives?

Numerous sociologists and industrial psychologists have conducted studies of the characteristics of national culture, religious culture and organisational culture. Hofstede defines culture as 'the collective programming of the mind which distinguishes the members of one group or society from those of another'.[53] Other writers refer to 'a system of shared perspectives or collectively held and sanctioned definitions' or, more simply, the customs, beliefs, practices, traditions, values and ideologies of organisations. Most cultures also have aspects of inclusion or exclusion of their members, rules and codes of conduct which govern member behaviours defining what is acceptable and what is not. Overall then, organisational culture includes such aspects as its philosophies, values, beliefs, work systems and practices, expectations and limitations on employee behaviour.

Examples of cultural issues in organisations might include dress codes, punctuality, formal (and informal) relationships between supervisors and subordinates, attitudes towards work and management, communication and participation. In one organisation or industry, hours of work may be rigid and enforced, in another quite flexible. Conflict between management and industry unions in one enterprise may be usual, while harmony and lack of union involvement is expected in another. The public sector in Australia has traditionally been more restricted by detailed policies and procedures than some of its private sector counterparts. Recent restructuring programs aim to provide more flexibility and discretion in this traditional culture.

Organisational culture is, of course, influenced by a large variety of factors, including the company's history, present management, size, structure, the nature of products or services, industrial relations activities and, above all, national culture. For example, US and Japanese national cultures influence the particular organisational cultures that develop in those countries. However, the type of culture which develops in companies such as IBM, McDonald's, General Motors or Remington will reflect these companies' particular histories, management styles and the nature of their industry. Similarly, in Australian industry, national culture strongly affects the attitudes of employees towards management (and vice versa), working conditions and expectations, and communication styles. But organisations as diverse as BHP, Telstra, the Australian Taxation Office and Sanitarium Health Foods have also developed distinct and identifiable cultures containing elements of national culture as well as those based upon their own industrial experience. The subsidiaries of multinational corporations often bear the cultural influence of their parent companies together with the influences of the countries in which they are located.

Writers such as Kabanoff have categorised all organisational cultures into four broad types:

- elite cultures
- meritocratic cultures
- collegial cultures
- leader-focused cultures.[54]

'Elite' cultures are 'top down' driven, while 'meritocratic' organisations involve heavy employee involvement and are equity based. 'Collegial' cultures assume cooperation and employee responsibility, while 'leader-focused' cultures require charismatic leaders and committed 'followers.' These cultures may develop over time as the result of organisational histories and structures, or they may be deliberately 'created' to enhance desired business strategies.

Both internal and external developments have necessitated major organisational changes to existing cultures aimed at greater flexibility, participation and overall effectiveness in a more competitive industrial environment. The reduction of middle-management levels (often called 'management delayering'), the streamlining of work processes, increased 'bottom line' accountability, and opportunities for employee consultation or participation have resulted in major modifications to organisational cultures.

The themes that appear to characterise the organisational cultures of the future, reflecting new global and industry requirements, include flexibility, agility, creativity, innovation, both quality and quantity aspects, responsiveness, high performance and a limited form of commitment from both employers and employees. As Parker and Inkson explain, this new form of organisational culture is likely to include a confusing and sometimes contradictory shift '… from long-term to short-term commitment, from non-contingent to contingent rewards, from company ownership to individual ownership of the career, and from permanent mutual loyalty to temporary opportunistic alliance'.[55] Organisations will be more likely in the future to assist the 'employability' of their workers rather than to guarantee their 'employment security'.[56]

In many cases, especially in e-commerce companies or where skilled employees are scarce, organisations may need to demonstrate their relative attractiveness to applicants, becoming the 'employer of choice' (see Chapter 6) by virtue of their more competitive cultures and conditions (e.g. share purchase schemes, autonomous work teams, exciting projects). In these cases the culture of these organisations will be determined as a compromise between the employer's needs and the employees' expectations within a competitive industry environment that may be local, national, or global. Goh and Fairhurst[57] describe such companies as having '… a shared understanding of company direction and brand promise; shared values and pride in the company; integrity; leadership, and a strong belief in product and service quality,' such as is demonstrated by The Ritz-Carlton Millenia Hotel (see 'Case 1: The Ritz-Carlton Millenia Hotel,' earlier in this chapter).

HR specialists have a major role to play in ensuring that an organisational culture conducive to the achievement of overall strategic objectives is developed and maintained. Lepak and Snell (1999) suggest that the roles of HR professionals in the management of culture change towards the achievement of desirable organisational objectives are broad and all-inclusive, involving the development of an 'HR architecture that aligns different employment modes, employment relationships, HR configurations and criteria for competitive advantage'.[58] Their analysis suggests that the task of the HR professional is both complex and contingent. The HR professional must ensure that the appropriate HR policies and systems are in place, that they are aligned with both organisational and employee goals, and that sufficient flexibility is built in to accommodate the changing needs of organisations and their employees.

Organisational and HRM policy

Policies are guides to action in organisations. They reflect management philosophies, principles and strategies, and form a bridge between strategies and operations.

In the complex web of interrelationships between organisational culture, strategy and structure, logic suggests that policies are developed to carry out chosen strategies and that they reflect cultural and structural realities. In practice, however, policies often precede strategic decisions and sometimes constrain them. Policies may be deliberately framed in order to modify organisational culture, or they may merely reflect it. Policies can be prevented by the structures of organisations or external pressures (legislation, awards, economic or social factors) or they may assist structural change. Policies can be broad (budgets, production levels, markets) or quite specific (study leave, accident reporting).

The Harvard model (see Exhibit 1.2) suggests that all HRM policies fall into four broad areas, namely:

- employee influence and involvement
- human resource flow
- rewards systems
- work systems.[59]

It further suggests that a strategic approach to HRM policy is fundamentally concerned with the reflection of management *choice* about how employees are managed – a choice about the nature of the employment relationship. Policy thus consciously reflects, or determines, organisational structure and culture, and puts overall strategies into practice.

There are, of course, many internal and external influences on the direction organisations may take with regard to their employees. Some of these aspects will be discussed in more detail in Chapters 2 to 4, but HR practitioners can choose to develop policies that will effectively reflect organisational objectives and ensure appropriate outcomes. We will use the above framework to examine HR policy in the context of contemporary Australian workplace relations.

Employee influence and involvement

The degree of employee involvement in organisational issues such as job design, work processes and conditions has been an issue for HR specialists since the early part of the 20th century, and both employees and their unions have begun to demand more employee involvement in many organisational activities. If HR policies are at least partially framed to influence organisational culture, then all policy statements can reflect organisational intent in the area of employee involvement. Thus, occupational health and safety, remuneration and rewards, training and development policies may include provisions for employee consultation with supervisors, or simply indicate who is responsible for allocating appropriate training courses.

Human resource flow

Policies in this area include recruitment, selection, appraisal, promotion, employment contracts, job security and retrenchment or outplacement – in other words, the movement (flow) of employees into, around and out of the organisation.

Central to HRM, such policies send messages to existing, new and departing employees about job security, productivity and teamwork expectations, and employee and organisational commitment. Thus, some organisations may choose to frame such policies indicating high organisational concern for their employees (e.g. promotion on merit, appraisal linked to career management, job security and voluntary redundancy). Others may prefer to keep employees 'on the edge' by a lack of job security (employment contracts rather than permanency), competitive promotional schemes and performance-based remuneration. The choice will depend on the nature of the organisation, its industry, desired outcomes, and cultural expectations of employees.

Reward systems

Arguably the most powerful messages to employees derive from employee rewards or remuneration policies. Do rewards, for example, recognise superior outcomes or merely reflect minimum requirements? Are rewards (income, benefits, careers) selective or universal? Do they incorporate employee commitment to organisational objectives or are they simply financial rewards for individual excellence? Appraisal schemes based upon direct financial rewards or bonuses often send the wrong messages to employees – quantity rather than quality is the criterion. However, in some cases (e.g. sales, production) they may prove very effective. HR policymakers need, therefore, to frame such policies in appropriate ways to reflect desired organisational outcomes.

Work systems

Policies in this area include job design, physical environments, and technical and information skills requirements. Messages sent encompass fundamental HR issues, such as the coordination between employees and their tasks, management concern for employees, and overall organisational efficiency in appropriately arranging tasks, functions and employees towards required outcomes. Thus, the important function of HR specialists is to frame policies that will both achieve organisational outcomes and ensure employee satisfaction, in association with other policies.

Human resource management – roles, functions and competencies

The roles, functions and strategies of HRM are many and varied, and depend heavily on the nature of organisations, the vision and skills of practitioners, and changes in the external environments of organisations. These aspects will be discussed in greater detail in subsequent chapters, but such features as organisational size, history and ownership, government legislation and political factors have a significant impact on the ways in which practitioners carry out their roles. The vision and skills of practitioners allow these influences to be seen as pressures and constrictions or opportunities and challenges.

The principal responsibility of HRM is to ensure that organisations have the right number, types and skill mixes of employees at an appropriate time and cost to meet present and future requirements. Thus, practitioners need to be aware of where organisations are going, the nature of the external and internal labour markets, and of the most effective strategies for matching labour demand and supply.

Practitioners need to operate at three distinct levels:

- strategic
- operational
- functional.

At the *strategic* level, practitioners are involved in corporate and human resource planning. At the *operational* level, they develop action plans to meet present labour needs. At the *functional* level, practitioners carry out the many activities that ensure employees are in the right place at the right time and for the right cost. All these roles will be examined in detail in subsequent chapters. As Dunphy suggests:

> HR management is about planning the optimum kind of workforce, hiring the best people, skilling them appropriately and shifting the mix of talent according to the demands of the marketplace. It is also about building a satisfied, productive and flexible workforce so that people like coming to work, are committed to their jobs and are prepared to innovate and change.[60]

Exhibit 1.7 resents the 'AHRI Model of Excellence' and its contribution to the achievement of an organisation's overall goals and objectives, as envisaged by the Australian Human Resources Institute. It sets out how skilled HR professionals can lead a business through a relevant body of knowledge to achieve human resource management solutions. In the model, HR roles include those of Strategic Architect, Stakeholder Manager, Workforce Designer, Credible Activist, Expert Practitioner, and Culture and Change Agent.

As Soo (2003) explains, SHRM '… has expanded to include issues that directly impact on an organisation's bottom line. These include improving productivity, quality of work life, workforce flexibility, enhancing legal compliance and, most important of all, gaining competitive advantage …'[61]

Exhibit 1.7 AHRI Model of HR Excellence

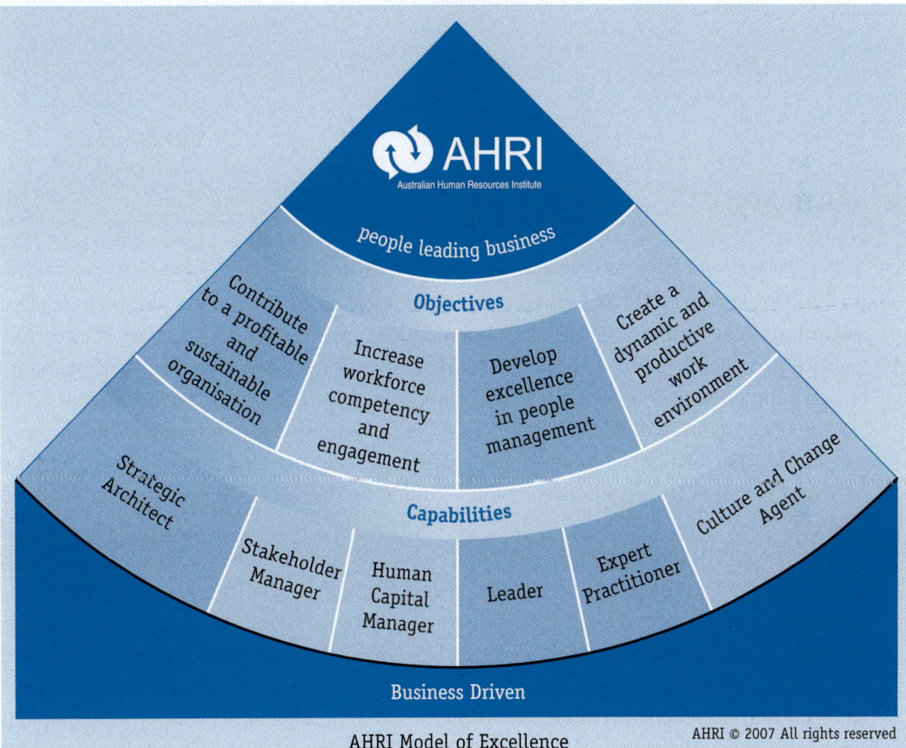

Source: AHRI Ltd 2007, www.ahri.org.au.

In the past it was usual for dedicated HRM professionals to assume the responsibility for all of these roles, with differing degrees of effectiveness. However, modern organisations recognise that HRM specialists neither possess all the required competencies to perform such broad roles, nor do they necessarily have the intimate knowledge of, or relationships with, employees in order to efficiently perform functions such as job design, recruitment and selection, human resource development, performance management, industrial relations and remuneration, especially at the workplace level. Thus, human resource management has become an organisational responsibility, shared between HRM professionals, middle and line managers, and sometimes external service providers, in the form of an 'HRM community' (Ulrich 1998), as illustrated in Exhibit 1.8.

While it is likely that organisations will differ in the ways that they allocate their strategic, operational and functional HRM responsibilities, depending on their history, ownership, industry type and relative expertise in these areas, the predominant HRM structures of many will conform with the above model, involving considerable communication and linkages between HRM professionals, middle and line managers, and external consultants. Professor Dexter Dunphy predicts that HRM professionals will become both a 'strategic partner' at senior executive level and '... an internal flying squad of change operatives',[62] while Elizabeth Gordon, Talent Director at Boeing, envisages that HR departments '... are likely to consist of a small strategic core supported by both internal HR generalists located close to the business, and outsourced HR specialists'.[63]

Exhibit 1.8   The HRM community

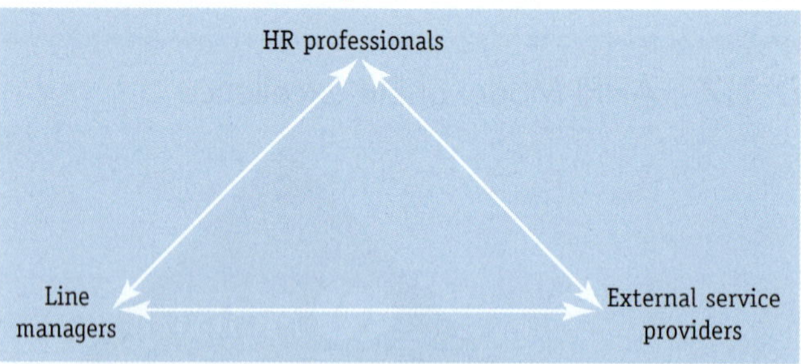

Source: Nankervis A. 2001. 'Restructuring the HR function: Strategic partnership or deconstruction?'
Human Resources Management Bulletin, CCH, Sydney, p. 10.

In this scenario, the roles and competencies of HRM specialists will include strategic planning, talent supply, 'vendor management' (i.e. the choice and control of external HR service providers), middle and line management training and support, management of the broad 'employment relationship',[64] and comprehensive HR auditing. Middle and line managers, on the other hand, will conduct their own job design, recruitment and selection; manage their employees' performance (including appraisals, job counselling and discipline); and monitor relevant remuneration and career plans, guided by overall HRM policies and supported by HRM professionals.

External HRM consultants will then provide specialised services such as executive or talent sourcing, some kinds of human resource development, HR information management systems (HRIMS – see Chapter 4), specific industrial relations advice, and payroll administration. Already, some large Australian banks and government departments have outsourced some, or all, of these HR functions, and BP has outsourced almost all of its HRM activities (payroll, recruitment, expatriation administration, records management, vendor management, and employee relocation services) in the US and UK to Exult.[65] The HR external service providers 'industry' is estimated to be worth more than A$55 billion globally, including such large consultancies as Kelly Services, Manpower, PriceWaterhouseCoopers, Accenture, Adecco, SHL, JobStreet.com, SyNet and Hudson.[66]

Exhibit 1.9 details the division of HR functions between line managers, HRM professionals, and outsourced specialists in this new 'HRM community.' It shows that a significant number of HRM processes (performance management, staff ownership of the organisation's strategy, knowledge management, team development, the facilitation of change management, leadership development, and workforce planning) have been, or are likely to be, shared with line managers in particular, and that the principal roles of HRM professionals will become HR measurement reporting, managing HR compliance, OHS standards, human capability profiling, HRD, strategic planning and induction. Some new research suggests that, contrary to previous assumptions, some line managers are '... keen to take on (HR) activities that relate explicitly to the development of their team'.[67]

Exhibit 1.9 Primary responsibilities for people management functions as mentioned by CEOs surveyed

Hr Functions	Line Managers	Human Resource Managers	Outsourced Specialists
Strategic HR planning processes	20%	77%	3%
Facilitation of change management	66%	33%	1%
HR measurement reporting	7%	90%	3%
Individual performance management processes	89%	11%	0%
Human capability profiling	15%	85%	0%
Leadership development	59%	40%	1%
Knowledge management	78%	21%	1%
Workforce planning	57%	43%	0%
Performance appraisal processes	59%	41%	0%
Recruitment and selection processes	41%	59%	0%
Induction processes	24%	76%	0%
Team development processes	69%	31%	0%
OH&S standards & policies	14%	86%	0%
Training & development programs	16%	81%	3%
HR compliance requirements	7%	90%	3%
Negotiating awards, EBAs & workplace agreements	22%	72%	6%
Risk management of human resources	28%	69%	3%
Staff ownership of the organisation's strategy	86%	14%	0%

Source: Mithen J., Edwards D. 2003. *HR: Creating business solutions*, Melbourne, AHRI-CEDA, p. 17.

Exhibit 1.10 below shows the comparative remuneration packages paid to HR Directors assuming new strategic roles, and Finance Directors, in a sample of global countries.

Exhibit 1.10 Comparative Remuneration Packages (HR and Finance Directors)

	HR Directors	Finance Directors
Country	Annual Total Cash (US$)	Annual Total Cash (US$)
USA	218995	324621
UK	202483	236607
Hong Kong	186586	212041
Australia	143431	175738
Singapore	155745	162931
India	55670	63806

Source: Adapted from Mercer HR Consulting 2006, 'Executive pay lowest in India,' *Human Capital*, April–May, p. 14.

The crucial issues in this new 'HRM community' are the capabilities of HRM professionals to assume their more strategic roles, with the associated business knowledge and skills; the willingness of middle and line managers to appreciate and accept HRM roles and functions; adequate provision of communication, training and support systems from HRM professionals to these managers; and clear and dedicated linkages between the professionals, line managers, and external service providers, in order to ensure the ongoing effectiveness of the entire HRM program.

Human resource management functions

HRM is concerned to resolve the following key issues:

- What quantity and quality of employees will be required now and in the foreseeable future to satisfy or exceed corporate objectives?
- Which strategies will be most effective in attracting, choosing and efficiently incorporating employees into the organisation?
- How can well-chosen employees be kept productive, satisfied and motivated to contribute to organisational growth and development?
- What methods are appropriate to maintain effective relationships between employees, jobs, work environments and management?
- Which strategies are required to ensure that all HR activities are linked and accountable?
- What systems are suitable for administering and evaluating the overall HR function?

The functional areas that constitute an HR program and contribute to the resolution of these issues include:

- human resource policy
- human resource planning
- human resource information management systems
- knowledge management
- work and job analysis, design and evaluation
- recruitment and selection
- diversity management
- career management
- employee and management training and development
- counselling, discipline and separation
- performance and quality management
- remuneration and benefits
- industrial relations management
- financial management of employee schemes and overall accountability and evaluation
- occupational health and safety.

These functions will be analysed in considerable detail in subsequent chapters, and will constitute the structure of this book. It is important to note that proactive/strategic human resource practitioners see their functions as parts of a whole or integrated approach. Each function should be clearly linked with all other functions in ways that are cost-effective and reflect organisational objectives.

Professionalism of human resource management

Due to changes in the workplace, in society, and among human resource specialists, human resource managers and their associations (e.g. the World Federation of Personnel Management Associations, Asia Pacific Federation of HRM, the Singapore Human Resources Institute, the Australian Human Resources Institute, New Zealand Institute of HRM) have begun to see themselves as part of a unique profession.

One of the characteristics of a profession is the development through research and experimentation of an organised body of knowledge. This knowledge is usually exchanged through conferences, seminars and workshops sponsored by professional associations. The latest information in the field is communicated through the literature published by professional associations, industry organisations and educational institutions (e.g. *Research and Practice in Human Resource Management* and *Asia Pacific Journal of HRM*). Other features of a profession include the establishment of a code of ethics (see the following section) and of accreditation requirements for its members. HRM can thus be seen as a credible and rapidly developing profession, although some observers suggest that its practitioners and professional associations will need to become more politically active in the future if it is to raise its public profile and that AHRI will need to police its codes of conduct more strictly. As an example, Professor Russell Lansbury, the Professor of Work and Organisational Studies at the University of Sydney, suggests that '… rather than criticise the (Australian federal government's *WorkChoices* legislation), … HR professionals in Australia … have been largely silent on the damage done to the nation's future workforce by the lack of a strategic vision for HR development and employment relations'.[68] While a contentious view, it illustrates the need for the HR profession to become more vocal and influential, individually and collectively, on such issues.

Ethics and HRM

A series of spectacular corporate collapses in Australia and around the world over the past several years have raised serious questions about the viability and relevance of the traditional roles of HRM. The unethical managerial practices that led to the collapses of Enron in the United States and HIH insurance, One-Tel and Ansett in Australia have signalled an urgent need for more integrity in corporate governance. A recent Aon Australia survey found that 'the impact of the Australian Stock Exchange best-practice recommendations on corporate governance (see later in this chapter) … and the introduction of International Financial Reporting Standards, as well as a myriad of other regulatory and compliance obligations, are top of the mind for Australian executives this year'.[69]

While corporate governance is usually the responsibility of senior financial managers in organisations, HRM is often seen as the most appropriate place for the 'ethical conscience' of an organisation to be located. The centrality of ethics in corporate governance makes HR the natural territory for ensuring integrity and ethics in the emerging strategies, behaviours and organisational processes. In many organisations, HR managers are being called upon to draw up blueprint ethical codes and standards of employee behaviour as well as implementing their compliance, and disciplinary and communication programs. Most HRM activities have an ethical dimension and therefore HRM should be the area where ethical culture is developed and cultivated. The contemporary issues of privatisation, re-engineering, mergers and diversity management present potential challenges for HRM managers that were not originally their responsibility.

Most people want to work for enterprises with high trust and a reputation for an ethical culture. Human resource roles such as recruitment and selection, staff development, enterprise bargaining, performance management, and workplace productivity improvements need an implicit and explicit underpinning of trust and ethics. Loss of this trusting culture leads to loss of reputation to attract the best people, markets and shareholder value. The importance of people as a source of competitive advantage becomes more evident as service oriented and knowledge based corporations dominate the economy. Recent corporate failures have contributed to employee demotivation, alienation and marginalisation, to the detriment of society.

In a study of HR professionals by Wiley (2000), the ethical codes of five US HR-related organisations were examined against six key 'stakeholder obligations.' The five organisations were the American Compensation Association (ACA), the American Society of Training and Development (ASTD), the International Association of Human Resource Information Management (IAHRIM), the International Personnel Management Association (IPMA) and the Society for Human Resource Management (SHRM). The six 'stakeholder obligations' were to employers, clients, colleagues, society, the profession and the professional societies. The study concluded by emphasising the need for a high level of integrity; respect for employees' rights and legal compliance; enhancing their professional competence; supporting the profession and not misusing professional affiliations; and guarding the confidentiality of privileged information, as illustrated in Exhibit 1.11.

It is now widely accepted that specific micro-level HRM practices are of limited value unless they are aligned to the macro-level 'big picture' frames of ethical reference. In issues such as downsizing, discrimination, confidentiality, anti-union practices, intellectual property rights, product safety, commercial dealings, negotiating techniques, and outsourcing, both macro-level and micro-level ethical principles need to be the guiding frameworks.

Exhibit 1.11   Five professional ethics items governing professional conduct in HRM

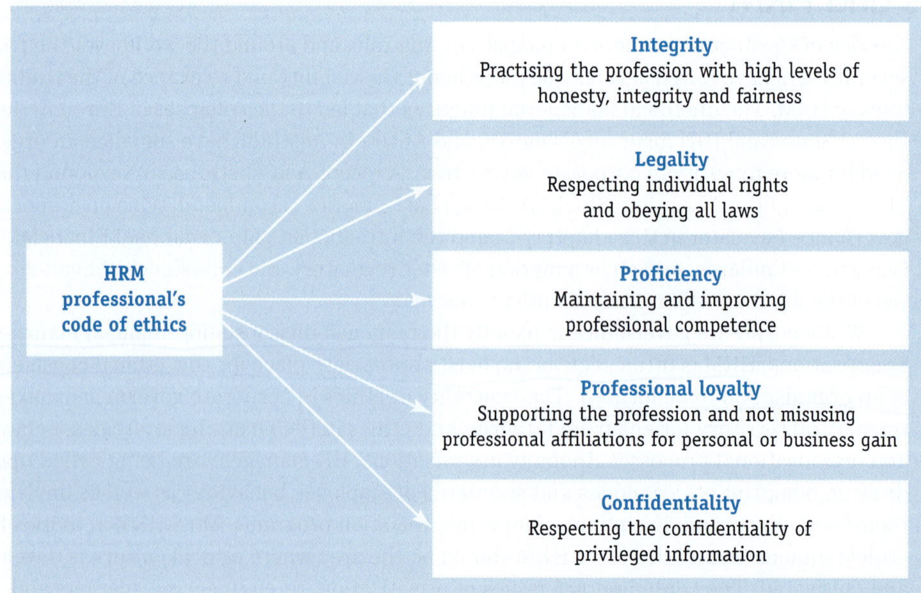

Source: Professor Samir Chatterjee, Curtin University of Technology.

Exhibit 1.12 Examples of HRM ethics

1 International and national human, civil and employment rights

2 Ensuring organisational and procedural justice for all employees

3 Compliance with legal and social responsibilities

4 Generation of social capital for common good through ethical conduct

5 Working conditions and occupational safety

6 Child labour, gender equity, sexual harassment, etc.

7 Differential pay and conditions of local expatriate staff

8 Dealing with 'whistle blowing'

Source: Professor Samir Chatterjee, Curtin University of Technology.

Some relevant examples of HRM ethical principles and issues are included in Exhibit 1.12. Strategic HRM, which views employees as a 'resource' to be utilised for meeting organisational purposes, raises many interesting ethical issues. How, for example, do such issues match with other contemporary imperatives associated with open communication, organisational development and change, empowerment, teamwork and 360° feedback? Lowry (2006) suggests that '… the recent industrial relations legislative changes in Australia (notably *WorkChoices*) arguably place greater responsibilities on HR managers, and raise issues related to the role they may or may not take in promoting fairness and justice within the workplace'.[70]

The establishment and promulgation of codes of ethical behaviour and standards of governance have been a popular response to the corporate scandals of recent years. But most codes are voluntary and unenforceable unless they are strongly aligned to the corporate culture. For example, Shell Oil Company uses performance management to integrate ethics and HRM.

In the final analysis, the principles of ethics may be similar around the world, but ethical practices are often culturally specific to a given society. For example, the HRM practices in China are dominated by the social *guanxi* (or reciprocity) and may appear unethical to many foreigners.

Summary

Human resource management is a complex and rapidly changing field of practice in Australian industry. Despite its comparatively recent origins, and drawing upon both overseas and local influences, HRM is a crucial factor in the success of Australian organisations.

Beginning in the 1940s as a series of functions, often neither integrated nor based upon solid conceptual foundations, modern SHRM is a dynamic specialisation in the process of refining its philosophies, practices and overall contributions to organisational effectiveness. In response to external influences, including legislation, award restructuring and enterprise bargaining processes, and to its own history, HRM is adopting a strategic approach to the management of human resources for corporate benefit. As with other professions, HRM confronts a number of difficult issues and dilemmas concerning ethics, roles, practices and the nature of its professional association. Further development of SHRM will eventually resolve these issues in creative and effective ways.

Key terms

employment relationship 11
'hard' HRM 12
human resource management (HRM) 4
personnel management 3
pluralist 11
'soft' HRM 12
strategic human resource management (SHRM) 13
strategic international HRM 23
unitarist 11
***WorkChoices* 3**

Key debate issues

1 The Australian federal government's *WorkChoices* legislation provides the perfect platform for the implementation of strategic HRM. Its managerialist bias enables organisations to benefit from greater employee flexibility and enhanced productivity.

2 Argue the cases *for* and *against*:
   a   the human resource specialist as manager of the employment relationship
   b   the human resource specialist as strategic business partner
   c   the human resource specialist as corporate ethicist.

3 HRM theories suggest that practitioners should devolve most functions to either line managers and/or external service providers, and focus on the organisation's cultural, structural, and change management issues. Discuss the benefits *and* disadvantages of this proposition.

4 'The globalisation of business demands new HRM models, systems and perspectives.' Discuss in relation to an organisation or industry of your choice. What are the roles of HRM professionals in strategic international HRM?

Student projects

1 Choose one journal article on the theory of strategic HRM from the United States, the United Kingdom (or Europe) and one from Australia (or New Zealand) and *compare* and *contrast* their explanations of the theory. If there are differences, why might this be so? In what ways are they the same? Is there 'one best way' in HRM, or does it depend on national or local factors? (Many suitable articles are included in 'Further readings' that follow.)

2 Draw up a set of ethical principles for an HRM function in a chosen organisation (without reference to examples in the text). Explain why these principles are important, and consider any practical dilemmas that they may pose for practitioners.

Exercise 1.1

Organisational and associated human resource strategies

Company A is a high-technology communications organisation entering a previously monopolistic industry. It is relatively small, financed by a consortium of multinational corporations, and aims to corner a specialised niche of the communications market. All staff have been recently recruited, and the company is keen to maintain an innovative, aggressive and flexible approach, with few levels of management, rapid internal communications and cost-effective procedures.

Company B is a large national confectionery manufacturer currently headquartered in Melbourne. It has previously been the market leader, but in the last few years its market share has been declining due to overseas competition. It plans to relocate its head office to Brisbane, to take advantage of less expensive overheads, and perhaps to reduce its manufacturing operations in Sydney and Melbourne. There are rumours that it may be taken over by a UK-based multinational. Some staff have already been offered redundancies, especially in middle-management positions.

Company C supplies computer support services to a broad and stable range of public service departments and statutory authorities. It has consistent, long-term contracts, and has regularly exceeded its profit goals. Employees are generally skilled, enthusiastic and productive. Turnover is unusually low, and morale appears excellent. Management has traditionally adopted a 'steady as she goes' approach.

Questions

1 Define the corporate strategy used by each company.

2 What potential issues and/or problems may be faced by each company in the near future?

3 What opportunities are available to each company, and how should they be maximised in the next few years?

4 Prepare an appropriate HRM strategy for one of the companies for the next one to two years.

Case study 1.1

Raffles International Limited

As the owner and operator of fine hotels and resorts, Raffles International delivers its promise of not only meeting but also regularly exceeding expectations. This plays a key role in fulfilling its credo of a hotel being more than its location, decor and amenities – a place where guests are treated so well that they want to come back. With its established brand name and excellent reputation, Raffles International is well recognised for providing the highest quality products and services.

Business strategy

Raffles International Limited is the hotel management subsidiary of publicly listed Raffles Holdings Limited. Its vision is to be the world-class Singapore-based company in the investment, operation and management of hotels and resorts, supported by a strong customer base and developing strong brand architecture under the Raffles International master brand.

In support of this vision, Raffles International Limited began to develop an international expansion strategy focused on obtaining a presence in capital and gateway cities in regions of Asia. To this end, it decided to acquire Swissotel Holdings AG at the cost of S$420.1 million. Through this acquisition, Raffles International gained ownership of the Swissotel brand and its trademarks and management contracts for 22 hotels including those of six majority or wholly owned hotel properties and minority interests in three hotels. The acquisition fits the group's strategic vision of obtaining a global 'footprint' through an enlarged portfolio of 38 hotels in 33 destinations that are business capitals, cultural centres and major leisure destinations. The acquisition of Swissotel achieves several of Raffles Holding's strategic thrusts – namely increased global reach, enhanced brand equity, economies of scale and 'value added' human capital.

Implementation of the acquisition process

Armed with a clear business expansion plan, Raffles Holdings set out to identify potential hotel operators for acquisition to complement its existing business. Once the target hotel operator was identified, Raffles Holdings immediately set up two task forces to conduct due diligence on the target hotel operator. The task forces were assigned according to specific tasks required in a due diligence exercise to ensure effective results.

One task force was specially assigned to look into the legal issues of each of the functional areas for their implication on the overall acquisition. This team, made up of key personnel from business development, finance, human resource, legal and sales and marketing locked themselves (away) with a myriad of files, documents, contracts, agreements, correspondence and notes to conduct detailed paper searches for any material evidence that would have an impact on or implication for the acquisition whether financially or operationally or legally. As this was a very daunting and challenging task, only the best people were deployed to this team.

The other task force was divided into project teams to gather as much information as possible on Swissotel in the respective functional and operational areas to aid the acquisition process. The project team comprising technical specialists in human resources, operations, marketing, finance and hospitality law were despatched to the various Swissotel operations spread across the USA, Europe/Middle East and Asia Pacific. These project teams were further complemented by Swissotel's Senior Regional Vice-President and the local general manager of the hotel in question.

Human resource management strategy and processes

In the case of the HR function, the following areas were carefully analysed and studied:

- employees' employment contracts and terms (e.g. notice of termination, severance pay, duration of contracts)
- employees' demographics, qualifications, skills, experience and competencies
- employees' remuneration details, costs of benefits and related costs
- pension and retirement plans and company's contractual agreements
- employer's liability – both written and implied
- agreements with unions and work councils.

Once the deal was concluded, management moved swiftly to integrate Swissotel's business, philosophies, people, policies, practices, systems and processes with that of Raffles International.

Communication

Tommy Ng said, 'We used emails, posters, dialogue and feedback sessions, committees and task forces, video tapes, telephone conferencing, state of hotel presentations and many informal settings to communicate our message but nothing beats face-to-face delivery.' To this end, the corporate HR team organised regular site visits, weekly teleconferences and quarterly video conferences to gather feedback and roll out systems, processes and initiatives. More importantly, corporate HR used these visits and conferences to strengthen relationships and create employee bonding. To further facilitate the communication process, messages were structured with consideration to sensitive issues such as culture, religion, anxiety, apprehension, language differences, different time zones and union and employee expectations.

Systems and processes

From a business standpoint, the group consolidated its global sales, distribution and marketing network and implemented uniform hotel operating standards and procedures. The integration of Swissotel allowed the group to realise synergies and create opportunities for shared services. The integration process further acted as a catalyst for the establishment and implementation of various systems and processes such as the customer relationship management (CRM) system, human capital management system (HCMS) and financial management information system (FMIS). These systems are the vital infrastructure to support the group's medium- to long-term business growth objectives.

People

The acquisition was that of an operating hotel and as such the employees in each operation were much needed to keep the operations functional. However, there was duplication of jobs in some areas such as Human Resources, where a team exists in both organisations. Raffles International was keen to promote a system of meritocracy and drove this philosophy by not making jobs redundant immediately. Job holders in duplicate jobs were reassigned and a period of six months was allowed for the incumbents to demonstrate their competence level, skills and knowhow. Being a Singaporean was not a criterion for retention and the final selection was based purely on merit.

Compensation and benefits

As much as it would like to streamline and harmonise policies and practices on compensation and benefits across the group, this was not always practical or feasible due to the difference in laws, cultures and norms. It was accepted that there would be differences across the group, but efforts were made to streamline practices within each SBU for control purposes. In one such streamlining exercise, it was discovered that some senior managers were paid above the market rate. This was subsequently streamlined to the standard of the company.

Other policies and practices

While it is preferred to keep HR policies and practices standard, the reality prevents such standardisation. Tommy Ng clearly understood this and issued a working strategy across the group to 'think global but act local.' This sensible approach helped make the integration process more seamless and lessened the resistance to change among employees.

Key success factors

And what were the three key success factors of a merger or acquisition? 'Strong leadership, communication and consistency on deliverables,' replied Tommy.

Source: Adapted from Case Studies Series 1/2003-11-13, *The Role of HR in mergers and acquisitions*, The Ministry of Manpower, Singapore, 4 September 2003, www.mom.gov.sg.

Questions

1 Outline the major business issues involved in this acquisition strategy.
2 Define the relevant HRM issues in the case.
3 Evaluate the effectiveness of the merger process, in both business and HRM terms.

Further readings

Baird M., Ellem B., Page A. 2006. *Human resource management: Strategies and processes – WorkChoices update*, Melbourne, Thomson.

Beer M. 1997. 'The transformation of the human resource function: Resolving the tension between a traditional administrative and a new strategic role,' *Human Resource Management Journal*, 36(1), pp. 49–56.

Beer M., Spector B., Lawrence P., Mills D., Walton R. 1985. *Human resource management: A general manager's perspective*, New York, Free Press.

Brewster C., Sparrow P., Harris H. 2005. 'Towards a new model of globalizing HRM,' *International Journal of Human Resource Management*, 16(6), pp. 949–70.

Hartel C.E.J., Fujimoto Y., Strybosch V.E., Fitzpatrick K. 2007. *Human resource management: Transferring theory into innovative practice*, Sydney, Pearson Education Australia.

Kulik C., Bainbridge H.T.J. 2006. 'HR and the line: The distribution of HR activities in Australian organisations,' *Asia Pacific Journal of Human Resources*, 44(2), pp. 240–56.

Losey M., Meisinger S., Ulrich D. 2006. *The future of human resource management*, Singapore, John Wiley & Sons (Asia).

Lowry D. 2006. 'HR managers as ethical decision-makers: Mapping the terrain,' *Asia Pacific Journal of Human Resources*, 44(2), pp. 171–83.

Macklin R. 2006. 'The moral autonomy of human resource managers,' *Asia Pacific Journal of Human Resources*, 44(2), pp. 211–21.

Nankervis A., Chatterjee S., Coffey J. 2006. *Perspectives of human resource management in the Asia Pacific*, Sydney, Pearson Education Australia.

Nankervis A., Compton R., Savery L. 2002. 'SHRM in SMEs: A general manager's perspective,' *Asia Pacific Journal of Human Resources*, 40(2), pp. 260–73.

Renwick D. 2003. 'Line manager involvement in HRM: An inside view,' *Employee Relations*, 25(3), pp. 262–80.

Sheehan C., Holland P., De Cieri H. 2006. 'Current developments in HRM in Australian organisations,' *Asia Pacific Journal of Human Resources*, 44(2), pp. 132–52.

Sheldon P., Junor A. 2006. 'Australian HRM and the *Workplace Relations Amendment (WorkChoices) Act 2005*,' *Asia Pacific Journal of Human Resources*, 44(2), pp. 153–70.

Whittaker S., Marchington M. 2003. 'Devolving HR responsibility to the line: Threat, opportunity or partnership?,' *Employee Relations*, 25(3), pp. 245–61.

Zanko M. 2003. 'Change and diversity: HRM issues and trends in the Asia Pacific region,' *Asia Pacific Journal of Human Resources*, 41(1), pp. 75–87.

Endnotes

1. In Wiesner R., Millett B. 2003. *Human resource management: Challenges and future directions*, Brisbane, John Wiley and Sons, pp. 293–4.
2. Lansbury R. 2006. 'Rethinking employment relations after WorkChoices,' *Human Resources*, 13 June, p. 8.
3. Dawson P., in Wiesner and Millett 2003, p. 306.
4. Bartlett C., Ghoshal S. 2003. 'Reinventing yesterday's managers,' *hrmonthly*, April, p. 13.
5. Ogier J. 2003. 'Advancing the profession,' *hrmonthly*, February, pp. 30–2.
6. Ibid., p. 31; Kelly D. 2003. 'A shock to the system? The impact of HRM on academic IR in Australia in comparison with the USA and UK, 1980–1995,' *Asia Pacific Journal of Human Resources*, 41(2), pp. 149–71.
7. Ogier J. 2003. op. cit., p. 32.
8. Hunt J. 2003. 'The anatomy of organisational change in the twenty first century,' pp. 3–4 in Wiesner and Millett, op. cit.
9. Erwee R. 2003. 'Integrating diversity management initiatives with strategic human resource management,' in Wiesner and Millett, op. cit., p. 59.
10. Kramar R. 2003. 'Changes in HR policies and practices: Management's dream come true?,' pp. 10–13 in Wiesner and Millett, op. cit.
11. Ulrich D. 2006, *Human Capital*, June, p. 3.
12. Rance C. 2000. 'Human resources – branching out to face the future,' *The Age*, 12 October, p. 1.
13. Willcoxson L. 2003. 'Creating the HRM context for knowledge management,' in Wiesner and Millett, op. cit., p. 72.
14. Grattan L. 2006, 'Social capital, innovation and the power of boundaryless cooperation,' *WorldLink*, 16(2), pp. 2–3.
15. Ibid.
16. Delahaye B. 2003. 'Human resource development and the management of knowledge capital,' in Wiesner and Millett, op. cit., p. 204.
17. Patrickson M., Hartmann L. 2001. 'HRM in Australia – Prospects for the twenty-first century,' *International Journal of Manpower*, 22(3), pp. 198–204.
18. Guest D. 1997. 'Human resource management and the legitimacy market,' *International Journal of Human Resource Management*, 8(3), p. 230.
19. Lees S. 1987. 'Human resource management and industrial relations,' *Journal of Management Studies*, 24(5), p. 504.
20. Baird M., McGrath-Champ S., in Kaye L. 1999. 'Strategic human resource management in Australia: The human cost,' *International Journal of Manpower*, 20(8), pp. 577–81.
21. Patrickson M., Hartmann L. 2001. op. cit.
22. Kaye L. 1999. 'Strategic human resource management in Australia: The human cost,' *International Journal of Manpower*, 22(3), p. 579.
23. Kelly D. 2003. op. cit., p. 150.
24. Lansbury R. 2006. op. cit., p. 8.
25. Legge K. 1995. *Human resource management: Rhetorics and realities*, London, Macmillan.
26. Martin-Alcazar F., Romero-Fernandez P.M., Sanchez-Gardey G. 2005, 'Strategic human resource management: integrating the universalistic, contingent, configurational and contextual perspectives,' *International Journal of Human Resource Management*, 16(5), pp. 633–59.
27. Tyson S. 1995. *Human resource strategy*, London, Macmillan, p. 30.
28. Rylatt A. 1999. 'Workplace learning: A new box and dice,' *Training and Development in Australia*, 26(3), June, p. 15.
29. Porter M. 1985. *Competitive advantage*, New York, Free Press.
30. Mithen J., Edwards D. 2003. *HR: Creating business solutions*, Melbourne, AHRI-CEDA, p. 5.
31. Chandler A.D., in Butler J., Ferris G., Napier N. 1991. *Strategy and human resource management*, Cincinnati, Ohio, South-Western, p. 18.
32. Ulrich D. 1998. 'A new mandate for human resources,' *Harvard Business Review*, January–February, pp. 128–30.
33. Tyson S. 1995. op. cit.
34. Legge K. 1995. op. cit., p. 172.
35. Martell K., Carroll S. 1995. 'How strategic is HRM?,' *Human Resource Management*, Summer, 4(2), p. 266.
36. Fisher C., Dowling P. 1999. 'Support for an HR approach in Australia: The perspective of senior HR managers,' *Asia Pacific Journal of Human Resources*, 37(1), pp. 1–17.
37. Tebbel C. 2000. 'HR just makes the grade,' *hrmonthly*, February, pp. 16–21.

38   Kramar R. 2000. 'Policies for managing people in Australia,' *Asia Pacific Journal of Human Resources*, 37(2), p. 52.

39   Howes P. 1999. 'Leveraging human resources effectively,' *hrmonthly*, November, p. 54.

40   Kramar R. 2000. op. cit.

41   Collins R. 2003. 'HRM in Australia', unpublished paper.

42   Sheehan C., Holland P., De Cieri H. 2006. 'Current developments in HRM in Australian organisations,' *Asia Pacific Journal of Human Resources*, 44(2), p. 141.

43   Ibid., p. 148.

44   Bamber G., Saffey R. 1996. 'Industrial relations reform and organisational change: Towards SHRM in Australia,' in B. Towers (ed.) 1996. *The handbook of human resource management*, 2nd edn, London, Blackwell.

45   Zanko M. 2003. 'Change and diversity: HRM issues and trends in the Asia Pacific region,' *Asia Pacific Journal of Human Resources*, 41(1), p. 84.

46   Welch D., Fenwick M. 2003, in Wiesner and Millett, op. cit., p. 36.

47   Brewster C., Sparrow, P., Harris, H. 2005. 'Towards a new model of globalizing HRM,' *International Journal of Human Resource Management*, 16(6), pp. 949–70.

48   Welch D., Fenwick M. 2003, in Wiesner and Millett, op. cit., p. 37.

49   Ibid.

50   Ibid.

51   Chandler A.D. 1962. *Strategy and structure: Chapters in the history of the American industrial enterprise*, Cambridge, MIT Press.

52   Department of Industrial Relations 1999. 'Work anywhere, any time,' *New Workplace*, 5(2), p. 1.

53   Hofstede G. 1985. 'Cultural dimensions in management and planning,' *Organisation Forum*, 1(1), pp. 12–31.

54   Kabanoff B. 1993. 'An exploration of enhanced culture in Australian organisations,' *Asia Pacific Journal of Human Resources*, 31(3), pp. 1–29.

55   Parker P., Inkson K. 1999. 'New forms of career: The challenge to human resource management,' *Asia Pacific Journal of Human Resources*, 37(2), p. 76.

56   Koh L.T. 2006. 'Employability and traits of Singaporean workers,' *Research and Practice in Human Resource Management*, 14(1), pp. 1–13.

57   Goh T., Fairhurst D. 2006. 'External image stands from internal drivers,' *11th World HR Congress 'Show Daily,'* 31 May, p. 5.

58   Lepak D., Snell S. 1999. 'The HR Architecture: Toward a theory of human capital allocation and development,' *Academy of Management Review*, 24(1), p. 32.

59   Beer M., Spector B., Lawrence P., Mills D., Walton R. 1985. *Human resource management: A general manager's perspective*, New York, Free Press.

60   Dunphy D., 1994. 'People wanted to manage people,' *Sydney Morning Herald*, 26 November, p. 27A.

61   Soo W. 2003. 'Strategic HR practices are here and now,' *Human Capital*, Singapore, SHRI, p. 14.

62   Dunphy D., 1994. op. cit.

63   Anonymous 2003. 'Tomorrow's people,' *hrmonthly*, June, p. 10.

64   Michelson G., Kramar R. 2003. 'The state of HRM in Australia: Progress and prospects,' *Asia Pacific Journal of Human Resources*, 41(2), p. 144.

65   Caudron S. 2003. 'HR is dead: Long live HR,' *Workforce*, January, p. 28.

66   Ibid.

67   Whittaker S., Marchington M. 2003. 'Devolving HR responsibility to the line: Threat, opportunity or partnership?,' *Employee Relations*, 25(3), p. 245.

68   Lansbury R. 2006. op. cit., p. 8.

69   Aon Australia 2006. 'Governance the biggest worry,' *hrmonthly*, June, p. 7.

70   Lowry D. 2006. 'HR managers as ethical decision-makers: Mapping the terrain,' *Asia Pacific Journal of Human Resources*, 44(2), pp. 171–83.

Online reading

INFOTRAC® COLLEGE EDITION
For additional readings and review on the evolution of human resource management, explore InfoTrac® College Edition, your online library.
Go to: www.infotrac-college.com and search for any of the InfoTrac key terms listed below:
➤ human resource management (HRM)
➤ personnel management
➤ strategic human resource management (SHRM)
➤ strategic international human resource management (SIHRM)

CHAPTER 2
THE CONTEXT OF HUMAN RESOURCE MANAGEMENT

The Australian Government's Intergenerational Report (IGR) projects that over the next 40 years, the proportion of the population aged over 65 years will almost double to around 25 per cent. At the same time, growth in the population of traditional workforce age – 15 to 64 – is expected to slow to almost zero. This will have a profound effect on the economy and, potentially, on our living standards.

Australia's demographic challenges, Commonwealth of Australia, 2004

While some HR managers may feel that the changes introduced by *WorkChoices* will give their companies an economic advantage, and even the capacity to be more internationally competitive, the danger is that the legislation may lead Australia down the low road, to a less skilled and less productive society.

Professor Russell Lansbury, 2006

Objectives

After reading this chapter, you will be able to:

1 Understand that human resource management operates within broader economic, social and political contexts.

2 Evaluate the current global and national economic and political contexts and the implications of each for strategic human resource management.

3 Recognise the impact of changing workforce demographics on the management of human resources.

4 Understand the significance of the shift in workforce participation and the implications for the development of human resource management policies and practices.

5 Explain the legal context of human resource management.

Introduction

As explained in Chapter 1, the essence of the Strategic Human Resource Management (SHRM) model presented in this text is the need to adopt a flexible and strategic perspective on the external environments of organisations to ensure 'fit' between HR strategies and business strategies. This chapter discusses those aspects of the external environment that currently impact on human resource management in Australia. As organisations do not operate in isolation from their environments, and as employees are drawn from these external contexts, this and the following chapter set the scene for the planning and practice of HRM (see Chapter 4).

There have been dramatic and significant shifts in the environment and external context in which HRM and business organisations operate and, arguably, some of these changes work in favour of the strategic HRM paradigm while others present new or ongoing challenges. The chapter begins with a consideration of the global economic context and its impact on the Australian economy. It then moves on to consider the changes in the labour market and the nature of employment in Australia. Here, the major demographic changes in Australia, including the ageing of the population, women's changing workforce participation and work–family and diversity issues are examined. In addition, the changes in employment relationships such as casualisation, outsourcing, offshoring and contracting are discussed as well as the pressures for flexibility. The chapter concludes with an overview of the political and legislative context for human resource management, while Chapter 3 examines the changing industrial relations context of human resource management.

The global economic context

A variety of political and economic events over the last few years have encouraged the convergence of different national systems and ideologies towards global market economies. At the same time, the emergence of local economies and cultures has seen forces for divergence, and even cross-vergence (that is, the transfer of management and HRM practices and techniques across the world). The collapse of socialist regimes across Eastern Europe in the early 1990s and the subsequent formation of the European Union (EU), the restructuring of the socialist economies of the People's Republic of China (PRC) and Vietnam, the resumption of Hong Kong and Macau by the PRC, and the surge, dramatic decline and gradual recovery of Asian economies over the last decade have resulted in aggressive competition on a global basis. Many observers predict that following the Asian economic crisis, India and China will emerge as the region's strongest economies.[1] To some degree, this prediction has already been realised, through the manufacturing and information technology sectors in China and India respectively, and many multinational organisations are leveraging on such developments to both grow their international markets and to restructure their global operations. As an example of this trend, IBM has recently increased its investment in India by US$6 billion, and Cisco Systems and Microsoft have expanded their Indian operations significantly, through new service delivery centres, innovation and research and development facilities.[2]

Globalisation is the term used to describe the increased pace of economic and cultural interconnectedness between different countries. The concept, however, is regularly challenged and debated, and there is considerable difference of opinion about the extent, cause and effect of globalisation. One of the main channels of globalisation has been the vast technological change that has enabled finance, information and goods to spread much faster than before. Additionally, the end of the Cold War and the spread of the political ideology of liberalisation have led, in some cases, to the removal of barriers to trade (e.g. APEC, the US–Australia free trade treaties), meaning that levels of foreign trade and investment have grown dramatically. There is general

agreement that globalisation is characterised by an expansion of markets and increased competition between companies and countries. Globalisation has thrust organisations into a more dynamic and competitive context and presented human resource managers with new and complex environments and challenges with regard to employing and managing workforces.

Growing competition has been evident in Australia's traditional markets (USA, UK, Europe), within the Asia–Pacific region, and even in Australia itself. The formation and growth of the European Union and the geopolitical grouping, and the Association of South East Asian Nations (ASEAN) have effectively excluded Australian companies from some export activities and joint ventures. While the establishment of the Asia Pacific Economic Cooperation (APEC) Forum and support from Japan and Malaysia for Australia's inclusion in ASEAN in the future holds some promise for Australian expansion into the Asia–Pacific region, the required reduction in tariff protection levels may disadvantage Australian organisations in the textile, clothing, footwear and automotive industries (see also Chapter 4). Since the early 1970s Australia's tariff structure for the textile, clothing and footwear (TCF) industry and the automobile sector have been under scrutiny. Dramatic reductions were made in the 1970s and 1990s and following reviews in the late 1990s and early 2000s by the Productivity Commission, further tariff reductions were proposed. However, after argument from trade unions and business that these industries may be disadvantaged with respect to regional competitors with markedly lower wage rates and conditions, the government announced a pause on tariff reductions in these industries. These debates highlight the increasing competitive pressure businesses face in Australia as well as the need to maintain reasonable standards of work and wages.

Although the influence of APEC has declined considerably since the Asian economic crisis (1997–8), Australian industry may be more significantly threatened in its increasingly competitive region by the rise of what some consider to be a new 'regionalism' in East Asia. Kelly[3] suggests that a new 'regional caucus,' comprised of the ASEAN countries, China, Japan and both North and South Korea, united by their 'Asianness,' may emerge to compete with Australia. Recent discussions within ASEAN, however, suggest that some opportunity for greater economic engagement between ASEAN and Australia and New Zealand may emerge over the next decade.[4]

In addition to political and economic pressures on Australian organisations, there has also been considerable penetration of internal Australian markets and entities by foreign competitors. Foreign interests have already taken substantial ownership of many Australian icons (e.g. Vegemite, Arnott's Biscuits, Tooheys, Speedo, BirdsEye, Peters, BTR Nylex, King Gee, Tom Piper and TNT) and incorporated many Australian hotels and resorts within their business portfolios.

The free trade agreement between the US and Australia, while controversial, is also of significance to Australia's international competitiveness. The agreement is said to improve access to, and facilitate trade with the US, Australia's largest trade and investment partner. The agreement reflects Australia's broad trade and economic interests by removing many barriers to the export of Australian goods to the United States. The aim of the agreement, on the Australian side, is to provide for a high degree of economic integration of both markets by creating immediate market opportunities in the US economy for various sectors of the Australian economy. The main sectors affected by the agreement include agriculture, manufacturing, services, financial services, government procurement, investment, telecommunications and e-commerce.[5]

With respect to human resource planning and management in Australia, these global pressures provide both challenges and opportunities. From the perspective of particular industries or organisations, key business products or services need to be identified, strategies refined, and the numbers and types of future employees (and their jobs) predicted. A global marketplace also greatly increases the potential labour pool, if organisations are prepared to operate internationally as well as locally. Furthermore, globalisation fosters the diffusion of human resource management practices within companies and between countries.

The Australian economy

The Australian economy fluctuates in response to domestic and global factors. In most recent years, the Australian economy has continued to perform well, despite some periods when international conditions were unfavourable. In particular, the economy continued on a path of growth during the Asian financial crisis of 1997 and 1998 and then through the recession in the US and Europe in the early part of this decade. Although the pace of growth has fluctuated, the Australian economy has been in expansion mode since 1991, making it a high performer when compared with other advanced countries. According to the Reserve Bank of Australia, average real growth of the economy in the past 10 years has been just under 4 per cent, exceeding the growth of most advanced economies but lower than the rates in regional countries such as China and India.

As a snapshot of the Australian economy in the period 1996–2006, inflation has increased from 3.1 per cent to 4 per cent; Gross Domestic Product (GDP) has increased; unemployment has fallen markedly from 8.4 per cent in 1996 to 4.8 per cent in 2006 (500 000 people); and company profits (per cent of GDP) have risen from 26 per cent to 30 per cent.[6] Approximately 63 per cent of Australians are reported to be in employment or actively looking for work, compared with nearly 80 per cent in China, 69 per cent in Singapore, 68 per cent in Canada, 67 per cent in New Zealand, 66 per cent in the United States, 63 per cent in the United Kingdom, and 60 per cent in Japan.[7]

The following section explains how industries and jobs have been changing in response to these global and national economic trends.

Changing industry and occupational structure

As in most developed countries, Australia has seen extensive change in its industry composition over the last few decades. The Productivity Commission reports that Australia's rate of structural change has been somewhat greater than the average for a selection of 15 OECD countries, although it has been below that of other countries in the region, including New Zealand.[8]

A combination of technological, economic and political factors has contributed to the changing distribution of employees across industries, as demonstrated in Exhibit 2.1.

In the past, Australia's agricultural sector was the most dominant sector of the economy, but by the middle of the 20th century manufacturing had taken this role. From the 1970s onwards, the services sector became the most dominant and important sector of the economy. According to the ABS, the service sector is '... the largest component of the Australian economy in terms of number of businesses, employment and gross value added'.[9] Services are now the fastest growing sector of the Australian economy, employing more than 75 per cent of the workforce and contributing more than 70 per cent of Australia's gross domestic product (GDP).[10] Comprised of retail, trade, property and business services, health and community services, and education, it is forecast to grow at an annual rate of 5.8 per cent over the next five years.[11] This phenomenon is common to all advanced economies. For example, 88 per cent of the US workforce is employed in the service sector.[12] Interestingly, but perhaps not too surprisingly, in Australia, there is almost equal representation of males and females in the services sector, with a relatively high proportion of part-time employees (34 per cent).[13]

Exhibit 2.1 Industry employment

INDUSTRY[1]	Employment	Employment Change				Projected annual jobs growth to 2010–11	
	Feb 2006	5 years to Feb 2006		2 years to Feb 2006			
	'000	'000	%	'000	%	'000pa	%pa
Accommodation, Cafés and Restaurants	480.6	11.5	2.5	9.5	2.0	9.0	1.8
Agriculture, Forestry and Fishing	360.2	–70.2	–16.3	–12.7	–3.4	1.1	0.3
Communication Services	181.5	–1.3	–0.7	8.4	4.9	2.1	1.1
Construction	878.6	221.9	33.8	98.9	12.7	15.1	1.6
Cultural and Recreational Services	269.3	45.2	20.2	29.1	12.1	5.9	2.1
Education	737.3	113.8	18.3	33.2	4.7	6.6	0.9
Electricity, Gas and Water Supply	87.0	21.0	31.8	13.9	19.0	–0.9	–1.1
Finance and Insurance	366.8	31.5	9.4	19.2	5.5	1.9	0.5
Government Administrative and Defence	451.9	79.7	21.4	5.6	1.3	5.1	1.1
Health and Community Services	1 035.2	156.3	17.7	68.7	7.1	31.6	2.8
Manufacturing	1 069.6	–36.6	–3.3	0.8	0.1	–5.9	–0.6
Mining	127.1	49.3	63.4	27.3	27.3	–0.2	–0.2
Personal and Other Services	396.9	55.1	16.1	26.3	7.1	8.5	2.0
Property and Business Services	1 205.6	117.0	10.8	87.8	7.9	30.4	2.3
Retail Trade	1 486.9	169.8	12.9	52.4	3.7	30.7	1.9
Transport and Storage	461.5	41.5	9.9	26.4	6.1	3.9	0.8
Wholesale Trade	425.5	–2.0	–0.5	–19.9	–4.5	–3.8	–0.9
Total (all industries)[2]	10 041.2	997.8	11.0	452.2	4.7		

[1] Industries are Division level of the Australian and New Zealand Standard Industrial Classification (ANZSC)

[2] Trend data, totals do not add

Source: *Australian Jobs 2006*, Department of Employment & Workplace Relations, copyright Commonwealth of Australia, reproduced by permission.

Exhibit 2.2 shows projected employment growth, especially in the service sector.

Another aspect of the transformation of the Australian economy, in line with the growth of the services sector, is the emergence of what has been called the 'new economy.' The new economy, also referred to as the 'knowledge' or 'information' economy and considered by some to be the vanguard of the services sector, is very evident in Australia. As mentioned earlier, the Australian economy grew at an average annual rate of around 4 per cent between 1996 and 2006. However, several industries grew faster than the economy-wide average. The fastest growth occurred in many of the industries identified by the OECD as knowledge intensive industries. For example, the communications sector grew at a rate of 10.4 per cent, while property and business services grew at a rate almost double the economy-wide average. Close examination of Exhibit 2.2 also demonstrates the growth of the knowledge economy. Technical specialists and professionals are in demand but clerical–administrative and processing jobs are in decline. In addition, the new economy has highlighted skills shortages in both professional and trades occupations, consequent on both associated technological and industry training developments. A recent survey conducted by the Recruitment and Consulting Services Association (RCSA) indicates that the 'Top Ten' occupations with skills shortages include non-building professional engineers, electrical trades (building), business professionals, building professionals, carpenters and joiners, and plumbers.[14]

Exhibit 2.2 Projected employment growth 2006–11 (top 10 industries)

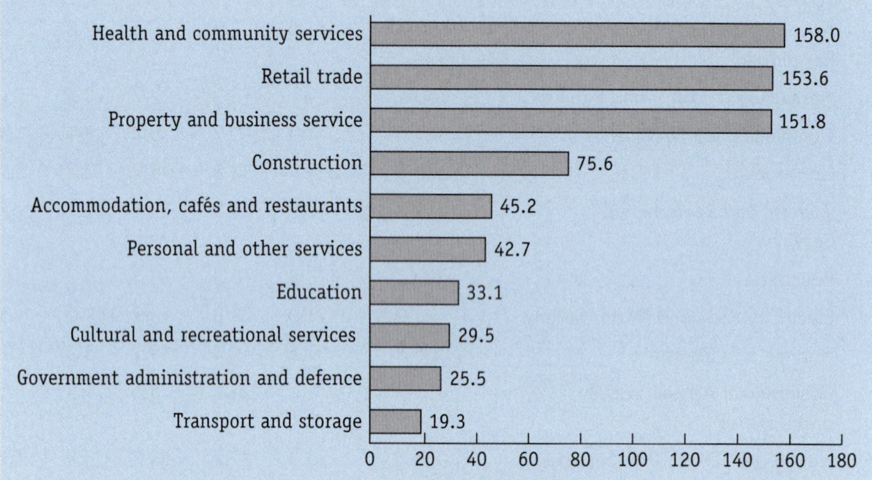

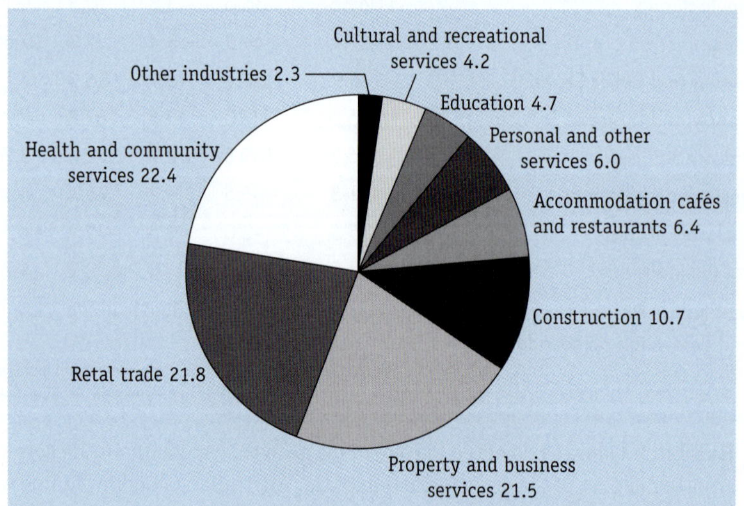

Source: *Australian Jobs 2006*, Department of Employment & Workplace Relations, copyright Commonwealth of Australia, reproduced by permission.

In addition to these industry shifts and structural changes, the impact of new technologies has often been to transform or even replace traditional industries with more flexible organisational forms, resulting in significant staffing implications. As examples, video shops, travel agencies, florists, and even pharmaceutical and medical services, have been complemented or replaced by Internet services, staffed by fewer and more specialised service providers, either onshore or offshore. News report 2.1 illustrates the effects of such organisational changes on traditional airline–travel agency–hotel relationships.

Jetstar to jettison agents via traveller booking site

Jetstar plans to cut out the middleman by letting travellers design and book holiday packages across its international and domestic network. The airline, which is due to unveil its international fares, will let passengers use 'dynamic packaging' technology to book flights, hotels and cars. They will then get the holiday at discounted package rates.

Chief Executive Alan Joyce said the airline hoped to introduce the international dynamic packaging later this year or early next year. 'That's something we've been working to build up. We've launched our Jetstar Holidays with technology on our website that packages domestic holidays. There are major system enhancements coming.'

Meanwhile, Indian software giants Tata Consultancy Services and Satyam Computer Services are neck and neck to win an application services deal with Qantas. With an estimated value of US$80 million (A$106 million), the contract covers the 300-person internal department that develops software for the airline.

Source: Adapted from Steve Creedy 2006, 'Jetstar to jettison agents via traveller booking site,' *The Weekend Australian*, 22–23 July, p. 33.

These developments have changed the landscape in which Australian organisations, and their human resource professionals, operate. The implications of these changes for human resource planners will include a need for innovative remuneration programs, talent management and retention techniques, attractive career paths, job and work redesign, and more flexible work schedules. In the leisure and hospitality industries in particular, HR managers will need to develop more integrated human resource management practices to ensure continuing productivity and profitability. Other relevant issues will include increasing skills flexibility, horizontal rather than vertical career mobility, and new industrial relations agreements.

Changes in the workforce and the nature of employment

Australia's population has now passed 20 million people and the workforce numbers approximately 10 million.[15] The composition of this workforce has changed in the past 20 years, especially in terms of age and gender distribution, and these changes have implications for all aspects of the management of human resources, from attraction through to selection, retention, development, remuneration and performance management. The following sections discuss the impacts of age, gender, education and the increasing consideration of employment conditions on HRM strategies and processes.

Age distribution

Worldwide, changing population profiles, in particular the ageing of the population, have become a critical issue of public debate and policy with significant implications for workforce planning, organisational HR policies and employees' quality of life. The ageing of the workforce is an important issue in all developing countries (e.g. the United States, United Kingdom, Japan, Australia, New Zealand and most EC countries), while it is less of a problem in countries such as India, Indonesia and Thailand which have considerably younger age profiles. As an example, more than 36 per cent of the Australian labour market was aged 45 years and over.[16]

The increase in fertility rates – or the 'baby boom' – that occurred after the Second World War created a substantial increase in Australia's population. Those born during this boom (1946–64) constituted a bulge in the age distribution of the population. As members of this group began to reach employment age during the 1960s, they created a similar bulge in the workforce. However, this generation is now approaching retirement age at a time when mortality rates and fertility rates are low. These trends signify a dramatic shift in the demographic shape of Australia's population[17] and present policy-makers and HR planners with a complex problem of an ageing and shrinking workforce if natural replacement alone is relied upon. In Australia, the total fertility rate (i.e. the average number of children a woman would have during her lifetime) is currently just over 1.7. This figure is down from 3.6 calculated at the height of Australia's fertility and is well below the rate needed to simply replace the existing population. However, this phenomenon is not restricted to Australia. Recent global evidence suggests that:

> within Europe, the number of workers aged between 50 and 64 (is expected) to increase by 25% over the next 20 years, while those aged between 20 and 29 will decrease by 20%. In the US the number of workers aged 55 to 64 will have increased by more than half by 2012 … (and) in Japan, almost 20% of the population is already over 65, the highest share in the world.[18]

The dual forces of the ageing of the population and declining fertility rates have emerged as significant policy issues, with implications for public policy as well as organisational policy. According to Peter McDonald (one of Australia's leading demographers), 'retention of people in the labour force as they get older, that is, a reversal of the trend to early retirement – is now a commonly recommended strategy to deal with ageing'.[19] This issue was the focus of a major federal government report released in early 2004. Entitled *Australia's demographic challenge*, the report canvassed, among other issues, the need to attract and retain older employees to the workforce and to adjust organisational policies and practices accordingly.

The changes in workforce participation rates among males and females, youth and aged, present a highly textured pattern of change. In Australia and throughout OECD countries over the last 30 years male labour force participation rates have declined while female participation rates have increased. The pattern is especially marked for older workers. In Australia, for example, in 1973, 88 per cent of males 55 to 59 years were in the labour force, compared with 72 per cent in 2006.[20] By contrast, labour force participation rates for married women in this age group increased from 20 per cent (1968) to 57 per cent (2006).[21]

The problem of Australia's, and indeed the developed world's, ageing workforce is usually expressed as one of labour force dependency, that is, the ratio of non-workers to workers. This ratio has altered considerably, with expectations being that in the next 20 years there will be a growing proportion of non-workers dependent on workers. In 2001, 12 per cent of Australia's population was over 65 and it is estimated that by 2020 this figure will rise to 18 per cent.[22] By 2030 it is predicted that at least 25 per cent of the Australian population will be 65 years and older and according to Peter McDonald, the 'ageing of Australia's population between 1970 and 2030 represents a very fundamental, historical demographic change'.[23]

In this context the issue of age discrimination becomes relevant. Age discrimination refers to 'any prejudice or discrimination against or in favour of an age group'[24] and potentially may affect employees at any stage of the HR cycle, that is, in selection for jobs or training, promotion, redeployment and performance appraisal. In Australia, legislation prohibiting age discrimination in employment exists in all Australian states and territories. It also exists in the Commonwealth jurisdiction with the *Age Discrimination Act 2004* making age discrimination unlawful in key areas of public life including employment and education.

While age discrimination as a concept is applicable to both older and younger workers, the ageing of the Australian workforce outlined above suggests that the issue may have considerable

resonance with the management of older workers. Although it is unlawful in most jurisdictions to discriminate on the basis of age, McDonald argues that there 'will be a need to change existing negative attitudes of many employers to older workers. Older workers must be seen as valuable workers. This means a shift in the psychology of employers but also a shift among older workers in the way they see themselves ...'[25] Teh suggests that 'management must view older workers as a discrete group with needs distinct from those of younger workers and as being integral to organisational productivity and profitability'.[26]

Other commentators suggest that workforce planners and HR professionals will need to face the increasing reality of intergenerational conflict in the workplace, due to the coexistence of four different generations – namely, 'veterans, baby boomers, Gen X and Gen Y. Each generation has its own values, view of career, learning and development, family, work–life balance, sense of loyalty, and expectations of leaders and the work environment'.[27] Consequently, HR policies need to be adjusted to take account of these issues and the requirements of an increasingly diverse workforce.

Some organisations have already adjusted their HR policies and practices. In Singapore and Hong Kong, labour-scarce service operations (e.g. McDonald's, Delifrance) have actively recruited 'seniors' both to fill job vacancies and to use the skills developed through experience. Proctor & Gamble has developed a dual career model for different workers and uses Yourencore.com to source experienced staff on demand; American Express and Deutsche Bank utilise intergenerative teams; and BMW's Leipzig (Germany) production site recruits only staff over 45 years old, using ergonomic design in its production systems.[28] Royle argues that in some instances these organisations may exploit the insecurities of older workers in order to access a more compliant workforce.[29]

In February 2004, Treasurer Peter Costello released a paper outlining the federal government's specific plans to deal with the changing Australian demography.[30] The treasury paper specifically considers the ageing population and argues that higher rates of economic growth can only be achieved by older people remaining in the workforce longer and by further deregulating the labour market to ensure people work harder and more efficiently. According to the Treasurer, Australian workplaces and the Australian workforce are likely to be very different in the future, with a large increase in the number of older workers and a strong demand for part-time work or flexible working hours.

This reconfiguring of the age distribution of the workforce has major implications for employers and HR planners as the interests of a workforce with diverse needs will need to be accommodated within the increasingly competitive environment in which business operates.

Women and work?

It has been argued that the 20th century was characterised by a separation between the economic and social spheres of life, where the corporation and men dominated the economic sphere, and family and women dominated the social sphere.[31] Similarly, Bailyn and Fletcher[32] argue that Western society was divided between the separate spheres of work and home and from this dichotomised structure emerged the notion of the 'ideal worker',[33] who was assumed to be a full-time male employee, and around whom pay, conditions, working time and organisational policies were based in most industrialised countries. In Australia, this model was epitomised in the Harvester decision of 1907 (*Commonwealth v Mckay*, 6 CLR 41) in which Justice Higgins of the Industrial Relations Court determined the living wage of a male with a wife and three children. While the historical context may have made this appropriate, this is no longer the typical family model in Australia.

Today, the 'male breadwinner model,' with the male in full-time employment and the female as the full-time housewife and carer is under question and the gendered construction of paid work and unpaid domestic work that largely dominated organisational thinking in the past is now under intense pressure to change. By 2002, the 'male breadwinner model' was the least common pattern in Australia, with only 27 per cent of couple families with dependents fitting this model. The dual earner family, either with the full-time working male and part-time working female, or dual career couple, is now the norm.[34]

Over the last 20 years, for example, female labour force participation rates have risen from 45 per cent to 55 per cent.[35] By contrast, the male participation rate stands at 77 per cent, down from 82 per cent 20 years ago. Women now constitute approximately 47 per cent of the total workforce and 42 per cent of the unionised workforce. Importantly, for the issue of work and family, 70 per cent of women in the prime child-bearing years (25 to 34) are in paid work. Further complicating the difficulties of balancing work and family for employers and employees, both males and females, is that 48 per cent of mothers are now in paid work and 45 per cent of mothers with children under the age of six are in the paid workforce. Offering flexible working hours and leave arrangements, improving paid maternity, paternity, parental and carer's leave entitlements, providing child care and elder care facilities and accommodating the return to work needs of women after childbirth are all issues confronting organisations and human resource managers in contemporary Australian society.

In response to the challenges presented by the increasingly blurred boundaries between the two spheres of home and work, some Australian organisations have introduced a range of human resource management policies which are variously referred to as 'family friendly,' 'diversity' and 'work–life' policies.[36] As Whitehouse and Zetlin argue, 'in a fundamental sense the most family friendly policies are … adequate wages, job security and the absence of work intensification,' but family friendly policies are typically considered more narrowly as organisational 'initiatives designed to facilitate the balancing of work and family commitments'.[37] They include leave provisions, flexible hours provisions, child (and elder) care provisions and support measures such as counselling and referral services. The Whitehouse and Zetlin study of Australian workplaces found that the provision of comprehensive work and family policies was uneven, particularly in the private sector. In another study examining the organisational characteristics associated with the provision of work and family polices, Bardoel found that 'large organisations with good track records in human resource management are more likely to provide work–family benefits'.[38]

Despite the increasing interest in and provision of work–family and work–life policies in organisations there remains concern about the ability of traditional institutions and policies to provide for a better balance between work and family. The changing demographics and social patterns have given rise to some important theoretical debates about women, work and family, which are having influence over Australian policy-makers within governments and organisations.

Following extensive focus group research on how employees with families manage the work–family-life interaction, Barbara Pocock[39] suggests that Australia has reached a critical stage where as a result of our traditional employment institutions and organisational values remaining unchanged, they now *collide* with the changed behaviours and expectations of employees and their families. She argues that work has essentially been designed for the 'care-less,' that is, those without immediate and direct responsibility for caring for others, but that this is no longer tenable given the changing involvement in paid work described above. While many Australian organisations profess to be family friendly, Pocock argues that the reality is more akin to 'the family-friendly/unfriendly iceberg': a small tip with good, workable policies, a large group below the surface that have not as yet addressed the issue or made appropriate changes.

Another theory which has attracted considerable attention is Catherine Hakim's Preference Theory.[40] Hakim, a British sociologist, hypothesises that based on their preferences, rather than their behaviour, women fall into three categories. Home-centred women, who represent approximately 20 per cent of women, have the home and family responsibilities as their major

preference, while another 20 per cent are work-centred, and these women put work and careers first. The largest group, which is approximately 60 per cent of women, is classified as 'adaptive,' and will move between home and work depending on the policy arrangements in place. It is argued that because women constitute a heterogeneous group, no single 'one size fits all' public policy is appropriate. In Australia, this approach has been used by the Howard government as justification for introducing a non-specific maternity allowance for all women, rather than a specific paid maternity leave scheme targeted at working women and recognising their dual roles in production and reproduction.[41]

Adopting a broader and integrated approach to work and family, the 'Dual Agenda' theory of Rapoport, et al.[42] argues that more than the introduction of family friendly policies is needed to meet organisational goals for efficiency *and* employee needs to balance work and family. In a similar vein to Pocock, this theory argues that current working practices are based on gendered assumptions of the male being the paid worker and the female providing home-based unpaid work. As discussed, this does not accurately represent the division of labour between women and men in advanced contemporary economies, and consequently a thorough questioning and altering of the assumptions underlying the organisation and allocation of work is required. In particular, questions such as 'Who is the "ideal worker"?' and 'What is "real work"?' need to be asked. The examination of such questions by organisations is most likely to come under the umbrella of human resource management, as they deal with the issues arising from the attention being focused on work and family today.

Maternity and parental leave in Australia

When many employees in market economies are time-poor, one of the most pressing policy concerns at national and company levels is family leave, including maternity, paternity and parental leave. While Australian federal workplace relations law (*Workplace Relations Act 1996* (Cth)) provides for 52 weeks unpaid parental leave, there is no universal provision for paid maternity leave, except for federal and state public servants. Federal public servants have had access to 12 weeks paid maternity leave since 1973, but the provision varies widely for state public servants. For example, Victoria and Tasmania provide for 12 weeks, New South Wales nine weeks and Queensland six weeks paid maternity leave for public servants. During 2002 the Human Rights and Equal Opportunities Commission (HREOC) brought the need for paid maternity leave to the public's attention and released a recommendation for a national paid maternity leave scheme for Australia.[43]

By international standards, Australia and the US are outliers, being the only two OECD countries without universal paid maternity leave protection for working women. As a result, in Australia, approximately 60 per cent of working women do not have access to paid maternity leave. For those who do have access to the entitlement through either public sector employment (where, as noted above, there is some legislative provision), or via awards, enterprise agreements or company policy, there is considerable variation in the provision.

One way of gaining paid maternity leave, as an employment entitlement and in addition to the government's recently announced maternity allowance (Budget 2004), is via enterprise bargaining, but as Baird, Brennan and Cutcher argued, the outcomes are highly variable and very few agreements provide the International Labour Organisation (ILO) standard of 14 weeks paid maternity leave.[44] The most recent data on paid maternity leave in enterprise agreements shows that progress through bargaining is still relatively slow and only 10 per cent of current agreements contain a paid maternity leave clause. However, since the heightened attention the work and family issue has received, there have been some promising moves in enterprise bargaining in terms of improving paid maternity leave entitlements, such as in the higher education sector (e.g. the Australian Catholic University and the University of Sydney).

Rather than negotiating improved entitlements with unions, some companies have unilaterally introduced improved conditions in company policy. IBM, for example (see News report 2.2), recently introduced 12 weeks paid parental leave, available for male and female employees. This is a significant improvement over the six weeks paid maternity leave and one week paid paternity leave formerly available. Although evidence to date suggests that men do not use parental leave widely,[45] the emphasis on work and family issues and women's and men's changing social roles may catalyse more men into taking parental leave, especially if it is paid. Business case arguments which stress the need to attract and retain valuable and scarce employees are usually employed to help justify such improvements in company policy. As shown in News report 2.2, Holden Australia claims that its 14 weeks paid maternity leave policy has greatly increased retention rates, validating the scheme's introduction.

NEWS REPORT 2.2

IBM Australia extends paid parental leave

Wednesday 17 March, 2004, 7.47 p.m. AEST

IBM has expanded the parental leave entitlements for its 10 000 Australian employees.

Under the company's new policy, the primary caregiver is entitled to 12 weeks paid parental leave. The entitlement is also available for adoption and to same sex couples.

Employees can also take the leave for up to 24 weeks at a reduced rate of pay and there is no qualifying period before they can have access to the leave.

Workers had previously been entitled to six weeks paid maternity leave and one week of paid paternity leave.

IBM said in a statement that 97 per cent of its female workers who take maternity leave return to work at the company. Some 30 per cent of the IBM workforce is female.

Alison Spencer, IBM Australia's manager of organisational culture and change, told *Workplace Express* that the company worked hard to attract and retain the best people. The extension of the leave provisions would help the company's attraction and retention, but was moreover 'the right thing to do.'

The company didn't expect to be overwhelmed by demand from male workers to take paid parental leave, she said. But she was aware that some men wanted to be more actively involved in parenting.

Many male employees were making extensive use of flexible work options to look after elderly parents, pick up children and fulfil their duties as single parents and she expected that in time more men would take on the role of primary caregiver.

Source: www.workplaceexpress.com.au.

NEWS REPORT 2.3

Paid maternity leave at Holden a retention winner

Wednesday 12 May, 2004, 5.53 p.m. AEST

Holden Ltd's introduction of 14 weeks paid maternity leave has had a dramatic effect on mothers' return to work rates – lifting them from 65 per cent to 100 per cent, according to the company's HR director.

Andrea Grant, who is on the company's board, told a session on women and work at the AHRI conference in Melbourne yesterday that Holden had been one of the first manufacturers to introduce paid maternity leave.

She had sold it to the board on the basis of the clear business case in favour of it – which had now been borne out.

Grant said the ground-breaking paid maternity leave provision, introduced in September 2002,

was part of a suite of measures to improve flexibility for employees.

The company had also introduced a 48/52 purchased leave scheme.

Grant herself has purchased an extra two weeks leave and hopes in the future to increase that to four weeks. The extra leave was important to her and other women because it removed 'mother guilt' – she now knew she would get a week off with the kids every nine or 10 weeks.

Asked whether at her senior level she could control her working hours, Grant conceded it had been difficult and that it had taken three years (since her appointment in 2001) and a lot of work to get to the stage where she felt she could manage her hours.

The key for her, Grant said, was to surround herself with a strong HR team and develop a good HR structure.

She said the younger generation of employees – including men – were seeking more flexibility in working arrangements, but that it had been a struggle at times to have managers embrace giving their staff more flexibility over working hours and working from home.

She cited the example of a young engineer who a couple of years ago wanted to work four days a week so that he could avoid putting his child into child care. The proposal had 'created an uproar' with the executive director of engineering digging in his heels in opposition.

But the director, Tony Hyde, had come around to the idea 'and now he flies the flag' on flexibility in his department, according to Grant.

She told the forum that Holden also faced a considerable renewal challenge because of its ageing workforce. Half of its senior people intend to retire in the next five to 10 years, she said.

Source: www.workplaceexpress.com.au.

Women in management

Although female participation rates have increased (as discussed above), women hold a very small percentage of the crucial decision-making roles in the organisations. Only 14 per cent of general managers are female, with about 22 per cent in middle management. The 2003 Equal Opportunity in the Workplace Agency (EOWA) census revealed that women hold only 8.8 per cent of executive positions in core business areas, which are the main feeder group for CEO and board positions. The representation of women on boards is no better, with EOWA reporting that women hold only 8.4 per cent of available board positions.

While these figures indicate an improvement in the work status of women, they still represent a major challenge for increasing opportunities for women at the highest levels, especially given that Australia is behind both Canada and the United States in the advancement of women in the workplace. In Australia, the situation is much better in the public sector where one in three board members is female. This is in stark contrast to the one in 10 in the private sector.

Despite the fact that anti-discrimination legislation, equal opportunity and affirmative action concepts have been around for 20 years, and that every Australian jurisdiction has embraced anti-discrimination legislation, change on the ground has been slow. This would indicate that time and legislation are not the complete answers to the problem. There is a need to question underlying assumptions about the division of work and an analysis of the systemic organisational barriers to women's advancement issues is also required. Career planning with a focus on the retention and advancement of women is paramount. Breaking down traditional workplace arrangements and allowing for flexibility is also the key to assisting the advancement of women to higher levels. Firms such as Deloitte Touche and Tomatsu have specific HR programs targeted at increasing opportunity for women at higher executive levels.

The representation of women at higher levels of organisations is not the only inequity faced by women in the workplace. Pay equity is also an issue that should be high on the agenda of firms seeking equality in the workplace. The 2003 EOWA census revealed that women's wages are usually only 84 per cent of men's wages. In the past, Australia's centralised wage fixing system assisted in regulating the gap between men's and women's wages, and while it was widely thought that decentralisation would increase wage inequities, for a complex variety of reasons, this has not occurred. One of the reasons is declining male wages at the lower end of the labour market, thus compressing the differential between average wages of males and females. For human resource managers and practitioners this issue is specifically related to job evaluation systems (see Chapter 5), which in the past have not adequately recognised the gendered distribution of work and tasks within organisations, often resulting in 'women's jobs' being undervalued.

Rising education levels

One of the most significant social trends is the rising educational level of employees. The parliamentary paper on the changing Australian demographic mentioned earlier in this chapter acknowledged that Australia's society is now more educated and better skilled than it was 40 years ago. Statistics provided by the ABS support this assertion. In 1993, 10.1 per cent of the population aged 15 to 64 had an undergraduate degree. This figure increased to 18.1 per cent in 2003.

Rising education levels, however, provide other difficulties, or opportunities, for HR planners. The more educated the workforce, the more employees demand fulfilling jobs, career progression and higher salaries. On the other hand, some employers have discovered that their employees are suffering from literacy problems which affect their performance. It has been estimated that between 10 per cent and 15 per cent of the workforce is semi-literate.[46] These problems for both employers and their employees may require literacy programs at the workplace. The challenge for HR managers and planners is to identify the future needs of each organisation and its employees and to ensure that they will effectively serve the long-term interests of the organisation while satisfying their own demands for job satisfaction, career opportunities and rewards.

Changes in work and employment patterns

Major changes in the working lives of Australian employees occurred during the last two decades of the 20th century, and these changes are both a cause and consequence of changing human resource management. The changes in the patterns of work were concentrated around three areas: jobs, hours of work and wages. The theme underlying each of them was flexibility. There were calls from employers and government for increased flexibility in the labour market, increased flexibility in working hours and increased flexibility in payment systems.

Flexibility

Flexibility in all aspects of the employment relationship has become the driving force for the restructuring of many organisations in Australia, New Zealand and throughout Asia, in order to assist in their change processes towards enhanced productivity, greater efficiency and effectiveness, and global competitiveness. Facilitated by government policies and industrial relations reforms (notably *WorkChoices*), flexibility initiatives have underpinned programs such as the introduction of new production systems, the reorganisation of jobs, the introduction of teams, downsizing, the devolution of HRM processes to line managers, individual contracting, outsourcing and contracting out of work. These changes have been theorised in a number of ways. One well-known model is Atkinson's[47] 'flexible firm model'

which distinguishes between core and peripheral workers. This model is shown in Exhibit 2.3. Core workers typically have access to valuable human resource policies; whereas peripheral workers, increasingly of casual or contract status, have limited or negligible access to the organisation's human resource policies.

Exhibit 2.3 Atkinson's 'flexible firm model'

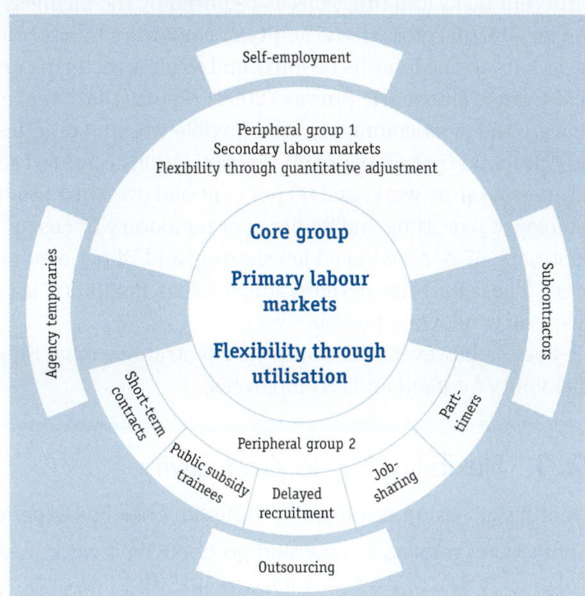

From the employer's perspective, the flexible firm allows the employment of staff under variable conditions, for different purposes and periods, and with quite disparate expectations. While 'core' workers may be employed on a permanent basis with generous rewards and benefits, others may be on renewable annual contracts, or on 'voluntary reduced worktime,' especially in seasonal industries, or on a casual, part-time or short-term contract. Other occasional staff may be employed by external agencies, outsourced or subcontracted. Decisions about the way in which an organisation's workforce should be configured are central to human resource planning, job design and work organisation, and depend on the business goals and strategies, as well as the nature of the firm's labour markets (tight or loose), and their core and peripheral work functions.

In recent years, industrial relations changes have facilitated the transformation of the organisational 'landscape,' to include five identifiable components of the workforce – namely, a shrinking proportion of permanent (or 'core') employees, supplemented by temporary staff, consultants, contractors and outsourced service providers.[48] The last four groups of employees are often referred to as the 'contingent workforce,' as they complement the core functions of organisations, and are usually employed on different terms to permanent employees, and may be employed by external service providers. A recent study estimates that the contingent workforce 'represents approximately 20 per cent of the average company's workforce,' and suggests that 'organisations that have determined how to recruit the right people, retain them past retirement age, and keep them engaged, motivated and productive, will realize distinct competitive advantages'.[49]

Australian employers have generally pursued three main forms of flexibility: numerical, functional and hours. *Numerical flexibility* refers to the ability to change the number of employees to suit the peaks and troughs of business. Considerable numerical flexibility has been achieved through the employment of casual and part-time workers, which has become a significant and growing employment trend in Australia over the past two decades and is discussed further below. *Functional flexibility* refers to the ability of employees to work across a variety of different tasks and functions as required by the business operations. Hours or *working time flexibility* refers to the ability of employers to alter the standard working hours of employees, to extend the lengths of shifts and to alter rostering arrangements.

The recent Cranet-Macquarie Survey (2006) reports that 'weekend work, shift work and overtime were the most commonly used flexible working practices used in Australian organisations'.[50] It found that 80 per cent of organisations required some weekend work, 70 per cent used some shift work, and 90 per cent had overtime provisions. In addition, 97 per cent employed part-time and 94 per cent temporary or casual staff; 74 per cent utilised fixed-term contracts; 57 per cent used job sharing; and 74 per cent employed staff on fixed-term contracts.[51] These findings perhaps suggest that 'flexibility' is perceived more from the employer's than the employees' perspective.

Exhibit 2.4 below, however, illustrates the HR strategies that Shell Australia has developed to facilitate flexibility for itself and its employees.

Exhibit 2.4   Flexibility, key to productivity

With a 105-year history as an employer in Australia, Shell has experienced many changes in the policies and procedures relating to how staff go about their work. Today's workforce of around 3 200 employees work anywhere from oil rigs to the office, retail service stations to refineries, trucks to terminals, and hotels to homes. In an increasingly global business, staff can be required to travel with their role or to work outside traditional '9 to 5.' Not to mention the desire from staff to have a sound work–life balance.

Shell Australia's flexible work policy is the result of an agreement reached between an employee and their line manager. If a role is suitable for flexible working, health, safety security and environment advice is provided to ensure staff will be working safely and ergonomically. It was discovered that with some planning and 'thinking outside the box,' many roles could be performed in more flexible ways than first thought, whether it is working 'non-traditional' hours, working partly from home, or working part-time. It was all about a change in culture from a supervisor, employee and peer perspective. Supervisors now appreciate that just because staff can't be 'seen' doesn't mean that they aren't working.

'Flexible work arrangements result in more satisfied staff which in turn leads to greater productivity,' said Shell Australia Chairman, Russell Caplan. To further assist employees, particularly in the work–life balance equation, a number of family friendly initiatives have been established. These include a dedicated child care facility in Melbourne where fees can be salary sacrificed, assistance with securing child care places in other locations where Shell has facilities, up to 12 weeks paid parental leave, carers/family leave to enable care for relatives or sick children, and study leave.

Source: Adapted from Anonymous 2006, 'Flexibility, key to productivity,' *The Age*, 29 July, p. 5.

Working hours

Another major change that has occurred in the working lives of Australians in the last decade is in relation to hours of work. In short, people in jobs are working longer and harder: 'The definition of what counts as the working day, the working week, has been profoundly reshaped during the last decades.'[52] This is particularly noticeable in the concept of the standard working week, that is, the 35- to 40-hour week. In 1990, 42 per cent of workplaces operated on standard hours but by 1995 this had declined to 31 per cent of workplaces. Research by the Australian Centre for Industrial Relations Research and Training[53] found that during the 1990s more than 50 per cent of full-time employees were working more than 49 hours per week, but by 2004, average weekly hours were estimated to be 45 for full-time male and 41 for full-time female employees.[54] The number of workplaces with extended hours of operation had increased as had the use of the 12-hour shift, especially in wholesale and retail trades. There was also an increase in the number of hours of overtime worked by Australians, with much of this unpaid, especially for white-collar employees.[55] These statistics are unable to factor in the amount of unpaid and unrecorded work undertaken by employees from their cars and homes, as a result of their use of computers and mobile telephones.

While the increasing flexibility of working hours provides managers with greater discretion over the allocation of work, it also impacts on employees, and the so-called benefits are now being contested. Although for some employees the flexibility of hours increases their ability to combine work and family, there is now growing recognition that this flexibility favours employers more than employees and is leading to work intensification and increased stress in the home and family.[56] This situation appears to have been exacerbated in the wake of the Australian federal government's *WorkChoices* legislation.

In a recent study, some 48 per cent of respondents claimed that more and more was expected of them. Sixty-eight per cent indicated that increasing work demands hindered their efforts to maintain a healthy work–life balance. From the organisation's perspective, work–life strategies continue to help the bottom line, with turnover down by 4.5 per cent, absenteeism by 3.5 per cent and return from parental leave up by 24 per cent.[57]

Casualisation

One of the major methods employers have used to achieve numerical flexibility has been to decrease the proportion of permanent employees and to increase the number of casual employees. Casualisation has become one of the most significant trends in the Australian labour market over the last decade or so. The increasing proportion of part-time (those workers who work less than 35 hours a week) and casual workers is largely associated with the growth of the service sector, the deregulation of the workplace, an increased number of women in the workforce, and the introduction of new technologies.

According to the ABS, the recent trend towards part-time and casual employment is a continuation of a longer term trend. Its statistics reveal that the number of persons employed part-time increased by over half (51 per cent) in the 10 years since October 1991. Over the same period, full-time employment increased by only 11 per cent. As a result, the proportion of total employment represented by part-time employment has increased from 22 per cent in October 1991 to 28 per cent in October 2001.[58]

A report by the Chifley Research Centre investigated this phenomenon and revealed that one in four Australians is now employed on casual terms.[59] The report also revealed that while casual workers are working for short periods in limited term jobs, there are many long-term casual employees in ongoing jobs. These employees are missing out on most of the important employment conditions and have limited access to other rights and forms of leave. One of the main problems with having such a heavy reliance on casual workers, apart from the human resource implications, is the inevitability of a deteriorating skills base, lower workforce stability and higher turnover costs. The Chifley report states that this is both inefficient and inequitable.

While creating opportunities for increased flexibility in the workforce, the casualisation of labour puts forth yet another challenge for HR practitioners in ensuring that the rights of these workers are met.

The new employment contract

Changing industrial relations legislation, the decollectivisation and decentralisation of industrial relations, the rise of individualised employee agreements, fixed term contracts and significant increases in part-time and casual employment have led to a remaking of the employer–employee relationship and increasing concern among employees about their job security. In Australia, these changes have largely been fuelled by government and employer demands for higher productivity and greater flexibility in the hiring and allocation of labour, most recently through the federal government's *WorkChoices* legislation. As a consequence, it is now widely acknowledged that the employment relationship has undergone considerable change over the last 20 or so years. Earlier employment relationships emphasised job security protected by strong unions and an institutionalised industrial relations infrastructure, long-term careers, promotion based on employee loyalty and commitment and employee benefits such as annual holidays, sick leave, generous superannuation, standard hours, overtime and penalty rates. Emerging employment contracts have scaled down these employee 'entitlements' severely, and now consider many of them to be negotiable rather than assured. As Kelly (2000) laments, '… concepts such as the family wage and the 40 hour week, which once seemed to be engraved in stone, have been swept unceremoniously away'.[60]

The political and legal context of employment in Australia

The Howard government and its predecessors under Hawke and Keating have, to varying degrees, emphasised the need for Australian industry to restructure its operations towards increased efficiency, enhanced product and service quality, and greater levels of national and organisational productivity. Restructuring has involved substantial micro-economic reform to remove traditional work processes and practices, to streamline production systems and distribution processes, and to adopt modern technological developments, to achieve these aims. These necessarily entail major changes to the work ethics, working conditions and overall cultures of all Australian organisations. Federal and state governments have also promoted the importance of quality enhancement and quality accreditation standards with the establishment of the Australian Quality Awards and international quality accreditation institutions.

Furthermore, significant changes to Australia's industrial relations system over the last 10 years at the federal level and in most states have led to increased diversity in employment arrangements, work practices and wage outcomes. The emphasis of the neo-liberal political philosophy has been on individualism, contractualism, choice and voluntarism in the employment relationship.[61] This has underpinned many of the legislative changes introduced in industrial relations legislation throughout Australia and which are discussed in more detail in the following chapter. The following section presents the contemporary framework for employment law in Australia. It has been contributed by Associate Professor Kevin Brown of the School of Business Law, Curtin University of Technology, Perth.

The legal context

In addition to understanding the economic and social contexts, human resource managers must be cognisant of the legal context. Law in Australia originates from two main sources: common law and statute law. *Common law* is the law created by judges and is identified by reading the decisions of judges. These create precedents that are binding on judges and magistrates in lower courts. *Statute law* on the other hand is law that is made by parliament, and in Australia there are six state parliaments, two territory parliaments and one federal parliament. Employment law is no different and the laws concerning employment emanate therefore from both common law and statute law, and in all the jurisdictions mentioned above. Consequently, there is a plethora of legislation covering the employment relationship. First, we shall consider the common law, and then statute law.

Federal workplace relations and state-based industrial relations legislation are discussed in detail in Chapter 3. These statutes coexist with the common law of employment. For approximately two-thirds of the Australian workforce, the terms and conditions of work are determined by awards, enterprise or individual agreements, which are formally regulated, codified and supplement the common law contract. The processes by which this is done in Australia and New Zealand are discussed in Chapter 3.

Common law

There are two main areas of common law where judges have made decisions that are pertinent to employment. They are contract law and negligence.

In contract law, decisions about who is or is not in an employment relationship is determined by the courts, based on precedent cases. Thus, early cases indicated that the nature of the relationship is determined by control and is explained as a relationship of mutual trust. The issue of whether a person is an employee or an independent contractor continues to be a continual source of litigation.

In the area of negligence, the courts have held that employers owe their employees a duty of care by virtue of their relationship. This duty is one that requires the employer to attain a standard expected of a reasonable employer. This has translated by case law into what a reasonable employer would provide in areas such as a safe system of work, safe premises, safe equipment and competent fellow employees. Failure to meet this standard will indicate a breach of the standard expected and any injured employee who can show the damage suffered such as loss of wages, medical expenses, pain and suffering or lost opportunities can sue for this loss provided that the loss is not too remote or fanciful. This is commonly referred to as a common law claim for damages, and most employees who are severely injured would consider pursuing such a claim.

Statute law

The other main source of employment law in Australia is statute law. The topic of employer and employee relations has long been the focus of the political divide between conservative and labour-oriented governments and this is often reflected in government approaches to employment statute law. There are many statutes that apply to employees. They cover:

* compensation in the event of injury (see Chapter 11)

* occupational safety and health (see Chapter 11)

* long service leave

* minimum conditions and superannuation

* legitimacy of trade unions

* mechanisms for dealing with industrial disputation

* provision for collective agreements, individual agreements and for the recognition of existing awards that contain terms and conditions of employment (see Chapter 3).

Exhibit 2.5   Relevant federal legislation

* *Workplace Relations Act 1996* – sets up the legal and administrative framework for the federal industrial relations system and includes the *WorkChoices* amendments that came into operation in 2006.

* *Occupational Health & Safety (Commonwealth Employment) Act 1991* – prescribes regulations and standards for the health and safety of employees.

* *Racial Discrimination Act 1975* – prohibits discrimination on the grounds of race anywhere in Australia.

* *Sex Discrimination Act 1984* – prohibits discrimination on the grounds of sex anywhere in Australia.

* *Disability Discrimination Act 1992* – prohibits discrimination on the grounds of physical or mental disability anywhere in Australia.

* *Age Discrimination Act 2004* – prohibits discrimination on the grounds of age anywhere in Australia.

* *Human Rights and Equal Opportunity Commission Act 1986* – sets up the principal legal and administrative framework overseeing equal opportunity at the federal level.

* *Equal Employment Opportunity (Commonwealth Authorities) Act 1987* – provides for a system of equal opportunity in relation to employment by federal agencies.

* *Income Tax Assessment Act 1936* – is the principal income tax statute.

* *Superannuation Industry (Supervision) Act 1993* – prescribes standards to be met by persons administering superannuation funds in Australia.

* *Workplace Relations Amendment (WorkChoices) Act 2005*

Exhibit 2.5 lists the relevant federal legislation pertaining to these issues. It is important to remember that legislation is enacted by state and federal governments. The exhibit lists federal legislation only.

Workers compensation

During the industrial revolution, when workers in Britain moved from agricultural work to work in factories, it became apparent that a significant number of employees in these factories were suffering injuries. These were usually a result of the activities within the factories. The British government passed legislation in 1897, which was refined in 1906, that required employers to pay compensation to their injured workers, whether or not there was any fault on the part of the employer or any employee (see also Chapter 11). This is known as 'strict liability' and generally workers are not excluded from a claim, even if they failed to take care themselves.

This style of legislation was adopted in the early 20th century in most state and territory jurisdictions in Australia and the federal government has passed similar legislation to deal with employees employed by the federal government and for seamen. However, the details of these statutes and how insurance is approached, and how much compensation is available, differs through the various jurisdictions.

Typically, the legislation requires a 'worker' (which often includes not only employees but independent contractors) who suffers a harm (typically described as an 'injury by accident') that is connected with their work to be paid compensation for lost wages and payment of medical expenses arising from the injury. Legislation has for some time provided lump sum payments to workers who have been injured and suffered a permanent loss to those parts of the body specified in the legislation. As certain diseases were identified as being caused by work-related activities involving certain processes or dealing with certain materials, such as asbestos, the legislation has evolved to provide compensation to employees who suffer a variety of industrial diseases, without necessarily having to prove a connection between the disease and the work-related cause of the disease. (See Chapter 11 for more details.)

Occupational safety and health

Until the mid-1980s safety issues were dealt with by legislation on the basis of relatively minor prescriptive regulations. These laws were aimed at shops, factories and some particularly dangerous activities such as timber mills and mining. Typically, they provided for relatively minor fines. A review of similar legislation in Britain resulted in a report by Robens that led to the introduction of general duty legislation, more commonly described as 'duty of care' legislation (see Chapter 11).

Each state and territory, as well as federal legislation for Commonwealth employees and maritime workers, provides for significant criminal penalties against employers, employees, self-employed persons, people in control of premises, manufacturers, suppliers, constructors and designers in relation to activities that may harm health or safety at places where people work. The legislation does not require a person to be injured or harmed for a breach to occur, although prosecution authorities are more likely to secure larger penalties from a conviction when a death or serious harm has occurred.

The legislation imposes opportunities for notices to be issued to improve or prohibit unsafe activities. Either inspectors or health and safety representatives, depending on the jurisdiction involved, issue these notices. The legislation typically provides that health and safety representatives are elected by employees to represent their issues and concerns and to bring such issues to the attention of management. Sometimes, this notification is achieved through the creation of safety and health committees. The sanctions in the legislation concentrate on fines but some states have introduced imprisonment for cases involving gross negligence causing death and others are considering alternative methods of bringing attention to the breaches that occur (e.g. industrial manslaughter – see Chapter 11).

Long service leave

Somewhat peculiar to Australia, each state and territory provides three months paid leave to employees after 15 years of continuous service. There is a pro-rata amount after 10 years in certain circumstances, including termination by the employer. Various agreements may alter these entitlements and some employees in the public sector obtain three months leave after seven years. In the construction industry, legislation in each state allows for portability of the entitlement by requiring employers to contribute into a central managed fund, even if the employee only works for that employer for a short period.

Summary

The economic, political and social environments, and the changes in these described in this chapter, highlight the dynamic context in which human resource management operates and some of the challenges. A strategic approach to human resource management requires practitioners to understand the external context of the organisation and the environments of their workforces.

Globalisation has led to increased competition and pressure on organisations to use their human capital as effectively and productively as possible and to compete in global markets for customers as well as employees. Transferred to the national context, these competitive pressures have seen successive governments introduce policies to re-regulate and deregulate the labour market, effectively increasing the prerogative of managers in relation to employment matters and enabling organisations to develop more specific human resource policies. While not all organisations respond strategically, arguably the opportunity is there in the current political environment for human resource management to take a proactive position on these issues.

Changes in the demographics of the population and the workforce, notably ageing, challenge human resource managers to seek ways to provide for the transitions in people's lives as they move from full-time work to retirement, or as they combine work and family responsibilities. This issue is also prominent in relation to the increasing participation rates of women in paid work. As women need to combine their reproductive and child caring roles with paid work, governments, employers and human resource managers also need to provide appropriate policies to enable employees to balance work and family. Men's roles, too, are changing. Combined with changed social attitudes, future generations of male employees may be expected to contribute more to caring responsibilities.

Ironically, however, just as business and human resource managers have advocated that employees are an organisation's most important and valued resource, employees have been subjected to increasing job insecurity, longer working hours, work intensification and workplace stress. One of the dilemmas for Australian human resource managers in this environment is to reconcile the often conflicting demands of the organisation with the needs of employees.

The changing context in which human resource management operates – globally and domestically, economically, politically and socially – has contributed to human resource management's rapidly changing role and responses. In terms of job design, employment patterns, employment relationships and reward management, significant changes are evident and these are discussed in subsequent chapters. Finally, this chapter has also outlined the legal context of managing human resources, an important and growing area of interest and concern. Various pieces of legislation emanating from federal and state governments impact on employment and one area that directly effects human resource management and employment matters is that which relates to industrial and workplace relations. This topic is the focus of the following chapter.

Key terms

Key debate issues

1 Flexibility imperatives in the workplace are heavily weighted in favour of employers rather than employees, and this has been further strengthened by recent Australian government initiatives.
2 Older workers are less productive and more resistant to change than younger employees.
3 Debate the pros and cons of family friendly work policies from the organisation's perspective.
4 Debate the qualities of the 'ideal worker.'
5 There is a great need for paid paternity leave in Australia: fact or fallacy? Debate.
6 Debate the pros and cons of casual employment from employer and employee perspectives.

Questions

1 What role does the global economy play in the Strategic Human Resource Management model presented in Chapter 1?
2 Consider the issues surrounding the ageing population. What are the main labour market implications of this demographic trend?
3 Discuss the implications of rising education levels for HR practitioners.
4 Discuss the concept of the 'new employment contract' and compare this to more traditional employment arrangements.

Case study 2.1

Ernst & Young

Ernst & Young is part of a global firm operating in 130 countries worldwide. Ernst & Young Australia is an accounting firm with a workforce of some 3700 people with clients based across the country. The firm has been 'good at recruiting' high-performing women with half the recruits being women. In spite of the high numbers of women recruited into the organisation only six out of 160 partners (4 per cent) were women in 1998 when Brian Schwartz commenced as CEO. Analysis showed that recruiting and nurturing a graduate into a senior role costs the firm about $300 000. A focus on retention simply made good business sense. 'Losing females costs the firm – quite simply – a fortune.'

How issues were addressed

There was a cultural shift made within the organisation after extensive discussions. One early initiative took a cross-section of senior and junior, male and female staff to a three-day forum and focused on the issue of retaining women in the workplace. This 'Accelerated Solutions Environment' worked through to a number of solutions which were then implemented in the organisation. Some of these solutions targeted women and others were common to men and women. Ernst & Young determined that a 'People First' strategy would put employees first and that 'high performing people' would lead to 'satisfied clients.'

The initiatives implemented include:

1   Ongoing performance measurement in Balanced Scorecard for Business Units including various diversity measures
2   Turnover, exit interview and workforce demographics analyses
3   Various flexible working arrangements including reduced hours, job-share, flexible start–finish times and telecommuting have been made available within the organisation
4   A Women's Leadership Forum based on a successful model from the US which aimed to provide role models, support networks and mentors for young women was instigated and has now been held on three occasions
5   Instigation of an externally judged award to recognise and celebrate individuals who promote the cause of women. This award was named the Lynne Sutherland Award, in honour of the first female partner in the firm who died in 1999
6   Instigation of a Women's Leadership Steering Committee to promote the development and retention of women in the firm
7   Family friendly meeting times were implemented
8   Easier remote access for people working from home was made available
9   Three months paid parental leave after two years service – covering maternity, paternity and adoption leave
10 Senior managers are held responsible for developing female employees, with performance measured in five areas including financial, operations, client relations, people and values
11 Management Key Performance Indicators include staff turnover and training input, each of which is analysed by gender
12 Women leaders have been sponsored to attend the US firm's Women's Leadership Conference
13 Ongoing staff satisfaction surveys.

Results

- The ratio of graduates recruited is 50:50 male–female.
- There are now two female partners on the board which is made up of 15 people.
- The first female partner to return from maternity leave working only four days per week has successfully maintained the same high-profile client for over three years without negative impact on the relationship. The client initially had some concerns as to whether this would be effective.
- One woman principal has an arrangement to be at home between 2.30 and 4 p.m. each afternoon and then to return to work after her children's father arrives home.

- A male partner is also working three days per week and so it is not just women who want to take advantage of the more flexible work options.
- Increased commitment and higher retention rates are being achieved from women returning to work from maternity leave. This results in keeping good people and not wasting 'millions of dollars invested in people' who leave the organisation.
- The presence of senior women at conferences and meetings is changing the dynamics of the meetings in a positive way.
- The percentage of female senior managers has increased from 35 to 44 per cent since 2000.
- The number of senior managers working part-time has doubled to 11 per cent.
- Three Ernst & Young employees (two female and one male) have been recognised with the Lynne Sutherland Award.

Source: Equal Opportunity for Women in the Workplace Agency,
www.eowa.gov.au. Copyright Commonwealth of Australia; reproduced by permission.

Questions

1 Examine each of the initiatives implemented by Ernst & Young from an HR perspective. Based on the ideas of Pocock, Hakim and Rapoport, which were summarised in this chapter, why did these initiatives produce the results they did?

2 Apart from the cost–benefit detailed in this case study, what other advantages can firms reap from policies targeted at the retention and advancement of women?

3 Consider the challenges that may be encountered with a program such as this. How would you, as an HR practitioner, deal with these issues?

Further readings

ABS 2006. *Australian social trends*, cat. 4102.0, www.abs.gov.au/ausstats/, accessed 14/8/2006.

ABS 2006. *Labour force, Australia*, cat. 6202.0, www.abs.gov.au/ausstats/, accessed 14/8/2006.

Baird M. 2003. 'Paid maternity leave: The good, the bad, the ugly,' *Australian Bulletin of Labour*, 29(1) pp. 97–109.

Baird M., Ellem B., Page A. 2006. *Human resource management: Strategies and processes, WorkChoices update*, 5th edn, Melbourne, Thomson.

Commonwealth of Australia, 2004. *Australia's demographic challenges*.

Kamoche K. 2006. 'Managing people in turbulent economic times: A knowledge-creation and appropriation perspective,' *Asia Pacific Journal of Human Resources*, 44(1), pp. 25–45.

Lansbury R.D. 2004. 'Work, people and globalisation: Towards a new social contract for Australia,' *Journal of Industrial Relations*, 46(1), pp. 102–15.

Patrickson M., Ranzijn R. 2004. 'Bounded choices in work and retirement in Australia,' *Employee Relations*, 26(4), pp. 422–32.

Pocock B. 2003. *The work-life collision*, Sydney, Federation Press.

Pocock B., Buchanan J., Campbell I. 2004. *Securing quality employment: Policy options for casual and part time workers in Australia*, Chifley Research Centre, April.

Waters M.A., Bardoel E.A. 2006. 'Work-family policies in the context of higher education: Useful or symbolic?,' *Asia Pacific Journal of Human Resources*, 44(1), pp. 67–82.

Watson I., Buchanan J., Campbell I., Briggs, C. 2003. *Fragmented futures: New challenges in working life*, Sydney, ACCIRT & Federation Press.

Websites

www.abs.gov.au for latest statistics. Use links to 'Key National Indicators,' 'Australian Social Trends,' and 'Labour Force, Australia.'

www.eowa.gov.au, Equal Opportunity for Women in the Workplace Agency.

www.austlii.edu.au for access to Australian statutes and case law.

Endnotes

1   Saywell T., Yau Z. 2000, 'Ready for the deluge,' *Far Eastern Economic Review*, 23 March, p. 45.

2   Rai S. 2006. 'IBM looks to triple investment in India,' *International Herald Tribune*, 7 June, p. 1.

3   Kelly P. 2000. 'United states of East Asia,' *Weekend Australian*, 29–30 April, p. 22.

4   Lyall, K. 2004. 'ASEAN trade door slides open,' *The Australian*, 7 May, p. 10.

5   www.austlii.edu.au/au/other/dfat/nia/2004/5.html.

6   Korporaal G. 2006. 'This party has got to end,' *The Weekend Australian*, 12–13 August, p. 33; ABS 2006. *Labour force*, cat. 6202.0, July, p. 1, accessed 14 August 2006.

7   ABS 2006. *Australian social trends*, 2006, cat. 4102.0, accessed 14 August 2006, p. 2.

8   www.pc.gov.au/research/commres.

9   www.abs.gov.au/ausstats.abs.

10 ABS 2005. *Australian labour market statistics*, cat. 6105.0, p. 11.

11 www.anta.gov.au/news.

12 Verma R., Boyer K. 2000. 'Service classifications and management challenges,' *Journal of Business Strategies*, 17(1), pp. 5–24.

13 ABS 2005. ibid.

14 Anonymous 2006. 'Skills shortage top 10,' *hrmonthly*, August, p. 7.

15 ABS 2006. *Australian labour market statistics*, cat. 6105.0, p. 5.

16 DEWR 2006. *Australian jobs 2006*, Canberra, DEWR, p. 4.

17 McDonald, P., Kippen, R. 1999. 'Ageing: the social and demographic dimensions,' in *Policy implications of the ageing of Australia's population*, Productivity Commission and Melbourne Institute of Applied Economic and Social Research, pp. 47–70.

18 Kuppel E. 2006. 'Is your organisation demographically fit?,' *The Official 11th World HR Congress Publication*, Singapore, SHRI, p. 13.

19 Ibid, p. 57.

20 www.abs.gov.au/ausstats/abs@nsf/mf/6202.0, accessed 8 March, 2007.

21 Ibid.

22 ABS 4102.0, 2002, p. 7.

23 McDonald P., Kippen R., op. cit., pp. 48 & 52.

24 Palmore E. 1990 in Snape E., Redman T., 'Too old or too young? The impact of perceived age discrimination,' *Human Resource Management Journal*, 13(1), pp. 78–89.

25 McDonald P., Kippen R. op. cit., p. 60.

26 Teh E. 1999. 'The aging workforce: some implications, strategies and policy considerations for human resource managers,' *Asia Pacific Journal of Human Resources*, 37(1), p. 73.

27 Henry A. 2006. 'Motivating and managing different generations at work.' Paper presented at the 11th World HR Congress, Singapore, June, p. 3.

28 Adecco 2006. 'Leveraging demographic change: Business strategies to deal with an aging workforce.' Paper presented at the 11th World HR Congress, Singapore, June, p. 17.

29 Royle T. 1999. 'Recruiting the acquiescent workforce, a comparative analysis of McDonald's in Germany and the UK,' *Employee Relations*, 21(6), pp. 540–55.

30 Commonwealth of Australia, 2004. *Australia's demographic challenges*.

31 Watson I., Buchanan J., Campbell I., Briggs C. 2002. *Fragmented futures*, Leichhardt, Federation Press.

32 Bailyn L., Fletcher J.K. 2002. 'Work redesign: Theory, practice, and possibility' *Working paper #C0004*, MIT Workplace Center, Massachusetts Institute of Technology.

33 Kanter R.M. 1977. *Work and family in the United States: A critical review and agenda for research and policy*, New York, Russell Sage Foundation.

34 Bittman M., Rice J. 2002. 'The spectre of overwork: an analysis of trends between 1974 and 1997 using Australian time-use diaries,' *Labour and Industry*, 13(1), pp. 91–110.

35 ABS 6203.0, trend series.

36 Lewis S., Smithson J. 2002. 'Developing working practices to support work-family integration and enhance organisational performance: An action research approach.' Paper presented at EURAM Conference, June.

37 Whitehouse G., Zetlin D. 1999. '"Family friendly" policies: Distribution and implementation in Australian workplaces,' *The Economic and Labour Relations Review*, 10(2), pp. 221–39.

38 Bardoel E.A., Tharenou P., Moss S. 1998. 'Organizational predictors of work-family practices,' *Asia Pacific Journal of Human Resources*, 36(3), pp. 31–49.

39 Pocock B. 2003. *The work-life collision*, Sydney, Federation Press.

40 Hakim C. 2000. *Work-lifestyle choices in the 21st century*, Oxford University Press.

41   Baird M. 2004. 'Orientations to paid maternity leave,' *Journal of Industrial Relations*, September.

42   Rapoport R., Bailyn L., Fletcher J., Pruitt B. 2002. *Beyond work-family balance: Advancing gender equity and work performance*, Jossey-Bass; Bailyn L. 2003. 'The equity imperative: Reaching effectiveness through the dual agenda,' *CGO Insights*, no. 18, July.

43   HREOC (2002a) *Valuing parenthood – options for paid maternity leave: Interim paper*. Human Rights and Equal Opportunity Commission, Sydney, April; HREOC (2002b) *A time to value*. Human Rights and Equal Opportunity Commission, Sydney, December.

44   Baird M., Brennan D., Cutcher L. 2002. 'A pregnant pause: Paid maternity leave in Australia,' *Journal of Labour and Industry*, 13(1), August, pp. 1–19.

45   Bittman M., Hoffman S., Thompson D. 2004. *Men's uptake of family-friendly employment policies, Policy Research Paper No. 22*, Department of Family and Community Services.

46   Cant S. 1992. 'Literacy problems a barrier to output,' *The Australian*, 1–2 August, p. 57.

47   Beardwell L., Holden I. 1994. *Human resource management: A contemporary perspective*, London, Pitman.

48   Joerres J. 2006. 'Optimizing and engaging the total workforce.' Paper presented at the 11th World HR Congress, Singapore, June, p. 4.

49   Anonymous 2006. *Engaging the total workforce*, Manpower, Milwaukee, p. 3.

50   Kramar R. 2006. *Cranet-Macquarie survey on international strategic human resource management: Report on the Australian findings*, Sydney, Macquarie University, p. 14.

51   Ibid, p. 15.

52   ACIRRT 1999. *Australia at work: Just managing?* Sydney, Prentice Hall, p. 119.

53   Ibid.

54   ABS 2006. *Australian labour market statistics*, cat. 6105.0, p. 57.

55   Ibid, pp. 101–25.

56   Pocock B. 2001. *Having a life: Work, family fairness and community in 2000*, Centre for Labour Research, Adelaide University.

57   'Long hours kill work-life balance without delivering productivity,' *HR Report*, Thomson CDP, 6 April 2004, pp. 1–3.

58   www.abs.gov.au/Ausstats/abs@.nsf/0/ef163e7fe2165aecca256b130075f601?Open.

59   Pocock B., Buchannan J., Campbell I., 2004. *Securing quality employment: Policy options for casual and part time workers in Australia*, Chifley Research Centre, April.

60   Kelly D. 2000. 'Employment and concepts of work in the new global economy,' *International Labour Review*, 139(1), pp. 5–32.

61   See, for example, Dabscheck's analysis of the increasing emphasis on contractualism in the management of Australian employment relations: Dabscheck B. 2001. 'A felt need for increased efficiency: Industrial relations at the end of the millennium,' *Asia Pacific Journal of Human Resources*, 39(2), pp. 4–30.

Online reading

INFOTRAC® COLLEGE EDITION

For additional readings and review on the context of human resource management explore InfoTrac® College Edition, your online library. Go to: www.infotrac-college.com and search for any of the InfoTrac key terms listed below:

➤ ageing
➤ globalisation
➤ intergenerational conflict
➤ labour market (s)
➤ work–life balance
➤ (workplace) flexibility

CHAPTER 3

INDUSTRIAL RELATIONS

employment practices which in turn would make our jobs as HR professionals harder.

hrmonthly, Dec05/Jan06

The workplace relations package released today does represent the most fundamental modernisation of our system yet seen.

The Prime Minister, John Howard, Press Conference, 26 May 2005

The Government's workplace agenda is not a plan to address the real economic priorities facing Australia. It is a radical plan to deliver workplace power to business and diminish the rights of every Australian employee.

Greg Combet, ACTU Secretary, 2005

HR will have a critical role to play … At the moment HR too often lets the unions fight the 'fairness' battles for the employees. HR has a vital role in ensuring the rights and needs of employees are protected.

hrmonthly, Dec 05/Jan 06

Employees who feel exploited do not perform well, nor do they offer loyalty to their organisation. This is going to be a major issue for the future. The proposed changes are unbalanced and would leave workers vulnerable to unscrupulous

Objectives

After reading this chapter you will be able to:

1   Understand the concept of industrial relations and its relationship to strategic human resource management.

2   Understand the framework that regulates industrial relations and the major institutions, parties and processes in that framework.

3   Recognise the differing views of the employment relationship.

4   Be familiar with major changes and debates that have occurred in Australia (and elsewhere) about industrial relations.

5   Understand the implications of these changes for strategic HRM.

Introduction

As the opening quotations show, *industrial relations* can be a very controversial and contested area of policy and practice. This is especially so at times of legislative change. In Australia, for instance, the federal government has recently introduced new industrial relations legislation which has been the cause of considerable debate. In Europe, many governments have been confronted with violent opposition to labour law changes, while in Asia, governments have sought greater flexibility in order to attract foreign investment, but at the cost of worker security. While industrial relations is a matter of national policy, it has implications at the societal, organisational and individual level. For this reason, it often brings out strong differences of opinion between people and political parties; and also because of this, it is important for human resource managers to understand the nature of industrial relations. While 'industrial relations' is a well-known term, other terms are also used to cover broadly the same subject area, with 'employment relations' being one of the most common. The term 'workplace relations' has been used for policy purposes in Australia for some time and is the name of the main federal legislation.

The 'industrial relations system,' more specifically, refers to the rules, regulations and institutions that govern the employment relationship and which set the terms and conditions of work and employment.[1] The major parties or actors involved in industrial relations are generally understood to be employers and their associations and employees and their trade unions. In Australia and elsewhere, governments play a significant role through the legislative changes they introduce. Furthermore, in many countries, governments also have an important role as employers.

Although the term 'the industrial relations system' suggests a stable network of social regulation, in reality industrial relations is a complex and power-ridden field and, at various times, not necessarily stable. Conflict between the industrial parties over power, control and the terms and conditions of work is not unusual. The ways in which conflict is manifested and the legislative requirements to resolve industrial conflict are discussed in Chapter 12. In this chapter, the focus is on the industrial relations system and how the employment relationship is regulated in Australia. A brief overview of changes in Asian and European industrial relations is also provided.

In Australia, this formal system of industrial relations has had a rich and complex history involving a century of government-sanctioned compulsory conciliation and arbitration. This provided a unique and centralised framework for determining work rules and resolving labour conflicts. During the 1980s, the perceived need for increased workplace and organisational flexibility, efficiency and competition led employers and the government to press for significant changes in industrial relations legislation and labour market regulation.[2] Further emphasis on change and deregulation has seen continued industrial relations change in Australia.

In Australia, government industrial relations policy has largely been about shifting the focus of attention from the national and industry levels to the workplace, and about transferring power from the collective associations of employers and unions to the individual employer and employee. Even the terminology is indicative of this shift in emphasis. Since 1996, the Australian federal legislation has used the term 'workplace relations' rather than industrial relations, reflecting a desire on the part of policy-makers in the federal sphere to emphasise the workplace or organisation level, rather than the national or industry level. To achieve these ends, the conservative government over the past two decades has introduced substantial legislative change which altered the bargaining framework in which employers, unions and employees operate.

Further significant changes occurred in Australia in 2005 with the introduction of the *Workplace Relations Amendment (WorkChoices) Act*. Despite strong opposition and a High Court challenge from the state governments on the constitutionality of the new legislation, the laws were passed and the new industrial legislation became operative in March 2006. As a consequence, Australia's industrial relations framework is now quite different to that which existed before: there are new minimum standards, new institutions and different processes are involved. The new legislation has an even greater emphasis on the direct relationship between employer and employees and a lesser role for third parties – including unions and industrial tribunals. Indeed, it could be argued that the emphasis is now shifting to the individual employee, rather than the workplace or organisation.

In addition to the considerable changes in the social, political and economic environments of business discussed in Chapter 2, the industrial relations changes have provided human resource managers with a new set of opportunities and challenges. The specific changes in Australian industrial relations over the last 20 years have meant that the options for determining the terms and conditions of employment are more diverse than ever before and the role of human resource managers potentially more important than before.[3]

This chapter outlines the new institutional structures, minimum standards and processes of regulation brought in by the *WorkChoices* amendments, paying most attention to those aspects that are newly created: namely, the Australian Fair Pay Commission, the new legislated standards of employment and the range of workplace agreements. The chapter also considers the role and place of human resource management in the new world of *WorkChoices*. Before discussing these issues, however, the link between strategic human resource management and industrial relations is explored.

Industrial relations and strategic human resource management

In the shift from personnel management to strategic human resource management discussed in Chapter 1, human resource management became closely aligned with the business goals and strategic interests of the organisation. Prior to this, personnel management and industrial relations were generally considered as separate functional entities in organisations, with neither of them closely integrated with business objectives. Strategic human resource management has sought to change this: first, by bringing the two fields of personnel and industrial relations together in an operational sense and often under the umbrella of human resources; and second, by aligning these spheres much more directly and closely to the organisation's business interests and strategies.

In Chapter 1 we also argued that the relationship between industrial relations and human resource management is often uneasy and contested. Some argue that the rules and regulations of industrial relations, which are often set outside the organisation, interfere with the organisation's internal human resource policies and strategies. It is also suggested that where industrial relations has a concern with 'third parties,' such as trade unions and government tribunals, it is at odds with the emphasis of strategic human resource management which is on the development of close direct relations between the individual employee and employer. Others go further, arguing that human resource management, in both theory and practice, is anti-union and explicitly pro-management.

Whichever perspective is adopted, understanding industrial relations and the regulatory framework remains important for the effective practice of human resource management and human resource management requires an understanding of all aspects of the labour relationship.

For many writers and practitioners of human resource management, 'industrial relations' refers specifically to the management of the employment relationship with the *unionised workforce*. In countries where unions and the industrial relations systems have historically had significant influence over employees' terms and working conditions, this has tended to be the understanding of industrial relations. Nevertheless, if human resource managers are to be effective managers of people they need to understand industrial relations and all that it covers: that is, the dynamics, contradictions and tensions of the employment relationship.

Exhibit 3.1 SHRM and the bargaining framework

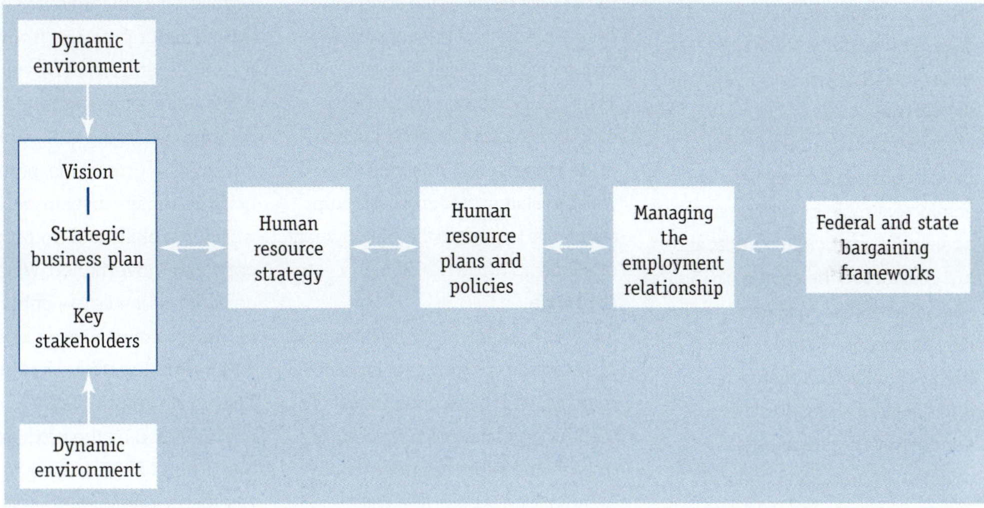

As Exhibit 3.1 shows, strategic human resource managers seek to link the way in which they manage industrial relations to the human resource plans and policies of the organisation. These, in turn, derive from the organisation's human resource strategy. This strategy must be cognisant of the business strategy and responsive to the dynamic environment in which organisations operate. This means that the responses to industrial relations issues may vary between organisations and over time. Later we examine the differing strategic responses of employers to industrial relations change. To conduct human resource management strategically, the legal basis of the employment relationship, and the regulatory framework of industrial relations which overlays this, must also be understood.

The bargaining framework in Australia

A bargaining framework is a concept used to describe the arrangements by which employers and employees determine and set the terms and conditions of the employment relationship.[4] Legislation is most important in setting the framework. Different countries, therefore, have different bargaining or industrial relations frameworks.[5] Furthermore, in response to movements in the economic, political and social contexts, governments often make changes to bargaining frameworks and such changes have been particularly apparent in Australia in recent years.

This section of the chapter describes the existing bargaining framework in Australia, with an emphasis on the federal system. An overview of changes occurring elsewhere is provided in News report 3.1.

NEWS REPORT 3.1

Changes in industrial relations in Asia and Europe

(1) Asia

In order to facilitate industrialisation and attract foreign direct investment, many Asian nations have pursued labour market reform by offering flexibility and increased deregulation.

(a) China

China's labour market reforms have been heralded as the shining example for other Asian economies, particularly India, and are considered the source of China's spectacular economic growth over the last decade. China, initially a highly regulated economy, has implemented a system of flexible employment contracts where millions of foreign and domestic employers independently determine wages, hours and working and living conditions. These reforms created a highly mobile workforce, although this came at the cost of mass layoffs and high unemployment. Recently, the high susceptibility to abuse of this system was recognised and labour reforms were proposed which, if implemented, would create a system of very minimum standards. These include (i) a presumption in courts, in the context of employment complaints, that the employee is correct unless an employer can rebut such a presumption with evidence, (ii) limits on probationary periods

when an employer can arbitrarily terminate an employee (iii) conversion of short term contracts to long term after a particular period and (iv) make the facts and realities, rather than terms of the contract, of an employment relationship key to litigating industrial disputes. Thus China has followed reforms promoting complete deregulation of the employment relationship with legislation creating minimum standards to govern the employment relationship (Brown 2006).

(b) India

India, at present, is on the threshold of introducing significant labour reforms, which are considered the key to promoting economic growth and reducing poverty in India. The labour market reforms, however, are at the centre of heated debate in India. While some argue that India's current restrictive labour laws create inflexibility in the labour market, which prevents economic growth, this view is contested by trade unions and workers who have vehemently opposed the introduction of the reforms (Sharma 2006). In India, reforms aimed at increasing flexibility with respect to termination, outsourcing and subcontracting were introduced in 2002 (Dutta 2006). These reforms created a dual structure of industrial regulation, under which

the significant portion of the Indian population engaged in the informal economy remained unregulated while the organised, formal sector, was subject to stringent regulation. Consequently, India is now under pressure from both the OECD and Asian Development Bank to implement labour reforms consisting of flexible termination provisions, restraints upon unionism, investment in workforce skills and training and corporate governance, which are considered the key to enhancing India's attractiveness as a venue for foreign direct investment. These reforms are likely to be implemented by the next election, due around 2008, although whether suggestions to add worker protections to the reform agenda will be heeded is unclear as yet (Sharma 2006).

(c) Malaysia and Singapore

Malaysia and Singapore, both states recovering from the Asian financial crisis, have followed the trend of other Asian economies and implemented flexible, deregulated labour market policies. Both nations' main industrial issue at present concerns the large numbers of unskilled illegal immigrants they attract. Both have implemented labour market reforms aimed at flexibility and productivity as

the key to boosting international competitiveness, particularly in the fields of value-added manufactures. Neither country is heavily unionised nor characterised by a significant degree of industrial disputation.

(d) Indonesia

Following the Asian trend, Indonesia's President, Susilo Bambang Yudhoyono, in May 2006 implemented labour reform laws which simplified Indonesia's complex labour laws, deregulated significant portions of the labour market and increased labour market flexibilities. In practice, this legislation meant the abolition of basic minimum standards such as laws requiring employers to pay two months severance pay for every year of a terminated employee's employment. The reforms were geared towards boosting flagging foreign investment. Critics however are concerned about the abolition of minimum employment standards in Indonesia, a country with no functioning welfare net.

(2) Europe

Although labour reform is definitively on the agenda of most European countries, the type of reforms being implemented reflect their significantly different context compared with, for example, Asia and Australia. Since 2000, the European Union (EU) has promoted the standardisation of labour market and industrial relations policy across the European states. The EU standardisation agenda, dubbed the Lisbon Targets, is intended to reform the labour market so that by 2010 Europe becomes 'the most dynamic and competitive knowledge-based economy in the world, capable of sustainable economic growth with more and better jobs and greater social cohesion' (Manpower 2005). The Targets focus on education and skills, the creation of a more diverse workforce and the achievement of full employment particularly, with the ultimate aim of standardising employment conditions across all 25 EU member states. Pursuing the standardisation agenda, the draft Agency Workers' Directive, aiming at standardising the regulation of temporary work across the EU was proposed in 2002, with controversial effect. The Lisbon 'agenda of labour reforms' is explicitly supported by major international institutions, such as the International Monetary Fund.

The member states of the EU have implemented the Targets differently, although all the reforms have in common a concern for limiting unemployment and increasing incentives for both hiring and entry into the workforce. In the past year, Spain, France, Germany and the Netherlands have all introduced legislation which maintain high levels of government involvement and specifically targets unemployment.

Firstly, Spain in July 2006 brought forth new legislation aimed at allowing thousands of employees on temporary contracts to upgrade to permanent contracts, albeit on strict terms and in exchange for less stringent regulation of terminations. The laws sought specifically to curb widespread use of short-term contracts which accounted for two-thirds of all new jobs being created in Spain. Contrary to Australia, the laws were passed after extensive consultation and with the agreement of the union movement.

Secondly, also in 2006, France's former Prime Minister, Dominique de Villepin, sought to implement legislation dubbed the 'first job contract or CPE' proposal, which would allow employers to dismiss staff under the age of 26 easily during a two-year probationary period. The proposed legislation, aimed specifically at reducing France's 24 per cent youth unemployment rate by providing employers with additional flexibility, was met with furious protests and rioting from angry students and unions. As a result of this vehement opposition, the Prime Minister ultimately withdrew the law.

Thirdly, exemplifying yet again Europe's emphasis on curbing unemployment and maintaining high degrees of labour market regulation, Germany introduced Hartz IV reforms, proposed in 2003–4 and implemented over 2005–6. Hartz IV aimed at providing incentives for the re-entry of the long-term unemployed into the workforce by combining welfare support and unemployment benefits so as to reduce welfare payouts. Hartz IV, though ultimately implemented as legislation, also met with protests and criticism from the German public. Finally, in 2004, the Netherlands introduced new labour rules reducing retirement entitlements.

Sources: Reuters 2006. 'Labour reforms in Europe,' www.reuters.com; ILO 2006. 'Labour and social trends in Asia and the Pacific 2006: Progress towards decent work,' International Labour Office, Bangkok, www.ilo.org; Sharma, A. 2006. 'Flexibility, employment and labour market reforms in India,' www.wiego.org/publications/EPW/Sharma%20Flexibility%20Employment%20and%20Labour%20Market%20Reforms%20in%20India.pdf; Manpower, 2005. 'Employment legislation update,' www.manpower.co.uk/news/legislation/000437_EmployBro_singlepp.pdf; Brown, E. 2006. 'Chinese labor law reform: Guaranteeing worker rights in the age of globalism,' www.worldpress.org/Asia/2574.cfm; Cotis, J.P. 2005. 'Economic policy reforms: Going for growth,' OECD, Press Conference, www.oecd.org/dataoecd/58/1/34514049.pdf; European Foundation for the Improvement of Living and Working Conditions, 2006. 'Collective dispute resolution in an enlarged European Union,' www.eurofound.eu.int/publications/htmlfiles/ef0642.htm; Economist Intelligence Unit, 2004. 'Economic outlook: Indonesia,' www.economist.com; Dutta, P. 2006. 'Trade protection and industry wages in India,' *Industrial and Labor Relations Review* 60(2), digitalcommons.ilr.cornell.edu/ilrreview/vol60/iss2/6/. All accessed on 16 January 2007.

The dimensions of the Australian bargaining framework to be considered are as follows:

1   The legislation. At the federal level the main legislation is the *Workplace Relations Act 1996* (the WR Act) amended by the *Workplace Relations Amendment (WorkChoices) Act 2005* (Cth).

2   The industrial relations institutions. These include the Fair Pay Commission (FPC), the Workplace Authority (formerly the Office of the Employment Advocate, OEA) and the Australian Industrial Relations Commission (AIRC).

3   The major parties or the bargaining agents in industrial relations. Individually, these are employees and employers; collectively they are unions and employer associations.

4   The industrial relations processes. Traditionally, the primary process for determining the terms and conditions of work for a majority of employees in Australia was collective bargaining or arbitration. Compulsory arbitration has been removed and collective bargaining has been displaced to some extent by the emphasis on individual bargaining.

5   The instruments of regulation. These are the legal and contractual outcomes of the bargaining. In the federal sphere they include workplace agreements and awards.

A summary of the Australian bargaining framework under *WorkChoices* is provided in Exhibit 3.2.

Exhibit 3.2 Australian bargaining framework

Legislation	*Workplace Relations Act 1996; Workplace Relations Amendment (WorkChoices) Act 2005* (Cth)
Institutions	Australian Fair Pay Commission, The Workplace Authority, Australian Industrial Relations Commission
Parties	Employers, employees, unions, employer associations
Processes	Collective bargaining and unilateral regulation
Instruments	Workplace agreements and awards

1. The legislation

Legislation is important for setting the framework for industrial relations, whether a country's approach to industrial relations is to be highly regulated or deregulated. With this in mind, it is clear that changes in legislation have a direct impact on the manner in which industrial relations is conducted. This has been clearly illustrated in Australia over the past few years where major changes in industrial relations legislation have occurred. Industrial relations policies also generate considerable debate and reveal differences in underlying philosophy – namely unitarist or pluralist approaches, as discussed in Chapter 1 – to the management and regulation of labour and the employment relationship.

When the Commonwealth of Australia was created in 1901, the Constitution empowered the federal government to settle interstate disputes by means of conciliation and arbitration while giving the government only limited power to directly enact legislation relating to industrial relations and employment matters. The Commonwealth Court of Conciliation and Arbitration, established in 1904, which was the forerunner of the current Australian Industrial Relations Commission, had the power to arbitrate the terms and conditions of employment by making *awards*. Similar industrial tribunals with similar roles were established for each of the states and throughout most of the 20th century these arbitration tribunals provided the main institutional framework for determining employment conditions in Australia. Consequently, Australia had separate industrial relations systems in each of the states and also at the federal level. (A summary of the state legislations is provided at the end of this section.) The systems in each jurisdiction generally reflected the political philosophies of the governments in power. Thus, labour governments tended to have laws that protected unions and workers and conservative governments introduced laws that benefited businesses and employers more directly. In 1996, the Liberal–National Party coalition introduced the first *Workplace Relations Act* and the Victorian state government ceded its industrial relations powers to the federal government, leaving the remaining five states with their own legislation. Since its election in 1996, the conservative federal government (Liberal–National Party coalition) has argued for a more 'unified' national system of industrial relations, and sees the latest amendments, *WorkChoices*, as delivering this. Others argue that throughout the last decade industrial relations and the labour market has been re-regulated rather than deregulated, and that this has been in favour of business and employers rather than employees and unions.[6]

Until the late 1980s, federal and state awards covered approximately 80 per cent of all wage and salary earners, although these tended to set only minimum rates of pay and conditions and permitted the parties to establish supplementary rates by additional collective bargaining.[7] Overall, federal and state governments and the industrial tribunals have been important in setting the agenda for Australian industrial relations and since the late 1980s governments have favoured a more decentralised, deregulated and organisationally specific approach to the management of the employment relationship. Many authors have commented on the transformation of the Australian industrial relations system. Wailes and Lansbury, for instance, have identified several phases of reform which gradually displaced the centralised system of industrial relations with firstly a period of coordinated or managed decentralism (1987–90), followed by coordinated flexibility (1991–6) and then a phase of 'fragmented flexibility' (since 1997).[8] These changes have also favoured individualised and non-union arrangements.

WorkChoices legislation

WorkChoices, or more properly the *Workplace Relations Act 1996* as amended by the *Workplace Relations Amendment (WorkChoices) Act 2005*, came into effect in March 2006. As the legislation is new, the full effect of it is yet to be seen. With this in mind, this section of the chapter is intended to provide the core information necessary to understand the industrial relations system.

The *WorkChoices* legislation establishes a new framework for employment regulation in Australia. It removes most of the tradition, practices and processes that were associated with Australian employment relations for much of the 20th century. Furthermore, it significantly broadens the reach of the federal framework of employment relations regulation.

Coverage

One of the main aims of the *WorkChoices* legislation was to bring more employers and employees under the federal legislation and establish one national system. This has not quite been achieved because some employees continue to remain under the state systems. However, *WorkChoices* has expanded the coverage of the federal system by using the corporations power. The federal system now covers the following corporations and employers:

- Trading, financial and foreign corporations (constitutional corporations)
- Employers in the Australian Capital Territory, the Northern Territory and Christmas and Cocos (Keeling) Islands
- The Commonwealth, including its authorities
- Employers who employ waterside, maritime and flight crew employees (and their employees) in connection with interstate, overseas, inter-territory or state–territory trade and commerce
- Employers in Victoria.[9]

By covering these groups, it is estimated that *WorkChoices* now has direct coverage of between 75 and 85 per cent of the Australian workforce. Those outside the scope of *WorkChoices* are principally those who are employed directly by the state governments or by non-corporate entities.

Definitions: Employers and employees

As a consequence of *WorkChoices*' use of the corporations power rather than the labour power, the employment relationship is now derived from the legal construct of the corporation. Thus, *an employer* is one who is legally recognised as a corporation and *an employee* is defined as a person who works for one of those employers.[10]

Exhibit 3.3 The *WorkChoices* changes summarised

Among the most important and far-reaching aspects of the legislation are the following:

- *WorkChoices* draws on the corporations power in the Constitution (s. 51.20) as opposed to the traditional, primary reliance on the labour power (s. 51.35).
- Partly through this mechanism, *WorkChoices* seeks to deliver a 'unified system' by overriding the power of the states and their industrial relations frameworks in relation to 'constitutional corporations' and their employees.
- *WorkChoices* removes the fundamental task of setting minimum wages from the Australian Industrial Relations Commission (AIRC) and gives that task to the Australian Fair Pay Commission (FPC), a new institution explicitly charged with privileging competitiveness and employment in its deliberations.
- *WorkChoices* introduces the first-ever direct regulation of conditions of employment by the Commonwealth Parliament. In addition to the minimum wage, it legislates for four minimum

conditions to be known as 'Australian Fair Pay and Conditions Standards' (AFPCS). These standards cover annual leave, sick leave, unpaid parental leave and maximum working hours.

- Together with the FPC's minimum wage, this set of conditions constitutes the five basic standards of employment. Everything else is negotiable, preferably at the organisational, workplace or individual level.

- There are several forms of workplace agreements, including Australian Workplace Agreements (AWAs), collective workplace agreements and greenfields agreements. The Act contains considerable detail as to the form, content and making of these agreements, including 'prohibited matters.' It also places new restraints on industrial action by unions.

- An Award Review Taskforce is working through all existing awards and their pay and classification scales to minimise and streamline them, with the aim being the provision of industry-wide common rule awards.

- Over time the combination of the new workplace agreements with the new minimum standards will all but end the traditional award system.

- Only those companies with 100 or more employees are now covered by the unfair dismissal regime.

The Australian Fair Pay and Conditions Standard

In a significant shift from past practice, under *WorkChoices* the federal government has legislated for a set of minimum employment standards to apply to employees in the federal system. These are called 'The Australian Fair Pay and Conditions Standard' (AFPCS) and are to be referred to as 'the Standard.'

The Standard covers five areas:

1 *A federal minimum wage*: To be determined by the Australian Fair Pay Commission (see section below).

2 *Maximum hours of work*: A maximum of 38 ordinary hours of work per week becomes the new Australian standard. However, these hours may be averaged over a 12-month period on agreement between the employer and the employee.

3 *Annual leave*: This standard provides for four weeks of paid annual leave (with an additional week for shift workers) but does not apply to casual employees. On agreement, employees are able to cash out up to two weeks of their annual leave.

4 *Personal/carer's leave*: Ten days of paid personal/carer's leave (including sick leave and carer's leave), with provision for an additional two days of unpaid carer's leave for permanent employees who have used all of their other leave and for casual employees. Employees other than casuals are also entitled to an additional two days of paid compassionate leave to visit a terminally ill relative or attend a funeral.

5 *Parental leave*: Fifty-two weeks of unpaid parental leave (including maternity, paternity and adoption leave) available to all permanent employees and casual employees with 12 months service with one employer.

Matters covered by the new standards are no longer 'allowable' award matters, and are being removed from awards as part of the Award Review Taskforce's role. Matters covered by the Standard can form part of new Agreements so long as they are equal to, or higher than, the standards set by the legislation.

While a floor of minimum standards has now been legislated, there is no agreement as to the efficacy of these standards for the whole community. For instance, the Australian Council of Trade Unions (ACTU), which is the peak union body, has produced a family impact statement which criticises the new standards.[11] Many employees may also feel that their conditions will be undermined, fuelling employee suspicion and mistrust and setting up a potential problem for HR managers and employers.

The state industrial relations systems

Whereas the above discussion covers the Australian federal legislation, there are still separate industrial relations laws in each of the states, with the exception of Victoria. Over the past decade all of the state governments have also initiated considerable legislative change in industrial relations, reflecting the philosophical and ideological persuasions of the governments in power. Exhibit 3.4 shows the most recent legislation in the state spheres.

The industrial relations laws of the states, all of which are governed by Labour governments at present, were changed in reaction to *WorkChoices*. In an attempt to pre-empt the contents of *WorkChoices* legislation, both Queensland and Tasmania amended their industrial legislation with the *Industrial Relations Amendment Act 2005* (Qld) and *Industrial Relations Amendment (Fair Conditions) Act 2005* (Tas) respectively. NSW and Western Australia followed suit, introducing amending industrial legislation, namely the *Industrial Relations Amendment Act 2006* (NSW) and the *Labour Relations Amendment Act 2006* (WA), after *WorkChoices* was already in force.

The amendments introduced by the states are similar in content and purpose. To varying extents, the state legislations incorporate provisions which aim to protect employees whose entitlements are arguably threatened under *WorkChoices*. To this end, the legislation includes provisions guaranteeing minimum entitlements. In Queensland, these minimum entitlements include a 38-hour ordinary working week, paid overtime, unpaid meal breaks of at least 30 minutes after five hours work, annual leave loading, casual leave loading, shift loading, overtime rates for public holidays as well as penalty rates and redundancy payments. In Tasmania, similar minimum entitlements were provided for as well as clarification of definitions of categories of employees (that is casual, part-time and full-time) in order to provide added protection for vulnerable workers and the inclusion of a requirement that the Commission ensure all enterprise agreements being certified do not disadvantage employees.

Western Australia has both introduced minimum entitlement provisions, focusing in particular on various forms of leave (parental, bereavement, annual, carers and sick leave), and enhanced the role of good faith bargaining. South Australia has also introduced amending legislation, namely the *Industrial Law Reform (Fair Work) Act 2005* which was the culmination of debate surrounding the Stevens review. The legislation, although introduced six months prior to the tabling of the WorkChoices Bill, similarly introduced provisions regarding minimum conditions, leave and pay equity. NSW amending legislation, rather than focusing on minimum entitlements, has focused specifically on providing extra protection for outworkers and incorporating provisions, which allow for the expansion of the Industrial Relations Commission's powers (which have been significantly diminished by *WorkChoices*) by written agreement between the parties. The NSW amendments reflect an emphasis on administrative compliance with *WorkChoices*, rather than a concern with protecting minimum entitlements as reflected by the other states. Finally, Victoria, which referred its industrial relations powers to the Commonwealth in 1996, is now entirely governed, in terms of industrial relations, by Part 21 of the *Workplace Relations Act 1996*, as amended by *WorkChoices*.

Associated legislation

One important role of human resource management is to ensure legal compliance. In addition to the principle legislation that regulates industrial relations, there are a range of other laws that

Exhibit 3.4 Industrial relations legislation in the Australian states

	Legislation	Institutions	Instruments of regulation	Bargaining agents	Industrial Disputes
NSW	• *Industrial Relations Act 1996* Amending legislation now incorporated in the Act: • *Industrial Relations Amendment Act 2005* • *Industrial Relations Amendment Act 2006*	• *NSW Industrial Relations Commission – non-judicial (conciliation and arbitration) powers – powers conferred by agreement where parties agree for dispute to be resolved by Commission (see Amendment Act s. 146A)* • *NSW Industrial Relations Commission in full session – enforcement powers* • *Industrial magistrate – enforcement powers* • *Inspectors – investigative powers*	• *Awards – last 12 months to three years – no limit on number of matters contained though must deal with certain issues (such as maximum ordinary hours, sick leave)* • *Recent amendments have led to some awards (applicable to employees of constitutional corporations) to be treated as enterprise agreements, and will expire* • *Enterprise agreements – union or non-union collective agreements – must be certified; prevail over state awards in case of inconsistency*	• *Employer associations* • *Unions* • *Anti-discrimination Board President (may appear at EBA hearings)*	Little scope for protected action – most industrial action is deemed unlawful (and injunctions against strike action are able to be taken out) • emphasis is on dispute resolution (with the Act containing mandatory dispute resolution guidelines) • especially broad powers to control any action taken in essential services industries
QLD	• *Industrial Relations Act 1999* Amending legislation now incorporated in the Act: • *Industrial Relations Amendment Act 2001* • *Industrial Relations and Other Acts Amendment Act 2005* • *Industrial Relations Amendment Act 2005*	• *Queensland Industrial Relations Commission – conciliation, arbitration and some judicial powers* • *Industrial Magistrate – enforcement powers* • *Industrial Court – appeals court with judicial powers* • *Industrial registrar*	• *Awards – no limit on number of matters contained, must not be discriminatory and must contain equal remuneration provisions* • *Certified agreements – union or non-union collective agreements, prevails over award in case of inconsistency*	• *Employer associations* • *Unions*	Some scope for industrial action during EBA negotiations (where advancing claims for proposed agreement or responding to industrial action of other party) – but cannot occur during life of an agreement. Validity of protected action dependent on ballot.

	Legislation	Institutions	Instruments of regulation	Bargaining agents	Industrial Disputes
			<ul><li>Queensland Workplace Agreements – individual agreements that can be negotiated collectively – more regulated than AWAs – operates to exclude awards but does not prevail against certified agreement in case of inconsistency</li></ul>		
SA	<ul><li>Fair Work Act 1994 (previously Industrial and Employee Relations Act 1994) Amending legislation now incorporated in the Act:</li><li>Industrial Law Reform (Fair Work) Act 2005</li></ul>	<ul><li>Industrial Relations Court of SA – judicial powers, appellate powers</li><li>Industrial Magistrate – enforcement powers</li><li>Industrial Relations Commission of SA (has IR and EBA divisions)</li><li>Industrial Relations Advisory Committee – statutory authority with advisory functions – assist in policy formulation</li><li>Employee Ombudsman – administrative functions</li><li>Workplace inspectors – investigative function (investigate complaints/ suspected breaches of Act and systematically audit compliance with the Act)</li></ul>	<ul><li>Awards – no limit on number of matters contained, must include equal remuneration provisions</li><li>Enterprise agreements – union or non-union collective agreements, prevail over award in case of inconsistency</li></ul>	<ul><li>Employer associations</li><li>Unions – one can represent all employees in workplace in certain circumstances</li><li>Employee Ombudsman – can represent employees in most legal proceedings (other than unfair dismissal) and has various investigative functions</li></ul>	<ul><li>Scarce reference to industrial disputation other than in relation to Commission's powers of settlement</li><li>Some scope for protected action during EBA negotiations</li><li>Act incorporates Federal secondary boycott laws</li></ul>
WA	<ul><li>Industrial Relations Act 1979 (part of Doplar Series of legislation)</li></ul>	<ul><li>WA Industrial Relations Commission – conciliation and arbitration powers</li></ul>	<ul><li>Awards – no limit on number of matters contained</li></ul>	<ul><li>Employer associations</li></ul>	<ul><li>Limited reference to industrial disputes</li></ul>

	Legislation	Institutions	Instruments of regulation	Bargaining agents	Industrial Disputes
	• Minimum Conditions of Employment Act 1993 (also part of Doplar Series of Legislation) Amending legislation now incorporated in the Act: • Labour Relations Reform Act 2002 • Labour Relations Amendment Act 2006	• WA Industrial Relations Commission in Court Session – also has judicial functions • Industrial Magistrates Court – enforce compliance • WA Industrial Appeal Court – hears appeals from WA Commission and Magistrates Court • Industrial inspectors – monitor statutory compliance	• Industrial agreements – union or non-union collective agreements • Employer–employee agreements – individual agreements that are more regulated than AWAs – operate to exclusion of award	• Unions	
TAS	• Industrial Relations Act 1984 Amending legislation now incorporated in the Act: • Industrial Relations Amendment (Fair Conditions) Act 2005	• Tasmanian Industrial Commission – conciliation and arbitration powers (non-judicial powers) • Full Bench of Tasmanian Industrial Commission – appellate powers • Magistrates Court – enforcement powers • Supreme Court – appellate jurisdiction (hear appeals from Magistrates Court and can review Full Bench decisions)	• Awards – no limit on number of matters contained, must deal with certain issues (particular minimum employment conditions) • Industrial agreements – union or non-union collective agreements, prevail over awards • Enterprise agreements – union or non-union collective agreements, must include minimum conditions	• Employer associations • Unions • Both Tasmanian Trades and Labour Council and Tasmanian Chamber of Commerce and Industry explicitly recognised by the Act • Non-union enterprise based employee committees may be formed	• No reference to industrial disputes
VIC	The *Employee Relations Act 1992* replaced the system of compulsory conciliation and arbitration with individual and collective agreements that were underpinned by a limited range of minimum standards relating to rate of pay and some forms of leave. In 1996, the Victorian Government referred all powers allowing the state to legislate on matters relating to industrial relations to the Commonwealth, facilitating the withdrawal of the Victorian state from industrial relations. *WorkChoices*, however, has introduced a new Part 21 which is now the primary legislation governing the operation of federal industrial laws in Victoria.			

NB: Neither the Australian Capital Territory (ACT) nor Northern Territory (NT) have specifically targeted industrial laws. Rather, they have more general laws such as the NT Work Health Act 1986 and the ACT Public Sector Management Act 1994 and Discrimination Act 1991.

impact on the employment relationship. These cover such matters as equality of opportunity, anti-discrimination and workers compensation. Exhibit 3.5 provides a summary of the associated legislation at the Commonwealth and state levels.

Exhibit 3.5 Associated employment legislation in Australia

NSW	Qld	SA	WA	Tas	Vic	ACT
Anti-discrimination Act 1977	Anti Discrimination Act 1991	Equal Opportunity Act 1984	Equal Opportunity Act 1984	Anti Discrimination Act 1998	Child Employment Act 2003	Discrimination Act 1991
Essential Services Act 1988	Child Employment Act 2006	Long Service Leave Act 1987	Long Service Leave Act 1958	Long Service Leave Act 1976	Equal Opportunity Act 1995	Long Service Leave Act 1986
Industrial Relations (Child Employment) Act 2006	Public Service Act 1996	Occupational Health, Safety and Welfare Act 1986	Minimum Conditions of Employment Act 1993	Shop Trading Hours Act 1984	Long Service Leave Act 1992	Occupational Health and Safety Act 1989
Long Service Leave Act 1955	Superannuation (State Public Sector) Act 1990	Public Sector Management Act 1995	Occupational Safety and Health Act 1984	State Service Act 2000	Occupational Health and Safety Act 2004	Public Sector Management Act 1994
Occupational Health and Safety Act 2000	Trading (Allowable Hours) Act 1990	Superannuation Act 1988	Public Sector Management Act 1993	Workers Rehabilitation and Compensation Act 1988	Public Administration Act 2004	Superannuation (Legislative Assembly Members) Act 1991
Public Sector Employment and Management Act 2002	Workers' Compensation and Rehabilitation Act 2003	Worker's Rehabilitation and Compensation Act 1986	Superannuation and Family Benefits Act 1938	Workplace Health and Safety Act 1995	Superannuation (Public Sector) Act 1992	Workers Compensation Act 1951
Shops and Industries Act 1962	Workers' Accommodation Act 1952		Workers' Compensation and Rehabilitation Act 1981		Workers Compensation Act 1958	**NT**
Superannuation Act 1916	Workplace Health and Safety Act 1995				Workplace Rights Advocate Act 2005	Anti Discrimination Act 1996
Workers Compensation Act 1987						Long Service Leave Act 1981
Workplace Surveillance Act 2005						Public Sector Employment and Management Act 2001
						Superannuation Act 1986
						Work Health Act 1986

COMMONWEALTH
Age Discrimination Act 2004, Disability Discrimination Act 1992, Equal Employment Opportunity (Commonwealth Authorities) Act 1987, Equal Opportunity for Women in the Workplace Act 1999, Occupational Health and Safety Act 1991, Public Service Act 1999, Racial Discrimination Act 1975, Sex Discrimination Act 1984, Superannuation Act 1992, Superannuation Act 1976, Superannuation Act 1990, Superannuation Act 2005

II. The industrial relations institutions

This section of the chapter outlines the main institutions regulating the employment relationship in Australia today. These are

- The Australian Fair Pay Commission (FPC)
- The Workplace Authority (formerly the Office of the Employment Advocate)
- The Australian Industrial Relations Commission (AIRC)
- The Workplace Ombudsman (formerly the Office of Workplace Services)
- The Australian Industrial Registry.

We focus on the Australian Fair Pay Commission because it is a new and vital institution created under *WorkChoices*. The Workplace Authority, the Australian Industrial Relations

Commission (AIRC), and the Workplace Ombudsman are briefly described. Exhibit 3.6 identifies the main institutions now operating and their principal functions.

Exhibit 3.6 Main institutions in Australia's industrial relations system

Institution	Function
The Australian Fair Pay Commission	Set and adjust minium wage
The Workplace Authority	Acceptance and lodgement of all workplace agreements, vetting of all agreements according to the new 'Fairness Test' (see later)
The Australian Industrial Relations Commission	Simplify and rationalise awards, regulate industrial action, resolve certain claims for relief from termination of employment
The Workplace Ombudsman	Audit and monitor workplaces and ensure compliance with workplace agreements, awards and the Standard.

The Australian Fair Pay Commission

The Fair Pay Commission (FPC) is a new institution in Australia's labour market and employment relations system. It is established as a statutory body independent from the Australian government, although the appointment of the Chair and Commissioners is by the government of the day.

In having authority over the setting of minimum wages, the FPC takes over a function previously undertaken by the Australian Industrial Relations Commission. The FPC is now the body which will set the legal minimum wage and set minimum award classification pay scales (based on the Award Review Taskforce). Minimum wages in Australia were previously set through award determinations, not by legislation, so the introduction of the FPC and legislated minimum wages represents a significant change from the previous minimum wage-setting mechanism in Australia.

The process by which federal minimum pay levels will be determined is also significantly different to that which previously operated through the AIRC. In the past, the 14 wage classification levels of the Metal Industries Award formed the basis of minimum wage adjustments and were determined by an annual safety net wage (or living wage) review. The lowest of these classification levels, C14, formed the federal minimum wage. In the 2005 test case (the final one under the old system), this was set at $12.75 per hour.

The main criteria for setting minimum wages in Australia through the award system fluctuated between the 'needs' of workers and the economy's or industry's 'capacity to pay.' For the FPC, however, arguments about the ability of the economy to pay and the labour market to create jobs for the low-skilled and youth entering the labour market take first priority. That these issues are now specifically mentioned in the FPC's parameters for adjusting minimum wages (discussed further below), reflects the increased desire of the federal government to connect welfare and work policies, and has led critics of the new system to believe that an opening is appearing for the creation of a 'working poor'.[12]

Apart from the criteria by which wages are set there has also been a significant shift in the level at which wages are set. As a result of changes in government policy over the past 10 to 20 years, the focus of wage-setting has been systematically moved from the national to the industry levels and then to the enterprise and, more latterly, to the individual employee. With the formal introduction of enterprise bargaining in 1991, the emphasis shifted from national or industry scale justifications to the capacity of single enterprises to pay. Since the introduction of the concept of the individual agreement (the Australian Workplace Agreement, the AWA) in 1996, the locus of attention shifted further to the ability of individuals to bargain. It is anticipated that this shift in emphasis to individual wage determination will continue.

Exhibit 3.7 demonstrates the shift from award-reliant employees to individual contracting over the past 15 years. While the data have had to be collated from various sources and are therefore not strictly comparable, clearly indicative trends are evident. In 1995, 33 per cent of workers had their pay and conditions set by awards; in 2004 it was down to 20 per cent and it is anticipated that the proportion covered by awards alone will continue to decline.

Exhibit 3.7 Breakdown of workforce employment arrangements – 1990 to 2004 and beyond

Arrangement	1990	1995	1999	2000	2002	2004	2010–15
Awards		33%	22%	23.2%	20.5%	20%	5–10%
Collective agreements	80%	No statistics					25% union: 15% non-union n/a
Registered			42%	35.2%	36.1%	38.3%	
Unregistered			No statistics	1.5%	2.2%	2.6%	
Individual contracts	20%	No statistics	No statistics				
Registered				1.8%	2.0%	2.4%	15%
Unregistered				38.2%	39.3%	31.2%	25%

Note: They also have 10 per cent on 'over-awards.'

Source: ABS, *Award coverage Australia*, May 1990, cat. no. 6315.0; AWIRS survey, cited in *Australian Industrial Law Newsletter*, 8/2000; Department of Employment, Workplace Relations and Small Business, *Award and agreement coverage survey*, 1999; ABS, *Employee earnings and hours*, May 2000, Australia, cat. no. 6306.0; ABS, *Employee earnings and hours*, May 2002, Australia, cat. no. 6306.0; ABS, *Employee earnings and hours*, May 2004, Australia, cat. no. 6306.0; based on Briggs C. and Buchanan J. 2005. *WorkChoices: Overview and likely implications*, Acirrt.

Structure of the Fair Pay Commission

The Australian Fair Pay Commission is based in Melbourne and is made up of the Chair, four Commissioners and a Secretariat. The Chair may be full-time or part-time and is appointed by the Commonwealth government for a period of no more than five years.

The four other Commissioners are part-time appointees and are selected from a broader range of backgrounds and experience than the Chair, including community organisations and workplace relations. Their terms are limited to a maximum of four years.[13] The inaugural Commission members were Professor Ian Harper (an economist) as Chair, Mr Hugh Armstrong (former National Executive President of the Australian Services Union), Mr Patrick McClure (CEO of Mission Australia, a large not-for-profit organisation), Mr Mike O'Hagan (owner and director of a company called 'MiniMovers') and Professor Judith Sloan (a labour economist and member of the Productivity Commission).[14]

The Secretariat provides administrative and research support for the Commission, including commissioning research, managing communications and coordinating consultation to assist in the wage-setting functions. The Secretariat is headed up by a Director who is appointed by the Minister for Workplace Relations. The key operating areas will cover policy and research, workplace relations law and practice, consultation and communication.[15]

Function of the FPC

The new Commission's main function is to conduct wage reviews and set wages, depending on the outcomes of wage reviews, with regard to wages in four areas:

1 The Federal Minimum Wage

2 Special Federal Minimum Wages for junior employees, employees with disabilities or employees to whom training arrangements apply

3 Piece rates of pay payable to employees or employees of particular classifications

4 Casual loadings.

There are particular wage-setting parameters within which the AFPC must work, and the objective of the FPC in performing its wage-setting function is to promote the economic prosperity of the people of Australia having regard to the following:

- the capacity for the unemployed and low paid to obtain and remain in employment

- employment and competitiveness across the economy

- providing a safety net for the low paid

- providing minimum wages for junior employees, employees to whom training arrangements apply and employees with disabilities that ensure those employees are 'competitive in the labour market'.[16]

The FPC's wage-setting decisions must be in writing, be expressed as decisions of the FPC as a body, and include reasons for the wage-setting decision. The Federal Minimum Wage must also be expressed as a monetary amount per hour. While these parameters provide some direction to the Commission in the setting of minimum wages, the Commission will still have considerable autonomy. It has authority to determine the timing, frequency and scope of wage reviews as well as the way in which the wage reviews are to be conducted. Also, the FPC can determine when wage-setting decisions are to come into effect and there is no guarantee that minimum wages will continue to be adjusted annually, as they have been in the past.

The FPC's wage-setting process

The process of FPC wage setting is very different to the process that was used by the AIRC to set minimum pay. Before commenting on the process by which minimum wages will be set, it is useful to be reminded of the FPC's functions.

The FPC is to do the following:

- Set and adjust the federal minimum wage.

- Set and adjust minimum classification pay scales.

- Set and adjust the federal minimum wage for juniors, trainees (including school-based apprentices) and employees with disabilities.

- Set and adjust minimum wages for piece workers.

- Set and adjust casual loadings.

The Commission's Chair has set out three important questions which will guide the Commission in its first wage-setting round. The questions, delivered to the Committee for the Economic Development of Australia by the Commission's Chair in Melbourne on 27 May 2006, are:

1 What do we know about the impact of minimum wages on employment and unemployment?

2 Who are the low paid in Australia and where do they work and live?

3 How are the incomes of the low-paid affected by changes in the minimum wage?

In its first round, the FPC cannot lower minimum wages below the levels set by the AIRC in its 2005 Safety Net Review. As noted earlier, this is $12.75 per hour and it is enshrined in the legislation as the base line for any subsequent wage adjustments. This hourly rate is thus the starting point for the minimum hourly rate of regular employees. As distinct from the operation of the AIRC in the former safety net review process, the Fair Pay Commission does not have to determine on the basis of presentations or evidence presented to it. Instead, the Commission can consult with the community, gather its own data and tender for research. Ultimately, the final decision is that of the Commission alone.

The FPC made its first decision in October 2006 and is due to make a second decision in late 2007. The first decision awarded a graded increase of $0.72 per hour to $13.47 an hour, or $27 a week for those earning less than $700 per week, and slightly less for those on higher wages. Reactions to the decision were mixed, with the union movement on the whole welcoming it (though not the need for the FPC), and employer groups suggesting the decision would cost jobs and drive up inflation.[17]

News report 3.2 is from the FPC's website:[18]

NEWS REPORT 3.2

Wage-setting decision

The Australian Fair Pay Commission's first decision was made in October and took effect from 1 December 2006. The decision has three main elements:

- an increase of $0.72 to the standard Federal Minimum Wage (to $13.47 an hour);
- an increase of $0.72 to basic periodic rates of pay in all Australian Pay and Classification Scales (Pay Scales) up to $18.42 per hour (i.e. up to around $700 per week based on a standard 38 hour week); and
- an increase of $0.58 to basic periodic rates of pay in all Pay Scales above $18.42 per hour (i.e. above around $700 per week based on a standard 38 hour week).

The increases flow on to junior employees, employees to whom training arrangements apply, employees with disabilities and basic piece rates of pay.

Source: 2006 Minimum Wage Decision Factsheet, Australian Fair Pay Commission, copyright Commonwealth of Australia reproduced by permission.

The Workplace Authority

The Workplace Authority was previously known as the Office of the Employment Advocate (OEA), first introduced in the first *Workplace Relations Act 1996* to oversee Australian Workplace Agreements (AWAs). The reduced role of the AIRC has to some extent been substituted by an expanded role for the Workplace Authority. The Workplace Authority now has a number of functions including the promotion and making of workplace agreements (see below for explanation of forms of workplace agreements); handling the acceptance and lodgement of *all* workplace agreements and notices about transmission of instruments and the collection of data and analysis of workplace agreements.

WorkChoices also requires the Workplace Authority to encourage the respective parties to agreement-making to take account of the needs of workers in disadvantaged bargaining positions (e.g. women, people from a non-English speaking background, young people, apprentices, trainees and outworkers) and also to have particular regard to assisting workers to balance work and family responsibilities and the need to prevent and eliminate discrimination because of, or for reasons including, race, colour, sex, sexual preference, age, physical or mental disability, marital status, family responsibilities, pregnancy, religion, political opinion, natural extraction or social origin.

The Australian Industrial Relations Commission

Over the course of the 20th century, the Australian Industrial Relations Commission (AIRC) became the primary tribunal resolving disputes and determining wages and conditions. *WorkChoices* changes its role considerably. The revised structure and functions of the AIRC are contained in Part 3 of the amended *Workplace Relations Act 1996*.

The AIRC's key functions are to rationalise and simplify awards and deal with unfair dismissal claims for businesses with more than 100 employees. It may also make 'Workplace Determinations' (but only if the Minister has issued a declaration on the basis that industrial action is threatening life, safety or is likely to cause significant economic damage) and perform limited dispute resolution functions (those conferred on it by agreement between employers and employees under workplace agreements); conciliate unlawful termination claims; negotiate agreements to the extent that the parties agree, regulate protected action where a secret ballot occurs; issue orders to stop unprotected action (must be issued within 48 hours, unless 'contrary to public interest') and revoke and suspend right of entry permits and resolve disputes over right of entry.

Most significantly, the AIRC has lost its wage-setting responsibilities by the transfer of its wage fixation power to the Fair Pay Commission (discussed above). As a result of the expanded role of the Workplace Authority, the AIRC no longer has responsibility for certifying collective bargaining agreements and furthermore it is not permitted to make any new industrial awards. The AIRC has also lost its compulsory dispute resolution functions as the new legislation encourages voluntary dispute resolution through the inclusion of a voluntary dispute resolution clause in all awards and agreements.

The Workplace Ombudsman

The role of the Workplace Ombudsman, formerly the Office of Workplace Services (OWS), is to provide inspectorate and compliance services. It provides advice and assistance to employers, workers and organisations about compliance and enforcement under the *Workplace Relations Act*. It may investigate claims of alleged breaches of federal industrial instruments and the *Workplace Relations Act 1996* lodged by employers and workers and where appropriate initiate litigation action in the courts to enforce workplace laws and enforce compliance with the *Workplace Relations Act 1996*. Workplace inspectors are able to enforce penalties for breaches of terms of the Australian Fair Pay and Conditions Standard, a workplace agreement, an award or order of the Australian Industrial Relations Commission, meal break entitlements, public holiday entitlements or extended parental leave entitlements.

III. The parties in industrial relations

In its simplest and most direct form, the employment relationship is a relationship between the employer and employee. Employment relations, however, are typically not so simple and are complicated by a number of other factors, including power relationships. When it comes to bargaining about terms and conditions of work, an employer generally has more power than an individual employee. For that reason, employees sometimes prefer to gain strength from acting collectively and from being represented by a third party in bargaining. Unions, representing groups of workers in a particular trade, occupation or industry, typically perform this function and engage in collective bargaining with employers.

In most countries, unions have been in decline. Despite this, they do still represent the collective voice of employees and understanding of unions and the union movement is crucial to understanding industrial relations.

Unions and the union movement

In 1894, Sidney and Beatrice Webb began their seminal work on trade unions with the following definition: 'A Trade Union … is a continuous association of wage-earners for the purpose of maintaining or improving the conditions of their employment.'[19] Today, the standard definition used by the Australian Bureau of Statistics is not very different: 'a union is an organisation, consisting predominantly of employees, the principal activities of which include the negotiation of rates of pay and conditions of employment for its members'.[20]

On the basis of these definitions we can see that a union is a work-based organisation, providing a collective voice for employees, and an institution whose purpose is to represent and defend those who work for someone else. The definitions emphasise a union's function as an organisation to defend, maintain and improve wages and working conditions through means such as bargaining, representation before tribunals and lobbying governments.

Early last century, H.B. Higgins, one of the founding fathers of Australia's unique conciliation and arbitration system, wrote that unionism should be fostered so that employers did not have to deal with the individual complaints of each employee. Instead, he maintained that employee concerns and grievances could and should be represented collectively through their union.

> The system of arbitration adopted by the Act [*Conciliation and Arbitration Act 1904*] is based on unionism ... It is, of course, better for an employer that he should not be worried by complaints of individual employees and that any complaints should be presented collectively by some responsible union.[21]

Support for unions as necessary and legitimate actors in industrial relations had declined dramatically by the end of last century. In part, this was aided by the emerging human resource management approaches which emphasised direct communication with employees and individualisation of the employment relationship. The changing view of unions was also fostered by governments which have had, as noted earlier in the chapter, a preference for deregulation of the employment relationship and less desire for third-party intervention or external regulation.

Despite the shifting political and economic contexts, Australian unions have been quite successful in achieving improved wages and working conditions for employees. Apart from ensuring that workers have entitlements such as paid sick leave and holiday leave, estimates show that wages outcomes in union-negotiated enterprise agreements are up to 17.5 per cent higher than non-union agreements.[22] However, in order to perform the functions described above, a union must have some degree of legitimacy. Employers and workers must recognise the union as the organisation that should represent employees in the bargaining over wages and conditions. Only when this recognition occurs can unions then proceed to bargain with management and represent the interest of their members. Gaining recognition is thus a very important aspect of a union's role and the ease with which this recognition is gained can be influenced by legislation and managerial policy. The federal government's latest changes to Australia's industrial relations legislation make recognition and bargaining even harder for unions. This is discussed in greater detail below. Furthermore, some managerial policies and human resource management strategies have taken advantage of the legislative environment to marginalise, avoid or exclude unions.

For unions to continue to represent and defend the interests of employees, they must also have members. This has become a complex and serious problem for unions in many advanced, industrialised nations. In Australia, for instance, unionisation rates have declined considerably since the mid-20th century. There are approximately 9 million employees in Australia and about 25 per cent of them are members of a union. Union membership is usually expressed as union density, that is, the percentage of the paid workforce belonging to a union. In Australia, these figures show union density to be falling. For instance, between 1990 and 2005 union density declined from 40.5 per cent to 22.4 per cent.[23]

There are some significant variations in union density between different sectors and segments of the labour force. For example, the following patterns in union density exist:

- a higher proportion in the public sector than in the private sector

- higher rates of unionisation among full-time workers than part-time workers

- slightly higher unionisation levels for men than women
- the highest rates of unionisation occurring in the sectors of power, water and gas supply, transport and government, administration and defence.

The decline in union membership presents a challenge for unions – and the union movement as a whole – and a great deal of research has been undertaken into union decline.[24] While there is still debate about the causes of decline in Australia, they may be grouped into two broad categories: those internal to unions and those external to unions. The internal causes relate to the unions themselves, their political alliance with the Australian Labor Party and their strategies over the past decade. The causes external to unions include the changes in the volume, structure and nature of work, as well as management and government strategies, which are discussed below.

The union movement

There are approximately 130 unions in Australia. These single unions have often defended their members by building alliances with other unions and becoming part of a 'union movement.' Unity and collective action are the foundation concepts of unionism. While a union may operate independently during the bargaining process, it often also shares power with other unions, acting in a coordinated way. In this sense, unions extend their unity and power organisationally as a union movement. Despite the changed political, economic and social environment, the union movement continues to play an important role in Australian society and at Australian workplaces and it remains an important part of Australian industrial relations.

The extension of unity through the union movement has given rise to a range of important inter-union institutions, generally referred to as peak bodies. In Australia, the peak national union body is the Australian Council of Trade Unions (ACTU). The ACTU was formed in 1927 and initially represented private sector, blue-collar unions. During the late 1970s and early 1980s, the white-collar and public sector peak union councils merged with the ACTU, so that it came to represent the vast majority of Australian unionists. The ACTU is now generally regarded as the 'voice' of the Australian union movement, although there are other peak bodies that operate at regional levels in places such as Newcastle and Wollongong, dealing with issues of specific relevance to workers in their geographic jurisdiction. In each of the states there are also peak union associations, for instance Unions NSW, the Queensland Council of Unions and the United Trades and Labor Council of South Australia.

The ACTU actively lobbies political parties and governments about a range of issues affecting the lives of workers and their families, both in Australia and internationally. For instance, the ACTU has taken an active stand on social issues such as paid maternity leave, on political causes such as independence for East Timor and the exploitation of child labour by multinationals, and on environmental issues such as atomic testing in the Pacific Ocean. Recently, the ACTU has forcefully opposed the *WorkChoices* legislation.

Union recognition

Australia's previous industrial relations system was based on conciliation and arbitration and could not function without collective organisations. Employer associations and, more particularly, unions, were component parties to a system which dealt with industrial disputes that extended beyond the limits of any one state. But a focus upon collective bodies – and unions in particular – has been in decline since a non-union stream of collective bargaining was added to the federal system in the *Industrial Relations Reform Act 1993*. The transformation of the legal framework gathered pace with the introduction of individual Australian Workplace Agreements (AWAs) in the *Workplace Relations Act 1996*. *WorkChoices* confirms the demise of a union-based system. It sets out to regulate the relationship between employers and employees, not between collective organisations.

Freedom of association

As noted earlier, unions gain legitimacy through official recognition and having a strong membership base. In order to recruit members, unions need to have access to them and employees need to be able to join unions. The concept of 'freedom of association' refers to the rights of employees to belong to a union or not to belong to a union. It was introduced in the *Workplace Relations Act 1996*. While *WorkChoices* retains these 'freedom of association' clauses, it does so in a slightly different form, and with the expansion of certain prohibitions, mainly directed at unions. *WorkChoices* says that people 'are free to become, or not become, members of industrial associations' and that no-one is to be 'discriminated against or victimised' for belonging to or not belonging to a union.[25]

Arguably, however, it is now more difficult to pursue claims under *WorkChoices* because when employees want to show that an employer has so discriminated against them on the basis of their union membership, they must establish that this was 'the "sole or dominant reason" for the action in question, not merely a reason'.[26]

Rights of entry

'Rights of entry' refers to the ability of union organisers to enter a workplace. Under *WorkChoices*, the rights of union officers to enter workplaces have been reduced, putting up additional barriers to union activities. Under the legislation:

- The requirements placed upon union officials seeking to obtain (and keep) an entry permit are more onerous than in the past.

- Unions can only gain access to a workplace to investigate alleged breaches of agreements or awards when at least one of the employees affected is a member of that union.

- The union must already have an agreement or award that gives it coverage of the employees whom officers seek to meet.

Exactly how all the changes will affect unions – changes to industrial action, freedom of association and rights of entry – remains to be seen. Unions may well find it more difficult to represent existing members or recruit new ones. There is no doubt that the new legislation is true to its goals of enhancing the individual employment relationships at the workplace. The legislation seeks to limit the extent of 'third party intervention' in very clear ways.

> The new union 'right of entry' provisions provide employers with far greater scope to resist or limit unwanted union influence at the workplace. Amendments to the 'freedom of association' provisions will restrict unions' capacity to engage in a range of tactics to support the collective representation of workers' interests, and limit their ability to block de-unionisation or individualisation strategies by employers.[27]

The decline in unionisation rates suggests that a significant shift in the traditional collectivist philosophy of Australian industrial relations has occurred. Nonetheless, most employees, even if they are not union members, have terms and conditions of employment that have as their reference point an award or a collectively negotiated agreement. These instruments of regulation are explained below, but before that we turn to employers and their associations, the other important parties to the employment relationship.

Employers and employer associations

In the past, just as employees formed unions, employers in Australia formed associations to represent them in multi-employer bargaining and before industrial tribunals. Under enterprise bargaining, however, the emphasis is on single employer bargaining, and consequently the role of employer associations as bargaining agents has also diminished. Sheldon and Thornthwaite

note that while there are hundreds of employer associations in Australia, very few provide an industrial relations service. Furthermore, membership of employer associations is declining, especially among firms with more than 500 employees.[28] Employers are performing their own negotiations with their employees and unions and, in many instances, this role would come under the human resource management portfolio. Furthermore, the environment in which the employment relationship is negotiated has changed considerably and the thrust of legislation has been to provide employers with greater choice and flexibility. Employers have responded to the changing political and union environments in a variety of ways. Some employers have taken the initiative to force change on their workforces and unions through limiting right of entry to unions, using tough bargaining tactics such as the lock-out and favouring various forms of individual contracts over more traditional collective bargaining processes. Other employers have adopted a softer approach and utilised the new industrial relations environment and enterprise bargaining to introduce more flexible work arrangements, family friendly initiatives and more satisfactory work organisation.

A review of some of the major industrial disputes over recent years suggests that a number of key employers in the mining and maritime industries have deliberately adopted a more aggressive or strategic approach to relations with unions while adopting a high commitment approach with their employees.[29] The result has been to attack union representation and collective bargaining while moving to individualised employment contracts.[30] In other industries (e.g. telecommunications, call centres and warehousing), employers have sought greater compliance from unions or tried to avoid them. Yet other employers have worked towards greater employee commitment and a degree of union cooperation (e.g. ICI/Orica, Colgate-Palmolive and Australia Post).[31] These different approaches illustrate the variety of industrial relations and human resource management models that currently exist in Australia.[32]

IV. The processes – collective bargaining, enterprise bargaining and industrial action

There are two key concepts in industrial relations that refer to the way in which employees and employers have determined wages and conditions of work in Australia. These are *collective bargaining* and *arbitration*. Together they have been the main processes used to resolve conflict between employers and unions and settle terms and conditions of work. In more recent times, the notion of individual bargaining has become more pronounced. An important distinction in industrial relations is between those matters that are subject to joint regulation (or bargaining and negotiation) and those that are determined unilaterally (or solely by managerial discretion or prerogative).

An early US text by Chamberlain (1951) stated that collective bargaining involves the 'agreement by employers and unions on the general terms under which employees would consent to work'.[33] Later, Clegg (1960) offered a classical definition of collective bargaining as the method used to resolve conflicts of interest between unions and employers, standing in contrast to methods of joint consultation, which are used where the interests coincide.[34] In both definitions, collective bargaining is understood to be inseparable from unionism. Since these early studies of collective bargaining there have been many developments in national systems of industrial relations and further refinement of bargaining frameworks, with consequences for the conduct of collective bargaining.

Arbitration is the process of using a third, independent party to unilaterally decide the resolution to a conflict between the two industrial parties of labour and capital. In some countries private and voluntary arbitration is encouraged, where the parties choose their own arbitrator; in others a publicly funded system of arbitration is provided. In Australia, under *WorkChoices*, the arbitral powers of the AIRC are very restricted and there is a much greater emphasis on direct bargaining between the employers and employees at the workplace level – a process that was for some time specifically referred to as *enterprise bargaining*.

Enterprise bargaining was a particular variant of collective bargaining, which dominated Australian industrial relations practice and theory during the 1990s.

Enterprise bargaining was formally introduced in Australia in 1991. The term 'enterprise bargaining' tends to be understood in two ways:

1   as the system of industrial relations currently in operation in Australia today, and contrasting with the former system of compulsory conciliation and arbitration

2   as one method of determining, through negotiation, the terms and conditions of employment for a specific enterprise or workplace. [35]

Apart from enterprise bargaining, there are two other variants of collective bargaining in Australia that have attracted some attention in recent years: *pattern bargaining* and *concession bargaining*. Pattern bargaining is defined as the 'imitation of collective bargaining settlements by parties not directly involved in the initial negotiations'.[36] The federal government in Australia, which is opposed to pattern bargaining, has defined it as 'a course of conduct, bargaining or the making of claims in a campaign or part of a campaign that involves seeking common outcomes in respect of wages or other employment conditions'.[37] The government's objections stem from its desire to restrict outcomes to a particular enterprise or workplace, and its opposition to the spread of outcomes from the stronger bargainers to the weaker bargainers. *Concession (or concessionary) bargaining*, a term that is more commonly associated with industrial relations in the United States during the 1980s, also emerged in Australia during the late 1990s.[38] In the United States it is understood as 'unions agreeing to wage cuts or freezes or in other ways, such as work rule changes, giving back to employers previous gains'.[39] In Australia it has been applied to the process whereby unions concede reduced terms of employment for new employees compared with existing employees – generally in return for job security – or where unions are forced to accept reduced terms and conditions in subsequent generations of the agreement, as per the US definition.

Industrial action

One way that unions and employers enforce their bargaining power is to take industrial action. In the traditional industrial relations and industrial sociological literature, industrial action is conceived of in broad and encompassing terms.

Under Australian legislation, however, industrial action and union activity is now heavily regulated and tightly defined. For instance, a secret ballot must be held in order to go on strike; a majority of the employees must vote in the ballot and of them, a majority must vote in favour of the action. Employees and unions may only lawfully take industrial action at certain times in bargaining and this is referred to as 'protected action.' There are heavy fines if these rules are not followed.

V. The instruments of regulation

As discussed earlier in the chapter, the objective of the federal government's industrial relations agenda is to encourage (perhaps even force) employees and employers to bargain directly with each other, either collectively or individually. Under the new bargaining framework there are now various options for formally codifying the terms and conditions of employment. These are Workplace Agreements – both collective and individual. No new awards are to be made.

All Workplace Agreements are legally enforceable documents. Additionally, outside the formal bargaining structure, individual contracts of employment made under common law are an option, as they always have been. There are six forms of agreement available under *WorkChoices* (set out in Part 8, Workplace Agreements). In addition, there are transitional arrangements to enable the move from the old to the new system.

Making agreements under *WorkChoices*

'Workplace Agreement' is the generic term for all forms of agreement under *WorkChoices*. Whether this broad terminology will help or hinder employers, managers and employees in understanding the processes remains to be seen. It is noteworthy that the term 'enterprise agreements,' for so long part of the language of industrial relations and human resource management, no longer appears in the Act.

There are six forms of 'workplace agreement,' and they are set out in the following order in the Act:

1 Australian workplace agreements (AWAs)

2 employee collective agreements

3 union collective agreements

4 union greenfields agreements

5 employer greenfields agreements

6 Multiple-business agreements.

All these agreements are to be lodged with the Workplace Authority and agreements operate as soon as they are lodged.

Australian Workplace Agreements

The new Act retains AWAs. These were first introduced in 1996. *WorkChoices* confirms recent jurisprudence in stating that 'An AWA may be made before commencement of the employment'; that is, employers can require new employees to sign an AWA as a pre-condition of employment.[40] AWAs are, plainly, the government's preferred option in agreement-making. AWAs override awards, other agreements and state instruments where there is an inconsistency.

Employee collective agreements

These non-union but collective agreements take over from the old non-union agreements. Employers may make such an agreement with employees in a single business or in part of a business.

Union collective agreements

These agreements, made between employers and 'organisations of employees' (i.e. unions) may be made when an organisation has at least one member employed in a single business (or part of a business) subject to the agreement to be made. The union involved must be entitled to represent that member, or those members.

Union greenfields agreements

As was the case before *WorkChoices*, what are now called union greenfields agreements may be made between an employer and 'one or more organisations of employees' if a new business is to be established. The meaning of 'new business' caused some dispute under the old Act. Under *WorkChoices* the definition is broad: for the purposes of these agreements, and for making 'employer greenfields agreements,' a 'new business' is a 'new business, new project or new undertaking'.[41]

Employer greenfields agreements

This is an entirely new form of greenfields agreement, one which an employer may make for a 'new business, new project or new undertaking' with no other party. The 'agreement' and its conditions are made unilaterally by employers. Employer greenfields agreements are written and lodged and then bind all employees as they come on stream. They can only last for 12 months.

Multiple-business agreements

Multiple-business agreements may take the form of any one of the collective agreements set out in *WorkChoices*' (that is, employee collective agreements, union collective agreements, union greenfields agreements or employer greenfields agreements). In some respects, it is surprising that multiple-business agreements exist in the Act at all, given the government's desire to focus on individual and single workplace agreements. These agreements are, less surprisingly, limited in scope in one important respect. This is that the Workplace Authority must not authorise the agreement unless satisfied 'that it is in the public interest to do so'.[42] It would then direct the employer to make an agreement in another way.

Required content in all agreements

All agreements will be read and understood in the context of the five minimum conditions of the Fair Pay and Conditions Standard (see above). Recent modifications to *WorkChoices* include a new 'Fairness Test' which amends some of these conditions (see 'Further changes to *WorkChoices*' later in this chapter). No workplace agreement or contract may exclude the minimum standards.

WorkChoices sets out four other items as 'required content':

- Nominal expiry date: one year in the case of employer greenfields agreements, but five years in all other cases.

- Dispute settlement procedures: if not included, then the 'model clauses' set out in the Act will apply.

- Protected award conditions which are listed in the Act. These relate to breaks (including meal breaks), incentive payments, annual leave loadings, days in lieu of public holidays, some allowances, loadings and penalty rates and special conditions for clothing outworkers.

- Content of other documents: other clauses from awards or prior agreements may, subject to some restriction, be 'called up' to a new agreement. Of these matters, the most contentious – and confusing – has been 'protected conditions.' These are taken to be included in new workplace agreements under *WorkChoices* but they can be overridden in subsequent agreement-making, so the protection is in fact limited to only existing agreements. (Clauses pertaining to outworkers are the only exception.)

Prohibited content

WorkChoices is highly prescriptive about matters that are not allowed to be included in any new workplace agreements. These are referred to as 'prohibited content.' These matters, which are not listed in the Act itself, but in the accompanying Regulations, include:

- payroll deduction of union dues

- trade union training leave

- paid union meetings

- the re-negotiation of a workplace agreement

- mandatory union involvement in dispute-settling procedures

- union rights of entry
- restrictions on engagement of independent contractors or their terms of engagement
- restrictions on engagement of labour hire of workers and requirements relating to their working conditions
- cashing out of annual leave other than that in accordance with the AFPC Standard
- provision of information about employees to a trade union other than that as required by law
- provisions encouraging or discouraging union membership or the employer supporting or not supporting the persons being union members
- terms permitting industrial action
- terms restricting or prohibiting disclosure of details of the agreements to the person bound by the agreement
- any remedy for unfair dismissal.

Exhibit 3.8 Terms prohibited under the Act

Terms which the Act prohibits from workplace agreements include those which:

1 provide for union training, deduction of union dues from wages or paid union meeting;

2 mandate union involvement in dispute-setting procedures;

3 restrict the use of independent contractors;

4 permit industrial action during the term of the agreement;

5 provide a remedy for unfair dismissal;

6 restrict AWAs; and

7 provide that any future agreement must be a union collective agreement.

Source: DEWR, 2006.

Awards

The role of awards, for so long central to employment relations in Australia, is all but ended:
- Minimum conditions are now set by the legislated standards and the AFPCS (discussed above).
- The abolition of the 'no disadvantage test' further weakens the award framework.
- The number of 'non-allowable' matters has been increased; in awards that do continue, some terms will no longer be enforceable.
- An award review task force has been set up to simplify and reduce the total number of awards.
- No new awards will be made except as a result of the task force's consolidation.

Transition arrangements

There are also special arrangements for the transition from state to federal systems. Those employers who are defined as corporations (and their employees) will initially be covered by 'a notional agreement preserving a state award' (NAPSA) or a 'preserved state agreement.'

Further changes to *WorkChoices*

In May 2007, after more than a year of controversy since the introduction of *WorkChoices*, the Commonwealth government announced further amendments to the *WorkChoices* legislation.

The changes included the introduction of a new 'Fairness Test,' the renaming of the Office of the Employment Advocate (OEA) to the Workplace Authority and the renaming of the Office of Workplace Services (OWS), to the Workplace Ombudsman. The roles of both institutions have also been expanded. The Workplace Authority now vets new agreements according to the 'Fairness Test' and the Workplace Ombudsman will conduct random audits of businesses.

The 'Fairness Test'

Much of the *WorkChoices* controversy was about which entitlements were actually 'protected by law.' Under the original *WorkChoices* legislation, 'protected' content was only 'protected' by default. Protected content included penalty rates, shift and overtime loadings, monetary allowances, annual leave loadings, public holidays, rest breaks, incentive-based payments and bonuses. These could, however, be legally removed in the making of a new agreement – either an AWA or a collective agreement. Employers were thus able to remove, in one step, any or all of the 'protected' entitlements, if the new agreement explicitly said they were not included. As data appeared, it became clear that many AWAs were, indeed, removing protected entitlements.

The Office of the Employment Advocate (OEA) released a sample of the impact of AWAs on 'protected conditions' and revealed that *all* the sampled AWAs removed *at least* one 'protected' award condition. Sixteen per cent removed all of them.[1] Further analysis, by academic David Peetz, showed that more than three-fifths of AWAs abolished penalty rates altogether and more than four-fifths of AWAs abolished or reduced overtime pay. Most AWAs also abolished or reduced meal breaks, public holiday payments and shiftwork loadings.[2] A later sample of AWAs, made between May and October 2006, showed that 45 per cent of AWAs removed *all* protected conditions. As well as still higher proportions removing loadings and penalty rates, incentive payments and bonuses were also being removed in 70 per cent of cases.[3]

In amendments to the *WorkChoices* legislation made in May 2007, a 'Fairness Test' was introduced. It replaces, in part, the former 'No-Disadvantage Test.' It is the responsibility of the newly named Workplace Authority (the former OEA) to conduct the 'Fairness Test.' This is to be done by taking into account both monetary and non-monetary compensation in place of lost 'protected' conditions. The Workplace Authority is to offer a pre-lodgement assessment of proposed agreements against the 'fairness test.' If the Workplace Authority deems the agreement does not pass the test, the employer and employee will be advised to consider ways in which appropriate compensation may be made. The nature of this compensation is slightly ambiguous, as it appears that it need not be financial, but could include more flexible working conditions, for instance.[4]

There remain some concerns with the 'Fairness Test.' It is not universal, and is only to be conducted on agreements for employees earning less than $75 000 per annum. It is not retrospective, so agreements lodged before May 2007 which have lost protected conditions will remain in force.[5] There is confusion about how the Workplace Authority will actually measure the fairness of lost entitlements and their replacements, with the Prime Minister saying that the 'good Australian commonsense' would be used.[6] There is also some uncertainty about who is actually covered by the 'Fairness Test.' The Deputy Leader of the Opposition and the President of the ACTU suggest that workers in new businesses, those on existing AWA individual contracts and people in award-free areas won't be eligible for protection by the new 'Fairness Test.' They imply also that workers in country areas or young people getting their first job are not guaranteed proper financial compensation

for losing their penalty rates, overtime pay, public holiday pay, annual leave loading or other award conditions. The Prime Minister disputed this, but did not clarify the position.[7] Employer groups were somewhat ambivalent in response to the changes. The Australian Industry Group, for instance, said they were not too dissatisfied, whereas the Chamber of Commerce said they were disappointed and that *WorkChoices* needed no change.

1   McIlwain, P. (2006) Evidence to May Estimates Hearing, *Senate Employment, Workplace Relations and Education Committee*, Canberra.

2   Peetz, D. (2007a) 'Brave New *WorkChoices* : What is the Story So Far?,' paper presented to Association of Industrial Relations Academics of Australia and New Zealand, 21st Conference, AIRAANZ, Auckland; see also Peetz, D. (2007b) *Assessing the Impact of 'WorkChoices' – One Year On, Report to the Department of Innovation, Industry and Regional Development, Victoria,* 19 March.

3   *Sydney Morning Herald,* 17 April 2007; see also *Sydney Morning Herald – Weekend Edition,* 21–22 April 2007.

4   Information provided on the Office of the Employee Advocate website http://www.oea.gov.au accessed 22 May, 2007.

5   Prime Minister, Mr John Howard, Transcript of Joint Press Conference Speech (With Mr Joe Hockey,) 4 May 2007 at http://www.ecruiting.com.au/express/200705/howardsafetynet.pdf

6   Prime Minister, Mr John Howard, Transcript of Joint Press Conference Speech (With Mr Joe Hockey,) 4 May 2007 at http://www.ecruiting.com.au/express/200705/howardsafetynet.pdf

7   Prime Minister, Mr John Howard, Transcript of Joint Press Conference Speech (With Mr Joe Hockey,) 4 May 2007 at http://www.ecruiting.com.au/express/200705/howardsafetynet.pdf

Implications: *WorkChoices* and human resource managers

The chapter has concentrated on the legislation and the bargaining framework for Australia, noting the importance of this for framing the way in which the employment relationship is regulated and impacting on the way HR is conducted.

The *WorkChoices* legislation changes the employment relations environment in Australia in two ways. First, it changes the macro regulatory context, that is, the rules of employment relations. Second, it changes the micro-environment of human resource management, by placing direct and complete emphasis on the employment relationship at the organisation level, not the national or industry level. As a consequence, there are new opportunities and challenges for the management of human resources.

The macro-context – or the rules of employment relations – can be summarised as follows:

- For the first time, federal legislation sets minimum standards of employment.

- The Act introduces new regulatory bodies, and restricts the functions of old ones.

- It curtails union presence at the workplace level and restricts collective bargaining.

- Employer prerogative is advanced.

- 'Third-party intervention' in the employment relationship is limited.

Many argue that the *WorkChoices* legislation is deliberately anti-union, that the environment has been re-cast in favour of employers and that individualism, flexibility and choice (as opposed to collectivism, stability and security) have become the dominant norms. Whatever view people take of this debate, there are implications for all aspects of human resource management. In short, *WorkChoices* puts the spotlight on the organisation and its human resource policies. In this micro-context there are new challenges and opportunities:

- The emphasis is on managerial prerogative and the associated rhetoric is about 'mutual benefits' rather than employee and union rights.

- The direct relationship between employer and employee is favoured, thus potentially influencing all human resource management functions over time, especially as the distinction between award-covered and non-award employees becomes more pronounced and the proliferation of employment types increases.
- The emphasis is on a workplace level agreement, individually or collectively bargained.
- The distinctive role of industrial relations (union relations) and industrial relations specialists is undermined, except for those areas where the award system remains unaltered – for instance, state public sector employees.

What does all of this mean for human resource management in Australia? There is, of course, more than one possible response. In the short term, human resource managers have the capacity to influence the transitionary arrangements, and thereby set the stage for the type of relationship they want to develop with their employees. This phase may also signal the nature of the future relationship with unions – if there is to be one at all. In the longer term, the human resource function has potential to take on a greater role. There is potential for change across all aspects of the human resource function: in influencing the types of contract employers have with employees; the selection and management of employees; the resolution of workplace disputes; and the provision of channels for employee voice.

Overall, there is also potential for a much more diverse set of outcomes from human resource management. Some organisations may take the high road of human resource investment; others the low road of labour-shedding and cost-cutting. In a political and economic context that allows this to occur, employers have increased opportunity to exercise 'strategic choice'[43] and to determine the parameters of the employment relationship.

At the same time, employers generally, and human resource managers particularly, must recognise the changing social and demographic characteristics of the Australian workforce. These changes may counter some of the freedom given to them by *WorkChoices*. Factors such as the declining size of the labour force relative to the population, the increasing demand for skills, the changing age demographics, the shifting mix of female and male participation in the paid workforce and the corollary of time and family pressure outside of paid work all create a labour market of great diversity and, in some situations, intense competition. Whichever the chosen course, human resource management has a role to play.

Exhibit 3.9 Decisions for managers

Under *WorkChoices*, managers will have questions both old and new to ask themselves:

- Should existing agreements be honoured in the transitional phase (i.e. for state awards) and thereafter?
- Options in the transitional phases: to re-negotiate terms and conditions comprehensively or to preserve as much as possible and settle on a pay and essential matters agreement?
- How should content that was covered by previous employment awards and agreements but are no longer covered by their award or new workplace agreement be dealt with?
- Do managers move to company policy and manuals or to memorandums of understanding with unions?
- How do managers now deal with unions who are parties to awards or enterprise agreements?
- Is there a need to include the new model dispute resolution procedure?
- What role will state tribunals have in the dispute resolution procedure?

- Grievance handling has now moved firmly back to the workplace, so supervisors and managers will have to deal with this. Are they skilled enough? Will training, re-educating and consulting with line managers about their role in dispute resolution be needed?

- Nominal terms of workplace agreements: what will managers actually want in these agreements?

It is too early to be certain about all the implications of *WorkChoices* for human resource management in Australia. It is also too early for the full effect of *WorkChoices* to permeate Australian workplaces and human resource management practice. Further uncertainty is provided by the unclear industrial relations policies of the Australian Labor Party, in view of the forthcoming federal election in late 2007. However, as to the latter effect, recent press attention to the decisions made by some employers post *WorkChoices* provides an indication of the direction some employers may take. (See 'News report 3.5: Amber and the juice bar squeeze.')

> It … remains to be seen just how quickly employers will move to exploit the
> opportunities the new legislation offers, given its complexity, opposition
> from unions, and indeed the natural conservatism of many managers – and
> whether this will prompt further intervention by a government that appears
> uncomfortable with leaving it to employers to make their own choices.

> Source: Stewart, A. 2006. 'WorkChoices in overview: Big bang or slow burn?',
> *The Economic and Labour Relations Review*, vol. 16, no. 2, May.

As to the impact of *WorkChoices* on human resource practice itself, a sense of this can be gleaned from the experience of other countries that have deregulated frameworks, such as the USA, the UK and New Zealand. The *WorkChoices* environment, with its emphasis on choice, has some parallels with the patterns observed by Kochan, Katz and McKersie of American employers in the 1980s.[44] Kochan and his colleagues wrote of the 'strategic choices' management could make in determining their relationship with unions and employees. They theorised that employers could choose from among the following options: with employees, they could choose to build high trust, high commitment relations, or they could opt for low trust, high control relations; with unions, employers could decide between avoidance, engagement or 'arms-length' arrangements.

By 1994 Walton, Cutcher-Gershenfeld and McKersie[45] observed that the choices for employers in their relations with unions were 'containment' or 'avoidance of unions,' 'arm's length accommodation of unions' or 'cooperation with unions.' With employees, employers were following strategies that produced relationships based on mutual compliance or mutual trust.

In this environment of strategic choice, however, human resource practitioners in the USA have struggled to find their place in organisations. They struggle to be both strategic business partners and to meet the needs of employees, and frequently fail on both counts.[46] With this US experience in mind, it may be the case that the *WorkChoices* environment will be similarly problematic for Australian HR practitioners, as they seek to find their strategic place and value within organisations at the same time as meeting the social and ethical responsibilities that often differentiate the HR role from other management roles in the business.

In the UK, studies show that a voluntaristic, organisational emphasis does not necessarily lead to better HR outcomes. Non-union firms show a 'bleak house' or 'black hole' outcome, where the HR practices and policies are of low quality, and where employee satisfaction and quality of work are lower than in unionised workplaces.[47]

Australia has been on the deregulation trajectory for some time, but the significant difference with *WorkChoices* is the philosophical and legal shift that underpins the changes. The Australian legislative framework for industrial relations had been moving from a centralised, regulated approach to a workplace and organisational focus, and has been accompanied by a deregulation of the labour market. Enterprise bargaining was introduced formally in 1991 and the *Workplace Relations Act 1996* consolidated the workplace focus.

As previous research has shown, aligned with the regulatory changes that occurred through the 1990s, the responsibility for the management of human resources was also moving to the workplace level and to partnerships with both line managers and senior managers.[48] With *WorkChoices* these shifts have been further consolidated; so what do HR managers in Australia think of the most recent changes?

A survey undertaken by the Australian Human Resources Institute (AHRI) in late 2005, when the proposed changes were widely canvassed but before *WorkChoices* came into effect, revealed some interesting responses from Australian HR managers. While most were in favour of a simplified, national system their responses to the role of unions and the need for tighter unfair dismissal laws was more divided.

NEWS REPORT 3.3

HR managers give strong endorsement to national IR system

Nearly nine out of ten human resource managers recently surveyed have endorsed the Government's proposal to move towards a unified national IR system.

Of the 782 respondents to a national survey of members conducted by the Australian Human Resources Institute, 87% indicated preference for a national IR system.

Nearly three out of four respondents also gave backing to the Government's approach on Australian Workplace Agreements, with 72% agreeing with the conditional proposition: 'If the making and approval of AWAs were simplified, business would introduce/increase its use of AWAs.'

In releasing the survey results, AHRI executive director Jo Mithen noted responses to a question on the proposed Fair Pay Commission. 'On this sample, a sizable 91% of our members are saying they want to see at least one commissioner with HR experience, while 77% are also saying they would like to see a union representative on the commission.'

On other survey questions, there was 86% approval for the idea that employees should be entitled to bring in a third party to assist in negotiating employment contracts or AWAs.

On the matter of unfair dismissal laws, however, there was some division with little more than half agreeing that the present unfair dismissal laws are hard on employers. A total of 53% agreed to the proposition that the present unfair dismissal legislation 'favours employees and is biased against employers,' while 47% disagreed with the statement.

On a related proposition that the new laws 'should disallow employees who are made redundant from bringing unfair dismissal claims,' 40% were in agreement with 60% disagreeing.

Respondents were evenly divided on the proposition that 'unions should be entitled to enter a workplace only after seeking a favourable court application,' with exactly 50% agreeing and disagreeing.

'These results show that our members, the HR and people managers with direct responsibility for putting workplace relations policies into practice, bring a healthy mixture of perspectives to the issue,' said Jo Mithen.

The survey was circulated during the latter part of September to a list of AHRI members who have a particular interest in employee relations and industrial relations matters.

Source: *hrmonthly*, December 2005.

The complexity and detail of the changes introduced by *WorkChoices* have specific implications for the management of the wages and conditions of work, as well as more general implications for the nature of the employment relationship. Whether it is general managers, line managers or HR managers, alone or in combination, who make the decisions about how to determine and formalise the terms and conditions of employment for their employees, a great range of issues now has to be considered.

These include:

- agreement making
- relations with unions
- relations with employees directly
- organisational policies and systems
- legal liability and compliance
- business and labour cost strategy.

Agreement-making

WorkChoices introduces more scope for change and employer choice in agreement-making. An extensive range of questions about the legal form, type and scope of agreements to apply to an organisation's employees arise. For example, these may include the following:

- Which form of workplace agreement is preferred?
- Are they to be union or non-union, individual or collective agreements?
- What transitionary arrangements need to be in place if transferring from the state award to the new federal system?
- What are the advantages and disadvantages of each?
- Who is to be covered by the new agreements?
- Are significant changes (reductions or increases) in pay and conditions to be made?
- Will the employer force the union into making concessions?
- Will there be trade-offs; for example, increases in pay in return for reduced leave entitlements?

Relations with unions

WorkChoices reduces the ability of unions to be present in the workplace and to represent employees. Employers have greater scope to influence the relationship they have, or do not have, with unions. This may involve a decision to continue bargaining with unions or to marginalise unions. Decisions about the direction an organisation takes in relation to unions will impact not only on the union–employer relationship, but will also send a signal to employees about what sort of human resource management model is to be followed by the employer.

Relations with employees

WorkChoices places emphasis on the direct relationship between the employer and employee. In a way similar to that advocated by much of the HRM literature, this is an opportunity for HR managers to influence relations with employees. But what form is this to take? Are relations to be based on commitment or control? In the medium term, there is also a sense that many employees could be suspicious of their employer's intentions and what they may be planning to do with the enhanced powers that *WorkChoices* gives them. Employees may feel less protected and more exposed to market forces. Levels of trust and security among employees may fall as a result. These are issues that human resource managers will need to consider and organisational avenues for employee voice may need to be reviewed. Certainly, dispute resolution processes need to be reviewed and possibly updated so that they comply with the new requirements. Alternative dispute resolution processes may also need to be examined and introduced. However, having a dispute resolution process that centres on the organisation does not, of itself, resolve the dispute or the problem! Managers will need to be skilled up to ensure that they can manage employee grievances properly and effectively.

Organisational policies and systems

As *WorkChoices* restricts the content of awards and prohibits from all agreements matters relating to union involvement at the workplace, there will be matters that need to find a new 'home.' Whether these are transferred to company policies is another issue that employers will need to consider. Company policies will have arguably more scope and reach than before, giving employers greater unilateral control over the terms of the employment relationship. Yet, as some have noted, this strategy contains certain risks as well.[49] Employers need to take care that they do not breach the duty of trust and confidence that is often written or implied in company policies. According to some commentators, this leaves open the possibility that employees could potentially sue for breach of contract and claim damages against their employer in the civil courts. Moreover, in relation to organisational policies, the integration and linkages between employment relations policies and other related areas should also be examined if the organisation is to follow best practice human resource management.

In some areas of workforce management, *WorkChoices* also requires further or different information to that which an organisation may currently hold. For instance, companies may need to collect data about the number of hours employees work in a week and calculate recreation leave on a monthly rather than an annual basis. These and other areas may require human resource managers to clarify the human resource information or payroll systems that are in place in the organisation to ensure that the right data is gathered.

Legal compliance

One of the standard human resource management functions is to ensure the organisation's compliance with employment relations laws. *WorkChoices* does not alter that responsibility and indeed there are some matters introduced by the legislation that may require immediate attention. For example, HR managers must ensure that the organisation complies with the new legislated minimum Standards and that the organisation is not in breach of the legislation in any other way, including the process of agreement-making:

Under the new *WorkChoices* legislation, the company will be liable for any breaches in the agreement-making process, not the individual who signs the declaration. Breaches will attract penalties in the order of $33 000. As a principal source of company advice and often with responsibility for signing-off agreements, HR managers are advised to be up to speed on their obligations under the Act.[50]

Furthermore, federal and state laws relating to anti-discrimination and occupational health and safety continue to operate, and *WorkChoices* does not reduce an organisation's obligations to comply with these laws.

Business strategy

WorkChoices enables employers to increase the range of possible responses they have to unions and employees and to have more choice about the business and labour cost strategies they wish to pursue. Strategies that focus on investment in human resources may be pursued by some companies; other companies may pursue different routes, because to some extent *WorkChoices*

allows business to reduce labour costs, if they so choose. The outcome is likely to see a greater range of human resource management responses. These may be influenced by a range of factors: for example, the industry sector in which the business operates, the size of the company, the responses of competing businesses or the tightness of the labour market. From a strategic HRM perspective, the changes introduced by *WorkChoices* set new challenges and options for business to consider and on which human resource practitioners need to advise.

HR responses

AHRI state councillor Janine Walker talks to labour law expert Mordy Bromberg about the future under the *WorkChoices* legislation

Janine Walker: Managing an organisation on a series of individual arrangements is very labour intensive. It seems very small organisations are most likely to do that. Medium to large employers would find your scenario theoretically interesting but, administratively, you can't run a business that way.

Mordy Bromberg: How will those employers respond? It depends on the nature of the relationship they want with their workforce. An employer who sees value in its workforce and wants to get loyalty and commitment isn't going to take advantage of its superior position – unless it's forced to. I think most employers don't want this legislation, but a lot will be driven into it by their competitors taking it up to get the benefits. It often only takes one bad egg and everybody else has to follow.

I'm not sure the administrative problems are as significant as you think. An AWA doesn't necessarily require individual bargaining or an individually tailored arrangement. Employers I've been involved with will prepare AWAs in standard form and negotiate as necessary. It requires more work, but it's not as if they're negotiating each and every part of the AWA.

I think most organisations will try to get a healthy mix of collective foundations and individualised add-ons, so we'll start to have a coexistence of those arrangements. You seem to see a much grimmer future.

Not necessarily. I think a lot of employers understand that collective arrangements are fair and want to treat their employees fairly. They understand that providing a workplace where basic rights are respected is likely to improve productivity and the capacity to attract and retain good employees.

A lot of employers will be completely frightened off by the complexity of this legislation. They will be unwilling to spend the $30 000–$40 000 plus, depending on the size of the organisation, to have lawyers tell them what the hell it all means. I can assure you, that's the cost they'll be looking at.

A lot of employers will want to opt out. I can see our workplaces dividing into two broad categories: industries where the sort of initiatives now at play will be either averted or utilised to a very minor extent; and workplaces where I fear this will provide an opportunity resulting in a great level of inequality and significant exploitation. If you take away the basic protections all decent IR systems are built on, you create an opportunity for market forces to take over in a way our society today would find unpalatable.

Source: Adapted from *hrmonthly*, April 2006.

Summary

With growing recognition that human resources are important assets of the modern organisation, managing the employment relationship has become a critical aspect of strategic human resource management. Influencing and determining the terms and conditions of work and understanding the industrial relations system and bargaining framework are critical to strategic human resource management.

In the last two decades there has been a transformation in the regulation of the employment relationship in Australia with a move away from the system of industrial relations introduced at the beginning of the 20th century. That system was based on compulsory conciliation and arbitration and the collective representation of employees and employers. Deregulatory moves have also occurred in China and are proposed for India. The European nations by contrast, have regulated in a different direction.

In Australia, the federal emphasis has shifted to individual bargaining between employers and employees at the level of the workplace. This has also meant a reduced role for third parties – unions and industrial tribunals – and an increased emphasis on non-union arrangements and individualising the employment relationship. In Australia, *WorkChoices* does indeed represent, as its architects say, a fundamental reshaping of the framework for the regulation of work and employment relations. It is very much meant to be different from past laws and practices and it is intended to make a difference to organisations and to the economy. It will take some years for the full impact to be felt and employer response and the economy will play their part in shaping exactly how *WorkChoices* plays out.

The role of human resource management in such a complex, fluid and contentious environment is difficult. It highlights not only the conflicting roles of HR managers, as agents of management and as advocates of employees, but also the need to remain alert to changes in the legislative and political contexts. The options for determining the terms and conditions of employment are more diverse than ever and as the focus continues to shift to the workplace and the individual, the potential for human resource practitioners and managers to influence the outcomes in the new bargaining regime is greater than ever.

Key terms

bargaining 73
industrial relations system 71
union 89
workplace agreement 95
workplace relations 71

Key debate issues

1 A good understanding of industrial relations is more important for human resource managers operating in Australia than in other countries. Discuss.

2 Debate the proposition that the decentralisation and deregulation of industrial relations in Australia has been more beneficial for business and employers than for employees.

3 Debate the view that third parties, for example, trade unions, can assist in developing better human resource management and improving trust between employers and employees.

Questions

1 What is individual bargaining and how does it differ from collective bargaining?

2 Who are the main parties involved in individual bargaining and what role can HRM play?

3 What is meant by the term 'third party' and who are typically the third parties? What are the pros and cons of third-party involvement in the employment relationship?

4 What are the implications for human resource management of the changes in the Australian bargaining framework since 2006?

NEWS REPORT 3.5

Amber and the juice bar squeeze

On 15 March 2006, 12 days before *WorkChoices* came into operation, 16-year-old Amber Oswald commenced work as a casual employee at the Pulp Juice Bar at Warriewood Square on Sydney's northern beaches. This business operated as a retail shop selling fresh fruit juices. Her employer was Pulp Juice Bars Operations Pty Ltd (Pulp).

Amber's terms and conditions of employment were set out in Pulp's enterprise agreement 2004, which was certified by the Australian Industrial Relations Commission on 24 February 2004. These terms and conditions included a starting pay rate of $9.52 per hour on weekdays, which would be increased to $10.05 per hour after a probationary period. She was entitled to penalty rates if she worked outside normal weekday hours ($11.90 on Saturdays, $14.27 on Sundays and $19.83 on public holidays). The enterprise agreement also provided for three-hour minimum shifts, various allowances, rest breaks and meal breaks and a dispute resolution procedure: disputes under Pulp's enterprise agreement 2004 would be referred to the AIRC for resolution.

On 24 March 2006, three days before *WorkChoices* came into operation, Amber's employer ceased operating. However, she was not informed that her employment had been terminated. On the very next day, a new owner, Pow Juices Pty Ltd trading as Pulp Juice Bars (Pow), commenced operating the juice business from the same premises, using the same staff, uniforms, stock and trading names and selling the same products.

Pow engaged consultants to prepare an Australian Workplace Agreement (AWA). This AWA provided a flat hourly rate of $8.57 for all hours worked, which was less than the prevailing New South Wales state award for shop employees. The AWA did not specify a minimum shift. Disputes under the AWA would not be referred to the AIRC for resolution. Instead, they would be referred to an organisation called Enterprise Initiatives, which acted as industrial relations consultant for Pow and was responsible for drafting the AWA.

Pow left generic letters of offer of employment for employees, known as the 'Pow Juice Limited Welcome Letter,' lying around the workplace. These letters were not addressed to anyone and did not contain pay rates. The letters did contain space for an employee to provide a signature to acknowledge that the AWA had been read and understood. However, the AWA was missing at the time that the letters were left.

It seems that Pow failed to put the AWA to Amber as a precondition of her employment. Amber was not personally issued with a letter. She never signed the AWA yet continued working at the juice bar for Pow.

At the insistence of Amber's father, Mr Oswald, Pow eventually provided an unsigned letter with blanks where the relevant address and pay rate details should have been provided. A Pow representative told Mr Oswald that an interim agreement regarding employees terms and conditions was being established with a more detailed agreement to follow. Mr Oswald was informed that Amber's pay rate going forward would be $8.57. Amber's boss was reported in the media as saying 'If they [15 to 20 staff at three Pulp juice franchise shops] don't want to sign, they can leave … it's not about what's fair, it's [about] what's right – right for the company'.[51]

With the help of her father and the Shop, Distributive Allied and Employees Association (union), Amber attempted to resolve her concerns informally with Pow.

Amber contended that under the transmission of business provisions of the *Workplace Relations Act*, she was still entitled to the benefit of the terms and conditions of Pulp's enterprise agreement 2006. After informal attempts to resolve the matter failed, the union, acting on behalf of Amber, applied to the AIRC to determine her dispute pursuant to the dispute resolution clauses in Pulp's enterprise agreement 2004.

Commissioner Lawson heard the matter on 26 April 2006. At the conclusion of the hearing, Pow gave undertakings to the AIRC to pay Amber according to the pay rates contained in Pulp's enterprise agreement 2004 with back pay for those hours she had worked at the AWA rate since the business was transferred.

During the hearing of the matter, Amber's representative,

Mr Bernie Smith, assistant secretary of the union, conceded that if Pow had properly carried out its plans to have all employees, including Amber, sign the AWA, the AIRC would not have had jurisdiction to hear the matter.

An article on page 2 of the *Sydney Morning Herald* on 28 April 2006[52] quoted sources from both sides of the political divide regarding Amber's dispute with Pow. A spokesman for the employer association, Australian Business Limited, noted that there were bound to be 'teething issues' following the introduction of *WorkChoices*. However, a spokesman for the NSW Industrial Relations Minister expressed concerns that once businesses fully understood how to exploit *WorkChoices*, more employees would have their wages cut and entitlements stripped.

Sources: Burke, K. 2006. 'Same work, $40 less: take it or leave it,' *Sydney Morning Herald*, Monday 10 April 2006, available at www.smh.com.au/news/national/same-work-40-less/2006/04/0009/1144521210927; Needham, K. 2006. 'Girl who took on boss squeezes more out of juice bar,' *Sydney Morning Herald*, Friday 28 April 2006, p. 2; Unreported, AIRC, Commissioner Lawson, Transcript of Proceedings, Shop, Distributive and Allied Employees Association and Pow Juice Pty Ltd, C2006/2484, Wednesday 26 April 2006, Sydney, available at www.airc.gov.au/documents/Transcripts/260406c20062484.htm.

Case study 3.1

Cleanslate – relocation options

The CleanSlate Company manufactures, markets and distributes a wide range of personal hygiene and household cleaning products throughout Australia and the Asia–Pacific region. It has operated in Australia for over 70 years and has strong customer and employee loyalty. Approximately 400 non-managerial personnel are now employed by CleanSlate in its Sydney factory and offices. They work across a range of occupations including manufacturing, transport and warehousing, research and development (R&D), and sales and marketing. The manufacturing, transport and warehousing employees are currently all members of the manufacturing workers union and work under a state award. The research and development and sales and marketing staff are on a mix of AWAs and individual common law contracts. For many years now the industrial relations at the site has been peaceful, but there was a time when the workforce was very militant. In some years up to 20 per cent of production time was lost due to strikes.

The Sydney site is old and requires considerable refurbishment. The company is planning to relocate all its operations and open a new facility somewhere else in Australia. It is not entirely sure where at the moment and has been considering whether or not to stay in NSW or move interstate, for example, to Queensland.

The move provides an opportunity to modernise the production process and the employment arrangements. It is envisaged that the new factory will require 20 per cent fewer production employees. It is anticipated that R&D and sales and marketing staff numbers will stay about the same. The production manager wants the new factory to run on two 12-hour shifts, rather than the customary three eight-hour shifts that operate in the Sydney plant. The HR Manager is also keen to introduce self-managed work teams and a different performance pay system at the new site. These changes mean that the organisation of work at the new factory will be quite different to the old factory and that the terms and conditions of work that now apply to CleanSlate employees may not be suitable for the new arrangements.

The HR Manager has been asked to present an options paper to the senior executive team. The timing is fortuitous as the new *WorkChoices* legislation gives her many more options to consider.

Exercise

As the HR Manager it is your responsibility to prepare the options paper assessing the various alternatives available to CleanSlate and recommending a course of action. You also think that in your role as HR Manager, you need to present options that best meet the needs of the company and the employees. On further reflection, you also think that not all the managers will see it quite this way, and will want to use the relocation to de-unionise the whole workforce.

Given this situation, how would you advise the senior management team about the following:

1   The issues that need to be considered before the move takes place?
2   The options for making workplace agreements and the advantages and disadvantages of each?
3   The pros and cons of trying to de-unionise the employees?
4   The factors that need to be considered in developing self-managed teams and an appropriate pay system?

Case study 3.2

The director's pay cut

Fatima has been the Director of the local school's after-hours care centre since it was established five years ago. She is in her mid-thirties, has children herself, lives in the local area and has the appropriate qualifications. She had a very good relationship with the previous management committee of the centre and there was considerable trust on both sides. Fatima was employed under a common law contract of employment, and was paid about $50 a week above the going award rate.

As in most cases, the management committee is made up of parents of children who attend the centre. At the commencement of 2006 many of the original management committee members left and were replaced by a new group of parents, most of whom are professionals and work in the city.

At their last meeting in May, the management committee decided to 'formalise' Fatima's employment contract by offering an Australian Workplace Agreement (AWA). Fatima was happy about this, until she realised that it also included a pay cut of $40 a week. Fatima is distressed and does not know what she should or can do.

Questions

1   What terms would have to be included in Fatima's new AWA?

2   What are Fatima's options in relation to her employment contract and the AWA?

3   What would you advise Fatima to do?

Endnotes

1   Dunlop, J.T. 1958. *Industrial relations systems*. Carbondale, Southern Illinois University Press.

2   Campbell I. and Brosnan P. 1999. 'Labour market deregulation in Australia: The slow combustion approach to workplace change,' *International Review of Applied Economics*, vol. 13, no. 3, pp. 353–94.

3   McGrath, Champ and Baird, 2003. 'HRM in an era of enterprise bargaining' in Burgess J., MacDonald D., *Developments in enterprise bargaining in Australia*, Croydon, Victoria, Tertiary Press.

4   Bray M., Waring, P. 1998. 'The rhetoric and reality of bargaining structures under the Howard government,' *Labour and Industry*, 9(2), December, pp 61–80.

5   See Bamber G., Lansbury R. and Wailes N. 2004. *International and comparative industrial relations: Globalisation and the development market economies*, Allen and Unwin, Sydney and Sage, London.

6   See Buchanan J. and Callus R. 1993. 'Efficiency and equity at work: The need for labour market reform in Australia,' *Journal of Industrial Relations*, 35 (4), pp. 315–37; Dabsheck, B. 2006. 'The contract regulation club,' *Economic and Labour Relations Review* 16(2).

7   Baird M., and Lansbury R. 2003. 'The changing structure of collective bargaining in Australia' in H. Katz, W. Lee and J. Lee (eds) *The new structure of labor relations: Tripartism and decentralisation*, ILR Press, Ithaca, New York.

8   Wailes N., Lansbury R. 1997. 'Flexibility versus collective bargaining? Patterns of Australian industrial relations reforms during the 1980s and 90s,' ACIRRT Working Paper no. 49, University of Sydney: Australian Centre for Industrial Relations Research and Training.

9   Australian Government, DEWR, 'WorkChoices, a new industrial relations system,' available at www.WorkChoices.gov .au/ourplan/publications/WorkChoicesandtheAustralianFairPayandConditionsStandard.htm, accessed 30 May 2006.

10   For a discussion of the implications of this, see McCallum R. 2006. 'Justice at work: Industrial Citizenship and the corporatisation of Australian labour law', *Journal of Industrial Relations*, 48(2), pp. 131–53.

11   ACTU 2005, *WorkChoices: Family Impact Statement*, 29 November, Melbourne, Australian Council of Trade Unions.

12   Edgar, D. 2005. 'Family impact statement on WorkChoices, the proposed new industrial regime', Unions NSW, available at www.unionsnsw.org.au/community/public/files/Family%20Impact%20Statement%20November%202005.pdf.

13   WRA Subdivision E, 38 (3).

14   For more information on the structure of the FPC see www.fairpay.gov.au.

15   Harper I. 2006. 'Ensuring fair pay: The first steps.' Speech by Professor Ian Harper, Chairman, Australian Fair Pay Commission, Thursday 16 February, available at www.fairpay.gov.au/fairpay/Media/AFPCReleases/ EnsuringFairPay-TheFirstSteps.htm.

16   WRA Division 2, s. 22.

17   The World Today (ABC): *'Fair Pay Commission delivers shock wage decision.'* Available at www.abc.net.au/ worldtoday/content/2006/s1774227.htm, accessed 21 January 2007; Grant Belchamber (ACTU Senior Industrial Officer), 'Making the boom pay: Securing the next generation of prosperity,' 4th Economic and Social Outlook Conference, The New Workforce, Melbourne, 2 November 2006.

18   www.fairpay.gov.au/fairpay/MinimumWageDecision/FactSheets/2006MinimumWageDecision.htm, accessed 11 January 2007.

19   Webb S., Webb B. 1894. *History of trade unionism*, London, Longmans, Green and Co.

20   Australian Bureau of Statistics, 1996. *Trade union statistics*, Australia, cat. no. 6323.0, p. 11.

21   Higgins H.B. 1922. *A new province for law and order*, Sydney. Constable and Company, pp. 15–16.

22   Australian Bureau of Statistics, *Survey for ACTU*, ACTU 2001. Press release, 30 April.

23   Australian Bureau of Statistics, 2005. *Employee earnings, benefits and trade union membership*, Australia, cat. no. 6310.0, 30 August.

24   See Peetz D. 1998. *Unions in a contrary world*, Cambridge University Press; Griffin G. and Svenson S. 1996. 'The decline of Australian union density: A survey of the literature,' *Journal of Industrial Relations*, 38(4), December, pp. 505–47.

25   WRA, s. 778.

26   Stewart, A. with Priest E. 2006. *The WorkChoices legislation: An overview*, at www.federationpress.com.au./pdf/Work ChoicesLegislation0206.pdf.

27   Forsythye A., Sutherland C. 2006. 'From "uncharted seas" to the "stormy waters": How will trade unions fare under the WorkChoices legislation?,' *The Economics and Labour Relations Review*, 16(2), p. 215.

28   Sheldon P., Thornthwaite L. (eds) 1999. *Employer associations and industrial change*, St Leonards, Allen & Unwin, pp. 4–5.

29   Ellem B. 1999. 'Trade unionism in 1998,' *Journal of Industrial Relations*, pp. 127–51; Ellem B. 2000. 'Trade unionism in 1999,' *Journal of Industrial Relations*, pp. 59–82.

30   Dabscheck B. 2001. '"A felt need for increased efficiency": Industrial relations at the end of the millennium,' *Asia Pacific Journal of Human Resource Management*, 39 (2), pp. 4–30.

31   Baird M., Lansbury R. 1996. 'Involving employees at Australia Post,' in E. Davis, R. Lansbury (eds), *Managing together*, Melbourne, Longman.

32   Kitay J., Lansbury R.D. (eds) 1997. *Changing employment relations in Australia*, Melbourne, Oxford University Press.

33   Chamberlain N.W. 1951. *Collective bargaining*, McGraw-Hill Book Company, New York, p. 3.

34   Clegg H. 1960. *A new approach to industrial democracy*, London, Blackwell.

35   Campbell I. 2001. 'The shock of the old: Conceptualising the shift to enterprise bargaining in Australia,' paper presented to Ten Years of Enterprise Bargaining Conference, 3–4 May, Newcastle.

36   Katz H., Kochan T. 2000. *An introduction to collective bargaining and industrial relations*, 2nd edn, Boston, McGraw-Hill, p. 460.

37   Deery S. et al. 2001. op. cit., p. 271.

38   B. Ellem, 2000. 'Trade unionism in 1999,' *Journal of Industrial Relations*, pp. 59–82.

39   Katz H., Kochan T. 2000. op. cit.

40   WRA, s. 326 (2).

41   WRA, s. 323.

42   WRA, s. 332.

43   Kochan T., McKersie R., Cappelli, P. 1984. 'Strategic choice and industrial relations theory,' *Industrial Relations*, 23 (1), pp. 16–39; Kochan T.A., Katz H.C., McKersie, R.B. 1986. 'The transformation of American industrial relations,' Basic Books, New York.

44   Ibid.

45   Walton R.E., Cutcher-Gershenfeld J., McKersie, R.B. 1994. *Strategic negotiations*, Boston, Harvard Business School Press.

46   Kochan, T. 2004. 'Restoring trust in the human resource management profession,' *Asia Pacific Journal of Human Resources*, 42 (2), August, pp. 132–46.

47   Guest D. 1999, 'Peering into "the Black Hole", the downside of the new employment relations in the UK,' *British Journal of Industrial Relations*, 37(3), pp. 367–89.

48   McGrath-Champ S., Baird M. 2005. 'The mercurial nature of Australian human resource management under enterprise bargaining,' *Asia Pacific Journal of Human Resources*, 43 (1), pp. 155–73.

49   Riley J. 2006. 'The evolution of the contract of employment post WorkChoices,' *The University of New South Wales Law Journal*, 29 (1), pp. 166–80.

50   AHRI e-newsletter, 22 February 2006.

51   Burke, K., 2006. 'Same work, $40 less: take it or leave it,' *Sydney Morning Herald*, 10 April 2006 available at www.smh.com.au/news/national/same-work-40-less/2006/04/0009/1144521210927.

52   Needham, K. 2006. 'Girl who took on boss squeezes more out of juice bar,' *Sydney Morning Herald*, Friday 28 April 2006, p. 2.

Online reading

INFOTRAC® COLLEGE EDITION
For additional readings and review on industrial relations, explore InfoTrac® College Edition, your online library. Go to: www.infotrac-college.com and search for any of the InfoTrac key terms listed below:
➤ bargaining
➤ industrial relations system
➤ union
➤ workplace agreement
➤ workplace relations

CHAPTER 4
HUMAN RESOURCE PLANNING IN A CHANGING ENVIRONMENT

HR has primary responsibility for activities that require long-term projections such as human resource planning. For the most part, these activities received high marks in terms of effectiveness.

Carol Kulik and
Hugh Bainbridge, 2006

The (HR) function is now expected to assume a more prominent position at the senior decision-making level and take a more proactive role in developing the organisation's people as a source of competitive advantage.

Cathy Sheehan, Peter Holland and
Helen De Cieri, 2006

Employer branding is about positioning your company as a place where talented people can achieve their career goals.

Wayne Beel, General Manager of HR,
Cement Australia, 2006

Objectives

After reading this chapter, you will be able to:

1 Define human resource planning (HRP) and understand its crucial relationship with strategic organisational planning.

2 Appreciate the links between HRP and strategic human resource management.

3 Understand the nature and role of Human Resource Information Management Systems (HRIMS) in human resource planning and SHRM.

4 Apply the techniques of human resource planning.

5 Discuss the advantages and disadvantages of HRP.

Introduction

In Chapters 1, 2 and 3 we discussed the theory of SHRM and some of its contextual influences. We also explored the fundamental relationships between broad organisational strategies and associated HR strategies, and their subsequent impacts on all human resource management functions.

The bridge between HR strategies and HR functions is the formulation of human resource plans that incorporate the desired outcomes of HR strategies, are responsive to continual changes in industry environments, and can be implemented through efficient and effective HR functions (e.g. job design, recruitment and selection, human resource development, performance management, rewards and employee relations systems).

The purpose of human resource planning (HRP) is to try to ensure that organisational objectives are met through the effective utilisation of the human resources of the organisation, taking into account changing circumstances within and outside particular organisations (see Exhibit 4.1). Thus, HRP is essentially an ongoing process, focused on the long term, but cognisant of contemporary changes in both the internal and external environments in which these organisations operate. In reality, human resource planning must be a series of processes, with long, medium and short-term contingency options, in order to comprehensively reflect HR strategies and to modify associated HR processes. Such plans are based inevitably upon efficient, effective and user-friendly Human Resource Information Management Systems (HRIMS), which collect, collate and analyse internal and external HR data. These are discussed later in this chapter.

Exhibit 4.1 Strategic alignment

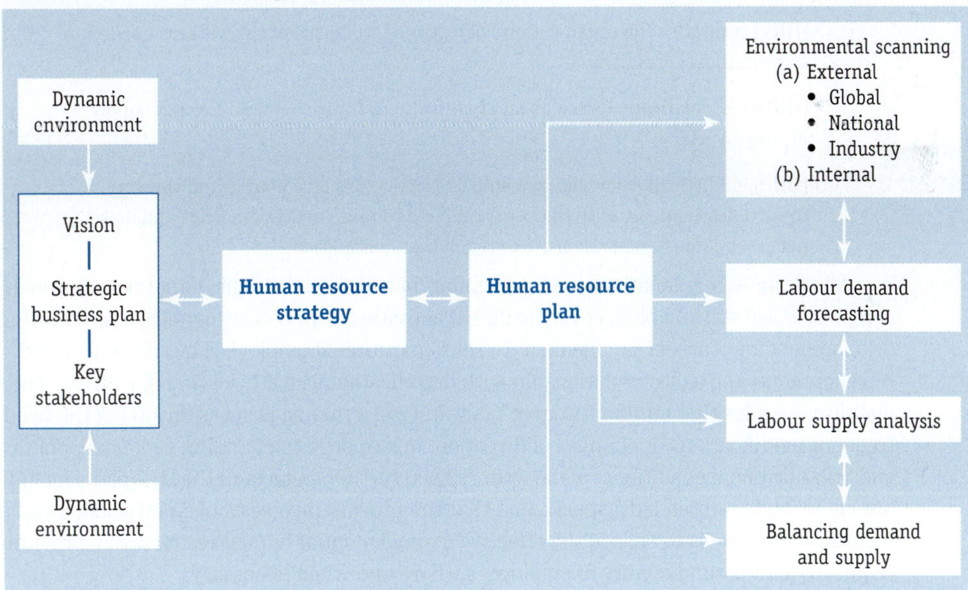

Importance of HRP

Planning is an essential process of management. Human resource planning provides the foundation for establishing an effective HRM program and for coordinating all the HRM functions. It also allows the HRM function to position itself to take the best advantage of fluctuations in the economy or labour market. The likely effects of future economic, social and legislative conditions, or organisational changes, can be converted from constraints and pressures to challenges and opportunities.

Astute human resource planners during the past few years may, for example, have been able to anticipate the benefits of recent restructuring initiatives of flexible work and job design and have developed training and career management action plans to take advantage of these opportunities. Similarly, the high costs of workers' compensation systems may have been converted to benefits by human resource plans concerned with health and safety promotion campaigns or accident prevention programs.

The failure to adequately plan for an organisation's human resources, on the other hand, can result in losses in efficiency and substantial costs to the organisation, through un-staffed vacancies, expensive replacement training, over-hiring or fragmented career management. The prevalence of employee retrenchment programs during the 1980s and 1990s in many Australian industries, and the more recent trends of business process outsourcing (BPO) and the extensive offshoring of service functions, could perhaps have been more effectively integrated in strategic human resource planning, which focused on retraining, multiskilling or early retirement campaigns. Such plans may have reduced the high financial costs (e.g. outplacement fees, termination and superannuation payments) and the adverse effects on community and employee morale of poorly planned redundancies or outsourcing programmes.

Human resource planning

Human resource planning has been explained in a variety of ways:

> [HRP] translates the organisation's objectives into terms of the workers needed to meet these objectives.[1]

> [HRP] systematically forecasts an organisation's future demand for, and supply of, employees.[2]

> [HRP] is a little like navigating a ship … (it) decides on a course and speeds toward destinations, with the constant need to take further readings and make necessary adjustments in order to reach that destination.[3]

All the above explanations contain similar features – a strategic, long-term approach; a comprehensive staffing plan, covering all HR activities from recruitment through training, development and career management, to the separation of employees by retirement and retrenchment; and a close relationship with organisational strategies and objectives. The last quotation implies that human resource planning is a dynamic process, involving the need for frequent modifications or changes of direction, in response to changing economic, political, social and organisational conditions. Some writers have further suggested that HR plans include both 'intended' and 'unintended' aspects, and that the process involves a blend of science and art.[4] Its overall purpose is to ensure the effective management of human resources by providing the required quantity and quality of employees where and when necessary.

HRP in practice, then, aims to '… manage … the pattern … that integrates an organisation's major goals, policies and action sequences into a cohesive whole'.[5] Towards this goal, HRP needs to undertake a systematic process of analysing organisational strategies and goals; conducting both external and internal environmental analyses (environmental scanning); and, subsequently, making a 'strategic choice' about the nature of HRM processes appropriate to identified organisational outcomes. As a recent research report suggests, HR professionals need to 'add real strategic value to the bottom-line, closely manage the employee–employer relationship and deal with a diminishing workforce'.[6] The changing characteristics of the Australian labour market and its dynamic industrial relations systems, and of those in our

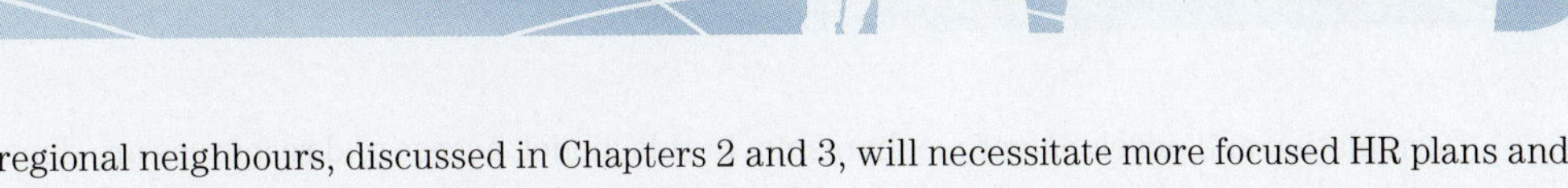

regional neighbours, discussed in Chapters 2 and 3, will necessitate more focused HR plans and more sophisticated HR modelling competencies.

Essentially, human resource planning is concerned with matching labour demand and labour supply projections within the internal and external contexts of organisations. Increasingly, human resource planners, rather than devising their plans in isolation, are involving organisational managers, employees, customers and suppliers in the formulation of their HR plans.

HRP and strategic organisational planning

In the past it may have been sufficient to rely on a loose relationship between the management of employees and organisational productivity or profitability. However, as noted earlier, competitive industrial conditions demand that practitioners undertake strategic human resource planning to anticipate, prevent and resolve staffing problems in order to ensure the achievement of organisational objectives.

Strategic planning is the process of setting major organisational objectives and developing comprehensive plans to achieve them. It involves deciding on the major directions of the organisation, including its structure, strategies, policies and the contributions of its various resources. An important part of the strategic planning process is the determination of necessary labour requirements and the prediction of likely sources. A strategic corporate planning process usually includes:

- a definition of the corporate philosophy
- scanning of environmental conditions (both internal and external)
- evaluation of the organisation's strengths and weaknesses
- development of objectives and goals
- the formulation of suitable strategies.

Similar approaches apply to human resource planning. A shorthand framework is the SWOT process, which seeks to analyse (in detail) the strengths, weaknesses, opportunities and threats facing organisations in the foreseeable future. In this process, strengths may include market position, global exposure, technological superiority, credit–debt ratios and the quality of human resources (number of employees, skills levels). Weaknesses could include inflexible organisational structures, poor market penetration, outmoded policies, a history of industrial action, or untrained and unmotivated employees. Opportunities might include the withdrawal of competitors, likely product or site diversification, newly discovered labour markets (e.g. university graduates, part-time workers, high unemployment levels, global recruitment). Threats often include restrictive government legislation or highly competitive labour markets (e.g. chief executive officers, chief knowledge officers, biotechnologists).

Effective links between organisational strategic plans and HRP are dependent on many factors, including mutual perceptions of senior management and HR specialists and the nature and stage of growth of the company. As discussed in Chapter 1, links between organisational and HR strategies depend heavily on the perceptions of senior and HR managers of the contributions that HRM can make to overall business success. Senior managers may adopt a 'monolithic' approach to their organisations, considering that line activities are the central functions, and that all other functions, including HRM, exist merely to service line managers' needs. In this kind of organisation, HR plans are unlikely to be well integrated with overall business plans. Alternatively, some senior managers may regard the HR functions as an important part of the organisation, but secondary to strategic plans. This is often called a 'functional' model.

Ideally, senior managers will see their organisations as pluralist, in which all parts (e.g. production, marketing, sales, HRM) are in constant competition with each other for scarce resources, but with legitimate access to formal organisational systems including strategy formulation and development mechanisms. In this model, access and resources are dependent on the clear contributions of each organisational function.

Exhibit 4.2 illustrates an ideal relationship between HRP and organisational strategic planning processes. The strategic HRM planning group effectively links all HRM functions with each other, modifies them in view of changing internal and external factors, and integrates the results with overall organisational functions and strategies. Production, marketing and financial management areas conduct similar planning activities, and compete with each other for scarce organisational resources and influence. Such a relationship is not common, nor always practicable, but many organisations are moving in this direction. The Australian Navy, the NSW Roads and Traffic Authority, Telstra and several private sector organisations (e.g. NRMA, BHP Billiton) have made significant progress towards such integration.

HR managers also need to recognise the need for closer integration between their plans and those of their organisations. In the past, lack of confidence, low status in organisations or skills deficiencies often prevented their involvement in effective HR planning. The growth of an HR profession in Australia, economic and social pressures, and more enlightened organisational attitudes towards HRM provide substantial opportunities for more mature relationships between HR and business plans.

The nature and stage of organisational development will also influence HRP and corporate strategic plan integration. When an organisation begins operations it is likely that HR planners will be mainly concerned with attracting sufficient numbers of employees with the right skills, and may be prepared to offer them higher than market wage and salary rates. As the organisation grows and prospers, the focus may change towards career management, specialised technical or professional recruitment, appropriate skills mixes and replacement (or succession) planning. If an organisation declines, merges with or acquires another organisation, or is affected by economic recession, emphases may be on identifying likely areas for retrenchment or restructuring.

Exhibit 4.2   Approaches to strategic human resource planning

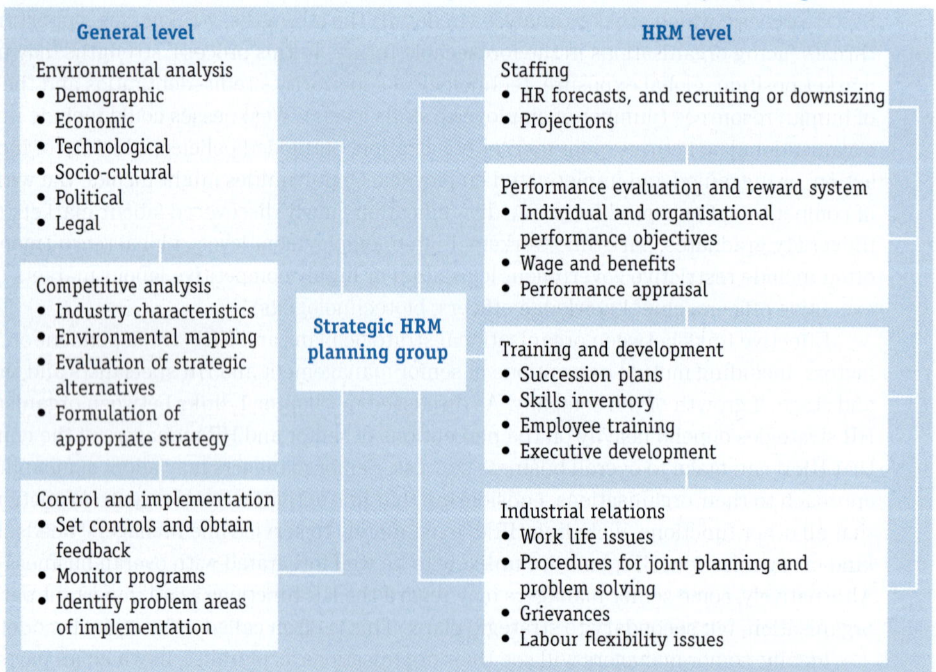

Source: From *Strategy and human resources management*, 1e, by Butler, Ferris & Napier, 1991. Reprinted with permission from South-Western, a division of Thomson Learning: www.thomsonrights.

News report 4.1 highlights the links between a business strategy of corporate restructuring in response to economic and industry threats, and HR planning. It also illustrates both the macro (e.g. structural, cultural and policy) and the micro components of HRP.

Human resource planning – the evidence

One Australian study suggested that while the majority of large organisations (88 per cent of companies surveyed) regularly develop formal corporate plans, 32 per cent of which have considerable input from the HR function, only 53 per cent formulated specific HR plans.[7] A more recent study suggested that 49 per cent of senior HR managers are 'actively involved in all types of strategic decisions,' with a further 36 per cent providing input or 'reacting to strategic decisions'.[8]

The Australian segment of the Cranet-Macquarie International Study (2006) also reported a healthy usage of both written (61 per cent) and unwritten (21 per cent) HR plans,[9] while an earlier study found that:

- 88 per cent of respondents draw up formal corporate/business plans

- 78 per cent use such plans to formulate and review workforce plans

- private sector organisations (83 per cent) were more likely than public sector bodies (75 per cent) to develop the strategic link between corporate/business and workforce plans

- of the organisations with human resource plans:

    - 59 per cent cover all employees, and the remainder focus on managers and professional staff

    - 51 per cent develop annual plans, 30 per cent for two to three years and 19 per cent for more than four years

    - 63 per cent of organisations use basic planning techniques (e.g. succession planning charts, manual records, etc.), whereas only 8 per cent report using more advanced techniques (e.g. HRIMS, supply and demand analyses).[10]

NEWS REPORT 4.1

Dixon cuts Qantas up into three

Qantas was not earning enough profits to sustain its 'existing and future investment needs,' Chief Executive Geoff Dixon said in a message to staff as he unveiled a major internal restructure of the airline. Just one week before the company's full-year profits are revealed, Mr Dixon said the airline needed to look at new ways to become efficient.

The restructure will divide the company into three business units: flying business; services (engineering, maintenance and airports); and associated businesses (catering, freight and Qantas Holidays). The memo said that managing the changes at Qantas had become a 'very complex task,' and that past organisational structures 'no longer deliver the outcomes required in this new environment.'

Each of the three business silos would have its own management and leadership, budgets, targets, and internal rates of return and accountability, although they will be served by the corporate office, IT and HR functions. While there is no mention in the memo of outsourcing or spinning off any of those businesses, some observers believe such actions are possible down the track.

Unions responded cautiously, saying that they had not been briefed by management. Australian Services Union airlines organiser Linda White said the proposal to 'cut it up into bite-sized chunks and divisions sends alarm bells to those of us who lived through Ansett ... The more divested you get, the

more companies you create, the employees are never sure where the assets are placed, which is the one with the money,' Ms White said. Qantas has already announced two programs to cut a total of $2 billion in costs. In response to the	current global economic downturn, SARS, the Iraq war and the success of discount carrier Virgin Blue, 1 200 of Qantas's 2 000 targeted job reductions have already been achieved, with the remainder to occur through attrition. Between	400 and 600 full-time jobs will switch to part-time, while a forced leave program in recent months has temporarily reduced staffing levels. Qantas has forecast a pre-tax profit of about $500 million, down from $630 million the year before.

Source: Adapted from Bachelard M. 2003. 'Dixon cuts Qantas up into three,' *The Weekend Australian*, 16–17 August, p. 36.

As the authors conclude, '... 57 per cent of respondents indicated that the emphasis on workforce/human resources planning has increased in their organisation. Providing this is done regularly and robustly, it can form the basis for more strategically relevant and effective' HRM practices.[11] Kulik's and Bainbridge's (2006) study found that HR professionals have the primary responsibility for human resource planning (nearly 76 per cent of their sample), but that it is also becoming a component of line managers' functions (24 per cent).[12]

Exhibit 4.3 illustrates the relationships between business and HRM strategies and plans.

Exhibit 4.3   A model of strategic human resource management

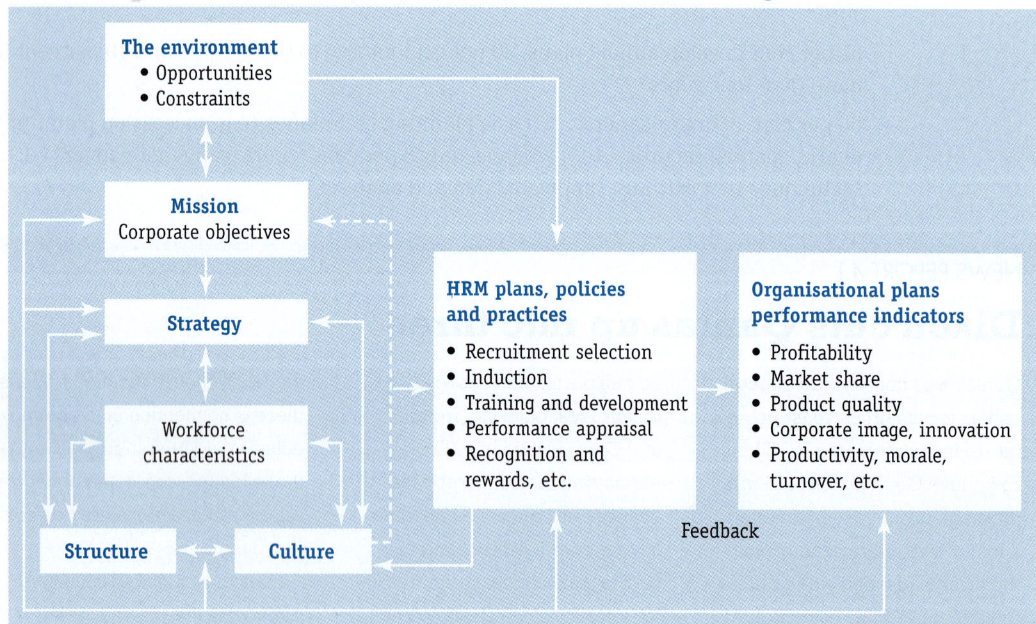

Source: Adapted from Collins R.R. 1994. 'The strategic contributions of the personnel function,' in A. Nankervis, R. Compton (eds), *Readings in strategic human resource management*, Melbourne, Nelson ITP, p. 42.

The factors that appear to influence both senior managers and HR specialists to more closely integrate HR and strategic plans include:

- *The nature of organisational environments*: Companies which are undergoing rapid technological change, or which operate in competitive environments, are most likely to possess integrative linkages.

- *Organisational size*: Larger companies are more likely to use strategic HR plans.

- *History, culture and philosophy*: Companies with dynamic, people-oriented and forward-thinking 'cultures' tend to recognise the need for integration.

- *The nature of business strategies*: Aggressive companies operating in dynamic environments are more likely to recognise the need for proactive HRP.

- *Location and level of the HR function*: Organisations which recognise the importance of human resources to organisational success are more likely to integrate HR and strategic plans.

- *Values and skills of senior HR managers*: Perceptive HR specialists have a considerable, positive impact on integration.

The process of human resource planning

HR managers usually employ a systematic process when undertaking HRP, as shown in Exhibit 4.4, including:

- labour demand forecasting

- labour supply analysis (including both internal and external sources)

- balancing supply and demand considerations

- the formulation of staffing strategies to meet organisational needs.

The process should be cyclical and ongoing, with the review providing feedback for subsequent forecasts. In practice, some organisations carefully forecast labour demand but neglect to accurately predict labour supply or monitor program effectiveness. Failure to do so will inevitably result in subsequent staffing problems (numbers, skills, HR costs), which will affect organisational effectiveness. We will now consider each step of the HRP process in detail. However, it is important to note here the key role that comprehensive, accurate and flexible HR databases, known as Human Resource Information Management Systems (HRIMS), play in all aspects of HRP processes. These issues are discussed later in this chapter.

Exhibit 4.4 Human resource planning model

Labour demand forecasting	Labour supply analysis	Balancing supply and demand
Considerations	**Internal**	**Recruitment (shortage)**
• Product/service demand	• Staffing tables	• Full-time
• Economics	• Markov planning	• Part-time
• Technology	• Skills inventories	• Job/work design
• Financial resources	• Management inventories	• EEO/AA programs
• Absenteeism/turnover	• Replacement charts	• Career management
• Organisational growth	• Succession planning	• Remuneration practices
• Management philosophy		
• Strategic plans	**External**	**Reductions (surplus)**
	• Demographic changes	• Dismissals
Techniques	• Education of workforce	• Retirements
• Trend analysis	• Labour mobility	• Retrenchments
• Indexation	• Government policies	
• Modelling	• Unemployment rate	
• Expert analysis		
• Delphi technique		

Source: From *Managing Human Resources*, 10e, by Sherman, Bohlander & Snell, 1996. Reprinted with permission of South-Western, a division of Thomson Learning, www.thomsonrights.com.

Labour demand forecasting

Labour demand forecasting is a key component of HRP. It involves estimating in advance the number and type of employees needed to meet organisational objectives. Highly sophisticated computer-based methods or simple 'rule of thumb' models may be used. The choice of method will depend on the expertise of the HR specialist, the complexity of organisational structures, market factors and the relative turbulence of the external environment. Forecasting, however, needs to take account of factors both within and external to organisations (see Chapter 2 and later in this chapter).

It is frequently more an art than a science, providing informed estimates rather than absolute results. The ever-changing environment in which an organisation operates contributes to this problem. In contemporary Australian industry, the effect of organisational restructuring, new industrial agreements and union amalgamations will inevitably influence demand forecasting, as will economic turbulence and consequent widespread retrenchments. The costs of inadequate forecasting are well demonstrated by the experience of one international airline, which was forced to rehire hundreds of flight attendants just months after encouraging a similar number to accept generous voluntary redundancy packages, presumably as the result of miscalculations in demand forecasts.[13] Large organisations such as the ANZ and Westpac banks, Telstra and Mt Isa Mines have been forced, for similar reasons, to rehire middle and even senior managers previously retrenched.

Techniques

There are two approaches to demand forecasting: quantitative and qualitative.

The quantitative (or top-down) approach involves the use of statistical or mathematical techniques. It is most often used by theoreticians and specialist planners. The complexity of some of these approaches can be seen in Exhibit 4.5. Methods can be effectively divided into indexation, trend analysis and simulation categories.

Exhibit 4.5 Labour demand forecasting techniques

	Indexation	Trend analysis	Simulations
Quantitative	• Production function (Leontieff's model) • Refined production function (Ghosh's model) • Work study model • Linear regression, linear programming, aggregate forecasting, extrapolative multivariate models	• Same as before (SAB) • Labour wastage analysis • Labour turnover analysis • Job matrix models • Actuarial analysis • Markov models • Cohort analysis	• New venture analysis • Change, optimisation and renewal models • Probability forecasts • Cross-impact analysis • Network analysis
Qualitative		• Rule of thumb • Delphi technique • Nominal group technique • Managerial judgement	

Source: From *Managing Human Resources*, 10e, by Sherman, Bohlander & Snell, 1996. Reprinted with permission of South-Western, a division of Thomson Learning, www.thomsonrights.com.

Indexation

- Forecasts of employment requirements in relation to one or several fixed organisational indices are known as indexation.

- The production function model (Leontieff's model) assumes a continuing relationship between output and employment numbers. Therefore, HR needs can be determined according to a simple equation:

$$\text{New HR} = \frac{\text{new output}}{\text{former output}} \times \text{former HR}$$

- Ghosh's refined production function model takes the further factor of productivity into account, producing a slightly more complex equation:

$$\text{new HR} = \text{change in productivity} \left(\text{old HR} \times \frac{\text{new output}}{\text{old output}} \right)$$

   This approach may be suitable for small organisations which can easily measure output and productivity within a relatively stable environment.

- Linear regression, linear programming, aggregate forecasting and extrapolative multivariate models use one or several variables (e.g. sales, investment) seen to be closely related to labour needs. Future needs can thus be inferred.

Trend analysis

- Forecasts of employment requirements in this method are based on a study of past human resources growth. The simplest form, often used in small organisations or in very stable business environments, is the 'same as before' (SAB) approach, which merely uses past levels of employment to indicate future needs. This is a reactive method and often fails to take account of changing requirements or opportunities for greater employee efficiency.

- Labour wastage analyses establish the trends (rises and falls) in employees leaving organisations, retirements, resignations, dismissals, often by section, job category and level, using the following simple equation:

$$\text{Labour wastage} = \frac{\text{number of leavers in a period}}{\text{total number of employees}} \times 100\%$$

   A refinement of this approach can be used to determine internal employee turnover (e.g. transfers, promotions) to assess the effectiveness of HR activities in these areas (see Chapter 13).

- Job matrix approaches consider labour movement by departments, job categories and through hierarchical levels.

- Actuarial approaches use statistical methods and models to predict future HR needs on the basis of averages and means.

- Markov models are more complicated statistical techniques that will not be dealt with in detail in this book.

- Cohort analyses single out specialist groups (cohorts) of employees and chart their progress through the organisation. The results of such analyses identify internal human resource movement through the organisation and, therefore, likely recruitment needs in the future.

Simulations and qualitative approaches

These techniques use computer-based systems to develop highly complex 'scenarios' for new HR options based upon multiple variables. Examples of these include new venture analyses, change/optimisation/renewal models, probability forecasts and cross-impact and network analyses.

Simulations, and the more complex forms of trend analyses, are usually only conducted by very large organisations with specialist HR departments.

Many small and medium-sized organisations prefer to rely on qualitative (or bottom-up) approaches to demand forecasting. While quantitative techniques rely on HR data analysed by specialists (including computer experts), qualitative approaches attempt to involve employees and their supervisors and managers in HR forecasting. Organisational 'experts' are consulted to assess anticipated developments and consequent future HR requirements. Three varieties of this forecasting method are the Delphi technique, the managerial judgement model and the nominal group technique (NGT).

The *Delphi technique* uses problem-solving and expert consultation methods in a structured manner. First, the forecasting problem is identified and divided into its component parts. Relevant data may be analysed and different perspectives of the problem sought from interested parties. Second, specialists in each part of the forecasting problem are consulted, using a structured and weighted questionnaire. These experts are deliberately kept apart to increase the breadth of forecasts. Finally, all responses are collated and returned to the individual experts for further comment. This process continues until consensus is achieved on all issues, and a cohesive demand forecast has been developed.

Managerial judgement is the approach in which supervisors and managers assess their own labour requirements, taking into account turnover, retirement, resignation, promotion and transfer rates, together with the effects of new technologies and work systems. Each section, division and branch of an organisation develops its own labour targets, which are then consolidated into an overall HR plan. It is essentially a bottom-up approach, useful in organisational restructuring or enterprise agreement negotiations. However, senior management may decide to hand down (top-down) quotas in line with overall budgeting priorities. This latter approach is often used in harsh economic times by the imposition of recruitment 'freezes' or moratoria.

The *nominal group technique* (NGT), in contrast, consciously uses 'group process' techniques to compare predictions on the required numbers and skills of employees in the future. Expert participants (including supervisors and employees) are invited to a meeting, and are involved in 'brainstorming' (non-judgemental listing of ideas) activities, followed by analyses of each listed idea or prediction. Group decisions are then made on the most realistic, ranked predictions.

The main advantage of qualitative techniques is the involvement in a part of human resource planning by people affected by subsequent HRM practices. Commitment to policies and practices is more likely to occur, as is better use of grassroots information. On the other hand, both the Delphi technique and the NGT are generally time-consuming and costly. The HR specialist should be the coordinator and consultant in all of these qualitative forecasting activities.

Ideally, HRP should use both quantitative and qualitative approaches. In combination, the two processes complement each other and provide a more complete planning coverage. Organisational restructuring and moves towards increased employee consultation in organisational activity may also be advanced by the inclusion of qualitative HRP forecasting.

Labour supply analysis

Once an organisation has forecast its future labour requirements, it must then determine if the number and types of employees required are available when and where they will be needed.

Labour supply can come from either internal or external sources. The process usually begins with an analysis of the existing supply of employees in the organisation. If current employees are not available to fill new job openings, the organisation will need to analyse likely external sources of human resources. There may, however, be conscious decisions to recruit externally, based upon the need to 'free up' organisational cultures or because specialist expertise is unavailable within the existing workforce. As an example, some parts of the Australian public sector have attempted to change traditional cultures by consciously recruiting from external sources for jobs above base level. These issues are addressed in more detail in Chapter 6.

Internal supply

An internal supply analysis usually begins with information from staffing establishment charts. These charts, especially in large organisations, indicate actual jobs, their present incumbents and present or likely future vacancies. In conjunction with establishment charts, skills inventories are valuable sources of employee information. Deriving from skills audits, which attempt to systematically establish the current skills levels of employees individually and collectively, and by inference, future skills requirements, skills inventories represent a comprehensive picture of the level of skills in an organisation. They have assumed greater importance in Australian organisations in recent years due to cross- (or multi) skilling programs. As retired Justice Macken has reflected, without effective skills inventories 'it is not possible to be sure that cross-skilling, multiskilling and career path development … will be effectively designed'.[14] Nonetheless, as earlier indicated in the CCH/AGSM study, the increase in usage of skills inventories has been very gradual.

Skills inventory

A skills inventory usually includes information on:

- employee job titles
- experience
- job history
- skills
- education
- duties and responsibilities
- assessment centre results
- languages, interests and hobbies (where relevant)
- licences, certificates
- future potential
- strengths and weaknesses
- training courses, seminars, studies
- career paths and job preferences
- geographic preferences
- subordinates
- project work and assignments.

Well-prepared and accurate skills inventories allow organisations to efficiently match likely job vacancies with appropriately prepared employees. From skills inventories, management and executive replacement (or succession) charts can be developed, enabling smooth and easy transition to crucial managerial and executive positions.

Exhibit 4.6 shows how an organisation might develop a replacement chart for the executives in one of its divisions. Note that this chart provides information on the current job performance and promotability of possible replacements. Replacement charts are very useful planning tools for locating hard-to-find employees or key management personnel.

Exhibit 4.6   An executive replacement chart

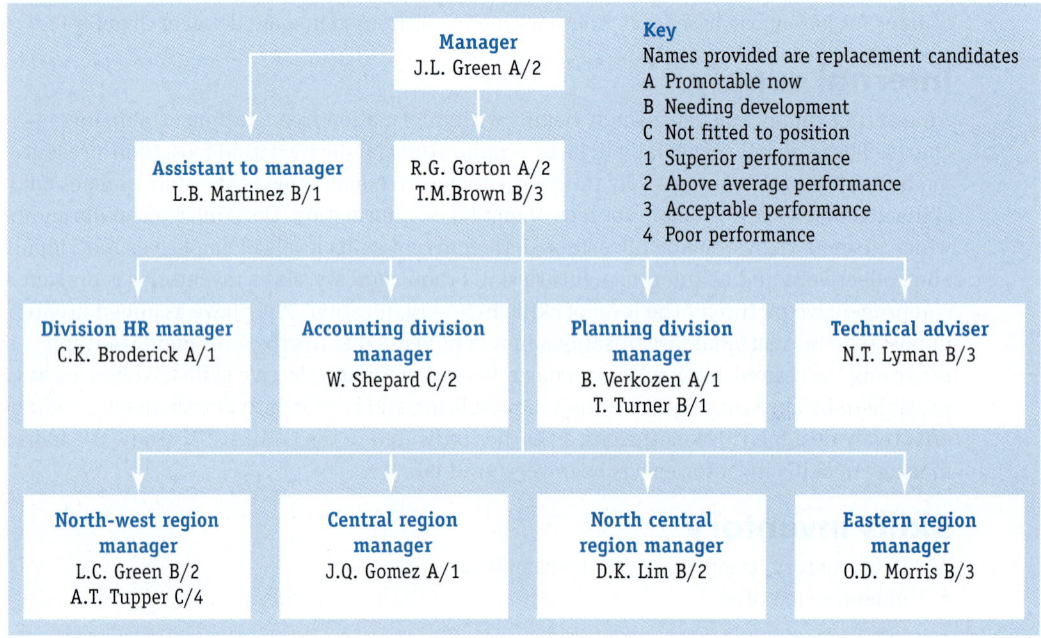

Some of the methods used in demand forecasting can also be useful in predicting future internal labour supply. Wastage analyses, if broken down into department, section and job categories, can be valuable in indicating high or low wastage levels, and thus whether actions need to be taken in the HRP process to redress them. High wastage (i.e. many employees leaving the organisation) may indicate low morale, lack of appropriate training or career opportunities, or merely the dynamic and competitive nature of the overall industry. Low wastage (i.e. the majority of employees staying with the organisation), on the other hand, can reflect high morale, job satisfaction or, conversely, stagnation and over-concern with job security.

Identification of the reasons for wastage, most effectively conducted by sensitive exit interviewers, will yield key information for HR planners. Future strategies may include more competitive remuneration programs, the development of clear career plans, tighter and more accountable appraisal schemes or more careful recruitment systems. Turnover analysis (i.e. the examination of employee movement within organisations by transfer, promotion or job rotation) can also provide useful information about the likelihood of a future internal labour supply with appropriate skills and experience, when required by the organisation. Problem areas can be rectified or new strategies adopted.

The following section explores the roles of HRIMS in the HR planning process in more detail.

Self-service in the new e-world

Traditional HR has been turned on its head by technology. Its impact is seen in the growing use of 'self-service' options by employees, the increasing use of line managers to handle their own people using e-technology, the development of e-recruitment and the growth in HR outsourcing.

And while most HR practitioners welcome technology's deft handling of onerous administration tasks, it has meant smaller HR departments that must reinvent themselves in order to meet the challenge of the new e-world.

For example, the HR centre of the ANZ Bank handles 250 000 telephone calls and 400 000 data-entry items across Australia and New Zealand each year. A program is currently underway to provide self-service options for employees to handle their own administration, as well as increasing the level of outsourcing, both of which are expected to significantly reduce the level of transactions incurred by the company.

Oracle's senior vice-president of human resources management systems development, Joel Summers, cites his own company's example of reducing HR costs by utilising self-service and line managers to transact HR functions. At Oracle, the ratio of HR representatives to employees is currently 1:2000 and the company is working towards making that 1:3000. The typical ratio in the USA is around 1:500.

According to Summers, self-service systems save on HR time and staff, and also have direct advantages for the corporation and the employee or user. He says that self-service increases employee satisfaction by giving employees an enhanced sense of involvement in their own career path and role within the company. In return, the system provides a greater understanding of employees by developing a database from their entries, leading to better information about the skills and needs of the workforce, locally or globally as required.

Self-service essentially makes the workforce of a company more 'visible' to the decision-makers within a company, Summers believes, and this leads to 'human asset optimisation' as managers scan and utilise the skills of their workforce.

Source: Victoria Steggall, *hrmonthly*, September 2000, p. 16.

Human resource information management systems (HRIMS)

The collection of information on aspects of work life as diverse as salary and payroll, compensation, leave, accidents, superannuation and employee benefits has always been part of the human resource manager's function. In the early history of personnel management, administrative aspects, including data collection, took up a great deal of time. Reviews of employee salary and leave entitlements often dominated the activities of earlier personnel officers, reflecting both management priorities and their own clerical backgrounds.

Such early information systems were manual, and were mainly used to notify employees of leave entitlements, to ensure accurate salary and wage payments and to process workers' compensation and superannuation claims. The data were seldom used to predict trends, identify problem areas and employees, or aid in the longer-term staffing process.

The complexity of Australian legislation governing employee working conditions reinforced this largely administrative focus of employee information. The clerical (or welfare) backgrounds of early personnel managers, reactive attitudes of management and the difficulty of handling large amounts of information manually often prevented more active uses of the data.

During the 1970s and 1980s, several factors radically changed attitudes towards human resource information management systems. The increasing complexity of payroll systems in this period demanded more flexibility in, and access to, information systems. These needs happily coincided with the development of increasingly sophisticated computer hardware and software systems. In large organisations, centralised payroll processing sections began to be separated from other human resource functions. Some organisations contracted their payroll responsibilities to external payroll bureaux with greater technological expertise, and at reduced costs.

Economic pressures on both small and larger organisations during the 1980s and 1990s led to permanent changes in the nature and uses of employee information systems. The need to measure, account for, and report on the costs of employee programs has been a strong influence on the development of sophisticated information systems.

Perhaps the most powerful influence on the development of flexible and comprehensive information systems has been the growth of federal and state legislation over the last decade in Australia. Governments now require not only the collection of new kinds of employee data (e.g. fringe benefits tax, equal employment opportunity, affirmative action, occupational health and safety), but also proof of contributions to organisational HR programs. Many information systems have been established as a response to government requirements in these areas. The impact of the recent Australian federal government's *Workplace Relations Amendment (Work Choices) Act 2005*, for example, has been to require considerably greater record-keeping functions from organisational information systems, including hours worked for employees paid less than $55 000, annual and personal leave and superannuation contributions.

United States and British experiences in the use of HRIMS encouraged their adoption in Australian HRM departments. Educational institutions and the HR professional bodies, recognising increased pressures for HR accountability and cost containment, began to emphasise the importance of HRIMS in HRM strategies. During the 1980s, HR managers began to see the value of computerised information systems in collecting data, and analysing trends in labour supply and demand. The HRIMS was becoming an essential strategic tool for HR planning and cost-effective human resource management.

Computerised HRIMS could also store employee data more securely, and allow easy access by HR specialists, senior and line management. Decentralised HR functions in very large organisations reinforced the need for HRIMS during the 1980s. Not only could trends in external labour markets, employee absence, turnover and wastage, and career paths be recorded in computerised information systems, but future costs could be determined. HRIMS provide a tool for developing closer links between HRM and HRP, between HRM and corporate strategies and, importantly, between HR managers, line and senior management.

As News report 4.2 illustrates, recent developments in information technology have not only transformed the nature and meaning of work, the numbers of jobs and the ways in which they are performed, as discussed in earlier chapters, but they have also radically transformed the nature and capacities of the HRM function.

Information technology, especially through the increasing use of organisational intranets, has enabled more HR information to be collected and processed more comprehensively and with greater accuracy and speed, and also enabled easier access to such data by HR specialists, managers at all organisational levels, employees themselves and sometimes their unions and associations. News report 4.2 outlines the benefits to HR professionals in terms of reallocation of their time, and the ability to devolve routine administrative activities to line managers or employees themselves, thus freeing them to focus on more strategic processes such as HR planning, knowledge management and career development.

As a contemporary example of the practical applications of modern HRIMS, the NSW government has developed a program for public sector reform using a jobs website (jobs.nsw) linking departmental intranets with the Internet, and incorporating 70 agencies and more than 300 job types.[15] In addition, an 'HR Expert System Project' provides departments with online access to the details of key employment legislation (see Chapter 2), and an 'EEO Good Practice' database offers a self-paced 'electronic refresher course' in merit-based selection.[16] AXA Australia has effectively integrated information management across four of its separate businesses by developing a corporate HR intranet called 'People Online'.[17]

For managers, direct access to employee information on both individual and collective bases allows them to better monitor past and present performance (e.g. leave, absences, productivity and cost factors), and thus enhances their capacity to develop timely and appropriate sectional HR plans in line with broader organisational plans. Employees can check the accuracy of their own HR data, update it where required, and in some systems obtain individual HR advice online. Neiger suggests that '… web-enabling, employee self-service and integration with back-end enterprise resource planning (ERP) are the "hot" features of IT for the human resources sector'.[18]

Self-service HRIMS or 'web kiosks' allow '… anyone with a web browser and appropriate permissions to access the system directly, [freeing up] HR to concentrate on strategic functions rather than spending time answering routine questions or preparing reports for line and divisional managers'.[19] In such systems, employees in organisations as diverse as Westpac, Pepsi, Wyeth Pharmaceuticals, the Australian Retirement Fund, the Australian Taxation Office, BHP, GPU PowerNet (Vic.), the Ford Motor Company, the WA Insurance Commission, AGC, UniSuper and Lend Lease can directly access information on personal details, staff benefits, awards and enterprise agreements, HR policies, leave entitlements, reports of staff satisfaction surveys, training details and planned organisational changes. Significant cost-savings can be achieve through the use of such employee kiosks, including reductions in HR time, printing and distribution costs, greater system efficiency and accuracy, and the scaling down of overall benefits transaction costs.[20]

Some organisations choose in-house HRIMS, linked with their existing email system, while others have consciously developed strategic partnerships with external 'application service providers' (ASPs) to provide some (and sometimes all) of their HR information services, as part of their 'outsourcing' strategies, as indicated in Exhibit 4.7. Many small or medium-sized enterprises (SMEs) have chosen external 'HR shared service/call centres' to reduce costs or to 'buy in' HR expertise on specialist matters such as payroll administration, industrial relations, enterprise agreements or occupational health and safety. As an example of the latter, IBM (UK) has developed AskHR, an HR 'client centre' that provides a broad range of HRM services for 90 000 organisations in 15 countries across Europe, the Middle East and Africa. It employs more than 80 people, and its stated purpose is to '… get the strategic (HR) people much closer to the grassroots than in the past, because they have more "intelligence"'.[21] Several authors have suggested that such HR call centres may in the future provide an entry point for HR careers.[22]

Larger organisations have tended to prefer the outsourcing of specific HR information services (e.g. payroll, recruitment, industrial relations) in conjunction with the maintenance of in-house HRM functions such as career development, human resource development and HR planning, often cemented through linkages between organisational intranets and ASP extranets. This option serves to maximise the benefits of costs and expertise, while minimising the possible disadvantages of the loss of a strategic HRM presence within the organisation, and avoiding the risk that '… their most confidential (HR) information will be located off-site and managed by a third party'.[23]

Exhibit 4.7 A model of strategic human resource planning using HRIMS

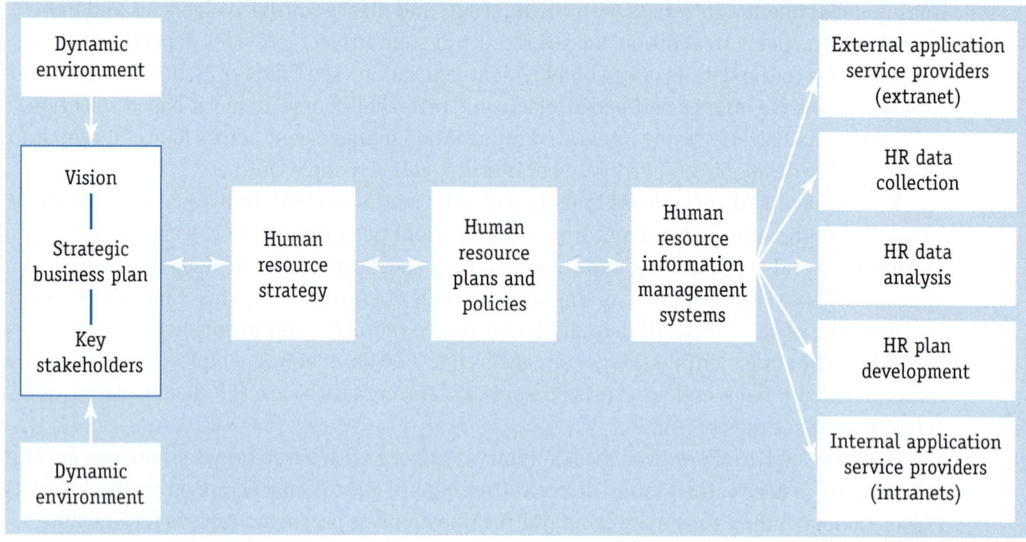

Regardless of the ways in which information technology and HRIMS may develop in the future, HR and information technology are inextricably linked: '… future generations will draw from the best features of organisational learning, IT infrastructures, performance support and knowledge management, and their hybrid vigour will dramatically improve organisational and individual performance'.[24]

Benefits and features of HRIMS

The specific benefits of HRIMS include:

- improved planning and program development using decision support software
- faster information processing and improved response times
- decreased administrative and HR costs
- accuracy of information
- enhanced communication at all levels.[25]

Not all systems fulfil all these requirements, nor is such a complete system suitable for all organisations. Essentially, however, all HRIMS contain information on:

- employees
- jobs and work conditions
- positions
- HR events (e.g. recruitment, training and development, performance appraisals, and terminations).

Exhibit 4.8 illustrates some components of HR information management systems, their interrelationships and the range of applications for which they can be used.

Exhibit 4.8 HRIMS overall scope

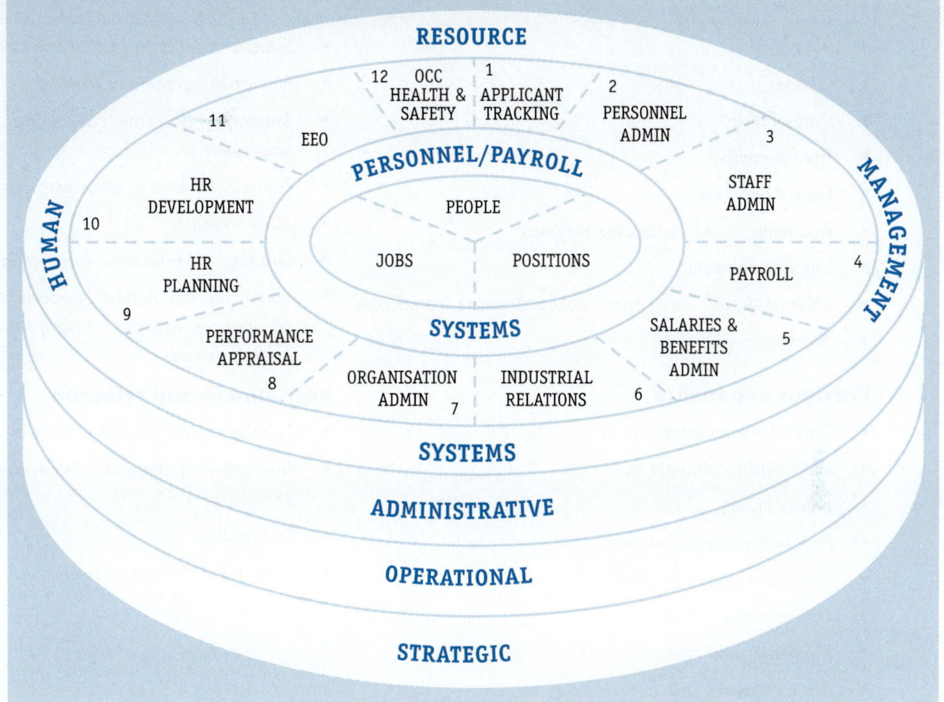

Source: Reprinted with the kind permission of Mr David Proud, Managing Partner, Puntimai Associates, HR Information Consultants.

Older forms of HRIMS were essentially 'relational databases' in which information on such HR aspects as the financial investment in training could be correlated by employee gender, or the number of sick days taken could be tied to specific age groups or job clusters. Newer forms of HRIMS allow such correlations, but also assist 'synthesis, analysis and consolidation'[26] of such data, an invaluable tool for strategic HR planning. As one author reflects, increasingly HRIMS are becoming '... databases on which decision support systems can be established'.[27]

Types of HRIMS data

As Exhibit 4.8 shows, information management systems contain aggregated records on all aspects of the employment relationship, for administrative, operational and strategic purposes. Administrative functions include records of industrial awards and agreements; HR policies; legislative, salary, leave and taxation details, superannuation and employee benefits schemes. Operational data include personal and job histories and records on recruitment and selection, training and development, performance appraisal, career and succession, absenteeism and employee turnover schemes. Strategic planning information includes administrative and operational records, together with data concerning staff positions, wastage, labour market trends, industry salary surveys, educational developments, employment and skills levels. Exhibit 4.9 shows the scope of employee information that may be included in a HRIMS.

Exhibit 4.9 Employee information details

Individual	Collective
• Name	• Establishment data (actual and occupied)
• Gender*	• Enterprise agreements (AWAs)
• Date of birth*	• Temporary, part-time, casual and contract employees
• Tax file number	
• Educational level	• Ratios of full-time to other employees
• Academic, trade certificates/degrees	• Skills inventory
• Union membership*	• Grading, classification, job evaluation data
• Other skills, e.g. languages spoken, licences, certificates	• Vacancies, e.g. number, department, occupations, reasons for advertising details, unfilled periods
• Work history	

Previous experience	**Recruitment and selection**
• Date of employment	• Number, ages, sources of recruits
• Initial and subsequent jobs	• Methods (including cost and evaluation of results)
• Salary history	
• Performance appraisal records	• Test results
• Training courses attended	• Interviewer training courses
• Career paths	
• Medical examination	
• Disciplinary records	

Conditions of service	**Career paths and succession plans**
• Individual employment contracts	• Promotions
• Annual leave	• Replacements
• Sick leave	• Training and development costs, numbers
• Long service leave	• Performance appraisal
• Leave without pay/special leave	• Salary data/packages
• Workers' compensation records	• Absenteeism, e.g. days lost, reasons, costs, ages, occupations
• Accidents and occupational health incidents	
• Equipment supplied	• Labour turnover
• Working hours	
• Employee benefits	
• Union membership*	• Workplace agreement conditions
• Workplace agreement conditions	• Legislated pay and conditions inclusions
• Legislated pay and conditions inclusions	

* These details may need to be collected and stored separately under EEO legislation.

Source: Adapted from Compton R., Morrissey W., Nankervis A.R. 2006.
Effective recruitment and selection techniques, 4th edn, Sydney, CCH Australia, pp. 212–13.

Strategic HR planning and HR information management systems

Proactive HR managers ensure that their HRIMS contributes to organisational performance. As Professor Boudreau points out:

> After all, more than any other resource, the 'human resource' embodies information-based characteristics such as knowledge, skills, capabilities and competencies. Thus, the value of the 'human capital' of organisations, and the method of managing it, depend on understanding and using information.[28]

A recent development in the uses of HRIMS in many Australian organisations has been the linking of 'benchmarking' practices to the design, choice and implementation of such systems as a directly strategic initiative. Integration with organisational strategic objectives is achieved by the subsequent establishment of performance targets and quantitative measures. As an example, Telstra is collecting relevant data from each of its organisational units and then establishing internal 'benchmarks,' which will, in turn, be compared with industry or international standards. Other organisations benchmark their overall HRM strategies in areas such as the attraction and retention of talent, performance management, leadership, rewards management, and cultural change, against their competitors or other industries.[29] Exhibit 4.10 illustrates the ways in which national and international benchmarks contribute to strategic HR planning.

Exhibit 4.10   The role of HR information in the HR strategic planning process

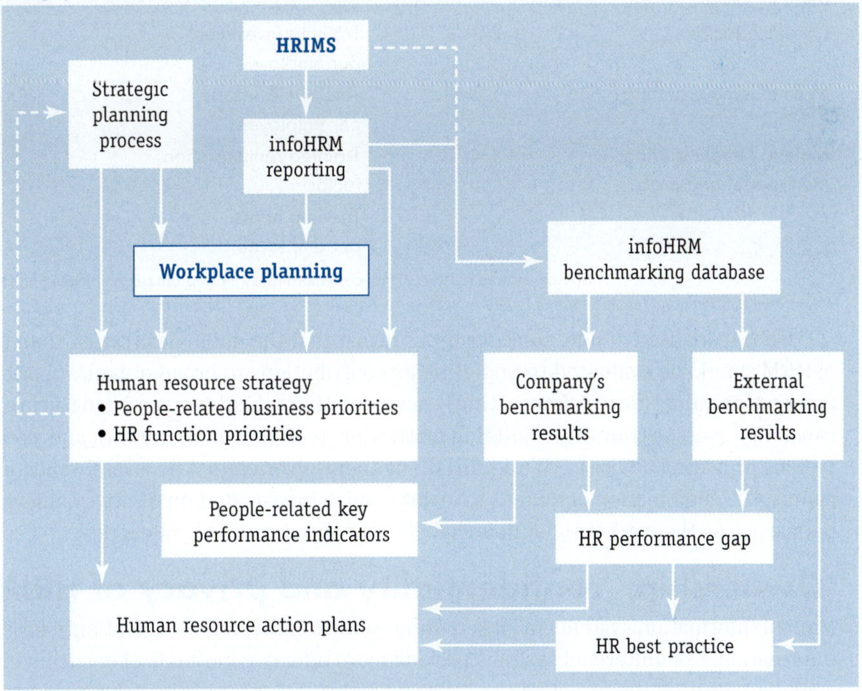

Source: Reprinted with the kind permission of Mr Peter Howes, HRM Consulting.

As a strategic 'tool,' HRIMS can be used to contribute to the development and modification of HR plans, on both quantitative and qualitative bases, and to feed into specific HRM processes. HR data, if collected effectively and contained within computerised, accessible systems, can compare organisational HR 'bottom line' outcomes by HRM process, between processes and with national or international performance 'benchmarks' (see Exhibit 4.11).

These comparisons enable the evaluation of the quantitative features of HR plans, as well as the subsequent promotion of the 'success' of strategies and plans to senior managers. They can also enable necessary modifications to HR plans and HRM functions according to movements in these statistics. Underperforming recruitment/selection processes or excessive termination costs (against predetermined benchmarks) can be targeted, or modified, in order to enable the achievement of HR and organisational objectives.

Exhibit 4.11   Key HR benchmarks, 1995

HR benchmark	All industry median	HR benchmark	All industry median
Revenue per employee	$104 650	Total unscheduled absence	3.2%
Expense per employee	$92 736	Dollar value sick leave per employee	$1 131
Profit per employee	$7 821	Total terminations	14.04%
HR expense factor	0.94%	Net recruitment rate	0.63
HR staffing factor	55.26	External recruitment rate	8.6%
HR managerial and prof. staffing factor	126.71	Internal/external ratio	0.96
Management staffing ratio	13.9	Time to fill	45.3 days
Overtime factor	2.01%	Training investment per employee	$797
Male to female staffing	1.8 : 1	Total OH&S costs per employee	$561
Male to female staffing, managerial and prof.	4.4 : 1	Training remuneration factor	1.8%
		Training hours per employee	25.08

Source: Howes P. 1996. 'Finance sector makes more profit per employee,' *hrmonthly*, August, p. 34.

On the qualitative side, some writers suggest that the outcomes (rather than the activities) of HRM should be evaluated to underline its contributions to broad organisational goals – that is, 'creating value' (versus forecasting), 'accumulating talent' (versus hiring/firing), 'building capability' (versus training), 'building motivation' (versus remuneration), and 'creating change' (versus providing advice).[30] While HRIMS by themselves cannot accurately substantiate these claims, the combination of quantitative data and demonstrated qualitative achievements are as persuasive as the marketing or financial plans of organisational colleagues.

'Ownership,' confidentiality and privacy of HRIMS data

Manual information systems in locked filing cabinets provided confidentiality for employee information. Computerised systems provide more effective methods of ensuring employee confidentiality, by the use of access keys and codes. All organisations, however, need to consider carefully which employee data are truly confidential and how they can best be protected. These are almost always ethical issues that should be considered before systems are developed.

As part of their outsourcing activities, some private sector organisations, and many federal and state public service authorities, have engaged specialist HRIMS providers to conduct their HR systems, and thence to supply ad hoc, operational and strategic HR data. These developments raise serious issues with respect to the 'ownership' and security of employee data, which may be held in disparate databases both within and outside particular organisations, and also with respect to the levels and methods of access to specific data by such diverse users as HR professionals, managers, employees and government authorities. As Internet and email systems are often essential components of 'self-service' HRIMS, employer–employee rights and obligations also require careful consideration.

On the issue of the 'ownership' of employee information contained in external HR databases, contracts with ASPs should explicitly ensure that all such data are, and remain, the property of the outsourcing organisation, that they should not be released to any unauthorised party during the period of the contract, and that they are returned to the employer on the expiration or non-renewal of the contract. These requirements are, of course, legally binding.

Australian legislation that may be relevant to ownership, confidentiality and privacy issues includes the *Crimes Act (Part VIIC) 1990* (Cth), the federal *Privacy Act 1988*, the *Privacy Amendment Act 1991*, the *Privacy Amendment (Private Sector) Act 2000*, various associated state acts and statutes (e.g. the *Privacy Committee Act 1975* (NSW)), and the freedom of information and anti-discrimination legislation federally and in all Australian states. Breaches can be dealt with by federal and state courts, and by the various privacy and anti-discrimination boards or commissioners.

While not directly related to HRIMS, the linkages between them and intranet or email systems also raise confidentiality and privacy concerns for many employers. Several authors[31] warn that Australian employers will need to become increasingly aware of their 'vicarious liability' for the content of their employees' email messages and Internet downloads.

Steggal,[32] for example, observes that Australia, unlike the US, has no constitutional privacy protection, no common law right to privacy and only limited statutory protection under the above legislative guidelines. She suggests that 'Australia is on the verge of a barrage of employee–employer cyber litigation'[33] as the result of disciplinary action taken against employees who abuse their access to email and Internet systems at work, or even at home, when using computers provided by the employer. Several Australian employers who fired employees for inappropriate use of their email systems (e.g. Rio Tinto (2003), *Ansett v Gencarelli* (2000), Telstra Victoria, CentreLink) have had their decisions questioned by the courts, especially where clear email policies and procedures had not been formulated and widely disseminated. On the other hand, the NSW Industrial Relations Commission recently found that a long-standing employee of NCR Australia who had collected pornographic material on his work computer was 'guilty of serious and wilful misconduct … and … had acted in breach of the company Code of Conduct'.[34] As Mike Toten[35] warns, all organisations will need to develop such policies in the future, both to inform employees of their rights and obligations in this medium and to protect themselves from expensive and disruptive litigation (see, for example, www.privacy.gov.au).

Successful HRIMS

The most effective human resource information management systems are those which:

- contain accurate employee and job data

- are sufficiently flexible to adapt to both present and future requirements

- clearly link with, and contribute to, HR plans

- are modular, but integrated in design, allowing multiple input and access

- allow clear control of human resource costs.

External supply

If an organisation lacks a sufficient internal supply of employees for promotion, or when staffing entry-level positions, it will need to consider the external supply of labour. Many factors influence external labour supply, including demographic changes in the population; national, international and regional economics; the education levels of the workforce; demands for specific employee skills; population mobility and government policies. In these circumstances, the human resource planner must gauge the most likely sources of employees within planning periods, according to trends in the relevant indicators.

HRP strives for an appropriate balance between labour demand and supply. Supply analyses determine how employees with the required qualifications and personal qualities can be attracted to fill job vacancies. Due to the difficulty of obtaining employees with advanced job skills and aptitudes, this phase of planning is becoming more crucial. Executive, managerial and technical specialist positions often demand specific job skills as well as broader qualities of flexibility, innovation and adaptation.

Other options to full-time permanent positions can also be considered, including casual and part-time positions, job-sharing and contract positions. Appropriate balance needs to be established between hiring new staff and retrenching existing workers, taking account of the effects on productivity, morale, career opportunities, and the demands of legislation such as equal employment opportunity and affirmative action. The environment of an organisation consists of the conditions, circumstances and influences which affect the organisation's ability to achieve its objectives. Every organisation exists in an environment that is both external and internal in nature, and both the external and the internal environment are composed of four or five elements: physical (internal only), technological, political, economic and social. A major challenge for employers and HR managers in particular is not only to understand and cope with both environments, but also to influence them. HR managers will increasingly become environmental scanners, searching for likely future changes in their internal and external environments, identifying pressures and opportunities, and developing HR strategies and plans to address them.

The external environment

The environment that exists outside the organisation is its external environment. The external political, social and commercial environment can have a significant impact on the policies, practices, strategies and plans of HRM. It helps to determine the values, attitudes and behaviour that employees bring to their jobs. By analysing the outside community and society, the proactive HR planner can assess likely current and future changes and determine possible impacts on the workforce and organisational plans.

External environments can be divided into three broad categories – global, national and industry contexts.

We shall consider each of these environments separately, but it should be borne in mind that many of the relevant organisational issues overlap both internal and external environments. Thus, imperatives for productivity, quality and effectiveness are global, national and industry-wide. And, as a recent study conducted jointly by the Committee for the Economic Development of Australia (CEDA) and the Australian Human Resources Institute (AHRI) concludes, there are seven crucial success factors for contemporary Australian business, namely:

- recruiting and retaining skilled employees
- increasing customer satisfaction
- employing and developing leaders
- sustaining a competitive advantage
- managing risk

- managing change and corporate culture, and
- becoming a more innovative organisation.[36]

These 'success factors' are associated with seven 'business challenges,' namely, skilled employees, customer satisfaction, leadership, competitive advantage, risk management, corporate change management, and innovation.

The global context

We all live and work in a global community, with global values, global perspectives and a global marketplace. Whenever the (US) Dow Jones index rises, the world's stockmarkets hold their breath, when the Japanese yen falls, ripples spread across the world's finance sector. The 'Asian economic crisis' of the late 1990s radically changed the nature of business relationships and profit expectations that existed beforehand. Since then, there has been a general economic shift from high to low inflation economies, with significant decreases in tariffs between countries, and a plethora of bilateral free trade agreements (e.g. NAFTA, US–China, US–Singapore, Singapore–Australia, New Zealand–Australia).[37]

Internet websites, cable television, mobile telephones, facsimiles and email communications ensure that we are reminded daily of our membership of a global community. Accessible international travel enables us to complement virtual reality with actual international experiences, and frequent flyer/customer loyalty programs encourage us to do so.

Technology, especially telecommunications and information technology, has enabled Marshall McLuhan's 'global village' to become reality. However, while technology has been a powerful medium for sweeping away our insular mindsets and replacing them with global perspectives, many other factors have also contributed. Any HR planner would be foolish to ignore the impact of these global pressures, which affect almost all the activities in which their organisations engage.

Globalisation and information technology

Globalisation and information technology represent the most potent forces for change in the nature and location of jobs, in the types of human resources required, and in their skills and competencies. In fact, modern forms of globalisation, involving the relocation of organisations, instantaneous communication within and between countries, and the formation of e-commerce companies or 'virtual organisations,' would not have been conceivable without the opportunities provided by the digital revolution involving the Internet, satellite links, cellular telephone networks, high-speed fibre optic cables and ICT infrastructure. It was estimated that there were more than one billion Internet users globally in 2005.[38]

Associated developments in biotechnology, alternative energies and nano-technology have not only radically restructured industry operations and priorities, but also transformed the nature of jobs, their locations and employment conditions, and produced new attitudes and mindsets among employers and their staff. As discussed later in this chapter, cost factors and new technology have resulted in a shift of traditional agricultural and manufacturing industries, either to automated operations or to countries with less restrictive labour conditions. Countries such as Australia, New Zealand, Singapore, Malaysia and Hong Kong are now firmly 'service economies' competing globally in the same information and telecommunications sectors.

While Western Australia, Victoria and New South Wales aspire to become leaders in information technology, and have the support of both federal and state political parties (e.g. the federal Coalition government's 'Information Economy' minister, the Australian Labor Party's 'Knowledge Nation' strategy), our Asia–Pacific neighbours, such as Malaysia (e.g. Cyberjaya near Kuala Lumpur), Hong Kong (e.g. new 'Silicon Valley') and New Zealand, have similar desires.

The Howard government in Australia has invested A$78 million on a Building IT Strengths Programme to assist start-up e-commerce companies,[39] and some state leaders have a vision to supply all homes with Internet access in the near future.

The impact of new technology on world economies is enormous and expanding, as is its contribution to productivity and competitiveness. Alan Greenspan, the former US Federal Reserve Bank Chairman, explained that the United States '… has been experiencing a higher growth rate of productivity-output per hour worked in recent years. The dramatic improvements in computing power and communication and IT appear to have been a major force behind this beneficial trend'.[40]

The implications for human resource management of the global surge in information and communications technology are immense in relation to new kinds of jobs, new forms of workplaces, radically changing and differential employment conditions, and heightened employee expectations of their roles, performance and entitlements. Many of these implications are discussed in detail later in this chapter and throughout the text. However, some of the major issues are briefly canvassed here.

At the macro-economic level, some industries (e.g. printing, clothing and footwear, agriculture) have relocated their manufacturing operations overseas or largely replaced previously labour-intensive processes with new technological systems. Some other industries (e.g. retailing, travel agencies, media) have chosen to engage partly (or wholly) in e-commerce activities (e.g. travelmart. com, flightcentre.com) or to form strategic partnerships with affiliated global organisations for economies of scale, the sharing of technological systems or knowledge transfer. The national tourism boards and agencies in almost every country in the world, hotel chains, airlines and many restaurants provide 'virtual tours' of their attractions and services, including price and booking functions online. Many other industries (e.g. telecommunications, banking) use 'shared service centres' or 'call centres' for similar purposes. Not only will this restructuring of operations result in fewer employees with more specialised skills, but it also suggests that larger organisations may lose talented and mobile professionals to their global or local competitors who can offer more attractive remuneration systems or more challenging projects. Lim Young-Hak, Executive Director of Internet Business, Samsung, has said that it is not easy to be creative when working for a big corporation.[41] HR planners need to build such realities into their future staffing plans.

One of the major issues confronting HR planners in this dynamic global context is that of the management of 'human capital.'

Human capital management (HCM)

Whereas SHRM proposes that the strategic management of skilled and adaptive 'human resources' (i.e. talented and skilled employees with the capacity for future development) is the primary source of competitive advantage in a dynamic global environment, human capital theory goes further, suggesting that the individual and collective impact of SHRM can and should be measured, and subsequently reported and marketed to the organisation's stakeholders, including its managers, shareholders and potential investors. As John Dyer, CSR Limited's General Manager HR, explains, 'all of our HR strategies should lead to improving the attractiveness of our stock, because the whole of HR is about leveraging performance through people'.[42]

Sexton (2003) reports that HRM issues influence more than three-quarters of the Dow Jones Sustainability Index criteria, and cites the findings of a US study which reported that '… 35 per cent of all investment decisions were based on non-financial data, of which more than half was HR-related'.[43] The HR practices most likely to attract investor interest include:

- executive remuneration

- succession planning

- organisational culture and management style

- the proportions of expatriate versus local staff

- staff turnover and wastage rates
- the receipt of 'employer of choice' awards
- industrial relations and occupational health and safety records.[44]

Kaplan suggests that 'high retention workplaces,' that is, those organisations which recognise the value of their human capital and which therefore exercise strategic staffing and employee retention plans, are more likely to attract the best candidates, to enjoy low absenteeism and turnover levels, to have greater customer satisfaction and loyalty, and to nurture 'innovation, creativity and risk-taking'.[45] In support of this contention, he cites the examples of Lend Lease, the Flight Centre, Nokia, AMP, The Body Shop, and IBM, which have been given awards as 'Winning Workplaces' by the Australian Chamber of Commerce and Industry in recent years.[46] The global integrated business solutions provider, Tectura, with 1 400 employees across the world, uses an annual 'Great Place to Work' employee survey and a half-yearly 'pulse survey' to measure staff satisfaction levels and to ensure that retention levels never fall below 95 per cent. According to its global Head of HR, Tectura's people strategies '… aren't about driving cultural change, but more about building relationships and leveraging Tectura's values – integrity, care, and results – as the common thread'.[47]

News report 4.3 below illustrates an interesting approach to HCM and HR planning in an unusual industry sector.

NEWS REPORT 4.3

Independence daily

One of the newest listings on the Australian Stock Exchange is Melbourne-based Daily Planet Limited, the first publicly listed bordello in the world.

The company has devised an HR strategy that is becoming more common in modern business – particularly among small and medium enterprises. It does not employ anyone. 'The Daily Planet has never employed anybody, except for a secretary,' says Andrew Harris, director and CEO. 'Everybody who operates in the Daily Planet is either a sub-contractor or independently licensed to operate on the premises.'

The business, which listed on the ASX in May, is actually the owner of the building in which the Daily Planet brothel operates, describing itself as 'Melbourne's only six-star hotel allowing sexual services on site.'

'The fact that (the staff) are contractors is simply a very good arrangement from a taxation point of view and a management point of view, because it makes them independent and us independent,' says Harris. 'We don't have problems associated with WorkCover, Workcare and all those other management issues that can arise from them. We don't have payroll issues, the girls have always collected their money direct and we don't even have to legally release their names.'

That doesn't mean that Daily Planet doesn't have their HR strategies though. Training and development is a priority, says Harris. 'Training is both requested and given at every level of staff; it doesn't matter if you're working as a shift manager, a receptionist, a hostess, barman, shower boy, doing administration, or you're one of the working girls, everyone in the establishment goes through a training program.'

But does Harris think that a sound human resources policy is something by which the company can leverage stock market interest? 'We're not sure yet, that will be up to the market,' he says. 'We do operate differently from any other brothel we know. We have nothing to do with the girls' money, we do have a proper development and training program, we do have a succession plan.'

Source: Sexton, F. 2003. 'How investors rate human capital', *hrmonthly*, August, p. 21.

Formulating human resource plans

Once labour demand forecasts and supply analyses have been conducted and compared, a series of integrated staffing plans needs to be developed, in line with corporate strategies.

Component parts of the human resource plan will include integrated plans for future work and job design; recruitment; selection; training, development, career management and succession; remuneration; separation and retirement/retrenchment; rewards systems and performance management. An integrated approach is essential not only for good human resource management practice, but also to ensure that organisational objectives, structures and cultures are effectively and efficiently aligned.

Effective HRP also inherently recognises that the best laid plans are likely to be disrupted by internal or external changes. Market shifts, technological changes, economic downturns, increased competition or industrial relations actions can severely inhibit HR plans. Thus proactive HR managers will take care to include a series of contingency plans in their overall human resource plan. HRP should also be cyclical, involving continuous monitoring and review. Like marketing, financial management or productivity plans, HR plans are seldom exact, but they generally involve a series of informed predictions of the future demand and supply of employees, and their likely costs and contributions to organisational effectiveness.

Drawbacks and benefits of HRP

Drawbacks

HR planning is sometimes avoided because it is time-consuming or just too difficult. Certainly, effective HR plans do take time and can be costly, particularly if specialists are required. In many large organisations, the complexity of internal and external factors may require whole sections to develop plans. HRP techniques can be complicated, and strategies may require long lead-times, during which economic or political conditions may change. Cultures may be immensely difficult to modify, structures seemingly impossible to alter. Adequate HR databases may not be in place or industrial conditions may be inappropriate for the proposed strategies. In many organisations, there are vested interests obstructive to new HR plans, and even top management may not recognise the need for change.

Benefits

Despite these drawbacks, a wide variety of benefits can be derived from well-prepared HR plans. Human resources in organisations will be better used, employee and organisational objectives can be more closely matched, and substantial improvements can be achieved in both productivity and profitability.

Employees can be recruited at the best time, for the right cost and in line with future organisational requirements. Idle labour, and under-supply of labour, can be efficiently avoided, and any labour surpluses can be used for the development of new markets or new products. Future skills requirements can be met by the timely training and development of employees, and their morale can be maintained by the smooth management of their careers. Likely redundancies can be anticipated and managed effectively with minimum disruption to employees, work processes and organisational objectives. Overall, HRP is a means of ensuring that all HRM activities are effectively integrated with business strategies, and that the HR function receives appropriate recognition by clearly contributing to the success of the organisation.

Effective HRP

As suggested, HR planning is a complex process, involving the use of qualitative and quantitative techniques supported by an effective human resource database. It requires the HR manager to be a strategic thinker, with close links to both senior and line managers, and up to date with the internal and external environments of their organisation.

Effective HR planning clearly depends on:

- top management understanding of, and commitment to, the HRP process and its outcomes

- the recognition of the equal importance of human and other resources

- an understanding of the crucial links between external and internal environments and organisational strategies

- effective linkages between HRP and HRM

- the provision of adequate staff, time and resources for HRP

- effective human resource information systems.[48]

Summary

This chapter examines the nature of human resource planning and its crucial relationship to organisational strategies and human resource management programs. It proposes a systematic approach, blending qualitative and quantitative HR planning techniques, supported by an accurate and comprehensive HRIMS.

The internal and the external environments of organisations increasingly affect the nature and complexity of HR plans, in positive and negative ways. HR planners need to act as environmental scanners, providing long-term and contingency strategies, to ensure that organisational and employee needs are effectively met. This flexibility is increasingly necessary as Australian work patterns and labour markets undergo dramatic changes. Towards the end of the chapter, the benefits and drawbacks of HRP are considered, emphasising its crucial contribution to organisational success.

Key terms

business process outsourcing (BPO) 114
career planning 124
employee kiosks 127
environmental scanning 114
establishment data 130
human capital management (HCM) 136
human resource information management systems (HRIMS) 125
human resource planning (HRP) 138
labour demand forecasting 120
labour supply analysis 122
offshoring 114
skills inventories 123
succession planning/executive replacement 116

Key debate issues

1 Strategic HRP is impossible in the changing internal and external environments of organisations, and with the short-term perspectives of most Australian companies and their governments.
2 Most Australian organisations are too small to be greatly affected by global issues. Only large companies with international subsidiaries need to build these factors into their HR plans.
3 Talent management and talent retention are the only priorities for HR planners in today's organisations.
4 Argue the cases for:
   a maintaining an HRIMS wholly within the organisation
   b an integrated HRIMS, including internal and external service providers
   c an entirely 'outsourced' HRIMS.

Case study 4.1

The past

The organisation is based in New South Wales and employs 2000 people in a variety of trade, professional and management roles. The company has enjoyed a monopoly position throughout its history but now faces keen competition following decisions by the ACCC. Market share is resting on 65 per cent but falling.

The organisation has had a small holding company and four business units, which are structured according to their function. Three of the four businesses are losing money. The executive has no appreciation of the core business concept even though a number of junior managers (many with business and MBA degrees) have suggested that this is a critical issue for consideration. They have argued that many functions of the organisation could be outsourced.

As a direct result, the workforce has been reduced from more than 5000 employees over the past two years and this has been achieved by voluntary redundancy. Unfortunately, many of those leaving the organisation have been those who could least afford to be lost. A great deal of corporate memory and intellectual capital has been lost forever. Employee training has been one of those areas severely curtailed as part of several rounds of cost-cutting exercises.

Leadership is predominantly in the hands of white, middle-aged males who have a long history of employment in the organisation. The seven-man executive group has no private sector experience. Each has come from the industry, with three of the seven beginning their careers as cadets with the organisation. Five are engineers and the other two are accountants. Leadership style could be described as transactional. The former CEO was one of the former cadet engineers and was the definitive transactional leader. He had little time for the 'warm and fuzzy' approach of the new-age leader.

The typical senior- and middle-level leader could be described as bureaucratic, risk averse, conservative and mechanistic in outlook. There has been no clear understanding of what type of leader might be required for the future. The future is seen as an extrapolation of the past. There is a cohort of young, fresh and well-educated middle managers who have the ideas and drive to help turn the organisation around but invariably they are blocked by their managers. Consequently, many have left or talk often of leaving the organisation. There is no succession planning. Most managers at all levels are working very long hours with little compensation, if any, and certainly little recognition.

The senior team spends much time selling the concept that 'our people are our most valuable resource' but the message received by the employees is that they are the organisation's most expendable resource. Trust and loyalty have largely gone as people wait for the next round of redundancies.

The predominant culture is bureaucratic although many people in lower-level positions can see the need for a major culture shift if the organisation is to survive. The business leaders argue that any attempts at organisational change must be rooted in the culture but the union counter-argues that management has already well and truly 'rooted' the culture. The need for a customer-focused culture is apparent to most but little is being done to address the issues.

The bulk of the general workforce is long-serving, with 15 to 20 years of service being the norm. People with 25+ years of service are common. The prevailing culture within this group is very paternalistic and this can be traced to management's past style. Their attitude can be summed up as one where the organisation owes them a living. Payday has always come each Wednesday and always will. The 'good old days' will soon return. If management wants a little extra then they will have to pay for it. Senior management is not trusted; any respect it once had has now been lost. Flexibility is talked of but is not apparent in practice.

Performance reviews have not been a priority in the past and are seen by current managers as a chore rather than as a strategic tool for aligning business and personal needs and objectives. The union has stated that it will cooperate only if salary increases are made an integral part of the performance review system.

The workforce and customer base is very diverse but the senior team does not reflect this nor understand the concept of diversity management. The concept is seen as one of those 'warm and fuzzy' HR fads.

The remuneration policy is 'one size fits all.' There is no clear link between pay and performance, although senior leaders have an 'at risk' component within their salary package despite the risk appearing to be minimal. Senior and middle managers can package their salaries and make use of salary-sacrificing strategies. The bulk of the workforce is paid under an award that by its operation is extremely rigid and is clearly one of the main barriers to introducing flexible work practices.

The industrial relations between the employer and the union are sensitive. The union has lost many members through downsizing and will resist any further attempts by management to reduce the workforce any further.

The present

A new commercially oriented board and CEO have at last been appointed by the shareholders and have come to understand that things must change rapidly if the organisation is to survive beyond another two years.

A few months ago the former CEO was moved on. His successor, Sally Yee, has identified certain major changes within the external environment that must be addressed. Specifically, she sees an organisation that has paid only lip service to customer focus and globalisation. She now wants to restructure the four business units based on their customer groups and to 'put a rocket up' senior leadership. Many have mistaken 'transparent' leadership with 'invisible' leadership. Remuneration must move towards an 'earned' culture rather than the 'entitlement' culture that has become entrenched.

Her view is that all non-core operations be outsourced and that only a small core of well-remunerated and highly developed full-time employees be kept on the payroll. Gaps will be filled by casual and contract staff. All full-time employees will be moved to individual contracts.

There has been an attempt to determine corporate values and to write a code of ethics so as to underpin strategy and culture change, but gaining commitment of senior leaders by way of their actions is proving a challenge.

A high-priced HR consultant has been employed over the past few months and finally has come to the CEO with a draft Corporate 'People' Plan for the next two years. Her task has been to identify the 'Big 6' issues that must be addressed immediately.

Question

1   Which 'Big 6' people issues/strategies do you feel must be included in the draft plan? Be prepared to justify your views.

Case study 4.2

You are the human resource manager for the following organisations:

*   a public service department which is about to be relocated from a capital city to a country area, according to state government policy
*   a Japanese multinational company which is keen to reduce staffing numbers and costs in its subsidiary on the Gold Coast
*   an inner-city manufacturing organisation which has experienced high levels of process workers leaving over the past couple of years (87 per cent annual average). Although it offers competitive salaries and rapid promotion, it cannot seem to keep its employees. To maintain its market position, the company needs to improve productivity levels.

Questions

1   What kinds of problems do you anticipate?
2   Are they pressures or opportunities? Can you convert the pressures to opportunities? How?
3   How will you cost-effectively address these situations?

Further readings

Boxall P., Purcell J. 2003. *Strategy and human resource management*, Basingstoke, Palgrave Macmillan.

Cascio W. 2005. 'From business partner to driving business success: The next step in the evolution of HR management,' *Human Resource Management*, 44(2), pp. 159–63.

Critchley R. 2004. *Doing nothing is not an option: Facing the imminent labor crisis*,' Mason, Ohio, South Western.

Kochan T.A. 2004. 'Restoring the trust in the human resource management professional,' *Asia Pacific Journal of Human Resources*, 42(2), pp. 132–46.

Kramar R. 2006. *Cranet-Macquarie survey on international strategic human resource management: Report on the Australian findings*, Sydney, Macquarie University.

Kulik C.T., Bainbridge H.T.J. 2006. 'HR and the line: The distribution of HR activities in Australian organisations,' *Asia Pacific Journal of Human Resources*, 44(2), pp. 240–56.

Lansbury R. 2004. 'Work, people and globalisation: Toward a new social contract for Australia,' *Journal of Industrial Relations*, 46(1), pp. 102–15.

Lansbury R., Baird M. 2004. 'Broadening the horizons of HRM: Lessons for Australia from the US experience,' *Asia Pacific Journal of Human Resources*, 42(2), pp. 147–55.

Meisinger S.R. 2005. 'The four Cs of the HR profession: Being competent, curious, courageous and caring about people,' *Human Resource Management*, 44(2), pp. 189–94.

Roberts R., Hirsch P. 2005. 'Evolution and revolution in the twenty first century: Rules for organizations and managing human resources,' *Human Resource Management*, pp. 171–6.

Sheehan C., Holland P., De Cieri H. 2006. 'Current developments in HRM in Australian organisations,' *Asia Pacific Journal of Human Resources*, 44(2), pp. 132–52.

Ulrich D., Smallwood N. 2005. 'HR's new ROI: Return on intangibles,' *Human Resource Management*, 44(2), pp. 137–42.

Endnotes

1   Robbins S.P., Low P.S., Mourell M.P. 1998. *Managing human resources*, Sydney, Prentice Hall, p. 108.

2   Werther W.E. Jnr, Davis K. 1989. *Human resource and personnel management*, 3rd edn, Singapore, McGraw-Hill, p. 92.

3   CCH Australia Ltd, 1986. *Australian personnel management*, Sydney, CCH Australia, p. 822.

4   Butler J.E., Ferris G.R., Napier N.K. 1991. *Strategy and human resource management*, Cincinnati, South-Western, pp. 22–3.

5   Quinn J. 1980. *Strategies for change: Logical incrementalism*, Illinois, Irwin.

6   Sheehan C., Holland P., De Cieri H. 2006. 'Current developments in HRM in Australian organisations,' *Asia Pacific Journal of Human Resources*, 44(2), p. 133.

7   Kane R., Stanton S., 'Human resource planning in a changing environment,' in A.R. Nankervis, R.L. Compton (eds) 1994. *Readings in strategic human resource management*, Melbourne, Nelson ITP, p. 217.

8   Sheehan et al, op. cit., p. 140.

9   Kramar R. 2006. *Cranet-Macquarie survey on international strategic human resource management: Report on the Australian findings*, Sydney, Macquarie University, p. 11.

10 CCH/AGSM 1994. *National survey of recruitment, selection and induction practices*, August, Sydney, CCH Australia, p. 2254.

11 Ibid.

12 Kramar R. 2000. 'In with the new,' *hrmonthly*, October, p. 49.

13 *Sydney Morning Herald* 1992. 'Now Qantas wants to hire more flight staff,' 2 May, p. 9.

14 Macken D.I. 1989. *Award restructuring*, Sydney, Federation Press, p. 60.

15 Porzolt V. 2002. 'Public e-service,' *hrmonthly*, November, pp. 40–1.

16 Ibid.

17 Perry D., Purcell J. 2000. *hrmonthly*, September, pp. 28–9.

18 Neiger D. 2000. 'Vendors weave web into new releases,' *hrmonthly*, September, p. 20.

19 Ibid.

20 www.kis-kiosk.com/apps/hr-kiosk.html, accessed 28/06/2006.

21 Pickard J. 2000. 'Centre of attention,' *People Today* (UK), November, p. 43.

22 For example, Pickard 2000. ibid; AIM 2000. *Online Management Newsletter*, Issue 9.

23 Neiger 2000. op. cit., p. 22.

24 Davenport T. 1999. 'HR and IT in wedded bliss,' *Think Tank*, June, p. 73.

25 Towers Perrin, 1995. *Priorities for competitive advantage*, US: Towers Perrin, p. 50.

26 Howes P. 1995. 'Multidimensional databases will be the key to new HR tools,' *hrmonthly*, December, p. 27.

27 Terrell J. 1997. '"Warehouse" aids conversion from data to decisions,' *hrmonthly*, March, pp. 32–4.

28 Boudreau J. 1992. 'HRIS: Adding value, or just cutting costs?,' *hrmonthly*, May, p. 8.

29 Collard R. 2006, 'Getting value from people measurement and talent.' Paper presented at the 11th World HR Congress, Singapore, June, p. 15.

30 Boudreau J. 1995. 'HRIS: Exploiting its REAL potential,' *hrmonthly*, August, p. 10.

31 For example, Williams D. 2000. 'Check your email policy,' *hrmonthly*, May, p. 35; Toten M. 2000. 'Privacy legislation privatised,' *hrmonthly*, June, p. 41; Steggal V. 2000. 'For whose eyes only?,' *hrmonthly*, June, pp. 16–21.

32 Steggal 2000. op. cit., p. 17.

33 Ibid, p. 16.

34 *Budlong v NCR Australia Ltd.* (2006), NSWIRComm 1075, 9/5/06, www.cch.com.au/aem, accessed 3 July 2006.

35 Toten M. 2000. 'New privacy guidelines,' *hrmonthly*, June, p. 21.

36 Mithen J., Edwards D. 2003. *HR: Creating business solutions – A positioning paper*, Melbourne, AHRI–CEDA, p. 8.

37   Hunt J. 2003. 'The anatomy of organisational change in the twenty-first century,' in Wiesner and Millett 2003. op. cit., p. 4.

38   Collard R. 2006. op. cit.

39   Howarth B., Skotnicki T. 2000. 'Who wins in the e-world?,' *Business Review Weekly*, 22(16), April, p. 111.

40   Margheris L., Henry D., Cooke S., Montes S. 1998. *The emergent digital economy*, Washington, US Department of Commerce, p. 1.

41   See Goad G.P., Lee C.S. 2000. 'Riding the Net,' *Far Eastern Economic Review*, 23 May, p. 8.

42   Sexton F. 2003. 'How investors rate human capital,' *hrmonthly*, August, p. 20.

43   Ibid.

44   Ibid.

45   Kaplan M. 2003. 'Sushi anyone?,' *hrmonthly*, February, pp. 36–7.

46   Ibid.

47   Donaldson C. 2006. 'Tectura: Working on the workplace,' *Human Resources*, 13 June, p. 12.

48   Kane R., Stanton S. 1994. op. cit., p. 232.

Online reading

INFOTRAC® COLLEGE EDITION

For additional readings and review on human resource planning in a charging environment, explore InfoTrac® College Edition, your online library. Go to: www.infotrac-college.com and search for any of the InfoTrac key terms listed below:

➤ business process outsourcing (BPO)
➤ employee kiosks
➤ human capital management (HCM)
➤ human resource information management systems (HRIMS)
➤ human resource planning (HRP)
➤ offshoring

HRM strategies, systems and processes

CHAPTER 5
WORK DESIGN CHALLENGES IN A GLOBAL ENVIRONMENT

Simply put, jobs as we know them are fast becoming relics of a bygone era. While employers, employees, paychecks and careers will remain, the rigid lines we draw around work itself will be gone.

Shari Caudron, 2000

Lets face it, the average computer user has the brain of a Spider Monkey.

Bill Gates, 2000

Big jobs usually go to the men who prove their ability to outgrow small ones.

Ralph Waldo Emerson

Objectives

After reading this chapter you will be able to:

1   Appreciate the contributions of job analysis and competency profiling to job and workplace design.

2   Understand the linkages between job analysis, competencies, position descriptions and person specifications.

3   Be aware of the changing nature of the role and use of job descriptions and person specifications.

4   Understand the value of competencies and competency profiling.

5   Appreciate the different methods of job design and the organisational benefits achieved.

6   Explain the challenges of the changing nature of jobs and the emerging trends in job design.

Introduction

The design of work to meet the needs of both the employee and the organisation is becoming one of the critical issues for employers today operating in a global environment. With the increase in educational standards and focus on knowledge-based work, employees are demanding more interesting work, with greater opportunities for skill enhancement and promotional opportunities, and employers have increased expectations relating to job flexibility, including multi-tasking, multiskilling and improved productivity. The federal government's introduction of the *Workplace Relations (Work Choices) Amendment Act 2005* also encourages employers and employees to directly negotiate and put in place the flexibility arrangements to both retain staff and to improve productivity.

Jobs are also changing on an ongoing basis, making job analysis a constant and dynamic process. There is a greater emphasis on matching competencies with productivity as well as on matching competencies with human resource development and new and future roles in the organisation. Organisational structures are also becoming increasingly flatter, with an emphasis on self-directed work teams and/or individuals operating as internal consultants and advisors to the organisation.

Jobs are also being redesigned to meet increasingly difficult human resource planning issues, particularly in the areas of labour supply and demand. In Australia, significant labour shortages are evident in occupations such as nursing, teaching, environmental science, engineering, town planning and the numerous trade professions. Human resource management professionals, at the senior levels, are also becoming increasingly scarce. These labour shortages are the result of numerous external and internal influences, such as economic conditions; a booming resource sector, particularly in Western Australia; changes to Australian federal industrial relations legislation; social conditions, such as ageing and the dynamic expectations of younger labour markets; the mobility of labour; and other demographic factors.

Job analysis

Jobs are considered to be the building blocks of organisations, with each job consisting of a number of outcomes, responsibilities, tasks and functions. These responsibilities and outcomes, along with the authority and responsibilities awarded to the job and the competency requirements in order to successfully achieve those outcomes not only define a particular job, but could also define a range, group or cluster of jobs. These then relate to other jobs within the team, section, business unit, department or division. As a total unit, all the jobs in the organisation, should, if designed accurately, achieve corporate or strategic objectives. To ensure that this is achieved, jobs need to be accurately analysed, designed and implemented. This process is referred to as job analysis.

Jobs are constantly changing. This is due to a range of internal and external factors, including economic, technological and market pressures. As such, the job analysis process is also ongoing, with competencies being reviewed to ensure that they remain relevant to the needs of the organisation and the position. This then leads to a review process for the two outcomes of the job analysis process: the job or person description (also known as duty statements) and the person specifications. Exhibit 5.1 reflects the strategic nature of this process.

Exhibit 5.1 Strategic model for job requirements

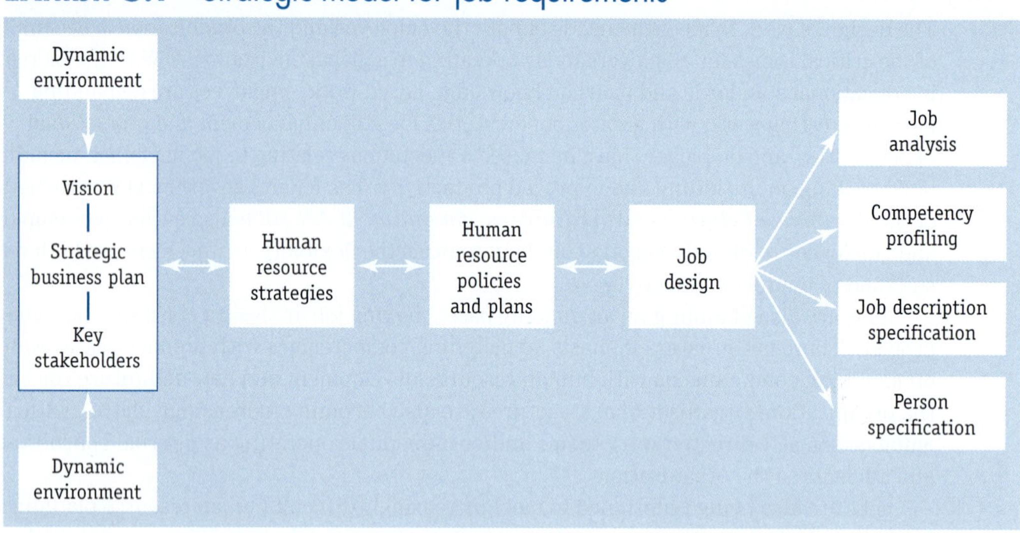

Human resource management and planning activities will determine and be influenced by the nature of present and anticipated jobs in organisations. HR plans that forecast increased or more highly skilled labour requirements to satisfy business strategies concerning product or market diversification result in changes to the number or nature of job requirements. Conversely, the downsizing, streamlining or restructuring of organisations requires their rationalisation, phasing out or modification.

Thus, there is a mutual relationship between the nature of jobs and human resource management, necessitating continual review of the nature, scope and components of jobs within organisations. Workplace bargaining efforts and increased government legislation (such as the *Workplace Relations (WorkChoices) Amendment Act 2005*) also emphasise the crucial importance of accurately describing and updating jobs, defining appropriate skills competencies and linking these to learning and development activities, career path opportunities and remuneration systems. Workplace agreements will be heavily dependent on the clear identification of job requirements.

Human resource managers are therefore well advised to maintain comprehensive HR information management systems (see Chapter 4) that include current data on the numbers, skills and qualifications, functions and performance criteria of all jobs throughout their organisations.

Linkage to HR functions

Job analysis underpins the critical human resource processes and functions involved in managing employees effectively. Exhibit 5.2 demonstrates the linkage of job analysis to other essential HR functions.

An analogy to demonstrate the importance of the relationship of job analysis to other human resource functions and processes is the structure of a house. The foundations of the home, concrete (known as the 'slab' in Australia), timber or some other building material can be compared to the job analysis. The walls, roof, windows and doors are the other HR processes and functions. In building or renovating a home, the foundations have to be right – if they are not level or structurally sound, the other components of the home – the walls, roof, windows

and doors will not fit properly and the house will be structurally unsound, leading to collapse of the structure or expensive repairs. This is the case for job analysis, if not carried out or not conducted accurately and comprehensively: the other HR processes will be ineffective and the cost to the organisation high – in terms of productivity and the ability to retain valuable staff.

Exhibit 5.2 Interrelationship of job analysis and HRM processes

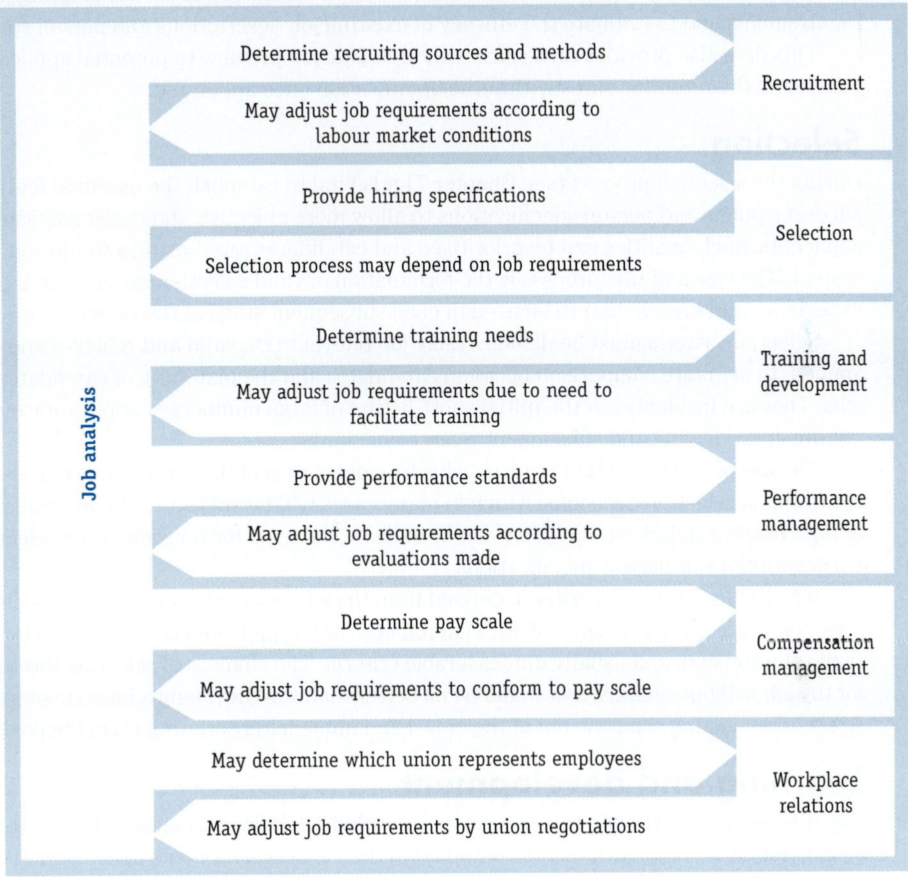

The following sections explain in more detail how job analysis underpins all other HRM processes.

Recruitment

To find the most suitable employees for jobs and thus for the organisation as a whole, those involved in employee recruitment (see Chapter 6) need to be fully aware of the relevant job description and person specifications, which are derived from comprehensive job analysis. A job description (or duty, role or goal statement) accurately details the component duties and activities of a job, the level of the job, the authority and responsibilities awarded to the job, and the conditions under which it is performed, while a person specification (or personal profile) establishes the specific personal qualities, attributes and competencies (e.g. qualifications and/ or training, work experience, work behaviour, skills, attitudes and abilities) of job holders. These allow those responsible for recruitment to devise suitable methods of attracting an appropriate pool of applicants, in line with specific job requirements and avoiding possible discrimination on unrelated skills and/or qualities. Thus, whether internal (e.g. memos, notice boards, intranet) or external (e.g. newspaper advertisements, university campus recruitment campaigns, Internet) recruitment methods are chosen, effective programs should attract suitably qualified applicants and discourage those who are unsuitable.

Accurate and detailed job analysis data should also indicate health and safety criteria and facilitate equal employment opportunity and affirmative action programs. If subsequent recruitment campaigns prove unsuccessful, it may be necessary to review existing job requirements and to evaluate the efficacy of existing job descriptions and person specifications.

This data also provides an accurate and realistic job preview to potential applicants, increasing the retention rates within the organisation once appointed.

Selection

During the selection process (see Chapter 7) it is vital to establish the essential features of job descriptions and person specifications to allow more objective and easier assessment of applicants. Such qualities can be prioritised and candidates rated using a weighting (e.g. points) system. The result of this process is the formulation of valid selection criteria (skills, abilities, experience and knowledge) to be used in each subsequent stage of the selection process.

Selection criteria must be demonstrably job relevant (i.e. valid and reliable) and equitably applied, to facilitate comparison between candidates and the matching of candidates with jobs. They are invaluable in the initial short-listing of large numbers of applicants, employment testing, interviewing and subsequent referee checking.

The use of valid selection criteria helps to avoid claims of discrimination and assists in the recording of selection decisions, which in many cases will be subject to the Australian *Freedom of Information Act*. Selection failures may indicate the need for revision of the selection criteria, job descriptions or person specifications.

Without such selection criteria, derived from the job description and person specification, the selection process is like a game of 'Russian roulette,' with applicants being selected by chance, on a range of unrelated, and usually unmeasurable criteria. The chances of selecting the best applicant for the job without such criteria would be no better than walking along a busy shopping mall or street and selecting someone out of the crowd and immediately offering them the position.

Learning and development

Any discrepancies between the experience, knowledge, skills and abilities demonstrated by a job holder and the requirements contained in the job description and specification or list of competencies for that job provide clues to developmental needs. As outlined in Exhibit 5.3. the gap between the needs of the position (job description and person specification) and the potential job holder, will result in the need for a human resource development plan. Conversely, the results of development efforts can be evaluated on the basis of progress made towards meeting these job requirements.

An integral component of wage determination in Australia is the clear relationship between identified job skills or competencies and learning and development programs, followed by appropriate career paths. If the remuneration policy adopted is linked with the organisation's strategic direction, this demonstrates a strategic approach to human resource management.

Career development, as part of the learning and development function, is concerned with preparing employees for advancement to jobs where their capabilities can be fully utilised. Formal qualifications and experience expressed in person specifications or competency profiles can determine how much learning and development is needed for lower-level employees to advance to those jobs. In some cases, these training and development needs may result in the adjustment of certain requirements for these jobs.

Exhibit 5.3 The relationship between job analysis and organisational learning

The 'gap' between what the job requires and the person possesses is the training gap.

Performance management

The job description and person specification, the result of the job analysis, provide the criteria for evaluating the performance of the holder of that job. For many jobs, these are often referred to as key result areas (KRAs) and key performance indicators (KPIs).

The results of performance reviews may, however, reveal that some job requirements are not completely valid. Therefore, adjustments in these requirements may be necessary. As already stressed, these criteria must be specific and job-related to avoid claims of discrimination. As an example, many manual labour positions have historically been occupied by males, due to tradition, and the need to lift heavy equipment or materials. With the widespread use of hydraulic equipment in industry, there is no longer a need to assess performance on the basis of ability to lift such weights. It would therefore be unlawful and ineffective to discriminate against females or slightly built males on this basis. A specific example is the job of a waste management officer. Traditionally, this role was usually occupied by males and involved the lifting of domestic bins and tipping the contents into the back of a waste management vehicle. Many of the local governments who employ these positions across Australia were facing spiralling workers' compensation costs due to accidents associated with lifting these bins, usually in the form of back, neck, shoulder and knee injuries. The introduction of European technology, in the form of the hydraulic lifting arms on waste management vehicles (referred to as 'one-armed bandits') meant that these waste management officers' jobs were redesigned to reflect a shift in focus to driving the vehicles, with the lifting being carried out by the vehicle itself. This has meant that males and females can equally occupy these positions with a distinct change in selection criteria to the possession of an appropriate vehicle driver's licence. In this way, performance appraisals may yield useful information for the modification of job descriptions and person specifications. This example also suggests that the job has been redesigned in such a way as to enable the contracting out of these positions altogether.

Remuneration management

Many workplace agreements emphasise the close relationship between job requirements, learning and development programs, career progression and appropriate salary and benefits systems. Accordingly, the relative worth (work value) of any job is directly related to its activities, duties and responsibilities. In many organisations sophisticated systems have been developed to relate payment to actual work requirements, enterprise or workplace negotiations and agreements, prerequisite qualifications and experiences, and the social issue of 'comparable worth' (see Chapter 10). In fact, many industries, particularly in the public sector, still have in place award systems defining classification descriptors which link directly to job descriptions and person specifications, which in turn determine salary classification levels. For senior positions, consultants can implement tailored package systems.

A continuing issue for women in Australia is that of equal pay for equal work. Currently, many women are not paid as well as their male counterparts in similar jobs (see Chapters 2 and 3). While this is both illegal and ineffective human resource management practice, some companies continue to pay similar employees differentially.

The same issue is currently being addressed over the question of equal pay for junior members of staff. Where their work is of equal value, so should their compensation. Objective job data help to ensure appropriate remuneration and consequent employee commitment and performance.

Inappropriate remuneration packages may reflect a need for a change in job requirements or adjusted pay scales, often in consultation with the relevant unions. Workplace bargaining provides substantial opportunities for equitable, and flexible approaches to remuneration based upon job competencies and skills.

Workplace relations

Accurate job descriptions, especially in written form and established as part of wage and salary negotiation processes, can be invaluable in reducing the level of industrial action. They can also assist in clarifying union representation and resolving subsequent employee grievances. In periods of organisational change, negotiation with unions may be necessary to adjust job requirements.

The job analysis process

Job analysis is the process of determining the requirements of jobs: the job outcomes; responsibilities, duties, tasks and functions; the complexity of the role; the authority awarded to the job; and the personal attributes, in the form of experience, knowledge, education and/or training, skills, traits, behavioural attributes, required to perform those jobs. Job analysis is integral to HRM because the information provided by this process is vital to the efficient and accurate implementation of all other HRM processes.

Human resource and line managers use collated job data for the development of job descriptions and person specifications. Comparing the skills possessed by employees with the results of job analysis can greatly assist the human resource manager to plan staffing strategies and restructure or redesign jobs to reflect economic, technological or organisational changes. In the shorter term, job analysis facilitates more accurate recruitment and selection practices, sets standards for subsequent performance appraisal, and allows appropriate grading or regrading of jobs and job categories for remuneration programs.

With the emphasis of Australian industrial relations legislation since 1996 on agreements negotiated with individuals or collectively, and based on issues often related to performance or productivity, job analysis is crucial to the identification of relevant skills and competencies and subsequent training and payment systems. Exhibit 5.4 illustrates the elements of the job analysis process and the functions for which it is used.

Job analysis is concerned with objective and verifiable information about the actual requirements of a job (and the person requirements) to meet organisational needs. It is therefore essential that the job being analysed is not considered in isolation to organisational planning strategies. Job analysts, whether they are from inside or outside the organisation, need to understand the importance of linking the process in which they are engaged to the strategic aims of the entire HRM strategy.

Exhibit 5.4 Elements of the job analysis process and its functions

Sources of data
Job analyst
Employee(s)
Supervisor(s)
Union/award

Methods of collecting data
Interviews
Questionnaires
Focus groups
Critical incident
Diaries or logs
Observation

Job data
Occupational
  health and safety
  requirements
Tasks
Performance standards
Responsibilities
Knowledge needed
Skills required
Experience needed
Job environment
Duties
Equipment used

Job description
Tasks
Duties
Responsibilities
Job environment

Human resource functions
HRP
Recruitment
Selection
Training and development
Performance appraisal
Salary and benefits
Workplace relations
Employee counselling
Enterprise bargaining
Skills audit
Remuneration
Authority relationships
Working conditions
Standards expected
Fringe benefits

Person specification
Skill requirements/competencies
Physical demands

Responsibility for the job analysis process

While the process of job analysis is usually the responsibility of HRM professionals and practitioners, the job holders, line managers and managers play a vital role in ensuring the accuracy and validity of the information provided. Job holders need to provide information on the roles they perform and the frequency with which they perform these roles; line managers need to also verify what is required to be undertaken; and the departmental managers need to verify all information in line with organisational and strategic objectives.

With large organisations, the job analysis process is often performed by specialist job analysts who are either part of the organisation's HR department or outsourced human resource consultants who specialise in such activities.

Data collection methods

There are a number of means by which data can be collected. The method selected will be determined by a range of factors, including the size of the organisation, the number of employees, the number of locations involved, the expertise of the HR department and organisational climate and/or culture. The method(s) selected should also relate to the nature of the job, the number of positions within the job category being analysed, and other prevailing circumstances.

- **Interviews:** The job analyst questions individual employees and their supervisors about the job under review. Standard questions regarding activities performed, priorities, time schedules, skills and qualifications required, responsibilities and technology involved (e.g. machines and computers) may be used, or more open-ended topics explored. When time is limited or when large numbers of similar jobs are analysed it is useful to conduct group interviews with job holders, their managers and possibly internal customers.

- **Questionnaires:** Structured, job-specific questionnaires are useful to job holders and their supervisors, especially where it is important to limit the time and costs of analysis. The results of these questionnaires may subsequently be tested on individuals or groups of job holders. Sometimes, when large numbers of jobs are being analysed, these can be standardised and computer-processed.

- **Job performance:** The analyst actually does the job being studied, to get first-hand experience of what it demands.

- **Observation:** The job analyst learns about jobs by observing job holder activities and recording them on a standardised form. Time and motion studies, derived from the early work of Frederick Taylor (see Chapter 1), were often used in the past and continue to be used, especially with manual or repetitive jobs, to ascertain specific job duties and the actual time taken for each task, during both busy and slow work periods. In other kinds of jobs, where quality is as important as quantity, it may be useful to videotape the performance of job holders for later study. Customer service areas (e.g. social security counters, airline check-in desks, hotel reception counters) particularly lend themselves to videotaping, as data can be obtained about the difficulties and skills of customer contact.

- **Diaries:** Job holders may be asked to keep diaries or daily or weekly logs of their activities during an entire work cycle. Seasonal aspects of jobs need to be reflected in the schedule for such diaries. If peak periods can be effectively determined, non-peak duties can be suitably timed. Diaries or logs are often necessary when analysing relatively unstructured management positions.

- **Critical incidents:** Jobs that require specified behavioural responses to crucial events (e.g. customer complaints, production breakdowns) may be analysed according to requisite skills and personal qualities. Job descriptions can then be developed to reflect these behavioural dimensions.

- **Focus and consultative groups:** After using these methods it may be useful for both accurate and acceptable analysis to talk with groups of affected job holders, their supervisors and customers about the results of such studies. This is particularly valuable for clarifying information, prioritising future duties and obtaining employee and union acceptance of anticipated job changes.

- **Existing HR records:** Conduct a review of the organisation's human resource records (HRMIS) (e.g. performance appraisal, productivity records) and existing job descriptions compared with similar jobs in other organisations. This could answer questions as to why the job was created, and how it has changed since the last review – essential information for wage and salary reviews.

If conducted by job analyst specialists, many of these data collection methods are computerised, allowing for questionnaires to be completed online, with results collated quickly and efficiently.

Future-oriented job analysis

The traditional process of job analysis assumes that a level of stability exists with the position being analysed. However, in today's increasingly turbulent global work environment, this is difficult to achieve, particularly with roles that are more impacted by such an environment.

Landis, Fogli and Goldberg (1998) explored a range of alternative job analysis techniques, in particular, Future Oriented Job Analysis (FOJA) and their success in a range of organisations studied.

They outlined the steps in the FOJA process, and these are summarised in Exhibit 5.5.

Exhibit 5.5   Steps in the future-oriented job analysis procedure

The steps outlined by Landis, Fogli and Goldberg (1998) are summarised as follows:

Step 1

Meet with all relevant parties involved in the change process to ensure an understanding of the proposed changes. A number of different perspectives can be explored and then a proposal agreed upon.

Step 2

Collation of all material related to the structure of the proposed jobs, decision-making on critical tasks in relation to the new organisational structure or strategy. An initial list of task statements and knowledge, skills and abilities (KSAs) are then developed for each of the jobs.

Step 3

More complete lists of task statements and KSAs developed and refined through group interviews and direct observations. Critical incidents are also generated and assessed.

Step 4

A set of task statements are then generated and a Task Sort Questionnaire (TSQ) developed. This data is then used to facilitate discussion with senior level management and the re-design team.

Step 5

The purpose here is to gather additional information about the likely nature of future jobs. Job analysis questionnaires are completed with respondents indicating the degree to which certain tasks would be required in future jobs and how important they are.

Step 6

Provides information regarding the most important KSAs for each job across major tasks. This assists in the development of selection tests.

Step 7

Meetings held with the management team to discuss results and areas of agreement and disagreement.[1]

Source: Landis R.S., Fogli L. & Goldberg E., 'Future Oriented Job Analysis', *International Journal of Selection and Assessment*, vol. 6, no. 3, July 1998, pp. 193–205. By permission of Blackwell Publishing.

While such a process is predominantly grounded in traditional job analysis methods, such as sourcing relevant information about the job and work observations, it also includes linking critical tasks to competency requirements as well as involving subject matter expert groups (SMEs) which could address changes in technology, job design and training issues.[2] There is also an emphasis on feedback mechanisms to deal with employee concerns which reduces the number of problems that may arise as part of the process.[3]

Competencies

In order to meet competitive challenges there is a focus on recognising the core competencies required by the organisation, seeking them out through recruitment and selection strategies and then retaining and developing them once in the organisation. Hagan et al. (2006) suggest that one reason for the popularity of competency programs is the belief that traditional job-based management systems may impede an organisation's ability to meet the challenges of a global economy.[4]

However, organisations are still grappling with the concept of what a competency is, how to define it, and how to address and recognise them in the contexts of attraction and retention. The continuous evaluation of the competencies required to meet organisational and competitive demands is also required.

What is a competency?

Much confusion exists as to what a competency is, how it is defined and what competencies lead to improved organisational performance and productivity. Zemke (1982), in Cooper et al. (1998), undertook a survey of 'experts' in the field in order to determine what a competency actually was and found the following:

> Competency, competencies, competency models, and competency-based training are all Humpty Dumpty words meaning only what the definer wants them to mean. The problem comes not from malice, stupidity or marketing avarice, but instead from some basic procedural and philosophical differences among those racing to define the concept and set the model for the way the rest of us will use competencies.[5]

Competencies were originally defined in the late 1960s by McClelland who set out to 'define competency variables that could be used in predicting job performance and that were not biased by race, gender, or socioeconomic factors'.[6] Hagan et al. (2006) described a competency as an individual characteristic existing on three levels:

- Knowledge and skills are on the surface as they are observable and measurable.

- Traits and motives are embedded deeply within an individual and tend to relate to their particular personality.

- Self-concept is found in between and includes an individual's attitudes, values and self-image.[7]

While this is a particularly personalised view of what competencies are, it reflects the importance of defining not only the attributes of the person required but those attributes that will reflect and match the organisational culture. Competencies benefit organisations when they can also provide customer value and enable them to create new business through product and service extensions and through innovation.[8] While there are many definitions of what a competency is, ranging from those that focus on personal traits to those reflecting broader work and job defined concepts, there is a common theme in that a competency, once correctly identified, will link directly with the achievement of organisational success.

In today's competitive work environment, organisations tend to either develop a range of generic competencies which fit the organisational culture, such as coaching, mentoring, team building, creativity and innovation, or develop job specific competencies which meet job outcomes, such as business or technical expertise and strategic planning. These can then vary depending upon the level and authority of the position being defined or analysed, particularly for managerial positions. The applications of competencies to human resource development (HRD) are discussed further in Chapter 8, especially the notion of Competency Based Learning (CBL).

Lee and Phan (2000) list a number of generic competencies for directors in global firms (see Exhibit 5.6) in order to improve recruitment and selection of senior staff for international firms:

Exhibit 5.6 Director generic competencies

1 Strategic perspective

Directors are expected to have the ability to see the macro perspective of an organisation based on patterns, trends and cause/effect relations so as to determine the raison d'être of the organisation. A director has to portray an understanding of a wide range of issues and their applications in different contexts that confront the organisation. This requires sensitivity to, awareness of, and an understanding of the business and market environment, and a practical grasp of the firm's core competencies. To formulate and agree on a corporate vision requires an understanding of the company as a whole in the context of the customer requirements, and stakeholder perspectives. The ability to think in terms of a systems perspective (i.e. the ability to see connections and establish relationships) is of significant value. A director with a strategic perspective can give meaning, direction and focus to the organisation by understanding the interdependence and interaction of external opportunities and threats with the internal competencies of the firm.

2 Business sense

Directors must be willing to take risks, be able to put oneself on the line to get something done. Directors need a sense of proportion, combined with the discipline to identify and prioritise what stakeholders, particularly shareholders, really care for. A sense of accountability to stakeholders and a willingness to put the responsibility of the company above self-interest is important.

3 Planning and organising

A director needs to be conversant with the planning process so as to identify the long-term goals that must be achieved, and to keep the board focused on those goals.

4 Analysis and judgement

A director needs to have conceptual flexibility to identify feasible alternatives or multiple options in planning and decision-making. When establishing strategy, a director needs to be able to focus on different options and to evaluate their pros and cons simultaneously.

5 Managing staff

A director needs to make considerable judgements of people, their capabilities, aspirations, motivation and limits when appointing the management team. Thus, directors must understand how best to harness managerial talent through direct involvement, empowerment and excitement.

6 Persuasiveness

As someone responsible for setting direction and obtaining support, a director needs to know how to use a variety of methods, such as persuasive arguments, modelling behaviour, forming alliances and appealing to the interest of others, to gain support for his/her ideas, strategies and values.

7 Assertiveness and decisiveness

Directors need to constantly focus on what needs to be achieved and to use an appropriate style to drive the attainment of goals. They need to try to build alliances that strengthen the firm. They must also understand the imperatives of the organisation in order to structure the task for the management team. This means that directors must be prepared to speak up on important issues and become recognised as advocates for a particular point of view.

8 Interpersonal sensitivity

Being able to involve others to build cooperative teams in which group members feel valued and empowered is a key competency that a director needs to have. Directors with this competency consistently seek to understand the viewpoints of others, as they try to foster teamwork in spite of the differences of opinion. Thus, directors need to know how to conduct open discourse, be responsive and attentive to feedback, and supportive of their stakeholders. This will allow them to understand the ideas, concepts and feelings of stakeholders and to comprehend events, issues, problems, and opportunities from the viewpoint of the other party. The quality of interpersonal sensitivity is required inside and outside of the boardroom. Thus, working with a team of fellow directors also requires tact, sensitivity, the ability to engender trust and respect, and the awareness of different perspectives, interests and values of others.

9 Communication

A director has to be able to present ideas clearly and with ease so that the other person senses the vision, inspiration, commitment and enthusiasm towards the firm. Thus, the ability to motivate and share the vision, goals, values and objectives of the firm are important.

10 Resilience and adaptability

Balancing the interests of the company's various stakeholders requires directors to have empathy for their issues, a willingness to make tough choices, and considerable diplomacy in the face of hostility. A director must be able to respond flexibly but in a disciplined manner so that he/she can push ahead with the strategic changes that different circumstances dictate. This competency requires a style of interaction and decision-making that is based on a 'win–win' mindset.

11 Energy and initiative

Directors must be action oriented. They must be able to take a stand on the issues and unhesitatingly make decisions when required to do so. While it is typical for the board to make decisions as a whole, individual directors must be willing to commit themselves and express confidence for the success of the actions to be taken.

12 Achievement motivation

A director must possess high internal work standards and set ambitious yet attainable goals to continuously improve. Directors must have the perseverance to follow through on a decision to make it succeed in spite of the initial obstacles. It means being willing to make unpopular decisions and sticking to them because they are right for the organisation.

Source: Lee, S.H. and Phan, P.H. 2000, 'Competencies of Directors in Global Firms: Requirements for Recruitment and Evaluation,' *Corporate Governance*, vol. 3, no. 3, July, pp. 207–8.

Exhibit 5.6 demonstrates that a range of competencies can be developed to suit the organisational culture as well as to meet the outcomes of the organisation. These can then be used to measure the performance of the employee as part of the performance management program. These competencies can readily be adapted to suit the outcomes of other staff or positions in the organisation as well as the strategic direction of the company as a whole.

For non-managerial staff, a number of the competencies identified in Exhibit 5.6 can be utilised along with a range of others and can include:

- planning and organising
- resilience and adaptability
- energy and initiative

- interpersonal skills
- written communication
- team work
- collaborative work ethic
- technical skills
- conflict management
- attention to detail
- compliance
- creative thinking
- stress tolerance.

This is not an exhaustive list, merely a guide as to how competencies can be delivered to meet individual, business unit and organisational needs. It is important that once identified, a descriptor of what the competency means, and how it can be achieved, is included. This assists with measuring performance and establishing targets against which the employee performs.

However, demonstrating a competence is not the same thing as demonstrating performance.[9] Rather, possessing a competence may lead to successful performance – it will not necessary result in it.

Gow and McDonald (2000) suggest that the use of a range of generic competencies for selecting staff and determining performance will not fully reflect the demands of the current or future job markets.[10] In order to test this assumption, Gow and McDonald surveyed 211 educators and managers from organisations and educational institutions throughout Queensland, Australia, to assess which attributes a sample of professionals who either educate or employ graduates considered to be essential to create or secure an income, either through paid employment, self employment, contract work or cooperatives.[11]

The study listed a total of 107 'Future Attributes' of which the participants had to determine how important these were for future work success. They were also able to list any further attributes they considered individuals would require. The findings of the study indicated that three key competencies needed to be demonstrated by graduates in order for them to generate an income:

1 adaptability to changing environments

2 business management skills

3 accountability.

There has also been significant discussion regarding the development of competencies for today's HR professionals. Research conducted by the University of Michigan Business School in 1993 suggests that HR's success is dependent on competency and specific skills in five key areas:

1 *Strategic contribution*: establishing business strategy, connecting organisations to their markets, anticipating change and putting systems in place to rapidly align employee behaviours with evolving organisational needs

2 *Business knowledge*: understanding how businesses are run and translating this knowledge into action

3 *Personal credibility*: demonstrating measurable value. While other skills may help HR professionals be part of the senior executive team, demonstrating measurable value will keep them there

4 *HR delivery*: providing efficient and effective service to customers in the areas of staffing, performance management, development and measurement

5 *HR technology*: leveraging HR technology and web-based channels to deliver value to customers.[12]

The development of competencies is integral to the job analysis process. Once the requirements of a job, or group of jobs, are determined, the competencies required to perform those functions, outcomes, tasks and responsibilities can be determined.

The term 'competency' is more than just a new word for a skill or attribute. A competency also reflects behavioural attributes and a more strategic view of skills and attributes required for successful performance of a role.

These competencies can then be linked to the design of jobs to ensure that the job holder has the capacity to demonstrate and utilise these competencies effectively. It is also vital that these competencies are measurable and achievable in the context of the organisational and strategic goals.

Competency profiling

A competency profile is a grouping of competencies, as demonstrated in Exhibit 5.6, which reflect the needs of the position and/or organisation in order to meet organisational outcomes. While many would argue that this is simply another term for job analysis, it does take the process further by actually identifying unique traits and characteristics that would result in improved performance. It is certainly a more personalised and humanistic approach, recognising the dynamic nature of organisations and the future challenges that lie ahead. For most organisations, competency profiling is necessary to ensure that their business outcomes are achieved. If standards and the means to achieve them are not well defined, an organisation is unable to deliver products and services to customers on quality, deadline and price.[13] For existing staff, knowing specifically what skills, knowledge, attributes and behaviours their employers seek enables them to assess their ability to provide them and gives them the opportunity to appreciate their own strengths and recognise development areas.[14]

In order for these competencies to be effective in achieving the organisation's strategic objectives, the following steps need to be taken:

- Identify the mission and key objectives of the organisation.

- Identify the skills (or competencies) needed by the organisation.

- Acquire these competencies by way of attraction, retention and learning strategies.

- Implement strategies that will reinforce those competencies so that they continue to be displayed by the employees who are already behaving that way so that other employees will start to model that behaviour.

- The reward system must reinforce these competencies by rewarding behaviour that the organisation values.

Shellebear (2002) outlines the advantages and disadvantages of competency profiling for organisations:

Exhibit 5.7   Advantages and disadvantages of competency profiling

Advantages

Sends a clear message about the behavioural indicators upon which staff will be assessed

Through getting involved, staff soon understand the objectives and processes of the business and their own roles and responsibilities relevant to it

Staff are able to track their competence development

Training needs are more easily identified

Assists managers in selecting and developing staff

Disadvantages
Some staff react to being categorised, particularly at a lower level than their colleagues and resent a perceived reduced status
Low management commitment, infrequent performance appraisals, and a lack of ownership can result in staff viewing it as a 'tick box operation' they conform to or seek to manipulate to justify a pay increase.[15]

Job descriptions

A job description is simply a written description of the job, the duties performed and the conditions under which they are performed. Traditionally, the following parts were essential elements in a job description:

- job title
- job identification
- accountability statements (who responsible to and who responsible for)
- roles and goals
- authority awarded to the role
- work environment.

Exhibit 5.8 provides an example of such a job description format.

Exhibit 5.8   A template for a job description

POSITION DESCRIPTION			
1 POSITION IDENTIFICATION			
Title	Environmental Planner	**Level**	
Service Unit	Planning	**Agreement/Award**	
Directorate	Planning and Development	**Date effective**	September 2006
Reporting to	Coordinator Environment	**Date last updated**	September 2006
		Position no.	00087

2   LIST OF DUTIES

- Develop and review environmental policies and strategies.
- Provide advice to consultants and customers on planning policies, strategies, structure plans and capital works projects.
- Assist the Coordinator in the preparation of submissions.
- Supervise teams.
- Supervise contract staff and consultants.
- Participate as a member of appropriate committees.

1   AUTHORITY STATEMENT

This position works under the limited direction of the Coordinator, Environment and has the authority to make decisions regarding project costing within budget parameters.

This position also has authority to sign correspondence and to give direction to members of the unit, contract staff and consultants in relation to environmental issues.

2   WORK ENVIRONMENT

Location: Perth.

However, job descriptions have changed tremendously over the past few years. This has been to reflect the dynamic and competitive nature of organisations as well as to provide a better match between organisational, strategic outcomes, business unit outcomes and individual position outcomes. As a result, job descriptions now often contain the following elements:

- job title

- job identification

- organisational chart representing accountability processes

- position purpose (or objective) statement

- key outcomes to be achieved

- key performance indicators

- competency requirements.

An example of the previous position description (Exhibit 5.8) in the changed format is provided in Exhibit 5.9.

Exhibit 5.9   An example of the new formats for position descriptions

POSITION DESCRIPTION			
1 POSITION IDENTIFICATION			
Title	Environmental Planner	**Level**	
Service Unit	Planning	**Agreement/ Award**	
Directorate	Planning and Development	**Date Effective**	September 2007
Reporting to	Coordinator Environment	**Date last updated**	September 2007
		Position no.	00087

2   PURPOSE OF POSITION

- To lead the activities of the environmental planning team to ensure environmental policies, strategies and programs are developed and implemented to address the range of strategic environmental issues.

- To participate in a multi-disciplinary team environment to ensure the strategic environmental objectives are achieved.

- To provide specialist environmental information and advice based on applied research and information gathering.

3   WORKING RELATIONSHIPS

Reports to: Coordinator, Environment

Responsible for: Contract staff, consultants, three administrative staff

4   BRIEF SUMMARY OF ACCOUNTABILITIES AND RESPONSIBILITIES

ACCOUNTABILITIES and RESPONSIBILITIES	KEY PERFORMANCE INDICATORS
OUTCOME: Environmental Planning and Project Management - Manage the development, implementation and review of an extensive range of environmental policies, strategies, programs and organisation practices including projects of significant complexity.	- Policies, strategies, programs are reviewed annually. - Identified programs are developed. - Advice provided is accurate and timely. - Submissions are timely.

- Provide specialist environmental advice and support in the development and review of planning policies, strategies, structure plans and capital works projects to ensure best practice environmental outcomes in a growth context.

- Contribute to and prepare submissions on state and federal legislation, policies and programs.

- Develop partnerships with key stakeholders to assist in delivering strategic environmental objectives.

- Lead, participate in and provide direction to multi-disciplinary teams, workshops and committees both within and outside the organisation.

- Provide supervision and direction to the Environmental Planning Team, contract staff and consultants.

- All legislative changes reviewed and advice provided to the organisation.

- Teams are communicated to regularly.

- Teams are aware of their outcomes and are equipped with the training to perform their roles.

- All legislation, codes of conduct, policies and procedures are complied with.

  Staff are employed in accordance with the competency requirements for the positions.

OUTCOME: Compliance and Legislative Knowledge

Comply with the code of conduct Policies and Procedures and relevant appropriate Legislation.

Occupational Safety and Health, anti-discrimination, equal employment opportunity and other legislation will be met in accordance with the parameter of this position.

Frequency key: D = Daily   W = Weekly   M = Monthly   A = Annually   * = as required

5   WORK RELATED REQUIREMENTS/SELECTION CRITERIA

Essential skills:

1. Tertiary qualifications in Environmental Science or a related field and extensive experience in environmental planning

2. Highly developed knowledge of and demonstrated ability to apply the principles of sustainability and in particular the ability to balance environmental and development interests

3. Highly developed written communication skills, including demonstrated skills in technical and other report writing

4. Highly developed oral communication and interpersonal skills, including the ability to deliver public presentations, facilitate meetings and forums, and liaise and negotiate with stakeholders

5. Extensive project management experience, including the ability to lead project teams and workshops, administer meetings and achieve project outcomes within time and budget constraints

6. Demonstrated ability to work constructively under broad supervision and as part of a multi-disciplinary team

7. Demonstrated ability to develop creative and innovative solutions to achieve environmental best practice outcomes within a growth context

6   POSITION DIMENSIONS

NUMBER OF STAFF DIRECTLY REPORTING TO POSITION	Three permanent positions, plus contract staff and consultants
EXTENT OF DELEGATED AUTHORITY	Operates with a high level of autonomy under broad direction
	Control over projects in accordance with agreed timeframes and budgets

6 POSITION DIMENSIONS	
EXTENT OF DELEGATED AUTHORITY	Required to use a significant level of initiative and judgement to resolve complex issues
	Negotiate acceptable outcomes with both internal and external customers
	Authority to give direction to members of the unit, other officers and consultants under the supervision of the position in relation to environmental issues
	Authority to sign correspondence in accordance with the organisation's policies, delegations or directives
	Provide recommendations on environmental matters
	Establish priorities and manage own workflow to achieve strategic objectives of the unit
LOCATIONS	Perth, Sydney and Singapore
ALLOWANCES/SPECIAL CONDITIONS	Nil
SPECIALISED EQUIPMENT OPERATED OR SPECIAL LICENCE REQUIREMENTS	'C' Class Driver's Licence
OTHER IMPORTANT DIMENSIONS	N/A

Job title

This provides a clear indication of the status and authority of the position as well as the job functions involved. For example, if the words 'Manager,' 'Supervisor' or 'Team Leader' appear in the job title, then the applicant or incumbent has a clear indication of the staff management responsibilities of the role as well as the status of the position within the business unit and/or organisation.

In accordance with Equal Employment Opportunity (EEO) and anti-discriminatory legislation, titles containing 'man' or 'woman' should be avoided. Examples include changing the titles 'Salesman' to 'Salesperson'; 'Barman' to 'Bartender'; and 'Airline Stewards/Stewardesses' to 'Flight Attendant.'

Job identification

The section not only covers administrative aspects for locating positions with position numbers for payroll and identifying the area where the position works, grading and level details, award or agreement linkage, but it also outlines reporting structures, including to whom the position reports and for whom (number and titles) the position is directly responsible for. This is often supported by the use of an organisational chart, providing an immediate visual picture of where the position sits, who it is responsible to and responsible for. This is not essential, but with complex organisational structures, it can provide an overview of the structure within the particular work unit or section.

Position purpose

There has been a trend toward including a succinct statement on the position objective or purpose. Why does the position exist and what is its primary purpose? This provides a clear understanding of the key outcome for the role. An example of this is provided in Exhibit 5.9.

Key responsibility/outcome statements

This is the most important section of the job description as it covers the actual responsibilities and outcomes against which the incumbent will be measured. These are normally listed in order of key importance and/or time dedicated to that outcome. Some job descriptions also include a percentage allocation of time against each outcome, adding up to a total of 100 per cent, to also give a clear indication of where most of the time is spent. This is becoming increasingly important in ensuring a realistic job preview (an accurate overview of the position, expectations and challenges) is provided. This can also prove to be problematic where jobs are more dynamic and fluid in nature and the actual time spent on particular functions or outcomes is difficult to quantify or it frequently changes. For example, the role of marketing manager may be able to provide an indicator of time spent on administrative versus marketing design and development during one particular month, but if there is a change in the nature of the client or size of the contract this may vary considerably.

The trend toward the use of outcome statements in job descriptions – away from a descriptive list of specific duties – assists in overcoming the problem of job descriptions limiting the type of work employees are involved with. Indeed, one of the common problems is the restrictive nature of the list of duties contained within the document and employees being unwilling to work outside of this structure. With the use of outcome-based statements, there is less emphasis on the performance of specific tasks and more on achieving results in line with business unit and/or organisational objectives.

Key performance indicators (KPIs)

KPIs are quantifiable, specific measures of an organisation's performance in certain areas of business and their purpose is to provide quantifiable measurements of what is determined to be important to the organisation's critical success factors and long-term business goals.[16]

The inclusion of KPIs in the job description creates a more seamless linkage to the organisation's performance management system (see Chapter 9). The employee is aware of the performance outcomes for the position when the employment commences, thus there is no confusion as to the expectations of the role. These KPIs can then be linked to the induction and learning and development programs.

These KPIs should be measurable and indicate the standard of performance required, as indicated by Exhibit 5.10.

Exhibit 5.10   Measuring KPIs

KEY OUTCOME	KPIs
Dealing with telephone and counter enquiries in a courteous and accurate manner	
1 All enquiries answered without referral to a senior officer.	
2 Number of complaints received.	
3 Ten to 15 minutes turnaround time for 80 per cent of all enquiries.	

If there is no standard performance management system in place in the organisation, these KPIs can then form the basis of such a system. If one is in place, the criteria against which employees are measured will have a tendency to be generic in nature. These KPIs complement the existing system and provide more meaningful and comprehensive feedback to the employee. These then form an integral link to the performance management system, with the KPIs being used as the primary measures of successful performance.

One of the challenges for the future is the development of broad job descriptions that can be applied to diverse, multiskilled jobs and can still provide important data for job evaluation, training, development and performance management. Williams (1999) cites an interview with author William Bridges who has proposed that there will be a continuing shift away from narrow job classifications and descriptions to a work world in which 'dejobbing' is prevalent and the emphasis is placed on the distribution of work.[17] Indeed, Bridges is further quoted:

> I don't want to say that no job will exist in 20 years. There's a continuum, with work at one end that probably needs to be spelled out in very specific duties. For example, nuclear power plant workers should have clear job descriptions – no messing around. On the other hand, there are whole industries, such as filmmaking and consulting, in which job descriptions don't play any real role. Jobs are not the way work gets done. Work gets done in cross-functional teams. It's outsourced to a group that isn't even made up of employees; it's done by temps. Now we can extend the word job to cover all those conditions, but notice what we're doing. We can't say, 'That's my job' anymore.[18]

Challenges for the future

With work and jobs changing frequently, and more significantly, the task of preparing relevant, up-to-date job descriptions will become more difficult and the need for it questioned more intently. This will be particularly the case in Self-Managed Work Teams, discussed later in this chapter.

Amazon.com, one of the leaders in e-commerce, employs 5 000 people and is an example of a new age organisation. The company does not have a complex system of job classifications, pay grades, promotional charts and job descriptions – it hires people to work, not to fit traditional job slots.[19]

Caudron (2000) investigates the work of the Center for Effective Organizations at the University of Southern California, where the new forms of work, and demands of today's organisations, had deemed the traditional job description as outmoded. Instead, person descriptions should be developed to allow companies to continually match and rematch employees to specific projects rather than jobs.[20] This is quite a departure from the current models which are in place but Caudron suggests that these 'err on the side of standardisation while paying little attention to individual differences … we encourage individual contributions, but we still hire, manage and compensate employees as if they came from exactly the same mould'.[21]

Leonard (2000) also agrees that traditional job descriptions lack the flexibility needed in today's workplace. She suggests that 'rapid corporate change, due to the influence of technology, flattening hierarchies and the lack of qualified workers, will not only make job descriptions obsolete before they are written, but may be a roadblock for HR professionals trying to orchestrate change within their organisations'.[22]

This shift in the way in which work is classified, evaluated and managed poses considerable challenges for HRM, particularly in the way in which outcomes are defined, managers are trained and work value is compensated. A greater emphasis on competency requirements and the contributions of individuals will play an even greater role.

Competency requirements

There is a general move away from using a separate job description to a person specifications document. The use of one, concise document saves time and becomes a more useful tool for both potential employees, present incumbents and managers and allows clear comparisons between the required tasks and employee competencies.

The replacement of selection criteria with competencies also highlights the importance of cultural fit to the organisation and the need to better match job outcomes with necessary competency requirements.

Job design strategies

While the job analysis process focuses on the business unit's and/or organisation's expectations of the role, job design focuses on meeting the needs of both the employee and employer. This is becoming a critical issue in the retention of employees in today's market, particularly with positions in limited supply.

Exhibit 5.11   Basis for job design

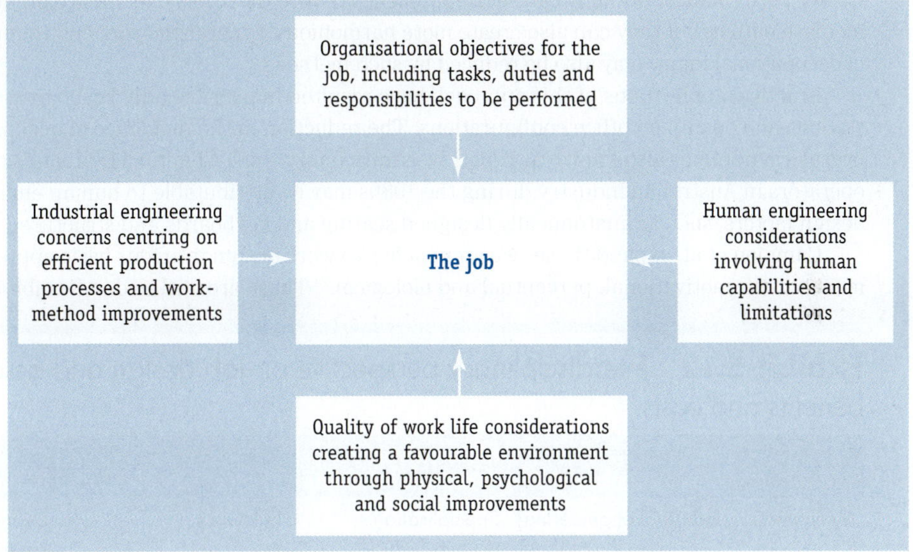

Exhibit 5.11 demonstrates how a contemporary approach to job design emphasises the improvement to quality of life rather than industrial engineering concerns. This reflects globalisation and human resource planning factors as well as new forms of work, individualised career paths and work–family issues.

Industrial engineering

The study of work is an important contribution of Frederick Taylor (Chapter 1) and the Scientific Management movement. Industrial engineering, which evolved with this movement, is concerned with analysing work methods and establishing time standards. Specifically, it involves analysing the elements of the work cycle that comprise a particular job activity. Often called functional specialisation, industrial engineering aims at faster production, high levels of specialist skills and uniform quality. Industrial engineers study work cycles to determine which, if any, of its elements may be modified, combined, rearranged or eliminated in order to reduce the time needed to complete the work cycle.

It is considered that industrial engineering lacks relevance to the new forms of work in place. The introduction of technology which replaces human beings in the manufacturing sector and enables staff to telecommute utilising technology to work in virtual teams all but removes the need for an industrial engineering approach to job design.

Job adaptation to employees' needs

Human engineering aims to identify and respond to worker's needs in the performance of their jobs. Influenced by the studies of pioneers such as Mayo and Herzberg of the Human Relations/

Behavioural Science schools (Chapter 1) and the work of Emery, Trist and Bamford of the Tavistock Institute, best known for the introduction of the sociotechnical (STS) approach to work design, the human engineering approach attempts to adapt the work, the work environment, technology and equipment to human characteristics. In short, it seeks to fit the machine to the person rather than the person to the machine, and is seen by many as a reaction to the dysfunctions of Scientific Management. Perceiving the relationship between the worker and the job as a system, job adaptation to employees' needs seeks to improve the efficiency of the overall system by preventing or minimising harmful effects of poor equipment or work station design on worker performance. Not only can such approaches reduce the levels of defective products and increase output, but they can also create more harmonious, synergistic work environments. Levels of occupational injury may also be reduced by such methods.

Practical applications of this approach have resulted in user-friendly keyboards, desks, work stations and open-plan office configurations. The reduction in the incidence of occupational overuse syndrome (also known as repetitive strain injury – see Chapter 11) among keyboard operators in Australian industry during the 1980s may be attributable to human engineering job design factors, such as anatomically designed seating and keyboards and structured rest breaks.

Campion et al. expand these two approaches to work design into four basic approaches: mechanistic, motivational, perceptual and biological.[23] These are outlined in Exhibit 5.12.

Exhibit 5.12 Interdisciplinary perspective on job design and associated benefits and costs

Model	Discipline base	Illustrative recommendations	Typical benefits	Typical costs
Mechanistic	Industrial engineering	Specialisation Simplification Repetition	Efficiency Easier staffing Reduced training	Decreased satisfaction Decreased motivation Training Errors Stress
Motivational	Organisational psychology	Variety Autonomy Participation	Satisfaction Intrinsic motivation Retention Customer service	Boredom Monotony
Perceptual	Human factors Experimental psychology	Reduce information-processing requirements	Reduced errors Fewer accidents Less mental overload	Financial costs Inactivity
Biological	Ergonomics Medical sciences	Reduce physical requirements Reduce environmental stressors	Physical comfort Reduced physical stress Reduced fatigue	

Note: These models are drawn from research in multiple disciplines that is exemplified by Taylor (1911) for mechanistic, Hackman and Oldham (1980) for motivational, Meister (1971) for perceptual, and Grandjean (1980) for biological. Recent evidence for the benefit and costs is contained in Campion (1988, 1989), Campion and Berger (1990), Campion and McClelland (1991, 1993) and Campion and Thayer (1985).

Source: Campion M.A. et al. 'Work Redesign: Eight obstacles and opportunities', *Human Resource Management*, vol. 44, no. 4, Winter 2005, p. 369. By permission of Blackwell Publishing.

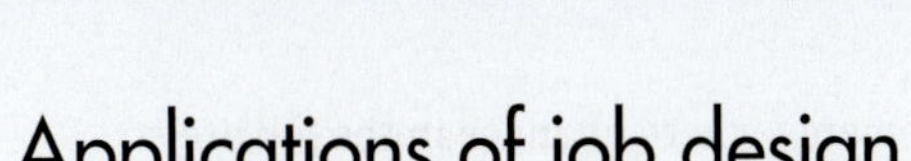

Applications of job design

Management uses of job design have evolved from preoccupations with work simplification, standardisation and division of labour to concerns with human needs in job performance. A major challenge confronting employers today is that of improving the quality of work life and a demand for work–family balance (see Chapter 2). These approaches to job design illustrate an important insight: the nature of work has a substantial impact on an employee's performance and attitude.[24] Increased globalisation, raised employee educational standards and consequent worker expectations, along with dramatic changes to health, safety and wellness legislation, have compelled managers to implement job design strategies aimed at the improvement of both the physical and psychological work life of their people. The main focus of these activities has been to make work more psychologically rewarding and to reduce anxieties and stress in the work environment. While job design assists in doing this, attention to managerial styles, communication strategies and consultation with employees will also improve the work environment and working relationships.

While there are some new trends in the design of work to meet the needs of both the employee and the organisation, the most traditional and most common are still:

- job enlargement
- job enrichment
- job rotation
- self-managed work teams.

Job enlargement

Sometimes called horizontal loading, job enlargement consists of increasing the number and variety of tasks of a job. While similar to current job duties, the new tasks offer additional variety, at the same level of complexity, to the job holder. Thus, a sales assistant job may be enlarged by the inclusion of stock control, some new worker training and weekly reporting tasks. Enlarged jobs help to relieve boredom by having the employee perform multiple duties. It is essential, however, that job enlargement is genuinely motivated by a desire to improve worker satisfaction, not simply to offload unwanted duties. A more cynical view is that job enlargement takes several boring jobs, and puts them together to make the new job several times more boring.

Job enrichment

Any effort that makes work more rewarding or satisfying by adding more meaningful, higher level and more challenging tasks to an employee's job is called job enrichment. A product of Frederick Herzberg's worker motivation studies, job enrichment aims to increase employee self-esteem and feelings of self-fulfilment, and hopefully long-term satisfaction and performance.[25]

Job enrichment (or vertical loading) may be accompanied by increasing the autonomy and responsibility of employees. Herzberg discusses five factors for enriching jobs and thereby motivating employees: achievement, recognition, growth, responsibility and performance of the whole, rather than simply parts, of the job. These motivational factors allow employees to assume more responsibility and involvement in decision-making processes, planning, organising, directing and controlling their own work. Job enrichment can also be accomplished by organising workers into teams and delegating greater authority for self-management to these teams.

In spite of the benefits to be achieved through job enrichment, it many cases it can often just lead to job enlargement. Managers and supervisors may be reluctant to grant employees more job responsibility and autonomy or decision-making opportunities, as these can challenge their power or threaten their own job security.[26]

Another problem with enrichment is 'job engorgement,' where changes in the job are so significant that the incumbent becomes overloaded with too many tasks to perform effectively, increasing role ambiguity, role overload and work stress.[27]

One recent form of enrichment is knowledge enrichment which involves adding requirements for understanding job-related procedures or rules.[28] This reflects the increasingly specialised and/or technical nature of work, particularly in knowledge-based, or learning, organisations (refer to Chapter 8). Campion et al. (2005) cite the research of Campion and McClelland (1993), where data from over 400 employees whose jobs had been redesigned (knowledge enriched) at a financial service institution were analysed to determine costs and benefits. The findings were that task enlargement resulted primarily in costs, whereas knowledge enrichment resulted in benefits.[29]

Job rotation

Employees experience job rotation when they do entirely different jobs on a rotating schedule. New employees may be introduced to different jobs and sections, either to give them an overall picture of the organisation, to aid subsequent cooperation between sections or for cross-skilling purposes. Graduate trainee schemes on rotating bases are frequently used to rapidly integrate employees into the organisation, to achieve the best fit for the new graduate or to indicate future career options.

In the past, restrictive awards have often prevented extensive job rotation schemes following induction. However, substantial opportunities now exist in Australian industry for more extensive job rotation programs linked to multiskilling, career training and development strategies, and career pathing plans.

The service sector, especially tourism and hospitality, provides significant avenues for job rotation (e.g. front of house, banquets, reception, housekeeping and administration) and thence a potential reduction in high turnover rates through more secure careers and increase in job satisfaction. Rotation can be on short-term (hourly, daily or weekly) or longer term bases (monthly, quarterly or half-yearly).

Self-managed work teams

Self-Managed Work Teams (SMWTs) address some of the difficulties of introducing job enrichment programs. Modern organisations have increasing levels of complexity and interdependence between workers. In enriching a particular job by adding higher order responsibilities and autonomy, other jobs are affected. This 'domino' effect means that to successfully address job design needs, the workers in the whole subsystem need to be included in the exercise. Combined with the need to consider individual differences of workers, this leads quite naturally to the adoption of a team-based approach. Thus, the SMWT (or work group) can be given authority to collectively make decisions concerning their production and work allocation processes.

The benefits of introducing SMWTs with their capacity to integrate tasks, flexibility, synergy and higher performance have enabled organisations such as BOC, Caltex, Bendix Mintex, Nestlé and DuPont to have great successes with this strategy over the past 10 years. Unfortunately, similar results cannot be guaranteed. Hockley claims that many attempts to form SMWTs have failed. He listed the following four factors as the main problem areas to be addressed:

1 SMWTs were formed to carry out narrow tasks with little complexity.

2 The SMWT concept was applied to work groups that are not teams.

3 Forming people into SMWTs is contradictory from the start. The first act of autonomy might be to reject the concept.

4 Lack of management resourcing, e.g. clear goals, training, freedom, negotiated accountabilities.[30]

Diversity management

Implicit in all changes to the nature of jobs, competency requirements and job design strategies is the need to effectively manage diversity. Diversity management has been called everything from 'just another HR fad' to 'just another name for EEO.' In its basic form, diversity refers to the variety of age, gender, race and cultural differences in the workplace. More recently, workforce diversity has come to include sexual orientation, physical and intellectual disability, together with other specific categories of employees, including the ageing.

All workplaces are diverse, but not all workplaces recognise the extent of their diversity nor do they have strategies in place to allow for the effective management of this diversity. It is a question of true inclusion rather than simply writing up more tokenistic policies on equal opportunity – because they are legally required to do this.

In reality, diversity management is no more than a strategy to create opportunities to attract the brightest talent from the entire human resource pool and to then develop and retain that talent in order to maintain a competitive position in the market. If organisations are to compete successfully in a turbulent global market they will need all the flexibility and agility they can muster (see News report 5.1).

Many shades of Big Blue

IBM: speaking from experience

IBM has been committed to workforce diversity for as long as anyone in the company can remember. 'We can trace it back to the very early years,' says IBM Australia chief executive Phillip Bullock.

Convinced that equal opportunity and fairness have both business and social benefits, he is modest about the company's reputation for valuing and promoting diversity. 'We always feel that we can do a better job, even if you think you have a good arrangement or a good process or mechanism in place, conditions change, people change and you need to rethink it.'

Nonetheless, he is often on the list of desired speakers when diversity conferences are planned. Managers from other organisations frequently consult with his small diversity team (headed by Alison Spencer) which has two-way benefits, 'You often learn as well as give.'

There is growing awareness that the business conditions are challenging, diversity and good management of people is important for sustainability and leveraging the skills available, says Bullock. He has no doubt that a business case can be made for diversity.

'At any point in time we would have 150 to 200 mothers on maternity leave. About 97 per cent come back and work for IBM, which saves considerable re-hiring costs. If you can have mothers resuming work in a fashion suitable for them and the business, you are already taking a significant step.'

Successful diversity initiatives are more than policies and goodwill. 'It depends on how the role of the manager is defined and structured. When someone in a team says she wants maternity leave, we try to work with her.

Typically, circumstances change. She realizes she needs longer leave or wants to work part-time.'

'That's the point where managers in many organisations say it is all too hard or the employee is too demanding. IBM managers look at options such as job share, part-time work, or some home-based work. They are encouraged to see flexibility as not just theoretically possible but practically do-able.'

'Senior management needs to create a climate of grassroots empowerment so first-line managers sense that if they create a flexible environment, they will be supported.'

Bullock chairs IBM Australia's diversity council, a group of professionals and senior and mid-level managers from across the business. It helps drive the diversity agenda and supports networking groups. The groups support individuals, report on barriers and difficulties, promote attitudinal change and reinforce that at IBM it's okay to be yourself.

When IBM's Asia-Pacific head visited from Tokyo late last year, he was invited to address the company's gay and lesbian, bisexual and transsexual group.

'We are serious about diversity,' says Bullock. 'It's part of our normal business.'

He has come to terms with the paradox of building caring, sharing workplaces in a volatile, sometimes hostile, global environment where downsizings and retrenchment are integral.

'It's a fact of life that business conditions are changing …

Promoting diversity helps ensure that you can attract and retain the best people, but you do it knowing you will still have to deal with uncomfortable issues that may cause heartache for a lot of people. When you are in that position, you have to make decisions consistent with your practices and policies in regard to the treatment of individuals and, of course, to diversity.'

Source: Carolyn Rance 'Does Diversity Pay?,' *HR Monthly*, April 2004, pp. 22–3.

It is, at the same time, a management philosophy that recognises and accepts that the external and internal workforce is changing along with the community, indeed the total environment in which they operate. Managing diversity is then the creation and maintenance of an environment in which each person is respected because of their results.

Summary

The design of work to meet the needs of employees and employers is one of the critical issues facing organisations operating in a global environment. Jobs are changing on an ongoing basis, making the job analysis process a constant and dynamic process. These changes are further exacerbated by issues associated with shortages of labour in a number of areas, as discussed in Chapters 2 and 3.

Jobs are the building blocks of organisations, and as such, need to be analysed, designed and implemented in an accurate and efficient manner. This is achieved through job analysis, which also remains a constant process due to a range of internal and external pressures as well as the changing nature of competencies demanded by organisations to remain competitive and viable. The job analysis process also underpins all other core HR activities and functions within the organisation.

There are a number of means by which data is collected as part of the job analysis process and the method selected will be determined by a range of factors, including the organisational culture, size, expertise and the nature of the job/s. The two tools produced through the job analysis process are job (or position) descriptions and person specifications. These two 'tools' then form the basis of job evaluation, recruitment, selection, human resource development and performance management.

In order to meet competitive challenges there is a focus on the development of competencies and competency profiling in organisations. The development of competencies, both 'generic' and those tailored to individual and organisational needs, is becoming a critical focus for most HR professionals today – for their own positions as well as others.

Job descriptions and person specifications are also changing, with many organisations combining the two tools into one meaningful and relevant document, inclusive of measurable outcomes and key performance indicators. However, the changing nature of work toward a more multiskilled and 'fluid' role has made it difficult for these documents to remain accurate and workable.

While the job analysis process focuses on the business units and/or organisation's expectations of the role, job design focuses on meeting the needs of the employee as well as the organisation. This is becoming a critical issue in the retention of employees in today's market, particularly with positions in limited supply. The move from industrial engineering to job adaptation to meet employees' needs reflects this and the focus is now on new forms of work, individualised career paths, and work–family issues.

There is also a focus on diversity management, which in today's competitive organisations is embedded in job description and person specifications competency requirements, recruitment and selection strategies, and career development plans. In reality, diversity management is no more than a strategy to create opportunities to attract the brightest talent from the entire human resource pool and to then develop and retain that talent in order to maintain a competitive position in the marketplace.

Key terms

ability 159
diversity management 173
job redesign 153
knowledge-based work 172
multiskilling 172
multi-tasking 171
productivity 149
skill 154

Key debate issues

1 The use of position descriptions to define jobs is limiting and acts as a disincentive for performance. They should be thrown away allowing roles to be more fluid.

2 What is important in determining competencies for jobs is related to personality traits and attributes. Qualifications, information technology and manual skills can be taught and are not essential to job performance – an ability to get on with people, be innovative and creative is essential and cannot be taught. How accurate is this statement?

3 The implementation of job design strategies is fine for organisations that are large and have the money to implement. It is too difficult and costly for small businesses.

4 Diversity management is no more than a matter of legal compliance.

Case study 5.1

Literacy test puts jobs at risk

An English literacy test which forced six non-English-speaking workers out of jobs at Malabar sewage-treatment plant was compiled not by a qualified educator, but by an engineer at the plant.

'The test that was given was an inappropriate one and it certainly was not designed to test the skills that those blokes would need to have to be able to do the job,' Mr Mark Millen, the Adult Migrant Education Service (AMES) teacher employed by Sydney Water to teach the workers, said yesterday. However, Sydney Water says AMES was shown the test in February and could have advised then that it should not be administered. The Director of Human Resources for Sydney Water, Mr Warren Hart, said it was crucial for employees to be competent in English for safety reasons.

'I'm quite confident that we are doing the right thing,' he said. 'I can't run the risk on safety of letting these people be a risk to themselves or other people that work there.'

Sydney Water administered the test to six employees of non-English-speaking backgrounds at Malabar treatment works after they had completed a 108-hour course with AMES. All six failed the 10-question test, which took some more than two hours to complete. As a result, they were told they would not be moved to new jobs, created as part of a restructuring at the plant.

Instead, they were to be transferred to a redeployment centre at Yagoona. When they refused, they were stood down without pay for 11 days. The Industrial Commission ordered that they be given work at Malabar while their union and the Board negotiated a settlement. However, they were again stood down for refusing to transfer.

Three hundred sewage-treatment plant workers will stop work for the second time on Friday in protest against the treatment meted out to their colleagues and have placed bans on training courses instituted by the organisation. They downed tools last Friday over the same issue. Sydney Water and the union will appear before the State Industrial Relations Commission again today in an attempt to resolve the dispute. Mr Hart said they would be taking the offer of further English training to the Commission. He said they would not back away from the test but would now emphasise the questions that tested safety in assessing a pass or failure. The employees would not be allowed back at Malabar until they had demonstrated their ability to communicate effectively in an emergency.

Mr Hart stood by the suitability of an engineer, the Malabar Operations Superintendent, to set the test. 'I don't regard that the setting of those aspects of the test dealing with the basic competency of taking messages in itself requires an expert,' he said. However, Sydney Water is discussing other aspects of the test with AMES. Mr Hart also said that since their plants had become more highly technical, it needed employees who were capable of being retrained.

One of the workers at Malabar, Mr Zdravko 'Ziggy' Trajevski, said he was capable of taking on the newly created position. 'I am 15 years there,' he said. 'I know how it works. I work as machinist fitter assistant for 15 years and have no problems. No have trouble. I don't know what is happening. I think it is 99% discrimination.'

One of the workers is on sick leave, citing stress as the reason. Another two have decided to accept the move, while a fourth is taking redundancy.

Source: Lewis J. 1992. 'Literacy test by engineer puts job at risk', Sydney Morning Herald, 30 June.

Questions

1   What are the issues in this matter?
2   What steps would you have adopted initially had you found yourself in the same situation as the Malabar operations superintendent?

Case study 5.2

The workplace of the new millennium

An increasing number of workers see themselves as overworked, underpaid and just fed up with the way their employers are treating them. They are having to work longer hours for less pay. And the job security they enjoyed just 10 or 15 years ago seems like a distant memory. The workplace that used to be 'one big happy family' is now the scene of stressed-out workers who fear for their jobs. As a case in point, IBM which had a 'no-layoff' policy through the late 1980s, has since discarded that policy and laid off hundreds of thousands of its employees.

In order to cut costs and improve productivity, most major corporations have instituted massive layoffs – on a magnitude not seen since the Great Depression of the 1930s. One in five employees today fears losing their job.

To improve competitiveness, firms are asking those employees who survive the layoffs to work longer hours and often for less pay than they made previously. The result is a workforce that is tired and burned out. A recent poll of workers found that 80 per cent of those surveyed described their employers as requiring them to work 'very hard'; 65 per cent had to work 'very fast'; and 42 per cent complained of being 'used up' by the end of the work day. Further research indicates that one in four sick days taken are used to catch up on family issues. To add insult to injury, employers are also increasingly replacing laid-off workers with part-time employees because the latter give management flexibility and often cost a lot less. Today, one out of every four workers is temporary.

Layoffs, pressures for higher productivity and replacement of permanent workers with temporaries are undermining employee loyalty. For instance, only one in four employees today say they are committed to their organisation. As employers have demonstrated by their actions that employees are expendable, employees are responding with a dramatic decline in loyalty to those employers.

The new workplace climate is highly threatening to people. When employees are asked what is important to them, factors like a better work environment, flexible jobs and understanding bosses are near the top of the list. But it is just these factors that are being undermined in many organisations as management tries to increase productivity.

Source: Reproduced from Robbins et al, *Organisational Behaviour*, 2e, © Pearson Education Australia, 1998.

Questions

1 Outline the competitive environment facing many firms into the new millennium.

2 Explain how these changes in the environment are affecting employees.

3 Is it possible for companies to be competitive and, at the same time, create a workplace that provides employee security? High employee loyalty? Family–work balance?

4 Provide a rationale as to why the current situation has come about.

Endnotes

1   Landis, R.S., Fogli, L., Goldberg, E., 1998. 'Future-oriented job analysis: A description of the process and its organisational implications,' *International Journal of Selection and Assessment*, vol. 6, no. 3, July, p. 194–205.

2   Ibid, p. 195.

3   Ibid, p. 196.

4   Hagan, C.M., Konopaske, R., Bernardin, H.J., Tyler, C.L., Fall 2006. 'Predicting assessment center performance with 360-degree, top-down, and customer-based competency assessments,' *Human Resource Management*, vol. 45, no. 3. p. 357.

5   Cooper, S., Eton, L., Kierstead, J., Lynch, B., Luce, S., April, 1998. 'Competencies: A brief overview of development and application to public and private sectors.' Public Service Commission of Canada, p. 4.

6   Ibid, p. 5.

7   Hagan, et al., p. 359.

8   Ibid.

9   Gow, K., McDonald, P., 2000. 'Attributes required of graduates for the future workplace,' *Journal of Vocational Education and Training*, vol. 52, no. 3, p. 377.

10   Ibid.

11   Ibid. p. 381

12   Meisinger, S. 2003. 'Adding competencies, adding value,' *HR Magazine*, vol. 28, no. 7, p. 8.

13   Shellabear, S. Aug. 2002. 'Competency profiling: Definition and implementation.' *Training Journal*, p. 16.

14   Ibid.

15   Ibid, p. 18.

16   Lockwood, N.R. Sept. 2006. 'Maximising human capital: demonstrating HR value with key performance indicators.' *HR Magazine*, vol. 51. no. 9, p. 2.

17   Williams, C.P. Jan. 1999. 'The end of the job as we know it.' *Training and Development*, vol. 53, no. 1, p. 52.

18   Ibid.

19   Caudron, S. Jan. 2000. 'Jobs disappear: When work becomes more important.' *Workforce*, vol. 79, no. 1, p. 30.

20   Ibid, p. 32.

21   ibid.

22   Leonard, S. Aug 2000. 'The demise of job descriptions.' *HR Magazine*, vol. 45, no. 8, p. 184.

23   Campion, M.A., Mumford, T.V., Morgeson, F.P., Nahrgang, J.D. Winter 2005. 'Work redesign: Eight obstacles and opportunities,' *Human Resource Management*, vol. 44, no. 4., p. 368.

24   Ibid, p. 367.

25   For Herzberg's original article on job enrichment, see F. Herzberg, 1968. 'One more time: How do you motivate people?,' *Harvard Business Review*, 46(2), January/February, pp. 53–62.

26   Ferris G.R., Gilmore D.O. 1984. 'The moderating role of work context in job design research. A test of competing models,' *Academy of Management Journal*, 27(4), December, pp. 885–92.

27   Campion, et al. p. 380.

28   Campion, et al. p. 380.

29   Ibid.

30   Hockley R. 1994. 'Self-managed work teams are a small part of the STS whole,' *hrmonthly*, November, pp. 12–14.

Online reading

INFOTRAC® COLLEGE EDITION

For additional readings and review on work design challenges in a global environment, explore InfoTrac® College Edition, your online library.

Go to: www.infotrac-college.com and search for any of the InfoTrac key terms listed below:

➤ competencies
➤ job analysis
➤ job design
➤ key performance indicators (KPIs)
➤ position descriptions

CHAPTER 6
ATTRACTING AND RETAINING TALENT

HR experts believe there are employment tests and software to accomplish any task ... including hiring 50 000 (anti-terrorist) workers overnight. It's not only a fallacy, it's a fraud. It just doesn't work that way.

Nick Corcodilos, 2003

The crisis that is hardest hitting business today, across the board, is recruiting and retaining qualified employees.

Shelley Langman, 2000

With most senior executive appointments there is a strong probability that the most suitable candidate will not even see the advertisement and may have serious concerns about confidentiality ... that is where executive search comes in.

Geoff Hines, 1996

Managers will find that the balance of power has shifted for the first time in three decades towards a seller's market for employees rather than a buyer's market for employers.

Phil Ruthven, 2004

Objectives

After reading this chapter you will be able to:

1 Understand the strategic nature of the recruitment process and its relationship to the vision, mission and strategic planning processes of the organisation.

2 Recognise the advantages and disadvantages of internal and external recruitment strategies.

3 Understand the emerging use of e-cruitment as a vital element in the evolution of e-business.

4 Be aware of the principal recruitment sources and appreciate when these resources might best be utilised.

5 Appreciate the benefits and disadvantages of using a recruitment consultant.

6 Understand the unique aspects of international recruitment.

7 Appreciate the importance of the retention of talent.

Introduction

Very few events of modern times have had anything like the impact of the catastrophe that was 11 September 2001. Countless people had their lives turned upside down by the direct consequences of that day, while many more felt and still feel the indirect flow-on effects over the ensuing years.

From an organisational perspective, arguably very few other professions have felt the impact in quite the same way as the human resources profession. Consider the negative impact on recruiting, education and development, succession planning and, of course, the vast loss of intellectual capital and corporate memory. Expatriate management has taken on a whole new perspective as people quickly were moved globally to fill gaps left behind by those many corporate people who lost their lives on that day.

Take the case of the US Transportation Security Administration which received orders from Congress to recruit more than 55 000 new people in 10 months. The goal was to rid the country of terrorism overnight.[1] Inadequate airport security was blamed as one of the key factors contributing to September 11. Then consider the immediate need to call out 125 000 members of the US National Reserve for off-shore service. No amount of people planning can hope to factor in this type of emergency situation.

From an entirely different perspective, consider the current global epidemic of diabetes and the predictions of the World Health Organisation that 300 million people will be affected by 2025. Consider then the challenges of Novo Nordisk, a Danish company leading the fight against this deadly disease. With 18 000 people in 68 countries, the company should have no problems in attracting the best talent from around the world.[2] In effect, Novo Nordisk is world famous only in Denmark! The challenge for management is to find the right recruitment strategies to attract the very best scientists in this field.

The strategic perspective

Recruiting is the process of attempting to locate and encourage potential applicants to apply for existing or anticipated job openings. Put simply, recruitment strategies attempt to create a pool of appropriately qualified and experienced people so that selection strategies and decisions can be initiated. During this process, efforts are made to inform the applicants fully about the selection criteria, that is, the required competencies, which will lead to effective performance and the career opportunities the organisation can provide for them. Thus, potential applicants can be motivated to apply for the positions that are open. Whether or not a particular job vacancy will be filled by someone from within the organisation or from outside will, of course, depend upon the organisation's HR policies, the requirements of the job to be filled, the talent to be found within the organisation and, often, the organisational politics surrounding the decision. Organisations can draw up the most elaborate recruitment processes but these can only minimise the political influences that will surround this critical aspect of human resource management.

The relationship between strategic employee recruitment and strategic planning is shown in Exhibit 6.1.

Before further meaningful discussion of relevant labour sources is undertaken, it is important to adopt a strategic orientation to the recruitment processes. Roger Collins[3] has argued that human resource managers must take on a much more strategic mindset than the operational one that may have served them well in the past. This shift in thinking has been significant as the profession has faced intense pressure to prove that it adds value to the organisation.

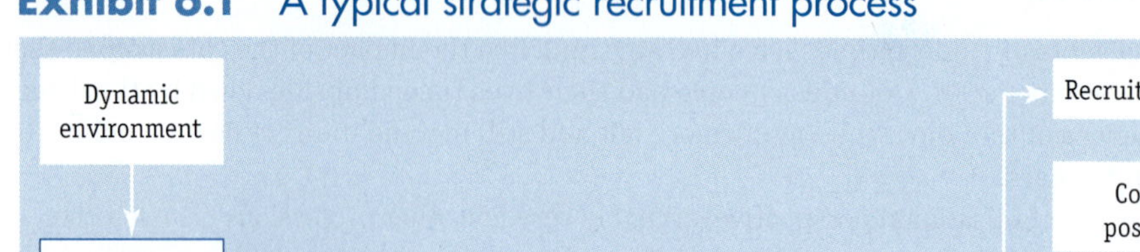

Exhibit 6.1   A typical strategic recruitment process

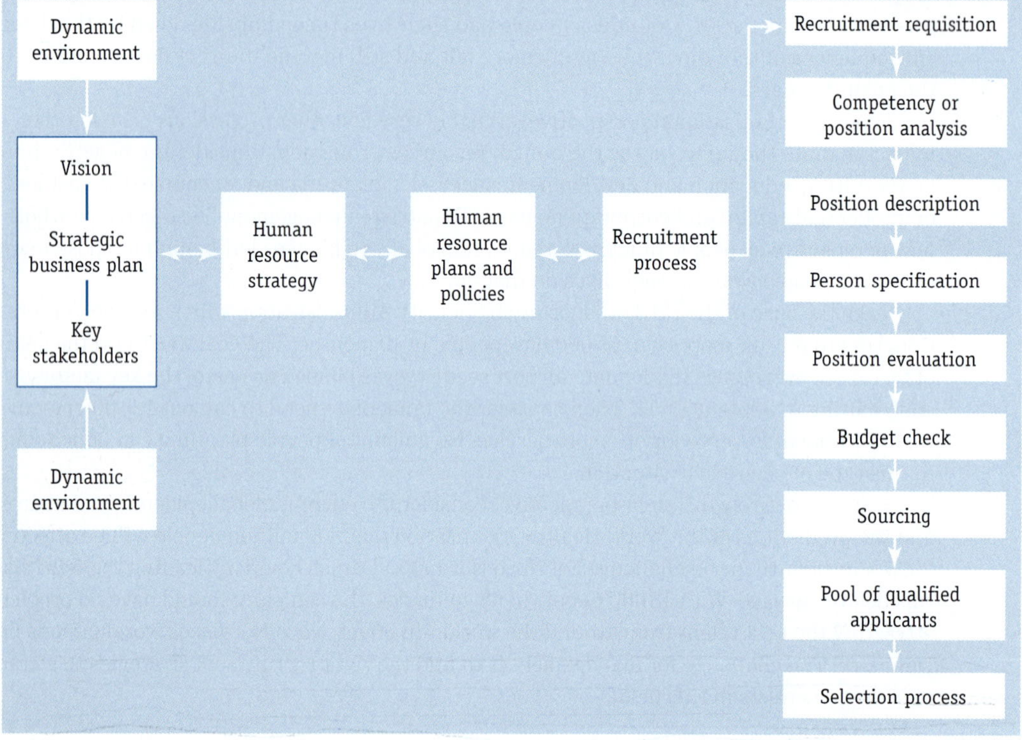

In terms of staff recruitment, HR managers must come to an awareness that their unique business environment calls for a situational approach to attracting employees. Those organisations adopting an organic, dynamic form of business strategy will seek out a different type of employee to those that are adopting more mechanistic or bureaucratic organisational strategies. The direction that a business takes, the culture that is being created or shifted and the competencies required all lead to an emphasis on internal or external recruitment at any particular time. The recruitment mix will change as indeed the same issues shift to meet the demands of an ever-changing marketplace.

The key point to be made is that recruitment strategies flow ultimately from the organisation's mission statement and strategic objectives. Recruitment strategies and processes must be compatible with higher level strategies. As a case in point, where the strategic direction is one of rightsizing it will make little sense for HR professionals to follow an external recruitment strategy except where there exists a watertight business case.

David Reddin, well-known international recruitment consultant, has contributed to the strategy debate by outlining his views on the features of strategic recruitment, which he claims are practised by only a handful of Australian organisations. According to Reddin, five key features are to ensure that:

- Human resource plans are linked to and support corporate plans.
- Human resource plans include people, developmental and succession plans.
- Recruitment strategies are in place and deliver against the goals of the organisation.
- Appropriate skills are in place to support the recruitment strategies.
- Subsequent induction, training, development and mentoring programs are available to add support to the recruitment program.[4]

Attracting key staff

Finding 400 prison officers is a tall order, especially when the public's perception of the job is unduly negative

It's the most challenging growth strategy Corrections Victoria's HR project team has ever faced – to attract, train and retain more than 400 prison officers and 150 clinical and administration staff this year.

The staff are needed for two new correctional facilities opened at Lara and Ravenhall. The newly created five-person HR team, situated within the Department of Justice, is not only taking recruitment. It is also out to change public perceptions of the prison officer's role and working in prisons generally.

The Victorian government has made a commitment to close some of the state's oldest prisons and change the focus of prison management to better case management and successful rehabilitation of prisoners to enable their return to the community. Amid record low levels of unemployment, the challenge is to attract suitable people who will be committed to a long-term career.

The change management model developed by the team has to withstand potential variables such as industrial action and adverse press at any given time. And throughout the growth and recruitment phase, stability of business operations can't be compromised. Prisons are required to maintain staffing levels at all times to ensure security and safety.

The reality is that nobody wants to grow up to be a prison officer. One of the project's biggest hurdles has been to change the public perception of prisons as places of violence and drug use, where the officer's role is little more than 'lock and key,' to one of a more humane and rehabilitative focus.

Taking a fresh approach, the HR team, working with an external recruitment provider, has developed and introduced what it calls three dimensional recruitment, using three methods:

- an online presence including a variety of areas/categories in job search engines
- press advertising to create awareness and lead to education about corrections and prison officers' roles
- closely timed post-advertising public presentations and information sessions.

The key underpinning of three-dimensional recruitment is the involvement of current staff in all communications and public presentations and creating staff advocates to encourage friends and job-seekers to consider applying.

There was an early decision not to avoid any sensitive questions raised at public information sessions, with fact sheets and brochures prepared to reduce applicants' fears. The sessions,

which began in January 2005, have enabled potential applicants to talk first-hand to people experienced in prison work. They have also given mature applicants considering a career change or a return to the workforce a chance to learn about such work and consider it as an option. Many had considered themselves too old to apply but they were precisely the kind of people with life experience that the recruiters were trying to attract.

It has become apparent from the information sessions that most people have little understanding of a prison officer's job and in the first instance did not recognise prison officers' uniforms. Nor do they realise the diversity of careers in Corrections. After visiting many prisons for research, the recruitment and marketing team moved away from a 'selling' approach towards highlighting the range of careers on offer in an honest way. For the first time, Corrections prison officers went as far as attending local festivals, markets and shopping centres to spread the message about what they do and what they are trying to achieve.

Weekly statistics have been used to assess the campaign and time its components. For example, the website has received an average of 250 visits per week, along with many job applications, after representation at community events. This direct method of recruitment proved successful in attracting a mature and diverse range of applicants. To date, the website has attracted more than 10 000 visits and almost 750 applicants have been completed online.

Historically, the ratio of applications to successful selections averages 8:1. Using the three dimensional recruitment method, the ratio has been 4:1, saving time and money. Prison officers have played an integral role with the recruitment provider and HR team in all aspects of staff recruitment and selection.

The five-month assessment schedule means many successful applicants will not begin work until later this year. Each month they are invited to a series of formal and informal gatherings with current prison staff so they can stay in touch and get orientated to their new location, role and training groups. Those unable or who choose not to attend are sent regular information by email or mail.

Source: Zemeel Saba, *hrmonthly*, May 2005. Zemeel Saba, MAHRI, is the prisons HR projects manager for Corrections Victoria.

After a decade of attempting to achieve some form of 'corporate anorexia' and then discovering that this approach did not work, organisations have again turned their focus to a recognition that people may well be their only source of sustainable competitive advantage. Carol Gill writes that globalisation may be the catalyst for this apparent refocusing on talent. She argues that with global competition, ideas develop quickly and people are more willing to change jobs more often. People are no longer seen as expenses and overheads but as strategic assets.[5]

Employers of choice

With this renewed interest in the so-called 'war for talent' has come a push by organisations to be known as employers of choice and in this way attract the best talent around. *Employers of choice* invariably recognise that a major priority for modern employees is the ability to balance work and home life while at the same time work for an organisation that will offer autonomy, meaningful work and opportunities for learning.[6]

Nicholas Way claims that this is a war that must be won but it is a battle with a difference because in many ways executives do not know how to go about it. Their old mindsets often get in the way of comprehending that they must treat skilled workers in a way that will at first attract them to a company and then make them want to stay.[7] NRMA's David Smith sums up the argument when he says that the war for talent is a reality in Australia, where there is now a better understanding that attraction and retention are the key to successful people management, but so too are developing and fostering internal talent. It comes down to a question of balance.[8]

Best employers

Interestingly, the Best Employers 2003 joint winners were the same two organisations that took out the 2002 award, Cisco and travel group Flight Centre. With some 160 entries, runners-up representing some very stiff competition included Virgin Blue, Lion Nathan, Nike, Johnson & Johnson, Diageo, Nokia and Macquarie Bank. Although it can be somewhat dangerous and prescriptive to look for cure-alls practised by such companies, a number of consistent themes did emerge.

The results show consistency in some key factors. The quality of senior leadership, a performance-driven culture where values are important and culture is aggressively managed by leaders; a passion for the organisation and the work employees do; and opportunities to grow and develop remained core attributes of the top list. The concept of employee engagement remains a key measure in assessing Best Employers. Engagement is a state of emotional and intellectual involvement or commitment.[9]

The judges were reportedly surprised by three elements of the data collected:

- Recognition is highly effective but still largely ignored by many organisations.
- Work–life balance 'is the pits' everywhere.
- The HR function is not well respected.[10]

The employers of choice of 2004–5 came as somewhat of a surprise as a number of 'new' organisations emerged with the top awards. Some of the major winners included Sensis, Snowy Hydro, Mounties and the Queensland Cancer Fund. Jo Mithen, the then Executive Director of AHRI, commented that innovation, top management support, alignment of HR strategy with corporate objectives and benchmarking were practices on display amongst the winners. Dr Brett White, a member of the national judging panel and Group Executive Officer with St George Bank, added that these organisations are really starting to 'move down a strategic pathway … looking to add value to the business'.[11]

The one final theme that emerges is that each organisation was aware that getting their credentials right will result in higher rates of attraction and retention of valued people.

A word of caution: in their search for talent, organisations must be wary of making promises that they simply cannot keep. Kieran Knowles writes that employers who promise the world and do not deliver will not only find a new source of discontent and turnover but may well be in breach of section 53B of the *Trade Practices Act*, where employees only need to show that an employer has made representations with respect to a future matter and failed to deliver.[12] Nor can employers dissociate themselves from the actions and promises made on their behalf to potential employees by employment consultants. The full court of the Federal Court has found that an employer cannot renege on promises made by a head hunter to a manager it sourced from a rival firm.[13]

NEWS REPORT 6.2

Australian HR awards 2006

Deloitte CEO Giam Swiegers was named the country's best HR champion at the Australian HR Awards 2006.

Held on Friday 15 September in Sydney, the awards recognise excellence across the entire spectrum of HR, with organisations from around the country competing in 17 categories.

Sponsored by Aon Consulting and organised by leading HR industry magazine *Human Resources*, winners included organisations such as Cisco Systems, Sydney Ports Corporation, PricewaterhouseCoopers and GM Holden.

Attended by 500 guests, Citibank Australia chairman Ron Bunker presented the keynote at the gala awards ceremony while entertainer and comic Peter Berner was MC.

PriceWaterhouseCoopers took out The MBA Connect Award for Best Graduate Intake Program for providing a good variety and depth of training and opportunities for graduates, while Sunstate Cement was recognised for its integrated and responsive strategy to business risk and objectives in winning The SageCo Award for Best Mature Age Workforce Implementation.

On an individual level, Alec Bachinksy, Deloitte's national partner for people and performance, took out The HR Partners Award for Best HR Director for his high level of innovation and commitment, while Deloitte's CEO Giam Swiegers won The Ipac HR Champion CEO Award for demonstrated commitment to HR in addition to leveraging the function to increase performance, profit and reputation.

'Winning these awards very much reflects the change management, people, strategies and ''can do'' attitude we have focussed on at Deloitte,' said Swiegers.

'Ultimately in professional services there is only one key differentiator – our people. With Australia's political and industry leadership increasingly focussed on better managing, training and retention of the country's skilled workforce, the Australian HR Awards 2006 are to be commended for their focus on best practice,' he said.

Bashinsky said Deloitte has worked hard to develop and enhance a range of people issues in the firm, with strategies for graduate and career development, cultural diversity, learning and development as well as executive coaching. A cost-saving program called 'Find Like Minds' has also saved the firm more than $1.2 million in recruitment costs over the past 12 months.

'Our focus has been on the high end value added HR strategies and partnering with our business leaders to achieve a stronger leadership and people focus within the firm. To me, this award is a confirmation that our people and performance strategy and execution is paying off and working more effectively internally within the firm,' Bashinsky said.

Developed in conjunction with leading academics and professionals from the HR industry, this year's selection and judging process included employee opinion surveys in addition to a two-tier nomination and selection process in which all submissions were reviewed by a shortlisting and final judging panel.

Company branding

The rush to become an employer of choice has seen a novel approach to employer branding, which has for so long been the domain of the marketing profession. In effect, corporate recruitment people have learned to draw from the experiences of their marketing colleagues in an effort to change the way that prospective and existing employees view the organisation. Employer branding is the sum total of a company's efforts to convince existing and prospective staff that this is an attractive place to work. It follows that all HR processes be aimed at world's best practice and the desired culture in place prior to jumping on the 'branding' bandwagon.[14]

The NRMA has for some years established processes and strategies to facilitate family and work balance. Cisco has a culture of strong leadership and open communication. Flight Centre offers autonomy and an empowered work culture where people can 'stretch' to achieve their full potential concurrently with company goals, whereas S.C. Johnson takes a holistic approach to branding by focusing on career development, leadership, accelerated development, employee recognition and work–family balance.

From a slightly similar perspective, Westpac has embarked on a campaign to recruit 900 older employees as financial planners and advisers. Concurrently, 40 per cent of Westpac branch employees have moved to the other side of the counter to meet customers at the front of house. With 45 years as the average age of Westpac customers and over-55s the fastest growing group, it made good commercial sense for staff to mirror the customer base.[15]

The retail industry has for many years suffered from a negative branding with school leavers taking on a 'job in a shop' either as a last resort or as a job that will provide some pocket money while they work through university or college.[16] See News reports 6.3 and 6.4.

In a recent research study, Roger Collins found that 58 per cent of respondents had undertaken a program to initiate and communicate a corporate brand while 36 per cent reported that their organisation had no such initiative. Collins argues that the key element in developing a corporate brand is the co-development of an employee value proposition. Only 30 per cent of respondents had taken this extra step. In addition, Collins reports that only 25 per cent of those who had gone down this path had attempted to evaluate whether the perceptions of employees were consistent with the employment brand.[17]

Shop tactics

Perceptions about pay rates, training and career paths have left retailers with a recruitment problem

The health of the retail industry is under threat. After years of neglecting employee training and development, the retail industry – which accounts for more than 7% of Australia's gross domestic product, and is the country's biggest employer, employing 14.5% of all workers – is facing a talent crisis. As the population ages, competition from all business sectors for young talent will increase. But many graduates believe the retail industry offers low wages, poor training and a lack of career opportunities, largely due to its status as a first job for many young people and because of the large number of casual and part time workers it employs.

The chief executive of David Jones, Peter Wilkinson, says the retail industry has tended to act 'as an industry of last resort,' allowing staff to drift into it rather than actively chasing talented young staff.

Deborah Davis, managing director of the retail industry recruitment firm Frontline Retail, says that one of the biggest challenges the industry faces is to overcome its image problem. She says there is a perception in the community that people work in retail because they cannot do anything else. 'People refer to jobs in retail as "just a job in a shop",' she says.

The associate director of retail and property at KPMG, Justin Ganly, agrees that the retail industry has an image problem, but says its lack of appeal to graduates also stems from other factors. These include the seven-day week of many retail chains, the slim profit margins of most retailers (which means they are often the first to feel the effect of an economic downturn and so are the first to cut costs), limited opportunities to move overseas, and the location of many retail head offices in suburban and industrial areas.

According to Davis, retailers should capitalise on the fact that many university students work as casuals in the retail industry. They can do this by selling the benefits of working in retailing to casual employees, and by offering their student workers full-time positions that utilise their education after they have graduated.

Michael Morrison, a lecturer in retail management at Monash University, agrees that the perception of careers in the retail industry is poor. He says: 'There is a mindset that retail is about standing by a checkout taking money.' Monash's faculty of business and economics offers a bachelor of business in retail management. Morrison says about 200 students are studying for the degree, which includes a range of business subjects, and retail subjects such as buyer behaviour and retail management principles.

'Most of my students doing the degree have worked in retail for years in some capacity,' Morrison says. 'So [retailers] have got people, trained on the shop floor, used to the culture of the organisation. You would think they should leverage off that, find out that they're doing a degree in retail and business and hire them. But they don't see that yet.'

Davis says few retailers devote sufficient time and money to training and developing their staff. 'If it doesn't become a priority we are weakening a weak chain,' she says. Ganly agrees, saying retailers need to improve their recruitment, training, staff development and career-planning programs. A survey of 100 applicants for retail positions conducted in 2001 by Frontline Retail found that only 8% of prospective retail employees did not regard training as important, and just 4% were not expecting to be trained by their prospective employer.

How real is the talent shortage in the retail industry? Consider recent events at Coles Myer, Australia's biggest retailer. In the past year, it has had to replace many senior executives, including its chief executive, the managing directors of its Target, Myer-Grace Bros and Kmart chains, its general manager of human resources, and its general manager of corporate affairs. None of the positions were filled internally. In every instance, Coles Myer recruited from outside the local retail industry.

Hiring John Fletcher, a former chief executive of Brambles, as the new chief executive was understandable, given the need to introduce massive changes at Coles Myer. But analysts say that Coles Myer's inability to fill other positions internally indicates a dearth of management talent:

- Kmart's managing director, Hani Zayadi, came from Wal-Mart (Canada) in July 2001.
- Myer-Grace Bros' managing director, Dawn Robertson, came from Federated Department Stores (United States) in May this year – after a seven-month search.
- Target's managing director, Larry Davis, came from Kmart (US) in August 2001.
- Coles Myer's general manager of corporate affairs, Pamela Catty, came from National Australia Bank in February this year.
- Coles Myer's general manager of human resources, Ian Clubb (who managed human resources for the Sydney Olympics) was appointed in January this year.
- Coles Myer's chief financial officer, John Schmoll, has announced his intention to retire in 2002. A replacement has yet to be found.

One insider says Coles Myer cannot keep good people because it does not nurture talent. For example, he says, the company has been unwilling to fast-track top performers – 'You have to serve your time in each role.' Salary increases have historically been set across departments, rather than determined according to individual performance. 'The incentive is not there to perform, which encourages mediocrity,' he says.

In February, the Australian Retailers Association and the federal Department of Employment and Workplace Relations released a report on finding and keeping talented staff in the retail industry. The report, which surveyed 60 retailers with a total of 278 000 employees, found that only 69% of retailers have a strategy to attract talented staff, and 72% have a strategy to retain good staff, through training and development.

Wilkinson, from David Jones, started his career in retailing when he was 12, working in his father's hardware store in South Africa. Although he has no tertiary education, Wilkinson believes that in the future, retail industry executives need a combination of shop-floor experience and formal education.

The highly competitive nature of the retail industry means that training and developing David Jones' 10 000 staff, and looking for the potential senior executives among them, is critical. During the past year, David Jones has found internal replacements for key roles that have included chief financial officer, chief information officer and general manager of human resources.

David Jones does not have a formal graduate program, but Wilkinson says it has no trouble attracting good graduates. Its in-house training programs include customer service, sales, management skills and leadership. The company also covers the cost of fees and books for staff in its stores and head office who wish to complete further study, provided the study is relevant to the business.

The managing director of the footwear and clothing retailer Colorado Group, Rowan Webb, agrees that the retail industry has not been a career of choice for top graduates. He says the industry needs to spend more on staff training and development, but says tight profit margins make that difficult for many retailers. 'With the pressure on costs, particularly rent, so intense, it is difficult for retailers to find the funds to increase investment in the area of human capital,' Webb says.

Davis, from Frontline Retail, says Colorado has a good reputation for its approach to training, but Webb believes it can do better. 'It is the one area we have not given adequate priority or investment,' he says. To attract the best candidates, Webb says, Colorado must demonstrate that it is an exciting company with a bright future, strong values, excellent training and genuine career opportunities for people who perform.

Earlier this year, Colorado launched a program called Colorado Campus, which will provide training for its 3000 employees. So far, leadership programs for senior executives,

run by the Mount Eliza Business School in Melbourne, have been developed, which can be used towards obtaining a masters degree in business administration. A training program for store managers is also being developed. In-store training is planned for store-based staff, and will be provided through the company's intranet.

Colorado actively recruits graduates for several positions, and, like Wilkinson, Webb believes the best employees have a combination of practical retailing skills and education. But Colorado also wants to develop employees who do not have degree qualifications. 'It is our first priority to identify these people and provide them with the coaching, training and career opportunities to realise their potential,' Webb says.

The managing director of McDonald's Australia, Guy Russo, says retailers need to offer a dynamic environment and culture to attract top talent. He says that training is not just about doing the right thing by your employees. 'It's going to flow through to our bottom line,' he says. Head office staff at McDonald's can complete post-graduate studies in business through Ballarat University in Victoria and Newcastle University in New South Wales. Executives can also complete management development programs offered by the Australian Institute of Management, and executive development programs through the Macquarie Graduate School of Management.

Most of McDonald's 55 000 employees work in its restaurants. Each year, the company hands out 90 'crew' education scholarships, valued at $1 500 each. Russo says more than $1 million has been given out since the scholarships started in 1994. 'It impresses upon staff that education is really important to us,' he says. Twenty-nine sports scholarships, also worth $1 500 each, are granted each year. Training for store-based staff includes certificates in retail operations and, for managers, certificates, diplomas and advanced diplomas in management.

In 1998, McDonald's became the first retailer to introduce a program, initially in Victoria, under which secondary school students could count their casual work with the chain and certificate-level training towards their school results. Although the program initially attracted criticism from the Australian Education Union and the media about the commercialisation of education, it has now been adopted in other states and by other retailers, including Woolworths.

To keep track of the skills and educational qualifications of the staff in its restaurants, McDonald's keeps a database with information about employees who are studying at university. The database is consulted whenever a vacancy arises to see whether there are suitable internal candidates. As a result, about 70% of McDonald's store managers and head office staff start in its restaurants, and have shop-floor experience. 'Zero cost, infinite gain,' Russo says. Staff who are ready for promotion are not held back. 'If we can't find a job for them in Australia, we will look overseas,' Russo says. As a result of this policy, former McDonald's Australia executives are now running operations for McDonald's in Europe, Taiwan and Indonesia.

Source: Hadden, M. 2002. BRW, 6–12 June.

Branding from the inside out

Many companies are as keen to market themselves to their employees as to their customers

In a recent television commercial for St George Bank, a woman is hosting a barbecue and asks one of the guests what he does for a living. He says he works for a bank, and everyone responds with a horrified silence, until the guest adds: 'St George.' Everyone laughs with relief. Like most of St George's brand advertising in the past, the ad was aimed at potential customers. But unlike most of the bank's previous brand advertising, the message – that St George is the best bank to work for – was also aimed at another audience: existing and potential employees. It is an approach that many companies are taking more seriously as they latch on to the concept of the 'employer brand.'

Until recently, an organisation's brand was mainly an asset communicated to an external audience, that is, the customer. However, senior executives have realised that the internal audience – employees – is equally important. In its advertising, St George tries to position itself as the bank that offers satisfaction to customers and employees.

Employer branding is the sum of a company's efforts to communicate to existing and prospective staff that it is a desirable place to work. It might sound basic, but human resources practitioners say it is remarkable how company management will push the many benefits of their brand to consumers but treat staff with disdain or even contempt.

A managing consultant with the human resources consultancy Hewitt Associates, David Brown, says: 'It is astonishing how many organisations still do not believe in the linkage between better business results and being an employer of choice and getting real value out of [employees].

'There is still a whole notion among these organisations of focusing on tangible assets and their impact on the bottom line,

rather than the intangible assets, which are people. One question we ask organisations is what they are spending on their human assets and what return are they getting, and it is not uncommon to get a blank look in return,' he says.

The rise of employer branding has been propelled by the shortage of talented staff in most industries. 'We know the war for talent is alive and well,' Brown says. 'It is driving companies to understand the cost implications of losing people, the cost implications of having employees who feel disengaged from their employer and are therefore underperforming, and the cost of having to hire new people to replace them when they leave.'

In February this year, Hewitt released a survey of the best employers to work for in Australia. Conducted in conjunction with the Australian Graduate School of Management and John Fairfax Holdings (the owner of *BRW*), the study is similar to a survey published each year by the United States magazine Fortune. Hewitt has conducted two surveys in Australia. The company that conducts Fortune's survey, Great Place to Work Institute, has been surveying employees for 20 years.

Hewitt surveyed 160 companies, ranging from those with fewer than 1000 staff to ones with up to 30000 employees. It found the best companies to work for shared four characteristics: people leadership (trusted leaders who

communicate with, and are more passionate about, their employees); a compelling employment offer; accelerated development (companies investing more in training and career development for staff); and good culture and values (a performance and results focus, an emphasis on fun and celebration, employee recognition and performance management).

Sceptics say the focus by Hewitt and other human-resources professionals on the employer brand is a fad, and even Andrew Bell, a practice leader at Hewitt, concedes that companies are hopping on the employer-branding bandwagon.

Bell says: 'What we see is companies like Lion Nathan [ranked fourth among companies with more than 1000 staff] that have been doing it for a long time. They have recognised that before they jump into the marketing side of the employment brand, it is vital to have all internal processes aligned with [the brand message]. The marketing should come last. But we also see companies jumping into the fad and doing the marketing first, which can cause a real problem. If the internal culture in the company is not right, then the brand standards are just not there.'

The director of Asia-Pacific sales for the human-resources management company TMP Worldwide, Tony Le Bars, says the brand image promoted to customers must be reflected in the operations and management style of the company. 'The employer brand, by definition, relates to the

values of the organisation, and those core values have to filter right through the organisation,' he says. 'If an organisation suggests to its customers that it is innovative and dynamic, and technologically number one, you would hope an employee walking in for the first time would at least get access to their own computer. It is amazing how many do not.

'The brand is not just the experience people on the outside have of an organisation, it is also very much on the inside. Employees and candidates now realise that it is a very competitive market from the employer perspective.

Go-go logo

How to develop a strong employer brand:

1 Understand your organisation: why do people join, why do they leave, what else are they looking for to connect them passionately to the company's strategy and goals, and what are the key people practices that will fuel organisational growth and value creation?

2 Create a 'compelling brand promise' for employees that mirrors the brand promise to customers.

3 Develop standards to measure the fulfilment of the brand promise.

4 'Ruthlessly align' all people practices to support and reinforce the brand promise.

5 Execute and measure. Stick at it: it will take 18 months to two years to see the results of the effort.

Source: Lloyd, S. 2002. *BRW*, 14–20 March.

Recruiting from within

Organisations will often try to follow a policy of filling job vacancies above the entry-level position through promotions and transfers. In Australia, a majority of jobs are filled without external advertising. By filling vacancies through promotions and transfers, an organisation can capitalise on the costs that it has invested in recruiting, selecting and training its current employees. Where much time and effort have been put into succession and career planning strategies, it will not make sense to continually recruit from external sources. Rather, promotions and transfers will be common outcomes of succession and career planning strategies. Promotion serves to reward the employee receiving the promotion for his or her past performance and, it is hoped, will result in continuing efforts by that individual. It also sends a positive signal to others that similar efforts by them will lead to promotion, thus possibly helping to improve morale within the organisation. This is particularly true for members of targeted minority groups who have encountered difficulties in gaining employment and will often have faced even greater difficulty in achieving advancement within an organisation. A non-discriminatory promotion policy is an essential part of the equal employment opportunity and affirmative action programs that most Australian organisations have now adopted.

To have maximum motivation value, however, employees must be made aware of the organisation's promotion policy and reward system. Such awareness can be facilitated through the preparation and dissemination of written statements covering these policies together with specific mention in any career workshops or induction and orientation sessions that might be conducted.

While a transfer lacks the motivational value of a promotion, it can sometimes serve to protect employees from retrenchment or broaden their job experience. Furthermore, the transferred employee's familiarity with the organisation and its operations can eliminate certain orientation and training costs that recruitment from the outside would entail. Most importantly, management has knowledge of the employee's performance record. This knowledge is likely to be a more accurate predictor of the candidate's success than the data gained about outside applicants through the selection process. Moreover, transfer between jobs facilitates current restructuring strategies such as multiskilling and career pathing.

In larger organisations, a common problem faced is that of 'silo mentality.' The separate business units or divisions can create artificial physical and psychological barriers to people mobility, thus working against what should be a seamless organisation. Transfers and cross-business promotions can help to break down these barriers and at the same time send out a powerful signal that this is one organisation.

Limitations of recruiting from within

Sometimes, certain jobs at the middle and upper levels will require specialised competencies and experience that cannot be obtained within the organisation and must be filled from outside. This situation is especially common in small organisations. For certain openings, it may be necessary to hire individuals externally who have gained from another employer the knowledge and expertise required.

Even though HR policy may encourage vacancies to be filled from within the organisation, potential external candidates should also be considered to prevent the inbreeding of ideas and attitudes. Applicants hired from the outside, particularly for 'rare category' positions, can be a source of new ideas and may bring with them the latest knowledge acquired from their previous employers. Indeed, excessive reliance upon internal sources can create the risk of 'employee cloning.' Furthermore, in the competitive field of high technology, for example, it is not uncommon for firms to attempt to gain secrets from competitors by 'poaching' their employees.

Where an organisation has engaged in competency profiling, it may well find that those competencies required to meet the organisation's strategic objectives are not evident within the organisation. In such cases, external recruitment will be essential. At the same time, developmental strategies must be put in place to allow internal people to be more competitive on future occasions where such competencies are sought.

In line with a change in strategic direction, an organisation may attempt to shift its workforce culture through an emphasis on external recruitment. In times of rapid 'whitewater' change, management may well decide that this strategy will bring the fastest results. There may not be sufficient time to shift existing paradigms in any other way.

The *potential* advantages and disadvantages of internal and external recruitment are shown in Exhibit 6.2.

Exhibit 6.2   Internal versus external recruiting

Sources of recruits	
Internal	
Potential advantages	**Potential disadvantages**
• May aid morale of employees	• Danger of inbreeding
• Easier to assess applicant's ability	• Discontent among those not promoted
• Good performance is rewarded	• Political infighting for promotion
• A succession for promotion developed	• Effective appraisal program required
• Necessary only to hire at base level	• Criticism from those outside organisation who cannot get in
• Avoids 'leak plugging' strategy	Old culture maintained
• Less costs involved in attracting a pool of applicants	Cloning by those doing the selecting

External	
Potential advantages	**Potential disadvantages**
• New ideas brought into the organisation	• Outsider may not fit in to organisation's culture
• No claims of favouritism from inside leading to resentment	• Morale of those passed over declines
• Forces insiders to compete – keep skills and education up to date	• More training and development required of new recruits
• More compatible with concepts of EEO/ Affirmative Action strategies	• A longer orientation period necessary
• Can be very effective in changing corporate culture quickly	• Can be a very expensive exercise, particularly where interstate or overseas recruits are involved
• Can provide for a more diverse workforce	• Evaluation of past work history more difficult

Methods of locating qualified job candidates

The effective use of internal sources requires a system for locating qualified job candidates and for enabling those who consider themselves qualified to apply for the opening. Qualified job candidates within the organisation can be located by computerised record systems, by vacancy bulletins or by recall of those who have been laid off.

Electronic record systems

With current Australian industry restructuring, many organisations are establishing data banks by way of a skills audit of staff. This audit provides for computerised information management systems – HRIMS (see Chapter 4). Specific HRIMS packages will allow an organisation to screen its entire workforce in a matter of minutes to locate suitable candidates to fill an internal opening. 'Resumix' is one such local software package.

These data can also be used to predict the career paths of employees and to anticipate when and where promotion opportunities for them may occur. Since the value of the data is contingent upon details being current, the record system must include provisions for recording changes in employee qualifications and job placements as they occur.

The intranet

Information concerning job openings may be communicated through the intranet in a vacancy bulletin or other form of newsletter. Other forms of communication include designated posting centres, employee publications, special announcement handouts and direct mail.

This system can provide many benefits to an organisation, but they may not be realised unless employees perceive the system as being administered in a fair and prudent way.[18] Therefore, in order to reap the full advantage of vacancy bulletins, organisations should consider the following when developing a system:

• competencies sought

• job content

• employee awareness

• posting periods

• applicant review procedure and feedback

• appeals procedure.[19]

Furthermore, job-posting functions more effectively when it is part of a career development program in which employees are made more aware of the opportunities within the organisation. Overall satisfaction with the intranet is also dependent upon the adequacy of the counselling given to system users and, of course, the visibility of the vacancies. This latter point is of particular relevance where a soft copy is used. Do all employees have access to a PC at work?

Recruiting outside the organisation

Unless there is to be a reduction in the workforce, any vacancy occurring within an organisation must eventually be filled with a replacement from the outside. Thus, when the organisation's CEO retires – or is retired – a chain reaction of promotions may subsequently occur. This creates other managerial, supervisory and staff openings. The question to be resolved, therefore, is not one of determining whether or not to bring people into the organisation, but rather one of determining the level at which they are brought in.

The labour market

The labour market, or the sources from which applicants are to be recruited, varies with the type of job to be filled and the remuneration for the job. Recruitment for executive or technical jobs requiring a high level of competence may be national or even international in scope. When staffing jobs that require relatively little skill, however, the labour market in which recruiting takes place may encompass a relatively small geographic area. The unwillingness of people to move may cause them to turn down offers of employment, thereby eliminating them from employment consideration beyond the local labour market. However, by offering an attractive level of compensation and by helping to defray moving costs, some applicants may be induced to move.

The ease with which employees are able to commute to work will also influence the boundaries of the labour market. The lack of suitable public transport or extreme congestion on the streets and freeways can limit the distance employees are willing to travel to work, particularly to jobs of low pay. Population migration from the cities to the suburbs has had its effect on labour markets. If suitable employment can be obtained near where they live, many people are less likely to accept or remain in jobs located in our central cities. Management will need to keep these factors in mind when deciding on the appropriate recruitment strategy to put in place.

In 2007, the Australian workplace passed the 10 million mark with unemployment falling below 5 per cent for the first time in 30 years. Phil Ruthven claims that this now means that the balance of power has shifted to a sellers' market with critical skills shortages appearing in a number of industries necessitating the import of labour from overseas. This trend is complemented by a fall in union membership to around 25 per cent of the workforce.[20] In essence, Ruthven is developing the same argument espoused in the federal government's *WorkChoices* reforms which are based on the notion that new working arrangements, based on a whole new mindset, must be developed by business. Alongside these trends, the current exit of the babyboomers and the emergence of Generation X and Y will require a complete rethink of current values and attitudes within the workforce.

Outside sources of recruitment

The outside sources from which employees are to be recruited will vary with the type of job to be filled. A computer programmer, for example, is not likely to be recruited from the same sources as a shop assistant. The condition of the labour market may also help to determine how productive a particular source will be. During periods of high unemployment, such as that in the early to mid-1990s (up to 11 per cent), an adequate supply of qualified applicants may be

obtained from among those who apply for work. A tight labour market may force the employer to advertise heavily or to seek assistance from local recruitment consultancies. The extent to which an organisation has been able to accomplish its affirmative action goals may be still another factor in determining the sources from which applicants are recruited. Typically, an employer at any given time will find it necessary to use several recruitment sources.

Furthermore, early studies have suggested that recruitment sources can affect an employee's subsequent tenure with the organisation. In general, applicants who find employment through informal sources, such as employee referrals and 'walk-ins,' tend to remain with the organisation longer than those employees recruited through the formal recruitment sources of advertisements and employment agencies.[21] These early findings, however, cannot be generalised to apply to all applicants. An organisation should conduct its own studies to determine the biographical factors that are related to employment tenure.

Recruiters also need to be aware of 'hot' areas within the labour market where there is a shortage in the supply of skilled people in a specific occupation. Faced with a critical shortage of qualified local lawyers, firms such as Allen Allen & Hemsley, PricewaterhouseCoopers and Freehills have pinpointed London and New York as places to source new recruits.[22]

Such 'hot' recruitment areas are not limited to the top end of town. Another area where shortages are well documented is the typical call centre. Not only is there currently a struggle to fill jobs but also to curb high levels of turnover associated with this area of work. Salaries are up, especially for call centre managers, alongside initiatives in development and career planning. Typical recruitment sources are being replaced with web-based recruitment technology. In addition, Prime Minister Howard has defended his *WorkChoices* legislation, in part at least, by pointing to the dire labour shortage across Australia.

Patrick Kiger provides the example of Chiron Corporation, a Silicon Valley bio-pharmaceutical company that requires recruits with scientific specialities so rare that only a handful of potential candidates in the world would qualify. Several of their recruiters spoke with the few specialist staff already employed to get their ideas on how or where such people look for work, if indeed they needed to look for work. The process arrived at was to establish focus groups whenever such a need arose whereby an image of the ideal candidate is developed right down to where they 'hang out' and which website they are likely to prefer.[23]

Advertisements

One of the most widely used methods for contacting applicants is through advertisements. While newspapers and journals constitute the media used most commonly, radio, television, billboards, posters, and even sound trucks have also been utilised. Advertising has the advantage of reaching a large audience of possible applicants. Some degree of selectivity can be achieved by using newspapers and journals that are directed towards a particular group of readers. Professional journals, trade journals and publications of unions and various non-profit organisations fall into this category.

The preparation of advertising copy for advertisements and recruitment literature is not only time-consuming, but also requires creativity when developing design and message content. Well-written advertisements 'highlight the major assets of the position, while being responsive to the job/career needs and concerns of the desired applicants.' An effective and attractive advertisement is important because, as one study showed, there appears to be a positive relationship between the accuracy and completeness of information being provided through advertisements, and recruitment success.

The aim of recruitment advertising is to make people aware that a vacancy exists and to persuade them to apply for the position. It is also an opportunity for the organisation to promote a specific corporate image.

Advertising can place a severe burden on the recruitment office. Even if the specifications for the openings are described thoroughly in the advertisement, many applicants who know they do not meet the job requirements may still be attracted. They may apply in the hope that the employer will not be able to obtain applicants who meet the specifications.

In times of high unemployment, it is usually necessary to insert into the advertisement a number of filters to prevent a deluge of unqualified applicants. David Wallage argues that during a recession, more than ever, advertisers must know their industry, audience and the status of the respective labour pool.[24] Exhibit 6.3 provides a number of ideas on how to get the best response to your advertisement.

Types of advertisements

Newspapers

The daily press is the most common and accepted method of recruitment advertising found in Australia. Nationwide dailies are the *Australian* and the *Financial Review*; metropolitan dailies include the Adelaide *Advertiser*, Melbourne *Age*, Brisbane *Courier Mail*, the *West Australian* and *Sydney Morning Herald*. A useful feature of these large-circulation newspapers is that they have specific employment sections with areas set aside for specialised fields of employment, such as hospital and medical, local government or computing. Another feature is the provision for display advertising. Such advertisements are found in the news sections as well as the classifieds.

Local suburban newspapers should not be ignored. While they have smaller classified sections, they are far less costly than the metropolitan dailies. For a fraction of the cost, a large advertisement can be run in the local press and, where employees are likely to be seeking work closer to home, it makes sense to use the local press. Once again, it is a matter of knowing your target market.

Professional journals

Whereas newspapers reach a mass market with a 'shotgun' approach, trade and professional journals reach a specific target group. Those reading the *Australian Accountant* will generally be accountants or employed in related jobs. The major problem with journals may be the time involved between the placement of the advertisement and its appearance. Some popular journals appear on a quarterly basis, which means a lengthy time lag that may not be possible to accommodate.

Exhibit 6.3   How to get the best response to your recruitment advertisement

Recruitment advertising has a more complex communication task than simply announcing positions that become available.

The best recruitment advertisement meets these essential criteria:

It must bring your recruitment message to the attention of as many members of the appropriate target audience as possible and motivate them to apply. In other words, it gets you the best possible applicants for the job you offer.

Sell the job

Your ads must seek out the best prospects, convince them of the benefits of working for your company, urge them to apply – and make applying easy. You must appeal to people in terms of their own interest. In other words, you must sell the job and sell your company department or section.

People will only accept a job for the benefits they get out of it.

The feeling of each ad must be one of people talking to people. To do this, a recruitment advertisement must be more than a 'job specification' – it needs to talk to the reader on a one-to-one basis.

Recruitment advertising acts as a form of corporate communication. It should project your company's corporate philosophy in a way that is inviting to potential applicants. The advertising should be seen to emanate from a 'people-oriented' company with the confidence to address the people it seeks with warmth and persuasiveness.

The advertising should reinforce the self-esteem of existing staff, at all levels. All employees like to see their employer look good – and your recruitment advertising is one more way to present your organisation well.

Copy style

The copy style should be friendly and informal, avoiding the 'job specification' stiffness which not only reduces the effectiveness of recruitment ads, but can portray the advertiser as aloof and remote, and therefore fail to attract the quality of applicant required.

- Write in the first person where possible. Use 'you' instead of 'the applicant' – he/she.

- Avoid cliches in the copy, e.g. 'applicants are invited,' 'write in the first instance,' 'a competent person,' 'we require the services' and 'the person we are seeking.'

- Remember your copy MUST BE gender neutral.

- Make it easy for the applicant to apply. List a phone number and a contact name so interested people can phone for more information.

    When advertising senior positions, put in an after-hours or weekend number for applicants to contact.

    The following copy checklist has been developed to help you prepare your recruitment advertising.

AIDA

Successful recruitment advertising has the same objective as all other advertising. It must SELL by attracting ATTENTION, stirring INTEREST, creating DESIRE, urging ACTION.

The acronym AIDA, formed from the words 'attention,' 'interest,' 'desire' and 'action,' will help you remember the basic selling aims of your advertisement.

COPY CHECKLIST

Name and logotype

Company name and address either at the top or base of your advertisement.

headlines

(Identification for your market)

- Write a headline. This does not necessarily have to be just a job title. However, to identify your audience it is better to use the job title as part of your headline.

- Job title. Some job titles are often not understood by people outside your company, e.g. 'Administration Officer Grade 3' has little meaning. Call the job what it is – 'Office Manager.'

Sub-head

- Location, salary or description of the department.

The job

- Size of the department (in relation to field of employment)
- Future projects/development
- Interest factors – facts about the company (don't assume that because you are a large organisation everyone knows what you do)
- Reason for appointment (promotion, expansion, new division)
- To whom responsible
- Duties
- Support (management and/or subordinate).

The requirements

- Education and training
- Qualifications.

Incentives

- Pay
- Benefits, inducements (overtime, bonus, car, pension, removal assistance, superannuation)
- Job satisfaction
- Working conditions/equipment
- Prospects/personal development
- Location and travel prospects
- Training
- Hours.

Action

Urge the reader to immediate action

- Call in person
- Telephone NOW for further information – area code in front of phone number, after-hours numbers for applicants to find out more
- Write.

Legalities

- Equal opportunity or anti-discrimination statement.

The above pointers are to help you prepare copy to get optimum response from your advertisement. Copy is only one of the elements of your advertisement; design and media selection are also paramount in reaching your target audience.

Your agency is always on hand to help you with all aspects of recruitment advertising.

– Neville Jeffress Advertising
Source: TMP Worldwide Advertising & Communications.

Recruitment agencies

Job Network

Until May 1998, each state maintained an employment service through the Commonwealth Employment Service, which was responsible for administering job search programs and unemployment benefits. From 1 May 1998 Job Network, a national network of specialist organisations, replaced the CES and now undertakes the placement of employees across a wide range of jobs throughout Australia.

Job Network consisted initially of more than 300 private, community and government organisations that competed to help people find the best possible position. The emphasis was and is on matching appropriately skilled and experienced employees to job vacancies, along with interview and job-search skills training.

Private consultants

As they charge quite substantial fees, private employment consultants are able to tailor their services to the specific needs of their corporate clients. It is common for some agencies to specialise in serving a specific occupational area or professional field.

Private employment consultancies differ in terms of services offered, professionalism and the calibre of their consultants. Where consultants are paid on a commission basis, their desire to do a professional job may be offset by their desire to earn a commission. Thus they may encourage jobseekers to accept jobs for which they are not suited and from which they may soon be terminated. When seeking the services of a private employment agency one should, therefore, exercise great care and caution (see Exhibit 6.4 below).

Most importantly, before signing an employment contract with an agency, a jobseeker should study the contract carefully, particularly the fine print.

Exhibit 6.4   Using consultants

When to use consultants	Tips for using consultants
High internal workload	Create a preferred supplier list.
Lack of specialised internal skills	Establish a strategic alliance.
Time constraints	Check credentials and track record.
Cost-effective	Big is not always better.
Short-term projects	Negotiate – you are in charge!
To free up internal resources for strategic purposes	Check on consultants' values.
HR manager may be too close to the problem	Talk to other clients.
Independence of the consultant	Seek lower rates for exclusivity.
No need to reinvent the wheel	Monitor and compare service provided.
Consultants may be seen as more credible	Consultants should make you feel that you are their only client.
Allows company to focus on core business.	Ensure the consultant takes the time to acclimatise.

Source: Bill Morrissey, Managing Director, Champion Pathfinder, Sydney.

Andrea Poe highlights the HR director's nightmare. The highly paid, widely sought new employee with the brilliant future has just decided to leave after a few short months. To make matters worse the exit date is just outside the 'warranty' period offered by the consulting company that has performed the recruitment exercise.[25] In such cases, the professional working relationship built up between the organisation and consultant will be tested. Typically, the consultant will want to maintain that relationship (and future contacts) and will be keen to come to a suitable agreement.

NEWS REPORT 6.5

Right for the job

There are telltale signs that show if your recruitment agency really has a talent for finding the right talent

What should clients expect from their recruitment agencies? Candidates to fill job vacancies, obviously, but it goes further than that.

Candidates with merely adequate qualifications aren't good enough when you are paying for a professional, specialised service. You should get quality talent that will stick around to improve the outcome of a project, or lift a team and the work environment if the placement is permanent.

The agency should take the pain out of the process with stringent applicant filtering that means you meet only the most suitable applicants. A strong agency may have a policy of sending no more than two candidates for a role unless a client requests otherwise. If it can't find a suitable candidate immediately, it should communicate the fact, not send through any resumes at all, and continue the search.

An approach like this builds loyalty and trust between client and agency. Once the tone is established, the client can feel confident the agency has their best interests at heart and is not looking for near-enough placements in the interests of a quick profit.

It is also important that recruiters care about everyone in their talent base – contractors as well as permanent placements. By having regular contact with contactors after they are appointed, agencies can identify issues before they become insurmountable. Meanwhile, the contactor feels like more than just another placement, increasing the likelihood of open communication and encouraging loyalty to both the recruiter and the client.

A key differentiator between a place-filler and a quality recruiter is the time they spend with clients defining jobs. Critical skills and qualities should be mapped accurately through probing discussion, even if the client can't pinpoint its requirements itself.

During the job-defining process, the recruiter should demonstrate sound industry knowledge and business acumen. Part of the recruiter's role is knowing what else is happening in the industry, which means attending events and briefings, reading publications and online outlets relevant to the sector and picking business leaders' brains on market issues. Ask your recruiter some broad, open-ended questions about what they see in the market and you'll soon find out if

they understand your business.

One a role is defined, an agency should act quickly and there should be constant, quality contact with the client. Progress updates should be offered with open discussion and questions on any issues that occur.

In a competitive market, value adding is another factor that separates run-of-the-mill suppliers from those striving to meet clients' needs. Value-adds that should be considered as core offerings include:

- the client's use of the recruiter's office for interviewing candidates
- fine-tuning of questions and style with the recruiter before interviews to ensure the candidates' strengths and weaknesses are probed effectively
- use of knowledge networks with access to industry and competitor information
- suggesting a different approach rather than persisting with the standard advertising model if it isn't bearing quality fruit.

If one person is carrying an account, the client is probably getting less than a comprehensive service. As well as the account

<table>
<tr><td>

manager and recruitment consultant, a back-office team should be dedicated to the task even if the account manager is the one point of contact (as is usual).

While the recruitment agency does the bulk of the work, the client's role is vital. Clients can help in many ways, such as by letting their recruiter know if they will have a position available in the future so talent can be 'pipe-lined.'

</td><td>

This is especially effective when seeing specialised or hard-to-find skills. Clients should make sure that, from the outset, they provide all the detailed information needed for the recruiter to do its job. Having to follow up for clarification is time-consuming, and missing information can lead to wasting time on unsuitable people.

If there are issues with the talent being sourced (or not sourced),

</td><td>

the client should let the recruiter know. How do you think the process is going? Is it on track? Are your expectations being met? The recruiting is aiming to keep you satisfied with quality placements and a smooth process, so if you'd like changes made to the process, suggest them.

Of course, the client also provides the budget, which should be sufficient for the task.

</td></tr>
</table>

Source: Deborah Howard, *hrmonthly*, May 2005.
Deborah Howard is managing director of the recruitment firm Diversiti, an Accenture business.

Executive search firms

In contrast to public and private employment agencies, the function of executive search firms (often called head-hunters) is not to find positions for jobseekers. Their role is to seek out candidates with the qualifications that match the requirements of the positions that their client firm is seeking to fill. Executive search firms generally do not advertise in the public media for job candidates, nor do they accept a fee from the individual being placed.

The fees charged by search firms may be about one-third of the annual remuneration package for the position to be filled. In the US this fee, or a major percentage of it, is paid by the client firm whether or not the recruiting efforts result in an individual being hired. In Australia, the situation is different in that few, if any, costs are paid unless an effective placement is made. In addition, most reputable search firms will 'guarantee' their selection, although the extent of this guarantee varies between companies. It is claimed that the majority of positions with packages in excess of $100 000 are filled by search strategies, but this claim is supported more by anecdotal evidence than academic research. Since high-calibre executives are in short supply, a significant number of the nation's largest corporations use search firms to obtain such executives.

Some authors claim that the most suitable applicants will often never see a newspaper advertisement, and that is where the advantage of search firms becomes evident. Search firms will use their extensive information networks to determine who the most suitable candidates are and then persuade them to make the move.

The approach taken by executive search and selection consultants Hamilton, James and Bruce is shown in Exhibit 6.5.

Educational institutions

Educational institutions are typically a source of young applicants with formal training, but with relatively little full-time work experience. Secondary schools are usually a source of employees for trainee professional, clerical and blue-collar jobs. TAFE colleges, with their various types of specialised training, can provide candidates for technical jobs. These institutions can also be a source of applicants for a variety of white-collar jobs, including those in the sales and retail fields. Some management trainee jobs are also staffed from this source. Some organisations target the part-time evening student, who may have up to 20 years' experience.

Exhibit 6.5   Executive search and selection approach

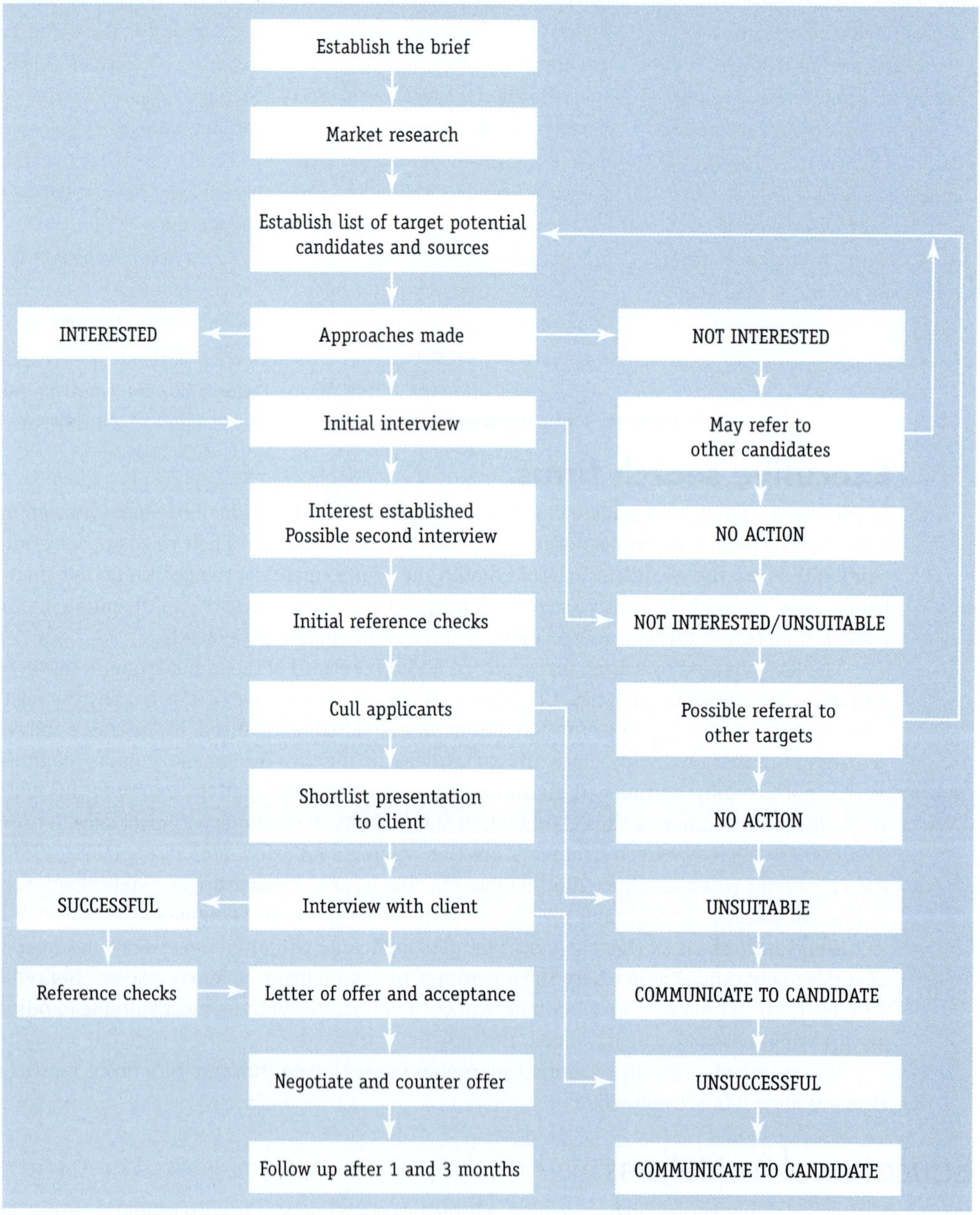

Source: Courtesy Hamilton, James and Bruce.

When filling technical and managerial positions, college and university graduates generally provide the primary source. Unfortunately for college graduates, the supply of applicants with undergraduate and even higher degrees is increasingly exceeding the available openings. Particular difficulty is experienced by graduates with degrees in the liberal arts, although some executives claim to prefer graduates with a broad background. The recruiters who represent these employers, however, tend to seek out people with specialised training who can make an

immediate contribution in the jobs where they are placed. Some liberal arts majors have also made themselves more attractive to employers by gaining work experience through part-time or temporary work.

The campus interview is the main strategy used to recruit college and university students. Major employer representatives attend each participating campus over several days, with final-semester students making appointments with them for interview.

Skilful solutions

What can organisations do to avoid skill shortages?

Bridget Hogg MAHRI

Principal Consultant, HR Development at Work

Today's HR manager needs to take a three-pronged approach to addressing skills shortages. Firstly they need to develop internal strategies to enhance attraction and retention. Secondly they should help senior managers understand why the national skills shortage is happening and the impact it will have on the organisation. And finally, they need to lead the charge in assisting the senior team to influence the macro-economic environment (via industry bodies, educational establishments and the government).

Retaining staff involves understanding and then meeting the expectations of the workforce. Developing employee value propositions (EVPs) is a good way to ensure that the organisation is considering what matters to its staff. EVPs can address key factors that impact on retention, such as career development, a sense of belonging and the need for flexibility. Propositions may include: 'Work here and you will have a senior manager as your mentor' or 'Work here and choose the hours that you work.' Once written, EVPs should then be communicated to staff in as many ways as possible (for example, on the company website, in advertisements, during interviews and induction) and, of course, the organisation must meet all the commitments made.

Effective organisations also find out why people leave (using surveys and exit interviews) and then address the issues raised. Key factors which contribute to high staff turnover include: an ineffective and aggressive management culture; lack of meaningful, interesting work; a perceived breach of the psychological contract; workplace bullying; and employees feeling neglected and unappreciated.

Organisations that will overcome the skills shortage will be those that have helped managers to accept their role in managing retention.

Kerry Fallon Horgon

Managing Partner, Flexibility at Work

These days retention is about more than money. The key to attracting and retaining the best possible staff is to create and sustain high-performing, flexible workplace cultures. These cultures include a purposeful, respectful, supportive workplace offering flexible work options as well as competitive pay and benefits.

Achieving work/life balance is a high priority whether the employee comes from generations X or Y, or is a baby boomer or older worker, and for many people this balance rates higher than salary or promotion. Nevertheless, for most employees experiencing work intensification and the expectation to work longer hours, work/life balance is more about rhetoric than reality. For the individual the results can be devastating – stress, burnout and associated health and relationship problems. For organisations, the long-term consequences include high staff turnover, lost productivity, increased workers' compensation claims and premiums, increased absenteeism and sick leave leading to skill shortages.

My recent research into strategies for managing excessive workloads has shown the need to address this issue at both the organisational-culture level and in terms of individual responsibility. The change required needs ongoing commitment, particularly by senior management, to address the underlying issues of values in action, attitudes, behaviours and what gets rewarded at work. This process of cultural change needs to be reinforced by an extensive performance management system that measures and rewards people in terms of climate, culture, values, diversity, succession planning and recruitment, supporting 'employer of choice' achievement.

An important starting point to facilitate such organisational change is senior management coaching at both an individual and team level.

Collin Beams CAHRI

Principal, WRDI (Workplace Relationship Development Indicator) Institute

Retention offers the highest return on investment (ROI) of any HR initiative. Notwithstanding this, many firms have historically adopted a reactive approach to addressing turnover – it has simply been accepted as the cost of doing business! Market forces (particularly given the imminent skill and talent shortages) will in future dictate a new retention mindset.

A key concept important in attracting and retaining skilled staff is the 'psychological contract.' It represents the mix of tangible and intangible factors that an organisation offers an employee (or 'the deal'). The tangible elements include things like pay, bonuses and superannuation. While businesses have to be competitive in terms of pay and other rewards, it's often the intangibles that are more important. For example, in the contemporary workplace, employees are seeing job challenge, a 'voice,' open communication, autonomy, opportunities to learn and grow, more flexible work practices and so on.

It is critical that firms deliver on 'the deal,' and that healthy dialogue is continually maintained between management and employees. To that end, recent advancements in HR metrics now provide firms with the ammunition to manage retention scientifically and proactively. Traditional exit interviews and focus groups are now regarded as limited or outdated methodologies. The HR metrics approach offers hard data upon which to identify organisational 'hot spots' and take confident action towards addressing retention risk. Turnover cost savings may be up to 2.5 times the salary of the job in question, but there are often other lasting organisational benefits as the key drivers of retention are also key drivers of performance.

Source: Interviews by Paul Somerville, *hrmonthly*, July 2005.

Employee referrals

Traditional recruitment strategies such as newspapers and the Internet have the potential to attract numerous applications, many of which may be unsuitable yet take great amounts of time to assess.

A more effective method may be to use a process of employee referrals. HR managers have found that the quality of employee-referred applicants is normally quite high as employees are generally hesitant to refer people who will not perform well once employed. Negative factors associated with the use of employee referrals include the possibility of 'inbreeding' and violation of equal employment opportunity policies. Since employees and their referrals tend to have similar backgrounds, employers who rely heavily on employee referrals to fill job openings may intentionally or unintentionally screen out, and thereby discriminate against, target group members. Stated simply, the status quo is maintained. Furthermore, organisations may choose not to employ relatives of current employees. The hiring of relatives, referred to as nepotism, can create charges of favouritism, especially in appointments to desirable positions. One creative approach encourages all employees to act as de facto recruitment consultants with effective (i.e. successful)

referrals rewarded by monetary payments. State Street Australia Ltd and JP Morgan pay their employees $500 per successful referral on the basis that the new employee satisfies probationary criteria. Employer of choice Cisco pays $1500 to employees for every successful placement.

Mulberger suggests a slightly different approach where organisations develop an 'alumni society' of former employees who will speak highly of the organisation as an employer of choice.[26] This approach will most likely be effective where employees leave with positive feelings towards their former employer. If this is not the case it is unlikely that anything positive will be passed on to prospective employees.

Unsolicited applications and résumés

Many employers receive unsolicited applications and résumés from individuals who may or may not be good prospects for employment. Even though the percentage of acceptable applicants from this source may not be high, it is a source that cannot be ignored.

Good public relations requires that any person contacting an organisation for a job be treated with courtesy and respect. If there is no possibility of employment in the organisation for the present or the future, the applicant should be tactfully but frankly informed of this fact. Telling the applicant to 'fill out an application, and we will keep it on file' when there is no hope of employment, is easy but not particularly ethical.

Professional organisations

Many professional organisations, such as the Australian Human Resources Institute, offer a placement service as one of their benefits for members. Listings of members seeking employment may be advertised in their journals and newsletters, or publicised at their local meetings. Current professional vacancies are shown in the same way.

Unions

In the past, unions have been a principal source of applicants for blue-collar and for some professional jobs. Some unions, such as those in the printing, shipping and construction industries, maintained hiring services that provided a supply of applicants, particularly for short-term needs. Furthermore, because of the power some unions exercised over hiring practices, employers who wanted to avoid confrontation found it prudent to use the union service. This has certainly been the case in the building industry in Australia. Legislation enacted and implemented in most states and federally, will modify, if not eliminate, this practice. The Howard government is committed to ending any practices that give any hint of compulsory unionism.

Executive leasing and contracting

In the past, temporary help has been restricted to office duties such as secretarial services. Over the past 10 years, this field has expanded to executive-level employees who come into an organisation on a short-term basis, often with a specific project in mind. Several large consulting firms, including Manpower, Drake, Mercer Cullen Egan Dell and Lee Hecht Harrison, have moved into this field in recent years. While the concept has advantages insofar as the arrangement can save money and recruiting time, and is extremely flexible in terms of what the leased executive is able to do, there may be problems concerning loyalty and commitment to the organisation.

With the dramatic increase in the number of organisations using outsourcing strategies, the use of contractors will add a new dimension to the flexible and mobile workforces that so many companies are attempting to build. As a case in point, in more recent times a number of public and private organisations have outsourced their entire human resource function to contracting organisations such as those mentioned above.

Deloitte Resources reports that of the 70 per cent of employers needing contract accounting, tax and finance staff have maintained or increased their use of such staff despite mixed economic conditions. It seems that while employers are looking for a more flexible workforce, employees are seeking more freedom and choice, leading to a win–win outcome.[27]

e-cruitment

After a slow start in Australia, online recruiting has finally become a significant option. Only a few years ago the ANZ Series was the benchmark in terms of the number of jobs advertised in daily newspapers but today measures such as the Olivier Job Index are given increasing attention. This index measures the volume of jobs advertised on the Internet and recorded a rise in almost every month of 2000. Indeed, advertising on the major sites – Seek, CareerOne and MyCareer – increased by 85 per cent during that year. Robert Olivier says that the future is clear – the Internet is replacing newspapers as the number one source of candidates.[28] The reasons for this drastic change in advertising behaviour seem clear. Kerry Sunderland suggests that there are three main advantages with e-cruitment:

- Lower costs – advertising online is often cheaper than in the print media.

- Increased exposure – online jobs can be viewed 24 hours a day, seven days a week.

- Speed – an almost immediate response by candidates is possible.[29]

The future of online recruitment seems assured with players such as Seek.com offering a whole new range of tools and services to both recruiters and jobseekers (see News report 6.7). For recruiters, Seek.com offers discrete zones in much the same way that newspapers segment the labour market with sections devoted to specific job/occupation groups. A profile section is also available where an organisation's detailed profile can be accessed, which also links to current vacancies and role statements. For the job seeker there is the benefit of having their résumé available online to both corporate recruiters and consultants, as well as the speed of job listing by email on a daily basis. All jobs listed have been pre-matched against personal criteria. In addition, applicants have access to online psychometric testing with many of the players.[30]

As a case in point, Stamford Hotels and Resorts, employing over 2200 people in 10 hotels across Australia, has pulled out of newspaper advertising entirely to focus on Internet recruiting. High turnover rates along with the high costs of newspaper advertising have led to their decision. Stamford has entered into a strategic alliance with Seek.com to provide the service required.[31]

NEWS REPORT 6.7

Nets catch the right people for the job

Companies are saving money and getting quicker results by using their intranets and websites to recruit staff

Increasingly, intranets and websites are being used to recruit staff, enabling some companies to reduce their dependence on classified advertising and recruitment consultants to fill positions. The pay-off, they say, is that positions are being filled faster and recruitment costs are much lower. The computer networking company Cisco Systems says its recruitment advertising costs are down more than 50% since 2000, when it started using its intranet to advertise positions.

When Alec Bashinsky joined Cisco two years ago as group manager of human resources, about 50 recruitment firms around Australia were providing candidates for about 95% of all Cisco positions. Bashinsky now uses only eight firms. 'I'm not very popular [with recruitment firms] as a result,' he says.

All positions at Cisco are displayed simultaneously on its intranet and public Internet sites. 'We have just upgraded our sites to include every position available at Cisco all over the world,' Bashinsky says. 'The only positions we advertise solely on our intranet are those that require Cisco-specific skills.' (An intranet operates like an Internet site. The difference is that only employees of the company have access to it. Intranets display information such as company news, rules and regulations of the organisation and, increasingly, staff vacancies.)

Bashinsky also established a staff referral program. 'Within six months, we were doing 55% of our recruiting through internal referrals,' he says. 'We offer $1 500 to employees for referrals and we find this a more effective method of sourcing candidates than educating a consultant about what we want. Once someone has been at Cisco for a while, they know the type of person we would be after.'

Cisco was never a large user of classified advertising. 'The IT [information technology] industry is very specialised and we found classified advertising just didn't work for us,' he says. 'We might run some graduate recruitment ads but that's all.'

Cisco's website allows applicants to build resumes and store them on the site. 'Having resumes stored in a set format allows us to be able to search by job role or skill set,' Bashinsky says. 'The difficulty other websites face is that they just ask candidates to send through a resume, and this makes it a monumental task to find the right person. In effect, because we now have a large database of resumes, we've become our own recruitment company.'

Bashinsky says one of the disadvantages of advertising on the Internet is that, when a position is posted globally, Cisco is inundated with overseas applicants who want to work in Australia. 'The issue for us is how to manage the global recruitment process,' he says.

In a study of the best employers to work for in Australia, released earlier this year by the management consultancy Hewitt Associates, Cisco ranked first among companies with fewer than 1 000 staff. Bashinsky says this has prompted an increase in the number of people wanting to work for the company. Cisco does not have a big turnover. Bashinsky says turnover has been 5 to 6% for each of the past six years (the information technology industry's average is 25%).

Another company that relies on its intranet to recruit staff is SingTel Optus. Julie Coleman, director of human resources at the telecommunications company, says it has been using its intranet to recruit staff for six years. It now spends 90% less on recruitment companies and classified advertising than it did two years ago. 'This reduction is very significant, especially in these times where cost-cutting is such an issue,' Coleman says. 'Around one-third of positions are filled through our intranet. The positions are also advertised on our public Internet site prior to using external sources.'

Coleman says the number of positions advertised on the intranet varies according to the time of year and how the economy is performing. Optus does not comment on staff turnover numbers. Late last year, Optus, to cut costs, announced a retrenchment program, Operation Win Through. In November, it said it would cut 561 jobs – 344 permanent, 217 contract – to reduce its costs by $100 million by 2003. This move followed the announcement in October of 350 redundancies in contract and permanent positions.

A year ago, Optus launched an employee referral program that offers incentives to staff if they recommend candidates for positions. 'Staff receive Myer-Grace Bros gift vouchers if they refer someone to us,' Coleman says. 'On average, 15% of new positions are filled this way.'

Coleman says Optus turns to external media such as newspaper ads to recruit staff only if it cannot fill the position via the intranet and Internet. 'As applicants apply directly to the Optus website, we have a huge database of candidates,' she says. 'When a position becomes available, we can review this resource and determine whether there is someone suitable.'

Speed is one of the key advantages of using an intranet to recruit staff. 'The average time taken to recruit someone is between two and three weeks, which is very quick,' Coleman says. 'We also make the recruitment process as transparent as possible, so candidates are confident all applications are being reviewed seriously. If any employee has applied for a position and is unsuccessful, they will receive a telephone call, not an email, to discuss which areas need development in order to help them be more successful next time they apply.'

Use of intranet and company websites to fill staff vacancies is hurting recruitment firms and newspaper publishers. But Phil Davis, the Australian and New Zealand managing director of recruitment company Robert Half International, says that, although more companies are advertising positions on their intranets, recruitment firms still have a big role. 'The reason recruitment companies are still prevalent is that they fill positions for a living and are good at it,' Davis says. 'A company's core business is not recruitment and the recruitment process is so important that it needs to get it right. If a company wants to be able to get the best candidates for a position, they are more likely to get them through using a recruitment company.'

Davis says people looking for jobs also need recruitment companies. 'If someone knows that they want to work for Telstra, then it would make sense for them to go direct to the company. However, if an accountant wants a general accounting position, then they would be better off registering with a recruitment company as it would have positions from a wide range of companies at its fingertips.'

Classified job advertising is a key source of revenue for many newspaper publishers, including John Fairfax Holdings, the owner of *The Sydney Morning Herald*, *The Age*, *The Australian Financial Review* and *BRW*. Nigel Dews, the chief executive of f2, Fairfax's online division, says advertising positions on intranets is an effective way for companies to recruit staff. 'However, you get the best people to fill jobs when you are advertising in the biggest market places, and this means in the classifieds and on sites such as mycareer.com.au [Fairfax's Internet job site],' he says. 'This way, you are not relying solely on people who may seek you out on the Web. People will fill jobs by advertising on their intranet or public Internet sites, but when you consider how busy the Web is, I'm not sure that they get the best candidates.'

That print classified job advertising volumes have been erratic over the past six months, says Dews, is attributable to the 'classic economic downturn' rather than an increase in the use of intranets by companies to recruit staff. 'The drop in classified advertising was brought on by a period of great uncertainty,' he says. 'In times of uncertainty, the first thing you do is rein in your advertising and your expansion plans.'

Intranets and company websites are not the only form of Internet-based recruitment. Sites such as Monster.com, Seek.com.au and mycareer.com.au carry many job ads. 'This week, we have around 22 000 on mycareer.com.au and last week we had 26 000,' Dews says. 'We tend to run about half this number in our newspapers. Although there are more jobs advertised online, this does not mean they are substitutes for what would have run in the newspaper. There were never 26 000 jobs [a week] advertised in the papers. Also, the cheaper cost of advertising online means companies advertise jobs that were previously uneconomical to advertise in newspapers.'

Dews believes that the print and online media work well together. 'You get different results from both,' he says. 'By advertising in the front section of *The Sydney Morning Herald* or *The Age* you can get people who weren't actually looking for jobs who see an ad and apply. By advertising jobs online you definitely get people who are focused on looking for jobs.'

Scott Mewing, a director of the recruitment company Michael Page International, says he is not worried about the impact of intranet job ads on his industry. 'Three years ago, people were saying the Internet would completely change the way people advertised for positions,' he says. 'However, it is apparent that the Internet has just become another tool, and it is not the tail wagging the dog. It has definitely affected us in a number of ways, in particular in the way we service candidates. We receive 300 applications over the Internet every day, so we need to work out how to service this number properly.'

Mewing says cost is encouraging the use of intranets to promote vacancies. 'Advertising a position on an intranet or a company's public Internet is free

to the organisation,' he says. 'This situation will put pressure on newspapers, although newspapers say one of their main advantages is that they are able to pick up the casual reader while not everyone has access to the Internet. Most companies use a number of tools. There is no one trend.'

Dews says that companies will use a combination of newspapers, Internet sites and intranets to find recruits. 'You want to make sure you are getting the best person for the job,' he says. 'The real cost is not whether you advertise with us or internally on your intranet; it is the cost of making the wrong hiring decision and having to go through the hiring process again in 12 months.'

Source: Gayle Bryant.

Exhibit 6.6   The Internet v. the newspapers

Year	Internet ads per year	Newspaper ads per year
2000	1 532 553	328 417
2001	1 272 893	240 574
2002	1 094 272	254 980
2003	1 167 876	249 396
2004	1 497 797	264 250
2005	1 935 296	253 827
Jan–Jun '06	1 447 692	140 982

Source: The Olivier Group, 2006.

Applications

Organisations generally make use of one or more methods of accepting employee applications. Whatever method is used, this should be spelt out clearly in the job advertisement along with the name of a fully prepared contact person who may be approached for additional information.

Applications made in person

This method is commonly used for short-term employment and also where large numbers of day labourers are sought. Where the applicant is successful, the new employee will commence work almost immediately.

In other cases, applicants 'drop in' to seek information about possible future vacancies. In such cases, no advertisement has been placed, but nevertheless a procedure is required to deal with this category of applicant. Certainly, they should not be ignored simply because they are operating outside the system.

Telephone applications

Where large numbers of applications are anticipated, it is generally wise to use the telephone as a screening device. Those persons calling in who do not match the predetermined selection criteria are politely turned away. This technique will, of course, require fully trained telephone interviewers who will most likely take the applicant quickly through a checklist based on the selection criteria.

Impulse applicants can also be persuaded to take their application further by the telephone interviewer. Many people will not commit themselves to writing, but will pick up the telephone.

Of great importance is the person chosen either as contact person or telephone interviewer. Organisations may spend thousands of dollars on advertising and placement only to have it all go wrong when the contact person picks up the telephone with minimal knowledge of the company and the job being filled. For those persons who 'survive' the telephone interview, application forms may be sent or résumés called for. In some cases, the applicant may be called in for a formal interview.

Application forms

Many medium to large organisations will have a specifically designed application form. In some cases several forms will be used according to the job to be filled and the type of information sought.

The main advantage of using an application form is that it will contain standardised information on each applicant and is subsequently of great use in shortlisting against selection criteria. Specific information can be found in the same place on each candidate's form. This is not always the case with résumés. Only essential information should be sought on an application form. Thirty years ago, it was commonplace to find questions pertaining to every facet of an applicant's life and many sought information on their parentage! Today, equal employment opportunity and privacy legislation has addressed these issues, and guidelines as to what type of information might be acceptably sought can be obtained from organisations such as the Human Rights Commission or the Privacy Committees (where they exist) in each state.

Résumés

In many cases, organisations will ask applicants to forward their résumé rather than have them complete an application form. It may be that the organisation sees this practice as being more professional or it could simply be a case of professional snobbery. Where senior positions are involved or where the information sought is highly varied, standard applications may be passed over in favour of a personal résumé. Where the decision is taken to ask for a résumé, the advertisement should be clear in terms of the information to be included. Requirements in terms of referees should also be clarified.

Response analysis

As mentioned above, it makes little sense to spend a lot of money on advertising in an attempt to attract a highly qualified pool of applicants only to have this good work undermined by a negative telephone response or no response at all. It is not only courteous but good public relations to acknowledge written applications. A simple envelope-sized card will suffice. Where e-cruitment is used instant feedback is given.

In addition, it is essential that recruiters collect and collate information on the source of applications. A yield rate on each source can be useful in later decisions as to where advertising may be placed. A simple question on the application form will tell recruiters where the applicant heard about the job.

Organisational recruiters

Who performs the recruitment function depends largely on the size of the organisation. There appear to be no strict rules here. For large organisations like BHP and TNT, professional HRM

recruiters are hired and trained to obtain new employees. In smaller organisations, recruitment may be conducted by an HRM generalist; or if the organisation has no HRM position, then recruitment is carried out by managers or supervisors.

General Motors (North America) has switched from a devolved to a highly centralised model to strengthen its employment brand in an effort to erase the image of GM as old-fashioned, highly bureaucratic and dominated by white males. At the same time, Kellogg with 14 000 employees across the world has commenced outsourcing the entire function![32]

Regardless of who does the recruiting, it is important to remember that recruiters have an influence on applicants' job decisions. Recruiters are often a main reason why applicants select one organisation over another. Recruiters who are enthusiastic, knowledgeable, friendly and prepared are more likely to be successful than those who exhibit negative personal characteristics. This occurs because applicants are likely to make inferences about the organisation and the recruiter's intentions that are based on the recruiter's characteristics.

Outsourcing recruitment

Over the past few years there has been a move towards outsourcing recruitment altogether. The concept appears to be one of freeing up internal HR people to get on with developing corporate strategy and policy and let the experts do what they do best. Another view is that recruiting is rarely ever going to be core business so why are we involved?

In 1999 the Department of Finance and Administration outsourced all of its HR services to PricewaterhouseCoopers, while in 2000 labour hire company Manpower won the Department of Defence recruitment contract. This followed on from a failed yet expensive campaign by the department to fill job vacancies.[33] The success or otherwise of such ventures will depend most often on the effectiveness of the strategic partnerships that are put in place.

Realistic job previews

Another way for organisations to increase the effectiveness of their recruitment efforts is to provide job applicants with a realistic job preview. A realistic job preview (RJP) informs applicants about all aspects of the job, including the desirable and undesirable facets of the position. In contrast, a typical job preview only presents the job in positive terms. The RJP may also include a tour of the work area, combined with a discussion of any negative health or safety considerations. Proponents of the RJP believe that applicants who are given realistic information regarding a position are more likely to remain on the job and be successful, because there will be fewer unpleasant surprises.

Some current research

Roger Collins and CCH Australia (2004) have studied the extent to which recruitment, assessment and selection practices are indeed strategic within Australian organisations. Only 37 per cent of respondents reported that they undertook HR planning and then linked the resulting plan with the organisation's strategic plan. Eleven per cent did not link their plans, 33 per cent relied on 'informal' plans and 18 per cent had no HRM planning.

Another area researched was the decision to 'make' or 'buy.' 'Makes' rely on strategies to grow their own people. 'Buys' are those recruited from external sources for a variety of reasons. Exhibit 6.7 shows the results of the research.

Additional findings show that 67 per cent of respondents reported that they did develop behavioural attributes as part of their recruitment and retention strategies.

Exhibit 6.7 Proportion of 'makes' versus 'buys' expressed as percentages for selected employee categories (N = 259)

Employee category	'Makes'	'Buys'	No preferred option	Not sure	Total (%)
Senior executive management	35	28	37	0	100
Middle management	58	14	27	1	100
Accounting/finance	19	51	29	1	100
IT	13	58	27	2	100
HR	24	40	31	5	100
Professional (eg lawyers)	7	53	23	17	100
Marketing	21	35	27	17	100

Print media still dominates as a strategy to attract candidates. Growth strategies were referrals, alumni referrals and poaching.

The Internet and intranet have also experienced rapid growth over the past five years with 81 per cent utilising these strategies.[34] Note that these findings are at odds with statistics shown at Exhibit 6.7.

In a separate study, Kramar (2006) reports that recruitment agencies and consultants were used for managerial (41 per cent) and professional/technical (39.3 per cent) positions while advertisements were most frequently used for clerical (38.4 per cent) and manual (38.4 per cent) positions. More than a third of organisations (35.9 per cent) used internal methods to fill managerial vacancies.[35]

These two studies show a consistency in terms of organisational level and referred recruitment channels. The following section explores the international dimension of employee staffing.

Exhibit 6.8   The international perspective

The main emphasis of this book has been on the domestic operations of Australian organisations. Increasingly, however, many organisations have begun to extend their businesses into overseas markets, with divisions, joint ventures or strategic alliances. Conversely, many foreign interests have bought into Australian companies as part of their global business strategies.

The reduction of some traditional Australian export markets and the expansion of others (e.g. Vietnam, the People's Republic of China); new regional trading groups (e.g. the European Union, ASEAN); new tariff agreements (e.g. APEC); and an overall focus on east and south-east Asian countries, have encouraged organisations to develop international business strategies which necessarily require accompanying international recruitment and retention strategies.

Multicultural workforces, both at home and abroad, require innovative HRM practices, and the management of Australian expatriates can demand quite diverse strategies.

SOURCES OF MANAGERS FOR INTERNATIONAL ORGANISATIONS

Exhibit 6.9 illustrates the interaction between the three dimensions of country, type of employee, and HR functions in IHRM. As it indicates, the three possible sources of multinational enterprise (MNE) managers are home country nationals (or expatriates), host country (or local) nationals, or third country nationals.

Home country nationals (HCNs) are managers from the organisation's headquarters, host country nationals are employees from the particular overseas country involved, and third country nationals may be natives of any country other than the home or host country. For example, a German national may be assigned as the manager of an Australian subsidiary or hotel chain in Malaysia.

Using each of the three sources of overseas managers presents advantages and disadvantages. These are some of the more important advantages:

- Home country nationals (expatriates) – talent available within company; greater control; company experience; mobility; experience provided to corporate executives

- Host country nationals (locals) – less cost; preference of host country governments; intimate knowledge of environment; language facility

- Third country nationals – broad experience; international outlook; multilingualism.

Most (MNEs) use all three sources for staffing their international operations, although some companies and countries exhibit a distinct bias for one of the three sources. Negandhi suggests that third country nationals are generally less frequently used, but that home country nationals are often chosen in the first stages of international business development, and host country nationals in subsequent stages.[36] Dowling and Schuler note that the choice of an overseas manager reflects the overall staffing policies of the MNE, the country of operation, and the desired attributes of their position.[37] Such policies can be ethnocentric, polycentric, regiocentric or geocentric.

Ethnocentric approaches are headquarters centred, with all key jobs being held by home country personnel. Thus many US and Japanese MNEs may recruit local employees at lower levels, but key managers come from the US or Japan. This is also usually the case for Australian organisations in their first overseas ventures.

Polycentric strategies treat subsidiaries as distinct national entities, employing host country nationals at senior management level.

Regiocentric policies are also locally based, but within broad regions or geographic areas. Some American hotel chains, for example, have regional offices for the Asia–Pacific region, with Australian managers based in Australia.

Geocentric approaches 'ignore nationality in favour of ability as part of worldwide business strategies'.[38] German organisations may employ Hong Kong managers (third country nationals), in Africa, Europe and Australasia. This option is likely to be the strategic choice of committed multinational organisations in mature stages of development. Each policy choice 'is not dictated by product-market or industry logic; each approach represents a different way of coping with the different socio-cultural environments of a multinational company'.[39]

Operationally, decisions regarding the appropriate source of manager will consider their technical competence, functional area of expertise, career plans, personal preferences, health status and personality attributes. These and other prerequisites for overseas assignments will be examined more thoroughly in the next chapter.

Exhibit 6.9   A model of international HRM

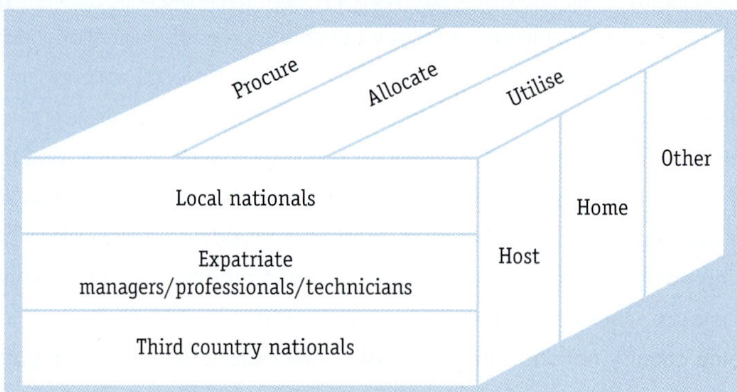

Source: Morgan P.V., 'International human resource management, fact or fiction?' *Personnel Administrator*, Alexandria VA, September 1986, p. 44. Reprinted with the permission of *HR Magazine*, published by the Society for Human Resource Management, Alexandria, VA; permission conveyed through Copyright Clearance Center, Inc.

Retention of key people

In the past, great emphasis has often been placed on attracting key people but there appears little research on the extent to which organisations go to retain those same people. With today's emphasis on the so-called war for talent it seems that many organisations have switched their efforts to this vital area of HRM. Attracting key people is only one dimension, the other is keeping them. It should go without saying that the starting point is effective recruitment and selection processes. An employee must 'fit' with the organisation's people and culture from the outset or very soon after.

Nicholas Way argues that there are three key requirements that organisations need to address if they are to retain their talent. They must create a great environment, great jobs and great leadership. Good people will no longer 'work for a jerk' if given the chance of something better, and leaders need to acknowledge this fact.[40] This is particularly true when attempting to attract and retain employees from Generation X and Y who no longer fit in or accept many of the paradigms of their leaders, who in a vast majority of cases will be from the babyboomer era.

What are the retention levers?

According to a survey conducted by Audrey Page and Associates, the key retention strategies are better work–family balance and career development opportunities. The survey concluded that organisations can either pay their people better or try to understand them better, with the latter being seen as more effective by those surveyed.[41]

Anderson and Pulich agree with these sentiments while reinforcing the view that younger workers now entering the workforce have different priorities to their older leaders. They will look for remuneration comparable to what their external peers receive but this alone will not retain them. They will look for respect and trust, professional growth, positive leadership and work–family balance.[42] This view supports the notion that no remuneration or incentive scheme will retain high performers who thrive on challenge and rapid change.

There are numerous strategies that employers can use to retain their key people but possibly the most effective is to simply sit down to a one-on-one session with them and ask what it will take to keep them. Given the costs, both direct and indirect, of first losing and then replacing key staff this concept seems all too simple but it also seems to be a far better approach than

conducting the traditional exit interview after the employee has decided to leave! Exhibit 6.10 shows those retention strategies often used in contemporary organisations while Exhibit 6.11 lists the direct and indirect costs incurred in losing and replacing valued employees.

Exhibit 6.10   How to retain key people

• Insider hiring – sweeteners to stay	• Variable remuneration
• Deferred bonus scheme	• Sabbaticals
• Off-shore business travel	• 3–4 day working weeks
• Career path	• Paid university education
• Work–life balance	• Create great work environment
• Create great jobs/leaders	• Remove the 'dinosaurs'
• Allow autonomy/stretch	• Frequent career 'fireside' chats
• Ask them!	• Packaged salaries

Exhibit 6.11   Cost of lost key people

DIRECT

- Recruitment/selection/orientation/training
- Loss of performance/productivity

INDIRECT

- Effects on workload
- Negative impact on colleagues
- Possible loss of customers

OPPORTUNITY

- Loss of intellectual capital
- Loss of corporate memory

Summary

Effective recruitment requires effective planning to determine the specific HR needs of the organisation on the requirements of the positions to be staffed that establish the qualifications of the applicants to be recruited and selected. Employers find it advantageous to fill as many openings as possible above the entry level by means of internal promotion. However, some jobs above the entry level require reliance upon outside sources.

These outside sources are also utilised to fill positions requiring special qualifications, to avoid excessive inbreeding, and to obtain new ideas and technology. The specific outside sources and methods utilised in recruiting depend upon the recruitment goals of the organisation, the conditions of the labour market, and the specifications of the position to be filled.

The legal requirements governing equal employment opportunity make it mandatory that employers exert a positive effort to attract and promote members of target groups so that their representation at all levels within the organisation approximates their proportionate numbers in the labour market. These efforts include recruiting not only those members who are qualified, but also those who can become qualified with reasonable training and assistance.

In addition, Australian governments and business organisations have come to realise that we are influenced by, and can have a significant impact upon, a growing world economy. 'Internationalism,' 'globalism' and 'new world order' are the buzz words of today. In our region the concepts of a Pacific rim and an Asian trading bloc have encouraged Australian organisations to review their alliances and economic priorities. The breakdown of the Eastern European bloc and the establishment of the European Union have provided new challenges and new opportunities for innovative Australian organisations. Current discussions at the highest level on free trade agreements with the People's Republic of China will open up markets never thought possible just a few years ago.

The effectiveness of our ventures in both Asian, the USA and European regions in many ways depends on the qualities of our human resource management programs and specifically those strategies designed to attract and retain key people.

Australian human resource managers will need to develop new and more appropriate programs to ensure that overseas divisions of Australian organisations are effectively staffed at both senior management and professional or technical levels. Relevant expatriate programs should include specialised recruitment, promotion, retention and repatriation schemes that are strategic, integrated, cost-effective and culturally appropriate. Human resource and senior managers are well advised to study the employment relations conditions and practices of countries in their trading region, and to adapt their programs accordingly.

Key terms

application form for employment 210
competencies 192
competency profiling 192
e-cruitment 206

Key debate issues

1 Organisations that need to recruit constantly from outside are admitting to failure – they also take a huge gamble on a largely unknown person.
2 There is no excuse for hiring a consultant. They cannot tell us anything we do not already know.
3 If our organisation is to have any hope of successful branding, we must centralise recruitment. Those business managers simply do not understand what needs to be done!

Case study 6.1

The firm

The senior partner studied the résumé for the hundredth time and again found nothing he disliked about Mitchell Y. McDeere, at least not on paper. He had the brains, the ambition, the good looks. And he was hungry; with his background, he had to be. He was married, and that was mandatory. The firm had never hired an unmarried lawyer, and it frowned heavily on divorce, as well as womanising and drinking. Drug testing was in the contract. He had a degree in accounting, passed the CPA exam the first time he took it and wanted to be a tax lawyer, which, of course, was a requirement with a tax firm. He was white, and the firm had never hired a black.

They managed this by being secretive and clubbish and never soliciting job applications. Other firms solicited, and hired blacks. This firm recruited, and remained lily white. Plus, the firm was in Memphis, of all places, and the top blacks wanted New York or Washington or Chicago. McDeere was a male, and there were no women in the firm. That mistake had been made in the mid-seventies when they recruited the number one grad from Harvard, who happened to be a she and a wizard at taxation. She lasted four turbulent years and was killed in a car wreck.

He looked good, on paper. He was their top choice. In fact, for this year there were no other prospects. The list was very short. It was McDeere or no one.

The managing partner, Royce McKnight, studied a dossier labelled 'Mitchell Y. McDeere – Harvard.' An inch thick with small print and a few photographs, it had been prepared by some ex-CIA agents in a private intelligence outfit in Bethesda. They were clients of the firm and each year did the investigating for no fee. It was easy work, they said, checking out unsuspecting law students. They learned, for instance, that he preferred to leave the Northeast, that he was holding three job offers, two in New York and one in Chicago, and that the highest offer was $76 000 and the lowest was $68 000. He was in demand. He had been given the opportunity to cheat on a securities exam during his second year. He declined, and made the highest grade in the class. Two months ago he had been offered cocaine at a law school party. He said no and left when everyone began snorting. He drank an occasional beer, but drinking was expensive and he had no money. He owed close to $23 000 in student loans. He was hungry.

Royce McKnight flipped through the dossier and smiled. McDeere was their man.

Source: Extract from John Grisham's The Firm, pp. 1–2, published by Century.
Reprinted by permission of The Random House Group, Ltd.

Question

1   Evaluate the key issues in this case.

Case study 6.2

Big, fast and easily bungled

Virtually overnight, the Transportation Security Administration had to hire more than 55 000 workers. Its problems with mishires and layoffs illustrate the issues inherent in fast large-scale hires.

Pity the poor Transportation Security Administration. It's easy to sympathize with the plight of this beleaguered group of airport-safety people. Last year Congress handed the TSA an order to hire more than 55 000 workers in 10 months. The administrator, Admiral James Loy, and his staff were expected to produce a first-rate nationwide team to rid the country of terrorism virtually overnight. To accomplish the task, the agency set up a multiphase screening process and enlisted some outside vendors to help out. After extensive interviewing, the TSA had thousands of people at more than 400 commercial airports x-raying carry-on bags, asking people to remove their shoes and waving hand-wands at those unfortunate passengers who set metal detectors screaming.

But things soured. The organization unwittingly hired a number of people with criminal backgrounds. As of 31 May, the airport-protection agency had fired 1 208 screeners for what Loy, at a recent congressional hearing, called 'suitability issues.' These mishires have caused an understandable ruckus among security-conscious citizens, and there have been some unhappy noises in Congress and in the press as well. Inadequate airport security was, of course, one of the factors that contributed to the 9/11 terrorist attack in the first place. The whole point of getting the agency quickly mobilized was to make airports safer.

Then there was the issue of cost. With a 2003 TSA budget of $4.8 billion, the security agency recently was forced to cut 3 000 jobs and plans to lop off 3 000 more by 30 September. Once this happens, its workforce will be trimmed by 11 per cent, which should save $280 million. The agency's problems with background checks and layoffs illustrate the troubles inherent in big, fast hires, particularly in a security-conscious environment.

Behind the screening

To get a sense of the nature of the TSA project, consider the experience of Covenant Aviation Security in Bolingbrook, Illinois. On 10 October 2002, the privately owned security firm won a contract to provide screeners for the TSA's pilot program at San Francisco International Airport. It was given 39 days to cobble together a workforce of 1 500 employees.

'Of the 800-incumbent screening force, only 127 employees were rehired, requiring us to initiate several job fairs to identify qualified applicants,' says Jim Brown, CAS's director of personnel and administration. 'As a result, we received over 22 000 applications for slightly more than 1 400 remaining positions, so the key for us was a thorough and effective assessment process that helped us quickly identify and select the best applicants in a short period of time.'

The rest of the process was like a steeplechase. Applicants had to prove that they were citizens and could meet the necessary federal requirements for employment. Then, Brown says, the people who passed the first stage 'began a myriad of physical, psychological and medical assessments to determine if they could meet the federally mandated airport screening position requirements.' The assessments included computerized tests, structured interviews, medical examinations, initial security checks and a drug test.

Thirty-nine days later, the TSA was so pleased with CAS's screening work that they asked the company to handle security operations at San Francisco International Airport and at Tupelo Regional Airport in Mississippi.

Though no one would argue that undertaking such a massive hiring job is anything short of problematic, not everyone applauds the TSA process. Nick Corcodilos, whose *Ask the Headhunter Newsletter* addresses opinions on the subject, says that the agency's employment predicament reveals a fundamental problem in the human resources industry. 'HR experts believe there are employment tests and software to accomplish any task – including hiring 50 000 workers overnight. It's not only a fallacy, it's a fraud.' Corcodilos says that the TSA should have 'hired more carefully and deliberately' and that 'there is simply no excuse for hiring people with criminal backgrounds in such positions.'

Corcodilos forces even the most sympathetic TSA-watcher to ask questions such as: 'Why didn't the TSA's vendors warn the organization about the dangers of speed-hiring?' And 'Shouldn't the TSA have asked for a more realistic deadline?' But such speculations tend to evaporate in light of the country's post-9/11 panic. Against this reality, it's difficult to imagine the TSA appealing to Congress for extra time. 'There is very little that TSA could have done differently and still meet the mandates given by Congress,' says TSA spokesman Robert Johnson.

Udo Trutschel of Circadian Technologies, a consulting business in Lexington, Massachusetts, disagrees. 'The staffing-level calculations are simply wrong.' He says that the TSA didn't take into account the variable nature of security screening, which changes with different arrival and departure times, plane size and the general time of day. A similar accusation come from Harold Rogers of Kentucky, a Republican congressman who recently told CBSnews.com: 'TSA threw money at the employee and screening deadlines in a shotgun fashion and overhired.' To be fair, Trutschel acknowledges, the golden rule of scheduling – 'Schedule people only at times and at places they are needed' – while seemingly straightforward, is in practice 'difficult to put in place.'

Reality check

Les Rosen, president and CEO of Employment Screening Resources in Novato, California, suggests that detractors of the TSA are too critical. 'Before blaming anyone for anything, let's do a reality check,' he says. 'Contrary to popular belief, there is no super-secret government background-checking computer where employers can submit a name and instantly get a thumbs-up or a thumbs-down.' Referring to the problems with reliability in conducting criminal-background checks, Rosen notes that official government rap sheets often have 'statistically significant miss rates.' Moreover, he adds, 'the difficulty is that there are some 10 000 courthouses in the United States spread out over approximately 3 200 state and federal jurisdictions, making finding a needle in a haystack easy by comparison.' He says that the agency's 'errors are not only possible, but also highly likely.'

'Here is a sobering thought,' he notes. 'If a 9/11 hijacker had faked a résumé in order to apply for a job in a sensitive industry, a criminal-record check may well have cleared him if he had not committed a crime in this country.'

By the TSA's account, it developed an effective background-check system to keep people with unsuitable backgrounds from becoming screeners. During the assessment process, candidates were fingerprinted and given the Questionnaire for Public Trust Positions. While candidates were being assessed, fingerprints were checked against a criminal database. Individuals who passed all tests at the assessment center and initial criminal-backgrounds checks were eligible to be offered conditional positions with TSA – conditional on the grounds that final background checks had not been completed. Next, the TSA hired a private company, ChoicePoint, to run criminal-history checks and verify references. Finally, TSA screeners went through the Office of Personnel Management investigation, a process that can take up to three months to complete for each individual, Johnson says.

The agency has informed Congress that it will have all phases of the background-check process completed by 1 October.

Avoiding trouble

As the TSA example suggests, there are many ways to bungle a big, fast staffing job. But there are also ways around these problems. Rosen says that the key to safe hiring is diversity in screening methods. To begin with, applicants should be informed that lying about their background will have severe consequences. He also recommends that interviewers ask 'a series of integrity questions routinely, designed to encourage applicants to be self-revealing.' For instance, an employer might say, 'Do you have any concerns about having your background checked?' And Rosen insists on calling past employers. This 'confirms the applicant's qualifications, demonstrates due diligence and, most critically, lets an employer know where a person has been, so the employer knows where to search for criminal records.' Without such a background check, 'you're hiring a stranger with no verifiable past.'

The TSA's hiring dilemma probably would not have happened to a private company. Roy Bordes, International Council vice president of ASIS, an association of security professionals in Virginia, says that the TSA situation was highly unusual. 'Private companies doing fast-paced, high-volume staff-ups will normally have the advantage of more time for the planning phase as well as the implementation phase,' he says. 'There are very few companies in the nongovernmental side that would not have these benefits, especially time controls.' And, he says, the TSA staffing requirements were unusually large. 'Very few companies have to hire 50 000 workers almost overnight.'

Corcodilos simply advises the business community to avoid mass hiring. 'You can't cram 10 people through a metal detector all at once and expect to know who's clean and who's not. Not any more than you can hire 50 000 people all at once and expect you're hiring the right people. It just doesn't work that way.' Good hiring involves plenty of time, savvy recruiters and an open channel to good people all the time. He urges human resources executives to become 'an active part of the community of people you will want to hire from.' The alternative, Corcodilos maintains, is 'to drive by street corners and pick up anyone who wants to work.'

TSA administrator for the day

Had human resources executives been in charge of hiring platoons of qualified airport screeners at the Transportation Security Administration instead of high government officials, they might have responded differently. Nick Corcodilos, editor of *Ask the Headhunter Newsletter*, calls the whole post-9/11 TSA enterprise 'a classic example of bureaucratic foibles,' and then says that the agency's assignment was chiefly a 'resources-allocation problem.'

He would have taken a two-step approach to quickly filling essential roles. First, he would have looked into 'renting, begging, borrowing people who have at least been vetted' by other government agencies – the post office, for instance, or the military. Step two: Corcodilos would have asked American business to identify good workers who were about to be let go for non-performance-related reasons unrelated to performance and signed them up.

Les Rosen is not intimidated by the idea of staffing the TSA. 'Over a 10-month period, the hiring needs come down to 5500 hires a month, or 250 people a day (assuming 22 workdays),' he says. 'Given the fact the workers are spread out across the United States, on the average that is only five hires per working day per state.' Rosen would have created a generic hiring procedure, and then had local human resources people do the actual hiring. Rosen's TSA would include an incentive plan for local recruiters. 'Since part of the fee would be based upon "success", the hiring professionals have an economic incentive to hire the best, not just move bodies.'

Roy Bordes, International Council vice president of ASIS in Virginia, suggests a straightforward, alphabetized plan that is impressively detailed, including a series of steps from A to J. He would have set up a series of committees, deadlines, and on-the-job training processes. (His inspiration comes from the military: 'The best way to know how to shoot a gun is to shoot a gun, thereby requiring limited class time and extended range time.')

Bordes says that the TSA should have worked with private industry from the very beginning. The agency, he reports, spent 'six months in getting each political appointee on board, most of whom were worthless.' He also maintains that the organization needed better crisis management. 'They had blow-ups every day in the beginning and really provided some dumb responses to the American people.'

Nonetheless, Bordes concludes that the 'TSA did a relatively good job in addressing the situation in light of the fact that they had to fight all of the political games occurring at that time. As a frequent flier (150000 miles per year) I have seen improvements in the overall screening process and in the attitudes of passengers toward that process.'

Source: Gordon K., *Workforce Management*, August 2003.

Question

1 Evaluate the key issues in this case.

Further readings

Bratton J., Gold J. 1999. *Human resource management*, 2nd edn, Hampshire, Macmillan.

Brewster C., Harris H. (eds), 1999. *International human resource management: Contemporary issues in Europe*, London, Routledge.

Buon T., Compton R. 1990. 'Credentials, credentialism and employee selection,' *Asia Pacific HRM*, November, pp. 126–32.

CCH Australia, 2001. *Recruitment manager: A user manual*, Sydney, CCH Australia.

Compton R.L., Morrissey W., Nankervis A.R. 2002. *Effective recruitment and selection practices*, 3rd edn, Sydney, CCH Australia Limited.

De Cieri H., Kramar R. 2003. *Human resource management in Australia*, Sydney, McGraw-Hill.

Dowling P., Welch D., Schuler R. 1999. *International human resource management*, 3rd edn, Cincinatti, South Western.

Hines G. 1996. 'Search process now fills most executive jobs,' *hrmonthly*, September, p. 22.

Reddin D. 1996. 'Strategy development builds for your company's future,' *hrmonthly*, September, pp. 20–1.

Stone R.J. 2005. *Human resource management*, 5th edn, Brisbane, John Wiley & Sons.

Way N. 2000. *Business Review Weekly*, 18 August, pp. 64–70.

Wiesner R., Millett B. 2003. *Human resource management*, Brisbane, John Wiley & Sons.

Endnotes

1   Gordon K. 2003. 'Big, fast and easily bungled,' *Workforce Management*, August, pp. 47–9.

2   Lachnit C. 2003. 'A people strategy that spans the globe,' *Workforce*, June, p. 76.

3   Collins R. 1988. 'The strategic contributions of the personnel function,' in A.R. Nankervis, R.L. Compton (eds) 1994. *Readings in strategic human resource management*, Melbourne, Nelson ITP.

4   Reddin D. 1996. 'Strategic recruitment builds for your company's future,' *hrmonthly*, September, pp. 20–1.

5   Gill C. 2000. 'Talent wins,' *hrmonthly*, April, pp. 34–6.

6   Tabakoff J. 2000. *Sydney Morning Herald* (My Career supplement), 16 August, pp. 6–7.

7   Way N. 2000. 'Keeping good staff outside,' *Business Review Weekly*, 28 April, pp. 134–8.

8   Centre for Professional Development, 'The retention levers,' *HR Report* 289, p. 3

9   Mithen, J. 2006. 'Australia's best people managers,' *hrmonthly*, November. pp. 20–1.

10   Ibid.

11   Ibid.

12   Knowles K. 2000. 'Promises, promises,' *hrmonthly*, August, p. 25.

13   See *O'Neill v Medical Benefits Fund of Australia* (2002) FCAFC 188. 17 June 2002.

14   Lloyd S. 2002. 'Branding from the inside out,' *Business Review Weekly*, 14–21 March, pp. 64–5.

15   Anon 2003. 'Westpac recruits older staff,' *HR Report*, Thomson CDP, 4 February, p. 8.

16   Hannen, M. 2002. 'Shop tactics,' *Business Review Weekly*, 6 June, pp. 58–61.

17   Collins, R. 2006 CCH/AGSM Survey on recruitment. CCH Australia.

18   Kleiman L.S., Clark K.J. 1984. 'User's satisfaction with job posting,' *Personnel Administrator*, 29(9), September, pp. 10–48.

19   Kleiman L.S., Clark K.J. 1984. 'An effective job-posting system,' *Personnel Journal*, 63(2), February, p. 205.

20   Ruthven, P. 2004. 'All change on the job front.' *BRW*. Sept–Oct. pp. 62–5.

21   Caldwell D.F., Spiver A.A. 1983. 'The relationship between recruiting source and employee success,' *Personnel Psychology*, 36(1), Spring, p. 6772.

22   Tabakoff N. 2000. 'Law firms fish for a pricey foreign catch,' *Business Review Weekly*, 20 October, pp. 96–9.

23   Kiger P. 2000. 'Search and deploy,' *Workforce*, June, pp. 65–8.

24   Wallage D. 1991. 'Writing job ads in an uncertain climate,' *hrmonthly*, May, p. 10.

25   Poe A. 1999. 'Recouping your losses when a new employee leaves,' *HR Magazine*, 44(5), pp. 82–90.

26   Mulberger R.D. 2001. 'Staff selection and retention: How to find, attract, hire and keep the winners,' *AFP Exchange*, May–June, pp. 18–22.

27   Centre for Professional Development 2002. 'Contractors the answer to staff turnover,' *HR Report*, no. 227, p. 7.

28   Sunderland K. 2000. 'The rise and rise of e-cruitment,' *hrmonthly*, December, p. 34.

29   Ibid.

30   Ibid.

31   Centre for Professional Development 2002. 'Hotel becomes online recruiter,' *HR Report*, no. 278, p. 3.

32   Martinez, M.N. 2002. 'Recruiting here and there,' *HR Magazine*, 47(9), pp. 95–100.

33   Centre for Professional Development 2000. *HR Report*, 30 May, p. 8.

34   Collins, R. 2006. op. cit.

35   Kramar R. 2006. *Cranet-Macquarie survey on international strategic human resource management: Report on the Australian findings*, Sydney, Macquarie University, p. 17.

36   Negandhi A. 1987. *International Management*, Massachusetts, Allyn & Bacon Inc., p. 310.

37   Dowling P., Schuler R., Welch D. 1998. *International dimensions of human resource management*, 3rd edn, Boston, PWS–Kent, p. 636.

38   Ibid.

39   Evans P. 1986. 'The context of strategic HRM policy in complex firms,' *Management Forum*, 6, p. 112.

40   Way, N. 2000. 'Keeping good staff onside,' *Business Review Weekly*, 28 April, pp. 134–8.

41   Centre for Professional Development 2003. 'The retention levers,' *HR Report*, 289, p. 3.

42   Anderson, P., Pulich M. 2000. 'Retaining good employees in tough times,' *The Health Care Manager*, 19(1), pp. 50–8.

Online reading

INFOTRAC® COLLEGE EDITION

For additional readings and review on attracting and retaining talent, explore InfoTrac® College Edition, your online library. Go to: www.infotrac-college.com and search for any of the InfoTrac key terms listed below:

➤ competency profiling
➤ e-cruitment
➤ employee retention
➤ employer branding
➤ employer of choice
➤ executive search
➤ selection criteria
➤ war for talent

CHAPTER 7
EFFECTIVE EMPLOYEE SELECTION

Faking personality tests is so widespread that it is amazing that test scores obtained under such conditions are taken seriously.

Professor Robert Spillane, 1985

The interview is an artificial situation. In an interview accountants do not account; programmers do not program; managers do not manage. They just talk about it.

Phillip Cohen, 1997

Another reason people lie, falsify or omit information is because they know that many companies do not have even the most basic controls in place to ensure a sound employment selection process.

Tammy Pratter, 2000

Past behaviour does not give a complete guide to future behaviour. It tends to deny the possibility that people's behaviour may change and develop over time, indeed that people can learn from past mistakes.

Jean M. Barclay, 2001

Objectives

After reading this chapter you will be able to:

1   Describe the factors to be considered and strategies used in reaching hiring decisions.

2   Define the concepts of reliability and validity.

3   Describe the three types of validity used in the selection process.

4   Distinguish between the different types of interviews according to the degree of structure.

5   Be aware of the pitfalls for selection interviewers.

6   Examine the key guidelines for the interviewing process that interviewers should know.

7   Identify the types of pre-employment questions that should be avoided during the interview.

8   Identify the types of psychological test, their benefits and disadvantages.

9   Appreciate the unique aspects of international selection processes.

Introduction

The recruiting process typically yields a number of applicants whose qualifications must be assessed against the requirements of the job. The selection of applicants from within or outside the organisation to fill existing or projected job openings is a major HR process that has far-reaching effects on the continued viability of the organisation.

Today greater attention is being given to the selection process than ever before. Typically, effective selection processes will begin with an examination of the organisation's strategic direction together with the accompanying human resource management plan (see Chapter 4). Where a change in corporate direction or simply a refocusing of the organisation's mission or purpose is indicated, it is incumbent upon HR professionals to ensure that all recruitment and selection processes link directly to such plans.

Peter Goldrick asks what makes a selection system best practice and concludes that it is the strategic perspective of employee selection. Does the selection system reflect the organisation's current vision, values and critical success factors? Only in this way can organisations select those who will participate in and champion their current culture and strategic direction. Goldrick asks whether people are hired on key competencies derived from the organisation's strategic planning process.[1] A more fundamental question might well be along the lines of: 'Do we know what the key competencies are?' A few even more fundamental questions are: 'What are the organisation's core competencies?' and 'What competencies will we build on in the future and which activities will we move away from, having decided previously that the organisation has no core competence in the area?' In essence, 'which activities will we retain as a business and which will we outsource?' Until these questions are posed and answered, strategic selection will at best be ad hoc, and success difficult to achieve.

SAP (Systems Applications and Products, an information technology business solutions provider), winner of the inaugural AHRI Best Practice Award (first awarded in 1997), has retained central HR control of the selection process to ensure that the process and sub-processes tie directly back to the corporate plan. Its view is that the recruitment and selection processes are far too important to leave to experimentation by non-specialists.

Where the job tenure of employees is protected by an enterprise agreement or by public service regulations or where unfair dismissal laws are at their most rigid, there is an additional incentive for management to achieve best practice selection policies and processes. It is typically more difficult to discharge unsatisfactory employees who have such protection.

The greatest impetus to improve the selection process may well have come from equal employment opportunity legislation and subsequent court decisions. What used to be the exclusive concern of the business unit managers or the human resources manager may now be carried into the various equal opportunity or industrial tribunals. The Howard government's *WorkChoices* legislation will also have an impact on selection decisions as will the chronic skills shortage faced by organisations during 2006 and 2007. All signs point to this shortage continuing for another 10 years resulting in a 'seller's' labour market. Such environmental forces need to be considered as integral to any strategic selection process.

While the selection process is typically the responsibility of the HR director or similar, managerial and supervisory personnel in all the business units of an organisation also have an important role in the selection process. The final decision in hiring will usually rest with them. It is important, therefore, that they understand not only the objectives and policies relating to selection but also the overall strategic direction of the organisation. They must be thoroughly trained in the most effective and acceptable techniques for evaluating applicants and must be motivated to use these techniques.

Pre-employment screening

It is assumed that individuals who are thoroughly screened against carefully developed position specifications (see Chapter 5) learn their job tasks readily, are productive and generally adjust to their jobs with a minimum of difficulty. As a result, the individual, the organisation and society as a whole benefit from a careful selection process. In addition, new recruit turnover will often be minimised. Currently, there is great concern within the HR profession that the massive increase in Internet recruitment is placing even more pressure on recruiters to ensure that claims made in an employee's résumé are accurate.

As a case in point, the head of the New Zealand Maori Television Service, John Davey, was sacked after it was found that his qualifications were bogus. His claims that he held an MBA degree and high level experience turned out to be fictitious. To make matters worse, he had been hired through a supposed professional recruitment consultancy. One writer has argued that the trend towards falsifying résumés is the reality and that an interview will only be granted if the résumé impresses organisational recruiters. People will also lie, falsify or omit certain information because they know that most companies simply do not have the most basic controls in place to ensure a sound selection process.[2]

Matching people and jobs

Those individuals who are responsible for making selection decisions should have adequate and accurate information upon which to make them. Information about the jobs to be filled, knowledge of the ratio of job openings to the number of applicants, and as much relevant information as possible about the applicants themselves are essential for making sound decisions.

Use of person specifications

In Chapter 5 the process of analysing and developing specifications for jobs was discussed, as was the newer process of competency profiling. Such requirements as skills, knowledge, attitudes, responsibilities and job conditions provide the basis for determining what types of information should be obtained from the applicant, from previous employers, or from other sources. The job specifications also form the basis for the administration of any applicable tests. Complete and unambiguous job information will help to reduce the influence of racial and sex stereotypes and helps the interviewer to differentiate between qualified and unqualified applicants.

Ordinarily, the managers and supervisors in an organisation are well acquainted with the requirements pertaining to skill, physical demands and other factors for jobs in their respective departments. Interviewers and other members of the HR department who participate in selection should maintain a close liaison with the various business units in order to become thoroughly familiar with the jobs and, of course, to be very aware of the strategic direction and needs of that business unit.

The selection process

In most organisations, selection is a continuous process. Turnover inevitably occurs, leaving vacancies to be filled by current applicants from inside or outside the organisation or by individuals whose qualifications have been previously assessed. It is common to have a waiting list of applicants who can be called when there are permanent or temporary positions vacant.

The number of steps in the selection process and their sequence will vary, not only with the organisation, but also with the type and level of jobs to be filled. Each step should be evaluated in terms of its contribution. The steps that typically make up the selection process are shown

in Exhibit 7.1. Not all applicants go through all of them. For example, some may be rejected after the preliminary interview, others after taking tests. In many cases, organisations will not use tests, either because of lack of knowledge, or because of suspicion of such tests. Where a panel interview is used, several interviews may be reduced to one interview.

Exhibit 7.1   SHRM and strategic selection

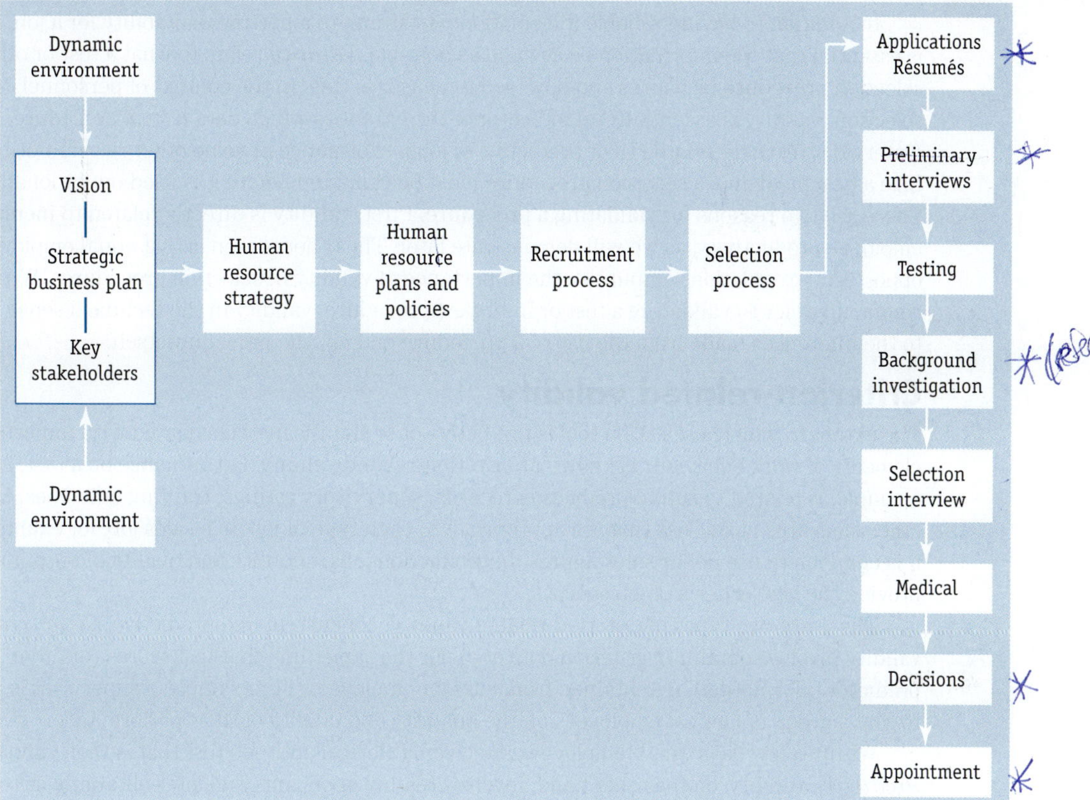

As shown in Exhibit 7.1, several different procedures are used to obtain information about applicants. These include the use of application forms, interviews, tests, medical examinations and background investigations. Regardless of the procedures used, it is essential that their use conforms to accepted ethical standards, including privacy and confidentiality, as well as legal requirements. Above all, it is essential to obtain information that has proved to be sufficiently reliable, valid and verifiable. In essence, selection is a negative process as its aim is to eliminate all but the successful applicants.

Obtaining reliable and valid information

The degree to which interviews, tests and other selection procedures yield comparable data over a period of time is known as reliability. For example, unless interviewers judge the capabilities of applicants to be the same today as they did yesterday, their judgements are unreliable. Likewise, a test that gives widely different scores when administered to an individual a few days apart is unreliable. Consistency is the aim.

Reliability also refers to the extent to which two or more methods (interviews, tests) yield similar results or are consistent. Inter-rater reliability, a measure of agreement between two or more raters, is one example where consistency is important. Where several interviewers are involved separately in the selection process, it is not difficult to foresee a situation where different results may be obtained. Unless the data upon which selection decisions are made are reliable, in terms of both stability and consistency, they cannot be used as predictors of future job success, which is, of course, what the strategic selection process is all about.

In addition to having reliable information pertaining to a person's suitability for a job, it is essential that the information be as valid as possible. *Validity* refers to what a test or other selection procedure measures and how well it measures this. In the context of personnel selection, validity is essentially an indicator of the extent to which data from a procedure (interview, test) are related to or predictive of job performance or some other relevant criterion. Like a new medicine, a selection procedure must be validated before it is used operationally. There are two reasons for validating a procedure. First, validity is directly related to increases in employee productivity, as we will demonstrate later. The other reason is that equal employment opportunity regulations emphasise the importance of validity in selection procedures. While we commonly refer to validating a test or interview procedure, validity in the technical sense refers to the inferences made from the use of a procedure and not the procedure itself.

Criterion-related validity

The extent to which a selection tool is predictive of or significantly correlated with important elements of work behaviour is known as criterion-related validity. Performance on a test, for example, is related to actual production records, supervisory ratings, training outcomes, and other measures of success that are appropriate to each type of job. In a sales job, for example, it is common to use dollar sales figures. In production jobs, quantity and quality of output may provide the best criteria of job success.

There are two types of criterion-related validity: concurrent and predictive. *Concurrent* validity involves obtaining criterion data at about the same time that test scores (or other predictor information) are obtained from current employees. For example, a supervisor is asked to rate a group of clerical employees on the quantity and quality of their performance.

Within a few days, these employees are given a clerical aptitude test that is then validated. *Predictive* validity, on the other hand, involves testing applicants and later obtaining criterion data after they have been on the job for some defined period. For example, applicants are given a clerical aptitude test, which is then filed away for later study. After the individuals have been on the job for several months, supervisors, who should not know the employees' test scores, are asked to rate them on the quality and quantity of their performance. Test scores are then compared with the supervisors' ratings. Regardless of the method used, cross-validation is essential. Cross-validation is a process in which a test or test battery is administered to a different sample (drawn from the same population) for the purpose of verifying the results obtained from the original validation study.

Correlation methods

Correlational methods are generally used to determine the relationship between predictor information such as test scores and criterion data. The correlation scatterplots in Exhibit 7.2 illustrate the difference between a selection test of zero validity (A) and one of high validity (B). Each dot represents a person. Note that in Scatterplot A there is no relationship between test scores and success on the job; in other words, the validity is zero. In Scatterplot B, those individuals who score low on the test tend to have low success on the job, whereas those who score high on the test tend to have high success on the job, indicating high validity. In actual practice, we would apply a statistical formula to the data to obtain a coefficient of correlation,

which is referred to as a validity coefficient. Correlation coefficients range from 0.00, denoting a complete absence of relationship, to a +1.00 and to –1.00, indicating perfect positive or perfect negative relationship respectively.

Exhibit 7.2 Correlation scatterplots

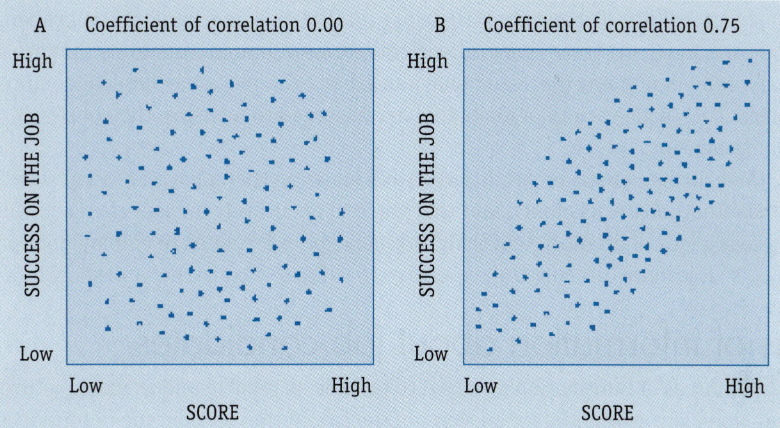

One of the authors has found a situation where test scores for admission to a management development program actually resulted in a negative correlation coefficient. Those who did best on the entrance tests did most poorly on the two-year program, and vice versa! Needless to say, the tests were replaced. This example shows the vital nature of validation for all selection methods.

Validity generalisation

For several decades, personnel psychologists believed that validity coefficients had meaning only for the specific situation (job and organisation). More recently, as a result of several studies (many involving clerical jobs), it appears that validity coefficients can often be generalised across situations – hence the term validity generalisation. Where there are adequate data to support the existence of validity generalisation, the development of selection procedures can become less costly and time-consuming. In Australia, the Australian Council for Educational Research (ACER) and Science Research Associates (SRA) produce test catalogues along with scales of norms for certain industry types. The idea is to match your organisation to one shown in the various tables, and then choose the appropriate tests. Both Dowling[3] and Hicks[4] have discussed the issue of generalisation and the need for caution.

Content validity

Where it is not feasible to use the criterion-related approach, perhaps because of limited samples, the content method can be used. Content validity is assumed to exist when a selection instrument, such as a test, adequately samples the knowledge and skills needed to perform a particular job.

The closer the content of the selection instrument to actual work samples or behaviours, the greater the content validity. For example, a public service examination for accountants has high content validity when it requires the solution of accounting problems representative of those found on the job. Similarly, asking an applicant to lift a 25-kilogram bag is a selection procedure that has content validity if the job description indicates that employees must be able to meet this requirement. Content validity is the most direct and least complicated type of validity to assess.

While content validity does have its limitations, it has made a positive contribution to improved job analysis procedures and to the role of expert judgement in sampling and scoring procedures. An assessment centre used for selection decisions is an example of such an approach.

Construct validity

The extent to which a selection tool measures a theoretical construct or trait is known as construct validity. Typical constructs are intelligence, mechanical comprehension and anxiety. They are, in effect, broad, generalised categories of human functions that are based upon the measurement of many discrete behaviours. For example, a mechanical comprehension test consists of a wide variety of tasks that are assumed to measure the construct of mechanical comprehension.

Measuring construct validity requires showing that a psychological trait is related to satisfactory job performance and that the test accurately measures this psychological trait. There is a lack of literature covering this concept as it relates to employment practices – probably because it is more difficult and expensive to validate a construct and show how it is job-related.

Sources of information about job candidates

Many sources of information are used to provide as reliable and as valid pictures as possible of an applicant's potential for success on the job. In this section, the potential contributions of application forms, résumés, background investigations and medical examinations will be studied. Because interviewing plays such a major role in selection and because testing presents unique challenges, there will be expanded discussion of these sources of information later in the chapter.

Of importance is the view that there is no perfect selection tool. From a strategic perspective, employers must ascertain the 'ideal' applicant in terms of the organisation's strategic direction and then choose a range of devices that hopefully will reduce the number of candidates until the final decision can be made.

In a similar vein, Barry Smith argues that the specification of the 'ideal' person must be formulated from both an organisational and individual career life cycle approach. In terms of the organisational life cycle, four distinct stages can be identified:

- starting up and getting in

- growing and making it

- maturity, holding on and levelling off

- decline, restructure and letting go.

The point made by Smith is that, for each stage of the life cycle, organisations must select staff who will fit that specific stage of the life cycle. Furthermore, individual career life cycles need to be analysed in an effort to ensure a good fit.[5] More recently, the realisation that major cultural and attitudinal differences existing between the babyboomers, Generation X and Generation Y, make the selection process even more interesting if not complex. As a case in point, Avril Henry has recently claimed that Generation Ys do not have a work life or a social life. They have a life! They are seeking great leaders, challenging work, mentors and mobility. Where this is not the case, they will go elsewhere.[6]

In a similar vein, Stephanie Dinnell supports this view arguing that Generation Ys now make up 20 per cent of the population and rather than being fickle, self-focussed and transient, they are in fact highly educated, ambitious and career oriented. Job security and long-term perspectives are foreign to them. They are quick to move on if their expectations are not fulfilled. These attitudes are in direct conflict with those generally held by babyboomers who in many cases will be leading their organisations for a few years yet.[7]

Recent research by Drake International into the Generation Y recruitment and selection 'dilemma' shows that 86 per cent expect to be promoted within two years (!), 63 per cent will stay less than two years, and 52 per cent see no problem in finding a new job. Richard Branson, Donald Trump and Bill Gates are seen as the most admired business leaders. Compare these attitudes with those held by the typical babyboomer and the issues surrounding recruitment, selection and retention of Generation Y and Generation X for that matter, seem obvious.[8]

At the other end of the organisation's food chain there are those babyboomers who currently are reaching retirement age – the first to retire having had access to superannuation for a large part of their working lives. This has brought forward a different phenomena – downshifting – a voluntary scaling down of one's career so as to enjoy a fuller life outside of work. An Australian study conducted in 2003 indicates that some 30 per cent of respondents had downshifted their careers in the previous 10 years.[9]

The point to all of this is that those conducting recruitment and selection campaigns must consider a much wider range of issues than ever before as they try to make the best 'fit' possible.

The Y front

With teenagers of yesterday becoming the workers of today, HR has to become adept at employing and retaining Generation Y

Having dealt with gender and cultural diversity in recent decades, HR professionals have started to focus on generational diversity. This year, the first of Australia's babyboomers begin to retire, and from 2008 more Australians will leave the workforce than enter it, creating a significant labour void. These factors, combined with 'transitioning' – Generation X moving into management roles, and Generation Ys commencing employment – will create a major shift in workforce dynamics.

As reported in April *hrmonthly*, it is projected that Generation Y (born 1980–94) will make up 40 per cent of the workforce within the next five years. HR professionals need to ask who these workers are, what makes them tick, and how they can attract, retain and get the best from them.

Just over 20 per cent of the population is Generation Y. Despite their reputation as fickle, self-focused and transient individuals, they are also highly educated, ambitious and career oriented. Having come of age in an era with little job security, competition is rife and profit is king. Gen Ys are simply a reflection of their times.

The attitudes, working styles and expectations of the leaders differ greatly to those of previous generations. If a role doesn't live up to their expectations, they are quick to move on. Gen Ys like employers who provide well rounded and evolving opportunities.

They want to make a difference beyond the financial bottom line and are more committed when corporate values resonate with their own.

The tenor of job advertisements is important. Drake International's latest research (a national survey of 3 000 Australians and a series of in-depth focus groups) shows that Gen Y responds best to adverts that convey a sense of fun, interest and variety. Salary alone is not a strong attractor for Gen Y hunters.

Given that today's 'now generation' relies heavily on efficient, one-stop solutions and straight-forward application processes, HR managers should place job adverts where Gen Ys are likely to look, such as online job boards and recruitment agencies.

Accurately selecting talented Gen Y employees can be a hit-and-miss process for HR managers. Drake research indicates that a bad hire can cost businesses between 30 and 200 per cent of a person's annual salary, without accounting for hidden costs such as lost productivity, low staff morale and poor customer service.

Difficulty in hiring talented Gen Ys is not because they don't exist, but because informal or poorly designed selection systems often fail to weed out the 'pretenders' from the 'real deal.' Gen Ys are interview-savvy and know how to dazzle employers. HR managers need to be wise to this and adopt best-practice selection methods drawing on multiple activities to assess relevant knowledge, skills and personality attributes. These include a clearly defined job description, objective ability-testing, assessment of cultural and personality fit, structured behavioural interviews and reference checks.

Many people leave their job not because there is a compelling reason to leave but because there is no compelling reason to stay. No previous generation has begun their working lives moving between jobs as frequently. Sixty-three per cent of those surveyed stayed less than two years with a single employer.

However, generation Ys are more likely to remain at companies that provide:

- **Professional growth and development** One of the strongest predictors of employee turnover – 90 per cent agreed that regular training would motivate them to stay with an organisation.

Gen Y is the most formally educated of the generational groups. They recognise ongoing training as the key to remaining relevant and effective in their current job and ensuring they stay employable.

- **Work/life balance** A career that enables Gen Ys to pursue other aspects of their life is highly attractive. Successful retainers of Gen Y employees have accepted the need to adopt flexible work practices such as unpaid leave, flexitime, work-from-home options and time in lieu.
- **Variety** It's the spice of working life for Gen Ys, who desire both challenge and change. Offering variety and flexibility in roles, such as with job rotation, helps maintain a multiskilled and stimulated Gen Y workforce.
- **Social interaction** Forty-two percent of Gen Ys surveyed placed 'relationship with peers' as one of the top reasons for getting or keeping their job. They are collaborative learners and enjoy working in teams, and favour a culture where interaction can take place and they can connect with older staff and customers.
- **Responsibility and input** They grew up with a say

in their own life choices, and want a similar voice in the workplace. Meaningful responsibilities and input into decision-making are highly regarded.

- **Reward and recognition** While money is important, they yearn for recognition to feed their self-esteem. Managers need to recognise and acknowledge the effort and performance of Gen Y employees on a regular basis.

Leadership plays a central role in employee retention. In a large analysis of exit interviews, about 70 per cent of departing employees cited leadership and management practices as their primary reason for leaving.

Gen Ys expect to be treated as equals. Ninety-seven per cent of those surveyed valued a leader-ship style that involved empowerment, consultation and partnership. They also value honesty, reliability, authenticity and loyalty in their leaders. They are very cynical of managers who don't live up to company and societal values.

Providing challenging, fun and stimulating work opportunities, with scope for professional development, are the keys to employing Gen Ys. It's generally a rewarding approach for Gen X, baby-boomers and management, too.

The generations defined sociologically

	Baby boomers Born 1946—1964 Aged 40s & 50s	Generation X Born 1965—1979 Aged late 20s & 30s	Generation Y Born 1980—1994 Teens & 20s
Prime Ministers	Harold Holt John Gorton William McMahon Gough Whitlam Malcolm Fraser	Bob Hawke Paul Keating	John Howard
Iconic technology	TV (1956) Audio cassette (1962) Colour TV (1975)	VCR (1976) Walkman (1979) IBM PC (1981)	www (early '90s) DVD (1995) Play station/X-Box
Music	Elvis Beatles Rolling Stones	INXS Nirvana Madonna	Eminem Britney Spears Puff Daddy
TV and movies	Easy rider The Graduate Jaws	ET Hey Hey It's Saturday MTV	American pie Pay TV Reality TV
Popular culture	Flare jeans Mini skirts Barbie, Frisbee	Rollerblades Hyper colour Torn jeans	Body piercing Baseball caps Metrosexual
Social markers/ landmark events	Decimal currency (1966) Neil Armstrong (1969) Vietnam War (1965–73) Cyclone Tracy (1974) Advance Australia Fair (1974)	Challenger explodes (1986) Halley's Comet (1986) Stockmarket crash (1987) Berlin Wall down (1989) Newcastle earthquake (1989)	Thredbo disaster (1997) Columbine shootings (1999) New millennium (2000) September 11 (2001) Bali bombing (2002)
Aspirational figures	John F Kennedy Audrey Hepburn Muhammad Ali	Bono (U2) Princess Diana Andre Agassi	Richard Branson Tiger Woods Paris Hilton
Influencers	Evidential Experts	Pragmatic Practitioners	Experiential Peers
Training focus	Technical Data/evidence	Practical Case studies/applications	Emotional Stories/participative
Learning format	Formal Structured	Relaxed Interactive	Spontaneous Multi-sensory
Learning environment	Classroom style Quiet atmosphere	Round-table style Relaxed ambience	Café style Music and multi-media
Sales and marketing	Mass/traditional media Above the line	Direct/targeted media Below the line	Viral/electronic media Through friends
Purchase influences	Brand loyal Authorities	Brand-switchers Experts	No brand loyalty Friends
Financial values	Long-term needs Cash and credit	Medium-term goals Credit-savvy	Short-term wants Credit-dependent
Ideal leaders	Command and control Thinkers	Coordination and cooperation Doers	Consensus and collaborative Feelers

Source: Drake International, published in *hrmonthly*, May 2006, p. 24; Table: *Generation Y – attracting, engaging and leading a new generation at work*, McCrindle Research and Courtney Roberts.

NEWS REPORT 7.2

Gen Y on the move

A survey of 3000 Australians born between 1980 and 1994 (Generation Y) has found that 86 per cent expect to be promoted within two years, 63 per cent stay less than two years with an employer, and 52 per cent think it's easy to find a new job.

The survey, by Drake International, indicated that HR managers who aren't up to speed on what drives and motivates Gen Y will lose significant competitive advantage amid a tight labour market, says Stephanie Dinnell, Drake's organisational psychologist.

Forty-two per cent cited poor management and leadership as the main reason they left previous jobs. Richard Branson, Donald Trump and Bill Gates emerged as the most admired business leaders.

Drake says the proportion of Gen Y employees is set to double from 20 to 40 per cent of the workforce in five years.

Source: *hrmonthly*, April 2006, p. 6.

A word of caution

Over the years, a great deal of research has been undertaken into the validity of the various selection devices commonly used by employers. In many cases, such research has found that most selection devices may have a probability of success that is little more than chance. Findings of similar research have been replicated internationally, but arguably the most quoted is Hunter and Hunter's 1984 study.[10]

Exhibit 7.3 shows the result of the Hunter and Hunter study. Twelve selection methods were tested for their predictive value as indicators of future job performance. Validity is expressed as a coefficient ranging from –1.00 to +1.00.

Exhibit 7.3   Selection methods

Selection device	Validity
Intelligence tests	0.53
Probationary period	0.44
Biographical history	0.37
Reference checks	0.26
Prior experience	0.18
Interviews (unstructured)	0.14
Training and experience ratings	0.13
Academic attainment	0.11
Education	0.10
Occupational interest ratings	0.10
General personality tests	0.10
Age	–0.01

Note: The conventional unstructured interview may have a probability of not much greater than chance in predicting successful job performance. Fortunately, where a structured, panel interview is used, the validity coefficient is often around 0.6.

Source: Sullivan P. 1991. Paper presented to IPMA Seminar, 19 September.

Though somewhat dated, these figures have been replicated internationally in hundreds of validation studies. There is no reason to believe that the Australian scene is in any way unique. Peter Sullivan of Morgan and Banks has concluded that, in view of such startling results, HR managers will have to rethink the validity of their favourite selection tools.[11]

Application forms

Most organisations require application forms to be completed because they provide a fairly quick and systematic means of obtaining a variety of information about the applicant. As with interviews, the various equal opportunity tribunals and privacy committees have found that many questions asked on application forms disproportionately reject females and minorities and are often not job-related. Application forms should, therefore, be developed with great care and revised as necessary. Because of differences in state and international laws, organisations operating in more than one state or globally may find it necessary to develop one form that can be used overall.

The information on the application form is generally used as a basis for further exploration of the applicant's background. It should also be used to provide as much information as possible that is predictive of job success. While application form data are usually evaluated subjectively, they can be scored in much the same manner as tests, with certain items weighted in terms of the most sought after selection criteria.

Even though applicants come armed with elaborate résumés, it is important to recognise that an applicant's résumé will tell us what the applicant wants us to know, not necessarily what we need to know. Many applicants engage the services of employment consultants to help them design elaborate, attractive résumés that extol their alleged virtues and abilities. These résumés are little more than tributes to the writing skills of the people preparing them.

Most large cities will have a consulting firm engaged in writing résumés for applicants. In reality the consultant is merely rewriting, usually in glowing terms, what the applicant has already provided.

Background investigations

In one Australian study, 90 per cent of responding organisations requested referees' reports in at least half of the applications they considered. Sixty-four per cent of the respondents reported that they never asked for written reports but preferred to make their own enquiries, usually by telephone.[12] Former employers, school and college officials, credit bureaux and individual referees may be contacted for verification of pertinent information, such as length of time on job, type of job, highest wages earned, academic degrees earned or credit rating.

In a more recent Australian study, Roger Collins has found that 63 per cent of respondents have moved to telephone background checking although only 12 per cent standardised their questions.[13] The consequence of not using standard questions is that valid comparisons are very difficult, if at all possible.

It is not safe to assume that the information furnished by the applicant is 100 per cent true. The most common ruse, according to employers, involves an exaggeration of one's educational background. 'I would like a dollar for every fake degree I have seen,' says Vince Murdoch of Murdoch Associates. 'With modern photocopiers, the process is very simple.'

A further word of caution is offered by consultants Morgan and Banks who argue that greed combined with a competitive market is forcing job seekers to fake résumés and qualifications. Their research has found that fudging employment details has become a part of a culture change in the job market and is most likely destined to stay.[14]

Checking references

Most organisations use both the mail and telephone to check references. Generally telephone checks are preferable because they save time and provide for greater candour. The most reliable information usually comes from supervisors, who are in the best position to report on an applicant's work habits and performance. It is often advisable, however, to obtain written verification of information about job titles, duties, and pay levels from the former employer's HR office.[15]

The notion of reference checking is based on the assumption that a person's future performance is linked closely to past performance. Reference audits thus are processes that attempt to gather relevant applicant data (education and employment histories, skills, character and interpersonal abilities) from people with whom the applicant has previously been closely associated. Often, sources can include school or university referees along with character references from local identities. Some employers will also go to the extent of a full security and credit check. Although this may seem warranted in some cases, care should be taken not to infringe human rights or privacy legislation. Requirements will vary from state to state, so those persons performing such checks should be conversant not only with federal legislation, but also that of each state within which the organisation operates.

Applicants will quite naturally provide the names of referees who will be favourable to themselves. It is generally useful to approach 'second generation' referees with the agreement of the applicant. Such referees are persons who have worked with the applicant but are not those who have been nominated.

Importantly, referees' reports should be requested in such a way that they address the specified selection criteria. Rather than have applicants produce reports, referees can be approached directly by employers who provide as much information as possible about the position and the person sought. This will then make possible a far more specific response from the referee.

Such measures will help to eliminate false claims, but for many employers this all seems to be too much trouble. A case in point involved a person who was chosen to run Sydney's Anglican St Luke's hospital complex. The successful applicant convinced the hospital board that he was a successful businessman, a university graduate and led a stable family life. In fact, none of this was true. He was a failed businessman, heavily in debt and with a mistress in Melbourne.[16] To make matters worse, it appears that a firm of search consultants was involved in the early selection stages (see Case study 7.2 near the end of this chapter).

In a more recent case before the NSW Industrial Relations Commission, a case for unfair dismissal was lost by an employee after it was revealed that a glowing referee's report was indeed written by the complainant's father. The employee had indeed worked for her father but at no time indicated such a relationship to her employer.[17]

Both cases bring into light the general notion of 'duty of care' when writing referee's reports. Once a reference is given, the law recognises a general duty, owed by the referee, to take reasonable care to ensure the report is accurate, true and fair.[18] Leading law specialist with Hunt and Hunt, Peta Tumpey, goes further to warn of increased fraud in the area of falsified backgrounds. As indicated above, the chronic skills shortage has led to a situation whereby employers are not being as vigilant as they might have been when the labour market was less tight. A check of overseas experience and education may well be tedious but the alternative is fraught with danger[19] – just another challenge for those organisations that are finding that they must engage in offshoring as a recruitment and selection strategy.

Medical examination

The medical examination is one of the later steps in the selection process because it can be costly. A medical examination is generally given to ensure that the health of applicants is adequate for the job requirements. It also provides a baseline against which subsequent medical examinations may be compared and interpreted. The last objective is particularly important in determination of work-caused disabilities under workers' compensation law. It is also particularly valuable in the placement of disabled persons.

In the past, requirements for such physical characteristics as strength, agility, height and weight were often determined by someone's unvalidated notion of what should be required.

Many such requirements tend to discriminate against women and some races, and have been questioned and modified so as to be more realistic in terms of typical job demands.

In a classic case before the NSW Equal Opportunity Tribunal, height and weight requirements were found to be discriminatory as they had no bearing on the job itself; that is, they were not a valid job requirement.[20]

A growing number of US companies, including 125 of the Fortune 500 companies, are trying to curb the cost of drug abuse in the workplace by requiring urine tests of job applicants. There are reports that sophisticated tests can detect marijuana up to 30 days after it is used, and cocaine up to three or four days. Drug testing is not widespread in Australia, but with growing concern about drug and alcohol issues, this is changing, especially in the defence forces and police services. Heavy transport, including bus and rail, is also employing random drug testing.

Employers will need to exercise care in the interpretation of medical results. Where, for example, an applicant has a partial loss of hearing or sight, any decision not to employ on these grounds may need to be defended. Most legislation now covers discrimination against persons with some form of physical or intellectual impairment.

The employment interview

Traditionally, the employment interview has had a very important role in the selection process. At the same time the interview is also considered to be not only an essential process but one that is fraught with potential traps and legal pitfalls.[21] A number of researchers claim that over the past 100 years the interview has been more widely researched than any other human resource process whereby the structure, reliability, validity and predictive power of the interview have been analysed and re-analysed by a myriad of researchers and scholars and where the same themes appear to be repeated in the outcomes of such studies.[22]

While researchers have raised serious doubts about the validity of the interview as a selection method, Arvey and Campion state that it is popular because it is especially practical when there is only a small number of applicants. It also does other things well, such as serving as a public relations tool. Other reasons include interviewers maintaining great faith and confidence in their judgements and, quite simply, applicants expecting to be interviewed. Finally, the interview has 'face' validity – it looks valid.

They suggest that researchers should focus on differences among interviewers rather than on the validity of the interview as a method. In other words, some interviewers' judgements are more valid than others in the evaluation of applicants.[23]

Other writers have argued that, despite the obvious problems with the interview process, the interview remains popular because of the social skills that may be displayed at the interview and their acceptability to managers and to applicants alike. They are also much more cost-effective than the alternatives of selection testing and assessment centres.[24]

Depending upon the type of job and the attitude of the organisation, applicants may be interviewed by one person, by several members of the organisation, or by an external consultant.

Interviewing methods

Employment or selection interviews differ according to the methods that are used to obtain information and to elicit attitudes and feelings from an applicant. The most significant difference lies in the amount of structure, or control, that is exercised by the interviewer. In the highly structured (or directive) interview, the interviewer determines the course that the interview will follow as each question is asked. In the less structured (or non-directive) interview, the applicant plays a larger role in determining the way in which the discussion will go. An examination of the different types of interviews (see Exhibit 7.4) will reveal the differences.

Exhibit 7.4   Types of interviews

Type of interview	For	Against
Directive or structured	• Consistent – all applicants treated equally • Usually more reliable • Time-efficient • All areas covered • Easier to compare applicants	• Can lack flexibility • Some areas ignored which should be followed up • Interviewer may dominate • Applicant may be overwhelmed by questions
Non-directive or non-structured	• Easier to explore leads and different areas • Applicant may be more relaxed • Can be tailored to individual situation	• Harder to control interview • May miss important areas • Harder to compare different applicants
Panel	• More impartial – group decision • Applicant closely observed • One panel member may notice or think of something missed by others • Suited to higher level appointments	• Cost • Applicant may feel outnumbered or intimidated • Panel may talk or argue among themselves • Less chance of establishing rapport
Stress	• Shows applicant's behaviour under conditions causing emotional strain • Can be suited to some high-pressure or unpleasant jobs	• Requires very skilled interviewer • May alienate and lose a suitable applicant • May affect company's public relations image • Relevant to only a few positions
Group	• Easier to compare applicants • Provides representative work situation • Suited to positions requiring managerial, verbal or interpersonal skills	• Expensive • Hard to assess • May not always relate to the job in question • Less personal contact

Source: Adapted from Compton R. L., Morrissey W., Nankervis A.R. 2006.
Effective recruitment and selection practices, 4th edn, Sydney, CCH Australia.

Non-directive interview

In the non-directive interview, the interviewer carefully refrains from influencing the applicant's remarks. The applicant is allowed the maximum amount of freedom in determining the course of the discussion. This is achieved by the interviewer asking broad, open questions, such as 'tell me more about your experience on your last job,' and by permitting the applicant to talk freely with a minimum of interruption. In general, the non-directive approach is characterised by such interviewer behaviour as listening carefully and not arguing, interrupting or changing the subject abruptly. It also involves using questions sparingly, phrasing responses briefly, and allowing pauses in the conversation. This latter technique is the most difficult for the beginning interviewer to master. The greater freedom afforded the applicant in the non-directive interview is particularly valuable in bringing to the interviewer's attention any information, attitudes or feelings that may often be concealed by more rapid questioning. This method is more likely to be used in interviewing candidates for high-level positions, as well as in counselling and grievance situations.

Directive interview

The most highly structured type of interview is the directive interview, which adheres closely to a highly detailed set of questions on specially prepared forms. A sample page from a directive interview guide is shown in Exhibit 7.5. The questions shown on the left are asked of each applicant. The 'Look for' sections on the right are designed to guide interviewers in those responses to which they should be alert. Another section of the guide provides advice on how to score each response. The interpretations are recorded later on a summary sheet that is completed on the basis of information obtained from the interview and other sources. The training required for the directive interview, as well as the fact that the procedure is standardised, has probably contributed to its moderate to highly valid results.[25]

Note that the interview form is based on competencies decided on through an earlier competency profiling exercise. In Exhibit 7.5, the competency is 'personal impact,' which is broken down into several elements. The specific element is 'a bias for action.' By developing such competencies initially, other HR functions such as training, appraisal and compensation are facilitated.

Exhibit 7.5 Personal impact – bias for action

Positive behavioural indicators	Sample questions	
• *Anticipates and responds to questions or issues* • *Spots opportunities and takes advantage of them* • *Seeks information from a variety of sources* • *Shows high energy, assertion and tenacity in actions* • *Thinks issues through and then acts purposefully* • *Is results oriented – lays claim to quantifiable results and achievements* • *Enjoys challenges, persistently pushes views, presses on against opposition* • *Solves problems without procrastination*	*1 Have you ever been in a situation at work where you've identified a practice or procedure that wasn't quite right? (Could be inefficient, untidy, unsafe, bureaucratic, etc.) What did you do about the situation?*	*Look for examples of:* • *person rectifying errors without procrastination* • *taking initiative* • *spotting opportunities and taking advantage of them.* *SCORE:*
Negative behavioural indicators	Sample questions	
• *Operates within rules and guidelines: does only what is required* • *Time pressures irrelevant to task* • *Backs off when challenged* • *Focuses on generating options rather than actions* • *Appears confused when explaining and outlining objectives* • *Only interested in contribution of own discipline* • *Procrastinates* • *Thinks things through without dealing with the practicalities* • *Misses opportunities* • *Afraid of failure* • *Will not commit to action.*	*2 Tell me about a proposal or idea that has been actioned primarily due to your own efforts.*	*Look for examples of:* • *making things happen* • *getting things done* • *implementing programs.* *SCORE:*

Source: Compton R.L., Morrissey W., Nankervis A.R. 2006.
Effective recruitment and selection practices, 4th edn, Sydney, CCH Australia.

Increasing use of highly structured interviews

More attention is being given to the highly structured type of interview as a result of equal employment opportunity and affirmative action requirements. For example, a structured interviewing process:

- is based exclusively on job duties and competencies that are critical to job performance, that is, valid selection criteria

- has four types of questions that may be used: situational questions, job knowledge questions, job sample and simulation questions, and worker-requirements questions

- has sample answers to each question determined in advance. Interviewee responses are rated on a scale defined explicitly in advance

- has an interview committee so that interviewee responses are evaluated by multiple raters

- is consistently applied to each applicant. All procedures are consistently followed to ensure that each applicant has exactly the same chance as every other applicant

- is documented for future reference and in case of legal challenge.[26]

The use of a highly structured interview is more likely to provide the type of information that is needed for making sound decisions. It also helps to reduce the possibility of legal charges of unfair discrimination. One must be aware that the interview is highly vulnerable to legal attack and that more litigation in this area can be expected.

Special interviewing methods

Most employment interviewers will use the methods that have just been discussed. However, there are other methods that are utilised for special purposes. One type of interview involves a panel of interviewers who question and observe a single candidate. This is called a board or panel interview and is used by government bodies, and increasingly by many private organisations.

Another type, which was developed during the Second World War as a technique for selecting military espionage personnel, places the candidate under considerable pressure and is therefore known as the stress interview. It usually involves rapid firing of questions by several interviewers who verbally attack the interviewee. While it may be useful in selecting personnel for intelligence or similar jobs, its use for most jobs is questionable. Frase-Blunt claims that throwing a Mensa-style question at candidates may be useful in high-tech hiring but one has to question the validity of such questions.[27] There is a real danger that such questionable techniques may well turn away the better applicants.

A group interview approach, sometimes called 'experiential recruiting,' entails shortlisted candidates spending a full day in the company of other competitors for the position and undertaking set exercises that have been designed to help select the right person for the position. Experiential recruiting puts people in real-life situations and tests social, interpersonal and problem-solving skills, along with endurance. Importantly, each and every exercise is tailored not only for the organisation but for the specific competencies required of the successful applicant.[28] In this way, the technique is tied closely to the strategic direction of the employing organisation.

Behavioural interview

Based on a thorough position analysis or competency profile the behaviourally-based interview (sometimes referred to as the situational interview) centres on the notion that future performance will be based largely on past performance. With a set of competencies

determined beforehand, the interviewer uses a critical incident approach to ask each candidate to relate, from their total lifetime experiences, situations that they have managed in the past that indicate the extent to which a specific competency has been attained. Consider for the moment that 'managing change' is a key competency for this position. The interview questions will be something like the following: 'A key competency for this position is the effective management of change. Can you relate to me from your personal experience a time when you have had to demonstrate this specific competency? What were the circumstances? What was the result?'

In this way, interviewers begin to obtain a picture of past success, or otherwise, rather than a series of claims as to what the candidate might do at some time in the future. The results can be verified through specific background checks.

This approach is at times referred to as behavioural selection, competency-based selection and targeted selection. In practical terms, they can be treated as synonymous. According to SDI Asia Pacific, their research indicates that 76 per cent of organisations use some form of behavioural selection process, with 50 per cent of the remainder indicating that they intend to use them in the future.[29]

The behavioural approach seems to rest very much on the assumption that future performance can be predicted by analysing past performance. This proposition may prove to be far too simplistic as some studies have shown that behaviour not only changes over time but that different candidates cannot always be compared in this way.[30] One writer has gone as far as to suggest that in most cases selection processes tend to lead recruiters to compare apples to oranges and this helps to explain why they get it wrong so often.[31]

What is wrong with the interview?

Considerable caution should be exercised in the selection of employment interviewers. Qualities that are desirable are: humility; ability to think objectively; freedom from over-talkativeness, extreme opinions and biases; maturity and poise. Most important is the ability and willingness to listen to what is being said and how it is being said. Experience in associating with people from a variety of backgrounds is also desirable.

A training program should be provided on a continuing basis for employment interviewers and, at least periodically, for managers and supervisors in other departments. Many books on employment interviewing are available as guides. For the HR specialist who wants to explore the topic in depth, a wealth of information is available in journals.

Five separate reviews of research studies on the employment interview have been published since 1964.[32] Each of these reviews discusses and evaluates numerous studies concerned with such questions as 'What traits can be assessed in the interview?' and 'How do interviewers reach their decisions?' The major findings of these studies are that information is available to help increase the validity of data gained from interviews. The studies conclude:

- Structured interviews are more reliable than unstructured interviews.

- Interviewers are influenced more by unfavourable than by favourable information.

- Inter-rater reliability is increased when there is a greater amount of information about the job to be filled.

- A bias is established early in the interview, and this tends to be followed by either a favourable or an unfavourable decision.

- Intelligence is the trait most validly estimated by an interview, but the interview information adds nothing to test data.

- Interviewers can explain why an applicant is likely to be an unsatisfactory employee, but not why the applicant may be satisfactory.
- Factual written data seem to be more important than physical appearance in determining judgements. This increases with interviewing experience.
- An interviewee is given a more extreme evaluation when preceded by an interviewee of opposing value.
- Interpersonal skills and motivation are probably best evaluated by the interview.
- Allowing the applicant time to talk makes rapid first impressions less likely and provides a larger behaviour sample.
- Non-verbal as well as verbal interactions influence decisions.
- Experienced interviewers rank applicants in the same order although they differ in the proportion they will accept. There is a tendency for experienced interviewers to be more selective than less experienced ones.
- Conducting interviews under guidance should be included in a training program. Practice interviews may be recorded on videotape and evaluated later in a group training session.

More recently, Milia and Smith[33] have revisited the debate in an effort to determine why Australian managers are so committed to a selection tool that is so obviously flawed. Their approach was to examine the selection practices of Australia's top 500 organisations. In essence, they concluded that, despite calls for better practice, little has changed. The preferred tools were still interviewing, reference checking and application forms, despite ample literature-based warnings that all three methods yield low measures of validity.

Essentially, the interview is an artificial situation with the players acting out the role expected of them.[34] This view has been expressed more recently by Cohen, who argues that accountants in an interview situation do not account, programmers do not program and managers do not manage. They just talk about it. Furthermore, those who do best at interviews are those who have had most practice at them.[35]

One has to ask why the interview remains popular, despite such findings. The research authors conclude that this is due to a belief among employers that the interview is the best way to assess the fit between individual and organisation.

Further and more recent research can be found at the end of this chapter.

Is there any hope for the interview?

A few ground rules for employment interviews that are commonly accepted and supported by research findings follow. Their apparent simplicity should not lead us to underestimate their importance.

- Establish the objectives and scope of each interview.
- Examine the purposes of the interview, and determine the areas and specific questions to be covered.
- Review job requirements, application form data, test scores and other available information before seeing the applicant.
- Establish and maintain rapport. This is accomplished by greeting the applicant pleasantly, by displaying sincere interest in the applicant, and by listening carefully.
- Be an active listener. Strive to understand, comprehend and gain insight into what is only suggested or implied. A good listener's mind is alert, and one's face and posture usually reflect this fact.

- Pay attention to body language. An applicant's facial expressions, gestures, body position and movements often provide clues to that person's attitudes and feelings. Interviewers should be aware of what they are communicating non-verbally. Research has shown that up to 90 per cent of meaning is reflected through one's body language.[36]

- Provide information as freely and honestly as possible. Answer fully, frankly and honestly the applicant's questions.

- Use questions effectively. In order to elicit a truthful answer, questions should be phrased as objectively as possible with no indication of a desired response (see Exhibit 7.6).

- Separate facts from inferences. During the interview, record factual information. Later, record your inferences or interpretations of the facts. Compare your inferences with those of other interviewers.

- Recognise biases and stereotypes. One typical bias is for interviewers to consider strangers who have interests, experiences and backgrounds similar to their own to be more acceptable. Stereotyping involves forming generalised opinions of how people of a given gender or race, appear, think, feel and act. The influence of sex role stereotyping is central to sex discrimination in employment.

- Avoid the influence of 'beautyism.' Discrimination against unattractive persons is a persistent and pervasive form of employment discrimination.

- Avoid the halo error. Judging an individual favourably or unfavourably on the basis of one strong point (or weak point) on which you place high value is the halo error.

- Control the course of the interview. Provide the applicant with ample opportunity to talk, but maintain control of the situation so that the interview objectives may be reached.

- Standardise the types of questions asked. Avoid discrimination by asking the same questions of applicants for a particular job. Additional probing questions may be used to draw out more information, or to deal with an evasive interviewee.

- Keep careful notes. Record facts, impressions and any relevant information, including what was told to the applicant.

Exhibit 7.6 Types of interview questions

Type of question	Purpose
Open	Useful in commencing the interview. These allow the applicant to do most of the talking. Aim at an 80:20 time ratio. Begin question with why, how, where, when, etc.
Closed	These are direct questions which usually result in a Yes/No response. Not a suitable choice when you want the applicant to talk. Can be used as part of a 'funnel' approach. Begin with open questions, then narrow down applicant's response with closed questions. Can assist in keeping interview under control. Also useful if you feel interviewee is being deceptive.
Probing	A question or series of follow-up questions which aim to elicit further response. Can be most valuable where applicant does not answer fully.
Hypothetical	A hypothetical situation might be presented to the applicant, followed by questions as to how he or she would respond to such a situation.
Fantasy	Of limited use, due to impossibility of verifying answers: 'What would you do if you won Lotto next week?'

Type of question	Purpose
Behavioural	Based on the assumption that future performance will reflect past performance, questions can be asked that require the applicant to demonstrate, with actual examples, his or her knowledge or skills in a specific situation: 'Tell me of an incident in your present or past job where ...'
Leading	These lead the applicant to the desired answer and as such are not recommended: 'You do not discriminate against women, do you?'
Loaded	These are generally not allowed in the courtroom and have no place in the interview room. These questions trap the applicant: 'Have you stopped malingering yet?'

Types of employment questions to ask

The entire subject of employment questioning is complex. There are differing and sometimes contradictory interpretations by the equal opportunity tribunals and state privacy committees about what is lawful and unlawful. There are no questions that are expressly prohibited. However, the tribunals look with disfavour on direct or indirect questions related to race, colour, religion, sex, national origin or sexual preference (see Chapter 2). Some of the questions that interviewers once felt free to ask can be potentially hazardous. As a general rule it is not unlawful to ask certain questions, but the action that follows may well be.

Several states have fair employment practice laws that are more restrictive than federal legislation. In general, if a question is job-relevant, is asked of everyone, and does not discriminate against a certain class of applicants, it is likely to be acceptable.

Particular care has to be given to questions asked of female applicants about their family responsibilities. It is inappropriate, for example, to ask 'Who will take care of your children while you are at work?' or 'Are you engaged?' It is, in fact, inappropriate to ask applicants, of either gender, questions about personal matters that have no relevance to job performance. Not only may employers be breaking the law, but they may be missing out on the best applicant. The answer is not to panic, but to review interviewing techniques. There is little information that you cannot obtain if it is job-related.[37]

Employers have found it advisable to provide those personnel conducting interviews with instructions on how to avoid potentially discriminating questions in their interviews. Exhibit 7.7 shows some examples of appropriate and inappropriate questions that may serve as guidelines for application forms, as well as for employment interviews. Complete guidelines may be developed from current information available from state Anti-Discrimination Boards or the federal Human Rights Commission. Once the individual has been hired, the information needed but not asked for in the interview may be obtained if there is a valid need for it and if it does not lead to discrimination.

Research conducted during 1994 found a significant increase in the use of standardised questions.[38] One could speculate that this result is in response to widespread criticism of the unstructured interview method as a valid selection process, together with pressure from the EEO movement to remove discriminatory practices from employee selection.

Employment tests

Since the development of the US Army Alpha Test of mental ability during the First World War, tests have played an important part in the HRM programs of both the public and private sectors throughout the world. Before the passage of the *Civil Rights Act* of 1964, over 90 per cent of US

companies surveyed by the Bureau of National Affairs Inc. reported using tests. By 1976, only 42 per cent were using tests. A survey in 1983 shows that one-third of the companies surveyed used commercially prepared tests. Of those firms, approximately 80 per cent used tests developed for office and clerical positions and 30 per cent used tests for professional and technical applicants, such as computer programmers, police and firefighters. A survey in 1985 revealed a continuing interest in tests, with 44 per cent considering increasing the amount of testing that they do.[39] Australian research findings will be discussed later in this chapter.

Exhibit 7.7 Employment questions to ask or not to ask

Inappropriate questions	More appropriate questions
Do you have any physical defects?	Do you have any physical disability or impediments which might, in any way, hinder your ability to perform the job for which you have applied?
Have you had any recent or past illness or operations?	Have you had any recent or past illness or operation which might, in any way, hinder your ability to perform the job for which you have applied?
What was the date of your last physical exam?	Are you willing to take a physical examination at our expense if the nature of the job requires one?
Are you an Australian citizen?	Do you have the legal right to live and work in Australia?
Date of birth?	Are you over 15?*
Age?	Are you over 15?*
Emergency information: (relationship)?	Emergency information: Name, address, telephone number.
Do you possess a legal driver's licence?	Only for applicants who desire a job driving a company vehicle. Do you possess a legal and current driver's licence?
What are your hobbies? Interests?	Do you have any hobbies or interests which have a direct bearing on the job you are seeking?
Have you ever been convicted of a misdemeanour or felony?	Have you, since the age of 18, ever been convicted of a misdemeanour or felony? (A conviction will not necessarily bar you from employment. Each conviction will be judged on its own merits with respect to time, circumstances and seriousness.)
Dates attended high school?	Did you complete high school?
Date graduated or last attended, high school?	Did you complete high school?
In what extracurricular activities did you participate? Clubs?	While in school, did you participate in any activities or belong to any clubs which have a direct bearing upon the job for which you are applying?
College or university subjects of interest?	While in college or university, did you take any courses that directly relate to the job for which you are applying?
What salary earnings do you expect?	If you are employed, are you willing to accept the prevailing wage for the job you are seeking?
Memberships?	Have you ever belonged to a club, organisation, society, or professional group which has a direct bearing upon your qualification for the job which you are seeking?

*** The minimum working age varies from state to state.**

Source: Adapted from Miller E.C. 1980. 'An EEO examination of employment applications'. Reprinted with the permission of *Personnel Administrator*, now *HR Magazine*, published by the Society for Human Resource Management, Alexandria, VA. Permission conveyed through Copyright Clearance Center, Inc.

Dowling,[40] Stone,[41] Compton[42] and Hicks[43] have each warned of the implications of testing in view of equal employment opportunity and affirmative action provisions. In essence, tests must be shown to predict future job success and be job-related.

One of HR's great challenges is in successfully navigating its way through the myriad of tests now available on the market while at the same time lacking the expertise and background in psychology to make a valid evaluation of the various tests employed by consultants and test vendors.[44] Many organisations utilise professional test consultants to improve their testing programs and to meet the equal employment opportunity requirements. While it is often advisable to use consultants, especially if an organisation is considering the use of personality tests, the HR staff should have a basic understanding of the technical aspects of testing and the contributions that tests can make to the HR program. The PA Consulting Group has a test aimed at making selection easier. The PA Preference Inventory is Internet-based and as such allows organisations to assess candidates anywhere in the world. PA claims Philips, Nokia and Email among its users.[45]

In particular, HR professionals must be able to define exactly what they hope to accomplish with a specific test and what competencies it purports to measure.[46] The world of work is now so vastly different that even positions with similar titles will differ so much that selecting a battery of tests for the most generic position will suddenly become a much more complex task than at first thought. Take the position of front-line manager as an example. Different knowledge, skills, abilities, attitudes and behaviours will be required depending on the organisation and its internal and external environment. Selection techniques such as testing must take account of such issues, otherwise the testing will in all likelihood prove to be invalid and unreliable.[47]

The nature of employment tests

An employment test is an objective and standardised measure of a sample of behaviour that is used to measure a person's abilities, aptitudes, interests or personality in relation to other individuals. The basic assumption behind such testing is that differences between individuals can be measured and related to future job success.[48] The proper sampling of behaviour, whether it be verbal, manipulative or some other type of behaviour, is the responsibility of the test author. It is also the responsibility of the test author to develop tests that meet accepted standards of reliability.

Data concerning reliability are ordinarily presented in the test manual. While high reliability is essential, it offers no assurance that the test provides the basis for making valid judgements. It is the responsibility of the HRM staff to conduct validation studies before a test is adopted for regular use. Other considerations are cost, time, ease of administration and scoring, and the apparent relevance of the test to the individuals being tested, commonly referred to as face validity. While face validity is desirable, it is no substitute for technical validity, described earlier in this chapter. Adopting a test just because it appears reasonable is likely to prove invalid, with poor correlation between test results and future performance.

While Dowling[49] claimed that there was moderate support for psychological testing in Australian industry, research conducted by Vaughan and McLean concluded that more than two-thirds of firms seldom or never used any tests.[50] The discrepancy here may be explained by Spillane, who suggests that some practitioners reject testing on the basis that it is a giant swindle perpetrated by psychologists and consultants. Spillane has focused specifically on personality testing and is quite damning in his criticism. His concern is that the test administrators obtain only the results that the individual is prepared to divulge:

> Faking personality tests is so widespread that it is amazing that test scores obtained under such conditions are taken seriously. Peak performance is the result of abilities, values and the ways in which people interpret social situations and choose strategies to achieve their goals. These human qualities cannot be dissected and packaged.[51]

Research by the Sydney Graduate School of Management's David Lamond has added to Spillane's work. His survey of hundreds of Australian managers has found little correlation between personality types and managerial behaviours.[52]

Dowling adds to the debate when he cites the work of W.H. Whyte, who, as far back as 1954, warned that many successful, dynamic business people would be walking the streets looking for a job if job testing were to be 'rigorously applied across the board today'.[53] In a similar vein, Spillane concludes his argument by claiming that many of history's leaders would not have made it to the top had personality tests been employed.[54]

Former NRMA director of human resources, Melanie O'Connor, takes a similar view by arguing that a person will often do well on a psychological test if they are good at doing such tests. In her view many people will do what comes naturally and try to pick what they see as the 'right' answers.[55] In the same vein, James Kirby has examined Australia's two most popular tests, the Myers Briggs Type Indicator (MBTI) and the California Psychological Inventory (CPI).[56] Questions such as 'What do you like about Alice in Wonderland?' and 'Should women be allowed in public bars?' or 'Do you like tall women?' each seem to be seeking a 'right' answer, but in so doing tempt the candidate to second-guess. Whether a true profile can be attained in this manner has to be open to question. Other tests popular with Australian managers include DISC, 16 PF, the Watson Glasser Critical Thinking test and numerous ACER applied reading and reasoning tests.

Other issues that need to be addressed include sloppy and inaccurate administration of the tests, storage of old test results and, of course, confidentiality. Guidelines established in September 1997 by the Australian Psychological Society should assist in cleaning up these issues.[57]

Individual managers will have to make up their own minds about the potential advantages or disadvantages of using tests. Managers must realise that the psychological test is but one of the tools available in the selection process and should be treated as such. The objective is to obtain the right fit between the organisation and the individual. If psychological testing can be shown to assist in this process then it has a valid place alongside tools such as interviewing and background checking.

A widely publicised case saw the resignation of ABC executive Hugh McGowan following his poor showing in the maths section of a psychological test. Before the NSW Industrial Commission, McGowan claimed that he was not promoted to director of television – a position he had been offered and had accepted – because of the test results (see News report 7.3).[58]

NEWS REPORT 7.3

Testing, testing

Psychological assessment of job candidates offers the promise of the perfect match. But do they work in practice?

The resignation of senior ABC executive Hugh McGowan in late April [2000] pushed the issue of psychological testing into the headlines. Four months later McGowan is deep in litigation, claiming he was not promoted to director of ABC television –

a position he had been offered and accepted before sitting for the tests – because of his results on a maths test. He is seeking $296 960 in compensation. The case will return to the NSW Industrial Relations Commission in November but already it is being seen in the industry as a possible test case. However neat a solution it may represent in the fraught world of recruitment and

selection, psychometric testing is highly controversial. Even experts, appalled by the publicity surrounding the McGowan affair and the effect on their booming business, warn that tests must be professionally constructed and administered to avoid problems. Be that as it may, testing is on the increase because screening large numbers of candidates quickly and efficiently is no longer a luxury for corporations desperate to cut the costs that result from inadvertently stuffing a square peg into a round hole. While it moves in and out of favour according to the state of the labour market, testing for job selection is common practice in the UK, Europe and parts of Asia. In the US, however, testing is out of favour after successful litigation citing discrimination based on test results has seen it labelled unconstitutional.

The fallout from McGowan's resignation has not surprised academic Professor Robert Spillane, from the Macquarie Graduate School of Management. He believes a high-profile case like McGowan's, if successful, could badly damage the thriving industry in psychometric testing.

It was only a matter of time before such an action occurred, similar to the case that killed off RSI (repetitive strain injury) litigation, he says. 'If it so happens your performance record is reasonable and you were dismissed because of this personality problem [recorded in a test result], it could be unfair dismissal and discrimination.'

The reason it hasn't happened until now is that we tend not to launch this sort of litigation here. 'We are litigious in certain areas but it tends to differ from the US,' Spillane says. 'Australian workers are more likely to sue the employer for making them stressed. We are reluctant to go on personality issues.'

Kevin Chandler, an industrial psychologist and managing director of human resources

consulting firm Chandler & MacLeod, dismisses such warnings and cites the growing sophistication of tests and the push for productivity improvements.

In a recent survey of Australian managers, his company posed the question: If you knew at the time of hire what you know now, would you hire the same people? Their responses were affirmative in only 68% of cases. 'What that means is companies that want to improve productivity have a third of their workforce that they would not rehire,' Chandler says. 'The 32% you wouldn't rehire were hired using bio-data and interviews and reference checks, and if that's the recruitment system in place it's making mistakes one in three times.'

Practitioners define psychometric testing as the measurement of an aspect of aptitude, personality, motivation or interest as expressed on a standardised scale – against the results for a similar group of people. Tests tend to cover three areas: intelligence and aptitude such as numerical and verbal skills, learning speed, problem solving, critical thinking and information processing; motivation; and personality. Hundreds of instruments are available, although the experts claim a relatively small number are professionally acceptable.

Supporters of testing say third-party assessment is a key reason for using the tests. Critics say it is no better than using an interview and proper reference check – and worse, it may be harmful and unethical. The corporate

world pretty much reflects this divide, with fans of testing such as Macquarie Bank using it extensively and others such as AMP having a policy against psychometric tests. Experts estimate about a quarter of Australian companies use testing in some way. Chandler & MacLeod has tested about 400 000 people in Australia over the past two decades.

The no-testing argument goes like this: respondents' own answers can be easily distorted, consciously or not; faking is common, and even if respondents are completely honest there may still be a gap between answers and actual behaviour; motivation factors – a popular focus of testing – don't necessarily correlate to required work behaviour; and testing is discriminatory and often misused or inappropriately applied.

Spillane, who once worked in the testing field, goes further and claims there is no proven link between personality and job performance.

Test advocates believe it is a useful adjunct to other assessment procedures, is more accurate than an interview, can screen many candidates efficiently, provides a high level of validity and reliability if professionally applied, may pick up factors not otherwise evident, and is sophisticated enough to pick up faking/enhancing by candidates.

McGibbon and Chandler can be expected to defend their trade. Both point to the careful use of validity and reliability in testing. Validity is more than just empirical back-up, with the need

to make a test 'feel right' and avoid confrontational questions.

The misuse of testing is one issue where both sides can agree. Thousands of tests are available and can easily be used inappropriately.

But claims and counter-claims about the quality, validity and reliability of tests are, according to Spillane, pointless unless a central issue can be resolved. 'Personality does not predict performance,' he says. 'I don't criticise the use of personality tests generally and debriefing can be very useful, but fortune-telling can be of use to people too.'

His main objections are the lack of technical evidence to link personality with performance in a job and the ethical implications of a third party being involved in personality assessment. These are, according to Spillane, some of the reasons so many Australians are concerned about the issue. Stereotyping from test results is a major worry, with candidates often reporting their concerns to him.

'Even if they find you are a 70% extrovert it doesn't tell you when your 30% introversion pops up,' Spillane says. 'These tests sentence people. I gave my class a personality test and the next week told them the results. Then I asked, "How many say this is very accurate?" and all but two of them said it was spot on. And it was exactly the same report.'

Chandler says things have changed since Spillane's work.

The sophistication of tests means the results can be highly accurate. 'That's the skill of the psychologist,' he says. 'If you ask questions that are face valid it's not going to measure your underlying personality – it will measure your political correctness or social acceptability.'

Chandler's latest work has moved into breaking senior jobs into competencies rather than using an 'omnibus personality test.' These instruments are much more accurate than in the past, he claims, and have very high success rates in pinpointing the right candidates.

Practitioners stress the need for qualified assistance in the field. They point to psychometrician Ian Kendall's compilation of a directory and website (www.opic.com.au) of occupational and vocational tests, with information on the purpose and application of instruments, as a step in the right direction.

Who's using

The ABC, undaunted by the McGowan affair, is asking its top executives to take psychological tests before appointments. It is one of several major organisations, including ANZ, Ansett, BHP, Coles Myer and Qantas, to use the tests.

Citibank uses personality testing but not at all levels or for all roles, according to the company's human resources director, John Eddy. It really depends on the purpose and different groups require a different approach. 'For some recruitment we would use them, we use the OPQ (Occupational Personality

Questionnaire),' Eddy says. 'It's the most validated and reliable test on personality.'

The bank uses tests mainly to identify the kind of people who will fit in. They are not used as the basis for a decision but to give a 'window' on the person. The weight given to the test results is 'about 10 per cent' in the final selection formula.

At Lion Nathan, group HR director Bob Barbour says testing is used to decrease the risk of making a bad hire. Introduced about two-and-a-half years ago, testing is only used in recruitment, not internally where Barbour says it can be damaging.

It seems to have helped prevent some costly mistakes. While recruiting a market research director, an apparently ideal candidate was tested to have a 3% score in numerical and critical reasoning. 'Those are pretty important skills for market research so we didn't make the appointment,' Barbour says. 'The tests are a good way of getting data on whether the candidates have the skills in those areas.'

Tests are also used to measure personal awareness because flaws in this area – such as failing to get on with the team – are the major reasons for people leaving within 12 months.

In addition, tests are also being tapped for 'talent audits' in organisations where major change is radically altering senior job requirements. Law firm Corrs Chambers Wesgarth conducted a talent audit last year using job analysis and executive assessment.

Source: Fox C. 2000. *Australian Financial Review*, September, pp. 38–43.

Similarly, on the industrial front, both BHP and the Dalrymple Bay Coal Terminal have faced industrial action over the use of psychological testing to decide which employees will have access to continued employment.[59]

Cynthia Fisher and Gregory Boyle offer a final word on testing when they argue for a cautious approach to personality testing. Such tests can complement but should in no way replace measures of ability. There are too many fraudulent claims and even more poor instruments.[60]

Classification of employment tests

Employment tests may be classified in different ways. Most of them are group tests, in contrast to individual tests, which usually require one examiner for each person being tested. Another classification relates to the manner in which the individual responds to the test items. For example, paper and pencil tests require the examinee to respond by writing or marking answers on a booklet or answer sheets. On the other hand, performance tests or instrumental tests require the examinee to manipulate objects or equipment. Paper and pencil tests are the most commonly used as they can be administered easily to groups as well as to individuals, with minimal cost.

Commercially available tests

In addition to the classifications mentioned above, there is a more fundamental breakdown of tests according to the characteristics that are measured. In Exhibit 7.8 the types of tests available from one commercial source are shown, along with what they are designed to measure and some of the jobs for which they are used. The publishers of tests in these various categories provide descriptions in their catalogues that are useful when making an initial selection of tests.

HR managers may obtain specimens of many paper and pencil tests for examination. These sets include a test manual, a copy of the test, an answer sheet and a scoring key. A test manual provides the essential information about the construction of the test, its recommended use, and instructions for administering, scoring and interpreting the test. Other tests are available only to registered psychologists; these tests are primarily those that purport to measure personality and intelligence.

Custom-made tests

Some large organisations do not rely upon commercial sources for tests. For various reasons, they develop their own tests. Probably test security is a major reason. Another good reason is that a tailor-made test is usually a better fit to the jobs and to the organisation. Most organisations, however, do not construct their own mental ability, aptitude and personality tests. If they do build tests, the tests are more likely to be job knowledge and job sample tests.

Job knowledge tests

Some organisations develop job knowledge tests, a type of achievement test designed to measure a person's level of understanding about a particular job. They are used to determine whether an applicant possesses the information and understanding that permits placement on the job without further training. Job knowledge tests have also had a major role in the enlisted personnel programs of the Australian army, navy and air force. They should be considered as useful tools for business organisations.

Job sample tests

Job sample tests, or work sample tests, require the examinee to perform tasks that are actually a part of the work to be performed on the job. They also have been devised for many diverse jobs: a map-reading test for traffic control officers; a lathe test for machine operators; a complex coordination test for pilots; an in-basket test for managers; a group discussion test

for supervisors; a judgement and decision-making test for administrators. A major Australian supermarket chain requires applicants for their meat department to carve up a side of beef.

According to an extensive Australian study, the use of psychological testing has increased significantly over the past decade. The major increase has been in personality/interest tests and in the use of assessment centres. As might be expected, the managerial and professional ranks reported the highest responses.[61]

As a final point it is worth noting the issue of potential cultural bias when utilising employment tests – specifically personality and intelligence tests. Chinese researchers have claimed that Western personality tests are biased in that they have 'blind spots' on measures such as cultural differences, harmony, face and family orientation. If this is the case then the finding may well be generalised across all Asian countries.[62]

For the future?

A survey of Victorian industry examined management selection practices in 39 targeted business organisations. While the sample is small, the researchers argue that general conclusions can be drawn.[63]

- Australian business firms have been no more than minimally attentive to the advice that has persistently issued from management journals and texts.

- There is a preference for ad hoc subjective assessment rather than systematic and standardised measurement and comparison.

- Selection practices revealed by this survey were technically and scientifically unsophisticated and highly susceptible to error.

- Most firms were strongly opposed to structured interview formats and even more reluctant to use partially structured interviews any more than occasionally.

- Most organisations seldom used more than one interviewer at a time, although most claimed to use more than one interview prior to a decision being made.

- There was a reliance on unsupported interview judgements, which were seldom checked against other sources of information.

- There was little use made of assessment centres (less than 10 per cent).

- More than two-thirds of the organisations never – or seldom – used psychological testing.

Many aspects of these findings are disturbing, to say the least. Additional research, using a wider sample of Australian organisations of all sizes and industry types, is urgently required.

Exhibit 7.8   Job-test validity chart (a guide to test selection)

Proper use of a selection system requires careful planning at every step. Outlined below is a basic approach for ensuring an effective program in your organisation, and some references where detailed information may be found.

1   Analyse the job. A job analysis is a breakdown of general job functions into distinct activities which are essential to performance on that job. Each activity is analysed to determine which human behaviours or characteristics critically affect successful completion of the activity.

2   Select the tests. Tests should be chosen to assess behaviours and characteristics that are relevant to the job (as shown through the job analysis). These may include knowledge, skills, aptitudes, values and interests. The Job-test Validity Chart can assist in the selection of tests which have been shown to be relevant to many jobs.

3   Administer the testing program.

   a   Instructions: Carefully follow all instructions for administering and scoring tests. Instructions are included in the Test Examiner's or Administrator's Manual. It is especially important that time limits be adhered to (when indicated) and that identical instructions be given to all applicants. The interpretation of scores, as provided in the test manuals, is based on these provisions.

   b   Test efficiency: Take advantage of the efficiency which a testing program offers. Test in groups whenever possible. When selecting groups of applicants for later placement, use tests as an initial screening device instead of costly and time-consuming interviews.

4   Select employees. Apply a standard rule for hiring all applicants. Apply each selection measure to all applicants consistently. Changing cut-off scores or varying selection procedures make it difficult to determine the effectiveness of the selection measure for your organisation.

5   Monitor the selection system. The selection system should be monitored to determine whether the system has an adverse impact on employment opportunities of any race, sex, or ethnic group. As a rule of thumb, adverse impact can be said to occur when the hiring rate (selection ratio) of a protected group is less than four-fifths of the hiring rate for the majority group. If adverse impact is found, you must either eliminate the adverse impact or validate the selection system.

6   Validate. While this step is required by law only if adverse impact results from use of the selection procedure, it is nevertheless always sound personnel management practice to validate methods of selecting employees. You as the employer bear the legal burden of proof for establishing the validity of your selection methods in the event of adverse impact. To validate means to conduct a systematic comparison between test scores (or other selection criteria) and job performance. Validation provides a measure of the predictive power of the tests in identifying successful performers, and establishes the range of scores obtained by high- and low-performing employees. These norms provide a valuable guide for selecting future employees.

7   References. Use these as other basic sources and a general guide for testing principles, job analysis, validation, and legal compliance issues:

   –   *Job analysis: Methods and applications*, by Ernest McCormick. New York, AMOCOM, 1979.

   –   *Psychological testing*, by Anne Anastasia. New York, Macmillan Publishing Company, Inc., 1982.

   –   *Employee selection within the law*, by M.G. Miner and J.B. Miner. Washington, DC, Bureau of National Affairs, Inc., 1979.

   –   *Science Research Associates Pty Ltd*, 84 Waterloo Road, North Ryde, NSW 2113.

NEWS REPORT 7.4

Finding a better fit

Employers need to look beyond material motivations if they are to retain talented workers who want for more out of life

Downshifters, sea-changers, cultural creatives … sometimes it's called getting a life. Around the world, more and more professionals are forsaking the 'rat race' and trappings of material gain to pursue a healthier, more balanced lifestyle.

The concept is not new. Before downshifting, there was a long history of 'voluntary simplicity,' which can be thought of as a radical type of downshifting with a political and/or spiritual mention. In 1977 Rosabeth Moss Kanter published *Work and family in the United States: A critical review and agenda for research and policy*, which brought the issue of work/life balance to the forefront of research. In the 1980s … companies slowly began to introduce work/life programs.

The term downshifting is widely attributed to John Drake, founder and former CEO of career management firm Drake Beam Morin. He defined it as 'changing voluntarily to a less demanding work schedule in order to enjoy life more.'

Downshifters want to slow down at work so they can upshift in other areas in their lives. Studies in Australia, the United Kingdom and North America have uncovered a number of primary motivations: a want to spend more time with family, or pursuing hobbies or creative interests, and a desire to have a less materialistic, more sustainable life.

Downshifters are people who 'make voluntary, long-term lifestyle changes that involve accepting significantly less income and consuming less,' said Clive Hamilton and Elizabeth Mail in their 2003 Australia Institute report *Downshifting in Australia: A sea-change in the pursuit of happiness*. They wrote that Australians were working longer and harder than they had for decades, and many were neglecting their families and their health as a result. The preoccupation with asset accumulation and consumption had come at an increasing cost, including record consumer debt and personal bankruptcies.

Hamilton and Mail's study revealed that, contrary to common belief, downshifters were as likely to be blue-collar as white-collar workers. Downshifting is not confined to a specific demographic group; it entices both men and women, with and without children, aged in their 30s, 40s and 50s.

Twenty-three per cent of adult Australians had chosen to downshift to a simpler lifestyle on less income in the previous 10 years, according to research for the 2003 Australia Institute study. In a 2004 US study, 19 per cent of adult Americans had voluntarily decided to reduce their income and consumption in the past five years. Similar findings have

been reported in New Zealand and Canada.

In a 2004 UK survey, four out of 10 people under the age of 35 said they planned to leave their high-powered, stressful jobs and downshift at some point in their careers. The 2004 US poll also found that 48 per cent of Americans had done at least one of the following in the past five years: cut back their work hours; declined or not sought a promotion; lowered their expectations of what they need out of life; reduced their work commitments; or moved to a community with a less hectic way of life.

A comparison of Australian and North American downshifters shows that Australians are much less likely to reduce their working hours and much less likely to take a job that pays less.

Every decision to downshift has a unique story behind it. Jodie Z, 41, was the HR director of a large bank when she downshifted to being a work-at-home mother. 'I always found HR to be a meaningful career but, like any job, I would spend half my day doing what I loved to do and the other half doing what the job description required,' she says. She loved the coaching and mentoring parts of HR, but not everything else that went with it. Last year she quit to establish a coaching and consulting firm that helps people reach personal and business success.

American Joe B, 35, a senior mortgage lender working in a small-town branch for a major US bank, rejected an offer of promotion to mortgage education trainer because he wanted to spend more time with his family. 'Rejecting the offer was a sacrifice in terms of money and position,' he says, 'but I look at it like this: spending more time with my kids is worth gold to me. I want to have the flexibility to drop my kids off to school in the morning, or even go home for lunch.'

From the corporate perspective, the emergence of downshifting is causing Australian organisations to rethink the very nature of work and work arrangements. For example, what is a full-time job as opposed to a part-time job? Who defines when and where a job is to be performed? By what measurements should companies remunerate their employees?

From an HR perspective, downshifting can be interpreted as the next level beyond work/life balancing. It requires companies to be even more creative in their understanding of what jobs are, the time it takes to do them, and what it means to integrate corporate needs with employee motivation, talent and the pursuit of individual happiness.

Clearly, if employees are overworked, unhappy and unfulfilled, they can't balance the rest of their lives, irrespective of how attractive their remuneration or how many fringe benefits they receive. Downshifters may not necessarily be cynical, angry or overly critical. They simply do not fit into the traditional fast-track mould any more. They are also measuring success by their own standards. In response, downshifters are increasingly expecting companies to be more flexible and accommodating of their needs.

'We're definitely seeing people who are not only interested in their careers, but also interested in being a whole person – having their work lives, their family lives and their community lives,' says the HR director at an Australian insurance company.

'A lot of people are involved in their communities,' says another senior HR manager. 'They may have a family or a family life, or they may take care of an ageing parent. In any case, they want to make a meaningful contribution to people around them. This is a very important aspect.'

Another HR executive, for a major retailer, says: 'We provide our managers with a lot of flexibility in creating an environment that works for people, rather than trying to fit people into a preset mould. The company optimises its talent focus by not having rigid policies. Rather, we allow managers to work with individuals on helping them succeed. The key issue is access to great talent and the flexibility around how to best access and retain that talent. I am not convinced that firm and inflexible policies would be the trigger for that.'

In the US, Chicago-based Morningstar has aimed at becoming an employer of choice by providing a relaxed workplace with dynamism and growth opportunities. 'People want to be seen as adults, capable of managing their own careers and lives,' says a Morningstar executive.

Corporate Australia has made some concessions towards work/life balancing with telecommunicating, job-sharing, part-time work, flextime and sabbaticals. However, downshifters are increasingly expecting more innovative solutions. Flexibility can create staffing challenges for management, and it is clearly limited in some companies and departments. For example, it's unlikely that blue-collar plant workers will be able to telecommute.

A Sydney media agency offers its employees flextime arrangements in the form of job-sharing and a condensed work week. Job-sharing arrangements are reviewed after six months. 'I would say to other HR professionals, be open to the flexibility concept and give it a try,' says a company HR executive. 'There are many rewards in it for all parties, and some benefits may not be visible up front.'

Where do you draw the line? That depends on what the business needs to accomplish. If you get away from why you are in business in the first place and focus too much on the needs of individuals, you don't balance what's really important for the business. 'It's a delicate balance between what needs to get done to remain competitive and successful, and the people you have behind to make it all happen,' says the Sydney executive.

Source: Dr Franco Gandolfi, *hrmonthly*, April 2006. Dr Franco Gandolfi is associate professor of management in the Department of Business Administration at Cedarville University, Ohio.

Reaching a selection decision

While all of the steps in the selection process are important, the most critical one is the decision to accept or reject applicants. Because of the cost of placing new employees on the payroll, the short probationary period in many organisations, and equal employment opportunity and affirmative action considerations, the final decision must be as valid as possible. This requires systematic consideration of all the relevant information about applicants. It is common to use summary forms and checklists to ensure that all the pertinent information has been included in the evaluation of applicants. A rating form based on valid selection criteria will assist the decision-making process.

Many employers have introduced a step in the selection process in which to determine more carefully how well the applicant understands what the job entails. A realistic job preview, covering in detail the nature of the work, working conditions, and the desirable and undesirable aspects of the job, may be included prior to final selection by the supervisor.

Summary of information about applicants

Fundamentally, an employer is interested in what an applicant can and will do. An evaluation of candidates on the basis of assembled information should focus on the two factors shown in Exhibit 7.9. The 'can do' factors include knowledge and skills, as well as the aptitude (the potential) for acquiring new knowledge and skills. The 'will do' factors include motivation, interests, and other personality characteristics. Both factors are essential to successful performance on the job. The individual who has the ability ('can do'), but is not motivated to use it ('will not do'), is little better than the employee who lacks the necessary ability.

Exhibit 7.9   Employers should consider 'can do' and 'will do' factors in selecting personnel

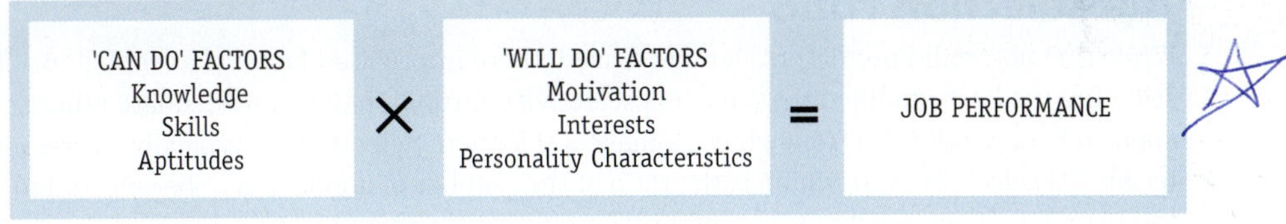

Decision strategy

The strategy used for making personnel decisions for one category of jobs may differ from that used for another category. The strategy for selecting managerial and executive personnel will differ from that used in selecting clerical and technical personnel.

While many factors have to be considered in hiring decisions, some of the questions that HR staff must consider are:

- How close is the 'job fit'?

- What effect will a decision have on meeting affirmative action goals?

- Should the individuals be hired according to their highest potential or according to the needs of the organisation?

- At what grade or wage level should the individual be started?

- Should initial selection be concerned primarily with an ideal match of the employee to the job, or should potential for advancement in the organisation be considered?
- To what extent should those who are not qualified but are qualifiable be considered?
- Should overqualified individuals be considered?

The answer to these and other questions will depend largely on the organisation's current strategies.

In addition to these types of factors, consideration must also be given to the approach that will be used in making decisions. There are two approaches to selection: clinical and statistical.

Clinical approach

In the clinical approach to decision-making, those making the selection decision review all the data on applicants. Then, on the basis of their understanding of the job and the individuals who have been successful in that job, they make a decision. Different individuals often arrive at different decisions about an applicant when they use this approach, as each evaluator assigns different weights to the applicant's strengths and weaknesses. Furthermore, personal biases and stereotypes are frequently covered up by what appear to be rational bases for acceptance or rejection.

Statistical approach

In contrast to the clinical approach, the statistical approach to decision-making is entirely objective. It involves identifying the most valid predictors and weighting them through sophisticated statistical methods. A comparison of the clinical approach with the statistical approach in a wide variety of situations has shown that the statistical approach is superior to the clinical approach.

Although this superiority has been known for many decades, the clinical approach continues to be the one most commonly used. This is a surprising circumstance in light of the widespread utilisation of technology in production, finance and marketing.

The selection ratio

While the most valid predictors should be used, there is a related factor that contributes to selecting the best-qualified persons. It is selectivity through having an adequate number of applicants or candidates from whom to make a selection. Selectivity is typically expressed in terms of a selection ratio, which is the ratio of the number of applicants to be selected to the total number of applicants. A ratio of 0.10, for example, means that 10 per cent of the applicants will be selected. A ratio of 0.90 means that 90 per cent will be selected. If the selection ratio is low, only the most promising applicants would normally be hired. When the ratio is high, very little selectivity will be possible as even those applicants of mediocre ability will have to be hired if the vacancies are to be filled.

Cut-off scores

The use of a statistical approach requires that a decision be made about that point in the distribution of scores above which a person should be considered and below which a person should be rejected. The score that the applicant must achieve is the cut-off score. Depending upon the labour supply, it may be necessary to lower or raise the cut-off score.

The effects of raising and lowering the cut-off score are illustrated in Exhibit 7.10. Each dot in the centre of the figure represents the relationship between the test score (or a weighted combination of test scores), and the criterion of success for one individual. In this instance, the test has a fairly high validity as represented by the elliptical pattern of dots. Note that the high-scoring individuals are concentrated in the satisfactory category on job success, whereas the low-scoring individuals are concentrated in the unsatisfactory category.

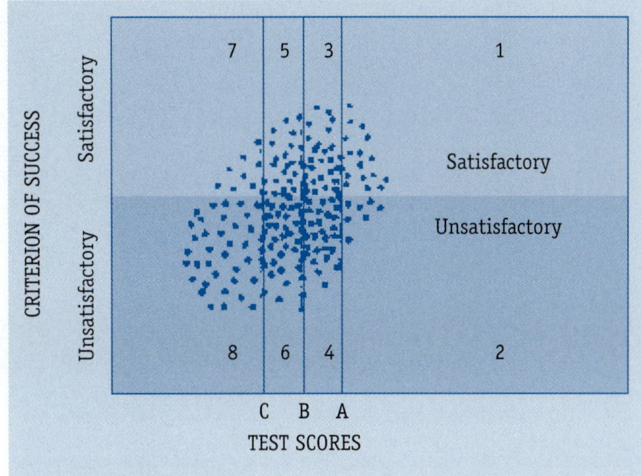

If the cut-off score is set at A, only the individuals represented in areas 1 and 3 will be accepted. Nearly all of them will be successful if more employees are needed (i.e. increasing the selection ratio), and the cut-off score lowered to point B. In this case, a larger number of potential failures will be accepted. Even when the cut-off score is lowered, the total number of satisfactory individuals selected (represented by areas 1, 3 and 5) is in excess of the total number selected from unsatisfactory (areas 2, 4 and 6). Thus, the test serves to maximise the selection of probable successes, and to minimise the selection of potential failures. This is all that we can hope for in predicting job success: the probability of selecting a greater proportion of individuals who are successful rather than unsuccessful.

Peter Dowling provides a clear picture of the use of cut-off scores when psychological tests are used. His concept, illustrated in Exhibit 7.11, can be used for any numerical score whether it be a test score or one taken from an interview rating scale.

The final decision

After a preliminary selection has been made in the employment department, those applicants who appear most promising are then referred to departments having vacancies, where they are interviewed by the managers or supervisors, who usually make the final decision and communicate it to the employment department. Because of the weight that is usually given to their choices, managers and supervisors should be trained so that their role in the selection process does not negate the more scientific efforts of the HR department. Alternatively, line managers may sit with the HR staff on a panel interview. A more reliable and valid decision is often the result.

Exhibit 7.11 Correct and erroneous selection errors

Notifying applicants of the decision and making job offers is generally the responsibility of the HR department. This department should confirm the details of the job, working arrangements, wages and so on and specify a time limit by which the applicant must reach a decision. If, at this point, findings from the medical examination are not yet available, an offer is often made contingent upon the applicant passing the medical examination.

The costs of getting it wrong

A number of authors have attempted in recent years to cost most aspects of the HR function, including that of incorrect selection decisions.[64]

The important consideration in costing out selection errors is to calculate not only the direct costs, but also the indirect costs. Poor decisions can incur:

- further recruitment costs
- training and orientation costs
- burnout costs
- lost opportunity
- reduced profit
- loss of competitive advantage
- impaired image, reputation
- reduced internal status
- impaired recruitment opportunity
- threatened company viability
- loss of other key staff.[65]

Some of these costs may seem intangible, but when the decision relates to a senior executive, the claims seem much more realistic. Peter Dowling takes this view when he argues that the costs associated with the erroneous selection of a senior manager can be considerable because of the 'disastrous strategic decisions resulting in a decline in organisational performance and valuable subordinates leaving to work for competition.'

In addition, Dowling argues that the problems can be further heightened in the case of an expatriate manager recalled from overseas due to poor performance. In such cases, the costs of air fares, personal expenses, salary and so on, can be added to the possible damage that may be done to relations with the host country government, local organisations and customers.[66]

Some recent research

In 2006, Professor Roger Collins and CCH Australia conducted the latest in their bi-annual survey on HRM practices in Australia.[67]

Exhibit 7.12 indicates the usage of various forms of selection testing reported by 259 respondent organisations.

Exhibit 7.12 Utilisation of various forms of assessment by selected employee categories, expressed as percentages for each category (N = 259)

	Senior managers	Middle managers	Professionals	Sales staff*	Graduates
Testing not used for this category	21	31	35	34	29
Intelligence tests	18	16	15	12	13
Aptitude tests	12	12	11	11	15
Attainment tests	3	4	5	6	6
Personality tests	29	24	19	19	18
Weighted applicant blanks	5	6	4	3	4
Ethical testing	2	2	2	2	2
Assessment centres	8	4	4	7	8
Not sure	2	1	5	6	5
Total %	100	100	100	100	100

*** In organisations employing sales staff, N = 89**

Source: Collins R. 2006. *CCH/AGSM Survey on recruitment.* CCH Australia, pp. 2–5.

Of note is the low number of organisations that still rely on such tests. This may be due to ignorance of the concept or may well indicate that organisations are more concerned by the nature of the debate that has raged over the use of employment testing. Of particular note is the very low utilisation of assessment centres as a method of selection.

Exhibit 7.13   Nature of training provided to selection interviewers, expressed as percentages (N = 259)

Of concern are the findings shown below. Ample evidence was provided earlier in this chapter on the value and validity of training interviewers. Yet the figures below paint a dismal picture. Only 13 per cent of respondents are providing what might be regarded as adequate training of their selection interviewers.

Nature of interviewer training	% of organisations	Nature of interviewer training	% of organisations
All interviewers have undertaken skills-based interview training.	13%	All interviewers have undertaken didactic (classroom) interview training.	7%
Most interviewers have undertaken skills-based interview training.	18%	Most interviewers have undertaken didactic (classroom) interview training.	8%
Some interviewers have undertaken skills-based interview training.	18%	Some interviewers have undertaken didactic (classroom) interview training.	10%
We provide no such training.	23%		
Not sure.	3%		

Source: Collins R. 2006. *CCH/AGSM Survey on recruitment*, CCH Australia, pp. 2–5.

Exhibit 7.14   Recruitment and selection metrics reported to senior management, reported as percentages (N = 259)

Metrics reported	Percentage reporting
Applicants per position	39%
Cost per hire	25%
Interviews per offer ratio	14%
Offer to acceptance ratio	11%
Quality of hires by recruitment source	15%
Number of hires by recruitment source	20%
Customer (line manager) satisfaction with the recruitment and selection process	22%
None of the above	44%

Source: Collins R. 2006. *CCH/AGSM Survey on recruitment*, CCH Australia, pp. 2–5.

At a time where HR professionals are more than ever being asked to provide evidence of value-adding services (see Chapter 1) it is quite astounding to note the figures above. The figures show not only a disregard for what are now seen as basic quality measures but also a disregard of well over 10 years of pleas from writers and professionals for HR to become more strategic.

The Collins/CCH survey has also found that 49 per cent of respondents use the panel interview, 34 per cent use sequential interviews while 8 per cent of respondents rely on evidence gained from a single interview. Standardised questions were used by 30 per cent of respondents while 28 per cent reported that they used such questions sometimes. Twelve per cent reported that they never used standardised questions.

A second survey has been conducted by Professor Robin Kramar from the Macquarie Graduate School of Management. Of note are the selection strategies used in Australian organisations.[68]

Exhibit 7.15   Selection techniques used

	Management	Professional/technical	Clerical	Manual
Interview panel	77%	65%	50%	32%
One-on one interview	53%	55%	61%	53%
Application forms	44%	51%	54%	49%
Psychometric tests	37%	26%	12%	5%
Assessment centres	6%	7%	9%	4%
Graphology	1%	1%	1%	1%
References	78%	78%	76%	59%
Other	5%	6%	5%	8%

Source: Collins R. 2006. *CCH/AGSM Survey on recruitment*, CCH Australia, pp. 2–5.

The figures vary slightly from those reported by Collins/CCH but the same trends are evident. Psychometric tests are used in a minority of organisations as are assessment centres despite evidence presented earlier in this chapter that assessment centres are often found to be the most valid and reliable form of selection.

Reference checks are used consistently but are still far from universal. Application forms are used by only half of the respondents and one can safely assume that résumés make up the difference given the popularity of the Internet and the need for a 'soft' copy of one's résumé (organisations now seek an electronic copy of résumés sent within a few days of advertising).

Fortunately, methods such as graphology seem to have almost disappeared along with such questionable techniques as astrology and phrenology.

Exhibit 7.16   The international perspective

The selection process

The first step in the selection process is to identify the job. If the job involves extensive contacts with the local community, as with a general manager, this factor should be given appropriate weight. A second set of factors relates to environmental variables. The differences between the political, legal, socioeconomic, and cultural systems of the host country and those of the home country should be assessed and rank-ordered.

If a candidate is willing to live and work in a foreign environment, an indication of his or her tolerance of cultural differences should be obtained. If local nationals have the technical competence to carry out the job successfully, they should be carefully considered for the job before the organisation launches a search (at home) for a candidate.

However, it should not be assumed from the above that most organisations take such a logical, rational approach to the selection of expatriate managers.

Emphasis must be given to different factors, depending on the extent of contact that the employee will have with the culture, and the degree to which the foreign environment differs from the home environment. Once an individual is selected, the amount of orientation required will vary. The nature of the orientation usually provided will be discussed in a later chapter.

Selection methods

The most common methods of selection used by MNEs are interviews, assessment centres and tests.

While some MNEs interview only the candidate, some of them interview both the candidate and the partner, suggesting that MNEs are becoming increasingly aware of the significance of the partner's adjustment to a foreign environment and its contribution to managerial performance abroad. Interviews are best conducted by senior executives who have had managerial experience in foreign countries. For example, at Mobil Oil (US) the manager of international placement and staffing and two assistants with foreign experience conduct a four-hour interview with the candidate and the partner to discuss all phases of the job. Emphasis is placed on the culture and the adaptability demands made on the candidate and their partner.

Assessment centres typically use individual and group exercises, individual interviews with managers or psychologists, and some personality and mental ability tests to evaluate candidates. Exercises that reflect situations characteristic of the potential host culture are usually included. The use of assessment centres has been shown to have high face validity and to be an effective tool for selecting from a large pool of international managerial candidates. A variety of psychometric devices, including personality inventories, are available to determine an individual's ability to adapt to a different cultural environment. Such inventories as the Minnesota Multiphasic Personality Inventory, the Guifford-Zimmerman Temperament Survey and the California Test (the Indirect Scale for Ethnocentrism) are among those frequently used. As with all such psychological tests they should be assessed for their reliability, validity and appropriateness to the designated overseas assignment.

Managing HR programs for international assignments

Effective management of overseas staff, especially those at management levels, requires a strategic, integrated and cost-effective series of HR programs before and after selection.

This initial HR strategy needs, of course, to be supplemented by an ongoing support program appropriate to the various phases of adaptation by new managers to their overseas cultural and geographic environment. It has been suggested that all overseas managers progress through a series of developmental phases, including an initial contact phase, disintegration, reintegration, autonomy and re-entry phases. HR activities should aim to both prepare the overseas manager for their likely occurrence, and provide ongoing support systems to reduce negative effects on performance and motivation.

Wendy Coyle, Director of Relocations at Dunhill Management Services, emphasises the need for ongoing 'caring' and practical support for both the expatriate and his or her family at several stages of the overseas assignment.

The family should be helped to make a 'game plan' for their new lifestyle. Portable skills and interests should be assessed and new directions planned. At the same time, training in cultural adaptation should be made available. It is the rebuilding of the family lifestyle and the integration into a new community which completes the relocation process.

A significant issue for HR specialists, at both selection and subsequent stages of expatriation, is the consideration of family attitudes to the overseas assignment. Partners of the prospective

expatriates may be unwilling to relocate overseas due to the potential harm to their own careers and lifestyles. In an era of 'dual careers,' a two- or three-year break in a partner's career can be disastrous, especially where it is not possible to pursue a similar occupation in the overseas location. In this situation, the 'trailing spouse' syndrome needs to be comprehensively discussed with the potential expatriates, their partners and children. Support is difficult to provide in some overseas environments, but should be actively sought (e.g. assistance with obtaining a similar position for the partner, discussions with the partner about the implications of the assignment, help to join social clubs in the host country, etc.). Similarly, children should be included in such pre-departure negotiations.

If Australian industry is to be successful in an increasingly global marketplace, human resource managers in joint ventures or multinational organisations will require highly sophisticated strategies to ensure the success of their overseas operations. Selection of appropriate managers is only the first step. Adequate training and development, ongoing career plans, specialised performance management and remuneration programs are also essential for international effectiveness.

Source: Kramar R. 2006. Cranet-Macquarie survey on international strategic human resource management: Report on the Australian findings, Sydney, Macquarie University

Summary

The selection process should provide as much reliable and valid information as possible about applicants in order that their qualifications may be carefully matched with person specifications. The information that is obtained should be clearly job-related or predictive of success on the job and free from potential discrimination.

Interviews and tests are customarily used in conjunction with application forms, background investigations, medical examinations and other sources of information. The interview is an important source of information about job applicants. Those who conduct interviews should receive special training that acquaints them with interviewing methods and equal employment opportunity considerations. The training should also provide for them to become more aware of the major findings from research studies on the interview and to apply these findings. While the popularity of tests has declined since the passage of equal employment opportunity laws, their value should not be overlooked. Tests are more objective than interviews, and can provide a broader sampling of behaviour.

In the process of making decisions, all 'can do' and 'will do' factors should be assembled and weighted systematically so that the final decision can be based upon a composite of the most reliable and valid information. While the clinical approach in decision-making is used more than the statistical approach, it lacks the accuracy of the latter approach. Whichever approach is used, the goal is to select a greater proportion of individuals who will be successful on the job.

Key terms

babyboomers 233
background investigation 235
behavioural questions 239
best fit 253
closed questions 243
downshifting 253
employment interview 237
employment testing 259
generation X 233
generation Y 233
interview questions 243
medical examination 236
open questions 238
reliability 227
selection 226
validity 228

Key debate issues

1 Professor Robert Spillane of Macquarie University has argued:

> Many of history's leaders and many of our folk legends including Bob Hawke, Winston Churchill, Gandhi, Napoleon, Helen of Troy and Joan of Arc would not have shown obvious management potential under the sort of personality tests used by corporate headhunters.

What are the issues here?

2 With many years of research findings indicating clearly that the selection interview is of doubtful value in predicting future job success, employers might do just as well to select directly from application forms.

3 A major public employer recruits and selects several hundred trainees, in a mass program, once or twice a year. Rather than spend much time and effort in screening applicants, the employer relies on a three-month probationary period to remove any undesirables. Do you think this is a more cost-effective approach?

Exercise 7.1

Avoiding discrimination in the selection procedure

In this chapter we have observed that the interview is used widely as a method for learning as much as possible about job applicants. While conducting an interview one must be very careful not to ask questions that are, or could be, interpreted to be discriminatory under equal opportunity or fair employment laws.

Study the following questions that interviewers might ask in the course of an employment interview. Evaluate each question in relation to equal opportunity employment laws. Is it acceptable or not? Rephrase those questions that you believe can be made generally acceptable under federal and state laws relating to discrimination in employment.

- Do you have any hobbies?
- From the ring on your finger, I assume that you are married. Am I correct?
- What type of work does your husband do?
- I notice on your application form that you are a college graduate. Did you take any courses that are related to the job you are seeking?
- Do you have any physical handicaps?
- Do you own your own home, or do you rent?
- Would you be willing to take a physical examination at our expense?
- You stated that you are a veteran. Did you have any experience in the military service that relates to the job we are discussing?
- Have you ever been arrested?
- This position will require interstate travel. Will your husband and family be able to cope?

Questions

1 What are the general rules concerning what may be asked of applicants in an employment interview?

2 How can an interviewer avoid asking questions that may be construed as discriminatory?

Case study 7.1

Working in harmony

The job of manager in a business organisation has frequently been compared to that of a symphony orchestra conductor. Both are concerned with getting each member in the organisation to play his or her part, and to blend each contribution into a team that works together productively and harmoniously. In order to produce the highest quality of music for its listeners, the San Francisco Symphony Orchestra (with more than 100 musicians) gives considerable attention to the recruitment and selection of personnel to fill vacancies in the various chairs. For 75 years, highly accomplished musicians have been striving to become a part of this organisation of world fame, and many of them have not achieved their goal.

Whenever a position in the orchestra becomes vacant, an announcement for musicians is placed in a local newspaper and in the magazine *International Musician*. Those who are interested in being considered for the position are requested to send a résumé. Upon receipt of the résumé, the applicant is sent a repertoire list and a list of materials to be included on a pre-screening tape. A committee of orchestra members listens to the tapes and invites qualified candidates to take part in the audition in San Francisco.

On the date of the auditions, musicians from all over the world arrive at Davies Symphony Hall. Numbers are drawn for the order of appearance. Candidates are then provided with practice rooms so that they can warm up for the audition. This stage of the selection procedure is the conducting of the preliminary audition, which, under the terms of the Master Agreement between the San Francisco Symphony Association and the Musicians Union Local 6, involves 10 members of the orchestra who listen to the candidates. Five of them are drawn from the principal chairs, and five are members-at-large from the orchestra.

When it is a candidate's turn to audition, he or she is ushered onto the stage behind a screen so as not to be seen by the members of the orchestra sitting in the auditorium. Each candidate plays the same selection designated in the repertoire for auditionees that was mailed to them. The repertoire typically includes a solo work designed to demonstrate the candidate's virtuosity. Immediately after a performance, which usually lasts about 10 to 15 minutes, the 10-member committee ballots on a 'yes' or 'no' basis. Ballots are collected and counted at once by the union steward and the symphony personnel manager. Candidates who receive six 'yes' votes are advised to be available for the final audition on the following day.

In the audition of the finalists, the music director joins the committee. The candidates again appear on the stage, one at a time, and play the prescribed selection; however, no screen is used. In evaluating the performance of the finalists, a discussion of each candidate follows the last audition. Committee members each express their opinions, and after they have finished, the music director states his or her opinions. Further discussion and then voting take place. Each committee member votes 'yes' or 'no.' Any candidate receiving six or more 'yes' votes qualifies. The music director does not vote, but can select or decline to select any qualifying candidate. (Additional provisions exist if a current member of the orchestra is a finalist, receiving eight or more qualifying votes.) If the music director selects a finalist for the vacancy, a contract is offered. Should the finalist decline, the music director may select any other qualifying candidate or may choose not to.

Questions

1 Why does the orchestra have candidates perform behind a screen for the preliminary audition? Would it be advisable to use this same procedure in the typical employment interview? What would be the advantages and disadvantages of such a procedure in the interview?

2 Why are candidates not permitted to choose their own music? How does this procedure compare with that used in evaluating job candidates in other types of organisations?

Case study 7.2

The conman of St Luke's

Sydney's Anglican establishment has been scandalised by the discovery that the man chosen to run its prestigious St Luke's hospital complex for the past year led a double life.

John Frederick Bundy hoodwinked the 13-member hospital board – which includes some of the most prominent names in Sydney medicine and business – into believing that he was a successful businessman, a university graduate and a man with a stable family life.

In fact, none of this was true, and when the board belatedly found out who the real John Bundy was, he resigned on the spot.

The bespectacled, apparently respectable 45-year-old businessman who was entrusted with the care of the 200-odd patients at St Luke's in Potts Point and its adjacent nursing home turned out to be a man with a history of business failure, a high-living pilot and part-time racing car driver who was two-timing his wife in Melbourne with a mistress.

Not only that, a routine check with a credit agency would have revealed that Bundy and his legal wife had court judgements for more than $6 000 worth of debts outstanding against them, some involving the operation of a business in the Melbourne suburb of Hawthorn, known as the Hotham City Diner and Bar, and others relating to his red-striped Beechcraft Duke, a six-seater twin-engine executive plane.

When Bundy told the board in 1990 that he had 'an impressive background in general management' he was, in fact, telling the truth – though not perhaps in the way those leading Anglicans imagined.

For much of the 1980s he was general manager of two companies which between them lost more than $30 million.

He claimed in his curriculum vitae to be a graduate in commerce from Melbourne University, and an associate of the Australian Society of Accountants. If the board or the headhunter had checked they would have discovered that the university had no record of Bundy graduating and Australia's two accountancy organisations had never heard of him.

In a brief autobiography in the hospital newsletter last year, Bundy made the false claims of commerce and accountancy credentials cited above and said that he brought to the job 'a very appropriate combination of recent experience in both the management of health funds and hospitals.'

He did not mention his first important business experience. In 1981, Bundy (according to a former director of the company) persuaded the Otto Corporation of Cologne, Germany – a waste management company best known for its 240-litre mobile garbage bins – to set up in Australia. A factory was built in Brisbane, and garbage collection contracts were signed up around the country, but although the company achieved a high profile, profits were elusive. In fact they were non-existent, and in the three years that he ran the company it lost (according to the records) several million. Eventually, Bundy left.

After Otto, Bundy – by now living with his wife, Lynette, in the Melbourne suburb of North Ringwood – obtained a job with Hospital Corporation of Australia, a subsidiary of the US HCA. His only experience in hospital management prior to St Luke's was about a year managing HCA's Warrigal Hospital in Melbourne. In 1986, he moved to Sydney where (according to the former boss) he became marketing director of HCA.

Bundy next popped up in the highly public role of general manager of Health Australia, an ambitious new health fund which began operations in 1987, the first 'for profit' private health fund in the country. At least, it was supposed to be for profit.

Mr Brent Walker, a principal at Tillinghurst management consultancy, who is an expert in health funds, says that federal government figures show that the fund lost $22 million in the three years that it operated. In the three months before it came to the brink of collapse in September 1990 it was losing an extraordinary $50 000 a day. Mr Walker, who examined Health Australia's books on behalf of a potential purchaser, says he was appalled by the lack of financial management, and valued the company at 'a negative, several million at least.' After unsuccessfully hawking the fund around the country, Switzerland had to pay the federal government's Health Insurance Commission to take it off its hands. It was eventually taken over by Medibank Private.

So, what went wrong? 'It was suicide,' says an industry insider. 'They advertised the cheapest rates and they promised the best benefits. It just didn't add up. They caused a lot of pain in the industry – everyone knew they were going to go bang, but how can you compete with fools?' On top of this, there was John Bundy's management style. 'He was flying round the country in his plane making these great plans – it was cloud nine stuff,' says the insider. 'He [Bundy] ruled it like a dictator. At one stage when he must have realised it was going down the drain, he just walked in and said "put the rates up eight per cent" and walked out again.' Bundy had resigned, once again, before the fund finally disappeared in October 1990, and he emerged in his new incarnation of general manager of St Luke's the following January. After an all-expenses-paid trip to the United States, he began to shake up the rather conservative and old-fashioned hospital, and to upset some of its prominent specialists by arbitrarily reorganising their access to operating theatres.

Bundy announced plans for doubling the size of the hospital – a new 300-bed wing, seven new operating theatres and a casualty section, although doctors at the hospital were puzzled about where the money was coming from. He spent more than $1 million rebuilding the hospital kitchen, hired a chef from the Regent, and began serving patients roast loin of Gippsland lamb and mango crêpes on Villeroy and Bosch china. He started a newsletter (Hosgoss) and he bought a 'percutaneous disectomy' machine 'using the revolutionary pulsating Holmium laser,' which was used to relieve pain in the backside.

Not all his whirlwind renovations were an unqualified success. He tried to make his nurses wear culottes, but they (the culottes) had to be withdrawn and sent back to the manufacturer because of 'quality problems.' And he decided not to proceed with plans for a social club at St Luke's after suggestions from the patients – some of them widows in their 90s – were found to include karaoke nights, B-52 parties, two-up poker, and 'let's get drunk and fall over parties.' But eventually, amid mounting concern from doctors and some board members, it all came to an end. 'Looking back on it,' said a rather shell-shocked senior surgeon, 'it was Walter Mitty stuff ... I'm afraid the board is going to have egg all over their faces over this.'

Financially, as well as with its image, St Luke's failed to benefit from Bundy's brief reign. In the year to 30 June, the hospital lost $22 000 compared with a surplus of $221 000 for the previous year. This was offset by $1.5 million given by more than 300 donors listed in the hospital's annual report.

As for Bundy, he has returned to Melbourne and the last known sighting was at the Hotham City Diner and Bar. He declined to return telephone calls from the *Herald*.

And that red-striped executive Beechcraft Duke: 'It has been repossessed, and is sitting in a hangar at Moorabbin Airport in Melbourne begging for a buyer at a mere $175 000'.[69]

Source: Adapted from Ben Hills, the Sydney Morning Herald, 21 March 1992.

Questions

1   What are the key issues here?
2   How would you have handled this assignment?
3   What safeguards would you have built into the selection process to minimise the chances of such problems arising?

Further readings

Arvey R.D., Campion J.C. 1982. 'The employment interview: A summary and review of recent research,' *Personnel Psychology*, 35(2), Summer.

Bernardin, H.J. 2007. *Human resource management*. 4th edn, Boston. McGraw Hill.

Cohen P. 1997. 'What's wrong with the interview?,' *hrmonthly*, July, pp. 20–1.

Compton R.L. 1996. 'Interviewing – facts and fantasies.' Paper presented to Recruiting to Gain the Competitive Edge Conference, Melbourne.

Compton R.L., Morrissey W., Nankervis A.R. 2006. *Effective recruitment and selection practices*, 4th edn, Sydney, CCH Australia.

Dessler.G, Griffiths, J., Lloyd-Walker. 2004. *Human resource management*. 2nd edn, French's Forest, Pearson Education.

Dowling P., 'Psychological testing in Australia: an overview and assessment' in G. Palmer (ed.) 1988. *Australian personnel management: A reader*, Melbourne, Macmillan.

Goodale J.G. 1982. *The fine art of interviewing*, Englewood Cliffs, NJ, Prentice Hall.

Kramar. R., De Cieri, H. 2005. *Human resource management*, 2nd edn, Sydney, McGraw Hill.

Nankervis A.R., Compton R.L. 1994. *Readings in strategic human resource management*, Melbourne, Nelson ITP.

Spillane R. 1985. *Achieving peak performance: A psychology of success in the organisation*, Sydney, Harper & Row.

Stone R. J., 2002. *Human resource management*, Brisbane, John Wiley & Sons.

Endnotes

1   Goldrick P. 1997. 'What makes a selection system best practice?,' *hrmonthly*, June, pp. 26–7.

2   Pratter T. 2002. 'Lies, lies and more lies,' *S.A.M. Advanced management Journal*, 67(2), pp. 9–14.

3   Dowling P. 1988. 'Psychological testing in Australia: An overview and assessment,' in G. Palmer (ed.), *Australian personnel management: A reader*, South Melbourne, Macmillan.

4   Hicks R.E. 1991. 'Psychological testing in Australia in the 1990s,' *Asia Pacific Human Resource Management*, Autumn, pp. 94–101.

5   Smith B. 1990. 'Dancing with the giants,' *hrmonthly*, November, p. 202.

6   HR Report 2006. no. 376, p. 4.

7   Dinnell S. 2006. 'The Y front,' *hrmonthly*, May, pp. 24–6.

8   Anon. 2006. 'Gen Y on the move,' *hrmonthly*, April, p. 6.

9   Gandolfi F. 2006. 'Finding a better fit,' *hrmonthly*, April, pp. 34–5.

10 Sullivan P. 1991. Address to IPMA Seminar, 19 September, p. 4.

11 Ibid.

12 Vaughan E., McLean J. 1989. 'A survey and critique of management selection practices in Australian business firms,' *Asia Pacific Human Resource Management*, 27(4), November, pp. 20–33.

13 Collins R. 2006. CCH/AGSM Survey on recruitment. CCH Australia, p. 4.

14 Compton R.L. 1996. 'Interviewing – facts and fantasies.' Paper presented to Recruiting to Gain the Competitive Edge Conference, Sydney and Melbourne.

15 Compton R.L., Morrissey W., Nankervis A.R. 2006. *Effective recruitment and selection practices*, 4th edn, Sydney, CCH Australia, pp. 94–6.

16 Hills B. 1992. 'The conman of St Luke's,' *Sydney Morning Herald*, 21 March, pp. 1, 11.

17 HR Report 2006. no. 384. p. 6.

18 HR Report 2006. no. 372. p. 6.

19 HR Report 2006. no. 383. p. 3.

20 *Dao v. Australian Postal Commission* 1987.

21 McConnell , Charles. R. 1999. 'A working manager's guide to effective and legal employee selection interviewing.' *The Health Care Supervisor* 17(4), pp. 77–89.

22 Buckley R, Norris A, Wiese, D. 2000. 'A brief history of the selection interview: May the next 100 years be more fruitful,' *Journal of Management History*, 6(3), p. 113.

23 Arvey R.D., Campion J.E. 1982. 'The employment interview: A summary and review of recent research,' *Personnel Psychology*, 35(2), Summer, pp. 281–322.

24 Barclay J.M. 2001. 'Improving selection interviews with structure: Organisations' use of behavioural interviews,' *Personnel Review*, 30(1), p. 81.

25 Bellows R.M., Estep M.F. 1954. *Employment psychology: The interview*, New York, Rinehart & Company.

26 Pursell E.D., Campion M., Gaylord S. 1980. 'Structured interviewing: Avoiding selection problems,' *Personnel Journal*, 59(11), November, pp. 907–12.

27 Frase-Blunt, M. 2001. 'Games interviewers play,' *HR Magazine*, 46(1), pp. 106–14.

28 Moodie A.M. 1997. 'Job candidates put to the experience test,' *Australian Financial Review*, 10 October, p. 66.

29 HR Report 1999. no. 206, 27 July, p. 5.

30 Barclay 2001. op. cit., p. 81.

31 Sturman M.C., Cheramie R.A., Cashen L.H. 2002. 'How to compare apples to oranges: Balancing internal candidates job-performance data with external candidates selection test results,' *Cornell Hotel and Restaurant Administration Quarterly*, 43(4), pp. 27–40.

32 Mayfield E.C. 1964. 'The selection interview – a re-evaluation of published research,' *Personnel Psychology*, 7(3), Autumn, pp. 239–60. See also Arvey R.D., Campion J.E. 1982. op. cit.

33 Milia L., Smith P. 1997. 'Australian management selection practices,' *Asia Pacific Journal of Human Resources*, 35(3), pp. 90–103.

34 Compton R.L. 1987. 'The selection interview,' *Personnel Today*, November, pp. 14–15.

35   Cohen P. 1997. 'What's wrong with the interview?,' *hrmonthly*, July, pp. 20–1.

36   Huseman R.C. 1992. *Business communication*, Sydney, Harcourt Brace Jovanovich, p. 272.

37   Gilchrist M. 1992. 'Queries employers should avoid,' *Business Review Weekly*, 20 March, pp. 74–5.

38   AGSM/CCH 1994. *National survey of recruitment, Selection and induction practices*, p. 2281.

39   Anon. 1985. Selected procedures and personnel records, *Personnel Policies Forum Survey*, no. 114.

40   Dowling P. 1988. op. cit., p. 70.

41   Stone R. 1987. 'Psychological testing – a modern checklist,' *Personnel Today*, July, p. 10.

42   Compton R.L. 1987. 'The selection interview,' *Personnel Today*, November, pp. 14–15.

43   Hicks R.E. 1991. op. cit., p. 94.

44   Bates S. 2002. 'Personality counts,' *HR Magazine* 47(2), p. 28.

45   HR Report 1999. no. 213, 2 November, p. 7.

46   Bates 2002. op. cit., p. 28.

47   Stevens C., Ash R. 2001. 'Selecting employees for fit: Personality and preferred management style,' *Journal of Managerial Issues*, 13(4), pp. 500–17.

48   Stone R. 1987. op. cit., p. 10.

49   Dowling P. 1988. op. cit., pp. 61–73.

50   Vaughan E., McLean J. 1989. op. cit., pp. 26–8.

51   Spillane R. 1985. *Achieving peak performance: A psychology of success in the organisation*, Sydney, Harper & Row, p. 59.

52   HR Report 2000. no. 239, p. 1.

53   Dowling P. 1988. op. cit., p. 61.

54   Spillane R. 1985. op. cit., p. 59.

55   Donaghy B. 1995. 'What's on your mind?,' *Sydney Morning Herald*, 28 October.

56   Kirby J. 1998. 'How new wave careerists unlock top jobs,' *Business Review Weekly*, 19 January, pp. 35–8.

57   Nance J. 1997. 'Our future may be in their hands,' *Sunday Telegraph*, 25 June.

58   Fox C. 2000. 'Testing, testing,' *Australian Financial Review*, September, pp. 38–43.

59   HR Report 2000. no. 236, 16 October, p. 8.

60   Fisher C., Boyle G. 1997. 'Personality and employee selection: Credibility regained,' *Asia Pacific Journal of Human Resources*, 35(2), pp. 26–40.

61   AGSM/CCH 1994. op. cit., p. 22–83.

62   HR Report 2006. no. 374. p. 5.

63   Vaughan E., McLean J. 1989. op. cit., pp. 29–32.

64   Fitz-Enz J. 1984. *How to measure HR management*, New York, McGraw-Hill.

65   Sullivan P. 1991. Address to Institute of Personnel Management Australia, Seminar, 19 September.

66   Dowling P. 1988. op. cit., pp. 63–4.

67   Collins R. 2006. CCH/AGSM Survey on recruitment. CCH Australia. pp. 2–5.

68   Kramar R. 2006. *Cranet-Macquarie survey on international strategic human resource management: Report on the Australian findings*, Sydney, Macquarie University, pp. 1–3.

69   Adapted from the *Sydney Morning Herald*, 21 March 1992. Original story by Ben Hills.

Online reading

INFOTRAC® COLLEGE EDITION

For additional readings and review on effective employee selection, explore InfoTrac® College Edition, your online library. Go to: www.infotrac-college.com and search for any of the InfoTrac key terms listed below:

➤ best fit
➤ medical examinations
➤ psychometric tests
➤ reliability
➤ selection interviews
➤ validity
➤ work sample tests

CHAPTER 8
DEVELOPING HUMAN RESOURCES IN ORGANISATIONS

A considerable amount of attention is being paid to knowledge management and intellectual capital ... through this connection knowledge becomes a product. The creation and management of knowledge within the system are captured through the idea of intellectual capital.

Garrick and Clegg, 2000

Whether it is called distance education, asynchronous studies, online instruction or e-learning, Internet-based training has gained a significant foothold in the realm of professional education.

Robb and Geffen, 2000

Human resource development refers to the integrated use of training and development, organisation development, and career development to improve individual, group and organisational effectiveness.

Noe, 2002

Objectives

After reading this chapter you will be able to:

1 Understand the nature and scope of organisational learning and development programs.

2 Describe the systems approach to learning and development.

3 Understand the preconditions for and basic principles of learning and development.

4 Identify the types of developmental methods used with non-managerial personnel.

5 Describe the methods used for identifying and developing management and leadership talent.

6 Explain the factors that should be considered in choosing and developing a career.

Introduction

The processes of recruiting and selecting human resources are only the initial stages in building an effective workforce. Managers, supervisors and employees also require continual learning and development if their potential is to be utilised effectively. The development of human resources should be viewed as beginning with their induction and orientation and continuing throughout their employment with the organisation. This is the essence of SHRM, as human resource development is the foundation for building human capital.

Organisations must continually be able to learn, adapt and grow if they are to survive and indeed prosper in turbulent environments.[1] In recent times there has been a great deal written about the concepts of knowledge management, intellectual capital and the learning organisation. Several writers have tied these concepts together so that knowledge becomes a product possessed by individuals that needs to be managed effectively. This then leads to the concept of an organisation's intellectual capital.[2] Importantly, knowledge management is about the knowledge in the heads and hearts of the people within the organisation and the management and retention of that knowledge.

Increasingly, lifelong learning has become vital to the success of modern organisations as rapidly changing technology requires that employees demonstrate the capabilities necessary to cope with new processes and production techniques. The growth of organisations into large, complex operations whose structures are continually changing makes it necessary for managers, as well as employees, to be prepared for new and more demanding assignments. As organisational strategies are renewed, human resources must also be renewed. Horwitz discusses the strategic nature of human resource development programs, concluding that a strategic approach necessitates increased intellectual and theoretical rigour, more comprehensive evaluations of claimed learning outcomes, and the determination of responsibilities for organisational leaning and development.[3]

In addition, there has been a distinct trend in recent years for organisations to take a broader view of human resources by creating career development programs. Such programs involve attempts to develop an employee's career in a way that will benefit both the organisation and the individual. Special attention will be given to those programs at the end of this chapter. Initially, our emphasis will be on such processes as the induction and orientation of employees, the design and evaluation of learning and development programs, and the application of learning theory. A major dilemma for organisations will be to what extent they expend resources on learning, development and career management programs while accepting the contemporary reality of mobile, short-term and casual employees.

Some initial definitions

Many terms are used to describe the strategies and activities undertaken within organisations to add value to their employees' capabilities, in order for them to contribute more effectively to overall organisational goals and imperatives. These include the broad umbrella term, *human resource development (HRD)*, which encompasses all such activities and provides a conscious alignment between an organisation's business and HRM strategies and plans: *training, learning, development* and *education*, among others.

HRD can be defined as '… the combined use of learning and interpersonal strategies and practices within an organisation to accomplish high levels of individual and organisational effectiveness'.[4] This definition encapsulates the strategic purpose of HRD as the integration of all learning and development activities for both organisational and employee benefit. 'Training' is a more specific term used to describe generally short-term formal and semi-formal methods of transferring basic knowledge and skills to employees. Thus, employees may be trained to operate machinery, to understand the implications of new legal or administrative procedures and processes, or to use particular computer software.

'Development,' on the other hand, is usually a longer-term process focused on the acquisition of more complex and deeper competencies, which may involve both formal training programs and on-the-job practical experience and mentoring. Employees may be developed into supervisors or managers by means of a structured series of on- and off-the-job activities, or cross-cultural skills may be developed through initial classroom training, supplemented with overseas assignments and mentoring from more experienced colleagues. 'Learning' is an ongoing process which applies to whole organisations (learning organisations) and their employees, and usually requires positive attitudes towards change complemented with structured learning programs.

'Education' traditionally referred to formal courses provided in primary, secondary and tertiary institutions, but has come now to encompass any broad learning systems which encourage the acquisition of conceptual, analytical and evaluative competencies within or outside organisations. Thus, some organisations encourage or sponsor their potential managers to undertake university degrees, in order to nurture their innovative and creative talents, for future benefit.

In this chapter, our focus will be primarily on the learning and development components of HRD, as these are the most common characteristics of contemporary organisational development. We will begin with a discussion of employee induction and orientation (sometimes called 'socialisation'), as it is the crucial foundation upon which all subsequent HRD activities are built.

Induction and orientation

The first step in the development process is to get new people off to a good start. Indeed, a formal induction (or orientation) program may well be the first and last chance to get a worker started on the right track.[5] Induction is defined as the formal process of familiarising (or 'orienting') new employees with the organisation, their job and the work unit. It should provide new employees with an understanding of how their job performance contributes to the success of the organisation and how the services or products of the organisation can contribute to society. Well-designed induction programs help in the reduction of new employees' anxiety, and can lead to the early development of positive attitudes, job satisfaction and longer-term commitment to organisations.

Exhibit 8.1   SHRM model of learning and employee development

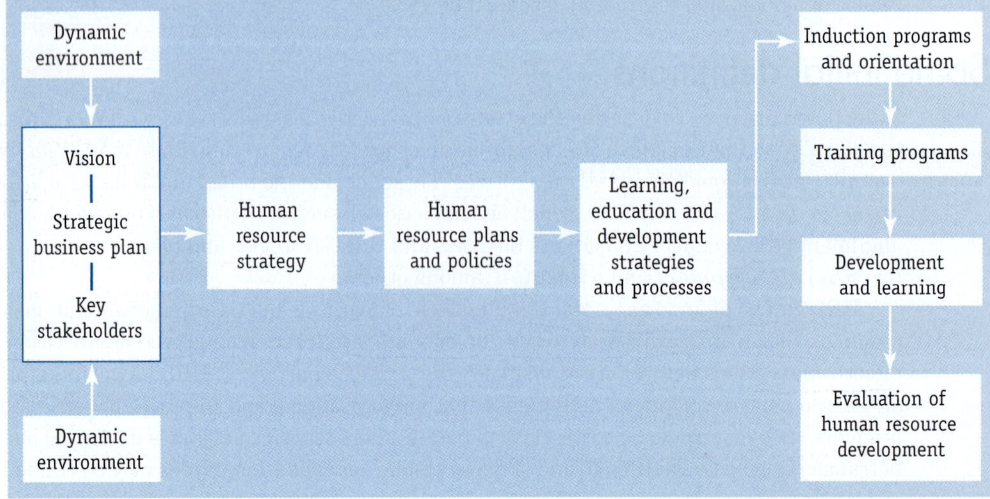

Induction provides the means by which new employees become 'socialised' to their organisations, and through which they acquire the knowledge, skills, attitudes and values that make them successful organisational members. When organisational socialisation is successful, individual and organisational goals unite. If such socialisation is ineffective, the result may be a rejection of the organisation by the new employee, often resulting in their departure.[6]

Reasons for induction

In some organisations, a formal employee induction program is almost non-existent or, when conducted, is performed in a haphazard manner. This is unfortunate since there are a number of very practical and cost-effective implications for conducting a well-run program. Some of the benefits include:

- increased employee retention

- enhanced productivity

- positive employee morale

- lower recruiting and training costs

- the facilitation of subsequent learning

- a reduction in the new employee's anxiety.

Thus, the more time and effort spent in helping new employees feel welcome, the more likely it is that they will become loyal and better adjusted employees. Of course, there can never be any guarantee that this will be the case. In order to achieve this goal, an effective induction program should be characterised by a continuous process, a cooperative endeavour, careful planning, and a follow-up and evaluation. This reflects a strategic 'investment' in an organisation's human resources.

Continuous process

Since an organisation is faced with ever-changing conditions, its plans, policies and procedures must change with these conditions. Unless current employees are kept up to date on these changes, they may find themselves embarrassingly unaware of activities about which new employees are being advised. While the discussion that follows focuses primarily upon the needs of new employees, it is important that all employees are continually informed about changing conditions and that all efforts *are* directly focused on the vision, mission and imperatives of the organisation.

Cooperative endeavour

For a well-integrated induction program, cooperation between HRM and the various business managers is essential. The HRM department is usually responsible for coordinating induction activities and for providing new employees with information about organisational directions, conditions of employment, pay, benefits and other areas that are not directly under a manager's direction. However, the manager has the most important role in the induction program. The new employee is primarily interested in what the manager says and does and what their co-workers are like. Before the arrival of the new employee, it is desirable for the manager to inform the work group that a new member is joining the work team.

The importance of the manager in the induction process cannot be over-emphasised. Since induction practices will have lasting effects on employee job performance, the manager plays a key role in reducing the 'first-day jitters' of employees while channelling their enthusiasm into productive activities. Managers should consider the orientation of all employees – new and old – to be one of their primary job responsibilities.

Use a checklist

To avoid overlooking items that are important to employees, many organisations devise checklists for use by those responsible for conducting some phase of induction. The use of a checklist compels the manager and the HR manager to pay more attention to each new employee at a time when personal attentiveness is critical to building a long-term relationship. Exhibit 8.2 lists suggested areas to include in an induction checklist for managers.

Focus on what's important

Those who plan induction programs often expect the new employee to assimilate readily all types of detailed and assorted facts about the organisation. While there are many things that the new employee should know, most of them can be learned over a period of time and in a series of meetings. It is customary initially to provide information about matters of immediate concern, as illustrated in Exhibit 8.2. New employees should have a clear understanding of the job, organisational requirements and any other important matters. The initial emphasis should be on the one-to-one relationship necessary to give a person a sense of belonging. Later on, attention may be devoted to informing them about those areas that have a lower priority or that require more time for presentation and comprehension. Items covered in later meetings may include the

Exhibit 8.2 Supervisory induction checklist

- a formal greeting, including introduction to fellow employees

- explanation of job procedures, duties and responsibilities

- further training to be received

- supervisor and organisation expectations regarding attendance, personal conduct and appearance

- job standards and production/service levels

- performance appraisal criteria

- conditions of employment, including hours of work, pay periods, overtime requirements, punctuality, etc.

- organisation and work unit rules, regulations and policies

- safety regulations

- anti-discrimination legislation, including sexual harassment and racial vilification issues

- those to notify or turn to if problems or questions arise

- chain of command for reporting purposes

- an overall explanation of the organisation's operation and purpose

- offers of help and encouragement.

organisation's history, benefits and structure.[7] Many Australian firms now produce DVDs or CD-ROMs covering these latter issues, while others include this type of information on their website. Induction sessions should be supplemented with a kit of materials that new employees can read at their leisure. Some materials that might be included are shown in Exhibit 8.3. Instructions to the employee on how to use the kit are recommended.

Sample orientation program

In addition to the manager's induction program, many organisations conduct a longer orientation program for all employees who have been with them for three to six months. This is an opportunity for management to ensure that all new employees have been inducted effectively and, some short time later, given the opportunity to sit with their peers and hear from a number of key employees within the organisation.

Exhibit 8.3   Items for a sample induction kit

- a current company organisation chart
- map of the facility
- organisation telephone/email directory
- key terms unique to the industry, company or job
- copy of policy/procedure handbook
- code of conduct/ethics booklet
- relevant confidentiality forms
- copy of workplace agreement or AWA
- copy of job description or duty statement
- organisation calendar, including scheduled holidays
- copies of performance review forms and procedures
- learning and development schedule
- sources of information
- detailed outline of emergency and accident prevention procedures
- copies of annual reports and newsletters (including website links)
- copies of superannuation and medical plans including information on choice of funds.

Source: Adapted from St John D. 1990. 'The complete employee orientation program,' *Personnel Journal*, May.

The following is a sample induction program.

9.30–10.00 a.m.	Welcome from the CEO – Our vision, mission, corporate direction, expectations
10.00–11.00 a.m.	Competitors, opportunities, threats – GM, Marketing
11.00–11.30 a.m.	Morning tea/coffee
11.30–12.00 noon	People issues/programs. Code of ethics – GM, Human Resources
12.00 noon–1.00 p.m.	Quality management – GM, Quality
1.00–1.30 p.m.	Lunch
1.30–2.30 p.m.	Tour of facilities
2.30–3.30 p.m.	Health and safety awareness – OH&S Manager
3.30–4.30 p.m.	Questions and answers

Reduce employee anxiety

The planning of an induction program should take into account the anxiety employees feel on their first day on the job. Time spent at the beginning of an induction period to reduce the anxiety level of the new employee will result in greater productivity and reduced HR costs. Where a checklist approach is used, it is helpful to divide the checklist into logical sections. With each section, include the name of the person responsible for covering each topic.

A possible problem with allowing employees to be inducted by their peers is the perpetuation of codes of conduct (for example, use of the Internet, timing of work breaks, dress codes) that do not conform to the organisation's policies. These informal, unwritten codes of conduct can undermine the organisation's formal operating procedures.[8]

Follow-up and evaluation

The manager should consult with the new employee after the first day and frequently throughout the first week on the job. When all the items on the induction checklist for the employee have been completed, both the supervisor and the employee should sign it. This record should then be placed in the employee's personnel file. After the employee has been on the job for a month and again at the end of a year, an HR staff member should follow up to determine the current effectiveness of the induction. Evaluations can then be conducted through in-depth interviews, unsigned questionnaires and surveys, and discussion groups. It is also vital to evaluate the induction and orientation program to effect continuous improvement.

Training, learning and development programs

Many new employees come equipped with most of the knowledge and skills needed to start work. Others may require extensive training and development before they are ready to make much of a contribution to the organisation. A majority, however, will at one time or another require some type of training, learning or development activity in order to maintain an effective level of job performance. While this may be accomplished on an informal basis, better results are usually attained through a well-organised, formal training program or a comprehensive on-the-job development program.

As discussed earlier in this chapter, training may be defined as a procedure initiated by an organisation to foster skill or knowledge development among organisational members. The primary purpose of such programs is to help achieve the overall organisational objectives. At the same time, effective training, learning or development programs must demonstrably contribute to the satisfaction of the employee's personal goals. Bartlett and Ghoshal make the valid point that successful learning and development programs may distinguish workplace competencies from the competition and thus contribute towards competitive advantage.[9] Development programs prepare employees with learning which will allow them to grow individually alongside the organisation itself.[10]

Scope of training programs

The primary purpose of training at the beginning of an individual's employment is to bring up to a satisfactory level the knowledge, skills and abilities (commonly referred to as KSAs) required for effective performance. As the individual continues on the job, training, learning and development provide opportunities to acquire new knowledge, skills and competencies. As a result, the individual may then be more effective on the job and may qualify for jobs at a higher level.

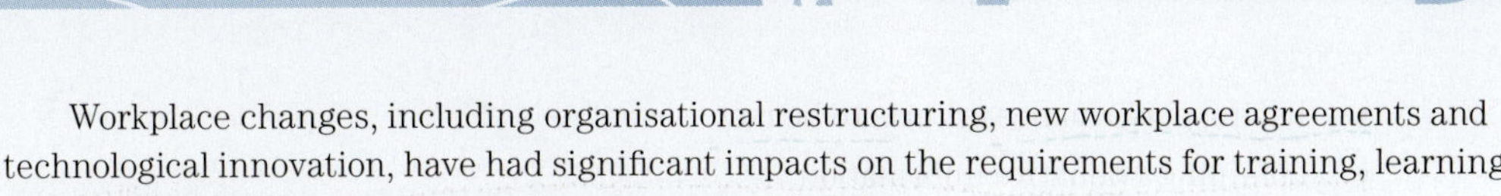

Workplace changes, including organisational restructuring, new workplace agreements and technological innovation, have had significant impacts on the requirements for training, learning and development programs, including the recognition that:

- Many jobs will be changed or enlarged, thereby requiring additional skills and knowledge.
- Other jobs will require a narrower range of skills.
- Many jobs will be replaced entirely by newly created jobs.

A key element of all such programs will be the need to develop a capacity for ongoing change and especially knowledge management, much of which will flow from forces in the external environment. These forces are likely to increase as competition – both global and domestic – accelerates the need to update and modernise an organisation's operations.

Exhibit 8.4   A contemporary training cycle

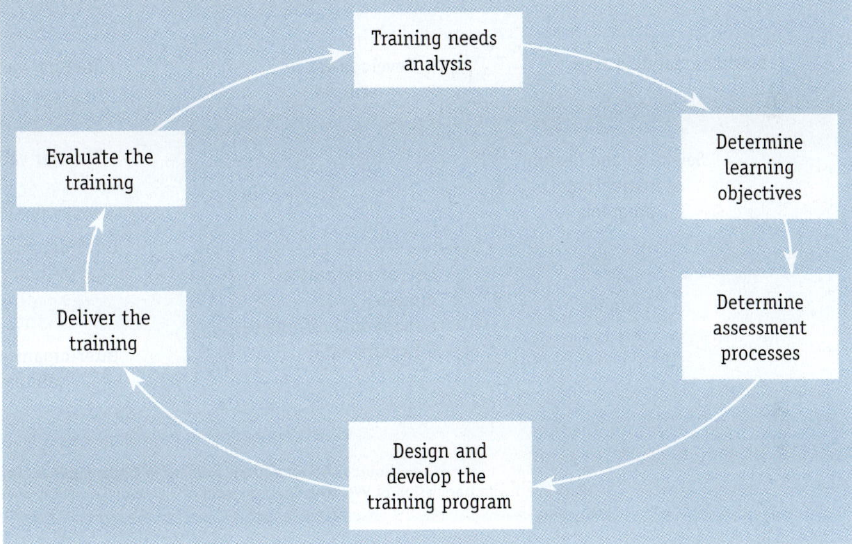

A systems approach to HRD

Since the primary goals of HRD are to contribute to the organisation's overall imperatives, as well as to the employees' career aims, such programs should be developed systematically. Too often one concept becomes the main focus of a program, or the objectives may be hazy. Effective behaviour-based evaluation is rare. Monk describes the typical, haphazard organisational approach as follows:

> (HRD) is an investment that organisations make, and while they watch their other investments extremely carefully, they are prone to disregard this very expensive one. They rarely insist on thorough evaluation of the actual learning that has taken place, the changes to employees' behaviours or performance, or to bottom-line results such as improved productivity, fewer accidents, better quality or improved morale.[11]

A recommended alternative to the haphazard approach is the systems approach, which emphasises:

- HRD needs analysis (or assessment)
- formulating instructional objectives
- developing learning experiences to achieve these objectives

- having performance criteria to be met
- obtaining evaluative information.

Exhibit 8.5 An instruction system model

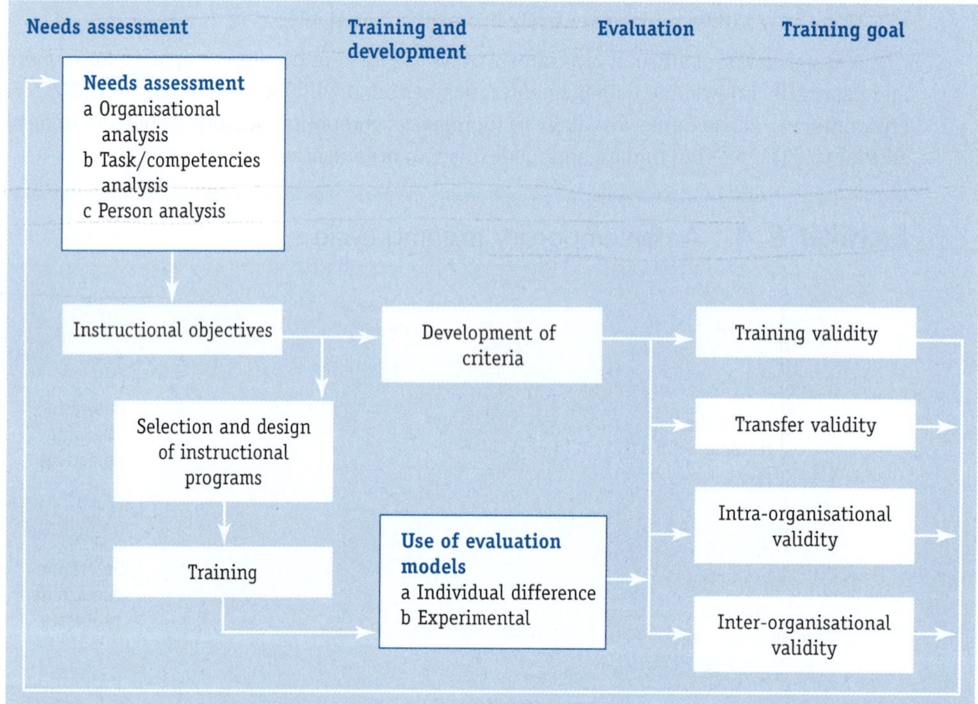

Source: Adapted from *Training in Organizations*, 3e, by Goldstein. 1993. Reprinted with permission of Wadsworth, a division of Thomson Learning: www.thomsonrights.com.

This approach also emphasises the complex interaction among the components of the system. A model of an instructional system that is useful to designers of learning and development programs is presented in Exhibit 8.5. Notice that the model consists of 10 phases within a continuous cycle, including comprehensive analyses of the learners; the work setting; the job, its performance objectives, measures and sequences; instructional strategies, materials and instructors.[12] News report 8.1 illustrates such a systematic approach to HRD in a large Australian organisation, and its component parts are discussed below.

NEWS REPORT 8.1

Telstra invests A\$67 million in training agreement with Accenture

Telstra has signed a five-year A\$67 million agreement with Accenture to introduce a new training program to Telstra's field services staff. Telstra Network and Technology Executive Managing Director, Dan Burns, said the Accenture agreement is an integral component of a broader staff training program. 'Telstra wants the best-trained telecommunications workforce,

whether it is field staff, network engineering or marketing, so that we are competitive and world class,' said Mr Burns.

Telstra Services Group Managing Director, Michael Rocca, said this arrangement would establish a new Telstra Learning Academy, which would design and conduct specialist training for its field workforce. 'Under this agreement, Telstra is using Accenture's global expertise so our field staff are skilled in new technologies and can deliver better service to our customers,' Mr Rocca said. 'Telstra is undergoing a major transformation with the introduction of many new products and advanced technologies. The new Telstra Learning Academy will help ensure that field staff have the skills to build, run and maintain these technologies. We want our staff to be able to do the best job for customers all the time.'

Academy staff will be based in existing Telstra training centres in Sydney and Melbourne, with trainers travelling across Australia to work with employees. Accenture's program will include development of training content with a focus on using real-life customer and network technical scenarios. 'As a result of this agreement, our field services staff will have greater skills and a better understanding of the network and advanced IP technologies,' Mr Rocca said. 'The Telstra Learning Academy is an investment in our people and the future skills of the telecommunications industry in Australia.'

Steve Willis, a partner in Accenture's Communication & High Tech operating group, said that 'Telstra's commitment to the development of its people's skills and the establishment of the Telstra Learning Academy, is an integral element of their overall transformation program.'

Source: Adapted from www.elearnity.com/A555F3/research/research.nsf, accessed 30/11/2006.

Exhibit 8.6 A performance gap

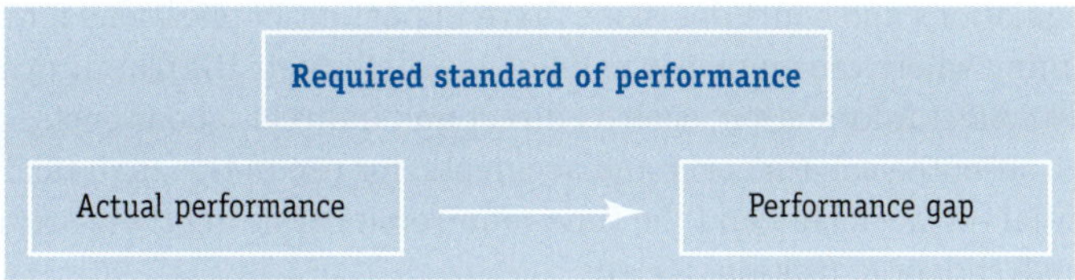

Source: Reproduced from Tovey, *Training in Australia*, 1st edn. ©Pearson Education Australia, 1997.

Needs analysis

A number of researchers have noted that needs analysis is inherently attractive to planners, as this signals the first step in any organisation's learning and development programs. Moreover, they argue that in gaining the interest of the organisation's strategic planners, needs analyses are more likely to deliver useful results in that their added value can be demonstrated.[13] All business managers and HR professionals should be alert for indicators of HRD needs. The failure of employees to achieve production or sales standards, for example, may indicate training requirements. Similarly, an excessive number of rejects or a waste of material may imply inadequate employee development. Excessive turnover in a business unit may reflect a need for supervisory training in interpersonal relations as might an attitude survey conducted with employees. One author argues that needs analysis will often be supply led or demand led. The former is largely driven by those providing the HRD and their vested interests in continuing to do so. Whether the organisation has its own internal professionals or uses the services of external consultants, there is a danger that in either case the HRD conducted will reflect the instructor's preconceptions of the job, which may not be accurate. The second approach is demand driven and has a business orientation in that all HRD programs flow from the strategic plan of the organisation. The strategic plan therefore provides the context for HRD and has a natural appeal to CEOs and senior managers.[14]

In order to approach learning and development needs more systematically, three different analyses are recommended for the assessment phase: organisational analysis, task analysis, and person analysis.[15]

Organisational analysis

An examination of the goals, resources and environment of the organisation to determine where HRD emphasis should be placed is called organisational analysis. The resources that are available to meet objectives such as equipment, financial and human resources must also be considered. Of particular importance in the organisational analysis is studying the impact of the organisational strategic plan on such activities. Typically, there are more HRD needs in organisations than there is budgetary capability. To avoid priorities for such decisions being made on an ad hoc basis, they can be set according to the degree to which the needs identified are consistent with the organisational strategic direction. As with other HRM activities, it is most important that the HRD function is integrated with the organisation's strategic plan.

A study in Australian companies found that competitive pressure was extremely important in focusing the minds of managers on the development of skills in their employees and organisations. 'It was the level of strategic response that they gave to those competitive pressures which really had the ultimate driving effect of making training happen.'[16]

HRM policies and organisational climate have an impact on the goals and methods of the HRD program. Similarly, external factors, such as public policy as reflected in laws, regulations and court decisions, have important implications for such programs in determining where the emphasis will be placed. In their HR planning activities, organisations typically collect information, such as direct and indirect labour costs, quality of goods or services, absenteeism, turnover and accidents, for use in the analytical process. Availability of potential replacements and the time required for training them are also important factors when analysing organisational needs.

Task analysis

Organisational analysis utilises a macro perspective on HRD needs analysis. Task analysis is the micro perspective. Designing a specific HRD program requires a review of the job description in which the activities performed on the job, and the conditions under which they are performed, are indicated. This review is followed by a task analysis that involves determining what the content of the program should be, based upon a study of the tasks or duties involved in the job.

The first step in the task analysis is to list all the tasks or duties that are included in the job. The second is to list the steps involved in performing each of the tasks on the list. Once a thorough understanding of the job has been obtained, the type of performance (i.e. speech, recall, manipulation), along with the skills and knowledge necessary for job performance, can be defined. Determining the types of performance skills and knowledge needed by employees can be done by observing and questioning skilled job incumbents or by reviewing the job description.[17] With this information, the selection of program content and learning methods is facilitated.

Person analysis

The third step in the process is to identify 'gaps' in the occupant of the position – gaps between the level of required skills and knowledge as identified in the task analysis, and those already possessed by the person. Assistance in identifying these gaps (i.e. learning or development needs) can also be provided by information recorded during the recruitment and selection system at the time of initial appointment; and later, data gathered during the performance review process. The needs thus identified can then be incorporated into training provided to the employee to increase their job proficiency.

Competency based learning (CBL)

Over the past few years, traditional HRD needs analysis methods have been enhanced by the advent of competency profiling, as discussed in Chapter 5. If this method is employed, once the organisational and task analyses have been completed it is necessary to determine the personal competencies required to effectively perform the job. This process determines the knowledge, skills and abilities required of people on the job. It is important to determine what prospective employees can and cannot do in order that the HRD program may be designed to yield maximum results at minimum cost.

From this base, it is then possible to progress to competency-based interviewing, learning and appraisal. A number of professions have moved this way, including hospitality, nursing, pharmacy, architecture, engineering, dietetics, occupational therapy, veterinary science and physiotherapy.[18]

Bassett's model shown in Exhibit 8.7 illustrates the links between the initial environmental scanning process and competency-based learning.[19] Bassett's model contains five steps.

- Organisational scan: Future directions, strategies, strengths, weaknesses, opportunities (SWOT analysis). In essence, what are we going to do? Where are we going?

- Strategic planning: How are we going to achieve our objectives? What strategies will be pursued?

- Competency profiling: What internal human resources are available to take us to our objectives? What competencies do they have? Which will they need?

- Competency gap analysis: What is the gap between those competencies required in order to attain strategic objectives and those possessed within the organisation?

- Competency development: How do we close this gap? Do we train, develop and educate our existing staff, or do we recruit new staff who already possess the competencies sought? Alternatively, should we bring in external consultants on a short-term basis?

When the decision is taken to develop existing staff, programs need to be put in place to close the gap between existing and required levels of competencies. As a case in point, one key challenge faced by many organisations will be in identifying potential managers and leaders from existing technical staff and then developing their managerial and leadership competencies to standards already determined by way of a competency profiling exercise.[20]

One point that should be emphasised is the strategic nature of the competency approach. Each step links back to the strategic direction of the organisation. Importantly, HR managers will be required to justify their CBL programs in terms of their contribution to organisational objectives.

The establishment of competency standards across Australian industry has been an integral part of the national training reform agenda – a series of measures introduced since 1989. The Australian National Training Authority (ANTA) defines a competency standard as 'the specification of the knowledge and skill and the application of that knowledge and skill across industries or within an industry, to the standard of performance required in employment'.[21] Subsequent to determining competencies for positions within an industry or organisation, delivery, assessment and certification of training is required.

Exhibit 8.7 Strategic model of competency-based learning

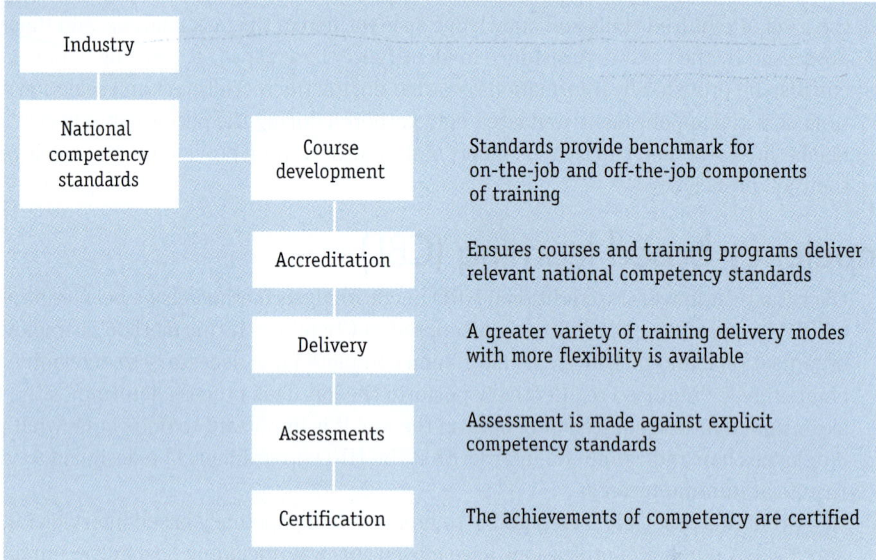

Source: Bassett B. 1990. 'Critical competencies for change,' *Training and Development in Australia*, Australian Institute of Training and Development, 17(4), p. 10.

Despite the relative popularity of CBL, observers have questioned some of its premises and processes. For example, Hager and Gonczi of the University of Technology, Sydney, suggest that:

- It is not valid to equate competence with performance. Other factors are important.

- There is more than one correct way to perform a task (the systems concept of equifinality).

- Competency-based learning may lead to a series of practical modules to the neglect of the mental processes underlying competence.

- The approach is claimed to be objective. In reality it is no more objective or valid than other methods of assessment. The process of validation is quite separate.[22]

Program objectives

After all the analyses have been made, a picture of the needs which may be addressed by HRD emerges. The desired outcomes of such programs should then be stated formally in behavioural-based objectives. Smith and Delahaye highlight the importance of instructional objectives:

> We cannot emphasise enough the necessity for defining training objectives first and defining them exactly. Training objectives come directly from the training needs analysis ... Any task is really made up of a series of behaviours. By desensitising these behaviours, you begin to arrive at terminal behaviour statements. A terminal behaviour is the basis for the training objective.[23]

One type of instructional objective, the performance-centred objective, is utilised widely because it lends itself best to an unbiased evaluation of results. For example, the stated objective for one HRD program might be that 'the employee will answer all telephone calls within three rings with a pre-prepared company welcome,' or 'serve all fast food customers in less than three

minutes.' Performance-centred objectives typically include precise terms such as 'to calculate, to repair, to adjust, to construct, to assemble, to classify,' and have three components:

- a statement of the terminal behaviour

- a statement of the standards that the employee is expected to attain

- a statement of the conditions under which the employee is expected to perform the terminal behaviour.

The delivery phase

Once the HRD needs have been determined and the instructional objectives specified, the next step is to develop the type of environment necessary for achieving these objectives. This includes formulating a specific HRD strategy and preparing instructional plans.[24] A major consideration in creating an appropriate learning environment is that of choosing a method or medium that will enable the employee to learn most effectively.[25] The methods that are commonly used in HRD at all levels – managerial, supervisory and non-managerial – will be discussed later in this chapter.

Evaluation phase

HRD, like any other HR function, should be evaluated to determine its effectiveness. Unfortunately, information about the achievement of objectives and the most effective methods to reach them are obtained in only a few instances, and then by research methods that are often inadequate.

While efforts at evaluation are evolving, too many decisions about HRD effectiveness are based upon anecdotal instructor and employee reactions. Subjective comments from employees are often 'glowing' and are easily gathered. Unfortunately, this information may not be very useful to the organisation because learning and development is not provided for its entertainment value. The real issue is whether the knowledge gained through HRD will be reflected in improved behaviour or job performance[26] or, in other words, whether there has been *knowledge transfer*. As Sofo explains, 'the most common complaint about (HRD) is that there is no "transfer of training" and that people's … habitual behaviour remains the same, largely unaffected by the "learning" experience'.[27]

Not only should employees be tested before and after participating in learning and development activities, but also the same tests or evaluations should be applied to individuals in a control group that has not received the HRD, and whose members reflect relevant variables such as experience, past training and job level. Some of the criteria that are used in evaluating overall HRD effectiveness are increased productivity, greater total sales, decreased costs and waste and, in recent years, the return on (organisational) investment (ROI). If a development program is designed to change the behaviour of supervisors, the evaluation should be in terms of observable (and observed) supervisory behaviours rather than acquired knowledge.

Planning the evaluation around specific questions or objectives increases the likelihood that findings will produce meaningful and concrete changes.[28] HRD managers have sometimes limited their influence in their organisations by not being able to prove their effectiveness objectively, and have consequently depended upon the goodwill of top management rather than on the strategic benefits of HRD to the organisation. Kirkpatrick's (1975) model of the evaluation of HRD, which has become a generally accepted approach, suggests the following phases:

Level 1: Reaction (What the learner felt about the activity)

Level 2: Learning (The increase in knowledge or capability)

Level 3: Behaviour (Extent of behaviour and capability improvement and application)

Level 4: Results (The effects on the business or personal improvement).[29,30]

Meeting learning and development goals

To help prove the effectiveness of learning and development, the evaluation phase must address the validity of the associated program. Goldstein describes four approaches to program evaluation:

- learning program validity – whether employees have learnt something from the program
- transfer validity – whether knowledge or skills transfer has occurred back in the workplace
- intra-organisational validity – whether new and more experienced employees share similar performance
- inter-organisational validity – whether a program validated in one organisation has similar results in another organisation.[31]

It may be argued that the second approach is the most relevant for most organisations, as discussed earlier in this chapter.

Cost–benefit considerations

The ability to measure the benefits derived from HRD varies according to the type of job. Where employees are performing relatively simple tasks, the effects of learning and development may show up quite dramatically. For more complex jobs, such as those at the managerial and professional levels, the benefits are more difficult to measure. It is generally found, however, that the benefits will far exceed the costs when the objectives to be met by an HRD program are clearly defined, when the most suitable instructional techniques are used and when employee motivation is high.

The benefits that are experienced by an organisation are similar to those found through a carefully developed selection program. Increased productivity and the ability of the competent employees to assume more responsible roles in the organisation are the major benefits. Reduction of waste, accidents and similar problems may also result from HRD programs.

The argument which the HRD manager must sustain is that the employee development program led to such improvements. In many areas of training, learning and development, many intangibles will arise that make measurement of results very difficult, although a number of researchers have addressed this key area.[32]

Principles of learning

The success of an HRD program depends upon more than the identification of employee needs and the preparation of the program. In order to maximise learning, careful consideration needs to be given to the relevant principles of learning. Two of the most accepted theories of the principles involved in adult learning are Knowles' (1984) theory of 'andragogy,' and Kolb's (1984) Learning Style Inventory (see Exhibit 8.8). Knowles researched the ways in which adults (and therefore employees) learn most effectively, concluding that, unlike children, adults are generally self-directed and expect to take responsibility for their own learning. As a consequence, adult learning and development programs should factor in explanations of the need to learn; provide frequent opportunities for learning by doing; and frame learning as a problem-solving activity. Therefore exercises such as role plays, case studies and group projects are useful in employee learning and development, and instructors act as facilitators rather than lecturers.[33]

Kolb's model illustrates similar features, with its four-stage cycle of adult learning – namely, *concrete experience, reflection, abstract conceptualisation* (the derivation of general rules) and *active experimentation* (developing future ways of building on learning).[34] More recent notions of 'single loop' versus 'double loop' learning, and 'deep' learning are applications of

these theories to organisational learning, conceptualised best in Senge's (1990) concept of the 'learning organisation,' or an organisation which systematically incorporates these adult learning principles into its routine problem-solving and decision-making techniques in an ongoing manner.[35] These principles are illustrated in the following discussion.

Exhibit 8.8 Kolb's Learning Style Inventory

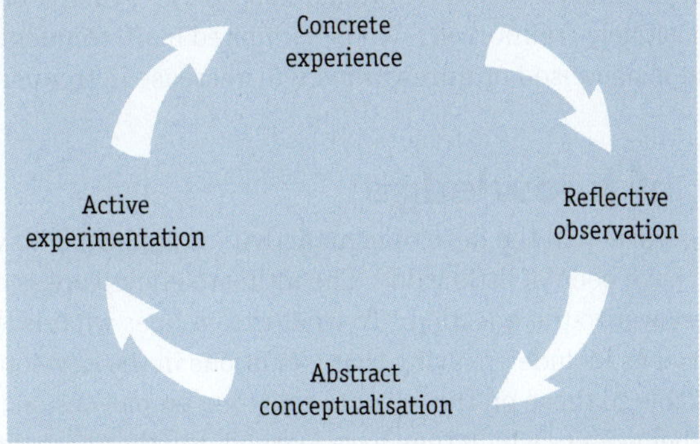

Preconditions for learning

Two preconditions for learning will increase the success of those who are to participate in such programs: employee readiness and motivation. The condition known as employee readiness refers to both maturational and experiential factors in the employee's background. Prospective employees should be screened to determine that they have the background knowledge or the skills necessary for learning what will be presented to them. Recognition of individual differences in readiness is as important in HRD as it is in any other learning situation. It is often desirable to group individuals according to their capacity to learn, as determined by scores from tests, or to provide a different or extended type of instruction for those who need it.

The other precondition for learning is that the employee be properly motivated. That is, for optimum learning the employee must recognise the need for acquiring new information or for having new skills; and a desire to learn as learning progresses must be maintained. While people at work are motivated by certain common needs, they differ from one another in the relative importance of these needs at any given time. For example, new recruits often have an intense desire for advancement, and have established specific goals for career progression. Objectives that are clearly defined will produce increased motivation in the learning process when instructional objectives are related to individual needs.

Some prerequisites for learning

After employees have been placed in the learning situation, their readiness and motivation should be assessed further. In addition, facilitators should understand the basic learning issues discussed below.

Meaningful materials

In accordance with adult learning theories, the material to be learned should be organised in as meaningful a manner as possible. It should be arranged so that each successive experience builds upon preceding ones so that the employee is able to integrate the experiences into a useable pattern of knowledge and skills. The material should have face validity.

Reinforcement

Anything which strengthens the employee's response is called reinforcement. It may be in the form of approval from the instructor or facilitator or the feeling of accomplishment that follows the performance; or it may simply be confirmation by a software program that the employee's response was correct. It is generally most effective if it occurs immediately after a task has been performed.

Behaviour modification, or a technique that operates on the principle that behaviour that is rewarded positively (reinforced) will be exhibited more frequently in the future, whereas behaviour that is penalised or unrewarded will decrease in frequency, is often used for such purposes.[36]

Transfer of knowledge

Unless what is learned in the development activity is applicable to what is required on the job, the effort will have been of little value. The ultimate effectiveness of learning, therefore, is to be found in the answer to the question: 'To what extent does what is learned transfer to the job?' Helpful approaches include ensuring that conditions in the development program conform as closely as possible to those on the job, and coaching employees on the principles for applying to the job the behaviours which they have learned. Furthermore, once formal instruction has been completed, the supervisor must ensure that the work environment supports, reinforces and rewards the employee for applying the new skills or knowledge.[37]

Knowledge of progress

As an employee's development progresses, motivation may be maintained and even increased by providing knowledge of progress. Progress, as determined by tests and other records, may be plotted on a chart, commonly referred to as a learning curve. Exhibit 8.9 is an example of a learning curve that is common in the acquisition of many job skills.

Exhibit 8.9   A typical learning curve

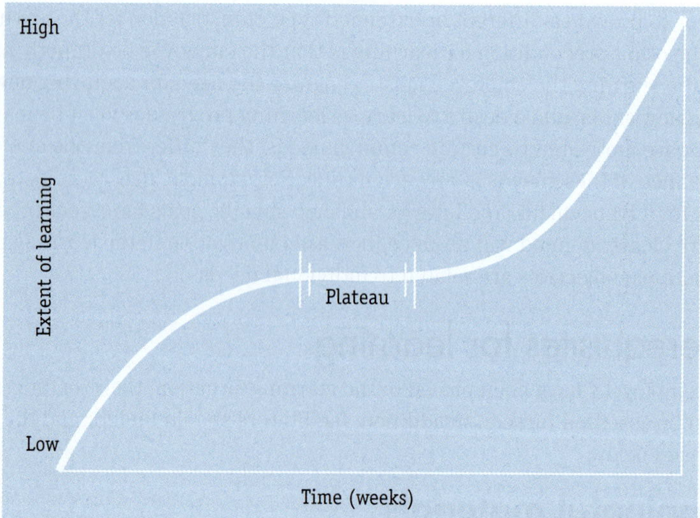

In many learning situations, there are times when progress does not occur. Such periods of no return show up on the curve as a fairly straight horizontal line, which is called a plateau. A plateau may be the result of ineffective methods of work or of reduced motivation.

Proper analysis by instructors and employees may reveal the cause of a plateau and may be overcome by such means as suggestions for new work procedures, or aid in establishing new incentives. Plateaux are to be expected and do not necessarily indicate failure of the program.

Distributed learning

Another factor that determines the effectiveness of learning is the amount of time given to practice in one session. Should training or development be undertaken in five two-hour periods or in 10 one-hour periods? It has been found in most cases that spacing out the activities will result in more rapid learning and more permanent retention. This is the principle of distributed learning. Since the most efficient distribution will vary according to the type and complexity of the task to be learned, it is desirable to make reference to the rapidly growing body of research in this area when an answer is required for a specific learning situation.

Whole vs part learning

Most jobs and tasks can be broken down into parts that lend themselves to further analysis. The analysis of the most effective manner for completing each part then provides a basis for giving specific instruction. Airline flight attendant jobs, for example, involve a combination of mechanistic (specific tasks that follow a prescribed routine), and organic (tasks that involve decision-making and individualised responses) duties, which are best learnt separately, and then combined to form the whole job responsibility. Thus, the prescribed takeoff and landing announcements, and formal safety procedures, are supplemented with separate learning activities about how to deal with difficult passengers or how to cope with food supply problems. In evaluating whole versus part learning, it is necessary to consider the nature of the task to be learned. If the task can be broken down successfully for part learning, it should probably be taught as a unit.

Practice and repetition

It is those things we do daily that become a part of our repertoire of skills. Employees need frequent opportunities to practise their job tasks in the manner in which they will ultimately be expected to perform them. The individual who is being taught to operate a machine should have an opportunity to practise on it. Similarly, the supervisor who is being taught how to train should have supervised practice in training.

Multiple sense learning

It has long been acknowledged that the use of multiple senses increases learning. Smith and Delahaye state that about 80 per cent of what a person perceives is obtained visually, 11 per cent by hearing and 9 per cent by the other senses combined. It follows that in order to maximise learning, multiple senses of the employees, particularly sight and hearing, should be engaged. Visual aids are therefore emphasised as being important to the learning and development activities.[38]

Developing non-managerial employees

Once the learning need is clear, the instructional objectives have been determined, and the principles of learning relevant to the situation have been identified, the most appropriate development method may be chosen.

A wide variety of such methods is available, some of which have a long history of usage. Newer methods have developed over the years out of a greater understanding of human behaviour, particularly in the areas of learning, motivation and interpersonal relationships.

More recently, technological advances, especially in electronics, have resulted in development strategies and techniques that in many instances are more effective and economical than traditional training methods.

On-the-job learning

The most commonly used method in the development of non-managerial employees is conducted by a supervisor or a senior employee who is responsible for instructing employees. It has the advantage of providing hands-on experience under normal working conditions and an opportunity for the instructor or mentor to build good relationships with new employees.

Although on-the-job learning (OJL) is used commonly by all types of organisations, it is often one of the most poorly implemented methods. Common drawbacks include:

- the lack of a well-structured environment

- poor supervisory development skills

- the omission of well-defined job performance criteria[39]

- wastage, or 'downline' effects or customer dissatisfaction because of mistakes made while the employee is learning on the job.

To overcome these problems, some experts suggest the following points for conducting successful OJL:

- Develop realistic goals and measures for each OJT area.

- Plan a specific development schedule for each trainee, including setting periods for evaluation and feedback.

- Have supervisors establish a non-threatening atmosphere that is conducive to learning.

- Conduct periodic evaluations, after the development has been completed, to prevent regression.[40]

Benefits of OJL training include:

- ease of organising and administration

- generally lower cost

- can be more timely (can quickly address an emerging performance problem).

Off-the-job learning

In addition to on-the-job learning, it is often necessary to provide employees with development opportunities in settings away from their usual workplace. Various methods are available for use within the organisation's facilities. Other methods involve having the employee travel to locations outside the organisation. In some cases, external training is obligatory, for example, TAFE apprentice training.

Conference or discussion method

The conference or discussion method of individualised instruction is frequently used when learning primarily involves the communication of ideas, procedures and standards. This method allows for considerable flexibility in the amount of employee participation that is encouraged or permitted.

Classroom and laboratory training methods

The maximum number of trainees may be handled by a minimum number of instructors in classroom or laboratory training. These methods lend themselves particularly to instruction in areas where information and instructions can be imparted by lectures, demonstrations, films and other types of audiovisual media. In some cases such training may be complemented with

the supervised use of computers or other equipment to enable employees to learn job-relevant skills such as particular software programs, ticketing procedures, retail scanning systems or production processes.

Programmed instruction method

Programmed instruction uses a manual, CD-ROM or software program to present programmed subject matter. A program represents an attempt to break down subject matter into highly organised, logical sequences that demand continuous responses on the part of the employee. After being presented with a small segment of information, the learner is required to respond to a question, either by writing an answer in a response frame, or by pushing a button on a keyboard. If the response is correct, the learner is advised of that fact and presented with the next step (frame) in the material. If the response is incorrect, further explanatory information is given and the learner told to 'try again.' In many Australian states, applicants for driving permits are provided with practice modules that use this method, for both learning and testing purposes.

A major advantage of programmed instruction is that the method incorporates a number of the learning principles discussed earlier. With programmed instruction, learning is individualised, employees are actively involved in the instructional process, and feedback on performance and reinforcement is immediate.

E-learning

As more and more employees are connected to either the Internet or the company intranet, organisations are increasingly discovering the power of the computer as a learning and development medium. Qantas has established an interactive Internet training facility to provide online training, which staff members can complete at their own pace. In addition, staff members have online contact with tutors.[41]

Cuscal (Credit Union Services Corporation (Australia)) has introduced an online, interactive induction program for staff in all Australian states.[42] The Internet has seen the development of the 'virtual' university and college from the older 'bricks-and-mortar' approach to learning (from 'bricks to clicks'). In addition to time and geographic flexibility, the learning modules can be varied to suit the needs of the learner,[43] with an 'anytime, anyplace' approach to learning.[44]

In addition, e-learning provides identical information to all of its users, and can reach huge numbers of potential trainees. The 'one-size-fits-all' approach to learning is no longer feasible.[45]

Simulation method

For some jobs, it is either impractical or unwise to train the worker on the equipment that is used on the job. An obvious example is the development of personnel to operate passenger transportation technology. The design of simulators emphasises realism in equipment and its operation at minimal cost and maximum safety. For example, NSW's Cityrail Tangara and Millennium train drivers receive their training through the use of a simulator, as do drivers on the Mass Transit Railway systems in Singapore and Hong Kong.

State-of-the-art computer simulation is also used to train airline pilots. Trainee pilots practise on simulators that reflect real flying conditions such as wind speed, turbulence and the lights at specified airports as the trainee attempts a landing.[46] The Royal Australian Navy is using the same type of technology to train its naval officers in the operation of warships and submarines.[47] A recent innovative example of the use of simulation technology in learning and development is the Mediseus Epidural, a unit that combines software feedback with an epidural simulator to assist in the training of clinicians and medical students in their epidural analgesia skills on virtual patients. Using the Mediseus, clinicians can practise on a simulator to a 'measurable level of proficiency' before carrying out the procedure on real patients.[48]

The major benefit of such training simulators is that while the experiences and conditions appear real, wrong decisions will not have the same dire consequences as they would if made on the actual job.

Apprenticeship training and internships

A system of training in which the new worker is given thorough instruction and experience (both on and off the job) in the practical and theoretical aspects of the work in a skilled trade is known as apprenticeship training. Apprenticeship programs are based on cooperation between management and labour, between industry and government, and between the company and the TAFE system. Although apprenticeship wages are less than those of fully qualified workers, this method does provide training with pay for individuals who are interested in qualifying for jobs as machinists, electricians, plumbers, panel beaters, motor mechanics and others. Such training systems for apprentices have recently been 'streamlined,' (e.g. shorter mandatory training periods and mixes of TAFE and workplace-based development).

Internship programs, jointly sponsored by colleges, universities and different organisations, offer students the opportunity to gain 'real life' experiences while allowing them to find out how they will perform in work organisations. Organisations benefit by obtaining student employees possessing new ideas, energy and a desire to accomplish a given assignment. Many Australian universities allow students to earn credit points based upon successful job performance and established program requirements and, in recent years, these have been supplemented by in-house, tailored undergraduate and post-graduate education programs conducted by universities in cooperation with industry.

Developing managers and supervisors

Many of the methods discussed in the preceding section may also be used in developing managers and supervisors. However, because of the broader knowledge and skills required of managerial and supervisory personnel, other methods are also used. In many cases, the emphasis is on learning, development and training.

Many studies of Australian and international organisations have found that competitive pressure is driving many decisions about their organisational learning and development strategies. These decisions relate to how competencies and skills inside the organisations are treated as a competitive advantage, and how they develop those skills.

On-the-job experiences

Management competencies, skills and abilities cannot be acquired just by listening and observing or by reading about them. They must be acquired through actual practice and experience in which a person has an opportunity to perform under pressure and to learn from mistakes. On-the-job experiences are used most commonly by organisations to develop executive personnel. Such experiences need to be well planned and supervised, and meaningful and challenging to the participant. Some of these methods include:

- *Coaching and mentoring*: involves a continuing flow of instructions, feedback, comments, support and suggestions from a chosen superior to subordinates. The coaching role of the manager gained renewed importance following the 'In Search of Excellence' research,[49] and the work of Henry Mintzberg.[50]

- *Understudy assignment*: grooms an individual to take over the supervisor's job by gaining experience in handling important functions of the job. Used extensively in the world of entertainment, organisations have found similar benefits flowing from this method.

- *Shadow executive*: involves a small group of high-potential junior managers forming a 'shadow' executive where they deal with real issues and feed their recommendations through to the organisation's formal executive.

- *Job rotation*: provides, through a variety of work experiences, a broadened knowledge and understanding required to manage more effectively.

- *Lateral transfer*: involves horizontal movement through different departments along with upward movement in the organisation.

- *Project and committee assignments*: provide an opportunity for the individual to become involved in the study of current organisational problems and in planning and decision-making activities.

- *Staff meetings*: enable participants to become more familiar with problems and events that are occurring outside their immediate area by exposing them to the ideas and thinking of other managers.

While the above methods have now been used for many years, a number of newer approaches have emerged in Australia over the past few years.

Off-the-job experiences

Conferences and seminars

While on-the-job experiences constitute core management development activities, certain methods of development away from the job can be used to supplement work experiences. These experiences may be provided on either an individual or a group basis and may be developed by means of special conferences or seminars.

A number of organisations now specialise in the provision of management seminars covering all aspects of organisational life but in some cases have questionable practical relevance. While this type of management development can be very useful in terms of updating knowledge, networking or acquiring new knowledge, its effectiveness will depend on the quality of the presenters, and organisations need to consider carefully the associated costs and benefits. In addition, it is quite common for the major professions to hold annual conferences for their members. These often will be complemented by monthly seminars or special interest group meetings.

Case studies

Case studies may be particularly useful in classroom learning situations. These cases, which have usually been developed from actual experiences within organisations, can help managers learn how to obtain and interpret facts, to become conscious of the many variables upon which a management decision may be based, and generally improve their decision-making skills.

The case study approach will often attempt to project the manager or supervisor into the case itself, and then ask them to analyse the facts, generate a number of possible solutions, and the consequences of each. The advantage of this method is that mistakes may be made without the consequences that might accompany the wrong decision if made in their organisations.

In most applications, the syndicate or small group discussion method will accompany the case study method. In this way, a number of skills, such as decision-making, interpersonal, communication and leadership may be assessed.

Barolsky suggests that many of the premier business schools around the world use the case study method, with the Harvard Business School being at the forefront, with a catalogue of over 4000 cases.[51]

In-basket training

Another method that can be used to simulate a problem situation is the in-basket technique. In this technique, the participants are given several documents, each describing some problem or situation, the solution of which requires an immediate decision. They are thus forced to make decisions under the pressure of time and also to determine the priority with which each problem should be considered. In-basket exercises are a common instructional technique in development and/or assessment centres.

Leaderless group discussions

A popular assessment centre activity is leaderless group discussions. With this technique, managers are gathered in a conference setting to discuss an assigned topic, either with or without designated group roles. The participants are given few or no instructions on how to approach the topic, nor are they told what decision to reach. Leaderless group participants are evaluated on their initiative, leadership skills and ability to work effectively in a group setting.

Management games

Learning experiences have been brought to life and made more interesting through the development of management games. Participants who play the games are faced with the task of making a continuing series of decisions affecting a hypothetical organisation. The simulated effects that each decision has upon each functional area within the organisation can be determined by means of a computer that has been programmed for the game. A major advantage of this technique is the high degree of participation that it requires.

Using computer technology similar to that used to train pilots and astronauts, managers and supervisors are introduced to a hypothetical market where they take on the role of business people and test their decision-making skills against the computer.

One of the best-known games is conducted annually by the *Financial Review* newspaper. Another is an annual competition run by Interstrat, based on a program developed by the International Business Management School in France. Australian firms competing have included Mobil, ANZ, Coca-Cola, Telecom, BHP, IBM, Westpac, Colgate-Palmolive and BP. Other Australian organisations that use a management simulation game developed by Abbott Training Systems include Alcan, Australian Airlines, and St George Bank.[52]

Role playing

Role playing consists of assuming the attitudes and behaviour of, and acting out the roles of, individuals (usually a supervisor and a subordinate who are involved in an HRM problem). Role playing can help participants improve their ability to understand and cope with the problems of the other person. Role statements are provided to each participant who is then expected to play that role. Problems will emerge when participants 'step out' of their role. Popular applications of this method include interviewing, leadership and decision-making skills.

Sensitivity training

This technique has as its primary goal the development of greater sensitivity on the part of its participants, including self insight and an awareness of group processes. It also provides the opportunity to improve human relations skills by having managers or supervisors better understand themselves and others. This is achieved by allowing the participants to share their experiences, feelings, emotions and perceptions about fellow employees. The ability to participate constructively in group activities is another benefit of this technique.

In recent years sensitivity training programs have tended to be modified to produce more organisation- and job-oriented discussions, with less probing into personal feelings and behaviour.

Behaviour modelling

Development programs designed simply to change supervisors' attitudes are no longer as necessary as in the past. Supervisors now must be shown how to put their attitudes to work. One approach is behaviour modelling, or interaction management. This approach emphasises the involvement of the supervisors in handling real-life employee problems and receiving immediate feedback on their performance.[53] The main purpose of behaviour modelling is to achieve behavioural change. There are four basic steps in behaviour modelling:

1 Supervisors view DVDs or video clips in which a model supervisor is portrayed dealing with an employee in an effort to improve or maintain the employee's performance. The model shows specifically how to deal with the situation.

2 Participants then engage in extensive practice and rehearsal of the behaviours demonstrated by the models. The greatest percentage of time is spent in these skill practice sessions.

3 As the participants' behaviour increasingly resembles that of the model, the participants provide such social reinforcers as praise, approval, encouragement and attention.

4 The principles of transferring the learning to the job are emphasised throughout.[54]

Does behaviour modelling work? Several controlled studies have demonstrated behaviour change on the part of supervisors, as well as measurable increases in worker productivity.[55] In one study, Meyer and Raich provided objective evidence showing that behaviour modelling training for marketing representatives actually resulted in increased sales.[56]

Orienteering programs

Orienteering (or outdoor physical training) has become a relatively popular means of developing work teams and grooming leaders, based on the belief that undertaking physical activities together in the bush or jungle builds skills which can then be transferred back into the workplace. Long used by the military and police services, it has also been used by organisations such as Robe River Iron Ore, Westpac, Tubemakers and BHP Iron Ore.

According to Cacioppe and Adamson, orienteering programs 'focus on personal and group development and take time to focus on management and behaviour principles and how they apply in the workplace'.[57] Miller and Rooke claim that employees and their managers are presented with opportunities to step outside their 'comfort zones' in pursuit of learning objectives.[58]

Outdoor exercises might include walking across a pole suspended by two others 1.8 metres off the ground. Others may ask learners to leap from a 1.2-metre pole on to a trapeze bar 1.85 metres away.[59] The promoted benefits include developing team leadership skills, problem-solving, building camaraderie and team bonding. Whereas providers talk of their particular program with zeal, not all consultants are convinced. Many argue that such programs represent little more than a management fad which in no way can be transferred to the workplace.

University and TAFE education

The TAFE network has offered business education for the past 50 years. Initially conducted at the certificate level, TAFE has expanded its courses into the Diploma and Advanced Diploma qualifications. In addition, most universities offer undergraduate degrees in commerce or economics, post-graduate degrees in business and commerce, and Masters of Business Administration (MBAs).

A management education at either level provides a broad treatment of skills and concepts, resulting in the exposure of employees, supervisors and managers to a wide variety of business issues. While management course curricula emphasise the development of practical industry skills, students should also develop a capacity to analyse contemporary business and social institutions from a wide variety of perspectives.[60]

In recent years, university and corporate consortia have developed hybrid programs which blend university course work with practical business applications. For example, Queensland Health (QH) engaged the Queensland University of Technology and the University of Southern Queensland to conduct a Graduate Certificate in Management course by distance education. Partially financed by QH, this qualification is designed to upgrade the management skills of its 450 middle managers who are spread across the state. The material used is normal university instructional material that has been contextualised to a health-care industry setting. Telstra, Westpac, Australia Post and Energy Australia have also entered into similar cooperative arrangements.

Trends in learning and development

Some observers have summarised the following trends in learning and learning technologies:

- *generic learning* – developing basic competencies across organisations
- *action learning* – learning by doing, and learning from actual events
- *self-paced learning* – using DVDs, CD-ROMs, e-learning
- *flexible/blended learning* – a mixture of instructor-led and learner-centred activities
- *technologically mediated learning* – allows learners to play and learn simultaneously
- *changing HR roles in HRD* – HR professionals as facilitators and internal consultants rather than trainers.

Management support

While it is acknowledged that many factors will affect the outcome of a learning or development program, one key issue will be the support or lack of support from senior managers, many of whom will see such programs merely in terms of their costs. This issue applies to any HRD program where time, and in many cases a large amount of money, will need to be spent.

Exhibit 8.10 Learning and attitude development continuum

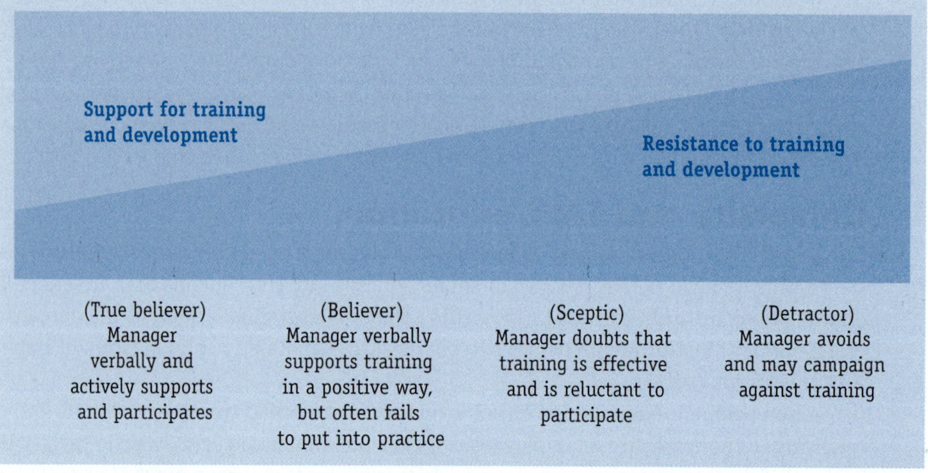

Source: Reproduced with permission from McDonald G., 'Manager attitudes to training,' *Asia Pacific HRM*, 27(4), © Australasian Human Resources Institute, 1989, by permission of Sage Publications Ltd.

McDonald's model (Exhibit 8.10) depicting management attitudes towards training and development[61] groups managers' perspectives into four categories:

- *true believer*: commitment and persistence shown by word and action
- *believer*: will support learning and development programs, but other priorities will dominate
- *sceptic*: doubts that learning will do any good. May well have had bad experiences along the way up the organisation
- *detractor*: open visible troublemaker. Detractors will spread negative comments about learning and development as often as they can.[62]

When HR practitioners can prove that their learning programs contribute to organisational profits, then they will be able to convert more managers to the status of true believer. In many cases, this time has already arrived, but in other areas, particularly with management education, there will often be too many intangibles for accurate evaluation and measurement. News report 8.2 presents a more positive example of one organisation's commitment to the development of engineering professionals into managers, taking into account their career aspirations as well.

'The team leader definitely needs some leadership skills,' Mr Vaughan emphasised.

'It needs to be someone who can see out front, can envisage where the project is going.' Communication skills are important, with an engineering team needing to manage customer needs, and quality, safety and environmental considerations.

'We're moving from managing design to managing the process of engineering,' Mr Vaughan said of the transition to management.

He noted, however, that Ford always had some engineers who wished to stay in technical roles for their entire careers.

After some mistakes in promoting the wrong people to management, the company created a career structure that allowed technical specialists to earn salaries equivalent to engineers in the management track.

'We had examples at Ford where we mistakenly promoted (technically-oriented engineers) to management positions – they weren't very good at being managers and didn't want to be managers.' Mr Vaughan partly attributes his own career success – he retired from Ford as senior vice president engineering and product development, reporting directly to Ford Australia's then president Jac Nasser – to the early completion of a Dale Carnegie management course.

'It's not just a public speaking course; it's about developing confidence.'

CELM's objectives are to influence the future career paths of engineers and, more widely, to promote the engineering profession.

Participants commented that engineers had slipped in community esteem since the early post-war decades, perhaps influenced by the economic rationalism of the 1990s. The decline in engineering enrolments at universities was a real concern.

The centre will arrange presentations for young engineers and short management courses with other professional bodies. The development of management competency standards for engineers is a related goal.

CELM's mission

- The Centre for Engineering Leadership and Management aims to help engineers progress from technical roles to management positions.
- It is being set up within Engineers Australia and will interact with technical colleges.
- The centre will run short management courses with professional bodies.
- CELM aims to develop competency standards in engineering management.

Source: *Benchmarking HR*, 4 April 2003.

Career management

The processes of human resource development discussed so far have a fairly long history. Typically, they have been carried out with organisational needs as the primary concern. However, since the mid-1970s increasing attention has been given to the employees' need to have satisfying careers. The term 'career,' as it is now used by professionals in HRM and related fields, refers to the sequence of jobs that individuals hold during their work histories regardless of their occupation or organisational level. No longer does the term pertain only to high-status or rapid-advancement occupations.

Increased competition for promotion, constant innovation in technology, more competitive and sometimes scarce labour markets, corporate rightsizing and restructuring and the consequent implications on employee commitment and loyalty are all major forces pushing organisations to offer career development programs.

Exhibit 8.11 An SHRM model of strategic career planning

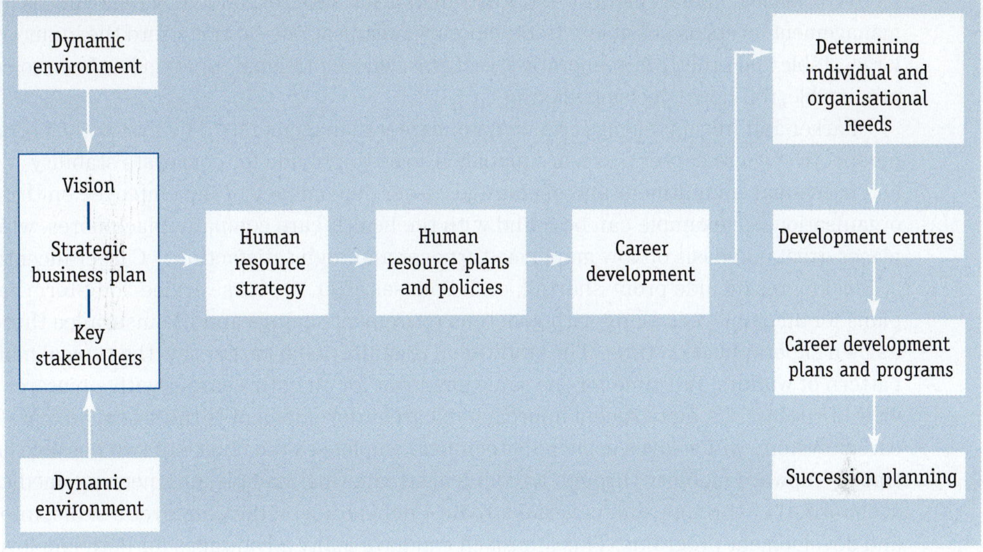

In addition, there is the vital need to retain key employees. The desire of employers to make better use of their employees' knowledge and skills and to retain those who are valuable to the organisation, its corporate memory and intellectual capital, is now recognised as an essential and strategic imperative. There is a growing awareness among employers that a career development program can benefit not only managers, supervisors and their subordinates, but the entire organisation as well.[63]

It is not so long ago that people joined an organisation for life. While there are 'lifers' in certain industries and specific organisations, the way forward today is to engage in what one of Australia's business leaders has termed 'career surfing' and to focus on employability and career positioning.[64]

A strategic perspective

Career development, as with each component of the HR 'package,' must take on a strategic emphasis. The management of careers in times of demands for more innovative, creative, and competitive organisations is one of HR's greatest strategic challenges. Many observers have suggested that the primary concern of all organisations is to attract and retain the best 'talent' in what is increasingly being seen as a global 'War for Talent,' and obviously therefore, career development is one of the important weapons in this 'war.'

Compton and Morrissey have argued that the paradigm for managing careers has shifted enormously over recent years. The traditional environment encouraged lifelong employment, numerous hierarchical layers, bureaucratic processes and many years of promotion through the hierarchy. Today there are fewer opportunities to advance through the ranks, as layers of management have been removed forever and democratisation of the workplace results in even fewer managers for the future.[65]

Similarly, James talks of 'flat earth' theory impacting on organisational hierarchies. Facing more volatile and competitive markets than ever imagined and an awareness of the success of more consensual management styles, Australian firms have responded by removing as many management layers as possible.[66] Contemporary organisations cannot afford the luxury of large, stable and orderly bureaucratic structures, whose principal function has been to ensure predictable, top-down decision making.[67]

Parker and Inkson discuss two views of career management.[68] The first is the corporate perspective where career paths are managed so as to provide for corporate stability and individual commitment and encourage career dependency of the employee on the organisation. An example can be found with the health-care company Blackmores, which places great emphasis on low employee turnover and high satisfaction.[69] Career incentives at Blackmores include profit-sharing, cash bonuses after 10 years service, long-term career plans for all employees along with generous retirement savings and life insurance through its own superannuation fund. The traditional organisational career saw the typical male pattern of working full-time for the same employer for an entire career with a hierarchical view of success.[70] A more recent approach to career development is the so-called 'parallel' career system, which gives especially technical employees the choice of two possible career tracks – upward mobility through a technical stream (for example, engineering, medical, accounting) or through a managerial stream – depending on the employee's skills, interests and development programs. This approach can have many advantages for both employees and their organisations.

A second view considers the organisation as a resource for individuals, which is the reverse of the traditional HR view of career management. In this scenario, employees (often the so-called Generation X and Y employees) sell themselves as a product and unashamedly pursue careers without boundaries. The emphasis is now on employability rather than employment security, which is arguably a more motivational situation for employees.[71] This newer view is supported by Kelly, who discusses a new career management paradigm where responsibility for career development rests with the individual. According to Kelly this is a departure from the traditional view held by employees as part of their psychological contract with their employers.[72]

Phases of a career development program

Organisations have traditionally engaged in HR planning and development. Historically this activity has involved charting the moves of large numbers of employees through various positions in an organisation and identifying future staffing needs. Contemporary career development programs, with their greater emphasis on the individual, introduce a personalised aspect to the process.

A common approach to establishing a career development program is to integrate it with the existing HR processes and structures in the organisation. Integrating the career development program with the overall HR program reinforces both. Exhibit 8.12 illustrates how HR structures relate to some of the essential aspects of the career development process. For example, in planning careers, employees need the organisational information that strategic planning, forecasting, succession planning and skills inventories can provide. Similarly, as they obtain information about themselves and use it in career planning, employees need to know how management views their performance and the career paths within the organisation.[73]

Exhibit 8.12 Two-way support: career development/human resources

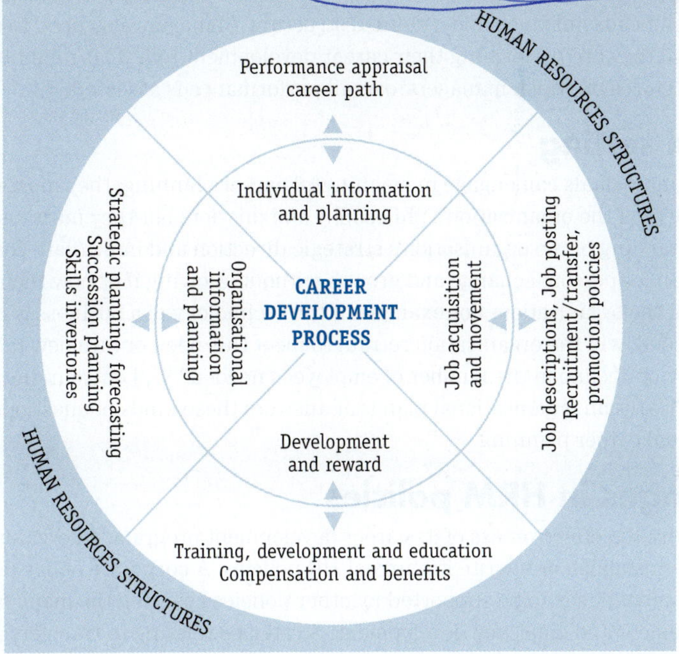

Source: Leibowitz Z.B., Farren C., Kaye B.L. 1986. *Designing career development systems*, San Francisco, Jossey-Bass, p. 41.

Determining individual and organisational needs

A career development program should be viewed as a proactive and dynamic process that attempts to meet the needs of managers, their people and the organisation. Individual employees are responsible for initiating and developing their own career plans. It is up to them to identify their knowledge, skills, abilities, interests and values and to seek out information about career options so that they can set goals and develop career plans. Managers are expected to encourage their subordinates to take responsibility for their own careers, while offering continuing assistance in the form of feedback on individual performance, information about the organisation, job and career opportunities that might be of interest. In turn, managers are similarly responsible for their own career development.

The organisation is responsible for supplying information about its mission, policies and plans and for providing support for employee self-assessment, learning and development. Significant career growth can occur when individual initiative combines with organisational opportunity. Career development programs benefit managers by giving them increased skill in managing their own careers, greater retention of valued employees, increased understanding of the organisation and enhanced reputations as people developers.[74]

As with other HR programs, the formulation of a career development program must be based on the organisation's strategic needs as well. Assessment of needs should take a variety of approaches (surveys, focus groups, interviews) and should involve people from different groups, such as new employees, managers, plateaued employees, and technical and professional employees. Identifying the needs and problems of these groups provides the starting point for the organisation's career development efforts.

For a program to be effective, leaders at all levels must be trained in the fundamentals of job design, performance appraisal, career planning, mentoring and career counselling. Line managers must be the heart and soul of a career development program. The average manager, however, needs guidance and a defined structure. Managers also need to receive feedback on how well they are performing their career development role. This might be one of the leadership competencies on which managers' overall performance is assessed.

Goal setting

Before individuals can engage in meaningful career planning, they must not only have an awareness of the organisation's philosophy and mission, but they must also have a clear understanding of the organisation's strategic direction and immediate goals. Otherwise, they may plan for personal change and growth without knowing if or how their own goals match those of the organisation. For example, if the technology of a business is changing and new skills are needed, will the organisation retrain to meet this need or hire new talent? Is there growth, stability or decline in the number of employees needed? Will outsourcing affect my business unit? Clearly, an organisational plan that answers these kinds of questions is essential to support individual career planning.

Changes in HRM policies

To ensure the effectiveness of its career development program, an organisation may need to either establish or rewrite its current HR policies. A corporate policy dealing with career development needs to be supported by other policies covering the many facets of performance management and employee development. Strategies relating to transfers and promotions require policy decisions as they impact on career development. These strategies may be used to move people out of their comfort zones into positions that will enhance their personal development.

A transfer is the placement of an employee in another job for which the duties, responsibilities, status and remuneration are approximately equal to those of the previous job. A transfer may require the employee to change work group, workplace, work shift or organisational unit and may even necessitate moving to another geographic area. Transfers make it possible for an organisation to place its employees in jobs where there is a greater need for their services and where they can acquire new knowledge and skills. A career downshift moves an individual into a lower-level job that can provide developmental opportunities and/or a better quality of work life, or possibly an alternative to retrenchment. Policy decisions relating to relocation and salary maintenance may be required.

A promotion is a change of assignment to a job at a higher level in the organisation. The new job normally provides an increase in pay and status, and demands more skill or carries more responsibility. Promotions enable an organisation to utilise the skills and abilities of its personnel more effectively, and the opportunity to gain a promotion serves as an incentive for good performance. In the past, the principal criteria for determining promotions were merit and seniority. The organisation determined how much consideration was given to each factor. Even when not restricted by a workplace agreement, management often found itself giving considerable weight to seniority because of the difficulties of measuring merit effectively and of communicating to employees that the measurement is fair. Today there is no choice. Promotion and other forms of career moves must be based on merit.

Gauging employee potential

The most important objective of any career development program is to provide the tools and techniques that will enable employees to gauge their potential for a successful career path. This objective may be achieved in ways that naturally involve the active participation of the

employees themselves. Informal counselling by HR staff and supervisors is used widely. Many organisations give their employees information on educational assistance, equal opportunity and affirmative action programs and policies, salary administration and job requirements. Career planning, work books and workshops are also popular means for helping employees identify their potential and the strength of their interests. Workshops have the advantage of providing a chance to compare and discuss attitudes, concerns and plans with others in similar situations. They can focus on current job performance and development plans. Others deal with broader life and career plans and values. Organisations such as AGC and Integral Energy conduct career planning workshops on a regular basis. These are supplemented by management training programs in mentoring and coaching skills.

Career counselling

Career counselling involves talking with employees about their current job activities and performance, personal and career interests and goals, personal skills and suitable career development objectives. Employees usually participate voluntarily, although some organisations make counselling a part of the annual performance review. As employees approach retirement, they may be encouraged to participate in pre-retirement programs, which often include counselling along with other helping activities. Career counselling may be provided by the HR staff, superiors, managers, specialised staff counsellors or outside professionals.

Organisations differ widely in the types of career development programs they offer. Some organisations have formal programs for all levels of employees covering a broad array of topics. Others are limited to career counselling that is incorporated into annual performance reviews. The more extensive career development programs also frequently include programs geared to special groups, such as management development programs, or programs for women, minorities or dual career couples.

The role of managers

Identifying and developing talent in individuals is a role that all managers should take seriously. As they conduct formal performance reviews, managers should be concerned with individuals' potential for managerial jobs and encourage their growth in that direction. There should also be others in the organisation who have the power to evaluate, nominate and sponsor promising employees. Those companies that emphasise developing human assets as well as turning a profit usually have the talent they need and more. Some companies have become 'academy' companies that unintentionally provide a source of talented managers to organisations that lack good management development programs.

Development centres

Core issues for any organisation are how to attract and recruit the best people, to deploy them so that they are working effectively, and to develop their skills for current and future challenges.

One rigorous and proven approach to addressing this issue is the application of development centre methodologies. Development centres have a long history in the field of applied human resource management. Strong statistical evidence supports the assertion that development centres are significantly superior to other techniques (e.g. interview, psychological tests, personality assessment, past performance) in selection, promotion and development applications.

What is a development centre?

In its simplest form, a development centre is a program (not a place) that involves individual participants undertaking a series of work-based simulations. The core concept is simulation.[75] These simulations reflect the job demands of a target role or position in the organisation. Participants in the simulations are usually observed (assessed) by senior managers, and possibly external managers, and their performance is assessed against a predetermined set of dimensions. The dimensions represent the characteristics that distinguish effectiveness in the target job or position. Once the simulations are complete, the observers meet to pool their assessments so that they can make recommendations and decisions on selection, promotion, learning and development needs, and career and succession planning. Finally, these decisions and recommendations are implemented by involving both the line managers and individuals.

Applications and advantages

Development centres involve people in performing activities that closely resemble the job they will be doing. When multiple observers assess this performance on clear, easily identified dimensions, the observations lead to more right than wrong decisions. The goal of the development centre exercises is to simulate the key roles and tasks of the target positions in order to provide candidates with the opportunity to demonstrate the extent of their competency in those roles.[76]

The applications of development centres are wide and varied. For example, a large diversified industrial company uses them to guide promotion from operator and leading hand to first line supervisor. Selecting partners is an application favoured by a major accounting firm. Several police services use development centres for managers progressing from middle to senior management level. The armed services have long used the approach at a variety of levels. Two of the major banks use development centres to guide the selection and promotion or career development of branch managers and general managers. Many organisations employ the approach for selecting graduates.

A leading multinational energy corporation uses development centres for guiding the careers of executive personnel throughout the Asia–Pacific region. The diversity of the Pacific Basin enabled this company to bring together cross-cultural observers and cross-cultural groups of managers with potential for future general manager or managing director roles. This approach allows the company to see how people perform across a variety of situations and cultures. Another multinational company employs the development centre approach for selecting management trainees. After selection and appointment of successful candidates, the company uses the information gleaned from the centre to guide job placements and to structure development opportunities.

Integral Energy uses a two-day development centre to develop not only their current senior leaders but to identify their next generation of leaders. Their approach involves both internal and external assessors observing across a range of competency-based, simulated exercises. A 360-degree feedback survey (see Chapter 9) is also incorporated. At the conclusion of each centre, participants are provided with both a centre report and a 360-degree survey report. Each is based on the organisation's leadership competencies but from two perspectives. Individual learning plans are then put in place.

Creativity and imagination seem to characterise best what is happening with development centres in Australia. Over the last five years, several common themes have emerged. It has become more common to see development centres applied with far greater flexibility, characterised by more openness, enhanced realism, and in many cases, with a primary focus on development initiatives.

In addition, companies are moving away from 'off the shelf' exercises and dimensions to develop their own organisation-specific competencies and simulations. Exhibit 8.13 provides a guide to how development centre thinking has changed over time.

Exhibit 8.13   Characteristics of development centre design

Centre type	First generation	Second generation	Third generation
Participant involvement	Minimal – participants simply tackle exercises	Feedback to participants at end of centre, sometimes after each exercise	Joint decision making on competencies displayed after each exercise
Exercises and tests	Off-the-shelf exercises and psychological tests	Mainly off-the-shelf exercises and psychological tests	Mainly real-life business problems
Development planning	Little – perhaps part of post-centre feedback	Some time given on the centre to planning, with monitoring and support afterwards	More time given on the centre, with significant monitoring and mentoring afterwards

Source: Griffiths P., Goodge P. 1994. 'Development centres: The third generation,' *Personnel Management*, June.

Disadvantages

The most commonly reported disadvantages of development centres are costs (both initial and ongoing), resource intensiveness and participants' perceptions of the process. The initial design and ongoing development and maintenance of a comprehensive program appear to be a costly investment, and this is enough to prevent many organisations even approaching the process. Those which do press ahead have found that the benefits far exceed the costs. Implementation is resource intensive, especially for administrators and observers, so if the commitment is lacking, the initiative is not worth pursuing. Finally, it is quite common for participants to be very fearful of the process when they believe it somehow disadvantages them. If their experience of the simulations is bad or they believe they have performed poorly, negative perceptions will be reinforced.

Despite these potential disadvantages, many companies believe that the benefits far outweigh the costs and they continue their commitment to the use of centres to assist in resolving human resource management issues.

Determining individual development needs

The requirements of each management position and the qualifications of the person performing it are different, so no two managers will have identical developmental needs. For one individual, self-development may consist of developing the ability to write reports, give talks or lead conferences. For another, it may require learning to communicate and relate more effectively with others in the organisation. Periodic performance appraisals can provide a basis for determining each manager's progress. Meetings at which these appraisals are discussed are an essential part of self-improvement efforts.

In helping individuals plan their careers, it is important for organisations to recognise that younger managers today seek meaningful development assignments that are interesting and involve challenge, responsibility and a 'piece of the action.'

In fact, the organisations with reputations for the best management make extensive use of job challenges to develop their executive talent. Positions that force managers to deal with sudden, unexpected changes are the jobs whose candidates require the most development.[77]

Younger managers today also have a greater concern for the contribution that their work in the organisation will make to society. Unfortunately, they are frequently given responsibilities they view as rudimentary, boring and composed of too many 'make work' activities. Some organisations are attempting to retain young managers with high potential by offering a fast-track program that enables them to advance more rapidly than those with less potential. A fast-track program may provide for a relatively rapid progression – lateral transfers or promotions through a number of managerial positions requiring exposure to different organisational functions, as well as providing opportunities to make decisions, preferably in profit centres. Access to the 'fast track' must be seen as fair.

Mentoring

When talking with employees about their employment experiences, it is common to hear them mention individuals at work who influenced them. They frequently refer to immediate superiors who were especially helpful as career developers. But they also mention others at higher levels in the organisation who provided guidance and support to them in the development of their careers. These executives and managers who advise and encourage employees of lesser rank are called mentors. The term 'coaching' is more commonly used for mentoring at senior management levels, and the advisors or coaches may be internal or external to their organisations.

Mentoring dates back to 800 BC when Mentor served as an advisor to the son of King Odysseus.[78] The concept of mentoring is based quite simply on the notion that people will often learn best when associating with others who have been successful. Forming alliances with such people who are genuinely interested and committed to professional development will help middle and frontline managers increase their visibility within the organisation.[79]

Hegstad argues that there are two types of mentoring, informal and formal. Informal mentorships are not arranged by the organisations but often will arise spontaneously due to similar interests or roles between the two parties.[80] Informal mentoring goes on daily within every type of organisation. Generally, the mentor initiates the relationship, but sometimes an employee will approach a potential mentor for advice. Most mentoring relationships develop over time on an informal basis. There has been a rapid growth of formal mentoring plans where mentors are assigned to those employees considered for upward movement in the organisation. Formal relations are managed by the organisation and often will be developed by assignment or mentor selection for an individual.[81] Under a good mentor, learning focuses on goals, opportunities, expectations, standards and assistance in fulfilling one's potential. The mentoring approach is used extensively by organisations such as Westpac, Australia Post, Qantas and DuPont. With this approach, a trained senior manager is selected by a person to act as their mentor. His or her role is to act as a sounding board for ideas and support when confronting new and demanding tasks.

The mentor reflects the original concept of the father figure, teacher, protector and trusted adviser. Although, in the past, junior managers may well have 'adopted' a mentor in an informal way, the formal mentoring approach relies on duplicating the conditions under which a successful informal relationship is likely to emerge.

The most successful of these relationships depend largely on a successful matching of personalities, values and perceptions. While self-selection of mentors would be ideal, this will not always be possible. The mentoring approach would appear to have much potential insofar as learning takes place on the job and role models can be established who will establish organisational norms for future performance.

Although the above-mentioned methods are frequently used in developing managers for higher-level positions in the organisation, they also provide valuable experiences for individuals being developed for other types of positions.

Mentoring has also been suggested as a way by which women can break through the 'glass ceiling.' Mentoring programs can be actively encouraged that provide female managers with the same opportunities as male managers, who have traditionally received this type of assistance and support.[82] Arnott's has adopted a mentoring scheme for new graduates and trainees. In light of the program's success, it has been extended to new team members and eventually all new employees.

Analysis of a large number of research studies revealed that mentoring functions can be divided into two broad categories: career functions and psychosocial functions. Career functions are those aspects of the relationship that enhance career advancement; psychosocial functions are those aspects that enhance the protégé's sense of competence, identity and effectiveness in a professional role. Both kinds of functions are viewed as critical to management development.

The days are over where employees progress simply by working long and hard. Today, both management and employees have a role to play – the key is to help employees develop their career preferences while meeting business goals.[83]

Jobs for the future

As discussed earlier, the traditional career is disappearing. Young people no longer start work with the expectation that they will stay for life but, rather, they see their career as their personal responsibility and actively market themselves as a product to be sold on a short-term, contractual basis. Employment security is not considered essential to their lifestyle; instead they cherish the concept of employability.

According to Schmidt, in the present and likely future workplace only two things will matter: people and knowledge. Sophisticated HR and knowledge-management skills already provide the competitive advantages of most contemporary organisations, and organisations are employing retention managers, knowledge directors and directors of intellectual capital to maintain those advantages. This has come about as organisations return to the reality that their real asset is their people and how those people are managed.[84]

Your new career

Jobs for life are out and 'baskets of skills' are in. The workplace of the future will be populated by specialists on short-term contacts, who hop from company to company – and often country to country – selling their skills to anyone who needs them. The traditional career, in which graduates joined a company and stayed for 20 years, working their way up the corporate ladder, is already disappearing. In its place are shorter stints of two or three years at different companies, building skills, changing direction and making contacts. Workplace experts say this trend will accelerate over the next few years.

A lecturer at the school of management at Queensland's Griffith University, Mohan Thite, says individual careers will be in a constant state of change, with frequent shifts in skills, responsibilities and income. He expects that workers will periodically backtrack their careers, changing from being an expert in one area to a novice in another to acquire new skills. He likens the new career to a jungle gym, with moves up, down and sideways, in contrast to the traditional ladder.

Thite says responsibility for career management has shifted from the employer to the employee. The old bond, in which employers expected loyalty, respect for rules and commitment in return for job security and steady career progression, is breaking. In future, work will be a short-term exchange rather than a long-term mutually beneficial commitment.

Thite uses himself as an example. 'The way I look at a job now is quite different to how I would have looked at it five years ago. Then, I would have applied for a lecturing position based on location, the chances for promotion, etc. Now, when I apply for a job I think about whether it will give me the kind of skills that are going to be in demand for the next five to ten years; how "e-enabled" is the university, how globalised is the university, can I teach the subject in a more technological way?'

For workers with skills, a good education and the ability to adapt, the new workplace will be liberating. The American magazine *Fast Company* talks about 'the hyphenated career,' in which smart people combine their education, skills and interests to become one-person, cross-functional teams.

Others will find it unsettling. The most important skill, according to Thite, will be self-management, including an honest self-assessment of technical and behavioural strengths and weaknesses, identification of personal preferences (such as

safety versus risk, or big company versus small company), and the ability to market oneself.

If this all sounds too hard, help may be at hand. The head of the online recruitment firm Seek, Paul Bassat, expects 'talent managers' to emerge. They will act as agents for individual employees, identifying career opportunities and helping with career development and training.

Companies will also need help to sell themselves to the skilled workers they need and to manage their diverse and changing workforces. The director of the Centre for Workplace Culture Change at RMIT, Professor Anna Bodi, refers to it as a 'dynamic jigsaw.' 'Companies must ask themselves why does someone want to come and work for them?' she says. 'The people they are trying to capture see it as an opportunity to improve their skill basket. What's in it for them? Everybody has to get something out of it and that doesn't mean them just receiving a salary each week. It is a marketplace on both sides.'

Thite says companies will adopt a new approach to recruitment that is portfolio-centred rather than position-centred. They will identify what they want the person to achieve and the portfolio of skills required, then find an individual with those skills and offer them a contract.

In this scenario, job titles become far less important. Employers are looking at skills and employability, not jobs. If they find a person with the right technical,

business, problem-solving and personal skills, plus initiative, that person may well call themselves whatever they like. Or they may choose to have no title at all.

Job titles of the future

Director of Intellectual Capital: collects, collates and categorises all the processes and knowledge of the company.

Data Mining Officer: extracts information on customers from vast databases.

Chief Futurist: identifies trends and helps companies predict changes.

Talent Manager: acts as an agent for individual workers, identifying career opportunities and helping with career development and skills training.

Retention Manager: develops strategies to minimise staff turnover.

Chief Evangelist: ensures that the company's vision is continually reinforced.

Financial Environmental Controller/Resource Allocation Director: allocates and manages scarce resources.

Director of People/Head of Human-Resource Capital Management/Head of Culture: makes sure that the company is a good place to work.

Head of People Processes: oversees the administrative parts of human resources.

Manager of Temps/ Manager of Contractors: looks after workers who are not part of the company's core staff.

Manager for Diversity: looks after the multicultural aspects of a workforce.

Privacy Officer: makes sure the company is not misusing customers' personal information.

Customer Resources Manager: makes sure the company is dealing with its customers effectively.

Trouble-shooter: has a wide range of skills that can be used in whatever area requires them.

Chief Ethics Officer: responsible for ensuring adherence to the company's code of ethics.

Job titles of the past

'Chief' anything (Chief Executive Officer, Chief Financial Officer): too authoritarian.

Knowledge Manager: will become intellectual capital manager.

Information Manager: will become information technology manager or systems operation manager.

Accountant: will become many new titles, such as resource allocation director or personal choice consultant.

'Human resources' anything (for example, Head of Human Resources): will become something warmer and fuzzier, such as director of people.

Some titles that are already here

The American magazine *Fast Company* has a regular feature on people with innovative titles. Examples include:

Chief Growth Officer: in charge of the company's overall growth.

Creatologist: rekindles the creative spirit, imagination and motivation of other people.

Culture Team Leader: helps new recruits succeed faster.

Director of Intelligence: maintains vast files on markets, clients and competitors.

Director, Department of the Future: develops marketing strategies to understand children and what they will buy when they reach their parents' age.

Messaging Champion: educates others about email, high-speed message switching and other forms of electronic communication.

Vice-President of Progress: changes people's attitudes and behaviour to reduce resistance to progress.

Apostle of Partners: acts as a middle-person between customers of a partner-loyalty network software developer and their 'channel partners.'

Source: Adapted from Schmidt L. 2000. *Business Review Weekly*, 24 November, pp. 64–5.

The final section of this chapter discusses in a little more detail the specific HRD issues associated with regionalisation and internationalisation, and the increasing demand for global employees with highly-developed managerial and cross-cultural competencies, whether they are required to live and work as expatriates, or whether their jobs and careers involve frequent travel to other countries as a normal component of their work schedules.

Exhibit 8.14   The international perspective

International learning and career development

Organisations that make comprehensive efforts to ensure that their employees understand, respect and can adapt to cultural differences will often experience substantial positive impacts on sales, costs and productivity. Ideally, learning and development programs for international or expatriate managers should begin with an extensive orientation to the geography, climate, customs, traditions, politics, potential problem areas and working conditions of the host country, continually supplemented by information and refresher programs, and completed by debriefing sessions following the overseas assignment.

While the costs of such extensive and continuing learning may appear excessive, a former manager of International Human Resources, Hewlett-Packard (US) asserts that 'the cost of training is inconsequential compared to the risk of sending inexperienced or untrained people'.[85] Apart from the financial and reputation costs of expatriate 'failure' to the employing organisations, the human costs to 'failed' expatriates and their families can be devastating.

Surveys in the United States, however, indicate that around 68 per cent of US multinationals undertake no such cross-cultural development programs.[86] It is likely that Australian organisations are even more remiss.

In view of US findings concerning the reasons for expatriate failure there is considerable evidence to support the view that the partners and children of expatriate managers should either be included in such development programs or have separate programs dealing with their own responsibilities. This is especially important in dual career families where the partner's career may be disadvantaged by international relocation.

Content of learning and development programs

Orientation programs need to be different in content according to the host country environment, the nature of the assignment and managerial role, and the type of business. However, there are broad general areas which all such programs must address, including the following:

- social and business etiquette

- history and folklore

- current affairs, including relations between the host and home countries

- the culture's values and priorities

- geography, especially the cities

- sources of pride: artists, musicians, novelists, sports, great achievements of the culture, including things to see and do

- religion and the role of religion in daily life

- political structure and current players

- practical matters such as currency, transportation, time zones, hours of business

- the language.[87]

Cross-cultural differences represent the most elusive aspect of international business. Often unaware of their own culture-conditioned behaviour, many people tend to react adversely to tastes and behaviour that deviate from those of their own culture. Styles of clothing, food, housing, and even the facial expressions and gestures in different cultures can be viewed as strange. Australians, especially in European and more recently Asian regions, may be in an advantageous position, due to an increasingly multicultural population, language and culture courses in schools and universities, and the propensity for Australians to travel the world.

In Australia's closest trading region, the Pacific Rim, very different customs, traditions, religions, work practices and societal values inevitably affect the negotiation of business contracts, the nature and conduct of training programs, and expectations concerning local employee attendance, performance, work conditions and employee rights. As examples, in some Muslim countries, employees may be entitled to flexible hours to allow for religious observances; in some cultures, female employees may be excluded or discouraged from certain occupations and work conditions; in others, recruitment may involve an element of 'nepotism' or 'corruption' generally unacceptable in Australian organisations.

Non-verbal communication, including handshaking, head-nods, physical posture and eye contact, has different meanings in different cultures. Accordingly, expatriate training programs should include some examination of verbal and non-verbal communication, cultural, social, political, economic, religious, geographic and work issues.

In addition, family support programs should address relevant issues such as the effects of the move on their career, lifestyle and family. A common experience of partners of expatriate managers is an excess of spare time in the host country. As an important cause of expatriate failure appears to be partner and family problems in the new country, attention needs to be given to how the partner will use his or her time in the host country, including developing relationships with local nationals.

Some research,[88] however, suggests that 'few Australian organisations provided post-arrival cultural awareness training' to either their expatriates or their families, and that the preparation periods for overseas postings were generally insufficient.

Learning and development methods

A variety of strategies, preferably integrated and ongoing, will need to be developed by the human resource manager in conjunction with senior managers, returned expatriates, and information from previous assignments. It is also valuable to consult with Austrade and the Department of Foreign Affairs and Trade for materials, programs and current information about the relevant countries. Readings, lecture discussions and DVDs about the culture, geography, social and political history, climate, and food and work regulations can be supplemented by simulations, sensitivity awareness training and exposure to the potential problem areas of host country environments.

Such development programs are, of course, essential prior to overseas appointment, but should continue as the assignment develops. Support to the expatriates and their families may include:

- initial assistance in preparation of the assignment

- a clear description of the objectives of the assignment

- appropriate status and recognition for the expatriate

- incentives, facilities and resources

- assistance with stress, fatigue, social support

- appraisal, career development and re-entry support.

Some researchers suggest that, while predeparture training is vital, it should also be supplemented by 'post-arrival training,' to ensure that cognitive learning is integrated with the experiential learning of the expatriate and his or her family in the overseas country.[89]

Predeparture training

It can be argued that the overseas assignment itself is perhaps the most useful development activity for home-country managers or professionals, especially for those whose future career is likely to be with the company. International exposure, however difficult, is bound to result in broadened perspectives of business and management skills in the handling of problematic situations with staff and valuable knowledge with respect to international customers and clients, their governments and cultures.

However, in order for prospective expatriates and their families to settle into the new host country environment as easily and quickly as possible, and for the expatriate manager or professional to perform at an optimum level, some form(s) of predeparture training can be very helpful.

For example, a parent company (or third country) employee who has significant overseas experience in similar locations (e.g. Hong Kong, Singapore, Malaysia) and an adaptable family, may require considerably less predeparture training for a six-month assignment in Indonesia than a manager from the home country with no overseas experience and a reluctant family, bound for three years to Thailand. In the former case, training might simply involve some basic language courses and information on relevant legislation, while in the latter it might encompass comprehensive skills, field trips and/or in-depth discussions with the expatriate and their family. In both cases, as Robock and Simmons note:

> However imperfect training may be as a substitute for actual foreign living experience,
> it is valuable if it can reduce the often painful and agonising experience of transferring
> into another culture and avoiding the great damage that culture shock and cultural
> misunderstanding can do to a firm's operating relationship.[90]

Given the relatively high failure rates and associated costs of expatriation discussed earlier, it makes good business sense to prepare expatriates properly for their overseas experience.

Naturally, all of these development methods have associated costs that will increase with the required level of 'rigour' and with the involvement of the chosen expatriates' partners and children, and companies will need to balance such costs against their anticipated benefits. In the case of European, Scandinavian and Australian companies,[91] a strategic business perspective needs to take these costs into account against the reported failure rates of expatriates. As 'failure' has so far only been measured in relation to premature return from overseas assignments, the potentially disastrous consequences of unprepared and disgruntled expatriates who remain in their overseas positions also need to be taken into account.

Apart from the cultural and linguistic characteristics of the new host countries, perhaps the most important feature of predeparture training and development for expatriates is concerned with 'cross-cultural' awareness. This can be achieved in a variety of ways, e.g. by 'attribution training,' direct 'cultural awareness' training and 'cognitive-behaviour modification,' 'experiential learning' and 'interaction training.' In some cases, all of these methods will need to be employed, in others one or two will suffice. Companies therefore need to ascertain the relative importance of each.

Special considerations

As well as the socio-cultural issues so far discussed, some special issues also require attention. These include risk to the expatriate's career development and managing personal and family life in an overseas location.

Career development

For executives with aspirations for head-office careers, international assignments may not be advantageous. Relocation to an overseas country may assist subsequent home country promotion or it may simply consign the executive to continual international relocation. Away from the organisation's headquarters, such managers may lose touch with domestic operations and changes, or their experience may be irrelevant to future organisational directions. Human resource managers need to ensure that their strategic plans include individually tailored succession programs for expatriates, and that international assignments are seen as valuable for subsequent career development.

Personal and family life

The most frequent cause of an employee's failure to complete an international assignment is personal and family stress. Culture (or eco-) shock – disorientation that may cause continual stress – is often experienced by people who settle overseas for extended periods. The employee's partner normally faces a much greater challenge than the employee. This difficulty may be compounded when the male or female partner has had to sacrifice their own career due to the relocation, often referred to as the 'trailing spouse' issue. Other factors include the age and educational requirements of children and the loss of important friendships and wider family contacts. The whole family must therefore be involved in the decision to relocate overseas.

HR programs should be integrated and ongoing, aiming to maintain the expatriate's personal well-being and work performance, and to avoid the phenomenon observed by Amant Negandhi:

> by the fourth or fifth country … he (she) locks himself (herself) with expatriate colleagues, and he (she) doesn't want to see anything of the local scene … for him (her), they are only 'these bloody people'.[92]

Summary

Because of rapid changes in technology and the growth of organisations into large, complex operations, HRD is vital to an organisation's success. In recent years, such programs have broadened their scope to include the career development of personnel at all levels. A development program begins with the important process of induction.

In designing HRD programs, a systems approach should be followed. This involves three phases: the assessment phase, the learning and development phase and the evaluation phase. From the wide variety of methods available for developing both managerial and non-managerial personnel, those methods should be selected that best meet the learning objectives and that utilise as many of the principles of learning as possible. While new methods must always be explored, the focus should be on the personal and strategic objectives to be attained. In planning and conducting such programs, instructors and facilitators should give special attention to the psychological principles of learning and the characteristics of successful facilitators.

Increased competition for promotion and advancement, the desire to get the most out of a career, better employee utilisation, and other demands, have resulted in the growth of career development programs. To succeed, such programs require management support, well-defined goals, effective communication and compatible HRM policies. It is essential that a career development program includes a comprehensive inventory of job opportunities, with carefully organised progressions from one job to the next. The process of choosing a career path should involve maximum participation of the individual concerned.

Career development programs often contain segments designed to further the advancement of special groups within an organisation. Management development programs, for example, help to provide a source of leadership talent that is custom-made for the organisation.

Managers should be trained to identify talent for further evaluation in assessment centres. The use of mentors to facilitate the career development process is a valuable and popular approach.

Special programs for women and minorities help overcome the barriers to advancement that individuals in these groups have traditionally encountered. The special needs of dual career couples must also be addressed in a manner that is satisfactory to both the couple and the employer.

To help employees achieve their career objectives, HR professionals should understand the process by which individuals typically make career choices and be aware of some of the more scientific approaches to career selection that may be used. Importantly, corporate leaders need to understand that today's younger employees hold a completely different set of values from their older counterparts and their career aspirations will be very different. This will require a radical shift in mindset for not only the organisation's leaders but also for its HR professionals.

Key terms

adult learning theory 286

ANTA 283

behaviour modelling 295

career plateau 288

competency based learning (CBL) 283

dual career couples 303

e-learning 291

expatriate 309

instructor (or facilitator) 288

KSAs 278

learning organisations 274

lifelong learning 273

needs analysis 281

parallel careers 300

ROI 285

sensitivity training 294

simulations 304

Key debate issues

1   The growing preference for managers with tertiary qualifications demonstrates that management positions require broad and complex competencies which cannot be solely developed on the job.
2   Employees learn more from practical work experiences and project participation roles than from classroom training, simulations or e-learning.
3   Competency-based learning is just training in 'new clothes.'
4   Generation X and Y employees are quite capable of managing their own careers. They don't need help from managers or mentors, especially as their commitment to organisations is at best transactional.
5   Cross-cultural learning and development for managers is largely unnecessary these days as business practices have become similar across the world.

Case study 8.1

Something about Harry!

Harry Halls, a prominent department manager of the Apex Machine Products Company, was being considered for promotion to division manager. He had a strong personality, ran a tight ship, clearly discharged his responsibility and was known as a good manager. Upon close inquiry, it became clear that he was 'carrying' all his section heads. They were weak 'yes' people, and none was remotely able to succeed the department manager. Harry was not appointed, and Susan Leigh, the CEO, was explaining to him why he was passed over.

'Harry,' she said, 'you should know that we all wanted nothing but success for you. You are well thought of among all the people I've talked to, and everyone wanted to see you get the chance at division management. This did not make the decision any easier for me, but I had other considerations to ponder. Basically, I was worried about the big risk of failure that you would run. In your present position you have carried the total load. I think this means that if you headed a business unit you would try to do the same thing, and you would surely fail and perhaps have a breakdown in health.

'Since you did not develop subordinate managers to carry the departmental load, I don't think you would or could use department managers properly. Then there is the problem of manager succession. We don't have anybody to take your old job, and you have not prepared any of your subordinates to do so. I'm afraid that the same thing would happen at the business level and we just cannot afford to take that kind of risk.

'I really don't know what the future holds for you. You are now 40 years of age. I don't think it is really possible for you to change your managing style. Maybe you can, but I feel that at the first sign of pressure, you would revert to doing all the managing yourself.'

'Well, Susan,' replied Harry, 'I can certainly see the problem from your point of view. What I don't see is why I have not been counselled on this point in the years past. I would have changed.'

'Would you really?' mused Susan Leigh.

Questions

1   Do you believe anything could have been done for Harry Halls? If so, what?
2   Is there anything that could be done now? If so, what?
3   What role should Susan Leigh play in Harry's future?
4   Are there any legal aspects to this case that Susan will need to consider?

Case study 8.2

The training and development dilemma at Whitney and Company

Company background

Whitney and Company is a global management consulting firm that has been growing rapidly, particularly in the United States and Western Europe. The firm provides comprehensive business planning and analysis as well as consulting in operational and technical areas such as finance, operations and information technology. Its client list includes medium-sized firms but its growth tends to focus on *Fortune* 1 000 companies.

Whitney clients include manufacturing and service organisations as well as government, health-care and religious organisations. The firm has offices in 24 US cities and offices in 16 other countries. With its world headquarters in Chicago, Whitney employs nearly 27 000 people, the vast majority of whom are young, aggressive professionals.

In light of the tremendous growth of the consulting industry, Whitney has ambitious plans for expanding the firm. It is estimated that in the next five years alone it will need 1 200 new managers and about 200 new partners. Because Whitney maintains a policy of promotion from within, these people will come mainly from the ranks of entry-level employees. There is plenty of incentive for these young professionals to do well; starting salaries for partners average US$250 000 (although normally individuals do not reach partner status until they have been with the firm for 10 years).

Training and development

Given the critical importance of professional talent, Whitney has devoted millions of dollars over the years to create in-house training facilities that are the envy of the industry. The most observable indicator of this dedication is the very plush Corporate Training and Development Centre (CTDC) in St Charles, Illinois, 30 minutes west of Chicago. The 100-acre centre provides living and meeting accommodation for approximately 500 persons and includes an impressive facility of classrooms, conference rooms, libraries and even a television studio. The centre also employs a staff of nearly 50 instructors, mostly field managers who rotate on a two-year basis into the CEDC.

Every new Whitney employee spends two weeks at CEDC before receiving a total of three additional months of training at one of nine other regional facilities in Atlanta, Boston, Cleveland, Chicago, Dallas, Denver, Los Angeles, Seattle and New York. All told, Whitney spends almost US$3 500 per employee for training and development each year.

The majority of this investment is on technical and systems training for entry-level consultants. Additionally, employees receive extensive training in the specific industries where they will predominantly work (e.g. oil and gas, telecommunications, banking, health care). The senior staff are particularly aware that Whitney's public image is largely a function of the actions and work quality of their first-level associates. Executives clearly recognise the importance of an expert workforce and spare no expense in this regard.

Employee performance

While Whitney affords many opportunities to its employees and spends a great deal of money on professional development, it expects a great deal from its employees in return. Especially in the first two years, it is not uncommon for a beginning associate to work 70-hour weeks. The schedules and travelling are often gruelling, and the rewards in the first few years are typically not commensurate. For example, salaries are generally in the mid-US$40 000s and the benefit package is only average from a firm of Whitney's size and reputation. The greater payoffs, as indicated before, come when one achieves partner status, but not much earlier.

Nevertheless, Whitney has little trouble attracting very aggressive, energetic students generally right out of college who are eager 'to pay their dues' for success in a major firm.

Occasionally, however, this aggressiveness has come across as being boorish and callous with clients, especially in the health-care industry. There are even situations where clients have discontinued business with Whitney, not because of concerns about expertise, but because of the 'fast-in, fast-out style of big-time consulting.' While in most cases, Whitney employees gradually learn to interpret the subtleties of client needs, occasionally (and increasingly) employees have been let go because of their lack of personal acumen.

In view of the importance of interpersonal competence at Whitney, some of the training staff have suggested that more attention should be placed on that part of the development of new employees. But others on staff point out that only two years ago a series of lectures was put into the training program dealing with clients and customer relations. The consensus has been that the program addition has not been well received. They simply do not feel the added expense would be justified. In fact, there is a growing group of senior partners who believe too much is already being spent on education and training since so many of those trained employees subsequently leave to take jobs with other companies.

The facts in this regard are clear. Only about 50 per cent of new hires stay with Whitney beyond their first five years. Approximately 90 per cent leave the firm within 10 years of employment. Most of these people either start their own firms or go to work for one of Whitney's clients. Comparatively few are fired. Many people think this turnover rate is terribly detrimental to the success of Whitney, especially given the immense expense for training and development. Many others, however, feel the departures are inevitable given the promotion-from-within policies. Some feel the turnover actually helps business since those who go to work for other companies often convince them to become clients of Whitney – the logic being that former employees are familiar with Whitney's procedures and generally will have respect for the quality of the firm's work.

The training and development dilemma

Not surprisingly, there is increasing debate regarding the role and importance of training and development at Whitney and Company. It is very difficult to know which parts of the current programs are effective and which are not. Likewise, there is the problem of determining if additional training is needed. As Anthony Blaine, one of the Training Directors, summarised: 'For years we've been throwing tons of training at these people, but we aren't sure if it's the right kind, if it's too much, or even if they're catching what we're throwing. We've got to start coming up with some good questions, and then figure out some pretty intelligent answers.'

Questions

1   What could Whitney do to enhance the value of training?
2   Is the company using the most effective techniques, especially with regard to training for client and customer service? What technique changes would you recommend?
3   How should Whitney decide specifically who needs training? Is it advisable, even cost efficient, to send everyone through the program?
4   How should Whitney specifically evaluate the programs?

Further readings

Burns R. 2002. *The adult learner at work*, Warriewood, Australia, Business & Professional Publishing.

Gibb S. 2002. *Learning and development*, Hampshire, Palgrave Macmillan.

Delahaye B.l. 2005. *Human resource development: Adult learning and knowledge management*, 2nd edn, Brisbane, John Wiley.

Jakupec V., Garrick J. 2000. *Flexible learning, human resource and organisational development*, London, Routledge.

Knowles M. 1984. *The adult learner: A neglected species*, 3rd edn, Houston, Gulf Publishing.

Kolb D. 1985. *Learning style inventory*, Boston MA, McBer and Company.

Mumford A. 1997. *How to choose the right development method*, Maidenhead, UK, Peter Honey.

Noe R.A. 2002. *Employee training and development*, 2nd edn., New York, McGraw-Hill Irwin.

Smith A. 1998. *Training and development in Australia*, Sydney, Butterworth.

Tovey M.D., Lawlor D.R. 2004. *Training in Australia: Design, delivery, evaluation, management*, 2nd edn, Sydney, Prentice-Hall.

Endnotes

1   Rhodes C. 2002. 'Facilitating learning organisations,' *Journal of Occupational and Organisational Psychology*, 75(2), pp. 252–4.

2   Garrick J., Clegg S. 2000. 'Knowledge work and the new demands for learning,' *Journal of Knowledge Management*, 4(4), pp. 279–86.

3   Horwitz F.M. 1999. 'The emergence of strategic training and development: The current state of play,' *Journal of European Industrial Training*, 23(4/5), pp. 180–90.

4   Sofo F. 1999. *Human resource development: Perspectives, roles and practice choices*, Sydney, Allen & Unwin, p. xxvi.

5   Frost M. 2002. 'Creative new employee orientation programs,' *HR Magazine*, 47(8), pp. 120–1.

6   Hiatt S.R. 1983. 'The effects of social orientation on socialisation outcomes of new nurses in hospitals,' unpublished dissertation, Arizona State University, p. 9.

7   Jones D. 1984. 'Developing a new employee orientation program,' *Personnel Journal*, 63(3), pp. 86–7.

8   Truell G.F. 1981. 'Tracking down the aroundhereisms, or how to foil negative orientation,' *Personnel*, 58(4), pp. 23–31.

9   Bartlett C., Ghoshal S., cited in Horwitz 1999, op. cit., pp. 180–90.

10   Wesley K.N., Latham G.P. 1981. *Developing and training human resources in organisations*, Glenview, Scott Foresman & Co., p. 6.

11   Monk R. 1997. *hrmonthly*, September, p. 26.

12   Rothwell W.J., Kazanas H.C. 1998. *Mastering the instructional design process: A systematic approach*, San Francisco, Jossey-Bass.

13   Leigh D. et al. 2000. 'Alternative models of needs assessment: Selecting the right one for your organisation,' *Human Resource Development Quarterly*, 11(1), pp. 87–93.

14   Chui W. et al. 1999. 'Re-thinking training needs analysis: A proposed framework for literature review,' *Personnel Review*, 28(1/2), pp. 77–90.

15   Goldstein I.L. 1993. *Training in organisations: Needs assessment, development and evaluation*, Monterey, Brooks/Cole Publishing, pp. 17–21.

16   Smith A. 1997. 'Training and building strategy: Building the links,' AHRI Annual National Conference, October, Brisbane.

17   Ribler R.I. 1983. *Training development guide*, Reston, Reston Publishing, pp. 7–22.

18   Hager P., Gonczi A. 1991. 'Competency-based standards: A boon for continuing professional education?,' *Studies in Continuing Education*, 13(1), pp. 24–39.

19   Bassett B. 1990. 'Critical competencies for change,' *Training and development in Australia*, Australian Institute of Training and Development, 17(4), p. 10.

20   Rifkin K. et al. 1999. 'Developing technical managers – first you need a competency model,' *Research Technology Management*, 42(2), pp. 53–7.

21   National Training Board 1992. *National competency standards policy and guidelines*, 2nd edn, p. 10.

22   Hager P., Gonczi A. 1991. op. cit., pp. 37–9.

23   Smith B., Delahaye B. 1998. *How to be an effective trainer*, 3rd edn, New York, Wiley, p. 83.

24   Caffarella R.S. 1985. 'A checklist for preparing successful training programs,' *Training and Development Journal*, 39(3), pp. 81–3.

25   Zemke R., Gunkler J. 1985. '28 techniques for transforming training into performance,' *Training*, 22(4), pp. 48–63.

26   Russ-Eft D.F., Zenger J.H. 1985. 'Common mistakes in evaluating training effectiveness,' *Personnel Administrator*, 30(4), pp. 57–62.

27 Sofo F. 1999. op.cit., p. 122.

28 Smith M. 1980. 'Evaluating training operations and programs,' *Training and Development Journal*, 34(10), pp. 70–8.

29 Kirkpatrick D. 1996. 'Ideas revisited: Revisiting Kirkpatrick's four level model,' *Training and Development*, 50(1), pp. 54–7.

30 www.businessballs.com/kirkpatricklearningevaluationmodel.htm, accessed 7 February 2007. See also, Kruse K. 'Evaluating e-learning: Introduction to the Kirkpatrick Model' (www.e-learningguru.com/articles/art2_8.htm, accessed 7 February 2007; McLoughlin C. 1999. 'The implications of the research literature on learning styles for the design of instructional material,' *Australian Journal of Educational Technology*, 15(3), pp. 222–41; Brinkerhoff R. 2006. 'Increasing impact of training investments: An evaluation strategy for building organizational learning capability,' *Industrial and Commercial Training*, 38(6), pp. 302–7; Bober C.F., Bartlett K.R. 2004. 'The utilization of training program evaluation in corporate universities,' *Human Resource Development Quarterly*, 15(4), pp. 363–83.

31 Goldstein I.L. 1993. op. cit., p. 27.

32 Fitz-Enz J. 1984. *How to measure human resource management*, New York, McGraw-Hill.

33 Knowles M. 1984. *The adult learner: A neglected species*, 3rd edn, Houston, Gulf Publications.

34 Kolb D.A. 1984, *Experiential learning*, Englewood Cliffs, NJ, Prentice-Hall.

35 Senge P.M. 1990, *The fifth discipline: The art and practice of the learning organisation*, London, Random House.

36 Luthans F., Kreitner R. 1985. *Organisational behaviour modification and beyond: An operant and social learning approach*, Glenview, Scott Foresman & Co., p. 127.

37 Robinson D.G., Robinson J.C. 1985. 'Breaking barriers to skill transfer,' *Training and Development Journal*, 39(1), pp. 82–3.

38 Smith B., Delahaye B. 1998. op. cit., p. 16.

39 Sullivan R.F., Milas D.C. 1985. 'On-the-job training that works,' *Training and Development Journal*, 39(5), p. 118.

40 Ibid., pp. 118–21.

41 Marshall K. 1992. 'Qantas puts a net under staff training programs,' *Australian Financial Review*, 19 December, p. 39.

42 Lane A. 1997. 'Online tuition cuts costs and lowers staff turnover,' *Australian Financial Review*, 8 December, p. 94.

43 Robb D., Geffen A. 2000. 'At home with Internet-based training,' *Risk Management*, 47(7), pp. 27–34.

44 Karr S. 2002. 'Anytime anyplace learning,' *Financial Executive*, 18(8), p. 38.

45 Pantazis C. 2002. 'Maximising e-learning to train the 21st century workforce,' *Public Personnel Management*, 31(1), pp. 21–6.

46 Gant S. 1992. 'Flying the decision simulator,' *Weekend Australian*, 23 May, p. 61.

47 Davis K. 1992. 'Program puts submariners in a class of their own,' *Weekend Australian*, 23 May, p. 61.

48 www.abc.net.au/newinventors/txt/s1725487.htm, accessed 11 December 2007.

49 Peters T., Waterman R. 1984. *In search of excellence*, New York, Harper & Row.

50 Mintzberg H. 1989. *Mintzberg on management*, New York, Macmillan.

51 Barolsky J. 1990. 'Case studies help improve training,' *Weekend Australian*, 11–12 August.

52 Moeller S. 1991. 'ATS training simulation a world leader,' *Weekend Australian*, 23 March.

53 Decker P.J. 1983. 'The effects of rehearsal group, size and video feedback in behaviour modelling training,' *Personnel Psychology*, 36(4), pp. 763–73.

54 Ibid, p. 763.

55 Wehrenberg S., Kuhnle R. 1980. 'How training through behaviour modelling works,' *Personnel Journal*, 59(7), pp. 576–80.

56 Meyer H.H., Raich M.S. 1983. 'An objective evaluation of a behaviour modelling training program,' *Personnel Psychology*, 36(4), pp. 755–61.

57 Cacioppe R., Adamson P. 1988. 'Stepping over the edge: Outdoor development programs for management and staff,' *Human Resource Management*, 26(4), pp. 77–95.

58 Miller E., Rooke S. 1991. 'Journeys towards excellence: The design of outdoor management development programs,' *Asia Pacific Human Resource Management*, 29(4), pp. 75–80.

59 Anon. 1991. 'Corporate training in the great outdoors,' *Weekend Australian*, 10–11 August.

60 Nankervis A. 1991. 'Human resource management education: Skill training or preparation for life,' *Asia Pacific Human Resource Management*, 29(3), pp. 41–8.

61 McDonald G. 1989. 'Manager attitudes to training,' *Asia Pacific Human Resource Management*, 27(4), p. 65.

62 Ibid, p. 64.

63 Hall D.T. 1976. *Careers in organisations*, Santa Monica, Goodyear Publishing, p. 36; Leibowitz Z.B., Farren C., Kaye B. 1986. *Designing career development systems*, San Francisco, Jossey-Bass, p. 7.

64 Kirby J. 1998. 'The keys to the best jobs,' *Business Review Weekly*, 19 January, pp. 35–8.

65 Compton R.L., Morrissey B. 1996. 'Career management in a new environment,' *Management*, March, pp. 11–14.

66 James D. 1995. 'The end of the career path,' *Business Review Weekly*, March, pp. 34–8.

67 Armstrong H., Gattegno G. 1993. 'How are you going to manage if the good old days don't come back?,' *Management*, May, pp. 11–14.

68 Parker P., Inkson K. 1999. 'New forms of career: The challenge for human resource management,' *Asia Pacific HRM*, 37(3), pp. 76–85.

69 Anon. 1998. 'A job that's too good to leave!,' *New Workplace*, 4(3).

70 McDermid S. et al. 2001. 'Alternate work arrangements among professionals and managers: Rethinking career development and success,' *Journal of Management Development*, 20(4), p. 305.

71 Parker P., Inkson K. 1999. op. cit., pp. 78–9.

72 Kelly R. 2003. 'Getting on with the job: Career management in a period of labour market restructuring.' Paper presented to the IERA Conference, July, Greenwich, UK.

73 Leibowitz Z.B., Farren C., Kaye B. 1986. op. cit., pp. 40–2.

74 Ibid., pp. 5–7.

75 Joiner D. 2002. 'Assessment centres: What's new?,' *Public Personnel Management*, 31(2), pp. 179–85.

76 Ibid., p. 179.

77 McCall Jr M.W., Lombardo M.M., Morrison A.M. 1989. 'Great leaps in career development,' *Across the Board*, 26(3), pp. 54–61.

78 Hegstad C. 1999. 'Formal mentoring as a strategy for human resource development: A review of research,' *Human Resource Development Quarterly*, 10(4), pp. 383–90.

79 McKenzie B. 1996. 'Mentoring frontline managers,' *Management*, March, pp. 9–10.

80 Hegstad C. 1999. op. cit., p. 383.

81 Ibid., p. 384.

82 Jameson, Caroll B. 1998. 'Mentoring: A way through the glass ceiling,' *Enterprise*, April.

83 Stevens P. 1994. 'Career development – up, up or away,' *hrmonthly*, September, p. 18.

84 Schmidt L. 2000. 'Jobs of the future,' *Business Review Weekly*, 24 November, p. 62.

85 Cascio W. 1989. *Managing human resources: Productivity, quality of worklife, profits*, 2nd edn, US, McGraw-Hill, p. 639.

86 Endel-Jakob K. 1985. *The environment of international business*, Boston, PWS-Kent, p. 420.

87 Copeland L., Griggs L. 1985. *Going international*, New York, Random House, p. 216.

88 Anderson B. 1998. 'The preparation of Australian expatriates for relocation to Southeast Asia,' *Asia Pacific Journal of Human Resources*, 36(3), p. 62.

89 Selmer J., Torbiorn I., de Leon C. 1997. 'Post-arrival intercultural training,' *BRC Papers on Cross Cultural Management*, Hong Kong, Hong Kong Baptist University.

90 Robock S., Simmons K. 1989. *International business and multinational enterprises*, 4th edn, Illinois, Irwin, p. 126.

91 For example, Dowling et al. 1998 cite several research studies which indicate that only 25 to 40 per cent of US companies offer such training. European, Scandinavian and Australian organisations do not seem to be much more proactive.

92 Negandhi A. 1987. *International management*, Massachusetts, Allen & Bacon Inc., p. 582.

Online reading

INFOTRAC® COLLEGE EDITION

For additional readings and review on developing human resources in organisations, explore InfoTrac® College Edition, your online library. Go to: www.infotrac-college.com and search for any of the InfoTrac key terms listed below:

➤ adult learning
➤ career management
➤ competency-based learning
➤ e-learning
➤ human resource development (HRD)
➤ knowledge transfer

CHAPTER 9
MANAGEMENT OF PERFORMANCE

Performance appraisal nourishes short-term performance, annihilates long-term planning, builds fear, demolishes teamwork, nourishes rivalry and politics.

W.E. Deming, 1982

We all constantly appraise, consciously or unconsciously, objectively or subjectively. We appraise ourselves and other people, we appraise behaviour, personality and systems.

John P. Wilson, 2001

Giving an employee bad news during a performance review is tough enough. So why make the job any tougher by saddling managers with complicated appraisal systems?

Lin Grensing Pophal, 2001

Employers who are serious about becoming employers of choice and who wish to retain their brightest talent cannot afford to demotivate them with a weak, ineffective performance review system.

C. Joinson, 2001

Objectives

After reading this chapter you will be able to:

1   Discuss the relationship between performance management and other HRM processes.

2   Describe the various objectives of performance management programs.

3   Discuss the primary performance review methods.

4   Describe the types of errors that arise in the use of rating methods.

5   Identify the different approaches to performance review interviewing.

6   Evaluate the unique performance management issues pertaining to international HRM.

Introduction

In the preceding chapters we discussed the programs that an organisation uses to attract and develop a productive, flexible and motivated workforce. In this chapter we turn to performance management programs, which must be developed if an organisation is to maintain and enhance its productivity. Of course, performance review takes place every day in every organisation whether there is a formal program or not. Supervisors are constantly observing the way their subordinates carry out their assignments and forming impressions about the relative worth of these employees to the organisation. We constantly appraise consciously or unconsciously, objectively and subjectively. We appraise constantly both personalities and behaviours.[1] This may well be one of the many challenges facing HR managers as they attempt to show that they do indeed add value rather than additional costs to their organisation.[2]

Recent research (2003) conducted by TPM/Hudson Global Resources, along with much anecdotal evidence, suggests that far too many organisations, and managers within those organisations, still regard performance review as an annual event that somehow must be tolerated.[3] They do not see the strategic links between this vital HRM process and the bottom line, nor do they appreciate the powerful management tool they have at their disposal.

Most organisations, however, do seem to use a formal program even if that system is not given serious thought in many of those organisations. In earlier research involving over 600 organisations, 85 per cent reported having a structured program.[4] In a later and larger survey of this type, while 96 per cent of respondents said they had a structured performance review, 30 per cent were dissatisfied with the system, 50 per cent only moderately happy and only 20 per cent claiming high to very high levels of satisfaction.[5] Further findings from this study will be covered throughout this chapter.

Separate research cited in the *Harvard Business Review* strongly suggests that companies using performance management systems perform better financially than those that do not.[6] The proposition is that companies that effectively manage the performance of their people will outperform on a wide range of financial and productivity measures those companies without such programs.[7]

Formal programs for performance reviews and merit ratings are by no means new to organisations. Performance review has been traced as far back as the third century AD when Sin Yu, an early Chinese philosopher, criticised a biased rater employed by the Wei Dynasty. Pre-scientific era manager Robert Owen used reviews in his New Lanark mills in the 1880s.[8] In the United States, the federal government began evaluation of employees in 1842 when Congress passed a law mandating yearly performance reviews for department clerks. Advocates have included eminent early management writers such as Drucker, Herzberg et al.[9] together with a number of contemporary writers such as Cascio,[10] who see performance review programs as the only logical means to appraise, develop and thus effectively utilise the knowledge and abilities of employees. Others, just as notable, see reviews as 'nourishing short-term performance, annihilating long-term planning, building fear, demolishing teamwork and nourishing rivalry and politics'.[11] Critics have even gone so far as to link performance review with employee burnout.[12] Other notable early writers to criticise specific aspects of performance review include Douglas McGregor[13] and Harry Levinson.[14]

As performance review has been around for so long there has been an enormous amount of research conducted, making this process one of the most praised, criticised and debated management practices for decades.[15] Despite all of the research, countless texts, articles and conference papers, performance review remains a major source of frustration for managers.[16]

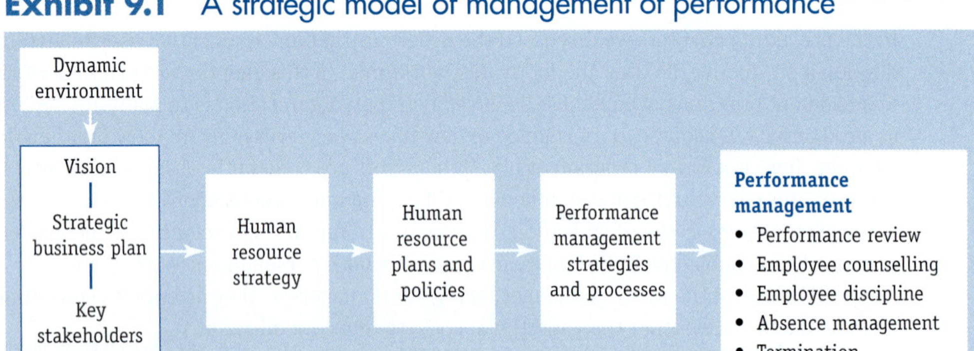

Exhibit 9.1 A strategic model of management of performance

Rapid and discontinuous change within organisations has led to workplaces that are now far more complex and ambiguous than at any time in our history. Organisations are being flattened, with spans of control being widened. Self-managing teams and other employee involvement schemes are becoming more popular. Organisations have embraced the concepts of 'employer of choice' and 'engagement' with enthusiasm. This is manifested in matrix and, more recently, network structures with a greater use of project management teams and loose relationships. There exists an exponential growth of specialised knowledge that managers simply cannot keep up with, and individuals working longer and harder for their own careers rather than as organisational clones.[17] These issues and more have led to a rekindling of interest in performance management strategies that work. While performance management schemes have been on the HR agenda for many years, the key issue is how to make them work.[18] A further complication appears when leaders recognise that their organisations now employ people from three eras; the babyboomers, Generation X and Generation Y, each with differing values and attitudes towards work and life generally. How does a performance review system cope with these added complexities? How does the system cope when these same people may be spread worldwide?

A strategic approach

Many different methods can be used to gather information about the performance of subordinates. Achieving an effective performance review can be difficult, so it makes sense to keep the system as uncomplicated as possible. If this is done, managers and employees alike should not hesitate to become involved and are likely to see the system as a tool for development and reward and not punitive in nature.[19] Employers who are serious about becoming employers of choice and who wish to retain their brightest talent cannot afford to demotivate them with a weak, ineffective performance review system.[20]

However, gathering information is only the first step in the review process. The information must then be evaluated in the context of organisational strategies and needs, and outcomes communicated to employees so that it will result in high levels of performance by means of developmental activities. Specifically, performance review must never be taken in isolation, rather, tied directly to the organisation's strategic plan and the strategies that make up that plan (see Exhibit 9.1). Linking a manager's performance agreement to the organisation's strategic plan is one way of ensuring that performance review takes on an essential strategic perspective.

From this point, the process can be cascaded down to each level within the organisation so that all employees are seen to contribute to the strategic direction of the company. Individual learning and development plans embodied in the performance review system will in turn emanate from the strategic plan. In this way the complete performance review and employee development processes can be directly linked to strategy.

Performance anxiety

The valuable task of performance management is more dreaded than embraced, but researchers and frontline professionals are identifying the problems and improving the strategies

A manufacturing executive in the United States wrote that, if he had the choice between a performance review and a paper cut, he'd take the paper cut every time. 'I hate annual performance reviews,' he said. 'I hated them when I used to get them and I hate them now that I give them.'

That sums up performance management for a lot of people. There's nothing much wrong with the theory, but for many companies a lot goes wrong in practice.

Out of nearly 1 000 HR professionals who responded to an AHRI survey, 96 per cent said they administered a performance management process. Thirty per cent were dissatisfied with it, half were moderately satisfied and only 20 per cent claimed high or very high satisfaction.

The results were no surprise to Alan Nankervis, associate professor of human resource management in the School of Management at Curtin University of Technology, who conducted the survey with Robert Compton, of the Australian Catholic University, in conjunction with AHRI.

'Dissatisfaction levels with performance appraisals, anecdotally and in research, tend to be pretty high,' Nankervis says. This is despite the fact that performance management is 'the jewel in the HR crown', being 'the way you link individual performance with organisational outcomes'.

Companies that tie individual workers' goals to their own business goals, that use performance appraisals as an ongoing and constructive dialogue with workers, and then complete the circle by investing in training and development, get the best out of their people and retain the best, giving them a competitive advantage, he says.

He puts the gap between theory and practice down to organisational culture and lack of training. In companies where performance management isn't working, managers and/or employees don't understand or appreciate the value of appraisals and don't 'buy into' the process. They do it grudgingly, because they have to, and they do the bare minimum.

The lack of organisational support is reinforced when managers fail to follow up. 'Nothing is done with the results. People don't get any training or development, or if they do, they don't get any outcomes in terms of promotion or salary increases.' That breeds cynicism, with employees writing the process off as a sham. 'Once bitten, twice shy,' Nankervis says.

Those implementing performance management systems often have little or no training. 'In this survey, there wasn't much evidence of the majority of people undergoing training,' Nankervis says. 'According to my data, 40 per cent of managers received it, yet virtually all of them do performance appraisals. Just 31 per cent of non-managers received training in performance appraisal. That's not a high proportion.'

Cynicism about performance management only builds further if support is not seen to come from the top. 'If CEOs aren't seen as also being appraised – fairly – then why should employees get involved?'

'People know the theory, they agree with the theory, but there's a big difference between the theory and implementing a highly practical solution that makes sense,' says Jeremy Nichols, the Empower Group's managing partner for Australian consulting.

Companies don't spend enough time in the development phase and don't do it well, he says. 'You have to start with where the organisation is and where it wants to get to, and the performance management process needs to link into ensuring the strategic objectives are achieved. A good diagnostic component is needed to determine "Where are we right now?", what the critical issues are and, importantly, what energy and focus the leaders have. People jump into design before they've done a good diagnostic.'

Once the designing starts, things get complicated. 'Organisations struggle with system design, then try to get that last 10 per cent absolutely perfect,' Nichols says. They keep adding to the system, while the leaders and employees using it struggle with a process that becomes too complicated for their needs.

'It's a case of finding a happy medium – being happy to say it's not perfect but it gets us 80 per cent of the way. That will give you a much greater return on what you are trying to do, which is help people know some key things: what's expected of me and my role, how am I going in that role, what can I do to improve, and how can you support me in my improvement?'

HR managers sometimes try to build too much into a performance management process, says Penny Lovett, general manager, HR, for health insurance provider HBA. 'We forget that the aim is really to create a tool to enable managers to manage effectively. Sometimes we get so caught up in the administration and design, we forget the end user.

'I've seen performance management systems that are technically perfect but far too complex – they become more of a burden than a help. When a system is over-complicated, people will deal with performance management as a once-a-year event that has to occur, rather than as part of a good dialogue between a manager and staff member that should be occurring throughout the year.'

In such circumstances, performance management comes to be regarded as something that takes too much time and distracts managers from their 'real' work.

That's where HR can add value, says Lovett. 'By having an effective performance discussion and using it as an opportunity to motivate staff members towards their goals, it can help managers achieve their own goals.'

Instead of being 'police officers' checking on managers' performance appraisals, HR professionals should be selling managers on their benefits, says Alexandrea Cannon, Coca-Cola Amatil's HR manager for South Australia and the Northern Territory. 'If they see the benefits, they'll do it. If they don't see the benefits, we're not using our influencing skills well enough.'

Managers should also be trained and coached in skills such as communication – especially those who feel more comfortable with the technical rather than the 'people' aspects of their jobs.

But Nichols says many managers are lucky if they receive a one-hour session on how to use a performance management tool, when in fact there's a 'whole subtlety' behind them. 'It's not just about using the tool. It's having the leadership skills to be able to listen, to question in the right way, and to build the confidence and capabilities of employees – as opposed to, "I've got through it, so I can tick that box."'

Nankervis also worries about mere form-filling. 'It's meant to objectify the experience, I suppose, but it's a very unreal way of operating. It's like passing an exam. It seems to me that you don't need the forms. If you have the relationships, and the right job criteria, you can do it informally and in a much more effective way than using complicated forms.'

At the Gold Coast City Council, HR manager Leigh Bernhardt has taken the controversial step of dropping the formal performance appraisal process, and the attendant paperwork, in the 800-employee engineering services division.

'We were having performance appraisals done by people who didn't want to do them and didn't have the communication skills,' says Bernhardt. 'So we negotiated with the union to drop them on the basis that each supervisor records in their diary at least once every

six months that they have sat down with each employee and asked ''How are you going? Is there anything we need to do? Is your training up to scratch?'' We've found that incredibly successful.'

In big companies, performance management can be regarded as something the HR department 'imposes' on operating managers, says Bernhardt, who has worked with Exxon, Mayne Nickless and others. Those uncomfortable with people management avoid 'part two' of performance appraisal – sitting down and chatting with employees.

Educating managers and supervisors in the subtleties of performance management would make a difference, he says. 'But do you really think we could release our people from operations for that sort of training, with all the other commitments on us?'

In the end, he says, managers and supervisors shouldn't need an annual appraisal process to identify areas of non-performance. 'As a manager, I can tell you who's performing and who's not, and what I've done about it.'

At HBA, Penny Lovett is introducing 'five-minute feedbacks' to make performance management a part of year-round behaviour. The mini-reviews are formally scheduled but not cumbersome, she says. 'They are very short and help managers and staff look at the key things. They also provide an opportunity to give feedback to a manager.'

HBA's recently revamped process also involves setting individual goals and career development plans at the beginning of each year, with a larger review every 12 months.

'Tools like five-minute feedback ensure that there are no surprises, that people are given opportunities throughout the year to realign themselves if necessary. They ensure that everyone knows where they stand,' says Lovett.

Coca-Cola Amatil has an annual performance planning session and a performance review, quarterly performance reviews against the annual plan, with adjustments if necessary, and monthly one-on-one informal discussions between leaders and team members.

Setting objectives at the planning stage is the key, says Cannon. 'You do that to get the strategic business plan to work. These things don't just happen. People need to make them happen.'

Cannon says she is passionate about performance management because it adds value to a business and assists people to feel good about what they are doing. 'Where it's not working, companies should knuckle down and have a look at what the problem is.'

Strategic shift

The Australian Human Resources Institute–Curtin University national performance study – the largest of its kind so far in Australia – came up with both encouraging signs and some disappointments.

Almost 1000 HR professionals, from a wide range of industries and companies of all sizes, responded to the survey, posted on the AHRI's website.

The results are still preliminary, but researcher Alan Nankervis says they indicate a slightly more strategic approach to performance management than surveys in 1990 and 1995. This is illustrated by the types of systems being used and the linking of corporate values into those systems.

In previous surveys, the decades-old 'management by objectives' process was clearly the preferred system; this time around, it accounted for just 7.2 per cent of systems. Sixty-four per cent of respondents said they used systems that linked individual and organisational objectives. The rest were evenly split between using 'hybrid' systems employing a number of techniques, and self-assessment.

'There's more use, for example, of the balanced scorecard approach, which is very much an integrated mechanism for performance and productivity', says Nankervis. A quarter of respondents are using this system now, and 41 per cent indicated they would in the future. While he doesn't particularly support the use of the balanced scorecard in this way, 'at least it attempts to link what the organisation is trying to achieve and what the individual is doing'.

On the negative side, most respondents still put their performance management systems to quite traditional purposes. For example, 89.2 per cent used them to determine training and development needs, and 88.9 per cent to appraise past performance. But barely a quarter nominated 'retaining high-calibre staff' as a purpose, while only a slightly higher percentage saw it as a tool to change organisational culture.

The minor use of innovative techniques, such as 360-degree feedback and peer and self-assessment, also disappointed. 'I had heard anecdotally that people were using team appraisals, or 360-degree appraisals, but that doesn't show up at all,' Nankervis says. About eight per cent of respondents used team appraisals 'fairly often or extensively', while about 14 per cent used 360-degree or 'multi-rater' feedback regularly.

Vox pop

hrmonthly asked a range of people for experiences of performance management:

'I've worked with some pretty tough people. If I'd given feedback to my boss telling him that I thought he was an incompetent people manager whose communication skills were abysmal – which was all true – it would have seen me out the gate.'

'My boss says that he doesn't give anyone a top mark. Well, how can you excel and do your best … that's a disincentive straight away.'

'For 12 months you've laboured under the view that you're doing a good job, then your boss calls you in and says you've done a bad job. Don't tell me that anyone walks out of one of those interviews and says, "I feel pumped. Now that they've brought it to my attention, I'm going to work harder."'

'It comes down to your personal relationship with the person who's doing the evaluation. If you have a good, healthy, open relationship –

you "click", you get on – it's a lot easier to give them some feedback. If you have a personality clash, you're going to put keeping the peace above the need for constructive dialogue.'

'I felt like I could be pretty open. But I didn't work that immediately with him anyway.'

'It is a chore, it is time-consuming and it takes people away from their day-to-day duties, and that's why people resent it. There's a lot of bureaucracy, there's a lot of form-filling.'

'You have these cosy chats, but you don't feel that anything comes of it. It clears the air for five minutes and he feels like he's done his bit, and you've got it off your chest, but nothing practical occurs.'

'It has these generic questions, and half the time they don't really relate to your job. You have to strain to think how that question might apply. It just becomes a total form-filling exercise.'

'Together there was a dialogue, give and take, where you'd say, "That's a little bit unfair, you've given me a 2", and they gave you a chance to defend yourself. Then together you'd formulate goals based on your assessment criteria. That was pretty constructive, it was all above board. I thought it worked really well.'

'There's no opportunity to give any feedback, there's no encouragement. It's ridiculous. A lot of the reasons you're dissatisfied might be to do with the management, the style of management, the lack of communication. It's almost as if they don't want to face that.'

'There is no performance targeting, as far as I'm aware, in the management tiers except for cost control – not how happy their staff are or whether they can retain good staff.'

'I don't know why people don't embrace it. Without systems like that, it's totally arbitrary. It comes down to your personal relationship with your manager, whether he likes you, whether you laugh at his jokes.'

Words can hurt

Managers responsible for performance appraisals need to think carefully about the way they communicate with employees amid campaigns to eradicate bullying from the workplace, says workplace relations lawyer Kathryn Dalton.

'One of the more recent issues we have seen arising in the performance appraisal area is the issue of workplace bullying,' says Dalton, of Herbert Geer & Rundle. 'While reasonable performance management can never be bullying, the manner in which a manager undertakes a performance appraisal could be said to amount to workplace bullying. Behaviour that is humiliating – sarcasm, insults or shouting – can expose the employer to a complaint.

'A manager may think they are giving constructive feedback, but it may be in a negative or humiliating way or in an inappropriate context, such as in front of other people or in the middle of a corridor.'

Legal pitfalls can arise when dealing with employees who fall

within the ambit of the *Workplace Relations Act* and who therefore have access to the unfair dismissal provisions, says Dalton.

'To avoid the risk of offending those provisions, the employer will need to show that the process they're involved in, if it ultimately results in termination of employment, wasn't harsh, unjust or unreasonable.'

Procedural fairness requires that an employee be given the opportunity to improve their performance, she says. 'You need to be specific about the areas of performance that require addressing, you need to give the person a reasonable opportunity to address the issues, and then you need to put to them again any concerns as to whether there has been an improvement.

'The potential consequences should also be understood – for example, that, if their performance doesn't improve, a possible outcome could be termination. If they're not aware of that, it puts a completely different complexion on what's going on, and that could be said to be unfair.'

Similar problems arise if negative feedback comes as a surprise at the annual performance review. 'Allowing a person to operate under the assumption that they're performing well is not an effective way of managing, and, if you were to terminate them for something they did six months earlier that you hadn't brought to their attention, that's not likely to be regarded as fair or reasonable either.'

If termination or a major change in the nature of the employment is contemplated as a possible outcome of an appraisal process, she says it is wise to have more than one person involved and to have notes taken.

Source: Lesley Parker, *hrmonthly*, December 2003.

Performance review programs

Advocates see these HRM programs as the only logical means to appraise, develop and thus effectively utilise the knowledge and abilities of employees. At the same time, other organisations install review systems for their symbolic value; that is, they indicate a progressive HRM function even though no-one appears to take the process seriously.

Appraisal systems have the capability to influence employee behaviour, thereby leading directly to improved organisational performance.[21] For the individual, appraisal provides the feedback essential to good performance. Newer approaches to performance appraisal stress training as well as development and growth plans for employees. A development approach to appraisal recognises that the purpose of a manager is to improve job behaviour, not simply to evaluate past performance.

Having a sound basis for improving performance is one of the major benefits of an appraisal program. Performance appraisal data may also be used to assess the effectiveness of other aspects of the HRM program. Performance appraisal reports have been found to be valuable measures of employee success that may be used in validating selection tests and in determining the relative worth of jobs under a job evaluation program. Such reports may be useful in defending HRM actions that have led to the filing of a grievance or a charge of discrimination. Finally, it is important to recognise that the success of the entire HRM program depends on knowing how the performance of employees compares with the goals established for them. This knowledge is best derived from a carefully planned and administered HRM appraisal program, which is compatible with the strategic direction of the organisation.

New demands for performance accountability, together with management obligations under enterprise bargaining provisions, have focused greater attention on performance appraisal. Although somewhat dated, Bernardin and Beatty discuss several relevant US developments that have arisen in response to these demands.[22]

The first development concerns the regulation of HRM functions. Due to government equal employment opportunity and affirmative action provisions, employers must maintain accurate, objective records of employee performance in order to defend themselves against possible charges of discrimination in connection with such HRM actions as termination, promotion and salary determination.

The second development is a response to employee concerns about the fairness and accuracy of performance appraisal as a basis for determining salary increases and promotions. Involving employees in the planning stage of the appraisal process and in helping to develop performance measures is a way of addressing these concerns.

The third development addresses the problem of increased costs and diminished organisational performance arising from under-utilisation or mismanagement of human resources. To attack this problem, organisations must develop appraisal systems that measure employee performance against objective, job-related standards.

The fourth development concerns the relatively low productivity growth of the United States over the past 15 years, compared to that of other major industrial countries. These developments have relevance to the Australian workplace, particularly with the move towards work deregulation associated with enterprise bargaining and globalisation. Strengthening appraisal systems by linking individual performance and rewards to measurable organisational goals is seen as one way to beat the 'productivity dilemma'.

Developing a performance review program

The HR department ordinarily has the primary responsibility for overseeing and coordinating the review program, but managers from the operating departments must be involved actively – particularly in helping to establish the objectives for the program. Furthermore, employees are more likely to accept and be satisfied with the performance review system when they have the chance to participate in its development. A sense of ownership on the part of employees is considered now to be an essential ingredient in an effective scheme.

The following objectives are suggested by Screwvalla on the grounds that appraisal should be made on the basis of scientific evaluation rather than on a casual basis:

* the assessment of past performance

* the encouragement of the deliberate managing of subordinates

* the assessment of potential for promotion or transfer

* the improvement of managers' motivation.[23]

    In addition, other common objectives include:

* strengthening of the relationship between employee and supervisor by bringing them together to discuss progress

* a means of obtaining feedback from employees, which may improve job design, the working environment, career path planning, etc.

* identification of potential for future management positions and promotions or transfers

* identification of training and employee development needs

* a source of information for workforce planning and career and succession planning decisions

* assisting the matching of employees with suitable jobs, in order to achieve better overall outcomes

* a source of information for decisions regarding wage and salary administration, as well as the allocation of various types of rewards

* an outlet for communicating grievances and either personal or work-related problems

- a means of maintaining performance levels, for example, by identifying deterioration before it becomes serious, and taking corrective action

- a means of assisting and encouraging employees to take their own initiative to improve job performance

- checking the effectiveness of other personnel policies, such as recruitment and selection, training and job analysis appraisal, as an interdependent component of the personnel function

- identification and removal of any obstacles to good job performance

- establishment and development of job competencies.[24]

Importantly, Screwvalla points out that care needs to be taken to ensure that the objectives identified do not conflict with each other.[25]

Exhibit 9.2   Interview with a Flight Centre representative – joint winner of Employer of Choice Award, 2003

Q. *Can you please give an overview of your company?*

A. Flight Centre Ltd has grown into a vast international network of more than 1 200 shops and businesses with operations in Australia, New Zealand, the United States, Canada, the UK, South Africa and Hong Kong. With a global workforce of 6 000 employees and an annual total transaction value in excess of AU$4.2 billion we expand at the rate of more than 20 per cent per year. Opening a new shop or office almost every working day, our company is recognised as one of the fastest growing of its kind in the world.

Q. *How would you describe the culture of the company?*

A. Youthful, dynamic, innovative, achievement-oriented, fun, supportive.

Q. *Why did you choose 360-degree feedback? What outcomes were you wanting?*

A. We believe 360-degree feedback is the only true and honest way to assess one's performance – it is in essence a reality check on our leaders.

Q *What were the key features of your implementation process?*

A. Being a profit-driven business we offer 360 as a service to our internal clients. It is a product that we market and on-sell.

Q. *What impact has 360 had in your company?*

A. Our leaders now look forward to receiving feedback from their direct reports, leaders and peers and use this in devising their business and development plans.

Q. *Can you define any benefits?*

A. A more self-aware workforce that is open to constructive feedback and more willing to learn and grow from the information it presents.

Q. *What do you think are the fundamental keys to success in presenting 360-degree feedback?*

A. Gaining ownership of the process by the participants – selling the benefits and having an impartial third party debrief the process.

Typical rating errors

With any rating method, certain types of errors can arise that should be considered. The halo error is also common with respect to rating scales, especially those that do not include carefully developed descriptions of the employee behaviours being rated.[26] Provision for comments on the rating form, as shown in Exhibit 9.3, tends to reduce halo error. In addition, those methods based on employee participation, such as MBO (management by objectives), BARS, and self-appraisal, tend to reduce rater error. Certainly, this is one of their major selling points.

Exhibit 9.3　An example of a rating form

Appraise employee's performance in present assignment. Tick (4) most appropriate source. Appraisers are urged to use the 'remarks' sections freely for significant comments descriptive of the individual.

1 Knowledge of work Understanding of all phases of his/her work and related matters	Needs instruction or guidance ☐	Has required knowledge of own and related work ☐	Has exceptional knowledge of own and related work ☐
	Remarks:		
	Is particularly good on gas engines.		
2 Initiative Ability to originate or develop ideas and to get things started	Lacks imagination ☐	Meets necessary requirements ☐	Unusually resourceful ☐
	Remarks:		
	Has good ideas when asked for an opinion, but otherwise will not offer them. Somewhat lacking in self-confidence.		
3 Application Attention and application to his/her work	Wastes time. Needs close supervision ☐	Steady and willing worker ☐	Exceptionally industrious ☐
	Remarks:		
	Accepted new jobs where assigned.		
4 Quality of work Thoroughness, neatness and accuracy of work	Needs improvement ☐	Regularly meets recognised standards ☐	Consistently maintains highest quality ☐
	Remarks:		
	The work he turns out is always of the highest possible quality.		
5 Volume of work Quantity of acceptable work	Should be increased ☐	Regularly meets recognised standards ☐	Unusually high output ☐
	Remarks:		
	Would be higher if he did not spend so much time checking and rechecking his work.		

It is common for some raters to give unusually high or low ratings. This gives rise to the leniency or strictness error. One way to reduce this error is to define clearly the characteristics or dimensions and to provide meaningful descriptions of behaviour, known as anchors, on the scale. Scale points with labels such as good, fair, and excellent, must be eliminated and replaced by meaningful anchors. After all, what is the real difference between 'good' and 'fair'? Another approach is to require ratings to conform to some pattern. For example, it may be required that

10 per cent of ratings be poor (or excellent). This is similar to the scaling requirement in some schools and universities where examiners grade using the 'normal curve' concept.

Raters who are reluctant to assign either extremely high or extremely low ratings commit the error of central tendency. To such individuals, it is a good idea to explain that one should expect to find significant differences in behaviour, productivity and other characteristics among large numbers of employees.

When the appraisal is based largely on the employee's recent behaviour, good or bad, the rater has committed the recency error. The resulting performance review will be biased either favourably or unfavourably, depending on the way performance information is selected, evaluated and organised by the rater. Without work record documentation for the entire appraisal period, the rater is forced to recall recent employee behaviour to establish the rating. The recency error can be minimised by having the rater routinely document employee accomplishments and weaknesses throughout the whole appraisal period. Rater training will also help reduce this error.

Furthermore, raters should be aware of any stereotypes they may hold towards particular groups (gender, race or other), because the observation and interpretation of performance can be clouded by these stereotypes. Two writers have proposed that individual differences in stereotypes of women affect performance ratings, and suggested that women evaluated by raters who have traditional stereotypes of women will be at a disadvantage in obtaining merit pay increases and promotions.[27] This problem will be aggravated when employees are appraised on the basis of poorly defined performance standards and subjective performance traits.

A performance appraisal that's better than ratings and rankings

In one author's opinion, an appraisal done in a question-and-answer format beats a ranking system hands down

Around the third or fourth century, the Chinese philosopher Sin Yu complained that the Imperial Rater of the Royal Court was showing favoritism in his ratings. It has been an uphill battle ever since.

Most people throughout history have despised appraising or being appraised at work. What's despised isn't so much the idea of a performance appraisal. Judging other people's performance, after all, is almost instinctive, and most of us probably sense the need for performance appraisals in organizations. What's despised is the way it's done, which is usually badly.

Long ago I played Captain Appraisal and took audiences on a 'time capsule' tour of at least 2000 years of human foibles in the ways, some quite bizarre, that performance appraisals have been done. They include two of the most problematic yet enduring ways: ratings and rankings. When you get an audience to laugh about the matter, you know that a deep-seated frustration has been tapped that needs venting.

Performance ratings, although almost universally loathed, still exist. When will we ever learn that dishonest ratings are inevitable because they're so easy to fudge and so tempting to fudge when they're tied to consequences such as bonuses and promotions? I've seen a rating distribution with 98 per cent of the people rated 'outstanding', the only people who 'stand out' being those who didn't get the fudged rating.

Rubber bands and bells

History is replete with doomed rating schemes and policies intent on foiling the Imperial Rater and placating the ghost of Sin Yu. A few examples are 'rubber-band rating scales', periodically stretched in trying to keep ahead of ratings creeping upward; the 'cracked bell', where ratings are forced into a bell-curve distribution; and 'group fudge', in which it's hoped that a truer rating will emerge from a circle of raters. These and other schemes are all part of the futile search for the Holy Grail of Honest Ratings.

Some organizations use rankings instead of – or in addition to – ratings. Rankings aren't even performance appraisals, however, because appraisals in their correct form don't rank people, but instead compare the performance of an individual against the expectations of performance by that individual. The worst flaw of rankings, though, isn't that they're not really performance appraisals but that forced judgments are required, and forced judgments will always have an arbitrary and unfair element to them. Thus, besides being invalid, rankings could also be considered an unethical practice.

Where does all of this leave us? Some critics argue for abolishing performance appraisals altogether, but that's not a viable option. Performance appraisals are an integral part of managing performance, and unmanaged performance simply can't be allowed to happen. The process of managing performance is essentially one of holding people accountable for their performance. It starts with the setting of performance expectations and ends with sanctions – rewards and penalties – on appraised performance.

20 questions

If we want to be responsible and get good performance, therefore, we're stuck with performance appraisals. What we sorely need is a more tolerable and honest way of doing them. One alternative that has been successfully pilot-tested by this Captain is asking a series of questions about performance. The questions require yes-or-no answers. Since performance has two parts – behavior and results – the questions must relate to each part. For example:

- Did you exceed any of your objectives?
- Which objectives, if any, were clearly exceeded, and what were the extra gains?
- Were any unexpected and very tough obstacles encountered?
- Are there any skills you want and/or need developed?

In all, about 20 short questions are needed, some of which are required to identify star performers.

While 100 per cent honesty in performance appraisal isn't possible no matter how well it's done, answers to yes-or-no questions ought to be closer to the truth than the ratings are. Here are four reasons why.

First, answering yes when the true answer is no is more than a fudge; it's a big, bald-faced lie, which requires considerable audacity to make, and isn't likely to be made.

Second, appraisals should be reviewed and certified, and people should know that the appraisals are being checked. This reduces the incentive to distort what they've accomplished.

Third, many of the answers are readily verifiable. For instance, you can verify whether an objective has been met or even exceeded by comparing the documented results obtained with the criteria that were stated in the written objective. As for the more sensitive and more subjective questions relating to behavior, there should be a paper trail showing any problems that the company and the employee have been working on as part of the performance-management process.

Fourth, a person's performance is often visible to colleagues – and it would likely take a conspiracy of two or more people to conceal a falsehood. This is possible, though not likely.

Whether yes-or-no answers are themselves indeed the answer to a 2000-year-old vexation is open to further debate and experience. In the meantime, remember to put performance appraisals in perspective. While they're necessary, they're less critical than the setting of performance expectations from which everything else follows.

Source: Brumback G. B. 2003. *Workforce Online*, July.

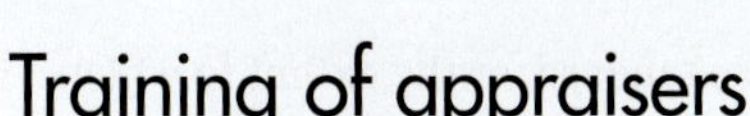

Training of appraisers

A weakness of many performance appraisal programs is that managers and supervisors are not trained adequately for the appraisal task and provide little meaningful feedback to subordinates. Because they lack precise standards for appraising a subordinate's performance, their appraisals often tend to become overly lenient to the point of having little meaning.

Latham and Wexley stress the importance of performance appraisal training by noting that:

> Observer bias in performance appraisals can be attributed largely to well-known rating errors that occur in a systematic manner when an individual observes and evaluates another. In order to minimise the occurrence of rating error and costly litigation battles, organisations, regardless of the appraisal instrument they use, are well advised to expose people who evaluate employees to a training program to minimise rating errors.[28]

Training programs are most effective when they follow a systematic process that begins with an explanation of the objectives of the performance appraisal system. The mechanics of the rating system are also explained, including how frequently the appraisals are to be conducted, who will conduct them, and what the standards of performance are. It is important for the rater to know the purpose for which the appraisal form is to be used and the benefits they might anticipate accruing from the scheme. For example, using the form for remuneration decisions rather than development purposes may affect how the rater evaluates the employee, and it may change the rater's opinion of how the appraisal form should be completed.[29] In addition, appraisal training should alert raters to the weaknesses and problems of appraisal systems, so they can be avoided.

Appraisal training should focus on eliminating the subjective errors made by managers in the rating process. Two of the authors have worked on a number of appraisal awareness sessions, complete with workbooks, to reduce the subjective errors commonly made during the rating process. As one study concluded, 'Rater training has generally been shown to be effective in reducing rating errors, especially if the training is extensive and allows for rater practice'.[30]

Finally, a training program for raters should provide some general points to consider for planning and conducting the review.

Local research indicates that those implementing performance reviews often have little or no training. According to the study, only 40 per cent of managers received this type of training, yet almost all managers undertake performance reviews. The figure for non-managers was a mere 31 per cent, even though they too had to perform reviews on team members.[31]

Establishing performance standards

Well before any appraisal is conducted, the standards by which performance is to be evaluated should be clearly defined and communicated to the employee. These standards must be based on job-related requirements. As discussed in Chapter 5, job standards should be based on job analysis or competency profiling and the resulting job descriptions and person specifications. When performance standards are properly established, they will translate job requirements into levels of acceptable or unacceptable employee performance.[32]

In establishing performance standards, there are three considerations:

- *Relevance*: This refers to the extent to which standards relate to the objectives of the job. For example, if a standard that 95 per cent of all customer complaints are to be resolved in one day is appropriate to the job of customer service representative, then the standard is said to be relevant to performance.

- *Freedom from contamination*: A comparison of performance among production workers, for example, should not be contaminated by the fact that some have newer machines than others. A comparison of the performance of travelling salespersons should not be contaminated by the fact that territories differ in sales potential.

- *Reliability*: This refers to the stability or consistency of a standard, or the extent to which individuals tend to maintain a certain level of performance over time. In ratings, reliability may be measured by correlating two sets of ratings made by a single rater, or by two different raters. For example, two employment interviewers may interview separately the same group of applicants and predict their job success. The interviewer ratings could be compared to determine interrater reliability.

Performance standards will permit managers to specify and communicate precise information to employees regarding quality and quantity of output. Therefore, when performance standards are written, they should be defined in quantifiable and measurable terms. For example, 'ability and willingness to handle customer orders' is not as good a performance standard as 'all customer orders will be filled in four hours with a 98 per cent accuracy rate'. Expressing standards in specific, measurable terms, and comparing the employee's performance against the standard results is a more justifiable appraisal.

It is conceded, however, that some jobs will involve tasks where quantitative measurement is difficult. In these jobs it may well be that success must be measured in how the work is performed rather than by the end numerical result. A case in point may be that of a drug and alcohol counsellor whose success will be measured in the quality and outcomes of counselling, rather than by the number of people seen each day.

Competency-based appraisal

The competency model has been discussed in Chapter 5. As a natural progression, appraisal may be based on those competencies identified, recruited and selected against, and then developed in employees. This process is shown in Exhibit 9.4.

Exhibit 9.4 Steps in competency-based appraisal

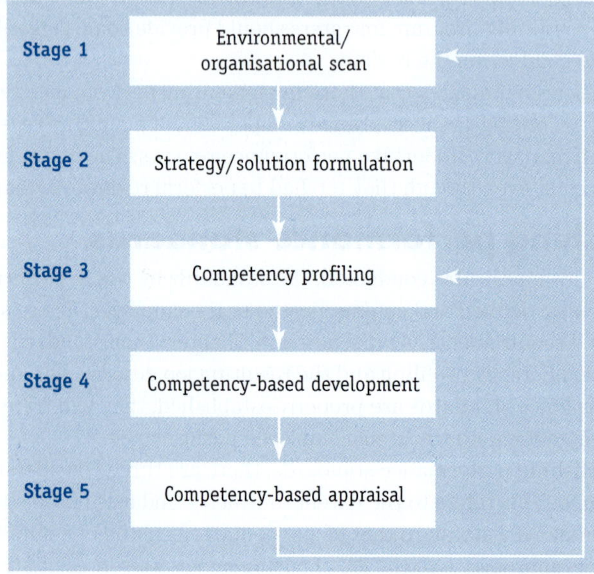

Source: Adapted from Bassett B., 1990. 'Critical competencies for change', *Training and Development in Australia*, Australian Institute of Training and Development, 17(4), p. 10.

Where a competency-based approach is used, the behaviourally anchored rating scale (BARS) method (discussed later in this chapter) is likely to be most appropriate.

Why performance appraisal programs fail

In actual practice, formal performance appraisal programs sometimes yield disappointing results, for a number of reasons. The primary culprits are lack of top management support, lack of job-relatedness standards, rater bias, excessive paperwork, and using the program for conflicting purposes. For example, if an appraisal program is used to provide a written appraisal for salary action and at the same time to motivate subordinates to improve their work, the two purposes may be in conflict. As a result, the appraisal interview essentially becomes a salary discussion in which the superior seeks to justify the action taken. Consequently, the discussion has little influence on the subordinate's future job performance.

As with all HRM functions, if the support of top management is lacking, the appraisal program will not be successful. Even the best conceived program will not work in an environment where employees are not encouraged by their leaders to take the program seriously. To underscore the importance of this responsibility, top management should announce that effectiveness in appraising people is a standard by which the appraisers themselves will be evaluated.

In addition, a policy statement signed by the chief executive officer must be a vital first step. Nankervis and Leece found that 34 per cent of surveyed Australian organisations using appraisals had no formal policy.[33]

Other reasons why performance appraisal programs can fail to yield the desired results include the following:

- Managers feel that little or no benefit will be derived from the time and energy spent in the process.

- Managers dislike the face-to-face confrontation of appraisal interviews.

- Managers are not sufficiently skilled in conducting appraisal interviews.

- The judgemental role of appraisal conflicts with the helping role of developing employees.

- Lack of commitment and a sense of ownership on the part of employees.

- Lack of interest by the supervisors.

- In the words of Douglas McGregor, 'a reluctance to play God'.

- Appraisal becomes a ritual, which neither party takes seriously.[34]

Performance appraisal in some organisations is a once-a-year activity in which the appraisal interview becomes a source of friction for both appraisers and employees. An important principle of performance appraisal is that continuous feedback and employee coaching must be a positive daily activity.[35] The annual or semi-annual performance review should simply be a logical extension of the day-to-day supervision process. There should be no surprises at the appraisal interview.

One of the main concerns of employees is the fairness of the performance appraisal system, since the process is central to so many HRM decisions. Employees who believe the system is unfair may consider the appraisal interview a waste of time and leave the interview with feelings of anxiety or frustration. Also, they may view compliance with the appraisal system as perfunctory and thus play only a passive role during the interview process. By addressing these employee concerns during the planning stage of the appraisal process, the organisation will help the appraisal program to succeed in reaching its goals.

Finally, organisational politics can introduce a bias even in fairly administered employee appraisals. For example, managers may distort ratings upward because they desire higher salaries for their employees or because higher subordinate ratings make them look good as managers. Managers may want to get rid of troublesome employees or, conversely, keep a valued employee by manipulating their ratings in some way. These are not errors in the traditional sense that we discussed earlier, since managers are well aware of what they are doing and the written rating is at odds with what the manager really believes about employee performance.

Performance review methods

Since the early years of their use, methods of evaluating personnel have evolved considerably. Old systems have been replaced by new methods that represent technical improvements and are more consistent with the purposes of appraisal. The discussion that follows examines in some detail those methods that have found widespread use, and briefly touches on other methods that are used less frequently.

Performance appraisal methods can be broadly classified as either relative judgement methods, such as individual rating scales and comparison methods, or outcome-oriented approaches, such as management by objective systems. The most current and popular methods will be discussed, including peer, self and upward appraisal and 360-degree feedback. Rating scales continue to be more popular despite their inherent subjectivity. The outcome-oriented approaches are gaining popularity because they focus on the measurable contributions that employees make to the organisation. Professionally designed systems used by Australia's large organisations use either. Exhibit 9.5 (see p. 341) shows the results of a recent comparative study into the types of appraisal schemes used both in Australia and in Singapore.

Peer appraisal

Occasionally, appraisals are made by persons other than a supervisor. Individuals of equal rank who work together are sometimes asked to evaluate each other. These peer appraisals provide information that differs to some degree from ratings by a superior. Peers can readily identify leadership and interpersonal skills, along with other strengths or weaknesses, of their co-workers. A commander asked to rate a police officer on a dimension such as 'dealing with the public' may not have much opportunity to observe it. Fellow officers, on the other hand, have the opportunity to observe this behaviour regularly.

One advantage of peer appraisals is the belief that they furnish more accurate and valid information than appraisals by superiors. The question might well be, 'who can most accurately judge job performance, the manager who often sees employees putting their best foot forward, or those who work with their fellow associates on a regular basis?'[36] Peer assessments are compiled into a single profile and given to the supervisor for use in the final appraisal.[37]

Despite the evidence that peer appraisals are possibly the most accurate method of judging employee behaviour, this system is not widely used in Australia. The reasons commonly cited include the following:

- Peer ratings are simply a popularity contest.

- Managers are reluctant to give up control over the appraisal process.

- Those receiving low ratings might retaliate against their peers.

- Peers rely on stereotypes in ratings.[38]

One overseas organisation tackles peer assessment in two phases. During the first phase of the review the team, minus the team member under review, agrees on a rating and produces a written report. In the second phase the full team discusses the rating with the reviewed team member and encourages him/her to respond. A trained facilitator participates in each phase.[39]

Employers using peer appraisals must also be sure to safeguard confidentiality in handling the review forms. Any breach of confidentiality can create interpersonal rivalries or hurt feelings and bring about hostility towards fellow employees.

Self-appraisal

A popular approach in Australia involves employees being asked to evaluate themselves on a self-appraisal form. Self-appraisals are beneficial when managers seek to increase employees' involvement in the review process. A self-appraisal system requires an employee to complete the appraisal form prior to the performance interview. During the interview, the supervisor and the employee discuss job performance and agree on a final appraisal. This approach also works well when the supervisor and the employee jointly establish future performance goals or employee development plans. Self-appraisal is most often used in combination with a management-by-objectives appraisal scheme and is particularly attractive where a participative culture is in place.

Upward appraisal

Upward appraisal by team members has been used in some instances to give managers feedback on how their subordinates view them. Subordinates are in a good position to evaluate their managers as they are in frequent contact with their superiors and occupy a unique position from which to observe much performance-related behaviour. Those performance dimensions judged most appropriate for subordinate appraisals might include leadership, communication, empowerment, coordination of team efforts, development of subordinates, planning and organising, budget control, creativity and analytical ability.

In a study including both profit and nonprofit organisations, three-quarters of the managers responding said they would value the feedback from employees for personal development issues. Over 70 per cent of the managers approved of subordinate appraisals when they would involve such issues as pay and performance and where the subordinate's input would count heavily in the appraisals of managers.[40]

Tony Beddison of the SACS Elite Consulting Group believes the main advantage is that 'the boss gets feedback often without learning who said what'. Beddison claims that the approach is spreading in Australia after success in the United States, as managers adopt a more open, supportive attitude towards their staff.[41]

360-degree feedback

Senior managers, HR professionals and consultants are under continuous pressure to come up with a new and better performance review model than that used in previous years. In recent years, organisations have pursued world's best practice, quality management, benchmarking and business process engineering, to name a few.[42] The danger here is that we will end up with a series of fads and fashions which come and go in quick succession. A sustained effort to provide accurate, objective and timely feedback on performance has seen the emergence of 360-degree feedback.

Whether we use the term 'multi-directional feedback' or '360-degree feedback' matters little – the concept is the same. Organisations will attempt to gather work performance data about an employee from as many sources as possible.[43] It has been suggested that multi-directional feedback is essential for overcoming leader blind spots and enhancing their overall emotional intelligence.[44] A relatively new approach for Australian organisations is the 360-degree feedback review, which usually requires six reviewers – two managers, two subordinates and two peers – to comment on an employee's performance over a range of predetermined criteria. This approach is used by many of our biggest companies, including Ampol, Big W, Citibank, Gillette, Yellow Pages, BP, Telstra, Qantas, Lend Lease, Toyota Australia and Integral Energy. The final report is a compilation and summary of the six individual reports, with feedback provided by a trained facilitator.

One Australian writer has commented on the intrinsic attraction of 360-degree feedback insofar as the theory looks right; by involving more than one person, the feedback process is likely to be more meaningful for both the supervisor and the employee.[45]

Given that over 90 per cent of the Fortune 500 companies are using some form of 360-degree feedback, it is interesting to look at the local context. A survey commissioned by Davidson-Trahaire found that 60 per cent of respondents had an ambivalent view of 360-degree feedback, with only 43 per cent having any experience in implementing 360-degree feedback systems. Only 37 per cent saw 360-degree feedback as a positive contributor to developmental needs. At the same time, 80 per cent saw development as a very important activity, while only 63 per cent felt that their current development processes were meeting their needs.[46]

The most recent Australian statistics indicate that only 14 per cent of companies have formally adopted this more innovative technique of gaining information and feeding it back to the employee.[47]

These statistics give the impression that too many of our organisations still remain reluctant to experiment with innovative approaches to managing their people. Instead, they remain with their conventional strategies while reporting dissatisfaction with current methods.

Peiperl argues that this type of resistance might be due in part to the nature of peer appraisal in that it tends to exacerbate bureaucracy, heighten political tensions and consume an enormous amount of time.[48] This can be true where trust is an issue, where the process is performed manually rather than electronically and where too many reviews are attempted at the one time. With six to eight people involved in each review, peer assessment and 360-degree reviews can virtually close the organisation down as people busily fill in the paperwork.

Given that peer assessment and 360-degree surveys appear to exhibit great potential in an area of HRM that has seen little change for decades, Gaskell and Flanagan pose the question: Why do we not see more multi-directional feedback?[49] Their explanation rests on the typical Australian top-down organisational structure where lines between management and worker have traditionally been drawn very clearly. There is a sense of vulnerability in most of us and it is this lack of security that leads to a defensive stance on anything new that might upset the manager–employee balance.

Finally, a word of caution before embarking on peer assessment or 360-degree review. The organisation's culture must be supportive of this type of strategy. Where trust, alignment, commitment and acceptance are present, the chances of success will be enhanced. Where these fundamentals are missing, success is likely to be very limited.

Rating scales

Rating scales are a very common method of performance appraisal. In one local research study almost 35 per cent of respondents reported using some sort of rating scale.[50] In the rating scale method, each trait or characteristic to be rated is represented by a scale on which a rater indicates the degree to which an employee possesses that trait or characteristic. An example of this type of scale is shown in Exhibit 9.3. There are many variations. The differences are to be found in the characteristics or dimensions on which individuals are rated, the degree to which the performance dimension is defined for the rater, and how clearly the points on the scale are defined.

In Exhibit 9.3 the dimensions are defined briefly and some attempt is made to define the points on the scale. Subjectivity is reduced when the dimensions on the scale and the scale points are defined as exactly as possible, rather than simply using a numerical scale with no descriptive anchors. This can be achieved by training raters and by including descriptive appraisal guidelines in a user-friendly performance appraisal reference book developed by the organisation.

Exhibit 9.5 Types of performance management systems

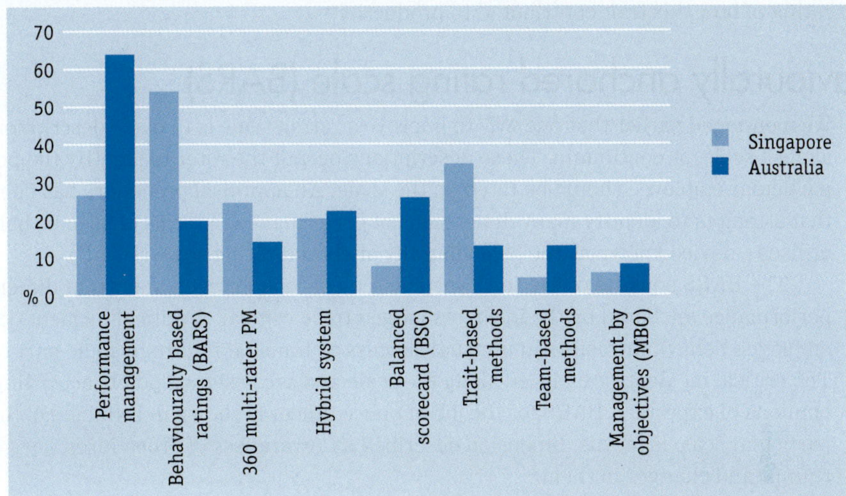

Source: Nankervis A., Compton R.L. 2006. 'Performance management: Theory in practice?', *Asia Pacific Journal of Human Resources*, 44(1), pp. 83–101.

The rating form should also provide sufficient space for comments on the behaviour associated with each scale. These comments improve the accuracy of the appraisal since they require the rater to think in terms of observable employee behaviours while providing specific examples to discuss with the employee during the appraisal interview. Space for employee comments is also highly recommended, if not essential.

Global rating

While a rating scale with several relevant dimensions is preferable, many organisations simply use a single rating of overall job performance, for example, appraising an employee's total performance as 'average'. Such a rating, commonly referred to as a global rating, is useful for making some HRM decisions, such as those concerning salary increases or promotions. It is, however, of little value to employees in understanding whether their specific job performance has been successful, and it is likely to be viewed as discriminatory. After all, what is the difference between 'good' and 'fair'?

Mixed standard scale

These are a modification of the basic rating scale. Rather than evaluate a trait according to a scale, the rater is given three specific behavioural descriptions relevant to each trait. For example, for the trait of cooperation, the descriptions might be as follows:

- Employee is extremely cooperative. Can be expected to take the lead in developing cooperation among employees. Completes job tasks with a positive attitude.

- Employee is generally agreeable. However, at times becomes argumentative when given job assignments. Cooperates with other employees as expected.

- Employee normally displays an argumentative or defensive attitude towards fellow employees and job assignments.

The descriptions for the trait reflect three types of performance: superior, average, or inferior. After the three descriptions for each trait are written, they are randomly sequenced to form the mixed standard scale.[51] Supervisors then evaluate employees by indicating that their performance is better than, equal to or worse than the standard for each behaviour. Once again, subjectivity is often a problem and claims of unfair discrimination are common. Also there is no rating of how this trait contributed to productivity.

Behaviourally anchored rating scale (BARS)

We mentioned earlier that one way to improve a rating scale is to place descriptions of behaviour along a scale, or continuum. These descriptions permit the rater to identify the point where a particular employee should be rated on the scale. An appraisal procedure has been developed that attempts to identify many dimensions of performance in terms of specific behaviours. It utilises a device known as the behaviourally anchored rating scale (BARS).

The BARS consists of five to 10 vertical scales – one for each important dimension of job performance anchored by the incidents judged to be critical. A critical incident occurs when employee behaviour results in unusual success or unusual failure in some part of the job. The critical incidents are placed along the scale and are assigned points according to the opinions of experts. A BARS for the job of police officer is shown in Exhibit 9.6. Note that this particular scale is for the dimension described as 'Awareness of procedures, laws, and court rulings and changes in them.'

Exhibit 9.6 A behaviourally anchored rating scale for a police officer

Job knowledge: Awareness of procedures, laws and court rulings and changes in them			
Could be expected to follow correct procedures for evidence preservation at the scene of a crime	Very high	9	Could be expected to be fully aware of recent court rulings and conduct him or herself accordingly
	——	8	
Could be expected to know he or she could break down a locked door while in hot pursuit and thus arrest a fleeing suspect	——	7	
	——	6	
Could be expected to have to ask other officers occasionally about points of law	——	5	Moderate
	——	4	
	——	3	
			Could be expected to search a suspect's car two hours after the suspect was booked
Could be expected to misinform the public on legal matters through lack of knowledge	——	2	
	——	1	Very low
Rater: ——			Ratee: ——

Source: Landy F.J. 1986. *Psychology of work behaviour*, 3rd edn, p. 185. Copyright © 1986, 1980, 1976 The Dorsey Press. By permission of Brooks/Cole Publishing Company, a division of International Thomson Publishing Inc., Pacific Grove, CA 93950 USA.

A BARS is typically developed by a committee that includes both subordinates and managers.[52] The committee's task is to identify all the relevant characteristics or dimensions of the job. Behavioural anchors in the form of statements are then established for each of the

job dimensions. Several participants are asked to review the anchor statements and indicate which job dimension each anchor illustrates. The only anchors retained are those which at least 70 per cent of the group agree belong with a particular dimension. Finally, anchors are attached to their job dimensions and placed on the appropriate scales according to values that the group assigns to them.

At present, there is no strong evidence that a BARS reduces all of the rating errors mentioned previously. However, some studies have shown that scales of this type can yield more accurate ratings.[53] One major advantage of a BARS is that personnel outside HR departments participate in its development. Employee participation can lead to greater acceptance and a sense of 'ownership' of the performance appraisal process and of the performance measures that it uses. BARS is particularly useful where the manner in which a job is performed is more important than the numerical output. One writer has claimed BARS to be MBO's (management by objectives) missing ingredient.[54]

The procedures followed in developing a BARS also result in scales that have a high degree of content validity. The main disadvantage of a BARS is that it requires considerable time and effort to develop. In addition, because the scales are specific to particular jobs, a scale designed for one job will not apply to another, that is, the scales are job-specific.

Management by objectives method

Management by objectives (MBO) is a philosophy of management first attributed to, and used by, Peter Drucker in 1954.[55] It seeks to judge the performance of employees based on their success in achieving the objectives they have established through consultation with their superiors. Performance improvement efforts under MBO focus on the goals to be achieved by employees rather than the activities they perform or the traits they exhibit in connection with their assigned duties.

MBO is a strategic system involving a cycle that begins with setting the organisation's common goals and objectives and ultimately returns to that step. The system acts as a goal-setting process whereby objectives are established for the organisation, individual departments, and individual managers and employees.

As Exhibit 9.7 illustrates, a significant feature of the cycle is the establishment of specific goals by the employee (step 3) using a broad statement of employee responsibilities prepared by the supervisor. Employee-established goals are discussed with the supervisor and jointly reviewed and modified until both parties are satisfied with them (step 4). The goal statements are accompanied by a detailed account of the actions the employee proposes to take in order to reach the goals. During periodic reviews, as objective data are made available, the progress that the employee is making towards the goals is then assessed (step 5). Goals may be changed at this time as new or additional data are received. At the conclusion of a period of time (usually six months or one year), the employee makes a self-appraisal of what has been accomplished, substantiating the self-appraisal with factual data wherever possible. The 'interview' is an examination of the employee's self-appraisal by the supervisor and the employee together (step 6).

Criticisms of MBO

The MBO system is not without its critics. One researcher contends that MBO is a lengthy and costly appraisal system with only a moderate impact on organisational success.[56] Another criticism of MBO is that performance data are designed to measure results on a short-term

Exhibit 9.7 Performance appraisal under an MBO program

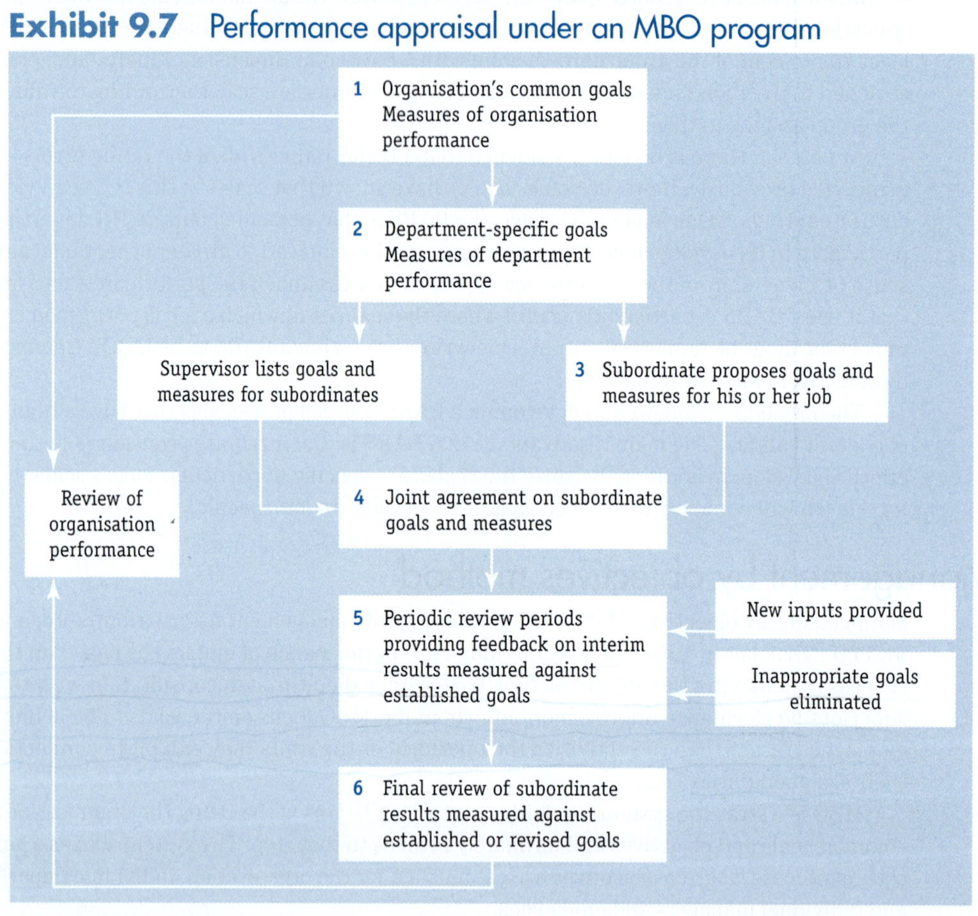

Source: Adapted from Odiorne G.S. 1979. *Management by objectives II*, ©1979 by Lake Publishing Company, Belmont, CA.

rather than a long-term basis. Thus, line supervisors, for example, may let their equipment suffer to reduce maintenance costs. In fact, in any job involving interaction with others, it is not enough to meet certain production or sales objectives. Factors such as cooperation, adaptability, initiative and concern for human relations may be important to job success. If these factors are important job standards, they should be added to the review. Thus, to be realistic, both the results and the method used to achieve them should be considered.

Some of the most damaging criticism has been from Levinson in his article 'Management by whose objectives?' where he argues, among other things, that the concept of mutual goal setting is a myth. Where the subordinate's objectives are inconsistent with the supervisor's, then the latter will prevail.[57] In addition, Deming, the father of total quality management, condemns MBO (and appraisal generally) as one of management's deadly diseases.[58]

One Australian writer has designed an appraisal system that allows for Deming's criticism, yet provides for an effective means of performance review.[59]

Exhibit 9.8   Example of a goal-setting worksheet

Universal Service Corporation

Employee's rating record

Name _________________________________   Date _________________________________

Job title _________________________________   Dept _________________________________

Appraised by _________________________________   Date started _________________________________

____

Summary of appraisal
Development needs

____

Major responsibilities and period goals   **Evaluation of attainment of goals**

____

Responsibility

....

Goal

____

Responsibility

....

Goal

____

Responsibility

....

Goal

____

Balanced scorecard

Imagine entering the cockpit of a modern aircraft and finding only one instrument there. Or trying to stop a charging bull by grabbing it by one horn. This is what we are trying to do by attempting to measure performance with limited criteria. This problem is addressed by the balanced scorecard approach to performance management.

The balanced scorecard was introduced to the popular strategic management literature by Kaplan and Norton in 1996.[60] This approach to strategy development translates an organisation's mission and strategies into a comprehensive set of performance measures that provides the framework for a strategic measurement and management system. The scorecard measures organisational performance across four balanced perspectives, resulting in a four-quadrant model. The four quadrants are:

1   financial

2   customers

3   internal business processes

4   learning and innovation.

Kaplan and Norton argued that the shortcoming of traditional performance measurement systems was an over-reliance on financial measures. The objective of the balanced scorecard is to measure financial and non-financial, forward-looking, predictive measures. The effective management of people, processes and customers is just as important.

This approach to strategy is then easily translated to performance management by setting mutually both short-term and long-term objectives for all employees across each of the four quadrants and then measuring success or otherwise in attaining those objectives. In so doing, performance review is far more likely to be linked to the organisation's mission and strategic plan than with any of the other systems discussed. In addition, the attraction of this approach to HR professionals will be in its emphasis on learning and growth goals not only for the person under review but also for that person's team members. It is also possible and highly practical to alter the headings on the four quadrants to reflect the strategic direction and objectives of individual organisations and also to better reflect the position being reviewed. As a case in point, ACU National is reviewing the use of the balanced scorecard for academic staff. Staff are reviewed and promoted on four criteria; scholarly achievements, teaching, contribution to the university and community engagement. The four quadrant model of the balanced scorecard seems to suit their purpose very well. Management staff may well use the original Kaplan and Norton criteria.

What about the new HR scorecard?

Review of an evaluator's appraisal

In most performance appraisal programs, an employee's immediate supervisor has the responsibility to appraise the employee's performance. Where a supervisor appraises employees independently, provision is often made for a review of the appraisals by the supervisor's superior. Having appraisals reviewed by a supervisor's superior reduces the chance of superficial or biased evaluations. Having said that, there is a growing trend towards 360-degree and 180-degree feedback systems, with claims that such approaches will further reduce bias by providing multi-directional feedback.

In an update to earlier research, Nankervis and Compton have published results of a 2004 study into Australian performance review systems. The results are very similar to those reported in 1990 and 1997, with the exception that organisations today are more likely to have a formal policy statement covering performance review.

Nearly 96 per cent of organisations have a formal system in place, with large organisations (more than 1 000 employees) more likely to have a formal system. Around 80 per cent expressed some level of dissatisfaction with their system's outcomes.[61] Purposes and key expectations of organisations of their performance review systems have been reported. Performance reviews are conducted solely by the employee's supervisor in 64 per cent of cases. Despite reported interest in team and peer appraisal, only 5.7 per cent reported appraisal by supervisor and teams/peers.

A majority of respondents appraise their people annually (59 per cent) with 38 per cent appraising on a six-monthly basis. Of interest is the steady increase in popularity of 360-degree reviews (14 per cent) and the Balanced Scorecard approach (25 per cent).[62] The following exhibits provide further details.

Exhibit 9.9 Managerial expectation for performance appraisal systems % (N = 992)

Performance requirements	Senior management	Middle managers	Supervisors	Other staff
objectives/targets	84.7	79.8	64.2	55.4
broad responsibilities and role	68.8	69.9	57.0	47.7
main job descriptions	41.8	56.0	65.6	67.6
written job descriptions	58.2	71.1	69.4	70.9
a set of competencies (linked to values)	39.4	41.2	36.5	35.0
a set of competencies (not linked to values)	20.0	24.7	24.6	25.9

Note. Percentages total greater than 100 as a variety of held expectations.

Source: Nankervis A., Compton R.L. 2006. 'Performance management: Theory in practice?', *Asia Pacific Journal of Human Resources*, 44(1), pp. 83–101.

Exhibit 9.10 Main purposes of performance management % (N = 992)

Aims of performance management	
Determine training and development need	89.2
Appraise past performance	88.9
Align objectives	75.5
Develop individual competencies	56.6
Assist career planning decisions	56.0
Link pay to performance	50.7
Assess future potential/promotion prospects	47.9
Discipline/dismiss non-performing staff	28.9
Change organisational culture	28.0
Retain high calibre staff	27.5
Other	4.2

Source: Nankervis A., Compton R.L. 2006. 'Performance management: Theory in practice?', *Asia Pacific Journal of Human Resources*, 44(1), pp. 83–101.

Further research

Kramar has conducted additional research as part of the Cranet-Macquarie survey on international strategic human resource management. This study is the third undertaken; Exhibit 9.11 shows statistics from 1996 to 2005.[63]

Exhibit 9.11 Percentage of organisations using performance appraisal for particular occupational groups

	2005	1999	1996
Managers	90%	96%	91%
Professional/technical	90%	86%	94%
Clerical	89%	77%	89%
Manual	61%	66%	47%

Source: Kramar R. 2006. *Cranet–Macquarie survey on international human resource management: Report on the Australian findings*, Sydney, Macquarie University, pp. 18–19.

These figures show a degree of consistency, apart from those relating to manual employees where the figures show a rising trend when those performed in 1996 are compared to those in 2005.

The information gathered from this study can be compared to those shown above from the Nankervis/Compton study:

- Input to HR planning – 69%

- Analysis of training and development needs – 96%

- Career decisions – 89%

- Remuneration – 74%

- Work design – 55%.

Finally, in 2005, the Performance Management Institute of Australia conducted a survey of Australian employees' attitudes towards performance management in the workplace. Their results are summarised in the following exhibit and show some interesting outcomes which complement the studies of Nankervis and Compton and also Kramar in that the survey takes a different approach with the questions posed.[64]

Exhibit 9.12 Employees' attitudes towards performance management

In your current role/last role how often do you receive a performance review?	%
Once a year	52.6
Twice a year	24.6
Quarterly	11
More frequently	5
Never	6.8
Over 50% of respondents receive a review once a year or less.	
Did your performance review focus solely on past results, or did it also look at setting goals and targets for the next review?	**%**
Review past results	14.3
Setting goals and targets for the future	16.4
Both of the above	69.3
The majority focused on both past and future, which is refreshing.	

Which of the following were assessed in your review?	%
Performance against business objectives	50.2
Performance against position description	59.6
Your personal development plan	65.6
Behaviours	53.3
Daily activities	66.4
Focus is widespread with an increased use of personal development plans	
If you were reviewed against objectives, were they related to the organisation strategy?	**%**
Related	66.2
Unrelated	33.6
One-third felt that their review was unrelated to strategy.	
Which statement do you feel best sums up your current review process?	**%**
I think it is essential for personal development.	59.6
I don't get any real benefit from it.	24.6
I don't know how it will help me get ahead in my career.	7.2
It's a nuisance.	8.3
40% see no real benefit in performance review.	

Source: Performance Management Institute Australia 2005.

An analysis of the above studies indicates that there has been an improvement in relation to performance review practices over the past 10 years but there is still a long way to go.

Appraisal interviews

The appraisal interview gives a manager the opportunity to discuss a subordinate's performance record and to explore areas of possible improvements and growth. It also provides an opportunity to identify the subordinate's attitudes and feelings more thoroughly and thus to improve communication.

The format for the appraisal interview will be determined in large part by the purpose of the interview, the type of appraisal system used and the organisation of the interview form. Most appraisal interviews attempt to give feedback to employees on how well they are performing their jobs and to make plans for their future development. Interviews should be scheduled far enough in advance to allow the interviewee, as well as the interviewer, to prepare for the discussion. Usually 10 days to two weeks is a sufficient amount of lead time.

Fundamental to the success of the appraisal interview is the relationship between the two participants in the process.

Areas of emphasis

Since a major purpose of the appraisal interview is to make plans for improvement, it is important to focus the interviewee's attention on the future rather than the past. The interviewer should observe the following points:

- Initially, emphasise strengths on which the employee can build, rather than weaknesses to overcome.

- Avoid suggestions about personal traits to change; instead suggest more acceptable ways of performing.
- Concentrate on opportunities for growth that exist within the framework of the employee's present position.
- Limit plans for growth to a few important items that can be accomplished within a reasonable period of time.

The appraisal interview is perhaps the most important part of the entire performance appraisal process. Unfortunately, the interviewer can become overburdened by attempting to discuss too much, such as the employee's past performance and future developmental goals. Dividing the appraisal interview into two sessions, one for the performance review and the other for the employee's growth plans, can alleviate time pressures. Moreover, by separating the interview into two sessions, the interviewer can give each session the proper attention it deserves. It can be difficult for a supervisor to perform the role of both evaluator and counsellor in the same review period. Dividing the sessions also may improve communication between the parties, thereby reducing stress.[65]

Improving performance

In many instances the appraisal interview will provide the basis for noting deficiencies in employee performance and for making plans for improvement. Unless these deficiencies are brought to the employee's attention, they are likely to continue until they become quite serious. Sometimes, underperformers may not understand exactly what is expected of them. However, once their responsibilities are clarified, they are in a position to take the corrective action needed to improve their performance.

Reasons for ineffective performance

There are many reasons why an employee's performance might not meet expected standards. First, each individual has a unique pattern of strengths and weaknesses that play a part. In addition, other factors such as the work environment, the external environment, including home and community, and personal problems have an impact on job performance. To provide a better understanding of possible sources of ineffective performance related to these environments, we have devised the comprehensive list shown in Exhibit 9.13.

It is recommended that a diagnosis of poor employee performance focus on three interactive elements: skill, effort and external conditions. For example, if an employee's performance is not up to standard, the cause could be a skill problem (knowledge, abilities, technical competencies), an effort problem (motivation to get the job done), or some problem in the external conditions of work (poor economic conditions, supply shortages, difficult sales territories). If any one of the three elements is deficient or unfavourable, performance will suffer.

Managing ineffective performance

The first step in managing ineffective performance is to determine its source. Once the source is known, a course of action can be planned. This action may lie in providing training in areas that would increase the knowledge and skills needed for effective performance. A transfer to another

job or department might give an employee a chance to become a more effective member of the organisation. In other instances, greater attention may have to be focused on ways to motivate the individual.

Exhibit 9.13   Sources of ineffective performance

Organisation policies and practices	Personal problems
• *Ineffective job placement* • *Insufficient job training* • *Ineffectual employment practices* • *Permissiveness with enforcing policies or job standards* • *Heavy-handed management* • *Lack of attention to employee needs or concerns* • *Inadequate communication within organisation* • *Unclear reporting relationships* • *Lack of clear job descriptions*	• *Stress* • *Relationship problems* • *Financial worries* • *Emotional disorders (including depression, guilt, anxiety, fear)* • *Conflict between work demands and family demands* • *Physical limitations including impairment* • *Low work ethic* • *Other family problems* • *Lack of effort* • *Immaturity* • *Drugs and alcohol* • *Health concerns*
Job concerns	**External factors**
• *Unclear or constantly changing work requirements* • *Boredom with job* • *Lack of job growth or advancement opportunities* • *Role ambiguity* • *Management–employee conflict* • *Problems with fellow employees* • *Unsafe working conditions* • *Unavailable or inadequate equipment or materials* • *Inability to perform the job* • *Excessive workload* • *Insufficient workload* • *Lack of job skills*	• *Industry decline or extreme competition* • *Legal constraints* • *Conflict between ethical standards and job demands* • *Union–management conflict*

If ineffective performance persists, it may be necessary to demote the employee, take disciplinary action or discharge the person from the organisation. Whatever action is taken to cope with ineffective performance, it should be done with objectivity, fairness and a recognition of the feelings of the individual involved. Any other approach may well lead to those legal problems outlined earlier in this chapter.

NEWS REPORT 9.3

Cutting the slack

What is the main cause of under-performing staff?

Paul Adams, CAHRI Human resources director, Tasmania KPMG

Why is it that high-performing individuals and teams set and achieve new goals with seemingly limitless energy and enthusiasm? And why are they able to do so without heavy-handed performance management systems or external accommodations to limitations? High performers seem to expect success and take personal accountability for their achievements, while seeking feedback from credible coaches to assist in their growth. They achieve their goals because they have faith in their capabilities and know that their environment will support them. If they fall short, they learn from the experience, envision the next desired outcome and acquire the new capabilities or competencies needed to deliver it. Their environment expects and encourages high performance.

Similarly, I believe that the main cause of under-performance is a direct consequence of the limiting beliefs individuals hold about themselves or their environment. If individual workers do not believe they can achieve change, the result is a reinforcement of the status quo and perpetuation of the problems. Unfortunately, in order to mitigate unfair dismissal risks,

many organisations' performance management systems often amount to little more than meticulously recording and restating the problems, which merely fortifies ineffective mindsets rather than building more effective thought patterns.

How do you break this cycle? Firstly, individuals must take personal accountability for their own growth and performance in order to achieve the changes in mindset required to perform at a higher level. Forcing them to change won't work.

Secondly, under-performing workers need credible leaders who provide firm, corrective feedback on inappropriate behaviour; leaders who inspire new and effective beliefs that drive the desired level of performance; leaders who support workers during their growth; and performance management systems where the focus is the desired outcomes and behaviours.

Finally, the organisational culture, systems and practices must support high performance and the pursuit of achievement.

Russell Varley, CAHRI General manager HR Elders Limited

The main cause of under-performing staff would have to be a lack of good

management. Providing regular feedback is a critical aspect of managing staff to help them perform at their peak. If employees are not provided with encouragement and coaching on areas for improvement, then how can they know when they are not achieving at the required level? Further, employees become de-motivated if nobody tells them whether their work is good, bad or indifferent.

While the formal process of performance management is important, managers should also offer regular feedback as informally as possible. A good manager will frequently ask staff if they have any issues and respond promptly if someone is under-performing.

Managers should also be aware that most workers seek skills development. In many cases of under-performance, employees don't achieve outcomes because they've not been given the skills or knowledge to accomplish the work required. Moreover, without development opportunities employees can become de-motivated. Most of us get out to bed every morning hoping that our job will provide some degree of challenge. But if work becomes boring or repetitious then people lose their enthusiasm and many become complacent or lazy. Good organisations will seek to

find systems or processes (such as automation) that eliminate the brain-dead elements of work.

Conversely, motivated workers are more likely to be found in organisations with a vibrant culture. Where there is a lot of employee interaction within a company, and a strong sense of direction from senior management, employees have a better sense of where they are going and are more likely to want to do their best.

Jen Sheridan, CAHRI Director Sheridan Winter, Learning and Development Consultants

The major cause of poor performance is a lack of role clarity. Role clarity involves people knowing what their job is, what they are expected to do and the standard to which they should do it – as well as where it fits in the bigger picture.

Often these things are not clear to staff due to poor induction and inadequate performance management. For example, I don't think managers generally use probation periods very well. It's all very well to cover the housekeeping and throw the induction file at a new employee and tell them to read it. But, right from day one, managers should set short-term objectives and outline some very clear indicators that will demonstrate whether or not the employee is on track. All too often at the end of probation, staff drift into becoming permanent without having their performance properly reviewed to discern whether they are the right person for the job and whether management has done all it can to assist them to succeed.

Another critical aspect of this process is ongoing feedback, including both the positive and the negative. Some managers avoid giving negative feedback because it is uncomfortable, but I also notice that positive feedback is very generalised. Employees are told they are doing 'a great job', without specifying what that actually means.

Managers can also help staff to perform better by finding out what helps and hinders employees doing a great job. This should happen at regular intervals in the performance management process, not just during appraisals.

I have also observed that training is often used as a solution to under-performance. While training is one valid part of a total strategy to lift performance, it is crucial that managers enable staff to transfer their new knowledge back in to the workplace.

Source: Paul Somerville, *hrmonthly*, May 2005.

Straight talk about job appraisal

Performance appraisals, while potentially a valuable tool for companies, have attracted much criticism, with some academics proclaiming that they nourish short-term performance, annihilate long term planning, build fear, demolish teamwork and encourage rivalry and politics.

Alan Nankervis, an Associate Professor and Research Director at Curtin University of Technology's School of Management, says: 'There has been an enormous amount of research conducted on performance management, making it one of the most praised, criticised, and debated human resource management practices for decades. But despite all the research, countless texts, articles and conference papers, performance review remains a major source of frustration for managers.'

Yet, done effectively, the tool has the potential to boost the overall performance of a business and the individuals who work for it. Indeed, research has shown, companies that manage the performance of their people effectively are more likely to outperform than those that don't.

Successful performance management can also help companies plan better, retain top performers and align individual goals with those of the organisation.

However, recent studies reveal that although performance management is widely embraced in Australia, its use remains problematic and companies struggle to implement it successfully.

The Hudson Report, which measures the hiring expectation of Australian employers, surveyed almost 7000 managers nationally and found that 45 per cent of Australian managers rate their organisation's HR and people management practices, including performance management, as average or below average.

The results, released at the end of April, also show that the key HR areas requiring the most attention include performance management systems, improved leadership capability and learning and development.

Another recent study – by Nankervis and Robert Compton, Senior Lecturer in HR Management at the Australian Catholic University, Sydney, in conjunction with the Australian Human Resources Institute – found that only 20 per cent of managers using performance management reported a high or very high satisfaction rate. Just over 30 per cent were less than satisfied while half were moderately satisfied.

Respondents cited the lack of links with organisational goals or with promotional and salary rewards as reasons for their dissatisfaction. Other factors included few participation or feedback opportunities, inadequate appraisal training, and implementation and administrative difficulties.

Nankervis says the use of performance management in Australia is becoming more widespread with 96 per cent of those polled in his latest study using it, compared to 85–86 per cent in studies done in 1990 and 1995.

Possible factors behind this rise include the need to bolster productivity in the face of greater competition, a rise in performance-based employment contracts and a more 'strategic' approach to performance management.

However, despite this growth in usage, Nankervis says satisfaction levels with present systems have deteriorated since his earlier studies. Training has also declined and the involvement of employees in the review of their own and their team's performance is not yet well implemented. Likewise, the message from management consultants is that there's still much work to be done.

'If you do a general Internet search on performance management, what you will come up with are articles on how to avoid problems,' says Melbourne-based HR consultant, Derek Stockley, highlighting just how difficult performance management can be.

Dennis Finn, Pricewaterhouse-Coopers' Head of Performance Improvement notes: 'People and organisations are getting better at doing performance management, but they still have a long way to go'.

Michelle Bourke, a Director within the Deloitte's Consulting Division, adds: 'While there is recognition of the value of performance management and its role in driving the business forward, many of the organisations we work with are struggling with their existing performance management systems and are looking for ways to improve them'.

So what goes wrong? In a 2002 Mercer Human Resource Consulting survey, managers listed inadequate manager skills in giving feedback, lack of follow-up of agreed actions and inadequate ongoing feedback as the major barriers to successful performance management.

Not setting the right objectives can also ignite problems, says Finn. 'What people find most frustrating about performance appraisals – when the appraisals are not working – is that they didn't get any input or didn't agree with the objectives set for them. They also say they had very little or no influence over those objectives or the objectives didn't reflect what they do on a day-to-day basis.'

Stockley adds: 'Companies are trying to relate the individual's performance to the organisation's performance – for example, their ability to achieve budget – but there are so many circumstances beyond an individual's control which can interfere with this. It's important to set objectives that people can actually achieve and over which they have control'.

Finn says: 'If the goals, measures and targets are too

loose and subjective, with no time scale set for when they are to be delivered, it will be extremely frustrating for the person who has to figure it all out'.

He notes that once objectives are set, there must be consequences for those who over or underachieve. 'The rewards given must be associated with whether that person is below target, on target, above target or even exceptional. Driving difference is crucial'.

Finn adds: 'Performance appraisals work best where the content of the performance management system is tightly aligned to the organisation's vision; and where this vision is broken up into goals, measures and targets that are then cascaded down through all areas of the organisation to those that can really influence them'.

Leaders have to spend time getting the key metrics right and then turn these into steps which are specific, measurable, time bound and objective. 'What often happens is that the manager drives the business based on the latest bushfire which leaves the company reactive and driven by short-termism and this leaves the employee frustrated,' says Finn.

'However, even when we know what we have to do, it's still hard to do. Most people gravitate towards the financial or numbers side, because these are easier to understand. Other aspects are harder to measure. But if you want to build up, say, leadership, you'll need to set non-financial targets such as the number of people ready to fill higher roles or the training and development available in the organisation per person.'

Sydney-based management consultant Wendy Cooper believes that in addition to boosting individual performance, the process should also include team-based objectives that promote teamwork and cooperation. This can be done by encouraging the group to buy into a new initiative such as installing a new software system, with shared rewards.

Cooper also cautions against putting too much emphasis on the negative during review. 'You should look at how staff can be supported and coached so that they can achieve their goals, rather than how they could be punished if they don't achieve them,' she says.

While the use of technology in performance management is growing, Stockley says nothing beats the value of a good face-to-face discussion. He acknowledges that most organisations need a more formal system, but says: 'The best system is a blank piece of paper and a really good one- or two-hour discussion'.

And, according to Finn, the more often it is done, the better. 'The tip is not to make it a one-off thing. Having a monthly one-on-one "mini-review" would measurably reduce the anxiety created at the end of the year and eliminate the surprise that is sometimes experience. You'd also correct what you need to earlier,' he says.

Source: Zilla Efrat, *Management Today*, August 2005. Zilla Efrat is a Sydney-based freelance writer.

Employee counselling

A quick perusal of current HRM texts indicates that the subject of counselling tends largely to be ignored by most authors. Employees are counselled from the day they join an organisation to the day they leave, yet most of this counselling is informal. There is usually no logical or structured technique in place, let alone a consistent approach to counselling issues. Most small- to medium-sized Australian organisations have no formal counselling programs, although there has been increased interest since the late 1980s.[66] Some 80 of our top 100 organisations now have a formal external counselling program in place.

What is employee counselling?

In counselling, a relationship is established where one person endeavours to help another to understand and to resolve a problem, whether it be work-related or personal.

This definition immediately raises the issue as to the role of supervisors and HR managers in the counselling process. Employee counselling must always focus on work performance rather than personal issues that are not affecting the employee's output. The exception is where the employee seeks assistance through self-referral to the supervisor or HR manager. The viewpoint adopted in this text is that personal problems not affecting work performance are not the business of the organisation. Only where performance is in some way affected should the supervisor intervene.[67]

Who should counsel?

Where a work performance problem exists, it is the role of the supervisor to investigate the extent to which work standards are not being met. This requires the supervisor to understand and to have communicated these standards to employees from the outset. Intervention by the supervisor must now aim at determining the reasons for the gap between standards and performance. Where the reason is found to be work-related, obviously the supervisor is obliged to take steps to correct the situation.

On the other hand, a supervisor who discovers that a personal problem is likely to be the cause of the deviation should exercise extreme caution in attempting to provide counselling. In such cases, the supervisor's role becomes one of detecting the problem, exploring with the employee the reasons for the problem, and, having discovered that a personal problem exists, referring the employee to either an internal, qualified counsellor or, where available, an external counselling service if this approach appears more appropriate. An overriding principle which is important to note here is that personal counselling must be voluntary; ethically an employee cannot be forced to undergo counselling sessions.

Who is the work-performance-impaired employee?

While many authors talk of the 'troubled employee', it should be made clear that this terminology seems to imply that an employee's private troubles are somehow the business of employers. In times when anti-discrimination literature uses terms such as 'hearing-impaired', 'intellectually impaired' and 'physically impaired', it seems appropriate to talk of the 'work-performance-impaired' employee. The sole aim of the employer in this situation is to bring a worker's performance back to an acceptable standard.[68]

Filipowicz cites a study by Ginzberg who found the following to be sources of tension in the workplace: isolation; tight supervision; work groups that include an increasing number of minority workers; a reduction in management's loyalty to older workers; displacement of higher echelon workers who have extensive organisational contacts; anonymity in rapidly growing organisations; excessive demands on young executives for mobility, with increased strain on marriages; technological advances that require employees to be better trained and educated; increased leisure time for workers who have insufficient resources to pay for recreational opportunities; and preference for hiring young workers, which results in increased pressures on older workers.[69] Other studies have added the following to the list: poor supervision; communication problems; discrimination; vague work descriptions; repetitive work; speed of work; job design; and lack of training.

The simple solution might be to discharge the worker, but this approach may not be appropriate for a number of reasons, the most persuasive being that the employee may be worth saving, especially when considering the high costs involved in hiring and developing workers. The 'problem' employee may well be a key member of the management team.

In a study carried out by one of the authors, a group of counsellors was asked to provide an outline of their caseload over a typical four-week period. The reasons for referral covered the following broad areas:

- financial
- grief
- gambling
- anorexia
- bulimia
- self-mutilation
- post-traumatic stress
- workload issues
  - underload
  - overload
- cross-dressing
- suicidal tendencies
- substance abuse
- pre-hospitalisation
- terminal illness
- self-image issues
- stress
- personality conflicts.

Confidentiality considerations do not allow more specific information to be released from this survey. It should be obvious that most of these issues are areas where supervisors should rarely venture.

NEWS REPORT 9.5

The new man at work: boss, I'd like to talk to someone about my emotional troubles

Men are greater users of workplace counselling services than women, and relationship troubles are their major woe. A study into the use of employee assistance programs in 650 Australian companies has found 55 per cent of the formal counselling sessions were run for men, just edging out their female colleagues.

Researcher Bob Compton, a senior lecturer at the ACU's School of Management, said the study dispelled the myth that men preferred to suffer in silence or seek advice from mates than see a counsellor. 'We thought we would find more women using counselling services but … it's pretty much evenly split,' Dr Compton said.

The top three reasons for seeing a counsellor were relationship problems, cited by one in five people, emotional disturbances or general feelings of stress (15 per cent of cases) and work–family balance (10 per cent). Stress caused by workplace bullying and conflict in the office made up only three per cent of cases.

Dr Compton said relationship stress had long been the biggest issue seen by workplace counsellors, who now provide services in more than 80 per cent of Australia's top 100 companies. Provision of employee assistance programs – usually outsourced to a private company with qualified psychologists and run off the

premises – has grown dramatically since 1985, when the NSW State Rail Authority and BHP were the only major organisations to offer a structured program. 'The issue is clear. If a valued employee has a personal problem, which is detracting from their focus at work, then work performance will most likely suffer,' Dr Compton said. 'People bring their emotional baggage to work with them. They cannot and will not simply switch off as they come through the door each morning.'

The study also found employees aged 30 to 49 were the most likely age group to use the services, making up 60 per cent of all counselling sessions. People in this age group were often feeling the twin pressures of high mortgages and juggling work and family responsibilities, Dr Compton said.

Nearly one-third of all people attending counselling were managers or professionals, with para-professionals making up a further 15 per cent. But the programs were used less by people from non-English speaking backgrounds, who made up only 10 per cent of attendees.

The next stage of Dr Compton's study will seek to determine whether employee assistance programs have helped relieve people's work and personal stress.

Source: Nixon S. 2003. HR Reporter, 7 April.

Employee assistance programs (EAPs)

A diverse range of organisations have established Employee Assistance Programs (EAPs) to provide free professional, confidential counselling to their employees and their families. Examples are the multinationals DuPont and 3M, large Australian companies such as Lend Lease and Qantas, and emergency services, hospitals and local government instrumentalities. Industrial Program Service (IPS) – Employee Assistance, Australia's largest provider of EAPs, has even established counselling programs with non-government organisations such as Greenpeace to provide assistance to their staff. In 1999, IPS – Employee Assistance established an EAP for the Sydney Olympics to cover both full-time staff and the 55 000 volunteers.

To some, EAPs can represent a 'big brother' meddling in employees' private lives.[70] To others, they are yet another management fad and a waste of time. A more positive approach is adopted by IPS, which sees an EAP as an effective strategy for assisting employees when personal or work-related problems are affecting their work. The programs are characterised by effective, early and minimum intervention. They offer a broad-brush strategy and aim at resolving problems such as those listed above.

A more formal definition is provided by Walsh as 'a set of company policies and procedures for identifying, or responding to, personal or emotional problems of employees which interfere, directly or indirectly, with job performance'.[71] The problem with this type of definition is that an EAP has to be more than policies and procedures; action must be taken to implement these plans. The second point that needs to be made is that EAPs cater for problems other than those affecting job performance. A person may self-refer to receive assistance with a personal problem that is not causing any deterioration in work performance.

It is important to note that the modern EAP aims at a wide range of problems. This approach varies from earlier approaches in the United States, the United Kingdom and Australia where the emphasis was placed solely on alcohol-related, and later drug-related, problems. The modern EAP has resulted from the failure of earlier drug and alcohol programs.

Philosophy of the EAP model

The early drug and alcohol programs were largely seen to have failed in meeting their objectives both in Australia and overseas. The programs generated a great many policies and procedures, but little action. From these early attempts emerged four principles, as outlined here.

The total person

One principle on which an EAP is based is the belief that organisations employ the total person, not just 40 hours per week of the person. Employees simply cannot – and do not – leave their problems at the front door on the way in and then pick them up going home. In addition, in most cases, employers are in many ways employing not one person but, indirectly, their partner and a number of children.

This view contradicts that of earlier management writers who saw individual needs as being subordinate to organisational needs. If it can be argued that job characteristics play a significant part in an employee's physical and mental health, then it is the total person who may need assistance from time to time. These problems may or may not be work-related but, in the final analysis, they may affect work performance.

Confidentiality

Confidentiality is crucial to EAPs. There must be no doubt in the minds of employees that their participation in the scheme is totally confidential. Any breach of trust will destroy the credibility of the program. A consequence of this requirement is that the company will, in many cases, know neither who is seeking assistance nor on what basis. Similarly, if the problem involves a supervisor, EAP counsellors may find their hands tied as they can hardly approach that supervisor and still maintain confidentiality (unless written permission of the employee is obtained).

Reactive and proactive strategies

The early EAPs tended to be reactive rather than proactive: action was taken after the problem became apparent. Employees either self-referred or were referred (voluntarily) to the program after performance had reached unacceptable levels. The belief was that if problem workers were recognised, aided and allowed to work out their problems, they would be salvaged and returned to a satisfactory position.

Today's EAP takes on both a reactive and proactive mode. Preventive services complement and extend the benefits derived from the program by advising on organisation methods to prevent personal or work-related problems and by actively promoting employee health, well-being and personal development. The types of programs offered can be broadly categorised into two areas: employee health promotion programs and employee development programs.

Employee health promotion programs address common concerns among employers, unions and employees. Programs include alcohol and drug education, stress management, heart disease prevention, AIDS education and quit smoking campaigns.

Specialist employee development programs are available where recurrent preventable problems have been highlighted through counselling or other assessment methods. Specific courses are then devised to meet the needs of the organisation. These include the management of problems associated with the organisation, such as:

- occupational trauma

- communication

- organisational change

- redundancy or retirement.

The emphasis in these programs is on teaching practical skills and, where appropriate, integrating with the EAP for individual counselling.

It should be made quite clear that management's legal responsibility is no longer limited to ensuring that fire extinguishers are full and machine guards in place. Physical and mental health are now covered by occupational health and safety legislation.

Professional counselling

Another principle of EAPs is professional counselling. While the success of all EAPs rests largely on the supervisors' observational skills (of work performance decline), there is great danger in assuming that they are able or even willing to ta ke on the counselling role. Speroff argues that supervisors should be taught to understand their fellow workers and to help them to the best of their ability. Their job should be to detect a work performance problem at the earliest time and offer referral to the person for assistance. This should happen only when two conditions are satisfied: first, the problem must be affecting work performance and, second, the employee must agree to accept assistance.[72]

The supervisor should not become involved in private matters which he or she is not qualified to counsel. If a private matter is not affecting performance, it is not the business of supervisors. The overriding principle here is that counselling must always be voluntary and provided by qualified and experienced professionals capable of working with a broad range of personal problems. The focus of the supervisor must always remain on the work performance of the employee.

This view is supported by Kuzmits and Hammons who agree that the supervisors are the key people in the program. They have the task of spotting the troubled employee, motivating the employee to seek professional help, working with the internal or external counsellors if necessary (and if appropriate) and, finally, monitoring performance levels following assistance.[73]

It should be remembered, however, that where an external agency is used and direct self-referral is available, the supervisors may not know the troubled worker is undertaking counselling assistance. Programs offer self- and supervision-initiated referral.

While supervisors are key people in any EAP program, counselling must be left to the counsellors. Supervisors should be made aware of their limitations in this field. One- or two-day staff development courses in employee counselling will most likely do far more harm than good. Such courses should be limited to teaching work performance monitoring and referral skills, rather than attempting to make expert counsellors of supervisors. Professional counsellors carry malpractice insurance whereas supervisors (and HR managers) usually do not.[74]

How does an EAP work?

A simple model of EAP operation is shown in Exhibit 9.14 and demonstrates the following requirements.

- If there is a problem related to a person's private life and it is not affecting his or her work performance, then it is not the business of the employer. The employer may be concerned, but has no right to become involved.

- The employer may provide a counselling service, but the decision about using it rests with the employee.

- It is important to provide the resources for people to seek help voluntarily, in a professional and confidential way.

- The basis of supervisory intervention is the recognition that employees have a responsibility to perform adequately on the job, and supervisors have the responsibility – and should have the training and support – to encourage and guide them to do so.

- The continued monitoring of job performance is the only method of assessment open to the supervisor or manager. When performance is below established standards, the supervisor or manager should discuss the facts with the employee and assist that person to return to an acceptable standard within the framework of the organisation's disciplinary policy.

- The referral for assessment counselling is made strictly on the basis of declining work performance every time a manager or supervisor formally approaches an employee about performance deterioration. This frees supervisors and managers from trying to assess personal problems.

- EAP supervisor or manager referral procedures should be tailored to fit the organisation's present policies.

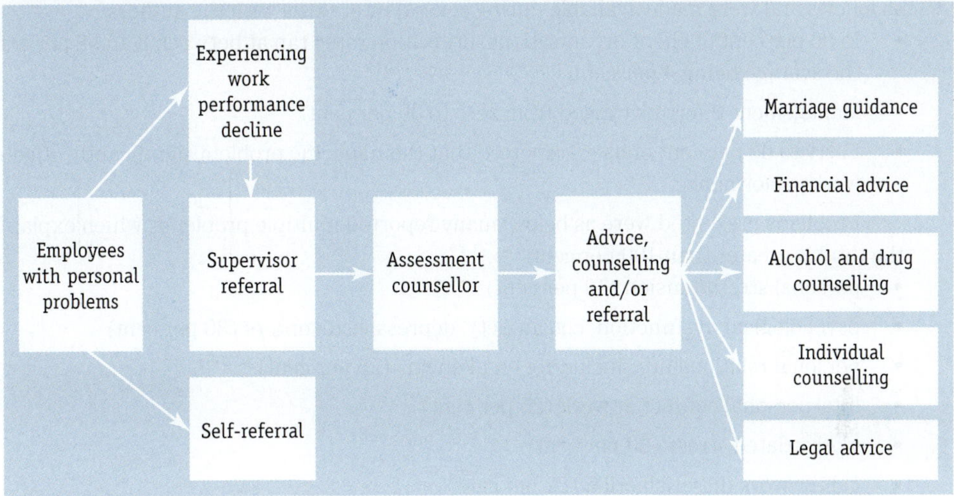

In a 1997 study of members of the Australian Human Resources Institute, Compton found that only 37 per cent of respondents had in place a formal counselling program. Of these organisations, 18.7 per cent were in the finance sector; 27 per cent in education; 18 per cent in government; and 11 per cent in manufacturing. A significant finding was that workplace counselling is far more likely to be found in larger organisations, with 82 per cent of those employing over 20 000 people utilising a workplace counselling service.

The main reasons given for introducing workplace counselling programs were as follows: union pressure (11.6 per cent); multiple workplace problems (23.2 per cent); keeping up with latest HRM trends (11.1 per cent); and as part of integrated HRM program (41.6 per cent). The most commonly presented counselling issues were: stress (26.75 per cent); relationships (25.08 per cent); retirement/redundancy (13.58 per cent); drugs of addiction (12.2 per cent); finance (5.95 per cent); grief (6.52 per cent); and gambling (2.93 per cent).

Interestingly, the study dispelled the popular myth that counselling services are only accessed by the lower levels of the organisation. Respondents reported utilisation rates of 6.65 per cent for senior management; middle management 10.6 per cent; first line management 12.5 per cent; administrative/clerical 24 per cent; sales 2.3 per cent; and manual 21 per cent.

On a less positive note, it was disappointing to discover that of those organisations that reported a formal program, the majority were staffed by unqualified counsellors. Where an informal program was reported, the situation was much worse, with 80 per cent of counselling being performed either by the relevant line manager, or the HR officer/manager. Of all respondents, only 25 per cent reported their counselling staff as holding a degree in psychology or similar. Of almost equal concern was a lack of any clear link between workplace counselling and other HRM strategies such as performance appraisal, career counselling, training and development or absentee control. At the same time, respondents perceived improvements to absenteeism (65 per cent); turnover (40 per cent); productivity (57 per cent); morale (65 per cent); and motivation (46 per cent). However, less than five per cent of respondents were able to specify how they intended to monitor any such benefits![75]

Davidson-Trahaire, a leading Australian EAP provider, conducted its own research in 1998 with more than 1 000 clients, covering both blue- and white-collar workforces. Their findings are as follows and were made available during several interviews with the authors.

- In 90 per cent of client organisations, utilisation rates ran at between 3 and 8 per cent with the average being 4 per cent.

- Management referrals ranged from zero to 30 per cent.

- Forty to 60 per cent of users reported that their specific problem significantly affected their work performance.

Problems presented were as below; many reported multiple problems, which explains why the total is greater than 100 per cent.

- personal stress/tension (40 per cent)

- psychological dysfunction, e.g. anxiety, depressive disorders (30 per cent)

- personal relationships, including breakdowns (25 per cent)

- interpersonal conflict at work (25 per cent)

- work-related stress (23 per cent)

- career/work dissatisfaction (22 per cent)

- child/family problems (10 per cent)

- alcohol use (8 per cent)

- legal/financial (5 per cent)

- other drugs (not alcohol) use (2 per cent)

In other cases, the problem presented was not diagnosed as the underlying condition but symptomatic of a deeper problem.

Statistics provided during interviews with IPS – Employee Assistance paint a similar picture. Using a sample of 10 000 clients from 600 different organisations, they found the most common problems were:

- relationship and family (38 per cent)

- work related (30 per cent)

- emotional (29 per cent)

- alcohol and other drugs (21 per cent).

Of new clients, 85 per cent were assisted through IPS counselling only, whereas others needed extended specialist help, for example, through the work organisation (5 per cent), community organisations (6 per cent) or through a specialist alcohol and other drug facility (2 per cent).

Current trends

Compton's 2003 study aimed to evaluate the effectiveness of the EAP approach to resolving workplace and personal stress. In a study involving a broad cross-section of 650 Australian organisations, it was found that 55 per cent of counselling sessions were attended by men and 45 per cent by women. This is indeed very close to the composition of the current workforce. The top three reasons for attending counselling were relationships (20 per cent) general feelings of stress (15 per cent) and work–family conflicts (10 per cent). The study also found that those people in the 30–49 years age group were most likely to go to a counsellor. Almost 33 per cent of those seeking counselling were managers or professionals, with another 15 per cent identified as para-professionals. Consistent with earlier studies, very few counselling sessions were attended by persons with a non-English speaking background.[76]

The modern EAP has continued the trend towards one-stop, broad-brush counselling services. It has matured and is now offering a more sophisticated and broad range of consulting and counselling services. A number of the major players have either merged or adopted an international strategy. Two of Australia's largest counselling organisations have just merged to form Davidson-Trahaire CorpPsych making it the largest supplier in the country. IPS – Employee Assistance, the oldest and formerly our largest supplier, has now changed its name to IPS Global to reflect its growing presence in South-East Asia.

It seems that today's HR professionals demand that their EAP providers offer them a one-stop cafeteria style of service. In addition they demand a service that is more proactive so that emerging problems can be addressed before they take on greater significance. Organisations want meaningful feedback regarding trends which are being detected by psychologists during their counselling sessions. HR managers are asking that their EAP act as an early warning system with demands for more analytical and interpretive data being made available on a regular basis.[77]

Critics of EAPs

There have been few critics of EAPs in Australia primarily because of the short history of these programs in this country. However, Dr Yossi Berger from the ACTU Occupational Health and Safety Unit argues that with EAPs, 'we have gone from bible-bashing fanatics warning against alcohol, to policy-flashing executives offering in-depth programs for personal problems often in revolting work environments'.[78] He states that a focus on the work environment must precede any personal problem exploration unless both occur simultaneously.

A dissenting report to the Committee of Review into Drug and Alcohol Services in New South Wales was critical of EAPs because of their focus on the individual and their supposed lack of preventive measures. These criticisms, however, are based on a limited understanding of EAP purpose and structure, and are really criticisms of the American EAP model, which is reactive rather than proactive.

Deves has questioned whether we always need to accept the 'expert' counsellors' assessment and indeed their level of expertise.[79] This view may well be supported where clinical psychologists, with limited exposure to organisational life, are employed as EAP counsellors.

Vickers and Kouzmin have raised the issue of 'big brother' and coercive counselling and asked whether EAPs are simply another form of employer surveillance of their staff.[80] However, their paper indicates little understanding of the contemporary nature of EAPs.

Evaluation of EAPs

EAPs have, in fact, grown out of historical traditions rather than empirical research. Much of the claimed cost benefits are based on US research that is, in many cases, rather suspect. A close reading of this material illustrates that much of the claimed benefits of EAPs are more rhetoric than fact. However, this is not to dismiss the beneficial report of EAPs' effectiveness in individual Australian organisations.

With this in mind, one study claims that EAPs save organisations $7.50 for every dollar spent. The claim comes from one of Australia's largest EAP providers, CorPsych. Its figures are based on a US study together with statistics from the 50 EAPs that it manages. Savings come from reduced absenteeism, increases in productivity, decreases in conflict and employees being better able to cope with change.[81]

Such claims must be questioned. The very confidential nature of counselling means that employers will not know who is attending counselling sessions unless the employee tells them. We also know that around 80 per cent of employees self-refer. This, in turn, means that evaluation of EAPs is very difficult to quantify in dollar terms.

Who needs an EAP?

The question 'who needs an EAP?' may well be posed. Unfortunately, there appears to be no typical profile of a corporate EAP user. Factors such as size, type of work, level of technology and composition of the workforce all seem to vary. The one constant factor is that EAPs are found in organisations that exhibit a genuine concern for their employees. Managers in such organisations show a readiness to invest in their people programs; they demonstrate a commitment to the well-being of their staff. Each organisation is different in its goals, culture, problems, technology, and so on, so there can be no single answer that will suit every situation. HR practitioners, given that they may well be placed in the key role of managing the scheme, will need to look carefully at the advantages and disadvantages of each approach. Finally, they will need to ensure that the EAP integrates with and builds upon existing human resource management programs.

Employee assistance programs will certainly be a key component of proactive human resource management operations of the future. Practitioners should take heed that in many ways the future is already with us.

Employee discipline

Disciplining employees who occasionally, or consistently, infringe organisational standards, is perceived generally by their supervisors as a difficult and unpleasant task. Growing concern with employee rights in the marketplace, discrimination, privacy and equity considerations appear to further complicate the disciplinary process.

The purpose of discipline in the workplace should, however, be perceived clearly as a genuine attempt to ensure that expected employee behaviour and performance are maintained to required organisational standards. Just as employee counselling seeks to identify personal problems and efficiently resolve them, discipline processes aim to recognise and correct unacceptable work practices for the benefit of the employee and organisation.

Links between discipline and employee dismissals are often overemphasised. A strategic approach to discipline will avoid the costs of dismissal, including possible claims of unfairness, by ensuring that early diagnosis and modification of worker behaviour results in corrected performance, not dismissal.

While unconnected processes, employee counselling and discipline actions may occur simultaneously. An identified problem with work behaviour may result in referral of the employee to a counsellor for personal problems, as well as disciplinary procedures in the workplace. Consistent infringements, or negligent behaviour (e.g. smoking in hazardous areas), may result in instant dismissal, based upon clearly established and union-agreed policies. These cases should, however, be rare.

The crucial elements of discipline processes include clear policies, equity across organisations and offences, union agreements, careful examination of the causes, well-documented records and appropriate appeals procedures.

Employee rights

Employee rights are the guarantees that employees expect from their employers, and are usually enshrined in industrial relations awards, Industrial Relations Commission determinations and legislation. The occupational health and safety, equal employment opportunity and affirmative action, and privacy legislation codify specific employee rights, along with leave, superannuation and workers' compensation entitlements.

The failure of employers to observe these requirements in their disciplinary processes may result in costly legal action, damage to organisational reputation or employee morale. On the other hand, any employer who fails to discipline wayward employees risks lost productivity, lowered morale and work satisfaction.

Organisations that establish programs of substance abuse testing, employee searches or surveillance, and associated disciplinary processes, should pay particular attention to employee rights (e.g. privacy, duty of care, equity) in their activities and records.

Disciplinary policies and procedures

Where disciplinary action is taken against an employee, it must be for justifiable reasons and there should be effective policies and procedures to guide its use. Disciplinary policies and procedures should cover a number of important areas to ensure thorough coverage. Exhibit 9.15 presents a disciplinary process model that illustrates the areas where provisions should be established. The model also shows the logical sequence in which disciplinary steps should be carried out to ensure enforceable decisions.

A major responsibility of the HR department is to develop, and to have top management approve, its disciplinary policies and procedures. Such development, however, must involve the participation of supervisors and managers who must carry out these policies. The HR department is also responsible for ensuring that both policies and disciplinary actions are consistent across the organisation and particular offences, and conform to legal and award requirements.

The primary responsibility for preventing or correcting disciplinary problems rests with an employee's immediate superior. The supervisor is the person best able to observe evidence of unsatisfactory behaviour or performance, and to discuss the matter with the employee. Discipline is but one of the components of a supervisor's performance management program.

Accordingly, supervisors should attempt to use a problem-solving, positive approach to discipline, aiming to uncover the reasons for the offence or behavioural problem, and to devise appropriate solutions. Often, the initial discussion with an employee may effectively resolve the issue.

Failure to confront the problem at an early stage may lead to its aggravation. Delays in taking such action make it more difficult to justify and may encourage other employees to feel that such behaviours are acceptable.

Exhibit 9.15 The disciplinary model

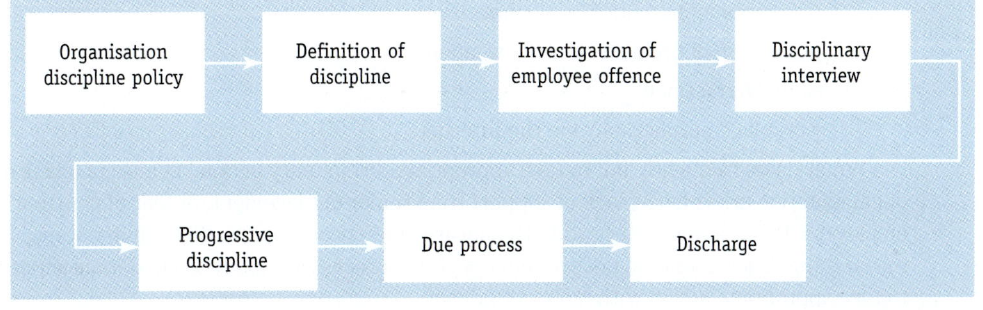

Common disciplinary issues noted by HR managers include:

- attendance problems
  - unexcused absence
  - chronic absenteeism
  - unexcused/excessive tardiness
  - leaving without permission.
- dishonesty and related problems
  - theft
  - falsifying employment application
  - wilfully damaging organisational property
  - punching another employee's time card
  - falsifying work records.
- work performance problems
  - failure to complete work assignments
  - producing substandard products or services
  - failure to meet established production requirements.
- on-the-job behaviour problems
  - intoxication at work
  - insubordination
  - horseplay
  - smoking in unauthorised places
  - fighting
  - gambling
  - failure to use safety devices
  - failure to report injuries
  - carelessness
  - sleeping on the job
  - using abusive or threatening language with supervisors
  - possession of narcotics or alcohol
  - possession of firearms or other weapons
  - sexual harassment
  - workplace pornography via the Internet.

Supervisors frequently fail to take appropriate disciplinary action because of a lack of documentation or evidence, lack of support from senior management, or fear of confronting employees. Policies that clearly state the nature of offences, specific disciplinary steps, researching aspects and the positive effects of this process are likely to encourage supervisors to take appropriate action with more confidence.

Organisational rules

Rules concerning expected standards of employee behaviour should ideally be widely distributed, periodically reviewed, and preferably written with adequate explanation and clear purposes.

Undertaking disciplinary action

Effective disciplinary action usually comprises four basic steps:

1   documentation of employee misconduct

2   the investigative interview

3   progressive discipline

4   correction or dismissal.

Each step will now be considered separately.

Documentation of employee misconduct

Many supervisors fail to effectively impose disciplinary procedures because they have insufficient records of an employee's misconduct. Failure to record such actions often results in the reversal of any subsequent disciplinary action. The maintenance of accurate and complete records is thus essential for effective disciplinary action.

Such records could include the date, time and location of the incident(s), the actual behaviour(s), witnesses, consequences of employee performance, prior discussions about the problem, disciplinary action taken and specific improvements anticipated, further proposed actions and follow-up dates.

Questions to consider in disciplinary investigations

1   In very specific terms, what is the offence charged?

–   Is management sure it fully understands the charge against the employee?

–   Was the employee really terminated for insubordination, or did the employee merely refuse a request by management?

2   Did the employee know he or she was doing something wrong?

–   What rule or provision was violated?

–   How would the employee know of the existence of the rule?

–   Was the employee warned of the consequence?

3   Is the employee guilty?

–   What are the sources of facts?

–   Is there direct or only indirect evidence of guilt?

–   Has anyone talked to the employee to hear his or her side of the situation?

4   Are there extenuating circumstances?

–   Were there conflicting orders given by different supervisors?

–   Does anybody have reason to want to persecute this employee?

–   Was the employee provoked by a manager or another employee?

5   Has the rule been uniformly enforced?

–   Have all managers applied the rule consistently?

–   What punishment have previous offenders received?

–   Were any other employees involved in this offence and possibly guilty?

6   Is the offence related to the workplace?

–   Is there evidence that the offence hurt the organisation?

–   Is management making a moral judgement or a business judgement?

7 What is the employee's past work record?
   – Years of service?
   – Years or months in present job?
   – Personnel record as a whole, especially disciplinary record?

The investigative interview

A good rule of thumb for supervisors is that interviews concerning employee misconduct should be held as soon as possible after the infraction. Using the so-called 'hot stove' rule implies an immediate reaction and the employee should be notified of their specific misbehaviour and appropriate remedial steps. This interview should focus on the particular problems, avoid discussion of personalities, and allow the employee adequate opportunity to explain his or her reasons. It may be useful to notify employees of their misbehaviour, in writing, prior to the interview and to consider permitting them to have a third party (e.g. colleague, union representative) present during this interview.

In many cases, the investigative interview may be all that is required to correct employee behaviour.

Progressive discipline

Progressive discipline is the application of corrective measures by increasing degrees. It is designed to motivate employees to correct their misconduct voluntarily. However, the sequence and severity of the disciplinary action will vary with the type of offence and its circumstances. Severe negligence (e.g. careless driving, violence) may result in dismissal following the initial interview; minor misbehaviours (e.g. absenteeism, productivity problems) may proceed to progressive disciplinary actions.

Typical progressive disciplinary procedures involve four steps:

1 oral warning (or counselling)

2 written warning(s)

3 suspension with (or without) pay

4 dismissal.

Records are usually made, preferably signed by both supervisor and employee, at the last three stages. The third-party representative may be present at all stages, and may witness (as an observer) all subsequent records.

Correction or dismissal

When employees fail, after frequent attempts, to conform to organisational rules and regulations, the final disciplinary action may be dismissal. As earlier stated, this stage should be avoided where possible but, if necessary, should be based upon comprehensive and justifiable grounds. Dismissal can be costly, not only in terms of separation payments, recruitment or replacement processes and the possibility of 'unfair dismissal' litigation (see Chapter 3), but also on the morale of remaining employees. It should therefore be demonstrably equitable, based upon job-relevant criteria and 'fair' processes.

Some useful guidelines for effective dismissal include:

- Focus on the dismissal and its causes.
- Present an objective, straightforward, firm decision.
- Hold a brief, businesslike and private interview.
- Avoid personal accusations and feelings.
- Provide information concerning severance pay.
- Give the employee information on the type of reference to be supplied.

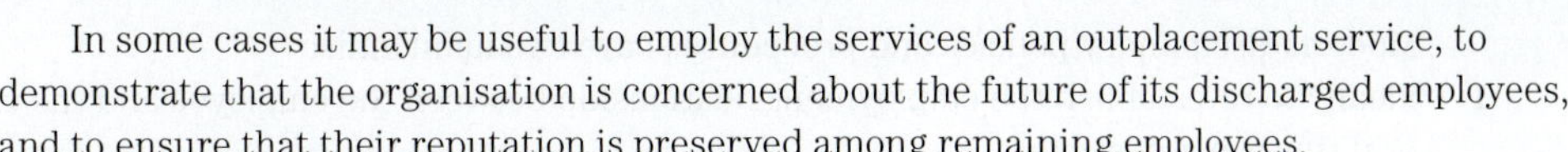

In some cases it may be useful to employ the services of an outplacement service, to demonstrate that the organisation is concerned about the future of its discharged employees, and to ensure that their reputation is preserved among remaining employees.

Appealing disciplinary actions

Effective disciplinary processes provide access to appeals mechanisms, to ensure equity and demonstrably 'reasonable' procedures. Such mechanisms may include reviews by higher or more neutral authorities (e.g. senior managers, HR managers); grievance procedures; or referral to external bodies (e.g. Anti-Discrimination Board, Administrative Decisions Judicial Review authorities). Ombudsmen, both government and private sector (e.g. the banking sector), may also be consulted by aggrieved employees.

All such options should be made available to employees who may feel disadvantaged by disciplinary actions. Above all, disciplinary procedures should be detailed in clear, explicit policies, and be distributed to all employees along with job-relevant behavioural and performance standards. The disciplinary process should be adequately defined for both supervisors and employees. Ideally, unions should be involved in the policy formulation, and supervisors trained in its application.

Discipline should be perceived as merely one of the tools available to supervisors for ensuring that all employees conform to (or exceed) section and organisational objectives, normally without excessive punishment.

The HR manager has a substantive role to play here in ensuring that policies reflect organisational imperatives, are consistent and equitable, and avoid costly legal challenges or adversely affect employee morale and productivity.

Legal aspects of disciplinary processes

In view of recent legal challenges to disciplinary procedures (e.g. Quinn; *Gorgevski v Bostik (Australia) Pty Ltd*), employers should carefully ensure that all proper and reasonable steps are taken for equity, and to avoid expensive litigation. In particular, where awards contain clauses specifying that 'termination of employment shall not be harsh, unjust or unreasonable' special care should be taken.[82]

Specifically, employers should ensure that new, or stiffer, penalties for prescribed types of misconduct are clearly justifiable, effectively communicated and understood by employees and their unions. Disciplinary policies and procedures should also demonstrate explanations of complaints and why they should not be dismissed. Summary dismissal (or dismissal without notice) is particularly prone to complaint, appeal or subsequent litigation.[83]

Despite these potential difficulties for employers, properly prepared, communicated and conducted discipline processes should avoid litigation and provide considerable benefits for both employers and their employees.

Termination of employment

(This section was contributed by Harry Anneveld)

Termination of employment can be initiated by either the employee or the employer. In this section we deal with terminations initiated by the employer. With the exclusion of redundancy, these fall into two main categories:

1   dismissal without notice, also referred to as instant or summary dismissal

2   dismissal with notice.

Modern disciplinary policies and procedures have two main aims:

1 ideally to re-establish the employment relationship between the employee and the employer, or if this is not possible,

2 to ensure that the employee is treated fairly and the employer terminates the employee for the right reasons and in the right way.

When replacement costs and the loss of experience are taken into account it is generally cheaper to re-establish the employment relationship than to terminate the employee. This should be taken into account before dismissing the employee. If there is any unfairness in the reasons for the dismissal or in the treatment of the employee this cost could, in certain circumstances, be increased by up to 26 weeks of salary payments. In a very small business this could equate to an amount that puts the viability of the business at risk – hence the debate in employer and conservative political circles.

Over the past 10 to 20 years there have been some momentous changes. These have included:

- structural change in many Australian industries

- a considerable move from employment in manufacturing to the service industries

- considerable improvement in the productivity of Australian businesses.

This was achieved across both Labor and Coalition governments at both state and federal levels. A substantial proportion of this productivity improvement was achieved through reductions in employee numbers, especially among older employees.

These governments also made changes to industrial relations legislation and systems. These changes, it could be argued, have mirrored the philosophical beliefs of the political parties concerned. Many of the changes have affected the balance of power between the players in the employment relationship.

In the latter part of this period, unemployment has reduced to levels not seen for many decades. Generations X and Y have joined the workforce and are gradually replacing the babyboomers. The new generations have not known high levels of unemployment. They are also more self-confident than their babyboomer parents.

The union movement continues to find it hard to recruit Generations X and Y employees in an era of dwindling babyboomer members. The unions are also grappling with adapting to the brave new world in relation to the tactics they employ, the institutions in which they must operate and their relevance to the new generations.

For many organisations there have been consequences:

- Employers have taught employees that they are expendable.

- Employers have lost the experience of older and long-serving employees.

- Employers have resorted to the documenting of policies, procedures, position descriptions, etc. to try and overcome the loss of experience.

- Employees' commitment to an employer is limited to what is good for their career.

- Employee initiative has suffered due to the limitations of over-documentation.

- Many employers have become as bureaucratic as they were before the need for structural change was recognised.

Included in the most recent changes in federal legislation has been the amendment to the unfair dismissal laws. The principle behind this was to protect small business from claims that could debilitate the business. It has been argued that, under the new legislation, 100 employees is not 'small business' and that the changes have gone beyond this principle.

The debate over the application of the new federal legislation to the states continues.

Exhibit 9.16   Managing employee performance overseas

The management of overseas employees raises many different and complex issues for human resource management, as discussed below.

The ultimate evaluation of the performance of expatriates and their workforces rests with the business results and outcomes achieved at the completion of the overseas assignment. Was the overseas operation effectively established (or has it grown)? Were new product markets successfully developed, and was the return on investment the best that could have been achieved during the period? Was the necessary network (e.g. customers, suppliers, governments) for future organisational growth established?

The answers to these broad business questions will necessarily depend on such factors as:

- the reality (or unreality) of business strategies

- the nature of the overseas venture (e.g. joint venture, strategic alliance, multinational) and the degree of support given by the parent company; the stability (e.g. social, political, economic) of the host country environment

- the relevance of staffing strategies (e.g. mix of home, host and third country nationals, skills and competency levels, etc.).

The standards of business performance (or benchmarks) against which such performance indicators are measured (e.g. regional countries, global standards, home country levels) also need to be factored into the determination of the effectiveness of the expatriate's performance. Are they too high, too low or just right?

As an example, an expatriate manager may be assessed as a very effective performer because they met (or exceeded) sales targets, even though they alienated their local subordinates or damaged good relationships with host country governments through overaggressive methods. Conversely, an expatriate manager may be regarded as an underachiever if they fail to meet financial goals because of problems with suppliers, local industrial relations difficulties or a focus on longer-term governmental relationships.

These examples suggest that the assessment of an expatriate's performance needs to take into account not only the outcomes they achieve, but also the environmental issues they face in diverse host countries, and the short- and long-term benefits of their activities. For host and third country nationals, performance appraisal and management schemes may need to be different from those familiar to the parent company, in order to appropriately reflect the different socio-cultural environments in which they operate.

Expatriate performance criteria and competencies

Mendenhall and Oddou[84] suggest that the broad international skills that expatriates must exhibit during their overseas assignment include:

- being able to manage a workforce with cultural and subcultural differences

- being able to plan for, and conceptualise, the dynamics of a complex multinational environment

- being open-minded about alternative methods for solving problems
- being flexible in dealing with people and systems
- understanding the interdependencies among the firm's domestic and foreign operations.

These broad expatriate performance criteria encapsulate the need for cross-cultural management competencies, and imply that the identified achievements of expatriate managers are directly transferable to the management of operations back in the home country. Organisations, therefore, which ignore or fail to appreciate the value of such competencies to home country operations do so at their own peril.

More significantly, Mendenhall and Oddou suggest that the relevant performance criteria for expatriates should include (at least) their 'technical information and expertise', 'adjustment to the new culture' and 'environmental factors'.[85] Dowling agrees with the need to factor 'environmental' issues (e.g. industrial relations, social and economic factors) into performance evaluation schemes, but adds that 'task' (i.e. the nature of the expatriate's job, the length of the assignment, the degree of required interaction with the host country) and 'personality' issues (i.e. qualities of the expatriates and their families relevant to the host country) may be equally as important.[86] The three writers emphasise that the appraisal of expatriates may need to differ from methods used in the home country, in order to properly take into account the diverse characteristics of the foreign environment.

Thus, the evaluation of expatriate performance may use different criteria or different levels of effectiveness in different countries of operation. An Australian company operating in Hong Kong, Indonesia, Singapore and India (for example) will need to set variable performance standards and to measure them sensitively in relation to developments in the diverse host countries.

Performance appraisal schemes for such expatriates will both (a) need to modify criteria to fit the overseas position and country characteristics, and (b) include an expatriate's insights as part of the evaluation. The latter aspect acknowledges that the performance appraisal of expatriates is ideally a joint process involving host country managers (and/or peers and subordinates), parent company senior managers and the expatriates themselves.

While all of these assessors may have inherent biases (e.g. host country employees will perceive performance from their own cultural frames of reference; parent company managers will often suffer from the 'tyranny' of distance; expatriates are likely to be highly subjective), the combination of views included is likely to be more accurate than the appraisal completed by a single parent company manager. In some countries, local employees may be reluctant to express their negative perceptions of expatriates due to 'hierarchical' or 'face' issues.

Appraisal of the expatriate is, however, an important function for the business itself and for the expatriate. For the business, it indicates some of the potential (or actual) problems likely to be faced in pursuit of its objectives and may suggest practical solutions or more appropriate criteria for subsequent expatriates. For the expatriates themselves, performance appraisals may influence their promotion potential and type of position received on returning home.

Appraisal of host and third country nationals

The criteria against which host and third country nationals are assessed are usually closely related to specific job (or task) criteria, although in the latter case, adaptability to the host country may also be included. Region-centric staffing strategies are usually based upon the demonstrated ability of third country nationals to adapt to the chosen host country, or previous experience in such operations. In such cases 'cultural adaptability' may form part of these appraisals, but technical expertise or managerial competence (as in the parent company) assumes more importance.

In the case of host country employees, there may be significant obstacles to the application of home country performance appraisal schemes due to the cultural barriers based upon 'collectivism', work and social ethics, or 'face' issues. As an example, it is often difficult to implement individual performance appraisal programs in countries such as Indonesia and the People's Republic of China because of the difficulty of giving employees 'negative' feedback. Similarly, assessments of 'leadership ability' may prove inappropriate in collectivist cultures such as Thailand and Malaysia, where such workplace qualities may not be culturally appropriate.

In such workforces, performance appraisals should still be conducted, but modified to conform to cultural demands. For example, rather than critiquing individual employee performance, it may be more appropriate to conduct generalised discussions on the levels of performance, and to identify positive solutions to productivity issues. The benefits of such modifications to workplace processes and procedures can then be emphasised, and subsequently reinforced with positive, future-oriented reward systems.

Designing performance management systems abroad

Earlier discussions suggest that performance management systems for both expatriates and their workforces need to be modified in order to reflect the influences of the host country environment on the overall performance of their companies. Performance management systems, incorporating performance appraisal, employee counselling and discipline, as well as access to career development opportunities, will depend upon the nature of the tasks involved, the required degree of interaction between expatriates and the host country environment, parent company perspectives and procedures, and the ability and desire of the parent company to adapt its appraisal schemes to host country operations. Each company will, of course, adapt its appraisal programs differently in diverse socio-cultural environments.

Summary

The success of an organisation depends largely on the performance of its human resources. To determine the contributions of each individual, it is necessary to have a formal appraisal program with clearly stated objectives. Carefully defined performance standards that are relevant and reliable are essential foundations for evaluation.

If appraisal interviews and any corrective actions are to be based on valid information, managers and supervisors should be thoroughly trained in the particular methods they will use in evaluating their subordinates. Participation in developing rating scales, such as BARS, automatically provides such training. Whatever the methods used they should meet the objectives of the performance appraisal.

The degree to which the performance appraisal program benefits the organisation and its members is directly related to the quality of the appraisal interviews that are conducted. Interviewing skills are best developed through instruction and supervised practice. In the interview, deficiencies in employee performance can be discussed and plans for improvement can be made.

Likewise, organisations need to consider the cost-effectiveness of introducing employee counselling programs. Where a strategic HRM package has been established, HR managers may find that the addition of an EAP will assist in establishing a climate where employees feel that they are more than mere numbers on the payroll.

Key terms

360-degree feedback 339
balanced scorecard 345
behaviourally anchored rating scales (BARS) 342
central tendency 333
disciplining 364
employee assistance program (EAP) 358
employee counselling 355
halo error 332
leniency 332
management by objectives (MBO) 343
peer review 338
performance management 347
performance review 329
rating scales 340
recency effect 333
self-appraisal 339
upward appraisal 339

Key debate issues

1 The search for the perfect appraisal form is akin to the search for the Holy Grail. In reality, the form used may well be a secondary consideration. Other factors will be of primary concern if the scheme is to be successful. Discuss.

2 'Employee counselling is just another example of management playing big brother. What possible good can a third party do? If employees cannot take the heat, let them get out of the kitchen!' What are the implications of this attitude?

3 Evaluate Deming's argument that MBO 'nourishes short-term performance, annihilates long-term planning, builds fear, demolishes teamwork, nourishes rivalry and politics'. Is there any place for performance review in a 'quality' organisation?

4 'In today's world of work, where a plethora of industrial legislation makes dismissal almost impossible, employers are better off not hiring in the first place.' Evaluate this view.

Case study 9.1

'Here, just sign the form'

'Tom,' said supervisor Nikita Houtgraff, 'would you stop by my office about 15 minutes before you clock out? I want to give you your annual performance appraisal. It won't take long, and I know you'll want to leave by five o'clock'.

Tom Blythe had forgotten that it was that time of the year again, but he was looking forward to the meeting because he wanted to discuss some new performance standards for his job. Also, he was slightly worried about the appraisal because he didn't think his performance had been up to par over the past year.

Promptly at 4.45 p.m., Tom knocked on Nikita's office door and was asked to come in. As he entered, Tom found his supervisor rushing to get some last-minute orders dated so they could be filled by the late shift. As Tom sat down, Nikita began, 'I've filled out your performance appraisal, so why don't you look it over and sign it. You'll see that I've given you excellent ratings on all the factors, but everyone in the crew got excellent ratings this year. I was really impressed with how everyone pitched it to get the Hobart order out this month. That order was really important to the company. I don't have anything else to add: just keep up the good work, and I'll get you a good raise.'

Tom looked the appraisal over and signed it. He could tell Nikita was really busy, so he thought he had better leave. Besides, he didn't want to ruin his chances for a salary increase. However, as he left her office, he felt disappointed with the interview.

Questions

1 Discuss Nikita's handling of Tom's performance appraisal interview.

2 Place yourself in Nikita's position, and develop a checklist to conduct the interview effectively.

Case study 9.2

'Just how good am I, doctor?'

Christian Simmons, a middle-aged man with several university degrees, had been employed by the government in a public health position prior to coming to General Hospital. At General, he served as the Mental Health Educator under Dr Janice Lee, Chief of the Mental Health Services Division. Christian's job involved giving lectures to schools, business firms and clubs upon request and conducting training classes on mental health education for new teachers, social workers and nurses. He was proud of his performance record, which contained mainly superior ratings and nothing below excellent. He liked his boss, too, not only because she had given him an opportunity to use his talents, but because she was always kind and considerate.

Performance evaluations at General were made every 12 months, and the customary procedure was for the reports to be prepared and placed in each employee's mail box. Employees could discuss them with their supervisors if they wished to do so, but they were expected to sign them. One day Christian found his appraisal in his mail box and became very upset over it. Instead of superior and excellent ratings on the scale, he found excellent and good ratings. There was no explanation given for the drop in ratings, only the statement that 'Mr Simmons continues to do good work as in the past'. Christian asked to see Dr Lee immediately.

The interview between Christian and Dr Lee took place that afternoon. Christian was quite blunt and wanted to know what was wrong with his work. Dr Lee explained that his work was fine and she could not understand why he was upset. Christian pointed out the difference in this last rating compared with others Dr Lee had given him in the two years he had been there, and asked Dr Lee to explain the difference. Dr Lee said that she thought it was a good appraisal and explained that she had changed her methods of appraisal. She refused to explain further, but assured Christian that his work was good and encouraged him to maintain this high standard. Christian did not want to sign the appraisal, but later conceded, inserting 'signed under protest' under his name. He then made plans for appealing against the rating to the Medical Superintendent, and if necessary the Hospital Board.

Questions

1　What are the issues here?
2　How would you advise Dr Lee?

Case study 9.3

'But I didn't mean any harm'

On 5 July 2000, Brett Warren was asked to resign his position, or be dismissed, following several claims of sexual harassment being levelled at him by a 25-year-old female colleague, Kate Lee, who had recently announced her engagement following a lengthy relationship. This action followed several lengthy investigations, both of which indicated that Warren clearly had breached not only corporate policy but also several pieces of state and federal anti-discrimination legislation – and to cap it off, the *Crimes Act*.

To make matters worse, prior to his termination Warren worked in the corporate human resource division from where the corporate policy had been formulated and all education programs emanated. His work station was some 20 metres from the Director of Corporate Human Resources, Robert Scott, and adjacent to Kate. The common perception was that Kate and Brett enjoyed a close but professional working relationship. There was no visible sign of conflict between the two, quite the opposite.

Warren's 15-year work record was excellent with no blemishes whatsoever. Married with two teenage daughters, Warren's behaviour at work was almost introverted and he was seen as a 'solid citizen' by their manager, Nicholas Min, whose work station was within earshot of both Warren and Lee. Needless to say, Nicholas Min was 'amazed' when these allegations finally surfaced. He has no idea that this behaviour had been occurring right in front of him over such a long period.

It was later revealed that the harassment had been occurring for some five years involving not only Kate but several female employees before her; each of whom had left the organisation due to the ongoing harassment. Not one had complained as they did not want to 'cause trouble' at a time when the company was going through massive downsizing. Specifically, they did not want to risk their redundancy money.

Robert Scott was even more amazed when six months earlier, Kate finally came to him with her first allegation. As Director of corporate HR, Scott doubled as Director of Affirmative Action and was not only responsible for corporate policy on harassment but had written the policy personally – such was his commitment to eliminating any such practices from the company. He had also personally conducted an educational roadshow right across the organisation some 12 months earlier. His was the public face of EEO/AA for the organisation and now he had what appeared to be the most serious complaint to date within his own division! And the alleged perpetrator was the most unlikely person to have engaged in such practices.

To say his head was spinning was a gross understatement. His informal practice was to resolve all such complaints prior to the end of the week so that people did not go home for the weekend to 'stew' over the issue and possibly blow it out of proportion. Kate Lee approached Scott at 4 p.m. on Friday 28 January.

Kate asked for a private meeting with Scott and as he showed her to a quiet meeting room he began to feel a sense of unease. Kate reported that her relationship with Warren had been very good for several years and they often engaged in many friendly discussions covering not only work-related issues but their personal lives. Kate had even been introduced to Warren's wife and teenage daughters on several occasions. When Kate announced her engagement she brought her fiancé in several times for lunch, at which time she introduced him to several people she worked with including Warren, Min and Scott.

It was at this point (her engagement) that her working relationship with Warren seemed to change. He seemed more distant but quite separately 'things' started to happen. She noticed that someone was leaving soft porn photos on her desk – the sort you would find in a number of popular and freely available men's magazines. She also found typed telephone messages asking her to call back. When she did the number was that of a local brothel. As time went on, the photos became more explicit and, moreover, Warren had begun to ask quite intimate questions about her relationship with her fiancé. When she declined to discuss her relationship, she noticed Warren's attitude towards her becoming more distant again.

This sequence of events continued for six months before Kate tried to raise the issue with her manager, Nicholas Min. However, she had no real evidence that Warren was behind the photos and telephone messages, which in turn were not only continuing but becoming more offensive. Kate had approached Min the previous December but declined to reveal her suspicions about who was behind the harassment. Min's response was quite simple: 'If you have no evidence you just have to put up with the situation until you do. In the interim, please focus on your work.'

The matter came to crisis point for Kate in early January, when for whatever reason, Warren became far more aggressive towards her, insisting she tell him about her sexual relations with her fiancé. Kate alleged he then went on to 'touch' her. At this point she claimed that she asked him in very clear terms to stop harassing her and he was not to touch her again under any circumstances. Kate then went on sick leave for two weeks in an attempt to avoid any further contact with Warren. She also needed time out to consider her next course of action as she knew that she had to act now or leave the organisation.

On her return she asked to meet with Scott. Having listened to the allegations, Scott decided on a private meeting with Warren whereby he outlined the claims made by Lee. Scott was more than a little staggered when Warren admitted to all claims without any argument. In fact, Warren's view was that Scott should dismiss him immediately as 'I will only do it again if you do not'.

Scott declined to do so as he did not want to be accused later of not following due process and he was more than aware of the implications of recently introduced unfair dismissal legislation. Indeed, he suspected that Warren was setting him up for a claim under that legislation.

Scott then called for Min to join him and outlined the claims. Min was both horrified and amazed that Lee could level such claims against someone as dedicated as Warren. He was even more horrified and amazed when Scott revealed that Warren had confessed to all claims. Their decision was that Warren be severely counselled and that Min watch the situation very carefully. This decision was privately communicated to Kate by both Scott and Min. While uneasy about remaining at work alongside Warren, Kate hoped that this would be the end of the matter. She even hoped that in time she could renew her previous working relationship with Warren.

On 5 July, Kate asked Scott again for a private meeting to which he agreed, albeit with a sinking feeling deep inside. Before they sat down Kate announced that the harassment had continued from the very day that they had last spoken and was now at the point where, if the company didn't take formal action, she would have to resign and take the matter to her solicitors. Kate then informed Scott that a number of other female former employees had rung her to tell her that they too had left the company because of Warren's harassment. They were also considering their options now that the matter had come out in the open.

Scott once again called Warren to his office. This time he gave Warren an ultimatum: resign now or be sacked. As Scott walked Warren to his car Warren's only comment was, 'I didn't mean any harm ... what will I tell my wife and daughters?'

Questions

1 Evaluate Scott's handling of this issue.

2 Evaluate Min's performance.

3 What steps must be put in place to ensure that this type of behaviour is not repeated?

4 What is likely to happen should Kate take her complaints to the Anti-Discrimination Board?

Further readings

Ainsworth M., Smith N., Millership A. 2002. *Managing performance: Managing people*, Frenchs Forest, Pearson Education.

Buon T., Compton R.L. 1990. 'The development of alcohol and other drug programs in the workplace', *Journal of Occupational Health and Safety*, 6(4).

Cascio W. 1996. 'Managing for maximum performance', *hrmonthly*, September.

Coles A. 2003. *Counselling in the workplace*, Berkshire, Open University Press.

DeCieri H., Kramar R. 2003. *Human resource management in Australia*, Sydney, McGraw-Hill.

Deming W.E. 1982. *Out of the crisis*, Cambridge, Cambridge University Press.

Dowling P., Welch D., Schuler R. 1999. *International HRM*, Cincinnatti, South Western.

Greenhaus J., Callahan G., Godshalk N. 2000. *Career management*, Ohio, South Western.

Levinson H. 1970. 'Management by whose objectives?', *Harvard Business Review*, July–August.

Maier N. 1976. *The appraisal interview: Three basic approaches*, San Diego, University Associates.

McGregor D. 1957. 'An uneasy look at performance appraisal', *Harvard Business Review*, May–June, pp. 13–38.

McGregor D. 1960. *The human side of enterprise*, New York, McGraw-Hill, p. 86.

Nankervis A.R., Leece P. 1997. 'Performance appraisal: Two steps forward, one step back?', *Asia Pacific HRM*, 35(2), pp. 88–92.

Wiesner R., Millett B. 2003. *Human resource management*, Brisbane, Wiley.

Endnotes

1   Nankervis A.R., Compton R.L., Baird M. 2002. *Strategic HRM*, Southbank, Thomson Learning, p. 390.

2   Wilson J.P. 2001. 'Performance appraisal: An obstacle to training and development?', *Career Development International*, 6(2), p. 93.

3   *HR Report*, 2003. Issue 307, Thomson CDP, p. 8.

4   Nankervis A.R., Leece P. 1997. 'Performance appraisal: Two steps forward, one step back?', *Asia Pacific HRM*, 35(2), pp. 88–92.

5   Nankervis A., Compton R.L. 2006. 'Performance management: Theory in practice?', *Asia Pacific Journal of Human Resources*, 44(1), pp. 83–101.

6   Rheem H. 1996, 'Performance management programs: Do they make any difference?', *Harvard Business Review*, September–October, pp. 3–4.

7   McDonald D., Smith A. 1995. 'A proven connection: Performance management and business results', *Compensation and Benefits Review*, 27(1), pp. 59–62.

8   Wilson, 2001. op. cit., pp. 93–4.

9   Herzberg F., Mausner B., Snyderman B. 1959. *The motivation to work*, New York, John Wiley.

10   Cascio W. 1996. 'Managing for maximum performance', *hrmonthly*, September, pp. 10–13.

11   Deming E. 1982. *Out of the crisis*, Cambridge, Cambridge University Press.

12   Gabris G., Ihrke K. 2001. 'Does performance appraisal contribute to heightened levels of employee burnout? The results of one study', *Public Personnel Management*, 30(20), pp. 157–72.

13   McGregor D. 1957. 'An uneasy look at performance appraisal', *Harvard Business Review*, May–June, pp. 13–38.

14   Levinson H. 1970. 'Management by whose objectives?', *Harvard Business Review*, July–August, pp. 125–34.

15   Glendenning P.M. 2002. 'Performance management: Pariah or messiah?', *Public Personnel Management*, Summer, pp. 161–78.

16 Lawler E. 1994. 'Performance management: The next generation', *Compensation and Benefits Review*, 26(3), pp. 16–20; Glover R., 1996. 'Why are we ignoring performance appraisal research?', *Parks and Recreation*, 31(11), pp. 125–8.

17 ACCIRT, 1999. *Australia at work*, Sydney, Prentice Hall.

18 Screwvalla Z.S. 1988. 'Performance appraisals: A framework for effective implementation', *Australian Institute of Management News*, 28 September, p. 47.

19 Grensing-Pophal L. 2001. 'Motivate managers to review performance', *HR Magazine*, 46(3), pp. 44–8.

20 Joinson C. 2001. 'Making sure employees measure up', *HR Magazine*, 46(3), pp. 36–41.

21 Taylor G.S., Lehman C.M., Forrde C.M. 1989. 'How employee self-appraisals can help', *Supervisory Management*, 34(8), August, p. 32.

22 Bernardin H.J., Beatty R.W. 1984. *Performance appraisal: Assessing human behaviour at work*, Boston, Kent, p. 39.

23 Screwvalla Z.S. 1988. op. cit., p. 47.

24 CCH Australia 1988. *Employee assessment, appraisal and counselling*, 2nd edn, Sydney, CCH Australia.

25 Screwvalla Z.S. 1988. op. cit., p. 5.

26 Jacobs R., Kozlowski S. 1985. 'A closer look at halo error in performance ratings', *Academy of Management Journal*, 28(1), March, pp. 210–12.

27 De Cotis T., Petite A. 1985. 'The performance appraisal process: A model and some testable propositions', in R. Lansbury (ed.), *Performance appraisal*, South Melbourne, Macmillan, pp. 18–35.

28 Latham G.P., Wexley K.N. 1981. *Increasing productivity through performance appraisal*, Reading, Addison-Wesley, p. 116.

29 De Cotis and Petite, 1985. op. cit., p. 22.

30 Landy F.J., Farr J.L. 1980. 'Performance ratings', *Psychological Bulletin*, 87(1), January–February.

31 Nankervis A.R., Compton R.L. 2006. op. cit.

32 Overman S. 1989. 'Best appraisals measure goals not traits', *Resource*, 8(2), February, p. 16.

33 Nankervis A.R., Leece P. 1997. op. cit., pp. 89–92.

34 McGregor D. 1957. op. cit.

35 Day D. 1989. 'Performance management year-round', *Personnel*, 66(8), August, pp. 43–5.

36 Edwards M.R. 1989. 'Team evaluation and management system'. Paper presented at 9th Annual HRSP Conference, Houston, Texas, 17–19 April, p. 1.

37 Edwards M. 1990. 'Joint appraisal effort', *Personnel Journal*, 69(6), June, pp. 12–28.

38 McEvoy G.M., Butler P.F. 1987. 'User acceptance of peer appraisals in an industrial setting', *Personnel Psychology*, 40(4), Winter, pp. 785–99; Wood et al., 1988, in G. Palmer (ed.), *Australian personnel management: A reader*, South Melbourne, Macmillan, p. 83.

39 Ramsay M., Lehto H. 1994. 'The power of peer review', *Training and Development*, July, pp. 38–41.

40 McEvoy G.M. 1988. 'Evaluating the boss', *Personnel Administrator*, 33(9), September, pp. 115–20.

41 Beddison T. 1992. 'Workers are now evaluating their boss', presented on Radio 2UE.

42 Holloway J. 1999. 'A vehicle for change? A case study of performance improvement in the "new" public sector', *The International Journal of Public Sector Management*, 12(4), p. 351.

43 McGhee K. 1997. 'Going full circle', *Sydney Morning Herald*, 25 January (Employment section), p. 1.

44 Green B. 2002. 'Listening to leaders: Feedback on 360 degree feedback one year later', *Organisation Development Journal*, 20(1), pp. 8–16.

45 Nagle R. 1997. 'The 360 degree feedback avalanche', *hrmonthly*, September, pp. 18–20.

46 Trafford C. 1997. '360 degree feedback provides tool to focus development efforts', *hrmonthly*, October, pp. 32–3.

47 Nankervis A.R., Compton R.L. 2006. op. cit.

48 Peiperl M. 2001. 'Getting 360 degree feedback right', *Harvard Business Review*, January, pp. 142–7.

49 Gaskell R., Flanagan P. 1995. 'Upward feedback: Directions in management development', *Directions*, Summer, pp. 10–12.

50 Nankervis A.R., Compton R.L. 2006. op.cit.

51 Benson P., Buckley M.R., Hall S. 1988. 'The impact of rating scale format on rater accuracy: An evaluation of the mixed standard scale', *Journal of Management*, 14(3), September, pp. 415–23.

52 Griffin M.E. 1989. 'Personnel research in testing, selection, and performance appraisal', *Public Personnel Management*, 18(2), Summer, p. 130.

53 Bernardin H.J., Beatty R.W. 1984. op. cit., Chapter 2.

54 Kearney W.J. 1979. 'BARS: MBO's missing ingredient', *Personnel Journal*, January.

55 Drucker P. 1954. *The practice of management*, New York, Harper & Brothers.

56 Daley D. 1988. 'Performance appraisal and organisational success: Public employee perceptions in an MBO-based appraisal system', *Review of Public Personnel Administration*, 9(1), Fall, pp. 17–27.

57 Levinson H. 1970. op. cit.

58 Deming. E.W. 1982. op. cit., p. 102.

59 Boswell J. 1994. 'Performance appraisals: Do they still fit in?', *hrmonthly*, February, pp. 15–16.

60 Kaplan R.S., Norton D.P. 1996. 'Using the balanced scorecard as a strategic management system', *Harvard Business Review*, January–February, pp. 75–85.

61 Nankervis A., Compton R.L. 2006. 'Performance management: Theory in practice'. *Asia Pacific Journal of Human Resources*, 44(1), pp. 83–101.

62 Ibid.

63 Kramar R. 2006. *Cranet–Macquarie survey on international human resource management. Report on Australian findings*, pp. 18–19.

64 Performance Management Institute of Australia 2005, Employee Performance Management Survey, pp. 1–3.

65 Slattery P.D. 1985. 'Performance appraisal without stress', *Personnel Journal*, 64(2), February, pp. 49–51.

66 Buon T., Compton R.L. 1990. 'The development of alcohol and other drug programs in the workplace', *Journal of Occupational Health and Safety*, 6(4), pp. 265–77.

67 Ibid, p. 270.

68 Ibid, p. 271.

69 Filipowicz C. 1979. 'The troubled employee: Whose responsibility?', *Personnel Administrator*, pp. 17–33.

70 Vickers M., Kouzmin A. 1999. 'Employee assistance programs: From crisis support to sanctioned coercion and panopticist practices'. Paper presented at the Millennium World Conference in Critical Psychology, Sydney.

71 Walsh D. 1986. 'Employee assistance programs', *Health and Society*, 60(3), pp. 483–517.

72 Speroff B. 1955. 'There's danger in trying to make every supervisor a counsellor', *Personnel Journal*, 33(10), pp. 37–57.

73 Kuzmits F.E., Hammons H.E. 1979. 'Rehabilitating the troubled employee', *Personnel Journal*, April, pp. 239–50.

74 Buon T., Compton R.L. 1990. op. cit., p. 271.

75 Compton R.L. 1997. 'EAPs: Big brother or strategic HRM?' in D. Mortimer (ed.) *Readings in contemporary employment relations*, Centre for Employment Relations, Sydney, pp. 339–48.

76 Compton R.L. 2003. 'Employee assistance survey launched', *HR Report*, Thomson CDP, Issue 299, July, p. 8.

77 Parry B. 1996. 'EAPs in Australia and the Pacific'. Paper delivered to the 3rd National Conference on Alcohol and Other Drugs in the Workplace, Sydney, 27–29 March.

78 Berger Y. 1989. 'Disaster cocktail: Alcohol, drugs and poor work environments'. Paper presented to the National Conference on Alcohol and Other Drugs in the Workplace Conference, September.

79 Deves L. 1989. 'Policy and action in occupational health', *Journal of Occupational Health and Safety*, 5(2), April, p. 110.

80 Vickers M. and Kouzmin A. 1999. op. cit.

81 *HR Report* 2000. No. 225, 16 May, p. 1.

82 Brooks B. 1979. *Contract of employment*, Sydney, CCH Australia.

83 Clark R. 1984. *Private sector employment: The law of dismissal*, Industrial Relations, Sydney, Research Centre Monographs.

84 Mendenhall M., Oddou G. 1995. *Cases and readings in international human resource management*, Boston, PWS-Kent, p. 383.

85 Ibid, p. 387.

86 Dowling P., Schuler R., Welch D. 1998. *International dimensions of human resource management*, 3rd edn, Boston, PWS-Kent, p. 636.

Online reading

INFOTRAC® COLLEGE EDITION

For additional readings and review on management of performance, explore InfoTrac® College Edition, your online library. Go to: www.infotrac-college.com and search for any of the InfoTrac key terms listed below:

- ➤ appraisal interviews
- ➤ employee counselling
- ➤ employee discipline
- ➤ performance management
- ➤ performance review
- ➤ performance standards

CHAPTER 10
STRATEGIC REWARD MANAGEMENT

> Money motivates ... by rewarding certain behaviours; it also motivates by showing people what is valued in the organisation – it provides a cognitive map of the path people must take to succeed: i.e. to make more money.
>
> *Gupta and Shaw, 1998*

> At their best, group incentive plans give employees a new voice and stake in company success and ask as much of their minds as their hands .... Properly designed and implemented, group incentive plans are a win–win proposition.
>
> *Jerry McAdams and Elizabeth J. Hawk, 2000*

> In the US, average CEO pay has gone from 82 times average earnings to 400 times but so what? The only issue is are they doing a good job and delivering for shareholders.
>
> *Peter Swan, 2006*

> Emphasizing large bonuses is the last strategy we should use if we care about innovation. Do rewards motivate people? Absolutely. They motivate people to get rewards.
>
> *Alfie Kohn, 1993*

Objectives

After reading this chapter, you will be able to:

1. Understand the strategic considerations, challenges and choices involved in employee reward management.

2. Appreciate the importance of reward management in contemporary human resource management strategy and practice.

3. Identify the four main elements of a 'total reward' approach, namely financial, developmental, social and intrinsic rewards.

4. Compare and contrast the main components of employee remuneration.

5. Critically analyse the main types of performance-related reward, including individual and collective plans, short-term and long-term plans, and the advantages and disadvantages of each.

6. Understand the processes and challenges involved in the review and development of strategic reward systems.

Introduction

As the above quotations suggest, reward management is one of the most important yet problematic and controversial of all strategic human resource management functions. As experienced HR managers know, reward management is very easy to do badly – and difficult to do well. In this chapter, we explore the key strategic aspects of employee reward management, as well as examining the main tools and techniques for configuring a strategically aligned and effective reward system. We begin by examining the definition and variety of employee rewards, as well as the main objectives of an employee reward system.

'Rewards' and 'total reward'

A reward may be anything tangible or intangible that an organisation provides to its employees in exchange for the employee's potential or actual work contribution, and to which employees as individuals attach a positive value as a satisfier of certain self-defined needs. As such, rewards can be seen as including not only financial rewards (that is, 'pay,' 'remuneration,' or 'compensation'), but also rewards of a beneficial non-financial nature. Such a broad definition means that the options for configuring a reward system are extremely wide. A holistic approach thus means choosing financial rewards compatible with the various non-financial rewards that the organisation may offer its employees. This is commonly referred to as the 'total reward' approach.[1]

As Exhibit 10.1 indicates, rewards can be divided into two broad categories: 'intrinsic' and 'extrinsic.' Intrinsic rewards arise from the content of the job itself, including the interest and challenge which it provides, the task variety and autonomy, the degree of feedback, and the

Exhibit 10.1 Elements of 'total reward'

Extrinsic rewards

Financial rewards/remuneration:
- Fixed/base pay
- Cash benefits
- Performance-related pay

Developmental rewards:
- Learning, training & development
- Succession planning
- Career progression
- Other indirect/non-cash benefits

Social rewards:
- Organisational climate/management culture
- Performance support
- Work group affinity
- Work/life balance
- Other indirect/non-cash benefits

Intrinsic rewards:
- Job challenge
- Responsibility
- Autonomy
- Task variety

Source: Bamberry, L. & Frino, E. 2006. ADAM Report, 51, December (published by the Workplace Research Centre, The University of Sydney). Extract reproduced with permission.

meaning and significance attributed to it. It follows that one of the most important determinants of the level of intrinsic rewards in any organisation is the way in which its jobs are designed (see Chapter 5). Extrinsic rewards arise from factors associated with but external to the job that the employee does; that is, from the job context. Some theorists[2] argue that intrinsic factors are the most powerful motivators of work effort. Extrinsic rewards are of three main types: financial rewards, developmental rewards and social rewards. Developmental rewards cover those rewards associated with personal learning, development and career growth, such as skills training and performance and leadership coaching. Social rewards are those rewards and 'indirect' (or non-cash) benefits associated with the organisational climate, performance support, quality of supervision, work-group affinity, and opportunities for enhanced work–life balance, such as flexible work time arrangements, staff sabbaticals, fitness and wellness programs, and the like. Financial rewards are of three main types: base pay (the relatively fixed component of total remuneration); performance-related pay (which by definition varies with measured performance); and 'direct' benefits, such as employer contributions to superannuation and personal health insurance. Later in the chapter, we shall examine each of these three main categories of financial reward or remuneration in more detail.

A key step in framing a total reward approach is to determine the respective roles of financial and non-financial rewards. This, in turn, may require an audit of the organisation to identify what non-financial rewards it provides and to ascertain the extent to which these may assist the organisation to attract, retain and motivate employees. Organisations that offer high job security, that enjoy a high level of prestige and public esteem, or that provide opportunities for 'in-house' training and development, may not have to offer as high a level of financial reward as do competitors that offer much less on the non-financial side. At the other end of the spectrum, an organisation experiencing high labour turnover and low productivity, perhaps because its employees find their jobs uninteresting, may opt to increase financial rewards substantially in order to meet staffing and performance requirements. Alternatively, such an organisation may choose to emphasise intrinsic rewards through job enrichment to make the work more appealing. In formulating an optimal approach to total reward management, then, each organisation will need to consider various combinations of intrinsic and extrinsic rewards.

While non-financial rewards do constitute an increasingly important aspect of a 'total reward' approach, it is almost always financial rewards that are of primary importance in reward management practice. For this reason, our consideration of reward management options and methods will focus primarily on financial rewards. Even here, though, human resource managers now have a wide array of choices at their disposal.

Reward system objectives

What is it that an organisation hopes to obtain by offering rewards to its employees; that is, what should a system of reward management seek to do? An organisation's reward system will have four primary objectives:

- to *attract* (or 'buy') the right people at the right time for the right jobs, tasks or roles

- to *retain* the best people by satisfying their work-related needs and aspirations and recognising and rewarding their contribution

- to *develop* (or 'build') required workforce capabilities by recognising and rewarding employees for knowledge, skill and ability enhancement

- to *motivate* employees to contribute to the best of their capability by recognising and rewarding high individual and group contributions towards meeting the organisation's strategic objectives.

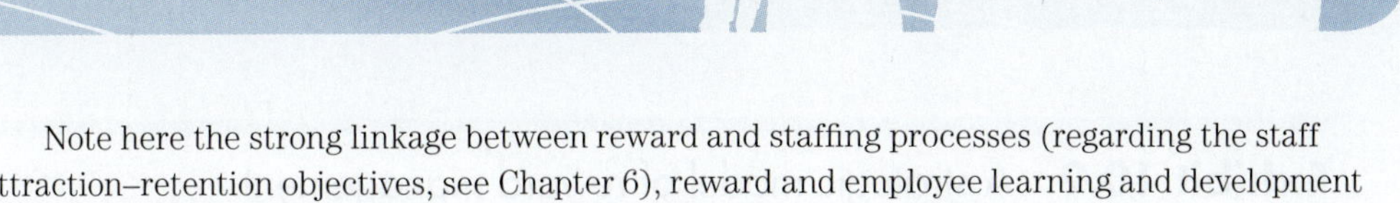

Note here the strong linkage between reward and staffing processes (regarding the staff attraction–retention objectives, see Chapter 6), reward and employee learning and development (see Chapter 8), and reward and performance management (regarding motivation, see Chapter 9).

A well-designed and administered reward system is also likely to have a number of important secondary objectives. In particular, it should seek to be:

- Need-fulfilling: the rewards should be of value to employees in satisfying relevant human needs.

- Equitable or 'felt-fair': reward levels should be seen as being both commensurate with individual contribution and appropriate by comparison with reward levels received by others.

- Legal: rewards should comply with relevant legal requirements regarding employee rights and entitlements, including mandatory minimum pay and benefits standards.

- Affordable: rewards allocated, and any associated on-costs, should be within the organisation's financial means.

- Cost-effective: there should be an appropriate 'return on investment' from total reward outlays.

- Strategically-aligned: the reward system should be configured so as to support the organisation's strategic objectives.

Taken together, this is a particularly exacting set of objectives and it is unlikely that any organisation will be willing or able to achieve all of them simultaneously. There is also considerable potential for conflict between the objectives themselves. For instance, one of the greatest challenges lies in reconciling perceived reward fairness with the objective of cost-effectiveness. Which is of greater importance? Dissatisfaction arising from perceptions of reward inequity can certainly lead to increased employee turnover and reduced motivation, but the costs and benefits of being a low payer will vary depending on the type of organisation involved. While some organisations may suffer serious performance impairment, others may be able to absorb these consequences and still meet their objectives. Tensions may also arise between the goal of cost-containment and that of offering rewards that are sufficient to attract and retain the right type and number of employees. From an organisational perspective, the optimal approach is not necessarily that which is cheapest. Rather, it is that which maximises the returns to the organisation for the outlay made – and this returns us to the vital matter of strategic reward management.

Strategic reward management

As indicated in Exhibit 10.2, a strategic reward management approach has two main requirements. First, the choice of reward strategy and practices should be informed by the organisation's overall human resource strategy, plans and policies. The reward practices applied should themselves be systemic (i.e. integrated and cohesive), as well as synergising with the wider set of human resource policies and practices. This alignment between practices and people management strategy/policy/practice, on the one hand, and organisational structure and people management culture, on the other, is known as 'internal fit.' Second, as a key element of the organisation's people strategy, reward strategy and practices should align with and support the organisation's overall strategic business plan (or 'competitive strategy') for effective operation in its dynamic environmental context. This alignment between competitive strategy and approach to people management is also referred to as 'external fit'.[3]

As noted in Chapter 1, there are a variety of competitive strategies that an organisation may choose to pursue. The critical message here is that one size does not fit all. While each organisation must ensure that it complies with its obligation to provide all legally mandated employee entitlements, above this mandatory baseline reward practices, like all other

Exhibit 10.2 A strategic model of reward management

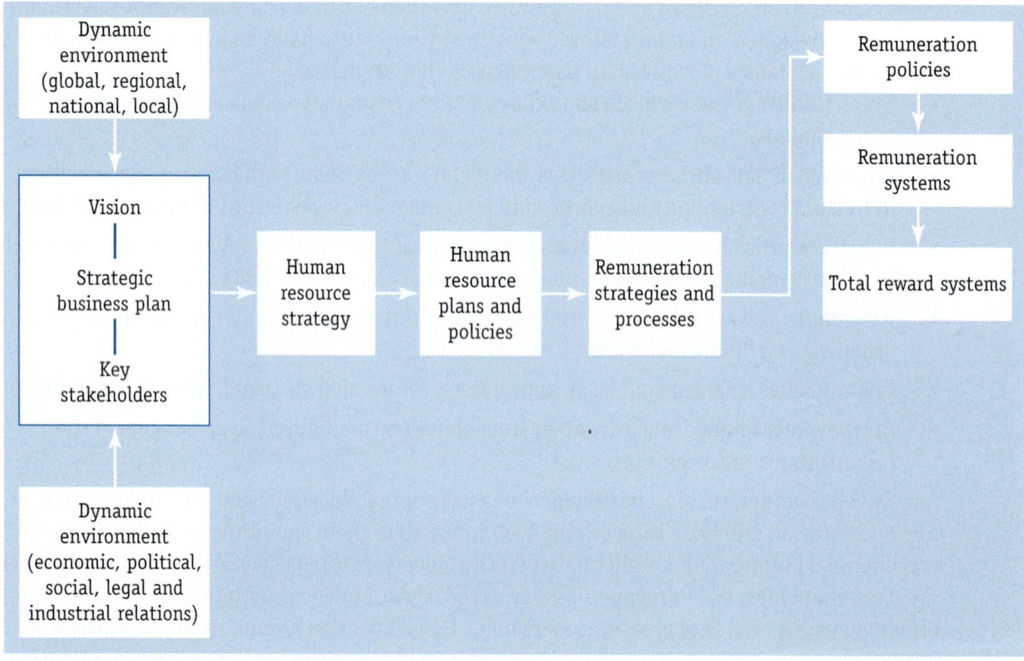

human resource practices, it should be tailored specifically to the particular strategy of each organisation and, where appropriate, to the specific strategies of distinct business units within the organisation. The aim is to develop and maintain a reward system that matches organisational and business unit performance factors (also known as 'success factors') and delivers the attitudes, competencies (i.e. knowledge, skills and abilities), work behaviour and results that the organisation requires from its employees.

Let us illustrate the way in which different competitive strategies accentuate different performance factors by considering briefly one of the most widely cited typologies of competitive market strategy, that formulated by US management theorists Raymond Miles and Charles Snow.[4] The Miles and Snow typology identifies three main types of strategy:

1 'Defender' strategy: Defenders are risk-averse and reactive and act to protect and preserve their market share from existing and new competitors. They will have only one core product or service line and focus on improving the technical efficiency of their existing operations. This may be achieved either by emphasising cost minimisation or quality enhancement, or a balance of the two. For instance, some automobile manufacturers tend to favour cost defender strategies, whereas others choose to compete on quality and to focus on high-end niche markets. As such, it is important to distinguish between 'cost defender' and 'quality defender' strategies.

2 'Analyser' strategy: Analysers are cautious diversifiers. They may have one or two core products or services and one or more non-core product lines that are spin-offs from the core business. An example would be a consumer electronics firm that has diversified into making movies; another would be an electricity supply firm that has added natural gas supply to its portfolio. Analysers are more likely to be market followers than market leaders and will also be inclined to compete on quality rather than cost, at least in the long term.

3 'Prospector' strategy: Prospectors are habitual diversifiers. They are proactive and perhaps aggressive market opportunists and risk-takers with a diverse and ever-changing portfolio of products and little loyalty to any particular type of product or service. They are constantly on the lookout for new and more attractive market opportunities, always trying to be first into a new product or service area, and ever-willing to take risks. The key success criteria are reduced product or service cycle times, adapting rapidly to environmental change and capitalising on new technical and product opportunities to achieve 'first mover' advantages in emerging markets.

Exhibit 10.3 summarises the combinations of key performance factors that are likely to be associated with each of the above strategies. To illustrate, let us compare the very different performance factors required by cost defender and prospector organisations. A cost defender will look to reward and other human resource practices that elicit and sustain high individual productivity and cost efficiency over the long-term. In general, cost defenders will also require their employees to maximise technical efficiency in job assignments that are individualised, narrow in task range, routine, low-skilled and closely supervised, with little involvement in organisational decision-making. Conversely, with prospectors the emphasis will be on speed, short-term results, agility, technological dynamism, flexibility and risk-taking, with employees having a high level of involvement in decision-making and being expected to apply a high level of technical skill and knowledge, exercise a high degree of autonomy across a mix of individual and group assignments, and demonstrate high 'organisational citizenship behaviour' (i.e. volunteering to 'go the extra mile' for the organisation).

Exhibit 10.3 Aligning strategy, structure, culture and performance requirements

	Cost Defender	Quality Defender	Analyser	Prospector
Citizenship behaviour	X	–	✓	✓
Technical knowledge and skill	X	✓	✓	✓
Individual results	✓	–	–	✓
Group/collective results	X	✓	✓	✓
Quantity/productivity	✓	✓	–	–
Cost minimisation	✓	X	–	–
Quality	X	✓	✓	–
Timelines	X	X	–	✓
Creativity/innovation	X	–	✓	✓
Risk-taking	X	X	–	✓
Short-term focus	X	X	–	✓
Long-term focus	✓	✓	–	X

Key:

✓ = Positive performance factor.

– = Neutral performance factor

X = Negative performance factor

Source: Adapted from Shields J. 2007. *Managing employee performance and reward: Concepts, practices, strategies,* Cambridge University Press, Melborne.

Later in the chapter, we shall consider how particular types and combinations of reward practice can be applied so as to elicit desired performance factors and, hence, to develop a strategically-aligned reward system. Before delving into the reward strategist's tool kit, however, in line with the model of strategic human resource management presented in Chapter 1, we need to consider how developments in the external operating environment also necessarily inform and influence the strategic reward choices made by individual organisations. In the Australian context, as detailed in Chapters 2 and 3, the most decisive developments in this regard in recent years have been those flowing from the transformation of employment relations law and regulation at the national level.

The changing basis of pay determination in Australia

For much of the 20th century, remuneration standards for the great majority of Australian employees were shaped by award determinations made by state and federal arbitral tribunals. Awards generally had industry-wide or occupation-wide coverage, with each award prescribing job-specific minimum rates of pay for standard hours worked, plus overtime and penalty rates for non-standard hours. From time to time, award rates were also subject to full or partial adjustment for changes in official cost of living indices. Over-award payments were also common in some industries. Yet, according to critics[5] the system of centralised award determination burdened employers with a degree of labour cost rigidity that minimised the scope for enterprise-specific pay 'flexibility' and managerial discretion.

While the award system retains considerable importance in Australian pay determination, as noted in Chapter 3, the last two decades have witnessed an accelerating trend away from the centralised system of pay setting and pay adjustment towards agreement-making at enterprise, workplace and individual levels. The move to enterprise bargaining and collective agreement-making began in the late 1980s and accelerated in the early 1990s, with union and non-union collective agreements now commonplace across the Australian workforce. The federal *Workplace Relations Act 1996* and the *Workplace Relations Amendment (WorkChoices) Act 2005* (see Chapter 3) have been designed to hasten the trend away from award regulation and, in particular, to institute registered individual contracts of employment in the form of Australian Workplace Agreements (AWAs), along with non-union collective agreements, as the dominant forms of pay setting for non-managerial employees. Unregistered common law individual contracts, previously confined largely to salaried executives, are also now coming to the fore for employees at senior manager level.

Exhibit 10.4 Methods of pay setting, Australia 2004

	Award only %	Collective agreement %	Individual arrangement or agreement[1] %	Working proprietors of incorporated business %	All methods %
All persons	20.0	40.9	33.7 (2.4)	5.4	100.0
Private sector	24.7	27.3	41.1 (2.6)	6.9	100.0
Public sector	2.3	92.2	5.5 (1.8)	0.0	100.0
Males	15.7	38.3	38.2 (3.0)	7.8	100.0
Females	24.4	43.6	29.1 (1.9)	2.9	100.0

	Award only %	Collective agreement %	Individual arrangement or agreement[1] %	Working proprietors of incorporated business %	All methods %
Managers & administrators	0.8	25.2	47.3	26.7	100.0
Professionals	6.7	55.8	32.8	4.7	100.0
Associate professionals	8.3	40.0	42.6	9.1	100.0
Tradespersons & related workers	22.5	34.6	35.2	7.7	100.0
Advanced clerical and service workers	8.2	30.2	51.8	9.8	100.0
Intermediate clerical, sales & service workers	25.8	38.4	34.6	1.2	100.0
Intermediate production & transport workers	17.3	50.0	29.8	2.9	100.0
Elementary clerical, sales & service workers	39.9	37.1	21.8	1.2	100.0
Labourers & related workers	37.9	36.8	24.5	0.8	100.0

[1] **Includes registered and unregistered individual agreements. Bracketed figure = % of registered individual agreements. Also includes employees receiving over-award payments by individual agreement.**

Source: *Employee Earnings and Hours*, ABS, Cat. No. 6306.0, May, 2004.
ABS data used with permission from the Australian Bureau of Statistics, www.abs.gov.au.

Exhibit 10.4 illustrates the changing methods of pay setting for various categories of employee in Australia as at May 2004. At that time, 20 per cent of all employees had their pay set by award only, 41 per cent by collective agreement and 34 per cent by individual arrangement, including 2 per cent under a registered individual agreement such as an AWA. Yet, as Exhibit 10.4 also shows, there was also considerable variation in pay setting method across different categories of employee. Pay setting by means of collective agreement was far more pronounced in the more highly unionised public sector (92 per cent) than in the private sector (27 per cent), while individual arrangements were markedly less significant (5 per cent in the public sector compared to 41 per cent in the private sector). Male employees were more likely to have their pay set by individual arrangement than were female employees (38 per cent compared to 29 per cent), while females were more likely to be covered by award-only pay setting (24 per cent compared to 16 per cent). Turning to pay setting by occupational category, individual arrangements were more prevalent among advanced clerical and service workers (52 per cent), managers and administrators (47 per cent), and associate professionals (43 per cent), while award-only pay determination was more prevalent among lower-skilled occupations, such as intermediate and elementary clerical, sales and service workers (26 per cent and 40 per cent, respectively) and labourers and related workers (38 per cent). Collective agreements were most prevalent for professionals (56 per cent) and intermediate production and transport workers (50 per cent).

Overall, despite marked sectoral and demographic unevenness, Australian employers are making much greater use of non-union collective agreements and AWAs in setting pay levels, making pay adjustments, and altering pay methods, a trend that is likely to gather pace under the radical changes to the industrial relations context under *WorkChoices*. There are a number of ways in which *WorkChoices* stands to transform reward determination in Australia. First, by instituting the Fair Pay Commission as the body with sole responsibility for determining and adjusting the mandatory minimum pay level, the legislation stands to privilege the notion of economic 'capacity to pay' over the more traditional principle of employee need in the setting of minimum pay standards. Second, by sanctioning the 'cashing out' or bargaining away of many pre-existing award entitlements, including overtime and shift loadings and penalty rates of pay for weekend and holiday work, *WorkChoices* stands to revolutionise the traditional approach to time-based remuneration. Third, as noted in News report 10.1, by encouraging the use of non-union agreements and AWAs, the legislation also affords employers far greater scope to experiment with non-traditional methods of remuneration in each of the three main categories of financial reward: that is, base pay, benefits and performance pay.

NEWS REPORT 10.1

Three key developments in agreement clauses

This issue of the *ADAM Report* takes a different angle in reporting on the latest innovations in agreements. Not only has *WorkChoices* fundamentally changed the bargaining landscape in agreements, we are beginning to witness a significant change in the rhetoric expressed within the *WorkChoices* agreements. The new rhetoric has a much stronger tendency than in the past to favour business needs over innovation. Commitment and innovation give way to flexibility and cost reduction …

While innovations are still found in the new wave of agreements, they appear to be mostly found within the unionised agreements. This dichotomous scenario confirms previous suggestions that the impact of *WorkChoices* is likely to be felt more strongly in the non-unionised sectors.

The new underlying current favouring business needs have been identified in four main areas: the reliance on company policy; wages and granting of wage increases; hours of work arrangements, overtime and penalty rates; and alternative dispute resolution procedures. Further details of these key developments are provided below, together with a compilation of the more traditional innovations.

Stepping outside the formal system – jumping out of awards and into company policy

The Coalition Government's *WorkChoices* legislation has managed to undermine the significance of, and substantially sidestep reliance on, the award system. The logical extension of this movement has been an increased reliance on a more informal system – company policy.

In past agreements, reference to company policy or HR manuals has not been completely unheard of. However, company policy tended to be invoked in relation to a particular matter or initiative only. In these cases, the enterprise agreement was supplemented by the policy as an attachment, effectively rendering the matter 'legally enforceable.' This use of company policy appears to be far more transparent when compared to current instances, given their open ended and directive nature. ….

Business needs drive wage increases

… the introduction of *WorkChoices* has seen a significant decline in the number of non-union agreements specifying a wage increase. Across all agreements in the database 59% of non-union agreements provide for a wage increase. In the September quarter only 36% of non-union agreements specified a wage increase. Amongst non-union greenfield agreements this drops to only 25%. It should be noted that employer greenfield agreements have a term of only twelve months and may not include a quantifiable wage increase over that period.

The most notable aspect of change in wages clauses is the growth in the number of agreements providing greater managerial prerogative in setting wage rates over the duration of the agreement.

Prior to the introduction of *WorkChoices* it was relatively common to find clauses in agreements that specified that wages would be reviewed annually, taking into consideration a range of internal and external factors such as CPI movements, overall economic growth and forecasts, industry developments and other key wage bargaining outcomes, company performance, and at times individual performance. The September quarter sees a greater focus on exerting managerial prerogative and direct 'business needs' as the key factors in considering any future wage increases. In a number of agreements a more open ended approach has been adopted where future wage increases are no longer guaranteed.

Extract four from the metal manufacturing industry, is an example of how vague and uncertain an employee's earnings growth will be over the life of an agreement. Consideration is made for an employee's performance, market conditions and business needs, however there is virtually no guarantee of any wage increase nor is there an indication of the frequency....

Extract eight, covering a labour hire company, specifies that any review undertaken will not necessarily result in a pay increase. The agreement also specifies that any bonuses and incentives are discretionary and the employer reserves the right to review, amend or retract any type of bonus or incentive at any time.

Extract 4 (metal manufacturing industry)

The employer shall conduct a periodic review of your performance which may result in an adjustment to your Wage Rate. This review will take into account relevant factors, including your performance and prevailing market conditions both generally and relating to the operational requirements of the business.

Extract 8 (labour hire)

1 PERFORMANCE REVIEW

The employer generally conducts reviews for all Employees. The conduct of such a review will not impose an obligation on the employer to increase your Wage Rate. The employer may, however, increase your Wage Rate after taking into account relevant factors, including your performance and prevailing market conditions both generally and relating to the operational requirements of the business.

25 BONUSES AND INCENTIVES

25.1 The employer may offer various types of bonuses and incentives to its Employees.

25.2 If you are eligible to receive a bonus, such a bonus or incentive scheme shall be communicated to you in writing in your Individual Letter.

25.3 Unless specified in your Individual Letter, bonuses and incentives are, in all cases, discretionary and the employer reserves the right to review, amend or retract any type of bonus or incentive at any time.

25.4 A bonus or incentive will only be paid if you are a current Employee as at the date a bonus is due to be paid and if you have been employed by The employer for a minimum continuous period of 12 months.

25.5 Employees who receive a bonus or incentive shall not have an expectation that a bonus will form part of their wages on an ongoing basis.

25.6 Should the Wage Rate paid to you over a 12 month period fall below the relevant guaranteed basic rate of pay forming part of the Australian Fair Pay and Conditions Standard, The employer may offset any payments made to you in accordance with this Agreement in order to meet the requirements of Clause 18.5(c)(ii).

Source: Bamberry, L. & Frino, E. 2006. ADAM Report, 51, December (published by the Workplace Research Centre, The University of Sydney). Extract reproduced with permission.

Base pay

Base pay can be defined as part of cash remuneration that is largely 'fixed' or 'guaranteed' and time-based rather than performance-based. It is the largest component of total standard pre-tax remuneration for most Australian employees: typically between 75 per cent and 80 per cent of the total, with benefits and variable/incentive pay making up the remainder.[6] As the primary or foundational component of cash reward, base pay serves as the benchmark for other cash components, including benefits and incentive pay, which are frequently expressed as a percentage of the base amount. In general, base pay is time-based rather than performance-based.

For each quantum of time worked, the employee receives a predetermined amount of pay. In broad terms, time-based base pay can be delivered either as an hourly, daily or weekly wage, or in the form of an annual salary. Time-based wages have traditionally been the main form of remuneration applied to manual and other 'blue-collar' jobs. In contrast, salaried employment involves annualised payment, typically carries no upper limit on hours to be worked, and is the main form of remuneration applied to executive, managerial and professional/'white-collar' positions.

Whether by necessity or choice, paying some base pay remains the rule rather than the exception. In many countries, legislatures or tribunals have prescribed payment of guaranteed minimum wage or salary levels. There are also some solid reasons why organisations may choose to offer generous base pay voluntarily. This is particularly the case in situations where qualified labour is in short supply. In such circumstances, base pay has a major role to play in attracting and retaining desired staff. Providing each employee with a guaranteed level of base pay demonstrates the employer's commitment to the employee, which in turn means that the employee is more likely to reciprocate. Finally, base pay is not incompatible with performance pay. Indeed, performance factors are playing an increasing role in decisions about how each employee's base pay level is adjusted over time.

Nevertheless, base pay systems are themselves quite diverse and there are three distinct approaches to building base pay:

- job-based pay
- skill-based pay
- competency-based pay.

As well as making quite different assumptions about what base pay can contribute to an organisation, and how it can do so, the above three alternative approaches entail distinct pay structures, evaluation (i.e. pricing) methods and processes, and modes of pay progression. Exhibit 10.5 summarises the three main base pay options, including the structures, evaluation techniques and progression modes associated with each.

Exhibit 10.5   Options for base pay

	Structures	Evaluation techniques	Modes of pay progression
Job-based pay	1. Pay ladders 2. Narrow grades	Market surveys and/or job evaluation	Seniority and/or 'merit'-based increments and promotion
Skill-based pay	Broad grades or job families	Skill assessment	Skill sets
Competency-based pay	Broadbands	Competency assessment	Competency zones or levels

Job-based base pay

The traditional practice has been to fix base pay according to the job or position occupied. This amounts to paying for the job rather than for the person who happens to hold the job. Payment according to the job or position held remains the dominant mode of remuneration in most developed countries. For instance, in Australia, standard time-based rates of pay for specific job classifications were enshrined in the plethora of occupational and industry

awards developed under the system of compulsory arbitration.[7] While the award-based system is now in decline, its legacy runs deep in Australian remuneration practice and is one of the main reasons why job-based pay still predominates in most Australian workplaces. In the job-based approach, positions of larger 'size' – that is, with a greater content of tasks, duties and responsibilities – attract higher levels of base pay, and employees can increase their base pay chiefly by ascending a hierarchy of job-related pay steps incorporated into either a ladder-like pay scale or a stairway of narrow job grades.

Pay scales typically consist of a hierarchy of position-specific pay levels, each comprising a sequence of flat pay rates, steps or points. Traditionally, step-wise pay increments within each level were based on seniority or service, with the increase occurring automatically after each year of service. In the past, service-based increments of this type have been a defining feature of public sector salary structures in many countries. More recently, though, many organisations in both the public and private sectors have adopted the practice of making within-level increments dependent on 'merit'; that is, on individual performance assessment. As such, pay for performance is assuming greater significance even in this most traditional of position-based structures.

A narrow grade (also known as a 'job grade') houses a group of jobs of similar size/value to the organisation and specifies a pay range for these jobs rather than a scale step or spot rate. Each grade will cover a group of jobs regarded as being of similar value to the organisation and therefore worthy of roughly the same range of base pay. Unlike simple pay scales, each grade allows for some variance in pay, but the range over which pay can vary is usually quite narrow. Each grade has a pay range that defines the minimum and maximum rates of pay for all jobs in the grade, with the pay range for each grade typically being 20 to 30 per cent. Each grade also has a range midpoint that usually serves as an internal 'control point' intended to regulate pay increases. The grade midpoint typically defines the pay rate for acceptable proficiency in the job.

In job-based systems, the two main techniques for job pricing are market surveys and job evaluation. Market surveys involve setting pay rates for particular jobs according to what other employers are paying for the same or similar jobs in external labour markets. Regular market surveys also allow organisations to monitor changes in market rates and adjust their own pay rates accordingly. As such, the approach emphasises 'external competitiveness' in determining the rate for the job. The organisation ascertains the range of amounts that other organisations are paying for jobs similar to its own, and then makes a strategic choice about where it will position itself relative to competitors. For this purpose, the market range for each position is commonly expressed as either percentile or quartile means. Rather than undertaking the data gathering themselves, many organisations utilise market data provided by specialist remuneration consulting firms.

Job evaluation, which is sometimes seen as an alternative to reliance on market data, involves determining relative pay rates by relating them to the importance or relative value of the job to the organisation. This is achieved by comparing jobs on a number of factors thought to be important in determining job value, such as skill, effort, responsibility or working conditions. Generally, job evaluation involves four main steps:

1   undertaking a job analysis, which provides data on the content of specific jobs

2   producing job descriptions, which summarise the core tasks, duties and responsibilities of each job

3   selecting and applying the most appropriate job evaluation method, then using job descriptions to evaluate the relative worth of each job to the organisation

4   creating a job grades structure based on job evaluation scores.

The end result of job evaluation is a hierarchy of jobs where all jobs of similar value to the organisation, no matter how different they might be in other respects, are placed at the same level in the job-based pay hierarchy. As such, job evaluation emphasises 'internal equity' in setting job-based pay rates rather than 'external competitiveness' per se.

Job evaluation methods are of two generic types: qualitative methods and quantitative methods. Qualitative methods generally involve non-analytical and whole-job comparisons and tend to rely on impressionistic and quite subjective judgements about comparative job value. Conversely, with quantitative techniques, jobs are disaggregated into component parts (or job 'factors') and numerical scores, or 'points,' are then assigned to each position according to the degree to which each factor is present in each job evaluated. For this reason, quantitative methods of this type are also known generically as 'points-factor' techniques.

One of the oldest and still most widely used proprietary points-factor methods is that marketed globally by consulting firm, the Hay Group. This is known as the Hay guide chart profile method.[8] As the name implies, with the Hay method jobs are evaluated by means of special guide charts. These provide for the evaluation of jobs according to three generic job factors, namely 'know how,' 'problem-solving' and 'accountability.' These are assumed to be components of all jobs. More recently, a fourth factor – 'working conditions' – has been added to the evaluation criteria. Separate guide charts are used for each factor and the factor scores are then combined to give an overall points score for each job.

As a means of valuing jobs and developing job-based pay structures, the points-factor approach has much to commend it. It can introduce order, rationality, strategic focus and consistency into potentially arbitrary pay structures by using transparent and clearly defined measures of job size and offering a consistent means of measuring relative job size/value. It also permits evaluation against a range of strategically relevant factors, and allows each organisation to ascertain the relative importance of its own specific jobs using those criteria most relevant to its strategic purpose. Further, the points-factor approach can also help to identify and eliminate inequities in the existing pay structure, as well as providing a rational basis for setting pay rates for new or changed jobs.

However, the points-factor approach also has some weaknesses and drawbacks.[9] In focusing on internal relativities and generic job content factors, it may downplay or even ignore critical market-related strategic success factors, a point actually conceded by commentators who assert its continuing relevance to contemporary reward practice.[10] According to Lawler,[11] points-factor methods privilege job size over job-holder contribution, emphasise internal equity over external competitiveness, and reinforce bureaucracy and hierarchy. Similarly, Emerson[12] contends that the Hay method has an inbuilt tendency to reinforce managerial hierarchy and traditional bureaucracy, especially by assigning large point scores to managerial 'know-how' as opposed to line-employee 'know-how'; by allocating large scores to jobs that directly affect financial results; and by awarding high points for supervising large numbers of people.

Perhaps the most appropriate conclusion here is that while points-factor job evaluation can never provide a totally objective or absolutely accurate way of valuing jobs, and while a poorly conceived and executed system of job evaluation can impair both internal equity and external competitiveness, carefully designed and properly administered and maintained points-factor job evaluation still has much to offer, certainly in comparison with relying solely on market rates. In practice, a well-managed system of job-based pay requires simultaneous attention to both internal equity and external competitiveness considerations.

However, critics suggest that job-based pay per se has a number of major shortcomings. While there may be some scope for recognising individual performance differences within each job grade, there is little incentive to improved contribution or performance in the job. Paying the job rather than the person provides employees themselves with little incentive to acquire skills and competencies which the organisation may need now or in the future. Pay based

on narrow job positions is incompatible with the new emphasis on task interdependence and teamwork. Further, by emphasising grade promotion, narrow job grades reinforce organisational hierarchy and can give rise to 'top-heavy' and costly management structures that are anathema to a high involvement management approach.[13] For similar reasons, job-based pay is unlikely to be compatible with a prospector competitive strategy. By the same token, the assumption of long-term stability in technology and job content, as well as the tight control that job-based structures allow over payroll costs, means that pay for the job will appeal strongly to organisations pursuing a cost defender strategy.

Partly as a result of the perceived limitations of job-based pay, organisations in many Western countries now structure base pay around the skills and competencies of the person rather than the 'size' of the job occupied. This is also known generically as 'person-based pay' and involves very different base pay structures to those characteristic of the older job-based approach.

Skill-based pay

By recognising and rewarding the acquisition of technical skills and job knowledge, skill-based pay is said to facilitate functional flexibility through multiskilling and teamworking. Multiskilling allows employees to be redeployed quickly without retraining delays. It also minimises down-time arising from the absence of required skills. By breaking down rigid job demarcations, it can enable a more flexible utilisation of the workforce as employees acquire a breadth and depth of relevant skills.[14] It is especially relevant to teamworking and in situations where maximum plant utilisation and speed of response are critical. It can facilitate systematic organisational learning and continuous improvement. Skill-based pay also lends itself to employee involvement in system design and administration. As such, exponents contend that it is ideally suited to high involvement management.[15]

The basic building block for a skill-based system is the 'skill set' or 'skill block.' A skill set consists of a bundle of related tasks and activities – or 'skill elements' – the mastery of which constitutes a finite and verifiable unit of learning on which training content can be developed and delivered.[16] Each skill set becomes a training module that must be completed successfully to warrant a further increase in the amount of base pay. For base pay determination purposes, associated skill sets are commonly housed in structures known as 'broad grades.' With broad grades, existing narrow grades are collapsed into a smaller number of grades with a view to widening the possible pay range for employees in each 'job family.' Such a structure allows individual employees to be recognised and rewarded for acquiring additional skills and knowledge associated with each job family. The pay range for each broad grade is typically 40 to 60 per cent; that is, some two to three times that of a narrow grade. Broad grade pay ranges are commonly set using a 'high–low' approach in which the minimum rate for the smallest reconstituted job is taken as the range minimum, while maximum for the largest constituent job becomes the range maximum. Monetary values are then attached to each skill set according to the estimated learning time required. As such, broad grades support functional flexibility, multiskilling and career-pathing for line employees.[17]

Yet skill-based pay also has a number of potential disadvantages. Equipping an employee with needed skills does not guarantee that the employee will apply them effectively. This is because skill-based pay rewards skill *acquisition* rather than skill *application*.[18] Skill-based plans involve complex procedures for skill training, assessment and accreditation; administrative procedures that can be very costly. A related problem is that of escalating training and assessment costs. When skill acquisition becomes the key to pay and career progression, the demand for training will inevitably increase. Training bottlenecks may be a major problem, particularly in the initial stages, where there may well be a short-term rush on available training facilities. The approach will also increase the pressure on supervisors, particularly regarding decisions about the allocation and scheduling of access to training programs.[19] Skill-based pay also carries some possible negatives for employees themselves. One of these is 'topping out.' Once employees have acquired all the skills they are required to learn, their pay will plateau, and they may lose task motivation and organisational commitment unless additional rewards, such as performance incentives, are made available. Then there is the problem of skill obsolescence. Since pay increases are based on the repertoire of skills that each employee accumulates rather than those that they actually use, any mismatch between learning content and actual requirements will undermine the system's efficacy. In the absence of opportunity to retrain, employees whose skills are no longer needed, say because of changes to product range or technology, may be exposed to pay reduction or even redundancy.

Given the focus on skill development and process improvement, broad grades will be particularly well suited to a quality defender strategy. The scope to facilitate skill diversification, multiskilling and teamworking means that broad grades and skill pay are also well suited to an analyser competitive strategy. The emphasis on training, multiskilling and teamworking also points to compatibility with a degree of employee involvement. The combination of broad grades and skill-based pay will be especially appropriate for roles with significant technical knowledge and skill requirements, such as process work, technical or para-professional roles, maintenance work and administration. In such roles, skills are relatively easy to identify, impart, assess and reward.

Conversely, skill-based broad grades will be less appropriate to higher-level professional knowledge work and managerial roles, since the chief performance capabilities here are 'soft' competencies rather than formal task-specific technical skills. Given its focus on hard, technical capabilities, skill-based pay has only limited application outside production line, maintenance and routine administrative work. Further, since pay for skill is necessarily a high-cost option, it would be unsuited to a cost defender strategy. By the same token, broad grades and skill pay would have only limited application to a prospector business strategy since in such firms product cycles may well be too short to accommodate internal training and retraining. Such organisations are more likely to look to external labour markets to satisfy their skill needs (i.e. a 'buy' rather then 'build' approach to staffing).

Competency-based pay

Some commentators suggest that a better means of configuring person-based base pay is to focus on assessing and rewarding deeply embedded abilities or 'competencies' such as self-confidence, achievement orientation, interpersonal empathy, persistence, composure, problem-solving ability, and the like. The appeal of the competencies approach lies chiefly in its focus on those personal attributes that are seen to be the most important and reliable drivers of high individual performance. As such, the suggestion that competency assessment should apply not only to performance management and development but also to employee reward has intuitive appeal.[20] Likewise, the competencies model is applicable to staff at all levels of the organisation, not just to skilled manual workers.

The defining features of competency-based pay are, firstly, a system of formal individual competency assessment (see Chapter 5), and, secondly, a 'broadbanded' pay structure. Broadbanding (also known as 'career banding') involves doing away with a large number of narrow jobs arranged in a steep hierarchy in favour of a much smaller number of job bands. Pay ranges are substantially wider – frequently 100 to 300 per cent – and the mode of pay progression is linked to either competency assessment or a combination of competency development and performance outcomes. A typical broadbanded structure will have between five and 10 bands. Progression within a given broadband may be linked either to competency assessment alone (i.e. competency-*based* broadbanding) or to a combination of competency assessment and individual performance outcomes (i.e. competency-*related* broadbanding).

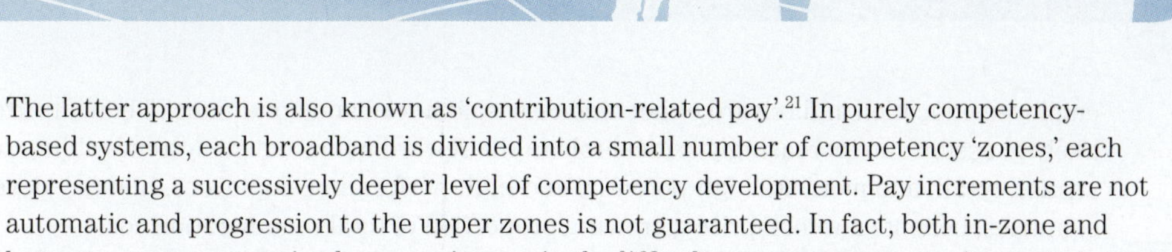

The latter approach is also known as 'contribution-related pay'.[21] In purely competency-based systems, each broadband is divided into a small number of competency 'zones,' each representing a successively deeper level of competency development. Pay increments are not automatic and progression to the upper zones is not guaranteed. In fact, both in-zone and between-zone progression becomes increasingly difficult as competency requirements become more demanding.

Competency-based broadbanding promises employers an unprecedented degree of flexibility in determining individual base pay levels. Exponents of the competency-based option[22] contend that broadbanding has many advantages over traditional graded structures. By flattening job hierarchies, it can redirect employees' attention away from competition for jobs and promotion and towards individual and group contribution to organisational success. Uncoupling promotion from individual career development and base pay progression redefines career 'success' from a vertical to a horizontal trajectory. This means that individuals no longer have to aspire to a managerial role in order to further their careers and base pay. By linking career development and pay progression to individual performance capability and achievement, broadbanding also supports a more strategic approach to reward management.

Yet competency broadbanding also has its drawbacks. Indeed, the enthusiasm initially associated with competency-based pay has, in recent years, been replaced by a healthy degree of caution.[23] Even if it were possible to accurately identify, select and assess deep competencies, there is no agreed or reliable way to price them. Competencies are commodities that have yet to be recognised in external labour markets. Far from simplifying payroll administration, broadbanding also stands to make it more complex and challenging, requiring considerably greater levels of remuneration expertise.[24] In the absence of clearly defined limits and 'control points' for pay progression, there is a danger of runaway payroll inflation. Further, the wide pay ranges characteristic of broadbands may create unrealistic expectations of pay rise opportunities, and this too can cause breach of trust and feelings of distributive injustice, especially if these expectations remain unfulfilled. The removal of promotional opportunities may also rupture trust. Overall, then, while broadbanding does hold considerable promise as a means of structuring person-based pay, its very complexity requires that it be handled with care, caution and, not least, patience.

The combination of broadbanding and competency-based or -related progression is of special relevance to organisations of the prospector type in which adaptability, timeliness, creativity and calculative risk-taking are of the essence. The competencies model is especially applicable in service, knowledge work and managerial roles. Conversely, the emphasis on wide role assignments and pay ranges would be incompatible with a cost defender strategy.

In sum, the design of a strategically-aligned system necessitates careful consideration of the options for building a suitable base pay structure and for managing pay progression within the chosen structure. In turn, a well-configured base pay system provides a solid foundation for each of the two additional remuneration elements, namely employee benefits and performance-related reward.

Benefits

Employee benefits may be either 'direct' or 'indirect' in nature. Direct benefits are financial entitlements that directly supplement cash base pay, including employer contributions to superannuation and health and medical insurance, paid leave, and the like. Indirect benefits cover a growing number of non-financial rewards, ranging from special unpaid leave provisions to the provision of wellness programs and advisory services. As such, benefits are a remarkably heterogeneous phenomenon. As the workforce becomes more diverse and as the level of employee education and reward expectation rises, financial and non-financial benefits are likely to assume an increasingly critical role in the reward management system's ability to attract, retain and motivate high-potential and high-performing employees. In many developed countries, benefits now comprise a growing proportion of total remuneration costs.

Direct benefits

As supplements to base pay, direct benefits can enhance the organisation's ability to attract and retain high-value employees. Such benefits include employer-funded superannuation savings, life, health and disability insurance, workers compensation, various forms of paid leave (e.g. annual, long-service, sickness, parental, carer leave), and severance pay. In the Australian context, employers are legally obliged to provide a number of these benefits, most notably superannuation contributions currently equivalent to at least 9 per cent of each employee's regular gross wage or salary. As we have seen, however, under the *WorkChoices Act*, some paid leave entitlements can now be cashed out or otherwise bargained away under an AWA.

In developed countries, employer-funded retirement or superannuation plans are now the single most important form of direct benefit provision for employees, as well as one of the largest additional costs to employers on top of wages and salaries, the main employment 'on-cost' for employers. Superannuation plans are of two main types: defined benefit plans, and defined contribution plans. Each may be contributory (i.e. employee-funded) or non-contributory (i.e. employer-funded), or both.[25] In recent decades, defined contribution plans have begun to replace defined benefit plans as the dominant mode of retirement planning in many developed countries. Defined benefit plans provide a predetermined amount of retirement income either as a lump sum or as a regular pension for the remainder of the person's life. Such an approach provides certainty as to the amount of entitlement at the point of retirement. Because such arrangements are not fully funded by contributions, it is necessary for the organisation to use actuarial calculations to ascertain the level of funding necessary to meet promised benefits. Defined contribution plans, also known as accumulation plans, specify the amount of employer and/or employee contributions but not the actual retirement benefit. Contributions are expressed as a percentage of the employee's annual remuneration, and employee contributions typically range between 5 per cent and 10 per cent, with the employer often contributing an equal or greater amount. In Australia, employees are also able to deduct their contributions from pre-tax income by way of a 'salary sacrifice' arrangement. The benefit may be paid either as a lump sum or as a pension where the employee uses the accumulated fund to purchase an annuity. The entitlement is calculated on the basis of accumulated contributions plus fund earnings over the period of contribution, with the latter determined largely by the changing state of returns on shares, real estate and other investments and, of course, the investment decisions made by the relevant fund managers. As such, employees have no guarantee of what their entitlement will be, so under such plans the employee assumes most of the risk.

Other direct benefits that employers may choose to incorporate in a benefits package include:

- discount loans
- housing or mortgage subsidies
- discount travel and accommodation
- product or service discounts
- free clothing
- subsidised canteens
- company cars and/or free parking
- club and gym membership
- self-education expenses

- school fees for dependent children
- notebook computers
- mobile phones.

Most such benefits are liable to taxation as a fringe benefit where such taxes exist, as is the case in Australia.[26]

Indirect benefits

In addition to monetary benefits, many organisations now offer employees a range of non-financial benefits. In essence, these are intended to make the organisation a more appealing place to work as well as to increase employee morale, job satisfaction, membership behaviour, organisational commitment and task motivation. In recent years, longer working hours and rising levels of workforce stress have prompted growing recognition of the importance of work–life balance and spurred some organisations to introduce non-financial benefits carefully targeted at enhancing employees' wellbeing. These benefits include, *inter alia*, flexible work-time arrangements, wellness programs and employee assistance programs. In part, these non-monetary plans are also targeted at reducing costs associated with compulsory financial benefits, including statutory sick leave and stress leave entitlements. The provision of targeted non-financial benefits, such as childcare facilities, may also support diversity management and equal opportunity. Most such initiatives amount to forms of social reward.

Flexible work-time arrangements are virtually limitless in their variety. With variable day arrangements, employees are able to vary the number of hours worked on any given day, providing they work the required number of standard hours per week and are at work each day during designated 'core hours.' Similarly, with a variable week arrangement, employees may work a long week or a short week, providing that they complete a standard number of hours each fortnight or month. Another variant is the rostered day off. A further option is flexible start and finish times, whereby employees nominate a daily start time and adhere to it for an agreed period. Job-sharing and permanent part-time work also increase the degree of time flexibility available to each employee, as, of course, do telecommuting and other work-from-home arrangements, which also give employees greater scope to better integrate family and work responsibilities both spatially and temporally. Unpaid parental and carer leave arrangements also fall into this category.

Employee wellness programs are designed to promote employees' physical and mental health and fitness. Examples include free medical check-ups, in-house gyms or subsidised gym membership, personal trainers, aerobics, yoga, Pilates and Tai Chi classes, in-office massages, stress reduction and relaxation sessions, ergonomic consultations, meditation rooms, staff health food canteens, nutrition seminars, weight control programs and quit smoking programs. As well as being inherently beneficial to employees themselves, health and fitness initiatives such as these can make a significant contribution to reducing absenteeism and raising productivity.[27]

The purpose of employee assistance programs (see Chapter 9) is to help employees to cope with and remedy personal problems that are interfering with their performance. Participation in an assistance program may be one of the items included in an action plan designed to remedy under-performance arising from a major personal problem.

Fixed vs flexible benefits plans

The content of benefits packages may either be 'fixed' or 'flexible.' They may have a standard content, with the composition being determined by legal requirement and employer choice. Alternatively, they may be flexible in content, with employees having a degree of choice in how best to configure their package within a range of options made available voluntarily by the employer. The latter are also known as 'flexible' or 'cafeteria' benefits plans. The logic of flexible packages is that one size does not fit all. Differences in age, family responsibilities, financial circumstances and lifestyle preferences mean that different employees will have different benefit needs, and the needs of any one employee will change considerably over time.

NEWS REPORT 10.2

Lend Lease

Beth Winchester is the Asia Pacific human resources manager for Lend Lease. The company has a cultural heritage of wealth creation for all staff and an innovative and egalitarian attitude to benefits, according to Winchester, in which everyone has access to the same benefits. Lend Lease was one of the first companies in Australia to offer in-house corporate childcare at its Sydney head office. Because it lacked the critical mass to provide a similar service in Melbourne or Brisbane, the company provided interstate staff assistance in finding childcare, then paid them a rebate equal to the benefit its Sydney employees received.

Winchester says that the key to Lend Lease's benefits package is flexibility. People are paid their package as either 100 per cent cash or cash plus benefits. Benefits include operating or novated car leasing, in-house childcare, laptops, salary sacrifice superannuation payments, access to financial planning services (the initial consultation is paid for by the company) and an employee share acquisition plan. In this plan, an employee can receive 5 per cent of their base salary in shares, which are held in trust. The employee receives annual dividend payments and only gets access to the shares when they leave the company, at which point tax is payable.

'The biggest challenge when offering any benefit is to keep up with the changes in legislation and the impact that any change has on the value of the benefit,' says Winchester. She says she hasn't noted any differences between blue and white collar employees or any gender bias when it comes to the benefits chosen, but that the difference lies in the current life cycle of staff. 'When my children were young, I used the child-care centre, but that's a benefit I'm no longer interested in. That's why any benefits package has to be flexible, so that people can choose benefits that are meaningful to them at certain stages of their lives,' she explains.

Winchester is continually reviewing Lend Lease's benefits offering. She is organising internal focus groups to discuss what's hot and what's not. In the past, she has commissioned a special report to benchmark the company's benefits in the Australian marketplace. She draws inspiration from networking, trade magazines, providers and employees when trying to discover what is new, different and cost effective in the market.

'The way you communicate a benefit is extremely important. A glossy 50-page flyer never goes down well,' Winchester has found. She advocates the use of a variety of media from electronic to print, access to answers about benefits right through the week, and to 'never underestimate the value of a good roadshow.'

Winchester believes that a competitive benefits package has a high impact on staff retention, although it is really the culture that keeps people in an organisation. Before designing a benefits package, she advises consulting staff on benefit preferences and fitting benefits to the size of your organisation. 'You should do a few things well, rather that trying to offer everything to everyone,' Winchester concludes.

Source: Russell, T. 2004. 'Financial benefits that make staff stick,' *Human Resources Magazine*, 19 October.

Overall, flexible schemes are likely to have greatest appeal to large organisations with highly diverse workforces, for which staff attraction and retention concerns are of paramount importance. Still, flexible benefits packages have some significant drawbacks for both parties. For the employer, cafeteria plans have high administrative costs simply because of the wider range of options that have to be made available, the sheer technical complexity of multi-plan schemes and the need to micro-manage each employee's package and frequent changes in their preferences.

For the employee, the array of choice available may be daunting and confusing. Poor or ill-advised choices may also compromise the employee's long-term security, especially if they result in the employee having inadequate health-care coverage or insufficient retirement savings.

Performance-related rewards: overview and arguments

Performance-related rewards (or 'incentives') are rewards given in recognition of past performance and in order to reinforce and enhance future performance. Performance pay, the most common form of performance-related reward, is usually an overlay to base pay and varies according to the level of measured or assessed performance. As such, performance pay is said to be 'variable,' 'contingent' and 'at risk,' rather than fixed or guaranteed.

From an employer perspective, pay-for-performance plans seek to reduce the degree of uncertainty associated with the nature of the employment exchange by specifying the basis of the transaction in more explicit terms. Performance pay can therefore be defined as any remuneration practice in which part or all of remuneration is based *directly* and *explicitly* on employees' assessed work behaviour and/or measured results (see Chapter 9). On the basis of this definition, it would be inaccurate to classify plans that focus on assessing and rewarding personal skills and competencies as performance-related reward plans since they focus on rewarding employees' productive 'inputs' rather than work activities/behaviours or outputs.

While performance-related reward plans can themselves be classified in many different ways, the four crucial considerations are:

1   What is being measured: behaviours, results or both?

2   Whose performance is being measured: individuals, large work groups (business units, plants, divisions), small work groups (teams), or the whole organisation?

3   Over what time frame is performance being measured and rewarded: over a short term (12 months or less) or a longer term (more than 12 months)?

4   What form does the contingent reward take: cash, company share equity, non-monetary?

Using these dimensions, we can identify three main categories of performance-related rewards:

1   Individual performance-related rewards. These are based on either the individual employee's assessed work behaviours or results, or on a combination of the two. These typically have a time-frame of no more than one year and, as such may also be described as a form of 'short-term incentive.' They may also be of a cash or non-cash nature, or both.

2   Performance-related pay based on the measured results of large or small work groups internal to the organisation as a whole. These may also be described as short-term incentives since the performance time-frame is typically between one month and one year. While rewards for group performance are generally monetary in nature, recognition for group performance may also be of a non-cash nature.

3   Collective performance-related rewards based on results achieved by the organisation as a whole. Where organisational results are defined in terms of financial accounting criteria (such as annual net operating profit) and the resulting payment is cash-based, the organisational performance plan would amount to a short-term incentive. However, where organisational performance is defined in terms of share market criteria (that is, movements in ordinary share prices and/or dividend payments to shareholders over a number of years) and the reward takes the form of actual or potential company equity, the plan equates to a 'long-term incentive.'

Exhibit 10.6 summarises the specific reward practices within each of these three broad categories. Each of these practices is examined in more detail below. First, though, it is instructive to consider the arguments for and against incentive plans in general.

Exhibit 10.6 Performance-related reward options

Who (= performance entity or unit) and when (= time frame for payout)?	How? (= behaviour)	How much? (= results)
Individual performance reward plans	• Merit raises or increments • Merit bonuses	• Piece rates • Sales commissions • Goal-based bonuses
		• Discretionary bonuses • Individual non-cash recognition awards
Collective/group short-term incentives (STIs)		• Profit-sharing • Gain-sharing • Goal-sharing • Team incentives • Team non-cash recognition awards
Organisation-wide long-term incentives (LTIs)		• Share bonus plans • Share purchase plans • Share option plans • Share appreciation and other rights plans

Incentives: for and against

While there are various economic and cultural reasons why organisations might choose to use performance-related rewards, the overarching reason is to increase employee motivation and work effort and, hence, desired performance outcomes. The assumptions underlying the motivation objective derive either explicitly or implicitly from one or other of the main 'process' theories of work motivation. These theories, which include agency theory, reinforcement theory, expectancy theory and goal-setting theory, all emphasise the centrality of employee cognitive processes to understanding and managing the relationship between rewards and task motivation.[28] Agency theory, which assumes a potential conflict of interest between 'principals' (i.e. owners) and self-seeking 'agents' (i.e. hired employees), prescribes performance-contingent pay as the most effective means of aligning employees' economic interests with those of employers/owners. Reinforcement theory posits that a timely reward for a given desired action will motivate employees to repeat the rewarded action, while punishment in the form of non-reward will extinguish misbehaviour. Expectancy theory holds that an incentive is likely to motivate higher work effort if: (a) the employee sees the promised reward personally valuable; (b) they expect that they can achieve the required level of performance; and (c) they trust the employer to deliver the reward in exchange for the achieved performance. Goal-setting theory suggests that employees will be motivated more strongly by performance targets that are specific, agreed and challenging and by feedback that is precise and instantaneous. A further common rationale for performance-related rewards is that they operationalise the 'equity' norm of distributive justice. Equity theory proposes, in part, that reward satisfaction stems from making employee outcomes (including pay level) commensurate with their individual inputs.[29] In short, high performers should be paid more

than low performers, with reward inequality being proportional to the difference in individual performance. This is a common normative justification for performance-related pay.

However, not all commentators are enamoured of incentive pay. On the basis of a survey response from 200 senior executives from 30 countries, Beer and Katz[30] even suggest that executives' belief in incentive efficacy is a 'socially constructed myth' chiefly of US origin. Undoubtedly the most thorough recent critique of performance-related rewards in general is that by US social psychologist Alfie Kohn. His argument, in essence, is that all incentive schemes are necessarily dysfunctional because they are based on supposedly invalid psychological assumptions.

Kohn[31] makes six main points against incentive plans in general:

1 *Incentives undermine intrinsic interest in the job.* Employees may see financial incentives as a 'bribe' and therefore suspect that 'If they have to bribe me to do it, it must be something I wouldn't want to do.' According to Kohn, workers not receiving any special reward may outperform those who do. Following Deci and Ryan's cognitive evaluation theory,[32] Kohn argues that the only genuine motivators are intrinsic; that is, interest in the job itself and enjoyment and satisfaction from a job well done. Pay bribes may actually cause people to lose intrinsic interest in what they do and reduce the quality of their work.

2 *Rewards motivate people to pursue one thing above all else: the reward.* Employees will demonstrate only the type of behaviour that attracts a reward. All unrewarded behaviour, including desired behaviour, is likely to be ignored. The resulting behaviour may well be wholly rational from the employees' perspective, but wholly dysfunctional for the organisation. The unintended consequence may well be to encourage misbehaviour.

3 *Rewards punish.* No one likes to be manipulated, and rewards, like punishments, are essentially instruments for manipulating behaviour.

4 *Rewards rupture cooperative work relationships.* By rewarding individuals and fostering individual competitiveness, merit pay may serve to undermine cooperation and teamwork.

5 *Rewards ignore underlying reasons for work problems.* Incentive pay addresses symptoms rather than underlying causes. Managers fall into the trap of relying on incentive pay as a substitute for effective management strategies, such as appropriate job design, providing meaningful performance feedback, providing adequate opportunity to develop skills and competencies, and giving employees more discretion and autonomy to be creative: 'If you want people motivated to do a good job, give them a good job to do.'

6 *Rewards discourage risk-taking.* Incentives reduce risk-taking and creativity and reinforce a narrow focus on expected behaviour – on compliance rather than creativity and initiative.

Kohn's arguments have themselves been challenged on both theoretical and empirical grounds. The proposition that incentive plans cannot be used to motivate desired performance is certainly contestable. Research shows that, under certain conditions (such as those prescribed by expectancy theory), incentives can exert a positive influence on behaviour and that extrinsic and intrinsic rewards can make a joint contribution to reward satisfaction and motivation.[33] Contesting the proposition that financial incentives are detrimental to intrinsic motivation Rynes, Gerhart and Park[34] offer evidence that incentives may enhance employee performance by two main means: first, by means of a direct 'incentive effect' on individual and group motivation and effort; second, by means of a longer-term 'sorting effect,' whereby employees more likely to be motivated by performance-contingent rewards will be attracted to workplaces with such practices in place while those not similarly motivated will be disinclined to enter or remain in such workplaces.

Perhaps the most meaningful conclusion to draw from these debates on the efficacy and fairness of performance-related pay is that pay for performance may have the potential to elicit higher levels of desired behaviour and results from participating employees. However, the effectiveness and felt-fairness of any such plan will be contingent on the mode of application, particularly the way the pay–performance linkage is configured, how effectively this linkage is communicated and accepted, and how appropriate it is for the organisational context involved. If Kohn is unduly pessimistic, then his opponents seem, at times, to be overly optimistic. As suggested below, some incentive plans may work well in some situations, while being ineffective or even dysfunctional in others.

Individual incentive plans

Merit pay

Schemes that reward individuals on the basis of formal performance appraisal scores are known generically as 'merit pay' plans. Typically, merit payments are based on performance grades determined by means of formal systems of behavioural observation and assessment. In traditional merit pay plans, payments take the form of cumulative additions to base pay. These additions are termed 'merit raises' or 'merit increments.' These reward employees for appraised performance in a previous time period – typically one year. An alternative approach is the 'merit bonus' method, in which the appraisal-based payment does not roll into base pay but, rather, stands apart from it and does not become an ongoing entitlement.

In a merit increment plan, merit payments are expressed as a percentage of base pay and calculated by means of a merit grid. The merit grid (or merit 'matrix' or merit 'guide chart,' as it is also known) specifies the precise link between the assessed performance grade, the employee's current position in the base pay range (also know as the 'compa ratio' – short for compensation comparison ratio) and the percentage performance increment. In essence, the merit grid is a 'ready reckoner' for awarding merit increases based, first, on assessed performance and, second, on current position in the pay range. Clearly, the higher the individual's current base pay level, the greater the monetary reward associated with a percentage increment. Merit grids are also intended to ensure that pay increases are applied consistently by supervisors throughout the whole organisation.

An example of a merit grid is provided in Exhibit 10.7. In this case, the pay range position is broken into quintiles (i.e. fifths) and percentage increments are prescribed for each quintile and each of five performance grades. Note that for each performance grade, progressively smaller percentage increases are given the higher the employee currently sits in their base pay range. This means that the higher the performance rating and the lower the existing position in the pay range, the larger the percentage increase. Conversely, the higher the existing position, the lower the percentage increase, which means that employees with the same level of

Exhibit 10.7 The merit grid

Performance grading	'Base pay range penetration' = current position in base pay range (quintiles)				
	Minimal quintile	Developmental quintile	Qualified quintile	Outstanding quintile	Exceptional quintile
Exceptional	6%–8%	6%–8%	4%–6%	3%–5%	2%–4%
Outstanding	6%–8%	4%–6%	3%–5%	2%–4%	2%–4%
Proficient	4%–6%	3%–5%	2%–4%	2%–4%	0%
Developing	2%–4%	2%–4%	2%–4%	0%	0%
Minimum	0%–2%	0%	0%	0%	0%

Pay range mid-point (compa-ratio = 1.00)

performance should receive around the same dollar amount no matter how large or small their existing base pay happens to be. The aim here is to promote relatively rapid pay acceleration for new job incumbents to the competitive midpoint but, at the same time, to control pay costs at the top end of the range so that the organisation does not become uncompetitive.

The danger in awarding lower percentage increments to those already positioned high in their base pay range is that the nominally lower reward can be demotivating to these employees. This, however, is largely a matter of perception. Much depends on whether employees value the increments in percentage terms or in absolute dollar terms. The crucial issue is how – and how effectively – the logic of the merit grid formula is communicated to the employees affected.

From an organisational perspective, merit increments have many potential advantages. Since pay increments are linked to achieved individual performance, the risk of the employer receiving no return on a pay increase is less than would be the case where pay is not directly performance-related, as in a traditional structure involving seniority-based pay scales. As such, merit increments increase performance-contingent flexibility in base pay adjustment. Merit increments signal the organisation's willingness to 'invest' in employees over the longer term. Likewise, because they increase base pay, merit increments can also reinforce staff attraction and retention.

On the other hand, merit increments are prone to the problems of validity and reliability associated with subjective performance assessment (see Chapter 9). Merit increments also combine performance pay and base pay, which means that employees may fail to see a clear and objective link between performance and pay outcomes. The size of the merit increase may also be too small to have any effect on motivation and performance. This is usually a symptom of inadequate budget allocation. As the following media report suggests, this problem may be particularly pronounced in national cultural contexts that place a low value on individualism. An important point of contrast between merit pay and many other forms of performance-related pay is that merit plans are not self-funding. This is because merit pay is generally based primarily on assessed behaviour rather than on 'hard' financial results. The major drawback, though, is that each merit increment amounts to an 'annuity'; that is, it becomes a permanent addition to base pay. This results in a compound growth in base salary, and the employee continues to receive past increases as annual entitlements irrespective of subsequent performance.[35] While the merit grid approach can control this to some extent, compound increases in base pay can compromise competitive strategy, especially that of the cost defender type.

Incentive pay needs a closer look; top performers not recognised adequately

The tiny gap in merit raises between highly skilled employees and below-average workers is a key reason companies lose talent to rivals, say compensation experts.

Differences in merit increases given to outstanding employees and below-average staff are minuscule in Thailand compared with other countries in Asia, says Pornpimon Maneewongwattana, a senior consultant at Hewitt Associates (Thailand).

The ratio of average merit raises based on performance-linked systems in Thailand between outstanding and average employees is 2.1 times, and 2.7 times between outstanding and bad performers, according to Hewitt's global survey of 162 leading companies worldwide.

In China, the average ratio of merit increases between outstanding and average staff is 1.5 times, while the outstanding below-average ratio is 5.6 times.

Comparable figures in India are 1.8 and 6.5 times; Korea 1.4 and 6.4; Malaysia 1.3 and 4.8; Singapore 1.9 and 9.1; and the Philippines 2.1 and 16.1 times.

Thailand is the only country where the differences in merit raises are almost insignificant.

'That's because it's Thai culture to be kreng jai,' Ms Pornpimon explains. 'So the bosses don't want to get into conflicts if they give the bad performers very low scores. That's one of the ways to lose the key talents who believe they deserve more to other firms.'

She suggests companies should pay higher than what is offered by rivals. 'Hence, it's necessary to study the market and set a benchmark to be followed,' she says, adding that the best way is to give the top talent the maximum the company can afford.

Montana Pornpunyalert, HR director at Deloitte Touche Tohmatsu Jaiyos Co, agrees. She says the gaps in merit raises between the top performers and average to low performers should be more pronounced through more transparent assessment systems.

As well, she says, rewards should be more flexible with a variety of options.

'It's the job of the company to find out what the real motives driving the performance of employees are. Money, particularly to the new generation, is no longer the only motivator driving

employees. Work–life balance, self-fulfilment and recognition are becoming more and more important today,' she said.

Hewitt's survey reveals other reasons for attrition. These include limited growth opportunities or role stagnation in a business (32%), external inequity of compensation (21%), conflicts with leadership or managers (10%), work–life balance (8%), lack of recognition (8%), and under-utilisation of skills (7%).

Across Asia, 98% of respondents said they had performance management systems. Eighty-nine percent link performance ratings to salary increases, 62% agree that performance ratings strongly drive merit increases and 74% say performance ratings strongly drive variable pay.

The countries with fully adopted variable pay systems are Australia, Hong Kong and Singapore, while the level in China is 68.4%, India 95.9%, South Korea 95.5%, Malaysia 80%, Philippines 81.8%, and Thailand 91.7%.

The survey also says that the most common types of variable pay are individual performance awards (77.5%) and stock options/ownership (60.8%).

However, the variable-pay schemes that have the most positive effect on business results … are gain-sharing or productivity payments (83.3%) and cash profit-sharing awards (66.7%). Stock

options, at 35.8%, actually have the least effect on business results, the survey said.

Though the use of key performance indicators (KPI) to measure an employee's performance is popular, it should be implemented with caution, particularly in large, conservative organisations, says Goanpot Asvinvichit, the director-general of the Government Savings Bank.

Take the GSB as an example, he says. 'I haven't dared to implement KPI as it would be too difficult for the employees, who are spread across the country, to comprehend. This is going to take some time, particularly with those who refuse to change.'

Kittiratt Na Ranong, the former president at Stock Exchange of Thailand, believes measuring performance by counting only the outputs is not a just practice.

'That's because there are times that the outputs can't be seen or measured within a few days or weeks. Sometimes it takes much longer,' says Mr Kittiratt, who is now a deputy director at the Sasin Graduate Institute of Business Administration of Chulalongkorn University.

In any case, he says, all HR people and company leaders need to come up with a system to fairly judge performance.

'Leading others the way you want to be led is the key to success,' he says.

Source: Siripunyawit, S. 2006. 'Incentive pay needs a closer look; top performers not recognised adequately,' *Bangkok Post*, 30 October.

The main alternative means of linking individual performance assessment and pay outcomes is the merit bonus approach, also know as the 'lump sum bonus' method. A bonus is a payment made quite separately from base pay. Merit bonuses do not become annuities and, to be retained, they must be re-earned. The critical difference between this approach and traditional merit increments is that the payments made are conditional rather than cumulative. In short, they avoid the annuity problem.[36]

Some merit pay plans combine increments and bonuses. The employee receives regular assessment-based increments only up to the midpoint of the relevant pay range. Once this level is attained, increments cease, and any increases in *total* pay beyond this level take the form of stand-alone bonuses that have to be re-earned each year to be retained. This means that while no employee can have a base pay greater than the midpoint value, there is still opportunity to receive additional amounts of pay related to individual performance.

Individual recognition awards

A key attraction of recognition awards is that they represent a flexible, low-cost and potentially effective alternative to regular merit increments or bonuses. Recognition for immediate past performance may involve rewards that are either financial or non-financial in nature. However, the cash and non-cash approaches are by no means mutually exclusive. Many such plans also involve nomination by peers and customers, not just by supervisors. Advocates argue that recognition should be both celebratory and fun: 'If you can reward a person and have fun in the process, you will satisfy two important desires of most employees: to be appreciated for the work they do and to enjoy their jobs and workplace'.[37]

The simplest form of cash recognition is the discretionary bonus. Discretionary bonuses are irregular lump sum awards for outstanding performance made at the discretion of the supervisor and/or senior management. Payment is kept completely separate from base pay, and the size of the payment is not tied in any arithmetic way to a performance measurement system. Discretionary lump sum payments, being highly visible, can communicate a strong performance message. By the same token, the absence of formal performance assessment means that award allocation may be seen as being arbitrary and with little clear link between performance and reward.

Recognition may also be of a non-cash nature. Non-cash rewards for high performance are also said to have a longer 'shelf life' than cash; that is, they have enduring 'trophy value'.[38] McAdams[39] identifies seven basic forms of non-monetary recognition:

1   social reinforcers: a public 'pat on the back' from the supervisor or peers, positive feedback, staff involvement in planning and decision-making (i.e. social rewards).

2   in-house learning and development opportunities (i.e. developmental rewards)

3   merchandise: either pre-selected items of significant monetary value or access to self-selected goods and services by means of shopping vouchers or certificates, retailer-specific debit cards, or printed or online catalogues from which specific items can be acquired by accumulating sufficient recognition points over a period

4   travel: all-expenses-paid trips for individuals, families or groups

5   symbolic awards: plaques, personal letters from the CEO, flowers, books, 'thank you' notes, publicity in in-house journals or the staff intranet, pins, gold watches, pens and desk-sets, books, CD and DVDs, restaurant meals, theatre tickets, tickets to sporting events, access to corporate 'boxes' at entertainment venues, T-shirts, embossed mugs, company umbrellas or hats, gym or sporting club membership, concierge services, massages, free parking spaces and the like

6   earned time off: time-off with pay additional to normal paid leave entitlements

7   flexible or family-friendly work schedules: ability to adjust working hours to fit personal needs and family commitments.

While many such rewards resemble the indirect benefits discussed above, the difference is that the former are directly performance-linked while the latter are essentially entitlements.

Advocates of the non-cash awards suggest that organisations should seek to recognise and reward performance excellence in more personalised, immediate and exciting ways. McAdams asserts: 'It is easier and more effective to promote the excitement of a noncash award than its cash equivalent. Noncash awards have built-in excitement and recognition factors that cash simply doesn't have'.[40] They are also likely to be less costly than cash. Still, non-cash recognition may also create an atmosphere of 'winners' and 'losers' (when the same few employees repeatedly get the award) or, alternatively, of 'everyone a winner' (where everyone takes a turn at receiving recognition). They may also be demotivating where employees feel that the reward is tokenistic and patronising ('beads and trinkets') and not worth the effort. Some rewards may also convey unintended messages. For instance, McAdams cautions against using earned time off to reward high performers since this may reinforce the perception that leisure is pleasure and work is pain.[41]

While academic research on the effectiveness of recognition awards is still in its infancy, and evidence of plan effectiveness remains largely anecdotal, as News report 10.4 attests, a well-designed and clearly communicated non-cash recognition plan can have a powerful effect on employee attitudes, engagement and performance.

NEWS REPORT 10.4

Insurance Australia Group

Australian insurance giant IAG has an online rewards system for its workforce called 'Reward Help.' Staff can go online at any time and nominate a fellow employee for helping others, for leadership, sustainability and innovation or other achievements.

A citation is emailed to the nominee's manager for approval, and they decide whether the achievement is worthy of an award. Successful nominees receive a thank you e-card or are rewarded with help points scaled from 20 to 150. With each point worth a dollar, employees can bank points or cash them in for a gift. The mechanics of the program are run by an external provider and gifts can be anything that the employee chooses, from theatre tickets and toasters to trips to Sydney's Blue Mountains.

Any company, especially a large one, needs to be careful about the values they reward.

'The awards are driven off "help" which the organisation tends to live by, so the link back to help is easy,' says Malcolm Green, IAG's human resources manager. Also important are 'transparency, honesty and meritocracy.'

The program was initially piloted in two units to create some champions who were keen to make it work and help in gaining buy-in from staff, says Green. 'All staff have access to the intranet so it actually got its own momentum once people understood.' The launch was also important, he adds, with significant effort put into the initial communication and lots of face to face and large meeting groups.

Business buy-in for the program was easy according to Green, as IAG has a long tradition of rewarding its staff and have always set aside a percentage of their salary pool for reward and recognition.

'[Our existing programs were] working quite well but we decided we needed to do something consistent across the group. On the communication side some managers did it better than others,' he says.

In order to measure effectiveness and return on investment, IAG conducts analytics around percentage of reward to salary bills, he says. 'We can satisfy ourselves it's working across the organisation.'

A big win for Green has been in employee engagement. 'We measure staff around engagement scores. We've found in parts of the business that use "Reward Help" effectively we've seen uplift in engagement scores. It may be due in part to some other factors, but there seems like there's quite a strong link,' he says.

The bottom line, according to Green, is that 'a clear link to a business objective is needed at the end of the day to do these things.'

Source: Brown, K. 2005. 'Shiny, happy personnel: Recognition and rewards,' *Human Resources Magazine*, 17 May.

Individual results-based incentives

Incentives geared to measured individual results, or individual 'payment-by-results' plans, are among the oldest and most enduring of all performance pay plans.[42] Included in this category are piece rates, task-and-time bonus plans (where employees are rewarded for completing a specified volume of work or a task in less than a 'standard' time), sales commissions and bonus payments to individuals for achievement of goals.[43] A major attraction of results-based plans for employers is that they offer greater certainty, immediacy and objectivity in the pay–performance relationship than that offered by other pay plans. Since desired results are frequently defined in measurable monetary terms, such plans also tend to be self-funding, which represents an important point of contrast with merit pay plans.

With results-based incentives, the result–reward relationship can be either fixed (i.e. a single rate of reward per unit of output) or configured according to a sliding scale, as in the case of progressively scaled payments, whereby the rate of payment itself increases as output rises. These systems may either be applied in conjunction with a guaranteed minimum base pay or, as in the case of pure piecework and commission-only work, as stand-alone reward plans. Piece rates and task-and-bonus plans were developed primarily for labour-intensive manufacturing jobs and had their heyday in the early to mid-twentieth century, when they were at the forefront of innovation in reward theory and practice in industrialised economies. However, interest in individual output-based incentives of this type has waned with the relative decline in manufacturing activity in Western economies since the 1970s. Sales commissions, of course, remain widely used in such sectors as consumer retailing, finance, insurance and real estate. Conversely, goal-based individual reward plans have become an increasingly important feature of white-collar professional and managerial work. For these reasons, we shall focus here on commissions and goal-based bonuses.

Sales commissions are the retail sector equivalent of piece payment and, like the latter, they may be flat-rate, scaled progressively (or in rare cases regressively), stand-alone (commission-only payment) or paid as an overlay to base pay. Typically, a commission payment will be expressed as a percentage of the sale made. This might be a flat rate of, say, 5 per cent of the value of each sale. Alternatively, the rate may be configured according to a progressive scale, say 3 per cent of the value of the first 10 sales per week, then 5 per cent for the next 10 to 19 sales, then 7 per cent each sale over 20. Commissions may also be expressed as flat dollar amounts rather than as percentages of sales revenue achieved. Whether the system is commission only or base pay plus commission will depend primarily on the nature of the product or service market involved, as will the proportion of total reward that is at risk via commission.

In general, commissions have the attraction of being simple to set and measure. They institute automatic task clarity and provide instant feedback and reinforcement. They substitute for direct supervision of sales staff, which is especially significant where staff are operating in the field rather than on the shop floor. Commissions are also likely to have a strong 'sorting effect' on staff profile, in that only the most effective sales workers are likely to stay on. Conversely, commissions may encourage aggressive, deceptive or negligent selling practices, including the sale of good to consumers who may be unable to service a consumer credit or loan debt. Similarly, individual commission payments may foster excessive competition among sales workers working for the same firm, leading to customer poaching and to the hoarding of market information. Commission-only sellers may neglect important tasks, such as good record-keeping, after-sales follow-up and the training of new sales workers.

Clearly, commissions are applicable only in sales roles. Goal-based bonus plans, however, are capable of being adapted to virtually any role. In essence, these plans entail annual or quarterly bonus payments linked directly to individual goal-setting. Goal-based bonuses may be based on either a flat scale or a sliding (progressive or regressive) scale. Exhibit 10.8 illustrates the difference between flat scale and progressive sliding scale bonuses. In each case the bonus paid for full goal achievement is $1 000. With the flat bonus plan, no bonus is paid unless the goal is met, and no additional bonus is offered for exceeding the goal. Either way, the absence of recognition for both 'near-miss' and 'over-achievement' performance may be demotivating to the individuals affected. An added problem with 'sudden death' plans of this type is that individuals falling just short of the target may engage in calculated dishonesty in order to improve their reward prospects. Sliding scale bonuses seek to avert this possibility. A threshold (or reduced) bonus applies where performance falls marginally short of the goal; the full bonus where the goal is fully achieved; and a premium bonus paid where the goal is exceeded.

Exhibit 10.8 Goal-based individual bonuses: flat and sliding scale plans

Goal achievement	Flat scale*		Progressive sliding scale	
	Rate of bonus payment	Amount of bonus paid	Rate of bonus payment	Amount of bonus paid
130%	100%	$1 000	300%	$3 000
120%	100%	$1 000	200%	$2 000
110%	100%	$1 000	150%	$1 500
100%	**100%**	**$1 000**	**100%**	**$1 000**
90%	0%	$0	60%	$600
80%	0%	$0	30%	$300
70%	0%	$0	0%	$0
60%	0%	$0	0%	$0

*Bonuses are paid out only if the performance target is achieved, which means that the organisation retains 100% of under-target performance improvement.

Goal-setting introduces a degree of transparency, ownership and apparent objectivity rarely possible with a behaviourally based appraisal. Even so, goal-setting is not without its risks. Where goals are either too loose/easy or too tight/hard, too few or too many, a goal-based bonus plan is unlikely to be effective. Where the goals are financial in nature, such plans are self-funding, which means that they avoid one of the major shortcomings of traditional merit pay plans, namely that of budget underfunding. By the same token, where the plan incorporates non-financial goals, such as those related to site safety or customer satisfaction, goal achievement on these criteria will require special funding, with all of its attendant challenges. A further potential problem with the goal achievement approach is that it focuses the employee's attention and effort solely on goals that attract a reward. As with sales commissions, rewarding only the hard, measurable results may encourage employees to ignore equally important but less quantifiable aspects of the job or role.

Collective short-term incentive plans

Most collective short-term incentive plans fall into one or other of four plan types: profitsharing, gainsharing, goalsharing and team incentives. In certain contexts, such plans may have decided advantages over individual incentives. Indeed, individual incentives may be quite dysfunctional in organisations where work is organised on interdependent and cross-functional lines and where results are predicated on a high degree of inter-employee cooperation. Interdependence

of this type is one of the hallmarks of teamworking and high involvement management. In such organisations, it may be neither possible nor logical to attribute performance to specific individuals, since what counts is collective effort and contribution. Collective incentives may encourage employees to work collaboratively to achieve goals that require teamwork and cooperation. Accordingly, collective incentive schemes are more likely to elicit a greater degree of organisational citizenship behaviour than are schemes of an individual nature. Collective plans are also likely to encounter less opposition from trade unions than are individual incentive plans. This is primarily because collective incentives focus on transparent results-based performance criteria rather than on individual behavioural assessment. In general, collective plans are also amenable to collective bargaining, employee involvement and more egalitarian pay outcomes. This is not to suggest that collective incentive plans are necessarily incompatible with individual performance pay plans. With careful planning, it is possible to combine the two approaches in such a way that they are mutually reinforcing. For instance, while the funding of a performance pay pool might be based on measures of improvement in collective results, the distribution of payments from the pool could be based on assessed individual contribution.[44]

Profitsharing

A profitsharing plan typically involves a formal arrangement under which bonus payments are made to eligible employees on a regular (usually annual) basis, based on a formula that links the size of the total bonus pool to an accounting measure of periodic (typically annual) profit, such as net profit (total income less operating costs) or net profit after tax. As such, profitsharing is applicable only to profit-making organisations and is not relevant to public sector organisations or non-profit entities. Payments usually take the form of a cash bonus, which may either be paid out immediately at the end of the relevant performance cycle (a 'current' plan), or set aside for future access at departure or retirement (a 'deferred' plan).

By allowing overall labour costs to be varied automatically according to the employer's 'capacity to pay,' profitsharing is seen as providing a form of organisational insurance against external contingencies, particularly fluctuations in product market demand and prices. As such, profitsharing is wholly self-funding. It may also increase employees' identification with and understanding of the organisation's financial circumstances, enhance citizenship behaviour and reduce industrial conflict.

At the same time, however, profitsharing has a number of potential drawbacks. Because profitability is influenced by many variables that are beyond employees' collective control, the line of sight between individual performance and reward is likely to be weak; that is, the 'instrumentality' nexus between effort and reward, as prescribed by expectancy theory, is at best very weak. For the same reason, profitsharing may give rise to 'free riding' or 'social loafing,' especially where payments are allocated on an equal basis irrespective of individual contribution. Profitsharing may also attract union opposition, especially where union members see it as a way for employers to substitute variable pay for fixed base pay and to undermine union rates of pay.

Gainsharing

Gainsharing is a form of collective performance-related pay in which management shares with all employees in a particular production plant or business unit the financial gains associated with specific measures of improvement in the results achieved by that work group as measured against an historical benchmark of the group's performance. Gainshare plans thus have four defining features:

1   A focus on measurable results that are within employees' collective control, such as labour productivity, unit labour costs, reduced materials wastage and the like.

2   The specification of a historical baseline of financial performance against which subsequent financial gains can be determined.

3   The use of a predetermined formula for sharing the monetary gains between the organisation and the participating employees.

4   A formal system of employee participation in making suggestions and decisions about ways to improve work group performance. In many (although not all) cases, gainshare schemes are designed, implemented and administered by joint management–employee committees.

Traditional gainshare plans emphasise 'hard' single-factor performance measures like labour cost reduction or labour productivity improvement. For instance, under the Scanlon Gainshare Plan, formulated in the USA in the late 1930s by sometime steelworker, unionist and university professor, Joseph Scanlon, productivity gains are measured in terms of shifts in the ratio of overall labour costs to the value of total sales, set against a carefully determined historical benchmark ratio. The lower the measured ratio in relation to the benchmark, the greater the labour saving and, hence, the greater the gain. Gains are calculated on a monthly basis and shared between employees and the organisation on the basis of a predetermined formula, typically in the ratio of 75 per cent to 25 per cent. Typically, all employees get the same percentage payout on their base pay, and payments are made on a weekly, monthly or quarterly basis. In many Scanlon plans, only 50 per cent of the gain is distributed automatically to employees. The remaining 25 per cent is placed in an equalisation fund to reimburse the company for any future 'negative gains,' with any excess remaining in the fund being distributed at the end of the year. The Scanlon model also places a strong emphasis on cooperative relations between management, workers and any unions that might be present and on employee participation in productivity improvement. A joint labour–management 'productivity committee' oversees scheme design, implementation and maintenance. Workers are also encouraged to submit suggestions for improving productivity and reducing costs, which are vetted by a special joint screening committee.[45]

One weakness in the Scanlon plan approach is a failure to factor out changes in sales value that are attributable to uncontrolled movements in external materials and commodity prices. More sophisticated plans, such as the Rucker and Improshare plans, seek to address this shortcoming.[46]

Like profitsharing, such plans are self-funding, but gainsharing also has a number of advantages over profitsharing. They can be targeted to particular plants, departments or divisions, or to discrete business units in the wider organisation. This compares with profitsharing, which is generally organisation-wide. Unlike profitsharing, they can be applied in public sector and other non-profit organisations. They also seek to reward only those results that are within the group's control. They can support a high-involvement culture through employee involvement programs and devolution of decision-making. They are also compatible with a unionised workforce and collective bargaining.[47] The emphasis on continuous improvement means that gainsharing is well suited to quality defender and analyser competitive strategies. Equally, they would be a poor fit for prospector strategies, since each change in technology, work organisation and product type will require recalibration of historical performance benchmarks. Like profit-sharing, they are also vulnerable to free riding. Finally, given the focus on 'hard' measures of cost and productivity improvement, traditional gainsharing plans ignore non-financial or 'soft' aspects of group performance, such as worksite safety, environmental compliance and customer satisfaction.

Goalsharing

Goalsharing is the collective equivalent of individual goal-based bonuses (discussed above) and, like the latter, it draws on the technique of goalsetting. As with goal-based individual bonuses, payments may be either flat-rate or geared (see above for discussion).

While goalsharing resembles gainsharing, it has several major differences. First, goalsharing is future-oriented, whereas gainsharing is tied to retrospective performance benchmarks. This makes goalsharing simpler to develop and more flexible, as well as wider in application and better placed to accommodate rapid changes in technology and product or service type. As such, it is particularly well-suited to a prospector competitive strategy. Second, goalsharing generally includes a combination of 'hard' and 'soft' performance factors, with the latter serving as deterrence to a narrow focus on hard results. For example, a multifactor goalsharing plan might include both financial criteria, such as controllable expenses and net revenue, and non-financial criteria, such as on-time delivery, customer satisfaction and product quality, with different weightings attached to each factor. Third, with multi-factor goalsharing of this type, the plan is generally not self-funding. Rather than creating a pool based on dollar value improvements above a performance baseline, goalsharing allocates a predetermined amount geared to the achievement of specific goals. A series of goals are established for the work group and a fixed, predetermined amount is paid to the group for each goal achieved or exceeded.[48]

Team incentives

Team incentives tend to be small group adaptations of single-factor gainsharing or multi-factor goalsharing. Team incentives emerged – or, more accurately, re-emerged – in the 1990s as the reward corollary of teamworking. Since they are targeted at the performance of small work groups they have greater potential to overcome the 'line of sight' problem so common in large group plans. However, the choice of team incentives rather than another collective incentive plan, such as business unit gainsharing or goalsharing, will depend primarily on how self-managing and autonomous the work teams are in relation to the rest of the organisation. If teams are largely self-managing, there is little interdependence between teams and the emphasis is on cooperation *within* individual teams, then team incentives may well be appropriate since each team will exercise considerable control over what it does and what it achieves. Conversely, where teams are highly interdependent and the emphasis is on cooperation *between* teams to achieve divisional, departmental or organisational goals, then a gainshare or goalshare plan pitched at capturing and rewarding the performance of the larger group may be more appropriate. In short, the greater the degree of inter-team dependence, the wider the coverage of the group performance scheme should be.[49]

Team incentives are well suited to organisations characterised by task interdependence, crossfunctionality, project work and participative management. This means that it is appropriate for both high involvement analysers and prospectors, but particularly to the latter, which typically have flat structures with networks of autonomous project teams. It may also be the case that team incentives will be less effective in a unionised setting. One reason for this may be that unionised employees are more reluctant to engage in peer monitoring and surveillance than non-unionists. Another reason may be that unionised organisations tend to be managed along traditional lines, leaving little scope for the potential benefits of employee participation.

Equity-based long-term incentive plans

Organisation-wide long-term incentive plans – more commonly known as employee share (or 'stock' or 'equity') plans – reward employees for improvements over time in the employing firm's share market performance. Such plans allow eligible employees access to share ownership in the organisation that employs them. Once confined almost wholly to executives, since the share booms of the 1980s and 1990s share plans have also assumed a significant role in non-executive reward practice, although their incidence varies considerably from country to country and industry to industry.

The potential rewards from share plans take four main forms: share price appreciation (or capital gain); annual dividend earnings; special bonus share issues; and special taxation concessions or exemptions. As such, share plans are seen as having a long-term benefit via the reinforcement of employee commitment to organisational success. Because they stand to foster an 'ownership' mentality among employees, share plans are also generally supportive of a high involvement culture. However, the precise attitudinal and behavioural outcomes will depend, *inter alia*, on the extent of employee eligibility and take-up and on the particular plan or plans involved. Shares may be issued to employees free of any charge (share bonus plans) or they may be sold to them at a discount on the market price (discounted share purchase plans) or using an employer-funded low-interest or interest-free loan. A third type of share plan – employee option plans – gives employees the option of acquiring a specified quantity of company shares at a particular price on or after a designated future date.[50]

Share grants

With share grants, or share bonus plans as they are also known, employees receive a gift of fully paid shares in the firm. Shares are 'fully paid' if the price of the shares has been fully met and no acquisition debt is incurred by the recipient. The distribution of shares to each employee is commonly based on a predetermined allocation formula – perhaps according to years of service with the company, position in the organisational hierarchy, on the basis of individual performance, or as an equal number or value of shares to each employee where the size of the grant is determined by group or organisational financial results, as in, say, a profitshare scheme. Some grants can also be traded immediately, which means that the grant is technically 'unrestricted.' However, it has become increasingly common for share grants to have certain limitations attached, which generally means that ownership does not transfer ('vest') immediately and/or that the shares are not be tradable immediately in the same way as 'common stock' (i.e. ordinary shares held by external investors). Conditional share grants of this type are known as 'restricted' share plans. While employees are not required to outlay any of their own money, they usually cannot sell their shares until a specified minimum period has elapsed.

For the company, share grants may encourage long-term employee commitment and membership behaviour, particularly where restricted shares and trust arrangements are involved. A firm may also issue shares as a way of securing employee acceptance of an organisational change strategy. In smaller companies, restricted share grants may also be a means of locking up company equity to prevent hostile takeovers. Equally, issuing share grants to employees may require a company previously managed along traditional lines to institute a new management system that is more 'open book' and participative. From the employee's perspective, share grants have the obvious advantage of being notionally cost-free, although grants are sometimes in lieu of an increase in cash remuneration, which means that an opportunity cost is involved. Regular share grants can serve as a convenient means for employees to supplement retirement savings although employee shareholders may well have a far higher risk exposure than will external shareholders since the latter are more likely to have a diversified share portfolio covering a range of sectors, industries and firms. Depending on the prevailing taxation regime, share grants may also carry tax advantages for share recipients, particularly where shares are received in lieu of additional cash remuneration and where tax liability on shares received can be deferred until retirement by being held in a managed trust.

Share purchase plans

With share purchase plans, employees have the opportunity to purchase part or all of a specified quota of shares in the company. Employees typically pay a small deposit on the full share purchase price with the balance of the purchase price repayable over a specified term. The plan typically

includes favourable purchase terms, such as a purchase price set below the prevailing market value and/or a low or zero interest loan from the company to fund the purchase. Some schemes allow the share purchase loan to be repaid from dividends so that the repayment period is open-ended and there is no employee outlay from personal savings. Other schemes involve employee savings plans and pay deductions to fund purchase. Legal ownership of the shares vests to the employee over time as the loan is paid off.

Share purchase funded by a company loan means that employees are indebted to the company for the duration of the loan and may thus be more accommodating of management initiatives. Also, where employees have had to pay for the shares, intrinsic or 'ownership' motivation is likely to be considerably stronger and more enduring than would be the case where shares have been received as a gift. By the same token, share purchase plans entail greater risk all round than is the case with share grants. In particular, by their very nature, share purchase plans expose employees to greater financial risk. Employees committed to repaying the principal on a company loan at a fixed purchase price will experience severe financial difficulties if the share price collapses and the debt is not renegotiated or forgiven.

Ownership in action

It was Karl Marx who suggested workers should own the means of production. More than a 100 years later, in a bastion of capitalism, ad agency Clemenger Communication Limited's 1212 staff are the means of production and most of them own the shop – 53.33 per cent of it at least.

Robert Gardner CPA, Clemenger's group accountant, says: 'Our company is a factory floor of people, we don't have any machinery. And if we can attract the best people, then obviously we are going to be able to produce the best work and pass that onto our clients.'

The US-based global advertising group BBDO, which first bought a 35 per cent stake in the company in 1972, owns the remainder.

In the fickle world of advertising, staff turnover is high and agencies fight to retain the star talent. The Clemenger scheme is designed to reward all staff equally.

Now that Australia has a buoyant economy, an ageing population and a skills squeeze, it's important for all companies to recruit and retain the best while increasing productivity.

BlueScope Steel, spun off from BHP in 2002, acknowledges a direct correlation with productivity improvements, although it is difficult to quantify precisely.

The company is typical in that most employee share schemes are within ASX-listed companies. Almost all 17 000 staff own shares in the company thanks to a plan that gifted staff shares to employees under Div 13A of the ATO's employee share acquisition scheme. The scheme allows companies to give $1 000 of shares tax free to employees each year.

In 2003 BlueScope gave employees the option to receive 200 shares at a share price of $5.00. In 2004 staff had the option to receive 150 shares at a share price of $7.86. This means that with capital growth and dividends, each employee has received $3 300 from the company. This year, BlueScope is inviting employees to buy $100 to $500 worth of shares, which it will boost by offering two shares for every one bought.

At Clemenger, the plan doesn't give freebies. Gardner says it's a way to reward and motivate staff and to help build their wealth. 'And it also brings a lot of stability,' he says.

Full-time or part-time staff can own the shares, including those at minority-owned companies, such as Hardie Grant Magazines, the publisher of *INTHEBLACK* for CPA Australia. Under the constitution the maximum staff shareholding is 5 per cent. The company's 04/05 annual report states that 441 staff own shares. Its share price has increased by 11 per cent to $2.47 and its dividend increased by 32 per cent to 36 cents.

The share valuation formula is spelt out in the constitution.

'The share price is purely based on the net assets and financial performance of the group and that's ratified by the auditors Ernst & Young every year,' Gardner says.

Usually about half the company's profits are paid as a dividend. That leaves the other half to be invested back into the company. If someone leaves the company, they must sell their share after the trade date of 1 December. 'The logic is that you should only benefit, if you contribute to the company,' Gardner says.

Clemenger has talked to many companies interested in replicating the scheme. 'We've had enquiries over time from funeral parlours to car dealers up in Griffith,' Gardner says. 'It's not the mechanics of the scheme that's the important part. The important part is to be able to retain good quality staff long term.'

Other companies that have ESOPs

Consulting engineers Ove Arup is owned by one Australian and two UK trusts. In 1968 the first trusts were established to gradually transfer ownership from the senior partners to the staff. This was completed in 1979.

Shepparton-based metal fabricators J. Furphy & Sons introduced an ESOP in 1997 as a way of involving the staff. Each year, 10 per cent of the company's after-tax profit is distributed. All employees who have been with the company for more than 18 months receive their bonus in tax-free non-voting shares.

Earlier this year DMC Outsourcing, a supply chain management operation, offered shares to anyone who had been with the company for more than a year.

Source: Extract from Charles, E. 2005. 'Share and share alike,' *INTHEBLACK*, November, p. 32.

Share option plans

An option plan grants the employee the right to buy a specified number of company shares at a predetermined price at a specified future date, such as the third anniversary of the option grant date. The price payable to exercise the option to acquire some or all of the shares – the 'strike price' – is commonly set at or below the market value of the shares at the time the option is granted. If the market price increases after the option is granted, the option-holder stands to make a net gain by exercising the option to acquire the shares, then selling some or all of them on the general market. An employee who expects a further rise in the share price may retain some or all of the shares acquired. Unexercised options carry no shareholders' rights and, unlike fully vested shares, options are not normally transferable.

Since the granting of an option does not confer immediate equity ownership, there will be no 'ownership' effect on motivation unless and until the option is exercised. Until the options are exercisable, the main behavioural effects will be twofold. First, restriction on exercise will reinforce staff retention, since the options are likely to be forfeited if the option-holder leaves the company. Second, during the holding period, the incentive effect will be largely extrinsic; that is, the holder will be motivated to improve company performance so as to strengthen market perceptions and increase the market share price with a view to maximising any capital gain when it becomes possible to exercise the option to buy and sell the shares involved.

However, with option plans the 'line of sight' between employee effort and financial reward is even more remote than is the case with share grant and purchase plans, since the realisation of any market-related rewards are significantly delayed. In 'bull' share market conditions, in which most companies are experiencing share price appreciation, options may confer unearned ('windfall') gains on some option-holders. For these reasons, it has become common practice for option plans to include exercise hurdles that make use of relative rather than absolute measures of a company's share market performance. For instance, the focus might be on how the company's share price performs relative to a group of peer firms, regardless of whether the share price trend for the group as a whole is rising or falling. As with all equity plans, options are 'fair weather' reward instruments; they may work well in time of share price growth, but can also compound a firm's problems if the share price falls, say in a declining ('bear') share market, and the market price falls below the option strike price. Option plans may also encourage a speculative outlook among employees rather than an ownership mentality.[51]

In general, employee share plans are particularly appropriate for organisations that are genuinely committed to a high degree of employee involvement and participation.[52] More specifically, given the accent on entrepreneurship, risk-taking and alignment with shareholder value, a broadly based option plan would seem to be a more appropriate choice for high involvement prospector organisations than for firms managed along more traditional lines and pursuing either defender or analyser competitive strategies, for which share grant or share purchase plans would be a better fit.

Executive incentive plans

While the incentive plans applied to executive-level employees, including salaried chief executive officers (CEOs), company managing directors and executive chairmen, resemble those applied to other employees, executive incentives are also sufficiently distinct in character to warrant separate treatment. By far the most important difference is that executive performance is almost universally equated with organisational results – and rewarded accordingly. Executive incentives are of two main types: short-term incentives; and long-term incentives.

Executive short-term incentives

Executive short-term incentives are awarded on the basis of one or more aspects of organisational performance over a short period, generally one year. Payments typically take the form of an annual cash bonus, and it is increasingly common for payment to be contingent on the executive achieving one or more targets related to the firm's absolute or relative annual financial or accounting performance. In essence, this amounts to reward-linked executive goal-setting, with the targets themselves generally focused on one or more indicators of the firm's annual financial performance; that is, on its internal accounting performance. Some widely applied financial measures include:

* operating expenses compared to budget

* revenue growth

* net earnings, or net income

* net operating profit after taxes (NOPAT)

* earnings before interest and taxes (EBIT), or operating income

* earnings before interest, taxes, depreciation and amortisation (EBITDA)

* earnings per share (EPS), or net income divided by the average number of shares outstanding

* return on assets (ROA), or net income divided by total assets

* return on equity (ROE), or net income divided by total shareholders equity

For the firm itself, the two main advantages of accounting-based measures are high 'instrumentality' (i.e. the relatively clear line of sight between executive behaviour, the performance indicator and the resulting reward) and the immediacy of the 'reinforcement' effect.

The chief drawback is their susceptibility to manipulation. Profit- and cost-related bonuses have particular problems in this regard. Indeed, they highlight particularly sharply the possibility that incentive plans may actually exacerbate rather than curb the 'principal–agent problem.' For instance, in order to achieve a bonus, the executive may be tempted to inflate the firm's paper profits artificially by postponing infrastructure investment, cutting back on research and development, retrenching staff to reduce payroll costs or divesting assets to raise revenue. Such actions will deliver a short-term personal gain but only at the cost of longer-term organisational performance and sustainability.[53] It is partly for this reason that firms typically apply both short-term and long-term incentives to their executive-level employees.

Executive long-term incentives

Executive long-term incentives tend to relate to organisational share market performance over a three-, five- or 10-year period, with rewards generally taking the form of company equity rather than cash, although cash payments based on multiyear performance would also qualify. The aim is to encourage a longer-term focus on improving organisational performance, particularly in terms of total returns to shareholders. Increasingly, such plans include both market-related performance targets and restrictions on the disposal of equity-based rewards.

The rapid growth in the remuneration of senior executives employed by listed companies in many developed Western countries since the early 1990s was driven chiefly by an explosion in the use of equity-based plans. Such plans come in an almost limitless variety of forms, but most existing plans fall into one of the following categories:

- restricted share plans

- option plans

- performance shares (or zero exercise price options)

- share appreciation rights.

Restricted share plans are variants of straight share bonuses or grants (discussed above). The executive receives the share free of charge, but full shareholder entitlement is 'restricted' in some way. For instance, the shares may be subject to forfeiture if the executive leaves the firm before the expiry of a specified period, a restriction commonly referred to as a 'golden handcuff.' Alternatively, or additionally, full ownership ('vesting') of the shares may be subject to the meeting of a performance target or 'hurdle' within this period. A commonly used market indicator is total shareholder return, which measures the additional wealth per share accruing annually to ordinary shareholders in the form of share price appreciation, dividend payments and any bonus share issues.

While executive option plans are similar to broadly-based option plans (discussed above), they also have some important differences. Firstly, companies in many Western countries are now required to report the 'fair value' of all new option grants to top executives and to 'expense' such grants against company income. Mandatory expensing is intended to counter the questionable belief that option grants are a 'nil-cost' means of remunerating executives. It is now widely agreed that option grants do impose various costs on the company and its shareholders.[54] There is the opportunity cost of income foregone by the company in issuing options to executives rather than, say, exchanging them for cash in a derivatives market. Shareholders may also incur an additional cost in the form of share 'dilution'; that is, a reduction in share price and/ or returns per share. This occurs when companies simply create an additional volume of shares for executives or when executives dispose of option-acquired shares in the general share market.

A second distinguishing feature of executive option plans is that it has become increasingly common for the option to purchase shares to be conditional on one or more performance 'hurdles' being met. One of the most commonly used relative performance hurdles in current executive option plans is the achievement of total shareholder returns (TSR) in excess of the

50th (i.e. median) percentile of returns achieved by a specified group of peer companies. That is, if the firm achieves TSR better than half of the comparator group, the options vest. Relative hurdles of this type also commonly incorporate performance-conditioned vesting. For instance, if the firm achieves TSR equivalent to the peer group median, the executive may receive 50 per cent of the full potential option entitlement; if its TSR performance exceeds the 75th percentile of peer group performance, 100 per cent of the entitlement may vest. However, there is now considerable evidence to suggest that market performance hurdles themselves are susceptible to executive manipulation.[55]

Risks in rewards

Poorly designed incentive schemes for chief executives can be counter-productive.

Boards have made much progress in measuring company and executive success. Accounting measures have given way to market measures – in particular, total shareholder returns (TSRs). Long-term incentive hurdles for chief executives have moved from absolute to relative measures (often TSR relative to peer companies) to reward or penalise chief executives on their performances, rather than at the whim of the market. Although some targets and constraints on long-term incentives (LTIs) and how these can vary with TSRs may sound reasonable, they can induce value-destroying behaviour.

The hurdles that most companies set on LTI plans require chief executives to achieve returns substantially higher than their peers in order to receive a maximum reward. For example, BHP Billiton and Rio Tinto pay the maximum under their LTI plans only if TSR is at least 5.5% and 5% (respectively) a year above the median of these companies' peers. One S&P/ASX 100 company has gone a step further and set itself a long-term target TSR of several times its cost of equity. Buoyed by its achievement of a five-year return exceeding three times its cost of equity, the company has set a goal of maintaining this performance. Sounds reasonable, but is it possible?

An AT Kearney study tracked most of the world's listed companies from the late 1980s to the early 2000s.

Not one company managed TSRs above its cost of equity for 12 consecutive years. Few managed three years, and even fewer five years.

AT Kearney's explanation of these results emphasised the difficulty of sustaining superior performance.

A company can earn TSRs above its cost of equity but market expectations are even more important. If investors expect it to earn more than its cost of equity, they buy shares and keep buying them (raising the price) until the expected TSR falls in relation to the cost of equity.

A company can exceed market expectations by creating nice surprises – for example, sales growth above expectations. It may do this for several years running, but as investors see sales growth expectations consistently exceeded, they will raise their expectations and bid up the share price. Eventually, expectations catch up to reality and TSRs fall in line with the cost of equity.

Even the few companies possessing sustainable competitive advantages that enable them to consistently earn superior profits on investment do not, on average, earn TSRs above their cost of equity. The market expects them to earn those superior profits, and factors this into prices.

The S&P/ASX 100 company cited earlier managed to surprise the market with a series of acquisitions and neat financial engineering. Although it may outperform market expectations for a couple more years, it cannot do so indefinitely – and this is no slight on the company.

The danger is that while the company continues to hold that lofty target, it must create bigger surprises each year to achieve it.

It must gamble on risky and big 'bet the company' moves or, preferably, abandon the target.

Exceeding the median TSR of peers by 5% in any one year may sound reasonable (although it is less than a one-in-three chance), but exceeding the median by 5% a year over five years (about 30% cumulative) is much harder. Performance hurdles substantially above the peer median can encourage dysfunctional behaviour.

The pressure for surprises can cause chief executives to mislead the market. Before the start of the TSR measurement period, a chief executive may play down the company's prospects (depressing the share price) to make the hurdle easier to achieve.

During the measurement period, the chief executive may take big risks against shareholders' interests, particularly if achieving the hurdle becomes more difficult. Towards the end of the measurement period, the chief executive may overstate company earnings or prospects to reach the hurdle.

Most Australian companies pay no LTI unless TSR exceeds the peer group median. Some companies (such as National Australia Bank) that previously set lower hurdles have since adopted this practice. But chief executives can usually predict reasonably well, at least one year before the vesting date, whether they will beat the median. Therefore, those with little or no hope of doing so (probably at least 25% of chief executives) have no effective positive incentive at all (only the negative incentive of risking getting fired). Resulting dysfunctional behaviour may include high risk-taking, delayed disclosure of positive news, earnings mis-statements or engineering value-destroying mergers to automatically trigger vesting.

Do you think your chief executive would not engage in such behaviour? Evidence suggests otherwise.

A recent study of hundreds of companies by Harvard University and Massachusetts Institute of Technology academics found that the stronger the link between chief executive rewards and shareholder value creation, the greater the incidence of earnings manipulation through discretionary accruals.

Chief executive compensation schemes will never be perfect. Sometimes it is sufficient simply to be aware of the imperfections and guard against the dysfunction they can cause.

But quick fixes, such as vesting some LTIs below the median, and checking for sanity the reasonableness of multi-year TSR targets, can be readily implemented.

Source: Kerin, P. 2006. 'Risks in Rewards,' *Business Review Weekly*, 29 June.

In recent years, many firms have replaced option plans with performance shares or zero exercise price options (or ZEPO plans). With such plans, the executive is allowed to take up shares at no cost but only on condition of a performance hurdle being satisfied over a designated performance period. In other words, the executive receives a free grant of shares subject to a hurdle. Since fewer ZEPOs will be needed to deliver a level of reward comparable to that of a fixed price option plan, there is less potential for dilution of ordinary shareholder wealth, especially when the shares themselves are acquired in the marketplace rather than being new issue. Unlike options, performance shares do not encourage speculative behaviour.

Share appreciation rights differ from option plans in two main respects. First, they take account of dividend earnings as well as share price appreciation per se over the designated grant period. Second, the executive is not required to take ownership of the shares; rather, the executive receives cash equivalent to the wealth that would accrue to ordinary shareholders via share price appreciation plus dividend earnings over the grant period, with the baseline typically being the market price at the date of grant. While rights payments are a direct cost to the firm, unlike unexercised option holdings, they allow the executive to share in the dividend stream flowing to ordinary shareholders during the period of the grant. The executive stands to receive a cash payment geared to the total returns to shareholders over a specified period in the form of share price appreciation plus dividends, whereas rewards flowing from an option plan will reflect share price movements only. In short, appreciation rights plans replicate the monetary gains accruing to ordinary shareholders but avoid the dilution effect common with option plans.[56]

Pay for performance or pay without performance?

Just how effective these executive incentive plans are in aligning executive reward with changes in ordinary shareholder wealth is a matter of ongoing empirical dispute. Studies conducted in the USA, the UK and Australia[57] indicate that executive reward levels are sensitive to prior changes in company performance, although in most cases the reported associations are weak. Critics like Bebchuk and Fried[58] argue that the day-to-day power and knowledge at CEOs' command continues to allow them to 'decouple' pay from performance and to extract 'stealth compensation' from unwitting or compliant company boards, including extravagant sign-on, termination and post-employment payments. Clearly, such effects will vary from country to country and company to company.[59]

Overall, the weight of evidence suggests that there is ample scope for company boards in general – and their remuneration committees in particular – to be more vigilant and robust in the approach that they take to linking executive reward to organisational performance. Contrary to the views of some apologists for spiralling CEO reward levels, it is also incumbent on human resource practitioners to alert boards to the possibility that the growing gap between executive and non-executive reward may, indeed, impair not only the motivation and commitment of line employees and managers but also the performance of the organisation as a whole. Cowherd and Levine[60] have found that the wider the pay differential between lower-level employees and senior managers, the greater the degree of lower-level dissonance and the lower the level of lower-level commitment, cooperation, effort and attention to quality. Byrne and Bongiorno[61] report similar findings. As such, the assumption that it is only the executive team that delivers 'shareholder value' is unsustainable.

Fitting it all together

Having examined the main elements of total remuneration and total reward, we can now turn to consider how best to combine these possible components into a strategically-aligned total reward system. As suggested above, there is no one 'best practice' reward system configuration. The aim should be to select and integrate those reward practices that best align with and support the strategy, structure and culture of the relevant organisation or, where appropriate, of its distinct business units. Developing a strategic reward system entails three key steps:

1   preparing a statement of reward philosophy and strategy
2   determining total reward mix
3   determining remuneration levels.

Statement of reward philosophy and strategy

Choosing the right reward mix requires that the organisation first establish its basic strategic requirements, particularly preferred employee attitudes, required performance inputs (i.e. skills and competencies), and desired work behaviours and results. It is the identification, application, measurement and reward of these human resource factors that holds the key to achieving strategic reward fit or alignment and, hence, to maximising the contribution of the organisation's human resources to strategic effectiveness and success.

Once the main human resource requirements have been identified, it is advisable to incorporate them into a brief statement of reward 'philosophy,' purpose and strategy. This may also form part of a wider human resource strategy statement (see Chapter 1 for discussion). The aim is to define succinctly the broad role that reward practices should play in assisting the organisation to be successful and sustainable and the values or 'philosophy' that will inform the approach taken. A reward strategy statement is basically a normative blueprint, or set of guiding principles, as to how associated practices will be applied to support the organisation's aims. This also presents the opportunity to define in broad terms the desired relationship between these and other human resource functions.[62] Most importantly, the reward strategy statement should indicate the primary purposes to which reward management will be directed. For instance, will the focus be on staffing (i.e. attraction and retention), on motivation, on cost-effectiveness, or on a three-way balance? A reward strategy that has a cost focus would be concerned, first and foremost, with controlling labour costs and keeping labour costs in line with industry levels and external labour market practices. A strategy that focuses on a staffing role would highlight the role of remuneration in attracting and retaining staff of the right type. A strategy that has a motivational focus would emphasise the role of financial and non-financial rewards in eliciting desired performance factors.

Exhibit 10.9 illustrates the form that a reward philosophy and strategy statement may take. In this example, the strategic requirements and performance factors are those of a high involvement prospector organisation (as described in Exhibit 10.3).

Exhibit 10.9 Example of a reward philosophy and strategy statement

At Dynastar, competitive success flows from our agility, adaptability, creativity and innovation – from our ability to anticipate market trends and to be the global leader in new product and service innovation. At Dynastar, we celebrate diversity both in our human capabilities and in the products and services that we deliver to our customers and clients in all parts of the world. We see the capabilities and contributions of our people as holding the key to success in our ever-changing competitive environment.

We offer our people work that is exciting, diverse and challenging, with a high degree of accountability and autonomy. To us, the essence of high contribution and performance is:

- ☑ self-management and growth of personal knowledge, abilities and talent
- ☑ championing our core competencies: citizenship, flexibility, creativity, market-focus, and ethics
- ☑ individual creativity and innovation
- ☑ strategic decisiveness and risk-taking
- ☑ timeliness and effectiveness in meeting challenging goals
- ☑ maintaining a positive balance between individual and team commitments
- ☑ demonstrating excellence, leadership and citizenship in every assignment.

At Dynastar, we offer work that is intrinsically exciting and rewards that recognize and celebrate individual and team excellence and that share the fruits of our competitive success. Above all else, our approach to employee reward will acknowledge:

- ☑ our strategic goals and priorities
- ☑ the worth of attracting the best available talent for as long as is mutually acceptable
- ☑ the importance of career self-management and portability
- ☑ individual creativity and contribution
- ☑ teamworking and citizenship
- ☑ the principal of reward for individual contribution and effectiveness rather than for seniority or position
- ☑ the importance of seeing our people as stakeholders and shareholders in our competitive success
- ☑ the importance of flexibility in reward choice
- ☑ the need to maintain fairness, transparency and consistency in reward administration
- ☑ the value of involving staff in system development and administration.

Source: Shields J. 2007. *Managing employee performance and reward: Concepts, practices, strategies*, Cambridge University Press, Melborne.

Determining total reward mix

The challenge here is to identify the bundle of reward practices that best 'match' or 'fit' the reward strategy; that is, to determine a 'best fit' reward configuration. This is really a multidimensional design challenge. On the widest scale, practices should fit organisation-wide strategy, structure, culture and life stage. At the same time, the practices should match the strategic and technical requirements of particular business units within the organisation, the configuration of particular work groups or teams within each business unit, the particular roles and occupations within the organisation and, as far as possible, the particular needs and expectations of individual employees.

The first design challenge is to determine an appropriate balance between the four generic reward types identified in Exhibit 10.1. Developmental and social rewards may be particularly effective in enhancing organisational commitment and citizenship behaviour since they address the so-called middle- and higher-order needs: the needs for social affiliation, esteem and 'self-actualisation' or personal growth. As such, developmental and social rewards can play a vital part in reinforcing the effects of remuneration. Financial rewards alone might not be enough to bind employees to the organisation or to elicit affective commitment to the organisation's success. O'Neal[63] also makes the point that non-monetary rewards may well hold the key to competitive advantage. Pay systems can be easily copied by competitors, but it will be far harder for them to emulate an effective system of developmental and social rewards.

In most organisations, though, the emphasis is likely to fall primarily on financial rewards, and this brings us to our second major design challenge relating to reward mix, namely the mix of remuneration plans. There are many questions that need to be addressed here:

- How much importance should be placed on base pay?

- How should base pay be structured?

- Does the nature of the work lend itself to skill- or competency-based base pay?

- What role should benefits play?

- Should benefits be fixed or flexible?

- How much emphasis should be placed on performance pay?

- Can the organisation afford cash incentives?

- Should incentives be individual or collective?

- Should incentives be cash- or equity-based?

- How should incentives be tailored to meet employee needs and expectations?

- What proportion of employees' total pay should be performance-linked and 'at risk'?

- What use should be made of non-cash incentives?[64]

The choice of pay mix will depend very much on the type of organisation and the type of employee concerned. Drawing together the insights offered in our discussion of specific pay practices, it is possible to sketch in the broad contours of best fit reward mix for each of our four archetypal competitive strategies. By way of illustration, Exhibit 10.10 summarises the key human resource requirements and best fit reward practices for each strategic orientation. Notice that there are substantial differences between the four cases in relation to each main area of reward practice.

With regard to base pay, pay scales and narrow job grades, with an emphasis on internal equity and progression based on seniority or merit increments and job promotion, are best suited to organisations with a cost-minimisation strategy and a traditional, low-involvement management approach. Base pay built around broad grades and skill-based progression would

Exhibit 10.10 Aligning strategy, structure, culture and reward practice

	Cost defender	Quality defender	Analyser	Prospector
Desired attitudes	Motivation; commitment	Motivation; commitment	Motivation; commitment	Motivation, short-term commitment
Desired behaviour	Task compliance	Task compliance; some citizenship	Citizenship	Citizenship
Results	Individual quantity or productivity; cost; long-term market share	Individual and collective quality; long-term market share	Collective quality; product diversification	Individual and collective short-term contribution, timeliness, creativity, successful risk-taking.
Performance unit	Individual; business units; whole organization	Individuals; work teams; business units; whole organization	Work teams; parallel teams; business units	Individuals, project teams, business units, whole organization
Performance criteria and measurement	Individual behaviour; results	Technical knowledge and skill; individual behaviour; individual and collective results	Technical knowledge and skill; cooperative behaviour; results	Soft competencies, results
Non-financial rewards	Few	Some intrinsic; developmental; social	Intrinsic; developmental; social	Intrinsic
Base pay structure	Pay scales; narrow job grades	Narrow job grades and/or broad grades	Broad grades	Broadbands
Base pay progression	Annual seniority or merit increments; scale or grade promotion	Skill-based pay for non-managerial staff	Skill-based pay for non-managerial staff	Competency-based pay for all staff
Benefits	Minimal, fixed	Fixed	Mix of fixed and flexible	Highly flexible
Individual incentives	Piece-rates; commissions; merit raises; non-cash recognition	Merit bonuses; commissions; non-cash recognition	Commissions; merit bonuses; recognition awards	Commissions; discretionary bonuses
Collective STIs	Cost-based gain-sharing; selective profit-sharing	Profit-sharing; multi-factor business unit gainsharing/goalsharing; team incentives	Goalsharing; team incentives	Team and/or business unit goalsharing

	Cost defender	Quality defender	Analyser	Prospector
Collective LTIs	Executive share bonuses	Share bonus or purchase plans	Share bonus or purchase plans	Share options, profit-sharing
Total remuneration level	Below market median (with high attention to internal equity)	Around market median (with moderate attention to internal equity)	Around market median (with moderate attention to internal equity)	Above market median (with low attention to internal equity)

Source: Adapted from Shields J. 2007. *Managing employee performance and reward: Concepts, practices, strategies*, Cambridge University Press, Melborne.

be best adapted to quality defenders and high involvement analysers, while a broadbanded base pay structure, with competency- and/or performance-related pay progression, would be a better match for high involvement prospectors, since these practices facilitate devolution, responsible autonomy and flexibility, and encourage informed risk-taking.

Turning to the choice of performance-related rewards, we can say that merit increments and results-based individual incentives will be a strong match for traditional cost-focused organisations, with a limited degree of profitsharing perhaps thrown in for good measure. Re-earnable merit bonuses offer a better means of rewarding individual excellence in quality defenders and high-involvement analysers, while goal-based individual incentives offer an ideal means of recognising and rewarding individual contribution in prospector firms. Collective incentives in the form of gainsharing, goalsharing and team incentives will be a good match for high-involvement analysers and quality defenders, especially given that work in such organisations will be interdependent and typically team-based. Broadly based equity plans are also well suited to all high-involvement organisations, particularly as a means of eliciting employee engagement and citizenship behaviour. For prospectors, where the emphasis is on innovation and agility, goalsharing and share options would be a strong fit.

Decisions must also be made about the target contribution of each main pay element (i.e. base, benefits, short-term incentives, long-term incentives) to the total remuneration of each distinct employee in each group. Here there are two widely followed 'rules.' First, the higher up the organisational hierarchy, the greater the proportion of total pay that can be performance-variable. Second, the higher up the hierarchy, the greater the proportion of total pay that can be linked to organisational performance.

Determining remuneration level

Having determined the proposed pay mix and component targets for each employee group, the next step is to set appropriate remuneration levels for particular jobs and employees. Whether the base pay structure consists of narrow grades, broad grades or broadbands, market-relative pay ranges must be established for each designated position. Essentially, this involves a choice about whether the organisation is going to pay at, above or below prevailing median market rates for comparable positions. This will depend largely on whether the reward strategy emphasises attraction and retention or payroll cost containment. A firm might choose to pay below market if it wishes to gain a cost edge over competitors in the product market. Alternatively, it may choose to pay above market if it wants to attract and retain employees capable of making a high contribution.

Again, the choice here should be informed by the competitive strategy. As indicated in Exhibit 10.10, a cost defender will be inclined to pay 'below market,' albeit with an accent on internal equity. In contrast, quality defenders and analyser firms may well be able to get away with matching the market median for the required skill labour simply because of the high level of intrinsic reward associated with work undertaken. In turn, prospectors will be inclined to opt for a high market relativity that maximises competitiveness in attracting and retaining scarce talent.

The choice of pay level will also be influenced by prevailing labour market conditions. Where there is a scarcity of required skills and competencies in relevant external labour markets, firms may have little option in the short term but to pay above market. Organisational life-cycle stage may also be a factor here. Start-up firms that are cash poor may have no option but to pay below market, as might mature defender firms facing competitive pricing pressure. Conversely, rapidly growing firms will be inclined to pay above the market median in order to buy-in competent staff, although, they may also choose to pay below market base pay but offer company equity as a trade-off. Such cash–equity trade-offs were common in the US information technology industry during the 1990s IT boom.

Summary

This chapter has explored the key concepts and practices associated with the management of employee reward, with a special emphasis on the selection and application of rewards that maximise the contribution of human resources to organisational effectiveness and success. We began by considering the distinguishing features of a strategic approach to reward management, the nature and importance of the 'total reward' approach, and the trend towards greater 'flexibility' in reward determination in Australia. Attention then turned to the three main elements of total remuneration, namely base pay, benefits, and performance-related rewards, the options and practices associated with each, and the organisational strategies, structures and cultures to which each might be most applicable. As well as comparing the wide range of incentive plans applicable to line employees – including individual versus collective plans, cash versus non-cash plans, and short-term versus long-term plans – we have also examined the controversial issue of executive incentive plans. Finally, we considered how the various reward options might best be selected and integrated so as to maximise the contribution of human resources to the achievement of the organisation's strategic objectives and to reinforce the desired organisational structure and culture.

Overall, designing and developing a strategic reward system – one that fits organisational requirements – is a complex and challenging process. Perhaps more so than with any other human resource process, it also allows the human resource strategist to demonstrate their vital worth to organisational effectiveness. Equally, effective reward management demands high-order competencies in organisational and behavioural analysis, as well as solid abilities in strategic decision-making, communication and human resource leadership. For these reasons, it can also be immensely rewarding in its own right.

Key terms

base pay 391
broad grade 395
broadbands/broadbanding 396
compa-ratio 404
competency-based pay 396
developmental rewards 384
direct benefits 397
discretionary bonus 407
extrinsic rewards 383
financial rewards 383
flexible benefits plans 399
gainsharing 411
goalsharing 412
indirect benefits 397
intrinsic rewards 383
job evaluation 393

Key debate issues

1   There is only so much that a reward system can achieve.
2   In setting pay levels, external competitiveness is a far more important consideration than internal equity.
3   The boom in employee benefits is attributable to demographic factors.
4   Non-cash recognition is just motivation on the cheap.
5   With results-based rewards, what does not get rewarded gets neglected.
6   With CEO reward, all that matters is whether the CEO delivers greater value to their shareholders.

Case study 10.1

(DE)motivation across cultures

Across cultures, what might increase job satisfaction and employee productivity? What motivates culturally diverse people to behave in productive ways? Can we use standardised approaches and generalise reward structures across cultures?

Let's look at some examples where over-generalising about culture had a negative effect and actually led to demotivation. A group of Indonesian workers in Sumatra who had their pay per hour raised in order to motivate them to work more hours actually worked less hours after the increase. As the Indonesians explained: 'We can now make enough money to live and enjoy life in less time than previously. We don't have to work so many hours.' The Australian head office hoped that by offering a financial reward, productivity would increase. Clearly this particular group of Indonesian workers were not motivated to work harder by a higher pay rate. Instead their reward was more time to enjoy life as they did not have to work as many hours to earn the same amount of money.

In another case an Australian manager working for a Korean company in Australia promoted a young Korean sales representative to Sales Manager to reward his good work. To the surprise of the Australian, the promotion had a negative impact on the new Korean manager's performance. Why? This Korean employee had a high need for harmony and status in the group he belonged to – and to fit in with his work colleagues. The promotion, an individualistic reward which in his eyes should have gone to the more senior and most respected member of the team, separated the new manager from the rest of the group, embarrassed him, and caused the more senior employee to lose face and therefore diminished the new manager's motivation to work.

A more complex example is the following: a Malaysian subsidiary of an American company was under serious threat by competition from other South East Asian countries. The US based headquarters sent their most experienced manager to turn the tide. The US manager set an ultimatum as part of an improvement program for the Malaysian managers (predominantly Chinese-Malay): Get your act together in the next six months, become profitable and improve quality or we will be forced to close the subsidiary. The Malay managers were also offered substantial financial performance bonuses. In some cultures this 'burning platform' approach (i.e. create a crises and most people will turn in the right direction to extinguish the fire) means creating the right needs (danger) and reward (safety). After six months however, the results were still below expectations. So what had happened? The US manager assumed that the Malay colleagues would be motivated by offering safety and financial rewards – as he would. He was totally unaware of the cultural differences. The leadership style applied by the American failed to motivate the managers for several reasons: it ignored the Chinese-Malay need for a more paternalistic management style; the six month turnaround project was not a realistic approach to the more long-term orientation of the Malay managers; the US manager made no attempt to become one of the management team – and missed the fact that the Malay managers responded more positively to orders given by those with prominent status in their own group rather than outsiders.

Ongoing cross-cultural research using existing motivation theories such as Maslow's Hierarchy of Needs, Hertzberg's Intrinsic vs Extrinsic Factor Theory and Vroom's Expectancy Theory, finds that those theories are very much culture-bound. That is, the theories fit best within the culture in which they were developed, or similar cultures. These research results also show that a person's frame of reference will determine the order of importance of his or her needs and rewards – and they guide their motivation. A person's frame of reference is in part determined by his or her culture. Thus, a person's needs and rewards are at least partially bound by their culture. Of course social needs, experience, skills, age, business travel experience, and overseas study to name a few, will all influence an individual's preference and order for needs and rewards.

Across cultures we find different needs and different rewards that drive people. Job security and life-long employment versus a more interesting and challenging job, the quality of life versus achievements and productivity, and social needs versus individualistic ego and self actualisation can vary enormously across cultures. A manager who deals with a new culture would do best to first observe which needs and rewards appear important to the individual, the team, or the organisation within that culture and not assume that existing culture-bound theories, and prior knowledge and experience with other cultures is simply transferable.

Source: Thissen, J. 2006. '(De)motivation across cultures,' Human Capital Magazine, October 2006.

Questions

1 Why are individualistic reward and recognition practices problematic in many non-Anglophone cultures?

2 This case refers to the failure of the 'burning platform' strategy adopted by one US firm as a means of achieving turnaround in its Malaysian subsidiary. Taking into account the remarks offered in the case concerning the strategy's cross-cultural shortcomings, what particular reward practices would have been a better fit for the particular organisational and cultural circumstances.

3 Rewards are sometimes seen as potentially powerful tools for driving cultural change in organisations operating domestically. Do rewards have any role to play in managing culture and change in firms operating internationally?

Case study 10.2

The dangers of the unearned bonus

Still red-faced over the $790 000 in bonuses paid to rogue traders Luke Duffy, Dave Bullen, Gianni Gray and Vincent Ficarra just before scandal broke, National Australia Bank is overhauling the way it dishes out the payments.

Australia's biggest bank has learnt some painful lessons about performance pay.

Protecting their bonuses was in part why traders entered into false transactions to conceal their losses and report profits.

Now, after a major review, the controversial payments will no longer be triggered largely on the basis of financial results such as meeting profit targets.

Instead of focusing mainly on how an individual has performed, the bonuses will be allocated according to how the group, team and business unit has done – as well as the 'people leadership' which staff demonstrate.

And there will be less management discretion in sharing out the bonus pool.

Industry insiders see this aspect as particularly significant.

'The sycophantic behaviour so often found in environments such as the NAB is encouraged and promoted by the large bonus payments that are subjectively determined by product or division heads,' said one high-flyer, who did not wish to be named.

'Throughout my [15-year] career in banking, the inner circle always received the biggest bonuses. Of course, the inner circle is often synonymous with the boys' club.'

The changes will apply to NAB's so-called financial market employees in the wholesale area, which includes staff in the high-octane world of money market, debt, and forex trading.

Ian Crichton, director of executive remuneration and share plans at Corporate Remuneration Advisers, is busy helping companies that are refining the way they award all forms of performance pay.

'There is a long way still to go, however,' he says.

To be sure, the bonus has backfired before.

Even in the booming 1990s and earlier this decade, when many employers could better afford to lavish splashy payments on their best and brightest, there were real problems.

Nick Leeson, who was responsible for bringing down the blue-blood Barings Bank and, more recently, in the US, jailed Allfirst currency trader John Rusnak, have been accused of trying to cover up trading losses to protect their bonuses.

But beyond these swashbuckling traders, there is a plethora of problems that companies across the country are dealing with when bonus schemes are not well designed.

Fat bonus cheques might be associated with the sexy side of the financial services industry, but in fact bonuses have reached most industries in Australia.

Paul Riggs, a principal with Mercer Human Resource Consulting, said that if anything, companies are extending incentive plans. In a surprisingly high finding, 92 per cent of companies Mercer surveyed had implemented such plans.

Bonuses are just one component of an increasingly complex remuneration picture. These days, the little yellow pay packet has been replaced by several components. On top of base pay, there is the international trend to variable pay. This in turn splits into short-term incentives – which include bonus schemes and sales commissions and are usually designed to meet short-term goals such as quarterly sales – and long-term incentives such as share options that vest over several years.

A broader range of employees are getting bonuses. Crichton says, 'Incentives are paid deeper in many more organisations today than say five years ago. That is, many more employees have an incentive opportunity available to them.'

Insurer IAG is just one company that confirms this trend. A bonus of up to 10 per cent of pay is available to all of its employees. The smaller cadre of selected senior managers and executives, comprising about 7 per cent of staff, are simply able to score bigger bonuses: between 20 or 30 per cent of their salary. The group executive for culture and reputation, Sam Mostyn, says the plan is designed to strengthen the link between performance and remuneration.

But as bonuses become more entrenched, the stakes only get higher, the dangers of them backfiring more apparent.

Riggs, who spends his days advising on remuneration, has noted the ways in which bonus schemes are vulnerable to manipulation. There's even a name for this – gaming.

'Gaming means playing with the bits under your control to get a better result – a higher bonus.'

By way of example, he cites a furniture department that passed all of its sales to one team member. There was a bonus for the one member for thoroughly trumping the sales target.

Then the team shared the spoils. 'If each team member accurately recorded their own sales, they all got small or zero bonuses for just reaching or just missing target. By pooling, they got a guaranteed share of a bigger pool.'

At its worst, Riggs says, employees will negotiate to set the target as low as possible 'so it will be easy to achieve.'

Peter Ryan, an associate with human resources consultancy Hewitt Associates, says the answer to the question 'How often [does] he [see] badly designed schemes?' is short. 'A lot. Over the past year or so we've been doing more consulting work on incentive plan design than probably the previous two or three years put together,' Ryan says. 'There's been an upsurge.'

The remuneration virtuosi know what they are talking about and now have a lot of history to draw on. With bonus payments a feature of remuneration since the 1980s, the debate has been raging for 20 years. Everyone agrees that when they are well designed, short-term plans deliver meaningful and competitive rewards to employees and thus drive better performance.

Says Riggs: 'There are hundreds of thousands, possibly millions of incentive payments paid every year in Australia across the total workforce. The number that are complained about is actually a pretty small percentage. But they are very imprecise mechanisms and they always will be, the assessment processes that lead to the bonuses.'

Consequently, the debate has now shifted to the way to best improve bonuses. It is also concerned with how to get the mix right between short and long-term incentives. This is especially true when employers want the loyalty and long-term outlook that long-term incentives promise, but today's mobile and restless worker wants the short-term reward for meeting annual – or even quarterly – objectives.

Companies are also concerned about moving away from awarding bonuses based on management discretion. To get around this discretion, they are increasingly basing their incentive plans on meeting very specific, quantifiable performance targets such as corporate, business unit or individual goals.

The director of reward practice with Hay Group, Graham O'Neill, cites the notorious example of the failed One.Tel. In that case, the multimillion-dollar bonuses to Jodee Rich and Brad Keeling were linked only to the share price and paid at a time when the company was hemorrhaging cash.

'When those things do occur, you really need to have a cap on the plan because you could have significant windfall gains which are not due to the behaviour of the person, but due to the stockmarket or exchange rates ... I think too often it tends to be, "we've got a spare hour, let's design an incentive plan and roll it out".'

Riggs says sometimes the targets are too quantitative – 'if it's all formula driven and very mathematical, it can get out of hand.' The problem with this is that employees get fixated on achieving the goals that will reap them bonus rewards.

But outspoken remuneration expert John Egan of Egan and Associates says part of the challenge employers face in improving bonuses is the sheer scope of the task. 'It's a big task for an organisation with maybe 2000 or 3000 receiving a bonus in what might be 100 different business units across Australia, across the northern hemisphere,' Egan says. ' ... Some very large companies, they would review these things every three years, just because they've got such a large amount of work on their plate. And if you are in a large company ... you might miss some of these things.'

Nevertheless, the Mercer figures suggest that about one in three companies will review their plans over the course of the year. Hints have begun to emerge that some of the schemes are undergoing transformations.

Some bonus babies now face caps on the amounts they can receive (although some will grumble this makes their reward scheme rather unrewarding).

There is also an increasing trend to companies starting to introduce a deferred component to the bonus payment, either by deferring the cash payment or delivering the bonus in shares.

Deferring part of the bonus acts as a 'golden handcuff,' effectively restraining the mobility of people between jobs. But more significantly, it leaves a claw-back option if the bonus later proves to be undeserved.

NAB had been deferring 25 per cent of the bonus payments to staff, but is considering increasing this proportion.

According to Crichton, this is designed to 'better align with performance.' But, he says, this technique is still very much in the minority.

'These changes are in response to shareholder [and] investor sentiment, greater focus and accountability on all remuneration components and general improvement in performance measurement techniques,' he says.

Source: Hepworth, A. 2004. 'The dangers of the unearned bonus,' *Australian Financial Review Weekend Edition*, 23–24 April.

Questions

1 Why are results-based incentives so susceptible to manipulation and why is the problem so pronounced in the financial services sector?

2 Why might deferring portion of an employee's results-based bonus have a beneficial effect?

3 Would it be better for results-based bonuses to be based on long-term as opposed to short-term results? Should they be based on group rather than individual results?

Further readings

Armstrong M. & Brown D. 2006. *Strategic reward. How organisations add value through reward*, London, Kogan Page.

Armstrong M. & Murlis H. 2004. *Reward management. A handbook of remuneration strategy and practice*, 5th edn, London, Kogan Page.

Armstrong M. & Stephens T. 2005. *A handbook of employee reward management and practice*, London, Kogan Page.

Bebchuk L. & Fried J. 2006. 'Pay without performance: Overview of the issues,' *Academy of Management Perspectives*, 20(1), pp. 5–24.

Bergmann T.J. & Scarpello V.G. 2002. *Compensation decision making*, Cincinatti OH, South-Western/Thomson Learning.

Bowen R. Brayton (2000). *Recognizing and rewarding employees*, New York, McGraw-Hill Professional Publishing.

Conyon M. 2006. 'Executive compensation and incentives,' *Academy of Management Perspectives*, 20(1), pp. 25–44.

Gerhart B. & Rynes S. 2003. *Compensation. Theory, evidence, and strategic implications*, Thousand Oaks CA, Sage.

Henderson R.I. 2006. *Compensation management in a knowledge-based world*, 10th edn, New York, Prentice Hall.

Heneman R.L. (ed.) 2002. *Strategic reward management. Design, Implementation, and Evaluation*, Greenwich, Connecticut, Information Age Publishing.

Heneman R.L. 2003. 'Job and work evaluation: A literature review,' *Public Personnel Management*, 32(1), pp. 47–71.

Kessler I. 2000. 'Reward system choices,' in Storey, J. (ed.), *Human resource management. A critical text*, 2nd edn, Thomson Learning, ch. 11, pp. 206–31.

Lawler E.E. 2000. *Rewarding excellence. Pay strategies for the new economy*, San Francisco CA, Jossey Bass.

Long R. 2006. *Strategic compensation in Canada*, 3rd edn, Scarborough, Ontario, Thomson Nelson.

Manas T.M. & Graham M.D. 2003. *Creating a total rewards strategy. A toolkit for designing business-based plans*, New York, Amacom.

Martocchio J.J. 2006. *Strategic compensation: A human resource management approach*, 3rd edn, Upper Saddle River PA, Pearson/Prentice Hall.

Milkovich G. & Newman J. 2007. *Compensation*, 9th edn, New York, McGraw-Hill Irwin.

Rynes S.L. & Gerhart B. (eds) 2000. *Compensation in organisations. Current Research and practice*, San Francisco, Jossey Bass.

Shields J. 2002.'Performance related pay in Australia,' in M. Brown & J. Heywood (eds), *Paying for performance. An international comparison*, Armonk, NY: ME Sharpe, pp. 179–213.

Shields J. 2007. *Managing employee performance and reward: Concepts, practices, strategies*, Melbourne, Cambridge University Press.

White G. & Drucker J. (eds) 2000. *Reward management. A critical text*, London, Routledge.

Zingheim P. & Schuster J. 2000. *Pay people right! Breakthrough reward strategies to create great companies*, San Francisco CA, Jossey Bass.

Endnotes

1 Fuehrer V. 1994. 'Total reward strategy: A prescription for organizational survival,' *Compensation and Benefits Review*, January–February, pp. 44–53; Kao T. & Kantor R. 2004. 'Total rewards: From clarity to action,' *WorldatWork Journal*, 13(4), pp. 32–40; Manas T.M. & Graham M.D. 2003. *Creating a total rewards strategy. A toolkit for designing business-based plans*, New York, Amacom; O'Neal S. 1998. 'The phenomenon of total rewards,' *ACA Journal/ WorldatWork Journal*, 7(3), pp. 6–18; Zingheim P. & Schuster J. 2000. *Pay people right! Breakthrough reward strategies to create great companies*, San Francisco, Jossey-Bass.

2 See, for example: Deci E.L. & Ryan R.M. 1985. *Intrinsic motivation and self-determination in human behavior*, New York, Plenum Press; Herzberg F. 1987. 'One more time: How do you motivate employees?,' *Harvard Business Review*, 65, pp. 109–20 (first published 1967); Kohn A. 1993. *Punished by rewards*, Boston, Houghton Mifflin; Kohn A. 1993. 'Why incentive plans cannot work,' *Harvard Business Review*, 71(5), pp. 54–63.

3 Shields J. 2007. *Managing employee performance and reward: Concepts, practices, strategies*, Melbourne, Cambridge University Press, ch. 4.

4 Miles R.E. & Snow C.C. 1978. *Organizational strategy, structure, and process*, New York, McGraw-Hill; Miles R.E. & Snow C.C. 1984. 'Designing strategic human resource systems,' *Organization Dynamics*, 16, pp. 36–52.

5 Plowman D.H. 1992. 'Industrial relations and the legacy of the new protection,' *Journal of Industrial Relations*, 34(1), pp. 48–64; Wooden, M. 2000. *The transformation of Australian industrial relations*, Sydney, Federation Press.

6 CSi – The Remuneration Specialists 2006. Australian General Industry Remuneration Report, CSi, Sydney, p. 16.

7 Hancock K.J. 1979. 'The first half century of Australian wages policy,' Parts I & II, *Journal of Industrial Relations*, 21(1 & 2), pp. 1–19, 129–60; Hancock K.J. & Moore K. 1975. 'The occupational wage structure in Australia since 1914,' in J.R. Niland & J.E. Isaac (eds) *Australian labour economics readings*, Melbourne, Sun Books, pp. 206–25; Hutson J. 1971. *Six wage concepts*, AEU, Sydney, pp. 132–242; Isaac J.E. 1986. 'The meaning and significance of comparative wage justice,' in J.R. Niland (ed.) *Wage fixation in Australia*, Sydney, Allen & Unwin, pp. 84–104; Shields J. 2002. 'Performance related pay in Australia,' in M. Brown & J. Heywood (eds). *Paying for performance. An international comparison*, Armonk, NY: ME Sharpe, pp. 179–213.

8 Armstrong M. & Murlis H. 2004. *Reward management: A handbook of remuneration strategy and practice*, 5th edn, London, Kogan Page, pp. 634–43; Holmes R.W. 1980–81. 'Job evaluation: Theory and practice,' Parts 1 & 2, *Human Resource Management Australia*, 18(4), pp. 42–9, & 19(1), pp. 45–52; Patten T. 1988. *Fair pay: The managerial challenge of comparable worth and job evaluation*, San Francisco, Jossey-Bass, pp. 192–201; Skenes C. & Kleiner B.H. 2003. 'The HAY system of compensation,' *Management Research News*, 26, pp. 109–15.

9 Lawler, E.E. 1988. 'What's wrong with pointfactor job evaluation,' *Compensation and Benefits Review*, 18(2), pp. 20–8; Long, R. 2006. *Strategic compensation in Canada*, 3rd edn, Scarborough, Ontario, Thomson Nelson, pp. 289–96.

10 Heneman R. L. & LeBlanc P. 2002. 'Developing a more relevant and competitive approach for valuing knowledge work,' *Compensation and Benefits Review*, 34(4), pp. 43–7.

11 Lawler, 'What's wrong with pointfactor job evaluation'; in E. E. Lawler 1990. *Strategic pay: aligning organizational strategies and pay systems*, San Francisco, Jossey-Bass, pp. 135–52.

12 Emerson S.M. 1991. 'Job evaluation: A barrier to excellence?,' *Compensation and Benefits Review*, 23(1), pp. 38–51.

13 Lawler 1988. 'What's wrong with pointfactor job evaluation'; Weiner N.J. 1991. 'Job evaluation systems: A critique,' *Human Resource Management Review*, 1(2), pp. 119–32.

14 Barrett, G.V. 1991. 'Comparison of skill-based pay with traditional job evaluation techniques,' *Human Resource Management Review*, 1, pp. 97–105.

15 Jenkins G.D., Ledford G.E., Gupta N. & Doty H. 1992. *Skill-based pay: Practices, payoffs, pitfalls and prescriptions*, Scottsdale, AZ., American Compensation Association; Ledford G.E. 1991. 'Three case studies on skill-based pay: An overview,' *Compensation and Benefits Review*, 23(2), pp. 11–23; Ledford, G.E. 1991. 'The design of skill-based pay plans,' in M. Rock & L. Berger (eds), *The compensation handbook: A state of the art guide to compensation strategy and design*, 3rd edn, New York, McGraw-Hill, ch. 15; Ledford G.E. & Bergel G. 1991. 'Skill-based pay case number 1: General Mills,' *Compensation and Benefits Review*, 23(2), pp. 24–38; Ledford G.E. & Heneman R.L. 1999. 'Pay for skills, knowledge and competencies,' in L.A. Berger & D.R. Berger, *The compensation Handbook: A state-of-the-art guide to compensation strategy and design*, 4th edn, New York, McGraw-Hill, ch. 11; Murray B. & Gerhart B. 2000. 'Skill-based pay and skill seeking,' *Human Resource Management Review*, 10(3), pp. 271–87.

16 O'Neill G. & Lander D. 1993. 'Linking employee skills to pay: A framework for skill-based pay plans,' *ACA Journal/WorldatWork Journal*, 2(3), pp. 14–27.

17 Shields J. 2007. *Managing employee performance and reward*, ch. 10.

18 Gerhart B. & Milkovich G. 1992. 'Employee compensation: Research and practice,' in M.D. Dunnette & L.M. Hough (eds), *Handbook of industrial and organizational psychology*, Palo Alto, CA., Consulting Psychologists Press, p. 505.

19 Dewey B. J. 1994. 'Changing to skill-based pay: Disarming the transition landmines,' *Compensation and Benefits Review*, 26(1), pp. 38–43; Greene R. J. 1993. 'Person-focused pay: Should it replace job-based pay?,' *Compensation and Benefits Management*, 9(4), pp. 46–54; Lawler 1990. *Strategic pay*, pp. 166–70.

20 Armstrong M. & Brown D. 1998. 'Relating competencies to pay: The UK experience,' *Compensation and Benefits Review*, May–June, pp. 28–39; Brown D. & Armstrong M. 1999. *Paying for contribution: Real performance-related pay strategies*, London, Kogan Page; Cira D.J. & Benjamin E.R. 1998. 'Competency-based pay: A concept in evolution,' *Compensation and Benefits Review*, September–October, pp. 21–8.; O'Neal S. 1995. 'Competencies and pay in the evolving world of work,' *ACA Journal/WorldatWork Journal*, 4(3), pp. 72–9; Risher H. 1997. 'Competency-based pay: The next model of salary management,' in H. Risher & C. Fay (eds), *New strategies for public pay*, San Francisco, Jossey-Bass, ch. 7.

21 Brown & Armstrong 1999., *Paying for contribution*; Armstrong M. & Brown D. 2006. *Strategic reward: Making it happen*, London, Kogan Page. pp. 132–5.

22 Abosch K. 1995. 'The promise of broadbanding,' *Compensation and Benefits Review*, 27(1), pp. 54–8; Abosch K. 1998. 'Confronting six myths of broadbanding,' *ACA Journal/WorldatWork Journal*, 7(3), pp. 28–36; Brown D. 1996. 'Broadbanding: A study of company practices in the United Kingdom,' *Compensation and Benefits Review*, 28(6), pp. 41–9; Gilbert D. 1994. 'Broadbands and winning in today's marketplace,' *ACA Journal/WorldatWork Journal*, 3(1), pp. 48–50; Hofrichter D. 1993. 'Broadbanding: A second generation approach,' *Compensation and Benefits Review*, 25(5), pp. 53–8; Risher H. 1995. 'Base pay: Rethinking the basic framework,' in H. Risher & C. Fay (eds), *The performance imperative: Strategies for enhancing workforce effectiveness*, San Francisco, Jossey-Bass, ch. 14; Risher H. 1997. 'Salary structures: The framework for salary management,' in H. Risher & C. Fay (eds), *New strategies for public pay*, San Francisco, Jossey-Bass, ch. 2; Rosen A.S. & Turetsky D. 2002. 'Broadbanding: The construction of a career management framework,' *WorldatWork Journal*, 11(4), pp. 45–55; Tucker S. 1995. 'The role of pay in the boundaryless organization,' *ACA Journal/WorldatWork Journal*, 4(3), pp. 48–59; Tucker S.A. & Cofsky K.M. 1994. 'Competency-based pay on a banding platform,' *ACA Journal/WorldatWork Journal*, 3(1), pp. 30–45.

23 Heneman R.L. & LeBlanc P. 2003. 'Work valuation addresses shortcomings of both job evaluation and market pricing,' *Compensation and Benefits Review*, 35(1), p. 8; Hofrichter D. & McGovern T. 2001. 'People, competencies and performance: Clarifying means and ends,' *Compensation and Benefits Review*, 33(4): pp. 34–8.

24 Stoskopf G.A. 2002. 'Choosing the best salary structure for your organization,' *WorldatWork Journal*, 11(4), p. 32.

25 Shields J. 2007. *Managing Employee Performance and Reward*, ch. 13.

26 Ibid.

27 Wells, J. 2004. 'Fit for work: Healthy workers are better business,' *hrmonthly*, June, pp. 36–42.

28 Shields, J. 2007. *Managing Employee Performance and Reward*, ch. 3.

29 Ibid, chs. 2 and 3.

30 Beer M. & Katz N. 2003. 'Do incentives work? The perceptions of a worldwide sample of senior executives,' *Human Resource Planning*, 26(3), pp. 31–4.

31 Kohn 1993a. *Punished by Rewards*; Kohn 1993b. 'Why incentive plans cannot work;' Davis J.H. 1995. 'Why rewards undermine performance: An exclusive interview with Alfie Kohn,' *ACA Journal/WorldatWork Journal*, 4(2), pp. 6–19.

32 Deci & Ryan, 1985. *Intrinsic motivation*.

33 Cameron J. & Pierce D. 1997. 'Rewards, interest and performance: An evaluation of experimental findings,' *ACA Journal/WorldatWork Journal*, 6(4), pp. 6–15; Gupta N. & Mitra A. 1998. 'The value of financial incentives: Myths and empirical realities,' *ACA Journal/WorldatWork Journal*, 7(3), pp. 58–66; Gupta N. & Shaw J. 1998. 'Let the evidence speak: Financial incentives are effective!!,' *Compensation and Benefits Review*, 30(2), pp. 26 & 28–32.

34 Rynes S.L., Gerhart B. & Park, L. 2005. 'Personnel psychology: Performance evaluation and pay for performance,' *Annual Review of Psychology*, 56, pp. 575–77 & 581–82.

35   Shields J. 2007. *Managing employee performance and reward*, ch. 15.

36   Lawler 1990. *Strategic pay*, p. 82; Schuster J. & Zingheim P. 1996. *The new pay: Linking employee and organizational performance*, San Francisco, Jossey-Bass, pp. 144–7.

37   Nelson B. 1994. *1001 ways to reward employees*, New York, Workman Publishing, p. 73.

38   McAdams J.L. 1996. *The reward plan advantage: A manager's guide to improving business performance through people*, San Francisco, Jossey-Bass, ch. 7; McAdams J.L. 1999. 'Non-monetary rewards: Cash equivalents and tangible awards,' in L.A. Berger & D.R. Berger, *The compensation handbook: A state-of-the-art guide to compensation strategy and design*, 4th edn, New York, McGraw-Hill, ch. 20; Nelson B. 1994. *1001 ways to reward employees*, New York, Workman Publishing; Nelson B. 1996. 'Dump the cash, load on the praise,' *Personnel Journal*, July, pp. 65–70; Nelson B. 1997. 'Does one reward fit all?,' *Workforce*, 76(2), pp. 67–70.

39   McAdams 1999. 'Nonmonetary rewards,' pp. 245–51.

40   McAdams, 1995. 'Rewarding special performance: Low-cost, high-impact awards,' in H. Risher & C. Fay (eds), *The performance imperative: Strategies for enhancing workforce effectiveness*, San Francisco, Jossey-Bass, p. 372.

41   McAdams 1999. 'Nonmonetary rewards,' p. 254.

42   Peach E. & Wren D. 1992. 'Pay for performance from antiquity to the 1950s,' in B. Hopkins & T. Mawhinney (eds), *Pay for performance: history, controversy, and evidence*, New York, Hawthorne Press, pp. 5–26 (special issue of the *Journal of Organizational Behaviour Management*, 12(1), 1992).

43   Shields J. 2007. *Managing employee performance and reward*, ch. 17.

44   Heneman R.L. & Von Hipple C. 1995. 'Balancing group and individual rewards: Rewarding individual contributions to the team,' *Compensation and Benefits Review*, 27(4), pp. 63–8.

45   Lesieur F.G. (ed.) 1958. *The Scanlon Plan: A frontier in labor–management cooperation*, Cambridge, MA, Technology Press of Massachusetts Institute of Technology; Miller C.S. & Schuster M.H. 1987. 'Gainsharing plans: A comparative analysis,' *Organizational Dynamics*, Summer, pp. 44–67.

46   Shields J. 2007. *Managing employee performance and reward*, ch. 18.

47   Dalton G. 1998. 'The glass wall: Shattering the myth that alternative rewards won't work with unions,' *Compensation and Benefits Review*, 30(6), pp. 38–45; Kim D-O & Voos P. 1997. 'Unionization, union involvement, and the performance of gainsharing programs,' *Industrial Relations/Relations Industrielles*, 52(2), pp. 304–32; Ross T.L. & Ross R.A. 1999. 'Gain sharing: Shared improved performance,' in L.A. Berger & D.R. Berger, *The compensation handbook: A state-of-the-art guide to compensation strategy and design*, 4th edn, New York, McGraw-Hill, ch. 19.

48   Shields, 2007. *Managing employee performance and reward*, ch. 18.

49   Gross S.E. 1995. 'Reinforcing team effectiveness through pay,' *Compensation and Benefits Review*, 27(5), pp. 34–8; Lawler E.E. 2000. *Rewarding excellence: Pay strategies for the new economy*, San Francisco, Jossey-Bass, pp. 193–219.

50   Shields J. 2007. *Managing employee performance and reward*, ch. 19.

51   Ibid.

52   Kaarsemaker E. & Poutsma E. 2006. 'The fit of employee ownership with other human resource management practices: Theoretical and empirical suggestions regarding the existence of an ownership high-performance work system,' *Economic and Industrial Democracy*, 27(4), pp. 669–85.

53   Shields, J. 2007. *Managing employee performance and reward*, ch. 20.

54   Bodie Z., Kaplan R.S. & Merton R.C. 2003. 'For the last time: Stock options are an expense,' *Harvard Business Review*, 81(3), pp. 63–71; Murphy K.J. 2002. 'Explaining executive compensation: Managerial power versus the perceived cost of stock options,' *The University of Chicago Law Review*, 69, pp. 847–69.

55   Aboody D. & Kasznik R. 1998. 'CEO stock options and corporate voluntary disclosures,' *Stanford Graduate School of Business Research Paper Series*, no. 1535, November; Yermack D. 1997. 'Good timing: CEO stock option awards and company news announcements,' *Journal of Finance*, 52, pp. 449–76.

56   Ellig B.R. 2002. *The complete guide to executive compensation*, New York, McGraw-Hill; Shields 2007. *Managing employee performance and reward*, ch. 20.

57   Conyon M. & Sadle, G. 2001. 'Executive pay, tournaments and corporate performance in UK firms,' *International Journal of Management Reviews*, 3(2), pp. 141–68; Jensen M. & Murphy K. 1990. 'Performance pay and top-management incentives,' *Journal of Political Economy*, 98(2), pp. 225–64; Lilling M.S. 2006. 'The Link Between CEO Compensation and Firm Performance: Does Simultaneity Matter?,' *Atlantic Economic Journal*, 34, pp. 101–14; Merhebi R., Swan P.L. & Zhou X. 2006. 'Australian CEO remuneration: Pay and performance,' *Journal of Accounting and Economics*, 46(3), pp. 481–97; Tosi H.L., Werner S., Kats J.P. & Gomez-Mejia, L.R. 2000. 'How much does performance matter? A meta-analysis of CEO pay studies,' *Journal of Management*, 26, pp. 301–39; Zhou X. 2000. 'CEO pay, firm size, and corporate performance: Evidence from Canada,' *Canadian Journal of Economics*, 33(1), pp. 213–51.

58   Bebchuk L. & Fried J. 2004. *Pay without performance: The unfulfilled promise of executive compensation*, Cambridge, MA, Harvard University Press; Bebchuk L. and Fried J. 2005. 'Pay without performance: Overview of the issues,' *Journal of Corporation Law*, 30(4), pp. 647–74; Bebchuk L., Fried J. & Walker D. 2002. 'Managerial power and executive compensation,' *University of Chicago Law Review*, 69, pp. 751–85.

59   Conyon M. & Murphy K.J. 2000. 'The Prince and the pauper? CEO pay in the United States and United Kingdom,' *Economic Journal*, 110, pp. 640–71.

60   Cowherd D.M. & Levine D.I. 1992. 'Product quality and pay equity between lower-level employees and top management: An investigation of distributive justice theory,' *Administrative Science Quarterly*, 37, pp. 302–20.

61   Byrne J.A & Bongiorno L. 1997. 'How ordinary workers feel when fat cats get the cream,' *Management reward Development Review*, 10(4/5), pp. 164–5.

62   Armstrong & Murlis 2004. *Reward Management*, pp. 533–5; Dolmat-Connell J. 1999. 'Developing a reward strategy that delivers shareholder and employee value,' *Compensation and Benefits Review*, 31(2), pp. 46–53; Long, 2006. *Strategic compensation in Canada*, pp. 187–213; Manas & Graham, 2003. *Creating a total rewards strategy*.

63   O'Neal, 1998. 'The phenomenon of total rewards.

64   Shields J. 2007. *Managing employee performance and reward*, ch. 21.

Online reading

INFOTRAC® COLLEGE EDITION

For additional readings and review on strategic reward management, explore InfoTrac® College Edition, your online library. Go to: www.infotrac-college.com and search for any of the InfoTrac key terms listed below:

➤ base pay
➤ employee incentives
➤ employee share (or stock) ownership
➤ internal/external equity
➤ performance-related pay
➤ reward satisfaction

CHAPTER 11

MANAGING OCCUPATIONAL HEALTH AND SAFETY

Healthier people cost less compared to people with more health risks, whether it's medical costs, absenteeism, workers compensation or presenteeism – regardless of the cost outcomes you use.

Dr Shirley Musich, Director, Wollongong University's Health & Productivity Research Centre, 2006

The Australian Government believes strongly that safe and productive workplaces rely on a cooperative approach between employers and employees to identify and eliminate hazards that may cause injury or death. The Government has always emphasised prevention rather than punishment after the incident as this fosters a workplace environment which promotes safety rather than allocates blame.

Hon. Kevin Andrews, former Minister for Employment & Workplace Relations, 28 April 2005

The Australian Council of Trade Unions (ACTU), the Trades & Labour Councils (TLCs) and unions will pressure governments to apply occupational health and safety lessons from effective enforcement in other areas, including visible, vigorous enforcement and recourse to penalties prior to incidents.

ACTU-OHS Program 2003–6

Objectives

After reading this chapter you will be able to:

1 Trace the development of OHS programs in Australian industry.

2 Understand the various perspectives of employers, unions and employees, and the influences of medical, paramedical and legal professions on OHS theory and practice.

3 Explain recent OHS legislation in Australian national and state government jurisdictions, and analyse its respective advantages and disadvantages.

4 Describe the scope of OHS programs.

5 Determine the roles of senior, middle, line managers and human resource management specialists in the management of OHS issues at the workplace.

Introduction

Earlier chapters emphasise the importance of economic security and psychological satisfaction to the effectiveness of employee work performance and productivity. Employees' needs for physical and emotional security demand equal attention.

HR managers and their staff, in liaison with both senior and line managers, are responsible for the provision of appropriate selection, training and appraisal processes to ensure the right employees are chosen, and then provided with the necessary support, to achieve individual and organisational objectives. The establishment and maintenance of a healthy and safe work environment for all employees and all occupations is not only desirable, but also a cost-effective means of supplementing more traditional HR activities. Occupational health and safety (OHS) issues pervade almost all aspects of HR functions: job design; quality of work life (QWL) programs; recruitment, selection, training and development; performance management; and remuneration systems all involve occupational health and safety issues.

During the last decades, health, safety (and welfare) issues have been highlighted by the development of comprehensive legislation in all states of Australia. The costs of accidents at work and diseases, both physical and psychological, incurred as a result of work activities, have begun to be calculated in terms of medical and hospital costs, time lost, replacement costs, rehabilitation and workers' compensation payments, and retirement and superannuation entitlements.

Recognition of the immensity of these costs to organisations and the prospect of cost reductions through healthy and safe workplaces have supplemented the external legislative requirements. Strategic approaches in OHS, as in other HRM areas, will ensure that occupational health and safety issues are paramount in the minds and plans of senior, line and HR managers (see Exhibit 11.1).

Exhibit 11.1   A SHRM model for managing occupational health and safety

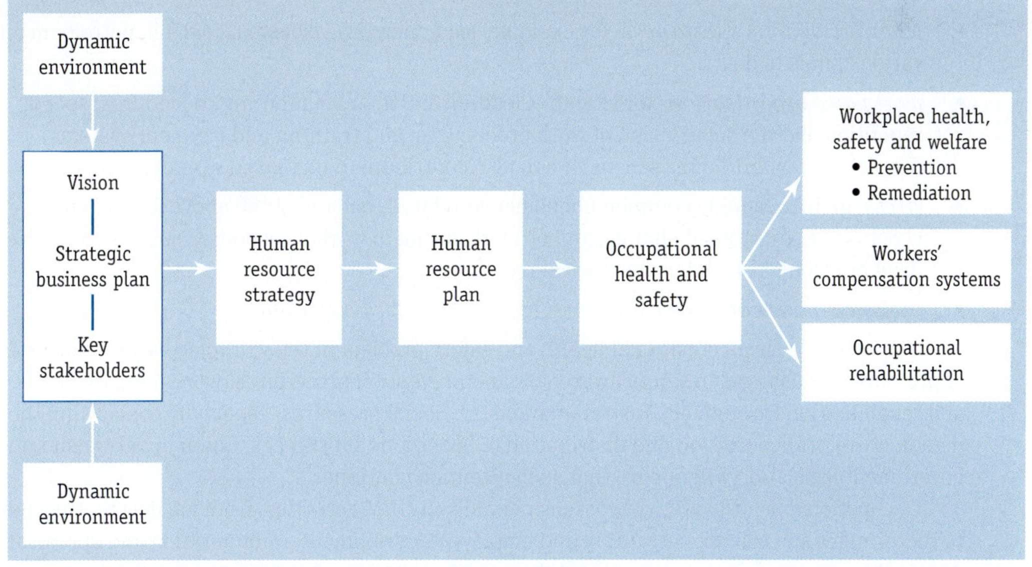

This chapter traces the development of OHS legislation and practice in Australian industry, analyses the perspectives of OHS specialists, and their impacts on the ever-growing variety of OHS issues. It also presents guidelines for the effective management of OHS issues, including the roles of senior and human resource management.

The extent of the problem

Estimates of the numbers and costs of industrial injuries and diseases vary, due to differences in the methods of data collection between the Australian states. However, recent data from the (former) National Occupational Health and Safety Commission (NOHSC) reveal that between 2001 and 2002 around 2000 Australian employees died, and more than 140000 were injured or became ill, as the direct result of workplace accidents, exposure to hazardous materials or dangerous work processes.[1] These incidents cost approximately '$4.7 billion in direct financial costs (workers' compensation paid and medical costs) ... (and) the estimated total cost for that year was over $34.3 billion or 5 per cent of gross domestic product (GDP)'.[2] According to the NOHSC report, the most dangerous industry sectors, in order, are transport and storage, mining, construction, manufacturing; and agriculture, forestry and fishing, with semi-skilled and skilled workers the most common victims.[3]

Direct and indirect OHS costs include sick leave, medical costs and rising insurance premiums, replacement salaries, equipment downtime, team and morale effects. Perhaps of more importance is the range of human and community costs, including the physical and emotional suffering of the injured employees, their families and dependants, financial disruption and often severe damage to employees' self-esteem and future work capacities.

The range of potential work hazards, both physical and psychological, is increasingly broad, encompassing:

- *physical factors*: for example, noise, vibration, excessive heat or cold and electro-physical agents. Ultraviolet and ultrasound, x-ray and laser technology, and mobile telephones have added to the existing potential risks in the workplace.

- *chemical agents*: for example, poisons, toxins, corrosive or irritant substances. In combination with some of the physical hazards above, chemical reactions can be both harmful and expensive.

- *other hazardous substances*: for example, lead, mercury, asbestos, coal, oil, petroleum and various kinds of dusts.

- *workplace organisation*: for example, loading and manual handling procedures; speed, repetition and the supervision of work procedures; and training and payment systems (especially reward/bonus schemes) can also contribute to increased worker risks.

- *stress*: an increasingly common phenomenon related to many of the above factors and constant organisational change, and often resulting in worker responses such as excessive drug or alcohol use and psychological reactions.

- *violence, physical or psychological harm from work colleagues.*

The extent of the occupational health and safety problem in the workplace is one of a series of pressures for changes in safety awareness and prevention procedures, work reorganisation and rehabilitation throughout Australian industry. Social pressures, especially concerning the manufacture, transportation and distribution of hazardous substances, union involvement and government legislation will ensure that such attention continues.

Occupational health and safety issues pervade all HRM activities, from job design, through to recruitment and selection, training and employee development, remuneration and appraisal. Thus, all human resource managers and their staff need to be alert to current and future risk factors in their workplaces and also to participate in the development of effective OHS management programs.

However, unlike many of the other HR activities, the management of OHS will involve considerable participation and consultation from managers, unions, employees and government agencies. The nature of this involvement is discussed in detail later in this chapter, but usual HR

roles in OHS include mediation between conflicting interests, policy and program development and coordination, the convening of consultative committees, and assistance in the compilation of relevant OHS data, for both preventive and rehabilitative purposes.

OHS and strategic HRM

Using OHS data, including financial costs, accidents, absenteeism and compensation statistics as part of an integrated HRIMS (see Chapter 4), HR specialists can adopt strategic interventions and use these as evidence of their contributions to business productivity and profitability (e.g. decreased costs, increased revenue).[4]

Thus, in the construction industry, a strategic HRM approach to OHS would focus on the common causes and trends of site accidents and injuries, assess the associated costs, human and financial, and develop appropriate preventive work systems or more effective administrative and rehabilitation programs. These initiatives would usually involve consultation with line managers, workplace committees, employees and their unions. In the hospitality industry, where minor cuts and burns are commonplace, precautionary measures may be implemented, at minimal cost, to enhance employee morale and organisational productivity.

Perspectives of OHS in Australia

Early developments in OHS awareness and prevention in Australia, like their precedents in the UK and US, were largely due to the pressures of the social reformers and the associated humanitarian movement in the late 19th century. Their concerns centred on the hazardous working conditions and increased risks associated with new manufacturing and mining industries, and in particular the use of child labour. Governments were, in general, very reluctant to pass protective legislation, considering that OHS was essentially a 'management prerogative'. Lack of regulations, and the costs of protecting workers, ensured that most managers paid scant attention to even the most obvious physical hazards until forced to do so by the growth in legislation as the 20th century progressed.

Fuelling this increase in legislative activity was the growth of a number of professions with an interest in occupational health and safety. John Toohey identifies the overall issues which became identified as central to the prevention of OHS problems:

- the correct perception of OHS issues and their causes

- the determination of the appropriate methodologies to address them

- adequate coverage of all occupations, industries and OHS issues.[5]

A variety of different professions began to express their interests in OHS issues during the 1970s and 1980s, each bringing with them their familiar perspectives and models of causes and solutions. Often the perspectives they brought to OHS were in conflict with those of other professionals. Leigh Deves suggests that each professional group aims 'to cultivate their own specialities, (their) interest groups are powerful and … (they) guard their turf jealously'.[6] Legislative developments, especially in the 1980s in all Australian states, only served to ensure their continuing interest in OHS issues, usually as consultants to industry or governments.

The main professions which have become involved in OHS in Australian industry include the medical profession, occupational epidemiologists, industrial hygienists, ergonomists, industrial psychologists and more recently, occupational sociologists. Management, unions and the legal profession have maintained an interest in such issues, especially since the 1980s. Each professional group represents a different perspective and will be considered separately.

The task of the human resource manager in OHS areas is thus made extremely complex, in coordinating and conciliating between these different professional groups, to ensure the most cost-effective approach to a growing range of OHS issues. Issues that highlight the differing diagnostic and management approaches of these professions include repetition strain injury (RSI), more commonly known as occupational overuse syndrome (OOS); stress; and sick building syndrome (SBS). These issues will also be considered as OHS case studies in subsequent discussion.

OHS and the medical model

Medicine was not traditionally involved in workplace issues such as accidents and disease. However, due to the negative effects of the Industrial Revolution in both the UK and Australia, the medical profession began to be consulted by managers and government agencies, searching for ways to prevent growing organisational and human costs.

Medical specialists naturally focused on the identification of the direct physiological effects of work on health. Aspects of workers' behaviour such as overexertion, the handling of toxic substances and the dangers of machinery preoccupied early occupational medicine practitioners. Links between the handling of toxic substances and the development of allergic skin rashes could be relatively easily determined and treated with appropriate medication. Trained to diagnose such relationships and prescribe accordingly, medical approaches to OHS quickly gained pre-eminence. OHS issues in the mining and construction industry during the 1970s and 1980s appeared to be easily resolved by medical diagnosis and treatment.

This so-called 'medical model' has been challenged by recent OHS studies of stress, occupational overuse syndrome and sick building syndrome. Medical or physical approaches often seem narrowly focused or unable to fully explain causes or to devise suitable preventive strategies. As Robert Spillane and Leigh Deves point out, medical diagnoses tend to favour managerial perspectives of the 'malingerer' or, even worse, to enhance employee feelings of 'patienthood';[7] that is, employees being encouraged to feel that they are helpless victims of work-caused illness. This can foster excessive worker dependency on medical specialists, and lead to ongoing treatment rather than encouraging a rapid return to work duties.

Occupational epidemiology

A sub-discipline of occupational medicine, occupational epidemiology 'explores the frequency of the occurrence of phenomena of interest in health care, and relates measures of their frequency to their determination'.[8] In other words, epidemiologists research 'epidemics,' or the incidence of diseases and illnesses in workplaces, and attempt to establish their causes and solutions. Occupational epidemiologists use mass scientific studies to determine causal relationships between work behaviours and occupational accidents and diseases. They may, for example, study the incidence of OHS problems such as asbestosis, toxic reactions, skin diseases or industrial deafness, and then suggest ways of preventing their occurrence. These approaches have been criticised for their over-concern with physical relationships and their pathological (or sickness) emphasis.

Industrial psychology

The application of psychology to the workplace, its accidents and diseases, brought a different perspective to their causes and treatment, emphasising behavioural rather than simply physical approaches. Applications of industrial psychology in Australian industry during the 1980s and 1990s include studies into worker stress and repetition strain injury/occupational overuse syndrome. Rather than merely relating these symptoms to the physical nature of the work, industrial psychology takes the view that they may be partly caused by individual psychological reactions to stressful, boring or repetitive work processes.

Industrial psychology has, however, been criticised for its over-concern with individual worker reactions to their work environments, and for its categorisation of workers into 'accident prone' or 'machismo' types. Macho workers are those who fail to take protective measures against risks because they feel them to be unmanly. Other critics suggest that industrial psychology tends to blame the victim, focusing on individual workers' (mis)behaviours rather than their work environments. As Michael Quinlan suggests, such approaches have often led to 'an undervaluing of the structural characteristics of the workplace which may be conducive to ill-health'.[9] Some of these perceived deficiencies of the industrial psychology perspective have been addressed by the views of industrial sociology.

Ergonomics and occupational hygiene

Ergonomics and occupational hygiene aim to eliminate risks and improve productivity by modifying the physical arrangements and conditions of the workplace. Usually employed by managers, these technical experts frequently undertake changes without consultation with either workers or their unions.

Ergonomics, drawing on Scientific Management theories, focuses on the physical features of the work environment (e.g. workstations, work processes and machinery), while occupational hygiene is more concerned with 'the identification, measurement and evaluation of hazards in the workplace, and the development of procedures for their control or elimination'.[10] Hazards can include physical, chemical or biological aspects, linked to specific physical illnesses and diseases.

Perhaps the best recent example of the contributions of ergonomics to OHS is its approach to occupational overuse syndrome (or repetition strain injury). During the 1980s and 1990s, ergonomists were often employed to prevent the rising incidence of OOS/RSI by designing workstations to minimise the repetitive strain on workers in selected occupations (e.g. telephonists, word processing operators). More comfortable chairs, modified keyboards and hourly rest breaks were instituted to reduce the physical and postural strains on such workers.

Occupational hygienists contributed to the reduction of asbestos-caused diseases by identifying high-risk exposure levels and limiting exposure with the provision of protective equipment (e.g. gloves, masks, suits and screens). With other potentially hazardous substances, hygienists have identified threshold limit values (TLV), short-term exposure limits and ceiling limits (STEC). Further examples of the influences of occupational hygienists can be seen in hospital radiotherapy units, where radiotherapists and their assistants are compelled to wear radiation measuring devices.

Both specialisations tend to focus on individual physical or physiological responses to specified work hazards, often at the expense of broader, more integrative approaches to the problems of occupational health and safety.

Industrial sociology

While recognising the contributions of medical and paramedical strategies to the resolution of OHS issues, sociologists have increasingly criticised their narrow focus on individual and physical factors, and their neglect of the importance of structural elements in the workplace. Sociologists suggest that such aspects as the lack of worker control in their work processes, 'production imperatives' and associated reward (or bonus) systems are significant contributors to OHS accidents and disease.[11] As an example, OOS/RSI mainly occurred in semi-skilled occupations (word processing, secretarial and telephonist positions) with little control over workloads and often bound by productivity-based bonus systems. Similarly, numerous research studies identify stress as a significant issue in manual rather than managerial positions, possibly due to employees' lack of autonomy or influence over their work processes. Dwyer proposes a four-level causative model of injury/disease, including:

- reward systems

- command (or hierarchical) structure

- work organisation

- individual factors.[12]

The union movement has, not surprisingly, been favourable to this sociological perspective, but has emphasised the consideration of many perspectives to resolve OHS issues. As John Toohey notes, the union movement has consistently encouraged 'multidiscipline, workplace-based research'.[13] He further suggests that 'many believe OHS provides an important and ideal vehicle through which to implement work reform strategies'.[14] Cynics have suggested that salary and wage agreements included in the former ALP federal government's Accord with the ACTU in the 1980s and early 1990s forced unions to embrace industrial sociology as a means of creating more substantive workplace bargaining issues. The impact of award reforms and enterprise agreements, which often include OHS issues, has been to encourage a more consultative approach between unions and employers with respect to OHS.

The legal profession and OHS

The growth in OHS issues has increasingly concerned lawyers and insurance agents, especially in the settlement of workers' compensation claims. Frequent disputes over OHS issues have ended up in both federal and state courts, resulting in payments to aggrieved employees or decisions in favour of employers.

The legal profession has a vested interest in occupational health and safety issues, and there are numerous examples of costly litigation as the result of employer negligence, or their failure to provide healthy and safe workplaces. Legal action has increased since the passing of more comprehensive OHS legislation in most Australian states during the 1980s. Arguments and counterarguments include reference to medical, ergonomic, occupational hygiene, industrial psychology or sociological perspectives, and may reflect managerial or union interests. The courts thus become mediators or arbitrators between the differing perspectives of OHS 'experts,' often at great cost to both employers and their employees.

Union approaches

Until the 1970s, most Australian unions showed only limited interest in OHS issues, preferring to concentrate on negotiations to obtain higher wages and more attractive working conditions for their members. Prior to the 1980s, 'danger' and 'dirt' money agreements were quite common components of industrial relations claims, especially in the mining, construction and manufacturing industries. Thus, unions have in the past been criticised for payment trade-offs in the area of OHS, rather than serious involvement in the prevention of accidents and diseases, or the rehabilitation of injured workers.

In part, however, union inaction in this area can be explained by a general community and industry ignorance of the causes of, or solutions to, OHS problems. Management refusal to allow union involvement in risk assessment or workplace redesign was also a contributing factor. Until the 1980s even the formal industrial tribunals generally avoided consideration of OHS issues in their conciliation and arbitration activities.

During the late 1970s and early 1980s, however, unions and their national representative body, the Australian Council of Trade Unions (ACTU), began to show more interest in, and growing knowledge of, these issues (see Chapter 3). The ACTU–ALP government Accord (1984), which restricted the wage and salary bargaining activities of unions, provided an opportunity

for them to branch out into other areas of workers' conditions, including health, safety and welfare. In 1983, the ACTU produced a comprehensive OHS policy and established a combined ACTU and Victorian Trades Hall Council Health and Safety Research Unit. Subsequently, most states developed their own health and safety information and training units. Some individual unions, notably the Australian Metal Workers' Union, also established OHS project groups or task forces. Most state capitals now have workers' health centres, or workers' health action groups, to promote OHS awareness and assist injured workers.

In the 21st century, with the significant restructuring of many Australian industry sectors, the impacts of new technology, and the emergence of individual employment contracts in response to the federal *WorkChoices* legislation, unions and their peak body, the ACTU, have heightened their awareness of and responses to the changing OHS issues in the workplace. The ACTU, for example, has developed a 'National OHS Strategy 2002–2012' which focuses on 'national action to address contemporary hazards such as work-related stress, dangerous working hours, violence and bullying; (the) health and safety impacts of labour market changes, such as casual and contract work; and (the) prevention of occupational diseases, such as cancer, heart and respiratory diseases'.[15] The strategy supports the use of regulation and enforcement for breaches of the OHS legislation, including criminal sanctions, public exposure, and even lobbying for 'occupational manslaughter' provisions for employers which breach OHS legislation (as already implemented in the Australian Capital Territory).

The ACTU strategy has been developed at least partly in response to changing employment relationships, and the impact of the *WorkChoices* legislation, and runs counter to the Australian federal government's preventive thrust in OHS. As the comment by the former federal Minister for Employment and Workplace Relations (Hon. Kevin Andrews) at the beginning of this chapter suggests, the government's position opposes further regulation of OHS and favours prevention rather than punishment in OHS. It aims to develop 'nationally consistent OHS arrangements' through its newly established Australian Safety and Compensation Council (ASCC), with priorities such as injuries and diseases of mature-aged workers, musculoskeletal disorders, and other injuries in the construction industry.[16]

News report 11.1 shows some of the potential OHS issues associated with the impact of more flexible employment conditions and practices, in this case the employment of foreign construction workers on temporary work visas.

NEWS REPORT 11.1

Skills shortages: foreign workers fall foul of safety laws

A $60 million construction project supported by the state and federal governments and employing foreign workers on controversial temporary work visas has been closed after it received 39 infringement notices. The workers are among 40 000 expected to arrive in Australia this year on the business visas designed for employers who cannot find local workers with specific skills.

Documents obtained by the *Herald* reveal that those at the site in Wetherill Park, where ABC Tissues is constructing a tissue-paper mill and plant did not meet the most basic criteria for eligibility for the so-called 457 visas. It is also understood that they were being paid in China, in breach of the visa conditions, by a Chinese Government-owned company acting as a labour hire firm.

The Australian Manufacturing Workers Union says that between their arrival in February and May the foreign workers were not covered by workers' compensation insurance, which is also a breach of the regulations. Workers on 457 visas should be skilled and fully qualified for their work, but at the ABC site there were forklift drivers and electricians without appropriate licences. Australian workers on the site said none of the Chinese workers could speak English, read safety signs or follow emergency procedures. Many had to be trained to perform the most basic tasks.

One Australian tradesman said he was stunned to see one of the guest workers make a non-compliant Chinese power tool fit a socket by stripping the cord and inserting naked wires straight into the plug. One local worker told the *Herald* that soon after they arrived the new workforce opened shipping containers stored on-site and unloaded masses of equipment shipped from China, including thousands of boxes of new tools, scaffolding, ladders and safety equipment that did not meet Australian safety specifications.

The Australian workers said it was impossible to maintain a safe site with two workforces labouring side-by-side unable to communicate. A spokesman for WorkCover said the agency was investigating the insurance and workers' compensation situation on the site, but could not say how they could prosecute a foreign company in the event it broke the law.

Source: Adapted from O'Malley N. 2006. 'Skills shortage: foreign workers fall foul of safety laws,' *Sydney Morning Herald*, 4 September, pp. 1 & 9.

Occupational health and safety, and HRM

As the above discussion suggests, OHS has become highly complex, especially since the 1980s, involving a diverse group of specialists, each with different perspectives, interests and objectives. Issues such as RSI/OOS and stress have illustrated the difficulty of establishing causes and appropriate solutions. Federal and state legislation has effectively emphasised the importance of OHS issues to the overall employment relationship. More than any other area of HRM, occupational health and safety requires substantial involvement from employees and their unions, supervisors, middle and senior management. This is not only legally required, especially where workplace consultative committees exist, but because OHS issues pervade all other HRM activities. Job and work design systems involve OHS considerations; recruitment, training and performance management programs will encompass OHS aspects such as employees' physical capabilities and general health status, previous levels of exposure to toxic substances, or stress factors. The HR manager will usually be involved in OHS issues at strategic, operational and administrative levels, in consultation with workplace committees, unions, managers and the broad range of OHS experts earlier described.

At the strategic level, HR managers will keep abreast of current OHS issues, legislation and strategies, analysing trends or accident rates, and workers' compensation costs, and projecting the impact of the introduction of new technology or new work processes on employee health and safety. In consultation with workplace committees, unions and managers, human resource managers may modify existing OHS policies or develop new policy directions.

At the operational level, HR managers may chair workplace committees or advise on procedures that are required to prevent accidents or injuries. They may also support supervisors and line managers in workplace redesign, provide safety awareness training or promotion campaigns, or advise on the relevant OHS consultants to resolve particular issues. Administratively, HR departments may coordinate the collection of statistics on accident rates and work-related diseases, or provide secretarial support to workplace committees.

OHS law in Australia

As indicated in Exhibit 11.2 below, Australian industry has been subject to a wide range of Acts and statutes concerning specific occupational risks and hazards. Common law (see Chapter 3) has been an additional avenue for injured workers to pursue claims.

Exhibit 11.2   OHS law in Australia

Commonwealth/federal

- *Occupational Health & Safety (Commonwealth Employment) Act 1991* (and Regulations 1991)
- *Occupational Health & Safety (Maritime Industry) Act 1993* (and Regulations 1995)
- *Safety, Rehabilitation and Compensation Act 1988* (and Regulations 2002)
- *Seafarers Rehabilitation and Compensation Act 1992* (and Regulations 1993)

Australian Capital Territory

- *Occupational Health & Safety Act 1989* (and Regulations 1991)
- *Workers Compensation Act 1951* (and Regulations 2002)

New South Wales

- *Occupational Health & Safety Act 2000* (and Regulations 2001)
- *Workers Compensation Act 1987* (and Regulations 2003)
- *Workplace Injury Management & Workers Compensation Act 1998* (and Regulations 2002)

Northern Territory

- *Dangerous Goods (Road and Rail Transport) Act 2005*
- *Work Health (Occupational Health & Safety) Act 2006*

Queensland

- *Workers' Compensation and Rehabilitation Act 2003* (and Regulations 2003)
- *Workplace Health & Safety Act 1995* (and Regulations 1997)

South Australia

- *Occupational Health, Safety & Welfare Act 1986* (and Regulations 1995)
- *Workers Rehabilitation and Compensation Act 1986* (and General Regulations 1999)

Tasmania

- *Workers Rehabilitation and Compensation Act 1988* (and Regulations 2001)
- *Workplace Health & Safety Act 1995* (and Regulations 1998)

Victoria

- *Accident Compensation (Occupational Health & Safety) Act 1996*
- *Accident Compensation Act 1985*
- *Occupational Health & Safety Act 2004*
- *Workers Compensation Act 1958* (and Regulations 1995)

Western Australia

- *Occupational Health & Safety Act 1984* (and Regulations 1996)
- *Workers Compensation and Injury Management Act 1981* (and Amendment Regulations 2005)
- *Workers Compensation and Rehabilitation Act 1981* (and Regulations 1982)

Source: Adapted from *OHS Alert*, www.ohsalert.com.au, accessed on 24 August 2006.

OHS legislation has always had three broad thrusts:
- *prevention*: to safeguard employees from real, or potential, health and safety risks
- *compensation*: to provide injured employees with minimum levels of monetary compensation
- *rehabilitation*: to assist the return to work of injured workers.

In practice, however, worker protection has often been limited to specific physical risks (e.g. toxic substances, machinery), and particular industries (e.g. mining, manufacturing). Similarly, until quite recently unions and their members have preferred compensation payments to comprehensive rehabilitation programs.

Historical developments

During the 1970s, growing costs associated with lost-time accidents and workers' compensation payments prompted criticism of existing OHS legislation. Specifically, that:
- The legislation did not cover all workers or hazards in the workplace.
- Risk standards were frequently inconsistent and multiple Acts applied within each workplace.
- Enforcement of the Acts was conducted by several government agencies, usually with severely limited resources.
- Established standards generally represented only the minimum requirements, and differed from state to state.
- No systematic reviews occurred, and updating of the legislation was largely ad hoc.[17]

Accordingly, unions, managers, OHS specialists and both federal and state governments were receptive to the findings of overseas authorities grappling with similar issues. In particular, the Robens Inquiry of 1972 in the UK, and the *Occupational Safety and Health Act* (OSHA) in the USA in 1970 attracted considerable interest, eventually leading to similar legislation in most Australian states during the 1970s and 1980s (see Exhibit 11.2).

Preventive OHS legislation

In the UK, Lord Robens examined existing OHS law and concluded that, like its Australian counterpart, it was far too fragmented, had a paternalistic or punitive focus and had largely failed to reduce accidents and injuries at work. He also concluded that OHS was not simply a legal or employer responsibility, but should also involve employees and their unions. Some critics of Robens suggest that he placed too little emphasis on the enforcement provisions of the legislation, preferring employer self-regulation.[18] In contrast, the US OSHA consciously developed mandatory health and safety standards, workplace inspection procedures and penalty systems.

In the Australian states, the explosion of OHS legislation in the 1970s and 1980s focused on the establishment of unified systems to cover a broader range of physical and psychological work risks. The concept of 'occupational well-being' and the inclusion of employee 'welfare' in at least some states signified a more preventive approach to OHS issues. The Williams Report, which established the NSW legislation, as an example, defines OHS as 'the protection and maintenance of the highest degree of physical, mental and social well-being of workers in all occupations'.[19] Leigh Deves suggests that the legislation provided:

> the opportunity to replace a fragmented and out-dated regulatory system
> that emerged from the social conscience of the previous century with a more
> positive and comprehensive legal framework that reflected contemporary social
> policies, and which conformed broadly to international conventions.[20]

Most Australian legislation followed the Robens and Williams approach to the enforcement of OHS legislation (i.e. self-regulation, cautions preferred to punishment), rather than the stricter US (OSHA) provisions. As discussed earlier, this perspective has been maintained by subsequent Australian governments,[21] despite the more aggressive position adopted by the ACTU. While some states (especially Tasmania and the Northern Territory) provided greater resources for their OHS inspectorates, many (notably New South Wales) remain under-resourced, and prefer to rely on informal sanctions (e.g. improvement and prohibition notices, injunctions, licence suspensions, or adverse publicity), rather than more stringent action for negligent employers.[22] Stronger organisational sanctions (cash fines, internal discipline orders, corporate probation, community service orders or criminal convictions) are seldom invoked.[23] Fines have been increased and in some states, the powers of OHS inspectors have been strengthened in recent years. As mentioned earlier, there have been campaigns in some Australian states and territories (notably NSW with its proposed OHS Workplace Fatalities Bill, and the Australian Capital Territory with an industrial manslaughter law) for amendments to OHS legislation to include new offences of 'industrial manslaughter' against negligent employers and their senior managers.[24]

As well as state legislation to deal with operational OHS issues, and regular inspections, the Australian government established the National OHS Commission (NOHSC) in 1985, as a tripartite policy review body. Now called the Australian Safety and Compensation Council (ASCC), it includes representatives from the Confederation of Australian Industry (CAI), the ACTU, and all state and territory governments. Its functions include setting advisory national OHS standards, developing national strategies and providing research, education, training and statistical support. It has recently released its National OHS Strategy which aims to reduce workplace injuries by 40 per cent and fatalities by 20 per cent by 2012.[25] It intends to develop 'greater national consistency for OHS and workers compensation,' with a specific focus on the construction industry.[26]

Workers' compensation and rehabilitation legislation

In the first two decades after Federation, most Australian states established some form of legislation to compensate workers injured at work. This legislation generally had little relationship to other safety law, and was primarily concerned with providing 'a specified array of hospital and medical expenses associated with their injury, as well as specified weekly payments in lieu of wages lost as a result of absence from work'.[27] Additional, so-called 'lists of maims' provided lump sum payments for permanent, total or partial incapacity.

Over time, workers' compensation systems exhibited serious flaws, which began to be recognised by management, unions and governments during the 1960s and 1970s. Not only was there a distinct lack of national coordination of systems, but the costs of both payments and premiums were escalating; claimants frequently experienced delays in the determination of their claims; not all workers were covered; and accident claims tended to be viewed more favourably than those for occupational disease. Differences also existed between states in such areas as eligibility (e.g. casuals and domestic workers were not always included), entitlements, definitions (e.g. 'disease,' 'injury') and insurance providers (e.g. public or private).[28] Furthermore, there appeared to be little incentive for the rehabilitation of injured workers, or even the prevention of identifiable risks.

During the 1980s, most Australian states began to modify their workers' compensation legislation to ensure more cost-effective, integrated and comprehensive compensation systems. Victoria passed Accident Compensation legislation in 1985, which, among other things, established the Victorian Accident Rehabilitation Council (VARC), setting up a 'network of government and licensed private rehabilitation centres' by 1989.[29] South Australia, in its *Workers' Rehabilitation and Compensation Act 1986*, established a Workers' Rehabilitation Advisory Unit, and New South Wales passed its own *Workers' Compensation Act* in 1987. New Zealand followed later with its *Accident Rehabilitation Compensation Insurance Act 1992*.

This legislation generally included changes in the structuring of benefits (emphases on weekly payments, and reductions or the removal of lump sum payments); insurance providers (e.g. government insurance office monopolies, or primarily privatised); and improved administration systems (streamlining of claims, reduction of cost structures). Most state legislation also introduced procedures to eliminate false compensation claims, and aimed to more closely integrate workers' compensation, rehabilitation and overall OHS preventive systems.

Some of the specialists involved in workers' compensation procedures simultaneously developed statements of professional ethics to ensure more effective and humane rehabilitation systems. An example of this is the code of the Australian Council of Rehabilitation Medicine which says that rehabilitation should be:

- *industry based*, with employers undertaking a critical role in supporting recovery, adjustment and resettlement back on the job

- *function oriented*, so that the physical, psychological and vocational impairment can be minimised

- *based on early intervention*, which enhances the chances of success, and maximises cost-effectiveness

- *multidisciplinary*, involving the best profession or person for providing a specific service, or making a relevant decision

- *based on a shared responsibility*, of all stakeholders (workers, employers, the compensation agency, professionals).[30]

It is perhaps worth noting that these points reflect the broad principles associated with the legislation. It also acknowledges the involvement of another series of vested interests in OHS, that of the rehabilitation and insurance providers. From an HR perspective, all these interest groups need to be consulted, coordinated and monitored to ensure cost-effective approaches to prevention, rehabilitation and compensation.

A recent Australian government report indicates that, while compensated employee fatalities are decreasing (from 398 in 1996–7 to 211 in 2002–3) and the total number of compensated claims is also diminishing (from 164 545 in 1996–7 to 134 480 in 2002–3),[31] it has been estimated that more than 300 000 Australian workers lodge workers' compensation claims annually, costing around $4.1 billion, and representing approximately 2.5 per cent of labour costs in workers' compensation premiums.[32]

These enormous costs have been exacerbated by the growth of global business, which entails frequent domestic or international travel, and which may lead to even greater insurance and workers' compensation risks and spiralling premiums. Transportation accidents, tropical diseases, deep vein thrombosis (DVT), fatigue and terrorist events are but a few of the increased threats to frequent business travellers. With respect to terrorism, most travel insurers are reluctant to provide coverage for its consequences, although most workers' compensation systems do offer limited protection for employees. As an example of the huge costs involved in such events, the 11 September attack on New York's World Trade Center reputedly cost the Marriott World Trade Center Hotel more than US$10 million in workers' compensation claims, as while only two employees were killed in the incident, another 146 filed claims for associated stress and trauma – 'the largest catastrophic workers' compensation loss in history'.[33]

Undoubtedly, such costs directly affect organisational profitability. It is therefore a crucial area in which human resource managers and their staff need to become involved, by analysing accident and workers' compensation trends and, through consultation with senior managers and workplace consultative committees, developing programs for addressing these issues.

Strategic approaches may include the redesign of work processes, the implementation of new technology for manual handling, or more effective safety training programs. OHS and workers' compensation provide the astute HR manager with significant opportunities to demonstrate their contributions to organisational success, by directly reducing costs (e.g. equipment downtime, compensation payments, and replacement costs), through more careful OHS management. More efficient rehabilitation programs, which ensure that employees return to work as quickly as possible, serve both employee and organisational interests. Roberts-Yates (2006) suggests that 'effective risk management, early intervention, a commitment by the injured worker to return to work, a non-adversarial context and competent injury/rehabilitation management at the worksite are critical factors to an early return to work. Clear communication and a rigorous quality service performance by the medical and vocational providers are seen by employers and human resource management as influencing successful rehabilitation and successful return-to-work outcomes'.[34] The following examples of health and safety, and rehabilitation policies (Exhibits 11.3 and 11.4) enshrine the cardinal principles of both OHS legislation and HRM practice.

Creating a safe and healthy work environment

We have seen that employers are required by law to provide safe and healthy working conditions for their employees. They are also required to compensate injured employees. The Australian Workplace Industrial Relations Survey (AWIRS) reveals some interesting findings about the application of OHS legislation at the workplace:

- 82 per cent of organisations have written OHS policies (compared with 71 per cent in 1990), covering 91 per cent of the workforce (compared with 83 per cent in 1990)

- 73 per cent of managers are responsible for OHS issues

- OHS committees exist in only 43 per cent of workplaces (compared with 41 per cent in 1990), more commonly in large workplaces and the public sector. Two-thirds of all workplaces have elected representatives, with or without a committee

- 38 per cent of employees received OHS training in 1994–5; this mainly involved permanent rather than casual employees

- stress was reported primarily by managers, professionals, clerks and para-professionals, with an imbalance towards female employees.[35]

Exhibit 11.3 Sample health and safety policy

It is our policy to provide safe and efficient systems of work, a healthy and safe working environment and the commitment that employees will not be expected to carry out work which is reasonably considered to be unsafe.

The key to our comprehensive health and safety program is the complete and sustained commitment of management and the involvement and responsible actions of every employee. Our goals in health and safety will be achieved through:

- injury prevention and loss control program

- environmental monitoring

- accident/near miss reporting and analysis

- rehabilitation programs

- medical surveillance and health promotion

- emergency and first aid procedures

- safety training and education

- safety systems for visitors and contractors

- safe working systems for employees

- fleet safety programs.

Your contribution to, and support of, our health and safety programs is essential if we are to be successful in preventing injuries and developing a work environment that is satisfying, efficient and safe for all.

Exhibit 11.4 Sample rehabilitation policy

Objective

The Company is committed to preventing work-related injury and illness through providing a safe and healthy working environment. This commitment is detailed in the Company Safety Policy and conforms to requirements of the *NSW Occupational Health and Safety Act 2000*. In the event of injuries or illness occurring, the Company is committed to providing a safe and early return to work commensurate with medical advice.

Program

In order to achieve these objectives, the Company will:

- Ensure that rehabilitation is the usual course of action immediately following work-related injury or illness.

- Assist an employee who has or is suffering from a work-related illness or injury to return to his/her pre-injury job or to other suitable employment through an individually planned program. An injured worker will not be prejudiced while undertaking rehabilitation.

- Maintain a network of support internally and externally to ensure rehabilitation is initiated, monitored and progressed to a satisfactory conclusion.

- Support rehabilitation by providing, where possible and practicable and when required, suitable duties for injured employees. However, there may be circumstances where suitable duties will not be available.

- Ensure that suitably trained occupational health personnel are made available to implement a program of rehabilitation.

  Employees will, where practicable:

- Take all necessary care in the performance of their duties to prevent work-related injuries to themselves and others.

- Support the principles of this rehabilitation policy.

- Actively cooperate in a program of suitable duties when this is recommended as part of the recovery process. It may be necessary to rehabilitate a person in another job classification irrespective of union coverage.

While the success of an OHS program depends largely on managers, supervisors, union representatives and employees themselves, the human resource manager can be involved in strategic, operational, coordinating and administrative roles that support all their activities. These roles will necessarily differ from organisation to organisation, and change over time as committees develop more comprehensive functions. We will now examine some specific OHS issues – accidents, smoking, stress, mobile phones, AIDS and the risks associated with international travel – and then discuss relevant management and HRM responses.

Issue 1: Accidents at work

As with other OHS issues, information on the extent and costs of accidents to Australian industry and society is imprecise because of differences in data collection methods between states, and often a failure to record indirect costs. One former Australian government minister suggested that costs to the taxpayer might be around $6 billion annually, but this is likely to be a conservative estimate.[36] In 1999, WorkSafe Australia estimated the cost of workplace accidents to employers and the community to be more than $27 billion annually.[37] A Western Australian study calculated that in 1989 there were 31 943 lost-time accidents in that state alone, resulting in 136 815 weeks of lost production, at a cost of $116.5 million in compensation.[38]

The major problem in reducing the impact of accidents is to identify their causes and to build in suitable preventive processes. Accidents generally occur as the result of unsafe acts or unsafe conditions. The most common accidents in industry occur as the result of manual handling processes, being struck by moving objects, faulty use of machinery or tools, and casual slips and falls.

Not surprisingly, the heaviest incidence of workplace accidents resulting in death or serious injury occurs in industries which use heavy machinery (e.g. manufacturing, agriculture) or which involve inherently dangerous work systems (e.g. mining, oil rigs). As examples, during 1998, more than 2 000 workers at BHP's hot briquetted iron project in Western Australia walked off the job after a crane 'sent a few tonne steel valve through the main reactor building from a height of about 40 metres'.[39]

WorkSafe Australia estimates that the mining industry has:

> … by far the highest incidence of workers' compensation cases of any industry, at 63 per 1 000, compared with the national rate of 27 for all industries … The industry had the highest incidence and frequency of fatal, non-fatal and injury compensation claims.[40]

Reported causes of such a high accident incidence include shifts from 'employee miners' to 'contract miners'; a loss of union influence on OHS; a decline in a safety and health culture; breaches of legislation and regulations; a lack of commitment and training in OHS; inadequate supervision and the (too) rapid promotion of inexperienced managers. Mines in New South Wales experienced three employee fatalities in the same period.

In most accidents, both immediate and longer-term factors tend to contribute. Accident investigations need therefore to examine the whole range of potential, or actual, causes. Exhibit 11.5 provides a framework for the effective explanation and prevention of workplace accidents.

It is evident from Exhibit 11.5 that simple explanations for the causes of workplace accidents are inadequate. Multifactor analyses of the causes, and multiple strategies for the prevention of future risks are required. Administrative actions might include accident trend analyses, changes in shift and rosters and more regular maintenance and monitoring procedures. Engineering approaches could involve workstation redesign, environmental programs or modifications to machinery or work processes.

Exhibit 11.5   Accidents in the workplace

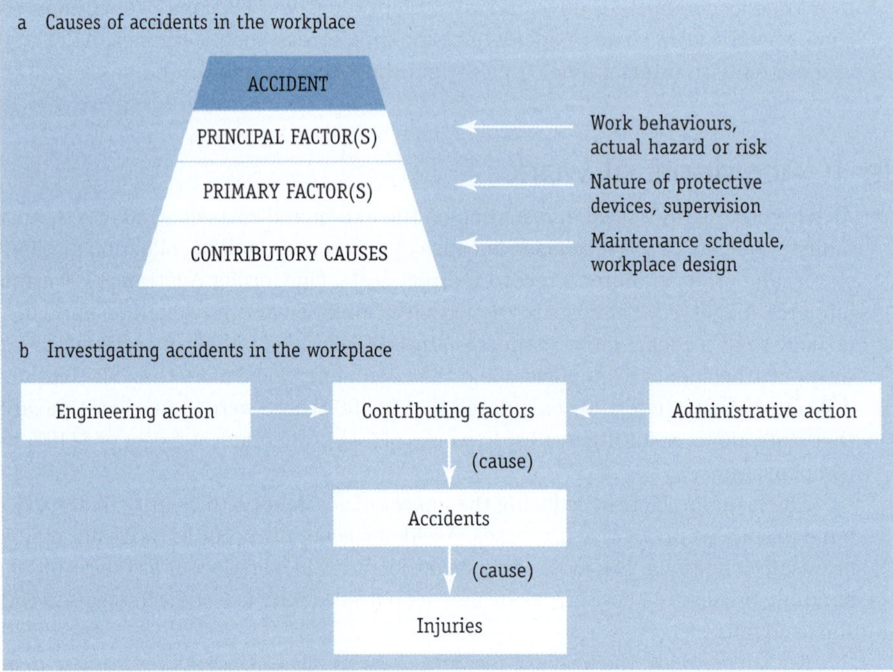

As suggested above, the trend towards the outsourcing of many non-core organisational functions has often included occupational health and safety issues. News report 11.2 shows some of the potential risks such as approaches used in the Australian Navy.

Some authors suggest that accidents are usually caused by the natural 'degradation' of one or more components of organisational 'systems' – that is, human resources, technology, the physical environment or process management – and that, accordingly, the prevention of likely risks is enhanced by the regular and routine maintenance of all components.[41] In the case of human resources, this means attention to procedural training, routine monitoring and effective safety rewards systems.

NEWS REPORT 11.2

Outsourced work 'reduced safety'

A fatal fire aboard the navy's biggest ship could have been avoided if HMAS *Westralia* had a tertiary-qualified engineer on board, the senior sailor in charge of the day-to-day running of the ship's engine room said yesterday.

Colin Bottomley, who was the deputy marine engineering officer, said a qualified engineer would have noticed the dangers associated with installing flexible fuel hoses, which are blamed for sparking the fire that killed four sailors.

Mr Bottomley told the coronial inquiry into the tragedy that he believed the navy's decision to outsource much of the maintenance and engineering work on the ship had reduced safety aboard *Westralia*.

The decision to install unauthorised flexible fuel lines is seen as the central issue in the re-examination of Australia's worst naval disaster for 30 years.

At the end of the first week of his inquest into the fire, West Australian Coroner Alastair Hope said yesterday he wanted to look into how the hoses came to be fitted.

He said the issue was at the 'heart of this case'.

'Four young people have died unnecessarily,' Mr Hope said.

'I want to find out exactly what went wrong.'

Mr Hope said a naval board of inquiry, which began days after the fire, had not examined the issue in appropriate detail.

The hoses, installed by a private contractor just weeks before the fire, were to stop constant fuel leaks. One was faulty and sprayed diesel fuel on to hot engine fittings, causing a fireball to erupt.

Mr Bottomley told the inquest this week that *Westralia* had been plagued by fuel leaks and he had battled for years for a new fuel system before contractors Australian Defence Industries had installed the flexible lines.

He said a contractor had assured him approval for the change had been granted and he believed supporting documents were readily available.

The ship had many maintenance problems in the two years before the fire, including a cracked deck, a breakdown near Darwin in 1996 and a minor explosion in the engine room while in Townsville.

An assessment before the fire had found 58 defects in one part of the engine room and had recommended that the ship enter dock and rectify the fuel leaks.

Mr Bottomley agreed it could take up to five years for approvals to make their way through navy channels.

'Quite often it's the only way you can get your ship to sea,' he said.

After the 1998 board of inquiry, personnel were warned they would face penalties if found to be taking short cuts.

Source: Carson V. 2003. 'Outsourced work "reduced safety",' *Australian*, May, p. 8.

Lin and Mills suggest that the major factors in accidents in the construction industry include a lack of safety training, company size, and the effects of competitive tendering.[42] They found that smaller companies are more accident prone, due to their tight profit margins, and perhaps less likely to rigorously monitor safety risks, and that self-employed building contractors are '… more than twice as likely to be killed at work'.[43] While Farraro notes that '… human behaviour is responsible for up to 95 per cent of all workplace accidents',[44] some others suggest that younger workers are injured more often than their 'silver collar' (older worker) counterparts.[45]

The Cole Royal Commission into the building and construction industry concluded that there was a need for a significant change to workplace cultures and safety behaviours, recommending a more integrated national OHS and workers' compensation system.[46] The Victorian government has already partially responded to these recommendations through its 'Strategy 2000,' attempting to reform its workers' compensation and OHS prevention programs, directing resources at the industries with the highest number of injuries (e.g. manufacturing, construction, transport and storage, meat and poultry, textiles and metal fabrication),[47] and the Australian Construction Industry Development Association has developed a Health and Safety Continuous Improvement Matrix, matched to the Australian quality assurance Standard AS 3901.[48]

As News report 11.3 shows, the precise identification of causative factors in accidents at work is crucial to their future prevention.

NEWS REPORT 11.3

Why efficiency is the enemy of safety

The commission of inquiry into a gas explosion at an Exxon-owned plant in Australia blamed both lack of training and lack of hazard identification. Professor Karl Weick explains that organisational failures, rather than poor preparedness, cause disasters.

On 25 September 1998, a gas absorber at the Longford Gas Plant, owned by Exxon's subsidiary, Esso Australia, burst, releasing a large cloud of hydrocarbon vapours. Seconds later, it exploded. Two staff were killed and four million people deprived of gas for about two weeks.

Esso placed the entire blame upon the control panel operator, Jim Ward, whom they said had ignored alarms and failed to follow procedure. The official inquiry, which released its report this month, blamed Esso for failing to ensure that Ward, and his supervisors, were aware of the hazards and knew the procedures for dealing with them.

The inquiry recommended the adoption of what is known as a 'safety case' system in which all potential hazards are identified, their likelihood of occurring calculated, and steps for mitigating the hazards specified along with the procedures for dealing with them. A government authority to monitor compliance with the system is to be established.

The safety case system was developed in Britain after the explosion of the Piper Alpha oil platform in the North Sea in 1988. However, the latest thinking about what makes complex workplaces reliable suggests that the approach is incorrect. It suggests also that the official inquiry failed to understand what caused the explosion.

Source: Uren D. 2000. 'Why efficiency is the enemy of safety,' *The Manager*, p. 1.

There are, however, a number of crucial activities which all organisations need to undertake, in order to cost-effectively reduce accidents at work. These include the provision of:

- comprehensive safety policies
- an occupational health and safety specialist function, either as part of the HR department, or within a strong OHS consultative committee
- safety awareness, prevention and training programs for all employees and their supervisors
- adequate medical, first aid and workers' compensation systems
- fire drills, protective clothing and equipment appropriate to organisational risks
- safety incentive and prevention schemes
- effective mechanisms for accident investigation, and the ongoing analysis of accident and injury statistics.

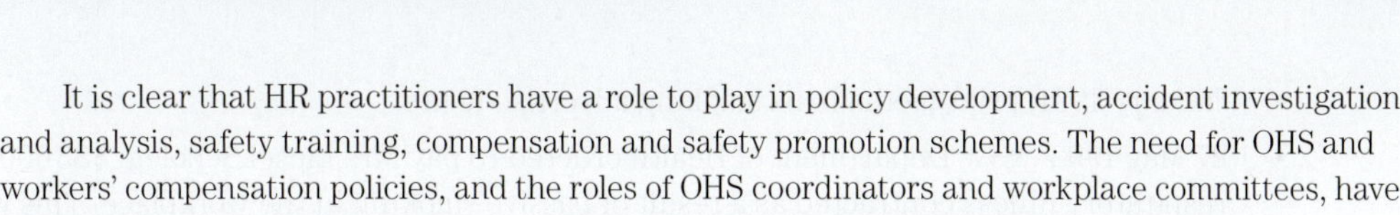

It is clear that HR practitioners have a role to play in policy development, accident investigation and analysis, safety training, compensation and safety promotion schemes. The need for OHS and workers' compensation policies, and the roles of OHS coordinators and workplace committees, have already been discussed. We will now consider the aspects of a successful safety program.

Safety awareness, promotion and training programs

Probably the most important role of a safety program is to motivate managers, supervisors and employees to be aware of safety considerations. If managers and supervisors fail to demonstrate this awareness, their employees can hardly be expected to do so. Some studies in Australia suggest that 80 per cent of organisational managers receive no training in overall OHS issues.[49] It can however be assumed that most line managers receive at least basic training in safety awareness and first aid. Just as important as safety motivation are knowledge of safety and an understanding of where to place safety efforts. Training can help personnel at all levels to understand the organisation's policy on safety, its safety procedures and its system of establishing accountability. An innovative development in training for the prevention of accidents at work is the establishment of advanced driver training courses for truck drivers, bus, taxi and forklift drivers provided by the Driver Education Centre of Australia (DECA) at Shepparton in Central Victoria. One company, Finemar's, has put 1 080 drivers through the program and it claims that 'driver turnover is down to about 12 per cent' (the industry average is about 30 per cent) and its accident rate is barely measurable.[50] In most organisations, the HR department will have some responsibility for the collection of accident statistics, the analysis of trends and the coordination of required training programs.

Accident investigation and records

Every accident, even those considered minor, should be investigated by the supervisor and the safety committee. Such an investigation may determine the factors contributing to the accident and may reveal what corrections are needed to prevent it from happening again. Correction may require rearranging workstations, installing safety guards or controls or, more often, giving employees additional safety training.

In most organisations, supervisors, specialist safety officers and workplace committees normally have the major responsibilities for designing and conducting these programs. However, the HR manager and their staff usually become involved as training adviser, program coordinator, resource provider and course evaluator. This joint involvement provides HR managers with opportunities to develop close links with supervisors, and to demonstrate their clear organisational contributions.

Issue 2: Smoking in the workplace

The major significant events in the history of smoking in the workplace are:

- 1962: Australian College of Physicians condemns smoking as a major source of lung cancer

- 1973: 'Warning – Smoking is a health hazard' label on cigarette packets

- 1976: tobacco advertising banned on television and radio

- 1977: advertising bans extended to theatres and halls

- 1983: ban on smoking in taxis

- 1987: ban on smoking in trains and on domestic airlines

- 1987: Justice Morling decision (NSW) on 'passive smoking' (*AFCO v TIA* 1987)

- 1988: Telecom, Australia Post, CSIRO, NSW Health and Education Departments and the Australian government public service introduce 'smoke- free' workplaces

- January 1991: print media bans smoking advertisements
- 27 May 1992: NSW Department of Health ordered to pay Mrs Liesel Scholem $85 000 for respiratory illness contracted as a result of passive smoking in the workplace. This was considered a landmark case
- early 1997: a NSW government committee (by a very small majority) refused to support a complete ban on smoking in licensed premises, including hotels and restaurants. Given the rising incidence of community concern about this issue, this position is likely to change over time
- *Health (Smoking in Enclosed Public Places) Amendment Bill 2003* (WA) smoking banned in enclosed public places, including workplaces. Most other Australian states have subsequently followed suit, notably Victoria in 2007.

Probably the most heated workplace health issue of the late 1980s and the 1990s concerns cigarette smoking in the workplace. Fuelled by overseas studies and, more recently, legislative precedents in NSW, Victoria and Western Australia, passive smoking (inhaling other people's tobacco smoke) has been linked with disease and death. Accordingly, many groups have successfully called for smoke-free workplaces.

The reasons for introducing smoke-free policies can be divided into financial, legal, health and corporate image factors:

- *Financial factors* include the impact of smoking (passive or active) on the use of sick leave by employees, cleaning costs, fire insurance premiums and higher air-conditioning costs.
- *Legal aspects* encompass increased workers' compensation costs, aggravated by legal precedents.
- *Health risks* are well researched, including emphysema and cancers of the lip, tongue, larynx, lung and stomach. The workplace effects of both active and passive smokers are evidenced in sick leave, invalidity retirement and rehabilitation statistics.
- *Corporate image*, often reflected in job advertisements emphasising that the organisation 'is a smoke-free workplace,' is important in attracting candidates concerned with their health. One study of New South Wales companies suggested that 53 per cent had smoke-free policies, 19 per cent were totally smoke-free, and 37 per cent simply had non-smoking, segregated areas.[51] In the future, and largely as the result of recent successful litigation on the issue of passive smoking, workplaces that permit employees to smoke at work will be the exception rather than the rule.

This OHS issue is, of course, sensitive in organisations with high proportions of smokers, and requires decisions on issues such as individual freedom (for smokers), aesthetics, fire hazards and cleaning costs, time lost for smoking breaks and appropriate action for non-compliance. The hospitality industry in particular has difficulty complying with smoke-free workplace policies, due to the assumed 'right' of their patrons to smoke, despite the likely harmful effects on staff and fellow customers. While large hotels and restaurants may be able to allocate smoking areas, smaller hotels and clubs may have neither the space nor the capacity to lose patrons as the consequence of such policies. However, this is likely to change in the short term.

Organisational policies on smoking in the workplace typically explain the reason for the policy, specify where employees can and cannot smoke, and state the penalties for violations. Procedures for resolving disputes between smokers and non-smokers are frequently included.

Efforts to help employees stop smoking are being promoted by many employers, although this is not the main thrust of such policies. Access to 'quit' programs, in employer or employee time, and the distribution of health promotion and lifestyle literature are common features of these policies. Human resource managers may be involved in the formulation of smoking policies, and the subsequent application of discipline or counselling strategies to smokers and their co-workers.

Issue 3: Occupational stress

Stress has become a significant OHS issue in Australian organisations in recent years, due to increased pressures on employees, legal precedents, and a series of research studies examining its causes, symptoms and effects. One report suggests that more than 20 per cent of all costs for workers' compensation claims in the Australian public service were for stress-related complaints.[52]

Another study found that more than 25 per cent of Australian managers feel some degree of 'stress' as the result of 'information overload,' office politics, loss of job satisfaction or, simply, too much work.[53] In this study, 62 per cent of managers who felt stressed reported actual ill-health and two-thirds had difficulties in their personal relationships. Similarly, an ACTU study of 10 000 workers reported that more than 70 per cent of workers suffer from stress-related health problems such as headaches, continual tiredness and anger, reportedly due to increased workload, organisational change and job insecurity. Organisational restructuring, downsizing and overall change strategies appear to be increasing employees' perceptions of stress, as explained in News report 11.4, and in the 1995 AWIRS study it was found that stress was the second most common cause of injury or illness in Australian workplaces, after dislocation and sprains.[54]

There is currently no clear, agreed definition of stress. Most definitions focus on either the stimulus (cause) or the response (symptoms), the individual worker or their environment.

Hans Selye uses two separate terms to distinguish between the positive and negative effects of stress on the individual, even though bodily reactions to the two forms of stress are similar.[55] 'Eustress' is 'positive' stress that accompanies achievement and exhilaration. Eustress is the stress of meeting challenges such as those found in a managerial job or physical activity. 'Distress' is when we feel insecure, inadequate, helpless or desperate as the result of too much, or too little, pressure or tension. Selye's stress and job performance model (Exhibit 11.6) applies this theory to job performance, suggesting that optimum stress (or eustress) may be achieved at work and reflected in job performance when jobs provide adequate challenges, but not too little or too much pressure. Exhibit 11.7 attempts to relate stress factors with particular kinds of jobs.

Exhibit 11.6 Stress and job performance model

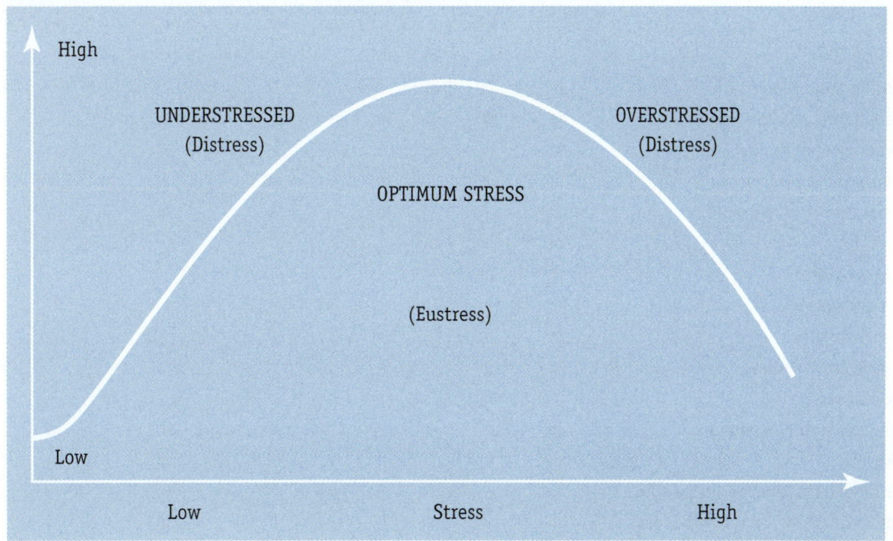

Source: Adapted from Selye H. 1974. *Stress without distress*, Philadelphia, Signet Books.

Exhibit 11.7 Stress and your job

Legend: **1** = Major stressors **m** = Minor stressors

	Risk of injury or disease	Long or irregular hours	Repetitive work	Distasteful work	Isolation	Performers	Low or no income	Helpers	Work under pressure	Red tape	Conflicting demands	Lack of autonomy	Poor public image	No security
Fire fighters	1	m		m					m		m			
Police	1	m		m					m	1	m	m	1	
Prison officers	1		m	1							m	m	m	
Security guards	m	1	m									m	m	
Ambulance drivers	m	1		1				m	m					
Cottage parents		m	m				1	m			m	m	1	
Doctors	1	m		m				1	m		m			
Ministers/priests/nuns		m	m	m	m	m	m	1			1			
Nurses	m	1	m	m			1	1	m		m	m		
Psychologists/counsellors		m						1						
Social workers			m	m			m	1		m	m	m	m	
Teachers	m	m				m		1	m	1	1	1	m	m
Youth workers		m					1	1			m	m		
Journalists	m	m	m	m			1		1	m	m	m	m	m
Lawyers		m	m	m	m				m	m	1		1	
Politicians		1	m			m			m		m		1	m
School principals		m	m				m		m	1	1	m	m	
Clerks			1								m	m	m	
Managers/executives		1						1	m	m				
Public servants			1								1	m	m	
Typists	1		m				m				m	1		
Union officials	m	m			m	m	1	m	m	m	1		m	m
Air traffic controllers		m	m						1		1	m		
Drivers (train/bus/taxi, etc.)	1	m	m	m			1					m		
Convenience store cashiers	1	m					1							
Small business operators		m	m	m			m		1	m	m			1
Farmers and rural workers	m	m	1	m			1		m		m			m
Miners	1	m	m	m										
Oil rig workers	1	m	m											
Foremen/women		m	m				m		m			1		
Process workers	1	m	m				1					m	m	
Construction workers	1	m										m	m	
Bank officers	1		m								m	m		
Share/commodity dealers		m							1		m			m
Actors		m			1	m			m		m			1
Entertainers/singers/media people		m				1			m					1
Creative artists/writers/composers		m			1		1		m					1
Orchestral musicians	1	m	m			1	m				1	m		
Professional sportspeople	1	m	m			m	m				1			m

A New Zealand researcher, Dr Phillip Dewe, provides perhaps the most comprehensive definition of stress, encompassing both stimulus and response aspects, the individual and their work environment: 'Stress is relational in nature involving some sort of transaction between the individual and the environment'.[56]

There is stress, and then there is stress

Stress is a common part of everyday life and is often beneficial. It is the overload of stress in the workplace, especially when the individual's total identity is linked with the organisation, that is counterproductive.

Thus it is useful to distinguish between good stress and bad stress, between stress in the workplace and stress caused by the workplace.

Bad stress arises from working under too much pressure, at a monotonous, thankless task, in a situation in which you have little or no control. Good stress is that associated with the effort required to do a task.

Gary Cox defines (bad) stress as 'a mismatch between a person's self image, their attributes and talents, and the organisational environment they work in'.

Bad stress may occur if a person is not a good fit for a task, or the work environment changes, or relationships on the job change.

Of good stress, Cox says: 'Every job carries with it a tension that leads to a heightened engagement of the person, a sharpened awareness, to get them going. This could be construed as good stress. The tension, the anxiety that is often a concomitant of a task-to-be-done, the dissatisfaction that attends incompleteness, is a variety of stress that pushes us to greater effort, closer and more intimate engagement with the task and, ultimately, higher productivity'.

A familiar example of this is the anxiety-ridden personality that puts off a task until the last possible moment and seems to require the rush of adrenalin to get the task done.

When there is the mismatch of person and work environment, the result is the bad stress caused by the workplace.

In a government agency in Melbourne's CBD works a middle manager and publications officer. She is responsible for the regular publication of two monthly journals, ongoing research for a yearly statistical report and the management of a shrinking number of uncertain, short-term contract staff. The result has been measurable forgetfulness, irritability, lower productivity, postponed deadlines, last-minute resolution of renewal of contracts and a spreading malaise throughout the entire workplace. As Cox says, 'One dysfunctional person will almost inevitably spread that dysfunctionality to others'.

The phenomenon of workplace bullying is both a consequence of stress and a stressor. Cox says: 'Although there might be various reasons for the bullying behaviours, people exhibit their most fundamental behaviours when under stress. Some will explode (perhaps becoming a bully in the process); others will implode and take it out on themselves'.

He says there is a point along the stress continuum at which a person will work at optimal performance, after which, if stress increases, performance declines.

Cox gives an example of this reciprocal interaction between the person and the workplace. 'Take an introvert who has to operate in an environment where it is necessary to exhibit many extrovert behaviours, for example, in a position that requires high-volume contact with people. The person will cope with it in the short term, but it quickly becomes wearing on them. Good stressors can become bad stressors when the person is overloaded. A balance is needed'.

Source: Kelleher P. 1999. 'Let me stress,' *Management Today*, August, p. 18.

Physiologically, stress is the body's reaction to a perceived threat that requires either 'fight or flight' in a stressful situation. The nervous system activates the secretion of hormones from the endocrine glands that places the body on a war footing. This response, commonly referred to as the alarm reaction, basically involves an elevated heart rate, increased respiration, elevated levels of adrenalin in the blood and increased blood pressure. It persists until the perception of threat reduces. This reaction may be valuable and life-preserving in physically dangerous situations, but is unhelpful as a reaction to most work stresses. However, if this physiological reaction to perceived distress at the workplace continues for prolonged periods, symptoms of fatigue, exhaustion and even physical or emotional breakdown may appear.

Medical, psychological, union and legal perspectives disagree about the definitions of stress, the links between stress and work factors, and between stress and disease, especially high blood pressure and heart disease. Research studies are inconclusive in these areas, permitting frequent litigation in workers' compensation arenas.

Sources of job-related stress

Stress at work can be attributed to the nature of the job and its environment, the individual worker, or a combination of these factors. As already discussed, industrial psychologists have been criticised for focusing on individual aspects – personality, behaviours – at the expense of work environments or processes. On the other hand, some industrial sociologists have perhaps overemphasised working conditions as a cause of stress, underestimating the role of individual workers. Several stress researchers suggest that the major causes, or sources, of stress in organisations – the organisational stressors – involve role, job, physical and interpersonal factors inherent in particular positions.[57] Exhibit 11.7 demonstrates this sociological approach to work-related stress in relation to particular kinds of jobs.

Distress in some jobs may derive from long hours, repetitive or distasteful tasks, isolation or actual job hazards. In others, a poor public image, a lack of job security or conflicting demands may result in stress symptoms and effects. A recent study of Victorian primary school principals attributes high levels of 'burnout' to a combination of factors, including role-based stress, task-based stress, 'conflict-mediating' stress (between pupils, teachers and parents), and 'boundary-spanning' stress (conflicting priorities and increasing responsibilities).[58] The effectiveness of strategies to reduce employee distress will inevitably depend upon the clear identification of distress symptoms and the accurate perception of sources. Exhibit 11.8 indicates the range of potential organisational stressors and appropriate prevention strategies in any workplace.

Burnout is the most severe stage of distress. Career burnout generally occurs when we begin questioning our personal values. Quite simply, we no longer feel that what we are doing is important. Depression, frustration and a loss of productivity are often symptoms of burnout. It can be due to a lack of personal fulfilment in the job, or a lack of positive feedback about performance. Both supervisors and HR managers have a crucial role to play in identifying jobs likely to result in employee distress or burnout and employees likely to suffer.

Tools they can use to prevent burnout include job redesign, the development of career plans, performance management and counselling systems. Award reform, consultative and employee feedback programs and enterprise agreements can contribute to more satisfying and fulfilling work outcomes. The HR manager should, of course, be involved with supervisors, employees and their consultative committees in designing and administering appropriate stress management programs. In this OHS issue, HR activities will include liaison with external or internal experts (e.g. industrial psychologists, sociologists, job designers), the development of stress management or stress reduction strategies, and referrals for employee counselling.

Exhibit 11.8 Stress in organisational settings

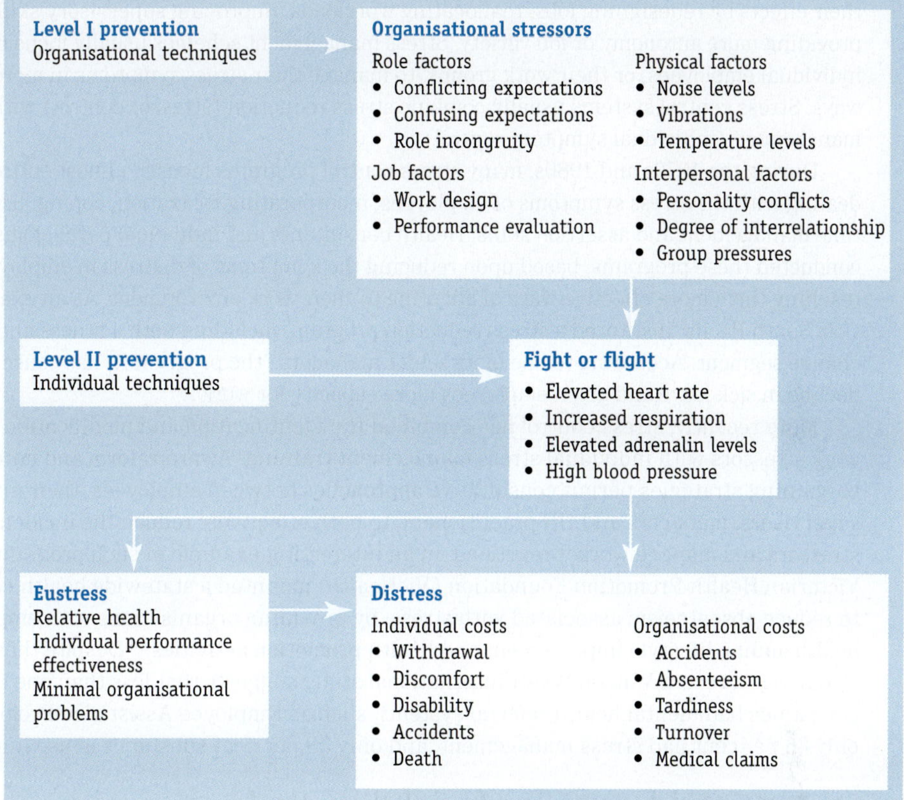

Source: From Quick J.C. 1979, 'Reducing stress through preventative management,' *Human Management*, 18(3). Fall, pp. 15–22 by permission of Blackwell Publishing.

Employer responses

Awareness of the legal and productivity implications of workplace stressors will help managers to initiate the most effective responses. Stress specialists suggest employers use the following five-step program:

1 Formulate a preventive strategy through analysis and forecasting of stress symptoms and trends.

2 Develop a stress diagnostic system to increase awareness and sensitivity to employee concerns.

3 Involve top-level management in developing priorities and procedures for correcting problem areas.

4 Evaluate current programs by determining if stress-related problems still remain.

5 Document what has been done to correct situations that result in stress, but be prepared to do something about them.

Training managers to recognise the symptoms of stress, to refer employees who may need professional help, and to implement programs for monitoring and treating problems is an important responsibility of the HR department.

Stress reduction and stress management programs

Stress reduction programs aim to identify relevant organisational stressors and thus to reduce their effects by redesigning jobs, reallocating workloads, improving supervisory skills or providing more autonomy or job variety. Stress management schemes usually focus on training individual employees, or their work groups, to manage their stress symptoms in more effective ways. Stress control systems usually combine stress reduction (stressor control) with stress management (individual symptom control).

During the 1970s and 1980s, many stress control programs focused almost entirely on dealing with the stress symptoms of employees, incorporating relaxation, coping, listening, time management and assertion skills. Health consultants and individual psychologists often conducted these programs, based upon reducing the symptoms of distress in employees and teaching them more effective ways of adapting to their work environment. As an example, Coca-Cola South Pacific instituted a stress reduction program, including both a fitness and a lifestyle change segment. According to one of its senior managers, 'the program ... has caused a sharp decline in sick leave and given employees more capacity for work'.[59]

More recently, stress control has combined the identification and modification of relevant work stressors with individual stress management training. Award reform and enterprise bargaining strategies permit consultative approaches between employees, their unions, supervisors, managers and HR practitioners, to both effectively reduce the incidence of stressors and manage worker reactions. In an interesting example of such programs, the Victorian Health Promotion Foundation (VicHealth) mounted a statewide health campaign to reduce absenteeism associated with stress, by providing organisations with employee health audits, lifestyle improvement and health promotion activities.[60] Despite these positive initiatives, a recent Watson Wyatt international study suggests that less than one quarter of companies had mental health referral systems, such as Employee Assistance Programmes, only 36 per cent had stress management, and only 38 per cent substance abuse initiatives.

Issue 4: Potential hazards of mobile telephones

The increasing use of mobile telephones by many employees as part of their daily work requirements has raised concerns about potential health hazards. While there is no conclusive research evidence on the dangers to employee health from frequent use of such devices, some studies have discovered relationships between exposure to electromagnetic radiation and the growth of lymphomas (cancers of the immune system) in mice. One Australian study, for example, found that mice that were exposed to digital mobile telephone frequencies for one hour daily '... developed lymphoma ... at double the usual rate'.[61]

Overseas, other studies have found some evidence of 'breaks in DNA in mouse brain cells,' links with other malignancies and even leukemia, in animal studies.[62] Telstra, on the other hand, reassures mobile telephone users by reference to over 40 years of research that humans have no such risks. Nevertheless, the Australian government allocated $4.5 million to fund further research into this issue.

Apart from the risk of cancer, other OHS issues (e.g. potential flammability of mobile telephones near petrol, accidents caused by their use while driving), deserve serious attention by employers.

Issue 5: Acquired Immune Deficiency Syndrome (AIDS)

In recent years, few social and community issues have received as much media attention as Acquired Immune Deficiency Syndrome (AIDS). Employee concerns, and associated legal and medical questions, have made it imperative for employers to address the issue in the workplace. Given the media coverage of AIDS, it is not surprising that employees and employers should have concerns about the potential risks from the transmission of HIV in workplaces.

There is no evidence that HIV or AIDS can be spread through casual contact in the typical workplace, but employee concern about contracting the disease has compelled many employers to develop AIDS programs and policies. In particular industries, such as health care, emergency and laboratory work, the risks may be greater. Certainly the incidence of 'needle-stick' injuries reported in hospitals has grown, albeit slowly, through Australian states in recent years.

Impetus for the development of policies, educational and preventive programs about AIDS in organisations has been provided by national initiatives in the 1980s. The Australian government spearheaded approaches to the AIDS issue by declaring a National HIV/AIDS Strategy in August 1989. This resulted from an earlier National Consensus Statement on AIDS and the Workplace (November 1988), the product of tripartite agreement between the federal and state governments and the ACTU. The National Consensus Statement follows (see Exhibit 11.9). Its broad principles encompass the protection of human rights and dignity, including the rights of healthy but infected workers to equal treatment, freedom from discrimination and access to normal rehabilitation and invalidity retirement processes. Confidentiality of HIV-infected employees' medical information and the reasonable protection of co-workers are also included.

It is important to note that, while all Australian states have anti-discrimination legislation which generally covers employees with HIV/AIDS, none have AIDS-specific legislation. This situation may soon change.

Exhibit 11.9   National consensus statement on AIDS

Policy Principles

Protection of the human rights and dignity of HIV-infected persons, including persons with AIDS, is essential to the prevention and cure of HIV/AIDS. Workers with HIV infection who are healthy should be treated the same as any other worker. Workers with HIV-related illness, including AIDS, should be treated the same as any other workers with serious illness. Most people with HIV/AIDS want to continue working, which enhances their physical and mental well-being, and they should be able to do so. They should be able to contribute their creativity and productivity in a supportive occupational setting. The World Health Assembly resolution (WHA 41.24) entitled, 'Avoidance of discrimination in relation to HIV-infected people and people with AIDS,' urged Member States:

a   to foster a spirit of understanding and compassion for HIV-infected people and people with AIDS

b   to protect the human rights and dignity of HIV-infected people and people with AIDS and to avoid discriminatory action against, and stigmatisation of them in the provision of services, employment, and travel

c   to ensure the confidentiality of HIV testing and to promote the availability of confidential counselling and other support services.

The approach taken to HIV or AIDS and the workplace must take into account the existing social and legal context, as well as national health policies. Issues regarding occupational superannuation and life insurance require further consideration.

Policy development and implementation

Consistent policies and procedures should be developed at national and enterprise levels through consultations between employers and employees and unions and, where appropriate, governmental agencies and other organisations. It is recommended that such policies be developed and implemented before HIV-related questions arise in the workplace. Policy development and implementation is a dynamic process, not a static event. Therefore, HIV/AIDS workplace policies should be:

- communicated to all concerned
- continually reviewed in the light of epidemiological and other scientific information
- monitored for their successful implementation
- evaluated for their effectiveness.

Policy components

a Persons applying for employment

- Pre-employment HIV/AIDS screening as part of the assessment of fitness to work is unnecessary and should not be required. Screening of this kind refers to direct methods (HIV antibody testing) or indirect methods (assessment of risk behaviours).

b Persons in employment

- *HIV/AIDS screening*: HIV/AIDS screening as part of an assessment of fitness to work should not be required, whether direct (HIV antibody testing), or indirect (assessment of risk behaviour).

- *Confidentiality*: It is important that confidentiality regarding all medical and personal information, including HIV/AIDS status, be maintained.

- *Informing the employer*: There should be no general obligation on employees to inform the employer regarding their HIV/AIDS status.

- *Protection of employee*: Persons in the workplace affected by, or perceived to be affected by HIV/AIDS, should be protected from stigmatisation and discrimination. Information and education are essential to maintain the climate of mutual understanding necessary to ensure this protection.

- *Benefits*: HIV-infected employees should not be discriminated against for example in access to and receipt of sickness benefits in general (as for other chronic infections), and training and occupationally related benefits.

- *Reasonable changes in working arrangements*: HIV infection by itself is not associated with any limitations in fitness to work. If fitness to work is impaired by HIV-related illness, alternative working arrangements should be considered where practicable.

- *Continuation of employment relationship*: HIV infection is not a cause for termination of employment. As with many other illnesses, persons with HIV-related illnesses should be able to work as long as medically fit for available, appropriate work.

- *First aid*: In any situation requiring first aid in the workplace, precautions need to be taken to reduce the risk of transmitting blood-borne infections, including Hepatitis B. These standard precautions will be equally effective against HIV transmission.

Employer responses

Most organisations which have addressed the issue of HIV/AIDS have done so in response to employee concerns. Their approaches have generally comprised the development of an AIDS policy, including the above principles; educational or information programs for supervisors and their employees; procedures to ensure employee confidentiality; effective accident management techniques; fitness assessment and access to appropriate rehabilitation; sick leave and retirement provisions.

HR managers have a role to play in ensuring that policies and procedures are rigidly adhered to, that educational programs are appropriate to the particular workplace and that counselling facilities, either on site or through external agencies, are available for both HIV/AIDS affected employees and their co-workers.

Issue 6: The risks of international travel

As News report 11.5 shows, flight attendants are concerned about their own exposure to the risks of domestic and international travel, as well as their increased responsibilities for the health and safety of their passengers. These risks include an increase in terrorism incidents, in the air and on the ground, as a result of the attack on the World Trade Center in New York and the bombing of the Sari nightclub in Bali; recent disease outbreaks, notably severe acute respiratory syndrome (SARS), in Singapore, Hong Kong, China and Canada; 'chicken flu' and deep vein thrombosis (DVT; or 'economy class syndrome').

'Deep vein thrombosis' refers to the possible health effects on such passengers and cabin crew of frequent airline travel in the relatively cramped economy class cabin. Although scientific evidence concerning this potential OHS problem is by no means conclusive, passengers can develop blockages in legs and arms, leading, in some cases, to 'deep vein thrombosis' from which there have been some associated deaths.

With the increase in the number of employees who are required to travel domestically or internationally as a normal part of their jobs (e.g. multinational corporate managers, consultants, engineering contractors, project managers, helicopter technicians, military personnel, university educators), these risks have assumed greater importance, for both the employees themselves and for their employers. For the employees, the likely dangers may deter them from travel, resulting in reduced career opportunities or even their inability to accept lucrative positions, or they may increase their stress levels and put pressure on their families. Negative mental or physical effects of terrorism or the contraction of diseases such as SARS can be even more harmful, especially as insurance companies are usually not prepared to cover such circumstances.

NEWS REPORT 11.5

Cabin crew's safety plea

Flight attendants want a greater voice about security and safety issues. The Flight Attendants Association of Australia is calling for more government and industry consultation on changes in policy and regulations. 'We're the ones who implement all of these cleverly devised and carefully crafted regulations and yet we're not considered primary aviation participants and consultation partners,' FAAA manager of safety and regulatory affairs Guy McLean said.

Mr McLean said the FAAA had worked hard to develop a relationship with the Transport Department and it had made some ground. But there needed to be more recognition of flight attendants' expertise and their primary role in ensuring the safety of passengers. 'It's time they realised that cabin crew are vital, critical members of an integrated operational safety team,'

Mr McLean said. The responsibilities facing cabin crews were increasing as aircraft got bigger, flight deck crews smaller and sectors longer, he said. 'If something happens on an aeroplane the aeroplane goes in to what they call a lockdown and those pilots are not coming out,'

Mr McLean said. 'The cabin crew have got to deal with it and their role has clearly evolved.'

The association is also worried about commercial pressures to differentiate airline products and moves to boost the proportion of the workforce working part-time. Pressures to differentiate products led to rapid changes in cabin layouts, often without guidance from a regulatory framework. 'Within CASA there are no cabin safety officials in the standards division,' Mr McLean said. 'The only cabin safety specialisation in CASA is in compliance.'

Source: Creedy S. 2003. 'Cabin crew's safety plea,' *The Australian*, September, p. 23.

For the employer, and their HRM specialists, apart from the loss of key employees and their talents, and adverse effects on morale, these risks may also involve potential international business failures, significant workers' compensation payouts, and even legal suits against the company. In order to protect themselves against such possibilities, employers are advised:

- to monitor the levels of travel required
- to develop alternative options (e.g. videoconferencing, electronic communication mechanisms) for the direction and control of overseas operations
- to establish codes of practice for travellers, and updated information on potentially dangerous countries or regions (e.g. most governments operate websites with updated terrorism warnings)
- to discuss risks personally with all travellers
- to examine and communicate the levels of insurance and workers' compensation entitlements it is able to provide.

Miscellaneous OHS issues

Office hazards

The hazards of office environments include air pollutants that come from building materials, furniture and furnishings, duplicating fluids, photocopier toners, rubber cement, correction fluids and other items commonly found in an office. Chemicals used in an office can also cause a variety of skin problems. Like factory workers, office workers are subject to hazards such as cuts, trips, falls, electrical shock, fires and noise.

Video display units

The expanding use of computers and video display units (VDUs) in the workplace has generated intense debate over the possible hazards to which VDU users may be exposed. Many fears about VDU use have been shown to be unfounded, but serious health complaints remain an issue, drawing attention to the need for more information, education and positive action. Problems that HR managers have to confront in this area fall into four major groups:

- *Visual difficulties*: VDU operators frequently complain of blurred vision, sore eyes, burning and itching eyes and glare.
- *Radiation hazard*: Cataract formation and reproductive problems, including miscarriages and birth defects, have been attributed to VDU use. The risks of exposure to VDU radiation have yet to be determined.

- *Muscular aches and pains*: Pains in the back, neck and shoulders are common complaints of VDU operators.

- *Job stress*: Eye strain, posture problems, noise, insufficient training, excessive workloads and monotonous work are also reported by VDU users.

To capitalise on the benefits of VDUs, while safeguarding employee health, organisations are advised to consider several strategies. These include educating employees in the proper use of VDUs; involving employees in system design; encouraging open-door communication with management so that concerns may be voiced and solutions found; using rest periods and job rotation; using ergonomically designed equipment; and ensuring that workstations have appropriate lighting.

Workplace 'bullying'

A newly recognised OHS issue, which is closely related to stress, is that of the 'bullying' of employees by their supervisors, by workmates, and sometimes by their clients. Sometimes called 'mobbing' or 'psychoterror,' it has been associated by some authors with recent downsizing and re-engineering imperatives, and was estimated in a German study to cause between 30 to 100 billion deutsche marks 'damage'.[63] Traditionally associated with manual workers, especially young apprentices, some authors have extended the incidence of 'bullying' to all workplaces,[64] including both physical and psychological intimidation at work within their definitions. According to these new interpretations, bullying is 'the repeated less favourable treatment of a person by another or others in the workplace, which may be considered unreasonable and inappropriate in the workplace',[65] and may be manifested by a range of behaviours ranging from physical violence to degrading or humiliating language or actions. Symptoms are reported to include increased employee turnover, higher absenteeism, stress claims, and a loss in productivity.[66] While legal action can be initiated against organisations and individuals through compensation laws in many states, '… more progressive employers are actively dealing with bullying, using internal surveys to provide their staff with examples of bullying behaviour, and to seek confidential feedback on its incidence'.[67] Legal action can be initiated against organisations and individuals through compensation laws in many states.

Repetition strain injury (occupational overuse syndrome)

In Australia, some of the potential problems with VDUs have been blurred, or even disregarded, as the result of the repetition strain injury (or occupational overuse syndrome) 'explosion' during the 1970s and 1980s. Ridiculed as 'retrospective supplementary income, runaway social invention, golden wrist, kangaroo paw, tenosynovitis, occupational neurosis,' RSI was an OHS issue that appeared especially among keyboard operators, telephonists, factory workers and public service clerks.[68] Its physical effects included sore wrists and arms, and solutions included workstation redesign, rest periods, counselling and medical treatment.

More recently, this OHS issue has arisen in the USA and the UK. In the USA, it has become known as 'cumulative trauma disorder' and has already cost more than US$27 billion annually. Considerable, and unresolved, debate continues about its causes and effects, between medical specialists, ergonomists, industrial psychologists, sociologists and lawyers.

Shiftwork

Award reform initiatives have focused not only on actual job requirements, but also on the conditions associated with work performance. Shiftwork, a common feature of many jobs, has become a focus of management, OHS and HRM concern. It has been defined as 'unusual or irregular hours, usually involving evening and night work'.[69] Research studies suggest that shiftwork interrupts workers' circadian (or body) rhythms, 'the light/dark cycle',[70] resulting in increased levels of workers' sickness (especially digestive and sleeping problems), and interruptions to productivity. Rotating shifts, which involve variable rosters morning, day and night – either week by week, or monthly – appear more associated with harmful effects on workers' health, accident levels and productivity.

Award reform and OHS initiatives provide employers and their HR managers with substantial opportunities to modify shiftwork arrangements to reduce adverse effects on shiftworkers. Rosters may be redesigned to minimise the incidence of night shifts or impose regular shift cycles. Ends of shifts can be moved forward (or backwards) to allow workers to avoid heavy traffic periods, and in some organisations, the lengths of shift periods have been increased to allow for four 12-hour shifts, rather than conventional five-day weeks.

Experts also suggest that where rotating shifts cannot be avoided (e.g. hospitality, manufacturing industries), they should move in a forward direction. That is, rotation from mornings to afternoons to nights, more closely reflecting natural bodily rhythms and social behaviours. Thus, OHS specialists, unions, employees, HR managers and their employers can adapt work processes and schedules to prevent likely risks and hazards, accidents and equipment damage resulting from shiftwork. Consultation with affected employees and their unions is essential in this area, especially as some shifts are particularly difficult to staff. As Coleman and Murphy suggest, '... health and safety can be maintained or improved by working less consecutive shifts and keeping rotations, if any, to a minimum ... The best cost roster for your facility must incorporate business needs, employee desires and health and safety'.[71] These difficulties may increase if enterprise agreements or changes to state government legislation restrict penalty rates for afternoon and night shifts.

Sick building syndrome (SBS)

A relatively new OHS issue in Australian industry, following US examples, is that of the so-called sick building syndrome. This refers to the feeling of a group, or groups of employees, that a part, or the whole, of their physical environment is unhealthy or psychologically unsuitable for their work processes. This may be due to faulty or inadequate air-conditioning systems, noxious substances associated with furnishings, or merely a distasteful atmosphere.

A study of apparent sick building syndrome in Melbourne concluded that 'up to three-quarters of all office buildings were affected to some degree by poor ventilation, badly serviced air-conditioning or noxious fumes from furnishings and construction materials'.[72] The recent fears of staff and students at RMIT University in the Melbourne CBD, due to possible electromagnetic radiation (EMR) contamination, based on six cases of employee cancers, were dispelled following extensive scientific studies, but might have been attributed to sick building syndrome.

Estimates of the costs to US industries of this phenomenon range to US$600 billion.[73] The implications of SBS for OHS experts, including hygienists, epidemiologists, psychologists and sociologists, as well as senior and HR managers, are likely to be immense, especially as its causes may be especially difficult to determine.

Employee personal problems

As mentioned earlier, the OHS legislation of some Australian states specifically includes the welfare, as well as the health and safety, of employees. Undoubtedly, the personal problems of employees aggravate, and are aggravated by, work issues. Job stress may result in substance (e.g. alcohol, drugs) abuse. Conversely, substance abuse adversely affects work performance. Recent research evidence suggests that alcohol-related hangovers alone cost Australian business more than $6.33 billion annually due to lost productivity, replacement and associated medical costs.[74] The Commonwealth Department of Human Services and Health estimates that total OHS costs to Australian industry are greater than $19 billion per year.[75] Anxiety, marital or financial worries may disrupt harmonious relationships with supervisors or colleagues.

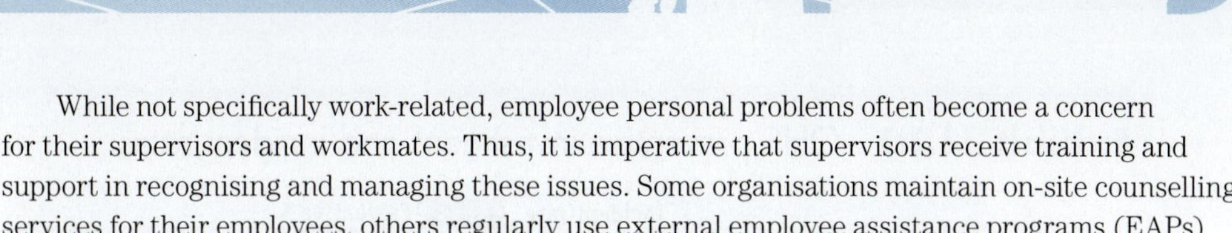

While not specifically work-related, employee personal problems often become a concern for their supervisors and workmates. Thus, it is imperative that supervisors receive training and support in recognising and managing these issues. Some organisations maintain on-site counselling services for their employees, others regularly use external employee assistance programs (EAPs). HR managers are usually involved in the coordination and evaluation of these programs.

Wellness programs

Previous discussions have largely concerned the identification of physical and psychological workplace risks and hazards, and attempts to minimise or prevent them. Following US examples, several large organisations in Australia have developed broad preventive programs concerned with overall employee lifestyle issues. The need for regular exercise, proper nutrition, weight control, and the avoidance of heart and lung disease, is emphasised in these programs, which often involve exercise schedules, aerobics classes and healthy nutrition regimens. The aim of these wellness or well-being programs is to encourage selected categories of employees to maintain their health and fitness. From an HR perspective, staff fitness or executive health programs represent effective investments in human resources, especially at managerial levels.

Managing OHS programs

With the high costs of occupational injuries, accidents, and disease to employers, employees and the community, there is no longer any excuse for employers to avoid their responsibilities in these areas. Legal aspects reinforce what is essentially a rational strategy for ensuring organisational productivity and profitability. As a consultation process involving senior managers, supervisors, union and employees, OHS management must necessarily also involve HR specialists in a wide range of activities. As Steve Wilson, an HR consultant, suggests, 'it's about working together as a group of people (not just a group of managers and employees) to implement the OHS systems required by legislation in a way that ensures that everyone is working safely'.[76] OHS issues pervade all HRM functions, and therefore HR managers need to operate on strategic, operational and administrative levels, creating links with all managers in their organisations. Their roles include liaison, OHS trend analysis, information dissemination, training coordination and evaluation, policy and program development, and the establishment of OHS accountability systems.

To be successful, OHS programs require:

- top management commitment

- extensive safety and health promotion, communication, training and development activities that are integrated and cost-effective

- adequate protective and medical/first aid diagnostic and treatment facilities

- risk management, recording, analysis and development systems

- consultative mechanisms to investigate, monitor, and prevent actual and potential workplace issues

- integrated approaches to accidents/injury/disease, rehabilitation and workers' compensation.

From a strategic HRM perspective, OHS provides an opportunity to protect employees and to save the associated costs of accidents and injuries, and to maximise their contributions to organisational effectiveness. As an example, one recent US study found that lost productivity cost US$99 million annually,[77] and another in the Intercontinental Hotels Group concluded that sickness absence cost around US$55 million per year, providing significant opportunities for the remediation of the underlying causes.[78]

Exhibit 11.10 OHS preventive investment and incident rates

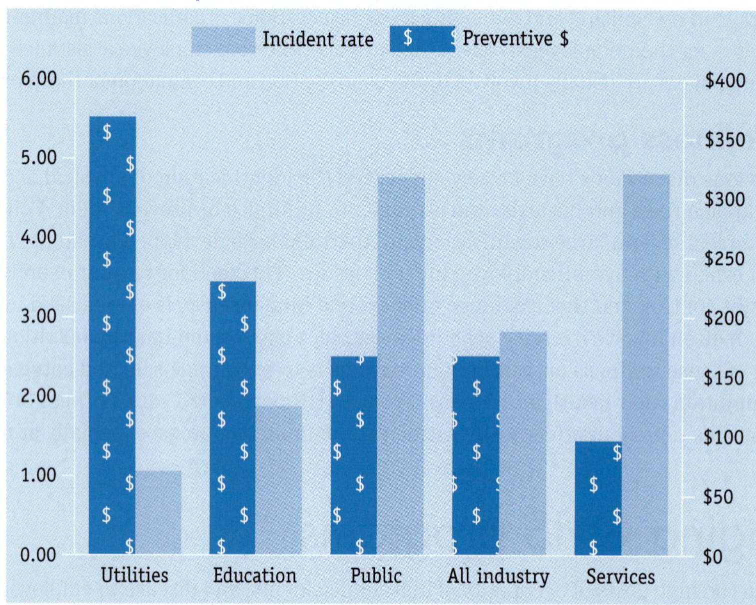

Source: Ellerby A., Barrett K. 2000. 'Data debunks widely held theories,' *hrmonthly*, June, p. 44.

Senior management, OHS specialists and HR managers all need to recognise that 'safety and health … (are) … an integral part of every job'.[79]

Presently, the implementation of Total Quality Management and Best Practice programs has also incorporated OHS initiatives and employee participation, in order to inculcate '… a culture of continuous improvement in the health management of employees'.[80] Strategic human resource managers will see this as a way of cementing their own positions and contributing demonstrably to organisational productivity.

As Exhibit 11.10 indicates, organisations which act strategically to prevent OHS problems by investing in preventive measures reap demonstrable and measurable rewards.

OHS information systems

As with the other components of a human resource information management system (see Chapter 4), an OHS database is a valuable indicator of organisational effectiveness, and provides essential information for both external reporting and internal HR management. OHS databases are compiled by supervisors, OHS consultative committees, senior managers and HR practitioners, and are often accessed by these people and other external users.

Effective OHS databases should include the following features:

* comprehensive data on all workplace incidents, not merely workers' compensation claims

* accurate records of workplace hazards and preventive measures

* effective cost-management of accident and disease (e.g. individual claims, medical and workers' compensation costs)

* control of cost reimbursement from insurance companies

- clear details of rehabilitation programs

- medical programs – pre-placement, first aid training, health monitoring

- interfaces with other HR processes.[81]

Both strategic and operational benefits can be achieved by an effective OHS database system, including the overall analysis of accident and disease trends, costs and benefits, the implementation of preventive measures and the identification of high, low and medium hazard and risk areas.

As examples, many large organisations have established OHS information and audit systems that contribute to the strategic management of OHS issues. These include the Du Pont System, the 5 Star System, the International Safety System (ISRS), Safety MAP (Victoria), and the Safety Achiever Bonus Scheme (SA).[82]

Sources of information and assistance

Specific assistance and information on the expanding range of health and safety issues in the workplace are now readily available from a variety of sources, including WorkSafe Australia, the Commonwealth Rehabilitation Service, WorkCover (NSW), WorkCare (Vic), state rehabilitation and labour councils, and workers' health centres in most states. HR managers are advised to consult with these agencies regularly, for current information and assistance with OHS policy and program development.

Summary

Occupational health and safety, more than any other HR issue in Australian industry, has experienced immense change and growth during the past decade. Due to a mixture of economic and industry factors, it has begun to occupy the minds and activities of a host of organisational and external groups, including employers, unions, state and federal governments, doctors, lawyers, industrial psychologists and sociologists.

Comprehensive OHS legislation in all Australian states during the 1980s, coupled with reforms in workers' compensation legislation, has compelled employers to examine their work practices and job design in order to ensure safer and healthier workplaces. This process has been increasingly consultative, focusing on preventive rather than merely reactive programs and strategies.

This chapter has critically explored the nature of current OHS legislation, the perspectives of the various vested interests, and a range of significant OHS issues, including workplace accidents, smoking, stress, AIDS, mobile phones and occupational overuse syndrome. Effective OHS management principles and sources of ongoing assistance for employers and HR practitioners are detailed. Strategic HRM approaches will ensure that the management of OHS is integrated with overall HRM functions in order to demonstrably contribute to an organisation's productivity and competitiveness.

Key terms

AIDS 464

DVT (deep vein thrombosis or 'economy class syndrome') 467

ergonomics 443

industrial psychology 442

industrial sociology 443

medical model 442

National Occupational Health & Safety Commission (NOHSC) 440

occupational epidemiology 442

occupational hygiene 443

occupational overuse syndrome (OOS) 442

quality of work life (QWL) 439

rehabilitation 449

Key debate issues

1 Occupational health and safety legislation is the result of the vested interests of doctors and lawyers rather than genuine concern for employee health or management excellence.
2 The medical model is the only appropriate, scientific method for resolving OHS issues. Sociology and psychology are largely unhelpful.

3 Occupational stress is more a psychological reaction to bad workplace management and conditions than a response to work overload or the challenges of increasing employee responsibility.

4 OHS management is an integral component of strategic human resource management.

Exercise 11.1

Occupational risk assessment

In groups of four or five, brainstorm all the possible health and safety problems for a chosen number of the occupations given below. List them for each occupation, and then rank them from 1 to 5 in order of seriousness for the organisation (1 is the most serious, 5 the least). What should employers do to try to prevent their occurrence?

Occupation	Health issue	Safety issue
Bank teller		
Beautician		
Auto mechanic		
Factory superintendent		
Airline pilot		
School teacher		

Exercise 11.2

OHS audit

In groups of four or five, undertake a comprehensive audit of a chosen part of your building and/ or its grounds. Each group should be allocated a designated area (e.g. one floor of a building, several classrooms, laboratories) and given 15 minutes to analyse all the possible OHS risks associated with it.

The group should then list all identified risks, and prepare a risk avoidance strategy for the organisation (e.g. preventive measures, priorities, costs and benefits, etc.) for subsequent presentation to the rest of the class. Presentations should be assessed on the comprehensiveness of the groups' analysis, the practicality of their remedial strategies and cost–benefit factors.

Case study 11.1

Safety squabble

Ray Walsh hurt his right wrist on the job. A doctor who examined him told him to keep the arm elevated and apply ice packs to it for 24 hours. The employer's policy in such cases was to try to get injured workers back at work as soon as possible, if necessary assigning them light duties that did not entail any undue strain.

About 19 hours after the accident, Walsh reported for work wearing tennis shoes rather than his customary work shoes. His supervisor, Doug Williams, told him to change into work shoes. Walsh complied, although he needed the help of another employee to lace up the shoes.

Williams then ordered Walsh to perform a routine equipment inspection of the department. However, Walsh refused to carry out part of this assignment that would have required him to descend a flight of stairs and inspect an area that was dimly lit and contained moving equipment. According to Walsh, his injured wrist deprived him of the use of his right arm, which made him fear for his safety in the event that he fell during the inspection.

Williams then made an appointment for Walsh to be examined by a doctor. The doctor cleared Walsh for return to work, but told him not to use his right arm for six days. When Walsh returned to the job site, Williams again ordered him to perform the inspection task, and again Walsh refused.

'No way I'm going to do that job … it's unsafe, especially with my arm out of commission,' Walsh said, 'I might be able to do a little bit of it, but you're going to have to find somebody else to do the rest.'

'That job's well within your capabilities and you know it,' retorted Williams. 'Since you're refusing an order, you can consider yourself suspended.'

With the help of the shop steward, Walsh filed a grievance that ultimately went to arbitration.

Questions

1   Do you believe that the company policy for such situations is sound? Why?
2   If you were the human resource manager for this organisation, what would you consider to be the implication of this incident for your safety training program for supervisors?

Further readings

ACTU 2003. *Occupational Health and Safety (OHS) – ACTU Program 2003–2006*, Melbourne, ACTU.

Bluff E., Gunningham N., Johnstone R.(eds) 2004. *OHS regulation for a changing world of work*, Sydney, Federation Press.

Casey A. (ed.) 2004. *OHS legal guide*, North Ryde, CCH Australia.

CCH Australia 2004. *Managing occupational health and safety: Basic legal requirements*, North Ryde, CCH Australia.

CCH Australia 2004. *Occupational health and safety: Legislative overview*, North Ryde, CCH Australia.

Department of Employment and Workplace Relations 2006. *Compendium of workers' compensation statistics Australia 2002–2003*, January, Canberra.

Oxenburgh M., Marlow P., Oxenburgh A. 2004. *Increasing productivity and profit through health and safety – the financial returns from a safe working environment*, 2nd edn, Boca Raton, CRC Press.

Peterson C. 2003. 'Stress among health care workers,' *Journal of Occupational Health and Safety – Australia and New Zealand*, 19(1), pp. 49–58.

Pocock B. 2003. *The work/life collision: What work is doing to Australians*, Sydney, Federation Press.

Productivity Commission 2004. *National Workers' Compensation and Occupational Health and Safety Frameworks*, Report No. 27, March, Canberra.

Quinlan M., Bohle P. 2000. *Managing occupational health and safety in Australia: A multidisciplinary approach*, Melbourne, Macmillan.

Roberts-Yates D.C. 2006. 'Employers' perceptions of claims/injury management and rehabilitation in South Australia,' *Asia Pacific Journal of Human Resources*, 44(1), pp. 102–22.

Taylor G., Easter K., Hegney R. 2004. *Enhancing occupational safety and health*, Oxford, Elsevier Butterworth-Heinemann.

Toohey J., Borthwick K., Archer R. 2005. *OHS in Australia: A management guide*, Melbourne, Thomson.

Watson I., Buchanan J., Campbell I., Briggs C. 2003. *Fragmented futures: New challenges in working life*, Sydney, Federation Press.

Wyatt A., Oxenburgh M. (eds) 2004. *Managing occupational health and safety*, North Ryde, CCH Australia.

Endnotes

1   Toohey J., Borthwick K., Archer R. 2005. *OHS in Australia: a management guide*, Melbourne, Thomson, p. 2.
2   Ibid.
3   Ibid, p. 3.

4   Nelson L. 1994. 'Managing managers in occupational health and safety,' *Asia Pacific Journal of Human Resources*, 32(1), pp. 13–28.

5   Toohey J. 1982. 'OHS research: A union view (2),' *Transactions of the Menzies Foundation*, 4, p. 188; Toohey J. et al. 2005, see pp. 7–15.

6   Deves L. 1990. 'Management and medicine: Some reflections!,' Editorial, *Journal of Occupational Health and Safety – Australia, New Zealand*, June, p. 292.

7   Spillane R., Deves L. 1987. 'RSI: Pain, pretence or patienthood?,' *Journal of Industrial Relations*, March, p. 42.

8   Quinlan M., Bohle P. 1991. *Managing occupational health and safety in Australia: A multi-disciplinary approach*, Melbourne, Macmillan, p. 45. See also Bohle P., Quinlan T. 2000. *Managing occupational health and safety: A multidisciplinary approach*, Melbourne, Macmillan.

9   Quinlan M. 1988. 'Occupational health and safety: New debates about "old" problems,' in G. Palmer (ed.), *Australian personnel management: A reader*, Melbourne, Macmillan, p. 281.

10 Quinlan M., Bohle P. 1991. op. cit., p. 6.

11 Quinlan M. 1988. op. cit., p. 282.

12 Dwyer, in Toohey J. 1982. op. cit., p. 187.

13 Ibid.

14 Ibid.

15 ACTU 2003. *Occupational Health and Safety (OHS): ACTU Program 2003–2006*, Melbourne, ACTU.

16 Andrews K. 2005. 'Key workplace OHS policy issues for the next decade'. Speech at the World Day for Safety and Health at Work, Melbourne Town Hall, 28 April.

17 Quinlan M. 1988. op. cit., p. 286. See also Bohle P., Quinlan M. 2000. op. cit.

18 Ibid., p. 289.

19 Williams T. G. 1981. *Report of the Commissioner of Inquiry into Occupational Health and Safety (NSW)*, Sydney, NSW Government Printer, p. 1.

20 Deves L. 1989. 'Policy and action in occupational health: A question of ideology,' *Journal of Occupational Health and Safety – Australia, New Zealand*, 5(2), p. 110.

21 Andrews K. 2005. op. cit., and ACTU 2003. op. cit.

22 Braithwaite J., Grabosky P. 1985. *Occupational health and safety enforcement in Australia: A report to the National Health and Safety Committee*, Canberra, Australian Institute of Criminology, pp. 31–2.

23 Ibid., p. 89.

24 Anon. 2003. 'Industrial manslaughter laws: Who will be the first?,' *HR Report*, issue 310, 12 November, p. 3.

25 Andrews K. 2005, op. cit., p. 2.

26 Ibid., p. 5.

27 Quinlan M., Bohle P. 1991. op. cit., p. 246.

28 Ibid., pp. 243–60.

29 Ibid., p. 275.

30 Ibid.

31 Department of Employment and Workplace Relations 2006. *Compendium of Workers' Compensation Statistics Australia 2002–2003*, Canberra, DEWR.

32 Ibid., p. 243.

33 Lipold A. 2003. 'The soaring costs of workers' compensation,' *Workforce*, February, p. 28.

34 Roberts-Yates C. 2006. 'Employers' perceptions of claims/injury management and rehabilitation in South Australia,' *Asia Pacific Journal of Human Resources*, 44(1), p. 102.

35 Morehead A., Steele M., Alexander M., Stephen K., Duffin L., 1997. *Changes at work: The Australian industrial relations study*, Melbourne, Addison-Wesley Longman, pp. 123–8.

36 Willis R. 1988. 'International Ergonomic Congress, Canberra,' August, in Pearson C. 1991, 'Accidents, a study and strategy for a safer workplace,' *Asia Pacific HRM*, 29(2), Winter, p. 89.

37 Robotham G. 1999. 'OHS makes slow progress,' *hrmonthly*, August, p. 30.

38 Willis R. 1988. op. cit., p. 89.

39 O'Meara M. 1998. 'Workers study report on BHP plant,' *Australian Financial Review*, 30 March, p. 17.

40 Davis M. 1998. 'Unsafe at any depth?', *Australian Financial Review*, 6 April, p. 2.

41 Mol T. 2000. 'Workplace accidents: The chaos theory,' *hrmonthly*, September, p. 34.

42 Lin J., Mills A. 2001. 'Measure the OHS performance of construction companies in Australia,' *Facilities*, March/April, 19(3/4), pp. 131–8.

43 Ibid.

44 Farraro L. 2003. 'The culture of safety,' *hrmonthly*, April, pp. 38–9.

45 Findley M., Bennett J. 2002. 'Safety and the silver collar worker,' *Professional Safety*, 47(5), pp. 34–8.

46 Evans L. 2003. 'Finding safety solutions,' *hrmonthly*, May, pp. 14–18.

47 Ibid., p. 14.

48 Lin J., Mills A. 2001. op. cit., p. 134.

49 Ruzek P. 1990. 'A stern test for tripartism,' *Personnel Today*, p. 10.

50 Tuckey B. 1998. 'Safety at work when work is on the road,' *Australian Financial Review*, 16 March, p. 48.

51 Smith R. 1992. 'Workplace smoking: Legal implications and workplace programs,' *Conference Proceedings*, Parramatta, 9 April, Industrial Program Service (NSW), p. 17.

52 Yaman E. 1994. 'Stress in 20 per cent of PS claims for compo,' *The Australian*, 5 November, p. 67.

53 1997. 'Information overload making us sick, survey reveals,' *hrmonthly*, March, p. 13.

54 Morehead A. et al. 1997. op. cit., p. 46.

55 Selye H. 1974. *Stress without distress*, Philadelphia, Signet Books, p. 83.

56 Dewe P. 1989. 'Developing stress management programs: What can we learn from recent research?,' *Journal of Occupational Health and Safety – Australia and New Zealand*, 5(6), p. 494.

57 Quick J. C., Jonathon D. 1979. 'Reducing stress through preventative management,' *hrmonthly*, Fall, pp. 15–22; Deves L., Spillane R. 1989. 'Occupational health, stress, and work organisations in Australia,' *International Journal of Health Services*, 19(2), p. 360.

58 Green R., Malcolm S., Greenwood K., Small M., Murphy G. 2001. 'A survey of the health of Victorian primary school principals,' *The International Journal of Education Management*, 15(1), pp. 23–31.

59 1992. 'How to manage workplace stress,' *Business Review Weekly*, 18 March, pp. 74–5.

60 Cant S. 1992. 'Health scheme attacks $7bn sickie problems,' *The Australian*, 19 December.

61 Davies A. 1997. 'Fear of frying,' *Sydney Morning Herald*, 3 May, p. 39.

62 Ibid., p. 43.

63 Heime H. 1995. 'An underestimated workplace terror: "Mobbing",' *Managing Office Technology*, 40(5), pp. 41–2.

64 For example, Phillips L. 2000. 'Behaving badly,' *hrmonthly*, September, pp. 36–7; Bolch A. 2000. 'Making bullies pay,' *hrmonthly*, September, pp. 40–1.

65 Phillips L. 2000. op. cit., p. 36.

66 Anon. 2002. 'Does bullying occur in your organisation?,' *hrmonthly*, July, p. 7.

67 Ibid.

68 Spillane R., Deves L. 1987. op. cit., p. 41.

69 1981. *Division of Occupational Health Newsletter*, p. 1.

70 Ibid.

71 Coleman R. M., Murphy D. 1994. 'Improve shift work rosters,' *Management*, June, pp. 14–15.

72 Cribb J. 1992. 'Big cost of sick buildings,' *The Australian*, 4 April, p. 49.

73 Ibid.

74 2000. *The West Australian*, 17 June, p. 3.

75 Peart T. 2000. 'What's your poison?,' *hrmonthly*, October, p. 44.

76 Anonymous 2006. 'Beyond compliance,' *hrmonthly*, July, p. 11.

77 Spooner M. 2006. 'Wealth in health,' *hrmonthly*, June, p. 34.

78 Anonymous 2006. 'Health in the hotel business,' *hrmonthly*, June, p. 36.

79 Boylson R. 1990. *Managing health and safety programs*, New York, Van Nostrand Reinhold, p. 5.

80 Yaman E. 1994. op. cit.

81 Coster D. 1989. 'Evaluating OHS software,' *Personnel Today*, July, pp. 22–3.

82 Sobieralski C. 1997. 'Does genuine need or vested interest drive funds for OHS auditing standard?,' *hrmonthly*, pp. 42–3.

Online reading

INFOTRAC® COLLEGE EDITION

For additional readings and review on managing occupational health and safety, explore InfoTrac® College Edition, your online library. Go to: www.infotrac-college.com and search for any of the InfoTrac key terms listed below:

➤ ergonomics
➤ industrial psychology
➤ industrial sociology
➤ medical model
➤ occupational epidemiology
➤ occupational hygiene
➤ stress

CHAPTER 12
CONFLICT AND NEGOTIATION PROCESSES

Let us never negotiate out of fear.
But let us never fear to negotiate.

John F. Kennedy, Inaugural Address,
20 January 1961

The most important trip you may
take in life is meeting people
halfway.

Henry Boye (no date)

Our legislation puts the emphasis on
direct workplace relationships, and
on the mutual interest of employer
and employee in the success and
prosperity of the enterprise.
The bill promotes a legislative
framework, without unnecessary
complexity or unwanted third party
intervention.

Peter Reith, 1996

Objectives

After reading this chapter you will be able to:

1   Understand the nature of conflict in the employment relationship.

2   Be aware of the alternative dispute resolution processes.

3   Analyse conflict resolution and negotiation strategies.

4   Identify and understand the situations in which to use the key conflict management styles.

5   Identify and understand the third party intervention processes.

Introduction

In Chapter 1, the pluralist and unitarist models of HRM were explored and applied to the employment relationship. The unitarist approach assumes common interests between employees and employers, with conflict often resulting from poor communications; while a pluralist approach acknowledges a divergence, or even a conflict, of interest between employees and employers, and the necessity to provide mechanisms and processes by which this can be resolved.

With the locus of control being increasingly passed back to the enterprise, its managers and employees, there has been a growing reliance on processes for reducing and resolving conflict within the workplace rather than relying on the resources provided by a third party, often in the form of an industrial tribunal or advocate. This change in focus has brought with it a need for line, operational and HR managers to develop skills in resolving conflict, especially industrial action.

These developments have encouraged the use of less formal methods of resolving conflict, such as mediation and process consultation. This is especially evident in organisations which rely on more educated and highly paid knowledge workers, or short-term and casual labour, rather than full-time permanent employees who often relied on their union representatives to provide support during times of conflict. Professionals and technical specialists have not only the skills to be able to negotiate independently, but are often in the strongest bargaining position due to the organisation's need for their labour. As examples, a significant number of professionals, including engineers, town planners, nurses, teachers, doctors and accountants, are in short supply, thus increasing their value to their organisations.

Not only is the absence of traditional collective bargaining and union representation evident among a range of occupational groups, it is also evident in a range of industries. One example is the phenomenon of call centres. Call centres were one of the fastest growing business activities in North America, Europe and Australia in the 1990s and the growth rates in Australia have risen from 20 per cent to 25 per cent annually.[1] In Australia, the industry currently comprises around 150 000 call centre seats in more than 4 000 call centre facilities, and is worth an estimated A$10 000 million per annum.[2] Waring and Bray (2006) also suggested that many of these call centres were set up as greenfield sites and their work practices were established without unions being involved in representing employees, and without formal regulation of wages and working conditions. In these instances employers used considerable 'managerial prerogative' to set the pay and conditions of the employees.[3] There are exceptions to this, and in many cases disgruntled call centre employees may deal with workplace conflicts simply by walking away, reflected in high turnover rates.

The nature of conflict

According to Wade, 'Conflict managers such as judges, mediators, conciliators, counselors, negotiators and lawyers are under constant pressure to provide more services for less money. Like Health services, there is taxpayer and consumer influence to cut down Rolls Royce service and "treat" more people with Volkswagen, accountable, quality-assured services'.[4] The trend towards leaner organisations, especially if it involves reductions in employee pay and conditions, can often lead to higher levels of conflict, particularly over issues such as workloads, the provision of resources, and remuneration and reward packages. Organisations are operating in an extremely competitive global environment where pressures exist to rationalise and to provide more efficient and productive services which co-exist with a shortage of qualified and experienced labour in a number of industries. In the case of

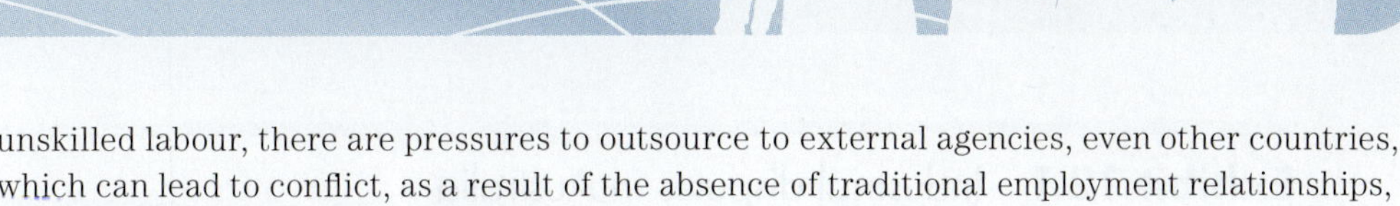

unskilled labour, there are pressures to outsource to external agencies, even other countries, which can lead to conflict, as a result of the absence of traditional employment relationships, cultural and philosophical differences.

While industrial conflict in the form of overt industrial action is declining (see Exhibit 12.1), conflict within organisations is not. Both the causes and nature of workplace conflict are changing in response to these industrial changes, and although the use of formal industrial tribunals is reducing, the use of alternative dispute resolution (ADR) techniques, involving mediators and facilitators to resolve conflicts is increasing.[5]

Positive and negative aspects of conflict

There can be a tendency to perceive all conflict as being destructive. However, there are also positive outcomes to conflict, which learning or knowledge-based organisations (see Chapter 8) characteristically harness to achieve higher levels of creativity and greater productivity: for example, Microsoft, BHP and Westpac. Yet most definitions of conflict are focused entirely on the negative aspects, and will include words which invoke strong feelings, such as 'clash', 'fight' or 'struggle'. Coser defined conflict as 'a struggle over values and claims to scarce status, power, and resources in which the aims of the opponents are to neutralise, injure, or eliminate their rivals'.[6]

Deutsch, Lewicki and others suggest that there are a number of negative consequences of conflict, including:

- increased competition between the parties which can hinder team cooperation

- heightened emotions such as anxiety, fear, irritation and frustration

- a breakdown in communication

- bias toward or exclusion of others

- divergence from the core issue

- lack of flexibility

- escalation of the conflict.[7]

Conversely, Tjosvold has focused on the positive outcomes of conflict. He has suggested that the following benefits emerge from a well-managed conflict situation:

- It heightens awareness of the issues among the parties.

- It can be a catalyst for organisational change.

- If handled in a cooperative manner, it can strengthen existing relationships and heighten morale.

- It promotes awareness of self and others.

- It enhances personal development.[8]

The key to achieving positive results from conflict is in managing the conflict effectively. This involves not only recognising the conflict early, but implementing appropriate strategies for resolution.

Industrial conflict

Lost time due to industrial conflict is reducing globally. This is due to a number of factors: the changing nature of work; increasing reliance on sub-contracted and casual labour; increased knowledge and skills of employees to negotiate themselves; and the use of individual bargaining processes, allowing the parties to determine terms and conditions which suit both parties. Exhibit 12.1 indicates that in Australia the decline in strike action over a 10-year period from 1993 to 2003 has reduced by almost 200 000 working days per annum. The impact of the *WorkChoices* legislation is likely to enhance this trend.

Exhibit 12.1 Industrial disputes in Australia

Year	Total number of disputes	Total employees involved ('000)	Total working days lost ('000)
1993	610	489.6	635.8
1994	560	265.1	501.6
1995	643	344.3	547.6
1996	543	577.7	928.5
1997	446	312.7	528.8
1998	514	347.0	524.9
1999	717	459.9	649.6
2000	691	324.8	465.3
2001	657	225.7	393.1
2002	766	159.7	259.0
2003*	642	275.6	439.4

***Series discontinued December 2003.**

Source: Industrial disputes in Australia, 1993–2003, ABS Cat. Nos. 6321.0 & 6310.0. ABS data used with permission from the Australian Bureau of Statistics, www.abs.gov.au.

Already the *Workplace Relations Act 1996* has restricted the ability of employees to take industrial action, and this has been further emphasised with the introduction of the *Workplace Relations (WorkChoices) Amendment Act 2005*. According to Harbridge and Walsh (2002), individual contracting in Australia grew by 75 per cent since 1996, from 20 per cent of the workforce in 1990 to 35 per cent in 1996,[9] as an illustration of the dilution of traditional employment relationships and formal bargaining structures.

In Australia, the acceptance of a pluralist approach to industrial relations and industrial conflict has been evidenced by the existence for almost a century of a model of conciliation and arbitration, which was introduced to resolve conflict between the parties.[10] Alexander and Lewer (2004) suggest that despite this structural recognition of the inevitability of conflict, the public has maintained a view of conflict as being negative, even though most people who have worked in organisations have experienced employer–employee conflict in some form.[11]

The following section of the chapter builds upon the detailed discussion of the *WorkChoices* legislation in Chapter 3 by illustrating its impacts on industrial conflict and conflict resolution mechanisms in Australia.

Industrial action under *WorkChoices*

Like the former Act, *WorkChoices* continues to recognise that employees and employers might resort to formal *industrial action* if they are unable to resolve disputes. Part 9 of the Act deals with this issue. The definition of *industrial action* in the Act has been amended by *WorkChoices* so that it is now defined by reference to certain types of action taken by either an employer or its employees.

Employer industrial action

An employer engages in industrial action only if it conducts a lockout; that is, if it prevents employees from performing their work without terminating their contract of employment. Other types of potentially industrially motivated acts by employers, such as redundancies or terminations of employment, are not industrial action within the meaning of the Act.[12]

Employee industrial action

Employees engage in industrial action if they:

1   Perform their work differently from the manner it is customarily performed or adopt practices which limit, delay or restrict the performance of their work.

2   Place bans, limitation or restrictions on their work performance, or on the acceptance of or offering for work.

3   Fail or refuse to attend for work or if they do attend work, fail or refuse to perform any work at all, although an employee who does not attend work on account of illness is not considered to be engaging in industrial action.

The Act exempts certain types of conduct from the definition of *industrial action* including where action by an employee is based on a reasonable concern about an imminent risk to his or her health or safety. An employee seeking to rely on this exemption bears the onus of proving that he or she had a reasonable concern.[13]

Exhibit 12.2   Exclusions from workplace agreements

Terms which the Act prohibits from workplace agreements include those which:

1   provide for union training, deduction of union dues from wages or paid union meetings

2   mandate union involvement in dispute settling procedures

3   restrict the use of independent contractors

4   permit industrial action during the term of the agreement

5   provide a remedy for unfair dismissal

6   restrict AWAs

7   provide that any future agreement must be a union collective agreement.

Source: DEWR, 2006.

When is industrial action prohibited?

Any industrial action taken during the life of a collective agreement or an AWA is prohibited under the Act. The Australian Industrial Relations Commission (AIRC) must hear and determine an application for an order to prevent or stop unprotected industrial action within 48 hours of the application being lodged. If the AIRC is unable to properly determine the application within this timeframe, it must make interim orders to stop or prevent the industrial action until such time that the matter can be heard, unless the making of such orders is contrary to the public interest.

Employees who engage in such industrial action may be subject to civil legal action and civil penalties up to a maximum of $33 000 currently.

Dispute resolution

WorkChoices introduces a new regime to the WR Act in relation to processes to resolve workplace disputes (Part 13). The objects of this Part are set out in s. 692 of the Act as:

(a)   encouraging employees and employers to resolve disputes at the workplace level; and

(b)   providing greater flexibility for the resolution of such disputes by allowing the parties to decide which is the best forum to resolve them.

Model dispute resolution process

The 'model dispute resolution process' (Model DRP) now applies to most disputes in the workplace and in particular those disputes concerning the application of:

1 awards

2 the Australian Fair Pay and Conditions Standard (AFPCs)

3 workplace determinations

4 workplace agreements (i.e. AWAs or collective agreements) where either the agreement expressly refers to the Model DRP as the agreed method for settling disputes or where the agreement does not provide for dispute settlement procedures

5 legislative entitlements to parental leave, meal breaks and public holidays.

The Model DRP encompasses a staged approach to settling workplace disputes. In the first instance the parties to the dispute must make a *genuine attempt* to resolve the dispute at the workplace level (s. 695). The Explanatory Memorandum to the Workplace Relations Amendment (Work Choices) Bill 2005 ('EM') notes that a *genuine attempt* to resolve the dispute would be evidenced if the parties engaged with each other in a cooperative and timely way (p. 343). The legislative notes to s. 695 explain, by way of example, that the affected employee might first discuss the issue in dispute with the relevant workplace supervisor and then with more senior management.

If this course of action does not resolve the dispute, the next stage is for the parties to refer the matter to an agreed body, such as the AIRC or a private organisation, for resolution by an *alternative dispute resolution process* (ADR) (s. 696).

Alternative dispute resolution (ADR) processes

According to the EM, 'An alternative dispute resolution process involves the parties seeking outside assistance to try to resolve their dispute'.[14]

Section 698 provides a non-exhaustive list of the type of procedures envisaged by the WR Act as ADR processes. These procedures include:

1 *Conferencing*: this procedure involves meetings between the parties and/or their representatives during which they discuss the matters in dispute with or without the assistance of a dispute resolution specialist and may combine facilitative and advisory dispute resolution processes, depending on the outcome sought.

2 *Mediation*: with the assistance of a mediator, the parties identify the disputed issues, develop options, consider alternatives and attempt to reach an agreement to resolve the dispute. The mediator does not advise on the issues in dispute or the potential outcomes but may advise on the processes.

3 *Assisted negotiation*: once having identified the issues to be negotiated, the parties seek the assistance of a dispute resolution practitioner to negotiate an outcome. Again, this person does not advise on the issues in dispute or the potential outcomes but may advise on the processes.

4 *Neutral evaluation*: the person assisting the parties to resolve the dispute considers the issues and provides advice on the facts, the applicable law and perhaps the possible outcomes and how these can be achieved.

5 *Case appraisal*: the case appraiser investigates the dispute and provides advice on possible and desirable outcomes and the means to achieve these.

6 *Conciliation*: with the assistance of a conciliator, the parties identify the disputed issues, develop options, consider alternatives and attempt to reach an agreement to resolve the dispute. The conciliator may assume an advisory role on the issues to dispute, but not a determinative role. The conciliator may also advise on processes,

make suggestions for settlement terms and actively encourage the parties to reach an agreement to settle the dispute.

7 *Arbitration*: the parties appoint an arbitrator who considers evidence and arguments presented by each party and makes a determination to resolve the dispute.

Evidence of what is said or done during the course of the ADR process is treated as being 'without prejudice'.[15] That is, such evidence is not admissible as evidence in any related court, arbitration or other proceedings unless the parties agree or the evidence is required to be admitted pursuant to the regulations.

Again, the parties must *genuinely attempt* to resolve the dispute using ADR. The purpose of this requirement is to prevent parties acting in a manner that could frustrate settlement of the dispute. According to the EM this would require the parties to make genuine attempts to agree on who should conduct the ADR.[16]

The role of the Australian Industrial Relations Commission (AIRC) in ADR processes

If the AIRC grants an application to conduct the ADR process, the AIRC's role is to *help* the parties reach their own dispute settlement, rather than being responsible for selecting processes to resolve the dispute or guiding parties to what the AIRC considers is the best outcome.[17] Where the parties agree, the AIRC can make recommendations, issue binding determinations or arbitrate. However, the AIRC is expressly prohibited from compelling any person to do anything, making orders or awards or appointing a board of reference.

The role of private ADR providers

If the parties nominate a private body as the ADR provider, it is a matter for the parties to agree on the parameters and limitations of that provider's functions and powers in respect of the dispute settlement processes.

Negotiation

There has been an increased focus, over the past decade, on determining the way in which the employment relationship is to be managed, as well as pay, working conditions, rewards and performance management systems within the organisation between the employee and employer.

Negotiation or bargaining skills remain an integral part of industrial relations and human resource management and are essential for resolving the conflicts that arise between employer and unions over the terms, conditions and organisation of work, or over the interpretation of awards and agreements.

The classic work on labour negotiations, *A Behavioral Theory of Labor Negotiations*, by Richard Walton and Robert McKersie, differentiated between four types of bargaining. The first, *distributive bargaining*, was most prevalent in the US at the time the book was written in the 1960s[18] and was descriptive of collective bargaining between unions and employers, where the parties were at 'arm's length' from each other's interests. Distributive bargaining is therefore bargaining or negotiation that results in a situation 'where one side's gain is the other side's loss' and is also referred to as win–lose or zero-sum bargaining.[19] Distributive bargaining is common, for example, where a union's demand for a wage increase for members comes at the direct cost to an employer's profits. The outcome is important for both sides, and leads to tough negotiations and adversarial relations.

By contrast, *integrative bargaining* is bargaining or negotiation that produces 'gains to both labour and management'. It is also known as mutual gains bargaining or win–win bargaining.[20] This can be achieved when it is recognised by both sides that negotiations can bring about improvements for all parties. For example, the introduction of new work arrangements that increase productivity for the employer and allow the employees to receive increased wages may be regarded as mutual gains, or integrative bargaining.

As negotiations in labour relations are generally conducted by individuals or teams of people who represent the interests of their side, either union members or organisational representatives, tensions can occur between each side. To settle these internal differences and to agree on the preferences between the bargaining sides requires *intra-organisational bargaining*.

The fourth sub-process of negotiations noted by Walton and McKersie is *attitudinal structuring*. This refers to the need for each side to manage the emotions, trust and uncertainty that are typical in the bargaining process. Labour negotiations are often about building long-term relationships, so attitudinal structuring is important to avoid compounding hostilities between the parties.

Definition of negotiation

Any formal or informal bargaining process in which two or more parties attempt to reach an agreement by successively narrowing their initial claims, through a series of offers and counter offers. The process of negotiation can be highly formalised (as in the case of arbitration) or it can be extremely informal (as in tacit bargaining). Negotiation can also occur unassisted (as in free collective bargaining) or it can occur with the support of an independent mediator (as in conciliation). Negotiation does not necessarily imply equality of bargaining power between the parties involved.[21]

Negotiation (or bargaining) involves the bringing together for examination, comparison and argument the opposing claims of employer/s and employee/s. The aim is to resolve or avert potential or actual industrial disputes by producing a solution that is finally acceptable to both and to which the parties will adhere. Negotiation varies in its degree of formality and occurs at all levels of industrial relations, from settling grievance disputes in the workplace to resolving wage claims or other industrial matters of organisational (and sometimes national) importance.

A number of aspects and approaches to bargaining have been identified and these are summarised in Exhibit 12.3.[22]

Negotiation skills

The freeing up of centralised arrangements since the early 1990s has moved the locus of the employment relationship to the enterprise or workplace, encouraging management to resolve disputes at the lowest possible level.

One consequence of the increased reliance on direct negotiation and bargaining between the employer and employee has been increased attention to the competencies of managers to successfully participate in these processes, and the acquisition of a range of skills to enable them to do so. These include:

- active listening skills
- verbal communication skills
- empathy skills
- strong interpersonal skills, particularly in the areas of persuasion, negotiation, mediation and facilitation
- problem solving and conflict resolution skills
- contractual knowledge and skills.

Exhibit 12.3 Approaches to bargaining

The *negotiation relationship* – negotiation and bargaining involve a relationship between parties. In the employment relationship (as opposed to other bargaining situations), this is ongoing and therefore requires managing both in the immediate term and for the future. The relationship is also multi-layered:

- There are inter- and intra-organisational relationships – between people representing different parties or organisations, and between people in the same organisation.

- There are interpersonal relationships, between people in the same organisation or between people in different organisations.

- Sometimes the personal relationships override the organisation and at other times, the reverse is true.

The qualities of a good negotiator include:

- Integrity – honesty and credibility are needed to build up goodwill, trust and durability of the relationship and commitment to the outcomes.

- Flexibility – negotiations are often subject to unpredictability and change. Flexibility is required to respond appropriately to see the situation in a different light if necessary.

- Communication ability – it is necessary to be convincing and to listen well, to understand the arguments and positions of the opposing party and to interpret, judge and consider responses.

- Personal detachment – it is necessary to separate the issue/s from the personalities of the negotiators and from one's own self-esteem.

Negotiating styles – while an individual may have a preferred style, a good negotiator will develop an ability to vary style to suit the occasion, depending on the relationship, the particular dispute or stage of negotiations. Negotiating styles include being obstructive, aggressive, cooperative or defensive. Since the opening exchanges in a negotiation are important to setting the tone, style should be considered before negotiations commence. (See below for further discussion of negotiating styles.)

Stages of negotiation – negotiations proceed through a series of stages; they may be telescoped into a 10-minute conversation or they may extend over months of discussion. The stages include:

- Introduction – introducing the parties involved, explaining the problem or issue and forming the agenda.

- Exploration – putting and probing the claims and arguments of the parties.

- Argument – the 'heartland' of negotiation: challenging and assessing the strength, position, perception and proposals of the other party; seeking answers and responses.

- Settlement – finding a solution and agreeing to complete the negotiations.

- Deadlock – a point in the negotiations where there is no movement on either side, and no resolution appears possible. This is a time to reassess, isolate issues, seek alternative views and inputs, or apply additional bargaining leverage.

- Completion and review – ensuring the agreement reached is clear and understood by both parties, is properly communicated to all and is accepted. It is advisable to put the settlement in writing, as a file note, a memo, an exchange of letters, or an agreement, depending on the issue in negotiation.

Tactics in negotiation – a number of tactics can be used in negotiations to improve the chances of success. These include careful use of the following:

1 People – who will be negotiating: one person or a team? If a team will be negotiating, allocate roles carefully, for example, 'tough' person, 'conciliatory' person.

2 Preparation – it is essential to be prepared and stay prepared, ensure the aim of the negotiations and the limits of bargaining are understood, know the maximum concessions to be made and be sure of the objectives of the negotiations. Plan the agenda and attempt to control the issues to be discussed.

3 Place and time – it is necessary to allocate space and enough time. If possible, it is also useful to be in control of where and when the negotiations are to take place.

4 Process – the bargaining will go through different stages as outlined above, and in the course of this, a variety of different processes may be used. During this time it may be tactical to do the following:

- be positive and constructive

- use concessions, compromises and packages of solutions

- use threats – carefully

- use variation, for example, change the pattern of argument, redefine the issues, review alternatives, have some time out.

Once concluded, it always useful to evaluate the negotiations, to recognise the weaknesses and strengths in style and tactics and to ensure arrangements are in place for the employment relationship to continue.

Source: Baird M., Grey I. 1986. 'Negotiating change: A practical guide' in D. Mortimer, P. Leece, R. Morris (eds), *Workplace reform and enterprise bargaining*, Sydney, Harcourt Brace, pp. 347–58.

Conflict management styles

Much of the literature covering conflict management styles has adopted, and adapted, the Pruitt and Rubin model,[23] which is a two-dimensional framework called the Dual Concerns Model (see Exhibit 12.4). On the horizontal dimension is the concern for the negotiator's own outcomes and on the vertical dimension is concern for the other's outcomes.

This model identifies five different management styles according to the degree to which the style is more concerned with achieving the parties' own concerns or those of others. Lewicki, Saunders and Minton[24] have clearly outlined the Pruitt and Rubin model and have listed the five styles that follow.

Contending

Contending is also known as competing, dominating or fighting. This is used by parties who are strongly self-interested and want to achieve their own outcomes at the expense of the other parties.

Lewicki et al. suggest that punishment, intimidation, threats and unilateral action are consistent with this approach. Wertheim et al. also argue that with this approach only short-term gains are achieved and relationships are likely to suffer.[25]

Exhibit 12.4   The dual concerns model

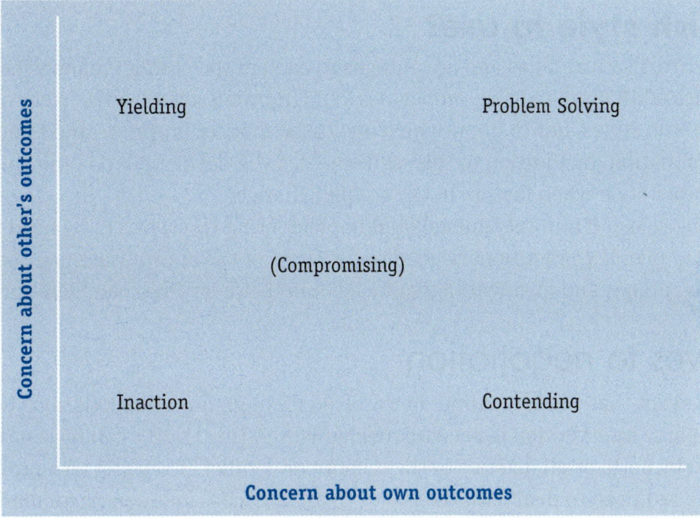

Source: Lewicki R.J., Saunders D.M., Minton J.W. 1997. *Essentials of negotiation*, New York, McGraw-Hill, p. 21. Adapted from D. Pruitt and J. Rubin 1986, *Social conflict: Escalation, stalemate and settlement*, New York, Random House.

Yielding

Yielding is also known as accommodating and obliging. From the model, it can be seen that this strategy suggests that there is little concern for achieving one's own outcomes or concerns. It can be seen as a submissive style, but there may in fact be situations where this resolves the conflict and pacifies others, particularly if the conflict is getting emotional or heated. However, as Wertheim et al. suggest, this may indeed lead to frustration as the actual issues and differences of opinion have not been discussed and resolved and the relationship may suffer.[26]

Inaction

This style is also called avoiding, or to use an Australian expression, the 'emu effect' (placing one's head in the sand!). This is self-explanatory and suggests little interest in achieving one's own outcomes, and no interest in assisting others to achieve theirs.

Unfortunately with inaction or avoidance, the conflict or issue often does not go away and may very well emerge again sometime in the future. However, this technique can be used effectively in situations where the conflict is perceived as trivial or minor and will resolve itself.

Compromising

As it can be seen, this strategy is located in the middle of the model and is often viewed as a bargaining style. Wertheim et al. also suggest that this is a 'give a little, lose a little' strategy, which is seen as displaying fairness in negotiations, but unfortunately only results in 'half wins' for both parties.

Problem solving

Problem solving is viewed as the most effective style and is also known as collaborating, integrating or cooperative problem solving. There is a high concern for achieving the outcomes for all the parties involved. The result of such an approach is considered to be 'win–win,' but does take time, energy, resources and most importantly a culture of trust between the parties.

Which style to use?

There are disadvantages and advantages to each of the conflict management styles discussed. A critical skill for managers, employees and HR professionals alike is not only to understand each of the styles, but to know which one is the most appropriate and effective to use in any given situation. In addition to this, skills need to be developed in being able to effectively change to another style when factors in the conflict change.

The role of HR in recognising and implementing the styles to be used is primarily an advisory one. HR practitioners need to be aware of the appropriate use of each style as well as the advantages and disadvantages of each and to advise line managers accordingly.

Alternatives to negotiation

In the event that conflict cannot be resolved through direct negotiations between the parties, third-party intervention is a useful mechanism. A third party can be seen as an independent person by both, or all, parties to the dispute or conflict. They can also provide the stability that may be required to deal with the issues in an impartial manner, particularly if high emotions are a characteristic of the conflict in question. However, the use of a third party may lead to a sense of failure for those who have been party to the conflict, reinforcing a sense of an inability to resolve the problem themselves.

There are two key forms of third-party intervention provided in the Australian institutional setting. These are conciliation and arbitration. Another form of third-party intervention, in dispute settling, apart from the active involvement of unions, is mediation.

Conciliation

In the context of the Australian industrial relations system, conciliation is often the precursor to arbitration. In conciliation, the independent third party 'seeks to bring the disputants to the point where they can reach agreement'.[27] If the conciliation process is unsuccessful, the dispute can be referred to arbitration.

Arbitration

Arbitration is defined as a process where the parties, after not successfully reaching a resolution, present their case to a third party who, upon hearing both sides, makes a ruling in regard to an outcome to the dispute.[28] Arbitration involves low levels of negotiator control, as the arbitrator makes the settlement decision. In Australian industrial relations, arbitration has generally been distinguished by its compulsory nature: the parties do not choose the arbitrator, they cannot opt out of the process and the decision is legally binding.[29] The introduction of the *Workplace Relations Amendment (WorkChoices) Act 2005* has meant a change in the focus of dispute resolution away from formal arbitrators such as the AIRC towards employers and employees without interference from third parties, including those sponsored by the government. Indeed, the new legislation introduced a model of dispute settlement that includes a range of dispute settlement options. This further reduces the role of government in the compulsory arbitration of issues. In other countries, particularly the European nations, private arbitration is much more common than compulsory arbitration. In such cases, the parties agree to choose the arbitration process, and a private arbitrator, as a means of settling their dispute.

Mediation

The term 'mediation' comes from the Latin root 'mediare' – to halve; in Chinese it means to step between two parties and solve their problems, and in Arabic it indicates manipulation.[30]

In the current Western context, mediation is deemed to be where a third party helps the two other parties to achieve agreement by guiding them. In some instances, this is becoming a more popular method for resolving disputes on an interpersonal, inter- and intra-organisational level.[31] Local governments are employing mediators to assist in the resolution of neighbour disputes and it is used in small claim cases and in marriage counselling and divorce negotiations.

One of the positive features of this method is that the parties themselves have control over the outcome and have high levels of input into the discussions. The role of the mediator is to identify the issues and concerns, assist in setting agendas and proposals and make suggestions for settlement.[32] However, the mediator is required to possess a sound level of knowledge and skill in communication, conflict resolution and problem solving.

Although all mediation processes involve the use of a neutral facilitator who does not issue a decision on behalf of the participants, there is no one prescribed way in which to achieve this – there are many forms of mediation. Coltri (2004) describes the basic distinction between mediation methods with the 'facilitative–evaluative distinction.' Facilitative mediation is where the mediator focuses on facilitating effective negotiations among the disputants and their teams whereas evaluative mediation emphasises the merits of each disputant's case by the mediator.[33] Facilitative mediation is one of the more common forms of mediation used in the Australian context, but there is certainly a role for the more formal evaluative process, which is often used when disputes are taken to court. Generally, there can be a blurring and mix of the two, depending upon the nature of the conflict and how the disputants relate to one another.

In the context of the Australian conciliation and arbitration system, mediation has a somewhat ambiguous role. Fells notes that mediation could be seen in two ways: as a 'distinct and independent process,' separate to conciliation and arbitration, 'with no clear next step if it fails'; or as 'another step towards arbitration' in which case the distinction between conciliation and mediation is unclear.[34] Although the federal government has in the past attempted to introduce mediation as a formal component of the Australian industrial relations legislation, the proposal was opposed by the other political parties.

Coltri provides a summary of the advantages and disadvantages of mediation compared to two other forms: litigation and negotiation.

Exhibit 12.5 Mediation vs litigation

Advantages of mediation compared with litigation	Disadvantages of mediation compared with litigation
Mediation is quicker and less expensive.	Mediation does not always result in settlement.
Mediation is more likely to encourage collaboration and cooperation.	Litigation guarantees some kind of outcome.
Resolution is more efficient and makes better use of parties' resources.	Unlike, litigation, mediation does not create legal precedent, which might prevent legal reform through the litigation process if mediation is coercive.
Mediation can address all issues, not just those for which a cause of action can be stated.	Incompetent mediators or mediators pressed for time may unwittingly contribute to the exploitation of a weak disputant by a strong one.

Advantages of mediation compared with litigation	Disadvantages of mediation compared with litigation
The whole conflict can be dealt with, including linkages and conflicts with non-disputants.	Because mediation is private, vindication and public reprimand may not be available remedies. This aspect of mediation makes it unpalatable for some disputants.
Mediation is likely to reduce meta-disputes, whereas litigation often creates more of them.	Because mediation is private, say some scholars, bigoted disputants, and mediators might be more likely to act on their prejudices than litigants and judges.
Mediation promotes greater quality of consent and psychological ownership, leading to greater satisfaction and voluntary compliance.	
Relationship advantages: 'competent' mediators help diffuse anger, improve communication, and specifically work on trust building.	
Mediation can 'transform' disputants by empowering them, teaching them negotiation skills and helping them see the other disputant's point of view.	
Mediation that does not result in agreement can streamline the dispute, clarifying and narrowing issues and making future resolution easier, quicker and cheaper.	

Advantages of mediation, compared with negotiation	Disadvantages of mediation, compared with negotiation
Mediation is better able to move disputants past impasse because it is better able to handle people problems, meta-disputes, and emotional factors.	Mediation is more expensive because it includes another professional.
The presence of a third party often alters the relationship dynamics that led disputants to impasse in the first place.	If negotiation is proceeding very well, it may be counterproductive to introduce a third person (the mediator).
Mediators can say things to the disputants that the disputants would reactively devalue if they had come from one another.	
Mediation is better at teaching disputants how to negotiate effectively.	
Mediators can usually address issues of trust, anger and communication more effectively than simple negotiation or lawyer-assisted negotiation can.	
Good mediators are usually more effective at diagnosing the conflict and choosing appropriate methods of addressing it than disputants and their lawyers.	
Compared with lawyer-assisted negotiation, mediation usually results in more creative resolutions better tailored to the interests of all disputants.	

Source: Coltri, L.S. 2004, *Conflict diagnosis and alternative dispute resolution*, Pearson Education Inc., New Jersey, p. 307.

Process consultation

Process consultation is a reasonably new intervention method and involves focusing not on the individuals and their issues but on the process itself. The aim is to focus on procedures rather than emotions and 'to create a foundation for more productive dialogue'.[35] The advantage of focusing on the procedure is to diffuse the emotional aspect of conflict and to improve communication between the parties.[36] A positive outcome of this process is that it provides the parties involved in the dispute or negotiation with skills in managing the issue more productively.

The tactics employed by process consultants include the following:

- separate the parties

- interview them individually and gain their view on the other parties as well as information on the history of the conflict

- structure a series of discussions/interviews between the parties to address the cause of past conflicts and perceptions

- create a strategy or format for dealing with differences in the future.[37]

Unlike mediation, the focus is not on a solution or outcome for the problem, but on looking at better and more effective ways to interact and control the agenda. This method, like the others, has limitations. It is only effective when the conflict has been long term and the parties can see no future except a continuation of that conflict, and that they also see that this is not an acceptable conclusion.

In the past there has often been a misconception that HR practitioners and specialists are in the most appropriate position to take on these roles, particularly mediation and process consultation. However, this chapter makes clear that these are unique and skilled roles that should only be undertaken by those with the necessary training. The role of HR is becoming more focused on the provision of advice in order to empower line managers to manage their own staff and to ensure that appropriately skilled professionals are brought into the organisation to assist in the resolution of conflict where necessary.

Conflict resolution processes

'Like packets of breakfast cereal, there is a large number of different products in the dispute resolution supermarket.'[38] In many cases, conflict may not be resolved through direct negotiations between the parties, and third party intervention can become a useful mechanism. Many of the models being used in Australia are commonplace and have been successfully used for some time, including conciliation, arbitration and mediation. However, there has been a significant increase in the range of dispute resolution services available which are quite new to the Australian setting and include 'arbitration of the papers, investigative tribunals, time limited judicial decision makers, specialist decision makers, early neutral evaluation, issue mediation, range mediation, med-arb, telephone mediation, baseball or best offer arbitration, and multiple models of counselling or therapy'.[39] It is not in the scope of this chapter to explain all of these techniques, but the med-arb is worthy of further explanation.

The Mediation Abacus (med-arb)

Developed by Gribben for the Bond University Dispute Resolution Centre, the Mediation Abacus (or med-arb), which is one of three models developed, is a visual model which demonstrates the many different ways in which a conflict situation or hearing can be dealt with and how the abacus 'bead' can be moved to adapt the service for all or some clients.[40]

Exhibit 12.6   The Mediation Abacus

Therapeutic	Non-therapeutic
Co-facilitator	Sole facilitator
Same gender	Different gender
Same professional orientation	Different professional orientation
Variable physical settings and protocols	Fixed physical settings and protocol
No intake process with individuals	Lengthy intake process
Separate intake worker	Mediator and intake worker are the same
No intake contact/documentation	Lengthy intake contact/documentation
No lawyers present	Lawyers necessarily present
Cooling off	No cooling off
No solutions suggested	Solutions suggested
Without prejudice meetings	Signed detailed agreements
Multiple meetings	Single meetings

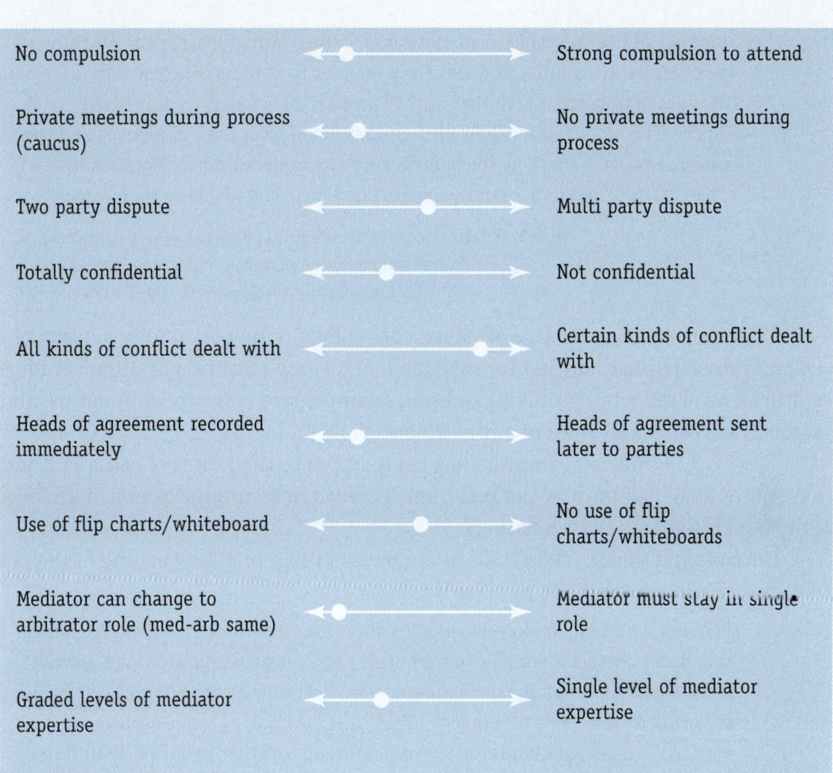

Source: Wade J. 'Current trends in dispute resolution in Australia,' *Bond Dispute Resolution News*, vol. 18, October 2004.

Larson (2004) suggests that dispute resolution practitioners and scholars have not been the fastest group to embrace technology and that compared to other professionals may in fact be one of the slowest groups.[41] During the last decade, the technological revolution has permeated various aspects of our lives so it seems logical that dispute resolution processes will be impacted by technology.

Cross-cultural awareness in conflict management

Western concepts of dispute resolution are based upon the belief that conflict is a natural part of life and that it empowers people to assert themselves and communicate in an effective and constructive manner, resulting in a positive sense of self worth and/or organisational effectiveness.[42] However, these assumptions are based on an individualistic orientation which often conflicts with countries that have organisational structures which reflect collectivist cultures. Noel, Shoemake and Hale (2006) outline an example of a typical Indonesian classroom situation, reflecting the communication culture that is practised and taught within the country:

> The teacher and her desk are located at the front of the room. The students sit in uniform rows facing the front and extending to the end of the classroom. The teacher occupies a space that is stage-like and raised about four to five inches above the space that students occupy. The teacher student ratio is usually about forty to one but can be as high as sixty to one. In many rural areas, teachers have several grade levels in one classroom. All attention is directed toward the front, with the raised position of the teacher's area

symbolic of her status. In most classrooms, the communication and learning are organized in a unilateral way from teacher to student. Students are disciplined to listen, memorise, and be prepared to repeat what is being taught. The teachers, for their part, are provided with their objectives and the information they share by the centralized education authority. As such, there is a 'disciplining' not only of the students but also of the teachers themselves.[43]

Source: Noel B.R. et al 2006, 'Conflict resolution in a non-Western context:
Conversations with Indonesian scholars and practitioners,'
Conflict Resolution Quarterly, vol. 23, no. 4, p. 430.

This excerpt suggests that Western concepts of teamwork and resolution of conflict in a collaborative manner may not be applicable in diverse cultural paradigms. Indeed, many Asian cultures, as is reflected in this Indonesian example, are collectivist in nature and have a strong, traditional respect for roles of authority and power.

However, significant attention has been drawn to the issues of cross-cultural conflict as a result of globalisation and the resultant increase in communications, both face to face and utilising technology, across borders.

Borisoff and Victor (1989) cite Ablamowicz (1993, p. 3) in warning of the potential for cross-cultural misunderstandings to occur:

The new communication technologies allow for efficient information exchange and closer contact among people from all parts of the world. However, having these means does not make communication better or more satisfying. They do not bring people close psychologically. While technology makes this contact possible, it does not guarantee success. Forcing together people with different values and lifestyles may turn a vision of global village into a nightmare.[44]

Indeed, as discussed in Chapter 5, national and international companies are rating the need for cross-cultural communication skills as one of the most important competencies required of senior managerial staff. Borisoff and Victor suggest that 'to interact with others in this integrated global arena, the individual must be able to communicate across cultures and with other minority subcultures within his or her own culture'.[45] They outline a five-point action plan in tackling misunderstandings that result from cross-cultural issues:

- Step One: assessment of the unique features of cross-cultural communication
- Step Two: acknowledgement
- Step Three: attitude adjustment
- Step Four: action
- Step Five: analysis.[46]

The global workplace is one in which the importance of cross-cultural negotiation and conflict resolution skills – for employers and employees – is high on the agenda. Indeed, jobs are designed to demonstrate the importance of this, and staff are employed with cross-cultural communication skills and are trained and performance managed against these criteria. The inclusion of cross-cultural mediation and negotiation mechanisms are thus essential to successful business relationships.

Summary

The underlying assumption of much of the public discussion about industrial relations rests on a dualistic notion of either conflict or cooperation, when in reality both are present in workplaces and society. In this chapter we have examined a variety of ways in which this conflict is manifested and managed in the organisational and industrial context. Changing industrial action patterns and the management of conflict via the mechanism of labour negotiations were discussed. The chapter has also raised the issue of managerial prerogative, which has been strengthened by the federal government's legislative changes, as a way of shifting conflict resolution away from institutional conflict resolution towards enterprise level negotiations.

Industrial and individual conflicts often occur when managers seek to introduce major organisational change. The chapter suggests that such change can be managed in a variety of ways, ranging from forcing to fostering, and involving different negotiation styles. The formal system of industrial relations in Australia had traditionally included two main dispute resolution processes, conciliation and arbitration. However, as a result of political and legislative changes in the past decade, compulsory conciliation and arbitration in Australia are now less favoured and the introduction of the *Workplace Relations Amendment (WorkChoices) Act 2005* has further shifted dispute resolution to the organisation and introduced a model of alternative dispute resolution. This context arguably promotes the role of human resource management, both as a means for providing alternative voice mechanisms for employees and for engagement in direct negotiations and other forms of conflict resolution.

The advent of the global workplace and alternative forms of working have meant that the way in which employers and employees resolve disputes has also had to change. This chapter has outlined a range of conflict management styles as well as a range of new forms of alternative dispute resolution methods which better suit these new working arrangements. Only time will tell if they achieve workplace harmony.

Key terms

arbitration 490

call centres 480

conciliation 490

enterprise 486

knowledge workers 480

managerial prerogative 480

Key debate issues

1   Conflict is inevitable in the employment relationship.
2   Third-party involvement is undesirable in the employment relationship because it deflects responsibility for decisions and behaviours away from the parties directly involved.

3   'Online dispute resolution will never be considered a legitimate form of dispute resolution by employers and employees – it is dangerous and takes away the human element, which is vital to achieving workplace harmony.'

Case study 12.1

Negotiations at St Jude's Community Hospital

Following the recent amalgamation between two small rural hospitals, the Northern Memorial Hospital and the North-Eastern Rural Hospital, to form St Jude's Community Hospital, a publicly owned, privately managed hospital, the unions and management are to negotiate the first enterprise agreement. The Australian Nurses Federation (ANF) and the Health Services Union of Australia (HSUA) will be parties to the collective agreement (it has been agreed that the maintenance unions will negotiate a separate agreement).

The amalgamation had led to the closure of the existing hospitals (which are slated for demolition and the land sold to create two planned rural communities) and the construction of a new hospital. St Jude's, 274 kms from Melbourne, is located 68 kms from the Northern Memorial Hospital and 97 kms from the North-Eastern Rural Hospital and is argued to be a 'hub' hospital meeting the needs of both communities as well as outlying areas.

The old hospitals had been operating for many years, with employees both living and working in the local area. Job satisfaction had been high, with fairly low turnover of staff – many had been employed for five to 10 years. Northern Memorial Hospital had been a 40-bed hospital, while North-Eastern Rural Hospital was a 50-bed hospital. The region has high levels of unemployment and an ageing population (as young people leave the area to gain employment). The closure of the hospitals, despite the building of the new hospital, is seen by some as yet another closure of a rural service, just like bank closures in recent years. This is felt particularly among members of the two communities who did volunteer work at the hospitals and had been involved in fundraising activities over the years. This may also mean there would be a negative community attitude to any outsourcing of services.

For the management company running the hospital, PrimeHealth, this is the first involvement in the provision of health services. The new CEO has an accounting background and has been employed because of his management expertise. Likewise, the new Human Resources Manager has considerable experience in human resource management positions but not in health, or related fields. The intent was to bring in a management team with 'fresh' ideas and with a commitment to change and client service rather than being tied to what has been done in the past. In accordance with this, all of the senior management team are employed on individual contracts with performance indicators determining performance-based pay, with a component linked to the profitability of the company. 'A new hospital in the new millennium' is management's mission statement.

St Jude's has 80 beds and provides the following services: surgical, medical, day only, post-natal, diagnostic (pathology and radiography) and allied health (social worker, physiotherapy). The coronary care and oncology services provided in the past at North-Eastern Rural Hospital will no longer be provided – St Jude's has entered into an arrangement with a private metropolitan hospital for provision of those services.

The amalgamation occurred fairly quickly, motivated in part by the need for repairs and renovations at Northern Memorial Hospital and the money for St Jude's being conditional on certain timelines being met. This meant consultation with staff was hampered by the speed at which the decisions were being made, with there being little over the actual design or construction of the hospital. Despite there being a commitment to no jobs being lost, there are concerns about people needing to relocate and, hence, redundancy. There are also concerns over the need for fewer management positions, such as Unit and Case managers, as jobs will be merged to avoid undue duplication, and the impact on promotion opportunities as well as concerns arising from the decision to not continue with some specialist services previously offered. There are also rumours that the management team thinks that some nursing management jobs can be done by non-nurses.

Catering and cleaning services, it is rumoured, may be outsourced, although they were not at either Northern Memorial Hospital or North-Eastern Rural Hospital. A metropolitan-based company, Cook'n'Clean, is apparently the favoured contractor as it has experience in the health industry. The unions are arguing to the contrary and are also wary of Cook'n'Clean being favoured as it is known that this is a company which prefers to hire new staff, and prefers to avoid dealing with unions, offering individual contracts and hiring people as contractors rather than as employees. Other rumours are that there may be the introduction of 12-hour shifts or split shifts (with two four-hour shifts over a 12-hour period comprising a single shift) for non-nursing staff. This is because the management wants to introduce rostering changes to increase staffing flexibility and has been prompted by a recent community emergency where a bout of influenza saw medical services being placed under great strain. A shift away from fixed to flexible nurse–patient ratios for nursing staff is also a priority: the management feels that on some shifts two nurses would be sufficient to look after 20 patients rather than the 5:20 ratio currently in place. Increased use of casuals, including nurses, or the contracting out of nursing have also been heard as possibilities, though the veracity of such rumours is unknown. This is felt to be a possible way of addressing the increased demand for services during the winter, given the proximity of St Jude's to a popular snow resort.

Relocation of staff remains the central issue. The increased travelling time experienced by many, and the lack of direct public transport, contribute to staff dissatisfaction. It is felt that there should be compensation for the costs incurred from the greater travelling time and an understanding of this when rostering is done. Because of this, the idea of split shifts is particularly worrisome, while others have found difficulties arising with their child-care arrangements in terms of dropping off and collecting children. Redundancies have already occurred, as specialist staff find they no longer have the capacity to work in their speciality or as a consequence of positions being merged.

There are some other problems facing St Jude's. There has been a spate of Workcover claims caused by people falling over on the slippery floor in the hospital foyer and in the corridors. To date, several employees have hurt their backs, one broke an arm after falling awkwardly while others have suffered minor muscle pulls while trying to stop patients slipping. Absenteeism rates have also increased, with associated rostering problems.

There are a number of issues the unions want to pursue: a wage increase, protection of nurse–patient ratios, improved redundancy provisions, 14 weeks maternity leave, consultation over outsourcing, rostering and shift arrangements, and a relocation allowance.

Union team

The team comprises:

1   If a team of three: two full-time union officials (one from each union, with the ANF official having previously worked at one of the old hospitals before being elected as a full-time official); one local delegate from the HSUA from the other old hospital.
2   If a team of four: two full-time officials and two local delegates (one from each union and one from each of the old hospitals).

There is also some tension about the union/s coming to tell the local members what they should do. Even though it is understood that the union/s tried to improve the degree of consultation over the amalgamation, there is still residual feeling that the union/s should have 'done more.'

The unions want to negotiate a 'short' agreement of 18 months to two years, so that matters can be renegotiated once the hospital 'settles.' A 4 per cent per annum wage increase is sought, plus a relocation travel allowance of $10 to $20 per week, an increase in paid maternity leave to 14 weeks), a better consultative process (such as a consultative committee with equal union–management representation), and improved occupational health and safety standards. Contracting out of catering and cleaning should be resisted at all costs. HSUA members in cleaning and catering, it is felt, would be vulnerable if having to negotiate an individual contract with a company like Cook'n'Clean.

Protection of nurse–patient ratios is one of the priority issues for the ANF and its members, while the relocation and redundancy issues are worrying for the HSUA members. The ANF is also concerned about the suggestion of non-nursing staff in nursing management positions, with industrial action already occurring over this matter at a metropolitan hospital. The HSUA is aware of the ANF and its members' antipathy to this issue and is not supportive of management's stance.

Management team

The team comprises the HR Manager, Director of Nursing, Director of Allied Health and Aged Care and either the Manager of Environmental and Hotel Services or the CEO.

The HR manager is still reasonably new in their job and is finding some difficulty in dealing with a CEO intent on introducing new practices and procedures irrespective of what were the previous practices and ways of doing things in a hospital setting. While supportive of change, the HR manager feels the CEO focuses too much on the 'bottom line' and on 'innovative' change without thinking through all the consequences (such as split shifts and non-nurses in nurse management jobs, the latter of which has led to industrial action at a metropolitan Victorian hospital). A greater emphasis on productivity is welcomed by the HR manager but preferably within a more consultative framework. Nevertheless, the HR manager is aware of the need to not be seen to undermine the CEO in front of the other managers (as well as the components of their contract dependent on cost-based performance indicators).

The various directors are constantly seeking a greater proportion of the budget for their divisions, with this always being seen as a competitive exercise. The CEO's suggestion of differential profit sharing for the divisions on the basis of efficiencies (i.e. cost-cutting) is seen as exacerbating this competitiveness with all directors harbouring unspoken reservations about the impact on patient–client service. The Director of Nursing is also concerned about the proposal of non-nurses in nurse management positions, though the Director of Allied Health Care and Aged Care sees promotion opportunities for staff in their division. A similar division of work being questioned is that of nurses giving injections, which the doctors feel encroaches on their job. The Manager of Environmental and Hotel Services, whose area of responsibility includes catering and cleaning, is aware of the outsourcing rumours but is not actively supporting Cook'n'Clean as the preferred provider.

The directions given to the management team are to negotiate a longer agreement of around three years, so as to provide some stability in the next few years, and for a wage increase staggered over that period of 5 to 6 per cent. A commitment to capacity for contracting out of all services is sought, as is introducing shift flexibilities such as 12-hour shifts or split shifts, together with flexible nurse–patient ratios. Some concerns have been raised about the likelihood of the unions seeking 14 weeks paid maternity leave for all employees; while the CEO thinks this might help with retention of female nurses, they think this may be 'excessive' for cleaning and catering employees.

Courtesy of Dr Cathy Brigden, Senior Lecturer, School of Management, RMIT University.

Case study 12.2

University of South Yuleton

At the University of South Yuleton, students have to register for courses, and pay fees, at the start of the academic year. Long queues form every year, which as a marketing academic, Michael Swanson, Head of the Business Faculty, regards as most undesirable: he believes that these students are the university's customers and potential customers, and thinks it possible that each year some get fed up and go down the road to a competing university, which offers similar courses. In any case, it creates a bad impression.

He also believes that some small organisational changes would make a big improvement. Examples include separating into a different queue the 20 per cent of applicants whose registration is complicated and who cause bottlenecks, and bringing all the Registry staff into the 'front line' at peak times, instead of, as now, having a proportion of them continuing with back office administrative tasks all the way through.

The problem, however, is that the Registry staff, and especially its Section Head, are very loath to change their systems in any way. Last year Swanson called a big meeting of several concerned academics plus the Registry staff, to try to get agreement on some changes. Unfortunately, the Registry staff quickly felt embattled, and became defensive, putting up objections to any plan that was suggested. The start of the academic year is approaching again. Swanson is still eager to do something about the problem.

Source: Guirdham, M. 1995. *Interpersonal skills at work*, 2nd edn, London, Prentice Hall, p. 366.

Questions

1 How would you advise Michael Swanson to proceed?

2 Would the use of a mediator improve the situation? Why or why not?

Further readings

Australian Government 2005. *WorkChoices – A new workplace relations system*, www.aph.gov.au/library/intguide/law/workchoicesbill.htm

Baird M., Grey I. 1996. 'Negotiating change: A practical guide', in Mortimer D., Leece P., Morris R. (eds), *Workplace reform and enterprise bargaining*, Sydney, Harcourt Brace.

DEWR 2006. 'Work Choices and industrial action', Fact Sheet 21, www.workchoices.gov.au/ourplan/publications/WorkChoicesandindustrial action.htm

Katz H.C., Kochan T.A. 2000. *An introduction to collective bargaining and industrial relations*, 2nd edn, Boston, McGraw-Hill.

Van Gramberg B. 2006. *Managing workplace conflict: Alternative dispute resolution in Australia*, Sydney, Federation Press.

Van Gramberg B. 2006. 'The rhetoric and reality of workplace ADR', *Journal of Industrial Relations*, 48(2), pp. 175–91.

Van Gramberg B. 2006. 'ADR and grievance procedures' in Teicher J., Gough R., Holland P. (eds), *Employment Relations Management*, 2nd edn, Melbourne, Pearson Education.

Endnotes

1   Waring P. & Bray W. 2006. *Evolving employment relations. Industry studies from Australia*. North Ryde, McGraw-Hill Australia Pty Ltd, p. 69.

2   Ibid, p. 70.

3   Ibid.

4   Wade J. 2004. 'Current trends in dispute resolution in Australia', *Bond Resolution News*, vol. 18, October.

5   Van Gramberg B. 2006, *Managing workplace conflict: Alternative dispute resolution in Australia*, Sydney, Federation Press.

6   Coser, L. 1956. *The functions of social conflict*. New York, Free Press, p. 8.

7   Deutsch M. 1962. 'Cooperation and trust: Some theoretical notes', in M.R. Jones (ed.), *Nebraska Symposium on Motivation*, Lincoln, NE, University of Nebraska Press, pp. 275–318; Lewicki R.J., Saunders D.M. & Minton J.W. 1997. *Essentials of negotiation*, New York, Irwin McGraw-Hill.

8   Tjosvold, D. 1988, *Getting things done through organisations*, Lexington Books.

9   Harbridge R. & Walsh P. 2002. 'Globalisation and labour market deregulation in Australia and New Zealand: Different approaches, similar outcomes,' *Employee Relations*, vol. 24, no. 4., p. 429.

10   Alexander R. & Lewer J. 2004. *Understanding Australian industrial relations*. 6th edn, Victoria, Thomson Learning, p. 250.

11   Ibid.

12   Australian Government, 2005, *WorkChoices - A new workplace relations system*, available at www.aph.gov.au/library/intguide/law/workchoicesbill.htm; p 27.

13   Explanatory Memorandum to the *Workplace Relations Amendment (Work Choices) Bill 2005*, p. 209.

14   Explanatory Memorandum, p. 344.

15   Explanatory Memorandum, p. 349.

16   Explanatory Memorandum, p. 344.

17   Explanatory Memorandum, p. 348.

18   Katz H.C., Kochan T.A. 2000. *An introduction to collective bargaining and industrial relations*, 2nd edn, Boston, McGraw-Hill, p. 176.

19   Ibid. pp. 176–7.

20   Ibid.

21   Sutcliffe P., Callus R. 1994. *Glossary of Australian industrial relations terms*, ACCIRT, p. 126.

22   Baird M., Grey I. 1996. 'Negotiating change: A practical guide,' in Mortimer D., Leece P., Morris R. (eds) *Workplace reform and enterprise bargaining*, Sydney, Harcourt Brace, pp. 347–58.

23 Pruitt D., and Rubin J. 1986. *Social conflict, escalation, stalemate and settlement*, New York, Random House.

24 Lewicki R.J., Saunders D.M., Minton J.W. 1997. *Essentials of negotiation*, New York, McGraw-Hill, p. 21.

25 Wertheim E., Love A., Peck C., Littlefield L. 1998. *Skills for resolving conflict*, Eruditions Publishing, p. 4.

26 Ibid, p. 36.

27 Ibid, p. 37.

28 Ibid.

29 Sutcliffe P. & Callus R., 1994. *Glossary of industrial relations terms*, ACCIRT, p. 12

30 Wall Jr J.A. & Lynn A. 1993. 'Mediation: A current review,' *The Journal of Conflict Resolution*, vol. 37, no. 1, p. 160.

31 Wertheim, et al. op. cit. p. 136.

32 Lewicki et al., op cit. p. 136.

33 Coltri. L.S. 2004. *Conflict diagnosis and alternative dispute resolution*, Pearson Education Inc, New Jersey., p. 307.

34 Fells R. 1999. 'Settlement process or tactical opportunity? Mediation in industrial relations,' *The Journal of Industrial Relations*, vol. 4, no. 41. p. 595.

35 Fells R. 1999. op. cit. p. 208; Lewicki, et al., 1997. op. cit., p. 208.

36 Ibid.

37 Ibid, p. 209.

38 Wade J. 2004, p. 15.

39 Wade J. 2004, p. 16

40 Ibid.

41 Larson D. A. 2004. 'Online dispute resolution: Technology takes a place at the table,' *Negotiation Journal*, January 2004.

42 Noel B.R., Shoemake A.T., & Hale C.L. 2006. 'Conflict resolution in a non-Western context: Conversations with Indonesian scholars and practitioners,' *Conflict Resolution Quarterly*, vol. 23, no. 4, Wiley Periodicals Inc., p. 430.

43 Ibid, p. 431.

44 Borisoff D. & Victor D.A. 1989. *Conflict management. A communication skills approach*, 2nd edn, Allyn and Bacon, Needham Heights, MA, p. 149.

45 Ibid, p. 150.

46 Ibid, p. 196.

Online reading

INFOTRAC® COLLEGE EDITION

For additional readings and review on conflict and negotiation processes, explore InfoTrac® College Edition, your online library. Go to: www.infotrac-college.com and search for any of the InfoTrac key terms listed below:

➤ alternative dispute resolution (ADR)

➤ conflict resolution

➤ industrial conflict

➤ mediation

➤ negotiation strategies

The effectiveness of HRM towards the future

CHAPTER 13
EVALUATING HUMAN RESOURCE MANAGEMENT

The future value of the HR profession hangs on understanding and supporting activities that create sustainable capability and external shareholder value.

Dave Ulrich 2006

To move to the center of the organization, HR must be able to talk in quantitative, objective terms. Organizations are managed by data.

Jac Fitz-enz 2006

I value the human resources role and I've chosen it as my profession, but I've always viewed myself as a business leader who just happens to be in a human resources position.

Brad Waite, 2003

Objectives

After reading this chapter, you will be able to:

1 Justify overall HRM strategies, policies and plans in relation to desired organisational outcomes.

2 Review the effectiveness and cost–benefit aspects of all HRM processes.

3 Appreciate the value of both quantitative and qualitative measures in the evaluation of the effectiveness of HRM.

4 Discuss the compliance and governance aspects of HRM practices.

5 Assess the success of HRM functions and tasks.

Introduction

Throughout this book, we have discussed the crucial role of the HR department in ensuring that organisational objectives are achieved through the effective and efficient management of its human resources. In the past, employees and human resource departments were often regarded as necessary but expensive overheads, the costs of which simply had to be borne by the organisation. A more modern view is that HR departments can both effectively manage their own budgets and structure all HRM activities to ensure that they cost-effectively contribute to the achievement of organisational objectives. In addition, they should add value to the legal compliance and corporate governance requirements of their organisation.

Professor John Boudreau suggests that all HR managers should seek to justify their HRM strategies by answering the following questions:

- Is the return to our expenditures on HRM programs adequate to justify these investments?

- Is it worth investing scarce financial resources to improve the quality of human resources?

- How can a manager choose between different options for managing human resources?

- How can HRM communicate its contribution to organisational goals in a way that is compatible with other managerial functions?[1]

In other words, 'How do you know if you are achieving maximum utilisation of your human resources?'[2]

Another author[3] suggests that HR professionals need to move from traditional 'cost centre' approaches (sometimes referred to as 'toxic accounting')[4] to 'profit/value centre models', which focus on the outcomes or contributions of HRM programs to organisational effectiveness rather than merely their costs. He proposes a strategic framework to ensure this desirable goal, which involves six 'core ingredients', namely:

- a mission that connects HR to the business

- measures that describe consequences, not costs

- business analysis that goes beyond traditional boundaries

- 'showcase' statistics that demonstrate the value added by HR

- service that 'makes a statement'

- a position in the hierarchy that enables action.[5]

This framework addresses many of Professor Boudreau's questions at an operational level, and clearly reinforces SHRM theory, as illustrated in Exhibit 13.1 and throughout the text.

In addition, the Australian Stock Exchange (ASX) has recently established a Corporate Governance Council, in order to inform organisations of their 'good governance' responsibilities, many of which are concerned with HRM functions.[6]

In essence then, if HRM is genuinely strategic in its focus, and managerial in its operations, it will account for its activities in similar ways to the managers of production, finance and marketing. In other words, a 'value-based, capital investment approach to HRM decisions'.[7] The notions of 'human capital' or 'human assets' reflect a quantifiable approach to the management of human resources, which is bluntly expressed by Jac Fitz-Enz:

> Profits aren't measured in terms of goodness, righteousness, or other aesthetics indexes. They are expressed in hard dollars. Therefore, if the human resource department wants to join the profit team along with marketing, manufacturing and the rest of the high status departments, it will have to start looking for and pointing out its contributions to profits.[8]

Exhibit 13.1 SHRM and evaluation

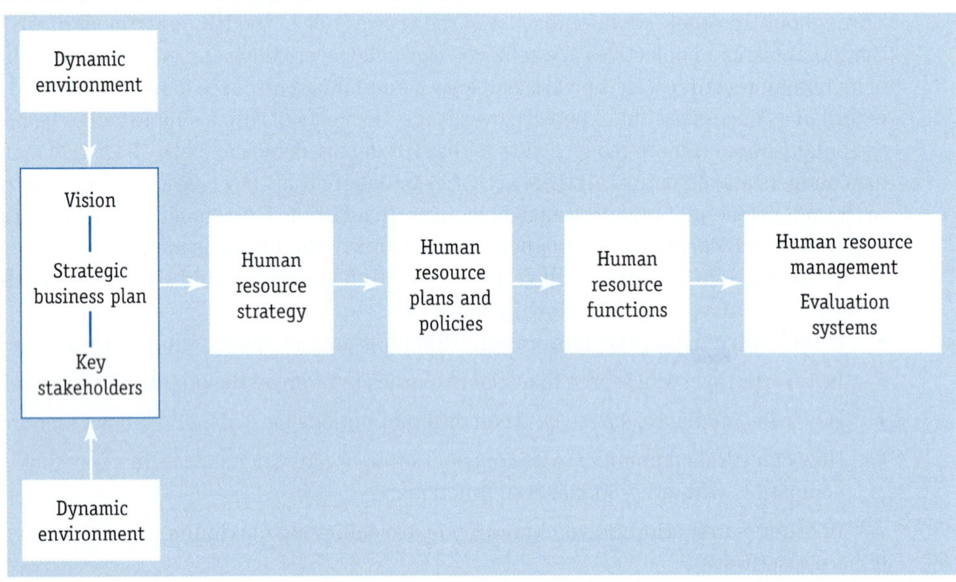

On the other hand, the importance of qualitative measures such as employee and customer satisfaction, legal compliance, corporate governance and corporate social responsibility (CSR) should not be underestimated.

The challenge for human resource managers is to account for both the short- and long-term costs and benefits of specific HR processes (recruitment, training, performance management), overall HR programs and proposed HR strategies. Many HR activities are, of course, difficult to quantify. While the costs of recruitment, training or occupational health and safety programs can be effectively quantified, their benefits in productivity or performance terms are more difficult to measure.

Recent economic history in Australia, however, suggests that the profitability of investments, mergers and acquisitions is also relatively unpredictable, at least in the longer term. Does this suggest that financial managers should neither plan nor account for themselves, or that production and marketing managers should not be held responsible for the success or failure of innovative work processes or marketing strategies? Proactive HR managers endeavour to measure the effectiveness of their programs and future plans in similar terms to those of comparable managers.

HR managers should be able to establish benchmark ratios for such aspects as annual HR department costs to employee, and HR costs to unit produced. HR department budgets can be expressed as a proportion of total company payroll. As an example, a survey of HR department costs in Queensland established an average annual cost per employee of approximately A$280 for the provision of their services.[9] A similar US study estimated the average annual cost at approximately A$325.[10] The comparison here was interpreted to suggest that Queensland companies were receiving inadequate HR budgets. It could also suggest that HR departments in the Australian study were more efficient than their US counterparts, or that the US companies had HR departments with excessively generous budgets. It should, however, be noted that HR cost-per-employee ratios 'should not be interpreted as a measure of the effectiveness of the HR function, but that (they) provide benchmarks, or standards for comparison'.[11]

Such measures are probably most useful when compared with like industries, or in the same organisation over historical periods. Broader cost–benefit measures of HRM may include considerations of the dollar value of the resources needed to implement programs, the 'number of person-years of workforce value affected ... (or) the change in the workforce value of those affected by the strategy, program or process'.[12] More recently, HRM academics such as Ulrich (2006) and Ulrich and Smallwood (2005) have suggested that the future of HR lies in 'understanding and supporting activities that create sustainable capability and external shareholder value',[13] and that 'organizational capabilities such as talent, speed, collaboration, accountability, shared mindset, learning and leadership are the deliverables of HR ... (which) contribute to an organisation's market value'.[14] These issues and the practical applications of HR information management systems are discussed in Chapter 4.

Purposes of measuring costs and benefits of HRM

The application of '... market dynamics to HRM costing ... is used to develop a theoretical basis for the above-normal profits that can result from strategic HRM action'.[15] Cost–benefit projections of HRM activity can assist and promote HR roles as the initiator, facilitator and enhancer of strategy.[16] More specifically, HR cost–benefit analyses can:

- aid overall HR planning and control

- emphasise the nature (and value) of people to the organisation

- provide a valid and reliable method of reporting cost and value

- assist senior and line managers to measure their own performance.

While traditional accounting measures focus on past performance, HRM costing is sufficiently flexible to assess 'how the business might perform in the future'.[17] Thus, Dow Chemicals in the United States measures the relative value of the centralisation versus decentralisation of its functions, IBM Corporation regularly evaluates the effectiveness of its US$1 billion annual training budget, and CIGNA focuses on the costs of its employee turnover/wastage rates, in order to make strategic decisions about future HRM practices.[18] As News report 13.1 below illustrates, some Australian companies are measuring the financial return on investment (ROI) of their HRM practices and reporting it to their shareholders as an indication of their overall corporate performance.

Westpac bank: intangible issues become tangible profits

Westpac (WBC) briefed the market on its approach to managing intangible value, arguing that these 'soft' factors are critical to delivering sustainable earnings performance and managing regulatory and reputational risk. Long a hallmark of the bank's strategies, management again reiterated its commitment to taking a longer, broader view as well as an ongoing commitment to better understanding the value linkages between the non-financial performance drivers and financial outcomes.

As tangible evidence of the benefits of its focus on intangible issues, WBC highlighted its 3.5 percentage point reduction in staff turnover (to 16 per cent) has lowered recruitment and other costs by an estimated $40 to $50 million. Further to this, if WBC could achieve ANZ's staff turnover levels of 11.6 per cent another $60 to $75 million would be available. As tangible evidence of the benefits of its focus on intangible issues, WBC highlighted the 6.1 percentage point reduction it achieved in lost time injury frequency has been worth $2.5 million over the past two years.

Engaged staff create sustainable financial advantage

As we have long argued, delivering on the 'soft' issues is a lead indicator of sustainable financial performance and a significant comparative advantage.

For example, Hewitt estimates that each additional engaged employee is worth $5000 per year in extra profits and high employee engagement correlates strongly with higher revenues, profits and total shareholder returns.

As the National Australia Bank (NAB) says, employee engagement is a 'tough measure' which goes 'beyond satisfaction' to gauge employees' intellectual and emotional connection to their work and their commitment to the organisation. High and improved employee engagement also leads to lower employee absenteeism, higher retention rates and longer tenures, which in turn leads to better customer satisfaction, and higher revenue productivity and profits. For example, US defence giant Northrop Grumman found that a 6 per cent increase in engagement led to 3 per cent lower employee turnover.

Source: Adapted from Anonymous 2006, *Westpac Bank: Intangible issues become tangible profits*, Macquarie Financial Services, 13 April, pp. 1–4.

However, even the most proactive HR practitioners will readily admit that measuring the costs and benefits of HRM activities is difficult, time-consuming and heavily dependent upon the accuracy of employee data from a well-designed human resource information management system (see Chapter 4). Despite the considerable advantages that accrue from the effective measurement of HR activities, some practitioners are reluctant to reduce the complexities of managing employees to a dollar contribution to organisational performance, or are dissuaded from so doing by workloads and lack of interest by senior management.

It should also be noted that 'dollars are not the only barometer of the effectiveness of HR activities. The payoffs from some activities, such as affirmative action and child care, must be viewed in a broader social context'.[19] Modern approaches to the evaluation of the effectiveness of HRM adopt broader perspectives which simultaneously encompass quantitative measures; and such qualitative assessments as 'managing talent … being involved in major change matters such as mergers and acquisitions … enabling staff to understand the business',[20] knowledge management, corporate governance and corporate social responsibility[21] (see later in this chapter).

However, the failure to measure the costs of such activities both prior to and after implementation would be foolhardy. Benefits of these programs may be more difficult to measure. Despite these difficulties, it should be remembered that the overall purpose of all these measures is to comprehensively account for, and subsequently to persuade management of, the value and contributions of the management of an organisation's human resources. Some authors suggest that not only can specific HRM processes (e.g. recruitment, human resource development, performance management) be assessed for their costs and contributions to organisational effectiveness, but that the value of 'knowledge capital' can, and should, be included on annual organisational balance sheets.[22] As Howes explains, 'the challenge for the HR professional is to develop processes to measure the value of the human capital of the firm'.[23]

The concept of *human capital management* has been discussed throughout this text, emphasising both its critical importance to organisational flexibility, competitiveness, profitability, and its inherent measurement difficulty. It has been defined as the 'sum total of all your employees' talents and capabilities (knowledge, skills, know-how and ability to innovate) serving to add value to the goods and services a company produces'.[24] Gallo and Thompson suggest that '… the use of HRM measures presents the greatest challenge. Credible, meaningful HR measures will be essential to the development of effective accountability systems and the

ultimate acceptance of the concept of HRM accountability'.[25] Some such measures may include 'human capital ROI' (the profit generated through investment in employees); revenue (or profit) per employee; labour cost as a percentage of revenue; or the voluntary separation rate.[26] Gallo and Thompson note that human capital management is the result of a shared responsibility between HR, senior and line managers, and between the HR and finance departments, and incorporates legal compliance, together with measures of the efficiency of HRM service delivery and the effectiveness of all HRM programs.

These measures need to focus on HRM programs which clearly contribute to and support strategic organisational goals and objectives. Hansen illustrates the crucial connection between the HR manager and the Chief Financial Officer (CFO): 'The CFO sets the overall human capital budget and then shares responsibility with HR for allocating that budget.'[27] Exhibit 13.2 shows the average proportion of organisational revenues spent on human capital in a selection of industries.

Exhibit 13.2 Spending on human capital

Per cent of annual revenues spent on human capital, selected industries	%
Financial services	43
Pharmaceuticals and professional services	45
Light manufacturing	32
Heavy manufacturing	25
Computers and telecom	37

Source: Mercer Human Resources Consulting/CFO Research Services 2003. Survey.

Jac Fitz-Enz has some interesting observations on the reasons why HRM has often failed to adequately account for its activities in the past:

- HR people do not know how to measure the costs of behaviour – many practitioners have little training, interest or encouragement in the use of quantitative techniques or statistics.

- Top management has accepted the 'myth' that HR activities cannot be evaluated in quantitative terms.

- Some HR managers do not want to be measured.

- A number of HR managers would like to apply some measures to their functions, but they haven't been able to do so.[28]

Approaches to HRM accounting

Employees have traditionally been regarded only as expense items, and HR departments as costly overheads, from an accounting perspective. Organisations during the 1960s and 1970s generally considered HR departments as necessary (if expensive) servicing functions, to recruit, train and pay employees, and more recently to administer legally required initiatives such as equal employment opportunity, affirmative action and occupational health and safety. The anticipated benefits were vague and apparently immeasurable.

With increasing HR professionalism, and the recognition of employees as human capital or value-added assets, together with growing employer acceptance of the ongoing costs associated with employment, approaches to HRM accounting have become a higher priority.

Several strategies have been adapted from accounting practice to the effective management of an organisation's human resources. These include the original cost, replacement cost, opportunity cost and economic value approaches.

- *Original cost* measures the accumulated costs associated with recruiting, selecting, inducting and training each employee, or groups of employees, at any time. In this approach, wages, salaries and employee benefits are considered expenses; training outcomes are expressed as benefits. Current value estimates are relatively easy to calculate.

- *Replacement cost* estimates the dollar value of replacing any employee, including separation payments and subsequent training costs. This approach fails to effectively distinguish between assets and expenses.

- *Opportunity cost* gauges the maximum value of the employee in an alternative use (i.e. what someone else would pay for the particular human resource asset) – a somewhat impractical approach.

- *Economic value* is based upon a goodwill method. This approach attempts to predict the value of employees in terms of likely future earnings. This strategy tends towards a 'theoretical rather than a practical management approach'.[29]

These approaches, often referred to as human resource costing (rather than human resource accounting), measure the economic consequences of employee behaviour, rather than simply their accumulated costs to the organisation. Costing should include both direct costs (e.g. payroll taxes, sick leave, company discounts, training, facilities) and the costs of the HR department. A further consideration for such costing is the distinction between controllable and uncontrollable costs for the employer. Controllable costs include employee wastage due to higher wages, and employee absenteeism due to poor or inadequate working conditions. Uncontrollable costs may include employee wastage or absenteeism due to sickness or death. The principal objective of human resource costing is to identify the controllable aspects of employee behaviour and their associated costs, and to design suitable programs to reduce these costs and improve consequent individual and organisational performance.

Some authors present a challenge for strategic human resource managers to '… develop a central analytical framework or technique – like econometric forecasting, the market share/operating margin matrix, or portfolio theory – to guide a firm's choice of human resource strategy'.[30] If such a framework can be developed in the future, it will radically enhance the reputation and perceived value of human resource management.

Some ideas towards such a framework include:

- *'HRM portfolio' concepts*: The function of the HR specialist here is to manage the 'portfolio' of crucial HR activities (e.g. recruitment, human resource development, performance management, culture change) in relationship to the organisation's strategic priorities, and with clear financial accountability.

- *'Flow' models of HRM*: As illustrated in Exhibit 13.3, this model focuses on the outcomes of HRM activities, both qualitative and quantitative.

- *HR stakeholder – HR success factor framework*: As Exhibit 13.4 shows, this framework involves a choice of HR strategies aligned with business strategies, the key component of SHRM. Again, the costs and benefits of each optional HR strategy can be evaluated in both qualitative and quantitative (financial) terms. As the figure suggests, a close alignment between HRM strategies, policies and practices and organisational outcomes can enable the evaluation of the qualitative directly in relation to the quantitative. Thus, if specialist technical recruitment is desired in order to transform an organisation's culture, the achievement (or otherwise) of this goal could be assessed against the HRM policies and processes adopted.

Exhibit 13.3 The human resource management model

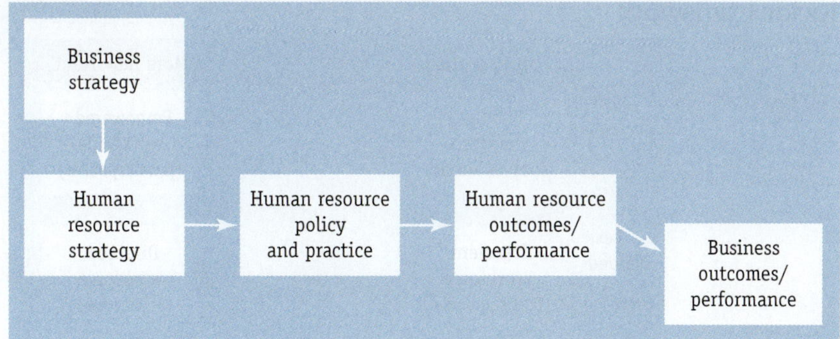

Source: From *Human Resource Management, An Economic Approach*, 2e, by Lewin & Mitchell, 1995. Reprinted with permission of South-Western, a division of Thomson Learning: www.thomsonrights.com.

- *Human/intellectual capital, people value measures*: As discussed earlier in this chapter, there is considerable debate about the need (and capacity) to develop accurate measures of the financial 'value' of human or intellectual capital, and its contributions to organisational balance sheets.

Though the debate is still in its infancy, some authors claim that appropriate measures can be developed. Howes, for example, has formulated an equation that may assist organisations to measure the current financial value of their human or intellectual capital:[31]

$$\text{Human/intellectual capital} = \frac{\text{Average market value} - \text{Average capital per employee}}{\text{Average workforce (full-time employees)}}$$

Although the equation may be criticised for its simplicity, and its inability to incorporate the qualitative dimensions of employee contributions, it nevertheless represents a useful starting point for the evaluation and promotion of the value of human resources to organisations. Another approach is provided by Schneier's People Value Add (PVA) model,[32] which uses a ratio that compares the economic value created against the dollars invested in employees.

Indicators of HRM performance

It is possible to assess the quality of the work environment, and therefore the effectiveness of HRM, by studying a range of indicators. They include employee turnover and wastage rates, absenteeism rates, injury and illness records, and the responses to employee attitude surveys and exit interviews. Gibbs suggests that there are two main dimensions of HRM program effectiveness: their 'internal fit' with organisational objectives, and their 'external fit' with industry best practice.[33] They should encompass both quantitative performance indicators and the qualitative assessments of HRM's internal 'customers' – managers and employees – obtained through consultation, communication and internal surveys.[34]

An example of HR measures used by Australian organisations is included in Exhibit 13.5. It covers a range of issues and measures, and assists with HR planning and management. The following section details the nature and types of quantitative HR measures – HR metrics – utilised by organisations to evaluate and demonstrate the value of their HRM activities.

Exhibit 13.4   The human resource stakeholder – human resource success factor framework

	Less important	More important
More valued	Entitled workforce (paternalistic)	Empowered workforce (participative)
Less valued	Transient workforce (transactional)	Directed workforce (structured)

Source: From *Human Resource Management, An Economic Approach*, 2e, by Lewin & Mitchell, 1995.
Reprinted with permission of South-Western, a division of Thomson Learning: www.thomsonrights.com.

Exhibit 13.5   HR measures

headcount	labour % of revenue	discretionary labour expenditure
workforce ratios	unplanned turnover	unplanned absenteeism
training course ratios	training expenditure	training hours
workers compensation	leave liability	internal communications
performance appraisals	exit interviews	remuneration
demographics	employee sourcing	succession planning
talent management	flight risk	knowledge management
payroll adjustments	performance-related pay	skills and competencies
vacancy duration rates	vacancy fill rate	occupational health and safety

Source: Lyle Potgieter and Peter Vlant, Peoplestreme.com, 2006.

HR metrics

HR metrics are quantitative measures of the costs or benefits of aspects of HR processes, and are becoming crucial to the strategic management of human resources towards organisational effectiveness. They provide measurement standards and benchmarks which demonstrate how HRM contributes to the desired organisational goals and outcomes. As Jac Fitz-Enz explains, 'to move to the center of the organization, HR must be able to talk in quantitative, objective terms'.[35] Consequently, many organisations have developed indices and benchmarks of HR metrics (sometimes known as Human Capital Management Metrics), including the Human Capital Index (HCI) from Hewitt and Associates, a widely used measure of how organisations manage their workforce in the United States. Similar indices have been developed by researchers at the University of NSW, with particular application to the investment, share market and funds management industry sectors.

HR metrics are used by a broad variety of organisational stakeholders, including investors and fund managers, organisational executives, HR managers, line managers and even employees,

sometimes for different purposes. As examples, investors and fund managers use them to compare their HR functions with those of competitors; executives can assess the congruency of HR processes with overall business strategies; HR professionals use such metrics to account for and promote the efficacy of their activities; line managers can ensure budgetary, operational and customer outcomes; and employees can better understand their individual and collective value to their organisations.

However, measuring the contributions of people, and linking HR metrics to organisational effectiveness, is quite a complex task, and perhaps the most difficult issue is that of causality. Thus, while most observers would agree that a well-managed workforce is more likely to result in a more effective and competitive organisation, clear linkages between HR metrics and organisational profitability are difficult to substantiate as there may be different interpretations of the data. For example, if annual employee wastage (see later) is calculated to be 15 per cent, should the CEO be concerned and take actions to reduce it? The response will inevitably depend on comparisons with wastage rates in competitor organisations, with overall labour market rates, or against the historical rates of the organisation. Similar dilemmas exist in relation to accident rates, absenteeism, sick leave and training. These are all strategic and operational issues which require comprehensive analyses of the data from HR metrics, and subsequent discussions between executives, HR professionals and line managers.

Some of the pitfalls associated with the use of HR metrics include the failure of HR professionals to clearly understand or promote the linkage between them and the organisational strategy; a lack of understanding of the potential value of HR metrics by senior executives and/or line managers; and overly complex and difficult to implement measures. Exhibit 13.6 illustrates the ways in which the BT (British Telecom) Group uses HR metrics to link its HR and business strategies.

Exhibit 13.6 Valuing human capital – BT's new initiatives

The BT Group is the world's leading provider of voice and data communication solutions throughout Europe, America and the Asia Pacific. In recent years it has undertaken sophisticated measurement techniques to assess the value of its human capital assets and to measure its contributions. While some measures have been employed throughout the business, BT introduced a comprehensive program which ranged from HR initiatives such as reducing absenteeism to value-orientated measures. It built a human capital balance sheet, applying financial reporting to its employee base. The analysis enabled BT to view employee value through fixed and variable cost perspectives. From the analysis, BT determined that employee absence was on average 13 days per year (approximately 89 million British Pounds), but that sick leave (as a significant component of absence) could be reduced to three days a year when work–life balance or remote working options (see Chapter 2) initiatives were implemented.

In addition, BT established 13 HR metrics to be used by all business units. These included the following:

- Human Investment Ratio

- Wealth created per full-time employee (FTE)

- Profit created per revenue created per FTE

- Cost per FTE

- Ratio of remuneration to revenue

- Average remuneration
- Absenteeism rates
- Voluntary resignation rates
- Executive stability rates
- FTE per department as a proportion of total FTEs
- HR departmental cost per FTE
- Graduate retention rate.

BT Group also adopted a technique which it called Economic Value Added (EVA), which aimed to measure the overall organisational performance against the cost of employed capital.

Source: Lyle Potgieter and Peter Vlant, Peoplestreme.com, 2006.

Employee wastage and turnover rates

There is considerable debate about the meaning of the terms 'HR wastage' and 'turnover'. Sometimes they are used interchangeably, and at other times wastage is not considered separately. 'Wastage' generally refers to the rate (or ratio) of employees who leave an organisation, through resignation, retirement or death during specified periods (i.e. movement out of an organisation). Turnover, on the other hand, concerns human resource movement within organisations (i.e. employees moving from job to job through transfer, promotion or relocation). Both measures can indicate the effectiveness of HRM programs and activities, as well as the overall health of an organisation, in satisfaction, morale and productivity terms.

The difficulty with both measures, however, is that each organisation will have different 'healthy' and 'unhealthy' rates of both turnover and wastage. Industry standards, often provided by industry associations – such as the Australian Chamber of Commerce and Industry and the Australian Bureau of Statistics – can be helpful in comparisons, but internal wastage and turnover analyses over historical periods are more useful, indicating employee trends in response to organisational changes.

It may, for example, be healthy to have high wastage levels in harsh economic times, or when many senior managers are simultaneously nearing retirement age. Opportunities for improved career paths, the introduction of new blood, or job rationalisation and cost reductions may be thus provided. On the other hand, highly competitive industries, such as the information technology sector during the 1980s and 1990s, may suffer from abnormally high wastage rates due to more attractive salary packages offered elsewhere. Similarly, employee turnover can be too high or too low, depending on career development programs, unsatisfactory working conditions and supervision, reduced promotional opportunities and high unemployment levels.

Human resource managers, in consultation with senior and line management and employees themselves, need to establish healthy levels of both turnover and wastage, in the context of internal and external factors; determine relevant costs and benefits; and design programs to ensure that wastage and turnover levels are kept within optimal limits. As Peter Howes suggests:

> using a combination of national and industry benchmarks and organisation-specific business knowledge, HR managers (should) be able to calculate the cost of employee-initiated 'turnover' (wastage) and identify the implications this has for the organisation.[36]

Costs of wastage

Replacing an employee can be time-consuming and expensive. Costs can generally be broken down into:

- separation costs for the departing employee
- replacement costs
- training costs for the new employee.

Several US studies have estimated wastage costs at two to three times the monthly salary of the departing employee. These do not include indirect costs such as low productivity prior to departure, lower morale and overtime for other employees. Consequently, reducing wastage levels can result in significant savings to an organisation. A study by the Australian Automotive Industry Council discovered wastage levels of 11 to 61 per cent annually among its members, with a median level of 28 per cent.[37] These levels increased in large, expanding organisations and decreased with industry downturns.

In this study, costs were estimated to be approximately $6 600 for non-trade employees, rising to $71 000 for managers.[38] An interesting outcome of the study was that wastage, combined with employee absenteeism, added an estimated $850 to the cost of each car produced in Australia. A similar survey in the Australian manufacturing industry calculates that each blue-collar resignation costs $5 000, and each white-collar worker $15 000.[39]

Exhibit 13.7 illustrates some of the positive and negative results of employee wastage.

Exhibit 13.7   Consequences of employee wastage

	Consequences for organisation	**Consequences for leavers**
Negative consequences	• Economic costs for separation, replacement, and training • Productivity losses • Impaired service quality • Lost business opportunities • Increased administrative burden • Demoralisation of stayers	• Forfeit seniority and fringe benefits • Transition stress in new job • Relocation costs • Terminate personal and family social network • Loss of valued community services • Disrupt spouse's career
Positive consequences	• Displace poor performers and employees with job burnout • Infusion of new knowledge and technology by replacements • New business ventures • Labour cost savings • Enhanced promotional opportunity for stayers • Empowerment of stayers	• Obtain better job elsewhere • Avoid stressful former job • Renewed commitment to work • Pursue outside endeavours • Relocate to a more desirable community • Improve spouse's career

Source: Mobley W. 1982. *Employee turnover: Causes, consequences, and control*, Reading, MA, Addison-Wesley.

Calculating employee wastage and turnover levels

The wastage and turnover levels of sections, departments and the entire organisation act as indicators of employee morale and job satisfaction. Accordingly, they also indicate the success, or otherwise, of HRM programs of recruitment and selection, training and development, career development and reward systems, and consequent organisational costs and benefits.

Turnover and wastage levels are usually measured by similar formulae:

$$\text{Turnover} = \frac{\text{Number of (internal) job leavers in period}}{\text{Average number of employees}} \times 100$$

$$\text{Wastage} = \frac{\text{Number of separations in a period}}{\text{Average number of employees}} \times 100$$

These rates may be assessed monthly, quarterly, half yearly or annually. Thus, if there were 25 separations during a month and the average number of employees was 500, the wastage rate would be:

$$\frac{25 \times 100}{500} = 5\%$$

Another method of calculating controllable wastage levels is to separate avoidable from unavoidable employee departures. Unavoidable separations are those occurring for reasons over which the organisation has no control (e.g. pregnancy, illness, death).

Controllable wastage rate is then calculated as:

$$\frac{\text{Number of separations – unavoidable separations}}{\text{Average of employees}} \times 100$$

This method yields what is probably the most significant measure of the effectiveness of the HR program, since it can direct attention to that proportion of employee departure which management has the most opportunity to control, by means of better selection, training, supervision, improved working conditions, better wages and opportunities for advancement.

The authors have experience of a manufacturing organisation in an outer suburb of an Australian capital city, which reported 87 per cent wastage rates annually among its process workers. The HR manager was, understandably, very concerned about the high rate compared to industry standards, but felt that her priorities had to be with constantly recruiting new employees to fill the job vacancies. She might have been more effective had she spent some time assessing the causes of this abnormally high rate.

A further indication of the health of the organisation may be gleaned by using a more positive stability index. This gives a picture of the proportion of employees who have stayed in the organisation over different periods and is calculated thus:

$$\text{Stability index} = \frac{\text{Number of employees with over one year's service}}{\text{Total number of employees one year ago}} \times 100$$

One Australian writer has suggested a formula for costing the dollar impact on organisations of employee wastage. He proposes the following equation:

Wastage cost = W\$ + D + R

where **W\$** = wastage dollars during the leaving period (including separation costs, time, etc.)

D = direct training costs (including trainers, consultants, room and equipment, wages and salaries, etc.)

R = recruitment costs (internal and external).[34]

Of course all these equations reflect quantitative rather than qualitative factors. The quality of employees is also an important consideration and requires attention in different ways, which will be discussed subsequently.

Determining causes of turnover and wastage

Many theoretical models attempt to explain the reasons why employees choose to leave their organisations, due to unfavourable jobs or workplaces, or more attractive alternatives. Some of these models have been illustrated (see Exhibits 13.8 and 13.9). All of them have common themes:

- that employees generally take some time to decide to leave, during which time astute employers can deal with their concerns (if so desired)

- that the intention to leave usually derives from dissatisfaction with the job itself (e.g. status, career opportunities, rewards systems, supervision or communication)

- that wastage is clearly related to the availability of alternative employment opportunities outside the organisation.

Exhibit 13.8   Investment model of turnover

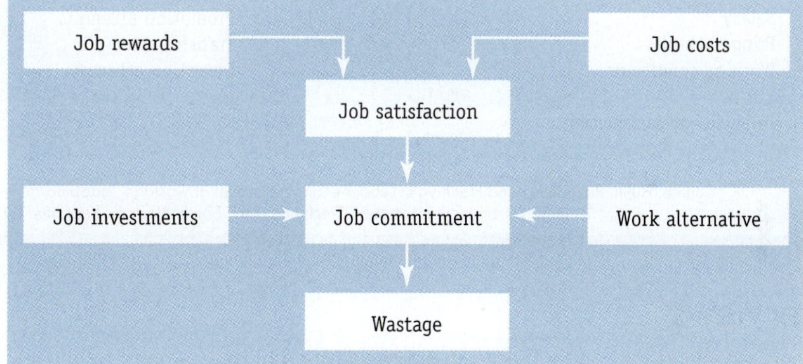

Source: Adapted from Rusbult and Farrell's 'Investment model of turnover' in Hom P., Griffeth R. 1995. *Employee turnover.* Reprinted with permission of South-Western, a division of Thomson Learning: www.thomsonrights.com.

As Exhibit 13.9 shows, however, relevant causal factors may be quite complex, and some employees may choose 'psychological withdrawal' rather than actual departure. This decision can cause even more harm to their organisation.

Some authors suggest that 'boredom' with the job can ultimately result in employee wastage, but that recognition of this cause can be effectively dealt with by proactive human resource management techniques.[40] As an example, the Australian Protection Service, which provides security services to airports and diplomatic consulates, has resolved problems of employee 'boredom' by an integrated program of communication between work groups and their supervisors, training programs for supervisors (e.g. conflict-resolution, coaching, mentoring, career development), increased work variety systems, and recruitment programs to clearly 'match' employee desires and skills with designated jobs.[41]

Two principal methods are available for organisations and their HR managers to determine actual (and potential) causes for employee departure:

- exit interviews

- employee attitude surveys.

Exhibit 13.9　Labour-economic model of wastage

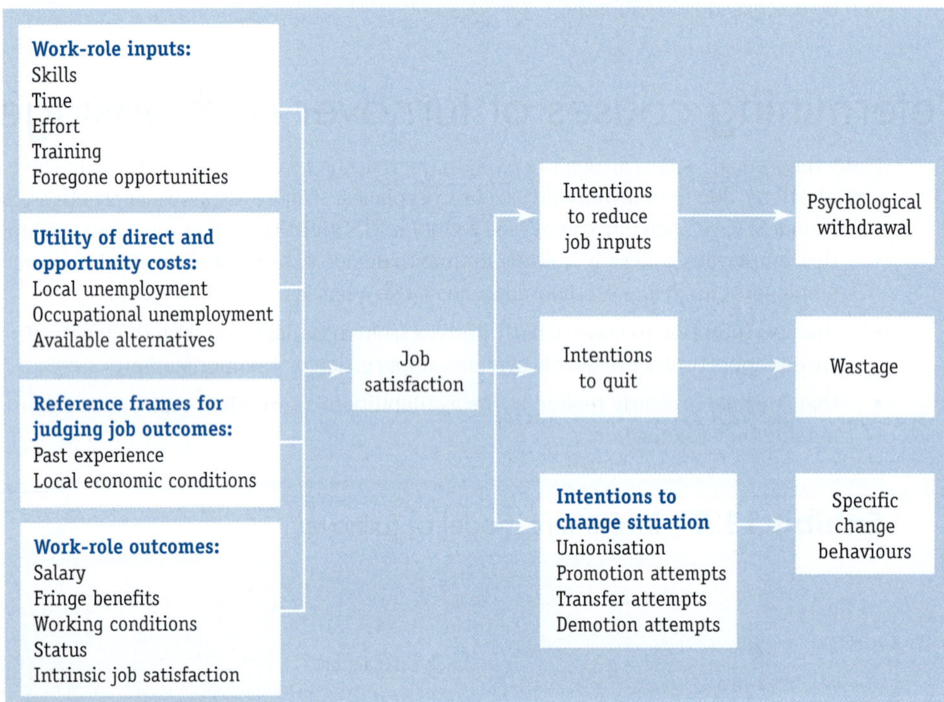

Source: Hulin, Roznowski and Hachiya's 'Labour-economic model of wastage', adapted from Hom P., Griffeth R. 1995. *Employee turnover*, Cincinnati, OH, South-Western. Reprinted by permission of Peter Hom.

Exit interviews

Some organisations conduct exit interviews with employees who have chosen to notify their resignation. They may include all such employees, or only the most crucial categories of employees.

Unfortunately, a large number of Australian organisations fail to examine why employees choose to resign, either because 'an employee's decision to leave is often regarded as a sign of infidelity or even treachery',[42] or through fear of confrontation. If exit interviews are not routinely conducted, the organisation may lose valuable feedback on its overall functioning, and the identification of problem areas. Exit interviews also provide an opportunity to 'coax back a good employee who may be reluctant to leave but is being driven by financial or career reasons'.[43]

Exit interviews are usually divided into two distinct phases: administrative and fact-finding. Administrative issues include details of severance payments, the return of identity cards, passes and keys. Fact-finding strategies, usually standardised for all interviews, cover areas such as:

- reasons for departure (positive and negative)
- relationships with supervisors
- fairness of pay, training, career development and performance appraisal programs
- working conditions
- things liked best (and least) about the job and the organisation
- communication issues
- suggestions for improvement.

A combination of open-ended, hypothetical and probing questions is likely to elicit the most useful responses from departing employees. The choice of exit interviewer is also important as 'the difficulty of obtaining accurate feedback from disgruntled employees is compounded if the exit interviewer is perceived as biased or inconsistent'.[44] Generally, the HR department, rather than the employee's immediate supervisor, is more suitable for conducting such interviews due to their perceived neutrality, and their ability to collate information from many exit interviews.

Exit interviews can be costly and time-consuming, but extensive and invaluable information can be collected by the astute HR practitioner for subsequent programs. It is also a way of gathering qualitative data, to be used in conjunction with quantitative information, for future and more effective human resource planning and management. The validity of the reasons given by employees for their resignations must be treated with some caution. Many employees prefer to leave on good terms and may consider frank discussion detrimental to their interests.

Some organisations employ post-exit interviews, conducted several months after employees leave, to overcome this problem. Response rates to such post-exit interviews, by mail or telephone, are often low and unrepresentative.

Employee attitude surveys

A qualitative method of gathering information about employee levels of satisfaction while still in their jobs involves the use of employee attitude (or opinion) surveys. Such surveys are potentially more useful than exit interviews as they can provide information on factors such as poor job design, inadequate supervision and communication. By identifying and rectifying problem areas, the tide of future resignations may be effectively stemmed.

Employee attitude surveys (EASs) are usually conducted on an organisation-wide or workplace basis, and may involve the administration of a questionnaire or the use of interviews. EASs have been reported to be quite widely used in US organisations,[45] and Australian organisations (e.g. Westpac, BHP, Lion Nathan, Johnson & Johnson) are increasingly taking advantage of this opportunity to audit employee attitudes towards organisational issues such as communication, motivation, the quality of supervision, pay and benefits. As evidence of this, there are now several HR consultancy companies in Australia that specialise in such surveys (e.g. Quantum Management International, Victoria; Hinds Workforce Research, NSW; Cammeray Services, Qld; and Indrad Services, WA).

Substantial benefits can accrue from a well-conducted EAS, including a large number of usable development suggestions, and evidence for changes in HR policy and practice. Perhaps most importantly, such surveys represent 'a clear demonstration of management concern and willingness to involve staff in the decision-making processes of the company'.[46] In an era of increasing employee consultation and participation on industrial relations issues, such surveys can aid employee commitment and enhance productivity.

To be effective however, EASs need to be more than simply window dressing. Poorly planned or administered surveys can, in fact, be counter-productive. An EAS requires a genuine commitment on the part of management and unions to survey objectives and consequences. Objectives must be clear, participants guaranteed confidentiality and outcomes seen to be acted upon. The timing of employee attitude surveys and the subsequent implementation of remedial schemes is also crucial. EASs naturally arouse employee expectations. If such expectations are not soon satisfied, employees may become even more cynical and less receptive to subsequent activities.

Lake also suggests that many EASs fail to achieve their objectives because they focus on the collection of information at the expense of consideration of its uses; the information collected is not adequately shared with line managers who must implement any required changes; and, due to their concentration on employees' attitudes, they sometimes neglect important practical issues such as the quality of customer service, delivery systems and operational processes.[47]

Absenteeism

While wastage and turnover rates are often significant indicators of the overall health of organisations and their human resources, the frequency of employee absences from the workplace may also indicate the state of the work environment and the effectiveness of the HR program. Absenteeism is difficult to define as it can be authorised (e.g. sickness, accidents), or unauthorised (e.g. long lunch hours, long weekends) and can be single or repeated, measured in minutes, hours, days or longer periods. Perhaps the most embracing definition of absenteeism is that it is 'any failure of an employee to report for, or to remain at work as scheduled, regardless of the reason'.[48]

This definition excludes programmed holiday or jury leave, but includes absences due to sickness and accidents. The task for supervisors and HR practitioners is to separate uncontrollable from controllable causes of employee absence, to measure the relevant rates, and to reduce the frequency, and associated costs, of unnecessary or avoidable absence. Some employers (e.g. Westpac) have changed their absence recording systems from daily to hourly periods to discourage unnecessary leave and to allow easier costing of its impact. Others have established unlimited sick leave systems (e.g. Optus, Integral Energy), based upon trust between employers and employees, and some of these have resulted in significant reductions in the frequency and costs of leave taken. The success of such a system will inevitably depend on the culture of the organisation.

Costs of absenteeism

Traditional accounting and HR information management systems often do not generate data that accurately reflect the costs of absenteeism. To call management's attention to the severity of the problem, and to promote HR accountability, absenteeism can be translated into dollar costs.

Some national surveys of absence rates in Australian industry have (conservatively) estimated average rates to be around 4 per cent annually,[49] with significant differences between sectors and within particular organisations. The costs of absenteeism include the pay and benefits of the absent employee, associated supervisory costs involved in counselling frequently absent employees, writing relevant reports and, in extreme circumstances, recruiting and training replacement employees. One study suggests that the overall costs of absenteeism in Australian industry in 1990 amounted to $3.2 billion for paid sick leave, $3.1 billion for permanent surplus staff, and $0.64 billion in overtime and temporary labour costs (overall $6.9 billion).[50]

A model for identifying the causes of, and the appropriate solutions to, employee absences (or labour withdrawal) is illustrated in Exhibit 13.10. The main principle behind this model is that modifications to HR practices such as work-job design, supervisory, training and career or remuneration systems will yield improved results in employee satisfaction, and thus less absenteeism or eventual turnover and wastage.

One way of estimating the overall costs of absenteeism to an organisation is based on the combination (hourly weighted) of average salary, costs of employee benefits, supervision and incidental costs. For a hypothetical company of 1 200 employees with 78 000 person-hours lost to absenteeism, the total cost was found to be $560 886. When this figure is divided by 1 200, the cost is $467.71 per employee per period covered.[51] (In this example the absent workers were paid. If absent workers were not paid, their salary figures are omitted from the calculation.)

Calculating absenteeism rates

It is advisable for management, and especially the HR manager, to determine the seriousness of absenteeism by maintaining individual and departmental attendance records and by calculating

Exhibit 13.10   Summary of labour withdrawal model

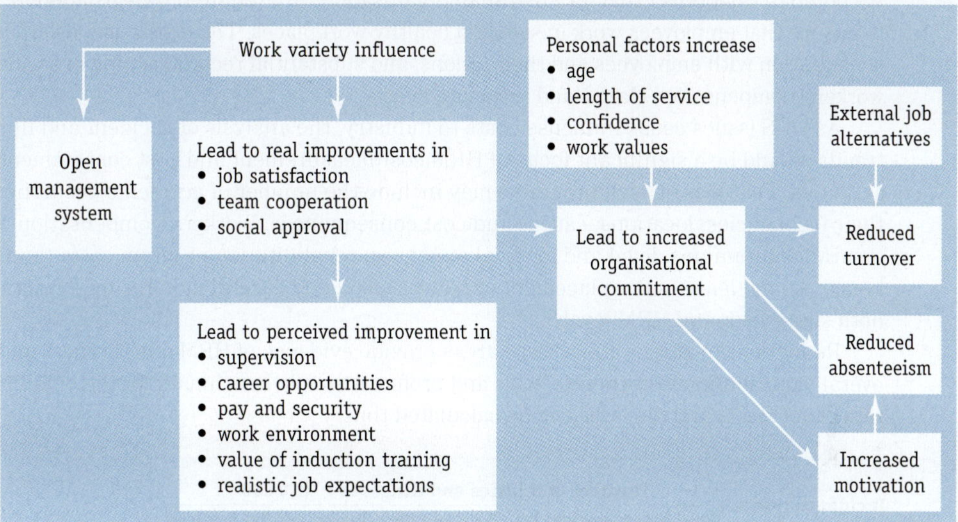

Source: Australian Manufacturing Council 1990. *Labour turnover on absenteeism costs and causes in the Australian automotive industry*, copyright Commonwealth of Australia, reproduced by permission.

absenteeism rates. The Productivity Council of Australia suggests that the following formulae may be useful:

$$\text{Absence frequency} = \frac{\text{total number of separate absences}}{\text{average strength of the workforce}}$$

$$\text{Absence rate} = \frac{\text{total labour hours lost}}{\text{total labour hours rostered}} \times 100$$

Thus, if an organisation registered 320 separate absences during a period when its employees numbered 160, then its frequency rate would be:

$$\frac{320}{160} = 2$$

If, of the 320 absences, each was of seven hours' duration, and the normal monthly hours for each employee were 160, then the relevant absence rate would be:

$$\frac{320 \times 7}{160 \times 160} \times \frac{100}{1} = 8.75\%$$

Reducing absenteeism

While an employer may find that absenteeism rates and costs are within an acceptable range, it is always advisable to monitor trends in employee absence, and isolate areas of high absenteeism.

Overall absence trend analysis is most effectively carried out by HR managers, using a comprehensive HRIMS (see Chapter 4), but supervisors play a crucial role in identifying frequent individual and group absentees and effectively correcting their attendance by timely and appropriate intervention. Such action may involve individual counselling, job and work redesign, supervisor training, career development programs and improved pay or working conditions.

Occupational injuries and illnesses

We noted in Chapter 11 that all Australian organisations are required by legislation in all states to ensure that employees work in safe and healthy workplaces. The legislation also requires consultation with employees and their unions, and substantial record keeping of accidents, workers' compensation claims and associated costs.

As OHS issues cause immense costs to industry, the analysis of accident and illness trends should be a significant focus of HRM cost measurement and cost containment activities. Features of such programs may include the number of accidents occurring, their frequencies, locations, causes and cost consequences. Workers' compensation claims, insurance premiums, legal and medical expenses, rehabilitation program costs (and dollar benefits), and leave and replacement expenses also need careful monitoring, preferably at both supervisor and HRM levels.

Reductions in any, or all, of these areas provide evidence of HRM effectiveness and their overall contribution to corporate goals and profits. A simple benchmark for the organisational rate of accidents and illnesses can be calculated thus:

$$\text{Incidence rate} = \frac{\text{Number of injuries and illnesses} \times 200\,000}{\text{Total hours worked by all employees during period covered}}$$

(Note: 200 000 equals the base for 100 full-time workers who work 40 hours a week, 50 weeks a year.)

Incidence rates can help to provide a basis for making comparisons with other organisations doing similar work, or for the same organisation over different periods. Sections, departments and branches of organisations can be similarly compared.

Auditing HRM

Australian management has been primarily concerned with the efficient and economic use of financial and material resources in the achievement of organisational goals. In the last two decades, however, increasing attention has been given to human resources and the contribution they make to the achievement of organisational success. The earliest approaches attempted to apply standard accounting techniques to human resource management programs – with limited success, as they failed to take adequate account of the complexity of HRM. Balance sheets could not, for example, account for the dollar value of employee morale, job satisfaction or communication factors.

More recent attempts to quantify, and justify, HRM programs aim to be broader in their approach. They include:

- human resource accounting
- traditional cost–benefit analysis
- global input-output ratios
- decision-focused cost–benefit analysis
- benchmarking
- behaviour costing
- program costing
- HR audits.[52]

Our discussion will be limited to the HR audit strategy, as other techniques are too complex for adequate discussion here. We will discuss program costing and benchmarking later in this chapter. A comprehensive HR audit will also use some (or all) of the above methods. Exhibit 13.11 displays an overall model linking methods of HR auditing with the audits of all other organisational managers, and overall organisational effectiveness.

Exhibit 13.11 Integrative model of HR effectiveness

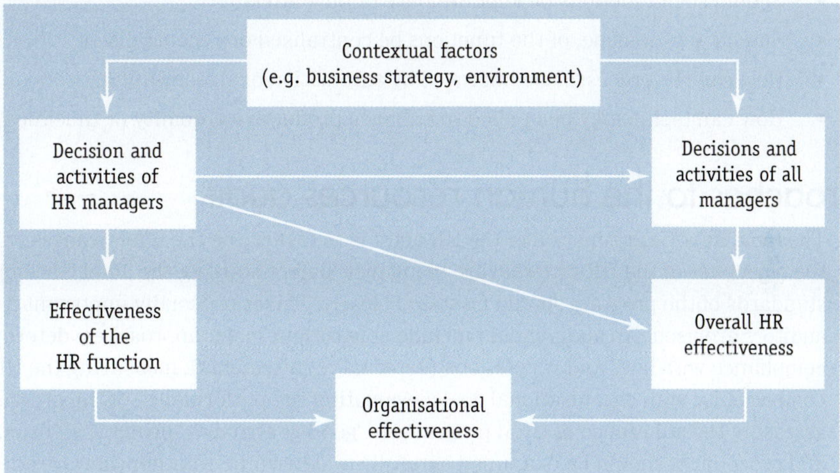

Source: Tsui A.S., Gomez L.R. 1988. 'Evaluating human resource effectiveness', in Dyer L. (ed.), *Human resource management: Evolving roles and responsibilities*, Washington DC, The Bureau of National Affairs.

Essentially, the HR audit is a systematic process of obtaining and evaluating evidence about the performance of human resource management, to ensure clear relationships between its goals and its outcomes. The HR audit can enhance the professionalism of the HR function and demonstrate its specific contributions to organisational effectiveness, productivity and profitability.

The HR audit provides an opportunity to:

- evaluate the effectiveness of HR functions, including cost-effectiveness

- ensure compliance with laws, policies, regulations and procedures

- set guidelines for establishing standards

- promote change and creativity

- assess the financial advantages and disadvantages of HR functions (against national and industry benchmarks)

- bring HR and line functions closer

- improve the quality, image and contributions of the HR function and its staff

- focus HR staff on crucial HR issues.

If an organisation is to remain competitive, it must undergo continual change. An audit of its HR program can help managers identify variations between actual and expected or desired conditions. The audit becomes a database stimulus for change. Not only can the audit facilitate change, but it can also be used as an instrument of change. For example, if it is desirable that the HR manager make changes in HR programs, an audit can be used as a neutral medium for the views of supervisors, peers and subordinates. Multiple pressures for change are thus brought upon reluctant managers.

In essence, the purpose of HR audits, especially in relation to the measurement and financial accountability of HR functions, is '… that it will indicate those areas of HR practice that have the most potential for return on investment'.[53]

The outcomes of HR audits can assist HR planners (see Chapter 4) by providing answers to the following questions:

- Should all current HR functions be maintained as they are, be modified or even be eliminated?
- Should such functions be kept in-house or outsourced?
- Should any, or some, of the functions be centralised or decentralised?
- How can HR processes be improved by automation or streamlining?
- How can technology be applied to enhance productivity, quality or timelines?[54]

Approaches to the human resources audit

The most important function of the HR audit is to determine the effectiveness with which the objectives of the HR program are being met. Before starting the audit, the objectives and standards of the program should be stated clearly. This is especially important if external auditors are used. An audit should include at least four major approaches: determining compliance with laws and regulations (external requirements); measuring the HR program's compatibility with organisational goals; evaluating the performance of the program; and assessing the adherence of HRM programs to 'good governance' principles. In addition, policies and procedures should be examined carefully to determine whether they are adequate in meeting objectives. Some audits may also include comparative analyses with similar organisations or industry standards, where available.

Determining compliance with laws and regulations

As we have noted throughout this book, the number of laws and regulations affecting HRM has increased dramatically in recent years. Organisations typically establish programs and procedures for achieving compliance with them. Top management needs to be aware of the manner in which managers at all levels are complying with the laws and regulations. Equal employment opportunity, safety and health, and superannuation programs are among the compliance areas often investigated in comprehensive audits.

Employers are required to maintain records for these programs in specified formats for examination by compliance investigators from Australian government and state agencies. In addition, many employers have learned to keep as much current information as possible about their performance in order to avoid last-minute crises in data-gathering projects.

Employers should take a proactive approach to compliance with laws and regulations. It is important not only to establish effective policies and procedures but also to make sure that subordinates understand them thoroughly. Too often it is assumed that workers know all about the policies and procedures that relate to their job or work environment. Just as employees are tested on their understanding of matters related to safety and security, their understanding of other relevant matters should be audited.

Measuring compatibility with organisational goals

For many years, managers of HR departments were viewed by top management as being out of touch with the goals of the organisation. In the past several years, however, labour costs, government intervention and recognition of the need for greater productivity have caused executives to revise their view of the importance of the HR function.

The process of setting goals requires close coordination with top management. This ensures that the policies and procedures of the HR department are consistent with top management's goals and objectives. The audit provides an opportunity to assess the extent to which objectives are being met and to revise policies and procedures accordingly.

Evaluating program performance

Each of the functional areas of HRM that have been described in detail throughout this book should help to meet the overall objectives of an HR program. It is important, therefore, to audit each of these functions to determine how effectively and economically they are being performed. Since it is not possible to discuss in this text all the details involved in the audit of each functional area, we suggest in Exhibit 13.12 the general types of questions that should be answered in an audit. As an example, an audit of employment contracts may reveal rigidity in their provisions, which makes it difficult for the organisation to recruit as flexibly as it may need to do in future economic and operating conditions. Similarly, a review of employee disciplinary procedures may indicate that supervisors do not understand or apply them effectively and thus impede organisational growth and development by maintaining negligent or inefficient employees. The sources of in-house information, usually records and reports that are available for use in the audit, are also included in the exhibit.

Exhibit 13.12 Auditing the major functions in HRM

Human resource function	Source of information
Planning and recruitment	
• Do job descriptions contain bona fide occupational qualification?	• HR budgets
• Are job descriptions accurate, periodically reviewed and updated?	• Recruitment cost data
• Are there any human resources that are not being fully utilised?	• Job descriptions and person specifications
• Is the affirmative action program achieving its goals?	• Hiring rate
• How effective is the recruiting process?	
• How productive are the recruiters?	
Selection	
• How valid are selection techniques?	• Employment interview records
• Is there evidence of discrimination in hiring?	• Applicant rejection records
• Are interviewers familiar with the job requirements?	
• Can interviewers recognise those questions that are unacceptable in a job interview?	• Transfer requests
• Are tests job related and free from bias?	• Discrimination complaints
• How do hiring costs compare with those of other organisations?	
Training and development	
• How effective are training programs in increasing productivity and improving the quality of employee performance?	• Training costs data
• Are there sufficient opportunities for women and minorities to advance into management positions?	• Production records
• What is the cost of training per person hour of instruction?	• Accident records
• What is the relationship between training costs and accidents?	• Quality control records

Human resource function	Source of information
Performance appraisal	
• Are the performance standards objective and job related? • Do the appraisal methods emphasise performance rather than traits? • Are the appraisers adequately trained and thoroughly familiar with the employee's work? • Are the appraisals documented and reviewed with employees? • Are the performance appraisal data assembled in such form that they can be used to validate tests and other selection procedures?	• Performance appraisal records • Production records • Appraisal interview records • Attendance records • Disciplinary action results
Salary and benefits	
• Does the pay system, including incentive plans, attract employees and motivate them to achieve organisational goals? • Is the choice of weights and factors in job evaluation sound and properly documented? • Do benefits and costs compare favourably with those of similar organisations?	• Wages and benefit data • Wage survey records • Turnover and wastage records • Cost of living surveys
Industrial relations	
• Are supervisors trained to handle grievances effectively? • Is there ongoing preparation for award restructuring and enterprise bargaining? • What is the record of the number and types of grievances, and what percentage of grievances have gone to arbitration? • What percentage of dismissals have been challenged?	• Grievance records • Arbitration data • Industrial action records

Source: From Suggett D., Goodsir B., Pryor S., 2000. *Corporate Community Involvement: Establishing a business case*, Canberra, Centre for Corporate Public Affairs, p. 57.

Most of the sources of information listed in Exhibit 13.12 yield statistical data that is readily available in many organisations. Where human resource information systems are being utilised, such information can be kept current for analysis and reporting, and should be used. We have made numerous references throughout the book to the increased use of HRIMS in HRM. One can expect even greater use of such information systems in carrying out the various HR audit functions.

As valuable as the information sources listed in Exhibit 13.12 are in measuring the effectiveness of the major HRM functions, over-reliance on quantitative measures may yield conclusions that seem objectively valid but fail to assess whether HR clients are really satisfied with the services they receive. Supplementary audit methods may include periodic studies of clients' perceptions of HR services. Clients may include line and senior managers, employees, applicants, customers or even union officials. User reactions may be obtained through employee and customer attitude surveys, discussions with employees, group meetings, manager and supervisor comments.

Corporate governance and corporate social responsibility

The twin issues of corporate governance and corporate social responsibility (CSR) have become important issues in Australia over recent years as a consequence of a number of company collapses (due in part to mismanagement or unethical behaviour); and a growing recognition that companies also have responsibilities to the wider communities in which they operate. There have been numerous examples in Australia and elsewhere of problems caused by abuses in the payment of CEOs and their boards, including unjustifiable bonuses, shareholdings and separation payments, during organisational downturns (e.g. Commonwealth Bank, HIH

Insurance, Ansett Airlines). To avoid future such occurrences, the Australian Stock Exchange (ASX) released a set of good governance principles for business. As the list below shows, many of the principles apply directly to HRM programs.

1 Structure the board to add value.

2 Promote ethical and responsible decision-making.

3 Safeguard integrity in financial reporting.

4 Make timely and balanced disclosure.

5 Respect the rights of shareholders.

6 Recognise and manage risk.

7 Encourage enhanced performance.

8 Remunerate fairly and responsibly.

9 Recognise the legitimate interests of stakeholders.

Source: Cooper J., Hogarth C. 2003. 'Good management', *hrmonthly*, October, p. 38.

An audit of HRM programs such as job design, recruitment and selection, HRD, performance management, remuneration and OHS would be incomplete, and even potentially negligent, without the evaluation of their adherence to good governance principles.

In addition to these ASX principles, Standards Australia has developed guidelines to '… assist HR practitioners to evaluate whether to implement a particular practice and to assist them in locating further information to build a business case'.[55] The Macquarie Graduate School of Management has recently established a body to assess the good governance and social responsibility ratings of Australian employers, along similar lines to the existing financial rating systems.

Corporate social responsibility is a newer concept which encompasses 'the commitment of business to contribute to sustainable economic development, working with employees, their families, the local community and society at large to improve their quality of life'.[56] It implies that companies should contribute to the economic sustainability of communities by considering the social and environmental consequences of their business decisions and practices. Typically, CSR strategies and policies are supported by 'triple bottom line' audits which include the financial, social and environmental impacts of organisations. There is now a Global Reporting Initiative (GRI)[57], and in Australia, a senate sub-committee (2006) has been convened. News report 13.2 illustrates the way in which some Australian organisations have implemented CSR programmes.

NRMA: being the service provider of choice

NRMA is over 75 years old. It was established as a mutual to assist stranded motorists and promote good quality roads. The organisation is now one of Australia's largest general insurers and financial service providers as well as being known as an inexpensive and efficient roadside service. Nevertheless, NRMA is still synonymous in peoples' minds with 'help' and accordingly receives a high volume of requests for donations and sponsorship.

The proposals mostly refer to NRMA's reputation for offering and providing help. NRMA has around 2.4 million members, 5000 employees, and comprises 20 companies with new businesses operating, outside of the traditional NSW home, in Victoria, Queensland, South Australia and Western Australia.

Community involvement objective

Sponsorships and community relations are regarded as a business strategy with both short-term and longer-term goals. Shorter term marketing and promotional outcomes are, for example, brand awareness and adding value to the brand. Longer-term outcomes are concerned with meeting community expectations, understanding and responding to social problems and developing staff teamwork and camaraderie.

The longer-term business benefits anticipated from responding to the social and political environment are to be 'the service provider of choice, the employer of choice, the neighbour of choice, and the investment of choice'.

Source: Adapted from Suggett D., Goodsir B., Pryor S. 2000, *Corporate Community Involvement: Establishing a Business Case*, Canberra, Centre for Corporate Public Affairs, p. 57.

Both good corporate governance and CSR can add considerable value to HRM functions such as recruitment and retention, especially in the global talent 'war', and can contribute to the minimisation of the adverse reputational impacts of corporate indiscretions. HR professionals will usually be involved in both issues in collaboration with other organisational managers. Donaldson suggests that their major contribution is to '… create a "success profile"… which includes the core competency set, organisational values (such as integrity) which help guide selection and assessment'.[58] In addition, '… if HR is going to help when it comes to governance, it needs to develop a people strategy that's aligned to the business strategy'.[59]

Measuring human resource program costs

Management is typically interested in the costs of activities required to meet HR objectives. Standard cost accounting procedures can be applied to all HRM functions. Cost savings may be demonstrated in wage and salary policies and procedures, employee benefits, recruitment, training and management development programs.

In establishing a program for measuring HR costs, it is important to enlist the participation of the HR staff. Many staff members will not be measurement-oriented. At first they may not accept that all HRM functions are measurable and that their cost can be determined and related to the benefits that accrue to the organisation. Through participative approaches the staff can identify a large number of measurable activities that can be included in formulae for measuring cost. Costs of induction, for example, can be calculated by employee and by department. The cost of various recruiting and selection procedures can likewise be computed. For example, the source cost per recruit (SC/R) can be calculated by the following formula:

$$\text{SC/R} = \text{AC} + \text{AF} + \text{NC/R}$$

where **AC** = advertising costs, total monthly expenditure (e.g. $28 000)

AF = agency fees, total for the month (e.g. $19 000)

NC = no-costs applicants, walk-in, non-profit agencies, etc. (e.g . $0)

R = total recruits (e.g. 119)

Substituting the example numbers in the formula:

$$\text{SC/R} = \$28\ 000 + \$19\ 000 + \$0/119$$

$$= \$47\ 000/119$$

$$= \$395 \text{ (source cost of recruiting per recruit).}$$

Exhibit 13.13   Key performance measures for HR functions

Recruitment and wastage		Training and development	
Recruitment rate (external)		**Training cost**	
Employees	• Number of external recruits hired divided by the average number of fulltime employees (FTEs) for the period (suggest quarterly basis)	Total training cost Employees Training time Total training hours Employees	• Total training costs divided by average number of FTEs • Total hours of training undertaken by all employees, divided by total FTEs
Recruitment efficiency		**Occupational health and safety (OH&S)**	
Recruitment cost External recruits	• Total external costs divided by the number of employees recruited by the organisation in a quarter	Total OH&S costs Employees	• Total OH&S costs, divided by the number of FTEs
Temporary factors		**Incidence rate**	
No. of temporary contractors Total employees	• Total number of temporaries or contractors to total number of employees (include temporaries/contractors) based on FTEs	Occurrence x 100 Employee	• The number of new lost-time deaths, injuries and diseases per 100 employees (quarterly)
Wastage rate		**Industrial relations disruption rate**	
External recruits Terminations	• Total external recruits divided by total terminations	Work days lost Total work days available	• The equivalent of total number of days lost due to industrial disputes, divided by total available work days by award FTEs (quarterly)

Source: Corrigan J., Daidonis M., Tibbits G. 1996. 'Accounting for Human Resources', *Management Accounting Issues Report 2*, March, Sydney, CPA, p. 6 (FTE stands for 'full-time equivalent' employees).

Exhibit 13.13 illustrates how simple costing formulae can be applied to HRM functions such as recruitment, training and development, occupational health and safety, and industrial relations.

While these formulae give a gross estimate of the overall costs of HRM functions, McBride and Dowling suggest an even more detailed approach, which involves identifying both the direct and the indirect costs of all the activities involved, assessing total annual, hourly and unit proportions.[60] As an example, they suggest that all recruitment programs involve a multitude of often hidden costs. These include supervisory and HR time and costs associated with:

- job definition, the preparation of job descriptions and person specifications

- advertising media choice, advertisement design and placement costs

- administrative activities (e.g. form preparation, handling applicant responses, acknowledgements and inquiries)

- short-listing, interviews, selection and notifications of successful and unsuccessful applicants

- testing (skills, aptitude and medical)

- induction and retraining programs

- pay and salary arrangements, relocation costs.

These can be largely considered direct costs of recruitment. Indirect costs may include the costs of workstations (e.g. furniture, equipment), office space and tools, as well as the ancillary facilities provided by the organisation for all employees (e.g. canteens, medical and welfare programs, payroll processing, and workers' compensation premiums). Total recruitment costs are then calculated by adding direct and (proportionate) indirect costs, and can be estimated for all annual recruitment, or per recruit.

With such accurate data, auditors can enable HR departments to develop more innovative, more beneficial and less expensive programs. Similar approaches are usable in all areas of HRM, including training and development, occupational health and safety, performance management, career development, EEO and affirmative action, and should ideally form part of strategic HR planning.

Data from effective HR audits can provide justifiable HR responses to senior management expectations, such as:

- 'Here's what we did for you and here's what it cost, and here's what you would have done without us and what it would have cost you.'

- 'Here's how much money we saved you in our benefits package by changing insurers.'

- 'Here's an idea that workers developed in a training program we led. It's now working and saving you $50 000 per year.'

- 'If you had not asked us to do this executive search, you would have had to hire an outside consultant at a cost of $30 000. We did it for $5 000.'

- 'In working with the union on a new agreement, we found a way to reduce grievances by 30 per cent, saving the company 6 429 hours per year in management time.'[61]

Cultural audit

With the increased interest in the area of organisational culture, it is only natural that this has also become the subject of audits. The cultural audit essentially involves discussions among top-level managers about the nature of an organisation's culture and the ways in which the culture may be influenced. It requires a serious examination of questions such as: What reports are filled out? What do employees spend their time doing? How do they talk with each other? Who is given what responsibility?

In studying organisational culture, the focus is usually on the underlying assumptions and orientations of employees. Conducting in-depth interviews and making observations over a period of time are the ways to learn about the culture. However, in studying the culture of an organisation, it is important to recognise the existence of subcultures. Subcultures within an organisation may well have quite different views about the nature of the work and how work is to be done.

Cultural audits have been commonly used in US organisations, but they are not yet common in Australian companies. This is likely to alter with the increasing recognition of the impact of culture on organisational change. Cultural audits necessarily have significant effects on the nature of HRM policies and practices.

Utilising audit findings

In the preceding discussion, we observed that there are many sources and indicators from which information may be obtained about the overall effectiveness of the HRM program.

Methods of analysing the findings

Several approaches may be used in analysing the information gathered from the various sources that have been described. These approaches include the following:

- Compare HR programs with those of other organisations, especially the successful ones.

- Base an audit on some source of authority, such as consultant norms, behavioural science findings, or an HRM textbook.

- Rely on some ratios or averages, such as the ratio of HR staff to total employees.
- Use a compliance audit to measure whether the activities of managers and staff in HRM comply with policies, procedures and rules.
- Manage the HR department by objectives and use a systems type of audit.

Where the comparison method is used, figures from outside sources are available. Data may be obtained from government agencies, reporting services, employer associations, industry trade associations, HRM benchmarking organisations (e.g. HRM Consulting, Qld) and consulting firms. Exhibit 13.13 illustrates some of the key HR benchmarks against which audit findings may be compared. Surveys conducted regularly by various organisations provide information that can be used to compare costs of the total program and its parts. Data on the salaries of HR professionals, department budgets and personnel staff ratios are reported periodically in journals and in reporting services' publications.

Costs of the HRM program

We noted earlier in the chapter that it is important to translate audit findings into dollar costs wherever possible. To say, for example, that turnover or wastage is expensive is not enough. When cost data are available, it is possible to make informed decisions about how much should be spent to improve existing programs or institute new ones, such as programs to reduce turnover or wastage. HR specialists should take the lead in preparing cost figures for as many of the HR activities as possible. With such figures the relationship between costs and benefits and between the costs and effectiveness of the proposed activities can be clearly demonstrated. A cost–benefit analysis is the analysis of the costs of a particular function (e.g. training) in monetary terms, compared with non-monetary benefits such as employee attitudes, health and safety. A cost-effectiveness analysis measures the costs of a particular function in monetary terms compared with monetary benefits resulting from increases in production, or reductions in waste and downtime.

If HR managers are to be effective and valued as part of the management team, they need to develop a measurement orientation. According to Jac Fitz-Enz, since value in organisations is most often expressed in financial terms, 'HR professionals are gradually giving up vague, subjective terms for the more specific, objective language of numbers'.[62] Innovative HR departments are increasing their influence within their organisations by moving beyond the traditional administrative role and practising 'human value management' – helping their organisations to achieve important human, production and financial objectives by using people's skills and talents to the best advantage. This is the essence of responsible and strategic human resource management.

Preparation of reports and recommendations

One of the most important activities of the audit team is the preparation of reports of their findings, evaluation and recommendations. The reports should include everything that is pertinent and will be useful to the recipients. One report is usually prepared for line managers. A special report is prepared for the HR department manager, who also receives a copy of the report given to line managers.

The value of information obtained from audits lies in the use made of it to correct deficiencies in the HR program. An analysis of the information may reveal that procedures for carrying out some of the HR functions need to be revised. It is even possible that certain parts of the total program should undergo a thorough revision if they are to meet their objectives. Finally, the policies and practices for each of the various functions should be examined to determine their contributions to the overall HR strategy.

Summary

Throughout this book, the importance of strategic and accountable approaches to HRM has been emphasised. Professional management of the crucial human resource requires demonstrably effective programs, which serve both employee and overall organisational needs.

In the past, both senior and HR managers have been reluctant or unable to quantify the use of their human resources due to a lack of will or the inadequacy of measuring instruments. In the 1990s, however, it has become imperative for HR managers to justify their strategies and functions in similar financial terms to their marketing and production counterparts. A variety of measures, from the application of traditional accounting approaches and the identification and analysis of HR trends such as absenteeism, wastage and turnover, to comprehensive HR audits, are now available to HR managers. Both quantitative and qualitative methods are useful in ensuring that SHRM meets the dynamic requirements of changing organisations. In addition, adherence to good corporate governance principles has become increasingly important. Employee attitude surveys and internal and external client research can supplement more quantitative data analyses.

The fundamental purpose of these techniques is to ensure that the HR department carries out its activities in a financially and socially responsible and innovative manner, towards the achievement of broad organisational objectives.

Key terms

absenteeism 522

corporate governance 528

corporate social responsibility (CSR) 528

employee attitude surveys 521

employee turnover 516

employee wastage 516

HR audits 526

HR benchmarks 533

HR metrics 514

triple bottom line 529

Key debate issues

1   While the costs of HRM functions can be measured reasonably accurately, the benefits are far too difficult to quantify, as they embrace quality of work life and long-term employee satisfaction issues.

2   The main purpose of using HR metrics is to speak the corporate 'language'.

3   Corporate governance and corporate social responsibility practices are good for business.

4   Measures of employee wastage, turnover and absenteeism are at best crude indicators of employee satisfaction, at worst, merely reflective of economic and social conditions.

5   Employee attitude surveys are unlikely to yield accurate information on morale and satisfaction as employees seldom reveal their true feelings due to fears of recrimination.

Exercise 13.1

The HR audit

As an external audit team (two to three people), you will need to contact the HR manager of a local organisation, and offer your services to audit one or two segments of their HR program.

Purpose

Your overall purpose is to analyse the effectiveness of present HR policies and procedures, and to suggest appropriate modifications to improve HR and organisational performance.

Method(s)

You may choose either a broad organisational issue (e.g. absenteeism, turnover and wastage, accidents) and the associated policies and procedures, or concentrate on a specific HR program (e.g. recruitment, training, remuneration). Your research should, however, be both quantitative and qualitative, and employ a variety of audit techniques: records analysis; comparative industry studies; employee and client attitude surveys; interviews or discussions with management, employees and relevant unions. As part of a group audit, individual members can be allocated to specific parts of the issue or program, or the entire audit can be conducted by the team.

Audit criteria

Above all, the audit findings should be reported in formal report style, and should demonstrate:

1   compliance with all legal requirements (e.g. EEO, OHS)
2   a strategic emphasis, linking program modifications with organisational directions
3   cost-effectiveness and accountable recommendations for change.

Confidentiality of material from the organisation should be strictly adhered to. It is also preferable that a report be prepared for the audited company.

Exercise 13.2

Evaluating the effectiveness of the HRM function

Students should use Exhibit 13.14 as a template against which to evaluate the effectiveness of the HRM function in an organisation of their choice. Each 'focus area' should be discussed in relation to the associated 'workplace behaviours'.

The exercise can be conducted in groups, using a different organisation for each group's evaluation, or as a class brainstorming activity focusing on a single organisation. In either case, students should consider the degree to which the chosen organisation(s) measure up against the ideal model, and where deficiencies are identified, suggest the causes and make recommendations for improvement.

Exhibit 13.14 Progressive practices

Focus areas	Workforce behaviours
Work life	• *Employees are valued as 'human' assets* • *Policies are in place to ensure individual needs for work–life balance are accommodated*
Work design	• *Focus on system performance rather than individual job* • *Emphasis on whole task, where doing and thinking are combined* • *Focus on team rather than individual* • *Decentralisation of decision making*
Employment security	• *Commitment to avoid downsizing and assist in re-employment* • *Focus on retraining, redeployment and employability* • *Selective hiring based on 'cultural fit' rather than specific job-relevant skills*
Employee voice	• *Business data shared widely through open-book management* • *Employee participation encouraged in a wide range of issues*
Compensation	• *Rewards reinforce group achievement and equity rather than awards geared to individual job evaluation. Examples include gain sharing and profit sharing* • *Equality of sacrifice in hard times*
Employee relations	• *Reduced status distinctions to de-emphasise hierarchy* • *Adversarial employee relations give way to joint planning and problem solving*
Leadership	• *Coordination and control based on shared goals, values and traditions* • *Supervisors facilitate rather than direct the workforce through their interpersonal and conceptual ability*

Source: Caro Gill, 'Talent wins', *hrmonthly*, April 2000, p. 35.

Case study 13.1

DaimlerChrysler Australia

The problem

DaimlerChrysler Australia has approximately 500 staff and is one of Australia's most successful importers of motor vehicles including commercial vehicles and trucks. The HR team decided to review its process of performance management because they found that the paper-based system was not providing the HR metrics which they needed. The major problem was that it was impossible to compile any meaningful data when every performance review required eight pieces of paper – meaning that someone had to compile data from a total of approximately four thousand pieces of paper, twice a year. The performance management system allows DaimlerChrysler to set performance goals for all staff.

The solution

The HR metrics required by the company included:

- rates of compliance with core behaviours
- level of achievement of business objectives
- distribution of learning and development objectives.

An automated system was implemented by a local consultant, which has allowed DaimlerChrysler to get a true grasp of compliance. With this new system, the compliance rate has jumped from 40% to 98%, primarily because of its ease of use, as the performance management process now requires access to only one screen. The HR metrics have assisted the organisation with talent identification, consistency and transparency, due to automated reporting. It is now obvious if one manager rates all their staff as outstanding, all of the time, which sometimes happens when the manager wants to maintain a good relationship with team members, or wishes to promote themselves. The new system has helped to drive a desired performance-oriented culture, and it is estimated that it has provided a 2% organisational benefit in the first 18 months.

Source: Lyle Potgieter and Peter Vlant, Peoplestreme.com 2006.

Questions

1 Why do you think this problem developed in the first place?

2 How should the HR manager use the new system and the associated HR metrics to promote the value of HRM?

Further readings

Anonymous 2006. *Westpac Bank: Intangible issues become tangible profits*, Sydney, Macquarie Financial Services, 13 April.

Bates S. 2002. 'Accounting for people', *HR Magazine*, 47(10), pp. 30–7.

Bezzina M., Gerstmyer S. 2003. 'Best practice guidelines', *hrmonthly*, October, p. 42.

Brockbank W., Ulrich D. 2005. *The HR Value Proposition*, Boston, Harvard Business School Press.

Cascio W. 1999. *Costing human resources: The financial impact of behavior in organisations*, 4th edn, Cincinnati, Ohio, South-Western.

Collins R. 2005, CCH/AGSM Survey on Recruitment, North Ryde, CCH Australia.

Donaldson C. 2005. 'Corporate governance: Does HR have a role?', *Human Resources*,18 October, pp. 12–13.

Hansen F. 2003. 'The CFO connection', *Workforce*, July, pp. 50–4.

Hom P., Griffeth R. 1995. *Employee turnover*, Cincinnati, Ohio, South-Western.

Howes P. 2000. 'Measuring human resources', *hrmonthly*, April, pp. 48–9.

Kramar R. 2006. *Cranet-Macquarie survey on international strategic human resource management: Report on the Australian findings*, Sydney, Macquarie University.

Lake N. 2000. 'Exploding the myths and monsters of employee surveys', *hrmonthly*, April, pp. 26–7.

McNulty Y. 2006. 'Understanding expatriate ROI: What it is, what it isn't'. Paper presented at the 11th World HR Congress, Singapore, 1 June.

Suggett D., Goodsir B., Pryor S. 2000. *Corporate community involvement: Establishing a business case*, Canberra, Centre for Corporate Public Affairs.

Ulrich D. 2006. 'The HR value proposition: A dozen things we know about organizations'. Paper presented at the 11th World HR Congress, Singapore, 1 June.

Ulrich D., Smallwood N. 2005. 'HR's new ROI: Return on intangibles', *Human Resource Management*, 44(2), pp. 137–42.

www.partnerships.gov.au/csr/corporate, accessed 13 September 2006.

Yen M. 2006. 'Providing the net between corporate and community', *Human Resources*, pp. 12–13.

Yeung A. 2006. 'Measuring and generating impressive returns on human capital'. Paper presented at the 11th World HR Congress, Singapore, 1 June.

Endnotes

1   Boudreau J. 1990. 'Measurement as a strategic human resource management decision tool'. Paper presented at the IPMA/IPMNZ Conference, Auckland, p. 2.

2   Corrigan J., Kaidonis M., Tibbits G. 1996. 'Accounting for human resources', *Management Accounting Issues Report*, 2, March, Sydney, CPA, p. 8.

3   Lake N. 1999. 'From cost centre to value builder', *hrmonthly*, July, p. 20.

4   Gill C. 2000. 'Talent wins', *hrmonthly*, April, p. 34.

5   Lake N. 1999. op. cit.

6   Cooper J., Hogarth C. 2003. 'Good management', *hrmonthly*, October, pp. 38–9.

7   Boudreau J. 1990. op. cit.

8   Fitz-Enz J. 1980. 'Quantifying the HR function', *Personnel*, 57(2), March–April, p. 42.

9   Trevor-Roberts B. 1984. 'An audit of personnel management activities in Queensland', *HRM Australia*, 22(3), August, p. 55.

10   Ibid.

11   Ibid.

12   Boudreau J. 1990. op. cit., p. 10.

13   Donaldson C. 2006. 'Intangibles crucial in HR's future', *Human Resources*, issue 107, 27 June, p. 1.

14   Kramar R. 2006. *Cranet-Macquarie survey on international strategic human resource management: Report on the Australian findings*, Ryde, Macquarie University, p. 7.

15   Butler J., Ferris G., Napier N. 1991. *Strategy and human resource management*, Cincinnati, Ohio, South-Western, p. 47.

16   Ibid, p. 53.

17   Bates S. 2002. 'Accounting for people', *HR Magazine*, 47(10), p. 33.

18   Ibid.

19   Cascio W. 1989. *Managing human resources: Productivity, quality of work, life, profits*, 2nd edn, New York, McGraw-Hill, p. 593.

20   Kramar R. 2006. op. cit., p. 27.

21   Gloet M. 2006. 'Knowledge management and the links to HRM: Developing leadership and management capabilities to support sustainability', *Management Research News*, 29(7), pp. 402–13.

22   For example, Howes P. 1999. 'Re-valuing the business', *hrmonthly*, August, pp. 38–39; Schneier P. 1997. 'People value add: The new performance measure', *Strategy and Leadership*, March–April, pp. 14–19.

23   Howes P. 1999. op. cit., p. 38.

24   Yeung A. 2006. 'Measuring and generating impressive returns on human capital'. Paper presented at the 11th World HR Congress, Singapore, 1 June.

25   Gallo J., Thompson P. 2000. 'Goals, measures, and beyond: In search of accountability in federal HRM', *Public Personnel Management*, 29(2), p. 241.

26   Yeung A. 2006. op. cit.

27   Hansen F. 2003. 'The CFO connection', *Workforce*, July, p. 51.

28   Fitz-Enz J. 1984. *How to measure HRM*, New York, McGraw-Hill, p. 28.

29   Clark R. 1992. *Australian human resource management: Framework and practice*, 2nd edn, Sydney, McGraw-Hill, pp. 82–3.

30   Lewin D., Mitchell D. 1995. *Human resource management: An economic approach*, 2nd edn, Cincinnati, Ohio, South-Western, p. 31.

31   Howes P. 2000. 'Measuring human resources', *hrmonthly*, April, p. 48.

32   Schneier P. 1997. op. cit., p. 14.

33   Gibbs S. 2000. 'Evaluating HRM effectiveness: The stereotype connection', *Employee Relations*, 22(1), pp. 58–69.

34   Ibid.

35   Fitz-Enz J. 2006, in Yeung, op. cit.

36   Howes P. 1997. 'Finding the turnover rate that's not too high, not too low, but just right', *hrmonthly*, October, p. 49.

37   Australian Automotive Industry Council 1990. *Study of the costs of labour turnover and absenteeism*, Melbourne, AMC, p. 2.

38   Ibid.

39   Anon. 1990. 'Employee turnover costs industry up to $1bn a year', *The Australian*, 8 June, p. 2.

40   McGhee K. 1997. 'Beating boredom', *Sydney Morning Herald* (Employment), 3 May, p. 1.

41   Ibid.

42   Nankervis A. 1990. 'Making a virtue out of necessity: Employee resignations', *Journal of Professional Practice Management*, Spring, p. 59.

43   Ibid., p. 60.

44   Ibid., p. 60.

45   'A survey of 429 HR managers reported 70 per cent usage at least once in the previous decade.' Gallup G. 1988, 'Employee research: From nice to know to need to know', *Personnel Journal*, 67(8), August, pp. 42–3.

46   Nankervis A. 1990. 'Productivity through participation', *Personnel Today*, May, p. 19.

47   Lake N. 2000. 'Exploding the myths and monsters of employee surveys', *hrmonthly*, April, pp. 26–7.

48   Cascio W. 1989. op. cit., p. 596.

49   Stone R. 1998. *Human resource management*, 3rd edn, Brisbane, John Wiley & Sons, p. 548.

50   Wooden M. 1992. 'The cost of time off work in Australia', *Asia Pacific Journal of Human Resources*, 30(3), Spring, p. 9.

51   Kuzmits F. 1979. 'How much is absenteeism costing your organisation?', *Personnel Administrator*, 6, pp. 29–33.

52   Boudreau J. 1990. op. cit., p. 11.

53   Howes P. 1997. 'Measurement is a prerequisite for auditing HR function', *hrmonthly*, April, p. 46.

54   Donahue M. 1996. 'Do your human resources add value?', *Management Accounting*, June, p. 47.

55   Bezzina M., Gerstmyer S. 2003. 'Best practice guidelines', *hrmonthly*, October, p. 42.

56   www.partnerships.gov.au/csr/corporate, accessed 13 September 2006.

57   www.en.wikipedia.org/wiki/Corporate_social_responsibility, accessed 13 September, 2006.

58   Donaldson C. 2005. 'Corporate governance: does HR have a role?', *Human Resources*, 18 October, p. 13.

59   Ibid.

60   McBride P., Dowling P. 1985. 'Costing HR: A guide for personnel practitioners', *HRM Australia*, November, p. 25.

61   Bellman G.M. in Cascio W. 1991. *Costing human resources*, 3rd edn, Boston, PWS-Kent, pp. 282–3.

62   Fitz-Enz J. 1984. op. cit., p. 29.

Online reading

INFOTRAC® COLLEGE EDITION

For additional readings and review on evaluating human resource management, explore InfoTrac® College Edition, your online library. Go to: www.infotrac-college .com and search for any of the InfoTrac key terms listed below:

➤ absenteeism
➤ corporate governance
➤ corporate social responsibility (CSR)
➤ employee attitude surveys
➤ HR audits
➤ HR metrics
➤ triple bottom line

CHAPTER 14
CHALLENGES FOR HUMAN RESOURCE MANAGEMENT

The next generation of HR professionals will need to be more externally focused and skilled at building networks and productive alliances with other groups and institutions, become more analytical and able to document the benefits associated with effective HR policies and practices, and be skilled at managing in an increasingly transparent society and information savvy workforce.

Thomas Kochan, 2004

The knowledge economy requires HR managers who can generate sustained organisational capabilities ... human capital stewards, knowledge facilitators, relationship builders and rapid deployment specialists.

Marianne Gloet and Mike Berrell, 2006

Our HCI (Human Capital Index) research has again demonstrated the strong link between effective human capital management and shareholder value.

Steven Dicker, Watson Wyatt, 2004

Objectives

After reading this chapter, you will be able to:

1. Identify future directions in SHRM theory and practice in the foreseeable future.

2. Understand the influence of workplace, national and international changes on SHRM into the new millennium.

3. Appreciate the priorities for SHRM research and practice in the future.

Introduction

Throughout this text we have emphasised the significance of the forces of globalisation and new technology on the nature of jobs, employee skills and competencies, employment conditions and workplace structures. This chapter attempts to identify the impacts of these irrevocable forces and, in particular, their effects on the further development of strategic human resource management.

While it is relatively safe to suggest that present organisational emphases on quality, productivity, innovation and efficiency will continue as industry becomes ever more competitive – and that labour flexibility and effectiveness will remain crucial towards those ends – the nature of the global, regional and national environments makes predicting the future shape of the Australian labour market more difficult. However, the replacement of ongoing employment relationships by enterprise and individual agreements under the impact of the *WorkChoices* legislation in Australia is likely to result in considerably less job security, shorter-term contracts with less 'allowable' conditions and benefits, and potentially fewer (and smaller) pay rises from the Fair Pay Commission. Some of these implications may be addressed differently by the new federal government after the 2007 election, whichever party is successful.

Organisations are likely to remain 'lean and mean' with the increasing automation of repetitive tasks in all industries, and the continuing outsourcing, contracting out and offshoring of non-core functions. Undoubtedly, however, new and more highly skilled positions will be required, spawning an increased 'war for talent' nationally, regionally and globally. Some industries (e.g. retailing, entertainment, tourism) may undergo fundamental changes towards their 'virtual' counterparts, and there is likely to be a further growth in service industries to accommodate new consumer needs. Knowledge management (see later) will increasingly become a major focus for HR professionals.

In addition, as organisations become increasingly more global, with the development of regional trading blocs and the establishment of overseas subsidiaries, multicultural or cross-cultural skills will be required both for overseas operations and for the management of diverse domestic workforces.

The devolvement of many traditional HRM functions to supervisors will provide HR specialists with challenges of coordination and accountability at organisational level, together with the responsibility for broad change management strategies, to align HRM and organisational objectives and strategies. As Ulrich suggests, the focus of SHRM in the future will not be on the functions of HRM, but rather on the 'deliverables' (or outcomes) in relation to desired organisational objectives.[1]

A series of likely external and internal influences on SRHM in the future are now discussed.

Environmental changes

Economic recessions, entrepreneurial collapses, persistent mergers and acquisitions, and the increasing internationalism of business have led to a turbulent industrial environment for Australian business, an environment that is likely to continue into the foreseeable future. Political changes in the European Union, and new economic and political groupings in the Asia–Pacific region, with dramatic increases in competitiveness, have forced Australian governments, business and trade union leaders to reconsider our place in the world, likely growth areas, and hence the nature of work structures, processes and human resource management practices. Traditional international influences from the United States and the United Kingdom are being supplanted by the regional pressures of Japan, Singapore, Hong Kong, China, Taiwan and South Korea.

One author categorises the major global 'drivers' of future industrial change as:

- the globalisation of markets and the internationalisation of business
- major political and social issues and trends
- advances in technology
- changing laws and regulations
- organisational growth and development
- fluctuations in business cycles.[2]

Others suggest that specific global issues confronting Australian organisations in the future include increasing globalisation; international 'megamergers,' the rise of regionalism (e.g. NAFTA, ASEAN) with the associated economic interdependence of member nations, further 'privatisation' of government entities, the 'Asian rebound' from crisis, and especially the resurgence of China, India and South Korea.[3] Some of these developments have already occurred, and while some provide significant opportunities for Australian organisations (e.g. globalisation, privatisation, new markets in China, India and Korea), others (e.g. international megamergers, Asian regionalism, excluding Australia) may threaten future growth.

As discussed in earlier chapters, the Australian economy is changing radically in response to both international pressures and domestic imperatives. Micro-economic reform is likely to continue, accompanied by corporatisation or privatisation in some industry sectors. The shift away from manufacturing and agriculture towards a multi-faceted service sector which employs both more highly skilled (e.g. property and business services, health, education) and more semi-skilled (e.g. retail, hospitality, tourism) employees is expected to continue, with many countries competing on the same industrial 'playing fields.' Recent statistics indicate that up to 88 per cent of the US workforce is employed in services[4] and that approximately 85 per cent of Hong Kong's GDP and more than 65 per cent of Singapore's business revenue derive from service-related industry sectors.[5] In Australia, an Australian Bureau of Statistics report asserted that the service sector is '… the largest component of the Australian economy in terms of number of businesses, employment, and gross value added,' comprising 65.5 per cent of all businesses and more than 73 to 75 per cent of total employment.[6] The implications of these statistics for human resource management are immense, in terms of recruitment and selection, human resource development, remuneration and career development strategies.

Social and demographic changes are likely to result in more educated and more highly skilled employees with increased job expectations vying for a smaller number of jobs and less access to long-term career paths within the same organisation. Schmidt agrees, suggesting that at the 'top' end of the labour market not only will employees be younger and more technologically literate, but they will change their jobs more frequently, and that their loyalty will need to be 'bought' by competing employers on the bases of interesting work projects and competitive employment conditions.[7] At the 'lower' end of the labour market, it is likely that – together with the continuous drive towards more flexible employment types such as part-timers, casuals, independent contractors, foreign workers on temporary work visas and agency 'temps' – more attention may need to be paid to work–life balance, family-friendly programs and more generous rewards and recognition schemes.

In addition, some employers will need to attract employees from less traditional sources (for example, 'teen entrepreneurs,' 'retiree entrepreneurs'),[8] and flexibility may encompass 'goodbye Christmas' and 'goodbye weekend' expectations[9] – in other words, the industry-wide implementation of '24/7' work schedules, already common in such sectors as information technology, telecommunications, hospitality and tourism. The challenge for HR specialists then will be to select the best candidates and to design mutually satisfying and stimulating work projects and rewards systems, with the recognition that employees will be unlikely to remain

with the organisation for long periods. Individual contracts, with enhanced benefits for employees based on agreed performance targets, will become the norm in many future organisations.

The general decline in union membership, together with a rise in Australian Workplace Agreements, as a consequence of the federal *Workplace Relations Act 1996* and the *Workplace Relations Amendment (WorkChoices) Act 2005*, has encouraged such changes. Lamenting the historically restrictive nature of industrial relations in Australia, a Business Council of Australia report suggests that:

> our industrial relations system has increased the cost of change … costs include lengthy and expensive negotiation and arbitral processes … When the cost of a change rises, rational managers either drop the change idea or give it a low priority.[10]

Industrial relations trends have already diminished the importance of the Industrial Relations Commission and state tribunals, replacing some of their functions with the Australian Fair Pay Commission, with an increasing emphasis on enterprise and individual agreements allowing negotiation over previously sacrosanct issues such as hours, leave provisions and overall working conditions. Some writers have gone so far as to suggest that trade unions already face a 'crisis of legitimacy' in this new environment.[11]

In this new environment HR professionals face many dilemmas with respect to their roles at the workplace. They may, for example, choose to become the 'head cutters' of the organisation, which brings with it the risk that unless they '… have a very good strategy for dealing with the longer term in the company … you will get a workforce that's as aggressive as hell.'[12] On the other hand, Russell Lansbury cautions that 'while some HR managers may feel that the changes introduced by *WorkChoices* will give their companies an economic advantage and even the capacity to be more internationally competitive, the danger is that the legislation may lead Australia down the low road, to a less skilled and less productive society'.[13] Lowry (2006) agrees, suggesting that HR professionals may choose to take the hard HRM route, or they may prefer to promote 'fairness and justice' in the workplace.[14]

Social factors and legislation

Social developments had significant impact on the nature and operations of Australian organisations during the 20th century. Such factors as the post-Second World War 'baby boom,' changing migration patterns, significant increases in education standards and associated employee expectations for job satisfaction, career development and more flexible remuneration systems heavily influenced HRM practices and processes. The increasing desire of women for full- or part-time work, equal payment and careers, now recognised by equal employment opportunity and affirmative action legislation at federal and state levels, necessarily affected HRM programs. Legislation in the areas of occupational health and safety, privacy, freedom of information and duty of care changed the nature of HRM practice, and this is likely to continue in Australia and all regional countries.

Social issues such as the ageing of the 'baby boomers,' coupled with reductions in the size of families and potentially reduced, if more specialised, migration programs, will have significant impacts on the nature of recruitment and selection, training and development, performance management and retrenchment programs. Recent debate over 'intergenerational tension' between the babyboomers, 'Generation X' and 'Generation Y' employees in competition for fewer jobs suggests that these issues will also need to be addressed through innovative HRM practices.

Future workforce trends, confirmed by Australian Bureau of Statistics reports, include reductions in the growth of the Australian workforce, a continued ageing of the population, a significant decline in the numbers of 'tradespersons and related workers' (e.g. mechanics, welders, electricians, carpenters and bakers), and a corresponding increase in the proportional representation of 'associate professionals' (e.g. radiographers, bank managers, chefs, customer service and hospitality managers) and professionals.[15] Associate professionals are now in the top four categories of employment in a majority of states, whereas tradespersons have declined in all Australian states, notably in the ACT. The introduction of new technology, industry shifts from primary and secondary to tertiary sectors, and increasing educational levels, especially at university level, have reduced the need for trades positions and increased the desire of employees for associate professional or professional positions and the associated working conditions. However, in recent times, governments and employer associations have become concerned about the scarcity of skilled tradespeople, and have implemented more flexible training programs to address these shortages.

These trends confirm earlier predictions of shorter-term careers, as professionals have the capacity to move between jobs to optimise their salary packages and to seek more challenging work tasks, and the imperative for continual change in particular jobs, organisational directions or work structures.

While opportunities for women have increased in professional categories, men still outnumber women by three to one in the 'managers and administrators' category in most Australian states, and more women are concentrated in part-time and casual positions and in declining industry sectors.[16] Diversity management strategies to incorporate more women in (especially) senior management positions in the future will require enlightened organisational approaches and relevant HR plans.

Trends which are likely to grow in the 21st century include limited but highly specialist recruitment programs; ongoing retrenchment and redundancy (targeted rather than voluntary) schemes; flexible and performance-based contracts and remuneration systems; and horizontal (rather than vertical) careers.

Given current industrial relations initiatives, notably the Australian *WorkChoices* legislation, such organisational structures will enable desired functional (multi- and cross-skilling), numerical (labour supply variations) and financial flexibilities. Already, as examples, some of the large telecommunications and transport authorities in all states are contracting out significant parts of their activities (e.g. workshops, road works, track maintenance, HR services centres) to private contractors and offshore service providers, and are contemplating the privatisation of their services. Such structural change is not only cost-effective, but also allows for flexible responses to external economic, social and political developments. It also portends immense changes in the nature of HRM activities, which are discussed later in this chapter. One observer summarises the broad implications of these developments for the employer–employee relationship thus:

> The decline in collective responses such as strikes to injustices in the employment relationship diverts attention to individualised responses to unbalanced exchanges with the employer. In this case, employees are redressing the balance in the relationship through reducing their commitment and their willingness to engage in organisational citizenship behaviours, which have been highlighted as important factors in an organisation's survival and wellbeing.[17]

Other continuing developments include further devolution of HRM responsibilities in many public and private sector organisations to regional, branch or line management levels, accompanied by zero-based budgeting. This has significant implications for human resource managers and their activities. Whatever the future holds for organisations and their managers, likely emphases will include ongoing change focused on human resource flexibility and the 'erosion of traditional job demarcations',[18] reduced labour costs and the more efficient allocation of employees. This will be achieved through improved employee participation, motivation and commitment, more effective industrial relations processes, environmental change and revised HRM strategies.

The future workplace

The consequences of the international, national and social influences described above on Australian organisations are, and will increasingly be, enormous. As explained throughout this text, not only is the nature of work itself undergoing a radical transformation, but so are the types of jobs performed, their requisite competencies and skills, employee qualities and expectations, and employment conditions. Schmidt suggests that future workplaces will be larger and more complex, but with many activities conducted through internal or external 'alliances, joint ventures and networks'; that they will need to be continuously responsive to 'dynamic consumer preferences and increasing product specialisation'; and that 'overseas revenues will overtake domestic sales'.[19]

Exhibit 14.1 illustrates some of the new jobs that accompany the so-called 'new economy' produced by globalisation and new technologies.

Kemske and others summarise the likely effects on workplaces of the future as:

- *global business*: global marketplaces, international workforces and cross-cultural competencies

- *workforce flexibility*: 'collaborative' cultures, creative employment contracts, a focus on performance not hours, employee choice and communication by intranet

- *workforce development*: lifelong learning (organisational and individual), multiskilling, team projects, JIT training

- *job definition*: pay linked to the value of the person (not the job) and organisational outcomes, versatility, challenges and a task focus

- *work and society*: work–family interface, dual career couples, 'cocooning' (through teleworking).[20]

Exhibit 14.1 The new jobs

- *Piracy/intellectual property managers*
- *Network security consultants*
- *Web developers*
- *Desktop, systems and network engineers, and support staff*
- *Bandwidth infrastructure engineers, and support staff*
- *Application service provider (ASP) support staff*
- *Testers*
- *Professional surfers*
- *Project managers/producers*
- *Copywriters/content producers*
- *Content managers*
- *Strategic sourcing consultants – managing delivery across vertical channels within a network as well as the traditional supply/value chain*
- *Relationship brokers*
- *Venture capital brokers*

Source: Sunderland K. 2000. 'Rising to the IT challenge,' *hrmonthly*, September, p. 32.

All of these changes to the nature of jobs, and the various workplaces in which they are performed, have been discussed throughout this text, but the future promises even more of the same. HR professionals will need to adopt appropriate new roles in order to ensure that these radical changes achieve their desired organisational outcomes.

SHRM in the future

As the future shape of Australian industry itself is unclear, so is the future of SHRM. However, many authors and practitioners share similar visions of the future, including themes of the 'transformation' of current paradigms, and of the development of 'strategic partnerships' between HRM and its organisations.

Professor David Ulrich envisions a broad 'HR community' within (and outside) organisations focused on the 'deliverables' of HRM. Tyson emphasises the need for '… strategic integration … winning (employee) commitment … partnerships with trade unions … (and) managerialism',[21] and Walker stresses that 'human resource activities should fit together as a system'.[22] Thomas Kochan goes further, to suggest that:

> HRM professionals will need to redefine their role and professional identity
> to advocate and support a better balance between employer and employee
> interests…to be more externally focused and skilled at building networks
> and productive alliances with other groups and institutions, become more
> analytical and able to document the benefits associated with effective
> HR policies and practices, and be skilled at managing in an increasingly
> transparent society and information savvy workforce.[23]

The major catalysts for these new roles are the long-term impacts of legislation such as *WorkChoices*; the community and business demand for enhanced accountability in HRM; and the ongoing global war for talent, all issues which have been discussed throughout this book.

The alignment of 'transformed' SHRM theory with SHRM practice will undoubtedly be the challenge for HR specialists in the future. The following section explores several conceptual models of SHRM in the future, and is accompanied by a subsequent section focused on future SHRM practice.

SHRM theory

The shift from personnel management to SHRM was required by the need for a more professional approach, and the increasing demand of organisations for more strategic, integrative and accountable approaches to HR activities.

The future will demand the further development of SHRM concepts to equip practitioners with more appropriate frameworks to guide their innovative practices. The immense changes in industrial relations processes in Australia during the last two decades demand a theoretical and practical accommodation of the relationships between HRM and industrial relations. Current debates suggest that unitarist managerial positions will need to be replaced by neo-unitarist or pluralist concepts that effectively embrace the conflicting needs of both management and employees. We may be moving towards a flexible notion of SHRM that accommodates 'the interdependence and complementary relationship of industrial relations and human resource management'.[24] Are industrial relations and HRM complementary, incompatible or simply coexistent?[25]

Additionally, HRM theorists and practitioners need to resolve the apparent contradictions between hard (i.e. effective, rational management of the human resource) and soft (i.e. emphasising the role of communication, motivation and leadership in achieving organisational goals) HRM notions.

This debate has been raised to the global level through the contributions of theorists such as Brewster, Sparrow and Zanko, who have speculated about whether there is an emerging 'universalist' model of HRM which spans all countries, societies and industries, or whether the different contexts of countries such as the United States, the United Kingdom, Australia, China, Indonesia and Japan will ensure divergent models which more appropriately reflect

their disparate cultures, values, industrial relations systems and managerial styles. Nankervis, Chatterjee and Coffey (2006) suggest that there may also be an emerging 'cross-vergence' in management and HRM theory and practice, whereby developing nations in Asia in particular are making their own contributions to ongoing developments in these areas.[26]

Two models of future SHRM

This section explores two related but different conceptual notions of SHRM theory in the future. The first is based upon an empirical study of SHRM worldwide, and it emphasises the transformation from 'functional specialist' to 'future business partner.' It is illustrated in Exhibit 14.2.

The 'transformation' model of HRM

This model proposes a broad and future-focused SHRM role, with most HR activities devolved to line managers, but with accountability to both line managers and strategic business plans. SHRM is a 'business partner' with a 'global perspective' and HR specialists will rotate between HRM and operational management. In many ways, this model reflects the SHRM theory discussed throughout this book.

Ulrich's HR competencies model

A second model, proposed by Ulrich, provides a multi-layered conceptual approach incorporating the management of strategic human resources, the management of firm infrastructure, the management of employee contributions, and the management of transformation and change (see Exhibits 14.3 and 14.4).

Exhibit 14.2 The Towers Perrin 'transformation' model of HRM

Human resource component	Current human resource functional specialist	Future business partner
• Nature of human resource programs and function	• Responsive	• Proactive
	• Operational	• Strategic
• Creation of human resource strategy and policy	• Internal	• Societal
	• Human resource department has full responsibility	• Human resource department and line management share responsibility
• Organisation of the human resource function	• Employee advocate	• Business partner
	• Functional structure	• Flexible structure
• Profile of human resource professionals	• Reporting to staff	• Reporting to line
	• Career in human resources	• Rotation
	• Specialist	• Generalist
	• Limited financial skills	• Functional expertise
	• Current focus	• Focus on future
	• Monolingual	• Multilingual
	• National perspective	• Global perspective

Source: Towers Perrin 1991. *Priorities for competitive advantage*, New York, p. 6.

In this model, HR specialists need to make choices between the presented options or to choose to implement all of them. As in the Towers Perrin model, the effectiveness of this model depends upon the breadth and depth of HR specialists' skills and perspectives, and their ability to develop sound relationships with both senior and line management.

Exhibit 14.3   HR roles in building a competitive organisation

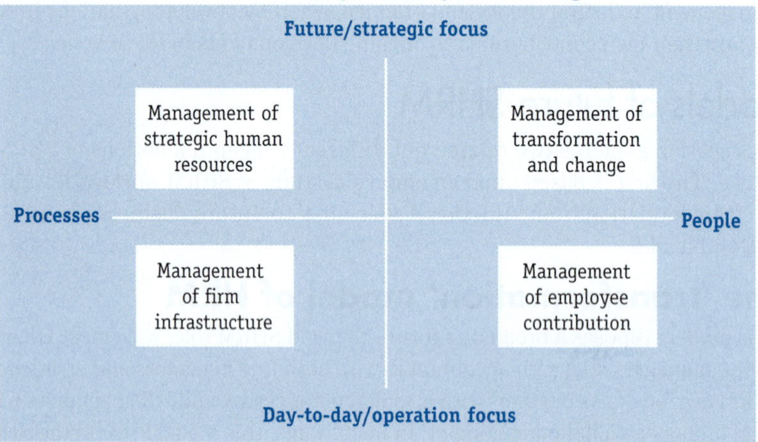

Exhibit 14.4   Ulrich's HR competencies model

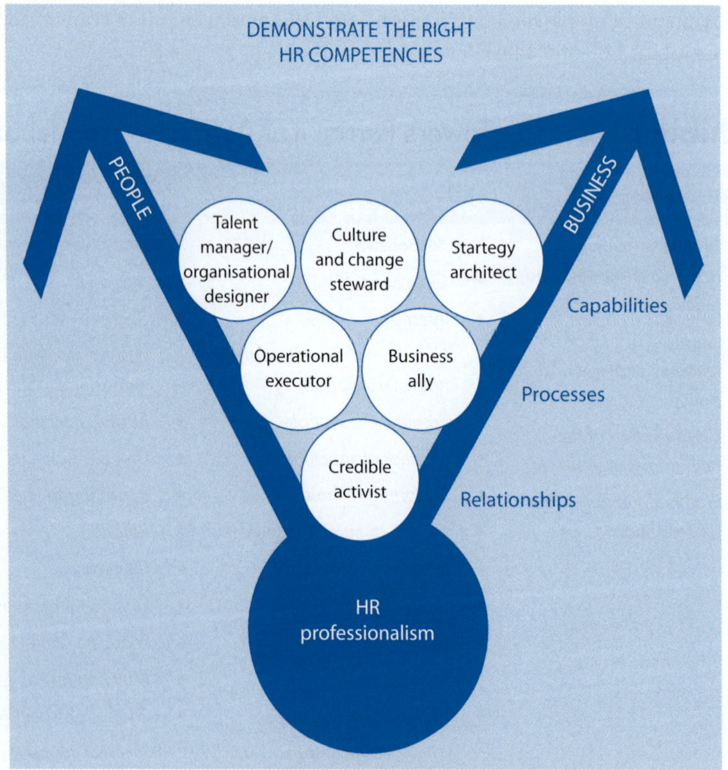

Source: Professor David Ulrich, Ross School of Business, University of Michigan.

The recent Cranet–Macquarie Survey on international strategic HRM (2006) found support for a view of HR 'leadership' that involves 'embracing concepts and responsibilities such as sustainability,

mental models and knowledge … concepts which move beyond traditional HR activities'.[27] The following section explores the links between sustainability, HRM and Knowledge Management (KM).

Sustainability, HRM and KM

In the knowledge-based view of organisations, knowledge is acknowledged as the most valuable organisational asset and the ability to manage knowledge strategically as the most significant source of competitive advantage.[28] In the wider search for sustainability, issues of context of culture and appropriateness are of paramount importance. In the realm of context, the focus should be on community as well as on process. The scope of knowledge management (KM) exists largely in the contextual filter that spans boundaries between various interactions between people, organisations, national cultures and international bodies. In the realm of context, KM can provide a range of boundary-spanning activities and support mechanisms. These include knowledge creation, knowledge sharing, appropriate frameworks, enablers, infrastructure, measurement, feedback, and learning and education, and are clearly in the HRM domain.

The application of knowledge and expertise, through KM and HRM, can act as resources to support sustainable organisational development. The deeper the intensity of knowledge and information exchange, the better the chances for developing effective management and leadership capabilities to support sustainability. In order to facilitate this, new modes of KM are required, as the drivers of the mainstream approaches to management development have largely reflected different visions and objectives. The focus must be on creativity, on internal organisational dynamics and the social processes of human interaction. Human interaction and how it occurs is central to knowledge creation and transfer. Organisations that develop unique capabilities in the management of knowledge processes can build distinctive competencies based upon exploiting the growing knowledge generated by these processes.[29] It is in the synergies between organisational capabilities and competencies, cultures and behaviours that the richness of the potential relationship between HRM and KM is displayed.

Strategic HRM can help to support sustainability through the identification of capabilities specific to sustainability and by seeking to align recruitment and selection practices to these capabilities. Through supportive learning and development programs these capabilities can be further developed. This includes identifying key individuals to be fast-tracked into sustainability roles, normally on the basis of their personal values and extensive networks and relationships. Sustainability goals can be built into the HR strategic plans to support the same goals in the overall business plans. Connectivity between sustainability, HRM and KM can be further leveraged through the inclusion of strategic provision for human capital development and the cultural infrastructure that supports knowledge-creation and sharing, communication, learning and networking and the formation of communities.

Source: Adapted from Gloet M. 2006. 'Knowledge management and the links to HRM: Developing leadership and management capabilities to support sustainability,' *Management Research News*, 29(7), pp. 402–13.

Other issues for the future

Two additional issues are relevant to the development of conceptual bases for HRM practice today. The first concerns the development of peculiarly Australasian models of SHRM. Much of our discussion of SHRM has been based on United States, United Kingdom, European and

Japanese influences. While these influences have been useful, and perhaps necessary for development, the challenge for HRM writers and practitioners in the future is to develop an Australasian concept of SHRM, reflecting our particular social, cultural, political, economic and industrial relations values, attitudes, practices and structures. Influences here could include a focus on the comparative HRM perspectives and processes of our regional neighbours; increasingly flexible employment contracts incorporating benefits for both employers and employees; emphases on the amalgamation of both 'soft' and 'hard' HRM; and true recognition and management of the diverse workforces of Australian organisations. Proper scrutiny and adaptation of overseas HRM trends and fads will also be required, rather than their mere adoption.

As suggested throughout this book, all of these are changing in response to international, regional and domestic imperatives, including a need for enhanced quality, productivity and competitiveness. The convergence of some of these features (e.g. management styles, financial and marketing strategies) together with regional trading initiatives (e.g. ASEAN, APEC) may encourage some similarities in the models developed in Australia, New Zealand and within the Asia–Pacific region.[30] At the same time, differences in industrial relations systems and working conditions are likely to persist for some time to come.

Another key issue concerns the roles of the HR professional associations, in particular the Australian Human Resource Institute (AHRI) and the Australian Institute of Training and Development (AITD). Both organisations have, until now, fulfilled relevant information dissemination, networking and accreditation functions. Their future challenge is to increase their profiles and activities in the areas of the development of SHRM concepts and philosophies; tighter monitoring of member ethics, and greater influence over federal and state HR programs and legislative initiatives. Increasingly, they will also need to further develop their international and regional alliances and perspectives.

Shared research activities, international and regional HR benchmarking and 'best practice' exercises, practitioner exchange programs and regional SHRM and HR development conferences and workshops are ways in which these crucial objectives may be achieved.

HRM practice in the future

As already suggested, HR specialists are faced with significant responsibilities in the future for the development of organisationally specific and strategic HR programs, predicated upon continual societal and organisational change and increasing productivity at all levels.

The current flexibility of industrial relations processes, coupled with the urgency of innovative and cost-effective HR programs, provide both pressures and opportunities. Human resource managers will need both to draw upon useful international techniques and to develop their own unique approaches in order to ensure that their activities demonstrably contribute to organisational performance and competitiveness.

Predictions about the likely future roles of HR specialists are divergent. As an example, the Dowling and Fisher research study suggests that career opportunities will increase, with greater professionalism, increased accountability and organisational recognition.

On the other hand, as a consequence of the devolution of many traditional HRM processes to line managers and supervisors and the outsourcing and 'offshoring' of others, some authors suggest that '… while some committed practitioners are working hard to establish HRM as a lifelong discipline … the very foundation on which their case is built is being eroded by changing values … technological and financial imperatives'.[31] In this scenario, line managers equipped with HR functional skills and outsourced service providers with sophisticated HRIMS will largely take over HR specialists' functions. Policy and strategic activities will be provided by 'HR elite consultants.'

This prediction is somewhat strengthened by contemporary developments including the decline in industrial relations activities in many Australian organisations, the production of more and more interactive HRM software (e.g. recruitment, training, payroll, career planning) and the significant increase in the numbers and functions of freelance HRM consultants. Recent research evidence also supports these trends.[32]

What these views have in common is a recognition that SHRM is a shared responsibility of all organisational managers, that there needs to be integration between HRM processes and strategies, and that all of these must be aligned with broad organisational strategies and objectives. Differences appear in relation to who will perform these functions in the future (i.e. line managers, consultants) and whether specialist HRM practitioner numbers will increase or decrease.

Future developments in HRM practice are likely to involve a concentration on the cultural elements of the employment relationship (e.g. building trust, more effective networks and specific culture change programs); knowledge management; and team-oriented work systems and multiskilling in preference to increasing specialisation. As HRM becomes increasingly valued as a crucial organisational function, it may be that managers 'rotate' in and out of specialist HRM positions as a normal part of their careers, as in Japan.

Other features are likely to include emphases on international best practice standards, performance targeting and ongoing productivity negotiations between employers, employees and their unions. Compton and Morrissey, however, warn that as well as developing new approaches, they should also '… get hold of the financials and understand what they mean. They cannot afford to conduct state-of-the-art people-development programs without understanding fully the cost implications of such programs'.[33]

Professor Ulrich provides a useful practical framework for HR professionals engaged in such imperatives:

*   Manage HR like a business.

*   Play new roles.

*   Respect history, create a future.

*   Build an infrastructure.

*   Remember the 'human' in HR.

*   Go global.[34]

Future directions in HRM research

In view of the likely future changes in the nature, functions and concepts of HRM, research by both academics and practitioners is crucial to effective development.

Academic research usually involves literature reviews, surveys, questionnaires, interviews, case studies and case histories designed to develop new theories, test existing theories, compare and evaluate conflicting theories, resolve contradictions or follow up previous conclusions. As such, this research usually requires rigorous attention to issues of validity (method, statistics, application), and draws upon previous research conclusions as well as applied studies.

Practitioner research is usually motivated by applied organisational need, to assess the nature and effectiveness of HRM programs, to establish modified activities, to resolve the competing interests of employers and employees and ultimately to meet government requirements or provide data for organisational reporting.

Common areas for both kinds of research include the effectiveness of SHRM programs, worker attitudes, job satisfaction, industrial relations processes, absenteeism, turnover and wastage levels, accidents, grievances, reward systems, and their impact upon organisational productivity and profitability.

Practitioners are usually most concerned with their own organisations, and academics with overall trends and their industrial or societal implications. Practitioner research results in HRM program modification, or justification, but academics are more concerned with broader societal and industry inferences. The two approaches are, however, complementary and should be seen accordingly.

Tools available to both kinds of researchers include interviews, questionnaires and surveys, data analysis (organisational, HRIMS, government data), literature surveys, professional association sources, HRM experiments, case studies and case histories. The choice of tool(s) will necessarily depend on the extent and purposes of the research, as well as its potential audience (within the organisation, or for publication). Professional journals such as the *Asia Pacific Journal of Human Resources* or *Research and Practice in Human Resource Management* offer opportunities for both academics and practitioners to promote their research findings. The publication of overall research findings may assist other practitioners as well as academic researchers. Research may also be pure (research for its own sake, usually theoretical) or applied (specific to an organisation), and reliant on primary (first-hand sources, e.g. case studies, survey and interview results) or secondary sources (e.g. literature reviews, other people's reports).

Primary sources are more credible than secondary material, but this will depend on the purposes of the research. Applied and secondary material may be most appropriate for practitioner evaluation of current HRM practices. The following list of HRM issues may stimulate future research which will contribute to the development of both theory and practice.

Future HRM research areas

- *The current state of SHRM*: Australia-wide; state comparisons; Asia–Pacific comparative studies; regional variations; industry and sector comparisons; organisational case studies; client surveys (e.g. trade unions, employees, managers), new roles (including relationships between HRM and KM)

- *Professional associations*: roles, functions, membership; state and national comparisons; future directions; accreditation guidelines, ethics and corporate governance issues

- *The management of diverse workplaces*: multiculturalism, intergenerational workplace issues

- *International SHRM*: overseas management programs (success or failure, different regions, countries, industries); comparative country or regional studies

- *HRM processes*: job design, recruitment and selection, flexibility and work–life issues, human resource development and executive development, performance management, remuneration systems, occupational health and safety, industrial relations, HRIMS; impact of recent legislation (EEO, AA, OHS, FOI, etc.)

- *Costs and benefits of SHRM*: case studies, cost-benefit analyses (all HR functions)

- *Industrial relations changes*: impact of award restructuring, Australian Workplace Agreements and enterprise agreements, union amalgamation and membership issues

- *Effectiveness of new techniques*: balanced scorecard, human capital management, performance-based pay, 360-degree appraisal, work–life programs

- *HRM broad issues*: absenteeism, turnover and wastage, employee attitude studies; performance, productivity, profitability; status, location and staffing of HR function, promotion strategies; impact of motivational and service/product quality programs, technological change, organisational change and development, organisational communication, employee participation, and consultation programs.

Summary

The future directions of SHRM are necessarily based upon both the historical development of the profession and the challenges posed by economic, social, political and cultural changes in the Australian industrial environment.

Recent industrial relations developments and ongoing organisational changes suggest that the principal focus of SHRM in the future will be that of change management, ensuring that organisations and their employees will be adaptive and responsive to both internal and external pressures and opportunities. Innovative and creative approaches to the management of an organisation's human resources will be increasingly required to effectively meet strategic and integrative objectives.

Flexibility is the main criterion for subsequent SHRM programs, in numerical, functional and financial terms. This will be achieved by adapting these practices to changes in the Australian industrial relations system, and thus ensuring effective relationships between HRM and strategic organisational objectives.

SHRM research, by either academics or practitioners, provides both guiding conceptual frameworks and practical applications for the entire professional association. The challenge is to draw upon the experience of the past and to integrate new approaches in view of social, political, economic and cultural changes.

Key terms

knowledge management (KM) 549
cross-vergence 547

Further readings

Avery G. 2005. *Leadership for sustainable futures: Achieving success in a competitive world*, Cheltenham, Edward Elgar.

Brewster C., Sparrow P., Harris H. 2005. 'Towards a new model of globalizing HRM,' *International Journal of Human Resource Management*, 16(6), pp. 949–70.

Chatterjee S., Nankervis A. (eds) 2006. *Asian management in transition: Emerging themes*, Basingstoke, Palgrave Macmillan.

Kochan T. 2004. 'Restoring trust in the human resource management profession,' *Asia Pacific Journal of Human Resources*, 42(2), pp. 132–46.

Kramar R. 2006. *Cranet–Macquarie survey on international strategic human resource management: Report on the Australian findings*, Sydney, Macquarie University.

Lansbury R., Baird M. 2004. 'Broadening the horizons of HRM: Lessons for Australia from the US experience,' *Asia Pacific Journal of Human Resources*, 42(2), pp. 147–55.

Lengnick-Hall M., Lengnick-Hall C. 2003. *Human resource management in the knowledge economy*, San Francisco, Berrett-Koehler.

Losey M., Meisinger S., Ulrich D. 2006. *The future of HRM*, Singapore, John Wiley & Sons (Asia).

Nankervis A., Chatterjee S., Coffey J. 2006, *Perspectives of human resource management in the Asia Pacific*, Sydney, Pearson Education Australia.

Nankervis A., Milton-Smith J., Miyamoto T., Taylor R. 2005. *Managing services*, Melbourne, Cambridge University Press.

Sheehan C., Holland P., DeCieri H. 2006. 'Current developments in HRM in Australian organisations,' *Asia Pacific Journal of Human Resources*, 44(2), pp. 132–52.

Sheldon P., Junor A. 2006. 'Australian HRM and the *Workplace Relations Amendment (WorkChoices) Act 2005*,' *Asia Pacific Journal of Human Resources*, 44(2), pp. 153–70.

Endnotes

1   Ulrich D. 1997. 'Long live the new HR,' *hrmonthly*, March, pp. 10–18.

2   Dawson P. 2003. 'Company change and human resources: In pursuit of flexibility?,' in R. Wiesner, B. Millett, *Human resource management: Challenges and future directions*, Brisbane, Wiley & Sons, p. 306.

3   Anon. 2000. 'Enter the brave new world,' *Workforce Online*, 79(4), April, p. 76.

4   Verma R., Boyer K. 2000. 'Service classifications and management challenges,' *Journal of Business Strategies*, 17(1), p. 5.

5   World Bank 2002. World development indicators 2002, www.worldbank.org/data/dataquery.html.

6   Matthews J. 2004. 'Innovation in services,' Paper presented to ANZIBA Conference, Canberra 5–6 November.

7   Schmidt J. 1999. 'Corporate excellence in the new millennium,' *Journal of Business Strategy*, November–December, 20(6), p. 40.

8   Challenger J. 2000. '24 trends shaping the workplace,' *The Futurist*, 34(5), pp. 35–43.

9   Ibid., p. 43.

10   Business Council of Australia 1989. *Enterprise-based bargaining units: A better way of working*, vol. 1, Melbourne, IRC, p. 72.

11   Lansbury R. 'Managing change in a challenging environment,' in A. Nankervis, R. Compton 1994. *Readings in strategic human resources management*, Melbourne, Thomson Learning, p. 135.

12   Kirby J. 1998. 'The firing squad,' *Business Review Weekly*, 2 March, p. 48.

13   Lansbury R. 2006. 'Rethinking HR after WorkChoices,' *Human Resources*, 13 June, p. 8.

14   Lowry D. 2006. 'HR managers as ethical decision-makers: Mapping the terrain,' *Asia Pacific Journal of Human Resources*, 44(2), pp. 171–83.

15   ABS Report 1997. *Our changing work profile*, Canberra, ABS.

16   Anon. 1997. *Weekend Australian*, 1 November, p. 4.

17   Coyle-Shapiro J., Kessler I. 2000, cited in Dawson P. 2003. 'Company change and human resources: In pursuit of flexibility?,' in Wiesner R., Millett B. 2003. op. cit., p. 312.

18   Schmidt J. 1999. op. cit., p. 40.

19   Ibid.

20   Kemske F. 1998. '60 HR predictions for 2008,' *Workforce*, 77(1), pp. 50–4.

21   Tyson S. 1995. *Human resource strategy*, London, Pitman, p. 80.

22   Walker J. 1992. *Human resource strategy*, New York, McGraw-Hill, p. 2.

23   Kochan T. 2004. 'Restoring trust in the human resource profession,' *Asia Pacific Journal of Human Resources*, 42(2), p. 132.

24   Gardner M., Palmer G. 1997. *Employment relations: Industrial relations and human resource management in Australia*, 2nd edn, Melbourne, Macmillan, p. 584.

25   Ibid., p. 12.

26   See Nankervis A., Chatterjee S., Coffey J. 2006. *Perspectives of human resource management in the Asia Pacific*, Sydney, Pearson Education; Chatterjee S., Nankervis A (eds) 2006. *Asian management in transition: Emerging trends*, Basingstoke, Palgrave Macmillan.

27   Kramar R. 2006. *Cranet–Macquarie survey on international strategic human resource management: Report on the Australian findings*, Sydney, Macquarie University, p. 28.

28   Barnes S (ed.) 2002. *Knowledge management systems: Theory and practice*, London, Thomson Learning.

29   Carlisle Y. 2000. 'Strategic thinking,' in Little S., Quintas P., Ray T (eds), *Managing knowledge: An essential reader*, London, Sage, pp. 12–38.

30   See, for example, Nankervis et al. 2006, op. cit.

31   Wittingslow G. 1997. 'The future for HR professionals: Line manager or policy-maker?' *Asia Pacific Journal of Human Resources*, 35(3), p. 108.

32   Kulik C., Bainbridge H. 2006. 'HR and the line: The distribution of HR activities in Australian organisations,' *Asia Pacific Journal of Human Resources*, 44(2), pp. 240–56.

33   Compton R.L., Morrissey W. 2000. 'Soft … hard … harder,' *Management Today*, December, p. 37.

34   Ulrich D. 1998. 'The future calls for change,' *Workforce Online*, 77(1), p. 90.

Online reading

INFOTRAC® COLLEGE EDITION

For additional readings and review on challenges for human resource management, explore InfoTrac® College Edition, your online library. Go to: www.infotrac-college.com and search for any of the InfoTrac key terms listed below:

➤ knowledge management

Glossary

360-degree feedback	A performance review process where an employee will usually choose up to eight other persons with whom they work, to review their performance. The employee will be required to choose several people employed above, below and alongside them. Often combined with self-appraisal
ability	A capability that an individual possesses; a quality that permits or facilitates achievement or accomplishment
absenteeism	The number of employees who are away from their jobs for explained or unexplained reasons during a given period
adult learning theory	Recognises that adults learn in different ways from children, particularly that they need to understand why the learning is important, and can participate actively in the learning. Sometimes called andragogy (as opposed to pedagogy)
AIDS	Acquired Immune Deficiency Syndrome
ANTA	Australian National Training Agenda, or the federal government's system for integrating high school, industry, and TAFE knowledge and (vocational) skills development
application form for employment	A standardised form used by organisations to obtain work-related and personal information concerning applicants for a vacant position
arbitration	The process whereby an independent third party makes a decision based on the merits of the evidence and submissions made to the tribunal. These decisions are legally binding for all parties involved
award restructuring	This emerged as part of Australia's structural efficiency principle (SEP) program during the late 1980s and the objective was to review awards, to remove outdated and outmoded provisions and make them more relevant to the needs of industry
babyboomers	Those persons born between 1945 and 1960
background investigation	A check by the employer into the background of an applicant for a position. Usually in the form of a check of written or telephone referees' reports. A method of verifying the details provided by the applicant
balanced scorecard	Based on a strategic management tool pioneered by Kaplan and Norton. Employees set goals and are assessed across four quadrants: financial, customers, internal business processes and learning and innovation
bargaining	In the industrial relations context, is also often referred to as collective bargaining or negotiation. These are terms used to describe the process whereby unions and employers determine the terms and conditions of work. More recently, there has been an emphasis on individual bargaining; that is, direct bargaining, without union representation, between an employee and the employer.

base pay — That part of remuneration that is largely 'fixed' or 'guaranteed' and time-based rather than performance-based. May be configured either according to the content of the job/position or on the basis of the performance capabilities (i.e. skills or competencies) of the individual employee

behaviour modelling — Using role models (e.g. supervisors and skilled employees) to reinforce desired workplace behaviours

behavioural questions — Sometimes referred to as situation questions as they seek information from the candidate as to what they would do in a specific situation. Each question is normally based on at least one competency for the position. Also referred to as competency-based questions

behaviourally anchored rating scales (BARS) — BARS is a contemporary rating scale approach to performance review that assesses how a job is performed rather than output; that is, behaviour is assessed. Very useful where quantitative approaches such as MBO will not give a valid result

best fit — A term used to describe the best candidate for the position. Is also used when describing best fit strategies

broad grade — A base pay structure commonly associated with skill-based pay progression that allows individual employees to be recognised and rewarded for acquiring additional skills and knowledge associated within a 'family' of combined jobs. The pay range for each broad grade is typically 40 to 60 per cent; that is, some two to three times that of a narrow grade

broadbands/broadbanding — A base pay structure commonly associated with competency- and/or performance-related pay progression in which a large number of narrow jobs arranged in a steep hierarchy are replaced by a much smaller number of pay bands, each with a substantially wider pay range – frequently 100 to 300 per cent

business process outsourcing (BPO) — The choice to use external service providers to perform selected organisational functions (e.g. IT, payroll, warehousing, logistics)

call centres — Primary function is to handle outbound and incoming communication from customers

career planning — Individual plans for employee careers

career plateau — Refers to a stage of an employee's career in which few future opportunities appear to exist

casualisation — A preference for employing staff on casual rather than ongoing or permanent contracts, for cost and staffing flexibility reasons

central tendency — This occurs where the manager rates employees as average across a five- or seven-point scale

closed questions — Require only a 'yes' or 'no' answer. Should be used sparingly to bring an issue to closure

compa-ratio — An index number representing the employee's position in their base pay range. Short for compensation comparison ratio

competencies — The skills, knowledge, attitudes and behaviours that will be required for a position

competency profiling	The process of defining and analysing the competencies required for a specific position
competency-based learning (CBL)	All learning is based upon the development of employee competencies (i.e. knowledge + skills + abilities)
competency-based pay	A base pay system which recognises and rewards individual employees on the basis of assessed embedded abilities or 'competencies' such as self-confidence, achievement orientation, interpersonal empathy, persistence, composure, problem-solving ability, and the like
conciliation	The process whereby a member of an industrial tribunal brings the parties to a dispute together with a view to having the parties themselves come to an agreement
corporate governance	Ethical and accountable standards of financial and operational management
corporate social responsibility (CSR)	Organisational contributions to the social and economic sustainability of the communities in which they operate
cross-vergence	The dissemination of management theories and practice from one country or region to others, used especially for the transfer of Asian management ideas to the Western world
developmental rewards	Cover those rewards associated with personal learning, development and career growth, such as skills training and performance and leadership coaching
direct benefits	Financial entitlements that directly supplement cash base pay, including employer contributions to superannuation and health and medical insurance, paid leave, and the like
disciplining	A genuine attempt to ensure that expected employee behaviour and performance standards are maintained
discretionary bonus	Irregular lump sum awards for outstanding performance made at the discretion of the supervisor and/or senior management
diversity management	The creation of an environment that allows all employees to contribute to organisational goals and experience personal growth
downshifting	A voluntary scaling back of one's career so as to enjoy a better mix of family/work priorities
dual career couples	Both partners in a relationship or marriage have their own careers, which can cause difficulties if one of them is faced with an interstate or overseas job relocation
DVT (deep vein thrombosis or 'economy class syndrome')	The formation of blood clots, often attributed to sitting in cramped conditions during long-distance flights
e-cruitment	Online recruitment processes via the Internet as contrasted to newspaper advertising
e-learning	learning methodologies using electronic technology such as the Internet or intranet

employee assistance program (EAP)	A particular model of employee counselling that has become increasingly popular since the mid-1980s
employee attitude surveys	Qualitative surveys which aim to elicit the degree of satisfaction of employees with jobs, employment conditions, workplaces and managers. Also called morale or climate surveys
employee counselling	A relationship where one person endeavours to help another to understand and resolve a work-related or personal problem
employee engagement	A state of emotional or intellectual involvement or commitment
employee kiosks	Intranet systems which permit employee access to their own HR records, allowing changes to their personal details, and freeing HR professionals to focus on more strategic functions
employee referrals	Applicants are referred to the organisation by internal employees; often a reward system applies where the referral is successful
employee turnover	A measure of the movement of employees through the organisation
employee wastage	A measure of the number and types of employees who leave organisations within a defined period. Usually focuses on analysing the reasons for their departure, with a view to retaining valued employees
employer branding	The sum total of an organisation's efforts to convince existing and prospective staff that the company is an attractive place to work
employer of choice	A concept that describes the strategies and processes put in place to attract, retain and motivate key talent
employment contracts	Formal or informal relationships between employers and employees which outline the expectations of performance, conditions and rewards; sometimes associated with 'psychological contracts' which infer employer–employee commitments and obligations
employment interview	Usually, a face-to-face meeting between the candidate and a representative or a number of representatives of the employing organisation. Can also be conducted by tele/video conference. Methods range from structured to unstructured
employment relations	A combination of HRM and industrial relations in a common framework
employment testing	A test that attempts to measure a person's ability against pre-determined selection criteria. Examples are: personality tests, intelligence tests, achievement tests and aptitude tests. Reliability and validity of such tests are of concern
environmental scanning	The process of analysing the external environments of organisations, in order to ascertain the potential and actual effects on organisational effectiveness
ergonomics	Studies the workplace physical equipment and facilities in relation to health and safety
establishment data	Records the actual numbers and requirements of employees and their positions at any point in time
executive leasing	A senior employee is contracted for a set period of time or to undertake a specific project. Usually contracted from a private consultancy

executive search	A process used by a private consultancy which aims at sourcing talent at the senior management layer of an organisation. Usually by direct approach rather than advertising
expatriate	An employee from the parent (home) country who is working for a period of time (usually more than a year) in an overseas (host) country
external recruitment	Any recruitment strategy that aims to attract talent from outside the organisation
extrinsic rewards	Tangible rewards arising from the factors associated with but external to the job that the employee does; that is, from the job context. Extrinsic rewards are of three main types: financial rewards, developmental rewards and social rewards
financial rewards	Rewards of a monetary/cash or near-monetary/cash nature. Also known as pay, remuneration or compensation, these rewards include base pay, direct benefits and performance-related rewards in monetary form
flexible benefits plans	Plans which allow employees a degree of choice in how best to configure their benefits package within a range of options made available voluntarily by the employer. Also known as 'cafeteria' benefits plans
forced choice method	A performance review system that provides several statements from which the manager must choose. Similar to a multiple choice examination
gainsharing	A form of collective performance-related pay in which management shares with all employees in a particular production plant or business unit the financial gains associated with specific measures of improvement in the results achieved by that work group as measured against an historical benchmark of the group's performance
generation X	Those persons born between 1960 and 1980
generation Y	Those persons born between 1980 and the present
globalisation	The expansion of organisational operations across national, regional and global boundaries, with its associated financial, marketing and HRM implications
goalsharing	Bonus payments linked directly to the achievement of group performance goals over a specified time frame
Gross Domestic Product (GDP)	A widely-accepted measure of national economic performance
halo error	Where one impressive factor overshadows the entire performance review. Can also be negative (devil error)
'hard' HRM	Emphasises employee productivity and performance measures, reflecting the transactional elements of the employment relationship
harshness	An error which involves an employee or employees being rated more harshly than those working for another manager yet producing similar outputs

home country nationals	Managers from the organisation's headquarters sent overseas as expatriates
host country nationals	Employees employed from within the overseas country involved
HR audits	A comprehensive assessment of the effectiveness of all HR functions against stated goals and outcomes. Can cover cost, compliance and governance aspects
HR benchmarks	Comparative quantitative measures of HR functions between organisations, often expressed as 'best practice'
HR metrics	Multiple quantitative measures of HR functions
human capital management (HCM)	The quantitative measurement of the value to the organisation of employee skills, competencies, and potential
human resource information management systems (HRIMS)	Databases designed to provide comprehensive employee information for strategic, operational and administrative HRM purposes
human resource management (HRM)	A long-term perspective which focuses on the links between personnel functions and their contributions to organisational goals and objectives
human resource planning (HRP)	The process of determining the numbers, skills and qualities of employees required to meet present and future organisational needs
indirect benefits	Cover a growing number of non-financial rewards, ranging from special unpaid leave provisions to the provision of wellness programs and advisory services. In essence, these are intended to make the organisation a more appealing place to work as well as to increase employee morale, job satisfaction, membership behaviour, organisational commitment and task motivation
industrial psychology	A focus on employees' psychological reactions to their workplaces
industrial relations system	The term comes from the seminal work of John Dunlop (1959) and refers to the context, rules, regulations and institutions that govern the employment relationship and which set the terms and conditions of work and employment.
industrial sociology	The study of interpersonal communications and relationships in the workplace
instructor (or facilitator)	Someone who is responsible for designing and conducting training and learning programs – instructors are usually associated with specific knowledge or skills training, whereas facilitators assist in adult learning and development, as mentors, coaches or supporters
intergenerational conflict	The potential difficulties posed by the diverse attitudes and work behaviours of employees from different generations (especially the 'babyboomers', and generation X and Y) in the workplace
internal recruitment	Any recruitment strategy aimed at existing employees; that is, transfer or promotion from within the organisation
interview questions	A range of questions put to the candidates for a position. May range from open to closed depending on the rationale for a particular question and/or the skill of the interviewer/s

intrinsic rewards	Psychological rewards arising from the content of the job itself, including the interest and challenge which it provides, the task variety and autonomy, the degree of feedback, and the meaning and significance attributed to it
job description	A statement that describes the job and the conditions under which it will be performed
job evaluation	Involves determining relative base pay rates by relating them to the importance or relative value of the job to the organisation. This is achieved by comparing jobs on a number of factors thought to be important in determining job value, such as skill, effort, responsibility or working conditions. Job evaluation emphasises 'internal equity' in setting job-based pay rates rather than 'external competitiveness' per se
job redesign	Changing the tasks or the way work is performed in an existing position or job
job specification	A statement that describes the 'best fit' person or ideal candidate for the position to be filled
knowledge management (KM)	The creation, dissemination and recording of knowledge, in both technological and human forms
knowledge workers	A term which evolved during the 1990s, it has been used to define a group of educated and/or a professional occupational grouping who meet their job outcomes primarily through the use of their knowledge and expertise
knowledge-based work	The primary focus of the role is on the reliance of information and knowledge to produce outcomes and results upon which performance is measured
KSAs	An acronym for Knowledge, Skills and Abilities (or Attributes)
labour demand forecasting	determining the need for employees in both the short and longer term. Can be quantitative and qualitative
labour market	The geographic area or demographic group from which employees will be sourced
labour supply analysis	Determining the possible sources of employees, either internally or externally
Learning organisations	A term coined by Peter Senge which describes organisations that develop systems to ensure that they continually learn from their own experiences and hence improve all their operations in an ongoing manner
leniency	A manager rates all employees at the high end of a rating scale
lifelong learning	The concept that learning should be a constant and ongoing experience at any stage of (employee and organisational) life
long-term incentives	Incentives awarded on the basis of individual or group performance over a period greater than one year, but typically over a three- to five-year period. Rewards generally take the form of company equity rather than cash, although cash payments based on multiyear performance would also qualify

management by objectives (MBO)	A performance review system that relies on the measurement of performance against mutually agreed objectives set at the beginning of the time period under review. Most useful where output is easily measured in quantitative terms (i.e. what has been achieved)
managerial prerogative	Managerial rights perceived by employers as being non-negotiable, therefore allowing management to make unilateral decisions
market surveys	Also known as salary surveys, these involve setting pay rates for particular jobs according to what other employers are paying for the same or similar jobs in external labour markets. Thus, the approach emphasises 'external competitiveness' in determining the rate for the job
maternity/paternity leave	Provided by some countries (paid or unpaid) to support and retain valued employees (female and male) who are starting families
medical examination	Often given in the latter stages of the selection process to ensure that the applicant is medically fit to carry out the range of duties and responsibilities set out in the job description. Care must be taken not to discriminate unfairly on physical and intellectual impairment
medical model	An emphasis on diagnosis and treatment rather than the prevention of illnesses and diseases
merit grid	The merit grid (or merit 'matrix' or merit 'guide chart', as it is also known) specifies the precise link between the assessed performance grade, the employee's compa-ratio, and the percentage performance increment
merit pay	Schemes that reward individuals on the basis of formal performance appraisal scores. Typically, merit payments are based on performance grades determined by means of formal systems of behavioural observation and assessment. In traditional merit pay plans, payments take the form of cumulative additions to base pay. These additions are termed 'merit raises' or 'merit increments'. These reward employees for appraised performance in a previous time period – typically one year. An alternative approach is the 'merit bonus' method, in which the appraisal-based payment does not roll into base pay but, rather, stands apart from it and does not become an ongoing entitlement
multiskilling	Training workers in a number of skills, enabling them to perform a variety of tasks or functions across job boundaries. Multiskilling may be horizontal, vertical or diagonal
multi-tasking	To concurrently carry out two or more tasks or the concurrent use of a single program that can carry out many functions
narrow grades	A narrow grade (also known as a 'job grade') houses a group of jobs of similar size/value to the organisation and specifying a pay range for these jobs rather than a scale step or spot rate. Each grade will cover a group of jobs regarded as being of similar value to the organisation and therefore worthy of roughly the same range of base pay. Each grade has a pay range that defines the minimum and maximum rates of pay for all jobs in the grade, with the pay range for each grade typically being 20 to 30 per cent

National Occupational Health & Safety Commission (NOHSC)	An Australian federal government research and planning agency, now renamed the Australian Safety and Compensation Commission (ASCC)
needs analysis	A system for evaluating the knowledge, skills and competency gaps of employees and their organisations
occupational epidemiology	The study of 'epidemics' (or the incidence of illnesses and diseases) in the workplace
occupational hygiene	Explores physical, chemical and biological hazards in the workplace
occupational overuse syndrome (OOS)	Also called repetition strain injury (RSI), it refers to the wrist and tendon pain experienced by employees in repetitive manual jobs such as word-processing
offshoring	The outsourcing of selected organisational functions globally
open questions	Often used to commence an interview. Questions ask 'what', 'why', 'how', 'when'
parallel careers	The development of two separate career options, usually through a technical or a managerial path
peer review	Persons of equal rank in the organisation are asked to rate one another
performance management	A number of strategies and processes which include performance review, employee counselling, disciplining and absence management
performance review	A formal review (often annually) of an employee's performance against pre-determined and mutually agreed objectives. Can also be informal on a much more regular basis
performance-related rewards	Also known as incentive plans, these are rewards given in recognition of past performance and in order to reinforce and enhance future performance. Performance pay, the most common form of performance-related reward, is usually an overlay to base pay and varies according to the level of measured or assessed performance. As such, performance pay is said to be 'variable', 'contingent' and 'at risk', rather than fixed or guaranteed
personnel management	A set of functions (e.g. recruitment, training, payroll) with a short-term administrative focus, and no clear links to organisational goals
pluralist	Contrary to the 'unitarist' view, this perspective assumes that the employer–employee relationship is inherently conflictual, and that their diverse interests need to be negotiated or bargained by representative bodies
productivity	A measure of efficiency, often considered as output per person-hour
profitsharing	A formal arrangement under which bonus payments are made to eligible employees on a regular (usually annual) basis, based on a formula that links the size of the total bonus pool to an accounting measure of periodic (typically annual) profit, such as net profit (total income less operating costs) or net profit after tax
quality of work life (QWL)	A range of measures intended to improve the satisfaction or contentment of employees in the workplace. May include job or workplace redesign, recognition and rewards systems, teamwork, flexible work schedules and new technology

rating scales	Any performance review system that relies on a rating scale to measure an employee's output
realistic job preview	Where applicants for a position are given a tour of the workplace and in particular shown their work environment and introduced to those with whom they will work
recency effect	An error that can occur when output across only the last few months of the rating period is taken into account
recognition awards	Financial or non-financial rewards given in recognition of outstanding performance by individuals or work groups. Rewards may be either financial or non-financial in nature, or a combination of the two
recruitment	The sum of activities and processes that aim to provide a pool of qualified persons from which the successful candidate may be chosen
recruitment agencies	Such agencies may include government sponsored networks, private consultants and executive search firms, each of which will provide assistance in employing qualified staff
rehabilitation	The process of assisting employees back to work following accidents or injuries
reliability	Refers to the degree to which two or more selection processes yield a consistent result e.g. consistency of results across a battery of psychological tests
restricted share plans	Share plans under which the employee receives the share free of charge but where vesting is conditional and contingent rather than guaranteed. For instance, full ownership ('vesting') of the shares may be subject to the meeting of a performance target or 'hurdle' within this period
results-based incentives	Incentives geared to measured individual or group results, including piece rates, sales commissions and bonus payments for achievement of goals
résumé	A personal document prepared by a job applicant that outlines information such as: personal details, work history, educational qualifications, competencies, professional memberships, interests and details of referees
retention strategies	Any strategy which aims to retain key talent within the organisation e.g. work/family balance policies, career planning
rewards	Tangibles or intangibles that an organisation provides to its employees in exchange for the employee's potential or actual work contribution, and to which employees as individuals attach a positive value as a satisfier of certain self-defined needs.
ROI	Return on (organisational) Investment, or the financial benefit of a chosen (HRM) activity
SARS (severe acute respiratory syndrome)	A virus spread through close contact with an infected person
selection criteria	Those essential and desirable criteria that will be sought and measured in applicants applying for a position

selection	A process that analyses and compares the applicants for a position against the selection criteria for the position. Often seen as a negative process as the aim is to eliminate all but the best qualified for the position. Also seen as naturally discriminatory and care needs to be taken that such discrimination is both fair and lawful
self-appraisal	The employee reviews own performance against performance standards and completes a report. The manager will do likewise and both then attempt to agree the result
sensitivity training	Can have many applications, but is often used to train managers and employees in understanding and empathising with employee problems or cross-cultural attitudes and behaviours
share appreciation rights	Surrogate share plans under which the employee is not required to take ownership of the shares; rather, the employee receives cash equivalent to the wealth that would accrue to ordinary shareholders via share price appreciation plus dividend earnings over the grant period, with the base line typically being the market price at the date of grant
share option plans	Provide eligible employees with the right but not the obligation to purchase a specified quantity of company shares at particular price on or after a designated future date
share (or stock) ownership plans	Provide eligible employees with access to share ownership in the organisation that employs them. Shares may be issued to employees free of any charge (share bonus plans) or they may be sold to them at a discount on the market price (discounted share purchase plans) or using an employer-funded low-interest or interest-free loan
short-term incentives	Incentives awarded on the basis of individual or group performance over a period of one year or less. Payments typically take the form of an annual cash bonus
simulations	Learning and development activities designed to replicate actual work situations within a safe learning environment. May or may not involve the use of simulators (technology)
skill	An individual's level of proficiency at performing a particular task; has been acquired through training
skill set	Consists of a bundle of related tasks and activities – or 'skill elements' – the mastery of which constitutes a finite and verifiable unit of learning on which training content can be developed and delivered
skill-based pay	A base pay system which recognises and rewards individual employees on the basis of the acquisition of required technical skills and job knowledge
skills inventories	Databases which include comprehensive information on the current skills, qualifications and competencies of employees
social rewards	Those rewards associated with the organisational climate, performance support, quality of supervision, work-group affinity, and opportunities for enhanced work/life balance, such as flexible work time arrangements, staff sabbaticals, fitness and wellness programs, and the like

'soft' HRM	Focuses on the communication, consultation, counselling and support elements of the employment relationship
strategic human resource management (SHRM)	Emphasises the close alignment between organisational and HRM strategies, processes, functions and outcomes
strategic international HRM	Strategic HRM in the international (or global) context. Sometimes referred to as 'strategic global HRM'
strategic reward management	The design and maintenance of an integrated reward system in which (a) reward strategy, policy and practice align with and support the organisation's overall human resource strategy, plans and policies which, in turn, support the organisation's overall strategic goals and objectives
succession planning/ executive replacement	Organisational plans for senior/executive career development
third country nationals	Employees from any country other than the home or host country
total reward management	A holistic approach to employee reward management integrating intrinsic and extrinsic reward elements
triple bottom line	An audit of the financial, social and environmental effectiveness of organisations
union (or trade union)	A work-based organisation which provides a collective voice for employees. It is an institution whose purpose is to represent and defend those who work for someone else. The Australian Bureau of Statistics defines a union as 'an organisation, consisting predominantly of employees, the principal activities of which include the negotiation of rates of pay and conditions of employment for its members'.
unitarist	A view of industrial/employment relations that assumes common interests and cooperation between employers and employees
upward appraisal	A method where team members will review and rate the performance of their manager
validity	Refers to what a selection process claims to measure and how well it is measured. E.g. does a psychological test measure what it claims to measure and to what extent is this trait measured?
war for talent	A term coined to describe the strategies employed by an organisation to attract the right talent to their organisation
WorkChoices	An abbreviated title for the Australian federal government's *Workplace Relations Amendment (WorkChoices) Act 2005*, designed to provide more 'flexibility' in employment conditions
work–life balance	Recognises that employees have different personal needs (e.g. childcare, ageing parents) which need to be accommodated in their work patterns. Also called work/family balance
workplace agreement	The generic term for all agreements that set out the terms and conditions of work under the *WorkChoices* legislation. It includes individual workplace agreements, known as Australian Workplace Agreements (AWAs), and also collective workplace agreements between unions and an employer.

(workplace) flexibility	Actions to improve the productivity and output of employees through reductions in rigid employment conditions on the one hand, and the accommodation of diverse personal needs on the other hand
workplace relations	Refers to the employment relationship as it constructed and managed at the workplace (or enterprise or organisation). Since the early 1990s this term has replaced industrial relations in many policy and legislative documents and is intended to convey a more direct relationship between a single employer and the employees at that workplace
ZEPO plans	Zero exercise price option plans (or 'performance share' plans) which allow employees to take up shares at no cost but only on condition of a performance hurdle being satisfied over a designated performance period

Index

L.M. Montgomery's Complete Journals

L.M. Montgomery's Complete Journals

The Ontario Years, 1922–1925

PUBLISHED BY
Rock's Mills Press

L.M. Montgomery's Complete Journals, The Ontario Years 1922–1925

For information, visit us online at www.rocksmillspress.com or email us at customer.servicerocksmillspress.com.

Contents

Preface

This new edition of *The Complete Journals of L.M. Montgomery: The Ontario Years* covers the final four years that Montgomery lived in Leaskdale, Ontario. It is a record of both the highs and the lows—and lots in between—from January 1922 to December 1925.

The highs include a trip to Bala, Muskoka, in the summer of 1922; a trip to Prince Edward Island in the summer of 1923 (and another trip there in July 1924 on a sadder occasion, the death of Montgomery's Aunt Annie); and a trip to Mammoth Cave in Kentucky in August 1924. During these years Montgomery composed *Emily Climbs* (1925), *Emily's Quest* (1927), and *The Blue Castle* (1926). She also received awards and recognition for her work as a writer, at home and abroad.

But these four years also saw many troubles, some new and some lingering. The most serious problem was her husband Ewan's mental illness—"melancholia" as it was known then—attacks of which occurred with little warning and could be alarming:

> Yesterday he sat or lay all day—unshorn, collarless, hair on end, eyes wild and hunted, with a hideous imbecile expression on his face. I cannot describe how repulsive he appears—I can hardly bear to stay in the same room with him. I can conceal this feeling but I cannot banish or control it. I am almost tempted to believe in that old theory of devil possession. (March 16, 1924)

Montgomery correctly understood Ewan's periodic instability as a psychiatric disease and looked for answers in medical books of the day: "I think I found in the book [*Hormones Regulating Personality* (1923)] a clue to the mystery of Ewan's personality. I believe his thyroid and pituitary glands are sub-normal. . . . . Possibly, too, it is some disorder in these glands that causes his periodic attacks of melancholia" (May 4, 1924). Her diagnosis was wrong, but a good attempt to manage a difficult situation (she gave him "thyroid pills" and tracked the unsuccessful results). Montgomery herself suffered from periods of acute anxiety. She knew that mental illness could be heritable and worried over her sons.

Other troubles arose. Not only did legal battles with her first publisher, L.C. Page & Co., continue, but a new lawsuit emerged. On June 16, 1921,

six months before this present volume begins, the Macdonalds' car—driven, as it always was, by Ewan—had collided with a car driven by Zephyr farmer Marshall Pickering. Both men were probably at fault. In the days before comprehensive traffic laws and seat-belts, car accidents were common, and the results could be grim. While in this case there were no lasting injuries, Pickering brought a lawsuit against Ewan for damages he claimed had arisen from the collision: an enlarged prostate gland and his wife's diabetes. The entire community was riveted by the lawsuit, with opinion divided (mostly falling in favour of the Macdonalds).

The community was also divided by Church Union. In the 1920s, rural congregations were declining and the cost of maintaining numerous small churches was too high. The remedy was the amalgamation of three churches—the Methodist Church, the Congregational Union, and the Presbyterian Church—into a single "United Church of Canada." While in parts of Canada this caused little controversy, in Ontario, many Presbyterian congregations did not want to become part of this larger United Church. A vote was held in each congregation on whether to remain independent or "go Union." In the Macdonalds' congregation, like many others, the debate grew bitter and divisive. "I feel harassed and depressed, when I get tired, over these unending lawsuits and Union problems," wrote Montgomery on August 17, 1924.

Montgomery's journals are a fascinating chronicle of national and international history, of social change, of local politics, and of family dynamics. It is also a unique record of Montgomery herself, a window into the personality of this complex, multi-layered, and deep-thinking artist.

***

The journals we have today, and upon which all the *Complete Journals* are based, were copied by Montgomery herself into ten uniform legal-sized ledgers.[1] They begin with an entry dated September 21, 1889, an announcement by the young Maud Montgomery (who in 1889 was 15 years old):

I am going to begin a new kind of diary. I have kept one of a kind for years—ever since I was a tot of nine. But I burned it to-day. It was so silly I was ashamed of it. And it was also very dull. I wrote in

---

1   These ten ledgers are now housed in the University of Guelph Archival & Special Collections.

it religiously every day and told what kind of weather it was. Most of the time I hadn't much else to tell but I would have thought it a kind of crime not to write daily in it—nearly as bad as not saying my prayers or washing my face. (September 21, 1889)

The record of Montgomery's life continues, finally ending in 1942 shortly before her death. By 1922, when this present volume begins, Montgomery had recorded a variety of life events. These include a year in Prince Albert, Saskatchewan (1890–91); a year at Prince of Wales College, Charlottetown (1893–94); a year teaching Bideford (1894–95); the publication of *Anne of Green Gables* in 1908; her marriage and honeymoon in England and Scotland in 1911; her move to Ontario midway through her life; the birth of her three children (and the death of one baby at birth); her travails as Mistress of the Manse; the effect of World War I on Canadian life; the death of her beloved cousin Frede Campbell in 1919; and her husband's recurrent mental illness.

This present volume opens shortly before Montgomery completed a monumental task: between 1918 and 1922 she copied all of her earlier journals to that date into the uniform legal-sized ledgers of 500 pages each that we have today.

Last winter I began to copy my whole journal into a set of volumes all the same size. My journal, beginning in the fall of 1890, has been written in various "blank books" of equally various shapes and sizes. I resolved to copy it as aforesaid. It will mean a great deal of work and will take a long time, for I can only spare fifteen minutes a day for it. But it will be a satisfaction when done. I shall be careful to copy it exactly as it is written but I mean to "illustrate" it as I go along with such photos of the scenes and people who figure in it as I possess. (September 2, 1919)

She finished the work of copying over three years later:

But today I finished copying my journal into uniform volumes. It has been a long piece of work but an interesting one. Perhaps a hundred years from now my descendants may read over this diary and regard it as an interesting heirloom … I *desire that these journals never be destroyed but kept as long as the leaves hold together*. I leave this to my descendants or my literary heirs as a sacred charge and invoke a Shakespearean curse on them if they disregard it. There is so much of myself in these volumes that I cannot bear the thought of their

ever being destroyed. It would seem to me like a sort of murder. (April 16, 1922).

From the first entry dated September 21, 1889, to the beginning of April 1922, Montgomery's journals comprise some 633,600 words—more than *War and Peace*. By 1942, that word count had more than doubled.

And this is not the only extensive copying task Montgomery undertook during these years. In this present volume, there is an extraordinary and unexpected inclusion of another diary in her handwritten ledger. On a visit to PEI in 1924, Montgomery records that her friend and cousin, Alec Macneill, presented her with his father Charles's old diary, composed between 1892 and 1896. Montgomery describes her delight at this diary, and a few months later copies the entire document into her journal. It is a big job, taking up 100 pages of her legal ledger. (Montgomery's transcription of Charles Macneill's diary is not reproduced here; given its length, it is available as a separate publication.)

Montgomery describes her work of copying the Charles Macneill diary "over several Sundays":

I have finished the old diary. It has taken me several Sunday afternoons and meanwhile I have been writing my journal entries separately and will copy them down later. To any other person in the world Charles Macneill's old diary would be tedious to read and unthinkably tedious to copy. But to me every moment I spent in copying it was a delight. I was back again in a world where happiness reigned and problems were non-existent—for me at least. I was so much at his home when a child and young girl that every word he wrote brought back vividly some sweet memory of those past days and childish frolics and delights. The most commonplace statement seemed like a finger touching the keys of an organ and evoking melodies of haunting sweetness—sights, sounds, of that old north shore farm that came back like the faint appealing voices of ghosts heard long ago many shadowy years agone.

In the weeks and months of early 1925, she describes herself as wrestling with some form of depression, likely related to ongoing anxiety over Ewan's mental illness. The soothing nostalgia of copying the old journal seems to have been at least in part therapeutic. But this diary and the long commentary that follows it is also a way of talking about her own artistic identity: her vivid imagination, her love of beauty, and her fascination with storytelling.

Montgomery notes that while copying Charles Macneill's diary, she had been "writing her journal entries separately," to be copied later into the uniform ledgers. In fact, we can speculate that Montgomery must have kept three years of notes "separately" while she was copying the first 33 years of her journals. There would have have been a point at which she finally caught up with herself as she copied out her earlier journal entries up to the present. (Or was there always a lag, from when she took notes on daily events to when she eventually wrote them up in her journal, mulling over how to shape them into the larger narrative?)

Montgomery asserts that her record is a "faithful" one, copied "exactly" as she had written it. We will never know how accurate a statement this is. There can be little doubt her journals are in the main very faithful to her lived experience, but she was also shaping a narrative about herself and her life.[2]

There are some fascinating moments where we can glimpse the creative process behind Montgomery's journal composition. They often seem to be written more or less immediately after the events of her life had taken place; however, we know that there was a lag at least part of the time. At the end of her handwritten ledger #3, for example, she writes:

> Another volume of my journal finished. … in those four years have been crowded a lifetime of emotions. Since I began this journal the war has ended—Frede has died. I will begin a new volume with the bitter certainty that in it there will never be any Frede, save in my memories.

That entry is dated December 21, 1919; Frede had died earlier that year, in January 1919. However, in a later entry dated February 19, 1922, Montgomery writes (presumably in an entry in her notebook to be later transcribed into the ledger), "I have been copying my journal of Frede's death and have lived it over." Here we see the three-year lag between writing about events as they happened and the transcription of this record into her ledgers. She could not have controlled where her original record of the past fell into the ledgers as she copied them, so her reflections of December 21, 1919, on "those four years" must have been added during the copying process, in 1922.[3]

---

2   Montgomery's biographer, Mary Rubio, believes that Montgomery was a scrupulously honest person—most of the time.

3   My thanks to Benjamin Lefebvre for this observation.

There is a connection between the journal writing endeavors of Montgomery and the title character of *Emily of New Moon* (1923), composed while Montgomery was copying out her journal. The young Emily has considerable literary talent, and wants to become a writer. The final words of *Emily of New Moon* echo the first words of Montgomery's own handwritten ledger: "'I am going to keep a journal, that may be published when I die.'" These words echo, in a more determined way, the young Montgomery's first entry into her handwritten ledger, noted above.

But journal-writing involves veracity, a tricky thing for a born story-teller. In the next novel in the series, *Emily Climbs*, some of the issues associated with journal-writing are drawn out. Emily's Aunt Elizabeth disapproves of her literary ambition. She and Emily come to an impasse: Aunt Elizabeth will fund Emily's education, but only on the condition that Emily give up writing. Emily claims that she would be unable to meet such a condition because writing is too much a part of her lifeblood. But ultimately the two settle on a compromise: Emily must promise that she will write only "what is true." She reluctantly agrees, reflecting that she can at least still compose "sketches of character—and accounts of everyday events—witty—satirical—tragic—as the humour took her."

Later Emily discusses the matter with her teacher and mentor, Mr Carpenter, who proclaims that such an exercise will be "excellent": "'Stick to facts for three years and see what you can make of them. Leave the realm of imagination severely alone and confine yourself to ordinary life,'" he tells her.

"'There isn't any such thing as ordinary life,'" returns Emily.

She reflects on her own position in a long line of ancestors who seem, like Aunt Elizabeth, to be making demands on her and limiting her freedom of expression ("'Cousin Jimmy says nobody can be free who has a thousand ancestors,'" she complains). Mr Carpenter points out to Emily that her ancestry is not limiting her; in fact, it is responsible for her willfullness and determination to succeed. (Here he uses a Latin term, *cacoëthes scribendi*, meaning "mania for writing"—a term Montgomery uses elsewhere to describe her own youthful determination to write.)

" . . . your ancestors don't seem to have wished any special curse on you. They've simply laid it on you to aim for the heights and they'll give you no peace if you don't. Call it ambition—aspiration—*cacoëthes scribendi*—any name you will."

Over time, Emily learns to value her ancestry. Along with the faithful curation of the details of her own lived experience, ancestry and tradition becomes a source of creativity and inspiration.

This may be how Montgomery was beginning to see her own journal-writing: "sticking to the facts" but embedding them with what she saw as her artistic lineage. Copying Charles Macneill's diary, and recording her own intense recollections of her childhood in Prince Edward Island, is part of this complex process.

During the four years covered in this edition, she finds creative connections to her ancestry. She looks back at her ancestors, but she also looks forward to her descendants, addressing them several times and wondering how they will respond to her journals. At the point that she describes finishing the task of copying her journals, she imagines her descendants looking back at her—as she will look back at Charles Macneill. How, Montgomery wonders, will she come across to an imagined "great-great-granddaugther of mine," a century in the future?

Will some great-great-granddaughter of mine ever bend her pretty young head over this page? If so—I salute you, dear! Here and now, across the gulf of generations, I put out my hand and say to you, "I lived a hundred years before you did; but my blood runs in your veins and I lived and loved and suffered and enjoyed and toiled and struggled just as you do. I found life good, in spite of everything. May you find it so. I found that courage and kindness are the two essential things. They are just as essential in your century as they were in mine. Here's to you, little great-great-grand-daughter, not to be born for a hundred years! I hope you'll be merry and witty and brave and wise; and I hope you'll say to yourself, 'If great-great-Grandmother were alive today, I think I'd like her in spite of her faults.'" (April 16, 1922)

The Ontario Years, 1922–1925

1922

Sunday, Jan. 1, 1922
Leaskdale, Ont.

Nineteen-twenty-two should have a gallant heart. It has a hard task before it. The world is, as I heard a man on the train say the other day, "upside down and inside out." Such a world is in a bad plight. Will 1922 be able to put it right—or even start putting it right?

Well, Lloyd George[1] will do what he can to help it!

Chester has been reading *Midshipman Easy*[2]—and has announced to me that when he grows up he is going to sea. I am quite accustomed to hearing him say he will be this or that—farmer, livery-keeper, garageman—according to the whim of the moment. I always laugh and say "All right, if you want to be." I said it today but I found it a little harder to laugh. For, some how, it gave me a nasty little sensation. Ewan's mother was a Cameron and the sea is in the Cameron blood. I wonder if Chester has it. I hope not. But I swear if he feels that way when the time comes to choose a career I won't try to hinder him. I have seen too much ruin and havoc come from parents forcing square pegs into round holes because of some selfish ambition of their own. But I sincerely hope it is only a passing whim born of *Midshipman Easy*. I shall put no more sea-tales in Chester's way—and I shall not fan the flame by any opposition.

I was helping Chester with some of the sums of his home work the other day. It amused me to find the problems dealing with the speed of automobiles passing each other. In my time it was railway trains. I suppose Chester's children will be ciphering out the speed of aeroplanes.

Friday, Jan. 6, 1922
The Manse, Leaskdale

I am famous—no longer is there any doubt of it! I have reached the stage where orphaned anecdotes in search of a parent are "mothered" on me, in the newspaper paragraphs. A friend sent me today a clipping from a western paper running thus:—

"Why She Refused to Offer Her Opinions."
Miss L.M. Montgomery Wanted to Remain Friends.

---

1   On Lloyd George, see note for October 21, 1922.
2   Frederick Marryat's novel for boys, *Mr Midshipman Easy* (1836); Marryat was a retired Royal Navy Captain.

Miss L.M. Montgomery, now Mrs. Macdonald, the well-known Canadian author, was once sitting in an editor's office when a young novelist entered.

"Miss Montgomery," said the novelist eagerly. "I value your opinion very much. Now, I want you to tell me candidly what you think of my new book?" Miss Montgomery smiled. "No, no," she hurriedly replied, "let us remain friends."

I was never guilty of this *bon mot!*

I also got two other amusing clippings which Alonzo Smith[3] sent me. They were not meant to be amusing—but I found them so.

There exists in New Glasgow, Nova Scotia, an editor named James Fraser—*en passant*, the father of Jen. He edits the New Glasgow *Chronicle*,[4] is a rampant Liberal, a virulent anti-unionist,[5] and easily first in the gentle art of making enemies. In journalism he is a hangover from the days of the *Eatonsville Gazette*,[6] and makes vitriolic abuse take the place of argument. Anyone who is opposed to him is on the side of the devil—nay, *is* the devil incarnate. Hitherto he has rather liked my books and has mentioned them favorably. But in the case of *Rilla* he sees red. From one brief sentence in the book, written by way of a joke on one of the characters, he infers that I am Unionist, likewise my husband. From another paragraph dealing with the Khaki election in 1917, he deduces that I am a Tory and he gets after me loaded for bear.[7] I just howled over the editorials. They do not belong to the kind that can really "get under my skin," so I must confess I found a sinful enjoyment in them.

---

3   Another Presbyterian minister, with whom the Macdonalds had become friends in 1921.

4   The *Eastern Chronicle* had been founded in 1843. James A. Fraser (1843–1937), a gold miner and Liberal politician, became manager/editor in 1881. At the time of writing this review, he was 79. Jen Fraser, his daughter, had been a friend and colleague of Frede Campbell while Frede was teaching at Macdonald College in Ste.-Anne-de-Bellevue, Quebec.

5   In the 1920s, small churches—particularly in rural districts—were struggling with declining membership. The decision was taken to amalgamate the Methodist Church, the Congregational Union, and the Presbyterian Church. In much of Canada this caused little controversy; however, in Ontario many of the Presbyterian congregations wanted to retain their independence. Each congregation held its own vote on whether to remain Presbyterian or to become part of the United Church.

6   From Charles Dickens' *The Pickwick Papers* (1836). The *Eatansville Gazette* (LMM spells it "Eatonsville") is the local paper in the fictional town of Eatansville; Dicken's account is a spoof on the biases of small-town news reporting.

7   The "Khaki election" refers to the December 1917 election where the issue of conscription was central to Canada's wartime politics. LMM had been one of some 500,000 Canadian women who cast their first ballot in a federal election. Prime Minister Robert Borden's Union government had passed the Wartime Elections Act, giving a vote to wives, mothers, and sisters of Canadian soldiers (LMM's half brother Carl Montgomery had enlisted). Liberal leader Sir Henri Charles Wilfrid Laurier, who had been Prime Minister from 1896 to 1911, correctly feared that conscription would alienate Quebec and divide the country. Montgomery's views of Laurier are reflected in her novel *Rilla of Ingleside* (1921), in which an overfed, poorly behaved dog belonging to the household of the despised, unpatriotic character "Whiskers-on-the-Moon" is named "Wilfrid."

Here are some choice tid-bits from them:—

"Possibly if there were more prayers and less stories in the Unionist minister's homes there would be less desire to throw away the church of their fathers—less of the spirit of Babel and more of Christ."

(Wonder what kind of prayers Jimmy F. puts up!)

"The series of Anne stories which are referred to *now and then* in the *cheaper* reviews."

(The italics are mine.)

"She is the wife of one of those transmogrified ministers[8] who clutter up the once proud and exclusive Presbyterian church in Canada."

What *is* a "transmogrified minister?" And could the bitterest enemy of the Presbyterian church say of it anything harsher than that it was "proud and exclusive?" Shade of the meek and lowly Founder!

"The writer alleges that Whiskers-on-the-Moon was the only Liberal in the valley where they lived."

Where do I allege it?

"The story is machine made and reads as if the machine was getting out of repair and consequently slipping cogs. But as the author has removed to Tory Ontario[9] it is probable that if she does not improve as a story writer she will at least enjoy her days in a bath of that Toryism in which she so delights to take readers and do lots of splashing. Well, let her splash in her own mud-puddle to her heart's content."

The joke is that I have always been a fervent Liberal and as bitter an anti-unionist as Jimmy F. himself. But I think I'll have to turn now. I don't want to be on the same side as he is.

Stuart is very indignant because the hens won't lay as fast as he wants them to. Today he came in and said despairingly, "Mother, can't you *make* those hens lay?" "*I* can't make them lay!" I said. "Why don't *you* make Paddy lay you some eggs?"

Stuart looked at me in disdain.

"Why, mother, Pat can't lay eggs," he explained. "*He* lays kittens."

---

8   "Transmogrified" is a term meaning completely altered, the implication being that Ewan Macdonald had become a lesser minister by virtue of being in support of Church Union. In fact both the Macdonalds (particularly LMM) wanted the Presbyterian Church of Canada to remain its own denomination.

9   In the election of 1917, Robert Borden's Unionist government (composed mostly of members of the Conservative party and some Liberal party members who had left the party) came to power, defeating Wilfrid Laurier's Liberal government. Borden was firmly pro-conscription, unlike Wilfrid Laurier. Ontario voted in favour of the mostly "Tory" (or Conservative) Union government, returning 62.3% in favour of Borden (Quebec, by contrast, was 24.7%). The Maritime provinces voting less enthusiastically (New Brunswick 59.4%, Nova Scotia 48.4%, and Prince Edward Island 49.8%).

Tuesday, Jan. 17, 1922
Leaskdale, Ont.

Last night we had our anniversary concert. Stuart recited "Seeing Things At Night."[10] It is an old piece and nearly everybody there had heard it two or three times. But he brought down the house. They clapped him back and he recited "A Little Boy Snake" concluding in a storm of laughter. He is really quite wonderful for six years of age. There he stood, rosy, handsome, perfectly at ease, smiling at everyone as if they were bosom friends with whom he was sharing a jolly little secret. What is before him, the little, loving starry-eyed fellow? Somehow I have always felt vaguely anxious about his future. He is so sensitive. Will the world use him gently? Will it love him too much—or not enough?

Friday, Jan. 27, 1922
The Manse, Leaskdale

I went in to Toronto Wednesday and came home tonight. I attended the Press Club dinner, at which I was guest of honor and spoke. I gave a talk on my experiences in climbing the ladder and some good advice born of my sorrows with the Page Co.[11]

In my task of copying my journals into uniform volumes I have reached the summer of 1918. Today a line, written blithely then, gave me a stab of bitter pain. Speaking of Frede[12] I said, "She goes soon to P.E. Island and we are hoping for one more happy vacation in the dear old spot."

We had it—it "was our blithest and our last."

That summer of 1918 was, I think, the pleasantest summer of my life. Never did I have such a delightful vacation as those six weeks on the Island— never can I have as dear a one again—for never can I have one with Frede. It will soon be three years since she went out that winter morning at Macdonald—Oh God, when I recall it I turn sick with pain.

Today I had a nice letter from Sir Ernest Hodder Williams (of Hodder and Stoughton[13]) and some English reviews of *Rilla*. All were kind but one which

---

10   "Seein' Things," a humourous poem about a young boy's struggle with courage by American poet and children's writer Eugene Field.

11   LMM had initiated two lawsuits against her publisher, L.C. Page & Co., in 1916. The first lawsuit was for withholding full royalties on *Anne of Green Gables*; the second was to prevent Page from bringing out an edition of *Further Chronicles of Avonlea*.

12   Frederica ("Frede") Elmanstine Campbell (1884–1919), LMM's cousin and beloved friend. LMM was heartbroken when Frede died of influenza in 1919.

13   Hodder and Stoughton, a London publishing house founded in 1868 (the business had roots in publishing for the Congregational Union in the 1840s), brought out the British edition of *Rilla of Ingleside* in 1921. Sir Ernest Hodder-Williams (1873–1941) was then co-owner of the firm.

sneered at my "sentiment." The attitude of some English critics towards anything that savors of sentiment amuses me. It is to them as the proverbial red rag to a bull. They are very silly. Can't they see that civilization is founded on and held together by sentiment. Passion is transient and quite as often destructive as not. Sentiment remains and binds. Perhaps what they really mean is sentimentality, which *is* an abominable thing. But my books are not sentimental. I have always tried in them to register normal and ordinary emotions—not merely passionate or unique episodes.

I had also two curious letters, one from a male prig and one from a female prig. The most humiliating thing about these letters is that the writers like my books. I wish they loathed them. The male prig says that my books have convinced him that "a real Christian can still write books" but goes on to solemnly warn me that my nefarious habit of marrying off my characters "tends to lower the conception of the holy state of matrimony." Whew! I wonder if he thinks it would be better if I let them mate up without marrying, or sent them into convents.

The female prig thinks "Mary Vance's"[14] talk is "vulgar" and that it should not be found in a book "written to influence young people." But then I don't write books for the purpose of influencing young people and I don't make children of the antecedents and upbringing of "Mary Vance" talk like "Elsie."[15]

The said prig also rebukes me gravely for letting Susan call the cat she "tried to kick with both feet" a *darned* cat. But the real old lady of the anecdote said bluntly that the animal was damned. Yet this terrible example did no harm that I know of.

I shall not bother replying to the male prig. But I intend to write a polite, carefully ironic letter to the female of the species.

I am re-reading Froude's *Elizabeth*.[16] His unsurpassable description of the long duel between her and Mary Stuart is as fascinating as fiction. He makes Elizabeth and Mary *live*—I feel as if I knew them both intimately. Whether his Elizabeth and Mary are the *real* Elizabeth and Mary cannot now be told but I believe they are, judging from the evidence of their letters and words.

It is odd—but I have always been on Elizabeth's side in that famous struggle. Why, I can't say. Most people seem to incline to Mary even those who

14   Mary Vance and Susan Baker are outspoken characters in *Rilla of Ingleside* (1921).
15   "Elsie Dinsmore" was the title of a series of didactic children's books, published between 1867 and 1905, by American writer Martha Finley (1828–1909), treating Christianity and familial loyalty.
16   *The Reign of Elizabeth* (1911) by English historian and novelist James Anthony Froude (1818–94) treats, among other topics, the relationship of Elizabeth I (1533–1603), Queen of England and Ireland from 1558 to 1603, with her cousin Mary Stuart (1542–87), commonly known as Mary, Queen of Scots. In 1587, Mary was beheaded on the orders of Elizabeth I on charges of treason.

admit her crimes. And I don't think I would have liked Elizabeth at all in the flesh. Nevertheless, I have always been on her side—have always felt sorry for her. Mary Stuart has intrigued the world's fancy by her charm, her passion, her tragedies, her misfortunes. Elizabeth, by contrast, seems sordid and shrewish. Yet in spite of all this I am glad she won. I think, though, she made a mistake in executing Mary. By so doing she set her up as a world's tragedy queen forever. Mary's death wiped out of recollection the crimes of her life and made a martyr of her. There is a fatal contrast between her dramatic exit and Elizabeth's pitiful death in old age.

Twenty years ago a travelling lecturer gave an entertainment in Cavendish Hall. I was not there, but later on I heard that one of the pictures he showed was Mary, Queen of Scots, and when it flashed on the screen, half the people in the audience exclaimed, "Why, that is Maud Montgomery."

I don't know which of the pictures of Mary it was. None that I have seen resemble in the least my face as I see it in the glass. And though Mary Stuart was a beautiful woman I have never seen any picture of her which I thought beautiful.

They certainly had colorful sovereigns in those days. What a difference between the Tudors and "Farmer George."[17] What a contrast between "Queen Bess" and "Victoria."[18] Nor do I think the contrast all, or even largely, in the latter's favor. Somehow, that splendid, impervious, stately, *human* Elizabeth is a very striking figure in history even if possessing none of the strange fascination that hangs around the name of Mary Stuart.

Monday, Feb. 13, 1922

For twenty-five years I have been trying to get into the *Ladies' Home Journal*.[19] At last I have succeeded. Years ago I used to try them vainly with stories. I

---

17   LMM is here comparing an assertive series of monarchs with a less successful king, as represented in the popular imagination of the early twentieth century. The House of Tudor ruled England and its traditional realm (Wales and the Kingdom of Ireland) from 1485 until 1603. This was a period of dramatic religious and political change, as well as national success. George III (1738–1820) was king of Great Britain from 1760 until his death in 1814. Despite periods of mental illness, leading to the establishment of a regency in 1811, the king's personal life was generally sedate. He came to be regarded as a homely country gentleman, and was nicknamed "Farmer George," partly due to a longstanding interest in agriculture.

18   "Queen Bess," the popular name given to Elizabeth I (1533–1603), Queen of England and Wales and Ireland from 1558, is contrasted to Victoria (1819–1901), Queen of the United Kingdom of Great Britain and Ireland from 1837 to 1901. Elizabeth was identified with an age of maritime adventurers and the defeat of the Spanish Armada; Victoria was remembered by LMM as an embodiment of staid Victorian sensibility.

19   The *Ladies' Home Journal* is an American women's interest magazine, founded in 1883.

have not sent them a story for fifteen years because I had not the leisure to write the type of story they want. But I have dangled a tidbit of verse before them now and again. Bite they would not. And now they have accepted a poem—"Farewell To An Old Room"[20]—and asked me for stories, assuring me that whatever I send them will be "carefully considered."

I feel a certain amount of quite childish triumph. It does not mean to me now anything as much as it would have meant fifteen years ago. The "wished-for comes too late," as the French proverb says. But it always gives me an intense satisfaction to succeed finally in anything I have tried for a long time to do.

Ewan has had some headaches lately.[21] But on the whole he has so far been much better than any winter since his trouble began. He has been fairly well ever since he got over that dreadful attack last fall. He has had no sleepless nights—at the worst he is dull and a little depressed. Perhaps the malady is wearing out. But I have hoped so often only to be cast down again.

Wednesday, Feb. 15, 1922

Today I finished *Emily of New Moon*,[22] after six months' writing. It is the best book I have ever written—and I have had more intense pleasure in writing it than any of the others—not even excepting *Green Gables*. I have *lived* it, and I hated to pen the last line and write *finis*. Of course, I'll have to write several sequels but they will be more or less hackwork I fear. They cannot be to me what this book has been.

Sunday, Feb. 19, 1922

Ewan has not been so well lately. He had one sleepless night when he had to take chloral.[23]

I have been copying my journal of Frede's death and have lived it over. It was bitter—bitter. Oh, Frede, if I could only *see* you for an hour—have one of our good old talks again!

20　In a letter to her long-time correspondent Ephraim Weber, dated November 1924, LMM describes receiving $35 for this poem. (See *After Green Gables: L.M. Montgomery's Letters to Ephraim Weber, 1916–1941* [University of Toronto Press, 2006]).

21　In 1919 Ewan Macdonald suffered from a major affective mood disturbance; see *The Complete Journals of L.M. Montgomery: The Ontario Years, 1918-1921* (Rock's Mills Press, 2017).

22　Published in 1923 by Frederick A. Stokes.

23　That is, chloral hydrate, to induce sleep. LMM notes many instances through 1919 where Ewan was given chloral to help him sleep.

Tuesday, Feb. 28, 1922

I have been considerably upset lately over several things. There is never any end to worry, it seems. If it doesn't come in one form it does in another. But there have been some pleasant things, too.

Ewan was away last Sunday and Capt. Smith[24] preached for him. He was here both Saturday and Sunday nights and we spent both evenings talking of a thousand subjects. It is such a delight to have a real conversation with a companion of intellect and sympathy. Captain Smith is one of the few people I have met with whom I can discuss with absolute frankness, any and every subject, even the delicate ones of sex. Sex is to men and women one of the most vital subjects in the world—perhaps *the* most vital subject since our total existence is based on and centres around it. Yet with how few, even of women, can this vital subject be frankly and intelligently discussed. It is so overlaid with conventions, inhibitions and taboos that it is almost impossible for any-one to see it as it really is.

Monday afternoon we went to Toronto, met Ewan and Mrs. Smith there, and went to hear Margot Asquith[25] speak in Massey Hall. She was not worth listening to and I had not expected she would be but I was extremely anxious to see her, after reading that amazing biography of hers. She was not worth looking at either. I never saw so witch-like a profile; and she was so flat you couldn't have told her front from her back if she had been headless. Neverthe-less, she was—Margot Asquith! She is a personality. You may hate—despise—deride—but you cannot ignore her.

We stayed all night in Toronto and came home next day.

Ewan was preaching in Markham.[26] It is vacant. It seems to me rather too good to be true that he could get a call there, but I heartily wish it for many reasons. I would hate to leave this dear old manse, my first *home* and my chil-dren's birthplace; but we will have to leave it some day and it would be wiser to go while the going is good. Ewan has not been contented here for a long

24   Edwin Smith, born probably around 1870 in Prince Edward Island, had (like Ewan) studied at Pine Hill Theological College in Halifax, Nova Scotia. Smith married in 1897 and fathered seven children. When war broke out Smith joined the Royal Navy Volunteer Reserve Force; records show he was a lieutenant in command of a Motor Launch (an originally Canadian-made small military vessel designed for harbour defense and chasing enemy submarines). As such Smith was one of many Canadians who served on motor launches during the war. He had been a minister in Prince Edward Island before moving to Tillsonburg, Ontario.

25   Socialite Margot Asquith, Countess of Oxford and Asquith (1864–1945), was married from 1894 until 1928 to H.H. Asquith (from 1908 to 1916 Asquith served as the Prime Minister of Britain). Her *An Autobiography* (1920) described a range of personalities in her life as well as her experience during the war years. Massey Hall, built in 1892, was a finely appointed music venue financed by businessman and philanthropist Hart Massey.

26   Markham, Ontario, was then a community located some 30 km/19 miles northeast of down-town Toronto; Cedar Grove is a community 7 km/4 miles southeast of Markham.

time. The congregation is not as strong as it was owing to deaths and removals. Zephyr, for one reason or another, has never been satisfactory. We have lost our best man in both sections and so find the work much harder. "Union"[27] seems to be "in the air" at Zephyr and if that should come to pass the congregation will be disrupted and we would have to leave, not knowing where to go—a prospect that always haunts me in my pessimistic, three-o'clock-in-the-morning moods. Ewan has been here twelve years—there is no one else in Lindsay Presbytery who was in it when he came save one and that one has changed congregations.[28] I think he has begun to feel an uneasy suspicion that people think he stays because he can't get any other place. This isn't so, of course—yet! Three years ago the Pinkerton[29] congregation asked him if he would accept a call. I was willing to go, though not enthusiastic, but he refused, for what reason I never could fully fathom. But it was well he did for it was only three months after that when his mental malady struck him down. It would have been much harder for me if we had just moved to a new place.

Then a year ago he would have got the call to Brooklyn and Columbus if Fraser[30] had not behaved so meanly. I shall never really forgive Fraser for that. It was an incredibly mean thing for a man to do.

Then, too, if Ewan "got a call" to a nice place the pleasant sensation might cure his malady. He has really been much better this winter and a "shock of joy" I verily believe might complete the cure and render it permanent.

All these things make me feel quite willing to "move," if we could go to a place at least as good as Leaskdale. I have never felt that it would be any use to hope or try for a much better place. There is too keen a competition in such places for a man of Ewan's limitations to have much chance of success.

Markham and Cedar Grove would, so far as we know, be a very nice place. Markham is a little town, or rather a large village, not so large as to preclude all hope of Ewan's being acceptable to it. The manse is fairly satisfactory and has electric light in it. Markham has a station and is only 25 miles from Toronto

---

27　Another reference to the possibility of three churches amalgamating: the Methodist Church of Canada, the Congregational Union of Canada, and the Presbyterian Church of Canada. See note 5, page 2.

28　Leaskdale and Zephyr were part of the Lindsay Presbytery (a system of management by the larger Presbyterian Church of Canada that oversees the congregations within its boundaries). It is likely LMM means that in 1922 Ewan was the only remaining minister on the original Lindsay Presbytery committee from the time he began there; all other ministers who had been on the committee had left that area by 1922 to serve parishes out of the vicinity.

29　A village some 80 km/50 miles north of Toronto.

30　James R. Fraser (b. 1867) was the minister at Chalmers Presbyterian Church, Uxbridge, from 1898 to 1921, then a widower with two young children. LMM describes this event in an entry of April 12, 1921; in LMM's account, Rev. Fraser took a position in Brooklyn and Columbus that Ewan Macdonald had hoped to obtain. (These are two small communities in Ontario roughly 60 km/37 miles northeast of Toronto.)

which would mean much to me. But the great thing which made me wish to go there was the fact that it possessed a High School. Thanks to this wretched school system of Ontario Chester will have to leave home in two or three years more to attend High School and this thought haunts me and worries me, because he will need home surroundings and restraints for several years more. If we could get to a place where there is a High School his inevitable going from home would be postponed several years—at least, until he is old enough to govern himself properly.

Mr. Rae of Unionville,[31] whom we know, is the moderator of Markham and so Ewan easily got a "hearing"—which is a hard thing to get in Ontario when this matter too often goes by "pull"—something which Ewan does not possess in many quarters.

Mr. Rae gave Ewan the first Sunday after the vacancy. I was disappointed in this. Mr. Rae seemed to think that he was thus giving him the best chance but Mr. Rae is a Scotchman and evidently does not understand how things go in Canada. It is very seldom that the first man on a leet[32] is called unless he is a very outstanding man. The last man has by far the best chance. Even though the people liked the first man the memory is blurred by succeeding candidates.

However, so it was and Ewan preached there last Sunday. We kept it secret of course. Owing to the system of settling ministers which obtains in the Presbyterian church—surely the worst system that was ever devised by the intellect of rational beings—it does a minister harm if it is known in his congregation that he has been "preaching for a call" and hasn't got it.

Ewan was quite encouraged by his day in Markham. He received so many compliments on his sermons that he thinks he may hope for a call. I cannot help hoping, too, though I try to suppress it, dreading increased disappointment. And now, I suppose, we must spend weeks in suspense, hampered in every respect by our uncertainty.

And now for the unpleasant things.

When we came home today we found a letter for Ewan from Marshall Pickering![33]

---

31   Rev. Frank W. Rae was minister at Unionville, 30 km/19 miles northeast Toronto until 1925.

32   A Scottish term for "list" (usually meaning a shortlist, cut down from a larger one).

33   On June 12, 1921, a car driven by Ewan Macdonald with LMM, her two sons, and two other passengers, Mrs Jake Meyers and her young daughter (both from Zephyr), had collided with a car driven by Zephyr resident Marshall Pickering; his wife, Sarah Pickering, was the only passenger. Both drivers were probably at fault. No serious injuries arose on either side from the accident. In an entry of June 6, 1921, LMM begins her account of the accident with these words: "We had a terrible accident last Sunday. It might have been a thousand-fold worse. I am thankful we escaped as we did. But it was horrible—horrible." Pickering was a member of the Methodist Church; there was traditionally a degree of ill feeling between Presbyterians and Methodists.

Marshall Pickering is the man whose car collided with ours that unfortunate Sunday last June. For this collision I consider that both men were to blame but that Pickering was more to blame than Ewan. And this I think is the opinion held by almost everyone. Ewan was guilty of decided carelessness in turning towards the side road without looking a *second* time to see if a car was coming from the north. He *had* looked once just before starting his car and, seeing no one, thought there was plenty of time to cross the road before any car

[Location of Macdonald/Pickering collision]

came—and so there would have been were it not for Pickering's furious driving. Pickering, on the other hand, was going at a furious rate—his own son when he heard of the accident said, "I suppose he was driving like the devil as usual"—right in the middle of the road and never slowed down or turned out an inch although by his own admission he had seen us for several minutes before we pulled out to the middle of the road.

Consequently the fair thing to do was for each man to pay for the damage of his own car. Eventually this proved to be about $50 for ours and $85 for his, ours being much lighter because we were on low gear, going very slowly, while he was tearing along at fully 30 miles an hour.

The morning after the accident we heard that Pickering had been taken ill in the night with stoppage of urine and had been taken to the hospital in the morning. Mrs. Meyers, who told me this over the 'phone, added that Pickering had had several of these attacks before. We heard this from several people afterwards also. Ewan went to see Mrs. Pickering that evening. She is a very ignorant, insolent, vulgar woman and was very insulting to Ewan but she never even hinted that the accident caused the attack nor did Pickering himself when Ewan went to call on him in the hospital. Moreover, a son of Pickering's, Wellington by name, was at the hospital and when he was talking to Ewan told him that his father *had intended to have the operation anyhow* the next week and had written him four weeks before asking him to come home for the summer and look after things while he was in the hospital. Ewan told me this when he came home from the hospital that night. Our minds were completely relieved and we heard no more of the matter.

One night early in December I had one of my queer "symbolic" dreams. I dreamed that I came home from Toronto and was told that Ewan had been *hanged* in the church shed by some unknown man and been cut down for dead but had come back to life after having been so cut down! I felt sure that

some kind of trouble was impending of which my subconscious mind was trying to warn me but I supposed it was connected with Ewan's malady and perhaps portended a new and unusually bad attack. None followed; but ten days later Ewan got a letter from Pickering stating that the accident had caused the operation, that it had cost him a thousand dollars, and coolly demanding that Ewan pay $500 of it.

I have seldom heard of such effrontery. If he had asked us to pay for the damages to his car there might have been some reason in it, and we would have done so to avoid trouble, even though he was equally to blame and a well-to-do farmer quite able to pay for his own car. But it was outrageous to ask Ewan to pay for the expenses of an operation which he intended to have anyhow—though *he* didn't know we knew that, I suppose, not having heard his son's conversation with Ewan. I suppose he thought he could "put it over us" quite easily. I might here say that the "operation" was the removal of an enlarged prostate gland which of course had been coming on for years.

Ewan wrote him back a temperate letter stating that as he considered they were both equally to blame for the accident he considered that it was only fair that each should pay his own damages. As for the operation he told Pickering that it was well known that he had those attacks before and had intended to have the operation anyhow. Probably this put Pickering into the rage of a man who has tried to do a detestable thing and has been found out. He is a very conceited, arrogant, bumptious man who cannot brook contradiction in anything.

But until today we had heard nothing more from him and had come to the conclusion that we never would. But today another letter came—the letter of a very angry man. I should not have been surprised at its coming for that morning in the hotel just as I woke up I heard a voice say distinctly "Marshall Pickering *has won his lawsuit.*" Evidently I had caught a thought wave!

Pickering denied that he had ever been ill before, said he would "prove by the doctors" that the accident had caused the operation and raved on generally and abusively through several very badly written and badly spelled pages. Among other things he said that he was "fourteen feet over on his own side of the road and going only at 15 miles as 20 witnesses could prove." This, of course, is absolutely false. Finally he wound up by declaring that if Ewan didn't settle for $500 before "a month from date" it would be settled in the courts.

The whole letter was evidently his own confused, ungrammatical, contradictory composition; but, as he stated fore and aft that it was "written without

prejudice"[34] it is evident that he has talked to some lawyer about it. I suppose he imagines that Ewan, being a minister, will submit to blackmail rather than be dragged into the worry and notoriety of a lawsuit. If so he does not know either of us. If, instead of writing insolent letters he had come frankly, as man to man, and asked for some assistance because of having been put to considerable expense, we would both have gladly done something for him. But this barefaced lie and demand is something neither of us can tolerate.

We will not be frightened into paying his bills. Nevertheless it has worried and upset me. I can never take things with the "easy-goingness" of Ewan. Ewan never worries over anything—except eternal damnation—but I do. It seems as if there could never be any end of worry for me. Just as soon as one thing passes, or grows easier, something else comes. I am somehow beginning to feel very restive and rebellious under it.

My own mail was not exhilarating. Mac sent royalty reports and the sales of *Rilla* are two or three thousand short of the sales of the other books. I had expected this. It couldn't be anything else in view of the terrible business depression all over Canada this past year.[35] Nevertheless, it was a bit disappointing.

Ewan went over to Zephyr to see Mr. Law,[36] the car agent and owner of the gas tank where we stopped. He is one of the two men who saw the accident. He told Ewan that Pickering was in the middle of the road and that he was willing to testify to that.

Now for weeks of worry! Does one ever get used to worry—hardened to it? Yes. I suppose we do. Once I couldn't have carried on the routine work of life at all, or enjoyed anything under the strain of all the worries I have had for the past seven years. But now I can and do, and have hours and days of contentment and even enjoyment sandwiched in between the active attacks of bother and unrest.

But I'm very tired of it.

Thursday, March 2, 1922

I slept poorly last night. Woke at four and couldn't sleep again—instead, I went through the details of several lawsuits with Marshall Pickering and was crossed-examined by lawyers without pity and without remorse. I saw Pickering producing hosts of doctors who swore that the smash caused the

---

34 A legal term meaning that the contents of a document, written in an attempt to settle a dispute outside of court (usually without a lawyer), cannot later be used in court.

35 The years 1920–21 had seen a sharp deflationary recession in North America as well other western countries. The effects continued to be felt into 1922.

36 William Law was the Zephyr Ford dealer; his son Ivan would marry Marshall Pickering's youngest daughter, Daisy.

operation—saw endless notoriety and unpleasantness—saw everything black and hopeless—but *still* said, away back inside, "We *won't* be bull-dozed."

Ewan is troubled with headache again. I had a touch of it myself all day.

This morning when I went to call the boys I found a placard hanging on their door whereon in big black homemade letters was inscribed the legend, "No entrance without our consent."

They are delicious. I was afterwards informed that *I* was not debarred, neither father. The prohibition was for Lily,[37] whom they both detest—for which fact I cannot greatly blame them. She is occasionally—*very* occasionally—half decent to Stuart but she never ceases to nag and persecute Chester. She has never said a kind word to him since she came. And he was such a pet with Lily Reid and Frede. But he is too independent to suit Miss Meyers.

[Stuart and Chester sleeping]

Friday, Mar. 3, 1922

Ewan seemed quite dull and miserable today. We both feel a little disappointed I suppose. Wednesday evening the Markham committee was to meet to make up the leet and Ewan thought it possible that they might decide not to have a leet but to call him at once. I didn't think this likely—and I thought I didn't hope it at all; but when no word came from Mr. Rae today, as would likely have been the case had they decided not to hear more candidates, I discovered by the keenness of my disappointment that I *had* hoped it.

Monday, March 6, 1922
Leaskdale, Ont.

Friday night I took ill with an attack of flu and was in bed Saturday and yesterday. I crawled up today but am very shaky. I was not, of course, anything like as ill as I was when I had the flu in 1918.[38] But neither then nor any other time did I ever feel such bottomless depression as I have experienced in this attack. It is a frequent accompaniment of influenza but has never been among

---

37   Lily Meyers, from Zephyr, had been LMM's maid from 1918 to 1925. Despite her long service in the Macdonald household, she and LMM had a rocky relationship.

38   Several waves of flu pandemics took place following the most serious pandemic in 1918, the so-called Spanish Flu epidemic; the outbreak of 1922 had a lower mortality rate.

my symptoms before. Never have I felt so utterly discouraged and pessimistic as during these past three days. Ewan is dull, too, so I am afraid another of his attacks is coming on. This, and the Pickering matter, intensifies my gloom. I can't see a ray of light—Ewan will never get a call anywhere—he will never be well—my children will be failures or worse—I shall be involved in lawsuits all my life—it is all dark and it will never be dawn. That is my feeling. I try to reason it away, but reason has no effect on it, any more than on Ewan's attacks of melancholy.

Tonight, as I sat in my room, feeling utterly wretched, Stuart, who was playing with Chester in the hall, came running in, his eyes shining, his cheeks flushed.

"Oh mother," he exclaimed, throwing his arms around me, "this is a happy life! I hope it will last always."

The contrast between my mood and his struck me rather bitterly. Dear little fellow, neither he nor anyone else can wholly escape unhappiness in life. But I do desire deeply that he may have on the whole a happy life. I try at least to give him a happy childhood. But is it any use

Stuart

trying to accomplish *anything* in this world? Are we not only puppets in the hands of destiny? (Yes. 1938)[39]

Tuesday, March 7, 1922
Leaskdale, Ont.

This has been a dark dull day, gloomy in every way. It has poured rain—the skies have been obscured by heavy clouds—the house seemed filled with shadows. Ewan is dull. I was too weak to work, so read Froude's history of *Bloody Mary*[40] all day. It was not a cheerful book but in my present mood I don't care for cheerful books. They are insulting. Poor Mary. In schooldays I learned to hate her; but now I think she was to be pitied. How very unhappy she was! If she had been happier she might have been kinder. On the other hand it might be as true to say that if she had been kinder she might have been happier. And can *anything* excuse the Smithfield fires? To *burn* a human being alive because he believed something different from you! It seems to us now

39   This parenthetical comment appears to have been inserted by LMM in 1938. She reread her journal at various points in her life, sometimes trying to get back in a mental frame to start a new book, and other times to ascertain the trajectory of her life. This comment was likely made at a time when she felt discouraged and depressed.

40   *The Reign of Mary Tudor* (1910) by James Anthony Froude (1818–94). Mary I (1516–58) was Queen of England from 1553 to 58. Mary was a staunch Catholic, and her reign saw considerable persecution of Protestants, who were considered heretics, guilty of treason against Catholicism. Estimates of those executed during Mary's reign range from 300 and 700. Many executions took place in Smithfield, London—hence LMM's reference to the Smithfield fires.

inexcusable. But is not that because we have ceased to believe in the reality of hell fire and ceased to believe that God would doom his creatures to everlasting torment because of an error in judgment or belief? Therefore it seems to us now incredibly hellish and cruel to torture to death anyone guilty of such error. But let us try to put ourselves in the place of one who did so believe. Come! *I* am a Catholic—I believe in everlasting hell—I believe that anyone who is not a Catholic will go there. I love my boys Stuart and Chester. A man comes who does not believe Catholic doctrine. He teaches what I believe a false religion. If Chester and Stuart should be led away into it I believe they will burn in horrible tortures for all eternity. Would I not feel that, in order to save *them* I *must* root out the abominable heresy? And, since ordinary death has no terror for the teachers thereof, I must terrorize them by the most hideous death possible—to save Chester and Stuart.

Yes, I think I can understand poor Mary Tudor.

Saturday, March 11, 1922
Leaskdale, Ont.

Ewan seems better. I am a little better too and have begun to write again. I had one of Ella's[41] hysterical letters again Thursday. She has not inflicted any of the kind on me since I pulled her up three years ago. I shall have to write her another bracer. If she goes on brooding in this way over old things she will go out of her mind. This letter, several pages long, seems to have been produced by the following facts:—Recently I sent Amy[42] a check for $8 to pay for a quarter's music lessons for her. This seems to have overwhelmed Ella and brought on an acute attack of remorse of conscience which in turn was responsible for the letter. It seems that, when I was down at Park Corner in the fall of 1920, helping Aunt Annie out with her business as administratrix of George's "estate," one night Ella chose, after her habit, to feel slighted over something that had been said or done—or *not* said or done—and had not "gone into the spare room to kiss me good night as usual." This offence is now preying on her mind and must be confessed and pardoned before she can feel comfortable over accepting the money. In a child this would be natural but in a woman of nearly fifty it betrays the weakness of mind that has always characterized poor Ella. The amusing part is that I never noticed the omission of which she was guilty, so little impression did her nightly pilgrimages to my room to kiss me good night after I was in bed make on me. Truth to tell, I dislike such

41   Ella Campbell, the widow of George Campbell, LMM's cousin from Park Corner.
42   Amy Campbell, one of six children of LMM's Park Corner cousin, George Campbell, and his wife Ella. (George Jr had died in October 1918.)

sentimentalities in mature women and had I noticed an absence at all I would have been relieved by it.

I shall write her, forgiving her fully and freely and give her a little plain advice about brooding over old shortcomings as she does.

Saturday, March 18, 1922

This has been one of the dull chilly weeks of early spring with bad, rough roads. We have paid several boring visits to crude and ignorant families in Zephyr. Ewan seems fairly well but I cannot shake off my flu depression. Life isn't really any harder just now than it has been generally for the past few years but I have not at present the strength to stand up to its problems, so it *seems* harder—seems impossible. I keep worrying over the possible effect on Ewan if Markham doesn't call him. The disappointment may bring on a bad attack of melancholia. Then, too, what is that beast, Pickering, going to do? Will there *ever* come a spring again that will for me be free from worry? I have not known one since the spring of 1914—the last spring of the old world.

Tonight, when I was pouring the tea something I happened to do suddenly recalled to me the memory of Amanda's[43] mother—Mrs. Wm. C. Macneill.

I happened to pour the cream into the tea-cups *before* grace was said. Instantly I remembered that Mrs. Macneill *always* poured the cream into the cups and then gave Wm. C. the signal for grace. It always seemed a bit strange to me in those days because everywhere else in my somewhat limited experience the ladies of the table waited until grace was said before doing anything.

Instantly I was back thirty or thirty-five years ago. I was sitting on the old sofa—I could see the very pattern of the brown-and-white cretonne[44] that covered it—in the sitting room of that old house. I always sat in its corner when I was there to tea.

x - window of old sitting room

43　Amanda Macneill was LMM's third cousin and had been her closest friend around age nine. In an entry dated November 29, 1910, LMM writes, "In my childhood there were ten families of Macneills living in Cavendish, eight of whom were 'our' Macneills" ("our" Macneills refers to the descendants of John Macneill, who had settled in Cavendish in 1790). Mrs. William C. Macneill, née Christy Ann Cameron (1833–1903), was Amanda's mother.

44　A heavy cotton material in colorfully printed designs, often used for drapery and slipcovers.

Behind me was the window with its muslin "lambrequin"[45] and the house plants on the sill. Before me was the table, set out with "Aunt Caroline's" famous old china set which they always used when they had company. I saw the quaint delightful shapes of cups and saucers and the peculiar ornamentation of spears and battle axes which were so arranged that a little distance away they looked like a conventional flower. I saw the dish of raspberry preserve, the little pat of butter on a small plate, the little cubes of cheese, the glass plateful of small squares of fruit cake and the invariable round thin cookies which completed the unchanging menu of a supper there—and always tasted good, too.

Old wrinkled Caroline[46] was sitting opposite to me, Amanda was beside me, young and girlish and ungnarled. Old William C. was at one end, making the grimaces for which he was noted—and close to me on my right hand at the other end sat Mrs. Macneill, pouring the cream into the cups with the air of a high priestess performing duly some significant rite. I could see her pale gentle face, hear her pale, gentle voice. Her voice *was* pale—her whole personality was colorless. I never heard her laugh in my life; and yet there was something about her I always loved. She *lived* for me tonight for a few seconds—she who has slept for over twenty years in the old Cavendish graveyard. She sat at the head of her table and poured tea in that quaint, prim, neat old room—a room which in spite of its quaintness and primness, had a dignity and reserve and charm which I never find in any modern room—and poured spectral cream into ghostly cups for me again tonight—that tall fair faded woman who never laughed and yet whom I remember so much more lovingly than many who were gay and mirthful.

Just a few seconds—then I was back again in the year of grace 1922, sitting at the head of my own table in Leaskdale manse and no one here knew of my flight over a thousand miles of space and an abyss of time.

Mr. and Mrs. Macneill and old Caroline are dead—Amanda and Tillie[47] are gone—Mac and Ham live there alone, two odd old bachelors. I wonder if, in the eons of Eternity that are to come, when we shall have completed some cycle too vast for our conception, I shall live this life of mine again and sit once more at that old table while Christie Macneill pours tea. In my mood of tonight I would like to think so.

---

45   Ornamental fabric.

46   Caroline was an unmarried sister of William C. Macneill (the "C" was for Cavendish). See also note 231, page 161.

47   Tillie was another daughter of William C. Macneill (that is, a sister of Amanda); Malcolm and Hamilton were two sons.

Saturday, Mar. 25, 1922[48]
Leaskdale, Ont.

A week of dull cold weather with the usual undercurrent of worry and suspense. But Ewan seems much better so that I think this attack is over and it was really a very slight one.

I feel horribly *stale* on everything this spring. It is just as if everything in life had gone utterly *flat*. I suppose it is the aftermath of the flu coupled with worry. But one pleasant thing did happen on Wednesday evening which sent a little thrill of courage and hope through my veins. It was Guild night and the subject was "Canadian Authors" which had been put on the programme at the suggestion of Margaret Leask.[49] I had written a paper on the subject and selected a programme of readings. I went to the church feeling very dull. It was a cold "dour" night, the walking was bad and I supposed there would be

Leaskdale Church

only the usual 18 or 20 of an audience. To my amazement the basement was full. The whole congregation had turned out. And when the programme was ended Margaret read to me a very nice address and Dorothy Lapp presented me with a bouquet of pink roses in the name of the Guild and as a tribute to their "Canadian Author."

The "address" read as follows:—

Dear Mrs. Macdonald:—

The members of the Guild decided that since this was to be "Canadian Authors' night" it would be a most fitting time to pay tribute to you as a Canadian authoress and also to show in some degree our appreciation of the wonderful interest which you take in our welfare.

As an Authoress, celebrated throughout the world, we are proud to

---

48   There are two entries for March 25, 1922, in LMM's handwritten journals. Her journal writing process, as she describes it several times, was to keep notes on events as they happened, and then write them up all at once as time permitted; this may be how the occasional date error slips in. The date of this entry perhaps should have been Friday, March 24, 1922.

49   George Leask belonged to the founding family of Leaskdale. George's son, George Jr., was married to Margaret Leask. Dorothy Lapp was the sister of Goldwin Dimma Lapp, who had been killed in the war, in 1917. Montgomery had dedicated *Rainbow Valley* (1919) to Goldwin as well as two other young men from her local community who had been killed in the war.

know you and honored to have you as the leader in our activities. Your leadership is a source of inspiration to all of us and under your leadership the meetings of the Guild are both interesting and instructive.

The outside world knows you as a brilliant writer but we know you not only as a writer but as a woman who has deservedly won respect and admiration.

We have met here many times during the years you have been with us and we have spent many hours in your home where we have enjoyed your gracious hospitality. We as a Guild ask you, Mrs. Macdonald, to accept this gift of roses with our best wishes for a long and happy life crowned with the glory your efforts deserve.

In future we want to show our appreciation not only with roses but with a happy willingness to assist you in every way in making our guild a success.

I confess I was pleased. I have worked hard, and with very little assistance, for ten years, to keep the Guild up; and I have thought sometimes that it was very little appreciated—at least, if appreciation was felt it was never uttered. So tonight's little tribute was very pleasant.

And yet there was a fly in the ointment, too. The plain truth is that Ewan wasn't overly pleased about it. He would deny this flatly— he would not admit it even to himself—but it is a fact for all that. I have always felt that Ewan never sympathized with or was pleased over any little compliment paid to me or my work in any department. I can't quite account for it but it is there and I have all too often felt the sting of it. Whenever we have been anywhere that an allusion was made to my literary success Ewan has invariably greeted it

My bouquet

with a little jibe or deprecating joke—quite good-naturedly—such as a parent might utter when a precocious child is praised. The child mustn't be made conceited—mustn't be allowed to think that it is really of any importance. Ewan's attitude to women—though I believe he is quite unconscious of this himself—is that of the mediaeval mind. A woman is a thing of no importance intellectually—the plaything and servant of man—and couldn't possibly do anything that would be worthy of a real tribute.

I *felt* this as we walked home together and something he said when we went to our room confirmed it. It gave me a very lonely feeling. It was not a pleasant thing to feel that my husband did not enter whole-heartedly into my little triumph—did not even say "You have deserved it" or something of the sort. Of course I have always known that Ewan has never had any real sympathy with or intelligent interest in my literary work and has always seemed either incredulous or resentful when anyone has attributed to me any importance on the score of it. But as he never sought to interfere with it in any way I would not let myself feel badly over this and have simply kept that side of my life and aspirations to myself and made it as unobtrusive as possible. But his attitude tonight hurt me and made me feel very solitary.

Saturday, Mar. 25, 1922
Leaskdale, Ont.

Ewan seems very well lately. But we are continually worried over this Pickering affair. The month of grace will soon be up and then I suppose we will know the worst.

Yesterday when Chester came home from school he informed me that he was slow in getting home because he had been "day-dreaming" along the road. In this dream he and Cameron and Douglas had "gone together to England in a big ship" etc. etc.—he had a whole string of imaginary adventures to relate.

Monday, Mar. 27, 1922

A miserable day—wet—raw—cold. The house was cold and uncomfortable all day. Ewan went to Whitby to consult a lawyer *re* the Pickering affair. At first he declared that if it came to a suit he would "conduct his case himself" but eventually I have been able to make him see the absurdity of this attitude and he has consented to see a lawyer.

Today I had a sharp, sudden spasm of *rebellion*—rebellion against worry! Everyone must have some worry in life—I am not such a fool as to be rebellious because I must endure my allotted share. But for the past twenty-three years—with the exception of the first three years of my marriage—I have had *ceaseless* worry. And today I felt as if I had reached the limit of endurance. I stood up and stamped my foot and flung defiance at the Powers That Govern, whatever they may be. I may have to go on suffering but I am not any longer going to believe that it is for my good. No; the Prince of Evil rules in *this* universe and when he tortures me I shall not insult God by attributing it to Him and "submit" in resignation. I shall stand up to and defy that Evil Spirit.

Sunday, April 2, 1922
The Manse, Leaskdale, Ont.

When Ewan came home on Tuesday he said that he had been advised by Judge McGillivery to retain a certain Mr. McCullough[50] of Toronto and had gone to him. He said McCullough heard his story and said, "If you can prove this Pickering hasn't the ghost of a chance."

So far, encouraging. But *can* we prove it satisfactorily? That is the point. And in any case even a successful lawsuit will be a worry and a very unpleasant thing for people in our position to undergo.

I was in Toronto for a few days shopping last week. Saw McClelland[51] and he told me that Wanamakers had closed their account with Page. This firm was his best customer and the loss will be a terrible blow to him.

Up to date we have had no bad news—and no good news. That is, Pickering has made no sign—and we have heard no word from Markham. I wish we knew definitely whether they will call us or not. I cannot make any spring plans—and certain plans should be made soon.

Monday, April 3, 1922
The Manse, Leaskdale, Ont.

Ewan had his handkerchief tied round his head again today. This always worries me. His attacks recently have been very light but one can never tell when a bad one will come again.

Stokes' royalty report came, too, and was not precisely cheering. *Rilla* fell a little short of my other books, but not, after all, as much as I had feared, considering the state of the business world.

Wednesday, Apr. 5, 1922

Ewan was very dull and gloomy today. I had a headache myself and though I cured it as usual with an aspirin I feel tired, stale, disheartened. We had a Missionary Guild tonight. The walking was bad and the attendance poor. Sometimes I almost give that Guild up in despair. Some of my loneliest moments are when I walk home alone from it in these dark cold nights.

---

50   James W. McCullough would become the Macdonalds' lawyer in the Pickering lawsuit; he had been a practising lawyer since 1886. His office was in Uxbridge.

51   John McClelland and Frederick Goodchild had established McClelland and Goodchild Ltd. in 1906. George Stewart came on board in 1913, and Goodchild left in 1918. McClelland & Stewart is now an imprint of Random House. Wanamakers was a popular American department store.

Thursday, April 6, 1922

We were at Wm. Lockie's to tea tonight.[52] It was a sort of martyrdom. Mrs. Lockie is a woman with whom I always feel wretchedly uncomfortable, as if I were in the presence of something essentially antagonistic. And her husband is the same type. They are both abnormal and their abnormality takes the form of their peculiar brand of so-called religion. Wm. Lockie is one of the two "leading men" in Zephyr church, because he is an elder and a large giver. Yet his giving does not spring from real liberality but from the same root as his abnormal views. He gives from a certain form of ostentation—"for his own glory" in short. He has done far more harm to Zephyr church than the most indifferent member in it. He will not accept any leadership or suggestion, even from his minister, but wishes to force his own peculiar viewpoint on everyone else. For instance—he thinks it wrong to run a church on business principles. There should be no "guaranteed" salary, no reports etc. People "should give as the Lord prospers them." In theory this position is quite correct and Will Lockie *does* carry it out. But human nature being what it is, a church would very soon die financially if run on that basis; and Zephyr church *is* dying financially because of it. Will Lockie has stubbornly blocked for years all effort to have it organized on a proper basis. The majority of the people realize this but are afraid to antagonize Will lest he withdraw his givings—as he always threatens to do when opposed—and leave them with a deficit to make up. He doesn't believe in prayer meetings, Guilds, Missionary societies or any organizations of that sort and has always opposed them. He has a colossal conceit and thinks he understands the Scriptures, church law, and church procedure far better than an educated and experienced minister. He has some of the most absurd ideas possible and I could shriek with laughter over them if the consequences of them were not so serious. I remember during the war hearing him berating the allies because they bombarded the German trenches before an attack, thereby giving the Germans due notice of their intentions. "Why," William used to demand, "don't they just slip over quietly by night and *take* the trenches?" At other times he would ask the world why the Allied aviators didn't set the Allied prisoners in the internment camps free by flying over the prisons and blowing them to pieces with bombs. It evidently never occurred to him that the prisoners would probably be blown to pieces too!

As for Mrs. Lockie, while she was airing some of her "religious" views I

52　LMM had a strong dislike of William Donald Lockie (1871–1964), a church elder, and his wife Mary Minetta Kennedy Lockie (1873–1930). The Lockie family were well-established in Zephyr, having emigrated from Scotland in the nineteenth century; the family had been among the founders of the Presbyterian Church in Zephyr. LMM and Ewan had always found relations with the Zephyr congregation more strained than those in Leaskdale.

was mentally recalling some tales I had heard of her from a lady in whose family Mrs. L. was a servant in her girlhood. She was a persistent thief of their jams and preserves—they could never be sure of finding a full jar in their cupboards. They had a terrible time with her. Yet this woman sets herself up as a model Christian and condemns anyone who doesn't agree with her on all points. I try to treat her courteously because if I offended her she would certainly try to make things unpleasant for Ewan; yet I question if it is not wasted patience. She *must* feel as I do the radical antagonism of our natures and dislike me quite as much as she could in any case.

Tonight William told us that they had given up the use of pork almost totally because it was contrary to Scripture, and that he never sowed mixed feed because it was forbidden somewhere in the Old Testament!

I was thankful when we got away. It was pouring rain and the roads were bad and our horse slow and we had seven miles of hills before us. But anything was preferable to the Lockies.

Wednesday, April 12, 1922
The Manse, Leaskdale, Ont.

The weather has been very wet and dull. April so far has been a "demmed, damp, moist, unpleasant"[53] month. We wait every day for the mail in mingled feelings of hope and fear—hope that there may be some good news from Markham—fear that there may be bad news from Pickering. And when neither comes relief and disappointment mingle, the one or the other predominating as other factors tend to raise or depress our spirits.

Chester has been taking Easter exams, and has done very well in all except hygiene in which he flunked for some reason. He did well in arithmetic this time but it is a subject that seems to bother him. He has a good memory but so far seems lacking in concentration. That may come as his mind develops.

Sunday, April 16, 1922
The Manse, Leaskdale, Ont.

I had one of my queer symbolical dreams last night and I take it to mean that we shall not get the Markham call, especially as I had directed my subconscious mind, when I was dropping off to sleep, to "listen in" at Markham and tell me what was in the people's minds.

I dreamed that I was pregnant and expecting the hour of confinement.

---

53   From *Nicholas Nickelby* (1838–39) by Charles Dickens (1812–70). The London-based characters of Mr and Mrs Mantalini are arguing; Mr Mantalini threatens to throw himself in the Thames and become "a demd, damp, moist, unpleasant body!" (ch. 34).

It came. I seemed to be ill for hours but no birth occurred. Then it was over but I had no child. I said to the doctor, "Am I going to have a child?" "No," he said. "It was a *false pregnancy* then?" I said. "Yes," he replied. I felt terribly disappointed—and then I woke with the thought of Markham in my mind. I never have those clear-cut symbolical dreams for nothing. I feel that I have been cherishing a false hope and the conviction has kept me feeling depressed and disappointed all day.

But today I finished copying my journal into uniform volumes. It has been a long piece of work but an interesting one. Perhaps a hundred years from now my descendants may read over this diary and regard it as an interesting heirloom. By that time they can give it to the world if they like. Everyone would be dead whom its publication could hurt and I would like it to be published in full *without omission*, save for this very paragraph I have just written. Cut it out, descendants!

This journal is a faithful record of one human being's life and so should have a certain literary value. My heirs might publish an *abridged volume*[54] after my death, if I do not myself do it before. It might be a good financial proposition for them. They should not include anything that would hurt or annoy anyone living.

I *desire that these journals never be destroyed but kept as long as the leaves hold together*. I leave this to my descendants or my literary heirs as a sacred charge and invoke a Shakespearean curse on them if they disregard it. There is so much of myself in these volumes that I cannot bear the thought of their ever being destroyed. It would seem to me like a sort of murder.

I do not yet know to which of my boys I shall finally bequeath this journal. Time must show which is the fitter to receive and guard it. Perhaps as yet unborn grandchildren and great-grandchildren will pore over these pages, with curious interest in a life lived so long before, in a world that will have so wholly passed away. Will some great-great-granddaughter of mine ever bend her pretty young head over this page? If so—I salute you, dear! Here and now, across the gulf of generations, I put out my hand and say to you,

"I lived a hundred years before you did; but my blood runs in your veins and I lived and loved and suffered and enjoyed and toiled and struggled just as you do. I found life good, in spite of everything. May you find it so. I found that courage and kindness are the two essential things. They are just as essential in your century as they were in mine. Here's to you, little great-great-grand-daughter, not to be born for a hundred years! I hope you'll be merry and witty

54   LMM began typing up an abridged version of her handwritten manuscript in 1930. Both the abridged and the handwritten volumes are in the University of Guelph Archival & Special Collections. (This present volume is based on the complete handwritten manuscript.)

and brave and wise; and I hope you'll say to yourself, 'If great-great-Grand-mother were alive today, I think I'd like her in spite of her faults.'"

[LMM in field of daisies]

Thursday, April 20, 1922
The Manse, Leaskdale, Ont.

April has really been a detestable month—so wet, cold, windy. Today seemed the climax of its wetness, coldness, detestableness. It snowed all day and was bitterly cold. We have been housecleaning all the week.

Ewan has been pretty well but not quite himself yet. Perhaps—let me hope it—this was the reason of a certain little occurrence today that hurt me keenly.

When the mail came Ewan took the Uxbridge *Times* and the *Presbyterian Witness*[55] and sat down in the kitchen rocker to read them. I was working at the dining room table. Happening to glance up I was arrested by the expression on Ewan's face—an expression it rarely wears but which I have seen on it sometimes when he had heard or seen something that annoyed him very much, especially something that had ruffled his *amour propre*. It was evidently produced by something he had read and I wondered curiously what it could be. When he finished with the papers he threw them down and went out silently, still with that expression on his face. I was curious enough to go out and scan the *Presbyterian*, thinking perhaps there was something in it regarding Markham. But though I searched it from cover to cover I could not

---

55   *The Presbyterian Witness* was a weekly publication that was independent of the Presbyterian Church, although the publication's content was related to the affairs of the Presbyterian Church and Presbyterianism in Canada. (The official publication of the Church was *The Presbyterian Record*.)

find anything to account for that bitter, disdainful, contemptuous look I had seen so plainly on his face and mouth. Then I looked through the *Times*. And there I found it—a brief little paragraph in the *Leaskdale Notes*.

"A pleasing event took place in our Guild lately when Mrs. Macdonald 'Our Canadian Authoress' was presented with a bouquet of roses. Mrs. Macdonald since coming to our midst has always given herself to everything that was worthy."

I went upstairs feeling very bitter. I was hurt—and I was worse than hurt—I was *ashamed* that my husband could be so small and petty as to look as Ewan had looked because his wife had been given a small tribute which in no way detracted from him. I wonder if other ministers feel that way when their wives are praised. I read recently an account of the presentation of an address and purse to some minister. In his reply to the address he said that he owed much to the assistance and sympathy of his wife. Ewan would *never* say such a thing to or about me—would never *think* it. And when others say something like that he is annoyed.

It has made me feel very lonely in soul.

I remember a bitter little experience early in our married life—one of those things that leave a scar forever. It was just after we came to Leaskdale and were getting the manse in order. One day Ewan came up from the Post Office with a letter from some stranger addressed to "Miss L.M. Montgomery."

He looked just about as he did today. "If you are going to go on receiving letters addressed like that you can get away from me," he said.

I was amazed. The thing seemed to me so trifling. And surely he had sense enough to realize that strangers who knew me only by the name on my books must so address me if they wrote at all. But he seemed to be absolutely blind to this; he sulked for three days. I let him sulk, too, for I myself was angry and disgusted. But I was also deeply hurt and it was long before I forgot it and the crude contemptuous way he had spoken to me. Eventually he got over his pet and resigned himself to seeing such letters occasionally. Less than a year ago something occurred that brought the matter up for discussion and Ewan owned quite frankly that he had been wrong and foolish—"I didn't know any better" he said.

But there is evidently some of the same feeling at the bottom of his mind yet—the mediaeval feeling that a woman has no business to have any separate individuality in name or attainment from her lord and master. I feel hurt— hurt. I have tried so hard ever since I came here to help Ewan in *his* work in every way in my power—and yet he feels and looks like this when a compliment is paid me on it.

Tuesday, Apr. 25, 1922
The Manse, Leaskdale, Ont.

Some malicious demon seems to delight in torturing me this spring. Life has been bitter of late. Last Saturday I took ill again with another attack of flu and I was horribly sick at night. I lay alone on the lounge in the dining room all the evening. Lily had gone home for Sunday before I became so ill and Ewan had gone out to spend the evening somewhere. If I had said to him, "I am sick and lonely. I want someone in the house to get me a drink when I need one or phone for the doctor if I get worse," Ewan would have stayed home willingly and been all kindness. But he never seems to *think* of anything unless it is suggested to him. When I was so ill with flu for three days in 1918 he never thought of suggesting a doctor until I roused from my stupor to ask for one myself.

I did not know he was going out until he had gone. Then I felt like *giving up*. I was so sick that I suddenly took it into my head that I was taking pneumonia—that deadly foe of my family. And if I did I would never recover—I would die and there would be no one to look after my children properly. I know now that I was a little lightheaded with fever. I ached all over; my throat was sore. I just got absolutely *babyish*. I wanted to be petted and waited on. I wanted someone to talk to me and cheer me up and make me laugh. I was so blue and lonely I cried pitifully. I had a miserable night but on Sunday I was able to get up and drag around to get meals. The fever was gone and I was no longer afraid of pneumonia but I was weak and wretched and hopeless. Yesterday I was a little better but very dull. Yet a letter that came—addressed to "Mrs. L.M. Montgomery" by the way!—made me feel ashamed of my depression. It was from a little girl of thirteen who had been thrown from a horse and had had to lie on her back for five months, with the prospect of so lying for seven more. And she had read my books *forty-two times over* and wanted to write and tell me that she could never have endured her lot if it were not for those books. Surely, when I can help and encourage people like this I can't be altogether useless and superfluous.

We had never heard anything from Pickering and were beginning to think he had come to his senses. But yesterday Ewan got a letter from Grieg,[56] a scratch lawyer at Uxbridge, demanding immediate payment of "$1,500" under threat of a writ. He has raised Pickering's original demand considerably—hoping to scare us a bit more I suppose. We are not so easily scarable. Moreover, we both feel that it is a matter of principle that is at stake. I suppose we

---

56   Willard F. Greig (c.1890–1964) served as a solicitor for the town of Uxbridge from 1919 until his death. (LMM consistently spells his name Grieg, after the composer Edvard Grieg, with whom the family claimed kinship.)

are in for a lawsuit now and in my present condition of weakness it upset me. I couldn't sleep all night but managed to go on with my work today. Yet tonight I feel a sort of desperation over my loneliness, problems, and lack of prospect. I can't *see beyond anything*. The landscape is blocked up and blocked out by these things.

Ewan went to see Law[57] today. He is our main witness but is desperately anxious not to get mixed up in a suit. Last week when he thought Pickering had given up he said to Ewan, "You were both in the middle of the road." Now he is not "certain that it was the middle of the road." It is all rather sickening. But we will not be blackmailed for all that.

Thursday, Apr. 27, 1922
The Manse, Leaskdale, Ont.

I have not been very well these two days—I have a racking cough and get tired so easily. The weather is bad and everything seems discouraging.

Ewan went to Toronto yesterday and saw McCullough. In order to put ourselves in a good position McCullough advised a small offer of settlement. So he has written Grieg saying that both were equally to blame for the collision. Ewan will agree to pool the damages and each pay half. As Pickering's were about $100 and ours about $40 this would mean that we would pay him about $30. I feel sure Pickering won't accept it. To demand $1500 and accept $30 would be practically to admit a frame-up and he will never do it. He will either send the writ[58] or drop the case altogether.

Ewan saw young Horner[59] in Toronto. He is a law-student there and was standing by Law at the time of the accident. He was not willing to give evidence, though he said Pickering was going at a furious rate. McCullough said he would do more harm than good as he seemed to have an entirely mistaken impression that Ewan turned his car to the left *after* he saw Pickering. This is absurd of course. Ewan had no time to do anything after he saw Pickering. Pickering's car struck ours and slewed it around to the left.

It is to be hoped Pickering won't get him. Old Horner, his father, a notorious old character, is very intimate with Pickering. But young Horner and his father are or have been on bad terms owing to the former's marriage. Young Horner doesn't want to be mixed up in the affair at all so may not tell the Pickerings what he thinks. I sincerely hope so, for if he swore to his statement regarding Ewan's turn it might do us a great deal of harm.

---

57   That is, William Law. See LMM's entry for February 28, 1922, and note 36, page 13.
58   A legal document issued to a lawyer, giving directions to prepare for trial; this would mean that Pickering had not accepted the settlement offered by the Macdonalds.
59   Mason Horner (1899–1961) had been called to the Bar in 1919. He was articled to W.F. Greig, and he would become a Queen's Counsel after World War II.

Friday, April 28, 1922

Had a poor night and a miserable day of worry and depression. But I feel a little better tonight. Ewan went to Zephyr and he and Mr. Law measured the road. They found that where the cars were was *not* in the middle of the road but better still, several inches over on our side. This is fine. Law seems quite willing to testify now. Ewan also heard of some man in Mt. Albert to whom Pickering told that he was going to have the operation anyhow. If this be so and we can get him it will be a good point for us. But rumor and witnesses are very uncertain. Of course we *know* Pickering meant to have it—his son told us all about it. But in the eyes of the law that is "hearsay evidence" and we cannot get it in.

Anyhow, we will soon know the worst since Grieg stated that he would send the writ in a week unless the claim was paid. The suspense will be over then and that is always the hardest to bear. But our whole summer will be spoiled. The trial will likely be in August and we can make no plans for any vacation or trip. Well, poor Ewan has paid bitterly for that carelessness of his on that fatal Sunday; and I have to pay, too.

Sunday, Apr. 30, 1922
The Manse, Leaskdale, Ont.

Yesterday and today I felt about as flat and discouraged and bitter as anyone could feel. But this evening Ewan and I motored over to Sonya to call on the Masons;[60] it was a lovely evening and the drive was so pleasant that it did me worlds of good. I felt like a different creature when I came home. A little tingle of pleasant sensation had run through my jangled nerves and brought them into harmony once more. I feel better tonight than I have felt since that last attack of flu.

Wednesday, May 9, 1922

A few days ago Ewan, who has seemed almost well for two months, had a return of headache and melancholia. In spite of past experience I had hoped it would not come back. So far the attack is a light one.

We are not to get to Markham. In the *Presbyterian Witness* today it was announced that they had called a young Mr. Auld—who, oddly enough, is a P.E. Islander too. Middle aged men have little chance against young men in the Presbyterian ministry. Hope has been ebbing steadily this past month when no

---

60   Sonya is a small hamlet some 7 km/4 miles east of Wick.

news came so it was not really such a disappointment to me as if it had come earlier. Besides, I never had any *real* hope since my dream.

Ewan seemed to take it lightly enough. But then he always takes disappointments lightly. The trouble is, I believe, that he won't *admit* they are disappointments. In the jargon of the psycho-analysts he suppresses them into his subconscious mind and later on they work out trouble for him. I can't help dreading the ultimate effect of this on him. Yet it may not have any at all. Ewan's reactions to anything are never those of the normal human being.

I had a good cry tonight over my lost hopes and then subsided into a sort of despairing determination to face a fourth summer of worry and misery. It seemed as if every scrap of hope that life would ever be any better or easier had vanished. Hitherto I have been kept up amid all my worries by a sort of secret hope or belief that there was something better further on—"around the bend" if I could only "carry on" until I reached it. Now this old belief seems to have gone suddenly and taken all my courage with it.

Thursday, May 10, 1922
The Manse, Leaskdale, Ont.

Busy housecleaning. Ewan has been just miserable enough. In the evening we made a couple of calls and he seemed better. We have decided that for the summer we will shake off our shackles of "going out to tea" and instead spin round a bit in the evenings, calling on two or three families instead of one and having a pleasant drive to compensate for the boredom.

When I came home I had an hour of reading Lecky's *Rise of European Morals*.[61] His discussion of the origin of conscience is interesting. He is opposed to the utilitarian theory[62] and thinks conscience is divinely implanted. Somehow, I cannot accept either of the theories *in toto*. It seems to me that there *is* implanted in us a certain feeling that we *ought* to do right and ought *not* to do wrong. So far I go with Lecky. But I believe that what we consider to be right and wrong is wholly a matter of education. We are trained to believe that a certain thing is wrong; when we do it therefore, *believing* it to be wrong, our innate sense that we ought not to do it vexes and reproaches us. Yet the thing in itself may not be wrong—may be absolutely right. Conscience is merely the result of our education in so called right and wrong and is not in itself

61   *The History of European Morals from Augustus to Charlemagne*, 2 vols (1869/1876) by Irish historian and essayist William Edward Hartpole Lecky (1838–1903).

62   Utilitarianism is a philosophy with roots in the Western tradition going back to the ancient Greeks. The basic argument of Utilitarianism is that the best action is one that promotes utility; that is, decisions should be made by seeking the action that promotes the maximum amout of well-being for the most people. Utilitarian philosophers include Jeremy Bentham (1748–1832) and John Stuart Mill (1806–73).

an infallible guide, though, since bitter experience has taught the human race the unpleasant results of certain deeds and courses of action (here I agree with the Utilitarians) it is a pretty safe guide, broadly speaking. Yet

> Christians have burnt each other, quite persuaded
> That the apostles would have done as they did.[63]

Lecky, too, discusses suicide in full. Personally, I have never felt the horror in regard to suicide that some feel. My attitude towards it is much what I found in Lecky, as quoted of someone.

"Life is forced on us; we did not ask for it; therefore, if it becomes too hard we have a right to lay it down."

But it is a cowardly thing to do if the doing of it leaves our burden upon others—ay, and a wicked thing. But if it does *not* I cannot see that it is wicked. It is a wicked and immoral thing to take *another* person's life, just as it is wicked and immoral to steal another person's money. But if the money is my *own*, and if I only will suffer from destroying it, it is *not* wicked to destroy it, though it may be a foolish thing to do.

I don't think *I* would ever be *really* tempted to commit suicide as long as I could get enough to eat and wear by any means short of begging. Life, with all its problems, has always been an extremely interesting thing to me.

Saturday, May 13, 1922

We finished cleaning the kitchen today, so housecleaning is over for another year. I am gardening now—I am glad—I love that. Ewan seems fairly well again. His attacks certainly are growing lighter. My tulips are out in full glory under the parlor windows.

The kitchen.

A corner of the garden.

We were out calling this evening. It was a perfect spring evening—the world was young and green and beautiful—and *clean*. Everything is always so clean in spring—no weeds—no

---

63　From Byron's *Don Juan*, Canto I, LXXXIII.

long grass—no fallen leaves. Think how many million springs there have been since "Creation's dawn" and all of them beautiful.

I enjoyed every minute of our drive and enjoyed it all the more because I had been re-reading a favorite old poem by Julia C. Dorr[64] and was haunted beautifully by it. Over and over in time to the beat of the engine I repeated it as we purred along through the green and amber dusk, some of the lines making an immortal melody through all the chambers of my being.

Oh, my garden lying whitely in the moonlight and the dew,
Far across the leagues of distance flies my yearning heart to you,
And I turn from storied castle, ivied fane[65] and ruined shrine,
To the dear familiar pleasance where my own white lilies shine—

With a vague, half startled wonder if some night in Paradise
From the battlements of heaven I shall turn my longing eyes
All the dim resplendent spaces and the mazy star-drifts through
To my garden lying whitely in the moonlight and the dew.

Friday, May 20, 1922
The Manse, Leaskdale, Ont.

I went in to Toronto yesterday. After shopping all day I went for a drive with friends out to Oakville through the misty spring evening. It was delightful—the white blossom glory of cherry and plum—the greenness—the cool gray mist—and the perfect comradeship. Next morning the drive back was just as lovely in the golden, fresh, dancing air.

Sunday, May 21, 1922

Today at dinner in the presence of a staid, solemn old minister Stuart looked up during a pause and said gravely, "Mother, do you think you'll ever have another baby?"

!!!

No, I never will. And as things are it is best. Yet that little unborn daughter of mine—how I would love her in the flesh. What would she have been like? Would I have seen my own girlhood again in her? Well, I shall have to hope for it in some little granddaughter—whom I may not live to see.

---

64   From "Lily Talks Lillies," by American poet Julia C. Dorr (1825–1913).
65   A "fane" is a temple or shrine.

I wish I had at least half a dozen children—or I would wish it if it were not for Ewan's terrible malady.

Monday, May 22, 1922

Began work today collecting material for *Emily II*.[66] I am sure I won't be able to make it anything as good as *Emily I* but the publishers want a series and it pays and so I'll carry it on. But I've a good idea for an adult novel,[67] of the light fairyland kind, and I'm going to go to work at it in the fall and see if I can go on with both at the same time. The experiment *may* be disastrous—I may "hate the one and despise the other." But I mean to try it.

There has been no word from Pickering yet. We expect it every day and it spoils the half hour before the mail. It is strange they don't either accept the offer or send the writ. We have found *two* men at Mt. Albert who were told by Pickering after the operation last summer that "the collision didn't cause his operation—he was going to have that anyway." They are reliable men and are quite ready to swear to this. This will be an immense help to our case and my mind has been much easier since we found it out.

This evening I spent gardening. Our lawn was green and blossomy. The sunset was exquisite behind the big maple trees. A peace long unknown to my troubled soul seemed to possess me. It shut out the world and corroding worries and discontents.

Corner of Lawn.

Paddy frisked about among the shadows. In the twilight—appropriately called the cat's light—is the only time when a cat reveals himself. At all other times he is inscrutable but in the hour of dusk and dew we can catch a glimpse of the tantalizing secret of his personality.

It was all so lovely that I loved the place and felt a foolish, irrational gladness that we had not been called to Markham and compelled to leave it. I had not only the beauty of this spring but of all the old springs here—especially my first spring here, I always remember that spring especially for the delight of having a garden again after having none for so long, mingled with the joy of my baby's anticipated coming. Yes, for a few hours tonight I was very happy.

I am feeling better anyhow. I seem at last to have shaken off the stubborn depression of the flu and am full of "pep" again. The old illusion that there is

---

66 *Emily Climbs*, published in 1925 by Frederick A. Stokes.

67 This would become *The Blue Castle*, published in 1926 by Frederick A. Stokes.

something good around the bend has come back to me. I know now that it *is* only an illusion but it helps me to live for all that.

Union is in the air at Zephyr. I don't know what the outcome will be. The Zephyr people want Union on a general scale but are with a few exceptions bitterly averse to union with the local Methodist church. I am not going to worry over it. We have plenty to live on no matter what happens. This "Union" matter has been a Dweller on my threshold[68] for years and now I'm just going to kick it out.

Thursday, June 8, 1922
The Manse, Leaskdalc, Ont.

This was a very hot day—phenomenally hot for so early in the season. But our weather lately has been lovely.

We have a new denizen of our household—a small scrap of a kitten which I picked up in an Uxbridge store, the poor pretty mite having been deserted by its mother. It is a "female" as Stuart gravely avers and we have named it "Queen." I have never had a female cat since old "Topsy" of childhood days, never feeling equal to coping with the nuisance of recurrent kittens.

There is one thing that has always been a matter of amazement to me—the wholly foundationless and absurd yarns that occasionally get into circulation in this community concerning me—yarns which have almost invariably had their source or their first circulation in Mrs. Alec Leask,[69] who, although she is friendly enough to me, has really caused me more annoyance than if she were my enemy. A few years ago she circulated a weird yarn that I was writing a book on *stepmothers* and meant to have it published *after my death*. I had never mentioned *my* stepmother to a soul in this province so what was the origin of the yarn I cannot imagine—if it had any origin outside of Mrs. Alec Leask's silly head. Soon after I came here the story was told everywhere that I had been born and brought up in the Anglican church and had told someone that I would *"never feel at home in the Presbyterian church."* The genesis of this *may* have been some joking remark of mine that "if Union went through I'd go over to the Anglicans."

Another of Mrs. Alec's fictions was that one day I had been informed over the 'phone that a certain check was coming to me and that I at once told the

---

68   A tongue-in-cheek allusion to one of LMM's early favourite novels, *Zanoni* (1842) by English author Edward Bulwer-Lytton. Book IV of *Zanoni* is entitled "The Dweller on the Threshold," a term from the Western mystic tradition that involves a haunting spectral figure; this reflects LMM's long-standing interest in mysticism.

69   The Leasks were a prominent family of Scottish extraction in Leaskdale, among its original founding members.

person 'phoning to "send it away for jewelry." This, of course, had no shred of foundation. I have never since coming to Leaskdale bought *any* jewelry except a pearl and aquamarine ring, price $14, and some bead necklets and pearl-bead earrings. And I did not order these over the 'phone!!

But the latest tale annoys me. It is to the effect that I have recently been left "a millionaire's estate" by the death of a relative. Mrs. A. Leask, it seems, was told during a recent visit in Toronto, that "a prominent Canadian author" had been left this and seems to have jumped to the conclusion that I was the lucky party. She has accordingly been diligently circulating the same. It is vexatious. Such a yarn will do neither me nor Ewan any good in the congregation. If a minister's wife "has money" some people seem to think that *he* doesn't need a salary at all. I have always been careful never to let anyone know how much money I really have made on this account. But this prudence has been defeated by the fictions that people make up. I could wring Mrs. Leask's neck with unholy pleasure—as well as those of all curiosity mongers.

I have been having a little trouble of late over some incidents in connection with Chester at school. Our teacher is a somewhat weak and inexperienced young girl and some of the older boys in school have been putting Chester and his classmates up to pranks. In some respects Chester is not an easy boy to train and Ewan makes no attempt whatever to help me in this matter. I told him he would *have* to help me in this affair and talk to Chester; he did so very reluctantly but in the end the disciplining was as usual left to me. There is nothing I miss more in my life than the aid of a wise and competent father in the bringing up of my children. It is absolutely lacking.

I had to "outlaw" Chester for a few days—that is, he was cut off from all the privileges of a son. I have found that this punishment is more effective than any other. Tonight I heard him crying in his bed. I went in and we "made up" and he promised to do better.

But these incidents make me very unhappy. I am afraid that my sons will come to regard me as the parent who is always correcting and punishing them and Ewan as the parent who indulges them and never punishes. It is not fair—and at times I feel very bitter about it.

Ewan went to Sutton today to consult with Dr. Boynton,[70] whom a friend told us might have been the doctor consulted by Marshall Pickering *before* the collision. He found out that Pickering had been to see Boynton in the middle of May, a month before the operation, and Boynton then diagnosed his trouble as enlarged prostate gland and advised an operation. This tallies with what Pickering's son told Ewan.

---

70   William John Boynton, MD, practised medicine in Sutton, a village located 2 km/1 mile south of Lake Simcoe and about 16 km/10 miles northwest of Zephyr, from 1899 to 1924.

I think Pickering wishes he were out of it. "Bill" Horner, his crony, went to Mr. McCullough[71] the other day and asked him to get us to "settle" it—a most extraordinary thing to do from every point of view.

Ewan's head has been bothering him of late. But I have not seen any indication of morbid thoughts. Yet the dread of their return always hovers in the background.

Monday, June 12, 1922

Ewan has been very dull and moody of late and that horrible sense of a *change of personality* in him has made itself felt these last two or three days. I can hardly bear to be in his company when I feel this. There is something in him then that is utterly repellent to me and I cannot overcome or smother the repugnance.

We were out calling this evening. The old lady of the house said some very nice things to me and I felt a warm glow steal over my forlorn soul, especially as Ewan was in another room and so could neither be annoyed nor derisive over her compliments. To be sure, she rather spoiled it by remarking, "Nobody ever need say anything against you or Mr. Macdonald to me"—thereby giving me the unpleasant feeling that people *had* been saying something to her. Probably she saw this significance herself for she added hastily, "They don't say anything—they don't dare to"—which didn't make it any better. I came away feeling that a thistle was sticking in my soul. My philosophy tells me that we can't please everybody and that it doesn't matter. But still the thistle pricks.

Tuesday, June 13, 1922
The Manse, Leaskdale, Ont.

Today was pleasant. I forgot all thistle pricks. We motored to Cannington[72] where I addressed the I.O.D.E. on Canadian literature. Later on we had tea with Mrs. McKinnon, the widow of a second cousin of Ewan's who was also a Presbyterian minister. Ewan seemed much better again and even seemed able to bear Mrs. McKinnon's telling him he had "an ideal wife" without resentment. I am very far from being an ideal wife and Mrs. McKinnon is a rather silly woman.

---

71   J.W. McCullough, the Macdonalds' lawyer, whose office was in Stouffville, a town about 33 km/20 miles south of Leaskdale. (His brother John McCullough, who would also be involved in the lawsuit, had a law office in Toronto.)

72   Village 32 km/20 miles northwest of Leaskdale. The Imperial Order of the Daughters of the Empire ("I.O.D.E.") was founded at the end of the nineteenth century by a Canadian woman, Margaret Polson Murray, in response to patriotic feeling associated with the Boer War; it began as a women's organization designed to give aid to soldiers.

When I got home I found a letter from a woman in Oshawa who wanted me to "select a verse that 'Anne' would have liked" for her darling baby's gravestone!

There is a pathetic side to this—and I've written her a nice letter; and yet it is an absurd thing to do.

Tuesday, June 20, 1922
The Manse, Leaskdale, Ont.

Marshall Pickering is like Ewan's melancholia. Just as soon as we begin to hope there is an end of him he comes back. Today Ewan got a letter from McCullough saying he had received the writ. Well, the suspense is over and we know the worst. The trial will not come off until the fall. I think Boynton's evidence will settle it in our favor—though I never recall that dream of mine without a qualm. We will just put it out of our minds till autumn and not let it spoil our summer. The talk and gossip it will make—and has made—is really the most disagreeable part. Almost everyone seems to sympathize with us and Marshall Pickering is universally condemned; but to feel that we are the centre of a whirlpool of gossip and surmise is very annoying—a whole bed of thistles.

Wednesday, June 28, 1922

I feel rather stiff today. Yesterday Lily and I spent the day picking wild berries on her mother's farm. It was hard work scrambling through the brush and being devoured by mosquitoes. I don't think I'll ever do it again, not even for wild strawberries.

Today was the last day of school and Chester passed all his promotion exams. I was very glad for I had been afraid of the arithmetic. Stuart had two "exams" also—arithmetic and reading and got 100 in the latter and 90 in the former. And he only six-and-three quarters. He is quicker to pick up a thing than Chester—but also quicker to forget.

Sunday, July 2, 1922

Cars are decent things—when they behave decently. After Zephyr service Ewan went to Mt. Albert and Mr. Dyer of Mt. Albert[73] came back here in our

---

73   Rev. C.E. Dyer (1891–1953) served as the final minister at Chalmers Presbyterian Church in Mount Albert (8 km/5 miles southwest of Zephyr). When Chalmers became part of Mount Albert United Church, Rev. Dyer moved to a congregation in a community some distance from Leaskdale.

car with his wife to speak at our missionary service this evening. Service was over at nine o'clock and the evening fine. I decided to "run over" to Mt. Albert with them to have the fun of coming back with Ewan. Which I did—and enjoyed it all very much and got back at eleven. But twenty years ago in the days of horses and buggies who would have thought of starting on a twenty-five mile drive after preaching "just for the fun of it?"

But the old days had their good points, too. And a six mile moonlit or starlit drive behind a spirited horse, with a pleasant companion, through the old fragrant Island woods, past the dim orchards and the dreaming fields, with the moan of the sea on a faraway shore sounding through the air, was a very pleasant thing. For, as Einstein says, Time is only relative.

We leave for Niagara in the morning, having promised the boys the trip all winter.

Saturday, July 8, 1922
The Manse, Leaskdale, Ont.

We had a splendid Niagara trip—good roads, good weather, and Lady Jane Grey-Dort[74] behaved herself much better than she usually does. We spent Monday night at Streetsville with the McKays.[75] The traditions of the pantry seem to be as lean as ever in that menage. I cannot understand how people can invite people to visit them, be, or appear to be, glad to see them, and then literally starve them. Seven of us sat down to a table whereon was just about enough food to supply three. I was as hungry when I got up as when I sat down; the boys were hungrier and I had hard work to make them shut their small mouths and refrain from embarrassing complaints. The McKay *menus* have been a standing joke among their acquaintances for years. I shall never forget some of our experiences when we were invited to supper with them when they were in Wick. Some of them were quite unbelievably funny. There are plenty of mean folks in the world but even mean folks when they invite you specially to supper will give you enough food to satisfy ordinary hunger. The McKays don't. We didn't have enough to eat until noon the next day when we got to Oakville and went to a hotel. Luckily I had a box of cookies along with me for the boys else I don't know what they would have done.

---

74   The Macdonalds purchased their Gray-Dort in 1921, one of the first cars to be manufactured in Canada. Gray-Dort Motors had been founded in 1915 when Robert Gray secured rights from Michigan producer Dort Motor Company to manufacture the car in Canada. One of the main characters in LMM's novel *The Blue Castle* (1926) calls his car, a Grey-Slosson, "Lady Jane."

75   The Macdonalds had been friends with the McKays when Rev. McKay was minister at a nearby church. The McKays had since moved to Streetsville, a village then 40 km/25 miles west of Toronto (now part of Mississauga).

We got to Niagara the next evening. After dinner we walked out and looked into that stupendous gorge where the maddened waters of the tortured river make their leap of supreme agony and the smoke of their torment goes up forever. Niagara is something it is futile to talk or write about.

We all went over the toll-bridge to the United States at night and saw two excellent movies. Next day we motored to Buffalo and back—a delightful drive—and then came as far as St. Catherines on the road home. Next night we reached Oshawa where the Smiths are living now and stayed all night there. We came home last night after a very enjoyable trip. Ewan was well, the boys good and interested, the weather perfect.

Saturday, July 15, 1922

I had a letter from Mr. Rollins[76] yesterday—like a voice from the tomb or an echo from ancient history. He says that "after long continued oral and written argument"—which is of ominous sound as bearing upon fees—he got the master to file a much better report than the first one but could not get him to file a really fair report (which is a euphemistic way of saying that the report was against us). The case was argued before Judge Hammond[77] in May and though the Judge said nothing either way he—Rollins—had a feeling that "he was impressed with our side of the case." But as the said Judge has gone to Europe there will be no decision till the fall.

Also, the Page Co. have appealed their libel suit against me to the Supreme Court.[78]

But I am not worrying over it. I got through with all that at once in those bad months two years ago. Herewith I dismiss the whole affair until the next letter from Rollins. Whiff—pooh—away it goes!

Tonight I was re-reading Mrs. Asquith's biography, keeping before me as I read the picture of that thin, witch-profiled woman on the platform of Massey Hall. The book is in bad taste of course—but things that are in bad taste are always intensely interesting. And some parts of it are very touching and beautiful. Tonight I read the chapter in which she watches at her sister Laura's

---

76   Weld Allan Rollins (1874–1952) was a lawyer specializing in corporate law who had represented LMM in her lawsuits against her publisher L.C. Page. For a complete account of LMM's legal encounters with Page, see Mary Henley Rubio's *Lucy Maud Montgomery: The Gift of Wings* (2008).

77   F.T. Hammond of the Suffolk County Court, Massachusetts, heard Rollins argue LMM's case in her two lawsuits against Page (establishing an injunction to prevent Page from publishing *Further Chronicles of Avonlea*, as well as a request for an account of the profits from LMM's books in the years before she broke away from them).

78   L.C. Page had sued LMM for "malicious litigation," a case dismissed in 1920 by the Massachusetts Supreme Court. Now, in 1922, Page was appealing the case to the U.S. Supreme Court.

deathbed. It reminded me so deeply of Frede's[79]—once more I stood in that dim sunrise room at Macdonald—once more I watched my darling's ebbing breath—saw it falter—fail—stop—once more my heart was rent with the torture of that awful hour—I flung the book away—turned out the light—cried myself to sleep. Oh, Frede—Frede! No, the dead never come back—or you would have come to me!

On every page of Mrs. Asquith's book I found myself wishing that Frede and I could have read it together. How we would have enjoyed talking it over—it is the sort of a book we could have discussed endlessly. It is at such moments I realize horribly how much Frede's death took out of my life on its intellectual side and how bare and desolate the finest chambers of my soul have ever since been.

Thursday, July 20, 1922
The Manse, Leaskdale, Ont.

Stokes' letter came to-day asking for the MS. of my new book. So I packed *Emily* off on her journey to the portals of the world—dear little "Emily" whom I love far better than I ever loved "Anne." I felt as if I were sending part of myself. Will she win a welcome? My original MS. of *Emily* I have put away. Some day it may have a certain value. I have the original MS. of *Anne of Green Gables* but not of some of its successors. I wish now that I had kept them all.

Anita Marcone is married again.[80] The announcement came today. So she must finally have got her divorce from Paul. This second venture is named Bernard Voelker. Sounds like another foreigner. Well, let us hope Anita will have better luck this time.

Tonight I was sitting on the veranda. Chester was playing about with a couple of girl chums and Lily was also there. Chester attempted to spring over the hammock in a running jump, caught his foot and fell, striking his head against the hard ground. I expected a howl of anguish for it must have hurt terribly. I exclaimed, "Chester, what have you done?" But Chester sprang up with a gay laugh—"Oh, nothing much, I guess"—and then bolted through the front door. I stepped in and heard muffled sobs in the library. He was curled up on the davenport crying into the pillows. The spunky little chap had braved it off

79　LMM had attended Frede at her deathbed in 1919; she gives a detailed account of this in *The Complete Journals of L.M. Montgomery: The Ontario Years, 1918–1922* (Rock's Mills Press, 2017).

80　LMM had met Anita Marcone in Boston in 1910, when visiting the Pages. In an entry dated November 29, 1910, she wrote, "I was not the only guest in the Page household. Mr. and Mrs. Paul Marcone of New York were there on their honeymoon. He is an Italian, his father a New York Banker, his grandfather a Sicilian count. Anita Marcone is a niece of the notable Senator Hanna and is a Philadelphian. In evening dress she is the most beautiful girl I ever saw. When she is forty she will not be beautiful—she will be fat and coarse. But just at present, in full toilette, she is something I could not keep my eyes off."

before others but as I sat down beside him and took his poor little head close to my heart he said piteously, "Oh, mother, it hurts!" So I cuddled him and kissed him and told him I was proud of him for hiding it from the world—and felt that this was what mothers are made for—to comfort behind the scenes.

Sunday, July 30, 1922
"Roselawn" Bala, Muskoka

We motored up here—85 miles—last Monday morning. Roselawn[81] is a boarding house on the Muskosh river,[82] kept by a Miss *Toms*. Old Mr. Toms, her father, is here too and her sister, Mrs. Brackinridge. They are very nice people.

We only room here. We get our meals up the street at a certain Mrs. Pykes who is a lady cumbered with much serving.[83]

The situation here is very lovely. The lawn runs down to the river where the bank is fringed by trees. It is beautiful at all times but especially at night when the river silvers under the moon, the lights of the cottages twinkle out in the woods along the opposite bank, bonfires blaze with all the old allure of the camp fire, and music and laughter drift across from the innumerable canoes and launches on the river.

Bala is a dear spot—somehow I love it. It has the flavor of home—perhaps because of its pines which are plentiful hereabout. The only drawback to the place is our terrible beds. They are those vile things—mattresses that have a hollow in the middle towards which sleepers insistently roll; and if

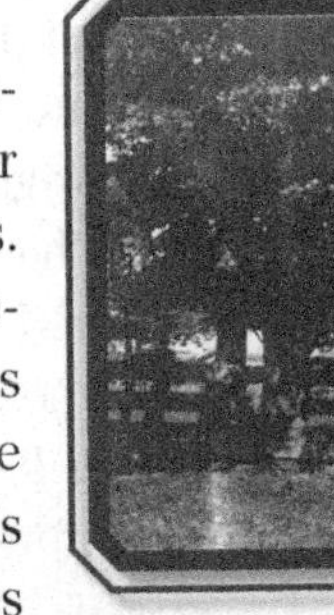

"Roselawn."

The Macdonald family starting for Bala.

---

81   The Macdonalds stayed at a tourist home in Bala, a town north of Toronto on the shore of Lake Muskoka. The popular tourist area of Muskoka lies east of Georgian Bay and includes Lakes Joseph, Rosseau, and Muskoka. "Miss Toms" may have been Katherine Burgess, a daughter of Roselawn's owner (Thomas Burgess). Burgess' grandfather, Thomas Burgess, had founded Bala in 1878.

82   This is now known as Moon River, flowing from Bala Bay to Georgian Bay. (There is a Musquash River starting about 9 km/5 miles west of Bala, at Moon Chute. The Musquash River would in coming years be made famous by the Group of Seven, notably by A.Y. Jackson's 1939 painting of it.)

83   Fanny Walden Pike was an eccentric Englishwoman who had formerly worked as a midwife. She served meals to summer visitors.

we put something between us to prevent this the beds are so narrow that the remaining space it too "cabined, cribbed, confined"[84] for any comfort. I haven't had a decent night's sleep since I came. Stuart was sick the first three days with an upset stomach and I had a secret fear that he was taking the measles, having been exposed to them two weeks ago. But luckily it was not measles and he is all right again and bathes in the Muskosh every day.

Ewan has been rather dull, too, bothered by headache and depression but seems better now. I read—do fancy work—correct a second MS. of *Emily* for my English publisher—and dream—lost but immortal dreams. I find that I can dream even yet in Muskoka.

What a lovely name is Muskoka! Music—charm—wonder—it suggests them all. Shakespeare nodded when he suggested that there was nothing in a name. There's a tremendous lot in it. Suppose Muskoka were called Udora! Or Stoufville?

Yesterday we motored up to Dudley and spent the day with John Mustard and his wife.[85] They

"Fringed with Trees"

"Come on in, the water's fine."

Dreaming.

---

84   From *Macbeth*, 3.4.25: Macbeth is feeling increasingly anxious, as events spiral out of his control: "But now I am cabined, cribbed, confined, bound in / To saucy doubts and fears."

85   John Mustard had been LMM's schoolteacher during her year in Prince Albert, Saskatchewan, in 1890–91. She described him as being moody, hot-tempered, and a poor teacher. Her account records Mustard beginning to "court" LMM, who rebuffed his advances. In an entry dated June 6, 1891, she wrote: "And then Mr. M. sheepishly informed me that he was thinking of going to Knox College and meant to be a minister. I don't know how I kept from laughing right out in his face. Mustard a minister!! Oh Lordy—how it will sound—Rev. Mr. Mustard. I pity the poor woman whose fate it will be to write 'Mrs.' before such a combination. I have a dim suspicion that Mr. M. intends asking me to accept that honor but I may be mistaken." In fact, Mr Mustard did become a very successful Presbyterian minister in Toronto.

have a cottage in an ideal spot on the bank of Lake Muskoka, buried in maple and oak trees. I loved it. The hot, noisy world was far away—cool silence was all around me—the gods of the wild wood welcomed back their own.

We had a nice afternoon. In the later part of it Ewan and the boys and Mrs. Mustard went fishing. I didn't want to go so I said I'd sit on the veranda and do fancy work. I wanted to be there *alone* in that lovely spot—to listen to the wind sighing and singing in the tree-tops to watch the beautiful zones of color on the lake—to dream out something very delightful. But John Mustard evidently supposed it wouldn't do to leave a guest alone and stayed, too. He bored me horribly; and, besides, I was rather disagreeably conscious of the *last* time we were alone together—that evening in the twilight in Eglinton Villa, Prince Albert, when he asked me to marry him. I wonder if he remembered it, too. There isn't the slightest thing about John Mustard to suggest that he recalls anything connected with those days—except *one* thing—the fact that he *never refers to them in any way.* If he were *not* self-conscious it would be the most natural thing in the world to recall a lot of the incidents of that year which had no connection with our "affair." *I* never refer to them—*he* never refers to them; the reason is the same in both cases.

Well, the world has changed so much since the last time we were alone together that it is rather hard to think it ever happened. It is rather as if two souls met in Eternity and thought but spoke not of some happening in some incarnation a score of lives before.

One thing I love about Bala is the roar of its falls. When I lie in bed at night it sounds exactly like the old surge roar of the Atlantic on some windy, dark-gray night on the old north shore.

Monday, July 31, 1922
Bala, Muskoka

Today we spent in making a boat trip over Lakes Muskoka and Rosseau. It was very lovely. The continuous panorama of lake and river and island made me think of Stevenson's lines.

> Where all the ways on every hand
> Lead onwards into fairyland.[86]

I had a very lovely forenoon. The boys were with Ewan so I sat alone—and—dreamed. I picked out an island that just suited me. I built thereon a

---

86   From Robert Louis Stevenson's (1850–94) poem, "Foreign Lands," first published in *A Child's Garden of Verses* (1885).

summer cottage and furnished it *de luxe*. I set up a boat-house and a motor launch. I peopled it with summer guests.—Frede, Aunt Annie, Stella, Bertie—Mr. MacMillan[87] (to whom I engaged Bertie!) We spent a whole idyllic summer there together. Youth—mystery—delight, were all ours once more. I lived it all out in every detail; we swam and sailed and fished and read and built camp fires under the pines—I saw to it that I had an island with pines—and dined gloriously at sunset *al fresco*, and then sat out on moonlit porches (well-screened from Muskoka mosquitoes!)—and always we talked—the soul-satisfying talk of kindred spirits, asking all the old, unanswered questions, caring not though there were no answers so long as we were all ignorant together.

Sometimes we varied it by going out to dinners and dances (for in my dream Ewan was *not* a minister!) at neighboring islands, enjoying them tremendously but always glad to skim back home over moonlit wonder-ways of soft, mysterious, dim silver, to our own dear bit of an island.

Some of us slept in the porches at night and some of us slept in the open, with the dark pines all about us, their crests in communion with the stars. (I don't know how we managed about the mosquitoes there but in a fairy dream one does not have to bother about things like that.) And what a perennial fascination there is in the thought of sleeping in the open under the stars for the heart of mankind!

"Soft, mysterious, dim, silver"

I dreamed it all out to the end of September. Then one night a storm came up. Our men and boys and Frede and Bertie had gone to the mainland in the motor launch early in the day. Aunt Annie and Stella and I waited in alarm for

87　Frede and Stella Campbell were LMM's cousins from Park Corner, Prince Edward Island; Aunt Annie was their mother; Bertie McIntyre was the daughter of LMM's father's sister, Mary Montgomery McIntyre; George Boyd Macmillan, who LMM called "my Scottish correspondent," was from Glasgow; he and LMM had been trading letters since 1903.

their return through the wild night while the hurricane shrieked through the channels and the waves dashed over the rocks to our very doors. At last, after anxious hours, they came, drenched and cold, but safe. And we joyfully pulled them in and shut the door on the storm; and we all sat down to a hot supper before the blazing fire in our big, timbered living-room, made all the cosier by the baffled, raging wind outside. And we talked—and drank of laughter—and were happy and triumphant, surrounded by the black legions of the storm. But under all our gayety we knew that our summer was over.

How silly it all seems written out! And how vital and delightful it all was in my dream! I woke from it when we reached Rosseau. And there was no enchanted island—Bertie and Stella were in different lands—Frede slept dreamlessly in her grave by a far-off ocean. Yet not two minutes before she had been laughing at me across our supper table in the firelight and I had heard the very cadences of her voice as she described their wild buffet through the storm and how she had been the first to see the lantern light I had hung on the pine tree by the boathouse for their guidance!

Thursday, Aug. 3, 1922
Bala, Muskoka

Today we motored to Pt. Sandfield,[88] taking Father Toms and Mrs. Brackinridge with us to see a certain garden there of which we had heard. It was an awful place to get to—I thought our car would be ruined. But it *was* lovely when we got

The view from the veranda

there—as lovely as my dream-built castle of last Monday. The view from the veranda looking over garden and lake was so lovely that it hurt me.

Friday, Aug. 4, 1922

Eight years ago today the world in which I spent my girlhood and young womanhood passed away forever in one sudden, overwhelming cataclysm. It seems impossible that it can be eight years. It seems as yesterday—it will always seem as yesterday—as the mountain always looks near though ever lengthening miles intervene. To me, those four years of agony seem an ever present thing. Yet in a letter I received the other day from a fifteen-year-old reader (who would of course be only seven when the war broke out) she told me how *Rilla* had made the years of the great war (which she only remembered dimly)

88   Port Sandfield is a community on Lake Rosseau some 20 km/12 miles north of Bala.

"seem so real to her." She belongs to a generation to which the Great War is only a name as well as all the other wars of the past.

The Manse, Leaskdale, Ont.
Aug. 6, 1922

We motored home yesterday, leaving "Roselawn" with real regret. Our vacation has been—as most vacations are—a compound of pleasures and discomforts. But the pleasures far outweighed the discomforts and we were sorry to come away—and then when we got home we were glad to get home. I

Roselawn. The lady in a white blouse on the veranda is me mineself.

was, anyway. It was so nice to see my own green lawn and maple trees again— my garden, my flowers, my house.

And *so* nice to lie gratefully down on a *good* bed at night.

The only shadow on our homecoming was the death of our poor gray kitty-cat, Queen. She was killed by a car night before last. Paddy, however, is well and catty and inscrutable.

Something that was said in our supper table conversation tonight reminded me of "Mad MacKinley."

"Mad MacKinley" was one of those eccentric creatures with which the P.E. Island countryside used to abound in my childhood. They are never seen now. Mad MacKinley was a very striking and picturesque figure.

He was one of the North River MacKinleys— an old and good family. In his youth he was brilliant and studied for the Baptist ministry, teaching school in order to pay his way through college and

A corner of my garden.

studying so hard at the same time that his mind gave way—and he became "Mad MacKinley." The insanity was concerned only with religion. In every other respect he seemed absolutely normal. But he conceived the idea that immersion was absolutely necessary to salvation and that anyone not immersed was damned. It followed that he must go forth and preach this to all at sundry times and in divers places.

His relatives had put him in the asylum once or twice but he always escaped; and finally, as he was quite harmless—they ceased to try to restrain

Old Presbyterian Church.
The x marks the spot where Mad McKinley always stood.

him and for many years he wandered over the Island continually preaching his warning—and he *could* preach, with a flood of eloquence and rhetoric.

He came very often to Cavendish, as several Cavendish people were married to North River people and he found a congenial atmosphere among the Cavendish Baptists, who were at that time very narrow and bigoted—believing, I think, in their secret souls just exactly as he did, although they were always ashamed of "Mad MacKinley" and his ranting.

We would be coming out of the old Presbyterian church some fine Sunday morning. Long before we who sat near the top got out we would hear shouts of exhortation rolling in—for Mad MacKinley always preached at the top of a sonorous voice. And when we reached the door there he would be, standing in the graveyard, haranguing the doomed Presbyterians eloquently.

He always took up his position in the graveyard because no one could molest him there. At first he had occupied the church green but some of the old Simpsons and Macneills, who were as bigoted as the Baptists—and who had not sense enough to leave a madman alone, had once hustled him roughly away. Then he resorted to the graveyard, standing just before the church door. He was quite an imposing figure, tall, always neatly dressed in a long black coat, with long gray hair and beard, clear-cut, intellectual features, and fine eyes where the light of frenzy burned. He would preach until the last straggler had gone. Then he would tuck under his arm the umbrella which he always carried—and which he waved wildly while preaching—and stalk off down the hill.

He would generally hang about the community for a week or so after that. He always visited the school and harangued the pupils on immersion. I remember two of these visits with especial clearness. One day he preached so long that the teacher became impatient and intimated that enough time had been lost. Mad MacKinley was very indignant. He turned and went out and ran around the school seven times. It was a very windy day and as he flashed repeatedly past the four low windows his long gray "duster" and long gray hair streamed out behind him like the robe and hair of some irate Hebrew prophet.

The other incident was still more comical.

It was the custom to have "Testament Reading" every morning at the

opening of school and each scholar had a "Testament." These Testaments, being very cheap affairs, wore out rapidly and were replaced by new ones, but the old ones remained in the desks. One spring Sarah Jack cleaned the school and collected about a bushel of old, torn, dog-eared, absolutely useless "testaments" and parts thereof out of the desks and carried them down into the bush where she dumped them under a tree. The very next week Mad MacKinley came around and, wandering through the bush, found this heap. He gathered all the Testaments up in the skirt of his gray duster, stalked up to and into the school and emptied the testaments down on the floor at the feet of the amazed teacher, exclaiming wrathfully,

"Behold how you Presbyterians treat the word of God!"

As there were as many Baptists as Presbyterians among the pupils, we Presbyterians felt very indignant!

Mad MacKinley often came to our place for his mail and frequently stayed for hours talking to Grandfather. Grandfather had once said to him, "Mr. MacKinley, you are welcome to come here whenever you like. But not one word are you to say of or about immersion under this roof." Mad MacKinley never did say one word; and he conversed with Grandfather on all subjects of world interest as rationally as anyone could. One day he came in and asked Grandmother if he might see a *Patriot*. Grandmother gave him one and he sat down in the kitchen to read it. He read silently for some time, neither speaking nor being spoken to; suddenly he gave a shout, threw the paper down, and rushed out of the house. He never came back again and we never knew why. Possibly he had seen something in the paper that displeased or upset him.

Mad MacKinley was a source of amusement to us young fry. We were delighted when he appeared, howling out his anathemas in the graveyard. We were too young to realize the tragedy in this wreck of a once brilliant intellect. To us, "Mad MacKinley" was a Roman holiday and nothing else.

He has been dead these many years. During his life he wanted his brother at North River to sell him a little bit of land on his farm and bury him there when he died, erecting a tombstone bearing nothing but the sole word *"Commissioned."*[89] This was not done, however.

I am reading Mommsenn's *Rome*.[90] The scholarship is no doubt amazing but the history is deadly dull. There is not one spark of imagination or insight to clothe the dry bones with life.

I had a delightful letter from a young girl in Washington State today. She lost her mother when a baby and said to me, "Your books are to me the mother

89   A term designating ministers approved by church authority as itinerant preachers.

90   *The History of Rome* (1854–56), a multi-volume work by German historian Theodor Mommsen (1817–1903). LMM misspells his name as "Mommsenn."

I have never known." Could anything nicer be said? It means much to me to know that my books have helped one human being as much as that.

I got another compliment tonight, too—Stuart looked up gravely into my face as I kissed him good-night and said,

"Mother, if you were a girl and would wait for me I'd marry you when I grew up."

Stuart is always saying funny little unexpected things. The other day he was going away for the afternoon and he said earnestly, "Good-bye, dear mother. Oh, I *hope you won't die before I get back!*"

Leaskdale, Ont.
Saturday, Aug. 26, 1922

Ewan has been very miserable these past two weeks—by far the worst attack since last February. He has been very melancholy and has suffered continually from headache.

I was in Toronto last Monday to discuss the new Stokes contract with Mac, missed my train—the very first time I ever missed a train in my life—and had to stay in over night. So I went to see the film *Orphans of the Storm*.[91] It was really the most wonderful thing of its kind I ever saw. I felt when I came out that I had *seen* the French Revolution. The guillotine scene, the storming of the Bastille, and the dance of the Carmagnole through the streets of Paris were very realistic and horrible.

What a way this will be to teach history to children when the Powers that run the schools wake up to it—in another hundred years!

Saturday, Sept. 2, 1922

A busy week. Monday we were occupied in preparing for the ministerial association which met here on Tuesday. On Wednesday we rose at 5:30 and left at seven, to have a day at the Exhibition for the children's sake. For the same sake we waited for the Grand Stand show in the evening—which was good.[92] I enjoyed the fireworks as much as the boys did. We left the grounds at eleven

---

91   *Orphans of the Storm* was a 1921 silent film depicting the Revolution in eighteenth-century France. The guillotine was a method of execution that involved decapitation. The Bastille was a medieval fortress and political prison in Paris that became a symbol of tyrannical rule by an out-of-touch monarchy; it was "stormed" by an angry mob on July 14, 1789. "La Carmagnole" is the title of a French song written during the French Revolution, celebrating the fall of the monarchy.
92   The Toronto Industrial Exhibition was founded in 1879 (it had been preceded by provincially sponsored fairs that were held in different cities, including Toronto); in 1912 its name changed to the Canadian National Exhibition. The Exhibition grounds cover 192 acres located along Toronto's waterfront on the shores of Lake Ontario.

and got home at 1:30. I enjoyed the drive home. The night was fine—Lady Jane behaved well for a wonder. I like travelling by night in a car that acts well. It always gives me the delightful sensation of being a comet, rushing through the darkness of space by my own light.

Lily, however, caught cold and has been laid up with tonsillitis the rest of the week, so I have been very busy. Ewan on the other hand is suddenly better and seems fairly well again.

Last night I heard an owl laughing out on one of the trees of the lawn. I shall never forget the first time I heard owl's laughter. I had often read of it but had never heard it. One night about eight years ago I was going up the road to make a call. It was a dark, still, autumn night with the first fine tang of frost in the air. Suddenly in the little copse of cedar trees on the side of the road to my right I heard chuckles of laughter. I thought it must be some of the village boys hiding there and felt annoyed at the thought that I might be the butt of their clownish amusement. But then it occurred to me that the laughter had in it something not quite human—some weird indescribable quality alien to our laughter—more akin to the Puckish mirth of fairy folk or fauns—with just a faint hint of malice in it. Now, unfortunately I can no longer believe in wood elves, so this laughter puzzled me. Until suddenly I thought of owls and knew it for what it was—a truly, delightful intriguing sound as if some unearthly survival of the Golden Age was chuckling to itself on a dark night.

Last night there was but one owl and he was certainly having a good time all alone over some owlish joke.

The Manse, Leaskdale, Ont.
Sept. 10, 1922

Cars sometimes become possessed of the devil—no doubt at all about that. Lady Jane had seven in her this week. She has worried our lives out. Of course she has never been really right since Pickering ran into us that unlucky Sunday last year. Besides the smashing up she got, everything else was jarred and loosened so that something has been continually going wrong ever since. But this week has beaten all records. It began last Wednesday when we went to Uxbridge. She stopped seven times on the way down without any reason that we could discover. Nothing we could do availed to budge her but always after about ten minutes she would apparently start of her own accord. Really, for all the world she acted just like a balky horse. At Uxbridge, a garage man thought, or pretended to think, that he had located the trouble and fixed it. Lady Jane came home properly. Thursday morning we had planned to go in to Toronto.

The Prisoner of Zenda[93] was being screened in Massey Hall and the manager had sent me four tickets. So I asked Mrs. Leask and Margaret to go in with us, desiring to put this treat in Margaret's way because she has always been such a cheerful, efficient helper in our Guild.

Lady Jane, however, had her own opinion on the matter and wouldn't start. It was noon before Ewan got her running and then she stopped three times on the road in. However, we did get there and Ewan took her to the Gray-Dort headquarters, thinking that they could surely discover there what was the matter with her. Mrs. Leask, Margaret and I got our dinners and went to Massey Hall.

I don't know whether I shall *ever* become sensible enough *not* to go to see screen versions of my favorite books. I am afraid I won't because I have been disappointed often enough to cure me of the foolishness if I were curable. I was very much disappointed in the film. "Rudolf" wasn't even good-looking and "Flavia" was merely a curly-headed doll with "goo-goo" eyes. The only live character was old "Sapt" who looked uncannily like what the real "Sapt" must have looked. He was convincing but nothing else was. I would resolve never to go to see another book-film if I thought I could keep it but I know I cannot. I will always go to them when occasion offers and always be sorry I did.

We got out at ten and tried to start for home. The Gray-Dort people had overhauled "Lady Jane" and charged Ewan nine dollars—and she wouldn't even start. Ewan worked over her an hour but in vain. The Gray-Dort garage was closed and no other was near except a little Ford all-night service station. Ewan got her towed there and then took the Leasks up-town to relatives, while I waited in the *Iroquois* lobby[94] and vowed that I'd never again invite anyone to go with us in a car—though I probably won't keep *that* resolution anyhow.

Next morning Ewan got Lady Jane overhauled again, paid some more cash and got away at ten. The brute stopped twice on the road home and we had four flat tires—or rather the same tire went flat for four times and no garage could discover what was wrong. However, we did eventually get home.

Tonight we started for Zephyr to attend a christening. Lady Jane stopped *eleven* times on the way over—and a thunderstorm came up and torrents of rain poured down. I was worn out when we reached there and dreaded the return home. But that absurd car came home without a spark of trouble. Of

---

93   Based on the popular adventure novel by Anthony Hope (1984), the 1922 silent movie by the same title was based on a 1896 play by Hope and Edward Rose. The film was produced by Metro Pictures Corporation.

94   The Iroquois was an elegant hotel in downtown Toronto, on York and King Streets, built in 1894. (It was destroyed by fire in 1975.)

course she is possessed—not a doubt of it. The Old Scratch[95] himself is in her.
    Tired? It is to laugh.

Sunday, Sept. 17, 1922
Leaskdale, Ont.

I have had a beautiful week. Really, I haven't had such a delightful ten days for many a moon.

Ewan left last Monday for a motor trip to Warsaw.[96] (This is not exactly the reason for my beautiful week!) He took Rev. Macdonald of Wick with him and if dear Lady Jane kept on with her antics as she did last week they'd have a charming trip but on the knees of the gods be it.

Lily also departed for her vacation and *this* is why I've had a nice time. Lily has really been intolerable for the past few months again. She was very good all winter, but by spring the salutary effect of the fact of Elsie[97] and its implications had begun to wear off and she slipped back gradually into her pre-Elsie habits. She was forgetful, lazy, neglectful, cranky and impertinent. So I hailed her departure with a secret exultation. The minute she was out of the house I fell upon kitchen, pantry and cellar cupboard; I put them in order and kept them so. I have had an orderly, peaceful, enjoyable week of it, with plenty of leisure made possible by system and the absence of any one to clutter up.

Kitchen.

I got up in the morning, got breakfast and "got" the boys off to school. Then I washed my dishes and sat down for a forenoon of writing. That done I got myself a "pantry bite," did what little tidying was necessary, dressed, did what tasks I had allotted to the day, cooked dinner at night, and then had a good evening of reading and fancy work. There was no abominable "visiting" to do and I was not plagued with aimless callers. When I felt so disposed I did a lot of fancy cooking by way of seeing if my hand had lost its culinary skill—it hadn't! I

---

95   A term for the devil that derives from the Middle English word *scrat*.
96   Ewan's brother, Angus Cameron McDonald (1865–1944)—the tombstone in the Oakwood Cemetery and obituary confirm the variation in spelling of the last name—was a prominent physician in Warsaw, a town in central Indiana. He had established the first hospital there.
97   Elsie Bushby, from a local farming family, would be the fourth maid at the Leaskdale manse.

revelled in my garden—which is splendid this year. All in all, I've had, as I remarked in the beginning, a beautiful week, with no alien spirit in the house to poison the atmosphere.

Monday, Sept. 18, 1922
The Manse, Leaskdale, Ont.

We had Mr. Carswell[98] for Sunday—a nice, ladylike old man of irreproachable soundness of theology. It would be impossible to dislike so harmless a creature but he bored me.

Today I wrote a poem, canned six jars of tomatoes and re-read *Trilby*.[99] One never hears *Trilby* mentioned now. It made the most tremendous sensation twenty years ago. One minister denounced it from his pulpit as "the apotheosis of the scarlet letter." Yet beside some of the heroines of today's novels "Trilby" was chaste as ice and pure as snow. Whatever she was, she was adorable and the book is full of charm from cover to cover and worth a thousand of the arid, sex-obsessed novels of today.

A question Stuart has just asked me reminded me of the hoods that were worn by children in my day. One never sees hoods now—except on young babies and then they are called bonnets. They are as out-of-date as crinolines.[100] Youngsters now wear "tams,"[101] which are really not half so pretty and can't, I'm sure, be as warm. Those old hoods were cosy things. Mine, I remember, were generally crocheted out of "cardinal" wool, with cardinal satin ribbon run through the holes, a perky bow of ribbon just over the forehead, and ties of ribbon. The last hood I ever wore was when I was twelve. Father sent it to me from the west. It was of cream wool and was very becoming. Really, I never looked nicer in anything.

I think it is a pity bonnets for elderly women have gone out. They were more dignified than the hats of today and much kinder to faded, wrinkled faces. Hats seem to emphasize hollow necks and sagging contours while bonnets minimized them. I remember that I liked very much to try on Grandmother's bonnets in the secrecy of the spare room. Grandma had irreproachable taste in bonnets and I thought they became me beautifully and looked forward with pleasure to wearing them when I grew up and married. Alas, I never did wear

98   David Carswell had been a missionary on the Prairies. Assigned to the Toronto Presbytery's supplementary roll, he did not have his own congregation.

99   Novel by British-French author George du Maurier (1834–96). LMM notes below that *Trilby* is compared to American novelist Nathaniel Hawthorne's 1894 novel, *The Scarlet Letter*, about a woman who is publicly shamed for committing adultery. LMM's early novel, *Kilmeny of the Orchard* (1910), was influenced by *Trilby*.

100   Stiffened fabric (or hoop) used as a petticoat to hold out a skirt.

101   A Scottish-style beret.

a bonnet—although the dressy little "toques"[102] which were in style in my early twenties were bonnets in every essential respect, lacking only strings. I remember one especially pretty one I had of black lace with a wreath of flowers. Those "toques" were very becoming to me and I have always cherished a hope that they would "come in" again. They never have. The vogue of big hats and engulfing turbans has continued for years and seems likely to continue—if hats don't "go out" altogether.

I have also been reading Emile Coue's book on "Suggestion."[103] I can hardly believe in all his miracles. If one could make oneself well and good by repeating over and over before going to sleep the mystic formula, "every day in every way I'm growing better and better" why couldn't one make oneself perfect or immortal? Still, I have proved in my own experiments that there is a great power in suggestion. I believe I have cured Chester of some annoying little nervous habits—blinking his eyes and tapping his teeth with nail of his forefinger for example—by bending over him every night after he had gone to sleep and suggesting to him aloud, three times, that he wouldn't do it anymore. At any rate the habits ceased abruptly after two or three nights. The headaches, too, from which he has suffered for years seem to have almost disappeared. Perhaps it was my "suggestion"—perhaps he is simply growing out of them. One cannot *prove* these things. I have been conducting a series of experiments on myself also but cannot as yet say whether they have affected anything or not. Some things happened—but then they might have happened anyway.

Last Friday a letter came from Rev. Mr. Lindsay of Erin, telling Ewan that he could have the last Sunday in September in Hillsburg—a vacant congregation in the Orangeville Presbytery.[104] He had applied for a hearing sometime ago and had given up hope of getting it. I at once telegraphed him and Saturday I had a wire saying he had sent word to Mr. Lindsay that he would go. From all we have heard of it I think it would be a nice place with some advantages that Leaskdale does not possess—and doubtless with some disadvantages. But there is a nice manse and quite a strong congregation where one would not have to worry over the removal of a family.

I had a letter from Ewan today. They reached Warsaw all right. Lady Jane behaved herself badly as far as Ingersoll where E. consulted an electrical expert who located the trouble in the coil. A new coil was put in and Lady Jane's insides troubled her no more. Ewan writes cheerfully and does not seem troubled by headaches or melancholy obsessions.

102	A toque in this usage was a small cap or bonnet having a narrow brim or no brim.

103	*Self Mastery Through Conscious Autosuggestion* by French psychotherapist Émile Coué (1857–1926). LMM does not write his name here or elsewhere with the French accents.

104	Hillsburgh is a community some 85 km/52 miles northwest of Toronto. The Scottish-born John Lindsay was moderator of the Orangeville Presbytery.

Saturday, Sept. 23, 1922
Leaskdale, Ont.

I feel as flat as a punctured tire, after the worry of the last twenty-four hours. Yesterday I expected Ewan home all day. He *had* to get back yesterday in order to catch the train to Hillsburg today. But the day passed and he did not come. I made pickles, canned tomatoes, cooked dinner for the boys and two of their school chums, and did not feel anxious until dusk. Then I began to feel anxious and continued to feel anxious until ten, when my anxiety passed into worry which deepened into a brainstorm as the hours crawled by and no one appeared. I had a wretched night. I was worried about the Hillsburg appointment but I was far more worried over the reason of Ewan's non-appearance for I felt sure some accident must have happened to delay him.

I stayed up till three when I took veronal[105] and went to bed. But even the veronal could not keep me soundly asleep. Every time a belated car purred past I sprang up listening, thinking it might be E. But morning came—no E.—noon—no E.! By this time I was really crazy—couldn't work—couldn't do anything but walk the floor.

At four o'clock Ewan walked in, tired, dusty, dishevelled.

On Wednesday night he had had a bad accident—an accident that might have been ten times worse. A car, *without lights* and on the wrong side of the road, had run right into him! Fortunately nobody was injured but Lady Jane was badly knocked up. It cost him seventy-five dollars, two days' delay and no end of worry to get her put into shape again. This accident was certainly not his fault in any way. Nevertheless it is enough to make one superstitious. Ewan *has* dreadful luck in the matter of cars. I think it is because he is a man who is slow of thought and cannot think quickly enough what to do in a sudden emergency.

Well, it boots not![106] The smash took place—and now what about Hillsburg? Ewan declared that he would motor there that night—84 miles—and keep his appointment. I flew round, got his supper, got out his clothes and hunted out his best sermons, while he washed and dressed. Then he started again on his long drive. But I have given up all hope of Hillsburg. He has a bad cold, is very hoarse, and is tired out. He will be very far from his best tomorrow and will not likely make a favorable impression. Well, so be it. In moments like

---

105　Veronal is the trade name for the barbiturate barbital or barbitone. It was brought to market by the Bayer company and remained a widely used sleeping aid until the 1950s. It was also used as a hypnotic drug to treat melancholia, or depression.

106　An archaic use of the word "boots" as a verb; the expression here means, "this does not help/ remedy the situation."

this when I am at my last gasp I fall back on kismet.[107] What is to be will be! Why worry?

Monday, Sept. 25, 1922
The Manse, Leaskdale, Ont.

It is late but I am going to sit up and write in this doomed book. I might as well for I couldn't sleep if I did go to bed.

Talk of blue Monday!

To deal with minor matters first:—Ewan came home tonight feeling quite sure that he had lost out in Hillsburg. And why? *Because he motored there*—or rather, because he has a car. It seems their last minister kept a car and by reason of it *spent too much time in Toronto.* So the people are prejudiced against a minister who has a car! The old folks with whom Ewan stayed were very bitter on the subject and plainly thought motoring a dreadful shortcoming in a minister.

Is it any wonder that young men are not crowding into the ministry?

But after all I suppose it is as well that Hillsburg is no longer one of our problems. For we have before us a fall of misery and worry.

Ewan was in Toronto on his way home and saw McCullough. Pickering is going ahead with his lawsuit and is claiming *eight thousand* dollars damages—one thousand for his operation, five thousand for his "sufferings" and two thousand for "injuries to his wife."

It is simply a conspiracy to get money out of us, nothing more or less. This man who wants five thousand for his "sufferings" is a well man today where for years before the accident he was miserable; his *own son* told Ewan that he had planned to have the operation the next week; as for Mrs. Pickering this is the first heard of *her* injuries. Pickering never referred to her in his letters. It is evidently a device of the lawyers who know that if Pickering was negligent *he* cannot get damages but that *his* negligence will not prevent *her* from getting them. Nobody heard of Mrs. Pickering complaining of any lasting injury before. At the time of the collision she had a tiny two-inch cut on her forehead which healed up in a week. On the other hand it is well known that she had been complaining of her health for years before the accident. Two thousand dollars is quite a large sum for a scratch that did not even leave a scar! But the woman is such a notorious person that she is capable of anything, so I feel more worried over this than over her husband's claims. Yet surely no court

---

107   Derived from the Turkish word for fate, "kismet" suggests a power that is believed to control events of the future.

would give her damages without medical evidence to her injuries. I would not think it possible, yet McCullough is evidently worried.

Well, we must fight. It is a hideous sort of predicament to be in but we are not going to pay the hospital bills of a man like Pickering unless we are compelled to. It is sheer blackmail and we will not submit to it as a matter of principle if nothing else. One comfort is that every soul in the community, outside of the Pickering clan—and indeed some in it—is on our side. Pickering is universally condemned

Scene of Accident

and we will not lose either caste or repute by fighting him when he drags us into law like this. Everyone knows that he has been ill for years and everyone knows, too, that he tore up Zephyr street like a madman and ran right into us, although he saw us plainly by his own admission. Of course Ewan should have looked a second time before he turned to cut the corner—and of course he shouldn't have been cutting the corner at all but that does not excuse Pickering for hogging the road at the rate of thirty to thirty-five miles an hour.

But oh, what a wretched fall I foresee!

Wednesday, Sept. 27, 1922
The Manse, Leaskdale, Ont.

Poor Ewan has begun his task of getting all possible evidence. We have already Mr. Law who will say that Pickering was in the middle of the road, did not turn out, did not sound his horn, was going very fast and was equally to blame. Then we have two men at Mt. Albert, Mr. Hugh Evans and Mr. Robert Wilson, both respected and reputable men who will testify that Pickering said to them shortly after he came out of the hospital, "The accident didn't cause my operation. I had to have that anyway."

Ewan also got several new witnesses today. Mrs. Jake Meyers, who was with us, says he was in the middle of the road—never tooted—and was going very fast. Another Mr. Meyers and a Mrs. Smith who saw him pass just before the crash say the same.

The Manse, Leaskdale, Ont.
Saturday, Sept. 30, 1922

We are having such lovely weather. If only we had "minds at leisure from themselves" to enjoy it! But I can think of nothing but the Pickering affair.

Many people in Zephyr think that it is Mrs. Pickering that put Pickering up to this. She is a woman notorious for bad temper, tyranny and stubbornness. She looks it—her very face is obscene. She doesn't seem to have a friend. She is Pickering's second wife—by the way, he "had to get married" as the country phrase goes, both times.

Other people think it is Grieg who has put Pickering up to it. Grieg has the reputation of taking up and pushing dirty cases. *I* think it is probably both Mrs. Pickering and Grieg. The latter evidently thinks, from things he has said, that *I* will settle the case rather than go to court. He little knows me. I have fought bigger and more hopeless cases than this rather than give in tamely to imposition.

Ewan went to Zephyr today to meet Mr. McCullough who wanted to see the ground for himself. He brought home two good bits of

The "Blind" Corner.

news. In the first place, there is no law against cutting a corner in the country. That is only a city ordinance. So Pickering can't catch us there. In the second place, the corner at Zephyr is a "blind" corner and the law is that anyone approaching such a corner must slow down to twelve and a half miles and blow his horn. Pickering certainly didn't do either. If he had the accident wouldn't have happened.

If—if—if! It's the most fateful word in the language. *If* I hadn't gone to Zephyr that Sunday—*if* Mrs. Meyers hadn't asked us to tea—*if* we hadn't been short of gas—*if* Ewan had looked a second time—*if* Marshall Pickering were a straight man instead of a crook—well, *if* Eve had never eaten the apple. Or, if you like it better, *if* the first ape who twisted off a bough and used it as a club had never thought of doing the thing. You can go very far back with your "ifs." But for all I'm glad the first ape *did* think of it—I don't know whether I'm even sorry that Eve ate the apple! After all, isn't it well "to know good and evil?" If we didn't what better would we be than babies or vegetables?

The Manse, Leaskdale, Ont.
October 1, 1922

Eleven years ago October first also fell on a Sunday. It was a day of pouring rain and I was blue and homesick. Eleven years—in those eleven years the world in which I was brought up has utterly passed away—humanity has had its heart broken—and Marshall Pickering has developed and lost an enlarged prostate gland!!

This fact just now looms largest in my consciousness, as a five-cent bit held close to the eye will blot out the hosts of heaven.

A man at Mt. Albert, said, when he heard that Pickering was suing us for $8000,

"Eight thousand! It's more than his whole damned carcass[108] is worth, let alone his prostate gland."

Of course Ewan and I know that even if Pickering won his suit he would never get anything like $8000.00—that it is the usual legal dodge to ask about four times what you have any real chance of getting. But our simple country folk, unacquainted with legal dodges, believe that if Pickering wins he will get the whole amount and they are horror stricken.

And they are also horrified at his suing "a *minister*." Evidently reverence for "the cloth" is not yet totally extinct in our land!

Mac writes me that *Emily* is a fine piece of work and "a great story." Let us hope my dear public will think so.

Wednesday, October 4, 1922

I felt very tired and depressed all day. But I fussed up a tea for two school-teachers—Miss Buckham of the North School and Olive Blanchard of our own.[109]

Ewan went to Toronto today to see his lawyer. Before he went he remarked on how well he was feeling this fall. And he *is*. He has never had a headache or any sign of mental trouble since August. He *seems* perfectly well but I have hoped too often to dare hope again. If the improvement only lasts until our lawsuit is over I will be thankful. I really think the fact that his mind is so taken up with the suit accounts in a great measure for the improvement. He cannot brood over religious phobias when he *has* to contemplate Marshall Pickering and his doings.

---

108   LMM's handwritten manuscript uses the British spelling "carcase" here.
109   During the years when LMM's sons were students in Leaskdale, no teacher remained for more than a year in either school.

Saturday, October 7, 1922

I had a nasty dream last night—one of my vivid, symbolic dreams that always mean something. I don't like it at all. I am sure it means trouble ahead.

I dreamed that Ewan was standing out on the road in front of Mr. Warner's house, talking to two men who were strangers to me. He was making some request of them which they seemed to grant, for he shook hands, smiled, and bade them good-bye. Then, as he turned away, the taller of the two men struck him a blow from behind and stretched him on the dusty road. Ewan sprang up at once and I had just time to think, "Oh, what a humiliation before the congregation," when I woke.

Every one of these vivid dreams that I have ever had has "come true" and I know this is a warning, let who will laugh.

Somehow, today was a peevish, *unsatisfactory* sort of day. Nothing very untoward happened—the usual routine went fairly well. But Ewan had one of his contrary moods on when he can't "ring in" with anybody. He is really a little sore over the fact that Hillsburg has called another man and has talked bitterly about the curse of the candidating system and the "tricks of the trade" involved. It is all quite true but cannot be helped so there is no use in railing over it. Normally I would have been disappointed but now it does not matter. If he *had* been called how could we have pulled up stakes in the mess we are in? It is so unthinkable that it was a special mercy of Providence that he was *not* called.

The days are getting very short and my long lonely evenings of autumn and winter have begun. But if I were not consumed by worry I could endure the loneliness cheerfully. After all I should be used to it. I have been lonely the most of my life.

Stuart, reading in a book today, came across the statement that all insects were hatched from the egg. He asked me if this were true. When I replied "yes" he said,

"But where would they get an insect to lay the *first* egg?"

Ay, there's the rub!

The Manse, Leaskdale, Ont.
Wednesday, Oct. 11, 1922

We have been shivering for two weeks for it has been quite cold and we have been unable to have a fire in the furnace because of some repairs that have to be made. But the man came up from Uxbridge today and finished the job. So we have a fire tonight and are physically comfortable, for which praise be. It is a little easier to bear one's worries when one is free from goose-flesh.

Ewan went to Toronto today. The "examination for discovery," as they call it, takes place tomorrow. Pickering's Toronto lawyer—Phelan, K.C., who is said to be one of the best lawyers in Toronto.[110] I am afraid Pickering has got ahead of us *there*—will examine Ewan and McCullough will examine Pickering and his Sarah.[111] We will then know what they mean to assert and try to prove. I wonder if Marshall Pickering will really swear to his falsehoods when it comes to a show down. Ewan thinks he won't but I feel quite sure he will. What else is there for him to do unless he backs down altogether which he certainly won't do now.

I have been writing every morning up to now but this morning I couldn't settle my mind to it. I kept worrying over tomorrow. Oh, if it were only over! I dread Ewan's return home.

The Manse, Leaskdale, Ont.
Thursday, Oct. 12, 1922

This has been a wretched day—dull, cold, showery. When I woke I said, "How can I get through this day?"

But I can always get through today. It is only tomorrow that I can't get through.

The day was one of silent worry—silent because I had no one to talk to. We cleaned the spare room. My worry deepened as the day wore on, closing down into the early darkness of a rainy night. At twilight I looked out over the dim landscape and shivered. The rain on autumn fields is a very sorrowful thing.

I helped Chester with his arithmetic and played dominoes with him and Stuart—and all the time I was fairly trembling with nervous dread. *Why* I should have been so nervous I don't know—I *knew* perfectly well what Marshall Pickering would say. I think at bottom I must have had a faint unacknowledged hope that after all he might back down when he saw Ewan would not buy him off and that I dreaded the extinction of that hope, even while I believed I did not possess it. At such times our minds seem split in two parts— one part a rational one which recognizes facts as they present themselves— the other an irrational one which persists in clinging to a blind, instinctive hope that *something* will turn up to avert the evil we shrink from and which trembles lest its hope be destroyed.

I was really cold with dread. I expected Ewan home by eight and got the boys off to bed that we might have an uninterrupted conversation. But he did

---

110   T.N. Phelan was a prominent Toronto lawyer who had been awarded the "King's Counsel" (KC) distinction, an honorary title meaning appointed by the Queen or King. Phelan had been hired—unbeknownst to the Macdonalds—to help Grieg.

111   That is, Sarah Pickering, Marshall Pickering's wife.

not come. It was pouring rain and I feared some accident for I couldn't see what else could delay him. I compelled myself to sit and sew until ten. Then I could not sit still any longer—neither could I read. So I fell to swatting flies! We have a fearful dose of them at present owing to the fact that Stuart left the screen door open today. For an hour I dealt death and destruction. Marshall Pickering was the doom of hundreds of flies tonight who might otherwise have lived several fly-years longer. At eleven the carcases of flies lay in drifts on the floor—the house was free from them—and Ewan came home.

He was blue enough, too. Like myself he had evidently been cherishing irrational hopes. Pickering swore to a whole catalogue of lies. He swore that he had never had *any* trouble before the collision—that he had never complained to anyone—that he had never consulted a doctor—in short that, as far as he knew, he was a perfectly well man until the night after the collision. When one recalls what his son told Ewan in the hospital it makes one wonder how a man *could* swear to such lies.

But that was not the limit of Marshall Pickering's fictions. He told an even more barefaced lie than that. He deliberately said that after the collision Ewan went up to him and said,

"This was my fault, Mr. Pickering, and I want to make it right"—that Ewan then reckoned up the damages—"the radiator will cost so much etc. etc." and that *he*, Pickering, then said,

"Well, Mr. Macdonald, this is Sunday night and we won't talk about it now."

Nice little dose of hypocrisy that!

Now, I was there and I heard every word that Ewan and Pickering said to each other. When they got out of the cars Ewan said, "Why, Mr. Pickering, is this you? I didn't know it was you."

"Neither did I know it was you," said Pickering.

"How was it we didn't see each other?" asked Ewan.

"Oh, I saw you—I saw you," exclaimed Pickering. "I saw you from the time you started from the tank."

"Are you hurt?" asked Ewan.

"No, *I'm all right*," said Pickering, "but Mrs. Pickering is a little hurt."

Then Ewan said,

"Well, that is the worst feature of this. As far as the damage to the cars go we can repair them in the garage."

Then Pickering went away with his wife and had no further conversation with Ewan. That is every word that was said—and yet he could go and swear—but there! He is a man who will stick at nothing!

Then Mrs. Pickering had her turn. She swore she was quite well before the collision and had never been well since. Questioned, she said "she had no

ambition and had to keep her daughters who had been working out, home to do the work." Admitted that she had not been to a doctor but was taking "a tonic." Both she and Pickering swore he was going "fifteen to twenty miles." Evidently their lawyers haven't yet seen the corner and don't know it is blind or they wouldn't have let him admit even that much. Pickering and his wife—they were examined separately of course—told different stories as to where their car was at the moment of collision—she saying they were away off on their own side of the road, he saying that he was on the middle of the road but turned out as much as the law required. This is just the opposite of what he said in his letters last winter. That man will say *anything* and if we cannot prove he is lying we will lose our case. The worst of it is that we cannot get what his son told Ewan in evidence. It is "hearsay" and so will not be allowed in. I daresay Pickering himself does not know that his son told Ewan that. If he *had* known I think even he could hardly have the face to make the claims he did. When he wrote his first letter to Ewan he thought Ewan knew nothing at all of his previous trouble or intentions and when Ewan wrote him that he knew (but didn't say who had told him) Marshall Pickering was so wild with shame over the thought that he had made such claims when Ewan knew the truth all along that he determined to stick to his lie to save his face if he could. He is a notoriously conceited man and it would make him writhe to think that Ewan *knew* he had to have an operation and that he was just putting a conspiracy over on us. So he has gone on, deeper and deeper, thinking Ewan would eventually pay something rather than be dragged into a lawsuit until he got in so deep that he could not back out without humiliation he could not bear. I think that is the real truth of the matter and explains the long delays that took place between each of his moves. He was afraid to go on and ashamed to go back. People in Zephyr, too, were constantly twitting him about it—asking him if he had given up the notion of suing Macdonald etc, and all this goaded him to carry out his threats.

Well, there is not much likelihood that he will retract now; and we will not. If he had not lied—if he had confined his demands to the hundred dollars that his car cost him—we would have paid the whole hundred without hesitation rather than be dragged into the courts, even though he was more to blame for the collision than we were. But when he tried to make us pay his hospital bills we simply would not do it and we both feel the same way about it. There is something in us both that will not submit to injustice even for the sake of peace.

But I will not sleep tonight.

The Manse, Leaskdale, Ont.
Friday, Oct. 13, 1922

This morning we went to Zephyr and I stayed with Lily Shier[112] while Ewan was hunting evidence. Rob said Dr. Johnson[113] was a witness for Pickering— having said that in his opinion the collision "produced congestion of the gland" and necessitated the operation. This is bad.

I went to see Mrs. Heath and when I told her that Marshall Pickering had sworn that he never had any trouble before the collision she threw up her hands and said, "Oh, Mrs. Macdonald, surely Marshall Pickering could never have sworn *that*. Why, he has been complaining and doctoring for years. And the morning after the collision my daughter, Mrs. Burnham, telephoned over to Pickerings and asked his daughter Verna how he was. When she heard he had gone to the hospital she asked if this was the result of the collision Verna said, 'Oh, no, it's only just pa's old trouble back again. He had to have the operation anyway.'"

I asked Mrs. Heath if Mrs. Burnham would give evidence to this. Likely Verna P. will be on the stand and we will be able to get it in. Mrs. Heath said she felt sure she would. So I came home in better spirits than I expected to.

This evening we went to a "Hypatia" social[114] at Uxbridge, held in Minnie Gould's house. I had expected I would be too worried to enjoy it but somehow I wasn't. To put on a pretty evening dress and then spin down to town over the good roads in the clear evening air, under a cloudless silvery sky, was so exhilarating that it made me feel almost happy for the time being. Besides, riding in a car always seems to cheer me up. It is as if we went so fast that we *left worry behind*. This impression seems to seize upon the imagination and produce for a time the effects of reality. I think this is why Ewan, when his attacks of melancholia come on, always seems to be so much better in the car.

The old Gould house is a spacious dwelling built in the days of large families, cheap lumber and cheap labor. We had a delightful evening. It was wonderful to have an evening with intelligent people who could really *talk* about something besides local gossip and politics. We had a good programme, a good supper and a jolly hour of after dinner speeches.

But of course this couldn't last all the way through. We left for home at one

112   Mrs Lillis May Reid, née Harrison, formerly a maid in the Leaskdale manse, left this position in December 1915 to marry Robert Shier of Zephyr.

113   Herbert Edgard Johnson (1885–1939) was a doctor from nearby Mount Albert.

114   Hypatia (c.350–415 CE) was a female philosopher and mathematician who became head of the Platonist school in Alexandria. The concept of a Hypatia Club, a self-improvement organization for women, dates to 1886. The Hypatia Book Club in Uxbridge continues to this day. Minnie Gould was a cousin of LMM's friend Mary Gould Beal from Toronto.

and just out of Uxbridge poor unlucky Lady Jane began to "act up." Out went our lights. Ewan couldn't locate the trouble and at that hour no help could be obtained. Luckily—yes, there *must* be such a thing as luck. Jacques Loeb[115] says the universe and all therein is the product of chance and at times I agree with him—there was clouded moonlight, so we managed to get home all in one piece by driving slowly. Luckily again we did not meet anyone. Yes, it was a charming evening and has restored my sadly impaired morale.

The Manse, Leaskdale, Ont.
Saturday, Oct. 14, 1922

This windy morning we went to Stouffville to confer with Mr. McCullough who was to meet us there. We called at Zephyr where Ewan asked Rob Shier just what Dr. Johnson said. It seems he said that he *thought* the accident must have caused Pickering's "spasm" that night but said he could not say so positively—many other things might have brought it on. This is not so bad as we feared.

We called for Mrs. Jake Meyers and then went to Mt. Albert where E. saw Mrs. Burnham. She was not very willing to testify. Her husband was away but she seemed to think he would be averse to it. However, E. pointed out how much it might mean to us and eventually she consented.

At Stouffville Mr. McCullough examined Mrs. Meyers and me and was pleased with what we could say.

I was woefully tired when I came home. The worst of it is that Ewan and I cannot stop talking about the case continually and discussing it from every angle. We vow we will not—and three minutes later break the vow. Day and night, out and in, at board and in bed, it haunts us. It is the Dweller on the Threshold and we cannot forget its grisly presence for an instant.

Sunday, Oct. 15, 1922

We have got an important piece of evidence. After church service in Zephyr today we went to see old Mrs. Alex Lockie who used to live across the road from Pickerings and is well acquainted with him. When I told her that Pickering had sworn that he had never had any trouble before the collision she stared.

"Why," she said, "in March 1919 he came to see my husband who was ill and when I asked him how he was he said, 'I feel very miserable. I am afraid

---

115   German-born American physiologist Jacques Loeb argued against progressive evolution, claiming instead that life evolves in terms of responses to unpredictable processes in a given environment.

I am going the same way my father did.'"

(His father died under an operation for enlarged prostate gland complicated with Bright's disease.[116])

We must get Mrs. Lockie as a witness.

Tonight I read Thomas Hardy's *Two on a Tower*.[117] I think I would like it very much if my mind was at leisure from itself. But the story ends abominably. When I am reasonably comfortable in mind and body I can endure a tale that ends sadly. But when, as now, I am in a chronic state of unrest and dread I want a fairy story where everything ends happily—something that will create in me the temporary illusion that there *is* "a destiny that shapes our ends"[118] and occasionally brings good out of evil.

The Manse, Leaskdale, Ont.
Monday, Oct. 16, 1922

This morning we went to Uxbridge and Ewan went to see Dr. MacClintock.[119] He was the doctor Johnson called in to help him when he found that he couldn't "relieve" Pickering. We have been afraid of MacClintock for we have had the impression for some time that he was antagonistic to us. But it seems he is not. He said that the prostate gland couldn't have been injured by the collision and that in his opinion the latter had nothing whatever to do with it. We will subpoena him—it will offset Johnson.

Nevertheless I am tonight tired, worried, blue, and about as composed as a flea. Ewan is away, having gone to Sutton on an evidence hunt. I don't know which is worse—talking about the affair to him or threshing it over in my own thoughts.

Tuesday, Oct. 17, 1922

I am excited tonight—happily excited. Ewan is home with a fine "kill" of evidence. One bit of it ought to win our case for us.

I was housecleaning all day, working feverishly to drug my worry. In the evening I put the boys to bed. Lily was out and I settled down to wait until Ewan came home. I trembled with suspense when I heard Lady Jane purring in. But Ewan came in, smiling.

---

116   Bright's disease is a historical term for a range of kidney ailments (the specific kidney disorder here is unknown).

117   *Two on a Tower* (1882), by English author Thomas Hardy (1840–1928).

118   From *Hamlet* 5.2.11–12. Hamlet says to Horatio, "There's a divinity that shapes our ends, / Rough-hew them how we will—"

119   Joseph A. McClintock served as a medical doctor in Uxbridge from 1903 to 1946.

"My search has not been fruitless," he said triumphantly.

We had been told by one of our people—who, by the way, are all eagerly hunting evidence for us—that she believed Pickering had been to Dr. Boynton of Sutton. So Ewan went to see him. And Pickering *was* there, in May 1922, about a month before the collision.

Boynton said,

"I didn't examine him but from the symptoms he described I diagnosed his trouble as an enlarged prostate gland and I advised an operation."

Moreover, Boynton has the date and name of Marshall Pickering entered in his ledger, though not, unfortunately, the nature of his complaint. But even so it is very good.

And Pickering swore that he never consulted a doctor. If this holds good—and it is documentary evidence—we can convict him of perjury.

Lily also tells me that her father went to consult Boynton in the spring of 1922 and saw Pickering in the office at the same time. He spoke of it to his family when he went home. But he is now dead so that is no help to us.

Another bit of good news was that Mrs. Alex Lockie is quite willing to give evidence. Joe Taylor saw the Pickering car pass "at thirty miles an hour if an inch" a second or two before the collision. And Mrs. Brigham told Ewan that in 1917 Verna Pickering told her that her mother had been to a specialist in Toronto and had been told that she had diabetes—the "sugar diabetes"[120] as it is called.

Now, if we can establish this surely we can corner Mrs. P. Yet that woman said in the examination for discovery that she never was ill before the collision. Surely, if we can show by medical evidence that both Pickering and his wife have sworn falsely the Judge will not believe that any of their tale is true.

The Manse, Leaskdale
Wednesday, Oct. 18, 1922

This was a nasty day—cold, dark, with a high wind and showers of snow. But when one is in a comfortable frame of mind the weather is only an incident. I worked with cheer today and performed all my little domestic rites in good heart. I haven't felt so well and easy since Ewan came home from Warsaw.

Thursday, Oct. 19, 1922

More ups and downs—fortunately the "ups" came after the "down." We had a letter from Mrs. Burnham imploring us not to subpoena her as a witness. Her

---

120   "Sugar diabetes" is a now-outdated term for Type 2 diabetes (also known as adult onset diabetes), in which the body fails to produce sufficient insulin.

husband she says will be dreadfully angry because their daughter is married to "the brother of the husband of a daughter of Marshall Pickering's." It will, she declares, brew up all kinds of family trouble for her. Well, it is hard on us but we will not take an unwilling witness. Anyway, Boynton's evidence is worth all the others put together. And Ewan has got another witness in Mrs. Burnham's place—Mrs. Bingham to whom Verna Pickering said the same thing. So I shouldn't feel blue but I do—a little. Perhaps it is because of something Velma Harrison said to Chester today. They had a spat. (Alas for first love! The said Velma is the girl Chester was in love with two years ago. *Now*, they are on chronic bad terms.) Velma, to taunt Chester, said something spiteful about me. Chester came home raging and told it as his justification for "pitching into" Velma. Of course nothing a silly little girl could say would worry me. But the sting lies in the fact that it is not a thing a child like Velma could think of herself. She must have heard an older woman say it—probably her mother. Her mother is a woman for whose opinion I care nothing. She is ignorant and odious. Yet the thing hurt me because it was as false and petty as it was malicious.

Well, this is only a pinprick. Yet, when we are employing all our powers of endurance to bear patiently a big worry and discomfort it hurts to have to detach even so much of that power as is necessary to endure a pinprick.

But against all this debit stands out one big blessed credit item. Today Ewan said,

"I haven't felt as well for five years as I do this fall."

And it is true. He *seems* perfectly well. If it were not for one thing I would say he *was* perfectly well.

He is away tonight on another trail. All our pastoral work is being hung up this fall because of this wretched worry. Fortunately our people understand. Everyone far and near is on our side, outside half a dozen birds-of-a-feather who herd with the Pickering crew. But "everyone" is not the Judge who will try our case. That Judge, by the way, will likely be Judge Lennox who is to sit on the Whitby circuit.

I am alone tonight and in one way it is a relief. If Ewan were here we would talk unceasingly and unavailingly about the case. At times I have to talk of it myself, or burst, but at other times I want a complete rest from it and I will have that tonight. I will go to bed early and have a good read. I won't enjoy the "read" wholly but it will drug my worry to a bearable point while it lasts.

The Manse, Leaskdale, Ont.
Friday, Oct. 20, 1922

Busy all day housecleaning, burning leaves—I do love the pungent reek of burning autumn leaves—and harvesting gladiolus bulbs. My glads were wonderful this summer. My rooms were full of them for nearly three months and I luxuriated in their exotic beauty. But this is the end of it for this season—and sometimes I feel drearily for all time. Will there ever be any beauty in life for me again?

Ewan came home tonight. He saw Dr. Johnson and Dr. J. said that in 1917 Mrs. Pickering consulted him in regard to certain symptoms. He diagnosed her trouble as sugar diabetes and sent her to a specialist in Toronto who confirmed the diagnosis. We have the address of this specialist and Ewan will see him.

One item of Ewan's report troubled me. Dr. Stephens, an expert who is interested in our case, saw Dr. Jones,[121] who performed the operation on Pickering and said to him, "Mr. Pickering is suing for damages for that affair." "Yes, and he'll get them too," said Jones.

This must mean that Jones' opinion is adverse to us and he will be on their side.

Long ago I read in D'Aubigny's *History of the Reformation in France*[122] a horrible tale of some poor creature who was tortured at an *auto da fe* by being lowered from a beam into a slow fire for a few minutes and then hoisted up again and so on. I think I have some idea of what he suffered. My torture at present is of the same nature.

Nevertheless I have never been able to agree that mental anguish is harder to endure than bodily anguish—that is, if it is of the same degree. Many people declare that it is—but it is my opinion that such people, while they may have suffered extreme mental pain have never suffered any extreme physical pain and so have no proper standard of comparison. I cannot believe that *any* mental anguish could equal the agony of a human being being broiled alive over a slow fire.

There *is* a devil and he is the Spirit of Cruelty that is rampant in the whole universe and that drags its bestial trail over every page of history. Cruelty is the very essence of sin.

---

121   Likely a reference to Toronto doctor Wellington Stephens (b. 1874), and to Dr Newbold C. Jones (b. 1880), a Toronto surgeon.
122   Swiss historian Jean-Henri Merle d'Aubigné's (1794–1872) *History of the Reformation in the Sixteenth Century* (1835–46); *auto-da-fé* derives from Portuguese, meaning "act of faith."

The Manse, Leaskdale, Ont.
Sat. Oct. 21, 1922

The Lloyd George Government has gone down—rather unexpectedly after all.[123] He has weathered so many crises that one expected him to weather this one also. But the man who has been the virtual ruler of the British Empire since the terrible autumn of 1917 has fallen. Perhaps it is well. Lloyd George was an indomitable fighter. He was the man for leadership in a great war. But I do not think he is a constructive statesman and that is what heaven and earth are shrieking for now—and failing to find.

But just now I am not interested in Lloyd George. Marshall Pickering is the man of the hour for me—the old devil!

Ewan talks of him continually. But it is better for his mind to be taken up with this than with his melancholic phobias. Even Marshall Pickering is not so bad as a dread that you have committed the unpardonable sin.

This morning Stuart gave us a laugh at the breakfast table. I was speaking of some woman whose badly spoiled children were dreadful nuisances. Where upon Stuart remarked gravely, "When I grow up I think I'll marry a wife without children!"

Thursday, Oct. 24, 1922

This has been a most unpleasant day. For the first time since I began housekeeping here eleven years ago I have had a quarrel with my maid.

I have known for some time that it was bound to come sooner or later. All last winter Lily behaved quite decently, evidently having learned a lesson from my getting Elsie when she was ill. But by spring the salutary effects of this had begun to wear off and several times through the summer she was exceedingly nasty. Since she came back from her vacation, however, she has been simply

---

123   Lloyd George, Liberal Prime Minister of Britain from 1916 until 1922, had led a coalition government through the second half of World War I. Lloyd George was considered to be a strong, decisive leader: in an entry of December 10, 1916, LMM wrote "I believe that Lloyd George is one of the greatest men Britain has ever produced." Two events in 1922, however, led to his downfall. First, news emerged that honours had been given to several rich businessmen in exchange for money. Second, and more serious, was the Chanak Crisis. This political crisis followed the end of World War I and the Treaty of Sèvres, in which Allied countries began a process of partitioning the Ottoman Empire; Turkey, the seat of the Empire, had fought on the losing side in World War I. The Treaty of Sèvres declared the Dardanelles and Constantinople (now Istanbul) a neutral zone. However, in 1923 Turkey began to march on Allied positions in the region, aiming to re-take key territory here. David Lloyd George called for war, but public opinion (as well as the British military) opposed armed conflict with Turkey. The situation resolved itself when Turkey, having overwhelmed Greek forces, received the territory it wanted through a negotiated settlement. On October 19, 1922, a group of Conservative Members of Parliament voted to end the coalition with the Liberals, and as a consequence Lloyd George's coalition government collapsed.

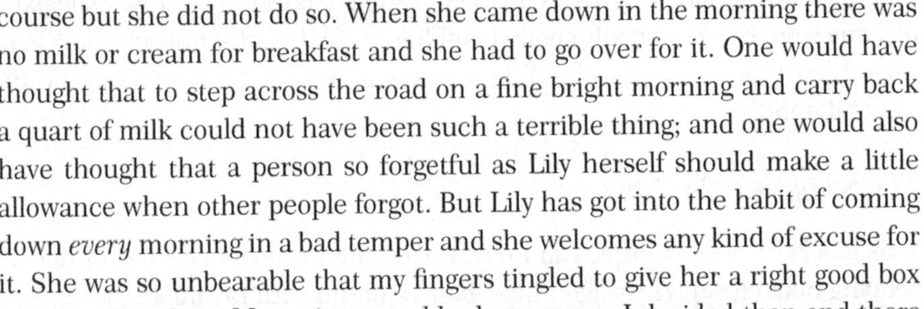

Lily

intolerable. I could have put up with her untidiness and forgetfulness but her bad temper and impertinence could not be endured and I knew that very soon we would have to have "a showdown." Lily must either be taught her place or leave.

I shrank from it. I hate to quarrel with a person I am living with. But Lily was making life so bitter for me in a hundred petty ways—and this, too, at a time when I am so harassed and worried—that I realized this sort of thing could not go on much longer. Lily had evidently come to the conclusion that I would put up with anything and that she could rule the house because I dared not quarrel with or dismiss her.

The limit of my endurance was reached one morning about a fortnight ago. Ewan and I had been away until late at night and Chester had forgotten to go to Mr. Leask's for the milk in the evening. Lily should have reminded him of course but she did not do so. When she came down in the morning there was no milk or cream for breakfast and she had to go over for it. One would have thought that to step across the road on a fine bright morning and carry back a quart of milk could not have been such a terrible thing; and one would also have thought that a person so forgetful as Lily herself should make a little allowance when other people forgot. But Lily has got into the habit of coming down *every* morning in a bad temper and she welcomes any kind of excuse for it. She was so unbearable that my fingers tingled to give her a right good box on her sullen face. My patience suddenly gave way. I decided then and there that I would put an end to this sort of thing. I have been patient for several reasons. Help is hard to get here; and Lily is the sort of girl who, if sent away from a place, would revenge herself by telling lies everywhere about the menage she had left.

But now nothing mattered except to rid myself of a nuisance that had become absolutely intolerable.

However, I did not say anything just then. I thought I could not have a domestic explosion when I am so upset over this lawsuit. It was unthinkable. So I decided that I would wait until the trial was over and then I would tell Lily plainly that she must behave herself or leave.

I felt very bitterly towards her. I have been very good to her—very thoughtful of her comfort and feelings. She is treated as one of the family and paid good wages for doing—and often doing very poorly—much lighter work than she had on the farms where she used to be hired. And yet now, when I am having such a hard and anxious time, she will not even refrain from adding to the misery and discomfort of my life by her unreasonable tantrums.

So I said nothing that day but events have forced my hand, and the long overdue storm burst today. Now that it is over I am glad. It has cleared the air and if Miss Lily chooses to go well and good. I am not dependent on her or anyone. Somehow, though, I don't think my lady has any intention of going.

We were cleaning the library yesterday and just before supper I asked Lily to wash the south window so that I could put the plants back on the sill, as I wanted them out of the way before I set the supper table. Lily answered in a rather impertinent tone that she wanted to finish rubbing down the furniture on the veranda and bring it in before dark. I ignored her tone, since her request in itself was reasonable enough.

"Oh, very well," I said pleasantly. "You can finish that first."

But Lily did not go back to the furniture. Whether she misunderstood me or not, she hurled herself out to the kitchen, got water, and went at the window in a rage. I shrugged my shoulders and said no more, but went to get a light by which to set the table. As usual I found that the lamps had not been cleaned or filled. I went to work and cleaned them. Lily saw me and seemed to be angrier than ever—because she felt, I suppose, that it put her in the wrong. Finally she came out—the window was only a ten minute job—and said in a voice that fairly trembled with rage, "Your window is ready for you."

Still preserving silence I put the plants back, while Lily made the pancakes for supper—and spoiled them also. They were scorched, and heavy as lead when she put them on the table. She slammed into her chair and began to drink a cup of tea. Stuart, who loves pancakes, said innocently, "Don't you want some pancakes, Lily?" "No," she snapped, "I don't feel much like eating anything."

Still I said nothing. I ate my supper, attended to the boys and ignored her—a proceeding that seemed to aggravate her still further. After supper she washed the dishes and went out as usual. I drew a relieved breath. The house seemed released from an incubus.

This morning I came down and found that Lily, having gone to bed in a bad temper, had evidently got up in a worse one. I was preparing Chester's school lunch and I asked Lily where she had put the butter. She gave me an impudent answer.

I laid down my knife and turned around. It was the last straw. I said, in a cold, measured voice,

"Lily, I have come to the end of my patience with you. I do not wish to quarrel with anyone but the time has come when you compel me to say to you that if you cannot behave yourself a little better than you have been behaving here for months you must find a place where the mistress will put up with that sort of thing, because *I* will not."

Lily's face turned crimson. I think she was utterly amazed at this turning of the worm. At first she attempted to speak but I silenced her and went on. I gave her such a dressing down as she richly deserved. She muttered sullenly that the boys wouldn't "obey her"—that she "couldn't get to sleep till all hours" because Mr. Macdonald and I were out late so often or sat up so late and that was why she was out of sorts in the morning—"you don't feel very good yourself when you don't get your sleep."

"No, I do not," I said, "but I do not visit it on those who live in the house with me and are not to blame for it. You are out late far oftener than we are. You knew when you came here that you were coming to the house of a minister and student who could not go to bed at nine o'clock as farmers do. You knew that Mr. Macdonald and I had to visit—and sit up when we were home to study and write. We make no loud noise when we come in and go to bed—there is no reason why it should disturb you."

"Even a person moving about the house keeps me awake."

"Then you must go where no one will move about the house. You can not find such conditions here. As for the boys, if you treated them decently you would have no trouble with them. You never say a kind word to them—you nag and rail at them from morning till night. You can not even speak civilly to them when they are not meddling with you at all. It is no wonder they will not try to please you. You have neglected your work recently to a ridiculous extent. In short we have come to the point where I must tell you plainly that you must either behave yourself or go."

"Perhaps I'd better go then if you're not satisfied," she muttered.

"You can please yourself about that," I said coolly. "I am not sending you away. I simply say that I will not have a maid in this house who isn't contented with her position. I have nothing to reproach myself with. I have been a good mistress to you. If you know of a place where you will have no inconveniences to put up with you had better go to it. *I* have never found such a place. But if you want to stay here I repeat for the last time that you must behave yourself properly and have done with these continual tantrums of yours and neglect of your work."

I left her there and went upstairs. I felt a great relief and I only regret that I did not speak just so to her long ago. Of course it has been a most unpleasant day. Lily has been very down but she has worked with a vengeance, doing everything quickly and thoroughly and in due season—as she *can* when she likes. I have ignored her completely.

I do not know what she will do. I think she will stay. She knows perfectly well that she can not get another place like this, with no outside work, near her home, good wages, and steady employment. But I would be just as well pleased if she did go. I shall never feel the same to her again.

Ay, di me![124] Life seems a very prickly, thorny wilderness to me at present with no oasis anywhere in sight.

Thursday, October 26, 1922
The Manse, Leaskdale, Ont.

For the first time in three weeks our house is warm—and consequently life is tolerable. We could not light a fire in the furnace because part of it was burned out and had to be replaced. And the evenings have been very cold of late. We have continued to exist by the grace of our coal oil heater. Said heater has saved our lives several times since its purchase, so I ought to be grateful to it. But I am not—I detest it.

All my life I have longed for an open fireplace. I suppose all my life I shall long for it and never get it—at least, until it is too late. If this house were our own I would have had one built in long ago. But in a manse this is almost out of the question. Though, had I known eleven years ago that we would be this long I would have put one in and felt that the delight of a fireplace for so many years would be sufficient recompense even if we did "move on" then. But one cannot know—and to go to all the trouble and expense of building a fireplace into a house and then possibly leave it in a year or so seems foolish. If the expense were all I would put it in—but it would mean so much bother and tearing to pieces. No, I am afraid I can never have my fireplace—can never sit before it on a cold evening, with my children and my friends, and talk as people *can* talk only before an open fire. A house without an open fire is a house without a soul. A black hole in the floor—ugh!

In the old home we had no fireplaces—they had been done away with when grandpa remodelled the house. But we had what was almost quite as good—the old-fashioned coal stoves whose open doors let out all the glow and warmth and friendliness within. Even the kitchen stove had a grate which radiated light and cheer. Nowadays there are no such stoves—even the kitchen ranges are ugly black boxes in which you cannot catch a glimpse of flame.

But at any rate we got the furnace fixed today and there is a very different atmosphere in the house tonight. I fear we shall have to burn wood this winter, owing to the coal strike in the U.S. and that will mean a good deal of annoyance from smoke since our furnace is not well adapted to wood.

Ewan has been talking lately of how well he is feeling. And he *is* well—perfectly well, whether it lasts or not. I am afraid to hope it will last but at any rate he is absolutely well now. I know this from a queer enough reason—*he doesn't "say his prayers"* any more!!

---

124 "Alas for me"; this term is used by the character of Frances Arabin in Frances Trollope's 1857 novel, *Barchester Towers*.

When I married I had a touching belief that ministers always prayed. Even I, who no longer believed many things of the old creeds, had never given up my habit of nightly prayer or lost a certain faith that there *was* a Power who would hear it. How much more, then, should a minister, who *did* believe the old creeds fully, still pray. It was a distinct shock to me to find that Ewan never prayed, except for the prayer at family worship. I think the truth is that he was never taught to pray in childhood and so never formed the habit. His parents were poor, his mother overworked and the whole atmosphere and tradition of the family the reverse of spiritual. Ewan, himself, normally has not an atom of spirituality about him, being a jolly, practical sort of man.

But from the moment his attack of melancholia came on in the spring of 1919, three and a half years ago, he has prayed, morning and night and often, when the recurring attacks were at their worst, through the day. Such prayers of course, did him no good and were only the instinctive cries of his irrational fear. Lately he has stopped them completely—never seems to think of praying. So I know that he is perfectly well for the first time since 1919. Oh, if it would only continue! If I thought the real worry he has had lately was the cause of his cure I would bless even Marshall Pickering. But it is probably a mere coincidence.

Friday, October 27, 1922

Today we got a letter from McCullough in which he seemed rather blue over our case. This worried me and I spent the afternoon in secret misery. I had to go to Alec Leask's to help with a quilting for the sufferers in the recent fires up north[125] and had to talk and smile to the women and endure the fox-like gnawing behind my cloak.

There is a wretched scandal just now, too, about a couple of our young people. The girl in question is such a nice girl and has always been such a help in our guild and church. It is a shame—and the gossip is sickening, especially among a clique which has always been jealous of her beauty and ability. Faugh! There are times when humanity stinks in my nostrils.

Lily, after sulking for two days—but *not* going—has suddenly become quite angelic and no one would ever imagine that there had been a word between us. I should have "spoken out in meeting" long ago.

I have the proofs of *Emily* to read but so far I have not been able to read them. I cannot settle down to mental effort of any sort. I am getting no work at all done this fall.

---

125   In October 1922, following an unusually hot and dry summer, a wildfire had destroyed an area of 1,680 square km/650 square miles in northern Ontario.

Saturday, Oct. 28, 1922
The Manse, Leaskdale, Ont.

We went to Stouffville today, through this faded autumnal land, and saw Mr. McCullough, who comes out there on Saturday afternoons. When McCullough heard of Boynton he became much more optimistic and said that evidence would go far to win our case. This cheered us up and we enjoyed the drive home through the clear frosty night, even though "Lady Jane" did "act up" all the way home. That car has been possessed of seven devils this fall!

Monday, Oct. 30, 1922
Leaskdale, Ont.

I am terribly upset and cannot sleep or rest. We went over to Zephyr this morning and I stayed at Rob Shier's while Ewan went up to take Boynton his subpoena. I soon made a ghastly discovery, which was confirmed when I returned.

It seems that Pickering heard in some way that Boynton was to be our witness—Boynton himself very foolishly told it. Pickering went to Sutton yesterday afternoon and told Boynton that he had never consulted him.

"Oh, yes, you did," said Boynton. "I have the record of your visit in my book"—and then, more foolishly still, he showed it to him.

Pickering looked staggered at first—then said,

"That must be my nephew, young Marshall Pickering."

This said young Marshall is a notorious scamp who got into some scrape this summer and has decamped no one knows where, so we cannot find him to disprove this. If we *could* find him I daresay he would be quite willing to help us for he hates his uncle. He is a young man of twenty-two and, as Boynton says, would never have an enlarged prostate gland, which is an old man's disease. But the trouble is that Boynton has been so befuddled by Pickering's positive assertion that he had never consulted him that he cannot swear to anything now. He told Ewan that he cannot remember the *face* of the man who consulted him and though he is "quite certain" in his own mind that it was Pickering he says he can't go on the stand and take oath to it. The entry itself proves nothing since there is nothing in it that shows *which* Marshall Pickering was there. Boynton says he is positive young Marshall never was to see him about anything.

We know old Marshall Pickering *was* there for Lily's father saw him in Boynton's office a month before the collision and mentioned it to his family when he came home. But he is dead and so we cannot bring the lie home to Pickering.

It upset me terribly and even some good bits of evidence we picked up to-day could not comfort me. We have got Arthur Smith who says he examined the tracks after the collision and at the point of collision they were in the centre of the road. This is good. Also Mr. and Mrs. Jas. Lockie were told by Pickering after he came back from the hospital that he had trouble before the collision. Mrs. Joe Taylor, too, was told by Ches Pickering the morning after the collision, "Oh no, the accident didn't cause father's trouble. He had to have the operation anyhow." But I suppose we cannot get the latter evidence in because Ches will not be on the stand. I shall not sleep again tonight. And there are two weeks yet before the trial comes on. It seems to me just now that I *cannot* live through them. When the worst comes I'll be able to bear it. But this suspense!

Tuesday, October 31, 1922
The Manse, Leaskdale, Ont.

I had a bad night—even veronal could not give me oblivion—and I had a worse day until dusk. I felt dreadfully worn-out physically and upset mentally. Ewan went to Zephyr in the forenoon to meet Mr. Button—McCullough's partner—and a surveyor who were coming out to make a chart of the road. I worked at routine tasks, sewed, mended, and tried to read proof but couldn't. Always I have taken delight in reading my proofs but this time I read them in torment.

Then the boys came home from school bent on having Jack-o-lanterns made for Hallowe'en festivities tonight. I couldn't disappoint them, so I went to work with two pumpkins and made jackies out of them, while I lived over the trial in my mind, saw our case lost, saw us having to pay out anywhere from three to six thousand dollars, and saw Marshall Pickering and that de-mon of a wife of his triumphant and boasting—which was the worst anticipa-tion of all.

Then Ewan came home and beckoned me into the library.

"I have good news for you." he said. "Mr. Button told me that McCullough had 'phoned out to him that Dr. Stevenson had managed to obtain a peep at the record of the case in the hospital and that it was *very favorable to us.*"

I felt as if I had been released from the rack. If there is a record of the case in the hospital—something we did not know before—I cannot believe that Pickering even now will really take this case into court after all. If he did and this record were produced it would prove him a perjuror. If the record is "very favorable"—and McCullough is not the man to overstate his case—he will

indeed be a fool to go on with this. Unless he has actually, through the effects of pain and ether, forgotten there was such a thing.

I haven't felt so care-free for a month as I felt tonight. Everything was transformed in the wink of an eye. An intolerable burden of worry and unrest seemed lifted from my soul. I was a child with the children and flung myself into the Hallowe'en sports without reservation. The village boys came in and Lily and I rigged them up in masks and ridiculous costumes and started them off. We had our gate posts adorned with two fine fiendish jacks and we went out into the crisp moonlit night and raked up fallen leaves and had a bonfire. I could hardly believe I was the same creature I

Hallowe'en masks and faces.

was in the afternoon—I felt so light-hearted, so joyful, so seized with the beauty of the night.

Then, when the fun was over and the boys in bed, I sat down and read my proof in enjoyment. Oh, I'm going to have a delightful sleep tonight.

This day week is the day of the trial. It will be over this night week. It seems impossible of belief.

Wednesday, November 1, 1922
Leaskdale, Ont.

I had my good sleep. It knit up my ravelled sleeve of care beautifully[126] and I have enjoyed the day and my work. We went to Uxbridge and E. subpoenaed McClintock. No doubt we will have Johnson and Jones against us but still he will help us a lot.

This afternoon Ewan went away after another hunt for evidence. He is not back yet. I always dread his coming for I am always in dread of bad news— such as the slump of another witness *à la* Boynton.

---

126   From *Macbeth* 2.2.35–38: "Methought I heard a voice cry, 'Sleep no more! / Macbeth does murder sleep'—the innocent sleep, / Sleep that knits up the raveled sleave of care."

Thursday, Nov. 2, 1922

Of course "Lady Jane" is possessed of devils—and at the very time when we need her most. Last night Ewan didn't come home. I waited up in anxiety until twelve when he 'phoned that he was at John Rynard's and couldn't get the car started. This morning he had to get the garage man to come up and tow it to Uxbridge. There it was found that the battery was stone dead—the result of something that same garage man himself had done to it recently. Ewan went on to Toronto from Uxbridge and will not be back till tomorrow night.

Today was dull, with frequent showers of snow. Somehow I got blue and discouraged again. This agony seems so long drawn out. For two months my very meat and drink have been flavored with Marshall Pickering—and a more odious flavor could not be imagined. Ugh!

Friday, Nov. 3, 1922

There are two adjectives that are never separated in regard to a November day—dull and gloomy. They were wedded together in the dawn of language and I shall not divorce them now. Today *was* dull and gloomy. And as night drew on my feeling of worry and unrest again became almost intolerable. I expected Ewan back this evening—and dreaded it lest he have bad news— but when Dr. Shier[127] 'phoned up at dark to say Ewan had 'phoned him he wouldn't be out tonight that was even worse, for I tortured myself with reasons as to why he had not come.

A spasm of rebellion seized me tonight—fierce rebellion that I should have been dragged into this wretched affair—forced into court and held up to the ribald gaze of a vulgar curious crowd—for, from all reports, the whole country side is going to the trial. It is true most of the onlookers are on our side and their curiosity friendly. It *is* curiosity, just the same, and I will be mouthed over afterwards in a hundred assemblages of gossip, and my looks, bearing, and evidence canvassed and detailed. It is indecent—indecent! I cried with the anticipatory horror of the hateful experience and felt as if I *could not* endure it. I couldn't get back my courage at all until I went up and lay down on the bed beside Chester and Stuart. Their arms around my neck and their dear little love-whispers helped me to get control of myself again and I set my teeth to endure and came downstairs again quoting an old parody on *Kathleen Mavourneen,*[128]

It may be for years but it can't be forever.

127　Dr Walter Columbus Shier was a medical doctor in Leaskdale and Uxbridge.

128　Originally a popular song composed in 1837, by 1922 several silent films titled *Kathleen Mavourneen* had been made. "Mavourneen" is derived from the Irish Gaelic ("my beloved").

This night week the torture scene will be over and there will be, whatever way it goes, an end of suspense—which is always the hardest thing to bear.

The Manse, Leaskdale
Saturday, Nov. 4, 1922

I had a nasty dream last night that Ewan came home and when I asked him about "the history of the case" said, "There is nothing in it." It was so vivid that it worried and depressed me and I was not surprised at the contents of a letter from Ewan at noon, saying that there was no history of the case after all, such being only taken when patients are in the wards. What Dr. Stevenson had seen was the report of the pathologist of Toronto University who dissected the gland and found that there was no congestion in it. As McClintock told us that if there were no congestion in the gland the accident had nothing to do with it, this is good: but the Pickering side knows nothing of this, so it will not prevent them from taking the case into court which was what I hoped.

Ewan got home at eight, having borrowed the car of a friend in Uxbridge—an old ramshackle affair. I shall not know an easy minute while we have it, lest something happens to it. Ewan has such wretched luck with cars somehow.

As soon as we got a bit of supper we started for Zephyr, as Mrs. Jas. Lockie[129] had 'phoned over in the afternoon that she wanted to see Mr. Macdonald as soon as possible. I had been half wild with nervousness before we started, after being cooped up here alone for three dark days with no one to talk to; but the cool fresh air and the agreeable sense of flying away from all earthly affairs which the car gave, did me a heap of good and made me feel quite full of spunk again. The tall mulleins stood up along our road in stiff, orderly ranks like companies of soldiers. I like best their vernacular name, "*devil's* candle-sticks." It is full of savor. And the trees and fields and groves were pleasantly suggestive and eerie as if full of elfish secrets. For a blessed short time I forgot everything but the lure of the night.

Mrs. Lockie's news didn't amount to anything much. It was only a wild yarn that has got around to the effect that Boynton has been "bought off" by Pickering. I don't believe *that.* He told Ewan that Pickering's act in bringing suit against us was "a dastardly deed" and hoped earnestly that we would "beat him." He told Mrs. Lockie some time ago that Pickering had been to him for treatment and that Mrs. Pickering had been to him in 1919 for diabetes.

Mrs. Lockie also told us that Ches Pickering told her in the March of 1921, three months before the collision, that his father was "very miserable" and

---

129   James Lockie (b. 1869) and his wife Mary (b. 1888); in an entry of February 14, 1926, LMM describes Mrs Lockie as "a terrible woman, noted for gossip and malice."

kept putting off having his operation, although he knew he ought to have it, because he was afraid it would "kill him as it killed his father." The whole Pickering family have talked of their father's condition for years, here and there, far and wide. But in the eyes of the law this is only "hearsay" and will not be admitted as evidence.

It is one o'clock. I am dead tired. But there must soon be and end of it.

Sunday, November 5, 1922
Leaskdale, Ont.

By next Sunday the suspense will be over. Ewan preached well today. One would not think any worry was hanging over him. But Ewan never worries over *anything*, except the things normal people do *not* worry over. I suppose it is as well; and yet I think it is better to worry a little more over real things and less about unreal things. It is not quite normal for anyone not to worry *at all* over troubles, even though they may not feel them so deeply as others do. Any normal person worries a little over real difficulties.

Monday, Nov. 6, 1922

This was Thanksgiving but I can't say the atmosphere of Leaskdale manse was exactly in accord with the spirit of the day. The weather was abominable. Showers of snow fell constantly and it was so dark that we had to light the lamps at 3.30. Ewan was not home either, having gone away on the trail of another witness. He got him, too—Lance Copelands, who asked Pickering after he came out of the hospital if the accident caused the operation and was told it had not.

Mr. Button 'phoned today that the trial would not likely be until Tuesday—another two days of suspense.

We also heard a rumor that Pickering has "a lot" of witnesses. We can hardly credit this. We know he has four—Mason Horner, Harry Risley, John Urquhart and "old Joe Profit." But still the rumor is a worrying one.

Mason Horner is the son of "old Bill Horner," Pickering's intimate friend. We know what Mason will swear to but we cannot find out what the others are going for. They are a fine assortment. Risley is a "home boy"[130] who used to work in Law's garage and was discharged last fall. He is notorious for his wild lies so will doubtless be quite ready to swear to anything he is wanted to. We

---

130   That is, a boy who has come from a home for orphaned (or otherwise vulnerable) children. Often such children were from the United Kingdom: between the 1860s and 1948, over 100,000 children of all ages were sent to new homes across Canada.

will see if the boast I have heard so many lawyers make that "they can always tell when a witness is lying" is justified by facts. Joe Profit is an old "bum" who has been living all his life on his wife's earnings as a scrubwoman. John Urquhart was in a scrape a few years ago for stealing oats out of the mill at Zephyr. A nice lot of witnesses! But they will stick at no lies and so are better for Pickering's purposes than truthful or honest people. This worries me for I have no faith in judges being able to tell when witnesses are lying anymore than other people. I have seen judges fooled by the lies the Pages told half a dozen times.

Tuesday, Nov. 7, 1922
The Manse, Leaskdale, Ont.

It is a curious thing that while Ewan has been scouring the country for witnesses one who could give most important evidence was living within ten minutes walk of our own door. We have always known that Marshall Pickering used to go down to see Lily's father when he was sick and talk to him of his trouble etc. but as far as Lily knew none of the rest of the family heard this. They only knew it because Mr. Meyers used to tell them about it after Pickering had gone. We had asked most of them but none had heard it for themselves. We never thought of asking Edith[131] as she was married and away from home long before her father became ill. And now it turns out that she heard a most important thing. One Sunday, May 15th, a month before the collision she was over to see her father and was in the room while Pickering was there. Pickering told her father that he had to have an operation himself "very soon," though he had been "putting it off as long as he could." Then he went on to ask her father about the expense, hospital etc.

This is excellent. We have nothing else so good, as all the other evidence is about what Pickering told various people *after* he came out of the hospital. It is a fortunate thing the trial did *not* come off today or we would not have had this evidence.

Wednesday, Nov. 8, 1922

Talk about Ewan being unlucky with cars! Today, just as he arrived home with the Thompson car, travelling at about 12 miles an hour on the perfectly smooth road outside our gate the crank shaft broke! It was no one's fault—the shaft had probably had an old crack in it. But here we are with no car and a lawsuit pending. And a borrowed car, too. But there is no help for it. It will cost us fifty dollars for repairs but that is a minor matter compared to our other

---

131   Edith Reid, Lily's sister, had been LMM's maid before Lily; Edith had married and left the manse in 1918.

worries. Poor Ewan phoned to the Sunderland garage, got them to come over and tow the wretched Chev back there, then borrowed Claude Morrison's car and started off.

Mr. Button 'phoned today that our case may not go on before Monday. Worse and worse! These repeated postponements are hard on the nerves. I spend these days listening miserably for 'phone calls—but I am thankful they *can* call us. Last week the line was out and nobody could get us and the worry of it added considerably to the sum total of all our other worries at present.

I am too restless these days to do any work requiring thought or concentration but I am getting a whole lot of odd jobs done that have hung fire for months waiting until I could finish them up. So thanks to M. P. for *that*.

Ewan went to Zephyr tonight with Claude Morrison's car and fortunately got back without any fresh mishap but with no new witnesses. But we picked up a couple of bits of gossip which agreed with us. Mrs. Lockie was listening on the phone the other day when Pickering was talking to his married daughter Mrs. Pete Arnold. (I fancy the Pickering ring is seldom heard these days when someone is *not* listening in.) Mrs. Pete asked him how he was. "Oh, I'm all in," he said. "Oh, don't worry over this," she said soothingly. "It is pretty hard to keep from worrying," was his response.

So *we* are not doing all the worrying. And if *he* is worrying so much he cannot be very sure of his case.

Then Marshall Pickering has been tampering with our witnesses. He has been to three of them and asked them out and out "not to tell any more than they could help." Surely this will score against him in the court's opinion.

Oh, if this were only over! Sometimes I feel that I *cannot* bear it a minute longer. Of course I *do*—and after all I've borne far worse things. And I don't think the outside world knows much of my worry. I keep a cool unmoved front outwardly. It is much to be thankful for that Ewan is so well—and I *will* be thankful for it when the smoke of conflict clears away and lets me see the stars that *are* shining in my dark sky.

Thursday, Nov. 9, 1922
Leaskdale, Ont.

We have got our own car back, thanks be! Not that she is such a comfortable possession but she is our own and therefore I am not so worried over possible damages to her as to other peoples' cars. Ewan brought Lady Jane home today. That she—demon was apparently all right; but when we went out after supper, intending to make a call she would not start—and did not. A malison[132] on all balky cars!

132　Archaic term for "curse."

Friday, November 10, 1922

We had the garage man from Uxbridge come up this morning and induce Lady Jane to go. When I cast up my accounts at the end of the year I feel sure the sum total of the upkeep expense of Lady Jane will drive me to home brew.

The trial is put off again until November 20th and is to be in Toronto instead of Whitby. These repeated postponements are hard to endure philosophically. As for the change of venue, it is more convenient for us in some ways but I believe we would have stood a better chance in Whitby. Our consolation is—not so many people will be able to go down from hereabouts.

Dr. Johnson seems to be out of conceit with Pickering at last. He has been rather backing him right along but he has found him out. Pickering disgusted him lately by going to him and begging him not to tell on the witness stand that Mrs. Pickering had diabetes! Johnson angrily told him that he would tell the truth to whatever was asked of him. Dr. Johnson himself told Rob Shier this.

We have subpoenaed another witness on our lawyer's advice but I don't know if it will do us any good. There is a certain Mrs. Taylor up at Shiloh[133] who is a Methodist and rather intimate with the Pickering clique. Soon after the collision this woman was at a Ladies' Aid meeting in Zephyr and said that she was sorry she had not insisted on the Pickerings staying to tea that afternoon—they had called at her place—because then the collision would not have taken place. But Mrs. Pickering had said, in refusing, that they must hurry home because Mr. Pickering was *feeling so miserable*. When we heard this Ewan went to see her but she would not admit she knew anything. But another Mr. Taylor there, a friend of ours, said to Ewan, "Take her down. She is a good woman and will tell the truth on the stand."

If she would give this evidence it would be very valuable as showing that Pickering's attack was coming on before the accident.

Saturday, Nov. 11, 1922
The Manse, Leaskdale, Ont.

Old Joe Profit has been forbidden by doctor to go on witness stand, owing to "a bad heart," so was examined by commission this afternoon. He told an undiluted lie. He said that he and Risley had heard Ewan say at Zephyr garage the morning after the accident, *"If I had been minding my business instead of talking to Law the accident would never have happened."*

Old Joe couldn't remember *anything* else—the time of the accident, whether it was spring or fall, not even the year it took place. His memory only retained one thing apparently. Risley, of course, will testify to the same lie. But

---

133   Shiloh was a small rural community northwest of Udora, 8 km/5 miles north of Leaskdale.

Mr. Law says Ewan never looked at or spoke to him after he started the car and Rob Shier was in the garage next morning all the time Risley and Profit were there and says that Ewan never said such words or anything like them. So it will be Ewan, Mr. Law, Mr. Shier, Mrs. Meyers and myself against Risley, the offspring of the London gutters, and the old village bum Joe Profit. And if the Judge believes them against us there is no such thing as justice!

Sunday, November 12, 1922

Somehow I feel better today than I have felt for a week. The suspense can not last much longer. I had a quiet, restful afternoon of reading.

We heard today that Mrs. Will Lockie sympathizes with the Pickerings. I could have told that without hearing it. That woman hates us and always has. Her hatred is a compliment. Will Lockie himself, odd as he is, seems to be on our side—at least he told Ewan recently that he hoped we'd beat Pickering.

Monday, November 13, 1922

I had a letter from Stell today which is in the nature of a portent. It was absolutely cheerful. She said in it that she was feeling fine—better than she had felt for ten years.

I suspect the recent rise in cotton has something to do with her cheerfulness. But whatever the cause I hailed it thankfully. One of Stell's howls of despair coming on top of all my present worries would be the proverbial last straw.

Lawyer Ormiston[134] told Ewan in Uxbridge today that Pickering has subpoenaed MacClintock and that he told Ormiston he was "going to contradict everything Johnson said." That is good, because it will come from Pickering's own witness. Though likely Grieg will find it out before he puts him on the stand.

Ormiston also told E. that he had asked Grieg why he didn't have a jury on the case. Grieg responded, "Do you suppose a jury would ever find against a Presbyterian minister?"

This convinces me of what I have felt all along—that we *should* have asked for a jury. But our lawyers thought a judge would be better, saying that a jury would be more apt to sympathize with Pickering's tale of woe etc. than a judge would. I have my doubts. But it is too late now.

---

134   William H. Ormiston KC was a prominent Uxbridge lawyer. He is only mentioned six times in LMM's entire journal record (three in 1922, once in 1923, and twice in 1924); it is not clear in what capacity he was involved with her legal matters.

Tuesday, Nov. 14, 1922

I have had another dream that means something. I dreamed I was in the old kitchen in Cavendish looking out of the west window at a hideous, pitch-black cloud that covered the whole western sky. I was dreadfully frightened of it, believing that some terrible destruction was coming upon me from it. But just as my dread was at its height—presto, there was no cloud—the sky was aswim with sunshine. I was in an incredulous daze. "It is impossible," I said, "that there was not even a drop of rain out of so black a cloud."

Then I woke. The dream has worried me. I believe it means we are to lose the suit. But in that case, how about the disappearance of the cloud and the absence of any evil consequences? To have to pay out anywhere from three to six thousand dollars would not agree with that. I can't understand it. But I feel sure trouble of some kind is ahead.

Tonight I finished reading Mommsenn's *Rome*. He is rather prosy but some parts are interesting. Nothing, however, "tastes right" to me nowadays. Reading hasn't the proper flavor—work is savorless. Oh, will it *never* be over?

Thursday, Nov. 16, 1922
The Manse, Leaskdale

Ewan met Marshall Pickering on the road today and was amazed to see how thin he had grown. We had been told this before but I thought people were perhaps exaggerating it to please us. It is true, however.

There was a cottage prayer-meeting at John Lockie's tonight and I permitted myself the satisfaction of snubbing Mrs. Will Lockie, as I have long yearned to do. I cannot make her any more my enemy than she really is and I consider that the time has come to put her in her place.

She was sitting beside me on the sofa. I happened to remark to one of the men on the fact of the Labour group in England having made such striking gains in the recent elections. Mrs. Will struck in:—"Well, I think Labour had better do something in this country. I'm getting tired working for nothing. I think I'll go to Toronto, too, and see if I can't get something done for the workers."

Mrs. Lockie is *jealous* of me because *I* keep a maid and so—as she fondly imagines—can "live without working." She was jealous when my children were born because I had a trained nurse. I remember the first time I was there after Chester was born she said, "We country women can't get a trained nurse. *We have to die.*"

I wanted to ask, "Has anybody died around here for lack of a trained nurse"—but I didn't. Neither did I say, "*You* have had three children. Yet you

are alive." But tonight I turned and looked Mrs. Will squarely in the face. "You have your U.F.O. government," I said. "I thought when you put it in it would do away with all the farmer's grievances."

There was a general laugh in which even Will joined. Mrs. Will is a great U.F.O. woman. She looked very silly and said nothing more. I ignored her for the rest of the evening.

I think little except our suit is talked of around here for a radius of twenty miles where two or three are gathered together. I can't exactly blame people. The fact of a minister being sued is a dramatic event to them—a veritable godsend in their humdrum, colorless lives. It is only natural they should make the most of it. But it is hard that Ewan and I should be butchered to make a Roman holiday![135] I feel all raw and bleeding, mentally and physically.

Friday, Nov. 17, 1922

Ewan was in Toronto today for a final trip before the trial. Mr. McCullough says that *if* our witnesses stand by what they have said we will win our case. This is encouraging. But one can never tell. I remember my dream of the cloud.

I have felt worried and nervous all day. It was dark and cloudy with frequent drizzling showers—so dark that I had to light a lamp at 3.30. This all made matters rather harder. Somehow I can't believe that we will win—it's "too good to be true." And I can't see *beyond* the suit—I feel as if it would *never* be over. Like Thomas Hardy, "I can't believe when it is raining that it will ever clear up." But it helps, as it always has done, to write it all out in this journal. It "gets it out of my system" to a certain extent so that it doesn't poison me totally.

At any rate we'll soon know the worst—"despair is a free man, hope is a slave."[136] When it is all over, no matter what the result is, I will be able to get back at times into my fairy world of dream and ideal. I am barred out of it now. I cannot escape from carking realities by an hour's sojourn in a land of faery, "where the rain never fell and the wind never blew."[137]

Lily, by the way, has been quite angelic ever since—to use a detestable slang phrase of the day—"I told her where she got off at." She is no tidier however.

Lady Jane Grey broke two of the leaves in her spring today. Dear Lady Jane!

---

135   From Byron's long poem, *Child Harolde's Pilgrimmage* (1812–18): "THERE was their Dacian mother—he, their sire, / Butchered to make a Roman holiday—" (Canto the Fourth, CXLI). In this metaphor, a gladiator expects to be butchered to provide pleasure for the audience.

136   This expression can be traced to medieval Islam.

137   From George MacDonald's 1871 children's novel, *At the Back of the North Wind*.

Well, I must go to bed. Fortunately I have been able to sleep pretty well right along in spite of everything. And oh, how gladly I always welcome the night after my strenuous days!

I have just had a bed-time snack of home-cured pork ham. After all, Marshall Pickering can't embitter everything. A good bite of pork ham still has some savor.

Monday, Nov. 20, 1922
Leaskdale, Ont.

A very dull, heartless sort of day. We had a lot of trouble getting a new spring in the car.

McCullough 'phoned that the trial will begin Thursday. I don't believe it. It will just be put off again—we can't really ever catch up with it. But I've been busy today getting ready for the trip—the most unpleasant expedition to Toronto I have ever taken.

Tuesday, November 21, 1922

I am feeling restless and worried. I do not know just why I should feel like this so much of the time. Even if we lose it will not ruin us. I think much of the unrest I feel and have felt all the fall, especially in the evenings, comes from the effect of the old Page lawsuits on my subconscious mind. All that old unrest I felt in Boston is registered there and gets stirred up when a similar worry arises.

It seems impossible that by this night week the trial will be over and the worst or best known.

I did a good deed today—I took in a poor starving homeless little gray cat and found a good home for it.

Our own cat, *Paddy*, is a very important member of our household. When Daffy died I felt that I could never care for another cat—and at first I was very indifferent to Pat. But he has made good. He is a handsome big fellow, a good deal like Daffy in appearance. He has not the intriguing streak of diabolism possessed by Daff—but he is a very lovable, velvety striped puss—I don't care a hoot about any cat that isn't striped—with engaging ways of his own and when I am not possessed by Marshall Pickering I take a great deal of pleasure in him and his soft furry flanks. We have got another

Paddy

witness—John Hall, to whom Pickering also told after his return from the

hospital that the accident did not cause his operation. He told him, "The trouble was coming on for some time—the collision may have hastened it a little." This makes eight good reliable witnesses to statements from Marshall Pickering's own lips.

We leave for Toronto tomorrow. If it were not for my thundercloud dream I should be hopeful enough. But at least it will be *over* after two more days of grim endurance.

Ewan looks very tired. He has had a strenuous fall. Yet he has been well and jolly through it all. If it only continues! I think if we win the trial the sense of success will scatter that dark complex of inadequacy in his subconscious mind which I believe is responsible for much of his trouble. But if we lose the opposite effect may be produced, and the complex intensified.

Sunday, November 26, 1922
The Manse, Leaskdale, Ont.

The suit is over—and we have *lost*, after a most unfair trial!

I suppose most people who have lost a suit are inclined to think that the Judge was unfair or prejudiced. That is natural enough. But I do not really think I am like that. When the Master, in my Page lawsuit, gave in a report that was mainly adverse to me I was disappointed but I did not think he had been unfair. He had listened to and weighed all my evidence, and when he believed the two Pages against my solitary assertion, unsupported by any other evidence, I did not blame him. The Pages were strangers to him and he had not the means of knowing them to be the liars they were.

But in this case the Judge *was* unfair. Everyone who heard the trial says the same thing. People who are absolute strangers to us and merely happened to be there said it. Even Mason Horner, a law-student and Pickering's star witness, said in Zephyr yesterday that it was "a very one-sided trial."

One-sided! I should say so. We simply did not have the ghost of a show. As soon as Judge Riddell[138] heard Pickering's story he made up his mind then and there, as everyone saw, and was determined not to change it. His conduct showed that plainly.

On Wednesday we motored into Toronto and took with us Edith, Mrs. Alexander Lockie and Mrs. Meyers. We spent the evening in John McCullough's law office[139] where all our witnesses were examined. I was dreadfully tired when it was all over and slept little that night.

---

138   William Renwick Riddell (1852–1945), a noted lawyer and Ontario Supreme Court justice from 1906, was also a prolific writer of books and articles, including a 1926 biography of John Graves Simcoe. A detailed history of the Pickering lawsuit and the trial itself is found in Mary Henley Rubio's *Lucy Maud Montgomery: The Gift of Wings* (2008).
139   John McCullough was the brother of J.W. McCullough, the Macdonalds' attorney.

Thursday morning we went to the court house but an unfinished trial took up the forenoon. I sat and listened to it. I did not just like Judge Riddell even then. He is a very eminent legal light but he is plainly a colossal egotist and thinks his own judgment quite infallible.

Our trial began in the afternoon. It all seemed a nightmare to me. The big courtroom was filled with people, nearly all of them Zephyr and Leaskdale people. Pickering went on the stand first and told the same string of lies as in his examination for discovery but made an important change in one respect. In the former examination he had stated that he had seen our car one hundred rods away. This time he said *Twenty rods*.[140] Confronted by Mr. McCullough with his preliminary answer he said, "*Well, if I said that I was wrong.*" I suppose his lawyer has told him that his former answer (which was the true one—or at least what he has said many times heretofore) was prejudicial to his case. One would think that a judge would conclude from this that a man who would swear to one thing in his preliminary exam and then contradict himself in the next examination, would very likely be "wrong" on other points also. But not so Judge Riddell.

Pickering swore he was going only 20 miles an hour. Asked by our lawyer if he didn't know that the law required a slowing down to 12 1/2 miles at a blind corner he retorted that it wasn't a blind corner. He said he had sounded his horn four times (another absolute lie) and he repeated his former falsehoods as to what Ewan said to him after the collision. He said that he had to be operated on not for *enlarged* gland but *for congested* gland and that the congestion was caused by the accident. He also said that he had *never* spoken of or thought of an operation!

Then Mr. McCullough began to cross-question him: "Did you say such-and-such to So-and-So etc.," as the laws of evidence require. Pickering denied flatly every allegation—he had never told Mr. Meyers he was going to have an operation—he had never complained to Mrs. Lockie—he had never told anyone that the accident hadn't caused his operation etc. At first he did it very brazenly but as the long string of witnesses was named off he began to go to pieces and finally admitted that he "might have said he had a burning sensation at times"—which of course was exactly opposite to what he said in the examination for discovery.

Then Mr. McCullough asked him if his wife ever had, or had been treated, for, diabetes. He said nervously, "She *had a little* of it a few years ago but she got some medicine from the States that cured her."

He was also compelled to admit that if he had slowed down to 12 1/2 miles he could have avoided the accident.

---

140   A rod is a unit of measurement that is rarely used noawadays. One rod is about 5 metres or 16 feet; twenty rods is appropximately 100 metres or 330 feet.

All through his cross-examination the Judge plainly favored him and checked Mr. McCullough repeatedly although Mr. McCullough asked nothing he had not a right to ask. When he began to ask Pickering about tampering with our witnesses the Judge stopped him at once and declared "it didn't matter." "Not matter?" said McCullough. "I think it was a most improper thing." "Not at all—not at all," said the Judge.

This was the first moment that I said to myself "The suit will go against us." A judge who could say that there was nothing improper in Pickering's going to our witnesses and asking them to keep back part of the truth was not a judge who would listen to *anything* that contradicted his pre-conception of the case, if he could get any legal excuse for refusing to listen.

When Pickering left the stand the Judge said to Mr. McCullough,

"I suggest that you do not put on those witnesses you mentioned," or words to that effect.

I felt thunderstruck. Mr. McCullough, too, was amazed and protested.

"Of course I don't tell you you can't put them on," said Riddell. "I merely suggest that you will save time by not doing it. I *shall give very little attention to such evidence.*"

I found it hard to believe my ears. This man was practically saying that he would not believe our witnesses, although he had not seen or heard one of them.

The Judge then went on to say, "The man has admitted that he had some trouble before the accident. What more do you want?"

Mr. McCullough was not quite quick enough here. He should have said, "I want to prove that he intended, before the collision, to have an operation."

Not that it mattered—not that anything he could have said would have mattered. The Judge had already made up his mind and decided the case.

But Mr. McCullough was so taken aback by the Judge practically barring out the very witnesses upon whom we depended to win our case that he was a bit rattled and said, "I want to test the credibility of the witness."

"Oh, I believe the witness. He is an honest man," said the Judge.

I knew that we had lost then and so did everyone else in the room. The Judge believed Pickering's story—that tissue of lies—and was evidently determined that we should have no chance of disproving it. He impressed me all through the trial as being determined to keep out or minimize *any* evidence that would make him doubtful in his own despite of the truth of the Pickerings' tale or render it difficult for him to decide in their favor.

"Call the doctors," said the Judge. "I see some of them here. Put them on."

It was evident that the Judge supposed the doctors were all on Pickering's side. Dr. Johnson went on first. He said he had been called in by Pickering had "found some congestion in the gland" and thought it must have been caused

by the accident as he could find no other reason for it. When it came to Mrs. Pickering he said he had treated her for diabetes and had sent her to a Toronto specialist who had confirmed his diagnosis.

We expected that Dr. Jones would be called after Johnson. One would have imagined that the specialist who performed the operation would be called on for evidence, whoever else was not. But he was not there at all. This shows, of course, that his evidence would not have been favorable to them. I wish now that we had subpoenaed him; but after his saying of Pickering, "He'll get it, too," we did not dare, supposing him to be on Pickering's side. I suppose he said that on purpose to prevent our subpoenaing him. They did not have Mc-Clintock either, evidently having found out that he was not on their side. Our lawyer did not call him either then, which I think was a mistake.

Johnson was the only doctor Pickering had there. Then Dr. Robinson, the Pathologist of Toronto University and the leading authority in his line in Canada,[141] went on. He stated that there was no congestion whatever in the gland and had the section of the gland there to prove it. Phelan quite lost his calm at this point. This evidence was evidently something totally unexpected by him, and it completely upset his plea that the congestion of the gland necessitated the operation. He asked angrily, "Is it customary to dissect the glands like that?" "Yes." "And are they open to the inspection of the public?" "Yes." Dr. Robinson furthermore said that an operation would have been necessary in any case in two or three months.

Then we had Dr. Powell and Dr. Stevenson,[142] both kidney disease experts, who said that diabetes was incurable and that the symptoms of Mrs. Pickering's complaint were the symptoms of diabetes. Then the court adjourned.

We did not know what to think. The Clerk of the Court, who seemed strongly in our favor, told us he could see plainly it was just a conspiracy to get money out of us. He said he believed Riddell would decide for us. He said he believed the reason Riddell had barred out the witnesses was simply that he had made up his mind that Pickering was negligent in not slowing down to the required legal speed and that therefore it did not matter whether the collision caused the operation or not—he could not claim damages. This encouraged us a little but I had a miserable night. I thought of my dream of the black cloud and felt sure it meant the loss of the suit.

Next morning court opened at ten. The first thing the Judge did was to make a suggestion that Ewan and Pickering go into a room together and try to settle the dispute "in Christian amity." Then I gave up hope utterly. If the

---

141   Likely John Livie Robinson, MD (b.1888).

142   Likely Newton Powell (1856–1935), former chair of Medical Jurisprudence and Clinical Surgery at Toronto General Hospital; Dr Stevenson is likely J.M. Stevenson, MD, CM (b.1862).

Judge had not already decided in Pickering's favor he would not have suggested "settling." That is, he had made up his mind to give P. the verdict *before* he had heard a single one of our witnesses, except the doctors. For anything he knew we might have been able to prove that the collision was wholly Pickering's fault and in that case to ask Ewan to "settle" would have been rank injustice. It is incredible to me that a judge could do such a thing.

Ewan went in with Pickering for form's sake but Pickering's "terms"—all the expenses and a thousand dollars besides—were not to be considered.

Mrs. Pickering then was put on the stand. She swore that she had not been "able to work" since the collision—had "no ambition" etc. etc. It really sounded awfully funny in that whining voice of hers—a voice assumed for the occasion as it is not her natural tone at all. In her preliminary examination she had sworn that her daughters had worked out *before* and had to stay home *after* the collision. She did not dare to repeat this lie, as she knew we had witnesses there to prove that such a statement was an absolute falsehood. Under cross-examination she admitted that she had never had a doctor or consulted one since the collision—which was rather odd in a woman as ill as she made herself out to be—and simply denied flatly that she ever had diabetes, although Pickering himself had admitted she had. *One* of them must have been lying, as any judge must have seen.

When Mr. McCullough tried to cross-question her about consulting various doctors for diabetes the Judge headed him off every time. When he referred to the specialist the Judge said, "This is the first time we have heard of the specialist"—although Dr. Johnson had told the whole story of sending her to the specialist on the stand. When Mr. McCullough persisted in asking her the Judge said, "I don't believe she ever had diabetes or if she had she is cured," and then he said to her, "You needn't answer any more of those questions."

I could never have believed any reputable judge would say such a thing. It was incredible. Dr. Johnson, Pickering's own witness, not ours, had sworn she had diabetes and that her specialist had confirmed it; two experts had sworn that the symptoms she complained of were diabetic; her own husband had said she had it once. And everyone knows diabetes is an incurable disease—or was up to a few weeks ago when Dr. Banting's discovery[143] was given to the world. And nobody pretends that Mrs. P. had taken the insulin treatment. And yet the Judge could say "She never had diabetes or if she had she is cured!!!"

Mason Horner was next put on the stand. He swore that Ewan turned

---

143   In the early 1920s medical research had determined that diabetes resulted from a lack of a protein hormone, insulin, secreted by the pancreas. In November 1921 Dr George Banting (1891–1941), along with the help of student Charles Best (1899–1978) and others, devised a means of extracting insulin from fetal calves. By spring 1922 he had established a private practice. In 1923, at the age of 32, Banting would be awarded the Nobel Prize in Physiology or Medicine along with J.J.R. Macleod, Professor of Physiology at the University of Toronto.

the *second* time across the road. Of course Ewan did nothing of the sort. Pickering's car struck ours and knocked it round. Mason Horner *may* have honestly thought that Ewan turned the car—but it is a little suspicious when Horner is the son of "old Bill Horner" who is supposed to have put Pickering up to the whole thing. Horner is a law student and couched his testimony in clear-cut legal language which seemed to make a very favorable impression on the Judge. Besides, Phelan staged a piece of acting in pretending that Mason Horner was "an unwilling witness." *We* knew all about what was behind this pretence for Horner is in the office next to McCullough's; but Riddell swallowed it whole and believed it.

Then Risley swore to his lie and old Jack Urquhart, the oat-stealer, swore to another, saying he had seen Ewan talking to Law *after* the car had started.

Our side went on then. Ewan went first and did very well—and *told the truth*. Then my turn came. It was the most horrible ordeal I had ever endured, standing there before that crowded courtroom of curious Zephyr gossips— even though they were on our side. I felt very nervous but I did not make any mistakes and Phelan let me off surprisingly easy in his cross-examination. Law gave very good evidence and Mrs. Meyers, but Joe Taylor made an absurd mistake through nervousness which robbed his evidence of all value. The rest of our witnesses were not put on. John McCullough wanted to put them on, but James McCullough did not because he thought the Judge would only be exasperated and besides, he, McCullough, was sure the Judge would give *us* the verdict because of Pickering's admission of not slowing down at the corner. I wish now we had insisted on their being heard but it is always easy to be wise after the event.

Then Riddell summed up and gave Pickering his verdict saying that his negligence in not slowing down was negligence to the public at large, or something like that, and not towards us, and that if it hadn't been for the collision he might have "gone on for years" without an operation. He gave Pickering a thousand for his operation expenses and five hundred for his *"sufferings"*— Pickering, who is perfectly well today after suffering for years!—five hundred for Mrs. Pickering, and "expenses."

We got up and left the court. We smiled gallantly and I don't think anyone saw much in our faces. But it was the most trying and humiliating moment of all. I bore up until we got to our room at the hotel and then I broke down and cried bitterly. I knew I would have to pay the three thousand for Ewan has only his $1000 Victory Bond[144] and our own expenses would amount to that. To pay out three or four thousand of my hard-earned money was not a pleasant prospect but I would have done it cheerfully for an honest debt and never

144   See note 103, page 125.

given it another thought; but it was the horrible *injustice* of it all that hurt me. This was just a conspiracy on the part of the Pickerings and old Horner to get money out of me. Everybody knows it—and there is something in me that revolts against it.

Then Ewan came in and said, "I shall never pay or let you pay a cent of money to Marshall Pickering."

"You'll have to," I said despairingly. "If you don't they'll sell up our furniture and garnishee[145] the salary. You know we can't let *that* happen."

"The furniture is yours," he said.

"Not in the eyes of the law," I said, believing this at the time.

When we were married Ewan had no money. He had had to pay some college debts after he got through and he had moved about a good deal. Besides, Ewan has certainly no "knack" of saving money. So I paid for all the furniture. I lent him the money for the Victory bond, too, but he paid *all* our living expense;—not merely *half*, as was our arrangement—until that was paid back. So the bond was his morally as well as legally. But I thought the furniture would be considered *legally* his and so could be seized.

"Well, I'm not going to pay it," said Ewan stubbornly. "If he garnishees my salary I'll give up the ministry and go into something else, before I will bow to such injustice. And not one cent of your money shall go for what was not *your* fault, whoever was to blame."

But I had no fight left in me just then.

We went up to our lawyer's office. Ewan told them how matters stood. Mr. McCullough laughed. "I'm *glad*," he said—"not glad, of course that you haven't anything but glad that scoundrel can't get it."

"What about the furniture?" I said. "It is really mine but can we prove it?"

"How was it paid for?" he said.

"By my personal check"

"Oh, then it is all right—that check can be got from the bank any time."

"What about my salary?" asked Ewan.

"Let your congregation pay it monthly in advance and they can't touch it."

This was news to me and gave me some courage to go on fighting. I know it will mean a lot of worry for us, perhaps for years, but as long as Ewan feels like fighting them I will do anything in my power to get the better of that pair of plotters and perjurers.

We decided to appeal. Of course there isn't much chance, since we haven't got our evidence in. McCullough said there was one chance in ten—which is probably an over-favorable estimate. But the point is—we'll get time to open the congregation's eyes diplomatically to what must be done; *and* we'll give

---

145   A debtor's wages may be legally intercepted—"garnisheed"—to recover the debt.

Mr. Pickering enough law to satisfy him. He must learn that man can go to law when he likes but can't always stop when he likes.

When we left the lawyer's office it was five o'clock and beginning to snow. I suppose the sensible thing would have been to stay in Toronto all night. But Edith wanted to get home that night to her children; and I had the instinctive and imperative desire of the wounded animal to crawl away and hide. So we started, having telephoned our party to meet us at an uptown garage—they were all staying far out in a suburb. About four or five miles up town in a residential district Lady Jane, true to form, stopped. Ewan discovered that the little reservoir in front was empty of gas. We could not get any from our tank so there was nothing to do but go for gas. He had to go a long way. I stayed there, alone and cold—for it was turning very cold. It was snowing thickly. Cars of gay people streamed past. I felt so wretched and crushed that I was numb. After about an hour Ewan returned with gas and filled the reservoir. Even then Lady Jane wouldn't go. He had to work with her for over half an hour before she would start. I stood and held the flashlight with freezing hands and feet. The snow was getting thicker—I began to fear we would be stuck on the road home. And at that moment Marshall Pickering was probably spinning homeward in great spirits. Well, never mind, Mr. Pickering. He laughs best who laughs last. You may find, dear Mr. Pickering, that getting a verdict is not quite the same thing as getting my money!

Finally Lady Jane consented to go. We reached the garage where our party was to have met us. They were not there—nor did they come for two whole hours, having waited to get their suppers. If they had told us they were going to do this *we* might have got something, too—but they hadn't. I went into a neighboring drug store and paced the floor, wishing sickly that I could get home—only get home. Ewan was cool, composed and in good spirits. When Ewan is normal *nothing* upsets him. He has a most enviable equanimity. And when he isn't normal he is entirely the opposite.

At last they did come. We started—the lights of the city slipped past us like the gleaming, hungry eyes of hundreds of great stealthy panthers. It was nine o'clock; I had dismal forebodings; the snow was thick and if Lady Jane "acted up" again on that desolate road at that hour of the night what could we do—especially with old Mrs. Lockie?

But our evil genius had decided to take a rest. All went well. The snow stopped, the road was good, Lady Jane skimmed along like a bird. And, as always in a car, my spirits rose. I ceased to feel tired—or rather, my tiredness showed itself in a certain exaltation of feeling and imagination such as I sometimes experience when I am much fatigued. I felt suddenly full of vim and *fight* again. We would get the better of Marshall Pickering yet.

The drive home was not the nightmare it had promised to be. But still I was

very thankful when we got home. I got our guests a lunch and got them to bed. Then I went to bed, too. I can't say I slept much but I rested at least. Ewan, strange man, slept like a top.

In the morning Ewan took Mrs. Lockie and Mrs. Meyers home. He came back with the news that Zephyr was in a ferment. The people are furious. They are ready to tear the Pickerings in pieces. When Marshall Pickering phoned to someone that morning that he had won the suit a listening woman cut in[146] with, "Yes, you've won the suit but *you've lost your soul.*" I don't envy Marshall Pickering his existence in that community after this. He is so hated that everyone will be glad to cast things up to him. After the trial Law went up to Pickering and said to him on the steps of the courthouse, "You *lied* on the witness stand." Pickering, it is said, made no reply.

Today was fine but cold. We had the ordeal of going out to church and enduring *sympathy*—or rather the expression of sympathy. I mean, by that, that one likes to feel that people *do* sympathize but it *is* an ordeal to listen to their attempts at voicing it. But Ewan preached a splendid sermon and I think a certain family of Methodists who came to hear what they could got an earful. One of the sons is engaged to Verna Pickering—who has a very rank reputation, it is said. So of course they are on Pickering's side.

When Ewan came back from Zephyr he had some more news. Mason Horner was out yesterday and was nearly mobbed. The boys of Zephyr shouted "*Lie*-yer—*lie*-yer," after him every time he was seen out. He himself said to someone that "the trial was very one-sided."

The Pickering gang are telling that *I* "tore my handkerchief to pieces when I heard the verdict." Their genius for lying is not confined to the stand, it seems.

Ewan still talks continually of the trial—its injustice and absurdities. But I feel as if I couldn't *bear* to talk of it, now that it is over and talking can do no good. It hurts me. I want to forget it and so be able to go on with my regular work, putting the devilish thing behind me. I am feeling very flat and spiritless in the reaction after the long strain. I am as firmly resolved to fight as ever but I have no stomach for it. Tonight for the first time since the trial I cried bitterly. It seems to me this thing will hang over us all our lives and in my present mood I cannot bear the thought of it. If Ewan would agree I would give in now, pay the money and be free. But Ewan is resolved and I know by experience that it is no use to try to move him.

---

146   In the days before wireless communication, telephony operated very differently than it does now. Up until a few decades ago in some rural regions, a neighbourhood would be connected to a single telephone wire, with specific rings to identify each house. Curious neighbours could easily pick up the phone and listen, even if they knew a given call was not for them.

Poor little Stuart! Yesterday morning at breakfast, when our visitors were joking over Marshall Pickering, saying he would have to seize the old cutter and Ewan's books, Stuart threw his arms around me and exclaimed, "Never mind, mother, Mr. Pickering can't take *me* from you."

No, he can't, darling. And I ought not to worry when he can't touch anything vital. But I've had so much worry and grief in these hard last five years that at times I feel as if I could not bear even an added pin prick. But these moods pass and I can always pick up and go on. What a blessing Ewan is so well this fall! If he had been as he was last fall what could we have done—except knuckled under and paid him all he wanted to get out of trouble,—him, the perjurer and blackmailer!

Monday, November 27, 1922
Leaskdale, Ont.

I slept better last night and felt today as if I were getting back to normal but still so tired—too tired even to realize yet that the trial is *over* and that no matter what comes the worst is past. I can't *feel* that yet; its incubus still burdens me. Tonight I could not help going over the trial in my mind and raging at the injustice of it. *That* is what hurts. If we had had *no* evidence I would not feel that the Judge had been unfair, but we *had* and he either barred it out practically or totally disregarded it. He gave that woman damages on her own say-so, although she had *no* medical testimony in her favor and we had the best against it. I have always heard that the plaintiff had to *prove* his injuries but in her case there was no proof of any kind. So I *do* feel that Riddell was very unfair.

Ewan went to Toronto today and Lily went home, so I am all alone and very heartsick. If I only had Frede to talk this out to! I could not talk of it to any other creature.

Tuesday, Nov. 28, 1922

I began writing again today and found that while I was at it I could abstract my mind from the real and live in the ideal. But as soon as I stop writing the real confronts me again.

Lily came back today bringing a flood of gossip about Pickering. One tale is that he had to borrow the money from old Horner to pay his lawyer. If he is in old Horner's clutches God help him. That old Jew lives only to make money by shifty tricks and cares no more for Pickering than for anyone else.

Ewan isn't home yet. I feel very lonely.

Wednesday, Nov.29, 1922

Ewan got home last night at twelve. We have entered our appeal. He also says that if it fails he will take the case to the Supreme Court at Ottawa.

I felt fairly well today until the early dark came—then I got very blue again. But I went out and led the Guild; then I walked home alone under the dark, cloudy sky and felt as if nothing good could ever happen to me again.

Saturday, Dec. 2, 1922
Leaskdale, Ont.

Thursday I went to Toronto to shop and stayed in until this evening. I had a rather miserable time. I can't as yet shake off the *effects* of over worry. I am nervous and restless much of the time, especially if I am away from home; and can't enjoy anything. The crowds of shoppers made me still wearier and I wandered around and did my buying without any of my usual pleasure in it. I stayed at a hotel, feeling that I *couldn't* visit friends and be asked about the trial a dozen times over. Ewan met me at Uxbridge this evening and we had a pleasant drive home in the mild wintery twilight. He said he had been to see James Mustard,[147] the Leaskdale treasurer, and Mr. Mustard said that if Pickering tried to garnishee our salary he could be "easily outwitted there." This raised my spirits. In my depressed state I had got it into my head that perhaps our people wouldn't back us up—a foolish fear, for I know exactly how they feel about it. But I knew Leaskdale would be all right. I wish I felt as sure about Zephyr. Of course, the Zephyr people are even more indignant at Pickering than the Leaskdale people, being nearer and hating him personally. But Will Lockie is treasurer there and he is such an oddity that there is no counting on what he will or will not do.

Monday, December 4, 1922

I have slept poorly for a week, waking at three, and not being able to sleep again. In waking hours I am restless and nervous, savoring nothing. But last night I slept better, not waking till six, and have felt better today than any day yet.

I was in Uxbridge today and met old George Allan Smith who had to stop me and ask all about the trial. I do hate talking about it. I would forget it—let it heal over—if people would let me—wouldn't tear the wound open with questions.

---

147   The Mustards were a prominent local family; Hugh and James Mustard were the brothers of John Mustard. (See note 85, page 43.)

"Well," said old George, when I finished, "everybody says he just tore up the street and run right into you. It's a funny thing that he could get damages for *that*."

Natheless, he did. The thing is so un-understandable to the simple country folk that they are all asserting that "Pickering bribed the Judge." This is absurd, of course. I do not think that Riddell, though egotistic and prejudiced, is the kind of judge who could be bribed—certainly not by any sum Pickering could be likely to offer. But the story shows how puzzled the people are over the verdict when they can only account for it by such a supposition.

Tuesday, Dec. 5, 1922
Leaskdale, Ont.

I am beginning to be able to *forget* for a few minutes at a time, which is a hopeful sign. Soon I'll be able to forget *all* the time except when some external incident or remark recalls it—of which there will doubtless be plenty for a time at least.

The most interesting department of *The Globe* now is the report of the appeals at Osgoode Hall. I study them with painful interest. I note that more of Riddell's cases are appealed than any other judge's. I note also that in almost every case he has given the plaintiff the verdict. It seems to be a habit of his.

Thursday, Dec. 7, 1922

Tonight we were at Richard Curl's in Zephyr and supped gloriously on venison steak—the said Richard being a mighty hunter in the season. He is also a bitter hater of Pickering and said "Don't you pay him one cent. Everybody round here knows that man and his wife have been doctoring for years. He always has been a notorious liar anyhow."

Saturday, Dec. 9, 1922

Last night I had my last ride in old Lady Jane. Today Ewan took her to Cannington and sold her. I saw her go with no regret. From first to last she has been a hoodooed car.

She really was my car of course, since I paid for her. But luckily she was registered in Ewan's name so was legally his. If she had been in my name Pickering could have come on me for his damages. I fancy his lawyers were a little disappointed when they found out she was in Ewan's name.

Wednesday, Dec. 13, 1922

Every time we go to Zephyr we pick up some new bits of gossip. Today Mrs. Bingham told us that Dr. Johnson told her that if the medical men who were at the trial banded together they could "make it hot" for the Judge. Of course I don't think they could do anything of the sort but it shows Johnson's opinion—and he was Pickering's witness. He is furious because the Judge believed Mrs. Pickering and not him in regard to her diabetes. In nothing more than in his treatment of Johnson's evidence was the Judge's bias so clearly shown. He believed the part that testified to congestion in Pickering's notorious gland and rejected the part that testified to her diabetes. Mrs. Bingham also said that the Zephyr boys would have pelted Mason Horner that day he was out with rotten eggs if they could have found any.

We hear that Mr. Pickering is "very mad" because we have appealed. Poor Mr. Pickering! I suppose he fondly dreams that no one should appeal to the law for justice but him. I expect he will be "madder" still before spring.

Saturday, December 16, 1922

Stuart has had a cold and sore throat for a couple of weeks and today I discovered that the gland under his ear was badly swollen. It worries me—although I remember that my worry over a similar gland in Chester's neck that terrible winter seven years ago was needless and I tell myself I am foolish. I was alone this evening and got very restless and depressed. I wildly wanted some of *my own gang* to talk to and laugh with—Bertie or Stell or Margaret. "Oh, for one hour" of any of them! But it cannot be!

The papers nowadays are filled with *radio*.[148] Dr. Shier has a set and he told me recently that last Sunday morning he heard a sermon preached in Pittsburg, Pa. in the morning and one in Chicago in the evening. It is all very wonderful—and I find it a little depressing. Is it because I'm getting on in life that all these wonderful inventions and discoveries, treading on each other's heels, give me a sense of weariness and a longing to go back to the slower years of old? Doubtless that has something to do with it. But I do really think we are rushing on rather fast. It keeps humanity on tiptoe. And all these things don't make the world or the people in it any *happier*. But I think this will go on for two or three hundred years—I mean the flood of great discoveries and inventions. Then probably the Zeit Geist[149] will get tired and take a rest for a

148   The first "wireless telegraphy" emerged in the late 1800s. When the US joined the war in 1917, however, it became illegal for private citizens to operate radios (radio usage was reserved for war communication). After 1919, the technology continued to develop, and early broadcasting stations came into existence, including KDKA in Pittsburgh and WDAP in Chicago.
149   *Zeitgeist* is a German word meaning "spirit of the time" or "spirit of the age."

few centuries and allow humanity to rest with him. But those of us living now have to speed on with him willy nilly.

In a generation or two *letters* will be obsolete. Everyone will talk to absent friends the world over by *radio*. It will be nice; but something will be lost with letters. The world can't eat its cake and have it, too. And none of these things really "save time." They only fill it more breathlessly full. That is all right for the young. But I look back to the old '90's with a feeling that they were a nice unhurried leisurely time. But perhaps that is only because I lived in a remote little country place eleven miles from a railway. Even today life is very unhurried and peaceful in Cavendish. Yes, I daresay that is the explanation.

I have recently been reading the life of Tennyson by his son.[150] It is a delightful book because of its atmosphere and background. It has always seemed to me that life among the "gentlefolk" of England must be—or was then—as nearly an ideal existence as can be found on this planet. I have always felt, when reading books reflecting it, that it was above all others the sort of life I should have liked to live—the one that most appeals to me. Today my reading Tennyson's life filled me with a sort of envy of that intercourse with congenial souls that was always his—going and coming. That is so wholly lacking in my life.

But if Ewan only keeps well I will be content—I will not complain of what is lacking. After all, books are wonderful companions.

I have been busy lately decanting "home brew." Last summer I made some red currant wine and some raspberry wine, from my recollection of Grandmother's method. Grandmother was famed for her currant wine. It *was* delicious—even Chateau Yquem[151] was not much its superior. I was doubtful of my success for I was not sure I remembered her whole process and I knew of many folk who had followed her recipe straightly and produced but a sorry beverage. But either I had good luck or I have inherited some of her brain cells for my "brew" is delicious—clear, ruby, sparkling with a quite sufficient "bite." I made it mainly for Ewan who seems to feel better and brighter after an occasional glass of it. But he doesn't need it now for he keeps perfectly well. Oh, if it only continues!

Friday, December 22, 1922
Leaskdale, Ont.

Had a letter from Stella today which did me good—she raved so wholeheartedly over Pickering. Stella's last few letters have been uncannily cheerful anyhow. She seems suddenly to have begun to feel very well and there isn't a growl

---

150   *Alfred, Lord Tennyson and his Friends* had been published in 1911 by Tennyson's son Hallam.
151   Château d'Yquem is a fine wine from the Bordeaux region in France.

in them. The difference between her recent epistles and all those of the past ten years is amazing and blessed and I pray fervently that it continues. But I have my doubts.

Chester has finished his school exams and got honors—78%. He started in by getting only 50% for writing and 56 for arithmetic—his poorest subjects—and I felt discouraged but after that he came right along. But, though a great reader, he isn't a student at all—at least as yet. Perhaps the desire will waken later—it did in both Ewan and me.

Tuesday, December 26, 1922

Christmas is over—a pleasanter Christmas than I have had for several years, as Ewan was well and cheerful. Stuart's neck is getting all right, too.

Lily was home for Xmas and brought back some gossip about Pickering. He is said to be "a changed man"—"looks miserable"—"doesn't want to talk" etc. I have heard this from other sources. I fancy he is feeling his loss of caste and standing. They say his perjury is constantly cast up to him and the boys hoot it after him on the streets. Many members of his Bible class have stopped attending, averring that they will not be "taught by a perjurer," etc. All this seems to have pierced even his iron hide.

Two men from Toronto, who were in Mt. Albert the other day, total strangers to both us and Pickering, said they were at the trial and never saw or heard anything so manifestly unfair and one-sided.

We certainly should have had a jury.

Thursday, December 28, 1922
Leaskdale, Ont.

I am feeling like myself again. Today for the first time in months I felt my old rapturous, *indwelling* sense of the imperishable beauty in life and in the world. It was glorious to experience it again.

We were out to supper tonight with a nice family and had a pleasant time. Mr. Barton talked of the trial and said that he had never known a trial concerning which there was such absolute unanimity of opinion. In most trials, he said, some would be on one side, some on the other, but in this everywhere there was just the one thing said.

"A trial like this," he said, "should be held in a place where a man is known. Up in Toronto they didn't know what sort of a couple Pickering and his wife are, so the Judge believed them. If that had been tried where they were known you would have won."

Very true; but the Judge didn't even give us any chance to show by our

witnesses that Pickering was lying. He didn't *want* to believe or to be compelled to believe that Pickering was lying because that would have made it harder for him to decide the case in P's favor. It was all simple enough if he could shut out any evidence that would prove Pickering was lying. Talk about justice! I *do* feel bitter when I think of that farcical trial.

Sunday, Dec. 31, 1922

The last day of the old year—the old miserable worried year. It closes in gloom again. All Friday Ewan's head trouble and melancholia returned with the uncanny suddenness of all his attacks. No doubt he will be miserable all winter now, in addition to all our other worries. I feel disheartened. It is all the harder to endure after this long time when he has seemed quite well and which led me to hope, in spite of the repeated experiences of the past four years, that this time he was really well. I have even dared to think that this Pickering trial was a blessing in disguise, since it cured him—a device of Ormuzd to hoodwink Ahrimanes![152] I feel that I *can't* face the winter. But of course I *will* face it—and live through it somehow. One has to.

152　Mythical figures from the spirituality of ancient Zoroastrianism.

1923

Tuesday, Jan. 2, 1923
The Manse, Leaskdale, Ont.

It absolutely makes me wince when people wish me "a Happy New Year." It seems such a mockery. I wish they wouldn't.

The holidays are over and the boys started to school again. I get up before daylight to get them and Lily up, prepare their lunch and get them off. If I were not unhappy and worried I wouldn't mind this. But somehow, as it is, it seems unreasonably nasty to get up thus in the dark and cold—a dark that reluctantly fades out into dull bitter gray. The manse is always bitterly cold these mornings. Owing to the coal strike last fall we could not get any hard coal and have to burn wood and soft coal. The furnace is not suited to this and the result is discomfort every way—a cold house—gas—smoke—dirt. Everything has a smear of fine black grime over it and the curtains and silver turn as yellow as brass in a few days. These in themselves are small things but it makes the big troubles harder to endure cheerfully when your flesh is goosey and your eyes are smarting with smoke.

I have been desperately lonely this evening. It is a cold stormy night and the snow is heaping up around the manse. I was all alone as usual after the boys had gone to bed—and I was tired after working hard all day and wanted some companionship. But there is none. Ewan in the grip of this horrible malady is as a stranger. He is interested in nothing—he is absolutely indifferent to me and the children. We mean nothing to him—in fact, I feel that he thinks our presence and existence irksome to him, as reminders of responsibilities he wants to forget or ignore. He has never actually turned against us—so far I have been spared that. He is simply indifferent to us and to all that concerns us and our home.

The heart asks pleasure first,
And then—excuse from pain,
And then—those little anodynes
That deaden suffering
And then—to go to sleep,
And then—if it should be the will
Of its inquisitor
The liberty to die.

So wrote Emily Dickinson bitterly—and I fear truly. I have got along to humbly asking for the "anodynes." Not yet have I asked to go to sleep or to die—no, life is too interesting in spite of its torture. And I want to live until my children can do without me. Sometimes when I get disheartened and discouraged in these gray, merciless days and worried nights I fear that I will not live—will have to leave my children without any real protector or guide. This is all foolish. So far as I know I am perfectly healthy and never felt better in my life. But at present I cannot believe that the "Inquisitor" is anything but capricious Cruelty.

Saturday, Jan. 6, 1923
The Manse, Leaskdale, Ont.

This has been a week of intense cold. Ewan has been very dull—much worse than last week. I have especially noticed this week the *repulsive* expression his features assume in these attacks. It changes his whole face. He is like a stranger. I cannot bear to look at him. That dull, sullen face, with its wild, haunted eyes, is so miserably unlike his normal cheerful smiling face with its dimples and roguish eyes. The change seems incredible.

Monday, Jan. 8, 1923

The bitter cold continues unbrokenly. But Ewan seems a little brighter and Stuart's neck is almost well.

Tonight I have been studying Emile Coue's book on "Auto Suggestion."[153] I believe a great deal can be done by suggestion, especially in the training of children. I always go in to Stuart and Chester every night when they are asleep and "suggest" various things to them. I have had a good measure of success, too, and cured Chester of some annoying nervous habits which all ordinary efforts failed to break. But I can not believe that it is the universal cure-all Coue claims. And I don't think that repeating "Every day in every way I'm getting better and better" twenty times before we go to sleep will make us all into angels.

Still, as I have said, I believe there is a good deal in it and I believe Auto Suggestion would help Ewan if he would try it. But he will not. This is the difficulty in his case. He will *not* believe there is anything the matter with him—he is, he insists, simply unforgiven for sin—and he will not try *any* method of curing himself. Besides, he seems incapable of making any continued mental effort. I have tried to "suggest" helpful ideas to him when he is asleep but the trouble is he always wakes up at once, he sleeps so lightly

153   See LMM's entry for September 18, 1922, and accompanying note 102 (page 55).

and my "suggestions" have no chance to work. Not that it matters much. I feel that Ewan's trouble is constitutional and too deeply rooted to be charmed away by formulae.

I read a book tonight that gave me much pleasure—*The Key of Dreams*.[154] In spite of its title it had nothing to do with dreams. I did not care for the love-story or the characters but I revelled in the exquisite descriptions of Japanese scenery and atmosphere.

Lately I re-read *Kate Carnegie*.[155] I don't think I've read it for fifteen years. The "Ian MacLaren" books had a tremendous vogue twenty years ago—and deserved it. There is a great gulf fixed between them and the nauseous sex stuff that pours from the press today. The atmosphere of *Kate* is delightful. I seemed to be back in the Cavendish of my childhood. There was the same tang and charm and simplicity in people, place and religion. One had a sense of "time to grow."

Friday, Jan. 19, 1923

We had very cold stormy weather lately. The days pass in a dull routine. On some days Ewan seems very dull, on others much better. We are beginning to expect the hearing of the appeal any day now and I find the suspense hard. I don't *want* to hope because I feel sure we can't win; and I can't *help* hoping, because it would be so heavenly to be freed from the whole wretched business. If we lose we will always have a sword of Damocles hanging over our heads. And it seems to me that I have had almost unbroken worry all my life since I was twenty. I want a change.

I had a dear bit of a walk all by myself tonight—in a soft white twilight under a young moon. The night was all my own and it was very kind to me. I bowed me down to my ancient gods. It was like a bit out of the olden years and lightened a little my present disgust of life. But the walk ended in an evening spent, in Jane Welsh Carlyle's splendid phrase, "under a harrow."[156] We were visiting a family where the ill-trained youngsters kept up such a ceaseless riot

---

154　Published in 1922 by Lily Adams Beck, *The Key of Dreams: A Romance of the Orient* explores Buddhism and the human emotion of love.

155　*Kate Carnegie and Those Ministers* is an 1896 novel by Scottish Presbyterian minister John Watson, who wrote under the pen name "Ian MacLaren." MacLaren's work included LMM's early favourites like *Beside the Bonnie Brier Bush* (1894); she wrote a paper on MacLaren while at Dalhousie University.

156　LMM likely knew literary figure Jane Welsh Carlyle through *Letters and Memorials of Jane Welsh Carlyle* (1883). In a letter dated August 27, 1843, Carlyle wrote, "I feel as if I had spent the evening under a harrow."

of yells and pursuit that I could hardly hear a word anyone was saying. And the people talked of Marshall Pickering *ad nauseam*. To be sure, they abused him whole heartedly but we have heard so much of that and it doesn't get us anywhere and keeps us all raw and sore. If only I might never hear Marshall Pickering's name again!

Towards the end of the evening I abstracted myself behind my knitting and while the children romped and yelled and their mother scolded them ceaselessly and ineffectively I deadened unpleasant sensations by formulating a

[Lottie Shatford's card]

theory of my own concerning life—what it was and how it entered into matter. But I shall not write it here. My descendents and readers can guess at it. It works out quite as reasonably as any other theory I have ever heard or read. One guess is as good as another at the ultimate mystery.

I was glancing over some old "autograph albums" the other night. There are no such things nowadays and they are generally mentioned as laughable and "Victorian" rural fads. Myself, I think they were rather nice, as so many "Victorian" things were. In one I came across Lottie Shatford's. It is so good that I retrieved it from the somewhat battered old album and I paste it here for preservation. It was out of place in that collection of rather silly and conventional verses. Lottie was a very clever girl but somehow the memory of our old acquaintance has no aroma. It is a mere dry, dead fact. She was not sealed of my tribe.

Sunday, Jan. 21, 1923
The Manse, Leaskdale

Ewan was at David Graham's in Zephyr this evening for tea and picked up some Pickeringiana. Marshall P. complained to Mrs. Graham not long ago that "No one congratulated him after the trial"—"they all crowded around Macdonald."

Poor Pickering! What could they congratulate him on—committing perjury? Mrs. Graham told him she had heard "Mr. Macdonald was so fixed he couldn't pay." "Oh," said Pickering. "Mrs. Macdonald will pay rather than

have the judgment hanging over them. If Mr. Macdonald had had nothing but his salary I wouldn't have sued him. But I knew Mrs. Macdonald had money."

Well, we have always known it was just a conspiracy to get money out of me but I am afraid Mr. Pickering will find I have no intention of paying his hospital bills. They say he is worrying terribly for fear he will lose the appeal or fail to get "his" money even if he wins. He is so changed that people who have known him for years met him recently and didn't recognize him. Verily, I believe in his heart he wishes he had never taken a step in the matter.

Wednesday, Jan. 24, 1923
Leaskdale, Ont.

Ewan was in Toronto yesterday conferring with the McCulloughs. John McC. told him that he had seen appeals won where there wasn't half so good a chance as in ours. I wish he would not say such things. They encourage us to hope in spite of ourselves and then failure will have an added bitterness. For myself I do not mind but I dread the effect on Ewan. He has been very dull lately. And yet sometimes I think these normal worries and disappointments do not affect him at all. His preoccupation of religious dread protects him from any annoyance from them.

This evening we went out visiting. When we started I felt dreadfully depressed and down-hearted. But as we drove on through the woods my spirits rose. It was a strange weird night—cloudy but with a moon behind the clouds—snowing softly and wetly but quite calm. We drove through woods and swamps where the trees were covered with white and looked like great ranks of spectres standing in sorrowful enchantment. There was something in the eerie beauty of the landscape that thrilled a chord in my spirit and my being responded to the music. So that, in spite of Ewan's gloomy silence and the monotonous evening with a family so dull that they make others dull sandwiched between our drives, I felt oddly happy and delighted, with a secret inner happiness and delight—as of a "fountain sealed" somewhere deep in my soul where no drop of poison from the outward universe could distill. "The kingdom of God is within you."[157]

We came home early. Ewan went to bed but I settled down for a bit of reading. Something I read suddenly recalled to mind a curious little incident of my childhood. I was I think about eleven or twelve. I was up in the loft of our "new barn," playing with a kitten. The loft was filled almost to the roof with wheat straw and I was on top of it about forty feet from the floor. I made a dive

---

157   Luke 17:21.

to catch my kitten, the slippery straw slid from under my feet and I shot head downward to the floor. Now, the curious thing about the experience was this. I could only have been one or two seconds in falling. Yet in that time I thought *five* distinct and deliberate thoughts with, so it seemed to me, quite a long interval between them. The first thought, as I felt myself falling was, "What has happened?" After what seemed an appreciable interval another part of me answered, "I am falling." Then I asked, "What will become of me when I strike the floor?" A second interval. The other part again answered, "I will be killed."

A third interval. Then I thought clearly and un-hurriedly, "Well, I do not care."

And neither did I. I knew I was going to be killed and it did not alarm me in the least. I was absolutely indiffer-ent. Then I struck—not on the floor but on a huge

The new barn.

pile of chaff. I was almost buried in it but I was not at all hurt save for the discomfort of chaff grains down my neck and in eyes, nose and hair.

I have never forgotten the experience and the strange leisurely way those questions and answers seemed to come in that brief moment. And the memory has always been a comfort to me. I do not think I will be afraid of death when it really comes. It will be just the same as it was then.

I think this explains the calmness and courage with which many have faced death in the past—as for instance the great Argyle[158] found soundly sleeping when the executioner came to call him—or, to take a totally different example, the composure of most criminals at the last. The courage of Argyle has been praised—and the courage of the criminal wondered at. But was it courage in either case? I think not—even though Argyle was a brave man. Courage must mean, if it means anything, facing bravely something we do dread. There is no

---

158   LMM, who traced her roots to Scotland, had a long-standing interest in Scottish history, particularly stories that for her were associated with Highland romance. Here the reference is to Archibald Campbell, the 8th Earl of Argyll and Chief of the Highland Clan Campbell. Born in 1607, Campbell was a Scottish nobleman and politician, as well as a leader of the Covenanters—a movement whose goal was to uphold Presbyterianism in Scotland. After several years of political turmoil following the Restoration of Charles II, Campbell was imprisoned in the Tower of London on charges of treason. In 1661 he was executed on the orders of Charles II. Argyll was famously calm and courageous in the days and hours leading up to his execution.

courage if there is no dread. And I believe nature simply did for those men at the last what she did for me—took away all the dread and left them indifferent to their fate as I was during that infinitesimal moment which seemed so long during which I was falling from the loft.

Thursday, Jan. 25, 1923
The Manse, Leaskdale, Ont.

It is four years today since Frede died. And tonight how fierce is my yearning for her. Oh, if I could only see that door open and Frede enter—sit down here beside me—talk, laugh. Oh, surely the jests of heaven have had more spice since she has shared in them. She can never come—the door can never open to her. Oh, my God, what a stab of pain comes with the thought! Oh, my friend—my friend! There isn't any *you*. You may be here in the spirit—but I want you in the flesh. I want you to grow old with me. Now, in old age, if I ever reach it, I shall have to remember things alone.

Sunday, Jan. 28, 1923

The bitter cold continues without any cessation. Ewan has been very miserable. On Friday he was about as bad as I have ever seen him. He could not even read—he walked the floor restlessly and looked wild and tortured. And there is no help. What help is there for a man who believes or fears that he is eternally lost.

Yet he preached quite well this morning. It is curious how he can. When he is compelled to do a thing he can do it and while doing it forgets all his dreads and terrors. Then, when it is finished, they return. While he is preaching or when he is out in company he can banish or control them. No one would then suspect his real condition.

The other day I received a letter from the Secretary of the Royal Society of Arts of Great Britain,[159] telling me that "the Council" had decided to invite me to become a "Fellow." This is a great compliment and one I certainly never dreamed of receiving. I am, it seems, the first Canadian woman to whom this honor has been offered. I wish Frede could have known of it. There is no one else to care very much, since my sons are not old enough to feel proud of it. Years ago I wrote in my portfolio that I meant "to climb the Alpine Path" and

159   Founded in 1754, the Royal Society is dedicated to "finding practical solutions to social challenges."

"write upon its shining scroll a woman's humble name."[160] I suppose I may say I have climbed it. After that humble name I shall henceforth have the right to write "F.R.S.A." But the real reward of the climb has not been the attainment of the crest but the wood violets and mountain fern gathered by the way—and the glimpses along the path of shining heights and golden valleys afar.

I have to go next week to Stratford and Mitchell to give readings.[161] I wish I did not have to go when Ewan is so miserable and when we expect the appeal some day next week. When I promised in the fall to go Ewan was so well. But I must go—and indeed I know I need something of the sort to pry me out of a certain rut of morbid feeling that I have got into this past month of cold and dread and petty annoyances.

Saturday, Feb. 3, 1923
Leaskdale, Ont.

I am home again. I had a delightful time while away and feel ever so much better, brighter and braver. I got back my proper perspective while away and can see *around* things now that have been blocking up my vision. The uplift of this ought to carry me through February at least. I felt dull enough when I left home last Tuesday. But I resolved that since I had to go I would *not* take my worries with me—I could leave them behind. Sometimes I cannot do this. At other times I can. This was one of the other times. I seemed to turn a lock on certain rooms in my house of life and did not enter them while I was away. The result was that I had a very happy and pleasant four days. Wednesday I spent in Toronto shopping and had lunch at the National Club with Mr. McClelland and Mr. Stewart.[162] This is something I always enjoy. The National is a nice place to eat and Messrs Mac. and S. are always agreeable companions. I went to Stratford that afternoon and spent the night at the manse there with Mr. and Mrs. Finlay Matheson—a delightful pair of people. Thursday morning I went to Mitchell a town twelve miles from Stratford. In the afternoon I spoke and read to the High School Students and in the evening at a "banquet" given

---

160   As a child, LMM pasted a poem entitled "The Fringed Gentian" into her scrapbook. The poem was from part of a longer narrative, *Tam, the Story of a Woman,* by Ella Rodman Church and Augusta De Bubna. In 1917, LMM published a series of autobiographical essays, "The Alpine Path," in the Toronto magazine *Everywoman's World.* In her own writing, LMM often referred to "the alpine path" as a metaphor for her own progress.

161   Stratford is a city some 200 km/125 miles southwest of Leaskdale; Mitchell is a smaller community to the northwest.

162   John McClelland and George Stewart were LMM's Toronto publisher (McClelland & Stewart). The National Club is a private club founded in 1874.

by the I.O.D.E.[163] About one hundred and fifty were present, half of course being men. I had never spoken to an audience of men before and I felt rather nervous at first but got on all right and everyone seemed pleased. We had a "spluxious" dinner and the Regent of the Chapter presented me with a bouquet of roses. On Friday morning I returned to Stratford and the Executive of the Canadian Club gave me a luncheon at the Windsor and another bouquet of roses.[164] In the afternoon I addressed the Club and enjoyed it. The audience seemed to also. But one lady told my hostess afterwards that she "really had not been able to listen" to what I was saying because she was "so taken up with *watching my beautiful hands and feet*"! Poor soul! I ought to wear brogans[165] and fur mitts the next time I speak.

I left Stratford—which must in summer be a wonderfully pretty place—at six and reached Toronto at 9.30 exceedingly tired. But I got a magazine and a box of my favorite candy (pecan roll, for the information of readers two hundred years hence!) and had a gorgeous revel of reading before I went to sleep. I came home this morning and on the train out unlocked the doors of my skeleton closet. I dreaded coming home. But Ewan seemed quite cheerful again and the appeal has not yet been heard so, if no news of success met me, I did not at least have to brace up against defeat.

I *wish* the appeal was over. We are awaiting it from day to day now and the suspense embitters life.

Tuesday, Feb. 6, 1923
Leaskdale, Ont.

I had a curious dream last night. I dreamed that a big box was delivered at our door "from Zephyr." I opened it and found therein a *coffin*. I opened the coffin and found it packed full of *candy*. I said, "Why, this is not a coffin at all. It is a Christmas box." Then I found myself in a strange room looking at another coffin which was on the table and which someone in the room told me "came from the direction of Peterboro." But as I looked at it, it faded away like mist.

The symbolism of the first coffin is plain enough. We will lose the appeal but the result will not injure us. But the meaning of the second coffin, which must refer to the appeal to Ottawa is not so clear. Why did it fade away?

163   See note 72, page 37, on the Imperial Order Daughters of the Empire (I.O.D.E.).
164   Founded in 1897, the Canadian Club organized speeches from a range of topics, notably politics, business, and the arts.
165   Brogans, or "Brogues," are sturdy, ankle-high boots, originally from Scotland and Ireland, for use in the marshy countryside.

In a magazine I was reading today I found a poem on a woman's favorite dresses—and a very dainty fanciful little bit of verse it was, too. It set me thinking of all the dresses I have had—and my favorites among them. Most of my dresses have been pretty ones. Grandmother had good taste in materials and I, myself, am not supposed to be lacking in the quality. But of course some I liked better than others. My first "favorite" dress was a silver-gray "pongee,"[166] trimmed with black velvet ribbon, which I had when I was about eleven. It was one of the prettiest dresses I ever had and I loved it all the more because it was a welcome change from the red cashmere which was the fashionable thing for little girls in my childhood. I had had several red cashmere dresses trimmed with plush or velvet—very nice dresses they were as dresses went then but I really never liked them, never having cared for red as a color. My shining silvery dress was very dear to my heart. My next favorite was a cream delaine[167] with a blue spot, trimmed with lace, which father sent me, followed in my affections by a dress of golden-brown material which I had when I went out west—very pretty material made in a very pretty way. I did not again have a favorite dress until my year at P.W.C. when I had a cream challie blouse[168] with a spray of purple violets in it, which, with its daintily puffed sleeves and lace bertha was one of the prettiest and most becoming things I ever had. It was made by Maggie Stuart, a Cavendish dressmaker who never had any training but was a born artist in her line. I've never seen her dresses equalled anywhere; and in those days of tightly fitting robes her ability to make "a perfect fit" was something uncanny. Her dresses always made you, in the country phrase, look as if you had been melted and poured into them. She, too, made my next favorite—a dress I had that miserable spring in Belmont, of some silvery-blue figured goods, with "bell" skirt and "butterfly" sleeves. It would no doubt look very funny nowadays but it was a beautiful dress in its time. My next dress love was a flowered organdy made up over yellow sateen[169]—a

---

166   Pongee is a type of woven fabric, often from "tussah" or raw silk, usually tan in colour, with an uneven or "slubbed" effect from the style of weaving. In the early twentieth century it was often woven in China.

167   "Delaine" is derived from the French word for wool; it is a fabric of high-grade woolen or worsted produced by finely combing wool fibres.

168   Challie—nowadays usually spelled "challis"—is a lightweight woven fabric, traditionally made from cotton or cotton and wool, a thin, soft drape with a matte texture. In an entry of June 8, 1894, describing a trip to the Opera House in Charlottetown for her graduation from Prince of Wales College, LMM described the blouse: "After tea we dressed in a flutter of excitement. I wore my cream challie with a bunch of pansies. Ida came along and we set out in great state for the Opera House."

169   Sateen is usually spun from mercerised cotton fibres (mercerisation is a treatment to make the fibre smooth); it is woven like traditional satin to give it a smooth, shiny look.

lovely thing and very becoming. Later on I had another something like it—my bridesmaid dress when Bertha was married—an organdy[170] with a purple flower and silk stripe. Two dresses that I got in Boston were lovely—my old rose "hobble skirt" dress and my apricot evening one. My trousseau dresses were all pretty and smart but the only one I really call a favorite was a black one of silk striped net. Two years later I had a lovely thing of brown charmeuse[171] with a jacket of heavy cream lace. My latest favorite was the French evening dress of shot old-rose-and-pale-green and Honiton lace[172] I got five years ago. I've never had anything since that I loved though I've had many pretty and becoming dresses. I think the fashions of today are very beautiful—the simple lines and classical effects which never look odd or queer—as do the crinolines, polonaises, bustles and huge puffed sleeves[173] and similar monstrosities of Victorian days—though some of the extremely short skirts look foolish enough on tall or stout figures. Well, most of those dresses of mine have been long outworn and gone into the limbo of forgotten things, with all their daintiness and beauty, along with the passions and hopes and fears of the years in which they were worn. *Sic transit gloria mundi!*[174]

My day for the frilly gowns of organdy and lace is over—henceforth I must wear the richer hues and materials of the matron. But I shall never be indifferent to dress. It is a very foolish woman who is—just as foolish as the one who makes it the foremost and only thing. Both are badly mistaken.

Thursday, Feb. 8, 1923
The Manse, Leaskdale, Ont.

We visited the Taylors of Shiloh tonight—a family of Zephyr congregation. Poor Mr. Taylor has been lying awake o'nights worrying over our case, believing that Mr. Macdonald would have to pay Pickering so much per month out of his salary or go to jail. When he found out that there could be no "jail," he

---

170   Organdy is a light, fine, sheer cotton fabric, with the strands twisted tightly and a "crisp" finish, often used for formal women's wear.

171   Charmeuse is a smoothly woven silk dress fabric.

172   Shot silk is a fabric woven from two or more colours, producing an iridescent appearance. Honiton lace is a traditional hand-made lace from Honiton, Devon, in England.

173   LMM is referring to a series of fashions from her own living memory. A crinoline is made from stiffened fabric (or a hoop) used as a petticoat to give fullness to a skirt. A polonaise is a formal dress with a draped overskirt. A bustle consists of a support framework, often made of stiffened fabric, designed to expand the fullness of a woman's dress at the back (Aunt Laura wears a small bustle in *Emily of New Moon*; Aunt Elizabeth disapproves of the style). Puffed sleeves were a fashion of the Edwardian age; Anne in *Anne of Green Gables* famously wanted a dress with "puffed sleeves."

174   "Thus passes the glory of the world" (Latin).

was enormously relieved. "I will be the proudest man on this earth, Mr. Macdonald, if he can't get one cent from you," he exclaimed.

Sunday, Feb. 11, 1923

Ewan did not sleep well last night. This is the first night he has been troubled with sleeplessness. We have had a dismal week of bitter cold and there has been a bad outbreak of flu all around us—the worst since the epidemic three years ago.[175] I suppose we will all have it and I dread it under the circumstances.

Monday, Feb. 12, 1923

Our intense cold continues and tonight is wild and stormy, with the wind howling around the windows and wraith-like whirls of snow. Somehow, though, I like a night like this and always have. I've always loved to cuddle down in a cosy lighted room or between warm blankets and listen to a storm. It seems to give me an exhilarating sense of victory—as if I were getting the better of some mighty foe. I even like being out in a storm if I can keep warm. It is pleasant to look forward through it to a warm shelter and a good table and a restful bed. It is pleasant to look at the houses we pass with their lights shining out through the tempest and picture the folks inside them as comfortable and safe, and little children, rosy and warm, their dear hands folded in exquisite slumber. And, apart from all this and under it all is some dramatic enjoyment of contrast which is too instinctive to be defined or expressed.

Sunday, Feb. 18, 1923

This has been a very dreary week—so dreary that my courage has ebbed low. It has been extremely cold; we are burning soft coal now, our wood being exhausted, and it is abominable stuff; it is a wonder we have not been asphyxiated with coal gas or blinded by smoke.[176] Our hard-coal furnace hasn't sufficient draft for soft coal; then everybody around us is sick in a widespread epidemic of "flu." I suppose we will all have it and I dread it. Two days we had no mail and the 'phone lines are all out owing to the storm. But then our 'phone service has been abominable all winter. Half the time we cannot get

---

175   That is, the 1918–19 influenza pandemic. The Centre for Disease Control estimates that one third of the world's population (some 500 million persons) were infected in this pandemic, with total deaths estimated between 20 and 50 million.

176   Coal gas is the product of combustion of coal (in this case, poor quality coal that produced more fumes than usual). There were newspaper accounts of entire families being asphyxiated by coal furnaces in LMM's day.

Central and the other half Central can't get us. Sometimes even the rings on our own line can't get in.

Then on Friday evening we got word that our appeal was lost. We had expected this but it didn't lighten the week's gloom any. All this was depressing enough but by far the worst is that Ewan has been very miserable all the week. It is the worst attack he has had for a year and a half and for a couple of days he was almost as bad as I have ever seen him—walked the floor, looked wild and haunted, declared he "wasn't worthy to speak to the people" when I reminded him that it was prayer meeting night in Zephyr. Poor Ewan! To hear him talking about not being worthy to speak to the Zephyrites would be ludicrous if it were not so hideously tragic. In his normal condition of mind he would laugh at the idea as a joke. But it is no joke now but horrible reality that for the time being he really feels that it is so, poor unhappy tormented soul.

When his attack came on in that spring of 1919—nearly four years ago now—he admitted to me that he had had three similar attacks. One in Glasgow—one when he went to Dalhousie—and one when he went to Prince of Wales. Yesterday, however, he admitted that he had had four, the first one being when he was about sixteen. It was induced, he said, by a sermon he heard on hell, preached by an old-style believer in fire and brimstone. It is useless to blame the preacher. He preached as he was taught by the church of his time. If the constitutional weakness had not been in Ewan the sermon would not have produced such an effect; and if the sermon had not done it probably something else would—he would at least have had the headaches and sleeplessness, with the depression, whether he had any definite "phobia" or not.

It has just occurred to me that when my sons read this journal after I am dead, if they ever do, they may possibly be inclined to blame their father for not telling me before our marriage that he was subject to recurrent constitutional melancholia. I do not want them to do this. I have never done so. Ewan did not *know* what his malady was—did not even realize that he had a malady. He believed—and believes still—that his attacks were—and are—the quite natural feelings of a soul under the wrath of God. He does not believe that his trouble is either mental or physical, save for his headaches,—does not believe, in short, that he is the victim of any mental unsoundness at all—and before the spring of 1919, when I insisted on his consulting a doctor, such an idea never presented itself to him. When he has recovered from an attack he believes firmly that he will "never feel that way again" and, indeed, seems absolutely to forget that he has had such attacks.

So I do not blame him for not telling me. I *do* think, however, that it was a very strange thing that his parents never discovered his real malady or obtained any medical advice for him. His father, at least, knew of his condition during

the two years at Dalhousie which it lasted, but never seems to have taken any notice of it beyond telling him "he would feel better soon." I simply cannot understand such conduct, except on the ground that old Mr. Macdonald, who was certainly a man of very mediocre intellect and narrow experience, did not know enough to realize what the trouble was, and that his mother who in her younger days was quite a bright woman naturally though with no advantages and little education, was so driven and harassed with the care of a large family and small means that she had not time to think about the minds or feelings of her children. At all events, whatever was the reason, nothing was done for him, although it is possible that proper treatment at the outset might have eradicated or subdued the evil tendency and prevented recurrence.

Therefore, as I have said, I do not blame Ewan for not telling me of his malady. Nor can I find it in my heart to wish he had, in spite of the agony I have endured in the past four years and the gloomy outlook of the future. If he *had* told me, of course I would not have married him. I could never have had the courage to marry a man under such a doom; nor, if I could have dared, would I have thought it right to do so because I hold that no man or woman ought to bring children into the world under the curse of such a hereditary tendency. And so Chester and Stuart would never have come to me and, under everything, is the basic conviction that that would have been terrible and that the fact that I have them makes up for everything else. If they escape their father's malady and grow up into good and useful men I shall always feel so, and be glad that Ewan did not tell me. But if they develop mental trouble as they mature or break my heart in some other way, as children so often do—oh, then I shall feel very differently about the matter.

So, all things considered, this has been a week with no gleams of sunshine to encourage me. I have felt very sad and lonely—oh, so lonely. I am strained for a talk—a laugh—with *my own people*—the race of Joseph—Stell, May, Margaret, Bertie.[177] They are the only ones I can really laugh with. But they are all too far from me. Sometimes this week I have felt that I could not endure it one moment longer—especially at night. But the morning would come and I would feel better and able to go on for the sake of my children—my dear boys with whom several times this week I have been too impatient about their little faults because I was so unhappy myself.

Ewan heard in Zephyr yesterday that Mrs. Pickering had been sick in bed

---

177   All friends and cousins associated with LMM's youth in Prince Edward Island: cousin Stella Campbell from Park Corner; friend and cousin by marriage May Macneill from Gartmoor Farm, Cavendish; native of Stanley, Prince Edward Island, Margaret Ross Stirling; friend and cousin Bertie McIntyre.

for two weeks with "Bright's Disease."[178] I suppose they can't conceal the fact that she is ill and dare not call it diabetes after what she swore to in the witness box. That perjury may cost her her life yet. If she had not been guilty of it she might go openly to Toronto now and take the new insulin treatment for diabetes and be cured. But now, if she does that, she must do it secretly and that is not easy or perhaps even possible. In spite of the fact that she is confined to bed they have not had a doctor for her—for fear, I suppose, that he would tell other people what her real ailment is. Certainly people are sometimes caught in their own trap.

This morning when we woke a snowstorm was raging and I got up prepared to face a lonely sunless day. But after all it has been a pleasant day. Owing to the storm there was no service and I, being exceedingly tired, resolved to make it a real day of rest. Ewan stayed in bed, the boys were both absorbed in a book, so I was free after a fashion. So I took the book Mr. MacMillan sent me at Christmas, and which I have never even had time to look over, and settled down for "a good read." I had it. The storm raged outside and the gray day wore to its sullen close but I was far away, a free soul, roaming amid the delights of *A Flower Patch In The Hills*.[179] It is one of a kind of books which seem to be quite common in England and Scotland but which United States and Canadian writers cannot or do not produce. I have often felt that I would like to write such a book and that I *could* do it but hitherto I have never had the time—for such a book would be a labor of love with love as its reward. It wouldn't "sell" here. Mr. MacMillan has sent me several of these books and I love them all but I think *The Flower Patch* is the best.

Monday Feb. 19, 1923
The Manse, Leaskdale, Ont.

Today was milder and Lily and I went to work to clean our pipes ourselves, driven thereto by the absolutely unbearable smoking of range and furnace. The pipes fill up so quickly as the result of burning soft coal. This being done and the pipes put up again we had some comfort the rest of the day.

Ewan went to Toronto today to see about carrying our case to the Supreme Court but came back this evening with the news that they had decided not to because in order to do so we would have to give a bond to pay Pickering's expenses if we lost. As we have no hope of winning it, since our evidence was not

---

178   Bright's disease is a historical term for a range of kidney diseases (the specific kidney disorder here is unknown).

179   *The Flower Patch Among the Hills* (1916) by English writer Emily Flora Klickman (1867–1958). Her books were a distinctive account of country life, with tales of local people, nature descriptions, anecdote, autobiography, religion, and humour.

half in, and only meant to take it there to give Marshall Pickering a full dose of the law he likes so much, we will not do this. McCullough should have told us of this condition before. He does not seem to have known of it himself, as he told us some weeks ago that it would be better to go to Ottawa than England because in the latter case we would have to give a bond. We have told several people that we meant to go to Ottawa and now we are put in a silly position which I resent. Besides, thinking there was plenty of time, Ewan had not yet concluded arrangements with the congregation for the payment of the salary in advance. This must be done right away. Also it is possible that Pickering will send the sheriff here at once. He can do it legally. Of course, he can't get anything if he does come since everything is mine but I hate the thought of it.

The mystery of the fading away of the second coffin in my dream is explained.

Wednesday, Feb. 22, 1923
The Manse, Leaskdale, Ont.

In spite of our pipe cleaning Monday the furnace and range began to pour out smoke today so we burned the flue out[180]—a horrible job. If Ewan won't see to getting it properly cleaned soon I'll have to. Perhaps we will now have at least one smokeless week.

I've been receiving several letters recently congratulating me on being elected to the F.R.S.A. Well, I wish being a "Fellow" conferred immunity from smoking furnaces, malicious law-suits, "flu" and bad 'phone service. But alas, it doesn't. I shall still have to shake down, and shovel coal into, the furnace o'mornings and o'nights just the same.

Ewan has been very dull lately. I have resolved to accept one fact—viz:—he will probably never again be really well. Intervals may come, when like last fall, he may seem almost or quite well; but these will be temporary and I must henceforth live my life alone as far as any real companionship and assistance from my husband goes and as far as the care and training of my sons is concerned. I refuse any longer to be tortured by alternate hope and fear and disappointment and suspense. "Despair is a free man, Hope is a slave."[181] From this out I will never again bewail his condition in this journal or my resulting loneliness and burden.

---

180   A "flue" is the pipe in a stove or furnace that exhausts the gases of combustion. In this case, the deposits in the flue were intentionally set fire in order to clear the sediment; this would reduce the tendency to "smoke."

181   Possibly a reference to American novelist Ellen Glasgow's (1873–1945) poem "Freeman": "The clankless chains that bound me I have rent, / No more a slave to Hope I cringe or cry; / Captives to Fate men rear their prison walls, / But free am I."

Saturday, Feb. 24, 1923

This week has been intensely cold and I am truly terrified lest we be found some morning all asphyxiated by coal gas. I read of similar catastrophes every day in the papers. I keep all the windows open at night but that in this 20-below-zero weather is a choice of evils.

The managers of both Zephyr and Leaskdale have paid Ewan's salary a month ahead and will continue to do so. They are all as anxious as we are to get the better of Pickering. This is a great relief to us. Now the next thing, I suppose, will be that Ewan will be summoned to examination as to why he did not pay up. After that they can do no more—except drag him up for examination every now and then. They would gladly do this to annoy him no doubt but they may be restrained by the fact that it will cost them a good bit!

Stuart, bless his sunny face, ensures us a laugh per day. Tonight at supper when Chester took a third tart Stuart looked at him and said severely,

"Chester, if you don't learn to stop eating when you've had enough you won't be a husband long to the person you are going to marry."

I *wish* it would get milder. We have hardly had a day above zero since December. The house is so bitterly cold in the mornings as we can't check the furnace, owing to the gas, so it burns out.

My geraniums are all dying from the effects of the gas.

Wednesday, Feb. 28, 1923
The Manse, Leaskdale, Ont.

It has been quite fine and mild since Sunday and consequently life has not been such a valley of dry bones. Ewan was in Toronto yesterday and brought home the typed evidence of our trial. We have been reading it. The amazing bias of the Judge is even more evident than it seemed during the trial. He asked several "leading questions" himself of Pickering and helped him out whenever he got cornered—also Mrs. Pickering. But he did not so help any of our side. But then *we* were *not* cornered. We were telling the truth so didn't have to cover up and explain. Every one of our witnesses told a plain straight tale and never once tried to hedge during cross examination. The Judge minimized our evidence all he possibly could and brushed aside what he couldn't. It is certainly all very curious. The medical testimony was all in our favor except Johnson's in regard to congestion and this was contradicted by Dr. Robinson's evidence and the gland itself—and yet the Judge paid no attention to it at all. I simply cannot understand it.

But oh, I am dreadfully sick of the subject and wish woefully that I might

never hear it mentioned again. And Ewan, since he has been reading the evidence, talks about it unceasingly. I am glad of this, of course, because it is much better that he should be thinking of this than of his morbid terrors, and so I discuss it with him readily—but all the time I feel as if I were being flicked and teased on some raw surface. The whole thing has been such a wretched, sordid, humiliating affair. I feel as if I had been dragged through a cess pool.

Today in Uxbridge Mr. Law told Ewan that he had been talking to Grieg who had told him that neither he nor Phelan believed Pickering's evidence. Grieg may have said this to placate Law to whom he owes money for a car and who is very angry because Pickering swore to a lie about him. But no doubt it is the truth. Both Grieg and Phelan must have known, after the medical evidence if not before, that both the Pickerings were lying. Grieg also told Law that he "never expected to win the case," which shows that the Judge's verdict was a surprise to more than ourselves.

When I get tired I sometimes feel as if I were in a prison and as if this Pickering affair will prick and sting me forever. It is the injustice of it that hurts me and makes me feel sore all over.

Well, never mind. Life will be easier when spring comes; and meanwhile it is very nice to have a small, blue-eyed son say to you as Stuart said today, "I hope if I am born again you will be born again as my mother."

Oddly enough both Chester and Stuart seem to have this idea of a succession of existences. I don't know where they got it for I have been exceedingly careful never to hint such a thing to them, preferring to leave them to work out their beliefs for themselves when they are old enough to. Likely Chester has read it somewhere and repeated it to Stuart. Chester is the deeper thinker, I believe, but Stuart is the quicker and more brilliant.

Monday, March 5, 1923
The Manse, Leaskdale, Ont.

Went to the Hypatia club today and read a paper on The Goddess Pasht.[182] Ewan was talking to Mr. Barbour today who told him, "Never pay one cent of that. It was an outrageous thing. I hate that Grieg." There does not seem to be a spark of sympathy for Pickering anywhere outside of his own clique.

Tuesday, March 6, 1923

Our bitter cold continues, also our bad 'phone service, our soft coal nuisance and all our other worries. But never mind. I dreamed last night that I looked

---

182   Pasht—now more commonly spelled Pakhet or Bast—is the Egyptian lion goddess of war.

at my opal ring and saw that the opals were gone and in my dream I said, "The opals are lost. I shall have no more ill luck."

I have no belief in the old superstition regarding opals. But the subconscious mind conveys its predictions to me through symbols and it has taken the opal as its symbol in this dream. I believe the tide has turned. I *want* to believe it, I suppose. These past seven years have been such an uninterrupted succession of worries and entanglements.

Ewan was at Presbytery meeting today. *Union* is the theme everywhere just now. A ceaseless conflict of letters to and from Unionists and Anti's rages in the press. I hate the thought of Union, especially as I fear Ewan will be one of the ministers who will be squeezed out and I dread the effect on his mind. But I decided one thing today and that is, I am not going to worry over Union any more, let it come when it will. As long as I am able to write we will not be dependent on Ewan's salary.

Saturday, March 10, 1923

A crowded week has ended. The big event of it was a huge missionary tea on Thursday for which Lily and I worked all day Wednesday in preparation and all day Friday cleaning up. This is an annual event and I always draw a breath of relief when it is over. We had a fine day and a big turn out—we always have when there is anything to eat! And we got several new members, who joined I think merely because they did not like to say "no" when I asked them.

Ewan saw Dr. Boynton today. He was raging at the Pickerings and declared the Judge *must* have been bribed etc.

I had a bit of a scare today. Soon after the women had arrived I happened to glance out of the library window and saw a man tying his horse to the gate and the thought darted into my mind, "It may be the sheriff." I turned sick with dismay. Ewan was away and the house was full of guests. What a flood of gossip would roll over Scott Township tonight if the sheriff came to the manse while the Auxiliary members were here. When the bell rang I trembled so much that I could hardly go to the door. Then, when I had opened it, it was nobody but Mr. Quigley with his coat collar turned up and a parcel he had been asked to leave!

I wish whatever is coming would *come* and have it over with!

Monday, March 12, 1923
The Manse, Leaskdale, Ont.

No sign of spring yet. This is unusual for Ontario. I feel quietly happy tonight—because of something I was able to do today.

This afternoon a certain Mrs. Widdifield of Sandford came here—coming herself because her husband was just recovering from flu pneumonia. She had a pitiful tale to tell. There was a mortgage on the farm for $5,000. Up to this year they had always paid the interest. Then a succession of misfortunes befell them—poor crop, poor prices, an operation on a daughter costing five hundred dollars. Consequently, they were six months behind with the interest and the mortgagor—backed by *Grieg*—was going to foreclose at once. A forced auction sale now, when the farmer's market is so low, would not bring more than two thirds of the value of the place and they would be turned out with nowhere to go. Her husband was worrying so over it that his recovery was retarded. She could not get aid anywhere in the present dearth of ready money in these parts and in her despair came to me. Would I lend them the money for principal and interest—five thousand five hundred in all—and take over the mortgage?

I felt really aghast. I could not do it. I would have to sell our Victory bonds[183] to get the money now and I will not do that for these Victory bonds are for my children, or for us to live on if anything should occur to prevent me from writing and I will take no risks with them. Besides I hate the thought of tying up any more money in mortgages. I have $5,000.00 in two mortgages now that have never paid a cent of interest for five to eight years and I doubt if I ever get even the principal back. I could not tie up another five thousand so. These people are honest; but their ill-luck might continue. I could *never* foreclose a mortgage and sell people out if I lost every cent. So the only thing to do was to tell her I couldn't and it was the hardest thing I ever did for there was something about this woman I liked. She tried to be brave—thanked me with a quivering lip for having listened so kindly to her story—and then broke down and sobbed. "I thought God would not let us be"—and stopped, unable to speak.

Well, I had to do something. I could not let that woman leave my door without some assistance—I could not nullify her faith in God. I would not have slept a wink tonight if I had done so. I had a sudden inspiration.

"I cannot take over your mortgage," I said, "but I will tell you what I will do. I will lend you enough money on your note of hand to pay the interest up to November. Then they cannot foreclose until the mortgage falls due and you will have time to get another crop and time to look about you to find someone who can take over the mortgage, with a better chance of succeeding, since you can say that you have always paid up the interest."

183   Bonds to raise money for Canadian participation in World War I began in 1914; the war bonds were named Victory Bonds from November 1917.

The change in poor Mrs. Widdifield almost made me cry myself. She tried to thank me, broke down again, sobbed out "God bless you" two or three times. When she went away she turned to me at the door and said, "Oh, Mrs. Macdonald, *I feel as if I could fly.*"

I have felt so happy all the evening that I was able to lift the worst of her burden from her and so thankful I could do it. Even if I never saw a cent of the loan again I would not regret giving it to the poor soul.

Stuart gave us another laugh at supper tonight. He was sitting, looking very grave; suddenly he drew a long sigh and said, "Oh, mother, I wish I was grown up and married and *had it over with.*"

It was very funny and yet I sighed a little behind my laughter. Stuart evidently has my tendency to cross bridges before he comes to them. It means a lot of unnecessary worry through life. And yet—I don't know. Perhaps it is the foresight and preparation induced by the worry that makes the bridge safe.

Later on in the evening Stuart pursued the same line of investigation.

"Mother, when I get married will I have to give her a ring?"

"Yes," I said.

"And is that the only one I will have to give her?"

"Well, it is customary to give your lady a ring when you become engaged to her."

"What is engaged?"

I explained.

"Will I have to kiss her?"

"It is not compulsory," I said gravely. "You need not kiss her unless you want to."

"I am glad of that," said Stuart in a relieved tone, "because I don't want to kiss any girl except my mother."

I think it highly probable that *this* is a bridge which Stuart will find it very easy to cross!!!

Thursday, March 15, 1923
The Manse, Leaskdale.

Wrestled most of the day with a smoking furnace and range. Oh, for spring! And yet I am forbidden to hope for spring because Ewan always has a bad spell in the spring and I dread it more than words can say. Always in prospect I feel that I *cannot* endure any more of these attacks of his. But when they come I can always endure them somehow.

Ewan was in Toronto today and came home with a bit of news—good if

true. Mr. McCullough told him that when he has been once examined he cannot be summoned to examination again without good reason. This is a relief to my mind. I thought he could be dragged to Whitby as often as they liked and Pickering is spiteful enough to do it. But perhaps Ewan misunderstood McCullough and what the latter said was, not that they *couldn't* but that they *wouldn't* take him again without good reason—because of the expense it would put them to.

I wish the examination were over. It is unpleasant to live like this expecting a summons from day to day.

Saturday, March 17, 1923

Yesterday, driven to desperation, I went out myself and got two Leaskdale boys to come and clean our chimney. It was almost full up. We soon had it cleaned. It left us with a filthy house but we have cleaned that up and are free from smoke once more.

Yesterday a big envelope came from Mr. Rollins. Dreading some ill news I did not open it till tonight—for we had to go out to tea last night and I didn't want to be upset for that and for the work I had to do today. So tonight after the boys were in bed and I was alone I set my teeth and opened it. But there was nothing definite. Last Tuesday the Page suit was argued in the Supreme Court of the United States but the decision will not likely be given for some months. Rollins says he "had a feeling" that the hearing went on "pretty well." I found the reading of the briefs and pleadings very interesting. The Deputy Marshall made affidavit that he had attached a "chip" as my property. I didn't know I owned a chip in Massachusetts!

In regard to *my* suit there is no decision yet. Rollins says it is most unusual for a judge to be so long in handing down a decision. He says French wrote the Judge the other day asking if he could not soon give his decision. It is possible that the delay means that the Judge finds a decision difficult and *may* give it in my favor. But I long ago gave up any hope that I could win the suit. Nor does it matter much now. The sale of the book has ceased now, and the injunction, which was all I ever expected to get, means nothing now. I only want to have it over with and wiped off the slate. It has been hanging over me, like a veritable sword of Damocles,[184] for three years and I never know where I stand or what bills I will be called on to pay.

184　A story from Roman mythology: Damocles, a member of the court of King Dionysis II, is allowed to sit on the King's throne. Damocles is surrounded by comfort and luxury, but—in order to illustrate the constant danger of being King—above his head hangs a sword, suspended by a single hair from a horse's tail.

Poor Ewan remarked today that he "felt no interest in anything." That is terribly true. He has never actually turned against me or the children—he is just absolutely indifferent to us. And if I did not insist on his doing certain things—visiting, going to Guild meetings etc.—he would never stir finger or foot to do them. The strange thing is that after I make him do them he feels much better for the time being and admits it. Yet next time it is just the same. Sometimes I get so disheartened that I feel it would be better to give up, get him to resign and cut him free from every obligation and responsibility. That would be by far the easier way. But from what Dr. Garrick[185] told me I fear it would not be the best thing for Ewan. So I struggle on, do what I can myself and *make* Ewan do what I can't do.

But he does not seem to suffer *acute* mental distress now, save for a day or so at the first of each renewed attack, and he has no sleepless nights. But I don't know if this is a good sign or not. I sometimes think that his heart or kidneys are not as they should be but he will never go and have them examined as I think he should.

I had a letter from Mrs. Wm. Laird today.[186] She lives in Vancouver and writes that Lem MacLeod's wife was in an asylum there, having gone violently insane last summer and that Lem, who has been living there, had been suddenly stricken with a severe attack of paralysis.

I feel dreadfully shocked somehow. I can think of Lem only as I remember him when I saw him last—a rosy-cheeked jolly boy. I cannot realize that he must be nearly fifty. But even so he is a young man to be attacked with paralysis.

Alas, how soon we grow old! At twenty we cannot believe we ever *will* grow old. It is an incredible thing. And it remains incredible until suddenly we wake up and find we *are* old. And it is just as incredible then because it never seems possible that so many years can have passed—we *feel* that it was only a few years ago when we were laughing, flirting boys and girls—only yesterday really. It cannot be nearly thirty years! I think it was one spring night only last week that Stell and I, standing out in the field behind Uncle John Campbell's barn, saw Lem's *gray horse*, about which I was always teased so much, flash past the red bend of the road beyond the pond and then heard the staccato beat of

---

185   Nathan Garrick was a professor of neurology at Boston University Medical School and later the Head of the Health Service; LMM had taken Ewan to see him during his attack of mental illness in 1919.

186   Mary Macneill Laird ("Mrs William Laird") was a long-time friend of LMM's, originally from Cavendish. Lemuel MacLeod was from French River. In an entry dated January 5, 1917, LMM gives an account of her romantic interests from a young age. "The next winter I was in Park Corner. Lem MacLeod and Edwin Simpson were both aspirants for the privilege of walking home with me from 'Literary.' I snubbed Edwin till he left me alone and went around with Lem."

flying hoofs across the bridge—Lem coming up to take me to Long River preaching.[187] I don't know why *that* memory should be so much more vivid than most of the others—I think the charm of the young year's soft gray evening cast a glamor over all the incidents of it which they lacked in themselves—for certainly there was no romance connected with my occasional outings with Lem. I liked him as a friend and that was all. But anything connected with those Park Corner days has a charm of its own. So often in these

By the Birches

gray, lonely, troubled winter days and nights I am *living* back in those spring evenings of long ago—evenings when the girls and I strolled over the Park Corner bridge, with the pond shining beyond us in the sunset like a great golden lily or played ball down on the green by the young birches. Evenings in Cavendish when Mollie or Pensie came "for the mail" and I "went a piece" with them through a dusk of lilac bloom and apple blossom and wonderful sunsets on New London harbor on long red roads, moist with clear, cold dews, and fringed with shadows. Oh,

those red roads through the spruces on a fine evening, with the different fairy-likenesses of the mosses on their hillocks! I hear again the wind whistling along them, sweeter than an old Cremona.[188] The thought of them brings an anguish of longing to my heart. I don't want youth again—but I *do* want those red springtime roads in the afterlight!

And yet—would they be quite the same without the joyous companions of old days? No, I fear they would be very lonely.

We are always hearing reports these days of Pickering telling people "I'll send the bailiff if Macdonald doesn't pay up." I don't know why he doesn't send him and have done with it.

A long red road

---

187   Long River is a community near Park Corner, Prince Edward Island; LMM attended church services in Long River while visiting Park Corner.

188   Cremona, Italy, was famous for violin production during the sixteenth to eighteen centuries.

Sunday, April 1, 1923
The Manse, Leaskdale, Ont.

This past week has been the coldest and roughest of the winter. One is tempted to think spring has forgotten us. I went to Toronto last Monday and stayed in till yesterday, shopping and having a pleasant change from the sordid life of the past months—though under it all I was haunted by the worry that the bailiff might come while I was away etc.

However, I had a pleasant time. While I was in, the Toronto *Star* published the results of a voting contest it recently had. "Who Are the Twelve Greatest Women in Canada?" I was one of the twelve! Such competitions are very silly and this is sillier than most for greatness has no necessary connection with fame. I am not "great" and neither are most of the twelve. But of course if the competition had been avowedly what it really was, a questionnaire as to the most *widely-known* women in Canada. I certainly am one and perhaps *the* most widely known.

I froze my ears going down Yonge St. on the 28th of March. This hasn't happened to me since Cavendish school days.

I had a talk with Mr. McCullough who is altering my will so that Mr. Pickering wouldn't be the gainer if I should suddenly drop out. I think we have got it fixed so that Ewan will really have what I want him to have and yet no one be able to touch it.

In speaking of the examination McCullough said rather doubtfully that he hoped we would be able to "maintain the ground we have taken." His uncertainty depressed me. There is one question which will be awkward if Phelan asks it—and ask it he certainly will.

The matter is this: When the big "fox boom"[189] was in swing on the Island and fortunes were being made overnight I lent Ewan a couple of thousand dollars to invest. He expected to double his money in the fall and pay me back. And he would have if the heir to the Austrian throne had not been assassinated at Sarajevo. The war came—the boom slumped—and Ewan was left with a lot of doubtful fox stock on his hands. It was thereupon agreed between us that I was to take the fox stock. I got whatever dividends were paid since—very few—but we never bothered with having them transferred to my name. This winter we *have* had them transferred. They are morally mine and McCullough says the fact that I have had the dividends will prove them legally mine, he thinks. Now, if Ewan is asked "Did you transfer any of your property

---

189   In the late twentieth century, fox farming became increasingly popular in parts of Canada, particularly Prince Edward Island. As the fox business expanded, the price of fox pelts skyrocketed; many fortunes were made selling pelts to large merchant companies like Holt Renfrew. As LMM notes, the "fox boom" came to an end at the outbreak of World War I.

to your wife since the accident" he will say "no," because that is the truth. But if Phelan asks, "Did you transfer any property from your name to your wife's," Ewan will have to say "yes." The fox stock is worth so little that it is hardly likely they will go to the expense of trying to get it; still they might, and even if we can "maintain our ground" as McCullough says, it will mean more trouble, worry and expense.

Chester MacClure, a second cousin of mine, was in Toronto visiting his daughter who is at the Conservatory of Music. He is a brother of my old friend of long ago, Vinnie MacClure. We had dinner at the King Edward. He told me he had been talking to a *Mail-and-Empire* editor who had been in court during our trial and who told him that anyone could see it was a framed-up job and that it was a shame that such a miscarriage of justice should be permitted.

Norman Beal[190] tells me that Riddell is said to be "crooked" and has been suspected more than once of accepting bribes. But I can't believe that Marshall Pickering could afford to give a big enough bribe to influence a man of Riddell's standing—unless Riddell was dreadfully hard up—which isn't likely. Riddell is known to have a keen grasp of "points of law" and he certainly used his knowledge to wrest his verdict in Pickering's favor, but I think it was through prejudice, not bribery.

Monday, April 2, 1923
The Manse, Leaskdale, Ont.

This morning when I got up I said to Ewan, "You are going to hear from Pickering soon. I dreamed last night that the bailiff came." Ewan laughed as usual but I felt quite sure. There was also something in the dream about "Tuesday or Thursday," but it was so confused I couldn't make that part out.

But this afternoon the bailiff did come at last—Mr. McCully from Blackwater whom we know. He was smiling broadly and seemed to look on the affair as a joke. He said he was deputed to come in the place of Sheriff Paxton of Whitby who was ill.[191] Perhaps the Sheriff *was* ill but I fancy he didn't like coming to a minister's house on such an errand, so shunted it over on McCully. McCully asked Ewan if he were going to pay the damages. Ewan gravely said he couldn't. Mr. McCully, with a twinkle in his eye, asked if he had any property. Ewan said "An old cutter and some theological books." This being done, Mr. McCully laughed over it all and said the story he had heard was that Pickering ran into us as we were backing out of a yard in Zephyr. This is a little more favorable to us than the real truth but shows the trend of public opinion.

---

190   The Beals were friends of LMM (see also note 453, p. 320).
191   John Franklin Paxton was Sheriff of Ontario County from 1887 until 1931.

Well, this is over. The next thing will be the exam and the sooner it comes the better. *Anything* is better than suspense.

Sunday, April 8, 1923

We have had a most unpleasant week of wind, snow and cold—bad roads—hideous landscape—soft coal smoke and gas. I set my teeth and endure. "It may be for years but it can't be forever."

This evening I read Gertrude Atherton's *Black Oxen*.[192] Like all her books it was charmless. She has neither atmosphere nor distinction of style but she can write an interesting yarn. In *Black Oxen* her heroine is a woman of sixty, who has been made young again by a certain gland treatment—which I believe is really being practised successfully in Austria. This woman becomes again beautiful and charming but alas, it is only her body that is rejuvenated. Her mind—her cynical, disillusioned mind—is still sixty years old. It works out very consistently.

Suppose I were able to take that gland treatment and be physically twenty years old again. Would I do it? Decide carefully. To be twenty again—oh, beautiful! But wait. Twenty—with a middle-aged mind—a *declassé*—cast out of my own generation because of my seeming youth—unable to find real companionship among the young because of my old mind. It would be horrible. No, no. I would not be twenty again unless all my friends could be twenty also. And even then—unless the clever surgeons of Vienna could blot out memory as well as years—I fear it would be but a sorry state of affairs.

Monday, April 9, 1923
Leaskdale, Ont.

This evening the constable of Uxbridge, yclept[193] *Smith*, came up and gave Ewan a summons to examination at Whitby on *Thursday*. (So much for my dream!) The joke is that he had also to give him six dollars of Marshall Pickering's cash, as it seems the law demands that the "judgment creditor" must pay the expenses of the "judgment debtor" to examination! This is really funny. It seems that Ewan will get more out of Pickering than Pickering will get out of him.

Ewan laughs over this. I can't. The whole thing is a nightmare and I dare not laugh till that examination is over. I am so afraid Phelan will ensnare

192   American novelist Gertrude Atherton's (1857–1948) novel, *Black Oxen* (1923) explores cross-generational relationships and youth culture.
193   Archaic term for "named" (from Old English).

Ewan into some answer that they can take hold of. And yet, in my dream of last fall, there was not a "single drop" out of the black cloud. If I could believe this absolutely I would not worry. And I should be able to believe in it for all my dreams of that kind have come true. Yet absolute certainty is not given by the gods and the glimpses beyond the veil are uncertain and dim. Yet that dream has been a great comfort to me and I don't see how I could have lived through the winter without it.

Now there are three more hard days to be endured and surely that will end our suspense. If only Phelan does not ask that one question! But he will—of course he will. And then—they may not dare to try to make anything out of it—and just for spite they may.

Wednesday, April 11, 1923
The Manse, Leaskdale

Mr. Cook[194] has been here for two days painting and staining hall and dining room. Consequently the house has been upset. And I have been upset. Now that the examination is drawing near I cannot settle to anything. I have worked hard both evenings making out an itemized statement of all money expended since last fall so that Ewan can account for every cent. I thank my stars that I have always kept a rigid account of all our expenditures every day. I have day books back to our marriage. We can show that the money we spent came to more than Ewan had from all sources and yet the expenditures are all entirely reasonable for a family like ours. Mr. Grieg may suspect that under ordinary circumstances Ewan would not have to pay all this—that I would pay at least half. But I am not compelled to pay half. If I choose to say sternly to Ewan, "You should wholly support your family as other men have to do. I will not pay for such support," no lawyer or judge on earth can condemn *me* for such a reasonable attitude! *I* don't owe Pickering anything—*I* am not responsible for his enlarged prostate gland! And if poor Ewan is cursed with a miserly wife who ties up her purse strings and makes him expend *all* his salary on keeping her and her children what can Mr. Grieg do but sympathize with him!!!

Moreover, if said miserly wife sometimes feels compunction and puts a certain sum aside in the bank for her husband to make use of if he will, said sum being equivalent to half our living expenses, that is still nobody's business but my own. *I* haven't got to account to Pickering in regard to how I spend my cash, whether wisely or foolishly. Oh, my dear Mr. Pickering, you or your legal

---

194   The Cooks were a well-established family in Leaskdale. Albert (1858–1924) lived beside the manse, and ran the Leaskdale store from 1899 to 1919, as well as being the Leaskdale postmaster from 1906 to 1919.

advisers put in a claim for damages for your wife because if *you* were negligent *she* was not and the law would not punish *her* for *your* fault. You must find it works both ways and neither will the law harass *me* because it has decided that my husband is liable.

Pickering is evidently worried enough; though I hear that Grieg keeps assuring him, "Oh, Macdonald will have to pay—don't worry over that." Pickering's frequent explosions bear testimony to his state of mind. His latest is that "if Macdonald doesn't pay I'll stop him from preaching." Just how he will do this Mr. Pickering has not condescended to explain. Perhaps he will stand at Zephyr church door with a broad-axe and brain anyone who comes to listen!

Ewan went to Toronto today and will go out to Whitby with Mr. McCullough tomorrow. I went to Guild tonight and ran it with outward composure and inward turmoil. Thank heaven that this time tomorrow night the examination will be over and we will know the worst or best!

Saturday, April 14, 1923
The Manse, Leaskdale, Ont.

We do not! But many things have happened whereof I shall now write. The old French proverb, "It is always the unexpected that happens" is about the only thing we can tie to on this planet. All the things that have happened since Wednesday night have been unexpected, both the good and the bad.

All day Thursday I was upset and could settle to no steady work, so did odd jobs. The mail came. There was a letter from Mr. Rollins. Instantly I knew that the Judge had given his decision at last on my suit—after three years!

Well, I dared not open it then. I expected and was prepared for failure but I knew the certainty of it would embitter my day, and as Mr. Cook was here working I did not want any additional nervous disturbance. So I put it away until night. At nine o'clock I was alone at last, Mr. Cook had gone home—Lily had gone out—the boys were in bed. I could open my letter and learn the worst.

I looked at it a little while before I opened it, telling myself that it really did not matter in the least that I had lost—nay, that, all things considered, it would be *better* if I lost. Then the thing would be ended for good and all, I would pay another big fee, charge up my expenses to profit and loss, and know where I stood at last. I would be *free*. On the other hand if I won—what? The injunction would be all I would likely get. After three years it would be a barren victory for the sale of the book is practically over. For all my expense and worry I should only have the satisfaction of beating the Pages. Then they would, of course, appeal—and that would mean more expense and worry. Yes, it would

be much better to lose—swallow the bitter dose—and henceforth be at peace. Yet there was something in me that grimaced at the thought of swallowing that draught of humiliation after my long fight.

"Well," I said, "let's take it and get it over."

I opened the envelope. There were two letters in it. The first I read ran thus:—

Dear Mrs. Macdonald:—

Judge Hammond handed down a memorandum of finding[195] yesterday construing the contract in your favor and directing a decree in accordance with the memorandum which I enclose. This decree will direct that the defendants pay you all profits made from the sales of the book.

I congratulate you on being at length successful in this long litigation and I trust that the profits will turn out to be something substantial. The defendant however takes the ground that there have been no profits.

I will in the course of time send you a copy of the Judge's opinion. It is pretty long so it will be some time before you get it.

The next step is for me to draft a decree and have it entered. I suppose the case will then go before a Master to ascertain what the profits have been from the sale of the book. This will be a proceeding where I shall try to ascertain all the gross income from the book and the other side will try to charge up as many expenses as possible. The defendant will have the right to appeal from the final decree but I do not anticipate that it will gain much by appealing. In the meantime the injunction will, as I suppose, be in force.

The second letter, evidently written a little later in the day than the other, read:—

Dear Mrs. Macdonald:—

I have just heard that, oddly enough, the Supreme Court in Washington also decided its case yesterday, this also being in your favor. I am not surprised that the decision should be in your favor but it is truly remarkable that two courts should decide the cases both on the same day after this great lapse of time. I am very much pleased that we are winning out.

At first I couldn't believe it. It must be a dream. Such things didn't happen in real life—not in my life anyhow. Then I went a little crazy I guess. I felt as I haven't felt for years—I felt *free*—I felt as if *all* my shackles had dropped off!

---

195   A "memorandum of finding" officially sets out a legal judgement.

They hadn't, of course—I knew that; the heaviest were still on me. But I did not feel their weight. I had wings for a few hours. How furious the Pages and French would be—French who had once laughed contemptuously as he spoke of the "injunction" and said he didn't take *that* seriously. I think I see his face as he listened to Judge Hammond's decision. I can't get over my amazement. The Master's report was in the main adverse to me and such reports are rarely disregarded. And how tickled McClelland and Stokes will be. I wrote them at once and told them the news.

This morning my wings had gone. I was back on earth again. The Page suit against me is done with; but they will certainly appeal the other and there will be more *expense* and *suspense*.

As for the profits, the book sold about 13,000 copies before the trial and they brought out a new edition while the trial was going on. But I feel sure the Pages will garble the accounts in some way and I doubt if I ever get a cent. Meanwhile, I know there will be another big bill of Rollins to pay.

It certainly was an odd coincidence that the suits should be settled the same day. My dream of losing my bad luck seems to have come true. But I am afraid the bad luck won't *stay* lost. The past four years have robbed me of most of my old optimism.

And then there was Ewan and his examination at Whitby. *It* couldn't have gone well, too. *That* would be too much good fortune to come all at once. There was a letter from him in the mail which I was afraid to open. If all had gone well and he was coming home that night why should he have written? I tore it open shrinkingly. It contained nothing but the cryptic announcement that "nothing had been done at Whitby." So I was left in suspense till tonight when he came home. It seems that ass, Grieg, had sent him merely a copy of the summons, not the summons itself. This wasn't legal and McCullough wouldn't let Ewan appear on it. The examination is put off till next Thursday. The joke is that yesterday would cost them about $25.00 for nothing. *And* they have to give Ewan another six dollars for next trip!

Phelan wasn't at Whitby, so it is evident that Grieg means to conduct the examination himself. I am very glad of this. Phelan is a keen clever lawyer but Grieg is an ass.

It is just as well the mistake was made. It will give Ewan time to hunt up his old bank books, which it seems he must have. McCullough never told him this. McCullough is certainly slack. If the examination had been today Ewan would not have had them and could have been made to attend again at his own expense to produce them. I like Mr. McCullough personally but I do think he is not nearly as keen as he should be.

It is not enough that we have our own worries. Others must dump their

financial troubles on us too. We had a pitiful letter today from Ewan's sister Christie.[196] They seem to be in a bad plight. I can't go into details—indeed, it was hard to make out what was the real trouble. It is because of their son Leavitt's doings. Poor Christie seems almost distracted. Her husband is very ill, too. She asked for a loan of $100. I sent it to her as a gift not a loan. I am glad to be able to help Christie. But she has two brothers, Angus and Alec, who are reputed to be worth a great deal of money. One wonders she would not apply to them instead of Ewan. And one more than suspects that it is because they know how to hold on to their money and are not remarkable for clannishness.

Tonight, after a long day's work was done, I read an hour in *Tommy and Grizel*.[197] The book has all its old charm. Yet I could always box Barrie's ears with a right good will because of it. *Sentimental Tommy* was a perfect book. Tommy was a delightful boy and Grizel an admirable girl, though I never had much use for Elspeth. But *Tommy and Grizel* is maddening. If Barrie wanted to depict the career and downfall of a weak man of genius—and nobody can deny that he has done it with uncanny penetration in "Tommy" and "Grizel"—why couldn't he have done it with a brand-new character and left our beloved Tommy alone? I shall never forgive Barrie for it. And Grizel! Such a nice child in the first book. Such an unlikeable, narrow, intolerant, silly girl in the second! I can't bear her and I think "Tommy" was much too good for her, with all his shortcomings.

Nevertheless, the book has much charm, especially as one can't help hoping all the way through—yes, though it were at the twentieth reading—that Barrie will "find a way" to end it happily. Barrie has to a superlative degree the power of creating atmosphere and character, so that his books give us the sensation of reading about people and places we have known well, and consequently have all the charm of a newsy letter from home. In a much smaller degree I have the same knack myself and that is why my books are liked.

I cannot help thinking that it was a great pity that Barrie forsook writing books and took to writing plays. His audience is much smaller and the life of a play short. He has cheated the world.

Somehow, I can never rid myself of the idea that Barrie was depicting *himself* in "Tommy." And was his wife drawn from "Grizel"? She divorced him—why, has never been satisfactorily explained. I hope I will live long enough to read a truthful biography (if there is such a thing!) of his life. Perhaps it will clear the mystery up.

---

196   Christie Macdonald McLeod, Ewan's sister, lived in Kinross, Prince Edward Island.
197   Scottish playwright and novelist J.M. Barrie (1860–1937) wrote many much-loved works, including *Peter Pan* (1904), *Sentimental Tommy* (1896), and *Tommy and Grizel* (1900).

Wednesday, April 18, 1923
The Manse, Leaskdale, Ont.

Spring comes slowly. April so far has been a cold backward month. Ewan left for Toronto this morning. Now for two days' worry.

I gave myself the satisfaction of phoning the news of my successful suit to the two Uxbridge papers. I do not usually air my private affairs thus. But at the time of the suit it got out and ever since at intervals someone asks me how it ended. So it will be just as well to let them know the result. If I lose the appeal they needn't know *that*.

And I think it will be a pill for Messrs. Grieg and Pickering! At least, it will show them that I am not afraid of litigation and do not easily submit to blackmail or threats.

Friday, April 20, 1923
Leaskdale, Ont., Can.

The long nightmare is ended. I can't realize it yet and will be able to draw breath only by degrees. Of course there is always a possibility that Grieg and Pickering may try to brew up some further devil's jorum.[198] But I imagine they have both learned an expensive lesson and may be inclined to let sleeping dogs lie henceforth.

Yesterday was a hard day. I worked doggedly but every minute seemed an age. This morning I was too worried even to work. Ewan came home at twelve. I was upstairs when he came in and I knew by the tone of his voice when he spoke to Lily in the hall that the exam had gone well for him. Nevertheless, I ran downstairs in a cold creep of suspense. We went into the library and he told his tale.

Grieg never asked the question we dreaded. He must be an ass *not* to have asked it, but the lucky fact remains that he did not. And he *did* ask some absurd questions. For instance he asked *three* times, "Had you any money in the *Leaskdale* bank?" When he asked it the third time Mr. McCullough said impatiently, "Mr. Grieg, Mr. Macdonald has told you twice that there is no bank in Leaskdale. Surely you ought to know that yourself after living only seven miles from it for several years."

It shows Grieg's calibre that he should ask such a question. I foresee that the Leaskdale bank will be a family joke in the House of Macdonald henceforth.

---

198   A jorum is a large bowl or jug used for serving drinks.

Grieg seemed to have the fixed idea that Ewan had had a lot of money in some bank—something he *never* had—and spent most of his time questioning along this line, after Ewan had repeatedly told him he had none. I feel a primitive desire to slap Grieg's insignificant face for him. Insolent cub, to doubt the oath or even the word of a Presbyterian minister. After he gave up the bank line in despair he began on the salary. When he was told that it was paid monthly in advance he was furious and could not hide it. I believe the idea had never occurred to him that the congregation would do that. I fancy Mr. Grieg is a sore and angry man tonight—and I don't envy him when he has got to tell his tale to Pickering. Some say he isn't paid in full by Pickering yet. If this be so, the odds are against his ever getting it.

I feel so relieved. It really seems too good to be true that Grieg never asked that one awkward question.

Nevertheless I shall feel uneasy for a time. They will leave no stone unturned to harass us. Pickering will be furious. And the announcement of *my* successful suit coming the same day will fill up the bitterness of his cup. He will be sure to imagine I have got thousands out of it.

I had a letter from Rollins today. He seems a bit downhearted. It seems he did not think the Pages would appeal because the expense of printing so much evidence would cost as much as they would have to pay us in profits. He does not yet know the Pages as I do. They would rather pay a lawyer ten thousand than me one thousand. They are going to appeal by a "bill of exceptions" which it seems is a tedious process and is a rare procedure. Rollins is so blue he suggests a compromise. I will not agree to this. For one thing I feel sure Page wouldn't compromise on any terms. For another I'm not going to back down now after fighting so long and winning the first round. Rollin's was so down three years ago that he wanted to settle because he thought Nay's[199] evidence would kill our case. But I refused and as a result I won despite Nay's evidence. Very likely I'll lose in the appeal but I will *not* knuckle down to Page.

Saturday, April 22, 1923
The Manse, Leaskdale, Ont.

I am feeling the reaction from the long strain of recent weeks. Today instead of feeling relieved that the exam was finally over I felt restless, unhappy, upset. Everything worried me. I expected the worst of everything. Marshall Pickering would sue us for conspiracy—or begin to worry our treasurers. Rollins'

---

199   Lawyer Frank Nelson Nay (1866–1942).

attitude got on my nerves, too. To add to the tension another distracted letter came from poor Christie. It is impossible to make out the rights of the matter but it is evident that Leavitt has landed them in a dreadful scrape of some kind. She wants me to lend them $5,000.00 on a mortgage. I simply can't do it. Poor Alex is dying—I have no confidence in Leavitt—if they failed to pay interest or principal I could never foreclose. I have $10,000 out now, some in mortgages and the rest on notes, from which I have never received one cent of interest and will not likely ever see a cent of my principal. I cannot tie up any more. One does not know what might happen.

Ewan has decided to run down to the Island for a few days and see how things are. He seems to think I should lend the money. I can't see it so. Angus[200] is Christie's brother and has three times as much as I have and he is the one who should lend it.

I went from bad to worse until the evening when I fled to my room, broke down and had a long cry. This served as a "went"[201] and I felt ten times better afterwards—snapped my fingers at Marshall Pickering and wrote Rollins an order for full steam ahead. I even began to think that, since poor Christie had to be rescued, I must see what I could do.

Monday, April 24, 1923

We were in Uxbridge today and Ewan heard a few interesting items from several people. Ormiston told Mr. Bennie that Ewan had made Grieg "fearfully mad" and that he (Grieg) "didn't know what to do now." Laing, a man connected with the livery stable, told Ewan that Marshall Pickering hadn't wanted to go on with the trial last fall but that he (Laing) had one day driven Grieg to five different places hunting for Pickering and when they found him Grieg urged him to go on with it until Pickering gave in. If this be true—and I don't doubt it for Grieg has the reputation of urging on cases whether good or bad— Grieg is a perfect devil. I hope he hasn't got his money from Pickering and never will.

Road to Uxbridge

---

200   Angus was a very successful medical doctor in Indiana. He had no children.
201   An older usage, from Scottish "went" (vent), as in an opening or channel to allow drainage or release of pressure. LMM also uses the term in the photo caption on page 251, as well as in two other instances in her journals.

Pickering, we were told, was very furious when he left Grieg's office last Friday and was breathing out threatenings and slaughter—"he would jail Macdonald etc. etc."

I *hate* those two men Grieg and Pickering viciously. I don't think I really hate any other human being—not even Louis Page or Mrs. William Lockie. I *dread* Page and I dislike her instinctively with every fibre of my being but it is repulsion not hate. I *do* hate the other two and I hereby devote them to the infernal gods!

Thursday, April 26, 1923
Leaskdale, Ont.

Our new car came today—a Dodge. [202] It is no more mine than the others were of course but it is in my name. Mr. Pickering will be furious when he sees us in it. I think Mr. P. will think twice before he brings another trumped-up suit against a minister with no money.

I hope we will have better luck with Dodgie than with poor Lady Jane. The trouble is Ewan can't take proper care of *anything*—from a pen knife to a car. He seems to have absolutely no idea of it naturally and was never trained to it. So we will likely have some trouble with it but surely not so much as Lady Jane.

Sometimes when I am working away at some prosaic task—as for instance today when I was washing paint—a memory picture and sensation comes vividly back to me—for no reason that I can perceive. Today—I was looking from my window at home on a spring evening when the world seemed holding its breath over a sudden perception of its own

My window at home.

beauty. I saw the cherry trees, the green fields, the long red hill road, and far over to the southwest the great clump of white wild cherries in the woods by Lovers' Lane. I saw all the incredible, indescribable, clear, dewy delicacy that thrilled me in those olden twilights. And for that one moment I shuddered with a pang of fierce homesickness.

---

202   Probably a Dodge 116, made in Detroit, and new on the market for 1923. The new Dodge, costing over $1000, had been given a new look, with a wider wheel base and lower appearance.

Monday, April 30, 1923

I went to Toronto Thursday to attend the convention of the Canadian Authors' Association. Had a very nice time and several nice social stunts, including a reception at Government House and a dinner at the Arts and Letters. At this latter function I saw for the first time in Canada women smoking in public. Of course women have smoked in Toronto for some time but I never saw them do it before at a dinner. I didn't like it. Not that I thought it the least "bad" or "fast" or even unwomanly. But it is *ugly*. Few women are so beautiful and charming that they can afford to divest themselves of any portion of their charm; so they are very foolish to do so by smoking. It doesn't matter about men. Men look ugly and silly, too, when smoking. But it isn't beauty that matters with them—only strength. So, dear grand-daughter, take it from me, you will be foolish to smoke. You won't look half as pretty while you're doing it.

One thing amused me at the convention. Invariably the least successful authors had the most to say and evinced the most determination to run everything and dictate all policies.

We had a breeze over the newly passed Copyright Bill.[203] Nobody can understand it. I believe it will kill out our young Canadian authors altogether and in the end our Canadian literature. Under the terms of it publishers will be afraid to accept the work of unknown authors.

Personally, I sat quiet and took it all in. But I did not find it unpleasant when Dr. Logan of Halifax[204] came up to me and said,

"Hail, Queen of Canadian Novelists."

Yes, I liked it.

I came home feeling anxious and fearful, as I have come home every time for four years, and especially this winter. Ewan seemed pretty well, however. But when we got home and went into the library he said, "I have news for you. There is to be a new trial."

My heart seemed to stop beating. I thought of course, that he was referring to Marshall Pickering and that he must be bringing suit for conspiracy or something like that. I turned absolutely sick. And then I heard Ewan say, "There's Rollins' letter." I snatched it, read it, and gasped with relief. It seems French has appealed to the Supreme Court for a *rehearing* of their libel suit. This was nothing like as bad as I had supposed. I didn't think it was possible

---

203   The Berne Convention for the Protection of Literary and Artistic Works had been introduced in 1886, establishing international standards for copyright protection. Canada had joined the Berne Convention in 1886 as a British colony, but the US had not. It had long been a matter of concern that authors whose works were first published in Canada had little protection under US copyright law. For this reason, Canada and the US signed a bilateral agreement, taking effect in 1924.

204   John Daniel Logan (1869–1929) was a specialist in Canadian literature, with a particular interest in the Maritimes.

to get a rehearing but it seems so. Rollins says there is no need to worry etc.

Yes, but I suppose it will mean more expense for me and that is what the Pages want. However, thank mercy it isn't Pickering. Ewan says he hasn't heard a syllable from or about him.

Tuesday, May 1, 1923

We went over to Wick manse to tea tonight. It is so delightful to be able to ride in our car again after the long cold winter of bad roads. One feels as if one had got out of prison. And Dodgie is a splendid car. Every time we go out in her we feel better satisfied with her.

I saw Dr. Shier today. He said he had never been so tickled over anything in his life than over hearing that Pickering hadn't been able to get a cent.

Wednesday, May 9, 1923
Leaskdale, Ont.

Ewan left for the Island tonight. We are in desperate confusion—the whole house torn up for the paperhanger. Owing to that detestable soft coal the paper all over the house is ruined and five rooms must be papered.

Wick Manse

May has so far been cold and wet—today we had two inches of snow. A letter from Mr. Rollins informed me that French's petition for a rehearing had been refused. So that's *that*, and no bother or expense for me. But there will be plenty of both before the other suit is finally settled—if it ever is! Rollins said he had been talking to Judge Hammond *re* the case and the Judge said that it was in Nantucket parlance, a "whale of a case" and that he had got intensely interested in it.

[Dodge]

Sunday, May 13, 1923

As today was Communion at Zephyr I went over with Captain Smith who is supplying for Ewan. Of course Mrs. Will Lockie gave me a slam—or rather

Ewan through me. She never fails to do it. When I said Ewan was so sorry to miss his Communion service Mrs. Curl said "Yes, and we missed him, too." But Mrs. Lockie said, "Oh, well, we had a very good sermon. Captain Smith seemed to take so well with the young people."

Of course that *is* a weak point with Ewan. He doesn't understand young people and never did, even when he was a young man himself. He never seems to know what to say to them and tries to carry off the situation by a misplaced jocularity. It is impossible for him to take them seriously as adolescence demands to be taken. But in Leaskdale where we have plenty of young people I fill this lack for I feel more at home with the young fry than with the older folk. And in Zephyr there are almost *no* young people. This is a fact. I never saw such a church. There are only about half a dozen "teens" in the congregation. Two of them are Mrs. Lockie's own and I don't think either Ewan or I "take" with *them*. Nor would we want to. They are as unattractive as their mother and the only two young people in both our congregations with whom I have never been able to "mix." I feel in their presence just the same feeling of secret enmity, dislike and resentment I detect in their mother. That woman *resents* any superiority in anyone—of education, dress, circumstances or personality. She resents my keeping a maid—having a car etc. It seems a personal matter with her. Of course she isn't normal—they say she is quite a bit "off" at times—but she is none the less disagreeable for that. She and her husband, in spite of their "fad" for giving and their "Pansy" type of religion, are the greatest drawbacks Zephyr church has. If they were not there the rest would go ahead and do something. But with their odd views they paralyze everyone else and blight the atmosphere.

Friday, May 18, 1923
The Manse, Leaskdale, Ont.

Poor Aunt Annie is in trouble again—no money to pay hired man's wages and buy clover seed. Here is where little Maudie's purse must come to the rescue once more. Well, I am very glad to open it to poor Aunt Annie. Only—I smile a bit, remembering certain things of long ago, when Aunt Annie's Clara and Stella were so often flung in my teeth because they were such splendid cooks and housekeepers and general hustlers. Yet today those same smart girls can't help their mother with a cent. It is to the despised dreamer she must turn for financial help. But while I do not forget this, I do *not* forget that Aunt Annie

was the only one of my mother's brothers and sisters who ever treated me like a human being, took my part, or seemed to have a spark of affection for me. She might condemn me herself as a foolish chaser of bubbles but she would not let anybody else "pick" on me and stood up for me valiantly. I remember a tale Frede told me. One day Uncle Leander and his second wife, Aunt Annie Putnam, and Uncle Chester and Aunt Hattie went to Park Corner for a visit and carried there some false yarns about me which had been told them by that old hypocrite, Aunt Ann Maria.[205] They took their tales to the wrong market. Aunt Annie rose up in her majesty and told them soundly that if they were going to listen to "Ann Maria's lies about Clara's[206] child they need not come to her house to repeat them"—and so sharply did she manhandle Uncle Leander that that gentleman actually dissolved in tears and admitted that he was wrong. He must have got a sound drubbing to surrender like that. But Uncle Leander *had* some genuine family feeling behind his autocratic exterior. Uncle Chester had none—though he was a more agreeable man exteriorly. But he seemed to have absolutely no affection for his sisters and brothers, even his father and mother. The *clan spirit* was totally lacking in him as in all the Woolners.

He might have been a different man if he had got a different wife. Aunt Hattie's selfishness raised a barrier between him and his kin which there was nothing in him to surmount.

Aunt Hattie, poor woman, is at present dying from internal cancer. Yet she has had *everything*—an unclouded existence, wealth, social position, a handsome, agreeable husband—no sad death, illness or worry in her whole 58 or 60 years. Now she must pay her debt to destiny in one huge lump sum. Pay we all must, it seems, sooner or later.

A wire from Ewan today states that he must stay another week.

Monday, May 21, 1923

A letter from Ewan. Things are worse than we dreamed of down there. Alec is dying.[207] Leavitt, who was running the store, has got them in for $13,000

---

205   This tale mentions three sons (and/or their wives) of LMM's maternal grandparents, Alexander Marquis Macneill and Lucy Woolner Macneill: LMM's Uncle Leander (1845–1913) and his second wife, Annie (1844–1902); Uncle Chester (1856–1942) and Harriet ("Hattie"); another son (not mentioned in the tale) is John Franklin (1851–1936), whose wife was Ann Maria.

206   LMM's mother, Clara Woolner Macneill (1853–76); LMM did not have a good relationship with her Uncle John Franklin or his wife Ann Maria.

207   Alec McLeod, Christie's husband; her son was Leavitt.

liabilities. Worse still, he has helped himself to $1500 of the post office money and has had to abscond to Boston. That is a penitentiary offense. Luckily Jack Whear, the Postmaster General for the Island, is married to a cousin of Christies and he has covered the matter up, on condition of Christie's paying the money back.

Ewan has addressed himself to the mess. He has induced the creditors to compromise for $9000, is raising five thousand by a mortgage on the farm and asks Angus for $2000 and the remaining $2000 from me. I have to sell out some Victory bonds to get it but of course it must be done for poor heart-broken Aunt Christie's sake. My heart aches for her. Beside such crushing troubles as her husband's fatal illness and Leavitt's scandalous behavior what are my worries—apart from Ewan's mental trouble at least. But I could horsewhip Leavitt with a right good will. To get his parents into a mess like that! He has disgraced his family and all who have the misfortune to be connected with him. But I must not be too harsh. I don't know how my own boys will turn out yet. The immediate thing is to save what we can out of the wreck for Christie.

Ewan seems wonderfully well. His mind is so occupied with this that he cannot brood on his old dreads. It is as it was last fall during the trial. 'Tis an ill wind that blows no good.

I have been rushing around all day arranging for the sale of the bonds etc.

Sunday, May 27, 1923
The Manse, Leaskdale, Ont.

For a wonder this was a fine Sunday and Mrs. Smith came up with the captain. We had a pleasant day, for Lily went home last night. In spite of the extra work this entails I am always heartily glad when she is out of the house, when I have my own friends here. We are free then to talk as we please with no outsider to hear, tattle, and pervert.

Mrs. Smith and I went to Zephyr and Mrs. Wm. Lockie surpassed herself. Coming out I met her in the porch and as usual said most graciously, "How do you do, Mrs. Lockie?" She stammered out "I'm glad to meet you" as if I had been some stranger to whom she had just been introduced. She *is* funny.

Monday, May 28, 1923

Ewan is not back yet but surely will be this week. Poor Alec died on Friday. We are about through housecleaning at last. It has been a more strenuous task this year than even ordinarily on account of the papering and the wet, cold weather. I had to dig and plant the whole garden myself but I've got it done at last. I feel rather in need of a rest. Luckily I keep well, energetic and fresh.

Thursday, June 7, 1923

I am really almost forgetting what Ewan looks like! He isn't back yet and won't be till next week. Meanwhile I write, garden, and run the affairs and societies of the congregation. As for the garden, alack! Tuesday morning my garden looked nice—rows of everything up beautifully. Tuesday evening it was a river of mud—the middle washed out. I have simply got out of patience with these Ontario thunderstorms. Every spring it is the same old story of washouts and floods, drat it! I have toiled for weeks in that garden and now I must toil weeks more to repair the damage.

Monday, June 11, 1923
The Manse, Leaskdale, Ont.

We had a Dominion Alliance[208] man here this Sunday—a Methodist yclept Rev. Ryerson Young. He is clever, deaf, *Methodistic*[209] and egotistic—the most egotistic man I have ever met I think. He is an unceasing talker and spent most of his time telling me all the wonderful things he has done in his career. He *has* done them too, I think. He is a veritable dynamo of energy—quite often misdirected—as, for instance, when he went out unasked and cultivated my aster bed, uprooting the ring of sweet alyssum I had planted around it under the impression that it was weeds. I think that incident extremely typical of the man. Before his sermon he gave me a horrible ten minutes by informing the congregation that the only reason he had come was because he wanted to see "L.M. Montgomery" and telling them they ought to be a highly cultured and bookish people when they had a "world famous authoress" among them. If Jenny Geddes' stool had been handy I would have thrown it at him with a right good will. Anything like that makes me wretchedly uncomfortable—it is in such bad taste. I never sped a parting guest so willingly for between his egotism and his deafness I was tired to death.

In all these weeks I have heard no more of Marshall Pickering than if he were dead. It is uncanny. I expected that after the examination he would go about breathing threatenings and slaughter as before. But he has kept an unbroken silence. I think there are two reasons for this and I wish I knew which is the more potent. One, I feel sure, is that he fears being hooted at for not getting his money after all and is keeping quiet to save his face as much as possible, since the less he says to people the less he'll be twitted. The other is

208   Established in the late nineteenth century, the Dominion Alliance for the Total Suppression of the Liquor Traffic was a Canadian organization that lobbied for prohibition of alcohol.
209   The Methodist Church of Canada, like the Presbyterian, was well established; the first Methodist preacher came to Newfoundland in 1776. Tension had long existed between the two churches. LMM's comments here reflect a Presbyterians tendency to see Methodists as lacking in social grace.

probably that Grieg has told him to keep quiet in the hope of inducing some of *our* people to talk and give away something of which they can make a handle. This is not likely to happen since the only two men who know anything that could harm us are very safe people who understand the art of holding their tongue. I have heard, since writing the above, that Marshall Pickering and his wife are both "very thin" and that Ewan's jaunt to Whitby cost him $60.

Tuesday, June 12, 1923

The General Assembly has voted for Union in the teeth of a large minority. I think it is a shameful thing and the coercive legislation which they are going to attempt to push through parliament is outrageous.

From all points of view I think it is a tragic blunder. The stately Presbyterian church, with its noble history and inspiring traditions, has been forced to commit suicide. The result will be strife, trouble and confusion for ministers and churches for twenty years. Nor, I believe, will the eventual result justify this wholesale uprooting. "Men and money" may be "saved" but the church will not be the gainer thereby. The money will stay in the pockets of the people and the men will go—forced to go—into other callings. The "United church" starts life with a combined deficit of nearly half a million. That will not be speedily made up by disrupted congregations half of whom are angry and sore over this compulsory "Union."

Personally, I refuse to worry. Union will probably complicate our problems here and if we are "squeezed out" and Ewan cannot get another suitable congregation we have enough to live on. Hundreds of poor ministers who trusted their fathers' church will be in a far worse plight. But I resent the high-handed way in which the so-called "leaders" have forced Union on to save their faces and I resent the feeling of "homelessness" it has brought me. I feel that I have no longer a church. My Presbyterian Church has gone—I owe and feel neither love nor allegiance to its hybrid, nameless successor without atmosphere, tradition or personality. I wish I were free to go over to the Anglican communion. It has always attracted me and I would feel more at home in it than I can ever feel in "the United Church of Canada"—a bumptious and arrogant title which it has no right to assume. Why should it call itself "the church of Canada" when Baptist and Anglican denominations are not in it?

Saturday, June 16, 1923
The Manse, Leaskdale, Ont.

Ewan got home today. He seems very well—if it would only last. He had a strenuous time down east but engineered things very cleverly. If Ewan had energy and ambition equal to his diplomacy and shrewdness in dealing with people he might have gone far. But he has always preferred to "take things easy" and for the past four years his mental disorder has intensified this to the

point of apathy. He is capable of a big *"tour de force,"* such as the remodelling of the old graveyard in Cavendish or inducing our congregation here to assume the support of a special missionary; but when it comes to steady routine work he does not like it. The missionary business has long since petered out, for instance.

He saw James Mustard this evening and the latter said some people thought Marshall Pickering was just keeping quiet in the hope of catching us at some weak point. This is no more than we think ourselves but it is always disagreeable to hear others say it. It gives one the feeling that perhaps they base their opinion on something they know or have heard, of which we are ignorant.

So far our new car is a beauty.

Speaking of the Mustards reminds me that Rev. John's son—who has always been a selfish, unmanageable boy—has broken his parents' hearts by suddenly without a word or warning, presenting them with a French Canadian Catholic wife whom he picked up in the mining regions up north.[210] It is a disgraceful way in which to treat his parents. He might at least have told them beforehand. It makes one feel that it is useless to toil and sacrifice for your children who may treat you with such ingratitude in the end—or disgrace themselves as Leavitt has done. Will Chester and Stuart break my heart thus?

I had a letter from Mr. Rollins today. French has asked Judge Hammond to reconsider his findings on some points.

Rollins says:—

> We went over to Cambridge to where Judge Hammond was to argue this and Mr. French argued an hour and three quarters . . . The Judge finally said that he had put an enormous amount of time on the case, more perhaps than he ought, considering the obligations he was under to other litigants, and that he had arrived at a definite conclusion which it would be impossible for Mr. French to shake.

Personally I think that Judge Hammond must be a very decent man! Of course, I would have had just as high an opinion of him had he found against me!!!

Sunday, June 17, 1923
The Manse, Leaskdale, Ont.

Rev. Mr. Macdonald of Wick preached here today and I went back with him and had tea there. He is a widower, a rather stodgy old fellow but with something very likeable about him. One feels at home with him, even if he is not

---

210   LMM here reflects an anti-Catholic and anti-French bias. John Mustard's son, Gordon Alexander (1899–1977) married Marie Larouche (1900–86) in Timmins, Ontario, in 1922.

brilliant company. I always enjoy a visit to Wick Manse. His daughter Jean is a nice girl, though we are too far apart in years to be "real company."

Ewan and I had a very nice drive home, purring along through the gentle spring night. He *seems* perfectly well now—I would believe he *was* perfectly well if he didn't still say his prayers!!!

Monday, June 18, 1923

I had a rare and real pleasure tonight. We went to call on a family up north and after I had done my duty talking to a woman who is in Milton's expressive phrase "stupidly good"[211] I decided to run over to the next farm and call on two women living alone there. I took a short cut through the orchard and across two clover fields and for fifteen minutes I was alone with nature again as I have not been, I think, for five years. It was unbelievably lovely. Solitude was with me like a sweet-lipped friend. A great fresh green world of springtime, fairy-blue hills and spacious fields, was all about me. Over me a violet sky, with a new moon low in the west. The wind was my comrade and the evening star my friend. I was knee-deep in clover and whispering grasses. I felt "an April-hearted thing"[212] once more—young, happy, care-free. My arid soul brimmed over. Ah, that it should be of such short duration. Too soon I had left my fairyland behind me and was listening to the rather weird conversation of an old lady whose mind is not quite rational where religion is concerned. I had to listen to her minute account of the death and illness of her husband— who was a miserly old curmudgeon, of no use to God or man, who never had a thought above the dollar sign in his life and would have sold his soul, if he had one, for thirty pieces of silver any day—and her reasons for believing that, in spite of all, "his name was written in the Lamb's Book of Life."[213] There was something pathetic and tragic in her efforts to convince me—and herself—that it was so. She was afraid in her secret heart that her husband had gone to hell—as logically he should have if the convictions she has held all her life were true—and she was also afraid that public opinion would think he had, which was a humiliating thing, even if he were really "saved." So the minister's wife must know how she had read the Bible to him and how he had said "Yes, ma," when she told him that these were the words of eternal life.

---

211   A slight misinterpretation of an expression in Book 9 of Milton's *Paradise Lost*. As Satan looks at the beautiful, innocent Eve (before she has been led astray), he momentarily loses his dark edge: "That space the Evil one abstracted stood / From his own evil, and for the time remaind / Stupidly good, of enmitie disarm'd, / Of guile, of hate, of envie, of revenge" (463–66).

212   From American poet Amelia B. Welby's (1819–52) "Seventeen" (1847).

213   Revelation 21:27.

No, I didn't laugh—even to myself. I didn't feel at all like laughing. I repeat that I found it pathetic and tragic; and I wondered what the God with whom I had been in close communion half an hour before on that windy green hill of clover would think of it all. Would He not have said, "Ye are all my children, blind, helpless, stumbling, mistaken, torturing yourselves with the creeds and dogmas of your own invention. In death I open a door and give you rest."

Thursday, June 21, 1923
The Manse, Leaskdale, Ont.

We were making calls in Zephyr tonight and of course the Pickering affair was dragged up everywhere while I secretly writhed in misery and humiliation. I hate to hear it talked about. The mere mention of it brings back all the wretchedness of those horrible months last fall.

John Rynard said that Risley had been telling that he had never been paid his witness fee yet. Risley is such a notorious liar that this is not necessarily true but it may be. If he hasn't then I fancy Grieg hasn't been either.

Ewan has had some headaches lately. I am afraid they herald another attack.

Thursday, June 28, 1923

We have had a very hot week and it has been hard on Ewan whose head has troubled him a good deal.

School is ended. Chester passed his promotion exams with honours—to our relief for as usual we had been afraid of arithmetic. It is very odd. He is not dull in understanding methods. It is just that he continually makes some silly mistake in adding or multiplying—sheer carelessness. And it seems that he cannot overcome it.

He will be in the entrance class to High School next year. It makes my heart sink to realize it. Oh, what will I do when my boys have to leave me?

I am very busy preparing for a trip to the Island. I don't feel enthusiastic about it some way. I think one reason is that I hate to leave Ewan here alone in case Grieg does or tries to do something—though what can he do? Nothing, that I know of. Yet there is always the dread that he will find out some legal twist through which to annoy us.

May jackals sit on his Grandmother's grave!

Chester

I have been reading Strachey's *Queen Victoria*.[214] Lord, how he smashes our old idols! When I was a child and young girl the Victoria myth was in full flower. We were brought up to believe that "the queen," from babyhood to old age, was a model for all girls, brides, wives, mothers and queens to follow. In those days every home boasted a framed picture of the queen—a luridly colored chromo, sent out as a "supplement" by a popular weekly. There was a crown and lace veil on her head, a broad blue ribbon over her breast, and jewels plastered on thickly everywhere. But the face! I looked at it in distaste and said, "Why, she's just a fat common looking old woman!" I shall never forget the look of horror on Grandfather's face. Talk of blasphemy—*lese majest-e*![215] I got a scorching rebuke, being told among other things that I should be ashamed of myself. I don't think I was. I only had an uncomfortable conviction that if Queen Victoria was really as "good" as she was said to be I must be very bad because I thought her ugly.

Strachey's book rather justifies me to myself. Poor Victoria hadn't any chance to be bad even if she wanted to be—and I *do* think she got tired at times of being so exceedingly proper. Prince Albert curbed her because she was unlucky enough to fall deeply in love with him. Mentally she was of very mediocre mould indeed, as anyone who read her published journals could see. But she had some qualities that helped to save her empire where a cleverer woman might have wrecked it. Her reign was a very wonderful epoch and its wonder made of a dumpy and dowdy little woman a symbol for a people who cannot do without symbols.

Sunday, July 8, 1923
The Manse, Leaskdale, Ont.

The past ten days have been a mad scramble. First there was a Sunday School convention here, with dinner and supper to be served in the classroom and endless committee meetings. Sunday was Communion Sunday—Monday we had company—Tuesday I had to go to Uxbridge—Wednesday the Missionary society met—Thursday we did some pastoral visiting—Friday we had a Mission Band quilting at Mrs. Leasks—Saturday the Mission Band met. And in my odd chinks and corners of time I have been getting ready to go east. I am about ready now and we leave tomorrow night.

Ewan has been very well this week. And he has given up saying his prayers! This is an excellent sign—as far as his mental condition is concerned at least.

---

214   British historian and writer Giles Lytton Strachey's (1880–1932) biography of Queen Victoria, published in 1921, was notoriously irreverent and witty.
215   An older term dating back to the Roman Empire, *lèse-majesté* refers to what was once the crime of undermining the dignity of a monarch.

How tragedy and comedy are mingled in this mad world!

I had a nasty dream last night. I'm sure it portends something disagreeable during my absence.

It struck me one day lately that I am beginning to look forward pleasurably to the daily arrival of the mail again. During the years of the war I dreaded it so that the feeling of dread persisted long after the war was over. Then I dreaded the mail because of what I might hear in regard to my lawsuits with the Page Co. And finally this past year it has been a torture because of the Grieg and Pickering matter. But lately there has been no particular reason to dread it and I find myself gradually slipping back to my old position of looking forward to mail time as a very pleasant incident of the day.

"Heart's Desire," Brighton, P.E. Island
Sunday, July 15, 1923

Monday night at seven o'clock we left Leaskdale manse. Wednesday night at about the same time we arrived at *Heart's Desire*—Fanny Mutch's[216] summer bungalow at Brighton. Our trip down was pleasant and uneventful. But one curious meeting befell me on board the car ferry.

I was crossing the lady's cabin when an elderly woman came up to me and said,

"I suppose you don't know me, Mrs. Macdonald."

For a moment I did not. I looked at the dowdy dress and hat, the untidy twist of gray hair with one forlorn end sticking out, the wrinkled, baggy face—and the cold, prominent, faded blue eyes. Where had I seen those eyes before? Then—I knew! One couldn't forget those eyes. They were bound up with some of the most disagreeable memories of my childhood.

Heart's Desire

"You are Mrs. Warren," I said, "once Miss Robinson."[217]

For it was she—that woman whom I have hated so bitterly for her old injustice and sarcasm. I had never seen her since she left Cavendish. She sat down beside me and talked to me all the time of our crossing. I had a queer feeling of unreality—I felt as if I had been hating a phantom—a creature that

216   Fannie Wise Mutch was an old friend from LMM's time at Prince of Wales College.
217   Isobel Robinson had been LMM's teacher in Cavendish, around the time LMM was 13.

never existed. This shabby bent old woman was not—could not be the bustling bitter young woman I remembered. I had a feeling that I had expended a great deal of passionate feeling on a very futile object. In brief it did not seem worth while to have hated her for over thirty years. My ancient grudge suddenly crumbled to dust.

At the same time I was feeling wickedly amused. This woman had evidently chosen to forget certain things and remember others which never existed. She spoke as affectionately of "dear old Grandmother and Grandfather" as if she had not bounced out of dear old Grandmother's house one night with Parthian insults,[218] and talked of both Grandfather and Grandmother afterwards in the nastiest fashion. She referred to my writing in those early years as if she had fostered my youthful talent and foreseen my future success before anyone else—she who had never noticed my scribbling save to sneer over it. As she maundered on with these insincerities, lavishing on me in twenty minutes enough compliments and praise for a lifetime, I was impishly recalling certain incidents of long ago and certain things she had said of me to others—"Her Satanic Majesty Maud"—"I never saw a child I disliked so much"—"one cannot teach one of her stripe anything"— and so on. I wonder what she would have said if I had suddenly mentioned these things. Denied them, probably. I have no doubt she utterly forgot them years ago. But she could not have forgotten that she left Grandfather's house in a senseless tantrum over a trifle and that he never let me go to school to her again. So one would have thought that some sense of shame or at least awkwardness would have prevented her from forcing herself upon me.

Fan met me at Borden and Margaret got on at Breadalbane and came as far as Hunter River.[219] She looks well but hasn't been at all well this past year—nerves bad etc. The menopause, in all likelihood.

Fan is big, fat, and as jolly as of yore. Her family are almost all grown up. I always liked Fan and she never changes.

Her little bungalow is beautifully situated, just where the North River empties into Hillsborough bay.[220] The sunset last night up North River was of a kind seen only in P.E. Island. We are situated here between two range-lights that burn enchantingly through the twilights, pearl-white against the ethereal

---

218　The ancient Parthians were famous for the ability of their horse-riding warriors to turn around and shoot arrows at a pursuing enemy. A Parthian shot (or insult) is a figurative expression for an insult hurled as the insulter is departing.

219　Borden, Prince Edward Island, was the ferry landing from New Brunswick. Margaret Ross was an old friend from Cavendish; she lived in Breadalbane, a community 36 kilometres/22 miles northwest of Charlottetown. She must have been on the train with LMM for 14 km/9 miles, the distance from Breadalbane to Hunter River.

220　The community of North River is across the North River from Charlottetown.

skies. Down the harbor there are more range lights and the big lighthouse and far out, seemingly in mid-harbor, shines the far-off light on Point Prim—a beacon "in fairylands forlorn."[221]

[Moonlight, North River, Charlottetown]

Next to us is a vacant lot full of daisies—a place of haunted loveliness in the twilights—and over the river daisied hayfields are as white as snow. I always come back to a realization of the Island's beauty with a certain amazement. I have always forgotten that it really is *so* lovely. There is nothing like it in smug opulent Ontario. I slip down to the shore sometimes in the late dusk, feeling how beautiful it is to be alone with the night again, with the stars all in their right places again over me and the white fields over the river lying lonely and lovely in the dim light, and gaze on water and field and hill with eyes that would devour them. In such exquisite moments I am a part of the sky and the night and the daisies blowing in the elfish wind.

[Stuart and Chester]

The boys go bathing in the river and Stuart is much intrigued with two adorable kittens of the establishment whose mother is named Nebuchadnezzar!![222] He takes them to bed with him and in the night I waken to hear old Nebby at my door, softly calling to her children in that nice throaty sound only a mother cat can make—really one of the nicest sounds in the world. The two kits answer—old Nebby springs up on the bed, and there is a glad and gay family reunion, with no end of the same pretty love-sounds. Then when the kittens have had their lunch away goes Nebby quite satisfied that her babies are in good quarters.

No doubt it is terribly unhygienic. Theoretically I sternly frown when Stuart pleads to have the kittens with him. But I notice that he has them for all; and I myself don't know of many nicer things than to waken up in the night and

---

221   From John Keats' (1795–1821) poem, "Ode to a Nightingale," a favourite of LMM. In the poem, the poetic voice addresses the nightingale, imagining the bird as an immortal being whose call has echoed through the ages: "The same [bird call] that ofttimes hath / Charmed magic casements, opening on the foam / Of perilous seas, in fairy-lands forlorn."

222   The name of a Babylonian King (in fact there were two "Nebuchanezzars"; the first lived c. 1125–1104 BCE and the second c.605 BCE–562 BCE).

put out a hand to feel a soft, warm, velvety purring little flank in the darkness.

Thursday evening we motored out to Winsloe to see Mary Campbell.[223] We had a merry evening; but there was something sorrowful about it. Dear old Mary looked so miserable. Her face haunts me. Truly it seemed to me like the face of a woman not long for this world. She has been ill for over a year—some kind of heart attacks. She is fretting too over her son Roland going west. He can't get on with his father—small blame to him for that—but he should not break his mother's heart. Youth never realizes—never understands.

[Stuart and kittens]

We had 'phoned out to Mary in the afternoon that we were coming and Maud had picked wild strawberries for us. They were delicious. And I had my own reasons for enjoying them doubly.

Saturday we went out to Earnscliffe with a picnic party.[224] The rest went digging clams and oysters but I simply sat on the river's bank and drank in the loveliness of the landscape, especially across the river with its high steep red banks and beyond them sheet after sheet of daisies and clover. Such clover! The red ones were as big as roses.

Oh, my Island is matchless—matchless. I feel that I did some violence to my spirit in leaving it. I *belong* here. It is *mine*—I am its own. It is in my blood. There is a part of me that *lives* only here. And to think that I did not really want much to come! How could I have been so insensible—I have been here only a few days but it seems as if I had never left it. Ontario—Leaskdale—they are dim and distant as a dream. This only is real—this colorful little land of ruby and emerald and sapphire.

Fan and I picked daisies for an hour today and knew we were *not* middle-aged mothers but gay, crazy college girls again, just loose from old P.W.C.

One exquisitely delightful thing about being here is that I am no longer surrounded by the miasma of Pickering. No one knows anything of it here—no one ever mentions it. After a year of stifling pressure this seems wonderful. I feel as if I had got out of some spiritual pest-house. The peace and beauty and happiness doesn't seem real.

223　Mary Campbell, LMM's cousin, had also been her roommate at Prince of Wales College.

224　Earnscliffe, Prince Edward Island, is on the south shore, some 25 km/15 miles southeast of Charlottetown.

[LMM and Fannie Mutch]

Cavendish, P.E. Island
Friday, July 20, 1923

How very natural it seems to write that.

Last Monday we went out to Kinross[225] and stayed there until yesterday morning. I had had a very nice time at *Heart's Desire*—and yet I was in nowise loth to leave!

Why?

Because both the children and myself were almost starved to death!

One could not believe, unless one had seen, the sketchy dabs of food that Fan called meals. She put on the table for ten people about enough for four— and most of it bought or canned stuff at that. I was in a state of chronic, gnawing hunger every moment of the time I was there. I could have endured it with a grin myself but it was dreadfully hard to manage the boys. They had the ravenous appetites of all sturdy boys and they were hungry all the time. I used to take them down to the shore—one dared not try to whisper in that thin, partitioned bungalow—and impress on them with threats of dire penalties that they must not ask for "pieces" or second helpings. They obeyed—but Stuart would sit at the table and look at me with the eyes of a hungry dog and sometimes whisper imploringly when Fannie had gone to the kitchen, "Mother, isn't there *anything* else?"

Had we been up town I would have sneaked them out to a hotel and fed them up or bought enough cakes to keep them in "pieces." But we were too far out of town for that and the "free-for-all" rooms of the bungalow precluded any private caches. So there was naught to do but endure. It spoiled my visit. I never want anything but plain food when I am a guest but I *do* want *enough* of it.

Aunt Christie's

225   Ewan's sister Christie lived in Kinross, a town 32 km/19 miles southeast of Charlottetown.

I don't know just where the blame lies. R.E. Mutch[226] has the reputation of being very mean. Fan is not mean but she is rather easy-going and does not try to make the most out of what R.E. allows.

The day we went to the picnic Fan took one small leathery lemon pie as her contribution—and there were eight of us. But the other cars took generous hampers and we had a feast. I was positively *faint* from hunger when I sat down to that picnic spread and I was ashamed of the way I ate. The boys got a filling up which enabled them to exist patiently until we got to Aunt Christie's Monday. Aunt C. had cold chicken and roast meat and biscuits and strawberries and cream—and she must have thought that Ontario people had awful appetites.

I hereby leave as a piece of valuable advice to my descendants this dictum—never starve your guests. No matter what you do *not* give them, give them enough to eat. Never mind frills if you can't afford them—they won't mind the absence of frills if they have enough to fill their stomachs. Man can't live by bread *alone* but bread he must have to begin with. Let no guest leave your doors with the gnawing sensation I had when I left *Heart's Desire*. You may have spoken with the tongues of men and angels but without sufficient meals you will be as sounding brass and twinkling symbols to your guests.

The Manse.

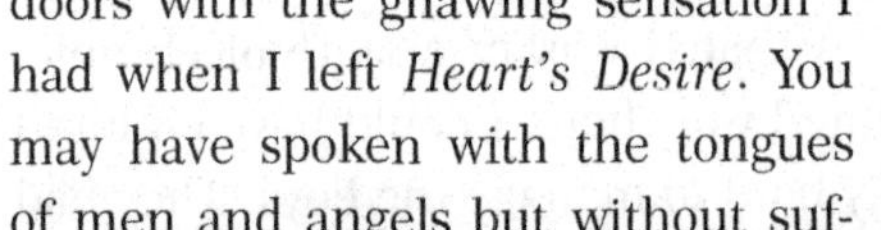

Entrance to Lover's Lane.

We had a very nice visit in Kinross and some lovely drives. The country was so beautiful and all along the wooded roads were little bays among the firs white with daisies. Yesterday morning we came to town and motored up to Cavendish. Last night there was a strawberry festival on the manse grounds and I saw so many old friends—some of them not seen for years. And yet "the old familiar faces" are growing fewer every time I go down. It is so delightful to be here. Some old gladness always waits here for me and leaps into my heart as soon as I return. I cannot describe how happy I feel. Today I went back to Lover's Lane. It looks much better than it did two years ago in the summer of the drouth. I missed some more old trees

226   Fannie had married Robert Everett Mutch in 1905; by 1923 he had become a successful businessman.

however. But I was very glad to see that any number of tiny birch and maple seedlings were springing up all along the fence side of it. Eventually if they have a chance to grow they will restore all its olden beauty to the lane. But will it be in my time?

The field beyond the lane was as lovely as of yore and so were all the silent remembered places. It is not only that I love these fields and woods. *They* love *me*.

The field beyond the lane.

Cavendish, July 21, 1923
Saturday

There is an amazing crop of kittens on the Island this year. Everywhere we go we find them—fat, fluffy, enchanting. Myrtle[227] has a dear thing called—ye gods!—*Savonarola*.[228] This beats even Nebuchadnezzar.

This evening was exquisite and I stole away for a walk. I find life here this summer easier than it has been in any of my previous visits. The boys are old enough to look after themselves and I do not have to keep tabs on them continually. Chester and Keith seem to enjoy each other's company this year and Stuart and Lorraine are cronies. In the evenings they join a crowd of Cavendish boys—the sons of my old schoolmates—and play baseball. This leaves me almost maiden-free.

So this evening I went over to the graveyard and kept tryst with my dead. The old spot was beautiful in the sunset light, with its plots snow-white with clover. And I did what sounds rather dismal but which did not seem dismal to me at all—I selected a plot for my own resting place. I want to be buried in Cavendish graveyard when my time comes. I want to lie among my kindred in the old spot I love so much better than any other spot on earth. As a minister's wife I shall not likely live long enough in any one place to make me feel

Stuart with Savonarola and Lorraine Webb

that I want to be buried there. Certainly I do not want to be buried anywhere where a Pickering could walk over my grave!

227　Myrtle Macneill had been born out of wedlock to a schoolteacher named Ada Macneill. Ada's aunt and uncle—Maud's Great-Uncle David Macneill and his sister Margaret—raised Myrtle, who was much beloved by them. In 1905 she married Ernest Webb, and the two inherited David and Margaret Macneill's farm.

228　Possibly after Florentine preacher Girolamo Savonarola (1452–98).

No, I belong here—this old Island gave me birth—it must give me a tomb. Here only can I rest at last—here it is fitting I should be buried. And it is fitting that Ewan should rest here, too. Cavendish was his first charge and it was he who converted the graveyard from the old jungle it once was into the orderly, well-cared for place it is today. One could say of him, buried there, as it is said of Wren, "If you seek his monument look around."[229]

I selected a plot on the crest of the hill, looking down on the beautiful scene I always loved—the pond, the shore, the sand-dunes, the harbor. On innumerable summer eves I have stood there and gazed on them, longing for some diviner speech to express what I felt. I want to feel that my last resting place is in sight of them.

It is rather odd that this plot should be vacant. It is one of the most desirable in the graveyard and all around it are taken up. I think it was predestined for me. There, sometime I shall lie and the wind will creep up from the sea to sing over me and the old gulf will croon me a lullaby—and

> "never a dream of the earth
> Shall break on my slumber with lure of an outlived mirth."[230]

Then in the afterlight I went halfway down the "Big Lane." It has grown very beautiful of late years because it has grown up so thickly with young spruces which when I left Cavendish were just feathering among the grasses. I walked among their shadows and found them better company than I find in the sunlight.

The evening was wonderful. A pale silver full moon shone in the sky. The roads were of that brilliant red peculiar to P.E. Island roads on a dewy evening after sunset. A break in the spruces on my left gave a sudden exquisite view of pond and dunes and harbor, all bathed in opal dust. A certain part of my soul, long starved, mounted up with wings as eagles. I was at home—heart and soul and mind I was at home. My years of exile had vanished—I had never been away.

Gartmore Farm, Cavendish, P.E. Island
Saturday, July 28, 1923

Tonight we came to Alec's. I was sorry to leave Myrtle's. We had a delightful visit there. I had such lovely walks through all my old haunts, bright with the beauty of the present and the iridescence of the past. One afternoon we spent at the shore. There's nothing in all the world like a sea wind. But one poetry

---

229   English architect Christopher Wren (1632–1723). Wren's remains are in St Paul's Cathedral; the English translation of the inscription on the plaque near his crypt reads, "Here in its foundations lies the architect of this church and city, Christopher Wren, who lived beyond ninety years, not for his own profit but for the public good. Reader, if you seek his monument—look around you."
230   From LMM's own poem, "A Request."

has vanished from the gulf forever. It is never now dotted with hundreds of white sails. The fishermen now have motorboats which chug-chug out in the morning and chug-chug back at night and are not on speaking terms with romance.

One evening I went down to Hamilton Macneill's[231] and told him I wanted to see the old place. Poor Hamilton was quite delighted. We sat awhile in the old sitting room where everything seemed exactly as it was forty years ago and therefore made me feel that I must be still a girl. Then he took me through the old garden and gave me a bunch of the old fat cabbage roses that I remember so well. Amanda used to bring bouquets of them to school to decorate our desk and old Aunt Caroline[232] always carried one to church. But the garden was overgrown and neglected—and full of ghosts.

x Stuart and the Webb children

Thursday I found a letter from Ewan in the box at the road. I carried it in, dreading to open it, for somehow I had the feeling as soon as I held it in my hand that there was something disquieting in it. There was. Ewan wrote that he had had a letter from Grieg "reminding" him that he had not paid the Pickering judgment and asking him to call at his office *at once* and pay it.

It was not Grieg's letter itself that disquieted me. Grieg knows well that Ewan has no money, so he cannot expect him to pay. But he must have had *some* purpose in writing it. The thought that worried me was that he must have found some legal device by which to annoy us and this letter was a necessary preliminary. I felt that my visit home, hitherto so lovely, was completely spoiled.

I had a hard afternoon and evening, trying to conceal my worry and talk naturally. I could not sleep at night until I took veronal. It seemed dreadful to be so far away from Ewan, unable to consult with him or help him if anything came up.

---

231   Hamilton Macneill, brother of LMM's childhood friend Amanda Macneill (Robertson).

232   In an entry for December 31, 1898, LMM describes "old Aunt Caroline," a sister of William C. Macneill ("William C." was the father of LMM's childhood friend Amanda) as a fixture in Cavendish: "She lived at Wm. C's and was his unmarried sister and household drudge. Poor old lady, I don't suppose there is a soul in the world who really regretted her or will miss her in any way. She was not an exhilarating person, being one of those unfortunates who are constantly worrying, not only about their own affairs but everybody else's as well, and will not give themselves or others any rest at all." See also note 46, page 18.

Friday morning Percy Turner came out to take me to Ch'town to speak to the Rotary Club.[233] I expected I would have a haunted day of it but the excitement and the necessity of concentrating my mind took my thoughts off my worry—I temporarily forgot it and had a nice time. I spoke on Canadian Literature and by way of dessert told of some amusing letters I had received from my readers. Judging from their peals of laughter the men enjoyed it. They gave me a big bouquet of roses and R.E. and Fan brought me out. It was pouring rain when I got back to Myrtle's and awaiting me was another letter from Ewan. This frightened me. If he had written so soon again there must be some more Grieg developments. I could not rush right upstairs to read it—I dared not open it in the presence of others lest it upset me completely. I knew I must not read it until I went to bed for if it were upsetting I did not want to have to talk to people until I had had the night in which to recover equanimity. So I sat and talked to the Webbs, giving an account of my day and all the time feeling as if I were in a bad dream. Finally I went to my room. I felt as if I could *not* endure any more bad news. Of course I *could* have—we always endure these things somehow. But fortunately I was not put to the test. When I said desperately to myself, "This has to be read. Open it!"—I opened it. Grieg *had* written another letter but when I read it all my worry ceased. It was a very different epistle from his former ones. Would Mr. Macdonald *kindly* call at his office and make some arrangement whereby the Pickering judgment could be wiped off?

Now, this letter carries its significance between the lines. Its real meaning is—"Pay us *something*—enough to cover the expenses of the trial and leave us where we were before it—and we'll let the rest go."

They cannot bring themselves to say this in plain words but there is no doubt that is what they mean. If Marshall Pickering could only get his expenses paid he'd be mighty glad to let the rest go—especially as he knows he hasn't any chance of getting it. Grieg would never have hinted at such a thing if he had any hope of finding a way to compel or harass us. So I felt quite easy again, went to bed and slept soundly and long, dismissing the matter from my mind.

Today the children and I had a lovely walk to old Deep Hollow and home through a path that, twelve years ago, was a mere trail through maple scrub but which now is wildly lovely with the maples grown into arching trees and the exquisiteness of wood blossoms all along it—Indian Pipes, star flowers, ladies' lips, rice-lilies.

We went back to the Hollow by way of Lover's Lane and I took a picture of the boys in it.

---

233   Rotary Clubs are an international organization designed to bring together business and professional leaders to provide humanitarian services and generally encourage ethical practices.

I don't know whether we shall enjoy our visit at Alec's as much as at Myrtle's. There are no children here for the boys to play with and I am afraid they will be lonely and I shall be kept on the job looking after them. Stuart was so lonely tonight that he cried. He missed Lorraine, I think.

But as for myself, it is lovely to be here again with May and Alec,[234] with the sound of the waves in my ears.

Chester with Stuart in Lover's Lane

Saturday afternoon, Aug. 4, 1923
Gartmore Farm, Cavendish, P.E.I.

We have had I believe even a nicer week than the one at Myrtle's. At least, I have enjoyed it even more for May and Alec are old cronies of mine, whereas Myrtle belongs to a generation a step removed from mine. Therefore there is more color and vivacity in our talks and we can discuss family folklore with the zest and spice possible only to genuine contemporaries.

Alec's place.
Gartmore Farm.

The boys, after one lonesome day, found themselves quite happy. They helped Alec coil and haul hay and occasionally went up the settlement to play with Cavendish boys and had a good time all round. Last Sunday it rained all day but the rest of the week it has been perfect—cool, clear, bright.

Our luck in kittens attends us. They have three beauties here of which one is the most oddly and beautifully marked cat I have ever seen—silvery gray with jet-black marks. The marks on his sides resemble a clover leaf with an M inside it and I said he would bring good luck so Chester suggested we call him that. I am going to try to take him home. I will not likely ever have such a chance again. Besides I want another cat from Gartmore Farm. The breed is good!

Stuart and Mike

234   Alexander Charles ("Alec") MacNeill (1870–1951) was the son of Mary Buntain (1828–1916) and Charles MacNeill (1831–1908), and the brother of LMM's childhood friend and cousin, Pensie MacNeill. (Alec's family spelled, and continue to spell, their name as MacNeill.) A second cousin to LMM and also an early romantic interest, Alec was married to May Hooper and lived in Cavendish.

One night Alec drove me down to see Lily Bernard,[235] over a road which Pensie and I often walked lang syne—poor Pensie, dead these twenty years but as vividly existent to me as if our schoolgirl frolics were of yesterday. Coming home it was dark and cloudy and rather cold and I revelled in it. There was something in that wild gray night with the fir trees tossing against a sullen sky that enchanted me. The wind's biting kiss filled me with a wild, lawless, secret, gypsy happiness, not to be translated into words.

I have always been glad that I possess the capacity to find the most intense pleasure in little things. Yesterday I was prowling about with my camera and I looked upon the little hill road east of Alec's and had one of my "flashes" of rapture in its beauty—rapture so poignant that I wrung my hands with the exquisite pain of it. It is in such moments as this that I know I can never die.

One night I had supper with Hammond and Emily[236] down in that old remote house by the Cove. Had a lovely time and came home around by the shore. I never felt happier than I did on that lovely evening by that blue majestic ocean. My own, own land!

When I reached Alec's Cove I heard gay voices up in the shore field and found the boys there helping Alec coil hay. I waited till they were through and then we went home in the clear afterlight with a little lad clinging to each hand.

Hauling in hay.

But, as always, the pleasantest hours of all were when the day was ended and the boys off to bed. Then May and Alec and I would get into the dining room and sit for a couple of hours around a lavish supper table—May is certainly a queen cook!—and eat and talk and laugh. Oh, laugh! It was delightful to be free to laugh with boon companions again. One evening in especial we laughed until we could laugh no more.

Alec produced a "diary" his father had kept for several years and we read it together. I don't think I ever read anything quite so delicious in my life.

Charles Macneill was an odd sort of a man, whom as a child I always loved because he was so kind to children. But I think that both as a neighbor and a father he left a good deal to be desired. He inherited from his mother—his father was not one of "our" Macneills but his mother was—a queer streak of the Macneill literary knack—a tiny thread of gold running through the slag of

235   Lily Bernard and her brother Oliver McNeil (1864–1943) were Cavendish neighbours, first mentioned in 1890 in LMM's journals. Oliver is mentioned often in the journal of Charles Macneill.
236   Hammond and Emily Mackenzie were long-time Cavendish friends.

a very commonplace character. It flashed out here and there in the diary in several naive, satiric entries which were so artless and spontaneous that I could actually hear old Charles Macneill uttering them. We laughed until the tears poured from our eyes.

The hill road.

Apart from the unconscious humor of the diary it gave me the keen, sad delight of a vanished world re-created. It made old Cavendish live again—the Cavendish of my childhood and girlhood. It was all there in those little shabby notebooks as no deliberate attempt at description could ever produce it. Men and women long dead lived there again as in yesterday. The little affairs of church and state in a remote P.E. Island farming community were reflected there as in a mirror. I looked in it and saw the world of my teens pass before my eyes again. Oh, yes, we laughed—but behind the laughter was a sigh—and that is the difference between the laughter of youth and the laughter of middle age.

I must finish the record of my visit with Alec and May in another volume. It is a long time since I concluded a volume of my journal in old Cavendish. This book holds the records of only four years—but they have been a very hard, bitter and difficult four years.

[END OF LMM'S HANDWRITTEN VOLUME 5]

[BEGINNING OF LMM'S HANDWRITTEN VOLUME 6]

Saturday, August 4, 1923
Gartmore Farm, Cavendish,
P.E. Island

[Gartmore Farm]

I always have a feeling of fate when I begin a new volume of my journal and look at its unwritten pages. *What will be written on them?* One always asks oneself that question and there is never any answer. With every succeeding volume I ask it more fearfully.

Again I begin a volume in Cavendish—this time at Gartmore Farm. Alec has discovered from some old papers of his father's that this was the original name of this farm. There are various spellings—Garthmore—Gartmoor etc. I like the custom of naming farms. It seems to give them a personality. It is a custom which has never obtained in P.E. Island—which is odd, because most of the early settlers came from Scotland and England where all the farms are named. And they named theirs to some extent—but their descendants dropped it.

My week at Gartmore Farm has been almost wholly delightful. The only annoyance has been the carloads of callers—generally perfect strangers—who have come to see "L.M. Montgomery" and have more than once upset plans May and I had formed. One of these, a severe maiden lady from Ontario, named "Bentley," informed me that she had a crow to pluck with me. It seems in one of my books "Miss Cornelia" mentions a man named "Bentley" who was a drunkard! Miss Bentley was pleased to inform me that "no Bentley ever was a drunkard."!!!!!

Another caller was a Mrs. Stirling McKay. I had a letter from her recently—very nicely written on correct stationery but signed with the damnatory signature of "Mrs. Stirling McKay." She wanted me to go to Summerside and spend a week with her! Considering that she is a total stranger to me I thought this an odd request. I had heard of her husband, Stirling McKay, a wealthy business man of S'Side and a friend of John Stirling's. But of her I knew absolutely nothing. I wrote back, courteously explaining that I had so little time to spend with my old personal friends that I could not include a visit to Summerside.

Well, the family came today in person. Mrs. McKay said she wanted to give

a lawn party in my honor when I was at Breadalbane and have me and the Stirlings in. I said I did not think I could go—I had only two days at Breadalbane etc. Oh, Mrs. McKay had already been to see Mrs. Stirling and had talked it all over with her. She did not exactly say in so many words that Margaret was eager for the party but she certainly contrived to give me that impression. So I yielded for if Margaret, after her shut-in winter among the aborigines of Breadalbane, was hungry for a little social diversion who could wonder? I told Mrs. M. I would go to her party and sent her away quite happy.

And now my visit in Cavendish is at an end. I go tonight to Park Corner and for the first time in my life I am dreading a visit there. It has been so beautiful here. And I know I will be lonely at Park Corner.

Everywhere I have gone this summer I have heard fulminations against Uncle John[237] for tearing down the old home. The Charlottetown people were especially indignant. They said it was the only "literary shrine" the Province possessed and it was a shame to destroy it.

For my own part, though I know as everybody else in Cavendish knows, just what Uncle John's motive was, I am well content that it should be torn down. It would not please me to think of it being overrun by hordes of curious tourists and carried off piecemeal. The Bentley party had their car full of some old junk they had retrieved from the cellar!

I have never seen the vacant place. When I have been anywhere on the road where I could see it I have averted my eyes.

Uncle John and Aunt Ann Maria look old and she is very failed. Ern has had a great deal of trouble with his wife. She is a nice little thing but her mind was badly affected for several years. Since the birth of her first child a year ago she has been much better. Lucy is a *grandmother*. The thought dazes me. Her only son married when he was seventeen and they did not know it for months. He has been a wild fellow, I understand. Ben Simpson's son would have small chance of being a model character, I suppose. But one never can tell, how children will turn out. One of my sons may break my heart, too.

Sunday Night, Park Corner
August 5, 1923

Last night Milton Green motored us over here. We called to say goodbye to Myrtle and I got *three* letters from Ewan. This fact spoiled my drive over in the

---

237   John Franklin Macneill (1851–1936), a son of LMM's maternal grandparents; relations between Uncle John and LMM had long been strained. He and his wife Ann Maria had six children, including Lucy (1877–1974) and Ernest (1884–1969).

Children at Park Corner.

Aunty and her hens.

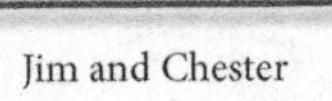

Jim and Chester

beautiful evening. They were all fat letters mailed the same day. My dread leaped at once to Grieg and Pickering. Something must have happened if Ewan had to write three letters so close together.

I dared not open them last night but this morning I shut myself up in my room, set my teeth and opened them. And the bogey my fear had created vanished. Two of them merely contained several letters to me from readers; and the one from Ewan himself contained nothing worse than some gossip re Pickering, who has broken his mysterious silence—evidently having concluded that it wasn't going to bring him any information—and is abusing Ewan everywhere and raving wildly, much to the amusement of the township.

But last night was painful to me. I found Aunt Annie[238] looking so thin. She seems fairly smart again and is beginning to sleep and eat well; but she has failed greatly since I saw her last.

And George's family are almost grown up. Dan is a man. Amy a big girl of twelve looking fifteen. Handsome—jolly—naive! Jim is a smart chap. He and Chester announced that they were going to sleep in the back bedroom and did so. They talked until three o'clock.

Maud and Georgie.

238　Aunt Annie was the daughter of LMM's maternal grandparents, Alexander and Lucy Woolner Macneill, where LMM had spent time as a youth. LMM's cousin George had passed away in 1918 during the influenza epidemic (as did a son, George Jr), leaving behind a wife, Ella, and several children: Jim, Donald (LMM and Frede called him "Dan"), Amy, Maudie, and Georgie. Aunt Annie's children, mentioned in the next sentence, were George, Frede, Stella, and Clara.

The birches behind the barn.

Maud is a very nice child and Georgie seems bright and sharp. Oh, they are all nice youngsters—but where are Clara and Stella, Frede and George? When I went to bed I was so lonely I cried half the night and couldn't sleep. Oh Frede, Frede, how I missed you last night! Here was the mirror that had reflected your face! Where were you? Where was the savor and vivacity of your speech? It seemed to me that I could *not* stay at Park Corner—that I must rush away in the morning—anywhere, away from this agony of loneliness.

Today was bearable however—days always are. Aunt Annie and Ella are so glad to have me here that their gladness surrounds me with a warm pleasant feeling. Old Park Corner is still beautiful—the birches down the lane and behind the barn are as white and stately as of old. There is an eternal triangle in birch trees—you so often see them growing in groups of threes.

Tuesday, Aug. 7, 1923
Park Corner, P.E.I.

In the days I am having a restful, quite pleasant time. But at night when the new family are asleep the ghosts come back and haunt me. They walk along the hall and tiptoe up the stairs and peep in at the door. Sometimes, indeed, even in the day, I have a ghostly

Birches down the lane

thrill for Dan's voice is so exactly like George's when heard out in the yard that I start when I hear it. Chester and Stuart are having a great time and the house is filled with laughter and frolic from dawn to dark. But not *my* laughter—not Frede's laughter. *That* laughter only echoes faintly in the darkness.

Last night Aunt Annie and I walked over to see Aunt Mary.[239] As we went along the road by Heath Montgomery's bush I happened to be telling Aunt Annie of an entry in Charles Macneill's diary:—"Today in the woods I cut down an old oak tree—the last of its race."

I said:—"I never knew that there were any oak trees on Prince Edward Island. I never saw one."

"Nor I either," said Aunt Annie.

---

239   Aunt Mary was the widow of Cuthbert Montgomery, LMM's father's brother.

Whereupon we both lifted up our eyes and there, right before us, were two big oak trees in Heath's woods. Talk of coincidence!

I had tea with Aunt Eliza[240] today and found Ellen Montgomery there—an old friend not seen for many years. She is seventy now but very bright and smart and full of the old, unmistakable, inimitable Montgomery flavor. I was always very fond of her and it was a pleasure to see her again.

Heath is a fine looking fellow. And he is going to make a wretched misalliance. It is too bad. He is going to marry a girl whose mother was a Hogan—a girl with no family or background. When I heard it I thought that perhaps she was pretty—or at least buxom and colorful. But she is almost repulsive. Not even a man could find her charming. And it is such a common, vulgar ugliness—not a striking or piquant homeliness. The only word that really describes her is the hideous one of *slob*. I can't imagine what possesses Heath. He is a man who could take his pick; and yet he is going to put that creature in the place of all the dear stately ladies of the old house. His mother, Aunt Eliza, is odd enough; but she is a lady. And Kate Hogan's daughter is to be mistress where Anne Murray and Louisa Cundall once reigned.[241] It is enough to make the old Senator turn over in his grave.

There is one house I will not visit this time—nor ever again probably—a house where hitherto I have always been a welcomed guest. Next farm, up behind the spruce bush, was William Ramsay's house. Mr. and Mrs. Ramsay were always friends of mine and many a jolly visit have Frede and Stell and I had there. Last winter Mr. and Mrs. Ramsay died within a few weeks of each other. The beautiful home was sold—and purchased by strangers of a totally different class. I feel so badly over it that I cannot even bear to look in its direction.

Every night poor Aunt Annie trots into the pantry and gets up a lunch for me. It pleases her so much that I make no protest though I am seldom hungry. I do not eat it in the pantry—I can't bear to. But I sit in the dining room *alone* and eat it and try to keep the tears back that Aunty may not see. For these solitary "snacks" are very bitter when those who once shared them with me are gone.

It rained heavily tonight. I love a P.E. Island rain.

---

240   Cousins on LMM's father's side. In an entry dated May 7, 1911, LMM had written, "Aunt Eliza is not liked by anyone. She has two children. Heath, the oldest, is a fine-looking young fellow, but reckless and dissipated. There are gleams of his father in him that warmed my heart to him, for I always loved Uncle Jim who so strongly resembled my father. But there was another strain I did not like."

241   Anne Murray and Louisa Cundall were two wives of LMM's grandfather on her father's side, Donald Montgomery (1808–93). Montgomery had been a politician, serving as a Conservative in the Senate of Canada from 1873 until his death in 1893.

The old pond is very lovely this summer. And on summer evenings the old back yard is full of frolicking children as of yore.

Wednesday, Aug. 8, 1923
Park Corner, P.E. I.

This afternoon I shut myself in the parlor and looked over a pile of old photographs of the vintage of puffed sleeves and pompadours.[242] Nothing has a more ghostly pleasure than this. One photo I came across was of Ed Simpson[243] taken some thirty years ago. Ed, by the way, has recently been on a tour around the world. His wife caught smallpox in Calcutta but has recovered. I heard this in Cavendish but nothing more except that Ed is very gray. Well, we are all getting gray but it must make a great change in Ed whose hair was so thick and dark. Poor Ed. The whole tale of that old affair seems so faint and far-off now that it has ceased to be anything more than a mere memory.

The old back yard.

Lem McLeod, too—he is on P.E. Island, a helpless charge on his brother's family. He is suffering from paralysis agitans[244]—but of a worse variety than Uncle Leander's. I wanted to go to see him but have been dissuaded. I am told that his look would haunt me. Nevertheless, I would have liked to see him.

Tonight Life Howatt[245] motored me up to see Aunt Emily.[246] We went up through Seaview and Darnley, over a road haunted by memories of Frede and Stella, who both taught in Seaview school.[247] There is one beautiful hill where we always met, when I, visiting at Park Corner, started in the late afternoon to

242   A pompadour was a style of arranging hair that dated back to the reign of Louis XV in eighteenth-century France; Louis' mistress, Madame de Pompadour (1721–64), popularized it. The style consists of hair swept upwards from the face and worn high over the forehead.
243   LMM had been engaged to Edwin Simpson in 1897; she broke off the engagement a year later.
244   That is, what would now be called Parkinson's Disease.
245   Eliphalet Howatt, a Park Corner neighbour.
246   Emily Macneill Montgomery, daughter of LMM's maternal grandparents, married John Malcolm Montgomery, one of LMM's father's cousins; the relationship between LMM and Aunt Emily had long been strained. Aunt Emily lived in Princetown, Prince Edward Island.
247   Seaview and Darnley are two small communities on the north shore, a few miles west of Park Corner.

meet one of them coming home. There was a magnificent sunset. The dream-like beauty of the landscape, unusually green for August, even in P.E. Island, was something not to be believed unless seen.

I found Aunt Emily not very well. She struck me as being very lonely.

Sometimes when I visit Aunt Emily she is so nice that I wonder why I ever thought she wasn't pleasant to visit. Other times she stings and slues[248] until I come away thinking I am justified in hating her. Tonight was one of her nice times and I enjoyed my chat with her.

It seemed nice to come back to Park Corner. After all, as long as Aunt Annie is here Park Corner will seem home to me.

Thursday, Aug. 9, 1923
Park Corner, P.E. Island

This morning when I wakened I found Stuart bending over me and saying in an eerie tone,

"Mother, we won't both live to get back to Ontario. We won't both step together into Leaskdale Manse."

The thing haunted me all day though I laughed at him and myself. I suppose he was worried because I was going away for the day. Stuart has been a haunted child ever since that night I spent at Amanda's. It was the first night he and Chester had been left without both Ewan and me away from home.

It seems he dreamed that night that the house where I was staying had been burned and me in it. Myrtle said he stood out in the yard next day and watched the lane all day until I came home. Since then he seems to dread my going anywhere and worries till I get back.

I went to Bedeque today to speak to a camp of C.G.I.T.s[249] there this afternoon. The camp is in a lovely spot and at first I felt as if I envied those girls. But on consideration I do not. I don't believe I'd care to be one of a camping crowd. I never liked a mob; and to live in the woods with several overseers to watch every step wouldn't please me at all. To be there alone with Frede or Bertie—oh, that would be the right sort of camping. To bask on the clover in the sunshine—bathe in the flaming river at sunset—loaf on the bracken in the woods—sit at nightfall by a camp fire—tell the stars at midnight over the dark woods—and feel always near at hand, within touch or call, the comrade who understood!

I spoke my piece—on *Friendship*—posed before twenty cameras—chatted with visitors—answered innumerable questions—and now and then looked

---

248 A nautical term meaning to swing around or otherwise change direction suddenly.

249 That is, Canadian Girls in Training, a church-based program for girls and young women between the ages of 11 and 17.

across the river to Lower Bedeque and the fields of the old Leard farm.[250] But those ghosts, too, are laid.

I was impressed by one thing—the plainness to the point of homeliness of those C.G.I.T.s. They seemed bright and jolly. But, with one exception, there was of beauty little and of charm not a trace. That exception was a little slip of a girl with brown hair, a delicious complexion, and a fillet of Junebell vine around her head that gave her the look of a young oread[251] or spruce-wood nymph. She was the only one I could conceive of a man's falling in love with. I think the sporting flapper of today has lost something. The girls of my day, as I recall them, had more lure and mystery.

I got home at dark, rather relieved to find that after all Stuart had not got drowned in the pond. Nobody ever *has* been drowned in that pond. I would have supposed that the mothers who brought up big families beside it would have been haunted by grisly worries regarding it but I don't remember hearing that they ever were.

Sunday, Aug. 12, 1923
Park Corner, P.E.I.

This morning I was in Long River church. I don't think there were more than fifty people there—and I was told there were more out than usual. I remember when that church was full every Sunday, gallery and all.

This afternoon Ella and I drove ourselves through to Long River to see her mother. The auto is all right for long journeys, bad weather, or a crowd. But for sheer simple pleasure I would choose a horse and buggy any time. I enjoyed every minute of that drive from the time we drove out through the old trees at the entrance until we returned through them. It was a gray gentle day, always looking like rain but never raining. We poked along and at every turn or curve

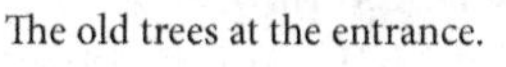

The old trees at the entrance.

one of the arch, provocative, elusive beauties of a P.E. Island landscape would reveal itself. Dan was at Long River and drove us home in the gray twilight. There is one of the most wonderful

250 The year she taught in Lower Bedeque (1897–98), LMM boarded with the Leard family. She fell in love with Herman Leard, a son of the family. The affair is described in a long entry of April 8, 1898.

251 From Greek mythology; an oread is a mountain nymph.

views on the Island from a certain hill back of Park Corner and the melancholy loveliness of the night wind off the sea sent an almost physical pang through me.

Monday, August 13, 1923

Little Hugh would have been nine years old today had he lived.[252] I wonder what he would have looked like.

Thursday, Aug. 16, 1923
The Manse, Breadalbane, P.E.I.

Tuesday was my last day at Park Corner. I felt very badly. In some ways my visit here has been sorrowful and yet there has been much pleasure and sweetness in it. And I felt so keenly over going away because I can never feel sure now that Aunt Annie will be here when I come again. She is 75. And at the best I cannot have many more visits with her in this dear old place. I might never have even another.

And she feels so badly over my going. She and Ella gave themselves up on Tuesday to preparing banquets for us, as if that were the only way they could

[Breadalbane Manse]

express their feelings, poor souls. A dinner of wild ducks—a supper of chickens—the old table groaned as of yore.

Stella and Clara want Aunty to go out and spend the winter in Los Angeles and Clara has actually offered to send her money for the trip. Friends of hers are going, too. I have been urging Aunty to go and promised her I would give her $100 to pay for her clothes. I don't know whether it is a wise thing. Certainly, once she was there, it would be splendid. She would escape the cold winter and get rested and built up. But such a long journey for an old woman who is liable to sudden attacks like hers is a serious thing.

Yes, Aunt Annie *is* an old woman. I can never believe it but it is true.

It was a hard parting. Heath motored us to Breadalbane. Margaret and I talked most of the night. On Wednesday the McKays motored out for us and Mrs. McKay's reception came off. Over 300 people came—the "old families"

252   A reference to LMM's second baby, Hugh, a stillbirth. He was born August 13, 1914.

to a woman. So she had her wish and was quite happy. Margaret and I had our own wicked private fun out of it all.

Among the guests were Oliver Macneill[253] and his wife who are living in S'side now. Oliver has changed a good deal. It was very funny to recall that the last time I saw him he was down on his knees imploring me to marry him— and that one part of me wanted to while the other part of me laughed at him. His wife is quite nice looking and the best dressed woman there.

When we were leaving Mrs. McKay gave me a parcel which she entreated me to accept as a "souvenir." As there was a crowd around I did not want to make a scene by refusing but I did not like to take it. It was as if she were trying to pay me for coming to her house. Margaret got a plate and Doris a vase and the boys balls and Mr. McKay sent a pearl handled knife to Ewan!!

When we got home I opened my parcel and saw cup, saucer and two plates of what I thought at first glance was Crown Derby[254] but on looking at the hall-mark discovered to be Crown Aynsley. By an odd coincidence it is the same pattern as a slightly larger plate of real Derby I have at home. I doubt if Mrs. McKay knew the difference.

Today Margaret and I had a delightful day of sheer *talk* and tasted every minute.

Tomorrow I leave P.E. Island. I shrink from the thought.

St. John, N.B.
Friday, Aug. 17, 1923

We left Breadalbane this morning of fresh August sunshine and reached St. John at seven. Had a hurried dinner, dressed hurriedly and went to a reception Mrs. Raymond, president of the Canadian club, gave for me. It was very delightful and I had a good time. As I went into the reception room I heard some woman behind me gasp,

"Oh, doesn't she look just like Queen Victoria!"

Her enraptured voice seemed to imply that she meant to be complimentary—but a glance at Queen Victoria's picture casts a shade of doubt on the matter!

---

253   Oliver Macneill was a second cousin who lived in the United States, an early romantic interest. In an entry of September 21, 1909, LMM wrote, "Tonight I realized clearly that Oliver Macneill is one of those men of whom I have met a few in my life—men who, without being able to inspire in me one spark of real love or even admiration, yet have the power to kindle in me a devastating flame of the senses. I have a horror of feeling thus towards any man I cannot marry." "S'side" is Summerside a town 60 km/37 miles northwest of Charlottetown.
254   Royal Crown Derby Porcelain is one of the oldest porcelain manufacturers in England; Crown Aynsley porcelain is of lesser quality.

St. John, N.B.
Saturday, Aug. 18, 1923

Dr. Mahoney[255] motored us to Hampton today where we had luncheon at the Wayside Inn, and came back to Rothesay to have tea at Major McLaine's. The house and grounds were beautiful. The Major has been a great traveller and has picked up some things, especially a certain screen of Chinese embroidery that smashed the commandment on coveting all to pieces for me. And yet when the owner of all this magnificence was introduced to me all he could find to say was, "This visit of yours to St. John will greatly help the sale of your books here."

Russell Macneill[256] himself could hardly have bettered that! Even wealth, rank, social position and globe trotting can't qualify for the clan Joseph.

Sunday, Aug. 19, 1923
St. John, N.B.

We had another delightful motor trip up the St. John river today. The Mahoneys are certainly showing me a good time. Mrs. Estey is thinner than when I saw her last but the same sweet woman. Maud is very pretty, very clever, very kind, with a bit of Mrs. Leo Hunter in her. I like Dr. Mahoney. He is a Catholic. Maud's marriage to him broke her father's heart. Mrs. Estey must feel it. But he is devoted to Maud, indulges her in everything and they seem very happy.

Aunt May[257] came to see me this evening and I enjoyed our chat. She has changed little save to get gray. We talked over those old Cavendish days. She brought me a real treasure trove—a letter written by my mother to Uncle Leander which she found in one of his boxes after his death. I was overjoyed to get it. I never had a scrap of mother's composition before. The letter was undated but must have been written when she was a very young girl, as she was going to school. It is a rather stiff little epistle, such as a letter written to a much older brother away at college or already in the ministry would be apt to be. It doesn't express any of mother's real personality but it is delightful to have it.

---

255   LMM had boarded with Mrs Ada Estey and her husband during her year teaching in Bideford, Prince Edward Island, in 1894–95. Ada's daughter Maud was now married to Dr Mahoney and had kept up the friendship with LMM. The identity of Major McLaine is unknown.
256   Russell Macneill was another son of May and Charles Macneill (that is, a brother of LMM's friend Alec). Here, LMM uses a favourite expression, "the race that knows Joseph," meaning a congenial soul.
257   Aunt May was the widow of LMM's Uncle Leander, a son of her maternal grandparents.

Saturday, Aug. 25, 1923
The Manse, Leaskdale, Ont.

How long will it be "the Manse, Leaskdale?" The answer to that depends largely on the "Church Union" question. The storm of conflict is plainly making itself heard in Ontario.

We came home yesterday. Last Monday I spoke in the Imperial Theatre at St. Johns and left for home that night, so exceedingly tired that I promptly took a bad cold, as I always do when tired. We had to stay overnight in Montreal so in the evening I took the boys to a movie. Just as we went up the hill from the Queen Hotel my heart gave a sudden painful throb. There was a church on the corner and in a corner of its grounds, raised from the street by a terrace of stone was a certain tree. Under that tree Frede and I once stood for hours, waiting to see Balfour and his party pass in the spring of 1917.[258] I recalled all the jokes with which we beguiled the time until that little green corner echoed to our unconquerable laughter. In the damp and darkness Frede stood under that tree and laughed to me over those six years of change and heartbreak.

The next day we came to Trenton and stopped off to visit Ralph and Laura.[259] Ewan arrived there the same night. He seems very well and this is a great relief for I had dreaded coming home and finding him dull and depressed.

Aylsworth Home.

We motored home from Trenton yesterday. On the way we were held up for a few minutes by some work on the road and one of the men came up and began talking to Ewan. Finding out who he was he said, "You're the man that was in that lawsuit last year. How did you get along?"

So I am back in the Pickering atmosphere again and must expect these reminders, like acrid stings. Ewan has heard nothing from

[Macdonald family and Aylesworth children]

258   Arthur James Balfour (1848–1930), who had succeeded Edward Grey as British foreign secretary in 1916, travelled to the United States to confer with American leaders in April and May of 1917. He also came to Canada to address Parliament on May 28, 1917, and to speak to the Montreal chapter of the Canadian Club two days later.
259   Laura McIntyre was the daughter of Mary Montgomery McIntyre (LMM's father's sister); she had married Ralph Aylesworth.

Grieg since those letters and nothing of Pickering.

Still, it is nice to be home. And yet—I'm horribly homesick for the Island and my friends there.

Wednesday, August 29, 1923
Leaskdale, Ont.

Emily of New Moon is out. I got two reviews today, both very favorable. The cover design of Emily is the prettiest one on any of my books I think. The little girl really does look as I imagined "Emily" looked. But there has been one weird mistake. The moon in the picture is an old moon, not a new one! Absit omen![260] The U.S. artist should really take a course in nature study.

I very seldom draw a character "from life"—"Peg Bowen" in the *Story Girl* is almost the only instance heretofore. But "Miss Brownell" of *Emily* is the Izzie Robinson of my own childhood. I gave myself that little bit of satisfaction!

New Moon is in some respects but not all my own old home and "Emily's" inner life was my own, though outwardly most of the events and incidents were fictitious. If poor George Campbell had lived to read *Emily*—or be told of it, for George never read anything—he would have laughed over the incident of the poisoned apple. He nearly frightened poor Heath Montgomery to death one evening when Heath was a small kidlet by telling him a big apple he had been eating had been poisoned for rats. That was George's idea of a joke.

The English edition of *Emily* has a plain cover but a pictured jacket. Somehow there is a certain eerie quality about the English artist's conception of "Emily" that I like. It is more *Emilian*. The English do these things better than the Americans.

I have been suffering all the week with an ulcerating tooth. It makes me homesick for heaven.[261]

I began work again on *Emily II*. Find it hard to get back into the stream of thought.

Thursday, Sept. 13, 1923

Lily is away for her vacation and Elsie is here—a most agreeable change. To be sure Lily, ever since that preachment I gave her nearly a year ago, has been quite amiable and well-behaved. But she continues to be hopelessly untidy, shiftless and forgetful—and unteachable. She is of the type that can't be

260　Latin for "may this (evil) omen be absent"; the expression, no longer very common, was used when referring to something undesirable, signalling a hope that whatever it was would not occur.
261　Before antibiotics and modern dental care, ulcerating teeth could lead to very serious infections, occasionally fatal.

taught anything and I have given up the vain attempt. A young fellow up the Seventh has begun driving her round and I sincerely and devoutly hope that he will marry her.

Today Ewan and I motored up to Bellhaven to visit Ferg Lockie's—old friends of ours who moved from Zephyr two years ago. It was a cold windy day but I enjoyed the drive. Ewan is so well. He seems—nay, is, perfectly well. I cannot hope it will last—he was just as well last fall—but it is much to have even a respite. He is taking a real interest in his work again—something he hasn't done since 1919.

For one reason I dreaded going to Fergus Lockie's. I knew the Pickering affair would be canvassed, since Ferg's mother was one of our witnesses. It was—and spoiled our supper for me. Fergus told us that Jake Meyers had been telling him that at a recent threshing[262] Pickering tackled him, trying to find out how the salary came to be paid in advance. Jake told him it was none of his business and gave him a proper dressing down. Pickering's psychology is curiously illustrated by this. Jake is one of our best friends and his wife was one of our witnesses. How could Pickering suppose he could find out anything from him? But the whole subject has such a horror for me that when Fergus began to tell what Jake told him I found my hands trembling so that I had to clench them together to keep them still. There *is* something for Pickering to find out, if he could. And if he did he could make serious trouble for us. It is not in the least likely he ever can or will find it out but the possibility keeps me worried.

I have just finished reading *Les Miserables*.[263] Oddly enough, I never read it before. I can hardly explain why. I heard about it when I was very young. I knew it was one of those books everybody ought to read—one of the acknowledged masterpieces of the world. Several times I had an opportunity of reading it but could I prevail on myself to begin it. I always meant to "some day" but the some day never came. What was the reason? I do not know.

But this fall I said, "Now, I'm going to *make* myself read *Les Miserables*." I *made* myself read the first few chapters. Then there was no further making. Or rather, the difficulty lay in making myself stop. I read hours when I should have been sleeping. One part of me enjoyed the book, another part shuddered in pain over it—but always it was fascinating. I am through with it—I don't think I'll ever want to read it again—but I would have missed a wonder out of life if I hadn't read it.

I have a busy fall before me. The Guild young people are going to get up a play and have asked me to attend the practices and stage manage the affair. I didn't feel that I could refuse them but I do grudge the two evenings out of

262	A process of separating seeds from the stalks and husks.
263	1862 novel by Victor Hugo depicting the life of impoverished nineteenth-century Parisians.

every week that I shall have to give to it. I will hardly have an evening at home for two months.

Saturday, Sept. 29, 1923
The Manse, Leaskdale

The mad rush has begun. Last Monday the township school fair was held in Leaskdale. Stuart was one of the competitors in the speech making contest and won first prize although the three other speakers were much older than he was.

I had ten people to tea that night and Elsie and I were dog tired when the last dish was washed up. Tuesday night we began to practise the play. It is a rather funny thing, simple and crude. It would be no use to try to get up anything else with the material we have or for the audience we will play to. Wednesday I went to Uxbridge, had company to tea and went calling once on the Fifth[264] in the evening.

Thursday I had a wire from Ella telling me that Aunt Annie was starting for California next Thursday. I knew she would likely go and I am glad but it gave me a horrible lost lonely feeling. Park Corner without Aunt Annie—without one of those who used to be there! It made me so lonely and homesick that I went to my room and cried.

Went to practice at night. Friday evening we were out calling. This is my first quiet home evening this week and I have answered a stack of business letters.

Saturday, Oct. 6, 1923
The Manse, Leaskdale

The rush continues. Monday I went to a meeting of the Hypatia Club at Mrs. Gould's[265] in Uxbridge and enjoyed it, but had to go to practice at night and came home with a headache. Aspirin and to bed.

Tuesday we had to take the boys to the Scott Fair at Zephyr and stayed for the concert at night. In the hall where the fancy work was exhibited I saw the Pickerings, man and wife, and looked them squarely in the face. They both look miserable enough. I fancy "if yesterday were tomorrow," as the old saying

---

264   That is, the Fifth Line road, a county road.
265   That is, Mary Gould Beal (see also note 453, page 320).

goes, Marshall Pickering would be very glad to find the whole thing a dream. Their presence poisoned the atmosphere for me. How they can have the effrontery to face their old neighbors after the lies they told puzzles me. But I suppose such people never feel shame.

Wednesday I went to the Missionary Society and had company to tea. Thursday night was practice—and a discouraging one, so many being missing. Of course in a play having twenty three characters one couldn't expect them all to be there every night—but there were really too few that night. Friday night we visited a couple in Zephyr whom we don't like and I called on the new Methodist minister's wife there—Mrs. Quaife, who doesn't apparently have any connection with the tribe of Joseph.

Last night there was a hard frost and my garden went. The glory of the cosmos has departed. It has been very beautiful.

This morning we went to Uxbridge and brought home a vociferous gray kitten in a small wooden box—Good Luck. We left him at Park Corner, having decided that we could not bring him home with us, owing to our stop-offs. Dan shipped him by express Thursday morning. He was brisk and happy and as beautiful as ever. Really, he is quite the most beautiful cat I ever saw. His markings are unique. Pat looks quite faded and ordinary beside him. Pat is very much peeved about this interloper and his language is terrible. Luck is quite willing to be friendly but Pat only growls and spits.

I haven't been feeling a bit well this week. I take dizzy spells—something strange for me. Then my tooth keeps plaguing me.

Saturday, Oct. 13, 1923
The Manse, Leaskdale

Still rushing, Monday evening practice—Tuesday evening pastoral calling.

Wednesday was a lovely day. We motored in to Toronto to hear Lloyd George in Massey Hall.[266] I had not expected to be able to get tickets but Mr. McClelland pulled wires and got a couple for me. There were 3000 tickets and 180,000 applications!

I suffered all night from an attack of bowel trouble and for any other person than Lloyd George would I never have got out of bed, much less motor to Toronto. But I was determined to see him if I could go at all, so I went with a jaw swelled out of all proportion by reason of that blessed tooth. We saw and heard the "little Welshman." I don't think he is as tall as I am—"from the neck *down*." He was hoarse and we could not hear all his speech. What we could

---

266   On Lloyd George, see LMM's entry, and accompanying note, for October 21, 1922.

hear was not so very wonderful. But it was the man himself—the man of the Great War. I think Lloyd George is and will always be considered one of the greatest men in the world and one of the most intriguing characters in history. He is essentially a fighter. He is lost without something to fight. He did more than any one man or score of men to win the war. But I think his day is done. He is not a constructive statesman, such as is sorely needed now. But he *had* his day—and did his work—and it was for this that we all sprang to our feet as he came out on the platform and shouted and hurrahed and clapped and stamped and *cried*—and would have flung ourselves down and let him walk over us if he had wanted to.

We stayed in all night. I felt better in the morning and spent the day shopping. We came home in the evening and I was so tired I would have given much to be permitted to go to bed. But I had to go to practice—and without anything to eat, as Lily, with her usual entire lack of foresight had gone to practice without leaving a thing ready for us to eat. For the first few years she was here I tried to induce her to realize that when we came home tired and hungry, we wanted to find our supper ready for us—and not have to wait an hour for it while she got it ready. But it was in vain. I have given up the useless attempt.

There was a wire from Stell, saying that her mother had reached Los Angeles safely, not even tired. Aunt A. is certainly a game old person. I was relieved to know she was safely there.

Friday night we had our Guild social. Today I had the Mission Band and tonight we went to Zephyr to attend a W.M.S. social where an address and present was given to a departing member. (N.B. I wrote the address last night after I came from Guild!!)

Of course, in all this I have little time for *living*. I cannot read, except for half an hour after I get into bed at eleven. I *should* go to sleep—but I have to read a little bit. By these half hour snatches I have just finished re-reading *Hypatia*.[267] I always like it.

Thursday, October 18, 1923
The Manse, Leaskdale

Haven't been well this week. Feel dull and headachy all the time and my ulcerating tooth still bothers me. But business as usual!

267	*Hypatia, or New Foes with an Old Face* is Charles Kingsley's 1853 fictionalised biography of the ancient Greek mathematician and philosopher Hypatia.

Today I had a letter from Ila[268]—who is in Oklahoma at present. Being a civil engineer's wife, there is never any knowing where she may or may not be. Her letter was about Carl and made me feel sick.

She writes:—

You were talking about Heath Montgomery's probable marriage. I don't suppose you know that Carl married a girl about three years ago and we never knew until Kate accidentally discovered it this year. It was a nasty shock. He has a little girl two years old, named Ila May after me, very sweet looking in her picture. They are not living together and it is all a horrid mess. There's nothing wrong with the girl (I haven't seen her myself) but she has very little education and of course I don't know why they quarrelled. It is too bad for the little girl's sake. Don't mention it, even if you ever write Carl, as he's fearfully touchy on the subject. I wished so much I had been in Winnipeg when they found it out as Carl will always listen to me to some extent but Kate always antagonizes him and he her. I imagine he did it when he felt utterly discouraged and down and out about his leg and so on. He always kept his friends sort of secret—a great deal because Kate and he quarrelled about them and I must admit he never picked the ones I would have chosen. The worst of it is that he had settled down so much in the past two years— has a good job and is interested in it. I had hoped he would marry some nice girl who could be "the makings of him." He is very responsive to affection but simply will not be driven. I hope he'll straighten out his life some way. I think they are going to get a divorce. What hurt most of course was his keeping it a secret. His wife finally got mad at him and telephoned Kate awful tales. Poor Kate was nearly distracted.

I should think it was a mess! Oh, and such a shame! Carl was such a dear—I feel wretchedly over the whole thing. I should think Kate *would* antagonize him—she wouldn't be her mother's daughter if she didn't. It's probably best to get a divorce—but divorces are not exactly part of our family traditions.

Well, as Ila says, we can't live other people's lives for them. For that matter most of us find it is about all we can do to live our own.

But this question of divorce is looming up as one of the problems of our age. I do not approve of lax divorce laws. But I do think our Canadian divorce law errs on the side of over strictness. Adultery is the only ground for divorce.

---

268   Ila May Montgomery was one of four siblings by Hugh Montgomery's second marriage to Mary Ann McRae; the other three half-siblings were Carl, Kate, and Bruce. Carl had fought in World War I and had lost part of a leg in 1917.

To this I think two others should be added and two only—incurable insanity and desertion for a period extending over three years.

Friday, Oct. 26, 1923
The Manse, Leaskdale, Ont.

Today was beautiful—warm, sunny, with a faint grape-like bloom over distant hills and fields. Lily and I spent most of it planting our bulbs and blanketing our perennials for the winter. It was delightful working out on the lawn, in the golden weather with the pussy cats frisking about us. Pat "first endured, then pitied, then embraced"[269] Luck. They are very good friends now and play together in the most

The Lawn

comical fashion. But Luck plays awful tricks on poor old Paddy. There is one especial chair both cats like. When Paddy is asleep in it Luck will jump on him and bite him all over, tearing great mouthfuls of fur out of poor Pat. Pat being older and fat and clumsy can't move quickly enough to defend himself so after a few vain attempts he flies leaving Luck in possession of the chair. Luck will look around with the most angelic, innocent expression and then curl down and go to sleep.

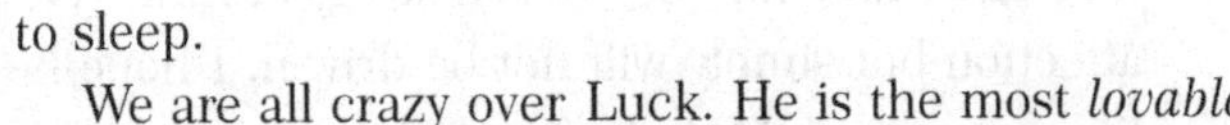

[Luck]

We are all crazy over Luck. He is the most *lovable* cat I ever had—even more lovable than Daffy II. He has the most engaging little ways and is a beautiful purrer. Old Daff was a most enchanting devil-cat and very dear to me for old sake's sake. But he was not at all the winning pussy Good Luck is. And Daff hardly ever purred— never except once in a while when he was hungry. As Paddy never purrs either I had concluded that it was because they were gelded. And I thought that was also

[Luck]

the reason that neither of them was affectionate or fond of petting. But Luck has been gelded, so that can't be the reason. It must just be their nature, just as it is Luck's nature to be the dearest cat that ever looked up at you with appealing eyes.

---

269   From Alexander Pope's (1688–1744) *An Essay on Man* (1733–34): "Vice is a monster of so frightful mien, / As to be hated needs but to be seen; / Yet seen too oft, familiar with her face, / We first endure, then pity, then embrace."

Luck is beautifully striped. I don't care a hoot for any cat that isn't striped. I never saw any markings like his, especially on the back. And his gray is so silvery that he makes Pat look brown and faded. But Pat is a pretty nice cat. I'm not going to go back on him for all the Lucks in the world. I shall never forget the evenings when he slept with his head on little Stuart's pillow with his paws around his neck, clasped tight in Stuart's arms. Pat is too big and grouchy to do that now but I'll always see him like that.

[Luck]

Saturday, Oct. 27, 1923

This evening Ewan and the boys and I motored down to Uxbridge to hear the radio. We hear music in Chicago and a speech in Pittsburg. It is a very marvellous thing and will probably revolutionize the world in another generation. But it made me feel a little unhappy and unsettled some way.

The real pleasure of the evening was our ride up and down lighted by an inglorious gibbous moon.[270] In a car you cannot feel the charm of the soft unfolding starlit night as you do in a buggy. But still it was pleasant to spin along and chat with the boys and Ewan. "Dodgie" has been such a lovely car. We have never had a single bit of trouble with her.

Wednesday, Oct. 31, 1923
The Manse, Leaskdale, Ont.

Sometimes this fall when I am rushing madly from one job to another, with never a moment to rest, read, or dream I feel rebellious and ask myself if this is the kind of life I was intended for. Then I recall last fall and the agony I endured all those months and I am ashamed. This year my worries are only external surface affairs. Last fall was the most terrible fall I ever spent in my life. My soul cringes when I look back on it. This day last year—Hallowe'en—was one of protracted torture.

Tuesday, Nov. 6, 1923

I am so sick of those practices. The play has ceased to have any meaning in my ears and I am discouraged with the stupidity of most of the performers. I tell them—I teach them—I show them—and then they will stolidly go on in the same old way. A few of the boys and two girls have discovered respectable powers of comedy but the rest are hopeless.

---

270   A waxing or waning gibbous moon is one in which the moon's face appears more than half lighted, but not full; that is, between the first quarter and the final quarter.

Last Sunday Ewan exchanged with Mr. Turkington of Whitby.[271] I went to Zephyr with Mr. T. and listened to a good sermon which Will Lockie praised unstintedly. It was a *very* good sermon—and it was taken word for word from a book of sermons, a copy of which Ewan has in his library! Of late years I have come to know that there is an immense lot of this done. Even Dr. Smith, the president of Westminister Hall, preached a sermon here which we found verbatim in a book we had. It is no wonder the pulpit is losing its influence over the pew. I really seldom enjoy a sermon nowadays. I'm always wondering if it is merely a recitation. It is this which makes the "calling" system such a farce. Turkington got the call to Whitby I suppose by preaching a borrowed sermon. So he has a town church and a splendid manse with electric lights and bathroom and hardwood floors. To be sure his people criticize his preaching as "dull." It is one thing to borrow another man's coat. It is another thing to wear it gracefully. Sometimes it doesn't *fit*.

Thursday, Nov. 22, 1923

I am quite sure I have never been so tired in my life as I have been yesterday and today. We had our Anniversary services on Sunday—very successful. Then Monday I spent all day in the church arranging it for the concert and had a final practice at night. Tuesday was a tremendous day of work, getting the tables set etc. I'm sure I went to and fro from the church twenty times carrying dishes etc. We had a big audience and our play went off with a bang. Everybody was delighted. What was odd was the way the performers waked up at the last. All at once they seemed to recall my instructions and act on them, with the result that, with exception of one or two absolutely hopeless ones, they all did amazingly well. When it was over George Kennedy came up to me and said, "Well, certainly, Mrs. Macdonald, we owe you a debt of thanks for all the trouble you've taken with us. You were very patient."

So I felt somewhat rewarded but I don't think the reward was quite enough to compensate me for all the extra work I've had. And I thought my feet would never be any more good. They ached so I couldn't sleep. Wednesday I had to let Lily go and help clean the church, so I did all the work at home, carrying everything back, washing almost all the dishes I possessed and putting everything back in place. I dared not stop a moment for fear I simply wouldn't be able to start again. My only comfort was those two blessed cats—it actually

---

271   Edward Turkington (1869–1928) had worked as a Presbyterian missionary in the Yukon Territory in the 1890s. He became a minister at St Andrew's Church, Whitby, in 1918. Turkington approved of Church Union but his congregation did not; he became a pastor at a United Church in Whitby.

rested me to look at those two peaceful unhurried creatures lying on their cushions in ease and grace. It made me feel happy to think that there really were creatures in the world who knew what leisure was. It gave me a feeling of comfort to stroke Luck's satiny coat as I scurried by. He has the softest silkiest fur I ever touched in a cat—Pat whose coat has always seemed fine, is positively rough by contrast. When people ask me what on earth I want to keep two cats for I tell them I keep them to do my resting for me. But there are times when I wish I could borrow a pair of their legs.

I was horribly frightened last week that Ewan was going to have another attack. He complained of headache one day—he was dull—twitched and sighed in his sleep— began reading the most dolorous of the Psalms at prayers—all premonitory symptoms with which I am painfully familiar. But they passed and he seems quite all right again. But I shall never be free from fear all my life again. Even if he gets quite well and stays so I shall always be afraid of a recurrence of the malady—and as every recurrence has been more severe than the earlier ones if he ever has another God knows what might be the result.

Practice must begin now for the Sunday school concert. Oh, for a lodge in some vast wilderness.

Have been reading, in the half hour before I go to sleep *The End of the House of Alard*.[272] Sheila Kaye-Smith is a favorite of mine. She reminds me of George Eliot. But her work is tinged—I had almost said tainted—with the pessimism of most present day writers of power. They reflect their age. It is hard to be hopeful today when one looks at the weltering world.

Tuesday, Dec. 10, 1923

Zephyr had its anniversary on Sunday. I had as usual the visiting minister to entertain and then spent Monday packing up all our play "properties" on the forenoon and helping arrange Zephyr church for it all the afternoon—and all the evening prompting and stage managing generally.

We ended up the play both in Zephyr and here with a very pretty tableau showing our two brides and their attendants. I got out my wedding dress and veil for Margaret Leask, who looked very pretty in it. My dress looks very nice still, only the cut steel trimming on it has turned dark.[273] I must replace it with something else. It quite spoils the look of it.

I couldn't get into that dress now. The disgraceful truth is that I'm getting terribly fat. Just at present I'm not *too* fat—but I've gained nearly forty pounds

---

272　English novelist Sheila Kaye-Smith (1887–1956) published *The End of the House of Alard* in 1923; the novel explores class and snobbery in English culture.

273　A replica of LMM's wedding dress is on display at her birthplace in New London, Prince Edward Island.

in the last two years and where will it stop? I must diet if I go much further. I was very plump in my teens. But I got thin that unhappy winter in Bedeque and never picked up again.

Today I came across an old letter from "Pastor Felix."[274] I had sent him a picture of Stuart at ten months and he wrote, "He has drunk himself full of sunshine and radiates it everywhere around him." Nothing could describe Stuart more happily. He does indeed radiate sunshine—the dear happy fun-loving, loving little lad.

I began writing again today. I haven't been able to write a line for over four weeks. I wanted to finish *Emily II* by Christmas but I can't now.

Thursday, Dec. 12, 1923
The Manse, Leaskdale

This evening I finished reading *The Mill On The Floss*.[275] I had actually thought Sheila Kaye-Smith was almost equal to George Eliot. Foolish creature! She has nothing of the breadth and power of George Eliot and cannot challenge comparison with her in regard to character drawing. *The Mill On The Floss* is my favorite among George Eliot's books. It is one of the few books which end sorrowfully and yet leave the reader with a feeling of satisfaction.

Friday, Dec. 21, 1923

The S.S. concert is over. The Zephyr concert comes off next week and then all such contrivances of the devil will be over for this year. But no doubt something else will come up to worry me. I have grown very pessimistic regarding the possibility of my ever having any lasting peace and freedom again. I had two dreams in November regarding Page that I don't like. I feel sure they presage something. I have been expecting word from Rollins regarding the appeal all the fall but have never had a line. In the spring he thought it would be settled in October. I suppose we shall lose. I can't feel any faith that I can in the end defeat those fiends or ever get free from their vindictive machinations.

And there is Luck, lying on the sofa, purring rapturously, a vision of beauty and grace, with his little stomach full of liver and not a care in the world. I could almost find it in my heart to wish I was a gray cat with a clover leaf and the letter M. on my side!

---

274   Methodist clergyman Arthur John Lockhart (1850–1926) was the uncle of Nathan Lockhart, one of LMM's childhood friends. He was best known for *The Papers of Pastor Felix* (1903).

275   *The Mill on the Floss*, published in 1860, explores a rebellious young girl growing up in a traditional family. LMM's misspelling of the author's last name as "Elliot" is silently corrected here.

Monday, December 24, 1923

We celebrated Christmas today, as Lily goes home tomorrow. The boys had their tree and a hilarious day. For myself, the day was pleasant. It was bright, mild and sunny. Ewan was well and I took a holiday from work and read and did fancy work. A grist of Xmas cards in the mail brought pleasant thoughts and memories of friends in many lands. A box came from Myrtle full of ground pine from Lover's Lane woods—as fresh and green and beautiful as when plucked. I decorated our dinner table with it and have a bowlful of it in every room.

Tuesday, Dec. 25, 1923

Officially Christmas! Luckily we had ours yesterday. Otherwise I fear we should not have had nearly so pleasant a Christmas day. Chester was ill with an upset stomach, Stuart suffered all day with toothache, I had a stiff neck. It didn't hurt me except when I turned my neck, but then I kept *wanting* to turn my neck. It was moreover a chill and melancholy day, so dark that we had to light lamps at half past three.

Our friend, Grieg, too, shot a tiny barb of malice into the day in the shape of the following letter:—

Rev. E. Macdonald:
Dear Sir:—
I was wondering if, at this Christmas season, you could see your way clear to dispense some happiness by way of a contribution toward the amount of the judgment and costs which my clients, Mr. M. Pickering and Mrs. S. Pickering hold against you.

Yours faithfully,
Willard Grieg.

It was beyond doubt Grieg's amiable intention to embitter, so far as he was able, our Christmas day. As we had our Christmas yesterday he failed; but the fact that he tried shows what his psychology is. A man who had any insight into human nature would not have antagonized the people he was making a request of by doing such a spiteful thing.

But it was in every way an extraordinary letter for a lawyer to write. Does Grieg imagine that we are so anxious to "dispense happiness" towards a man and a woman who hounded us with an unjust and iniquitous claim and swore to falsehood after falsehood in the witness box?

Then there was a letter from Ella. Dan had quarrelled with the hired man—Dan has no patience and his father's bad temper—the hired man had

gone and they had no money to pay his wages. Would I "lend" them a hundred? Aunt Annie had told them when she went away "if they had any trouble to write to Aunt Maud!"

I wonder what they would do if there was no "Aunt Maud." I will send the money—that will be three hundred for 1923—but I am beginning to think that it is pouring water into a sieve to try to save Park Corner. Dan went out with some wild companions Hallowe'en night, got into a scrape and was hauled into court by an irate householder. Ella had to borrow money from her brother to pay the lawyers. If Dan is going to begin like this there is no use in trying to help him. I am feeling disgusted. As for the hired man they do not need a hired man from the first of December to the last of April. Dan should be easily able to do all that has to be done then, as a regular thing, and save a hundred and fifty dollars. But Dan is not fond of work—I saw that when I was there this summer.

Between Grieg and Ella I feel old and depressed tonight. But maybe my neck has a good deal to do with it.

Thursday, Dec. 27, 1923
The Manse, Leaskdale

Thank mercy the last of those contrivances of the devil—church concerts—is over. Today was rough, windy and uncomfortable. We went out to dinner, christened a baby and had a nice time as it was with a family we have always liked. Then we went to Zephyr, had tea with another family and christened another baby. I had a frightfully dull time. Then we went to the Sunday School Concert at Zephyr church. It wouldn't have been so bad if I hadn't been so awfully tired. I think a Sunday School concert has its place. But we have had so many church affairs this season that I'm simply "fed up" with them.

Monday, December 31, 1923
The Manse, Leaskdale

Today we went to Uxbridge with the horse. I expect the car season is finally over. We ran Dodgie longer this year than ever before. I hate to give her up. It is so comfortable and quick in cold weather. But needs must. We had tea with Mrs. Hugh Mustard, who lives in Uxbridge now. She was always a good friend of ours. At the supper table she was talking about *Emily* and the humor in it and remarked, "I often say to the girls, 'We never see the funny side of L.M. Montgomery'"—*apropos* of some joking remark of mine to the girls that a minister's wife didn't get invited to parties!

There are a good many of L.M. Montgomery's sides they don't see!

This is the end of 1923. The first months of it were harassed and wretched. But in thinking it over it occurs to me that, since April, I have really been happier than I have been for several years, as far as every day life goes. I have had no great worries and some very pleasant times. Of course, at one time of my life, I would have regarded my present existence as anything but a desirable one. But all goes by comparison in this world. And, compared to the years since 1914, the last two thirds of 1923 have been quite a happy time—so peaceful and unworried that I have an uneasy feeling that it can't last long. I am entirely convinced that there can be no *lasting* peace or freedom for me.

1924

Saturday, Jan. 5, 1924
The Manse, Leaskdale, Ont.

My doleful presentiment proved only too well-founded. I knew those dreams of mine in November meant something. Today a letter came from Mr. Rollins. I opened it with a grim determination to hear we had lost the appeal. I don't know but that that would have been better than what it really contained. There were three letters or copies of letters. Here is the gist of them.

Mr. Rollins to me:—

The appellate proceedings have been backing and filling here in your case against the Page Co. Mr. French prepared a bill of exceptions[276] in which he collected all the pieces of evidence favorable to his side and left out most of those favorable to us. I thereupon redrafted it, leaving in everything he had and putting in the things favorable to us. This was not at all satisfactory to Mr. French who applied to Judge Hammond. Not getting any relief from him he wanted a conference with me. We had the conference but did not get anywhere and he applied to Judge Hammond[277] again, and again got no relief. There the matter has stood until today. I received a letter from Mr. Morrow.[278] Apparently Mr. French like other great generals has felt the force of the maxim that "attack is the best defence." They have therefore started proceedings for libel against you in New York, getting jurisdiction there, or trying to, by attaching the sums due you from Stokes for royalties. No doubt the ground on which they rely as supposed libel is the averments[279] about secret copies in the bill of complaint by which we started our proceedings here; in other words just the same as the supposed cause of action in the Federal Court here which was disposed of.

I suppose that it will be necessary to employ a New York lawyer now to defend this New York suit."

Letter from Mr. Morrow to Mr. Rollins:—

---

276   A formal statement of the objections made during a trial stating any objections to the decision, with the relevant facts and circumstances.
277   See note 77, page 40.
278   Mr Morrow was a representative from Frederick A. Stokes, LMM's New York publisher.
279   A legal term that means a positive affirmation or statement of fact.

I am writing to tell you that our treasurer was served with a copy of Warrant of attachment[280] in the libel suit of L.C. Page and Co. against Lucy M. Macdonald ordering us to safely keep so much of her property within this county as Mrs. Macdonald has or may have at any time before final judgment in the action.

The warrant was served on Mr. Dominick by a deputy sheriff who asked if we had any property of Mrs. Macdonald's. Mr. Dominick answered no on the grounds that as our books stated there is nothing owing to her. There is of course accrued royalty on her books up to December 31, but the amount is not known to us since our books are not yet made up and that royalty according to contract is not payable until May 1, 1924. . . .

What on earth does this suit mean anyway? Is it merely one step in a legal battle or is it just spite work?"

Mr. Rollins to Mr. Morrow:—One paragraph from letter:—"We were successful in the litigation here and the Page Co. have been trying to take it to the Supreme Court on appeal; but I judge from your letter that they do not think their chances are very good, and that they therefore developed this back fire idea of bringing this suit against Mrs. Macdonald in New York."

There doesn't seem much to say except that there is apparently no end to the deviltry the Pages will attempt and no end to the kinks in the U.S. law that enable them to do it. It is an iniquitous law that permits a person's property to be attached before a case is even tried. There is no end to the injury such a proceeding might work to an entirely innocent person.

I know the Pages will move heaven and earth to prevent my case going before a Master[281] to find the profits on the book. They have told their counsel there is no profit and they will hate to be found out in a lie by him, apart from everything else. And of course they are determined to have revenge on me to the limit. It must have been a bitter disappointment to them to find there was nothing due me until May. Their own system is to account for royalties only once a year on December 31st. If this had been Stokes' system they would have made a big haul. But luckily Stokes pay in May and November. So by November I had all my regular royalties to date and my $5,000. advance on *Emily* as well. So I shan't be much embarrassed immediately by this step. As for the future—well, "never give up; the other man may have a fit!"

---

280   A warrant of attachment is an authorization allowing the seizure of property (in this case, LMM's royalties).

281   A master is a court-appointed official who helps the court carry out a variety of special tasks in a specified case. For example, the master may take testimony or permit discovery of evidence.

But I feel upset and worried. This will mean more expense and trouble and uncertainty. The only bright gleam in it is the fact that, as Rollins says, it is evident they have not great hopes of the success of their appeal. They therefore want to get this hold over me to compel a compromise that will save their face. I swear that I will fight them all my life before I will allow them to thus bully me. Before the other suits were settled French told Rollins they would drop their suit if I would drop mine. Of course I refused. No doubt their motive is the same now. But their first shot has missed fire.

Sunday, Jan. 6, 1924
The Manse, Leaskdale

Last night at three o'clock I was down and out. But as always I feel more courageous in daylight. The unrest and worry of yesterday has passed away. Page's doings upset me now for a few hours, instead of weeks as formerly. One *can* get used to anything—if you live long enough.

There is something brewing in regard to Marshall Pickering. I am sure of it. I had an odd dream regarding him and his wife a few nights ago. I don't know what it means—it didn't exactly seem menacing; on the contrary it seemed rather encouraging. But one thing I feel certain of—we shall hear some news of or from them before long.

Monday, Jan. 7, 1924

Another letter from Rollins—a very reassuring one:—

For your comfort of mind I may say that such investigation as I have made into this burst of activity on the part of our friends leads me to infer that the Pages will not get along in New York any better than they did in the United States courts. I find it stated in an authoritative book that the New York courts refuse to retain jurisdiction of an action of tort between non-residents on a cause of action arising outside of the state unless special reasons are shown to exist which make the retention of jurisdiction necessary and proper etc.

This *is* a comfort. I know from the relief it gave me just how greatly I was dreading another lawsuit and appearance in court.

But I can't help fearing it is too good to be true.

Wednesday, Jan. 9, 1924

A third letter came from Mr. R. today—still more reassuring. He had received a letter from Mr. Von Briesen—Stokes' attorney and presumably a good one— and writes:—

"Mr. Von Briesen thinks that the case will be dismissed on motion on the grounds stated in my letter to you. I asked him if the sheriff could go around and get the royalties on each accounting day after May 1, 1924, until he had received the amount of the ad damnum[282] in the writ, $30,000; and he said he could unless the case is dismissed in the meantime."

Well, here's hoping.

Thursday, Jan. 10, 1924

An oft-quoted proverb is that "It is always the unexpected that happens." The unexpected *has* happened—not only the unexpected but the unthought of!

This doesn't mean that Louis Page has withdrawn his suit or written me a humble letter beseeching forgiveness. Oh, no, that is beyond the realm of even unexpectness.

No, what has happened is this. *Mr.* Marshall Pickering has been in the hospital in Toronto for nearly three weeks *taking the insulin treatment for diabetes.*

It is really an almost incredible thing. If it had been *Mrs.* Marshall, it would have been only what everyone has been predicting. But that *he* should have diabetes! In mediaeval times it would have been considered a direct judgment of God upon him for the lying evidence he and his wife gave about her condition. I don't think that at all but it is an odd coincidence. The insulin treatment will probably restore him to health but he will have to continue taking it at intervals all his life and it will give him something to think about.

He swore on the stand that his wife had a "little diabetes" at one time but had been wholly cured by "some patent medicine from the States." Now, why couldn't he have cured himself by the same means and saved himself the expense of the insulin treatment?

For it *is* rather expensive. No wonder Grieg wanted us to "dispense some happiness" in the shape of cash. But Marshall Pickering is a well-to-do farmer and is quite able to pay his own bills. *We* did not compel him to go to law.

"The mills of the gods grind slowly"—but it can't be denied that they do "grind exceeding small."[283]

---

282   From Latin, *to the damage*; a legal term for the damages being claimed in a given lawsuit. Page was seeking $30,000 in damages for "malicious litigation"; to recover this money, he tried to stop LMM from receiving royalties from her New York publisher, Stokes.

283   A favourite expression of LMM; one source is second-century Sextus Empiricus in *Adversus Grammaticos*, which translates as "The millstones of the gods grind late, but they grind fine."

Friday, Jan. 11, 1924
The Manse, Leaskdale

Chester and Stuart have got the results of their Christmas Exams. Stuart led his class with an average of 80 5/7. Chester also led his class but had an average of 68 2/9. This was not really so good as last year but it must be considered that this year he wrote on questions taken from old High School entrance exams, which were therefore much harder in proportion. The odd thing is that he made 82 in arithmetic which has always been a poor subject with him, and only 58 in Literature. I suppose the improvement in Arithmetic is due to the fact that for two years I have worked with him in the evenings helping him with it. It is odd that a son of mine should be poor in *Literature*. But Chester is like his father in this respect. Ewan has absolutely no feeling for or understanding of literature at all. I think I never met anyone so absolutely lacking in it—at least, among educated people. Chester seems to lack it, too, in spite of his fondness for reading. But possibly it may develop in him later.

Chester is beginning to mature physically—too young I am afraid. It will be a reason of anxiety for me. If he has inherited Ewan's tendency to melancholia it will probably show itself during the years of puberty. I have had to talk to Chester lately about certain habits to avoid. His father should do this but he is not a man who can do it, so, as all else, it falls to me. I have always tried to talk simply and truthfully to my boys about sex matters when they came to me with questions. The way in which such matters were treated in my childhood disgusted me. I was told all manner of silly lies. I was *never* told anything of the truth. All sex matters—the basic matters of life—were taboo—evidently something too vile and shameful to be spoken of. What a conception to plant in a child's mind concerning such things. A certain "doctor's book" in the house, a clean, sensible volume, where sex was explained excellently, was forbidden to me sternly. It should have been put into my hands. Of course I read it by stealth and I have never felt that I did wrong to do so. I know I learned things there that safeguarded me and saved me in many situations of after life and spared me many a worry.

The present generation has saner views of sex and its presentation to the young. There are several excellent books which make a parent's duty somewhat easier. I gave one such to Chester today. I hope he will be guided by its teachings.

Sunday, Jan. 20, 1924
The Manse, Leaskdale, Ont.

We have had a great deal of gray depressing weather.

Tuesday I had a letter from Mr. McClelland. He said he had heard that N.Y. courts were "years behind" in their judgments and consequently it was

unlikely they would take jurisdiction of my case. This is comforting—or meant to be. But if through some twist of French's infernal ingenuity they do take jurisdiction, my royalties will be tied up at least two years and likely three or four. Well, I have my dreams to comfort me. They foretold all this and they were distinctly comforting.

Had a very nice letter from the editor of *The Delineator*[284] this week, saying that *Emily* was "the most charming story she had read for years."

Thursday I finished *Emily II*. I haven't decided on a title yet. By dint of writing three hours per diem whereas I formerly wrote only two I am getting a bit ahead of my work and losing that hateful feeling of breathlessness I have had for years. Of course *Emily II* isn't half as good as *New Moon*. The second volume of a series, especially if it deals with a very young girl, is the hardest for me to write—because the public and the publisher won't allow me to write of a young girl as she really is. One can write of children as they are; so my books of children are always good; but when you come to write of the "miss" you have to depict a sweet, insipid young thing—really a child grown older—to whom the basic realities of life and reactions to them are quite unknown. *Love* must scarcely be hinted at—yet young girls in their early teens often have some very vivid love affairs. A girl of "Emily's" type certainly would. But "the public"— one of the Vanderbilts once said "Damn the public."[285]

I'm just saying what one of the Vanderbilts said. I'm not saying it myself.

I can't afford to damn the public. I must cater to them for awhile yet.

Friday I went to a Presbyterial meeting at Lindsay[286]—drove seven miles to Blackwater station over wild rough roads—then home at night again. I was tired by now—"the way was long, the wind was cold"[287]—I was expecting a letter from Rollins and dreading it. I found the drive dismal and courage ebbed low. But there wasn't any letter—and there were two rosy little sons and two adorable gray cats—

Chester and Stuart

Two pussy cats

---

284   A monthly women's magazine, published in New York, that ran from 1875 until 1937.

285   An interview with railroad magnate William H. Vanderbilt published in the October 17, 1882, Chicago *Daily Tribune* had reported him as saying, "the public be damned."

286   LMM likely attended this meeting without Ewan. A "Presbyterial" was part of the larger Women's Missionary Society structure (usually related to fundraising for missionaries).

287   From Sir Walter Scott's long poem, *The Lay of the Last Minstrel* (1805). LMM had indeed seen an arduous journey that day, driving herself with a horse and sleigh some 12 km/7 miles to Blackwater Junction. From here she took the Whitby/Port Perry/Lindsay line to Lindsay, Ontario, a community that was home to Lindsay Presbytery (some 43 km/26 miles west of Leaskdale).

and a volume of Hume's history[288] which I am finding very interesting.

But the letter from Mr. Rollins came yesterday along with one from Mr. Von Briesen—on the whole comforting. Rollins writes:—

As to whether the N.Y. courts will take jurisdiction or not, the result of my investigation is that it is wholly discretionary with the court. . . . Jurisdiction will be refused unless some special circumstances are made out. I suppose that Mr. French will have all of the special circumstances that he can and will be very ingenious about it. The most obvious consideration of this sort is that if the plaintiff is not allowed to sue in New York he will have to go to a foreign country. In as much, however, as the foreign country is not much further from Boston than New York is I should not think that this would be very convincing. My impression, without having seen the complaint as yet, is that the New York court will decline jurisdiction. This also is Mr. Von Briesen's idea.

Mr. Von Briesen writes in part:—

The attachment has as yet reached no existing indebtedness to Mrs. Macdonald. Consequently, if there is a default on the part of the defendant in the libel action the plaintiff under the judgment thus obtained could only take that property which the attachment has reached, i.e. nothing. The fact that some indebtedness may accrue next May does not help the plaintiff. The plaintiff's best course is to abandon his present proceeding until May 1st and then issue a new warrant of attachment and reach the debt which will then exist from Stokes to Mrs. Macdonald. If however the plaintiff does abandon the present proceedings and the attachment is vacated then Stokes & Co. by an advance to Mrs. Macdonald, say next April, in anticipation of the amount due in May may so shape the situation that there will again be a condition such that Stokes & Co. owe Mrs. Macdonald nothing. If on the other hand the plaintiff does not abandon the present proceedings then the plaintiff under our rules must proceed to effect service on the defendant by publication, as provided by the statutes of New York. If the plaintiff completes its service in this manner then the defendant should appear specially and move to dismiss. . . . If the motion is unsuccessful then the case goes on our general calendar and is not likely to be reached for two years. . . . Unless the plaintiff effects service on the non-resident defendant and does it properly the whole action collapses by itself. . . .

So that's that! It is my opinion that Page will *not* abandon the "present proceedings" because he knows quite well that if he does Stokes will pay me in advance and so leave him in the air again. On the other hand he *may* think

---

288   Scottish historian David Hume's (1711–76) *The History of England* (1754–61).

that, since he got nothing by this attachment and since the appeal will probably be settled in March before he can get another attachment, it is useless to go on, since he can't hold it over me to compel me to settle my suit before the appeal. This would influence any ordinary man. But Page's vindictiveness is abnormal and will carry him to any length, since he is rich and can afford it. So I prepare for the worst and dare not hope for the best.

Ewan *is* very well. I realized this very clearly tonight at the supper table. We were, as usual, playing the game of "The Clergyman's Cat." Stuart loves this and I encourage it because I think it is a very effective way of stocking the boy's vocabulary of adjectives. We were in "d" and had used so many adjectives that the supply was running low. Finally when Ewan's turn came he said with a deprecatory grin, "The Clergyman's Cat is a *damned* cat"—and joined in the laughter that followed.

Now, if any trace of his melancholia still lingered in him he would never have said this and if anyone else had said it he would have flinched as if a deadly sore place had been touched. He would have felt, not the normal distaste of a mind averse to vulgar profanity, but the abnormal horror of a mind to whom the idea of "damnation" was too real and awful to put into words.

But our cats are not damned! They are elect animals.

Saturday, Jan. 26, 1924
The Manse, Leaskdale, Ont.

This has been a week of bitter cold and storms—also of unpleasantnesses. Monday I was ill all day—it stormed—and there was the Annual Congregational meeting with its usual tale of deficit. Thursday we visited in Zephyr and had supper with a family who are ignorant and narrow. Really, only one thing they said was interesting! That thing being that our friend M.P. is home for two weeks, at the end of which time he has to go back to Toronto to begin taking the insulin treatment. He has been on a diet hitherto. Of course, this is a "judgment" on him. We hear that everywhere. It is odd how firmly the idea of "judgments" is lodged in the mind of the average man. I don't think there is any judgment in the matter; but I daresay that Pickering's worry and sense of humiliation in failure has so affected his system that he has fallen an easy prey to disease. A good many "judgments" are doubtless of this nature.

We had a dreadful drive home over those interminable Zephyr hills in the teeth of a thick driving snowstorm. I was tired out next morning but had to drive down to Uxbridge to sign an affidavit for Stokes in regard to my income tax in the U.S. When I was in Mr. Ormiston's office he said that the night before he had got a letter from Blake, Lash and Cassells (Page's lawyers in Toronto) asking, on behalf of Mr. Asa French[289] if I still lived in Leaskdale. I

---

289   Asa Palmer French (1860–1935) was the lawyer representing the Pages.

don't know why this should have depressed me as much as it did. It carries no additional significance, being merely one of the necessary steps to "effecting service"; but somehow it did upset me and I have been about as composed as a flea ever since. One reason, I suppose, is that I hated to have Ormiston or anyone round here get wind of this new suit. I had hoped to keep it secret and not have it talked of. Then again, it seems to me *too good luck* that I should both escape this suit and win the appeal too. It simply seems to me that such good fortune couldn't happen. And just now, in this cold, stormy imprisoning weather I feel as if I *couldn't* face the winter of suspense before me, with every day bringing its fresh dread of what the mail may bring. It seems to me just now that I *can't* open another letter of Rollins!

I am worried over Stuart, too. The child isn't well. He has been pale and languid for two months, with poor appetite. I rather think the real source of the trouble is the ulcerating tooth that has worried him ever since Xmas and has now culminated in a badly swelled face. I wanted the dentist to take it out in November but he thought it better not, since it was a milk tooth and its extraction so early would permit the gum to shrink.

It has been storming ever since Thursday and bitterly cold—28 below zero[290] this morning. All these things combined make it a little harder to throw off my worries re the Page suits.

On Wednesday came news of the death of Lenin[291]—one of the most extraordinary men of any age. He made the most tremendous experiment ever attempted and shed the blood of millions ruthlessly to further it—and failed. Even Lenin could not conquer or change human nature. Matters in Russia are pretty much as they have always been. One tyranny has been substituted for another, that is all—a tyranny just as merciless as the former, it would seem.

In Britain they have a Labour Government[292]—which some, of course, regard as the end of the world. But I am sure it cannot make a worse mess of

---

290   Until 1970, Canada used the Imperial system; -28°Fahrenheit is equal to -33°Celsius.

291   Russian communist revolutionary and political theorist Vladimir Lenin (1870–1924) died on January 24, 1924. LMM, like many observers of the time, had worried about the rise of Russian "Bolshevism." Following Russia's 1917 withdrawal from the conflict in World War I, the "Red" army, led by Lenin and Leon Trotsky, took power. The new regime established *soviets*—worker's councils—across the country to improve working conditions. Lenin was head of the government of Soviet Russia (1917–24) and of the Soviet Union (1922–24).

292   The Labour Party in Britain is traditionally centre-left, representing trade-unionism as well as social-democratic and socialist outlooks. A general election in the UK, held in December 1923, had resulted in a "hung parliament"; the Conservatives did not win enough seats to form a government. In January 1924 Labour Party leader Ramsay Macdonald formed a government with support of the Liberal Party. Macdonald would be the first UK Labour Prime Ormister. Given his working-class background, eyebrows across the world were raised when he became Prime Minister. His ministry lasted only nine months.

things then recent governments have made and may easily do better. As for the end of the world *that* came in 1914—the end at least; of one world—and those who shut their eyes to that fact are blind and foolish.

I have been reading Mrs. Moodie's *Roughing It In The Bush*.[293] This is one of our Canadian classics which I have been told repeatedly "I ought to read." There seems to be something in me that resents being told I "ought to read" a book. I find that I never buy or seek out that book; but if it is put into my hands I read it to get rid of it. Mac sent me a new edition of it in his Christmas parcel and I find it delightful from cover to cover—fresh, witty, vivid. I shall put it on my shelves to read again when opportunity offers. When I read of Mrs. Moodie's trials and difficulties I am ashamed to grumble about mine. But, really, she was never persecuted by demons like the Pages!

Sunday, Jan. 27, 1924
The Manse, Leaskdale

It was 28 below zero this morning! But then there are no mosquitoes!

The candlesticks

Good Luck belied his name this evening. The little devil contrived to knock down and smash to bits three pieces of my treasured bric-a-brac—one was the little bronze statuette of "The Good Fairy"[294] which was Frede's first wedding present, and one was one of my beautiful Bristol glass candlesticks. The odd thing is that both these things were broken before but a magician in Toronto mended them so beautifully that you wouldn't have known it. And now they are broken again. Is it predestination? Or devilment? On the chance of it being the latter I'll have the Good Fairy mended once more but I fear the candlestick is done for. I could spank Luck with a shingle!

Monday, Jan. 28, 1924

I don't recall so "gray" a January even in Ontario. We have hardly had a day of sunshine. This is very characteristic of an Ontario winter and I always find

---

293   Author Susanna Moodie (1803–1885) was born in England and settled in the Province of Upper Canada (Upper Canada was part of British North America that would now be considered southern Ontario), near Peterborough. She published a narrative of her experiences in *Roughing It in The Bush: or, Forest Life in Canada* in 1852.

294   This was a statuette that had belonged to Frede. At the time of Frede's death, LMM described it as "a pretty little bronze statuette called 'The Good Fairy' which had been given her by two of the staff. Being her first wedding gift it seemed to have a special significance. She always kept it on her bureau. I shall put it somewhere where I shall see it often and perhaps in days to come it will give me pleasure and not pain" (February 7, 1919). The statue was manufactured by Jessie McCutcheon Raleigh Nelson in 1916. It was sculpted by (and rarely credited to) Josephine Kern (Mrs James Mapes Dodge). See lmmontgomeryliterarysociety.weebly.com.

it has a very depressing effect on me, especially when I am worried. There is something in a storm that stimulates and provokes to combat, but dull, unvarying grayness soaks into and colors your soul. Besides, this has been a hard day—a day full of pinpricks. Stuart's face is swelled so badly from his aching tooth that he had to stay home and wailed dismally much of the time. Then there was a letter from Mr. Morrow saying that Page had been trying to find out from Mr. Burt about the facts and figures concerning the reprint editions. He *didn't* find them out—but what new deviltry is in the wind now?

Again Ewan complained of his head today and has been a little dull and contrary for a couple of days. This may pass off as it did in November—or it may remain and grow worse. The very possibility makes me sick with fear. Then there were two or three bits of congregational gossip that were worrisome. Such are always cropping up of course. Usually they turn out to amount to nothing and normally don't worry us. This has been a hard year on our farmers round here. Buying prices very high—selling prices very low. As a result half of the farmers in Scott[295] are financially embarrassed and a few are utterly down and out. This of course reacts on church work and finances.

I feel dull and unhappy.

Last Friday was the anniversary of Frede's death. It is five years since she went from me. What hideous years they have been. I had a little respite the latter half of 1924 but now the torture has recommenced—and is harder to bear than if it had never ceased. I *cannot* have any faith that the Page suit will be dismissed. And then for years of worry!

Wed., Jan. 30, 1924
The Manse, Leaskdale

For a wonder today was mild and sunny. It made such an immediate difference in my outlook. As usual I dreaded the mail. There *was* a letter from Rollins—and I betook myself to the spare room to read it—that being the only place I can be secure from interruption. But it was merely a note to say he

The spare room.

had asked Von Briesen (Stokes' lawyer) to handle our N.Y. suit. I think this is all right. Von B. must be a good lawyer, or Stokes would not have him, and he will have a personal interest in the case on account of Stokes.

Then I had a letter from Alexina Wright. In it she says;

---

295   That is, Scott Township.

Poor Laura is, I guess, a busy woman.[296] She is still in Saskatoon. Andrew lost his position there and came down here to secure work. So he is clerking for Joe Kernaghan in the hardware business. I feel so sorry for them. . . They find it pretty hard getting along and their boys have been anything but a help to them. Gerald and Jack particularly are pretty wild and give their parents many heartaches . . . Laura at present has her house full of boarders and roomers. I feel sorry for Andrew having to live away from home at his age.

All this sent me upstairs to cry. It is a shame that dear Laura, who has always been a most unselfish and generous and hard-working creature, should be in such a position at her age and through no fault of her own. I feel ashamed of worrying over my own troubles. They are not as bad as hers. But then she had nearly forty years of happiness and freedom from care and I never had that. Oh, well, I must stop growling. But then it's a relief to get it out of my system in this journal. Nobody ever hears me growl outside of it.

Friday, Feb. 1, 1924

Yesterday we visited a family in Zephyr whom we neither like nor trust. They are the kind of people before whom you must always say everything over to yourself beforehand to be sure it is safe and harmless. We have always felt they were not with us though we have never found them out in any overt act or speech. There are very few like them in either of our congregations fortunately. We had a long rough drive there and back.

Ewan seems all right again. There has been no further headache.

Saturday, Feb. 2, 1924

Gray—gray—gray! And a letter from Mr. Morrow in which he says:—

"In my last talk with Mr. Von Briesen I found he was not quite so confident as at the beginning that the N.Y. action could be dismissed. I know he would advise opposing the efforts of the Page Counsel but I think he feels that it is by no means a sure thing that the opposition would prevail."

This is what I have felt all along but it has upset me woefully and I have been good for nothing all the rest of the day. I can't understand why Von Briesen should be so confident at first and then change around like this. A lawyer of his standing should not have been encouraging at first if he had not known the situation thoroughly.

---

296   LMM had befriended Laura and Will Pritchard during her year in Prince Albert, Saskatchewan, 1890–91. Alexena (sometimes LMM spells it "Alexina") was another friend from Prince Albert.

Well, I suppose the state of things must just be *faced*. If there were a witch handy I would go to her and get her to put a curse, not loud but deep, on Louis Page and George, his brother. Then, if she had one left, I should have her clap it on Asa P. French!

Sunday, Feb. 3, 1924
The Manse, Leaskdale

This has been a mild day—but of course *gray* and sunless. I had a white night[297] and had to take veronal but today I feel calmer and able to *endure*. Endurance! That has been my life since 1919. But no doubt it also expresses the lives of a good many people besides me.

Lately I have been corresponding with Mrs. Hotaling, editor of a N.Y. magazine regarding a curious case of parallelism. She wrote me a distracted letter several weeks ago, saying that the editor of *Modern Priscilla*[298] had recently written her that one of his readers had written him that her story "Avis Lindsay" published in the January *Priscilla*, was simply the plot of *Anne's House of Dreams*. Mrs. Hotaling was in a bad way, and assured me she had never even read *Anne's House of Dreams* and had taken the idea of her story from a news clipping regarding a shell shocked soldier. I knew quite well that there could be no plagiarism for Mrs. Hotaling is quite incapable of that and besides, morality apart, has too much sense to steal a story from so recent and well-known a book. I wrote her and assured her that I believed in her entire innocence. And I do still. Yet, when I read the story—she sent it to me—I was almost "dumfounded." It *was* a deadly parallel sure enough, and I do not wonder that the unknown reader who protested thought it must have been stolen. Not only was the central idea the same but setting and characters had a marked resemblance. Perhaps Mrs. Hotaling's subconscious mind fished my ideas out of the pool of world subconsciousness!!

Oh, heigh! I wish my heart were a little lighter. It is very heavy. It seems long till Friday when I expect a letter from Mr. Rollins in answer to the one I've written him about Morrow's letter.

Monday, Feb. 4, 1924

A bad bad day every way. It was cold and east-stormy. In the morning I wrote and felt fairly. But a letter from Mr. McClelland upset me. He said he was going to mail me a check for my royalties at once lest Page attach my Canadian

---

297   LMM's term for a sleepless night. On veronal, see note for it on September 23, 1922.
298   *Modern Priscilla* was a magazine devoted to women's home life that ran from 1887 to 1930.

royalties also. I felt desperate and hopeless. If Page can do this I shall have to surrender. I can hardly believe it. I have always understood that in Canada no attachment can be made until a debt actually exists—in a case such as this, until the case is tried and a verdict for damages obtained. I think Mac *must* be mistaken and yet he ought to know.

Heaven grant me patience!

There was also a letter from Rollins with a gleam of sunshine. He wrote:—

"Mr. French and I have at last apparently agreed on a Bill of Exceptions, of which I will send for a copy when the printing has been completed. I think that that case is probably in more favorable shape than it has been at any time up to date."

Mr. Rollins is generally right in his conclusions, so this is hopeful.

Tuesday, Feb. 5, 1924
The Manse, Leaskdale, Ont.

How hard it is to hear little worries where we have big ones! When I have no big worries my smaller ones sit lightly on me—Lily's inefficiency, gray stormy days, getting up before dark[299] on cold mornings, coal oil lamps because my gas lamp is balking just now, a furnace with water pan burned out, a front door that *won't* shut and a storm door that *won't* open, green wood for the range and so on and so on. Normally I "say Oh and let it go." But nowadays these midges annoy me unbearably. I want *all* my endurance for the big worry.

Today we had the worst storm of the winter. The mailman did not come so I could not get off an urgent letter to McClelland entreating him to let me know clearly if my Canadian royalties could really be attached. This will prolong my suspense—and suspense is the one thing I have never been able to bear.

Wednesday, Feb. 6, 1924

The storm is over and the mail came. We even had half an hour of sunshine. So I felt better and was able to work and write.

This evening I went down to the rink to see Chester and Stuart skate. There is an open air rink in Leaskdale this winter. I had never seen them skate before. They do very well. It seemed quite wonderful to see Stuart darting about in the crowd like a bird. I felt an odd wistfulness as I watched them. I used to wish so much when I was a girl to be able to skate but I never had any chance to learn. I walked back home in the dark and snow, with the laughter

---

299   LMM likely meant getting up in the dark, that is before sunrise.

of the skaters ringing behind me and felt very lonely and hopeless. *I* have no friends here—no congenial companionship of my "race of Joseph." When I am not worried I find enough pleasure in my household interests and books; but just now I can enjoy nothing.

Friday, Feb. 8, 1924

Verily, this has been a hellish day. Worries are falling on us "thick as Autumn leaves in Vallambroso."[300]

This forenoon the *bailiff* appeared again and handed a legal document to Ewan which proved to be a notice that on Feb. 19th Grieg would ask Judge Ruddy of Whitby for an order to summons Ewan to a second examination "touching his means and estate since last examination."

I should have known this was coming. One night not long ago I dreamed that Lily asked me if Grieg had "sent a service" and when I said "no" she said, "Well, it's coming soon." Two days later the Page service came and I thought the wires of the subconscious had got crossed and the warning referred to this. So I was woefully upset. Of course, it is nothing like to be dreaded as the first one was. Ewan has got nothing but his salary and has used it for our living expenses. But he hasn't yet been paid for February and if there is a shortage in the treasury there may have to be a little more manipulation and I hate that—and dread it. For though only two reliable, tight-lipped people know of it there is always danger of a leak.

I may be mistaken but I believe the psychology behind this second attempt is this. Rumor persists in asserting that Grieg has never yet been paid by Pickering. Last week in the *Times*, one of the Zephyr "notes" was that M.P. had been in the hospital for diabetes. Now, M.P. is a man who is never willing to admit that there is anything the matter with him or his family and I feel sure he has never told Grieg that he is ill. Grieg has seen this "note" and is afraid that M.P. will drop off some of these days, leaving his debt to Grieg unpaid. Then Grieg, to get it, would probably have to *sue* the widow and family—something he would be very unwilling and ashamed to do. Hence he is making a desperate attempt to get *something* from Ewan while Pickering is still living.

Today was dreadful. The Session met here this afternoon and the wives came also and stayed to supper. By chance or God's grace the bailiff came in the forenoon. If he had come in the afternoon when they were all here it

---

300   A famous line from Milton's *Paradise Lost*. God casts Satan, Beelzebub, and other former angels (those angels who had rebelled against God) out of Heaven and into Hell. Satan regroups, summoning his injured troops from the flaming lake into which they have been cast: "His Legions, Angel Forms, who lay intrans't / Thick as Autumnal Leaves that strow the Brooks / In Vallombrosa" (I.299–304). Vallombrosa is a Benedictine Abbey in Tuscany, Italy.

would have been unbearable. As it was, we had a little time to recover our outward composure. But I was busy with preparations for supper—was making a salad when the bell rang—and I found it exceedingly difficult to go on with my compounding and planning. Then the mail came and there was a big fat letter from Rollins. Its corpulency alarmed me. Something, I thought, must be amiss when he had to write so long a letter. Of course I did not read it then. But the knowledge that it had come and must be read before I went to bed haunted me all day. Between the two things I was almost crazy.

But I finished my salads and preparations. I made a pretence of eating dinner. I dressed myself. I received my guests. I sat and talked to them the whole afternoon. I set the table and presided over it. I don't think any of my guests noticed that I wasn't eating any supper. Then I sat the evening through and talked small talk to those four good dull women.

I am not sneering at them. They *are* good—I like them. It is not their fault that they are dull. The lives they lead necessitate that. Usually I can chatter away to them of small local happenings, fancy work, house plants and hens, and find it easy, though not stimulating. But today it was torture. And this evening it was really dreadful. They were talked out—they were tired and waiting impatiently for their husbands to go home. But said husbands were having a fine time talking politics and Church Union in the library and wouldn't budge. I thought the evening would never end. But of course it did and at nine they went. Lily and the boys were out skating. Ewan settled down to read. I flew to the spare room and determinedly opened Rollins' letter.

But it, at least, was almost reassuring. Its bulk was due to the enclosure of a letter from Von Briesen. Rollins does not seem to think that I need take Morrow's utterance too seriously. From Von B's. letter it is evident *he* wants to try his hand at "compromising" the Boston suit with Pages. This, of course, is because he wants to get Stokes out of the nuisance of the attachment. No doubt Morrow's letter was to prepare me for this and influence me to consent.

Both letters are too long to copy but I will jot down the important passages. These are mixed—good and bad.

"Even though the N.Y. courts take jurisdiction of the suit in New York it does not follow that there would ever have to be a trial on the facts. It may be that the Court there can see on inspecting the plaintiff's declaration that it has not stated a case."

Good!

"As to when we will find out whether the case is to be dismissed or not I cannot tell you. I presume a motion to dismiss will come on within a few months and then . . . the defeated side can appeal."

Bad—very bad! I had hoped the motion for dismissal would come soon and I would *know* what I had to face.

"In regard to your suit here I suppose the printing will be done in time to have the argument in March . . . . moreover I judge that Mr. French wants to press it along. So the probabilities are it will be heard in March."

Good!

"But law cases always string out longer than one thinks they are going to. If it is not heard in March it will not be heard until October."

Bad!

"But my impression is that it will be heard in March and decided a few months afterwards."

Good—*and* bad. Those "few months" are depressing. In Canada appeals are almost always decided on day of argument—or at most a few days afterward. Certainly the States are criminally slow in their work.

"Mr. French volunteered the remark to me that he did not expect to win in the Supreme court of Massachusetts."

Good—very good—superlatively good!

"Talking to Mr. French I threw out the suggestion that you were being persecuted. He said that, while he did not think so, he had mentioned to his clients the advisability of not protracting the litigation but that they gave no hint of desiring a settlement."

On the whole bad—as showing that the Pages are just as determined as I have always known them to be! But with a shade of comfort, as indicating that at least French is not urging them on.

In Mr. Von Briesen's letter only one sentence is worth recording.

"In the New York suit we are quite certain that the plaintiff will never recover anything."

Good in the superlative again.

I think the "goods" have it. The relief given by the letter was so exhilarating that for the rest of the evening I felt quite at rest, not even worrying over Grieg's doings. I sat in the parlor with Ewan and our pussy cats and read with enjoyment.

Saturday, Feb. 9, 1924

I had a good sleep last night so felt better able to grapple with my dour fate today. Ewan left in the morning for Stouffville to interview McCulloch on this new development. I spent the morning writing in full to

A corner of the parlor.

Rollins and the afternoon conducting the Mission Band. A letter from Margaret was a pleasant thing, bringing with it a breath of comradeship and P.E.I. peace. I spent the early evening reading a delightful book Mr. McMillan sent

me at Christmas, *Between the Larch Woods and the Weir*, by the author of the book which delighted me so last year, *The Flower Patch In The Hills*.[301]

Then Ewan came home. McCulloch says that the order may not be given by the judge. He says E. cannot be taken for a second examination "except for good cause"—and no good cause has arisen since the last time. But Grieg may trump up some assertion to influence the judge. I know he wants to get a chance to badger Ewan with questions in the hope of getting some hold on him. Fortunately Grieg is such a fool he can't devise much deviltry. He can't do anything without a mistake, it seems. In the document he sent E. he wrote *Thursday*, the 19th of Feb. The 19th of Feb. is on Tuesday.

All this is encouraging. But so beaten down do I feel after the hammering of these past four weeks that I am hopeless of anything. I don't *dare* hope because the acute pain of hope destroyed is worse than the dull ache of constant despair and I can't face it. So I accept the fact that Grieg will get his order. But I do think it is the last time he will try it, unless he gets hold of some very real "good cause" indeed.

Pickering will of course have to pay for this new move. It will cost him at least thirty or thirty-five dollars. I suspect Grieg has compelled him to pay this by threatening to make him pay the whole thing. I would like very much to know what goes on between them but I shall never have that satisfaction.

Oh well—"it may be for years but it can't be forever" as Clara used to say. But the years are flying and we have not so many before us as we used to have. I have often felt, as I did after the trial, that it would have been wiser, despite the humiliation and rank injustice, for Ewan to have let me pay the $3600 involved and be free from worry henceforth. But he never would or will. Nothing can move him when he has made up his mind. And if it were not for my own problems I would be quite ready to help him fight to the bitter end. But I confess that so much piling up all at once has rather broken my *morale*.

It is an odd coincidence that both Ewan and I should have so much trouble with litigation. Dear knows, our life is not such an easy one, apart from this, that the fates need pile Ossa upon Pelion[302] in this fashion.

Sunday, Feb. 10, 1924
The Manse, Leaskdale

Reading *Adam Bede* today I found a sentence:—"There is nothing that is not bearable as long as a man can work." That is absolutely true.

---

301   See note 179, page 120 (Feb. 18, 1923). Emily Flora Klickman (1867–1958) wrote books about country life; *Between the Larch Woods and the Weir* had been published in 1917.
302   Ossa and Pelion are two mountains in Greece; the expression suggests adding complications to a matter that is already challenging enough.

As I read *Adam Bede* I laughed again at myself for thinking Sheila Kaye-Smith[303] a rival of George Eliot. She is but as a shadow. I do not think there is in all fiction anything of its kind more poignant and tragic and terrible than the picture of poor helpless betrayed "Hetty" wandering alone over England in her desolation and despair. Sheila Kaye-Smith couldn't have done anything like that. She would have smirched it with a dash of sex and left us feeling that Hetty deserved all she got, the little hussy! In the pages of *Adam Bede* we are wrung with sympathy and pity for her!

But then Sheila Kaye-Smith would *never* have committed the horrible sin of making "Adam" fall in love with and marry "Dinah"—and within eighteen months of his tragedy! I can never forgive George Eliot for that and the averred fact that Lewes put her up to it doesn't excuse her.

We have had so many stormy Sundays this winter. Today was the stormiest of all and Ewan could not get to Zephyr. There would be no service, so consequently there will be less money in the treasury to pay the salary—and this is so important just now.

We had something for supper tonight I never had before, and never expected to have—a roast of buffalo meat! It is a portion of the buffaloes slaughtered in the Government's park in Alberta last fall. It was delicious—tender and of excellent flavor—very like beef with just the merest suspicion of wildness.

I am depressed and dull this evening and dread the coming week. Some day in it we will get the copy of Pickering's affidavit spoken of in Grieg's writ. Heaven knows what is in it. He will swear to anything.

Monday, Feb. 11, 1924
The Manse, Leaskdale, Ont.

Today was a rarity—fine, mild and sunny. I felt ever so much better—worked like a beaver—and really did not worry at all, until "dark came down." But I grew a little dull in the evening—and *restive* under this long slow torture.

I have to go to Kitchener[304] this week to address the Canadian Club. I wish I did not have to be away this week of all weeks. I had been looking forward to it all winter but now all pleasure in its anticipation will be gone. Perhaps I *will* enjoy it, though, if I do not get any bad news before I go.

I have learned that Page *cannot* attach Canadian royalties so *that* worry has vanished.

303　*Adam Bede* (1859), by English novelist George Eliot. On November 22, 1923, LMM records reading Kaye-Smith's *The End of the House of Alard* (see note 272, p.186).

304　Kitchener is a city 110 km/68 miles west of Toronto. The Canadian Club, founded in 1897, promotes new ideas in the Canadian community.

Saturday, Feb. 16, 1924

Wednesday morning I left for Kitchener. No word came from McCullough on Tuesday, so if I had no good news there was at least no bad. It was eighteen below zero[305] and the roads were very heavy so that the drive to Uxbridge was not very pleasant. Ewan, too, talked constantly of Pickering and the injustice of the trial. When anything occurs to recall it he canvasses it as if it had happened but yesterday. This hurts me—it is like opening an old wound.

But I *did* have a very nice time in Kitchener and was too busy to think of my worries. I stayed with Mrs. Kaufman, whose husband is a manufacturer of Kitchener and must be very wealthy for they had one of the loveliest homes I was ever in, with every comfort and luxury.[306] I came back yesterday. On my way through Toronto I called to see McClelland and Stewart. The result was rather depressing. They have had a very poor business year and have lost money—instead of making any profits. They are reducing their staff and lopping off everywhere possible. And it is said most of the other Toronto publishers are in even a worse plight. The business depression[307] of the last two or three years has had a very marked effect on the publishing trade and better things cannot be hoped until the country is past the crisis—and no one can predict when that will be. I grew rather nervous as I listened. What if they were to go bankrupt? Well let us hope things will brighten up a little in 1924. It is never forbidden to hope.

As I drew near home I dreaded what I might have to hear. But as Ewan took my grip he said with a laugh, "I have something to tell you," and I knew that whatever news there was was not bad. McCullough had sent the copy of Pickering's affidavit. *Such* an affidavit. When I got home and read it I laughed too. Laugh! One might howl over it! Surely nobody but Pickering and Grieg could concoct such stuff.

But it was no laughing matter to get home. It was bitter cold—twelve below zero—and such heavy roads that Teddy could only walk. I grew woefully tired—for on roads like that I am always trying to *help the horse*. At least, that is the only way I can describe my feeling. I seem to be making a continual mental effort to *push the sleigh*, and it tires me almost as much as if I were actually doing it.

When I got home, got warmed and fed I settled down to enjoy Pickering's affidavit. Here are the choice portions:—

---

305   -18°Fahrenheit is equal to -28°Celsius.

306   Alvin Ratz Kaufman was the owner of Kaufman Rubber Company.

307   The years 1920–21 had seen a sharp deflationary recession in North America and other western countries. The effects continued to be felt into 1924.

I. "Since the date of the said examination I *am informed and believe* that the said judgment debtor has been *bequeathed certain property, estate or effects* by a friend or relative in *one of the Maritime provinces*. I am further informed and believe that the said judgment debtor has been making away with his property in order to defeat and defraud his *creditors in general* and myself in particular.

II. That I am further informed and believe that the *wife* of the judgment debtor is *paying for the upkeep* of the judgment debtor's house and in other ways relieving the said judgment debtor of his domestic financial obligations in order that the said judgment debtor may have more money *wherewith to enjoy himself* and to spend in *unnecessary ways*."

The italics are of course mine.

I suppose Pickering has been hearing some irresponsible gossip born of Ewan's trip to P.E.I. last spring when poor Alec died! Poor Alec, who died thousands of dollars in debt and to whose widow I had to lend money to help her out!

Creditors in general! Who are they I wonder. Ewan doesn't owe a cent to a soul in the world. But perhaps this is merely a necessary legal phrase.

The cream of the whole thing, however, lies in the last paragraph. Really, it is hard to believe a lawyer would draw up such a nonsensical statement for anyone to sign. Why, don't the fools realize that if I *were* trying "to defeat and defraud" I could do it quite legally and safely by making Ewan pay *all* our expenses, as far as his salary went, and then *giving* him as much of my money as I wanted to to enable him "to enjoy" himself. In fact, this is exactly what our arrangement has been and there isn't a legal flaw in it. A man is bound to support his family—*I* am absolutely free, as far as Marshall Pickering is concerned, to spend my money exactly as I choose.

That phrase "enjoy himself" will be another family joke, on a par with the *Leaskdale bank*. Henceforth, I shall tell Ewan sternly, when I see him having a good time, that it is illegal for him to enjoy himself as long as Mr. Marshall Pickering can't get that $2600 he is yearning for.

The affidavit is a great relief to us. Knowing how unscrupulous both Pickering and Grieg are we were afraid Pickering would swear that the salary was unpaid or something like that. And in doing so he would have made it awkward for us, because Zephyr is two weeks behind and though it will be easy to get that before the examination, it would not be possible before Ewan makes his counter affidavit tomorrow and so he could not have sworn that it was false. Then there would be no hope of escaping another examination.

It seems to me there *should* be a hope. If they can get a second summons on *that* affidavit then the "good cause" plea is a *farce* and *anyone* could get a

second summons on anything. But I am not going to let myself hope. I shall decide that they are sure to get the second order. There is no real reason to dread it for nothing has occurred since the "last" examination that Ewan has any cause to dread being questioned on. It is only the nuisance and humiliation of being dragged again to Whitby, especially at this season of the year, and the uncertainty of the time etc. But once it was over it might really be the best thing for us. Pickering would have to pay at least thirty dollars for it and he would not be likely to repeat that a third time on the sinking sand of floating gossip or his own wild surmises.

They say he has to go to Toronto every fortnight to take the insulin treatment. Probably he will have to keep that up as long as he lives.

I also found a letter from Rollins—brief but encouraging:—

"You will see the end of this matter in the course of time. Indeed, it seems to me that it has a little different feel to it now from what it used to have."

Rollins' *feelings* have generally turned out pretty accurate.

I read an old letter today—written in 1874 by Uncle Leander[308] to my mother just after her marriage. It gave me a strange sweet ghostly feeling and took me back to that old white farmhouse of fifty years ago. Uncle Leander is dead, the young bride and bridegroom to whom the letter was written are dead—almost everybody mentioned in the letter is dead. Yet they seemed alive as I read it; and that life, so different from the hustling, tip-toe restless life of today, seemed around me once more. It was as if, for a few moments, a door into the past had been opened.

It made me homesick—as if I had *suddenly breathed in a fragrance* from some sweet, haunted pleasance where bloom all the roses of yesteryear.

Monday, Feb. 18, 1924
The Manse, Leaskdale

Today was fine but bitterly cold. However, we got the house comfortable by night and had a nice home evening, reading in the parlor— the boys, Ewan and I, Pat and Luck. Not that Pat and Luck read. But they slept and purred and played and added greatly to the pleasure

The Parlor

and *homeyness* of our evening. We use the parlor as our "living room" in the winter. Carpets and upholstery suffer but that is a minor consideration. The library is too cold in winter and the dining room too small and crowded. So we

---

308   Leander George Macneill (1845–1913) was an older son of LMM's maternal grandparents; that is, an older brother of LMM's mother, Clara Macneill.

use the parlor. Tonight we were cosy and happy. The moon shone bluely on the frosted window pane and outside was a cold, white, beautiful, austere world; but inside was warmth and light and laughter.

I was re-reading *Zanoni*.[309] I have not read it since I was married. When I was a child I read it until I could repeat whole chapters off by heart. The book was one of the few novels in the house at that time—Uncle Leander had left a paper-covered copy there. It had an incredible fascination for me. When I took up *Zanoni* I seemed to open a magic door and step at once into a world of enchantment.

I did not expect tonight to find much of the old delight or magic in the book. For one thing, I was so *saturated* with it in childhood that I expected to find it palling. For another, so few of Lytton's books have stood the test of years with me that I felt afraid I would find *Zanoni* wanting, too.

But I did not. I read the book with just the same pleasure as in those old years—with just the same sense of enchantment. The magic door still swung open and through it I still made my escape from the real. I loved and joyed and sorrowed with the characters as keenly as ever; and as ever the pathos of that last interview between "Zanoni" and "Viola" in the prison cell of the Terror left me in a passion of tears. Much of the pathos in many of Lytton's books is false and strained. But *that* scene rings true.

Zanoni entered largely into my childish life. I was always *living it*—reconstructing parts of it to suit my wishes. Sometimes I was "Viola"—but not the Viola of the book, whom I always thought a foolish weak creature, utterly unworthy of "Zanoni." I adored "Zanoni." *He* was always my dream lover. I could never forgive "Viola" for her desertion of him. Nothing could excuse it. In my dream we were parted but not through any fault of our own—and at the last we met again, escaped the Terror and "lived happily for ever after."

Just as often I was not "Viola" but myself—not in love with "Zanoni" but the pupil of "Mejnour." I quailed not at the "Dweller of the Threshold"—I failed not in any of the tests—I attained the Great Secret—the first woman who ever "passed the ordeal."

Sometimes I re-wrote certain parts of the novel. For instance I made "Glyndon" survive the ordeal and win the boon for which he thirsted. Then I always added a codicil in which "Mejnour" suddenly appeared in the last chapter, when "Viola" is found dead, adopts "Zanoni's" child and brings it up to be a second "Zanoni." It always worried me terribly to think of that poor baby alone in the world—especially the world of the Terror. I used to lie awake at nights in

---

309   One of LMM's early favourite novels was *Zanoni* (1842) by English author Edward Bulwer-Lytton. The novel explores aspects of the ancient tradition of theosophy and occultist philosophies, where characters seek knowledge of the mysteries of life and nature.

that old look-out room—I was sleeping in the look-out room in the years from nine to twelve—and rescue it and build up a wondrous life for it.

I have read no book which influenced my inner life as did *Zanoni*. There were some sentences in it especially which, in themselves and quite apart from their context, held an indescribable charm for me. They hold it still—I found them tonight as subtly delightful as of yore—as full of romance, suggestion, poetry, gramarye!

"Monuments of murder, how poor the thoughts, how mean the memories ye awaken, compared with those that speak to the heart of man on the heights of Phyle or by thy lone mound, gray Marathon!" . . . "Child of heaven and heir of immortality, how from some star hereafter wilt thou look back on this ant-hill and its commotions, from Clovis to Robbespierre, from Noah to the Final Fire." . . . "Between the assassin and his victim rose a form that seemed almost to both a visitor from the world that both denied—stately with majestic strength, glorious with awful beauty." . . . "So smiles the eternal Nature on the wrecks of all that make life glorious. And not a sun that sets not somewhere on the silenced music—on the faded laurel." . . . "If, on the contrary she fall to me I know not what may be her lot; but I know that there is an ordeal which few can pass and which hitherto no woman has survived." . . . "A moment in the life of ages, a bubble on a shoreless sea—what else to me can be human love?." . . . "All his early aspirations, his young ambition, his longings for the laurel, were merged in one passionate yearning to overpass the bounds of the common knowledge of man and reach that solemn spot, between two worlds, on which the mysterious stranger had fixed his home" . . . "he would have surrendered all that mortal beauty ever promised, that mortal hope ever whispered, for one hour with Zanoni beyond the portals of the visible world." . . . "As he gazed, a star shot from its brethren and vanished from the depth of space." . . . "Age after age wilt thou rue the splendid folly which made thee ask to carry the beauty and the passions of youth into the dreary grandeur of earthly immortality" . . . "and the moon seemed to smile back its answer of calm disdain to the being who perchance had seen the temple built and who in his inscrutable existence might behold the mountain shattered to its base" . . . "Ho, ho, Zanoni, man of mystery and might, who hast walked amidst the passions of the world with no changes on thy brow, art thou tossed at last upon the billows of tempestuous fear?" . . . "Ha, young Chaldean—young in thy countless ages—young as

The "look-out"

when, cold to pleasure and to beauty, thou stoodest on the old Fire-tower and heardest the starry silence whisper to thee the last secret that baffles death" . . . "Though mine art fail me, though the stars heed me not, though space with its shining myriads is again to me but the azure void, I return but to love and youth and hope. When have they ever failed to triumph and to save?" . . . "And above this roar of the lives and things of the little hour stood he on whose starry youth the clouds of ages had rolled in vain" . . . "Ha, ha, thou who wouldst baffle death, learn how the deathless die if they dare to love the mortal!" . . ."Falls, oh stately column, over which stars yet unformed may gleam—fall, that the herb at thy base may drink a few hours longer the sunlight and the dews." . . . "He was there—there in all the pride of his unwaning youth and superhuman beauty." . . .

I do not know why these fragments should mean to me what they do. But I know they do.

Tues., February 19, 1924

Today was very different from last night. I was not the bride of Zanoni—the Mistress of the Stars—but the harassed mistress of a very cold country manse. It has been a miserable day—bitterly cold and raw, with a wild penetrating east wind. We couldn't get the house warm. Ewan went to see Wm. Sellers today and they fixed up the salary matter safely. But it is humiliating. Stuart has a very bad cold and is thin and dull-eyed. I can't get him built up and it worries me. As the day wore on I got very nervous and depressed. I suppose the matter of the order is settled by now as this was the day they were to go to Whitby. Oh, I wish we knew what was done. One can face what one knows. Well, I suppose we will hear from McCullough tomorrow. I dread the suspense of the mail.

The Manse, Leaskdale, Ont.
Feb. 20, 1924

I needn't have dreaded it—there wasn't any mail.

Last night a furious storm of wind and snow came up. I never heard the windows pound and rattle so. I could not sleep; and then about three, just when I had fallen asleep I heard Lily out in the hall saying that she heard a cat crying outside and was afraid it was Pat as she had hunted the house over and could not find him.

I knew Luck and Pat were in when I went to bed but Lily had come in after that and Pat might have slipped out. If one of our pampered cats was out in that terrible storm it would freeze to death, since it could not get into any shelter. So I shiveringly crept out and got a light. We had plastered up the

doors with coats and cushions to keep out wind and snow, so did not want to open them unless obliged to; but at first we could not find Pat and thought we would have to. At the last minute we found him curled up cosy and snug on the boys' bed! So we went to bed again but I did not sleep.

A terrible storm raged all day today. When we gave up hope of the mail Ewan telephoned Mr. McCullough, while I waited, cold with suspense. The connection was very poor—all Ewan could make out was that "it had been *postponed*" and he would "write us."

This has worried us all the evening. *Why* has it been postponed? We cannot imagine. Grieg with his usual incorrectness had written in his summons "*Thursday*, February 19th." But *Tuesday* was the 19th and McCullough said the date of the month was the one to go by. Is it possible that Grieg still thought Thursday was the nineteenth and never turned up at Whitby at all? I can hardly believe that possible. Besides, if that were the case why wouldn't McCullough say so? Why be so mysterious about it?

Friday, Feb. 22, 1924

The storm is over but it is still bitterly cold. There was no mail yesterday either so our suspense continued. It got on my nerves and I began to imagine all sorts of things. If Grieg were there why should it be postponed? *He* would not ask for a postponement. It must then be McCullough who had asked for it and that could only be because Grieg had sprung something new and unexpected on him.

Today the mail came and Ewan went down for it. I waited miserably. But when he came back—no word from McCullough. I can't understand it.

Saturday, Feb. 23, 1924
The Manse, Leaskdale

Today was still very cold but the sun shone and the drift stopped. There was still no word from McCullough. This means that nothing untoward has happened, because if it had he would have written at once. But it is odd he wouldn't write anyhow. Surely he must know we would want to know the reason for the postponement whatever it was. However, we feel quite easy again and I enjoyed my work all day and my evening reading.

The storm of Wednesday is said by the papers to have been the worst in fifty years. The amount of snow is tremendous and the roads are terrible. February has been a very cold and rough month all through. Oh, how I long for spring and the measure of freedom it will bring.

Chester had a test exam this week in arithmetic and made 90% in it. This

is encouraging. I have worked with him in the evenings for two years and he seems to be overcoming the carelessness that caused his mistakes. Perhaps, too, my nightly suggestions in his sleeping ear, *à la Coue*,[310] have helped.

Tuesday, Feb. 26, 1924

Today I had to go to Uxbridge. I go as seldom as possible this winter but we needed some things Ewan couldn't get, so I went today. It was by way of being an ordeal. Bitterly cold and such bad roads. I was so tired when I got home that I could not even read this evening, though I was renewing my youth in *Ben Hur*[311] and found the "orchard of palms" as charming a spot as ever.

Sunday, March 2, 1924

This has been a hard week. Fine but so cold. Bad roads. The sudden death of our next door neighbor, Mr. Albert Cook,[312] a good friend of ours and a man we liked very much. A nasty dizzy *tight* feeling in my head for three or four days which I don't like. All these things have made life unhappy and unsatisfactory. I feel very tired and dull today. But I have the "missionary tea" here on Tuesday so I must bestir myself tomorrow.

Ewan was in Toronto Wednesday and found out about the "post-ponement." Of course, as is usual, it was the last thing we would have thought of. McCullough didn't go to Whitby at all. He simply 'phoned Grieg the day before and asked him if he was willing to put the hearing off until "better weather." Grieg was willing and so the matter stands.

I don't know what McCullough wanted to put it off for. It would have been better to have got it all over with. Now we will have it hanging over us all winter, for the hearing won't be until the last of March. However, I've had one or two comforting dreams lately so I'm not going to worry anymore over the matter. We have nothing to fear, even if Grieg does get his order for examination, since the salary is paid up and Ewan has not had any "legacies." But it's the *humiliation* of being dragged down to Whitby at Grieg and Pickering's whim and wish!

I've been reading "Vanessa"—Marjory MacMurchy's story[313]—this week. It is not bad reporting but Marjory cannot create. Still, of its kind, it is quite well done.

---

310   See note 103, p. 55.

311   Lew Wallace's (1827–1905) *Ben Hur: A Tale of the Christ* (1880).

312   Albert Cook (1858–1924) and his wife Sarah Elizabeth Town (1866–1944) lived next door to the manse. See also note 534, p. 426.

313   *The Child's House: A Comedy of Vanessa from the Age of Eight* (1923) by Canadian journalist and writer Marjory MacMurchy (1870–1938).

Had a letter from Stella on Wednesday. Lots of complaints as usual. But still I do like to get a letter from old Stell. Between the complaints there's always a lot of the true Josephian flavor which is to me as manna to a hungry soul.

One bright spot in all these drab days is the fact that Ewan is so well. It will soon be a year since his last serious attack of headache and depression. Almost I dare to hope that he will remain well—at least for some years. I cannot hope he will never have another attack. Probably when he is about sixty another will come. Yet it is possible this may be the last. When I think of the past five years!

The snow is piled up all around us. I feel like a prisoner. One has to be young to enjoy winter.

Sunday, Mar. 9, 1924
The Manse, Leaskdale, Ont.

This has been a bitter week.

Ever since Ewan took his first attack five years ago I do not think it has once failed that, if I venture to express to myself or write in this journal, the hope that he was permanently well, another attack would follow immediately. On Monday Ewan seemed perfectly well; on Tuesday I went into the library and found him sitting there, a handkerchief tied round his head, his eyes wild and terrified, his face repulsive with the vacant almost imbecile expression so characteristic of these attacks at their worst.

It is very disheartening. I feel as if I had not, and could not, gather together enough courage to undergo the weeks before me. Ewan will *never* be well. Why was I so foolish as to hope it? But it seems harder to bear after the comparative happiness of the past six months.

I have felt better myself this week—have not been troubled by dizziness. But I feel uneasy about the fact of Chester's development. On Monday, when Ewan was well, I wanted him to consult a doctor about it but he pooh-poohed the idea. *He* had matured at twelve, therefore it was all right for Chester. But this fact, which assures him, alarms me. I am afraid that Ewan's early maturity may be linked up with his constitutional tendency to melancholia. Chester is not delicate physically. He is robust, rosy, and sturdy. But is there any lurking mental unsoundness? The next six years will answer that question.

I had a letter from Bertie[314] on Monday which filled me with delight. She is coming east this summer. But now the delight has paled. If Ewan is not well there will be no pleasure in her visit. But I must try to think he will be better. I suppose things might be much worse. It is well that this attack did not come earlier, when I was in the acute stage of worrying over the Page lawsuits. And

---

314   LMM's friend and cousin, Beatrice ("Bertie") McIntyre.

it is well, too, that McCullough did ask for a postponement of the hearing. Otherwise this would probably have been the very week that Ewan would have had to go to Whitby. Perhaps, coming now, the worst of the attack may be over before spring work begins. He will be better in the car season, too.

It has seemed this week that spring may be coming. We had a thaw and several mild days. The big drifts have shrunk and bare spots have appeared in the fields.

The Missionary Tea came off Tuesday—and it was very hard for me to have it that day of all others. My mind was preoccupied with Ewan's condition when I wanted to concentrate it on the problem of *feeding* thirty guests. I never *enjoy* the Tea and always have a sigh of relief when it is over. But I find a certain enjoyment in doing everything necessary competently and efficiently—making a success of it, in short. But this year I longed only to have it over, to get them all away, and be alone to face the facts of existence.

One of the facts was a disappointing report from McClelland. I had expected it but not quite so discouraging a one. *Emily* sold only about 8500 copies where *Rilla* sold 12,000.[315] As *Emily* has done just as well as my other books in the States it can't be because it wasn't an *Anne* book but simply because of the rotten business conditions prevalent in Canada for the past year. I must share in the general slump of course. But it isn't exhilarating coming along with everything else.

The hardest thing about this week was that we had promised, before the attack came on Ewan, to go out to tea on three consecutive evenings, being anxious to overtake our allotted "visiting" before the spring break-up.[316] We went but the evenings were torture. I tried desperately to keep talking, to conceal Ewan's silence and depression; and he himself always tries when out in company, to affect cheerfulness. I think the effort is good for him; but there is always a reaction as soon as we leave. The drives home, over the bad roads, have been dreadful, the horse plunging in the holes of the track, Ewan sitting beside me in unbroken silence. Friday night I cried silently all the way home. My nerves had been under such a strain all the evening, trying to talk brightly and naturally, that it was a relief to cry it out in the dark. Ewan never suspected my tears. He was wrapped in his own gloomy meditations to the exclusion of all else.

Well, in a few days I shall have adjusted myself to these conditions again and be able to endure them calmly.

---

315   LMM's novel about World War I, *Rilla of Ingleside* (1921).

316   With the coming of spring and the frost leaving the ground, gravel and dirt roads in the Ontario countryside were rendered virtually impassable by ruts, potholes, and mud. Even today rural roads often carry load restrictions that are in effect in March and April.

Yesterday I finished my second revision of *Emily II*. It is now ready for the typist. I have called it *Emily Climbs*—a vile title, but the only one I can think of which includes "Emily's" name. It has been hard to do these revisions when ever since New Year's I have been so upset and worried. And yet, whenever I forced myself to sit down to it, I found solace and escape—I was free from my bonds and torments and roamed in an ideal world—coming back to reality at the end of my three hour's "stint" with renewed courage and "grit."

Ewan has been very miserable today and made a mess of preaching. But he did well to preach at all. Yet he is always better when he forces himself to do his work. When he gives himself over to inactive brooding it intensifies his conviction of his "lost" condition.

A curse on the devilish theology that implanted such ideas in his consciousness! But had he been a normal man they would not have taken such hold on him; and I suppose if it were not this delusion it would be something else.[317]

I read two books this week—*Waverley* and *The Blind Bow Boy*![318] The gulf between them is as wide as the gulf between sanity and degeneracy. The latter book is an incredible compound of stupidity, vacuity and nastiness. Yet is has been praised in reviews as "exceedingly clever and brilliant." *I* should class it with the dull, dirty things obscene little boys scribble on the walls of water-closets. Faugh! I flung the thing into the furnace when I had finished it and washed my hands to get rid of the atmosphere of putrescence. To turn from it to *Waverley* was like coming out of a pigsty to a blue moorland hill swept clean by the winds of heaven.

It is a dull day but mild. The afternoon is a symphony of beautiful grays and smokes and pearls. One feels that spring is hiding around the corner. Oh, if it were only here.

I am writing with Luck curled up on my lap. We are all quite silly over that cat. He is so *lovable*. I never in all my experience with cats have known one so much so. Everybody who comes to the house raves over him. The girls who were here Tuesday burned incense at his shrine. I suppose something will happen to him erelong. I have grown so cringingly afraid of fate that I dare not hope that anything so beautiful and charming as this little purring cat will long escape the devil.

---

317   Nowadays Ewan Macdonald's "malady" would likely be described as a major affective mood disturbance, resulting in depression, loss of normal involvement, and a sense of guilt. Here LMM blames the doctrine of "predestination"—that is, the belief that God is all knowing, and thereby already knows which individual human beings are among the "elect" souls destined for heaven and which are doomed to hell.

318   *Waverley* (1814) is one of Scottish poet and novelist Sir Walter Scott's (1771–1832) most famous historical novels, a long-time favourite of LMM's; *The Blind Bow-Boy* (1923) is a novel by American writer Carl Van Vechten (1880–1964).

Sunday, Mar. 16, 1924
The Manse, Leaskdale, Ont.

This has been a dreadful week. Just at present I feel at the end of courage and endurance.

Ewan has been most miserable since Wednesday. I do not think he was ever worse even during his first attack five years ago. It has been most difficult to conceal his real condition from the community and the congregation. I do not know what to do.

He made a dreadful mess of preaching today. He was absolutely puerile. In these attacks his mentality seems to be that of a rather backward boy of about twelve. I writhed in humiliation and came home at the point of tears. I found Ewan in the library in a very bad condition. As usual in these attacks he was convinced that he would always be like this. Nothing is more curious than the way he forgets, in these attacks, the fact that he has recovered from many similar attacks during these five years—nothing, except the way he forgets, when he is well, that he has ever had such attacks at all.

But he wanted to "resign"—"get away." Now, as far as I myself am concerned, I would be very glad if he did resign. It would mean escape from the many intolerable conditions of recent years. And then, too, I have a large income, quite enough to support us all, in vastly greater comfort and amid far more congenial surroundings than is possible here.

But this is the trouble:—if Ewan resigned and then became quite or almost well again in a few weeks or months, as is quite probable, he would be most unhappy to find himself with no occupation and living on his wife's earnings. He would be miserable until he got to work again and then, even if he secured a congregation even as good as this one, it would be just the same thing over again.

I literally do not know what to do. The manifestations of Ewan's malady are so unaccountable that it is impossible to see what is best to be done.

I have been trying this afternoon to finish a letter to Bertie MacIntyre but gave it up. I began it two weeks ago when Ewan was quite well. Bertie had written me that she was coming east this summer and I was overjoyed—then. Just now, I feel that I do not want to see her.

When Ewan was well we had planned a motor trip in August to Kentucky to see the Mammoth Cave[319]—something I have always wanted to see since childhood, when I read a most amusing story the scene of which was laid in Mammoth Cave. I wrote and asked Bertie to go with us. Now I don't know what to do. We *must* make our plans soon, in order that Bertie may arrange

---

319 Mammoth Cave is part of the longest cave system on earth. LMM details her trip there, below.

hers. If Ewan's malady runs on, more or less, all summer as it did in 1921, there would be no pleasure in going. I can never forget those miserable motor trips to and from P.E.I. And yet it is just as likely he may be quite well in August—or at least well enough to go and enjoy it.

The suddenness of these attacks is so uncanny. Two weeks ago Ewan was well, jolly, and care free—a fine looking man with a pleasant, open face and friendly, twinkling eyes. Yesterday he sat or lay all day—unshorn, collarless, hair on end, eyes wild and hunted, with a hideous imbecile expression on his face. I cannot describe how repulsive he appears—I can hardly bear to stay in the same room with him. I can conceal this feeling but I cannot banish or control it. I am almost tempted to believe in that old theory of devil possession. There *is* an alien personality in Ewan during these attacks. He is an utterly different creature from the man I married. The touch of his hand on me seems like the profanation of a stranger.

I wrote once in this journal that I did not mean to write anymore concerning my feelings during these attacks. But I find it too difficult to keep this resolution. I have no friend—no confidant. I find that "writing it out" here helps me to endure. When I feel that I have come to "the end of my rope" I write it here—and find at the close of writing that the rope has lengthened a little and I can go on.

And yet—to face years, perhaps, of this life, never knowing what day the malady may recur! But one must not think of it. When I do I feel that I can't face it. When I *don't* think about it I can go on.

There are thousands of other people far worse off than I. But I have never been able to find much comfort in this fact.

Life has, of course, gone on this week in spite of its dreadfulness. The routine of existence doesn't stop because one is miserable. There have even been some moments not altogether bad.

Last Sunday evening I was sitting in the parlor feeling that, somehow, I just couldn't go out to Guild—just couldn't, that was all. Then Luck and Pat got up on the rocking chair and began one of their funny performances, half-play, half-fight. Pat was so indescribably comical in his antics that I burst into laughter—and laughed until the tears stood in my eyes. Suddenly I was able to go to Guild and read my paper.

Stuart has begun "writing stories," modelled—bless us!—on "Peck's Bad Boy."[320] And they are quite good, too, much better than I could have written when three or four years older than he.

320　Henry Peck, here referred to as "Peck's Bad Boy," is a character created by author George Wilbur Peck (1840–1916), published in a series of novels between 1883 and 1908. The first was *Peck's Bad Boy and His Pa.*

And yet I don't think I want him to be a writer—at least, not primarily. I know too well the difficulties and discouragements of such a career. The reward is brilliant when success really comes—but it often seems a mere toss-up of fate whether it comes at all or not. I have always loved my work—I have been happy in it—I would not have exchanged it for any other. And yet I hope that Stuart will not be possessed, as I was, of the *cacoethes scribendi*.[321]

Tuesday I wrote a little poem—"Canadian Twilight." When I write such poems I am always back in Cavendish. It was twilight on the old St. Laurence Gulf and the sand-dunes that I was really describing.

It has been bitterly cold these past four days. Nothing springlike in the air or landscape yet. Oh, for spring! When Ewan is able to get out in his car he will be better. And I will have some temporary escapes, too, that will help over the dark hours.

I read a weird "story" about myself in a Toronto paper lately. It ran as follows:—

When L.M. Montgomery, author of *Anne of Green Gables*, lived as a child at Prince Albert, Saskatchewan, she had not then decided whether to be a great writer or a great actress. The actress career had a little the best of it, owing to the copy of a thrilling melodrama having fallen into her hands.

One day a citizen heard the most blood-curdling screams coming from little Miss Montgomery's father's woodshed. Now the Canadian woodshed has long enjoyed a prominent place in the correction of children's misdemeanors, so that such sounds from such a place were not unusual. But so awful were the shrieks of terror the man was sure no childish crime required such punishment. Hurrying, bent on interfering, you can imagine his surprise at seeing a little girl of twelve alone in the shed.

The villain had dragged the ragged heroine to the precipice and was about to cast her over so that he could inherit the Montmorenci millions. So intent and wrapped up in the part was the maiden that she never noticed the intruder. He retired, amused instead of horrified, but ever since has felt that even if literature gained a successful author, the stage lost a wonderful emotional actress.

There isn't a word of truth in the yarn. My father never had a woodshed and I never did "stunts" like that anywhere. I never had the slightest hankering for the stage and my dramatic performances were confined to humorous dialogues for school concerts, which I never practised alone. However, the

---

321   Latin for "an uncontrollable urge to write."

fake anecdote is harmless if silly. But it annoys me to have misleading things like that published about me.

One day this week something recalled to my mind my old trick of "seeing" wall-papers.[322] It occurred to me to try if I could still do it. I could; and what is odder still, I found that I could bring the miniature wallpaper much *nearer* to my eyes than I could in youth. Formerly the nearest I could bring it was about a 1/2 yard from my eyes. Now I find that I can bring it to within about an inch—and the pattern is exquisitely tiny and fairy-like. I wish I could find out the reason I can see it so at all—and if anyone else ever had the gift. I find I can do it as well with one eye shut as with both open—and with either eye. I have just stopped and done it—right before me, two or three inches from my eye, was the dining room wallpaper in miniature apparently as solid and real as the wall itself. I have also discovered another strange thing. When I have once produced it by the muscular effort I can *look away* at something else and then look back and find *it still there* without any repetition of the contraction. But if I let it slip back to the wall while looking at it I have to repeat the contraction to produce the illusion again. It's very odd but I suppose I shall never know the reason or cause of it.

I had a letter from Myrtle Thursday—rather depressing, too. They are having very hard times on P.E.I. and she writes as if they might have to give up farming and try something else. Times are hard everywhere. Conditions here in our community have been very bad these past three years. The farmers are going to the wall everywhere—especially those who bought farms at war time prices. Something *must* give way before long. Either prices for machinery and clothes *must* come down or prices for farm products *must* go up. This state of affairs has made our work in the church much harder for two or three years. And it worries us to see people we like and are interested in, as is the case in regard to most of our families, crowded to the wall.

I had a letter from Irving Howatt[323] this week. He is still on the rocks. I think I might as well wipe the four thousand I lent him and Mort off my books. He has never been able to pay a cent of interest on it and I feel sure I shall never see a cent of the principal. What is worse, Stella made her mother send the $400 she inherited from Grandmother's estate to Irving for investment and

322   LMM describes her ability to "see" wallpaper in the air in an entry of September 5, 1918. A similar description is found in chapter six of *Emily of New Moon*: "Emily had discovered that she possessed this odd knack when she was six. By a certain movement of the muscles of her eyes, which she could never describe, she could produce a tiny replica of the wallpaper in the air before her—could hold it there and look at it as long as she liked—could shift it back and forth, to any distance she chose, making it larger or smaller as it went farther away or came nearer."

323   Irving Howatt was a neighbour who lived near Park Corner. He had been an early romantic interest of LMM; later he was engaged to her cousin Stella for 15 years before the engagement was broken off and Stella married another man.

I doubt if she ever gets any of it back. Yet, if I would lend her the money, she would be into some wildcat investment tomorrow. She never learns anything from past mistakes.

There, I'm getting bitter. Just now I take a jaundiced view of everything. I'll stop. But I feel better than when I began. I've got quite a bit of resentment and rebellion and discouragement out of my system. And Ewan *may* be almost well this day week. It is never forbidden to hope.

Sunday, March 23, 1924
The Manse, Leaskdale, Ont.

No, it is never forbidden to hope! But sometimes it seems almost impossible to do it.

This has been another wretched week. Ewan has been most miserable. This is by far the worst attack he has had since the initial one five years ago.

Oh God, if he is going to go like that again!

He has not slept well all the week. Some nights he could not sleep at all. I have kept up the treatment advised by Dr. Garrick but I never can see that it has the slightest effect. The attack runs its course and, as far as I can see, the treatment neither helps nor hinders.

We had a retired Methodist minister from Uxbridge take the services today. And of course every soul in the church came up to me and asked me if I "had tried this or that." Everyone has a remedy that cured *him* or *her* of headaches! As if we had not tried everything over and over! But of course they mean well and they do not guess that headache is but a symptom of Ewan's malady. If his torturing thoughts would vanish his head would be all right.

This has happened at the worst time of the year. The roads are all but impassable. Mr. Edmonds started with a buggy today and had to exchange it for a cutter en route. The ground everywhere is mud and slush—the landscape hideous. Ewan cannot get out to divert his mind in any way. *I* can't get out to gain a brief release from nervous strain.

Last Monday, on the last of the roads, I went to Uxbridge and read a paper before the Hypatia Club on "Problems of History." I haven't been anywhere since. Yesterday and Friday I was miserable physically—felt a nasty *tight* heavy feeling in my head all the time and could not take an interest in anything. I feel better today however.

Eight years ago the symptoms of the menopause began but the menopause itself did not come until two years ago. During those years, in which a woman should be free from worry and strain, I had the worst worry and strain of my life. Yet I never had better health. The menopause was absolutely normal with me. I had no disturbing symptoms of any kind. I hated to see it come—I think

a woman always does. It seems as if a gate were shutting between her and youth forever. But at least it brought me no suffering of any kind.

But, although the actual menopause occurred two years ago, still regularly every month I experience certain symptoms which always characterized the monthly period. I always have a "sick headache" and I always have one, or sometimes two days, when I feel "blue," depressed, nervous and indifferent. When not aggravated by any worry or strain these feelings are not *very* marked or uncontrollable; but when, as this week, they happen to synchronize with worry and trouble they are very hard to bear and I found it almost impossible to endure them. *Everything* seemed dark, dreary, hopeless and I could not bear looking forward to years of life such as the past five years have been. I lived them all at once, so to speak. But today these symptoms have vanished and I feel more courageous.

In *Anne of Green Gables* I made "Anne" exclaim once, "Isn't it a splendid thing that there are mornings."

Just at present I can't feel that anything is "splendid." But I am thankful that there are "mornings." Every night this week I have gone to bed feeling "down and out" but always in the mornings I find it possible to go on.

I read two books this week, a new one, *The Gods of Pegana* by Lord Dunsay and an old one, *Ardath* by Marie Corelli.[324]

I don't know what I thought of *The Gods of Pegana*. I don't know whether I thought it very clever or very foolish. But when I shut it up I thought, "Oh, if I could only talk this book over with Frede!"

As for *Ardath*! I bought the book twenty-seven years ago. I paid twenty-five cents for it. The same book today sells for seventy-five cents. Two years ago it sold for a dollar.

I always liked to read Corelli's earlier books. She had almost every conceivable fault as a writer but she could tell a story. In her later books she repeated herself and grew very shrill and hysterical. The first two thirds of *Ardath* is a good yarn. The remaining third is a badly written tract. But the book helped me because its fantastic imaginations were a good antidote to the carking reality of my present life.

Mingled memories came to me with *Ardath*. It recalled Cavendish and the friends to whom I lent it and with whom I discussed it. It was not so pleasant

---

324	Published in 1905 by Anglo-Irish writer Lord Dunsany, *The Gods of Pegāna* generated much attention for the unique fantasy world it depicted. English novelist Marie Corelli (1855–1924) had been a very successful writer. Although Corelli was generally disliked by critics, LMM admired her storytelling ability. *Ardath* had been published in 1889. By coincidence Corelli would pass away in June 1924; see LMM's entry for June 6, 1924.

to remember Edwin Simpson.[325] The book was full of him. I lent it to him that spring of 1897. I was then at the stage when one underlines books violently. I had much underlined *Ardath*. What I didn't underline Ed did. On every page some sentence he had marked flashed out at me with a sardonic reminder.

I wonder what Ed's life has been. I think likely it has been happy, though his childlessness must have been bitter to him. *I* have certainly had little happiness. But still I have never at any time been as unhappy as I would have been as Edwin Simpson's wife.

One sentence I had marked was *"Fame—fame—next grandest word to God!"* I was very ambitious then. Ed did not agree with me. He said it should be *truth* instead of *fame*. I retorted by saying *God* and *Truth* were synonymous.

Well, I no longer think *fame* a grand word or fame a very important thing. It certainly does not confer or increase happiness or goodness or usefulness. My work has brought me fame of a sort but the real reward of the work was in the pleasure it gave me to do it. And the fact that my name and my books are household words in all English speaking countries doesn't make it a bit easier for me to shake the furnace down or keep my patience with Lily's forgetfulness and untidiness!

For four winters I have had to look after the furnace—and it is really no job for a woman. But it was harder to get Ewan to do it than to do it myself. But this winter until three weeks ago Ewan always attended to it and it really was a great relief. But since his attack came on he has not done it. He won't get up until the middle of the day and he goes to bed too early. So I do it; but after all that is a trifle in itself. The trouble is there are so many of these trifles, each so inconsiderable in itself that one is ashamed to mention it, yet the cumulative effect of them all is not inconsiderable. Ceaseless pinpricking gets on the nerves after awhile. Every day from dawn to dark seems full of petty annoyances—and they drag my spirit down and make me feel petty too—as if I were a poor fly smothered in cobwebs.

Stuart has discovered that he likes my books and has been greedily reading them all these past two weeks. He is such a comfort to me—the dear, bright, merry little fellow. He has never been anything but a joy to me from the moment of his birth.

I shall now stop carping. This weekly growl in my journal is always a great help to me. After I get it written down I always think things are not so bad and that I can manage for another week.

---

325   LMM had been engaged to her cousin Edwin Simpson. In an entry of January 22, 1898, she details how the relationship ended.

Monday, March 24, 1924
The Manse, Leaskdale

Ewan slept fairly well but wakened early from a horrible dream. He said he dreamed that he was sitting at a table beside James Mustard[326] and that he suddenly found himself *cutting James Mustard's throat*. Surely a horrible dream indeed. To me, the worst horror of it is that I fear this dream was caused by a self-destructive impulse trying to struggle up from the sub-conscious mind into the conscious, and being there converted, by that very "cowardice" Ewan confessed to me in his November attack of 1921, into a murderous attack on his best friend.

It is a curious fact that Ewan seldom dreams when he is well. It is only when these attacks come on that he dreams. I read not long ago that a total lack of dreams was a sign of a tendency to mental disorder.

Ewan was very dull all day and had a restless spell in the afternoon. I tided him over it with a bromide.[327]

Tuesday, March 25, 1924

This has been a terrible day. Last night was also dreadful. Ewan could not sleep and two doses of chloral had no effect on him. This makes me feel very apprehensive. Never before has he been so bad that chloral would not make him sleep. What shall I do if it continues to be inoperable?

At six o'clock this morning he had the worst attack he has ever had at any time. He got so restless he insisted on getting up and going down to the library "to be by himself." I hardly knew what to do. I was afraid to insist on going too, lest he turn violently against me. So I let him go down alone. But in a few minutes he came up again. I never saw anything look like him. His face was absolutely livid, he was shaking from head to foot, his eyes were glaring like a tortured creature's—he said he was "almost gone"—his heart had "almost stopped beating"—"he was *lost*," he was going to everlasting perdition.

I would have been terrified to death had I not seen him almost as bad as this in Dr. Garrick's office five years ago.[328] That time I *was* terrified; and even the doctor was alarmed. He sprang up and tried Ewan's pulse, then said, rather sternly, "Mr. Macdonald, your pulse is strong and normal. There is nothing the matter with your heart. This is just the effect of your nerves."

---

326   The Mustards were a prominent local family, with whom LMM and Ewan were friends.

327   Bromide compounds were used as over-the-counter sedatives and headache remedies.

328   During Ewan's first bout of mood disorder in June 1919, LMM took him to Boston to consult mental health experts. Nathan Garrick was a professor in neurology at Boston University Medical School and would become the Head of the Health Service there.

In a few moments the fit passed and Ewan was comparatively normal. Remembering this I took courage. I got the distracted creature into bed, got him warmed, gave him bromide *and* encouraged him to talk all his terrors out. Usually it is very hard to get him to do this. Ewan has always been unable to face any unpleasant reality, or what he thinks is a reality. He evades it in every way possible and if compelled to put it into words, clothes it as euphoniously as possible—as, for instance, "I am becoming a fatalist"—"My work will not be accepted" and so on. But this morning he was so wild with terror that it all came out—he was going to be lost—God hated him—he was doomed to hell. It was dreadful to listen to this string of mediaeval superstitions which to him at the moment were hideous realities. It almost made me physically sick. But it did him good to drag them into light and face them. In a few minutes his shakings ceased, the livid hue left his face and he was calm.

I sat all day by his bed, talking to and trying to encourage him. It was a dismal task for reason has no influence on insanity. At nine, at twelve and at three he had restless spells but an early bromide got him past them without any repetition of the awful experience of the morning.

His kidneys are not acting right, as is always the case in these attacks. His breath reeks with urea. I have begun giving him kidney pills and making him drink water copiously. I think his liver is disordered, too, for his skin is such a bad color. It is strange that his stomach and digestive apparatus never go out of order, even in his worst attacks. He can always eat quite normally. I read recently in a book on insanity that melancholiacs *never* had a good appetite or proper digestion. But he has.

The roads are bad, the weather gloomy, and there is no stirring out. But I suppose this is just as well. It prevents people from coming to the manse which is certainly a blessing just now. It would be almost impossible to conceal the real cause of Ewan's indisposition if people saw him.

I dread the night. I am so very tired after last night's sleeplessness and the unceasing watchfulness and anxiety of the day.

Wednesday, Mar. 26, 1924
The Manse, Leaskdale, Ont.

Last night the chloral made Ewan sleep, much to my relief and I got a little rest too. But he was very miserable all day. Had many restless spells and was tortured with his dread of having committed "the unpardonable sin."[329] He

---

329	The "unpardonable sin" is blasphemy against the Holy Spirit. In Mark 3:28, Jesus is quoted as saying, "Truly I tell you, people can be forgiven all their sins and every slander they utter"; but there is one exception: "Whoever blasphemes against the Holy Spirit will never be forgiven; they are guilty of an eternal sin."

stayed in bed till noon and then got up. He could not read. Generally in these attacks he can, except during his restless spells, read light fiction and divert his thoughts a little but this time he cannot. At six this evening he was much better and I knew by experience he would be all right for the evening. So I went out for an hour and called on an old couple in the village. They are futile, uninteresting creatures and it was hard to talk to them. But the atmosphere about them was sane and normal and did me good. I escaped for a breathing spell from the poisonous miasma of poor Ewan's horrible phobias. I came home feeling a little more courageous. Ewan seems fairly well now. Perhaps the worst is over.

I grasp at certain hopes. I know they are almost certainly illusory but we must get strength somewhere, if only from an illusion. I tell myself that since this is by far the worst attack since the initial one, five years ago, that it may be the *last*—the final "kick" of the departing demon. And I recall, too, a mysterious dream I had about the first week in February—one of my vivid, symbolic dreams. I dreamed we were visiting the Taylors. There was a house across the road and just as we were coming away Mrs. Taylor said, "Aren't you going over there to see your mother, Mrs. Macdonald? She is very ill." I said, "Why, Mrs. Taylor, my mother died years ago." "Oh, no," said Mrs. Taylor, "that is your mother sitting over on that veranda. She has been there quite a time and I do not think the people she is with are very good to her." Accepting the fact, as one does in dreams, I went over and said to the sick woman, "Mother, I never knew you were here. I thought you were dead."

"No, I am not dead but I am dying," she said. "I have only a few months more to live." "Why didn't you send me word?" I said reproachfully. "I would have come and taken you to my home. You must come right home with me now." "Then you must take me away from these people or they will not let me go," she said.

I awoke and puzzled a good deal over this dream. I have had dreams of this type before though different in content. For instance, a few weeks before the Pages entered suit in New York I dreamed that I held in my arms a child I thought dead and presently found it living. I have come to understand that such a dream invariable means that *something I have thought was at an end is coming up again.*

In this instance it evidently foretokened a resurgence of Ewan's malady. What then? *It is dying.* There will be an end of it this time, perhaps at the close of the "few months" mentioned in the dream.

One hugs *anything* that promises a little relief from horror!

Thursday, March 27, 1924
The Manse, Leaskdale

A dreadful night followed by a *hellish* day. Undoubtedly the worst day I have ever had in my life. If Ewan is no better tomorrow I must have assistance. I dare not remain here alone with him if he continues like this. The responsibility is too great and the strain too awful.

Ewan could not sleep all night nor of course could I. I gave him two doses of chloral. They might as well have been water. He stayed in bed till eleven when he got up and went out to feed the horse. (Since Mr. Cook's death we have no neighbor to help us out in this matter.) When he came in I was alone in the kitchen. I saw at once that he was in the throes of another attack. He was shaking from head to foot—his work was done—he was lost forever—God hated him—he might drop dead any moment. He walked up and down wildly.

Fortunately Lily was upstairs.[330] I shut the door, hurriedly got a bromide ready and made him take it. In half an hour it took effect or the spell was over and he was calm. I got him to lie down. After dinner he dozed off a little but woke at three very restless. Lily had gone to visit friends for the afternoon and evening and I was most thankful she was out of the house. From four to six Ewan was terrible. It was the worst attack he has ever had—nothing five years ago was comparable to it. He walked the floor—he could not rest—finally at six o'clock he declared he must get out—he could not stay in the house another moment. I had to let him go. The roads were a mass of mud and slush—I could not go with him and I knew he did not want me to go. I let him go—I watched him stride in along the side road in the dull March twilight as if pursued by furies—I got the boys' supper and ran every few minutes to the front door to see if he were coming back. I was cold from dread and worry. At last I saw him coming back. I knew then how frightened I had really been.

He came in—still hunted—still frenzied. He was dying—he couldn't live longer than a few minutes! I felt his pulse. It was strong. I got him into the library where the children couldn't see him. I thought I must 'phone for Dr. Shier. He isn't much of a doctor—none of the Uxbridge doctors are. And if he came the secret we have tried to hide—the secret Ewan wants to hide as much as I do when he is in his senses—would be the property of common gossip. But I felt I could bear this alone no longer.

Then, all at once Ewan's mood changed. *He burst into tears!* This is something that never happened before. For a little while he cried bitterly. Then he seemed almost normal. The demon left him wholly—for a time at least. He

---

330   Lily was a huge gossip; because she came from Zephyr, where Marshall Pickering lived, LMM worried that her tales would soon have reached the wrong ears.

lay quietly on the sofa all the evening. His breath was suddenly quite wholesome. He even spoke of things he must soon do—have his teeth attended to, etc.—this from a man who twenty minutes before had believed himself dying!

These "spasms" of Ewan's are something I can never quite understand. I have read a great many books on melancholia and neurasthenia[331] in these past five years and it always seems to me that his attacks are more like neurasthenia or, indeed, hysteria than melancholia, which seems generally to be a fixed idea, remaining about the same all the time. Dr. Garrick himself told me that it was very difficult to diagnose Ewan's case. If it were not for the notion about the unpardonable sin, which is the hall-mark of melancholia, he would be inclined to think the malady was neurasthenia. Myself, I believe it partakes of the nature of both. Whatever it is, it is devilish and nothing more terrible, both for the sufferer and his friends, can be imagined.

Oh, what am I to do if this goes on? How can I face tonight? And tomorrow?

Friday, March 28, 1924
The Manse, Leaskdale

Hell is absolute but heaven is comparative. There is only one degree of torture that constitutes hell—the unbearable. But there are scores of degrees of heaven. Therefore, today, *compared with yesterday*, was heaven. The torture was *bearable*.

Last night at nine I gave Ewan chloral. No effect. At eleven I gave him five grs[332] of veronal. He went to sleep and slept till seven. I slept too, and so gained a little strength and energy. But before I slept I suggested to Ewan, "à la Coue" several things, repeating them softly over and over into his ear—"You will have no more headaches"—"You will sleep well every night"—"You will always feel well and happy"—"God loves you and all will be well with you." It can do no harm and may do good.

Ewan seemed better this morning but took a restless spell at 10. Very bad till eleven but nothing like yesterday. He would not get up and I thought it best not to urge him. I sent round to Dave Lyons to come up and feed Teddy. Ewan lay in bed all day and read very fitfully. His head bothered him considerably but he has had no more restless spells. I grasp at this fact as encouraging. Tonight his teeth are bothering him as well as his head.

I spent the day sitting in the hall just outside our room, doing routine bits of sewing and mending and watching him closely. Today has been much much better than yesterday. But what about tomorrow?

331　"Neurasthenia" described a basket of symptoms, including fatigue, anxiety, and depression.
332　"Grs" is an abbreviation for grains, a now rarely used unit of measurement; one grain is 1/15th of a gram.

Later on. Bedtime.

At eight o'clock Ewan grew restless and took a bromide. But he says he has felt better today than for several days. I do not dare hope. I seem to be in a sort of trance of watchful endurance. I am fighting a subtle and terrible foe with all the weapons at my command—drugs and suggestion. Which will win?

Saturday, March 29, 1924

A day or two ago I read in a book on neurasthenia that *blue pills*[333] had a good effect sometimes in regulating the liver. I knew E's liver was in a bad state so I sent to Uxbridge for blue pills and gave him one last night. Also, I gave him 5 grs. of chloral and he slept 1 1/2 hours. But this was not enough. I knew if he lay awake all the rest of the night thinking he would be worse again today. So I gave him veronal and he slept till 8.30. Today he got through the whole day without either restless spells or bromides. This *is* an improvement. But his teeth have been troublesome all day. In a way though, this seems to divert his thoughts from imaginary horrors. I kept hot applications to his face all day, as this was the only thing to bring relief. There is no cavity in the tooth—he had it examined by a dentist two weeks ago. Probably the trouble is an abscess at the root caused by pyorrhea.[334]

But in spite of the improvement I have found this a horrible sort of day. I had hardly any sleep. And the weather has been terrible. Dense black clouds—so dark we had to light the lamps in the afternoon—high, violent wind, bitter cold—showers of sleet—and, of all things, a wind-up this evening of thunder and lightning. This means at least two weeks of cold backward weather.

I see nothing from any window but a frozen hideous landscape. I am spiritless. I wish *just one* little pleasant thing would happen to give me a fillip.[335] As it is I feel down and out.

Today Lily's constant muttering to herself nearly drove me distracted. She has developed the habit in the past two years and is growing worse all the time. I can seldom catch a word, though I have often tried to. I don't mind a person *talking* to herself as she goes about her work—I do it myself a little. But indistinct muttering is a very different thing. I don't suppose she is abusing me and my method all the time, though certainly she does part of the time, thus working off resentment she dare not show openly. I think she is railing at everybody

---

333   "Blue pills" or "blue mass" is the name of a medicine formerly used against a range of complaints, including syphillis, tuberculosis, constipation, and toothache. The pills typically contained one grain (64.8 milligrams) of mercury, a known toxin.

334   Pyorrhea is a now-outdated term for what dentists call peridontal (or gum) disease.

335   That is, a thing or event that acts as a stimulus or boost.

and everything in her ken. Anyhow, it is unbearable just now when I have so much to contend with. I have mentioned it to her once or twice, jokingly, but she only stares and denies it. One can't do anything with a person like that. A young fellow has been going with her all winter and I have been hoping he would marry her. But he seems to be cooling off. Nobody can really endure her long. She is always being dropped and it doesn't improve her nerves or her disposition. I ought to pack her off of course. But it is so hard to get any kind of help here; so I put up and put off. But there are times when I would like to turn my sulky, muttering madam over my lap and give her a sound spanking.

Sunday, March 30, 1924
The Manse, Leaskdale

Last night E. slept an hour and a half without any drugs. This is the best for a week. Then his teeth wakened him and I gave him veronal. He has suffered greatly from his teeth all day but seems quite cheerful—laughs a little at jokes and shows some interest in affairs. This is a good sign. The blue pill has cleared his skin certainly—the livid dusky hue has gone and his face is clear and wholesome looking.

This morning, though, he complained of "hearing voices inside his head" whenever he shut his eyes. One voice said "A house divided against itself cannot stand."[336] I do not like this.

Altogether it has been a hard day—cold, damp, snowy. Mr. Edmonds preached again.

I feel a little encouraged but afraid to hope.

Monday, Mar. 31, 1924

March is ended. It has been a dreadful month.

Last night I gave E. veronal but the pain in his teeth kept him from sleeping. I fear he will have to go to Uxbridge and how he is to go in his present condition and in the state of the roads I really do not know. As he couldn't sleep I couldn't either and was badly prepared for the day. Ewan's teeth have been bad all day but mentally he has seemed almost cheerful.

Today the temperature was at zero. Not much flavor of spring about that. I never longed so for spring. The wind was high and the house was cold all day. Our coal is done and we have to burn green wood[337] which is almost worse than nothing. I feel miserably tired and depressed.

---

336   Mark 3:25.

337   That is, wood that has been recently cut and not allowed to "cure"; as such, it still retains sufficient moisture that it makes a poor fuel.

Tuesday, April 1, 1924

Last night I 'phoned Dr. Shier and asked him if it would be safe to give Ewan seven grains of veronal. He said it would. As a result Ewan slept well all night but this morning his teeth were so bad that we had to decide to go to Uxbridge. I dreaded the drive both for him and myself. The wind was high and bitter and I thought the hard frozen, only half bare roads would be terrible. But we went—and positively I enjoyed the drive! The buggy top protected us from the wind, the roads were smooth and good; even the wild showers of snow that swept over the landscape at intervals weren't so bad. The dentist found a cavity in E's tooth after all, treated it and relieved him promptly. All the drive home Ewan was quite cheerful—even joked about Pickering. This evening he read all the evening.

Wednesday, Apr. 2, 1924
The Manse, Leaskdale

Both Ewan and I got a good sleep last night. He has been quite calm and rational all day, though his head troubled him somewhat. I feel such a relief. Life seems almost sweet once more.

But I can't yet settle down to do any writing. I feel barred out of my kingdom when I cannot write.

Chester told me tonight he had decided to try the entrance. He has been in the entrance class but we had not intended him to write the exams till next year. But the teacher seemed disappointed so I told him he could please himself. I am afraid he will fail in arithmetic, though he has been doing much better in it lately.

It seems but as yesterday when *I* was taking the P.W.C. entrance and worrying because I feared *I* had failed in arithmetic. I recall the summer night down by the shore that evening after the results came out in the paper. How very happy I was! This has brought the past back to me with a quick rush, and a sweetness it did not possess even at the time.

Thursday, Apr. 3, 1924

Ewan hadn't a good night. Had to take chloral but even then slept restlessly and wakened at six. He said he heard voices—one said to him "The time has come." He was rather restless all day and once had to take a bromide but the attack passed very swiftly.

Today was the first *nice* day we have had—I *tasted* spring. The sunset tonight was all soft misty pinks and blues behind the Leask trees. Well, the sky is still as much mine as anybody's!

Friday, Apr. 4, 1924

E. had to take veronal again last night but seemed pretty well all day and talked of things he meant to do "when he got better." This is a great advance on last week when he was never going to be better. I kept cold wet cloths on his head all day and it kept in check the "burning sensation" he complains of. This evening he said he felt better than he had for weeks.

Saturday, April 5, 1924

No doubt Ewan is *much* better. He went to Uxbridge today for another treatment of his tooth and has seemed quite cheerful. But now that the worst of the strain is over I feel the reaction. I have been terribly tired all day—just as if I had been *flattened down* to earth by some terrible beating storm. And my soul is washed empty of every wish and hope and desire except just to be *let lie there*—not to have to get up again and stagger on. House cleaning, gardening—all the spring "jobs" are looming up before me and I haven't strength or energy for them.

Read *Life and Confessions of a Psychologist*.[338] Very interesting in some parts—very dull in others.

"Mother," said Stuart, coming in this morning, "don't you think crows have a *very quaint* way of sitting?"

Wednesday, Apr. 9, 1924

Ewan has been keeping better—and I feel better. Pleasure in my work is coming back to me—at least in the mornings—but as the day wears on I get very tired and discouraged again. The weather keeps so cold and dark. Ewan went to Toronto today and will stay till tomorrow. He is quite well enough to go now and I think it will help him. And, to be candid, *I* was glad to have him away for a day or two. When he is home, the house is, so to speak, saturated with him—or with the abnormal exhalations of his present personality.

Thursday, Apr. 10, 1924
The Manse, Leaskdale

I had such a glorious good unbroken sleep last night. But today was not easy, somehow. It was a dull cold day with showers of snow. I did some work on

---

338   American psychologist and educator Granville Stanley Hall (1846–1924) became the first president of the American Psychological Association in 1882, at a time when the field of psychology was still relatively young. Hall would pass away just 19 days after this entry by LMM, on 24 April.

a book I'm trying to write, *The Blue Castle*,[339] but couldn't get in the proper mood. And I rather dreaded Ewan's return home. I know he meant to see McCullough and did not know what he might hear. And I thought perhaps he might go to a specialist to have his heart and kidneys examined. They were all right five years ago but sometimes I have thought they were not as they should be. I have often suggested to him that he have them tested but when he is well he laughs at the idea and when he is not well he has not the energy to decide on doing it. But a few weeks ago when this attack first came on he promised me he would when he went to Toronto.

And my fear today was that he might discover there was something not right and this would depress him so in his present state.

But when he came home he was quite cheerful. He *hadn't* seen any doctor however. But he had seen McCullough who said he had sent Ewan's affidavit to Grieg as soon as he got it but had never heard a word since. I really believe we will hear no more of it—though I suppose as soon as we think that pop will go the weasel again.

I looked at Ewan as he sat at the table tonight eating his supper—a fine looking man, with a clear healthy skin, cheerful, rational, talking interestedly of domestic things—and contrasted him with that livid, shaking, terrified, haunted creature of exactly a week ago. It seemed impossible that they could be one and the same. Of course, Ewan is not well yet—and he will likely have relapses. But, if one can judge from past experiences he will not be so bad again during this attack at least.

Sunday, April 13, 1924

Ewan preached today—that is he read an old sermon. But he got on fairly well. He never recovered so swiftly from such a bad attack before. Is it suggestion—blue pills—or just predestination? Who knows? He has been sleeping very well lately and seems tolerably cheerful. I suppose he will be dull and idle for weeks, perhaps months; but so long as he is not as he was that awful week—!

Sunday, April 20, 1924

Ewan had a slight relapse the first few days of the week. Could not sleep without veronal and was dull and "heady." Heard voices "inside his head" again. But the past three days he has been quite better again and preached a new sermon today quite well. I am feeling better, too, and have had several temporary escapes that helped me.

339   *The Blue Castle*, set in Muskoka, Ontario (where the Macdonalds had enjoyed a holiday in summer 1923) would be published in 1926 by Frederick A. Stokes.

We have got Dodgie out again and Wednesday evening we went over to Zephyr to visit and "tea" with a family. The roads were splendid and it was delightful to spin along them. I felt as if I had got out of prison again. Ewan, too, as always felt much better. I think the car gives him a sensation of *escaping* from his haunting demons.

But our sojourn with the Walker family was not a good thing for him. Mrs. Walker is the woman who once told me all the tales of women who had died in childbirth before Chester was born. Tonight, by a sort of devilish felicity, she chose the very subject of all others I dreaded to have Ewan hear discussed—viz; suicides of the unsound in mind! Mrs. George Longhurst of Zephyr took Paris green[340] Saturday and was saved only by the fact that she took too much. Mrs. Walker went into all the gruesome details with a relish. When she finished I tried to turn the conversation but she had found a congenial subject and meant to run it down. Next came a meticulous account of the suicide of "a cousin's daughter" who drank carbolic acid[341] and an uncle who hanged himself! Ewan got so restless that he had to get up and go out while I sat in nervous apprehension. However, he soon came back and as Mrs. Walker could not think of any more horrors just then I got the conversation switched to something more agreeable.

We heard that Mrs. Marshall Pickering is also in the hospital now being treated for diabetes! The woman who swore that she never had diabetes! She must be pretty bad when she would give up and admit it. Pickering himself it seems is not taking the insulin treatment but is dieting.

Well, they will be able to compare symptoms!

Later On

Just as I had concluded writing Ewan came in and suggested a ride over to Wick, as we hadn't seen the Macdonalds for months. So we all went and had a nice call and drive, although the night was bitterly cold. Coming back I let Chester sit in front and I sat back and cuddled Stuart, listening to his little confidences and dreams. "Do you think my fancies *too extravagant*, mother?"

Sunday, Apr. 27, 1924
The Manse, Leaskdale, Ont.

Monday night I went to Toronto for my semi-annual orgy of household shopping. It was not enjoyable but it was a change of tribulation. I came home

---

340   Paris green, a higly toxic insectide containing arsenic, had been used in suicides since its development in the nineteenth century.

341   Carbolic acid, or phenol, is a highly toxic substance discovered in 1834 that causes the nervous system to collapse (it would be used as a means of execution in Nazi Germany).

Friday night with dread but found all fairly well. Ewan slept well all the week except Friday night when he had to take veronal.

I brought home a minute puppy for the boys—a smooth-haired Airedale. I wanted a chow but couldn't get one and I have been putting off the boys too long. Boys should have a dog. Stuart particularly is fond of dogs. Our cats don't like "Dixie" any too well but must resign themselves to him. We have quite a menagerie.

I have never had much to do with dogs. When I was a child we had an old black smooth-haired dog called Gyp—a nice old fellow. After his death we never got another. I was very fond of "Rex" the beautiful Gordon-setter we had in Prince Albert, and of "Laddie," a Scotch collie belonging to one of the men in the *Echo* office,—beyond question the finest and most beautiful dog I ever knew. I like big dogs; but in our small lot a big dog wouldn't do. My own choice would be an English bull-dog; but what would the congregation think?

I am reading *Youth* by Conrad.[342] The first thing of his I've ever read. He has some compelling qualities but overloads his stories with detail. I fancy the more one reads him the better one likes him; and I think I will enjoy *Youth* when I read it the second time much better than I am doing it in the first.

Sunday, May 4, 1924
The Manse, Leaskdale

All this week we have been housecleaning. We had to paper and paint which always confuses and delays things. Then it is hard to get Ewan to do certain things this spring. He went to Toronto for Thursday and Friday and so we could not get the library carpet beaten[343] or the heavy furniture moved. However, yesterday we got the room finished and it looks very nice. I go and sit in it a few minutes when my soul wearies of the disorder of some other rooms. If Lily had an ounce of sense in her puerile, stubborn head we could make housecleaning much easier and less exhausting.

Ewan has been about the same this week. Some days better, other days very dull. When he went to Toronto I wanted him to see a good specialist about his kidneys. Instead he went to a "chiropractor" and threw away five dollars on a worthless quack treatment. It does make one feel a little impatient at times.

Everywhere we go this spring people are putting in hardwood floors. I

342　Joseph Conrad (1857–1924) was a Polish-British writer; "Youth" is technically a short story, written in 1898. LMM may have read it in a collected 1902 edition, *Youth, a Narrative, and Two Other Stories*. Another writer to pass away shortly after LMM records reading him/her; Conrad died of a heart attack on August 3, 1924.

343　Before the invention of vacuum cleaners, carpets or rugs were taken outside, hung over a clothesline, and beaten with wire carpet beaters to remove the dust.

cannot help contrasting them with the miserable floors in this manse—soft wood, worn, warped, cracked, stained and disfigured in every way, necessitating constant painting. No idea of putting hardwood floors in the manse ever occurs to them. I've been painting and staining floors all the week and I'm so tired of it that I'm disgusted with our congregations!!!

On Tuesday I read in the *Guardian* of Aunt Hattie's[344] death. She has been ill for three years with internal cancer. I never liked Aunt Hattie—none of us did, for that matter. Yet I felt oddly sorry and downcast to hear of her death. I think this must be because it seems, somehow, to remove that old life, of which she was a part, still further away. It doesn't seem to me possible that it is nearly forty years since that summer evening when Uncle Chester brought his bride to the old home in Cavendish for her first visit. I can see her very clearly as she stepped out of the buggy—tall, handsome, very fashionably dressed. Aunt Hattie was always in the forefront of the fashion and every fad that came along was eagerly adopted by her. In spite of her imposing exterior she was a child in heart and brain. She had neither intellect nor charm. She was, I think, the most absolutely selfish and coldly calculating being I ever knew and I have not one single pleasant memory connected with her personally.

Nevertheless it spoiled the day for me when I read of her death.

I read a most absorbing book this week—stealing time from sleep for the reading—*Glands Regulating Personality.*[345] It is an amazing thing. I cannot agree with all the writer's conclusions and theories. Even those that are very likely correct will take a great deal of proving. But the *facts* concerning the endocrines are marvellous enough, all deductions apart.

I feel that we are on the threshold of a new and amazing revelation. The world needs it. The older revelations have exhausted their mandate. I believe the next one will come through science. What form it will take I cannot guess. But I am sure that the next two or three hundred years will bring it. Perhaps it may come sooner. Perhaps it will come along the very lines hinted at in this book. Or perhaps it will come in one grand burst of discovery by some master mind. Two thousand years ago Jesus burst the bonds that were stifling the human race. Now those bonds are tightening around us again—outworn dogma, dead superstitions. It will take something as tremendous as his message of spiritual freedom to destroy those bonds again. But it will come. The whole world is chaos; the Spirit of God again broods upon the face of the waters; and presently there will be light.

---

344   Aunt Hattie was the wife of LMM's Uncle Chester Macneill.

345   American psychologist Louis Berman (1893–1946) published *The Glands Regulating Personality: A Study of the Glands of Internal Secretion in Relation to the Types of Human Nature* in 1922, a summary of research on "internal secretions" (i.e. glandular secretions that we would now call hormones, such as testosterone and estrogen) on growth, health, and behaviour.

I think I found in the book a clue to the mystery of Ewan's personality. I believe his thyroid and pituitary glands are sub-normal.[346] The symptoms given in the book have always characterized him. Possibly, too, it is some disorder in these glands that causes his periodic attacks of melancholia.

Friday came a bulky parcel from Mr. Rollins. Of course it would come on a day when we were all torn up by the roots. At night when alone and quiet I opened it. I had expected that it would contain the news that the appeal had been decided. Nothing of the sort. The Bill of Exceptions was not printed in time for the March court so now it must go over to the fall. The fine Italian hand of the Pages and French is clearly visible in this. They could have had that printed in time easily enough. But they are determined to string the affair out as long as possible. I shall *never* be free from it.

Mr. Rollins also enclosed a copy of the argument used by Mr. Von Briesen when moving to have the N.Y. suit dismissed. It reads well and seems unanswerable to me. But I refuse to let myself hope. I dare no longer to be optimistic. This past winter seems to have killed the faculty of hope in me. I cannot throw off the horror of those three weeks when Ewan was so bad. I cannot believe that life can possibly hold anything for me except ceaseless and ever-recurring worries and misfortunes.

Having written that I looked up—and saw on one hand an exquisite gray cat regarding me with intriguing mystery in its eyes and on the other hand a flower dish full of sky blue grape hyacinths and golden daffodils. A piercing pleasure filled my soul. Such temporary escapes as this make it possible to go on—as if one had got a brief glimpse of some fair enchanted land where we might find all our lost days.

Saturday, May 10, 1924
The Manse Leaskdale

This week has given us abominable weather—cold, wet, windy. Some days I have really been tempted to yell to Baal.[347]

Ewan has been very miserable too—worse than he has been since March.

---

346   Ideas taken from Berman's *The Glands Regulating Personality* (see note 345, above). Berman compares thyroxine to the accelerator of a car: "One may sum it up by saying that the thyroid secretion is the great controller of the speed of living: the less one has, the more slowly one lives" (48); it is also associated with melancholia. Berman describes the pituitary gland as the "controller of growth, but also the controller of the initiation of that most mysterious process, puberty" (65). LMM had observed Chester's early maturation and may have been particularly interested in this as a hereditary factor. Berman argued that the life of every individual in every stage is "dominated" by his glands of internal secretion, which may have had a "controlling influence" on individual psychology. Two of these were "thyroid centered" and "pituitary centered."

347   "Baal" is a word for God, originally from ancient Semitic language (here used tongue-in-cheek to suggest a pagan god).

There were three nights he could not sleep and in the days he has sat about and looked hunted. This evening he took a turn for the better again and said he hadn't felt so well for a long time.

I had a doleful letter from Ella on Monday. I had sent her a hundred dollars to get a new buggy—their old one being completely done. She was very grateful, poor creature, but thought she ought to tell me that Dan is pretty wild and may not "make good." I did not need her letter to tell me this. I saw enough last summer. Dan is lazy and self-indulgent, bad-tempered and impatient. Moreover, he seems to be following in his father's footsteps—low dances, raffles and—I suspect, drinking. One would think his father's career might have warned him. But there is a sort of "invincible ignorance" in some of those Campbells. Since Aunt Annie went away there has been no check on Dan. His mother has no influence over him. She implores me to write him "advice." Not I. What would be the good? He wouldn't take it.

Ella implores me frantically to burn her letters. I do not do it. I do not ask her to write me these details and since she does I shall keep her letters. I may find them convenient as a weapon of defense some day. Some bitter experiences have taught me that it is wise to keep certain letters. Then people cannot deny what they have written and put falsehoods in my mouth.

It is a pity Jim is not the oldest. He is a real Macneill—a worker and manager. He would bring back Park Corner prosperity and revive the old traditions. But he is only twelve and Aunt Annie and Stella are besotted on Dan—whom they have helped to spoil.

Sometimes I think our Dixie dog is an unmitigated nuisance. We have had an awful time teaching him to eat. And at night, until recently, he has howled for hours, "like a lost soul in agony" as Stuart gravely declares. (Unluckily he got this off before poor Ewan on whose morbid mind it fell like the flick of a whip on a wound.) Then the little beastie is so dirty, never having had any training. I have never had anything to do with bringing up a dog in the way good dogs should go but it is never to late to learn. There is something—comical, wistful, entreating—about the little dog's face that makes me love him in spite of his nuisances and indicates that he has the root of the matter in him in spite of appearances. Luck has kissed and made friends but Pat swears vilely whenever poor Dixie toddles near him. Pat for some mysterious reason has lately taken to sleeping at the foot of our bed—something he never would do before. But Luck has ousted him from the boys' bed and downstairs smells, I suppose, of dog. So Paddy comes to us. Last night he came up before we put our light out and took one of his weird "dancing" spells. I laughed until the bed shook. I never saw a cat go through such a performance before. There was really something weird about it; it was quite indescribable!

We have been housecleaning all week, hampered by the bad weather. To-night is fine, so perhaps we will have a few nice days now.

Why have some lines of poetry a potent and indescribable influence over us—an influence that is not conditioned by their merit? There are four lines of Mrs. Hemans which have always, from the time I first read them as a child, opened the doors of magic to me.

> The sounds of the sea and the sounds of the night
> Were around Clotilde as she knelt to pray
> In a chapel where the mighty lay
> On the old Provençal shore.[348]

Today they recurred to me and I shivered with profound delight. Why? They are not great poetry—they do not possess the intrinsic sorcery of Keats' "magic casements" or Milton's "aery tongues."[349] These latter thrill my mind and fancy. But Mrs. Hemans' lines make my *heart* ache with a supernal fleet-ing ecstasy. Is it because of the picture they paint? Is it because "the sounds of the sea and the sounds of the night" were around me in childhood? Is it because of the romance always associated with "the old Provençal shore"? It does not seem to me that the secret is in any of these things. It goes deeper still—to some former life and some intense moment in that life—perhaps!

Sunday, May 11, 1924
The Manse, Leaskdale

A depressing day. E. seemed dull again and moaned dismally on coming from church about "preaching to people who were better than he was." Then my Sunday School class seemed a little duller and stupider than usual. I have been teaching Ewan's class since his attack. He began it last fall when he was feeling well but cannot teach it now. I do not like it. Years ago I taught a Sunday School class in Cavendish for several years—up to the time of my leaving—and liked it. My class was of boys with a sufficient leavening of bright and intelligent pupils to make the work interesting. Besides I was not so afraid of an occasional lapse into heresy then as I have to be now. The consequences would not have been so disastrous. But as far as that goes I believe I might

---

348 From English poet Felicia Dorothea Hemans' (1793–1835) long narrative poem, "The Lady of Provence."

349 From Keats' poem, "Ode to a Nightingale": "The same [bird call] that ofttimes hath / Charmed magic casements, opening on the foam / Of perilous seas, in fairy-lands forlorn." "Airy tongues'" is from Milton's *Comus* (1634): "A thousand fantasies / Begin to throng into my memory, / Of calling shapes, and beck'ning shadows dire, / And airy tongues that syllable men's names / On sands and shores and desert wildernesses."

teach sheer paganism here and if nobody heard me but those five girls it would never be suspected. I could not have believed that girls of fourteen, who had been going to Sunday School all their lives, could be so stupid and ignorant. Ewan found them so too. For several weeks our lessons have dealt with incidents in the life of Moses. Yet today when I asked "Who led the children of Israel out of Egypt into the Promised Land?" not one of them could tell me. And yet two of those girls were in their first year at High School. I can rarely extract an intelligent answer to the simplest question from them. All this rather gets on my nerves when everything else is so discouraging.

Then Ewan came home with some discouraging reports from Zephyr—when did any other kind of reports originate in Zephyr?—and altogether I feel that the sands of time are sinking.[350]

Tuesday, May 13, 1924

I am reading, in that precious hour between ten and eleven, Guizot's *History of France*.[351] It is very interesting. But a prolonged dose of history like this always breeds pessimism in me. The unceasing succession of crimes and brutalities and treacheries and horrors that make up "history" make me feel that it is impossible that there can be any "personal" God—or any Power that can or will protect or defend the individual. I can, of course, see clearly in all history a certain Force struggling upwards out of darkness and horror into light and sanity; but it seems to me a blind, impersonal force to whom the individual is nothing. And when I feel this I descend into the deeps.

Friday, May 16, 1924

I see by *The Guardian* that John Stirling[352] has been called to Montague. This will be so nice for Margaret. She has been buried alive in Breadalbane, with no congenial friends or pleasant surroundings.

We had Guild this evening. Some of our Guild meetings are good and encouraging. But this one was a failure. The subject was "John Keats" and nobody cared anything about it. The readings were dull. Ewan read his paper wretchedly—when he is melancholy he reads as badly as a schoolboy of eight. I felt ashamed and humiliated. I wanted to throw a book at him and howl.

---

350   *The Sands of Time Are Sinking* is a nineteenth-century hymn by Anne Ross Cundell Cousin.

351   French politician and historian François Guizot (1787–1874) had published *The History of France from the Earliest Times to 1848* in 1895.

352   John Stirling and his wife Margaret Ross were long-time friends of the Macdonalds (John had presided over their wedding). Stirling had been minister in Breadalbane, Prince Edward Island.

But of course I didn't. I sat decorously, read my own paper—and came home alone. It was a beautiful night though cold—moonlight, clear sparkling air, luminous stars. The beauty soothed and calmed me. If I had had some of the race of Joseph to run with me under the moon I could have been happy for a few minutes. But I was alone.

Saturday, May 17, 1924
The Manse, Leaskdale

Have been housecleaning all the week and trying to garden. But the almost constant rain makes both difficult. I am very tired. Ewan has slept all the week without having to take anything even once. This is the best record since February. But he is very dull and quiet and will not do *anything* until he is compelled to.

Sunday, May 18, 1924

One thing today made today worth living and writing about. It poured rain until two. Then it cleared and became clear and bitterly cold. We all went to Zephyr and after service got Mrs. Rob Shier and went up to Belhaven to visit a former Zephyr family. We stayed there until eight then came home. Nothing in all that, except a dull day spent amid stupid people, shivering with the chill of fireless rooms most of the time. But when we dropped Mrs. Shier at Zephyr, Chester and I sat together in the back seat and talked all the way home. *Real* talk. Chester's mind is developing rapidly just now. We flew along. The moon flooded the bare spring hills with light. The pine stump fences writhed up along the roads like the stark skeletons of creatures that had died in torment. We talked. Chester discoursed on transmigration and told me some remarkable dreams he had had as we cuddled together in the dimness with our arms about each other. I cannot describe the charm of it all—you cannot photograph starlight. But we were perfectly happy for a little while. "What a nice little mother you are," said Chester.

Sunday, May 25, 1924

Another week of rain, cold, and hard work ended. But I am glad to say the housecleaning and gardening are about done. They have never been so hard as this year. Ewan has slept well all the week and some days seems fairly well, on others dull. It is only in the car that he seems quite well. The minute he is out of it he is down again.

I don't know whether our dog is a darling or an unmitigated nuisance—

"Airy voices"

Dreaming of Bubastis.

or both. Sometimes I love him—sometimes I want to wring his neck. Luck remains entirely adorable and all the legends of old springs hover around him as he listens to "airy voices" on the fence of the lawn or basks inscrutably in our scanty hours of sunshine, dreaming perchance of Bubastis and his fellow-gods in "the land of the river."[353]

The Church Union bill[354] after being the storm centre for weeks in Ottawa has been given a two years hoist. Meanwhile, "the courts" have to decide on the constitutionality of it. If they decide against it that is the end of it. If they decide for it it becomes law in July 1926. There's a nice muddle for you. It won't please anybody. But a good deal of water will flow under the bridges in two years and the ghost of Mr. Micawber[355] broods over the troubled waters.

Monday, May 26, 1924
The Manse, Leaskdale, Ont.

This morning I resumed work on my third *Emily* book[356] and this afternoon Lily and I cleaned the horse stable. I have been at Ewan all the spring to clean it but he kept saying "Yes, yes" and never doing it. It has never been cleaned since February—in other words since the inertia of his melancholy came upon him. As our horse was here until May 1st its condition may be imagined. It *had* to be cleaned before we could put our setting hens[357] in it so today we did it. To do Lily justice, she never balks at a job of this kind. She seems, indeed, to like it, having had plenty of it to do on the farms where she worked before coming here. But it was a hard, dirty and unpleasant job. But we did it thoroughly and tonight, though my back aches and my feet moan, I feel the satisfaction of "something attempted, something done." It has certainly "earned a night's

353   Bubastis was a city in ancient Egypt along the Nile River that was a centre of worship for the feline goddess Bast.

354   In 1924, The United Church of Canada Act was passed, incorporating three major denominations into one, the "United Church of Canada." It had been a hugely divisive issue throughout society; only two thirds of Presbyterian congregations voted to merge into the United Church.

355   The reference here is a fictional character in Charles Dickens' novel, *David Copperfield* (1850). Wilkins Micawber was incarcerated in debtors' prison.

356   *Emily's Quest* (Frederick A. Stokes, 1927).

357   That is, the hens that were going to set on their fertilized eggs and hatch them.

repose"[358] but whether I shall have it or not is a question. I am too tired to sleep, I fear.

Of course I put on, for the task, clothes that couldn't be materially injured by it; and as, arrayed thus, I carried out forkful after forkful of manure I grinned to myself as I wondered what my readers—ay, and my publishers, too, for that matter—would think, if they could see me. Judging from the letters I get, my readers, at least the young and romantic portion, seem to imagine that I never do anything, except sit, beautifully arrayed, at a desk and "create" "Annes" and "Emilys"! They might admit that I sometimes washed dishes or dusted a room but I'm sure they'd never think I cleaned horse stables!

Wednesday, May 28, 1924

Yesterday afternoon we motored to Newmarket where I was to give an evening of readings for some C.G.I.T.s. It was a warmer day than we have had, the young leaves and blossoms were coming out, Ewan seemed fairly well and so I enjoyed the drive. It was certainly much pleasanter than cleaning the horse-stable!

We had supper at the manse. Mrs. Mann is one of those very gushing prayerful women whom I find fearful bores. While we were sitting in the church—which is a very nice one—she whispered to me her tale of woe regarding her first Sunday there. She was aghast to discover that the stairs, leading from the schoolroom up to the church were "excessively narrow." This was terrible. She did not see how she could endure it. "Oh, Mrs. Macdonald," she whispered fervently, "you don't know how I felt! Only my habit of constant prayer carried me through. As I went up and down those terrible stairs I kept saying over and over, 'Oh, God, help me to be brave. Oh, God, help me to be brave.'"

I found it hard to repress a whoop of laughter in the good lady's face. If she had come to a manse with no sanitary conveniences—if she had to clean out horse stables because her husband was too melancholy to do it—I wonder if she would have thought narrow stairs required so much courage. The stairs, by the way, are gone. God—or Mr. Mann—put it into the heads of the congregation to do them over and widen them. Who says prayer is never answered?

I wore my batik silk dress and my black and gold lace scarf. After the programme the girls gave me a beautiful bouquet of roses. As I held my roses and bowed I saw a picture of myself in the "rig" of yesterday popping in and out of that stable with unending forkfuls of manure. The contrast struck me

---

358　From American poet Henry Wadsworth Longfellow's (1807–82) "The Village Blacksmith": "Each morning sees some task begin / Each evening sees it close / Something attempted, something done, / Has earned a night's repose."

so forcibly that I grinned—and Mrs. Mann assured me afterwards that never had she seen so charming a smile as that with which I rewarded the bouquet givers!

Thursday June 5, 1924
The Manse, Leaskdale

Last Saturday, just as we were leaving to attend a ball game up at the north school I got a letter from Stella saying that her mother, after being perfectly well all winter and gaining 25 lbs., had had another of her bad attacks and had been so ill that she alarmed them, but seemed getting better and they hoped the worst was over. I felt anxious for these attacks of Aunt Annie's seem to get worse and worse as time goes on. She had such a bad one about this time last year. I was sorry, too, because I feared she would not be able to go home this summer now. She had been planning to come the last of June. We went to Uxbridge after the game and while there I got a wire from Stell:—

"Mother very very ill. No hope of her recovery. General break down of the mucous membrane of stomach and bladder. Chills, high temperature and hemorrhage. Let me hear from you."

I don't know how I got home. The drive was like a nightmare. But when I got here I found that a very curious thing had happened. *I had ceased to feel.* I can only express it that way. I never felt just the same in my life before. It was just as if something in me had said, "I refuse to be hurt. I *will not* suffer more pain." Fancy continued to picture the further impoverishment of life if Aunt Annie died, mind suggested a hundred problems and perplexities in regard to that helpless family at Park Corner—but nothing gave me pain. I wept no more. I went to bed. I did not sleep, it is true; but there seemed no reason why I could not. I was calm and composed and—detached. Ay, *that's* the word, exactly. Some vital connection between perception and feeling had been cut—whether temporarily or permanently I could not say. All day Sunday the numbness continued. It was merciful—and yet I did not like it. Not only the ability to feel pain seemed gone but the ability to feel anything. I thought of the incident I read not long ago in a book on psycho-analysis; a man hated his wife—hated her so intensely that he wished he might never see her again—wished it so intensely that the wish came true. He *went blind*; not only could he not see his wife but he could not see anything. My mental condition seemed to correspond to his physical one. And I felt curiously cut off from my kind. I felt neither fear nor love nor ambition, nor any desire save to lie down and be let alone. I did not even dread the 'phone ring, though I expected it every moment.

Sunday night I slept well. Monday morning the 'phone rang. As I went to it my mind and feelings were quite calm but my legs trembled and I turned sick at my stomach. The wire was:—"General condition much the same. Pulse remains good. Temperature still high at intervals. Very slight chills continue but not so severe. Cannot give definite encouragement yet."

Tuesday the wire was:—"The doctor feels much elated over mother's condition. She is still very very ill."

Today's wire was:—"Cannot see much change but she is holding her own well. Temperature still high."

It may be she will again recover. But I doubt if she will every again be able to return to Park Corner. And that, for me, will be just as if she had died.

Ewan left Monday morning for P.E.I. He will be away a month. I have to say that his going was a relief. For three months he has just hung around gloomy and unhappy, casting a blight on everything. Sometimes lately, when I have been so tired and over worked I have felt as if it were the last straw to sit down at the table and look at his dull downcast face without a trace of interest or animation in it. This is the bitterest thing in mental disorder. In physical illness our household intimates are still the same; but in this they are changed into alien personalities.

Besides, the trip and concentration on Christie's business troubles may help him. I thought it did last year: but that may only have been co-incidence.

Of course, compared to what he was in March Ewan is almost well. He sleeps well and is quite cheerful in company. He is just dull, and lifeless day in and day out at home and seems to think everybody else should feel as dull as he does. He has no affection at these times for either the children or me. We mean nothing to him. He has no interest in any of the things we are interested in. Poor, poor Ewan! Why should he be cursed with such a fate?

The ball game last Saturday was between Leaskdale school and the "north school." They played a ball game and a football game. Leaskdale lost in both, alas. But they have only been organized for a week whereas the north school has been playing all the spring. Chester was one of the nine. As he stood at the bat I suddenly remembered something that Frede had said one day twelve years ago as she bent over sleeping "Punch" on the veranda: "I would come from the ends of the earth to see him play his first football game."

Leaskdale trial

Well, Chester was playing his "first football game" and I was there to see it. But where was Frede? Not even from the ends of the earth could she come. Her journeying had led her far beyond "the utmost rim of sinking stars."[359]

"Oh death, where is thy sting? Oh, grave where is thy victory?"[360]

Paul never lost anyone vitally

"Let her went"

"Wait till *I'm* old enough."

dear to him or he would not have written that. He would have known *then* that the sting of death and the victory of the grave is in the *separation for this life* and nothing can avert the agony of that lifelong loneliness. It is *here* we want our beloved—not in some far-off heaven.

In fancy Frede sat by me through all that game. I could hear her laughing, applauding, cheering. Well, perhaps she *was* there. Perhaps as Stuart sat upon a post and howled for Leaskdale Frede stood beside him and sent her ghostly cheer across the playground.

But no:—Frede would be in Los Angeles where brave old Aunt Annie is making what may be her last fight with our grim enemy—or perhaps our best friend. Yes, I think death is our best friend; and that most of us could not live if we did not know that death was certain.

"Luck"

Catch-as-catch-can.

---

359   A possible misquotation of one of LMM's favourite meditations on death, Tennyson's poem *Ulysses*: "To follow knowledge like a sinking star, / Beyond the utmost bound of human thought."

360   1 Corinthians 15:55. In this passage Paul meditates on the Resurrection and how it helps Christians be less afraid of death. Jesus' death and resurrection is like a bee that has lost its sting.

My garden, long delayed by the wet and cold, is coming up. I never fail to find renewed pleasure in it each year. I walk up and down the rows every morning and evening attended by two cats and a dog. They are not such good friends as the expression implies. But Luck tolerates Dixie and Pat ignores him having found Dixie profanity-proof.

A dog.

Friday, June 6, 1924
The Manse, Leaskdale

I had a letter from Stella today, written, of course, at the time of her first wire, and so very hopeless. It has been discounted to some extent by the succeeding wires. Nevertheless, I do not like Aunt Annie's symptoms. The doctors say that they think it is either an infected gall bladder or cancer of the stomach. I do not believe for a moment that it is the latter. Aunt Annie has never had the slightest trouble with her stomach or her digestion. She has been perfectly well all winter and has gained twenty-five lbs. But it may be the gall bladder and very likely is, since she has had gall stones for years. I fear it is a serious thing.

Marie Corelli is dead.[361] The news affected me somewhat. When I was a girl she was in her hey-day and her books always made a tremendous sensation. The critics abused her lavishly and everything they said was true. But she could tell a story and her books were read by millions. I used to read and discuss them with my friends so that Corelli's name was linked with much of the happiness of youth and her death seems therefore to have a personal meaning for me.

This evening I was reading *The Diary of Marie Bashkirtseff*.[362] This book came out when I was a young girl and made a tremendous sensation. It was discussed in all the reviews. I longed to read it but books like that never penetrated to Cavendish and I could not afford to buy it. Recently a new edition was brought out and I sent for it. If it were published today for the first time it would hardly cause a ripple. We have had book after book of these intimate chronicles far more frank and sensational than poor Marie's passionate longings for fame and success. The diary is interesting at first but one tires of it as one reads on because it is just the same all the way through. It is a pitiful tragic record. I do not think Marie was a very agreeable person to live with.

---

361   See note 324, page 227.
362   Ukrainian artist, writer, and sculptor, Marie Bashkirtseff (1858–84) kept a diary from age 13; it was published in 1887.

Her excessive craving for fame and worldly success was abnormal and affected me unpleasantly, like a morbid thirst. Most of us feel, whether mistakenly or not, that fame and success are pleasant things but few seem to crave them as poor Marie did. She wanted them too much ever to have them. I think the intensity of her desire was a symptom of the disease which killed her. Her subconsciousness knew her inherent tendency and realized that life might be short; hence it imbued her with a feverish desire to attain before death overtook her.

I think her book will live because of its painful sincerity.

Monday, June 9, 1924
The Manse, Leaskdale, Ont.

On Saturday a letter from Mr. Rollins came. I felt sure that it contained news about the New York suit and I decided not to open it until today. Mr. Lord was coming that evening to preach and I did not want to be upset while he was here. Nevertheless I worried about it all Sunday and dreaded this morning when it would have to be opened. I felt that, somehow, I really had not the courage and strength to open another of those missives that have come at intervals for four years. But I had a dream last night that made me feel that the news the letter bore was not bad. I have often had this type of dream when I was dreading something that turned out a mere scarecrow after all. I dreamed that the garage was on fire and Lily and I were trying to put it out. *We succeeded*. I woke and said "There is good news in that letter." Nevertheless I opened it with trembling fingers:—

Dear Mrs. Macdonald:—
I have just received a telegram from Briesen & Schrenk, reading as follows:—'Page vs. Macdonald dismissed for want of jurisdiction.'
I am glad we have been successful, but suppose the other side may appeal.

Today's mail brought another letter, enclosing one from Mr. Von Briesen, giving details. He writes:—

We believe that the plaintiff will undoubtedly appeal and will probably apply for a stay of proceedings pending the appeal. If the plaintiff pursues this course the payment of the money accumulated with the Stokes Co. will be held up pending the appeal but we are hoping that our adversaries may possibly make a misstep which will allow us to have the money sent to Mrs. Macdonald before any stay is obtained. In the meantime sufficient for the day are the good decisions thereof.

Mr. Rollins writes:—

I cannot help having the feeling that although the other side appeals which is probable, the decision of the trial court will not be disturbed—my process of reasoning being that the matter having been one of judicial discretion, the decision of Judge McGoldrick will not be overruled unless plainly wrong and that it is not plainly wrong.

This has lifted a tremendous weight from my mind, which is especially a thing to be grateful for just now when I have so many other troubles. Of course Page will appeal and my money will still be tied up—for I do not share Mr. Von Briesen's pious hope that Page's lawyers will make a misstep; but that will not seriously inconvenience me and I have no fear whatever that the appeal will succeed.

So that's that, Louis P.!

Tuesday, June 10, 1924

This has been a lovely day—the most delightful day we have had since last summer. It was warm enough to be pleasant. We have had such a phenomenally cold spring. But then there have been no mosquitoes. During these last five years the mosquitoes have been dreadful and last spring we were almost eaten up alive. This year we have had no trouble. I hate mosquitoes. One mosquito in my room at night can keep me awaker than a bad conscience.

This has been a happy day of a peace and quiet long unknown to me. There was no word from Aunt Annie and in such a case as this "no news is good news." I finished a short story in the forenoon—"Some Fools and a Saint"—and spent the afternoon and evening working in my garden, enjoying every minute. People say:—"It must be a great deal of work to keep such a large garden." Of course it is; but then it is such delightful work—out in the open, under the lovely spring skies with the young green leaves unfolding on every hand. What a change from my prison of the winter.

And I have the best garden I have ever had. Everything came up and there have been no bad thunderstorms to wash it out—another advantage of the cold spring. I have rows upon rows of delightful possibilities—corn, cucumbers, poppies, gypsophila, cosmos, peas, asters, gladiolii, beans, sweet peas, parsnips, sweet sultans, radishes, balsams, zinnias, beets, carrots, pansies, egg plant, parsley, nasturtiums, watermelons, lettuce, onions, cabbages, cauliflowers and tomatoes. I prowl about, weeding, watering, transplanting. My cats frisk around me, my small dog, of whom I am getting very fond, chases the cats and gets his ears boxed—by the cats—for his pains. And we are all so temporarily happy together that life seems good.

Then follows a long delightful evening of reading, since there is no "visiting" to be done. Tonight I read *Barabbas* over again.[363] I like it the best of Corelli's books because having a miracle ready to her hand in the Resurrection she does not have to invent one and is kept within reasonable bounds by the limitations of the gospel story. I enjoyed the book. Nevertheless when I had finished it I had to get out Strauss' *Life of Jesus*[364] and read some of it for an antidote.

Saturday, June 14, 1924
The Manse, Leaskdale
Ten o'clock, A.M.

I had a very remarkable experience this morning—so remarkable that I hasten to set it down here while it is still fresh in my memory. I have never had anything of the kind before. I have had strange predictive dreams but this was not a dream.

I wakened early—too early to get up, so I tried to go to sleep again. I was not actually asleep. I was quite conscious that I was lying there in bed, that the boys were talking down the hall in their room—arguing over something—and that Dixie was howling dolefully at the kitchen door. I seemed to be just on the border line between sleeping and waking. Suddenly I heard a voice. It was as clear and distinct and audible as any voice I ever heard in my life;—"*This is the last of the series of misfortunes that have come upon you like a rage*" was what the voice said.

I awakened up wholly as it pronounced the last word—wakened up with a strange peaceful feeling that has persisted ever since.

I don't know what to make of it.

But I believe it. I believe that my misfortunes are at an end—this "series" of them at least. But the conviction does not elate me. Because I know Aunt Annie is not going to recover. I feel sure of it.

"This" refers to her illness, I know, and it will terminate in her death, for otherwise it could not be called one of "my misfortunes." No, Aunt Annie is going to die and this is to be the last of the "series of misfortunes." *Series* is the right word. Whatever intelligence uttered that sentence was an artist in words, and it has indeed fallen on me "like a rage." For the past five years I have been smitten with blow after blow as if some angry Taskmaster were buffetting me. It began with Frede's death. Then came the terrible months of

---

363	*Barabbas: A Dream of the World's Tragedy*, by Marie Corelli, published in 1893.
364	German writer and theologian David Friedrich Strauss (1808–74) wrote about the "historical" Jesus, arguing that Jesus was human, with no divine nature.

Ewan's first attack of melancholia; then lawsuit after lawsuit with the Pages; then the horrible year of the Pickering affair; then this attack of Ewan's this winter; and now dear Aunt Annie's illness—yes, and death.

But it is ended. Frede's death began it—her mother's will close it. Henceforth there will be peace—and desolation.

Monday, June 16, 1924

Today I had three letters from Stella—all written nearly a week ago. In the first two her mother's serious symptoms continued but in the third and last she spoke of marked improvement and hoped her mother had taken a turn for the better. I cannot hope it—have not hoped since I heard that mysterious voice Saturday morning.

Poor Stell; her letters are very hysterical. It is natural and not inexcusable that she should deplore her mother's danger as if no one on earth had ever loved and lost a mother before. But it is disgusting to read her rants against the nurse, with whom she fights continually. One would think that even Stella could keep from fighting with the nurse at such a time.

I expected a wire from her today for I dreamed last night that Grandmother Macneill[365] and I were roaming about a strange city looking for some person we could not find; and Grandmother's face was so old and wrinkled and distressed, as it never was in real life.

Tuesday, June 17, 1924
The Manse, Leaskdale, Ont.

The wire came this morning; as I was writing in the parlor the 'phone rang. I went to it. The station master—a telegram from Los Angeles:—

"Mother is gradually sinking. Everything is being done but without avail. Danny wants to come but I don't know what to tell him. It might be too late when he got here. Please wire him what you think best to do. Stella."

The strange numbness which has possessed me since the Saturday of the first telegram suddenly broke and was swept away in a torrent of sorrow and desolation. Aunt Annie dying! Impossible! Aunt Annie could not die—*could not*. I had a bad afternoon. Oh, these bereavements are hideous things.

This evening I sent a night letter to Stell; "Have wired Dan not to go. He is too young and can do no good. You must bring your mother home. I cannot face Park Corner alone or attend to the business there. I will pay your expenses."

365   LMM's maternal grandmother, Lucy Ann Woolner Macneill (1824–1911).

Stella has written in one of her letters that she did not know what they would do if Aunty died. Clara is running a big private hotel and could not leave it; and she—Stella—could not afford to come. This was a hint for me, of course. And of course I took it. I would do anything in my power that dear Aunty would like me to do. Oh, how thankful I am that I have always helped Aunt Annie with money cheerfully and ungrudgingly. She never came to me for help in vain. I made her last six years on earth tolerable.

And I cannot—I *cannot* go to Park Corner for that ordeal alone. That helpless family—the ghastly loneliness with no Aunt Annie! *No Aunt Annie at Park Corner*. I cannot realize it. I cannot picture Park Corner without her. She has always been there—she was always the centre around which everything revolved—even at an age when other women are relegated to the chimney corner. I could scream at the very thought of going to Park Corner and not finding Aunt Annie there. I was never there in my life that she wasn't there.

I shall have some days of hideous suspense now. This evening the station phoned up again—another telegram. I went down with shaking knees—but it was only a business wire from New York.

It is dark; the house is quiet—the boys asleep. I am writing in the library. I dread to stop, for then the pangs of my grief will pounce on me like wolves again. With the exception of Frede's death this is the most bitter sorrow that has ever come to me. It will take more out of life than anything else, save Frede's loss, has taken. Oh, but I lived through *that*—so I can live through *this*.

I lifted up my eyes at supper time and saw the picture of Park Corner on the wall. There it was—the big beautiful, orchard-bowered house that was the wonder castle of my childhood, where Aunt Annie reigned as queen, dispensing the lavish and gracious hospitality for which she was famous. And she will never be there again—never.

What will happen at Park Corner I don't know. Oh God, I can't endure this heartache. I wish that merciful numbness had lasted. Oh—oh—oh—this is too great a price to pay for the boon of human love.

The Manse, Leaskdale, Ont.
Wednesday, June 18, 1924

Last night was possessed of a devil in Leaskdale manse. I went to bed very tired and hoping for a good sleep which might give me enough strength to carry on with. I was just falling asleep when I heard Lily calling out agitatedly, "Where's the flashlight? There's some kind of an animal in the yard." Inwardly cursing Lily and her mare's nests[366] I roused up and got her the flashlight.

366　Traditionally, this expression means either a hoax or a fuss over nothing.

Was just lapsing into slumber again when Lily returned, announcing that she could not see anything. Once more I wakened and once more I fell asleep. Re-enter Lily; agitation more marked: the mysterious animal had returned and had got into the hen pen; she believed it was a fox after the hens; wouldn't I dress and go out with her—she was afraid to go alone.

I got up, dressed and went out. If it really were a fox my hens must be saved. As we approached the hen-pen an old yellow dog, who had been gnawing a bone flung to the chickens dashed madly off in terror. I returned to bed, thinking things not lawful to be uttered.

Again, for the last time, I grew sleepy and was just "off" when I heard an anguished meow. The next moment a little distracted animal landed on my bed, still piteously entreating. I put out my hand—touched it—what on earth? I sprang out of bed and lit the lamp. I saw a sight that doubled me up with laughter. Poor Luck had evidently got into the pantry, got caught in and pulled down the long sticky "fly stop"[367] hanging there; then he had got it wound around and around him from tail to nose. I had to separate the poor cat from that miserable girdling. His fur is coming out and it pulled off in big bunches. Then most of the mucilage remained on him and made the remaining fur stick out all over him in grotesque spikes. By the time I had finished I was past sleeping and spent the rest of the night tossing restlessly and thinking wildly.

All day I dreaded hearing the 'phone but no message came from Los Angeles. I spent much of the day in my garden, weeding and thinning. I have a wonderful garden this year. I have never had one so good. Everything came up and there has been no "wash-out" to ruin it, as generally happens. I hate the thought of going away from it.

Thursday, June 19, 1924
The Manse, Leaskdale

No word yet. This suspense is very hard to bear. And one *cannot* keep a torturing hope from creeping back—perhaps, it whispers, she may rally after all.

I had a good sleep—the best for a long time. But for the first time I could not write this morning.

There was a letter from Stell, written while she still had hope. And full of ravings against Clara. I always discount Stella's utterances largely but it does seem that Clara really has behaved in a strange and unfeeling manner during her mother's illness. Even so, one sister should not rail at another so at such a time.

Ewan also wrote and says he feels much better then he has felt for a long time.

---

367   That is, fly paper, for catching insects.

Friday, June 20, 1924

It is ended.

This morning at eleven the message came. Aunt Annie died yesterday June 19 at 12.30.

I spent the afternoon writing letters and telegrams. Sometimes I had to walk the floor in bitter tears and sorrow, mingled with the stubborn incredulity with which we always face the fact of death. Aunt Annie could not be dead—she *could* not.

Saturday, June 21, 1924

A busy day—pierced through every little while with stabs of anguish so dreadful that if I am alone I shriek aloud. Between these stabs I am numb and calm.

This afternoon I went back with the boys to their swimming pool in Leask's woods. It was a beautiful afternoon and for a brief space I didn't believe any more that Aunt Annie was dead. So I was quite happy.

Swimming pool.

Stuart is quite a fish. He can swim and dive amazingly. Chester, of heavier and less elastic build, doesn't do as well. Can't swim yet without a plank under him.

It was beautiful there in the sunlight and shadow. But this evening was hard.

Monday, June 23, 1924
Walker House, Toronto

I came in today to see Mrs. Meloney, the editor of *The Delineator*. She is much in love with "Emily" and I am to arrange four stories from the first and second *Emily* books for publication next year. For these four stories, which are already written, I am to get sixteen hundred dollars! Yet twenty years ago I wrote many stories just as good—better—for which I was glad to get fifty or sixty apiece. Mrs. Meloney was nice but couldn't realize at all just what my life is and couldn't understand why I couldn't get time to write more short stories etc. I gave up trying to explain. She is an inhabitant of a different world, and we do

not talk the same language. I could not tell her the nature of my husband's illness or make her see the necessity for my doing so much church work.

And, of course, I didn't tell her I ever cleaned horse-stables!

Thursday, June 26, 1924
The Manse, Leaskdale, Ont.

Am very busy getting matters arranged so that I can go away with an easy mind. I don't know when I will have to go until I hear from Stella. Mrs. Alec Leask was down this evening and I walked up the hill with her. It's odd about Mrs. Leask—she has spasms of exasperating foolishness—she is eaten up with unholy curiosity about everything that doesn't concern her—I wouldn't trust her around a corner—and yet there is a tang of the race of Joseph about her.

I walked back alone, attended by the goblin lanterns of the fireflies under a cloudless silvery sky, haunted by the legends of old forgotten springs.

It is the brooding season, haunted and sad and dear
When vanished things return not with the returning year.[368]

Ah no, they do not return. Aunt Annie has gone on and she will not return. She will not come as a guest to my house again—I will not go to hers. Between us now is a silence that will never be broken. Yet she was with me as I walked down the hill to the leafy corner where my home was. I heard her voice and saw her smile. Her foot kept step with mine. Aunt Annie was always too vital and vivid a personality to die quickly. It is her type that is the genesis of ghosts.

[Looking north through Leaskdale; the house in the right foreground is the Manse; the white building in the distance is the store.]

Friday June 27, 1924

After all the Church Union Bill is passed—the "Coercion Bill" as it has been well named. The Commons disregarded the recommendations of the Committee completely and passed the bill *in toto*. Well, we will see what will come of it. No church, founded on such a deed of injustice will ever prosper.

368　From "A Sailor's Wedding" by Canadian poet Bliss Carman (1861–1929).

Monday, June 30, 1924

The end of June. It has been a strange month. In one way a time of bitter suspense and grief; in the other a peaceful, pleasant month. It seems a horrible thing to say that a month has been peaceful and pleasant because my husband was away. Yet it is true. Those months before June were so terrible—the whole house seemed so saturated with that repulsive personality which replaced Ewan's normal self—that it was a relief when he went away. I have read and worked and slept, free from that sense of an ever-present strain and horror. Ewan's letters lately have been quite cheerful. He seems much better.

I packed for my journey today. I leave next Thursday night. Stell wants me to go down and help Ella with the arrangements. I feel reluctant to do so but it is best.

Wednesday, July 2, 1924
The Manse, Leaskdale

Ewan came home last night. He seems pretty well. This morning we took Chester down to Uxbridge to begin taking his High School entrance exams. I was reminded of that morning so long ago when I went to Prince of Wales to write my entrance. "Like leaves on trees the race of man is found."[369]

He thought he had got on all right this evening. He will go tomorrow and Friday. I am sorry I have to go before he finishes. The arithmetic will be his danger point, just as it was mine.

Ewan still says prayers night and morning, so he is not well. But I am relieved that he is well as he is. Otherwise I would be wretched at the idea of going away.

I have been much troubled by headache myself this week. And I feel so tired all the time.

Park Corner, P.E. Island
Sunday, July 6, 1924

I am here again in the dear old spot, so changed and lonely for me. I had a hot, unpleasant journey down. Life[370] met me at Kensington last night and we came down the old beautiful road, fragrant with the wild-fern scent of a warm summer evening. There were a few terrible moments when I reached Park Corner and Ella came to meet me—but no Aunt Annie—for the first time in all my life no Aunt Annie.

---

369   From Book IV of Alexander Pope's translation of Homer's *The Iliad*: "Like leaves on trees the race of man is found, / Now green in youth, now with'ring on the ground: / Another race the foll'wing spring supplies, / They fall successive, and successive rise" (181–85).
370   That is, Eliphalet ("Life") Howatt, a neighbour and friend from the Park Corner area.

Since then I have got on fairly well. Last night I slept alone in Stella's old room upstairs. I had expected it would be a ghostly night. Last summer I felt and recorded it in this journal, that at night the old house was thronged with phantom presences. I felt it so keenly that I almost was compelled to believe it. And I feared it would be even worse now. But there was absolutely no such sensation, though I lay awake for a long time. *The ghosts were gone*. They came only because Aunt Annie was here. She is not here now—and they come no more. They will never come again. This sounds very nonsensical—but it is exactly what I feel. And who knows?

[Park Corner]

[Stella Campbell, Park Corner]

This has been a dull day. Ella and I planned out everything. I think it is well I came. Poor Ella is so helpless and inadequate. It is farcical to see *her* in Aunt Annie's place. And yet I am fond of her and sorry for her. It is not her fault that she is only a grown-up child. It was a grim joke of Fate to cast her for a part which requires unusual powers of organization, will and judgment. Anything so helpless as Ella in the midst of the problems that surround her could not be imagined. And her plaintive whines are almost more than I can endure. Donald[371] is one of her problems. He will never make a farmer, that is certain. He is as lazy—as Ella herself, to put it plainly. And she has no control or influence over him. Jim should be the farmer. He would restore the Park Corner traditions if anyone would. But the child is only twelve and Ella cannot run this place. They have a good hired man this year but even so a farm must have a head. Dan is bad-tempered and fights with his help. Bad temper has been the curse of this family. Yet Aunt Annie and Uncle John[372] were the best natured people alive. The situation is beyond me and I am inclined to wash

371   LMM normally refers to Donald Campbell as "Dan."

372   Aunt Annie had been married to Uncle John Campbell (1834–1917). At his passing LMM had written, "Uncle John Campbell was a man I always loved deeply. For no other uncle, of marriage or blood, did I have such an affection. He was the kindest, most hospitable of men. I never heard a harsh word from him" (December 19, 1917).

my hands of it, having problems enough of my own. Perhaps when Stell comes we can think of a way out.

I went over to see Aunt Eliza tonight.[373] As usual she told me how beautiful my mother was and added that I didn't look a bit like her!! Heath's wife is there and, from all appearances, is not going to let the family die out.

Monday July 7, 1924

A hot and busy day. I think I have got things planned out pretty well. I went over to see Aunt Mary tonight.[374] She is the only one of our old circle left.

Park Corner
Wednesday, July 9, 1924

Yesterday afternoon Heath motored me over to Cavendish, and I stayed there until this evening. A brief visit but a very pleasant one. I stayed last night at Webbs'[375] and had a delightful walk through Lover's Lane and Deep Hollow last night. A terrific storm last fall played terrible havoc with what was left of the old trees. The poor old lane has some remnants of beauty here and there but it is sadly unlike what it was twenty or even ten years ago.

This morning I went to Alec's and had dinner with them and a lovely time. *As yet*, change has not touched that home. Alec and May have a car and they brought me back this evening.

One thing depressed me very much—Cavendish is getting so shabby. Almost all the houses are unpainted and dowdy. Alec's looks nice and snug but everywhere else the places seemed down-at-heel. Times are hard, of course, but I fear there are other reasons—indifference, the dying out of the old families. The manse in particular looks dreadful and gives a poverty-stricken look to the whole landscape around it. No one has lived in it since the Stirlings left and the people are quarrelling over the question whether to build a new one or repair it. There is something wrong somewhere.

Thursday, July 10, 1924

I had a restless night. Today was very hot, made hotter by the frying of a big batch of doughnuts. I had excellent luck and was pleased. The funeral baked meats must not disgrace the old traditions. I found the pantry lamentably empty but I went to the local store and stocked it up. This evening I copied

---

373　See footnote 236, p. 170.
374　Aunt Mary was the widow of Cuthbert Montgomery, LMM's father's brother.
375　That is, Myrtle and Ernest Webb.

some recipes from Aunt Annie's old cook-book. It spoke very eloquently of her. Never was such a cook as Aunt Annie. Almost every page recalled some feast of the past.

I had letters from Chester and Mrs. Meloney today. Chester thinks he passed. Mrs. Meloney writes me that, after all, she dare not use the "Father Cassidy" story in the *Delineator*. Because of the Ku Klux Klan she is afraid to publish a story in which the "hero is a Catholic Priest!"[376]

Yet we live in the year of grace 1924! Well, it would seem as if, in spite of all our vaunted democracy, nine tenths of the human race must always be in bondage to some form of tyranny.

This vexes me. I shall have to write a new story to fit into that particular place in the series. And this will be very difficult to do, much more so than writing an independent story. Besides it will take a good deal of time.

Sunday, July 13, 1924
Park Corner, P.E.I.

It is all over. "Ashes to ashes and dust to dust." Aunt Annie sleeps with her own.

Friday evening Cuthbert[377] took me up to Kensington. Almost everybody in Park Corner went up. The train came at 10.40. Stella and I came home together—a strange drive through the dark scented summer night. Stella does not seem to have changed a bit in her looks. We talked everything over. On our way we passed the team wagon in which was the big steel box inside of which was Aunt Annie's coffin. It gleamed weirdly in our car lights as we swept by. So came Aunt Annie home.

We gave supper to twenty five people that night. I do not say it was for the sake of that supper so many went to Kensington and attended us home. No, I believe they would all have gone even if they had known they would have no supper. They were kind neighbors who loved Aunt Annie and were all anxious to help us in every way they could. But they enjoyed the supper for all that. Ella and I had seen that it was a good one—cold chicken a-plenty, biscuits, preserves, pies, cakes galore. Even Aunt Annie herself would have accorded it her approval I think. I had an uncanny feeling that Aunt Annie herself should be sitting at the head of the table, pouring the tea and smiling on the circle as she had always done of yore. But Mrs. Howatt was sitting there—and they

---

376   A Ku Klux Klan movement had been founded in the southern US in 1915; based on an earlier movement, the group flourished across parts of the south and midwest until the mid-1920s. Among other things, this white nationalist group opposed Catholics and Jews.
377   Cuthbert Montgomery was the younger brother of LMM's father.

were bringing Aunt Annie into her home by the front door. I heard the sounds under all the hum of conversation. But I could not go in until Ella came to me and whispered, "Won't you go and see her now, Aunt Maud? She looks lovely."

I went in. I had been afraid that we would not be able to see Aunt Annie—and I had felt that I could not bear it if I did not see once more that kind face which had always looked upon me with a smile. I wanted to see her just once more—yet I feared some terrible change.

Aunt Annie, lying in her steel casket in that softly lighted old parlor was the most beautiful thing I ever saw. There *was* a change—the change from age to youth. She looked like a young girl. Her dark hair, in which there was hardly a thread of silver, was waved over her forehead as she always wore it. There was not a wrinkle on the peaceful face; and she wore a little dress of white silk.

I do not remember Aunt Annie young. As far back as I can recall she was a stout middle-aged woman, with a lined face, soberly clad in dark dresses. Now I saw her as a girl. Beautiful—I was thankful to see her once again and so lovely. And yet it is not as that marble-white bride of death that I shall remember Aunt Annie. No, I shall think of her as an old woman in a gingham apron coming out of her pantry or feeding her chickens. Aunt Annie always seemed to be feeding *something*—human beings or animals. She was always *giving*. She had had much sorrow in her life and many disappointments but nothing had

[Aunt Annie feeding her chickens]

ever broken her spirit or embittered her heart. Death gave her back her old beauty and—perhaps—her old happiness. At least, peace and rest.

Stella and I talked late that night. When I heard Aunty was dead I wired Stella to have a post mortem. The immediate cause of Aunt Annie's death was an infected liver which in turn was caused by an infected gall-bladder. But she had also Bright's disease[378] and serious heart disease. It is a mystery how she could have been so well all winter, with such conditions. She *was* well and gained twenty-five pounds.

The result of the post mortem was a relief to me. When Aunt Annie asked me last fall if she had better go to Los Angeles as the girls wanted her to, I told her I thought she had better—though I did not urge it. And since her illness I

---

378   Bright's disease is a historical term for a range of kidney diseases (the specific kidney disorder here is unknown).

have been tormented by the thought that if I had advised her against going—and I know in that case she would not have gone—she might not have become ill. But now I know that it would have been the same had she been home, for the gall-bladder condition was of long standing. I am so glad she went. She had one happy carefree winter and she had every care and attention at the last.

The funeral was yesterday. There have been eight funerals in that house, since it was built about fifty years ago—and only one wedding—mine. Aunt Annie never saw one of her daughters married. I was the only bride of that old house.

[Geddie Memorial Church]

Aunt Annie was buried in the cemetery behind the old Geddie Memorial church.[379] And this morning Life motored Stella and me down again to put flowers on the graves. I stood by Frede's and wondered if she and her mother had met once more—or if they both slept dreamlessly on "the shore of Acheron."[380] We cannot *know*. "Oh death, *there* is thy sting! Oh grave, *there* is thy victory."

Stella and Life

There lay Uncle John, George, Frede, Aunt Annie. Stella, I suppose, will be buried on the shore of another ocean. But I hope that I shall lie not very far away from them—just over the harbor in the old burying ground in Cavendish. So, in death as in life Frede and I will be near each other.

Frede's Grave

Oh, Frede! Frede! If you were here tonight. My darling—my beloved friend.

---

379   Located on the north shore overlooking New London Bay, Geddie Memorial Church was built in 1836–37 as a meeting-house style of church. Frede Campbell was buried here in 1919. It remains a local landmark.

380   Acheron is a river in northwest Greece that is mentioned in ancient Greek myths. It is one of the five rivers of the Greek underworld; the newly dead are ferried across the Acheron and the Styx by the ferryman Charon.

The Manse, Leaskdale, Ont.
Tuesday, July 22, 1924

I am thankful to be home again. Though I am conscious of a bitter desolation.

Last week was a sorrowful one. Stella and I went over the old house, where everything was linked with the old life and dreams. We left things pretty much as they were. Everything looked as it always did. It seemed to me so inadequate that everything should look so much the same when Aunt Annie had gone forever. But she had gone—and the old home was *dead*. Its soul went with her.

We tried to solve the "problem of Dan." Stell soon saw for herself, and Life emphatically told her, that Dan would never make a farmer. We decided that she should take him away with her, for a year at least, and see how he gets on at something else. If he likes it and doesn't want to come back some arrangement can be made to tide matters over until Jim can take hold. I feel that I can do no more from a financial point of view for Park Corner. I have given Aunt Annie hundreds of dollars since George died. I am glad I did—glad that she never came to me in vain and that I always gave it to her freely—glad that I often sent her money unasked. But I cannot keep this up. They must learn to rely on themselves at Park Corner. They have a good farm and should be able to get a living off it. I may be able to do something for Maudie. Everybody, including Donald himself, was pleased over the plan and I hope it will come out right. Stell can manage Dan. He likes her and respects her and if anybody can make a man of him she can.

One evening Charlie MacKay motored us up to see Aunt Emily[381] who is not very well. The drive was pleasant and the unbelievable loveliness of the wild green growths in the fir woods along the way gave me some of my old thrills of supreme delight. And it was good to be with old Stell again. She seems better and happier than she has been for years. There were none of the old complaints. I think she is quite happy with her husband now. She has a dear little boy. Ewan Campbell Keller is a most attractive little chap. He isn't a bit like our clan in any way, so must take after the Kellers. Stell makes a very good mother, too.

One evening I went through to Long River with Dan to see Ella's mother. The drive home was beautiful and I felt a sorrowful pleasure in it. It was a clear moonlight night and we came home by that lovely hilly "upper road." The country around us was full of the indefinable charm of a P.E. Island landscape and at one point there is a most wonderful view. Then we came out to

---

381　Emily Macneill Montgomery, daughter of LMM's maternal grandparents, married John Malcolm Montgomery, one of LMM's father's cousins.

the hill where we heard the breakers tumbling on the shore and saw the dark groves around Park Corner. But no Aunt Annie was waiting for me when I came in.

Thursday night was probably the last night that Stella and I will ever spend together at Park Corner. It was a melancholy thought. The wind howled around the eaves in a ghostly fashion and I could not sleep. Friday Stella and I went to tea with Aunt Mary—again likely the last time we three would be together. Then we walked home across the old bridge *for the last* time. These last times are very bitter things when we know they are the last. How often Stella and I had walked together over that

The old bridge

bridge. We are the last of the "race of Joseph" now and our homes are a continent apart. I recalled the last time Frede and I walked there—that dark November night of '18. Little had changed in the scene—and the sea was gleaming in the sunset below the pond—our old sea with its memories, its music, its winds, its magic. I felt very sick at heart.

But I thank God for all those years of Aunt Annie. Nothing can take *them* from me.

Dan drove me to Kensington that evening and I spent the night with Tillie Bentley.[382] Sunday morning I reached Montreal and spent the day with Fred Macneill[383] and his wife who are living there now. Mrs. Fred is by way of being a bit of a freak. She is trying desperately to simulate a youth that has passed away. She has a fretful faded face and perhaps it was the contrast with what she saw in her mirror that kept her exclaiming at intervals all through my visit, "Oh Maud, you look *so happy*." "You *do* look so happy."

Well! I suppose I do look happy—partly because I have always determined that the world should not know of my troubles and trained my face to wear a smile, partly because I have trained my muscles to look pleasant; but after all perhaps it may be—a little or a great deal—because under everything in the core of my heart I have always had and been conscious of a certain subtle happiness the world never gave me and could not take away. With the exception

382   Tillie Macneill Bentley was Amanda Macneill's sister.

383   In a long retrospective entry of January 7, 1910, LMM writes of Fred Macneill, a childhood friend and cousin in Cavendish: "I remember the thrill of pride I felt one day when I caught quite a large trout as large as some caught in the pond. Fred Macneill was with me and I felt that I went up ten percent in his estimation. He respected me much more thereafter. A girl who could catch a trout like that was not to be altogether despised."

of a few tortured hours now and then it has always been with me, sustaining and nourishing. Kingdoms illimitable, starry or stormy, have been mine in that secret realm of imagination and insight. Even when fears and worries have dogged me like wolves I could find escape from them there. And so perhaps in spite of all the tragedies and sorrows of my life, I am, at heart, happy.

Ewan and Chester met me in Toronto in Simpson's rest room. As Chester came towards me he pulled an envelope from his pocket and handed it to me proudly. It contained the announcement that he had passed his entrance. So we were very glad and happy together.

[Chester]

The marks of successful candidates are not given, which is one of the defects of the Ontario system. They should be. A candidate would like to know his weakest points— and also, his relative standing. We have no idea whether he passed well, fairly, or just scrapingly.

Ewan seemed pretty well. I was shocked to hear that Aunt Flora was dead.[384] She had had a paralytic stroke in June but was thought out of danger when I left home. And now she was gone—good, kind, affectionate, loyal Flora.

We got home in the evening and though I had only been away a little over two weeks I had the sensation of having been away a long long time. I found my cats, dog and garden fine and dandy. It is nice to be home again. But somehow I feel rather tired and discouraged.

Wednesday, July 23, 1924

Zephyr had its garden party tonight. I spent the evening washing dishes for the gorging crowds, inwardly resentful of the fact that I must waste my time thus, when I had so much work to do of my own. A church that cannot pay its way without an annual garden party is a farce.

But I had a delightful drive home with my two kiddies.

Ewan says he thinks Zephyr will go Union. The Senate by the way amended the bill, to allow congregations to vote on the question whether they should go in or stay out. Zephyr is an unaccountable place. Three years ago when Ewan and Mr. Roach tried to bring about a co-operation arrangement whereby the two Zephyr churches should join and Leaskdale and Sandford unite—a

---

384   Flora Macdonald Eagles (1862–1924) was the only child and namesake of Ewan's father Alexander and his first wife Flora (1833–1860). She married New Brunswicker Amos Eagles (1853–1941); they lived in Braintree, Massachusetts, a town with a population of about 10,000 located 16 km/10 miles north of Boston. LMM had stayed with them twice in 1919: first, in January, during her lawsuit with the Pages, and a second time that summer during Ewan's mood disorder.

really good arrangement for all concerned—the Zephyr Presbyterians voted it down. Now they have swung around to Union—at least a good many. This will leave Leaskdale in the air, no matter whether it votes in or out—and we will be on the road. Well, let it come. It is all of a piece with life these past six years. And yet I did feel badly when Ewan told me this tonight.

From now on the Union Question will be the burning one everywhere. I dread all the talk of it. The feeling in Ontario is very intense. No matter what happens our Presbyterian church can never be what it was. We have to choose between staying in a broken, crippled church—which would be my choice were I free to choose—or going into a hybrid nameless "United Church."

Sunday, July 26, 1924
Leaskdale, Ont.

Last night we motored down to Uxbridge to meet Bertie.[385] She has changed a good deal and looks older than when last I saw her—a good deal older. Only when she laughs youth pops out through her eyes and flashes over her face. Bertie has a won- derful smile.

Bertie

Sunday, August 17, 1924

It is very quiet here tonight. This seems rather strange after two weeks of excitement. If I were not so tired I think I should like it. Existence has been so hectic since May. But I *am* tired—and, perhaps because of that, rather dis- couraged and hopeless.

On Monday morning, July 28, we left for our motor trip to Kentucky. We ar- rived back Thursday evening, Aug. 7, after a very delightful motor trip of 1817 miles. Yes, it *was* delightful, though there were hours and moments in it when I was ready to vow I would never, no, never go on a long motor trip again. But there were other hours and moments which made up for everything.

Our first day was very pleasant. We went from Leaskdale to Sarnia—a good lap.[386] Roads were excellent, weather perfect, and companionship *mostly* agreeable. I say "mostly," because along in the afternoon we, in the goodness of our hearts, picked up an Irish lady who wanted a chance to a summer resort near Sarnia where she was going to work. She was an odd body and though we laughed heartily over her afterwards we were very thankful when we got rid of

---

385   Beatrice ("Bertie") McIntyre was a friend and cousin, the daughter of Mary Montgomery McIntyre (LMM's father's sister).
386   Sarnia is roughly 350 km/240 miles southwest of Leaskdale, lying at the northern tip of Lake St Clair, and bordering the state of Michigan. From Sarnia, Detroit (the largest city in Michigan) is roughly 100 km/62 miles southwest.

her. A few miles out of Sarnia a heavy thunderstorm came up. We popped into a barn close by the road, with a handy open door and stayed there for half an hour. Then the shower being over we made Sarnia unhindered. And that was the only drop of rain that fell on us or near us in all those eleven days on those 1817 miles. This was such good luck as to be positively uncanny.

The only real drawback in the pleasure of our trip was the hot nights. The days were of course hot, too, but the motion of our car created a breeze that kept us cool and we felt the heat only when we stopped for meals. But at night we felt it severely. That first night in a small-roomed hotel in Sarnia was anything but pleasant. However, we were so tired that we slept and felt quite fresh and adventurous next morning. We crossed into the U.S. and got to Detroit for dinner. We got *into* Detroit easily enough but I thought we would never get out of it. We wandered round for what seemed like hours and really was one before we could find our road out of its swirl of traffic. This delay prevented us from reaching our objective, Fort Wayne, that night. Darkness overtook us at *Hicksville* and at Hicksville[387] we stayed.

I don't know what Hicksville is like—I did not see much of it. It *may* have every virtue. In it people may live, pure of soul, lofty of aspiration. Mute, inglorious Millions may throng its streets; gems of purest ray serene may sparkle in its social galaxy.[388] But for me Hicksville will always connote—*bedbugs*!

No, no, let me be just—exact. Let me not exaggerate. *One* bedbug.

Bertie and I discovered him in our room, peacefully traversing a pillow. Naturally we went mad. We fell upon that bed and tore it to pieces. I flew to Ewan's room and dragged everything off the beds there. But we found no more. Evidently that poor solitary creature had been left there by some traveller and when we appeared came gladly out for company. Bertie, however, would not get into bed but slept on the floor. I was too tired for even my horror of bedbugs to keep me awake. I flung myself on the bed and slept. In the morning we had a worse fright than the bedbug one. When I had dressed and went to get my packet of money out of my chatelaine to slip it into safety between my breastbone and corsets—it was gone. Ensued agonized searching. We rummaged everything. Found it not. What a plight. Stranded in a Hicksville, penniless—for Ewan carried only a little loose change. He is so apt to lose money that I always take charge of the funds on a trip. And here I had lost everything we had. It must have been stolen! Then when I gave up in despair—of course—I found it—just where it ought to be. I had put it in its place as soon as I donned my corsets and there it was all the time!

---

387   Hicksville, Ohio, is some 43 km/27 miles northeast of Fort Wayne, Indiana.

388   A reference to English poet Thomas Gray's (1716–71) "Elegy in a Country Churchyard": "Some mute inglorious Milton here may rest, / Some Cromwell guiltless of his country's blood."

We never told Ewan about it.

We reached Warsaw at noon and had dinner with Angus and Edith[389] at their pretty summer cottage at Winona Lake. I had never been in Warsaw since the fall of 1916. My horror of Edith's fussiness was always so great that I could never bring myself to go back. But our brief visit was very pleasant and Edith gave us a delicious dinner. Though Bertie and I did have a laugh to ourselves over the fact that when we went into the spare room we found the bed carefully covered with newspaper—lest we lay some dusty profaning article on the spread, I suppose.

Angus' cottage

We left at three and got to Indianapolis that night. The scenery down through Indiana was monotonous. Any one place was pretty enough but it was all fatally the same—mile after mile of fertile farms and little villages with hanging baskets. But we made our own fun and enjoyed the road until about five or six. Then invariably

En route

every evening the testing time came. We suddenly became aware that we were tired, hungry and disgruntled. At least I always felt so and I have no doubt Bertie and Ewan felt just the same. I can't be quite sure of course—for none of us ever failed to emerge victoriously from the test. No one ever exploded. So I think we did remarkably well for if things got on their nerves as things got on mine we must have been three combustible creatures under our exterior calmness and courtesy. At such times I wished I had never left home and vowed that I would *never* start on a long motor trip again. What fools people were to go whirling over the continent in this crazy fashion, getting dusty and dirty—oh, how dirty!—and scandalously tired. The ceaseless questions of the boys drove me frantic and a certain little schoolmarmish tendency in Bertie to look upon all the world as a school of small children whom she must admonish, direct and guide became temporarily quite intolerable. At other times I

---

389   Ewan's brother, Angus Cameron McDonald (1865–1944)—the tombstone in the Oakwood Cemetery and obituary confirm the variation in spelling of the last name—was a prominent physician in Warsaw, a town in central Indiana. He established the first hospital there. Winona Lake is just outside Warsaw. He and his wife had no children.

didn't mind it at all, merely noting it with amused tolerance, since everybody has some foibles. But in these dark hours of early evening I used to set my teeth and grind them lest I say something sharp that would leave a blister on our friendship forever. Yes, a long automobile trip in the heat of summer is as good a test as I know. People who can pass it successfully need not be afraid of any other.

Then we would get to our hotel, get bathed and dressed and sit down to a good meal. Presto change. Everything was all right. A motor trip through strange lands was a delightful thing—Bertie was a dear witty companionable creature. The boys were regular little bricks of travellers. And so to bed.

I recall especially a wonderful firefly illumination in the fields as we went along that evening. It began at sunset when the firefly lanterns were a peculiar green colour. Bertie and I watched them in delight. I shall never forget those wonderful Indiana fields of fireflies and the cool, elusive night smells along the road. It was certainly a night that belonged to the fairies, with a clean love-ly wind blowing through it. The fatal hours of four to six had passed. Night had restored our nerves and we felt good and happy and affectionate.

We had a nice hotel in Indianapolis[390] but the heat was so intense that we did not sleep well.

Thursday—what a day that was! All went well to Louisville and for some miles beyond. The prairies were behind us and the Kentucky hills were around us. The scenery was beautiful and the roads fair. *And* they were of our own bright Island red. This amazed me. I had never heard that Kentucky had red roads. But it has! And I shall never forget them!

Beyond Camp Knox the Dixie highway[391] was closed being under con-struction. We had to make two detours—forty-five miles in all. I never was on anything in my life like that detour. The mountain road in Maine, where our Gray-Dort broke down on that trip east, was terrible. But it was as a boule-vard compared to that awful Kentucky detour of hills and sloughs, bumps and rocks. Darkness overtook us on it. It seemed as if it would never end. What if our car broke down—as break down it *must* on that awful road. *No* car could get through it and live! And what would we do? We were twenty miles from a garage—from any kind of help.

Dodgie *did* get through. Not a thing happened to her or us.

Some things are foreordained—and other things are just darn sheer luck.

The next day at the cave we heard lurid tales of what had happened to cars

390　Indianapolis is the capital of Indiana, some 900 km/560 miles southwest of Leaskdale.

391　Probably Fort Knox, an army post just south of Louisville. The Dixie Highway was part of a new automobile route designed to connect the midwest to the southern states, and was constructed between 1915 and 1927.

on that road. One party of tourists were out all night on it and had to be towed back to Louisville the next day!

It was ten o'clock when we got to Cave City and found what we had not expected to find—a good hotel, with delightful darky waiters[392] and southern cookery. I shall remember forever, the corn fritters in syrup and the hot biscuits. Never did anything taste so good. We resolutely barred our minds to the thought of that unspeakable road. We would *not* go back over it. If there were no other road from the Mammoth Cave region we would just stay there forever and live on corn fritters.

The night was so hot we did not sleep well and my head seemed full of wool when I got up next morning. But another delicious Southern breakfast heartened us up and we were as keen as ever when we started for the Cave. We had ten miles of bad rough road before we got there—and were waylaid by the "New Mammoth Cave folks" but escaped out of their clutches. And finally we got to Wonderland.

I find it difficult to write sanely of Mammoth Cave. It cast a spell upon me and I shall be its prisoner forever, no matter where I live. I have been home-sick for it ever since I left it. It cannot be described.

If Mammoth Cave were in the Old World what legends and myths would have pertained to it. Epics would have been written on it—operas composed about it.

The primitive little hotel and office are in a grove of pines. There are four "routes" in the cave. We had only time for two. We were short a day because we had to be back for a wedding. But the two

Mammoth Cave Hotel

we saw were the most important, though I think we missed one or two good things—especially the flower avenue. But some day perhaps I will go back and see that.

The first thing to do was rent and don the "Cave costume." When I put mine on Bertie declared I had it hindbefore. Agreeing, I reversed it. But it was hindbefore-er than ever. So I turned it again. One bloomer leg was so loose it insisted on slipping down to my ankle. I couldn't be continually pulling it up so I went through Mammoth Cave with one leg up and 'tother leg down. I must have looked very weird. But everything there was weird and nobody cared what anybody else had on.

---

392   That is, dark-skinned; this term is now out of use.

There were about forty in our party, with two guides—negroes. Each pair of us was given one of the odd little lanterns used in the cave. Some caves in that region are lighted with electric light. I am glad Mammoth Cave is not. Half its charm, I think, is due to those flickering little lights and the resultant shadows; and nothing in the cave impressed me more than that long line of lanterns strung out along a river bank in that Stygian gloom[393] or winding up the long flights of rock stairs, or flickering through stately palaces of eternal night.

L.M.M.

Bertie

We went down the pine clad hills by flights of stairs to the steep valley where the mouth of the cave is. We went down another long flight of stairs to the grated iron door. Here a tremendous wind met us—a terrific wind, seeming by contrast with the sultry air of the Kentucky afternoon as icy cold as "the wind that blows between the stars"—and yet a clean, lovely wind. It is only just at the entrance you meet it. In winter, I understand, it blows inward. The temperature in the cave itself is the same the year round—54 degrees. It is just comfortable and the air is peculiarly bracing and pure—not in the least damp or mouldy as I think I half expected in a realm 300 feet underground.

I also had a vague idea that Mammoth Cave was simply one enormous cave with various avenues leading out of it. But it is a series of caves, all enormous, connected with each other by all sorts of passages—great shadowy, mysterious avenues—winding stairs

[Entrance to Mammoth Cave]

cut out of solid rock—narrow passages—low passages—tiny slits through which you can hardly squeeze. On that first route we walked five and a half miles and it seemed but a stroll for the love we had for it.

I cannot describe those wonderful miles in detail—I must "hit the high

---

393   A word derived from the River Styx, said to be the river that forms the boundary between Earth and the Underworld.

spots," taking them higgledy-piggledy as they present themselves to my mind. The guides flung blazing balls of cotton waste up on the ledges of rock, illuminating the vast amphitheatres or filling with huge whirls of light and shadow the deep pits over which we crossed. At such times I recalled Milton's description of hell in the first canto of *Paradise Lost* as the only thing approximating to what we saw around us.

A dungeon horrible, on all sides round.
As one great furnace flamed . . .darkness visible,
Regions of sorrow, doleful shades . . .[394]

One drawback was the size of our party. So many were young boys who kept up a racket of yells, howls and hoots. I wanted to go through that cave in silence—nothing else was fitting.

All my life I have heard preachers and teachers holding up the fish in the rivers of Mammoth Cave as horrible examples of what happened to creatures who neglected to use and cultivate their powers—they lost 'em. The fish in Mammoth Cave are blind—eyeless. One variety has a place for eyes but no eyes; another variety, still further sunk in sloth and wickedness have not even a place for eyes. And they are quite white.

The Bridge of Sighs crosses the Bottomless Pit. I grew almost dizzy here and was glad of the stout iron railing. The boys were much delighted with the grotesque figures of birds and animals formed by deposits of black oxide of manganese on certain white limestone walls and also with the odd stalactites some small, some quite tremendous, of which the Bridal Altar and Jenny Lind's armchair were the most striking. And of course the Fat Man's Misery and the Tall Man's Misery and the Grecian Bend were very funny indeed and shrieks of laughter echoed along them, while the shadows held a sort of Witch's Sabbath all around us. But I liked best the long, lofty galleries where time meant nothing—where joy had no meaning and sorrow became only the mere ghost of grief.

I would like to go through Mammoth Cave *alone*—or with only Bertie or Frede. It is of course impossible—but it would be the only way to see the Cave properly. A riotous laughing crowd is out of keeping with it. The moments I enjoyed most in the Cave were those when Bertie and I lingered a minute or two behind the others and stood together in silence looking about us. Then we "sensed" the Cave—its grandeur, its compelling charm—its magic—its devilry. For it isn't altogether holy. No, it is a very Pagan place. The old gods of the underworld rule it.

---

394   From Milton's *Paradise Lost*, Canto 3, lines 61–63.

And it has a River Styx. The original Styx could not possibly be Styxier. I shall never forget that black sullen stream between its steep sheer banks of rock. The Echo River[395] is really much more human. As we went down the steep slope to it the effect of those before us getting into the boat with their lanterns was wonderful. Was old Charon[396] there to ferry us across? We all got into the boats—the guides propelled them by simply touching the roof of solid rock over head. Along we went; the guides made various noises—bells, trumpets, etc. and we sang. The reverberations were—wonderful. That word will be worn out before I finish this account. But I can't help it. It is the only one that fits. Everything in and about that place was wonderful—nothing more or less.

At the end of our route came "The Corkscrew."[397] I don't think I shall try to describe the Corkscrew. Nobody would believe me if I did. Stuart thought it delightful. So might I had I been forty years younger or forty pounds lighter. But as it was—well, if I ever go back to the Cave, I shall not, I think, attempt the Corkscrew. I'll walk back two miles and get out the other way.

We all got up it and through it, however—and there was the iron gateway and beyond the world of light. But first we had to climb that long entrance stairway. Coming so soon after the Corkscrew it almost laid me low. I got to the top of it absolutely breathless. Yet there remained the terrace stairs.

In due time I did get up them. Then we realized how tired we were. We had never thought about it before. Tired! I was so tired that I was afraid to sit down for fear I should never be able to get up again!

And after all I've forgotten to mention the Egyptian Temple[398]—the wonderful*est* place of its kind on that route. But I can only mention it—I can't describe it—those mighty encircling columns—that tremendous dome, all sculptured by the torrents of ages agone. No, there is no use to try to write of it. Milton might have—but I cannot.

We had supper—a delightful meal of chicken and corn fritters and hot biscuits in a primitive dining room. We had chicken for every meal at Mammoth Cave. The hens in that region must go in terror of their lives. But it was delicious.

Our rooms were small and hot. But we slept, oh, yes, we slept. You sleep after you have been through Mammoth Cave. Stuart slept outside under the pines and I envied him but was not small enough to curl up on the seat of the

---

395   Echo River runs through Mammoth Cave; this river is inhabited by blind fish.

396   See note 393, p. 275. Charon is the ferryman who takes the newly dead across the Acheron and the Styx to the Greek underworld.

397   The "Corkscrew" was a notoriously difficult, winding passage through the loose rocks of a great tumbledown taking visitors between different levels.

398   In a large dome-shaped area there are six columns.

car as he did. He was up bright and early and declared he was "hungry for the Cave." We all felt that way. Even Ewan was captivated by Mammoth Cave—and Ewan seldom seems to take much pleasure in the things that please others. I may say in passing that Ewan was perfectly well all through our trip and enjoyed himself.

That morning's route was shorter, being only about three miles. It was the more enjoyable that there were only a few in the party. It was quiet and we got "the feeling" of the Cave, as we had not the previous day. The Star Chamber and Martha Washington's Statue stand out in memory of that route.

The Star Chamber was wonderful. We all sat down on a wooden bench—you can't sit for any length of time on the *rocks* in Mammoth Cave. They are too deadly cold. So we sat on the bench. Away went the guide with his gasoline lantern. He had made us put out all ours. Slowly it grew dark. All at once—we were not sitting in a huge cavern 300 feet underground. Not at all. We were sitting in a deep canyon with walls of rock towering above us—and far beyond the rocks a clear night sky. I never saw so perfect an illusion.

Then the light disappeared altogether. Absolute darkness. I never knew what it meant before. And absolute silence. No night on the surface of the earth is absolutely silent. There is always some little remote detached voice of the night—some sigh of wind—some rustle of leaf or grass. Here there was nothing. Silence reigned unbroken as it had reigned for thousands—perhaps millions of years.

Then suddenly in the "sky" above us shone myriads of stars. This illusion was caused by the crystals shining in the roof as the guide shifted his invisible light. It was very beautiful but not so perfect as the one of the sky had been. I was conscious of the black rock roof—I could not quite lose it.

Then the guide brought back the light slowly from another angle imitating the first faint rays of dawn breaking far down among the rocks. He also imitated other things—capitally. We heard a man chopping wood—dogs barking—cattle lowing—roosters crowing—finally a most realistic cat fight. The cats snarled and swore and spit—and rent the eternal silence by the final wild shriek ere joining battle. By this time it was daylight—and our guide was back smiling to receive our plaudits.

"Martha Washington's statue" is another illusion and an extremely beautiful one. It was discovered by accident and is caused by a light falling through a hole in the rocks on the white limestone wall down at the far end of a dark avenue. There it stood—a lovely, gleaming, white beauty against the background of darkness. It was hard to believe it was only an illusion.

"Lover's Leap" stands out in memory, with the wild flare of the guide's torch behind it and the long slope below.

There was no Corkscrew exit this time, praise be. We came back to the Grand Gallery and so out to the gate where no Cerberus[399] barred our escape. But of the two I'd rather take my chances with Cerberus. Oh, that Corkscrew!

I forgot the Christmas turkey! Some elfin artisan of the cave carved it once and hung it from the roof and forgot it. The gnomes missed their Xmas dinner. But perhaps they got enough to eat in the Bacon Chamber where the hams and shoulders have been drying for a few thousand years. Those stalactites made me feel young—a mere child. They grow an inch in a hundred years!

When I left Mammoth Cave I said to Bertie, "I am coming back here some-time." And as I spoke I was possessed with the feeling that I couldn't bear to come back without Bertie and Ewan and Chester and Stuart. I couldn't go through the Egyptian Temple and over the Bottomless Pit and along the Echo River and down Lover's Lane and through the Gothic Chapel without them. I could not bear those haunted chambers alone. The feeling was so poignant that I shuddered. Mammoth Cave must be terribly full of ghosts. Everyone who goes through it leaves something of himself there—a little bit of his soul—his personality. And he always wants to go back and find it. But does he ever go? Somehow, I fancy very few people revisit Mammoth Cave. It mightn't be safe. Suppose it kept too much of you?

We left the cave after dinner and motored to Hodgenville—almost every place in the south is a "ville." We went by the Jackson highway.[400] It was not as bad as that detour but it was next to it in my Expurgatorious Index of awful roads. Most of it was the "cobblestone" variety. We toiled slowly over it, wondering how the natives put up with such roads at all. Once in a long while we would come suddenly and unexpectedly on a wee bit of new macadam or cement—perhaps a mile or two. We would pounce on it with a simultaneous yell of delight and tear over it like mad.

And yet those roads were unbelievably beautiful. I shall forget their awful-ness before I forget their loveliness. Over hill and through valley and along the sides of mountains where the trees hung over the road. Once a short detour led us right up the bed of a shallow, wide stream. I thought we would sink to our hubs but we splashed serenely on. We spent the night at Hodgenville[401] where we found delicious Southern food. All next morning the roads contin-ued naughty and charming but we reached Lexington at noon and our worst

399   Cerberus is the three-headed dog that guards the gates of the Underworld to prevent the dead from escaping.

400   A relatively new highway at the time, the Jackson Highway connects Chicago and New Orle-ans via Nashville, Tennessee. "Expurgatorious Index" refers to a list of books the Catholic Church forbade its members from reading.

401   Hodgenville is some 69 km/43 miles north of Mammoth Cave. Lexington, in the next sen-tence, is 205 km/128 miles from Mammoth Cave.

troubles were over. From there to Cincinnati[402] the roads were quite good. But night came on long before we reached Cincinnati—a dense, black night. And of course we struck a detour—not such a bad road but long—so long that half the time we were in agony lest we had got on the wrong road altogether. On and on we went through endless twists and loops and woods—all woods. And yet somehow it was very wonderful in its way and weirdly beautiful. Bertie and I began to sing, "Lead Kindly Light,"[403] which seemed particularly appropriate—though I couldn't exactly enter into the spirit of

> I do not ask to see
> The distant scene—one step enough for me.

I would have given a good deal to be able to see "the distant scene" and get some small idea where we were and what was before us.

But when we came to the last verse,

> So long thy power hath blessed me sure it still
> Will lead me on
> O'er moor and fen, o'er crag and torrent till
> The night is gone

Something entered into and possessed our souls and the night became holy and the dark woodland a temple of the Almighty. Moments like that were the high lights of our trip and catch our eyes as we look back.

And after all we were on the right road and at ten o'clock we finally reached Cincinnati and considered ourselves "back north" again. On Monday we motored all day and reached Marion. On Tuesday we motored all day and reached Conneaut. We enjoyed those days but there is nothing especial to say about them.

Wednesday we reached Buffalo and crossed over. "Ah, there's *something* in Canadian air," said Ewan exultantly as we "hit the pike." It was cool, at least, and that was delightful after the sultriness of Ohio and New York. We got to Niagara at sunset—and the gods handed us out another special favor.

A thunderstorm came up—the worst electric storm that has been known at Niagara for thirty-seven years. We saw another indescribable thing—the Horseshoe Falls by lightning.

---

402   Cincinnati, Ohio, 453 km/282 miles south of Detroit, Michigan.

403   A hymn written in 1833 by English cardinal John Henry Newman. The story associated with this hymn, which LMM may have known, related to a group of miners trapped underground following an underground explosion. Thirty-four men and boys in the mine had found a pocket of clean air. They had to remain in almost total darkness for 14 hours before rescue. One miner began humming "Lead Kindly Light," and the rest joined in with the words, "Lead kindly light amidst the encircling gloom, lead thou me on, / The night is dark, and I am far away from home."

The first storm was over and Bertie and I were sitting together on a bench under one of the shelters, looking at the American Fall and telling each other what a pity it was that the Canadian Fall was not similarly lighted. We could see nothing of it, save off to our right the great mist wraith that rose in the darkness.

Then another storm came up—and for half an hour Bertie and I sat there, spellbound, rapt, gazing on such a sight as we had never seen or deemed it possible to see—the great Canadian fall, lying under the ghostly shimmering blue-white gleam of that lightning while athwart the mist tore zigzags of living flame as if some god were amusing himself hurling thunderbolts into the abyss. No, I shall never see the like of that again. But I have seen it once.

Old Nature can turn a trick or two yet. One could not believe unless one had seen it how unspeakably *tawdry* the illuminated American Fall seemed beside that unearthly splendor of the Horseshoe.

The next day was fine, cool and altogether delightful. We motored home by lakes of faint blue loveliness and through contented old harvest meadows, mellowly bright and serene.

On the way we stopped and had some hot dogs.

All along our route we were beset with signs offering hot dogs. None of us had ever eaten hot dogs and we decided that before the trip was over we *must* sample a hot dog. But we kept putting it off from day to day in hopes of cooler weather and now on our last day it was "now or never." Luckily the day was cool and we were quite hungry. So we pulled up by a roadside booth and ordered hot dogs for all. We enjoyed them too.

Does some incredibly ignorant great grandchild demand "What is a hot dog?"

A hot dog is simply a savoury fried sausage, smoking from the pan, imprisoned between the two halves of a fresh roll. I recommend them if you are hungry.

We got home Thursday night.

[travelling group]

And there was a big fat letter from Rollins for me.

I wonder if the time will ever come when it will be possible for me to come home from a trip without the dread of finding a letter about that miserable lawsuit. And they always come just at a moment when I would especially desire not to have such missives.

I did not open it til Saturday afternoon, after Bertie had gone, en route to

England. I would not have opened it then, for Stella and Dan were coming at night and I dreaded being upset for their visit. But I thought it might be something that would require an immediate answer.

It was a bill from Briesen and Schrenck for a thousand dollars for getting that suit dismissed. I really think that is exorbitant for so little work. What on earth would it have been if we had had to fight the suit? There was also another bill for $400 from Rollins but this was reasonable for the work he did.

Well, I can pay it, but it will leave me woefully short of ready cash for the year.

Stella came that evening and stayed till Wednesday when I went to Toronto with them and saw her off sorrowfully. We must live so far apart—and in spite of everything Stell is a jolly soul and of the race of Joseph. Only she and I are left of it.

I came out Wednesday night and drove home under a very strange splendid sunset. Ewan seems very well. The strange summer of mad rushing about is over. It is nice to be quiet and peaceful again; and yet it is lonely. I feel harassed and depressed, when I get tired, over these unending lawsuits and Union problems. But I must get down to work. I have got terribly far behind with everything.

We heard this week that Zephyr is likely to vote into the Union. This will leave Leaskdale in the air, whether it goes in or out, and the congregation will be broken up. Zephyr is a most unreliable quantity. Three or four years ago Mr. Roach—the then Methodist minister at Z.—and Ewan endeavoured to arrange a co-operative scheme whereby the two Zephyrs would go together and Sandford unite with Leaskdale. This would have been a very good arrangement. But the Zephyr Presbyterians would none of it. And now they will go in for Union.

Monday, Aug. 18, 1924

Mr. Gray told Ewan yesterday that the feeling in Leaskdale was strong against Union. Also Will Sellers said there was a great deal of opposition to it in Zephyr. The fact is, each person interprets the situation in the terms of his own prepossession. It is impossible to say which way it will go. I have got to the point where I would not care a pennyworth were it not for the possible effect on Ewan.

Neither Ewan nor I try to influence the people in any way, either for or against, nor ever have. We believe they should be left free to decide for themselves.

But I wish it were all finally settled. I am so tired of confusion and suspense.

Tuesday, Aug. 19, 1924
Leaskdale, Ont.

I began work today on that short story for *The Delineator*. This evening when we were out calling I noticed to my horror that Ewan's head was bothering him again. I gave him a thyroid tablet. Last spring I decided that Ewan has always been a sub-thyroid and that any depressing event or situation, as well as epochal periods in his sex life, interfered with the functioning of the thyroid gland still further and produced his attacks of melancholia. I decided that when his next attack came on I would try the effect of some careful doses of thyroid.

Sunday, Aug. 24, 1924

Ewan has been a little dull this week but his head seems better. I have been very busy with a score of different things. Tonight we thrashed out the Union problem. Ewan said he had made up his mind to remain in the Presbyterian church. I was glad to hear him say this. I have never tried to influence his decision and have told him I would of course follow him whatever course he took. As a minister's wife, there could be nothing else for me to do.

There is some talk of Leaskdale uniting with Mt. Albert if Zephyr leaves it in the lurch. This would make a good strong congregation. The worst drawback would be the distance apart—twelve miles. And in any case, Ewan would probably have to resign. Mt. Albert would want to choose its own minister. So, no matter where I look, I can see no chance of anything save of being torn up by the roots. And that is a process that is always very painful to me. Especially when one hasn't the least idea where one will be transplanted to.

Monday, Sept. 1, 1924
The Manse, Leaskdale

This has been a very busy week filled with many small duties. I got a good idea for the second story of the *Emily* series early in the week and have been working at it. Ewan has been very well lately and does not say his prayers. Is it the effect of the thyroid extract or did it just happen so? He has often these slight attacks which seemed to pass away of themselves.

Stuart is reading *Kilmeny*[404] today and is very much absorbed in it. He runs to me every few minutes to read me some passage that has struck his fancy.

---

404   One of LMM's first novels, *Kilmeny of the Orchard*, was published in 1910.

Have recently been re-reading Arthur Machen's story of *The Bowmen*[405]—the original of the amazing myth of the Angels of Mons—a myth that sprang up full-fledged in a few weeks and is sworn to and believed by many people to this day. Truly, human credulity is a fearful and wonderful thing. If you *want* to believe a thing you can very easily find proof for it that will satisfy you.

Thursday, Sept. 11, 1924

In 1892 or thereabouts, when I was a very young girl, the United States and Canada were convulsed over the famous "Lizzie Borden" murder case in Fall River, Mass.[406] The papers were full of it and people all over North America who had never heard of Lizzie Borden took sides for and against her and thrashed the case out day after day. I remember some of the Cavendish boys driving home from prayer meeting one night singing that horrible quatrain which was broadcast at the time.

"Lizzie Borden took an axe
And gave her mother forty whacks,
And when she saw what she had done
She gave her father forty one."

Lizzie Borden was found not guilty and returned home. From that day to this I have never heard or seen reference to her. A few days ago something, I do not remember what, recalled her to my mind and I thought, "I wonder if she is living still and if she was or was not guilty." The very next day, by one of those curious coincidences that so frequently happen, I read a review of a new book bearing the idyllic title *Studies in Murder*, in which one of the cases described was the Borden Murder. I sent for it and this evening I read it.

There is no doubt in my mind that Lizzie Borden was guilty. Because there was simply no one else who *could* have committed the double murder. And yet it is almost as impossible to believe that she *could* have done it. It is one

405   Welsh fantasy author and mystic Arthur Machen (1863–1947) published a short story, "The Bowmen," on September 29, 1914, in the London *Evening News*. The story was based on one of the early engagements in World War I. On August 22–23, 1914, the British Expeditionary Force had suffered heavy casualties outside of Mons in southwest Belgium, followed by a retreat in the face of a well-armed and organized German division. In Machen's story, phantom bowmen from the Battle of Agincourt (a 1415 English victory against the French in the Hundred Years' War, aided by the use of the English longbow) summoned by a soldier calling on St. George, appeared mysteriously and helped the English soldiers. This was the origin of the name, "The Angel of Mons." The story was (perhaps mistakenly) published not as fiction but as fact. The tale seized the imagination of many, and in spite of Machen's efforts to dispel the myth, continued for some time to be taken as fact.
406   Lizzie Borden (1860–1927) was acquitted for the murder of her father and stepmother in 1892.

of the most remarkable—nay, *the* most remarkable—psychological problems I have ever read of. My own idea is that Lizzie Borden murdered her father and stepmother and that the servant girl, Bridget, was an accessory after the fact, being bribed by Lizzie to help her conceal or destroy all traces of the crime. This would account for the fact that no trace of blood was found on Lizzie Borden's clothing and no instrument discovered that could be shown to have inflicted the wounds. For there was really no scrap of *real* evidence at the trial to connect Lizzie Borden with the murder. One cannot blame the jury for finding her not guilty. Yet guilty she must have been.

She is living today, in a comfortable home, on the money inherited from her murdered father. She must now be about 64 years old. Will she ever confess? Has she ever felt remorse for her crime? I confess I would like to see this woman—talk with her.

Another interesting case in the book, "Mate Bram," had a double interest for me in the fact that the lawyer for the defence was my own dear Mr. Asa P. French.[407] Really, Mr. French is to be congratulated on his clients. He seems to have a liking for defending scoundrels.

Saturday, Sept. 13, 1924
The Manse, Leaskdale

Read a little booklet today, *Daedalus*[408]—a volume of scientific prediction. Some—perhaps all—of the things the writer predicts may come true. But if they do I think I am glad the present scribe will be dead. I don't think I would like to live in the world *Daedalus* foretells.

Saturday, Sept. 20, 1924

I have been feeling uneasy again about Ewan this week. On Tuesday he complained of his head "feeling sore" again and it has bothered him some ever since and he is rather quiet and dull. I had a letter from Stella today. Here is one paragraph:—

"Clara told Lowry when he was there the other day that she was going to divorce Fred and marry Kennedy. Now Kennedy is about 26 or 27, not a day older. This has been going on for two years now." . . .

---

407   Thomas M. Bram was the first mate on a cargo ship named the Herbert E. Fuller bound for Argentina. On the night of 14 July, 1896, the captain, his wife, and second mate were killed by axe. Although evidence pointed to another member of the ship's crew who had been institutionalized five years earlier for a violent psychotic episode, Bram (who was of mixed race) was convicted. For this trial, French was a junior counsel defending Bram. Bram was pardoned in 1919.
408   *Daedalus; or, Science and the Future* (1924), by British scientist J.B.S. Haldane, on the future of science.

This was simply disgusting. I could never have believed Clara could be such a fool, though she never had any judgement at all. She is at the so-called "dangerous age" now, about forty six or seven, and there is no knowing what crazy thing she will do. Clara was kind and good-hearted but she never had, in the homely old phrase, "any gumption." I shall be very sorry if she makes herself miserable by divorcing her husband and marrying a mere boy. However, it is not done yet and Stella never understates things.

Wednesday, Sept. 24, 1924

Last night the first hard frost caught my garden and killed most of the flowers. I feel this with more than usual regret. I may never have another garden here. And my garden has meant so much to me, especially in these last dark hard five years.

I feel very unhappy and worried. Ewan could not sleep last night and has been dull and restless all day. I have begun giving him the thyroid extract again.

Friday, Sept. 26, 1924

Yesterday Ewan felt very miserable all day and admitted that his gloomy dreads had returned. I had to give him chloral last night. Then he slept restlessly while I lay awake and cried. I have *no* courage—I *cannot* face another six weeks like those last spring. My very soul grows cold and sick at the thought. And yet E. has got bad so rapidly that I fear the attack will be a severe one. I had ventured to hope that he would be well all the fall at least as he has been these two last falls, and we would have that much of a respite. But it is of no use to hope *anything* in connection with his horrible and unpredictable malady.

Sunday, October 5, 1924
The Manse, Leaskdale

Soon after my last entry Ewan seemed to recover completely and has been splendid ever since. He never before got over an attack that began so severely so quickly. Can it be the thyroid? If I could believe that the attacks could be controlled and headed off by giving him the thyroid extract, the greater part of the dread that has hung over my life like a black cloud for five years would be removed. Ever since the beginning of the attack I have given him a thyroid pellet twice a week and a blue pill the next night.

I never heard Ewan preach better than he did today. And he seems so jolly and cheerful. But will it last? I have grown afraid to hope.

Friday, October 10, 1924

I went up to North Bay[409] Tuesday and spent Wednesday there. Spoke to the girls in the Convent school in the forenoon. They gave me a bouquet of roses in a handpainted vase. The Reverend Mother and Sister St. John were very sweet and interesting women. In the afternoon I had a motor drive, spoke to the students in the Collegiate and then to the Canadian club. Left North Bay on the night train, expecting to be in Toronto by seven and catch the morning train out home—which I was very anxious to do, as I felt that I had so much work to do at home that I must get back as quickly as possible. So much for my plans.

A short distance from North Bay we came up to a disabled freight train, which had lost a wheel off its locomotive. We were hung up six hours and as a result never reached Toronto until twelve. There was no way of getting anything to eat till we reached Allandale at ten,[410] when we were given a few minutes at a restaurant there. But by this time I was past eating and could not swallow a mouthful. By the time we reached Toronto I had a dreadful headache and the very thought of food nauseated me. I went to the Walker,[411] got a room, took aspirin and went to bed. I fell asleep and slept till six when I woke up, feeling quite all right but inclined to be very disgruntled over missing my train home and losing a day.

Now, mark! Had I caught that train home I would not have had a wonderful pleasure.

After I got some dinner—the first food I had eaten since supper the evening before—I decided that I would go to see George Bernard Shaw's play, *Saint Joan*.[412] I had been wishing to see it but had not supposed it possible. I saw it—and never did I have such an evening of enjoyment. Julia Arthur played Joan. The critics praised her but I cannot echo their praises. Joan was never such a pink-and-white golden haired, brilliant, beautifully clad person. Only when I shut my eyes and listened to her wonderful golden voice did I get the conviction of the Maid. But the rest of the cast—the Archbishop of Rheims, the Bishop of Beauvais, the Earl of Warwick, Parson Stogumber, the Chief Inquisitor and above all the Dauphin were exceedingly good. Oh, if Frede could only have been sitting beside me while I saw that play.

One thing impressed me especially—the beauty of the costumes of that age. Even the suits of armour, which I had always supposed must be awkward heavy things were beautiful. In the epilogue when "a gentleman of 1920" ap-

409   North Bay is a city 270 km/168 miles north of Leaskdale, on the shore of Lake Nipissing.
410   Allandale Station was a large train station located in Barrie, Ontario.
411   The Walker House hotel, built in 1873 and demolished in 1976, was an elegant hotel located in downtown Toronto near the train station.
412   *Saint Joan* (1923), by Irish playwright George Bernard Shaw (1856–1950).

peared, clad in the conventional costume of today, with a high crowned beaver hat, he looked so absurd and eccentric that I joined sincerely in the laughter of the assembled ghosts at his appearance.

Shaw's play is a ripe and wonderful thing; but I don't think his Joan is the real Joan either. That Joan is still an enigma.

Ewan said today he hadn't felt so well for a long time.

Sunday, October 12, 1924
The Manse

I have been re-reading Frede's letters. I have not read them since the winter she died. But I have been so hungry for her lately—especially since seeing *Saint Joan*—that I had to get out the letters. Last night when I went to bed I thought I would read just one. Then I said "Just one more"—and that went on till twelve o'clock. It was always "just one more." I was like a famished creature pleading for just one more bite of food.

In one way Frede was never as good a letter writer as Stella. She had not Stella's knack of filling in all the small details which are so interesting. Frede only "hit the high spots" where she was telling you about anything—her letters were impressionistic to the last degree. But she had, more than anyone I ever knew, the power of infusing her personality into her letters. Such letters have a terrible resurrective power. While I read them Frede sat before me in the flesh. I saw her smile, heard her ready laugh, heard her voice uttering those poignant sentences. It was impossible then to believe her dead—impossible not to feel that she was still somewhere in the world and that I was reading a letter that had just come from her, still warm with the touch of her hand.

There is a great sadness in some of her letters. When you met Frede she was always so bright and funny that you never suspected the undercurrent of unhappiness and sorrow. But it betrayed itself in her letters. Both Frede and I hated to wear our hearts on our sleeves—to take the world into our confidence. It was part of our code that we must always present a front of laughter and satisfaction. Even with each other, as a rule, we kept this up. Nay, with each other it was not pretence—it was reality. For so dear we were to each other, such pleasure and satisfaction we found in each other's company that for the time at least we *were* happy and joyous, knowing neither loneliness nor disappointment nor regret.

Sunday, Oct. 17, 1924

Today we motored to Stouffville, through a brilliant sunlit autumn landscape, to have lunch with Mr. and Mrs. MacCullough. Dr. and Mrs. Freel were there too and we had a very enjoyable time. It is very nice to meet people now and then who can talk of something besides crops and Church Union.

I had a letter from Myrtle Webb[413] when I got home. In it she said "About a month ago John F. Macneill[414] was thrown from a truck wagon and very badly hurt. He is only now getting able to move a little."

The curious thing about this is that about a month ago I had a very vivid dream about Uncle John. I dreamed that he fell off his barn loft and was very badly hurt. At first they thought he was killed; then one of the men who were carrying him out of the barn said to me, "He is not killed, only badly injured." When I woke I told Ewan the dream and said I felt sure I would hear that Uncle John had met with some accident.

And yet there are people who will say there is nothing in dreams. Well, I thought that myself once. I used to laugh at it as mere superstition. But I know better now. I have had too many telepathic and predictive dreams to doubt.

We have had so far a most beautiful October. Very like my first October here, thirteen years ago. Is this to be my last? The thought casts a little shadow of loneliness and dread over everything.

Monday, Oct. 20, 1924

"How easy it is to spoil a day"—the line from an old bit of newspaper verse comes back to me. Today was spoiled for me by the fact that Chester made only 30% in his composition exam.—the lowest but one in the school. It is a bit of irony on Fate's part that the son of L.M. Montgomery should do so poorly in composition. Of course Ewan has no gift or knack of literary composition whatever—I don't think I ever knew a person who had less. But I had hoped that Chester would at least inherit enough of my power of expression to get along respectably in his classes, even if he did not possess it to the full.

Stuart has been reading my old short stories lately—the "pot boilers" I wrote so many years ago. He has just gravely asked if I will "leave them to him in my will."

Tuesday, Oct. 21, 1924
The Manse, Leaskdale, Ont.

Today I finished re-reading Frede's letters. And I feel as if I had lost her over again. Life seems desolate. While reading them the impression of her being still alive was so strong that a dozen times I found myself thinking, *"When I write Frede* I'll tell her this-and-that."

413   Myrtle Macneill, a long-time friend of LMM, had been born out of wedlock to a schoolteacher named Ada Macneill, and had been raised by LMM's great-uncle David Macneill and his sister Margaret.
414   LMM's Uncle John Franklin Macneill (1851–1936). See note 237, page 167.

But I cannot write to her. And no message can come from her to me. At least, none has ever come.

Wednesday, Oct. 22, 1924

We have had an ideal October. So like my first October here thirteen years ago. Tonight was clear, crisp, starlit. The boys had raked up the fallen leaves and Lily was having a bonfire of them outside the gate. But Chester and I prowled up and down the road star-hunting. We re-found Aquarius, Fomalhaut, Aquila, Corona, the Pleiades and the Hyades.[415] I recalled the days of fourteen or fifteen years ago when I prowled over Cavendish hills and fields in spring and summer and autumn twilights star-hunting. Tonight I had one of those hours when the enchantment of the past falls over me once more. I saw the gulf waters silver under the moon. I saw old familiar red-ploughed fields on a frosty autumn night, gardens by the sea that have in them something no inland garden can ever have, beautiful young eyes that once looked up on those scenes with me. All about us, beyond the flickering light of the burning leaves was the strange, deep sadness of a dead landscape on a late fall evening. But its darkness was peopled for me with ghosts of a far land. The lad at my side did not see them. He saw only the stars and the bonfire and the two pussy cats that chased each other in and out of shadows.

But we had a lovely time.

I have been re-reading Mrs. Gaskell's wonderful life of Charlotte Brontë.[416] It is a fascinating book. Perhaps because it is so full of mystery—the mystery of those three strange Brontë women—those "gray sisters" and their weird lives.

[looking north in Leaskdale; repeat of photo on page 260]

When E. and I were in England we went to Haworth[417] and saw the church and the graveyard and the parsonage. Much to my disappointment we were not allowed to go inside the house. But I stood in the graveyard and gazed my fill on it. It had been changed a little—not much—a bay window or two had been added at the corners—in an attempt, I suppose, to make the house

---

415   This is a list of constellations in the night sky; LMM had long been a student of astronomy.

416   Elizabeth Gaskell's (1810–65) biography of English novelist Charlotte Brontë, *The Life of Charlotte Brontë* (1857). Brontë's (1816–55) novels include *Jane Eyre* (1847), of which there are echoes in LMM's own character of Emily.

417   Haworth, England, in West Yorkshire, is the location of what is now the Brontë Parsonage Museum, a writer's house museum that is the former home of Charlotte, Emily, and Anne Brontë.

more habitable. It certainly didn't improve it architecturally. I stood there and thought, "In that house Charlotte Brontë wrote *Jane Eyre*. There Emily Brontë and she died. In that room they walked at night and talked over their hopes and ambitions and plans."

I can well remember the impression *Jane Eyre* made on me when I first read it—an impression that has remained and deepened with every re-perusal.

It is customary to regret Charlotte Brontë's death as premature. I doubt it. I doubt if she would have added to her literary fame had she lived. Resplendent as her genius was it had a narrow range and I think she had reached its limit. She could not have gone on forever writing *Jane Eyres* and *Villettes*[418] and there was nothing in her life and experience to fit her for writing anything else.

Emily Brontë[419] is a mysterious figure. The impression of her left from reading the *Life* is an unpleasant one. She seemed to have no friends. Yet Charlotte loved her devotedly and said she drew her character of "Shirley"[420] from Emily. The picture drawn of her stubborn, gallant, senseless heroic fight against death is a wonderful one. Nothing in literature is more poignant and pathetic than her sudden, useless capitulation at the last moment—"If you call a doctor I will see him now." Too late—too late. But probably no doctor could have saved her. Her genius was really greater than Charlotte's—and even narrower. But the world did not know it when she died. Strange Emily Brontë.

There was a marked masochistic strain in Charlotte Brontë—revealing itself mentally not physically. This accounts for "Rochester." He was exactly the tyrant a woman with such a strain in her would have loved, delighting in the pain he inflicted on her. And this same tendency was the cause of her cruelty to "Lucy Snowe"—who was herself. She persecutes "Lucy" all through *Villette* and drowns her lover rather than let the poor soul have a chance of happiness. I can't forgive Charlotte Brontë for killing off M. Paul Emmanuel. I don't know whether I like "Lucy Snowe" or not—but I am always consumed with pity for and sympathy with her, whereas Charlotte delights in tormenting her—a sort of spiritual, vicarious self-flagellation.

Speaking of masochism:—I think that normally I am entirely free from it. But all through the years of my sex life there was always one day or two every month when I became very nervous and somewhat depressed. During this

---

418   *Villette* is a novel written in 1853 by Charlotte Brontë, in which the character of Lucy Snowe (mentioned below) leaves her native England to travel and live in a fictional French-speaking city, Villette. There, Lucy meets an autocratic, chauvinistic teacher named Paul Emmanuel.

419   Emily Brontë (1818–48) is best known for her novel *Wuthering Heights* (1846).

420   *Shirley* (1849) is a novel set during the industrial depression around 1812, during the Luddite uprisings in the Yorkshire textile industry.

time a mental masochistic tendency made its appearance in me and I heaped all sorts of misfortunes on myself in imagination—*and enjoyed it*. At such times I could not bear to imagine the gay and brilliant adventures I ordinarily revelled in. Pleasure became pain and pain pleasure—as if my nature were turned inside out.

There are many things about Charlotte Brontë that remind me of Frede—although in other respects no women could be more dissimilar. But I always rise from a perusal of the *Life* with a vivid feeling that I have known those three girls of the old grey parsonage on the steep hill very well.

Thursday, Oct. 23, 1924
The Manse, Leaskdale

Today was one of mild excitement in our small berg. The plebiscite election[421] was held. We are a pretty "dry" community—in more senses than one. Out of one hundred and twenty eight votes polled only sixteen were wet. We have been conducting an intensive campaign of exhorting and canvassing for weeks and I am glad it is over. Personally, I think it a pity mankind cannot be the master and not the slave. But since it is so weak we must sheer it up with props like the O.T.A. and similar measures. They are not very effective but still a speed law is better than none. We do not yet know how the province went but the reports coming in tonight are rather depressing. The wets are leading. But of course we expected they would in the cities.

Friday, Oct. 24, 1924

The O.T.A. has carried—though by a very much smaller majority than last time.

We are busy housecleaning. I keep wondering rather sorrowfully if this is the last time I shall clean this old manse. I would be very unhappy if I let myself dwell on this thought. As a rule I determinedly and successfully refrain from thinking along this line at all but every now and then I am stabbed with a pang of realization.

I had a letter from Kate today. She is to be married on November 19 to a Scotchman named Sinclair McKay. Ila wrote me several years ago about their engagement. I don't think he is much of a match from a worldly point of view

---

421   On October 23, 1924, a referendum was held in Ontario on the issue of repealing the Ontario Temperance Act (LMM refers to this as the "O.T.A."). Voters chose between two questions: (1) "Are you in favour of the continuance of the Ontario Temperance Act?" and (2) "Are you in favour of the sale as a beverage of beer and spirituous liquor in sealed packages under government control?" "Dry" communities were in favour of the Act—that is, prohibition—while "wet" communities wanted it repealed. As LMM rightly notes, cities with larger urban populations voted predominantly in favour of question 2. It was a close vote, but a small majority voted in favour of retaining the Act.

but he may be very nice. Kate is 36—just the age I was when I married. I remember how her mother used to gibe at "girls who didn't go off very soon." I cannot feel much interest in the marriage somehow. It is like that of any other stranger. But I hope she will be happy.

Ewan and I motored over to Zephyr tonight. The drive was enjoyable. As we spun along people were burning piles of potato stalks in the fields and the night seemed full of magic and engaging devilry. Bonfires in the darkness are always pagan and belong to the old charming gods.

Something else belongs to them too—the thistles and mulleins along the road in the car-light. In daylight they are thistles and mulleins. In car-light they are troops of Pan.[422] Such eerie, gnomish things and creatures flashing up out of the shadows and sinking back again as we go by. They make our autumn roads a continual procession through elfland.

Sandwiched in between these two drives were two or three calls where Church Union was the most cheerful subject discussed. Oh, for a lodge in some vast wilderness where the name of Union was never heard and the thought of Union never thunk!

Saturday, Oct. 25, 1924

These are the days of raking leaves and burning them at night. The boys rake them up when they come from school and throw them over the fence on the roadside. Then we burn them by starlight. Tonight we had a corn-roast and the boys had some of their boy chums over. We sat on boxes around the fires and ate our roasted corn and candy, told jokes, sang community songs and had a very hilarious time. Overhead the Eagle flew and off in the south Fomalhaut[423] smouldered in the autumn mists. I wonder if around those mighty suns revolve planets whereon are inhabitants who have corn-roasts. But it was a nice bit of fooling and I enjoyed it and was as crazy as the rest of them.

Monday, Oct. 27, 1924

Our beautiful weather continues. This morning Ewan left on a motor trip to Boston on business connected with Christie's affairs. I hope it will do him good. He has not been perfectly well this past week. In his sleep he has moaned a great deal and occasionally I have seen him putting his hand to his head. If he is like this when he comes back I must see what the blue pills and thyroid extract can do again.

---

422   Pan is a character from Greek mythology, the god of wilderness, wild animals, and music. His unseen presence was said to arouse panic in those who traversed his realm.

423   Fomalhaut is one of the brightest stars in the night sky. The name derives from the Arabic *Fum al Hut* ("Mouth of the Fish").

Tonight we had a toast roast at our bonfire and drank tea with it. Hot tea and toast around a bonfire on a frosty starlight night is very delicious. Why do things always taste better out of doors around a camp fire?

Wednesday, Oct. 29, 1924

Today a fat letter came from Mr. Rollins and spoiled my afternoon and our potato roast at night. I went through the motions with the rest but my soul wasn't in them. When everybody went to bed I opened it. But it was only the printed copy of his brief for the Supreme Court which is to be early in November—so he says.

I have been re-reading *The Gayworthys* by Mrs. Whitney.[424] She had a great vogue when I was young but nobody reads her now apparently. Yet *The Gayworthys* is a very charming book. Mrs. Whitney preaches and moralizes too much but between the preaching and moralizing her stories are delightful. At least *The Gayworthys* is. I enjoyed it for three reasons. 1. It brought back the old days when I first read it many years ago; 2. It is clean, wholesome, entertaining; 3. Mrs. Whitney had the gift, for which all other shortcomings are forgiven, of making her characters live. You feel they are real people whom you know. Therefore every trivial fact about them is interesting. Mrs. Whitney is at her best in describing country life. She bores you when she takes to the sea and the town. "Hilbury" seems to me a place I have lived in. "Jane Gair" is a masterpiece. If Anthony Trollope or Jane Austen had created her she would be one of the famous women of literature, instead of being forgotten by all save a few who like myself read and loved the book of old. "Gay" is a dear but I never had any use for "Gershom Vorse." "Gay" was far too good for him. Mrs. Whitney might have let *one* of her pairs of lovers have an early and happy mating. That proportion would not have been untrue to life. There was no real reason why "Gabriel" and "Joanna" mightn't have married years before they did—no reason whatever except that Mrs. Whitney was resolved not to have it so. But with it all I recommend *The Gayworthys* to any of my descendants who can get it and want to know what life was like forty years ago in the farming communities of New England and the Maritimes.

Thursday, Oct. 30, 1924

Today I was amazed and alarmed by a bulky letter from the "L.C. Page Co." I opened it gingerly. It was a screed from George Page—Louis knows better than

---

424　American poet and writer Adeline Dutton Train Whitney (1824–1906) published more than 20 books for girls that expressed a traditional view of women's roles. LMM also mentions English novelists Anthony Trollope (1815–82) and Jane Austen (1775–1817).

to write me!—asking me if I would "co-operate" with them in getting out a little brochure of my life and literary career, to be used for the information for customers seeking it.

I can't understand the psychology of those men. Here they have been hounding me through the U.S. courts for years and at this very moment have a suit against me in New York—a mere "spite" suit—and have tied up my royalties and worried me half to death. And yet they coolly ask me to help them get up something solely for their own benefit and convenience—for I get nothing out of it.

This has worried me all the evening like a pinprick. I don't want to have *any* communication with them. I "co-operated" with them over that book of short stories in 1919 and look what came of it. I think I'll send the whole precious bundle of letters and "brochures" to Mr. McClelland and ask his advice.

Tuesday Nov. 4, 1924

These days have been dull, cold, gray. I have felt curiously dull and depressed. I dread the winter more than I can say. It will be just what all the winters lately have been, I suppose, full of inescapable worries snapping and snarling at my heels. All the fall when Ewan was well I did not worry over anything. But as soon as his trouble returns then all the other worries that lurk in my path become unendurable—especially when I wake up in the night or the hopeless lifeless hour proceeding dawn.

Ewan is *not* well. He returned from Boston Saturday night and has been dull and depressed ever since.

Our evening "roasts" are over I fear. The evenings are becoming too cold for them—and all the leaves are burned.

Corn Roast

Lily and I worked hard all day cleaning up the yard finally for the year, raking, burning and tidying generally. I am overtired tonight, and perhaps that is why I am so discouraged.

Wednesday, Nov. 5, 1924
The Manse, Leaskdale

Ewan is wobbling again in regard to Church Union. I expected that when his melancholia returned. He has never any energy then. Well, I am ceasing to care. What matter what church he is in? If he continues as he has been he will have to give up the ministry. I am so sick of the whole thing—the sordid

struggle between "Unionists" and "Antis"—the ceaseless battle in the papers, the bitterness and hard feeling engendered. It is horrible and if God ever does laugh He must be laughing now. What things are done said in His Name!

But one dear pleasant thing happened today. I thought I had read all Frede's letters. Today in looking over my letter trunk I found another packet and pounced on them as a miser on an unexpected or overlooked nugget of gold. Tonight after everyone went to bed I read them. They opened the locked years for me. After all, life *was* beautiful once. There is at least the *possibility* if I cannot feel the *hope* of it becoming so again.

Saturday, Nov. 8, 1924
The Manse, Leaskdale

Thursday we heard that Herbert Pearson was in Port Perry Hospital for a very serious operation—appendicitis and adhesions. H. is one of our finest young men and ever since we came here was our right hand in Guild work. His sudden illness—he had been apparently in the best of health until a day or so before his attack—and danger was therefore a personal matter to us. We went right down to Port Perry and saw him for a few minutes. The nurse seemed very pessimistic. She said his bowels were paralyzed and gangrenous spots had appeared in them. Dr. Archer, who operated, said he had never had a patient in that condition recover.

It was all very depressing. I made up my mind that I would try to save Herbert by "mental treatment." It could do no harm and might do good. I fell asleep Thursday night "willing" that Herb should recover. Nevertheless, yesterday evening just as we sat down to supper Dr. McClintock phoned up from Uxbridge that Herbert was dying and that Ewan had better go down as soon as possible. I broke down and cried. Coming after a hard day, when Ewan had seemed duller and gloomier than any day yet, it seemed the last straw.

I decided to go to the Port with E. It was a night of terrible wind. I never saw a worse hurricane. The roar of it against the hooded car was so loud that we had to shout to each other to be heard. The dust blew from behind us in clouds that were worse than fog. Crowds of dead leaves flew over the ground before us like fleeing armies of frenzied mice. It was a strange, weird drive over the nineteen miles to the Port.

The nurse met us with a whispered "I suppose you know there is no hope for this young man." We went in. Herb knew us, though drowsy with morphine, and said he felt "much better." The nurse accounted for this by telling me that the morphine had allayed the pain. Ewan read and prayed. Then we sat about and waited. I sat in a corner by myself and concentrated fiercely on "willing" Herb to live. It all depended seemingly on the bowels. If their

paralysis could be removed nature would do the rest. If ever mental treatment could do anything surely it could do it here.

We were there from 8.30 to ten. At 9.30 Dr. Archer came in. He was amazed at the condition he found. Herbert's temperature was normal. He told us that he had hope once more. The nurse turned us all out and gave Herb an enema. Then she came out with a bright face. "I got results," she said triumphantly. "The bowels are beginning to act."

Of course it might all have happened anyhow. We can never *know*. That is the pity of it.

This morning the word was that Herb was showing "decided improvement."

Nevertheless I have felt very depressed all day. It has been cold and dark. Neuralgic toothache has vexed me. Stuart has been ill with a slight attack of cystitis. Ewan has been gloomy. Ah, *that* is what darkens everything.

Sunday, Nov. 9, 1924
The Manse, Leaskdale

I fancy that few people in Leaskdale will ever forget this Thanksgiving Sunday. It has been one of the days people will tell their grandchildren about. It dawned inauspiciously. Just as I came downstairs at 7.30 our phone call rang. I went to it with a premonitory sensation of dread. I knew no one was ringing us up at that early hour for good news.

It was from Laura Colwell. Herbert had had a relapse and was sinking fast!

I went to church bitterly. So much, I said, for "mental treatment." It was all a farce!

The church was full. The devotional exercises were over. Ewan announced his text; but his sermon has not been preached.

Reuben Harrison ran in, white-faced, whispered to his father and Alex Mustard who got up and went out.[425] Already Reuben's entrance is become shrouded in myth and legend. Some people aver he had his hat on. Others aver he had not. Some declare he was "white as chalk." Others are equally certain he was "red as fire." So much for evidence.

A whisper flew over the congregation like a wind—or flame. "Will Cook's house was on fire." In two minutes the church was empty and a stream of cars was pouring in along the side road. Ewan got our car and we started, too, desperately hoping that the fire might be only in a small way and easily conquered.

---

425   Reuben Harrison, 17, was from a local family (LMM mentions his sister Velma twice in this journal as well as Mrs Edith Harrison, "a notorious gossip" [p. 325]). Allan Alexander Mustard, 28, was the son of her friends, James and Jennie Mustard.

Will Cook has been one of our problems for the last two years. Ever since the shock of his father's death he has been "melancholy." Very like Ewan in fact. Wouldn't work—worried over imaginary financial difficulties instead of theological ones. He was worse than E. in some ways—tried to hang himself once. Yet out in company nobody would have supposed there was anything wrong with him. His poor wife has had a dreadful life of it these two years.

About two months ago Will suddenly got well. He began to work and seemed entirely normal. We were all glad and relieved.

And now this! It would, we feared, set him back worse than ever.

As we whirled up the hill by the schoolhouse we saw the house, away up on the hill along the sixth. It was wrapped in flame—flames were pouring from the roof. Nothing could be done.

The contents were saved. We could do no good and E. had to go to Zephyr so we came home and I got E. his dinner. I was alone all the afternoon as Lily was over at Will's. I shut myself in the parlor and "willed" Herb's recovery all the afternoon. At nine o'clock Velma Harrison ran in. Her brother had just come up from Port Perry. Herbert was "much better." The paralysis had passed off. There was "good hopes."

This day of depressions and alarms and exaltations has been rather too much for me. I think I'll go to bed.

Saturday, Nov. 15, 1924

"The melancholy days have come, the saddest of the year."[426] So many days this week have been dark and consequently depressing. E. keeps dull but there does not seem much change either way. I am vaguely anxious all the time.

The practice on Saturday afternoons for the S.S. concert began today. I have to attend in order to keep the pupils from tearing the church down. Most of them are decent kids enough but there are a few wild hyenas from poor and ill-bred families who will not behave except when they are made to and infect the others with their devilment. There are plenty of people in this village who have more time than I have and could very well go there and keep order. But if anything can be shuffled over on the minister's wife let it be shuffled.

Herbert Pearson is recovering and Will Cook continues quite well.

Sunday, Nov. 16, 1924
The Manse, Leaskdale, Ont.

We had Mr. Anderson, a missionary from India, here today preaching. Most of the missionaries we have had here have been delightful and interesting men.

---

426   From American poet William Cullen Bryant's (1794–1878) "The Death of the Flowers."

But Mr. A. certainly is not. He is dour, silent, uncommunicative, with nothing whatever attractive in his personality.

It turned very cold today and a high wind rose. Tonight in Guild it wailed and moaned about the church. It made me think of Park Corner. When I can help it I never think of Park Corner now. To think of it without Aunt Annie hurts me unbearably. But tonight in Guild I couldn't help thinking of it, with anguish. I recalled the many nights Frede and I had lain together in one of those big rooms and heard the wind swoop up the pond from the gulf and wail and sigh around the house and thrash through the great maple grove.

I have never heard a line from Park Corner since I left it. Ella can only write apparently when she wants money. She has not, I hear, been very well but some of them could write if she felt unable to. But what matter? There is no one there now that matters to me or for whom I care vitally. That it should be so at Park Corner!

Sunday, Nov. 23, 1924

I went in to Toronto last Monday morning for a shopping spree. I enjoyed the first three days very much. I like shopping. Those big department stores delight me. I like to buy pretty things and take them away from the glitter and noise to a real home. All this at first. Then I get tired and loathe the stores with their noise and mobs.

I went to Hamilton[427] Thursday night and spoke to the Business Women's Club there. I had a very nice time. The reporters descended on me in swarms and all wanted to know what I thought of the present day girl, smoking for women—and *Flaming Youth*.[428] I said that I thought the present day girl exactly like the girl of yesterday—the only difference being that the girls of today *did* what we of yesterday *wanted* to. I said I thought smoking was harmless but made women look ugly; and that *Flaming Youth* was a book haunted by the imaginations of hell. They reported me with fair accuracy except that one lady wrote me down as saying that smoking did no harm—in moderation.

One undertook to describe me and my dress: "Often when a woman carves for herself a definite and very prominent place in the world of art or literature the effort by which she has attained that position leaves its mark on her. Mrs. Macdonald is an exception. When she graciously permitted the *Spectator* to interview her at the Connaught last night the interviewer found her altogether a delightful person—rather above medium height, with thick hair slightly

427   A large industrial city in Ontario located at the west end of Lake Ontario.
428   American novelist Samuel Hopkins Adams' (1871–1958) *Flaming Youth* (1923; also known as *Yankee Whores*); the book treated aspects of female sexuality and caused much outrage.

graying, which she wore waved and coiled becomingly about her well-shaped head. Her face was unlined and she smiled easily. She wore a frock of delicate lavender flowered silk, caught at one side with a rhinestone buckle. Her hat was of gold cloth with lace falling softly over her face. An exquisite scarf of gold lace was about her shoulders and her brown satin slippers were buckled with rhinestones. The large pearls which she wore in her ears accentuated the clear whiteness of her skin."

Now, over and against the above ought to be set a description of me cleaning out the horse stable last spring or "rastling" with the furnace this fall!!

Friday I lunched with Messrs. McClelland and Stewart and spoke to the girls at McMaster.[429] Yesterday I came home and went to bed with a horrible cold. When I got home I found—of course—a letter from Rollins. But it was only to say he had just argued our case before the Supreme Court that day. As the judges said nothing he couldn't "tell how it hit them." He also enclosed French's brief—which I haven't read. It would do no good to read it and it would only make me blue and miserable because it would seem so unanswerable. And I am blue and miserable enough without that.

Mon., Nov. 24, 1924

I had a white night last night. Couldn't sleep and everything looked black. But I felt better today, being able to work again. We went over to Sunderland this evening and called on the Dudgeons—the new Methodist minister and wife. He is not bad, though I don't fancy a certain Methodistical cant about him. Her I don't like at all and am disappointed for I had hoped I might find an agreeable friend.

The Union battle rages wordily still. I am sick of it. I am training a lot of boys and a lot of girls in two dialogues for the S.S. concert. And I am sick of that. I cough and sniffle constantly—and I'm sick of that. There are some things I am *not* sick of however and one of them is Jane Austen's novels. I've been reading *Emma*. When I think of it and *Flaming Youth* the contrast is as between a mad-house and a decent home.

Wednesday, Nov. 26, 1924

Was busy all day preparing to have the Dyers to supper tonight.[430] He is the new minister at Greenbank and we have hitherto liked them both quite well, though Mrs. D. is shallow and he is a conceited youth who has no aversion

---

429   McMaster University was founded in 1887 in Toronto as a Baptist college; it was at that time located on 273 Bloor Street West (McMaster moved to Hamilton, Ontario, in 1930).

430   At the time of church union, Rev. Carmen Dyer and his family left Mount Albert for Greenbank, a village some 13 km/8 miles southeast of Leaskdale.

to giving advice to older and more experienced men. I like entertaining and I looked forward to a pleasant evening. It was a nightmare. Dyer spoiled supper by arguing furiously with Ewan about Union through the whole meal. Dyer is an apostate. He was a strong Anti while he was in Mt. Albert, an Anti congregation. Now that he is in Greenbank, a Union charge, he has turned his coat and like all renegades is determined that everyone also should follow his example. He did more to confirm Ewan in his Anti-ism than all the Anti arguments have done. Ewan has no liking for being herded along a road, willy nilly, by brash young ministers who "know it all."

The Dyers brought 3 children under six and I thought they'd tear the house down. Mrs. Dyer and I simply could not converse at all and finally I gave up the attempt. Dyer sat calmly there and preached Union without making the slightest attempt to control or check his riotous offspring until they wound up by smashing literally in pieces one of my good Hepplewhite parlor chairs. Then he rebuked them mildly. I was thankful to see the last of them, and I am so exhausted that my thoughts are flying around in my head without order or sequence. I know I shall not sleep.

Thursday, Nov. 27, 1924

I have been giving Ewan thyroid for a month—three tablets a week. He still keeps dull and I cannot see any effect whatever. But it is possible that he might be much worse without them. I am going to stop giving them for a month and note if there is any change in him, either for the worse or better. I dread the winter so. I am so afraid he will have another attack like last year. I *cannot* face it.

Today was so dark I had to light a lamp at eleven in the forenoon to see to write. Such weather is bad for the nerves. And we all have such terrible colds; which do not seem to improve no matter what we do.

But it is a nice thing to feel a dainty little cat jump up on your bed in the dark and snuggle down beside you, purring. That happened last night. And there are some other nice things. I am finding much pleasure writing my new book *The Blue Castle* and getting ready to write Emily III.[431] All these things help. But sometimes it seems to me as if my life now were little else than a search for anodynes. There is always some gnawing mental pain or anxiety to be temporarily obliterated by an opiate.

Saturday, Nov. 28, 1924

This evening after everyone was in bed I read over a packet of Will P.'s let-

---

431   *The Blue Castle* would be published in 1926, and *Emily's Quest* in 1927.

ters[432]—and could not believe they were written thirty years ago by a boy who died twenty seven years ago. There was for me a bitter delight in them. They brought back all those laughing boys and girls of the long ago. They were full of our old jokes and phrases and catchwords—that have no meaning now to anybody in the world but me.

Saturday, Dec. 6, 1924
The Manse, Leaskdale, Ont.

This has been, I think, the "darkest" week I ever put in. I mean it literally not figuratively. Almost every day has been so cloudy that it was absolutely necessary to light the lamp at eleven in the forenoon to see to write—and at four in the afternoon to see to do anything. This of course is not stimulating and disagreeable things are harder to bear in the absence of light.

We are practising for our annual nightmare—the S.S. concert. I go on Saturday afternoons to the general practice at the church to help generally and keep the children in order. Not an easy task. There are three or four boys from poor and ignorant families that are as bad and "nasty" as they can be and incite the others to riot. The girls of the concert committee can't do a thing with them so I have to go to overawe them. Which I do effectually.

Then I am drilling the girls in one dialogue and the boys in another. They meet here alternate evenings to practice and hammer nails in my coffin. The boys are doing fairly well. Perhaps because Chester and Stuart are in it and, knowing by grace something of acting, incite the others to emulation. But the girls seem hopeless. The only two who have any idea of expression and acting have such weak voices. It seems wasted time to work with them. And I have so much to do.

We were over at Richard Curl's one evening this week for our annual supper of venison steaks. We always go when Richard comes home from his hunting "up north." The venison was delicious and the Curls, though ignorant people as you could find, are yet oddly easy to talk to. We like them both, feel a real friendliness in the atmosphere, and always enjoy our evening there.

Ewan had a Session meeting Thursday evening to arrange for the Vote on Union. He says he thinks there is no doubt Leaskdale will go Presbyterian. I wish we could feel as sure of Zephyr. Counting vote by vote we think Union will lose. But I will not hope it. Hope has fooled me too often. The Session in Z. are for Union. But that does not matter especially as they are men who have always been out of sympathy with the congregation on every point and have little or no influence over it. They have blocked Ewan consistently and

---

432   See note 296, p. 203.

persistently ever since he came in any effort to build up the congregation or inspire it. They don't believe in prayer-meetings or special meetings of any kind. They never approved of our Guild. They are bitterly "down" on Christmas trees or Sunday School concerts. This year I offered diplomas in Zephyr S.S. and the result has been an increased attendance but that does not allay their opposition. The Leaskdale Session has always been so different. Ewan has found it a pleasure to work with them.

I have been re-reading *John Ward, Preacher*.[433] It is years since I read it. I enjoyed it. The parts I like best are those dealing with the Ashurst life and people. These are delightful. I never had much sympathy with the tragic story of John and Helen Ward. "John Ward" was a fanatic of a type never found nowadays. But given his belief and premises he was logical and consistent. I dislike but respect him. "Helen" I consider a goose. She had no common sense. If she had she would have known that when she married a Presbyterian preacher she must hold her tongue about her heresies and not air her opinions to the people of his congregations. If she were not prepared to do this she should not have married him. The theological bogies she destroys are powerless nowadays but once they were of power and she should have recognized her position. But then Margaret Deland would have had no story.

Hugh Walpole's *The Old Ladies*[434] is a very gripping book and I enjoyed it. Its truth is painful. There must be thousands of just such unhappy women. I feel honestly ashamed of my growls. But for how long will I be ashamed?

Sunday, Dec. 14, 1924
The Manse, Leaskdale

It is snowing thickly today and is very cold. I fear winter is really settling in. I wish it could have kept away until all the concerts are over.

Today the announcement of the meeting to consider the vote was read in church. It must come in two or three weeks now. As Ewan said the other day, "Isn't it like a nightmare?" It truly has been. The bitterness and controversy— the unbridled letters from both sides filling the daily papers. It is all disgusting and disheartening. The Unionists have been up to some very dirty propaganda in this Presbytery. There is no doubt that the Unionists, whether they realize it or not, are trying to establish a clerical domination over the people of the church, who are simply to do what they are told and make no protest. In all old established churches there is always a tendency to this and in the "United

433   American novelist Margaret Deland (1857–1945) had published *John Ward, Preacher* in 1888; the book treats social and religious problems, taking a particularly critical view of Calvinism.
434   English novelist Hugh Seymour Walpole's (1884–1941) *The Old Ladies* (1924).

Church" the drift is very pronounced and will become intensified. But it is too late in the day of history for that. The human mind will not submit again to such tyranny. Nevertheless the condition of our disrupted church is deplorable.

I wonder if it would be such a terrible thing if "the church" ceased to influence people at all. I do not think so. The Spirit of God no longer works through the church for humanity. It did once but it has worn out its instrument and dropped it. Today it is working through Science. That is the real reason for all the "problems" we hear so much of in regard to "the church." The "leaders" are trying to galvanize into a semblance of life something from which life has departed. Visible decay has not yet set in—"tis Greece though living Greece no more"[435]—and those who love her will not believe she is dead.

Well, the long agony will soon be over though its concluding pangs will be the worst. We will soon know the result here and elsewhere. And when you know a thing you can meet it.

If it were not for Ewan's mental malady, I would not care a fig which way it went as far as I personally am concerned. But I cannot help dreading the effect disruption may have on him. He seems better and more cheerful this week. But when we were out to tea one evening this week and he was reading the Scripture lesson he came to the word "hell" and fumbled over it with almost inaudible voice. No one else noticed it but I knew it betokened the unhealed sore in his mind. Even the word terrifies him and he shrinks back from it like a child shrinking from a bogy in a dark room.

Still, I am thankful he is as well as he is. If I could only hope he would be no worse this winter. I wonder what life would be without fear.

I cannot see that the stopping of thyroid tablets have made any difference one way or another. I have begun making E. take a couple of yeast cakes[436] a week for the sake of the vitamines. I say "make" advisedly for it is a hard task to get him to take anything. I have been taking yeast for three years and the difference they have made in me has been amazing. As the slang phrase of the day goes, "they pep you up." Ewan certainly needs "pep" but it is a question whether vitamines can supply it in his case. However, they may help him a bit.

---

435   From English poet Lord Byron's (1788–1824) *The Giaour*: "'Tis Greece, but living Greece no more! / So coldly sweet, so deadly fair, / We start, for soul is wanting there."

436   In an entry of October 24, 1921, LMM recorded that she was eating yeast cakes: "One of the recent discoveries of science is vitamines. Yeast cakes are full of them." (LMM used the spelling "vitamine" as it had been popularized in the early twentieth century.) Yeast cakes, a source of B vitamins, were small pressed cakes wrapped in foil.

The Manse, Leaskdale, Ont.
Sunday, Dec. 28, 1924

These past two weeks have been one of those nightmares of which the recent years have been so full. Nothing in 1924 was worse except those terrible two weeks with Ewan last March.

Monday, Dec. 15 led off in the dance of devilry. It was a bitter cold day and we went to Uxbridge in the morning. Passing the window of a drug store I saw a *Delineator* hanging up with my name on the cover as a noted contributor. That is the first time it has happened in magazinedom. How it would have delighted me twenty years ago! "The wished-for comes too late."[437]

After dinner the mail came. For me there was a great brown full envelope from Mr. Rollins—exactly the sort of parcel I would expect the decision of the Supreme Court to be enclosed in. I took it for such and decided I must not open it that day. If the news were bad it would upset me mentally and render the school concert that night a misery. So I locked it away in the desk and tried to forget it but could not. It spoiled the afternoon and evening for me. In the evening we went to the school concert. It was not an affair a mature mind could find a great deal of pleasure in but to the children it was a won-derful event and hence we, as parents, had a sort of vicarious enjoyment in it. Chester and Stuart did very well in their respective parts. But I don't think the teacher we have this year is much good. Chester is certainly not learning anything from her as far as I can see. I hear the other parents saying the same.

Tuesday Ewan went to Presbytery. At first I had decided not to open Rollins' letter until Wednesday morning, as I had to go to the Zephyr Sunday School concert at night and take part and did not wish to be unnerved for it. But after dinner I suddenly resolved to open it and learn the worst. It was unnerving me as it was, rendering me unsettled and apprehensive and quite unable to settle down to work. So I got out the packet, reminded myself that even if I had lost the appeal the affair would be ended and that would be a blessing—gathered up my courage—slit it desperately open.

What did I find?

A copy of the *Boston Evening Post* with a marked paragraph regarding a certain book which Mr. Rollins thought I might find interesting!

So much for my twenty-four restless hours and my desperate resolution!

And it will all have to be gone through again when the decision really does arrive. It disheartens me to think of it. I have received so many upsetting let-ters from Mr. Rollins during the last five years that with every fresh one I feel as if I could *not* bear one more.

Zephyr concert was very good and I enjoyed it. The boys did well in their

---

437　A line from Thomas Carlyle's (1795–1881) *The French Revolution: A History* (1837).

readings and both were encored. But it was very late when we got home and I was exceedingly tired. Thankful however that two of the concerts were over.

I might here mention that the crossword puzzle infection which has swept like an epidemic over North America has at last struck Leaskdale manse in its most virulent form. Chester developed the first attack. For several days he worried me to death with appeals for "words" and as I had a thousand things to do I felt I could not spare the time to puzzle over them. Then, all at once, the germ laid *me* low. I became an idiotic as Chester and stole time from eating and sleeping to solve crossword puzzles. It is maddening to find oneself the slave of such a silly craze. But I suppose the fever will run the course and leave me convalescent. I really think it is a capital amusement for children. It must have a tendency to enrich their vocabulary and fasten a great deal of information in their minds which might never otherwise be obtained. But for such as me crossword puzzles are a device of the devil!

Wednesday, Dec. 17, Ewan left for several places on church business and did not return until Friday night. All that day Lily and I agonized over the cutting and making of the costumes for eight boys in a "rooster drill." We have been toiling for three weeks over them. We shouldn't have to do it at all—the two girls who wanted to have the drill should have seen to it. But, like most things, it was left to us and I have had more bother and worry over it than over anything of the kind I ever attempted to do.

Thursday, Dec. 18, was fine and coldish. I had a letter from Ella at last—the first since I was in Park Corner and full of complaints and some innuendoes. Oh, I *would* like to get a real cheerful letter from *somebody*! I am getting that I am afraid to open a letter—*any* letter. I get rather "fed-up" with having everybody's troubles heaped on my own. This is what comes of a certain resolution I made when I was a very young girl. To wit:—that I would never inflict the tale of my woes and worries on other people, who had plenty of their own to bear. I wrote them out in this journal but to the world and to my friends I invariably presented a smiling front. Now, the consequence has been that I am supposed never to *have* any troubles or anxieties—I never get any sympathy—and everybody hastens to dump their own upon me. No, in my present mood of discouragement and protest I aver that it doesn't pay to be invariably cheerful.

Neither do I altogether believe that it is a wholly desirable thing to have a sense of humor. Most women have not and the lack saves them. The few who possess it have no refuge from the merciless truth about themselves. They cannot think themselves perennially misunderstood. They cannot revel in self-pity. They cannot comfortably damn everyone who differs from them. No, we women with a sense of humor are not to be envied it!

I had two dialogue practices Thursday—the boys after school, the girls in the evening. The boys did well but the girls giggled so continually and inces-

santly that I had to grit my teeth to keep from hurling the book at their heads. They made the same mistakes of omission and commission they had made from the beginning; they made eyes at Chester instead of attending to their business. Oh, they were an aggravating set of young minxes!

Up to Thursday I had for six weeks been feeling exactly like a cat one jump ahead of a dog. But until then I had kept the one jump and hoped to be able to. Thursday night the dog caught me.

Lily took to bed with "tonsillitis"!?

She was in bed for three days. I had everything to do and her to wait upon. Ewan being away I had to attend the furnace. By Friday night I was too tired to sleep. Lily wanted the doctor in the afternoon—she had about a dozen different diseases besides "tonsillitis"—a new one every half hour. The doctor came—said there was no tonsillitis about her—merely a sore throat and a slight temperature. She was to stay in bed a few days and she would be all right.

Saturday Dec. 20 was very cold and squally. As I had to attend practices both afternoon and evening I got Elsie to come up for the day. I would have kept her for a few days but at this time of the year she could not stay. I did a days work in the forenoon. When mail came there was a box from Marian Webb full of the little green ground spruce of the Lover's Lane woods. As green and fresh as when they left the old farm. I went to practice feeling a bit encouraged. But half an hour dispelled that. We had a most discouraging afternoon. *Everything* went wrong. It was the last practice but half the children weren't there. The basement was bitterly cold. We sewed and pasted wildly trying to finish the heads and tails of those accursed "roosters." Everybody was discouraged. I came home on the point of tears, got supper, and prepared for the evening practice of the grown-up performers. Stuart was crying with "a pain"—said pain being a little attack of cystitis[438] to which he is rather subject. I put him to bed with a hot water bottle. Ewan's head was bothering him too. It is about three weeks since I gave up giving him thyroid. The effect of the last tablet will therefore be ended now. So it would seem as if they had done some good. Or it may be only coincidence. But I will begin giving them again and noting results.

The evening practice went off better than the afternoon but I was miserably tired. I came home alone under a sky blazing with stars. I never saw them of such brilliancy. If it had been warmer I would have lingered to study them but it was too cold. I came home feeling chilly and with the beginning of a sore throat myself. Stuart was asleep but Lily terrified me by a yarn that he had a "lump" or swelling on his abdomen, just on the spot, according to her description, where the swelling in appendicitis comes. The child was asleep

---

438   Inflammation of the urinary tract and/or bladder, usually caused by a bacterial infection.

and my hands were cold so I decided not to disturb him by any examination that night. But between this new worry, and my over fatigue I could not sleep. It was a long, cold, dark, dreary night when every worry of my life snapped and snarled at me. It was vain to tell myself that Lily is always a calamity-howler, making mountains out of molehills, I knew that but I couldn't suppose she had entirely imagined that "swelling." As soon as Stuart woke in the morning I anxiously examined him. There was no trace or sign of any swelling and the pain was gone. Really, Lily is a most consummate fool.

Sunday, Dec. 21st. was exceedingly cold. I could not go out to church and was not sorry as Ewan was going to speak on Church Union, giving his reasons why he meant to remain in the Presbyterian church, and somehow I didn't want to be there—though I can't just analyze my reluctance. I suppose it is just the shrinking from having a sore spot touched that makes me dislike all reference to it.

Sunday night my throat was worse and I had a bad night with cystitis. It is years since I have had an attack. It came on suddenly as it always does and all the week I have been most miserable with it. It seems a year since last Sunday. I have never had any ailment which makes me more abjectly miserable for the time being. Ewan had to go away again Monday morning on church business and did not get back until Tuesday night. Lily got up but only wandered around complaining of everything. The day was gloomy and cold, and the night most wretched. I could not sleep and my ailment got on my nerves to an unbearable extent. All Tuesday forenoon I was most miserable and when at ten a 'phone came saying that a couple of men from Toronto were on their way to see me re the reorganization of an insurance company in which I am shareholder, I felt that I could *not* see them. Yet it was necessary that I should. Fortunately I felt much better in the afternoon and got my conference over without too much misery. When they had gone Ewan came home and opened a letter that had come in the mail for him. It proved to be from a certain George Furness in Toronto inviting himself out for Xmas. Neither of us knew him. He is the brother of the husband of Ewan's niece on the Island. Ordinarily it would have been all right. I would have been glad to have him come. But now it seemed the last straw. We had been planning since we were both so miserable that we would have a Xmas tree for the boys and postpone our dinner to the last of the week. But now we would have to have it.

By this time I was quite miserable again but had to go to the concert. It was necessary for me to go but it was not necessary for Lily who would have been much wiser to stay at home. Go she must, however. The evening seemed like a long nightmare to me. The concert was good after all in spite of all our trials. The boys did splendidly in their dialogue; and so did the girls. They no longer giggled and ogled but applied themselves to the business in hand and seemed to remember all at once all my hints and instructions. The famous rooster drill

was a huge success; but I asked myself if it had been worth while to have all the trouble and worry I had had about it to give that audience five minutes of laughter; and I emphatically answered "no."

Ewan had driven us up and back in the car; but nevertheless I must have caught cold for I had a dreadful night. My throat got so bad it was agony to speak or swallow and at dawn I had the worst attack of cystitis I ever had. Nevertheless I had to get down to work and get the house put in order for the coming guest. After dinner I had to rest awhile, being utterly exhausted. Then I got up, resolved to make a batch of doughnuts, as we had no cake in the house. I planned to begin at two and get through at five but a caller came and stayed an hour. It was almost dark when she left for the day was very cloudy. But I set my teeth and went to work at the doughnuts. Finished them at six. Then supper had to be got ready. I was holding myself to the task by sheer will power but the special demon who had been set to plague me that day had another trick up his sleeve. He must have been a young devil, on probation and very anxious to win promotion. It was not enough that I should have a throat that made every word a torture and that nerve-wracking cystitis besides. I developed a strange sore foot. The soft muscle at the side of the Achilles tendon began to pain me. At first it felt exactly like a bad bruise though I had not hurt it in any way. It got worse rapidly. By the time I had supper ready I could not bear my shoe on. A phone came saying that the train was late and they would not be home till ten. I took off my shoes, lay down and fell asleep at once. When I was wakened by the car coming in I sprang up but fell back with a cry of pain. I could hardly endure to move my foot. Again I set my teeth, welcomed our guest, sat at the supper table, helped wash and put away dishes, then decorated the Xmas tree and put out the presents—all the time hardly able to move. It was now twelve. I got a pail of hot water, soaked my foot for an hour and then went to bed. I do not recall a harder and more exhausting day in my life. I had had no sleep for three nights and I was "all in."

For a mercy I slept well but at seven the cystitis returned and from then till ten I was in misery. My throat was still bad but the pain was gone from my foot which was only very stiff. It was the most peculiar seizure I ever had and I cannot understand it.

Christmas day was bitterly cold. We got the dinner. Then had just time to get dishes washed up before we had to get supper. At nine o'clock I sat down for the first time that day, except at meals. It was a terribly cold night with a high wind—the coldest Christmas we have had for years. I have never put in a more miserable one physically.

But we did not get any Xmas card from Friend Grieg. I had been expecting it would come, to add to the enjoyment of the day. But it came not. The little devil had done his best but he forgot that.

Friday morning I had another bad attack but felt pretty well until evening. My throat began to get better and I got the house straightened up. Yesterday I was still better save for one bad attack. Mr. Furness left yesterday afternoon. I think he had a good time. He is one of the nicest little fellows I have ever met—easy to entertain—good company. If I had been well I would have enjoyed his visit tremendously. But as things were never did I speed a parting guest so gladly.

I have felt better today but far from well.

Ewan heard today in Zephyr that the Will Lockies are going to vote Anti. They have always been Unionists. I wonder if it was Ewan's exposition of his reasons for remaining Presbyterian that turned them. But they are unstable as water. Probably Mr. Armstrong will turn them round again. What a nightmare the whole thing is. But then has my life been anything but a succession of nightmares?

Monday, Dec. 29 1924
The Manse, Leaskdale

A dull gray day, bitter cold. Had a good night but was miserable all the forenoon. Tried to write a little but made a poor fist of it. Lily complains ceaselessly of a hundred aches and pains but went to the rink tonight and skated till eleven. She gets on my nerves dreadfully just now. When she is not growling she seems to be in a sort of cold tantrum, working fiercely and snapping the head off anyone who dares speak to her. Ewan, too, is certainly not so well. He is dull and gets off by himself to brood. I have begun the thyroid tablets again. If they check the attack I shall take courage. If they do not—*can* I face another time like last spring? It will take a week or ten days before they will attain a maximum effect.

Thursday, January 1, 1925
The Manse, Leaskdale, Ont.

Nineteen-twenty-five! I shrink back from it. Another year of misery? I have lost the power to hope for anything else. I actually cringe when anyone wished me "a happy New Year." It seems such an impossible thing.

Perhaps it is the dark hour before the dawn. One *must* cling to a little hope, else it would not be possible to live.

Lily went home last night for New Years and the house has really seemed exorcised of an evil presence today. She has been unbearable lately. Of course, her nerves are bad; but she is so foolish. Out every evening till eleven o'clock, skating or visiting. No wonder she is in bad shape. I don't know what to make of her lately. She will not take any advice or suggestion—complains ceaseless-ly—yet if you try to pin her down to a definite statement of what is wrong she cannot tell you.

I have felt better physically today and hope the cystitis is wearing off. But I feel "no good." Last week took more out of me than ordinary years.

But the New Year did give me *one* gift. Another little packet of Frede's let-ters. They were like a message from beyond the grave. In one of them, written in the spring of 1918, she was planning our summer on the Island. "We will have one more ramble together about all our old Park Corner haunts," she wrote. "Somehow I have a feeling that it will be the last for many years."

Your premonition was true, Frede. It *was* our last—not only for many years but for all time. And yet Paul asked of the grave where was its victory![439] He never loved and lost!

If Frede were only in the world—to write to—to get a word of sympathy and appreciation from—what a difference it would make to me! Oh God, it will soon be six years since she died—since that awful morning in Macdonald college when I stood beside her bed and watched her die!

And this is the first Christmas that there was no Aunt Annie to send a gift and a letter to. No Aunt Annie! No one at Park Corner of the old circle. I will not think of it! Life has enough pangs at present without that. I must bear and endure a little longer for my children's sake.

My dear children! That comical little rascal Stuart. Tonight when I let him and Chester off with a mild rebuke for some bit of mischief, Stuart exclaimed,

---

439   From 1 Corinthians 15:55. See note 360, p. 251.

"You are the *dearest* mother. Any other mother would have sentenced her sons *to immediate death.*"

I had to laugh over it. And the laugh curdled in my throat and turned to a gasp as I remembered how Frede would have laughed over it.

Frede!!

Saturday, Jan. 3, 1925

Yesterday at supper Lily who had been in a vile temper all day took something very like a fit of hysterics. I told her I thought she had better go home for a month and have a good rest. I also told her to go to her room and lie down and I would wash the supper dishes. She flung off to her room but she neither rested nor lay down. She strode about her room for two mortal hours, doing I know not what, and then went out somewhere till eleven o'clock. This afternoon Ewan took her to see the doctor at Sunderland, who couldn't find anything wrong with her. Told her her nerves were bad and to take a rest. She came home and though she could not wash the supper dishes she could go to the rink and skate till eleven o'clock. She told me she only looked on and did not skate but the boys told me she skated all the evening. Chester also overheard Gerald Collins asking her why she hadn't been down to see the hockey match that afternoon and madam responded, "I was in bed while the hockey match was going on," whereas she had been to Sunderland. The fact is one cannot believe a word she says. She has got so on my nerves lately with her tantrums and her dozen new symptoms every day that I shall be heartily glad to get her out of the house. The real secret of her "nerves" is that she has no "beau" and cannot get one apparently. I would really feel sorry for her if she would behave herself but it is difficult to feel much sympathy for such a creature.

I am glad to say I am feeling better myself but still not up to par. I get so blue and discouraged. And as yet the news on the Church Union voting is depressing.

Sunday, Jan. 4, 1925

I had a bitter spell of crying after I went to bed last night and didn't sleep well. This morning I went to Sunday School and church. The announcement of the voting was made. When Ewan came home from Zephyr he said Mr. Armstrong was strongly in favor of Union and is trying to influence all the people to vote that way. This is unfair when Ewan has never made any attempt to influence anybody one way or another. He announced his own determination to remain Presbyterian and told them all to vote as their conscience dictated. But have the majority of the Zephyr people any consciences? I have never seen any indication of it. Mr. Armstrong's conscience is his own stubborn conviction

that he knows more than anyone else in the world and must be right on every question. He has from the first blocked and hindered Ewan's efforts in every way, and frowned upon every attempt to improve matters. He was superintendent of the S.S. until his illness last year and almost ruined it. The children would not go to it. When he became ill Ewan took it over, as no one else could be got to do it, and as a result by introducing some up-to-date methods, it has come right up and is a good Sunday School. Mr. Armstrong resents this. He is the type of man who can't forgive one who succeeds where he failed. His wish for Union is a purely economic one. He thinks it would be easier to raise the minister's salary if they went in with the Methodists. Though a few years ago this same Mr. A. declared that if Union went through he would never go to the Zephyr Methodist church but would drive to Mt. Albert.

Lily went home today and I drew a breath of relief. It is so nice to be alone for a little after such a six weeks as I have had.

The Manse, Leaskdale, Ont.
Monday, Jan. 5, 1925

This morning I rose at six, got breakfast, put out the washing by eleven o'clock, got dinner and went to Uxbridge. Came home and did odd jobs till eleven o'clock. The vote on Union was a shade more encouraging today. The results of the little mission fields out west continue to swell the Union list but the results of the self-sustaining Ontario churches are beginning to come in and I fancy they will tell a different story.

This evening I was glancing over some of my old schoolbooks and smiling—a little bitterly I fear—over some of the things scribbled on their fly leaves. I was a shark for writing on my fly leaves in those days. A blank sheet of paper was always a temptation I could not resist. In particular I was addicted to mottoes. There were two I had adopted as my own and I wrote them on the fly leaf of every schoolbook I owned. Well, they were very good mottoes and I believe I can say I have lived up to them. One was,

In everything you do aim to excel
For what is worth doing is worth doing *well*.

The other was,

Never say that fate's against you,
That you cannot conquer luck,
For there's no such thing as either,
All depends on work and pluck.

But I no longer believe whole-heartedly in the latter. I am convinced that there *is* such a thing as "fate" and that sometimes it brings all "work and pluck" to naught.

Nevertheless, it would not do to sit down and fold one's hands!

Those old fly leaves bore, too, many scraps of rhyme and verse which came to me at some inspired moment and were jotted down "lest I forget." Seldom did I make any further use of them. They were of all varieties. Some very moral and didactic. For example,

Perchance some word of thine may echo back
In far eternity upon thine ears.
Perchance some thought thou deemest lost may live
To shape the destiny of unborn years.

or

Ambition, sin by which the angels fell,
Ambition, power by which the race is raised
Ambition, voice that in our lightest hours
Shames us from trifles, calls us to the heights.

But I never wrote any more of the poem on ambition!

When tossing nightly on a restless couch,
Staring through darkness with far-seeing eyes,
Hearing the waves of Time that break upon
The shores of vast Eternity

is a pretentious fragment of some forgotten design. But I know more now than I did at fifteen about "tossing on a restless couch"!

And Spain in triumph welcome back
The son she once refused to own . . .
And future ages read his story
Who trod the dizziest heights of glory

I wonder what I meant to do with those. But there was one verse—I remember the moment I composed it. Sitting out on the "side bench" in a grammar class, thinking out the lines between bouts of analyzing. I never finished it:—

A wild red rose in a grass-grown lane
A shy red rose, a sweet red rose,
Nodding to every wild wind that blows
As its shadow comes and its shadow goes,
And it blossoms there in the grassy lane
Kissed by sunshine and wet with rain.

Not so bad for fifteen. The rose that inspired the little verse has faded long ago—long, long ago. But can beauty ever really die? Is not that rose's beauty somewhere?

Tuesday, Jan. 6, 1925
The Manse, Leaskdale

A very busy day. I fell upon my house furiously and got it all put in proper order for the first time since early December. An anxious day too for Ewan went to the meeting in Zephyr church called to arrange for the vote. I fairly trembled when I heard him return. He had a chancy time enough. Mr. Armstrong made all the trouble he could and would have prevented the vote after all if he could have but Ewan got his way in the end. The result however will be very doubtful there. There are some we *know* will vote Union. Some we *know* will vote Presbyterian. But there are half a dozen who are uncertain. And they may—nay, will turn the scale. Ewan and I spend half our time figuring out the Zephyr vote. We *think* we are sure of a majority but Zephyr is and always has been a broken reed. One could not imagine two congregations so different in all essential respects as Leaskdale and Zephyr.

Thursday, Jan. 8, 1925

Exceedingly busy, getting ready for Guild executive which meets here tomorrow night. I swept and baked cake, cookies and date loaf. And worried over the Union vote at Zephyr and at large. I dreaded the coming of the mail in the same miserable suspense I used to await the war news. But the news was reassuring. The pendulum is swinging our way. And the first congregation in our Presbytery to vote has voted out. Kensington on the Island has voted in. I fear the Island will go mainly Union. They are so far away from the centre of things and do not understand the tremendous issues at stake. But the vote was very close at Kensington and the "antis" are going to organize a Presbyterian church of their own. This is one of the dreadful things about the disruption that has been forced on our church by impatient "leaders" "drunk with sight of power."[440] Congregations torn up or rendered bitter and sullen, old friendships broken, old ties sundered. I could "weep my spirit from my eyes" as I think of it.[441]

Friday, Jan. 9, 1925

Last night Ewan came home from Zephyr with the wretched and amazing news that Mr. and Mrs. Will Sellars are going to vote for Union. I could hardly believe it. They have always been so bitter against it. I have heard them say repeatedly that if Zephyr went for Union they would leave and come to Leaskdale. And now they have turned around. It is depressing. They have always

---

440   From Rudyard Kipling's (1865–1936) poem "Recessional" (1897).
441   From *Julius Caesar*, 4.3.102–103.

been our best family, both to give and to work—one of the few reasonable families in that odd, Lockie-cursed church.

And John Lockie and his wife are also going Union, it is said. Their argument is the economic one—"it will cost less." And after all Mrs. John used to say about the Zephyr Methodists.

Mrs. Sellar's father George Allan Smith of Uxbridge, has recently turned over for Union and I suppose has swung his family over.

I was up at daylight this morning to make pies, cake and date loaf for to-night. The miserable suspense at mail time today was almost as bad as in war time. But the news was good—the churches are voting out everywhere. But the sad thing is that many congregations are splitting up and being spoiled. The minority won't give in and stay by their church. This is a pity. It would be much better for them to stick together whatever way it went. But some of the tactics and propaganda employed by the Unionists are disgusting. It must be a poor cause that has to be bolstered up by props such as that.

I had the Guild executive here tonight and we had a very nice meeting.

Monday, Jan. 12, 1925

Elsie Bushby[442] came last night and will stay with me till Lily can come back. This morning I took up work on my *Blue Castle*. The air is full of rumors about Union. I am so sick of it all. Ewan seems much better since I began giving him thyroid again.

Tuesday, Jan. 13, 1925

Today the balloting closed in Leaskdale which voted to remain Presbyterian by 63 to 11. I don't think any of the eleven will leave the church. They are not cranks and there has been no bitterness. But Zephyr is a different matter.

Long River and Clifton on the Island have voted Presbyterian, also the Kirk in Charlottetown.[443] The Alberton and Kensington Antis are organizing a Presbyterian church of their own. But it is wretched to see such congregations split up. And the bitterness everywhere. It is so terrible that it is getting on my nerves and I cannot shake it off.

I had a letter from Hattie Gordon Smith[444] today, telling me that she had had to divorce her husband, who had ruined her life by his dissipated habits. I

---

442   Elsie Bushby, from a local farming family, would be the fourth maid at the Leaskdale manse.

443   Long River and Clifton (now known as New London), two communities near Cavendish. The Kirk of St James Presbyterian Church on Fitzroy Street in Charlottetown was built in 1878. Alberton and Kensington, in the next sentence, are two other PEI communities.

444   Harriet ("Hattie") Gordon Smith had been a favourite schoolteacher of LMM in Cavendish in 1889; she was an inspiration for the character "Miss Stacy" in *Anne of Green Gables*.

had been thinking for several years that there was something agley[445] there for she has never mentioned him in her letters and recently she has been living with a brother in B.C. "Dear, oh dear," is there no happiness anywhere? Yes, of course there is. Only it doesn't seem to come to me or my friends. Hattie's family—two daughters and a son—are grown-up and married, so she is practically alone in the world.

Monday, Jan. 19, 1925

We have been having a very cold snap—and Leaskdale manse is not a comfortable place in a cold snap. But it relented a little today. Several of our Presbytery congregations voted out—Kirkfield—Glenarm—Fenelon Falls.[446]

Dr. Anderson is dead.[447] He was an old man—in the eighties. He seemed an old man thirty years ago at P.W.C. owing to his snow-white hair and beard. The news of his death saddened me and lent an added note of depression to a day that needed no more.

Tuesday, Jan. 20, 1925

Zephyr voted out—23 to 18. Ewan is very jubilant tonight but I cannot feel so—though I am glad we have won out, technically at least. He thinks the Pros will accept the situation. I cannot think so. Armstrong will never forgive the fact that Ewan prevented him from getting his own way and there are at least two other families who will follow him. If the church could afford to lose them it would be much better off without them for they have always been wet blankets in every respect. But it cannot—and what will be the result! The church will dissolve—Leaskdale will be left in air—we will have to move. Of course it will not be hard to get a congregation in the Presbyterian church. But I hate the thought of leaving Leaskdale. It is home to me now and though I know there are many nicer places to live, yet *we* cannot be sure of getting one of them.

Stuart, when told that Zephyr had voted out said, "Hurrah! Now we won't have to leave." Stuart is like me. He gets deeply attached to his home spot and dreads the thought of being uprooted. I am sorry for it. I wish he had taken after his father in this respect, instead of me. He would likely be so much happier in his life—unless he can select his home and stay there—what I can never do.

---

445 "Agley" is a Scots word meaning awry or askew; here it recalls Scottish poet Robert Burns' poem, "To A Mouse, On Turning up in Her Nest with the Plough, November, 1785": "The best laid schemes o' Mice an' Men / Gang aft agley, / An' lea'e us nought but grief an' pain, / For promis'd joy!"

446 Congregations within Lindsay Presbytery.

447 Alexander Anderson (1836–1925) was Principal of Prince of Wales College from 1868 until 1901, when he became Superintendent of Education for Prince Edward Island.

The Guild fry want to get up a play and have asked me to be "coach" again. I must help them—but I dread it, when my mind is so constantly worried and my spirits depressed.

Malpeque[448] has voted "in" but there is a big minority and it is said the church is hopelessly split. What a shame! That old historic congregation. One of the finest—no; *the* finest rural church on the Island. Torn into shreds!

Saturday, Jan. 24, 1925

We all suffered a terrible disappointment this morning—a disappointment in which we had goodly fellowship. For the first time in a very long period Ontario was to have a total eclipse of the sun.[449] It was total in Toronto but not quite so here. It seemed extremely aggravating to be so near a total eclipse and miss it. Had it been summer we could easily have motored in. But the roads and weather are so terrible that I reluctantly gave up the idea of going in by train the night before—as was necessary, as it began at eight.

Alas! Thick clouds covered the sky the whole forenoon. At ten it was so dark in the house we lighted a lamp. Outside it was twilight. That was all. We sorrowfully put away our equipment of smoked glass[450] for the next eclipse— which is due in about a hundred and thirty-five years or thereabouts!

Tonight six years ago I watched by Frede's deathbed and saw the being I loved most among women slowly gasping her life away before me. That night and the awful dawn that followed it shattered my heart. Before that the world was good to me, no matter what happened, just because she was in it—that girl who loved wonder and beauty and laughter.

Sunday, January 25, 1925

It is six years since Frede died.

All the "pros" were out in Zephyr church today. This is encouraging. But I shall not breathe easy until the annual meeting is over. Ewan seemed very dull again today and Stuart was in bed all day with a recurrence of that pain. I cannot help feeling afraid of appendicitis, though I think it is really too high up in his little anatomy for that. And he never has any fever with it.

---

448   Another community on the north shore of Prince Edward Island that LMM knew well.

449   A total eclipse of the sun took place on January 24, 1925. "Totality"—in which the moon passes between the earth and the sun, completely obscuring the sun from a viewer on earth—occurred in regions of Canada and the United States.

450   Smoked glass was a home-made approach to safe viewing of eclipses that involved allowing a candle to lay a deposit of soot on a piece of clear glass.

Tuesday, Jan. 27, 1925
The Manse, Leaskdale, Ont.

We have had very cold rough weather. Today it was 35 below zero[451] in the forenoon. Ewan has been dull and complaining of headache again. I feel as if I were in a cage with people poking sticks at me between the bars.

A letter from Lily today asking if I can get along until Feb. 15th as she is "feeling better but not well." I hear she is running all over the country to parties etc. so I doubt much if she is very ill. I am beginning to wonder just what madam means.

Sunday, Feb. 1, 1925

These past days have been hard. Ewan is quite miserable. I feel downhearted and discouraged over his condition. Yesterday I had to give him bromides. His symptoms point to another attack like last winter's.

I have been reading Dr. McMechan's *Headwaters of Canadian Literature*.[452] One thing in it amused me very much. He said my writings plainly showed the influence of my having "married a minister." I raised a laugh over this. My "marrying a minister" had absolutely no influence in any way upon my writings. Critics generally imagine a good deal of nonsense.

Monday, Feb. 2, 1925

Ewan went to the annual meeting at Zephyr today and came home with bad news. Armstrong and Will Lockie are going to leave and likely John Lockie, Will Rynard and Will Sellars also. This will ruin the church—which is exactly what Armstrong wants. There will be only thirty families left, and they will be too discouraged to try to keep it up. These five were the best givers—and they state frankly as a reason that they are going into the Union church so they will not have to give so much. A church founded on such a motive will hardly be a force for righteousness.

I was sadly upset. The practice for the play was here tonight and I felt as if I was in a nightmare. Ewan is miserable, too, and had one of his nervous chills tonight.

451　-35°Fahrenheit is equal to -37° Celsius; readings on the two scales coincide at -40°.

452　Archibald MacKellar MacMechan's (1862–1933) *Headwaters of Canadian Literature*, published in 1924, was one of the first books to argue that there was an existing literary tradition in Canada. Of LMM he wrote, "A special significance of Gordon's fiction and of Miss Montgomery's is their Scottish atmosphere. Both writers are of Scottish descent. Gordon is a minister, and Miss Montgomery married a minister. In all they write the influence of the minister is either actual or implied." (212).

Tuesday Feb. 3, 1925

I sometimes feel like giving up this diary altogether. It seems such a monotonous record of worry and sorrow. But it is the only outlet I have.

I slept poorly last night and could not write today. I had a letter from Mary Beal, full of woes and asking for a further loan of $300.[453] I *would* like to get a cheerful letter from *somebody*. Of course I must lend her the money. But I am miserably short just now of ready cash and this will further inconvenience me. She has not paid the last interest on her former loan yet. But she got a new car last summer!

Well, she is the only congenial friend I have anywhere near me and I want to help her if I can.

Sunday, Feb. 8, 1925

This has been a hard week but the weather has been mild. Some days I felt a little more cheerful, others very dull, tired and hopeless. Ewan has seemed a little better.

On Wednesday I finished a novel, *The Blue Castle*—a little comedy for adults. I have enjoyed writing it very much. It seemed a refuge from the cares and worries of my real world. I shall still have a good bit of work revising it.

I burned my hand quite badly one day this week kindling a fire and suffered keenly for a day or so. I have been very fortunate in this respect at least during my life. I recall no other painful burn except the one long ago in childhood at Grandfather Montgomery's.

I had a curious dream about Mr. Armstrong last night. I feel sure it has some reference to the Zephyr church matter but I cannot understand it.

Tuesday, Feb. 10, 1925
The Manse, Leaskdale

Life grows no easier. I have not felt well this week and Ewan seems worse again.

Today I began a certain bitter task. To wit; making out a list of the things I must do and get for Chester when he goes away to school next fall. It hurts me horribly but it must be done. And it seems so brief a time since he was my wee white baby of that happy summer.

---

453   Mary Gould Beal was originally from a prominent family in Uxbridge (in fact Uxbridge had once been named "Gouldville" after the family). She was a founding member of Uxbridge's literary society, the Hypatia Club. Her husband Norman Beal and his brother had owned a successful wholesale leather business. Following the end of World War I, however, the business went downhill. It finally failed during the Great Depression. Beal then sold life insurance until his death in 1938. The Beals maintained their earlier lifestyle partly with loans from LMM.

I *do* resent one thing keenly and that is that almost all the years of my boy's childhood which should have been my happiest years I have been so unhappy and worried over Ewan's malady. It has poisoned everything for me. And now Chester must soon go and will never belong really to the home again. Only coming home for vacations.

Wed., Feb. 11, 1925

Ewan did not sleep well last night and today he had many of the symptoms that ushered in that dreadful attack last year. Must this go on all the rest of my life—this ceaseless dread and secret anxiety? I have kept up all winter. But this evening when Ewan had gone gloomily to bed with a towel round his head and I was alone in the dining room I broke down. "Oh, not again, God—not again," I pleaded and sobbed. And truly I feel that I cannot face it *again. Everything* seems dark. There is not a gleam of light anywhere.

Sunday, Feb. 14, 1925

Ewan has seemed better again. But I have had a sort of break-down and a return of the condition of mind and nerves I suffered so many years ago that terrible winter down home. On Friday night we went over to tea with Jas. Lockies. It was a terrible evening. They voted "out" but to hear them go on one would think they repented it. We had to sit the whole evening and listen to a constant stream of discouragements, complaints, forebodings and veiled insults or what seemed so. Mrs. Lockie even said that "what had ruined Zephyr congregation was Ewan's asking for money for missions." This is so ludicrous that I could have laughed in her face had I dared. She is a terrible woman, noted for gossip and malice and she is never twice the same. One day she is cheerful and friendly and ready to look on the bright side. The next she will be as she was last night. I have been under a miserable strain all winter and this was the last straw. I came home,

> too sick at heart to war
> With failure any more.[454]

and since then I have not slept at nights and by day am a prey to a horrible, unreasoning nervous unrest. Yesterday was really a dreadful day. I could not work and had a wretched sensation in the solar plexus. I can't describe it but it is very dreadful.

This afternoon Lily phoned over and said she could not come back this week. I asked her bluntly when she expected to come. "Oh, she didn't know—wouldn't be any use if she was here"—and similar vague statements. I hung up the receiver, knowing at last what I have suspected all along. Lily is not

---

454   From Canadian poet Bliss Carman's (1861–1929) poem, "A Song Before Sailing."

coming back—and had no intention of coming back when she left. She has taken this way—and a mean way it is—to get away. I knew she was discontented ever since Earl Thompson stopped driving her around last summer. One day she said to me half jokingly that an aunt of hers had sent her word that she was staying too long in one place—that she'd never "get a man" if she didn't go to a new place.

Well, if poor Lily but knew it I would have been very glad if she had said she wanted to go. I have been wishing she would go for some time. But I feel hurt that she should behave in this way for she has been very well treated here and I had a right to expect squarer dealing from her. But one should not expect anything else from her class. If I can only get another maid all will be for the best. I will keep Elsie if she can stay, though I fear she is not overly strong.

Monday, Feb. 16, 1925
The Manse, Leaskdale

I slept a little during the first part of the night but wakened about three and could not sleep again. I felt that I could *not* get up and face life, but when I got up and got to work I felt better until twilight when my nervous unrest and depression returned.

The one bright spot on my dark horizon is that Ewan has been real well these past few days. Better than he has been any time since last October. It makes such a difference in life when he seems something like his old self. It has been the dread of another March like last March hanging over me all winter that has made life so intolerable and robbed me of courage to face and overcome all the other worries and stings.

Wednesday, Feb. 18, 1925

Last night I had to take chloral before I could sleep. I felt a little better today. This evening at the Guild social I gave a talk on our trip to Mammoth Cave. But when I came home I was very "blue" and downhearted. Life has been such a drab, worried affair ever since November that I can't conceive of it ever being anything else.

Thursday, Feb. 19, 1925

Wretched night. Woke at four and could not sleep again. Everything presented itself in its darkest shades. I lived over all my past misery and all my possible future misery. This is always one of the characteristics of these attacks of neurasthenia.

This evening we had promised to go to tea at Will Sellars. Always before we have enjoyed going there. We felt that they were our friends and they have

always backed us up in everything. But now all is changed and we felt uncomfortable and awkward. But they were very nice and the evening passed off well on the surface. We never mentioned the church matter of course but when Ewan went out to get his horse something Mr. Sellars said seemed to signify that they are not going to leave the church. This revived a little hope in my heart for if they stick I believe the church can get along.

Oh, if Ewan could only get well and *keep* well! We could go to some other congregation then and be rid of Zephyr forever. But what would be the use of going to a new place if Ewan continues as he has been for six years. It has been *I* who has kept things together here—*made* Ewan visit and preach—run all the societies—planned out the work and so on. And I haven't the heart or courage to tackle such an effort in a new place—in fact, in a new place I could not do it as I have done it here, where the work was already organized.

But I am very morbid just now owing to this attack of neurasthenia. I can't take an all-around view of anything.

Friday, Feb. 20, 1925

I slept well last night and so got through today fairly well. We had another drive over to Zephyr tonight to visit Fred Walkers. They were agreeable and nothing nasty or discouraging was said there. But they are not among our workers or givers and are interested only in making money. Very few of the Z. families in either the Presbyterian or the Methodist churches take any *real* interest in their churches. They are not of the type that does.

Saturday, Feb. 21, 1925

Had a poor night. Today was dark with showers of rain. I worked at the revision of *The Blue Castle* but always with such an undercurrent of unrest and depression that I could not enjoy it or forget myself in it. Tonight Stuart had another attack of that pain—this time in the region of his stomach. But it did not last long after I applied the hot water bottle. Soon after I went up to ask him how he was and he said cheerfully, "Oh, *life* is *bearable* now."

I wish I could say the same. My life this winter is *not* bearable. I wish just *one* little pleasant thing would happen to give me a fillip that would enable me to "carry on." Really, not *one* pleasant thing has happened to me since last October—not one. Just a succession of monotonous duties, illnesses, worries, stings, small vexations, and over all like a starless sky over a wintry earth the ceaseless gnawing dread that Ewan will have another attack like last winter.

Lily, I hear, was at a dance at Sandford last night and told someone present that the doctor had told her she "shouldn't work for a year." Why didn't she tell me that? Because the doctor didn't say anything of the sort to her. She has

thought this up since. I mean to write her at once and ask her plainly if she means to come back or not. I am not going to be played along in this fashion. A girl who is able to dance all night is not ill.

Thursday, Feb. 26, 1925
The Manse, Leaskdale

Sometimes lately I have almost decided to give up writing this journal altogether. I am tired of this monotonous record of misery and unrest. But on the other hand, it is the only relief I have. If I did not write things out in this journal I could not bear my life at all. So I shall keep it up for a while longer at least.

Sunday was a dreary day of frequent showers. But I had slept fairly well and felt better, with no attacks of nervous unrest through the day. Ewan stayed for supper at John Rynard's and had a few bits of encouraging news when he came home. But I cannot bring myself to hope that any good thing can come out of Zephyr.

Monday morning we went to Uxbridge as I had not been down for some time and had to go. But it began to rain on the way down and continued to pour all day and we had a terrible trip there and back. We have had more of these dreadful drives this winter than ever before. The roads have never been good since November. But I felt fairly well all day until twilight when I had a return of nervous unrest, coupled with a nasty feeling of being *hemmed in*— imprisoned, with no hope or prospect of escape. But I was able to banish it by reading.

I wrote to Lily that evening asking her plainly if she intended to come back or not. I told her I would keep the place open for her if she wanted to come back but if she didn't I thought I had a right to know.

Tuesday evening we had to go to tea at John Taylors. Dreadful roads but luckily not far—only three miles. But we had a dull tedious evening with nothing but Church Union to talk about and I was very tired and depressed.

Yesterday I got a letter from Lily which she had written before she got mine. In it she said I had "better not depend" on her coming back. So that is settled.

It is best. Lily had been here quite long enough. Yet one cannot live seven years with a person and not feel some pain at parting—at least, I cannot.

Elsie is going to stay. I think she will do fairly well but I do not expect to find her altogether satisfactory. In some ways she will suit better than Lily, in others not so well. And I will have to teach her a great deal. But then she seems very willing to learn. She will not, I think, have the tantrums and cranky spells of Lily but neither will she be the good company Lily was *between* her tantrums. Lily had an almost Josephian sense of *jokes* and was not at all bad company when in good humor. And so devoid is my life of all congenial companionship

that even this was a boon and was the strongest reason why I put up so long with other things that were very annoying. So her letter added a little to my depression of yesterday.

We had to go over to Zephyr to have tea at Herb Warrens. The roads were dreadful. We had to go in a buggy as the greater part of them were bare but there were some places where there was a great deal of snow and I was in terror lest we capsize altogether.

Then we had a dreadful evening. We heard nothing but gossip re Church Union and discouraging gossip. And it began to pour rain and we could not think of coming home over such roads in the rain. We had to stay all night and I was so depressed and worried over the gossip and general atmosphere of the family that I could not sleep at all. As a result my nerves have been dreadful today. We came home this morning. Another very unpleasant drive in a high wind. I worked all the afternoon at revising *The Blue Castle* but could not lose myself in it or enjoy my work. I tried to sleep but could not. There were no letters—nothing pleasant at all to break the dead monotony of bad weather, worry and neurasthenic wretchedness. I have been most miserable this evening and have felt that it is simply impossible to go on living. I am literally obsessed by the Zephyr situation and the Union mess. My intellect tells me it is nonsense to take it so seriously and presents a score of reasons why it need not worry me at all. But this has no effect on my feelings. I am exactly as I was that miserable winter down home so many years ago. Not quite so bad yet—but I soon shall be if this goes on.

Friday, Feb. 27, 1925

Last night I took veronal and slept so I felt better today and was able to work. But it was cold and stormy and tonight I feel restless again.

Mrs. Harrison of the store—a notorious gossip—asked Elsie today if she got up before I did. She said Lily had told her that she was *always up and had all her work done before I got up.*

I have always known Lily told falsehoods but it is hard to believe she could have told so brazen a one as this. She never, since she came here, got up before I did. I have *always* been the first one up, rising at 7.15 and calling Lily. Then I got the boys' school lunches ready while she got breakfast. The rest of the work had to wait until she had gone down to the store and stayed there for the most of an hour gossiping.

It is well she is gone. But I suppose she will tell all kinds of falsehoods about me and my household all over the country. In my present state of nerves this worries me more than it should. But everything worries me now. I am terribly morbid. When I lie awake at night everything looks dark. I cannot see a ray of hope anywhere. I cannot believe that life will ever become liveable again. I can

see nothing before me but worry of one kind or another all the rest of my life and it takes the heart out of me.

Saturday, Feb. 28, 1925

Last night I had a good natural sleep and felt better today—able to work, which is all I hope for now. Ewan remarked today on how well he was feeling. But this does not cheer me because I have found that whenever he speaks of feeling well in a few days a change will come and one of his attacks come on.

We had a slight earthquake shock tonight.[455] At 9.30 I was sitting by the dining room table reading when I felt a queer sensation. I thought "Am I dizzy?" Then I realized that it was my chair that was wobbling, not me. At the same moment the dishes in the cabinet behind me began to rattle and jingle as if someone had collided with it. This went on for several seconds. I wondered if it were an earthquake but was not sure until I 'phoned to Uxbridge and found out that reports of it were coming in from all over the country.

Earthquakes—eclipse of sun—disruption of the Presbyterian church—what further signs and wonders in this year of grace 1925?

Sunday, March 1, 1925
The Manse, Leaskdale

I have felt better today than for a long while. But there is nothing especial to write of and I am going to spend the afternoon and evening copying into this journal for preservation Charles Macneill's old diary. It is such a curious record of the life of a farmer on the North Shore of P.E. Island thirty or forty years ago. As such it will have a certain value in the future. May lent me the old notebooks when I was home last summer but I have never had time to copy them and I must soon send them back to her:—

---

455   This earthquake, known as the "Charlevoix–Kamouraska" earthquake, struck northeastern North America on February 28, 1925, causing damage mostly in Quebec. It was one of the most powerful quakes measured in Canada in the twentieth century.

Copy of Diary Kept by Charles Macneill, farmer, of Cavendish, P.E. Island in the years 1892–[1898][456]

"Sunday, Aug. 7, 1892

Came to Charlottetown. Went to Zion Church. Heard Mr. Brewster, Methodist minister, preach a sermon on The Great King, the Lord Jesus."

"Monday, Aug. 8

Went to see Dr. Taylor about my eye. He said he thought it a —[457] and did not operate on it but told me to come back whenever I felt it sore. It does not feel well to-day."

"Monday, Aug. 8

Took the cars at Charlottetown for Hunter River at 3 o'clock Standard Time. Had a nice drive on the cars. Met a Mr. Alex Bernard of Richibucto in town. Came out on the train with him. He left his vessel and went home by steamer. I walked home from Hunter River. Got home about 10 o'clock."

"Tuesday, Aug. 9, 1892

At home to-day. Poor weather for hay-making. Raining hard this afternoon."

"Wednesday, Aug. 10

Fine day. Cut the hay seed in the forenoon. Put hay in in the afternoon. Put up a stack. Did not finish it."

"Thursday

Rain to-day. Sent and got 3 deal to fix the horse-stable floor. Paid 63 cts. for them. Got 2 bundles of shingles for Albert. Paid $1 per 100."

"Friday, Aug. 12

Poor weather for haying. Trying to stump. Beginning of storm. George Mackay's schooner is ashore at Rustico."

"Saturday, Aug. 13

Storm not over. Going to try the stumping."

"Sunday, Aug. 14

Preaching at Rustico to-day. Commenced to rain at 12 o'clock to-day with thunder. The people got caught in the rain coming home from church. My eye does not

---

456   Charles Macneill (1831–1908) was the father of LMM's friend and cousin Alec Macneill. Here LMM copies out the entirety of his journal; space does not permit recreating her record of these entries (the total word count for the Charles Macneill diary is 28,130 words; it takes up some 100 pages of her handwritten journal). To give a sense of the enormity of the task of recopying it, however, the first month—August 1892—is printed here.

457   Here LMM inserts a dash, perhaps to indicate she could not read the diagnosis.

feel well to-day. Is very sore by times. Louisa Donald and her boy were here to-day. They were great strangers. Donald Smith of Clinton and his wife were here to-day."

"August 15

Raining hard to-day. Very poor weather for wheat and hay. My eye is very sore."

"Monday, August 16

Rain all day."

"Tuesday, August 17

Stumping."

"Wednesday, August 18

Cut hay down on road. Put up a stack of hay in Montana for Alexander."

"Thursday, Aug. 19

Commenced harvest. Cut 2 ¼ acres of mixed feed."

"Friday

Albert went to Kensington after Binder Twine. Got 50 lb. at 13 cts. per lb. $6.50."

"Saturday, Aug. 20th.

Very dull weather. Stumping in forenoon. Cutting round field of oats in afternoon.

"Sunday, Aug. 21

Went to hear Mr. Allan Simpson preach on behalf of Halifax College. He says we ought to help. Expects this congregation to give twenty dollars. My eyes are very sore to-day. Alexander and Pensie and Maud[458] went to the English church to-day. Mrs. James Craswell and Mary Ellen Mutch was here to-day. Wind north east. Prospect of storm. A lot of grain ripe both oats and wheat. Minnie and Lorenzo was here to-day."

"Monday, August 22

Fine clear day for harvest cutting. Wheat up at the back field pretty fair crop. Machine doing fairly well. Eye very sore."

"Tuesday, Aug. 23

Cutting oats. Doing well so far."

"August 23, 1892

Fine bright day. Going to try and finish cutting oats."

"Wednesday, Aug. 24

Finished cutting the field of oats. Moved the binder over to Albert's. Cut his field of oats."

---

458 Pensie and Alec Macneill, Charles Macneill's daughter and son. The "Maud" here is LMM.

"Thursday, Aug. 25

Finished cutting Albert's oats. Taking in the mixed feed."

"Friday, Aug. 26

Alexander went to Kensington for deck springs. Did not get them. Got 2 balls of twine. I cut around the field on the road. Very cold."

"Saturday, Aug. 27

Cut Albert's wheat. Put in oats. Not very dry."

"Sunday, Aug. 28

Rain to-day at preaching. Albert and Alexander heard Mr. Spurr preach."

"Monday, Aug. 29, 1892

Cleared up fine. Going to cut the field of oats on the road farm. Don't expect to have a good time at it."

"Tuesday, Aug. 30

Fine day. Finished cutting the field on the road at noon. Came home and mowed around the wheat field and started the binder."

"Wednesday, Aug. 31

Finished cutting the wheat and stooked it up complete and mowed ½ acre of new land. Took in three loads of oats. Not too dry."

**

I have finished the old diary. It has taken me several Sunday afternoons and meanwhile I have been writing my journal entries separately and will copy them down later. To any other person in the world Charles Macneill's old diary would be tedious to read and unthinkably tedious to copy. But to me every moment I spent in copying it was a delight. I was back again in a world where happiness reigned and problems were non-existent—for me at least. I was so much at his home when a child and young girl that every word he wrote brought back vividly some sweet memory of those past days and childish frolics and delights. The most commonplace statement seemed like a finger touching the keys of an organ and evoking melodies of haunting sweetness—sights, sounds, of that old north shore farm that came back like the faint appealing voices of ghosts heard long ago many shadowy years agone. Pensie was alive to run with me under the moon and together we slipped back into that garden where the sword is set and mortals may not pass—the Eden of childhood.

I have copied the diary faithfully. Occasionally there is a mistake in the date or a mistake in spelling. But very few. Charles Macneill was a remarkably

good writer and speller for a man who had had so little chance. Almost his only grammatical error is to use "was" with a plural subject. None of his family could do so well. They all seemed to take after their mother who was very illiterate, loveable and kind though she was.

Yes, every line has its charm for me. Charles writes that it is raining heavily. I am standing with Pensie at the front door of the little hall looking out over eastern Cavendish. The rain is coming down steadily over the wide green fields and the dark groves of spruce and the little golden dells between them. Far down "Angus MacKenzie's house" comes out against its emerald hill. Off to the left runs the sea, gray through the mist of rain—how did Tennyson put it?—"The sea's long level dim with rain"[459]—I recalled that line often when I looked at the sea from that old house on a rainy day. And the long red road growing darker and redder and richer under the wet. Sometimes he adds that it is thundering and I see the huge black clouds riding up over the tiny house and the great willows behind it and Pensie and I run from the door and crouch in the parlor that has grown almost dark, and out to sea a shaft of lightning pierces the sky and the woods have grown dim in their skirts of shadow. Or he complains that it is very poor weather for haying. I see the great hayfields— riffling in the wind—lying in lustrous, fragrant swaths after mowing—covered with "coils" in the light of July sunsets—haunted and still on nights of white moon splendor. "Down home" the neat little cones into which the raked hay was hurriedly made up when rain threatened were always called "coils." Here in Ontario, that name is unknown. They are called "cocks." Many a time I have helped "coil" the hay, when a fine afternoon gave promise of a sudden shower and everybody was pressed into service to get the hay saved. It was not hard work—and the surroundings made it pleasant. I remember that Pensie and I coiled a whole field of hay one evening when the men were away and a thunderstorm was brewing. I don't think our coils were as perfectly shaped as Mr. Charles' would have been but they served. And now Pensie has been dead nearly twenty years.

"A fine clear day for harvest"—I see the sunlight falling over the fields "ripe unto harvest." I see the rows of "stooks"—"shocks" they call them here. I have "stooked" grain in my time, too—I see the bare stubble land after the big loads of grain have been hauled to the barn. I used to build a load now and then myself. There was an art in it. If the load were not properly built it was apt to collapse before it got to the barn and cover the builder with ignominy. Of course I never had much of this sort of work to do but almost every summer

---

459   In fact these lines are from the first stanza of American poet John Greenleaf Whittier's (1807–92) poem, "The Last Walk in Autumn": "O'er the bare woods, whose outstretched hands / Plead with the leaden heavens in vain, / I see, beyond the valley lands, / The sea's long level dim with rain."

there came an afternoon when rain threatened and men were scarce and "we youngsters" were pressed into emergency service. I never "built" a load of hay. But a load of sheaves was not such a hard thing to build if you were careful to "bind" it properly with the end sheaves as you went along and didn't get it too wide or too narrow or too top-heavy or too loose.

Or perhaps the "rain" comes on Sunday, while the people are at "preaching." I am back in the old Presbyterian church in Cavendish. I am sitting in the pew between Grandmother and Grandfather. Right before me in the front pew sit Amanda and Tillie and old Aunt Caroline[460] of the quilted black satin bonnet. Far back under the gallery in one of the post seats Mr. Charles is sitting, his shock of bushy gray hair standing stiffly up above his gray bearded face. Everybody else is there. Folks dead and buried for a quarter of a century hurry out of their graves and come to fill their pews just because I read in an old diary that it "rained at preaching." Not one is missing from "old McKinstrie," in the front centre pew to "old Willie Makum," twisting his face into weird grimaces away up in his gallery pew. Mr. Archibald is preaching and the choir are all in their places in the front pew of the gallery. Rain is beating against the high, narrow white-glass windows. The wind is wailing mournfully around the church. I look out of the window so blessedly near our pew. The long grasses in the graveyard are tossing in the wind or lying down wetly under the down-pour. The pond is gray down in the valley, the sand hills can be hardly seen for rain—the sea beyond moans on its rocky shore. The horses tied to the graveyard fence don't like the rain. But the wet landscape has a charm all its own. After all, I rather like it when it "rains at preaching."

Old Cavendish Church

Or perhaps it is just "blowing hard." Perhaps the wind is north. Then it comes swooping up from the shore right through Charles' yard and whistles about his doorstep. Away out the gulf is dotted all over with white caps. Near in to shore just beyond the green fields is a line of breakers under a mist of foam. But if it is northwest or west the little house is so well sheltered by the "bush" to the back of it that we don't feel the wind. It only thrashes the tops of the trees and howls in the dog-woods. But it may be south or southwest and then it is a lonesome thing, purring softly down over the slopes behind the

460   Aunt Caroline was Charles Macneill's unmarried sister. See note 9, page 18 (July 28, 1923).

house and laughing in the garden and blowing leaves crazily across the yard. Or it is east—sad, mournful, blowing up from "a gray and haunted shore." And night comes down with the blackness of the wild autumn storms and Pensie and I scurry into the house and shut the door, laughing, in its face. Pensie with her pretty auburn curls and her roguish face. Who said she was dead? I saw her but a moment ago. As Kipling says, "The Lords of life and death shut the doors behind us"[461]—but sometimes they swing open for a minute and the ghostly hands of winds that blew forty years ago play with our hair again.

Or it is "a fine bright day." Who should know better than I what "a fine bright" August day on that old north shore was? Air crystal and golden. Vast sky gardens where white cloud flowers bloomed. Great golden fields with the magic of dark spruce woods behind them. Musky, spicy garden flowers. Triangles of sea shimmering into violet; faint blue loveliness over New London harbor: "authentic music of eternity" echoing up from the rocky shore. Yes, it is indeed a fine bright day. There are days like that there yet. We never have just that kind of day inland. Only the sea can give them.

Or a November entry says "snowed in the night." The first snow of the winter that is to be. At sunset the world was gray and ugly. At sunrise it is a fair white thing and the sea looks blackly gray and dour by contrast. The ploughed fields are all dimpled; the spruces and firs are as white palms; the apple trees still holding their withered leaves look blossom-gay again. Only they are all white. There are no pink hearts. But as the day wears on it gets "sloppy." The snow melts and the beauty vanishes.

In December there is "a fine day with squalls of snow by times." Yes, I remember that kind of day, too. Ground frozen hard. Biting wind in spite of the sunshine. Up comes a big black cloud. A wave of gray shadow goes over the world. Then the stinging drive of sudden snow. The air is a wild white blur with it. The fields whiten, the hills grow pale. Presto, the cloud is gone. The sun is out. But winter is a little nearer. Then comes an entry, "Froze hard last night. Roads very rough." Bumpy driving over them now. Pensie and I give up our out door prowls and keep to the house when I visit there. But when I go home in the wintry twilight there is something nice in tramping along over the hard firm road. No mud now. Household lights gleaming warmly out along the road. Melody of storm in the wind that is swooping down over the sleeping fields; a big round silvery moon floating up over a frosty hill; the gnomish beauty of dark lombardies against the moonrise; bars of moonlight and shadow on the road under the trees and Pensie beside me—always laughing. Do the dead laugh?

In January are many "cold" entries. "As the days begin to lengthen the cold

---

461   From Rudyard Kipling's short story, "The Finest Story in the World," from his 1890 collection, *Indian Tales.*

begins to strengthen" says Grandfather Macneill, quoting a saw of his father, who doubtless had it from *his* father. I wonder who first invented the little rhyme. I recall the odd sudden childish rebellion that always flamed up in my soul when I heard it. I hated it; and yet it *was* true—for a time. The cold *did* strengthen in January and February; and the storms came whirling over the fields and heaping drifts along the fences and fiercely bombarding the little house crouching against its friendly sheltering "bush." But they died at its door. Inside it was always the cosiest, warmest, snuggest, little place. Sitting room and parlor heated by roaring stoves. What matter if it were "very cold" outside?

But even in January comes sometimes "a mild day" and "a white frost." What a pretty name is "white frost." And the thing itself—lovely as some whim of wildwood god. Every tree a miracle—every dead weed and blade of grass a wonder. The great willows arching over the little house things of silver and pearl; the shrubs in the garden and the underbrush in the grove fairy jungles.

Then in March come the "blustery days"—"the windy days," "the mild days." April brings rain and bad roads; and in May there is a "foggy day." How I used to love foggy days. For me there was always a beauty and a mystery in the fog of that north shore. An evening fog filled me with a strange deep joy—that mournful ghostly thing hanging low over the fields and drifting in phantom-like waves through the spruces. But Pensie is laughing. I hear her telling a joke. An old man drives into the yard and greets her father. "Fogging, sir." We have never heard "fogging" before. We think it is exquisitely funny. Thereafter we never meet each other on a misty day without saying "Fogging, sir." And why not? As well as raining and blowing? Yes, I loved days when it "fogged."

"Mr. Charles" has "built a stack." Again a host of memory pictures. One never sees stacks in Ontario. The barns here are so large they can hold all the hay and grain. The smaller P.E.I. barns could not and when there was a generous crop some of it must be "stacked." Sometimes the stack was built in the field itself and hauled home by sleighloads in winter. Often the grain or hay was hauled to the farm-yard and a group of stacks built in some sheltered place. These groups had a certain fascination for me, especially in a winter twilight when they were coated with snow and seemed to shoulder each other in the shadows. Or at night with a pale moon-glow behind them. I never took part in building a stack—that was only for experts; but I recall one afternoon when Pensie and I climbed up on a half-finished stack and lay there in the fragrant clover talking girlish secrets with the blue sky over us and the cool delicious gulf breeze blowing around us, bringing with it all kinds of elusive whiffs from all the little dells and slopes of the old farm.

One day Mr. Charles has one brief entry and one alone. "Stumping."[462] After a man had been stumping all day he did not feel much like diary writing. He was thankful to go to bed, feeling that some stumps attempted, some stumps done had earned a night's repose. Mr. Charles "stumped" a little every summer and cleared a bit more fertile land. But there were always enough stumps left in the "back fields" to provide delightful berrying grounds for us. Nowhere were there more delightful spots than among the stumps, nowhere places were berries bigger and redder or more abundant than among the long grasses and the clumps of fern.

One day he "puts up a stack of hay in Montana." Montana! That was what they called the acres of stumps over grown with a second growth of young maple at the "backest back." Why, I don't know. But I knew every winding path and maple clump and young fir group and fern-filled hollow in that beautiful place and I am in it again just because of its mention in Mr. Charles' diary.

"Albert went to Kensington after binder twine."[463] An entry that connotes a certain change that had come into farm life, doing away with much hard work and also with much romance and beauty. The advent of the "self-binder."

I do not of course remember the day of the reaping hook. But when I was a very small girl Grandfather had an old-fashioned mowing machine. On it were two seats—one for the driver, the other for a second man, holding a wooden rake in his hand, whose duty it was to rake off the sheaves, using his own judgment as to when enough grain had fallen on the board from the knives to make a sheaf. I have heard Grandfather say what a wonderful invention they thought this when it came first. But it was now out-of-date and very soon a new mower was bought, with revolving rakes that went round and round until, when the driver touched a spring, one rake fell lower than the others and swept off the sheaves. This was thought another wonderful contrivance. But the sheaves had to be bound and for this extra "hands" were hired—mostly black-eyed French girls who bound quickly and chattered ceaselessly in their patois. I found a great fascination in watching them and I longed to know how to make the "bands" but nobody ever would teach me. A girl would catch up a cluster of grain, twist it with another cluster in a special knot, gather up the sheaf and knot the "band" around it in a twinkling. They did it so quickly my eye could never follow the motion and to this day the secret of the knot is unknown to me. I wonder if anyone living knows it or has it become one of the "lost arts."

Then came the self-binder—and the laughing, chattering "binders" vanished forever from the harvest fields by the gulf. The day of "binder twine" had come—and one more bit of poetry vanished from the world. And was any-

---

462 Stumping consisted of removing tree stumps to enlarge fields for tillage.
463 Used to fasten hay or straw into bales that could be stacked in a barn.

body a whit the happier for the self binder? As for all the flood of machinery inventive "genius" has let loose upon the world?

"Alexander and Pensie and Maud went to the English church to-day." This is the only time I am mentioned in the diary. A reference elsewhere to "Maud playing the organ" is meant for Maud Macneill. But it is the mention of the English Church that touches the secret spring. The English church—as it was always called then. It is Anglican now;[464]—was at South Rustico about half way between Cavendish and Charlottetown. It always had a charm for me—an old gray church set back on a side road amid big trees, with a graveyard all around it. I did not get there very often but sometimes Alec and Pensie and I drove down to it on a summer Sunday evening. Great Grandfather Woolner[465] was buried there and his wife. I remember that on this particular evening Mr. Charles commemorates it began to rain and we had a wet drive. But I do not recall that it damped our spirits in the least. It seems to me that, when Alec and Pensie and I were on any jaunt, we laughed incessantly. Well, in those days most people with whom I foregathered did laugh, if they were any connection of the race of Joseph. I take some credit to myself for it. I had a knack of saying funny things about everything we saw or heard that kept my companions in agonies of mirth—and no jokes ever got by me. I think I have some of the power left yet; but I seldom get any chance nowadays to exercise it. Only when I go back to Cavendish and sit with Alec and May around their supper table do I discover that I can still make people laugh.

Mr. Charles has several references to "the road farm." This is another phrase which, quite pithless to most readers, is a master key for me, opening another door into the past. This road farm was "a parcel of land" lying along the side road that led from the "Rustico Road" down to the eastern shore where were the remote farms of the Bernards, the Flemings and "Sandy Laird on the Capes." This road led through woods and clearings almost its whole length and was a wild and beautiful spot. I remember the first time I saw it; and that is linked with another memory. Pensie and I are sitting together in school one rough winter day. Amanda is not there. Very few pupils are there. So Pensie and I are sitting together in the old "back seat" where the desks were so high that almost anything could be done behind them. But Pensie and I are not doing anything very dreadful. We are writing "letters" to each other on our slates. I don't know why we are not doing arithmetic or studying our lesson. Let the teacher answer. We finish the letters and exchange slates. Pensie writes me about a certain plan of ours—to wit, that when spring comes we will walk down to Oliver Bernard's (Oliver was married to her sister Lily).

---

464   St. Mark's Anglican Church in South Rustico, established in 1848; it was torn down in 2016.
465   Robert Chester Woolner (1787–1860) was born in Dunwich, England, and emigrated to PEI.

Pensie describes the road we will take—"such a pretty road"—ferns all along it, trees meeting overhead etc. I am intrigued. From that moment I look forward hungrily to our walk. In due time it comes. One rare spring day we walk down. For once realization is every whit as sweet as anticipation. The road *is* lovely. Ferns in clumps and ferns in curly masses and lonely upstanding brackens; masses of purple rhododendrons—"sheep laurel." Mayflower stars along the way; blue and white violets; strawberry blossoms; clumps of young maple; slender firs; bird calls; wild fragrances; squirrels chattering secrets of Polichinelle;[466] stipplings of sunlight along the moist red road; wine of spring in the crystal air; hill glamor and upland magic; an immortal spirit of beauty brooding over everything; Pensie and I faring on together, feeling adventurous and expectant. No cares—no worries—not a bit afraid of tomorrow.

But Pensie is dead; and I am inclined to think that the road has been "cleared" and is nothing now but a road instead of being, as it was then, a highway in the land of faery.

Mr. Charles has "stooked" a wheat field up complete. I see it, lying in autumnal sunlight, dotted over with the golden stooks—"shocks" they call them in Ontario. I have done a little "stooking" in my time too. It was not hard work. A field of stooks in moonlight was always a place of faery and gramarye.[467]

"Taking in wheat from the old place." Chas. Macneill was a thrifty soul and he had accumulated goodly acres. Besides the "home place" he had the "road farm" and "the old place" which is now Alec's farm. It was called the old place because his uncle, "Old Chas." Macneill, had once owned it. Before this time he had also owned the farm which is now Albert's and after this he rented the "old Ewan McKenzie place." He was a tireless steady worker and a good manager. I know of no man who enjoyed farming more truly than old Mr. Charles. He rose while it was yet night and looked well to the ways of his farmyard and stables. One record has it that he got up at 2 o'clock to take in a field of wheat because it looked like rain.

One entry "got the mill for to thrash" revives another host of memories. In those days in Cavendish everybody had his crop thrashed by a little two-horse-power "threshing machine." I think most of them have gasoline engines now. Here in Ontario all the threshing is done in a day or two by a gang and a steam engine.

In those old days we small fry were vastly excited when the threshing days came. Generally we had to stay home from school to "tramp straw." Albert Macneill had a mill and he went around to thresh for his neighbors. His job was to "feed the drum." Sometimes he cut the bands also and then someone

---

466   "Polichinelle" is the name of a character from Italian *Commedia dell'arte*.

467   "Stooking" referred to creating a field stack of small rectangular bales of hay or straw. "Gramarye" is a Middle English word for occult learning or magic.

had to pass him the sheaves one by one from the piles in which they were pitched down from the loft. I often did this and loved to do it. To watch the great ravenous teeth of the "drum" catch and rend and tear the sheaf as Albert "fed" it had a terrible fascination for me. So many sheaves made a "rally"—I don't know how many. After each "rally" horses and men had a rest of ten minutes or so. But perhaps I was not passing sheaves but was "tramping" straw in loft or outside stack or shed. This was necessary in order to pack the straw and make room for it all. It was gorgeous fun. I loved it all—the whir and roar and dust—and the clouds of grain pouring out of the drum, while the straw was coughed furiously out beyond to the waiting man with the fork who tossed it to us. The only drawback to it all was the mice. There were always legions of them, especially when the lower layers of sheaves were reached.

Pensie and I, I remember, loved to get on the wooden tread of the mill, when it would be standing idle before their barn, and make it go. We always had to get one of the boys to start it first but once started we could keep it going as long as our legs lasted. If we had been compelled to do this we would have howled in protest; but when it was play—why, it *was* play. And if I had "growing pains" that night when I went to bed—why, everybody had to have growing pains. One must grow.

There are some rather pathetic little entries about his eye. Eventually he lost the sight of it completely but then it ceased to be painful and the other remained good to his end. In one entry he writes "It is hard to be afflicted thus." No doubt it was. And yet Charles Macneill had a life almost free from trouble and illness. I never knew of his being ill until the time of his death came and this trouble in his eye was the only physical affliction he ever had. His family all turned out decently and there was no break in it until Pensie's death which came a year or two before his own. His life was a very narrow one but in its groove, it was as happy, peaceful and prosperous a one as I ever knew.

The entry "hauling old longers for firewood" reminds me of the fact that I have never heard the old rails of fences called "longers" (pronounced longgers) any place outside of P.E. Island. I have never come across it in any literature, not even in dialect. Yet they were always called so on the Island. The derivation must have been English or Scotch. Yet I suppose neither in England nor Scotland were there ever any fences of that kind, so one is forced back on an American or Canadian derivation. The "poles" which Mr. Chas. often cuts in his diary, were much slighter, shorter affairs, used for the ends of the "longers" to rest on. In my childhood these pole and longer fences were all there were, save back in the clearings where some "stump fences" were found. Occasionally some fiendish creature built what was called a "picket fence" or a "pitchpole" fence. This was built entirely of "poles" driven into the ground at an angle, their sharp points sticking up all along the top. You couldn't climb it or wriggle through it. Therefore we berry pickers hated it and anathematized

the builders thereof. Then "board fences" came in but were too expensive to oust the longer fence entirely. And then the hideous, horrible barbed wire, which being cheap was soon met with everywhere. I *have* managed to climb a barbed wire fence but it was not a joke. And it was impossible to slide between the wires as we did in the plain wire fences of a later day.

The old "snake" longer fence was a beautiful thing in its way, though wasteful of land. In the angles formed by the longers such beautiful things grew. Long, purple-plumed wild grasses, ferns, bracken, strawberry vines, daisies, fireweed, farewell-summers, yarrow, "life-o'-man" and great armies of golden rod. Even in winter the gray-headed golden-rods stuck up through the snowdrifts that always filled up those corners.

There were stone "dykes" there, too, and they were beautiful things when they grew old. The custom was brought out from Scotland. The dykes were built of layers of the red stones picked off the fields alternated with layers of sods. Soon the grass growing from the sods covered the stones, and if it didn't mosses and lichen did. Then dear things took root in the crevices among the stones and wove beauty about the old dykes—flowers and ferns and mosses and berries. An old dyke was an amazing place for strawberries, with stems so long that you could pick a "bouquet" of them. And there were always bird's nests in the holes among the stones. A low fence was built along the top of the dyke or a hedge of spruce trees planted. If they were not planted they sprang up and grew anyway. Oh, those old dykes were the most lovable things. Our old farm was full of them. A dyke ran down right from "Jimmy Laird's line" along the main road to our gate. Another one, covered with wild rose bushes, bounded the field by the church. Our front orchard was surrounded by one, so old and overgrown that it looked like a bank of earth and huge trees grew out of it. The whole road down to the shore had a dyke along one side of it—a dyke where I have picked quarts of strawberries on summer evenings. Amanda's old lane was dyked on both sides—a dyke famous for the "sours" which we loved to eat. To speak of a barbed wire fence in the same breath with one of those exquisite, poesy-haunted old dykes were to commit sacrilege.

Verily, the fact that Mr. Chas. "hauled longers" one day over thirty years ago and wrote it down has led me far afield—into old fields, lying in the light of faraway summers, hemmed in by dykes or silver-gray longers and gaining from them a certain racy individuality and charm no wire-girdled meadow could ever know or possess.

The cheapness of things in those days is a constant marvel to me now. One day Mr. Charles went to the shore and bought three mackerel. For these three mackerel he paid the huge sum of 8 cents. They would make a good dinner for his whole family. Today those same three mackerel would be at least a dollar and probably more.

It is odd how our tastes change as we grow older—not only mentally but physically. When I was a child I could not eat mackerel—fresh mackerel at least. I always loved the delicious broiled salt mackerel. But the fried fresh mackerel which almost everyone thought so delicious I could not eat at all. Now I love it. I always liked fresh codfish. No one knows what fresh codfish is really like except one who has eaten it with only an hour between sea and pot. Those great snow-white slices of codfish served up with Grandmother's "drawn butter" sauce.[468] Food for gods! Nothing to equal them save the trout Uncle Leander caught in the pond. There is a flavor about salt water fish that no fresh water fish ever possesses. Codfish dried and broiled was a great breakfast and supper dish. They were spread on constructions called "flakes" and turned carefully until dry. It was an art not to let them get "sunburned" which ruined them.

People who have been dead and forgotten for a generation live in this diary of old Mr. Charles. He mentions "James McKinstrie"—and instantly I see him. A little white haired old Scotchman sitting every Sunday in the "top middle pew" of old Cavendish church. He was born in Scotland and never lost the Lowland "brogue." He was an eccentric individual and there was always some tale of "old McKinstrie's" utterances floating round. He had considerable native intelligence but was entirely uneducated. In short, he might have stepped out of one of Scott's novels. The type is never seen today.

Scattered all through the diary are the French names—Mr. Charles does not always spell them right—which were so well-known to my childhood. Gautiers (we called it "Goachy"), Peters, Blacquiere (Blackair), Pineau (Mr. Charles has it Penowe), Gallant (Gallong), Doucet, Doiron, Poirier (Perry), Buote (Be-ot) and so on. And the first names. Silvien, Francois, Maxim, Peter (Peter Peters was a red-headed Frenchman who used to work for Grandfather), Leon, Napoleon (generally "Pullyong"), Zebedee (always "Zeb") and a host of Scripture names—Moses, Jeremiah, David, Matthew, Paul etc. etc. etc. Grandfather always had a "hired boy" in the summer. From May to November the wages paid those boys in those days were $36. Thirty six dollars for a whole summer. Nowadays they want that a month! Nor did they think themselves abused. I always liked our French folk. They were generally a good-natured, happy-go-lucky obliging lot. The only thing I disliked was a certain smutty streak which was carefully concealed from our older people but was now and then allowed to peep out before us children.

"Cleaning out the greenhouse" does not refer to a conservatory. The "greenhouse" at Mr. Chas. was a deep pit dug in the ground with a wooden roof built over it, in which vegetables were stored, generally those intended for the stock. People did not have cement stables in those days and the cellars of

---

468   A sauce made with butter, onions, and cornstarch.

the houses could not hold all the crop. So they built what were called "green-houses," though the name was certainly a misnomer.

"Nobody travelling. Times very dull." Mr. Charles did not like it when nobody was travelling. No one liked better than he to see folks drop in. He counted that day lost whose low-descending sun had not shone on some begging or borrowing Frenchman, some strolling peddler, or some neighbor, even if he might write a sarcastic sentence about them in his diary that evening. He loved to talk to everyone, getting all the local news. You always heard all the current gossip at "Charles's." They were not malicious. But they never read books or papers and their only amusement was their interest in the doings of their small world. They had a spy-glass in the house and it was invariably trained on everybody who walked or drove down the road. I never went down that road in daytime without feeling that spy glass focused on the small of my back. It was a local joke.

Mr. Charles buys "a load of seaweed" from a certain Toph Pinneau—"Toph" being short for Theophilus. In the autumns of those days everyone had to haul or buy seaweed to "bank the house for the winter." It was a November job. The whole house was encircled by a girdle of sea-weed, held in by stakes and "longers." The more seaweed you could command the higher and wider your "banking." I remember Uncle John Montgomery up at Princetown used to have the house banked to the windowsills. It certainly made it warm for the winter. I don't really know if they bank with seaweed on the Island now or not. A great many people "bank" now with sods or clay—as the unfortunates of forty years ago who lived too far inland to get seaweed had to do them.

"Took the sleighs out of stable, box and wood."

There were three classes of "sleighs" in common use in those days. The "jaunting sleigh"—the name "cutter" was never heard then—which was used for light travelling and always by canoodling couples. The "box sleigh"—or "pung" as it later came to be called. A rather comfortable affair which might have a seat in front or might have no seat at all. In that case it was filled with straw, covered with a buffalo or rug. You all hopped in and squatted down— half a dozen of you. I've had more fun in those old "box sleighs" than in any other form of conveyance—especially on moonlit winter nights on the road to some party or "meeting," when everyone in the sleigh was under twenty. The "wood" sleigh—so called because used for hauling wood, was merely a low frame on runners, sometimes with a loose board or two laid on it, with stakes at the four corners connected by chains. When the sleigh was empty the driver rode standing and it must have been quite an art to balance yourself. There were also "mud" sleighs—wood sleighs with huge wooden boxes very deep, on them, used for hauling home the loads of mud which were dug from the oyster beds in winter. Later on "toboggans" became very fashionable—not quite so "classy" as jaunting sleighs but much "classier" than the box and much affect-

ed by young lads who could not aspire to a jaunting sleigh but wanted some vehicle to drive their lady friends about in. At Charles', Alec drove the jaunting sleigh, Russell drove the toboggan and the old folks were generally contented with the homely reliable "box."

In winter days Mr. Charles spent much time in the woods cutting firewood. They never burned anything but wood. The woodpile was always to the left of the kitchen door. In the tiny kitchen was an old Waterloo Stove. When Pensie and I came in from coasting or sliding with cold toes we sat before it and warmed them on the hot hearth. Sometimes we roasted corn cobs over the glowing coals. That little house was plain and homely but it was snug and warm. The "sitting room" and parlor were heated by stoves with doors that slid open revealing the glowing flames within. They were quite as beautiful and companionable as fire places. Off the parlor was the "spare bedroom." The tiniest place. Behind the door the bed filled up the whole side of the room. The bureau was in the corner opposite the door. There was one window looking out under the big willows into the garden. Many a night Pensie and I spent in that cosy bed, talking over our girlish secrets. And I have one sweet memory that seems to stand out more clearly than all the others. To this day it gives me the most delightful feeling whenever I recall it.

It was a cold winter night and good "Mrs. Charles" had come in with her candle to see if we were warm enough before she went to bed. Pensie was asleep but I was not, though I pretended to be, curled down among my pillows with closed eyes. Mrs. Charles bent over us. "Dear little children," she said gently and tenderly.

That was all. Mrs. Charles has been for many years in her grave. She was a very illiterate, simple-minded woman from whose lips no pearls of wisdom or jewels of inspiration ever dropped. But I have forgotten most of the wisdom and culture I have listened to; and I shall never forget those three simple words of love. I came from a household where affection was never expressed in words. Stern Grandfather, reserved Grandmother would never have said to me "dear little child" even had they felt it. And I loved such expression—I craved it. I have never forgotten it.

Poor Mrs. Charles never got over Pensie's death. Pensie was the only one of her family who had died. Whenever she saw me afterwards she would talk to me by the hour about her—"because you and her were such friends." She and Pensie are together now—if indeed "there be a land of souls beyond that sable shore."[469] And, if there be, I hope Mrs. Charles will come to me there, with Pensie, and look lovingly at us and say "dear little children" in just the same tone she said it that winter night of long ago. Oh, people should say things

---

469   From Byron's *Childe Harold's Pilgrimmage*, Canto II, stanza 8.

like that to children—little speeches of love and tenderness. They are more precious than rubies to small souls.

Mr. Charles never expressed his affection—if he felt any. One would never guess from his entry, "Ren Toombs' child died to-day,"[470] that the said child of the said Ren Toombs was his own grandson. This curious indifference runs through all his entries regarding his family. Perhaps it was only because he "being Scotch" could not put his feelings into words, especially cold-blooded written words. But somehow I do not think he was very deeply attached to anyone even his own children, despite his hospitality and kindness. Whenever "ma" went away for a day or two he wrote nasty little slurs in his diary about her. He seemed to resent her absences, instead of being glad that the poor soul had those few brief and seldom releases from the monotony of her busy days. But perhaps I am unjust to him in this. It maybe that these little spiteful entries of his concerning poor "ma's" little holidays were merely the result of his loneliness when she was away. Perhaps he missed her so much that he resented the pain and transferred his resentment unconsciously to her. He would never admit, not even to himself, that he missed her unbearably but his discomfort had to have this queer distorted outlet. Believing this I can laugh over the entry, "Ma not home yet. Nearly as crazy as the Toombs." And a day or so later, "She'd better stay with the Toombs altogether."

Minnie's baby—her first-born—had died and her mother was staying a few days with her to help and comfort her. I fear we can't exonerate Mr. Charles completely from the charge of selfishness!

And he was always very satirical about his boy's little outings. He had an odd habit of writing that they had "gone on a mission" to the Scotch or "the American Jews" when they took some of their lady friends driving. Those boys were all steady hard-working fellows whose liveliest dissipation was a concert or pie-social. But Mr. Charles always waxed sarcastic when they had driven off and he sat him down to write in his little diary. I suppose they did run around a good deal. After working hard all day they wanted a little amusement and as they cared nothing for books had to seek it elsewhere. But it is killing to read all the "old man's" biting sentences about their gadding!

His three sons and his three daughters all married and "settled down" near to him. None of them ever seemed to have any desire to go afield—except Robbie. "Rob" was the second oldest boy; and he went clear across the continent to the Pacific coast and settled on a farm in the state of Washington. He was never home but twice afterwards. I do not think he has done any better or is any better off than if he had stuck to the old Island. Rob was more like his father than any of the others—which was probably why he could not get on as

---

470   Lorenzo Toombs was a Cavendish neighbour.

well with him. At all events, he left home because, he said, he could not "get a square deal."

"Took a load of wood to Alexander M. Macneill's."[471] Mr. Chas. brought us up a load of wood every winter in return for sundry bags and baskets of apples in autumn days. But the peculiarity of this entry is that Grandfather was Charles' uncle and one wonders why he did not write "Uncle Alexander" as he always called him. Did he feel that it would be tempting who knew what principalities and powers if he wrote too familiarly of his relatives?

Mr. Charles had his share of the Macneill jealousy. He did not like to think that any of his circle was doing better or even quite as well as he himself was. Not even when it was his own son-in-law. This is why, when he writes that Oliver Bernard was "hauling mud" he adds dryly, "Expects to be rich soon."

Of course Oliver Bernard *was* a terrible "blow" and none of his wife's family ever liked him. They were not at all well pleased when Lily married him, though he was a steady fellow with a comfortable home. They just didn't "like" him, that was all and they never did like him. But that didn't justify a "poison mean" trick that Albert played on him once when he was courting Lily. It was Henry MacLure told me this. One night he went home with Albert from some revelry and stayed all night with him. It was late—about twelve o'clock. Everyone was in bed except Lily who was "sitting up" with Oliver B. in the parlor. Albert inferred this because a brand-new overcoat of Oliver's was hanging on the sitting room wall. Albert went into the pantry, brought out a big bowl full of beets in vinegar and poured the whole mess into one of the pockets of the overcoat!

What was the sequel, if any, I never heard. Probably Oliver swallowed the insult for love's sweet sake. Anyhow, nothing redder than the beet vinegar flowed because of it. Yet dynasties have fallen for less.

Mr. Charles liked a sly slap at a minister now and then. One entry reads, "Mr. George was here to-day. He talked politics most of the time he was here. Did not say anything about religion or the one thing needful."

Mr. George was the minister who "supplied" Cavendish the winter after Mr. Archibald went away. As for Mr. Charles, he was by no means the spiritual person one might suspect from that entry. Religion to him meant going to church on Sundays and paying so much to the minister's salary. If Mr. George had talked religion to him he would have been the most uncomfortable man alive. I fancy Mr. George's complexion in politics did not commend itself to Mr. Charles!

Some of Mr. Charles' entries regarding "pigs" and "sows" are amusingly naive. Mr. Charles generally kept what was alluded to in a hushed voice—among

---

471   That is, Alexander Marquis Macneill (1820–98), LMM's grandfather.

women folk at least—as a "boar." This involved various mysterious visits from neighbors and Mr. Charles has them all marked down in his diary. Probably his reason was to keep track of such services until the fees were paid but they make rather comical entries, cheek by jowl with his hints about religion and his Sunday texts!

Mr. Chas. had his own private nicknames for people. Who "Long 5 axe handles" was I have no earthly idea but I strongly suspect that "Johnny Big-eyes" was Uncle John F.

"Too much bushel for a small canoe" was an old Indian proverb. I had heard it in my childhood but had forgotten it until it popped up again in the diary. Very expressive I think. Today we say "he bit off more than he can chew" but I like the Indian version better. I think the entry he makes regarding Russell, "too big for his pants," was of native manufacture. Certainly Mr. Chas. does not in this diary appear to be an overfond or over-proud parent.

"Hauling dulse" brings a whiff of salt air from the gulf. Two kinds of things were called "dulse." One was the long semi-transparent ribbons of real dulse which were regarded as quite a dainty. We picked them up on the shore, wet and glistening and ate them. Many people really liked them. I only pretended to.

The other dulse was the heaps of sea-plants that piled up on the shore after certain storms—mostly I think from the east. It was composed of real dulse, kelp—how pretty some forms of kelp were, especially the long strips that looked like shirred brown silk ribbon—Irish moss and all kinds of sea-weeds, and was an excellent fertilizer. When the word came that dulse was "in" every farmer whose land ran out to the gulf hurried to the shore with carts and hauled industriously.

Very delicious blanc-mange could be made from the Irish Moss—which was a pretty feathery thing when it was fresh and wet ranging through all colors—green, brown, pink, cream. Another variety of sea-weed bore bunches of little bladder-like fruit which burst with a report when you squeezed them. And there was a kelp like a long brown sea-snake.

An April entry, "Ice on shore," brings me back to the gulf. Springs in Cavendish were late or early according to the time the ice "went out." All winter the gulf was white with ice. But when spring winds began to blow a blue rift appeared here and there; and some fine day with a strong wind from the south away it all went. As long as the ice was "on shore" the weather would be cold and the green of field and woods reluctant to appear. Sometimes after the ice had been gone for two or three weeks we would see an odd, white streak far out on the northern horizon and say with a shiver, "The ice is coming back." Sometimes it would come clean into the shore again. And when it did it generally brought seals with it and the farmers would chase and capture them. The

skin of that kind of seal was of no value but enormous quantities of oil could be obtained from the carcass and a farmer was lucky if he captured a seal or two. I recall a particularly huge one Grandfather caught. Its white and gray hide was nailed to the side of the barn to dry and I always see it when I hear the expression, "There'll be hides on the barn-door."

When Mr. Charles wished to express neighborly kindness in any way he "said it with wood." When anyone was sick Mr. Charles took them a load of wood. When anyone died Mr. Chas. sent them a load of wood. Well, a load of Mr. Charles' good hardwood was not a bad thing to have on hand—especially when much cooking had to be done for a funeral! It would really be of much more use than an anchor of roses or a pillow of white hyacinths.

He frequently uses the word "chores." I think they were the only family in Cavendish that used that word. Everywhere else the expression was "turns." It was only after some of the girls who had gone to Boston to work came back with new words that "chores" came into general circulation. The older folks did not adopt it, except Mr. Charles. No "Yankeeisms" for them. Grandfather and his contemporaries "did the turns" to the day of their deaths.

One Saturday Mr. Chas. cuts wood "for Sunday." Of course this was always done. One might cook a big dinner on Sunday and have half one's friendly circle in to help eat it but it was an unpardonable sin to cut wood on "The Lord's day." I remember a clan story that was always being told of Grandfather Montgomery. He was the soul of hospitality and always had a houseful of guests on Sunday. One Sunday an appalling discovery was made. By some oversight the wood had not been chopped on Saturday. There was no wood to cook the dinner. Grandfather rose to the occasion. "Boys," he said quietly to my father and Uncle Jim, "go out and *break a little with the back of the axe*"!!!

I don't know who the "two she-weasels" were who were around asking for money to buy the minister a fur coat! Either Mr. Charles did not like parting with his hard earned dollars to buy fur coats for ministers or—as was more likely—he did not like the ladies themselves. But he would be very agreeable to their faces, for all that and would send them on their way rejoicing. Then he would relieve his feelings and escape a complex by calling them she-weasels in his diary! Perhaps he was in a bad humor that day. Next day or so two other ladies arrived collecting money for a present to the school teacher. Mr. Charles let them off with "beggars." Somehow, "beggars" sounds very savorless after "she weasels."

One naive little entry amused me. "Letty was here to-day. She is very smart. Gave her ten cents for Christmas." Letty was his little granddaughter, then about two or three years old. "Ten cents" does not seem a very lavish Christmas gift. But I recall that when I was a small girl ten cents seemed a quite munificent sum indeed. In fact, as far as actual money goes it was worth as

much as thirty or forty today, and to have a whole "ten cent piece"—one never heard of dimes in those days—to spend and no questions asked was wealth.

Mr. Charles gives poor Aunt Ann Maria a fearful slam in one of his entries. She has "got a new fur coat and if she could get a new set of brains might do very well for a while."

Well, brains were certainly not poor Aunt Ann Maria's long suit. She had absolutely none. But she was a splendid cook, and a gracious hostess, and had it not been for the basic flaw in her character, incurable deceit, she would have been an admirable and lovable woman despite her lack of intellectual brilliancy.

Mr. Charles occasionally uses the word "calie"—the Gaelic word for a visit or friendly call. Mr. Spurr, the Baptist minister,[472] introduced this word into Cavendish. When he came over from Nova Scotia he brought it with him and it soon became quite at home in our vocabulary. "Off on a calie" or "gone calie-ing" is a common expression there to this day. Of course that is not the right way to spell it. I like the word myself. It has a pleasant, homely, friendly sound to me—perhaps because I heard it so often on the lips of old friends who sleep in Cavendish churchyard—Mr. Charles among them. It brings to mind many a delightful autumn or winter afternoon when I took my fancy work and "went on a calie" to the home of some girl friend. "Calies" were sociable things.

Mr. Chas. faithfully records all the bushels of grain sown each spring and harvested in the fall. Of course this sowing was done by the seeder then and for many years before. But I well remember the years before the "seeder" came into its own. When I was very small there were no "seeders." All the grain was sown by hand. I can recall very vividly seeing Grandfather striding across the red fields scattering seed from a particular kind of basket slung from a rope around neck and shoulder. There were people I believe who had the knack of "sowing with both hands" but I never saw any of them at work. Such gifted individuals could of course sow a field in just half the time required by the others.

One spring day Mr. Chas. "ploughed the little field." Well do I know that "little field." It was on the left hand as one entered the gate, filling up the space between the road and the barns. As the barns were slightly higher the drainage from stables and manure sheds seeped down into that field making it "rich beyond the dreams of avarice" as far as soil went. Consequently its crop was always a bumper one, grain growing there higher than a man's head. Mr.

---

472   Rev. Spurr was the adoptive father of LMM's childhood friend, Nate Lockhart. Nate's father, Nathan Joseph Lockhart, was a sailor who had died at sea shortly before his son was born. Nate's mother Nancy remarried a Baptist minister, John Church Spurr, who eventually adopted Nate (even so, at some point Nate began to go by his father's name, Lockhart). The correct spelling of "calie"— that is, a Scottish country dance—is ceilidh.

Charles indulged the peculiar whim of building his barns and all other out-buildings between his house and the main road, so that all comers had to pass along his lane through a passage formed by the barns on the left and granary, greenhouse, pighouse and "boiler house" and hen house on the right. But nobody ever seemed to mind that when the friendly eye of the little white house beyond winked genial greeting. The real drawback was that the barns to some extent spoiled what would otherwise have been a glorious unhindered view of the gulf from the doorstep of the back door. And that was a pity, nice barns as they were. Very nice and very neat. Always beautifully whitewashed with red painted doors and windows. Mr. Charles had a passion for whitewashing. Every spring he whitewashed not only his house, well-house and outbuildings, but the fence posts down the lane. Nobody else in Cavendish ever went as far as that, though most people whitewashed their houses and barns, if they were not painted. When I came to Ontario the big gray, unpainted barns gave me at first a certain impression of shiftlessness. A P.E. Islander was considered "shiftless" if his barns were neither painted nor whitewashed. And I must say I do not think Ontario's gray barns add much to the beauty of her landscape or her farmsteads.

Certainly all through his diary Mr. Charles does not impress one as a man who was at all proud of his family, whether it was a Scotchman's affected humility or not. But one of his gloomy predictions at least did not come true: "The boys are not likely to make good farmers. Too much hurry sometimes." They all turned out excellent farmers, industrious and hard working and no one would ever accuse them of being in a hurry over anything.

"Pensie gone after Jacks to shear sheep" evokes a host of quaint old memories. The sheep-shearing was an annual event on Cavendish farms and was a mixture of interest and horror to us young fry. Large flocks of sheep were kept in those days and the evening gambols of the lambs around the fields were delightful to see. The "Jack girls"—"Old Margaret" and her niece Sarah—went around sheep shearing. They arrived on the morning of the eventful day carrying their shears and their "sheep shearing" clothes in a bundle. These they promptly put on—and very dirty, greasy, unpleasant garments they were. Shearing unwashed sheep was a dirty job—and in those days the sheep were never washed before shearing. The Jack "girls" were not noted for their beauty at any time and in those shearing togs they were good understudies for Macbeth's witches.

The sheep were driven into the sheep house and a shearing table was erected. Maggie, with fatal eye, selected and seized a sheep, swung it to the table, hobbled its legs and began shearing. Clip-clip went the skilled shears. The fleece fell away, so white and clean and silvery on its under side. The sheep emerged from it, an odd bare figure, scampering away in amazement at

her escape and transformation. I often wondered what a sheep thought about while she was being shorn. They generally lay very still. Was it the calm of despair? A "good" shearer never wounded the sheep. But sometimes with even the most expert the shears bit too deep and the sheep scampered away with a red stain on her flank. At the end of the day the shearers were paid at the rate of 4 cents a sheep. Not too much surely. I would not have sheared a sheep, even supposing I had been able to, for 4 dollars much less cents.

The "horror" of the day centred about the lambs. Those poor pretty frisky lambs who had never known pain. How my heart bled for them. Their tails were cut off that day. I was told it had to be and I suppose it had, though to this day I do not understand why it was necessary. Oh, those poor little bleeding lambs, running to their mothers to be comforted, bleating pitifully. The wounds seemed to heal quickly and next day the lambs would seem normal enough. But I don't think they ever scampered around the fields at sunset quite so light-heartedly again.

After the sheep shearing the wool-washing was a day's work. It was always done outside. A fire was kindled under the big potato boiler, the tubs were taken out and the wool washed and spread on the grass to dry. When dry it was bagged and carried away to the carding mill, whence it came back in those beautiful soft glossy rolls of floss. Grandma spun them on her little spinning wheel. She never used the large wheel. At Park Corner they spun in the garret. They had two large spinning wheels which are there to this day. Women like spinning. I think I would have liked it myself if I had ever had a chance to learn it. But grandma had given up spinning long before I grew up. Spinning went on at Park Corner till Aunt Annie's death. Stella and Frede were expert spinners.

Then came knitting and weaving. Very few people weave now on the Island but when I was a child many did. Amanda's mother always wove up in their garret. What a fascination it was to watch her. A great many people, however, hired "the Jacks" to do their weaving for them. As I recall it those Jacks were really very useful members of the community. They spun and wove and sheared sheep, planted and picked potatoes, bound sheaves, and plaited hats from the wheat straw. Somebody was always getting the Jacks to do something—there were three of them. "Old Jane," Old Margaret and Sarah, who was young then but is old now. Margaret died last year—nearly a hundred years old. But Jane died over twenty years ago. And they sent for me to take a picture of her in her coffin!!! It was a ghastly performance. The coffin had to be propped up almost on end before the window. The resulting picture, however, looked exactly like old Jane—who looked no weirder in her coffin than she did in life. What a craving the human heart has to keep some poor "counterfeit presentment" of its loved and lost. It is a little hard to conceive of anyone loving Jane Jack but

no doubt her sister and her parents did. Old Mr. Jack died before my recollection but I remember old Mrs. Jack, who was not at all a bad-looking old lady and must have been quite comely in her youth. She was always spinning at her little wheel with a white frilled cap around her face. How odd it would be to see an old lady nowadays with a cap! Yet I do not know that our old ladies have gained so much in giving up caps. They were quite becoming to lined faces and graying hair. And the caps for state occasions were very "dressy" and becoming. I remember (Step) Grandmother Montgomery was noted for her smart caps. When she went to an evening festivity she always carried her cap in a box with her. Old "Grandma Campbell"—Frede's grandmother—and Great Aunt Ellen always wore little hood-like caps of black net with a black ruching around the face. But these were thought old-fashioned by up-to-date old ladies who perched little confections of lace and ribbon on the top of their heads and called them "caps," much to the scorn of still older dames who condemned such new-fangled vagaries and predicted dire things of the state of society which permitted them. What would they have said if they could have seen the lady I saw in church last Sunday—sixty if she was a day and her white hair bobbed. And am I in my turn as antiquated as those scornful dames of long ago when I assert that I thought she looked very pitiful and ridiculous? The present mania for bobbed hair is becoming to young fresh faces. But I think it is very cruel to the faded and aged—and indeed to all who are past their first youth.

"Mercy me," as those ladies of the last century would have said. Where have I wandered to from Mr. Charles' sheep-pen? Let us get back to our muttons and see if "the Jacks" have finished his sheep. Yes, and been paid 88 cts. only, having shorn 22 sheep. Sweet be their slumbers.

(Step) Grandmother Montgomery

But on that very eve it "looks like rain" and Mr. C. predicts the "sheep storm." Evidently it did not come just then but come it certainly would. The "sheep storm" never missed. It had nothing to do with the sheep but it was a June storm, invariably coming soon after the sheep were shorn. The wind would set in from the northeast, bitterly cold and blow hard from that direction for two and sometimes three days, with driving stinging rain. The unlucky sheep, their warm coats reft away, would feel it bitterly. Hence the name. I am afraid I did not sympathize properly with the poor animals for I always liked the sheep storm. There was such a bite and tang to it. I would like to see a sheep storm again. They never come in Ontario.

On Wednesday, July 13, 1898, there is a curious entry about a wedding. There is not a word in it to indicate that it was his own daughter Pensie's wedding. Mr. Charles was evidently very inarticulate when it came to the great changes of life.

I remember that I felt very sore over that wedding. Pensie and I had been intimate friends all our lives. But she never even told me she was going to be married. Everybody knew it for her dressmaker had given the secret away. Two or three days before her wedding day she came up for the mail and as usual I "went a piece" home with her. But she might have been a hundred years away from getting married for anything she said. Two days afterward she was married, having only two or three of her cousins on the spindle side[473] in to see her.

I was deeply hurt—and the hurt remained for a long time. I think I was justified in feeling hurt. It was a strange way for Pensie to behave. But the pain has long vanished and I can make excuses for Pensie now which I was too sore to make then. She had some of her father's odd streaks in her and one of them was an inability to tell or talk of any such matter—just as the very entry in his diary about her wedding shows. I did not understand this then and I resented Pensie's silence for a long time. I went to see her once in her new home; but New Glasgow was seven miles away and it was not easy for me to get over. I suppose I did not try very hard, after her strange behavior. But I am glad to think that in the year before her death we met oftener and the old friendship put forth an autumnal blossom again. The old bitterness had worn itself out. The last time I saw Pensie was one winter evening. I went over and spent the whole evening with her. She was in bed but did not know her condition was so serious and hoped to recover. I knew better and under my outward gayety I felt very sad. We had one of our old evenings of chat and gossip and jokes. She died very soon afterwards. She has been dead nearly twenty years. But while I have been writing this she has been alive. I have heard her laughter, seen the flash of her blue eyes, the toss of her auburn curls. She is gone—and Mr. and Mrs. Charles have gone—and the old Cavendish has gone. But it lives again in Mr. Charles' old diary and I am loth to cease writing of it. It has been a refuge—an escape from the bitter, worried present; I hate to leave it and come back to 1925! For life now is a bitter harassed thing for me, always in bondage to a great dread; and there are times when I envy Pensie, asleep in her unmarked grave on the New Glasgow hillside. "The one shall be taken and the other left."[474]

---

473   That is, on the female side.

474   Matthew 24:40: "Then shall two be in the field; the one shall be taken, and the other left."

Monday, Mar. 2, 1925
The Manse, Leaskdale

Elsie and I worked hard all this cold, blustery day, preparing for the big annual missionary "Rally Day" tea here tomorrow. I have rather dreaded it with a new maid but I think we have got everything pretty well in hand. By night I was very tired but I had to brace up, as we had play practice here tonight. I was a nervous wreck when it was over—and so discouraged. They don't begin to know their parts even yet and what with drilling, prompting, and reading absentee parts I felt exhausted when they left at 11.30, leaving a house all torn-up which had to be put in order before I could go to bed. It is now 12.30 and I have that big day ahead of me tomorrow.

Tuesday, Mar. 3, 1925

Thanks be, it's over. And well over, too. Elsie did very well in spite of inexperience. We worked all the forenoon getting things in readiness. A blue letter to Ewan from Scott of Cannington,[475] bewailing the loss of fifteen Unionists who had left his church in a body and gone over to the Methodists, owing to the interference of outside Unionists, contributed the accustomed note of worry and depression to the day but I had no time to think of it when the women began to come. We had forty here and served three tables. When they were finally gone, the dishes washed and put away, I thought I might have an evening's rest. But I am one of those in whose stars no rest is written. I found old Miss Lindsay on my hands for the night—a wandering old maid of endless tongue who had missed her chance to her interim home and had to stay all night. She talked incessantly until bedtime and I tried to sit quiet and listen. But at moments it seemed to me that I *must* break loose—and run to the end of the world to escape this horrible existence.

I never felt more utterly weary and hopeless in my life than I do tonight. I am like a creature caught in a trap. I cannot get out and somebody is always poking sticks at me through the bars.

Thursday, Mar. 5, 1925

Tuesday night I had to take veronal in order to get a little sleep. So I obtained a few blessed hours of forgetfulness. I spent yesterday morning cleaning the house up. Mail came. A letter from Rollins. No doubt the long-deferred

---

475   A community some 30 km/18 miles northeast of Leaskdale.

judgment of the Appeal Court.[476] But I dared not open it for I had to go to Zephyr to attend the prayer service of the W.M.S. there and I dared not risk being upset by it.

To Zephyr I went. The service, owing to the Union situation was a period of mixed sensation for me. But outwardly everything went off very well, though I had, as I always have in Zephyr and never anywhere else, the feeling that everyone was looking at me through a microscope.

We had to stay over for the evening for a presentation to some people that are leaving Zephyr, and got home at twelve, played out as usual. However, I had a good sleep and felt better this morning though very tired and fibreless. It would take a score of good sleeps to put me on my feet. And one cannot sleep well if one is always afraid of tomorrow.

As soon as Elsie and Ewan got off to Uxbridge and I was alone I opened Rollins' letter:—

> The Supreme Court has just handed down its decision in your case against the Page Co. The opinion is by the Chief Justice himself and uses up ten typewritten pages. He says there is no ambiguity about the contract and that it did not give the defendant the right to publish its 1912 copies; furthermore, that having used the wrong material the defendant should account for profits. The defendant's exceptions were overruled. In other words you are completely successful.

I had a half hour of exhilaration after this but I am too thoroughly depressed for it to last long and soon slumped again. Page and French will only hatch up some new devilry to prolong the agony. It will never be ended. I felt terribly tired all day. Ewan came home with some new Union gossip that was worrisome and spoiled our evening.

Ewan is not so well again. Just as I expected after his being so well last week. Yet he is not and has not been nearly so bad as he was this time last year. If only March were over! It was in March he was so bad last year. If he gets through March without a really bad attack I will have a little hope and that will help me along, even though I don't have any *real* confidence in hope now. It has proved illusory too often.

Friday, March 6
The Manse, Leaskdale

I had only a fair sleep last night because Ewan did not sleep any too well. He has seemed dull and "heady" all day and I am cold with dread. But I am not

---

476   That is, the Massachusetts Supreme Court, giving a finding in LMM's lawsuit against Page for the publication of *Further Chronicles of Avonlea* in 1920.

so neurasthenic as I was last week. I am able again to lose myself in work or in a book and forget my worries to a certain extent. This gives my nerves a chance to heal up.

I read tonight in a delightful book of astronomy by Camille Flammarion.[477] He is a poet as well as a scientist and his book is charming. As I roamed with him among the stars I felt that, after all, Zephyr is not the universe.

But a pea held close to your eye can blot out the sun! And a grain of dust *in* your eye can make you temporarily oblivious to the Milky Way and the Orion nebula.

Never mind! If Ewan only keeps fairly well I shall not succumb to worry over the Union question. It is only its possible effect on him that worries me.

Oh, I am so tired—tired—tired! I was out this evening to see the trousseau of a bride who is to be married Wednesday. As I looked at her pretty things and her radiant face I wondered if I had ever been so hopeful and happy. It seems so long since I dared to feel hope about anything.

Her mother said to me, "I hope Mary's married life will be as happy as mine has been," and I found myself looking at the woman with a sort of wondering awe. She is a stupid, narrow-minded, selfish woman. Yet she has been happy! Why should she have had a happy life and I such a miserable one? These past six years with their nightmare dreads and horrors and sorrows have seemed to spread their blackness all over life, past and future. They have made me superstitious. I feel that I must be one doomed by fate to misery. That it is useless to hope that I will ever be free from it—that all the rest of my existence must be one of worry and humiliation and disappointment. Ashes for meat, wormwood for drink.[478] One can struggle on when there is a little hope of escape *sometime*. But when there seems to be none—when every year adds new worries and bitterness and strips away some little thing that helped to make existence bearable, it is very difficult to endure.

Tuesday, Mar. 10, 1925
The Manse, Leaskdale

I have been feeling better of late. The weather has been mild and springlike and has had a good effect on me. I have finished revising *The Blue Castle* and have it ready to be typed. I am sorry it is done. It has been for several months a daily escape from a world of intolerable realities.

Ewan came home from Presbytery tonight feeling very unhappy. The way the Unionist ministers have acted has been terrible. The rankest injustice

477   French astronomer and writer Camille Flammarion (1842–1925) wrote more than 50 books in his career, on topics as varied as popular science, astronomy, science fiction, and psychic research.
478   Probably quotations remembered from the Book of Lamentations.

and underhanded devilry has been practised. Several of them have lost their congregations by reason of the latter voting to remain Presbyterian, and seem determined to destroy what they cannot carry with them. The United Church will be fortunate in her men. But where in all this is there any spirit of the Master they profess to follow? Thank God, they will be out of the Presbytery after June 10. But meanwhile old friendships are torn asunder and bitter heart burning, and resentment substituted.

Mr. Macdonald of Wick,[479] who for six years has been a fast friend of ours is an enemy now because he has taken it into his head that Ewan tampered with the Anti-Unionists in his congregation—something Ewan never dreamed of doing. Indeed, when some of them came to Ewan to ask his advice in regard to taking the matter into the courts Ewan tried to dissuade them. But I understand they are going to do it. Wick voted in by a majority of two because Mr. Macdonald would not let several people vote who had an indisputable right to vote. He simply removed their names from the communion roll without any authority whatever. I am amazed that Mr. Macdonald could stoop to such a dirty piece of work. The bitterness in Wick is dreadful. It was one of the nicest rural congregations in Ontario and now it is ruined whichever church finally gets it. And that is the story everywhere.

Sunday, March 15, 1925
The Manse, Leaskdale

Things have been going on as usual—hard work, much driving about on bad roads—bitter cold after a false promise of spring, great tribulation drilling the play-actors, many unsettling "Union" rumors, a few minutes escape into a fascinating volume, *History of Religion*[480]—ice-storms—Mission Bands—fairly good royalty report from Mac—a bit of encouragement in that Ewan seems very well again and preached today as he has not done for a long time.

And another letter from Rollins. To wit:—

I enclose a copy of letter from the Chief Justice to Mr. French who, apparently, wrote the court that they had made a serious mistake. Mr. French did not send me a copy of his letter to the court so I do not know what the alleged mistake was. But he told me some time ago that he thought the Court had not apprehended the distinction between a character *appearing* in a book and being *mentioned* in a book. etc.

The letter from the Chief Justice to Mr. French was as follows:—

479　Another minister at a local village some 11 km/7 miles east of Leaskdale.
480　*History of Religion: A Sketch of Primitive Religious Beliefs and Practices* ... by Allan Menzies (1845–1916). The first edition appeared in 1895, the fourth in 1911.

Dear Sir:—

Your letter of March 6 respecting opinion in Macdonald V. Page Co. has been received and given careful attention by all the justices sitting in the case. The opinion does not rest upon any mistake of material fact. No change is made in the opinion. Treating your letter as a motion for re-argument, it has been considered by the full court and is denied.

Mr. French is surely the gallant leader of forlorn hopes.[481]

It is idle to wish the end of this will come. It is endless. One must just endure. But I *can* endure only if Ewan keeps well.

Wednesday, March 11, 1925

This morning I tried to write a little again and succeeded. To my joy, I was able to *lose myself* again in my writing and forget reality. As long as I sat there writing I knew that though my body might dwell amid these distractions of time my spirit inhabited Eternity. This cheered me up a little. I have had a horrible feeling lately that I would never be able to write again.

But the rest of the day I felt very flat and toneless. I went to Mary Oxtoby's wedding[482] and seemed like a weary ghost among mundane revellers.

In the evening I went to play practice but not a quarter of the cast was there. The rest had gone to the station to see the wedding party off. The remainder might as well have gone for all the good they did. They could talk of nothing but the wedding and the practice was a farce.

Thursday, Mar. 12, 1925
The Manse, Leaskdale

The *Guardian* brought today the news that Zion Church, Ch'town, had voted Presbyterian. This was welcome news as we had been much afraid we would lose it. Both the Charlottetown churches have voted out now. Montague, where the Stirlings are, voted in, after a very bitter fight, by a majority of one. Margaret has owed me a letter since last November. I suppose she has been too upset and worried about the Union affair to write letters. She always disliked the thought of Union but of course John was an ardent Unionist and Margaret would have to go with him.

We went to tea at Jake Myers in Zephyr tonight and then to a prayer-meeting.

---

481   "Forlorn hope" is an expression of Dutch origin; it describes a band of soldiers who take part in a doomed military campaign.

482   LMM and Ewan Macdonald had boarded with Mary and Lizzie Oxtoby when they first arrived in Leaskdale. In her long retrospective entry of September 24, 1911, LMM described the Oxtoby sisters as characters "who would have delighted Dickens."

Zephyr air had its usual effect on me and I came home worn out and dispirited.

Sunday, Mar. 15, 1925

Yesterday a letter came from Rollins but as I had a busy day on with Mission Band in the afternoon and play practice at night I didn't open it till this afternoon when Ewan had left for Zephyr. It was unimportant—merely a copy of the appeal court's reply to Mr. French's request for re-argument.

I had a pleasant afternoon, copying Charles Macneill's old diary and living in the past, followed by a rarely restful evening reading in the parlor. I have not enjoyed such an evening for a long time. Ewan seems very well again so I dare to hope that he is not going to have a dreadful attack this March. He preached unusually well this morning I thought.

Monday, Mar. 16, 1925

We went to Uxbridge in a buggy today. The snow has gone very early this year. This evening came the welcome news that Quaker Hill congregation had voted out 48 to 26. This is fine. We had felt very doubtful about it for old George Allan Smith is one of the elders there and has "run" it all his life to suit himself. He has worked tooth and nail for Union so that if the Presbyterians won at all they hoped only for a bare majority. But 48 to 26 is a fine result and Quaker Hill is safe. The question now is—what will George Allan and his five married sons do? Will they leave? Or will they stay? Ewan thinks they will stay because they have always been much attached to Quaker Hill church. But if I know old George Allan, they won't. *He* won't anyhow. He will be furious because Quaker Hill went against HIS opinions. Two of his sons have always been opposed to Union but voted for it at his behest. It seems, although he bought each of them a farm, he has not given any of them the title and so all have to do just as he says. And if all the Smiths go Union Mrs. Will Sellers will, too. *This* is the consideration which makes the Smith decision of painful interest to us.

Wednesday, Mar. 18, 1925
The Manse, Leaskdale

This was a Zephyr day which means I am a discouraged creature tonight. I went over to a meeting of the Zephyr Women's Institute this afternoon, having promised to read a paper. Of course, it is undenominational but I felt surrounded and inhibited by Methodists who are very "sore" at Ewan and me because we haven't "gone in" with them. No matter what I say they make me feel it is the wrong thing.

And the Unionists poisoned the atmosphere worse than the Methodists. I *sensed* their resentment like a tangible thing. *And*, that nothing might be lacking, that sister of Satan, Mrs. Marshall Pickering, and her three daughters, were there.

But did I wilt in this air? Not I. I "hilt up my head" and kept my flag flying. Chatted pleasantly and composedly with everyone—except the aforesaid P's. Read my paper coolly and impressively. And wished myself a thousand miles away.

But I had one inward snicker of genuine amusement. The Roll Call was to be answered by the name of "a famous Canadian woman." When Mrs. Julius Rynard's name was called she promptly answered with "L.M. Montgomery." Mrs. J.R. is a Methodist but rumor has it that there is no love lost between her and Mrs. Marshall P. And I firmly believe she answered with my name to annoy that amiable lady. If such was her friendly idea she succeeded admirably for the Pickering countenance was exceeding grim.

After the Institute I was in at Rob Shier's for a few minutes and Mrs. Weldon was there with some more depressing Union gossip. I came home blue over bad, rough, icy roads and went to Guild. Very few were out and it was flat. I came home flatter.

Thursday, Mar. 19, 1925

A bad day. Last night there came an awful storm of rain with a wind that was bound to get inside. It clawed at the windows, shrieked at the eaves, and rattled and banged at the shutters the whole night. I could not sleep. Took an attack of cystitis and was more miserable. Towards morning fell into a very brief nap and had a horrible dream of Luck coming home with his tail cut off! Got up feeling useless and felt so all day. Ewan was rather dull and heady, too.

In the evening we had to go over awful roads to a to a wedding reception on the fifth. It was a dull affair for us and we had a wretched drive home in the pitch black night, especially through a long swamp where the road was half under water and so narrow that when we met a couple of buggies we had a serious time getting by. Luckily I had my flashlight or we should all have gone into the ditch.

Saturday, Mar. 21, 1925
The Manse, Leaskdale

Two nasty days. Much bothered with cystitis. I am so dull and lifeless I cannot feel pleasure or interest in anything.

[Lucky]

Sunday, Mar. 22, 1925

I always dread Ewan's return from Zephyr whenever he goes there. Nearly always there is some bit of news to depress us. Today was really bad. John Lockies are going to "go Union" and likely John Lowries, too. I feel very badly over this. Mrs. John Lockie was a great help in our church. John was a good giver, though no help in any other way. And they had children who would soon be of help in the Sunday School. They were against Union until very lately and no one knows why they turned. But I think I have a pretty good idea. In the voting for two new elders which was held a few months ago John Lockie was *not* voted for. He really did nothing for the church except pay pretty well. There were two Lockies already on the session and the congregation would not stand for any more. The Lockie men are detested in Zephyr. William Weldon and Will Sellars were elected—and wouldn't accept the eldership because they felt they couldn't get on with the Lockies. But I've *felt* ever since that John Lockie was secretly very sore because he wasn't in and Weldon was. I am quite certain this is at the bottom of his change of coat.

There is not *one* of those Zephyr people who are going into the Unionist church from a proper motive. Not *one* is going in because he sincerely thinks it is the right and Christian thing to do. If there were I would respect him at least. But we know the motives that are prompting them. John Lockie says he is going because it is "too much of a financial struggle" to keep up the Presbyterian church. Will Lockie is going "because he isn't going to be connected with a dwindling church." Old Armstrong is going because of the financial struggle too. Mrs. Will Rynard has always wanted Union "because the Methodists have a nicer church and a bigger Sunday School." If Will Sellers goes he will go because he is under his wife's thumb and she will go because her father tells her to. And so on. Well, from one point of view, it is not much difference where such people go. But when we are striving to hold Zephyr for the sake of Leaskdale we feel badly over the situation. But my real worry is—how will it affect Ewan? If it did not aggravate or prolong his malady I should care very little if everybody in Zephyr went over to the Unionists.

Monday, Mar. 22, 1925

This has been a bad day. I could not sleep last night and all day I suffered from nervous restlessness without cessation. I have felt dreadfully morbid and cannot see a ray of hope anywhere. Ewan was dull and gloomy all day. The papers were full of the bitter battle which is being waged between Unionists and Anti-Unionists in the Legislature. There was nothing cheering anywhere and a letter from Mr. Rollins did not lighten the gloom. He thinks the N.Y. appeal will be argued in April and he says,

I assume that you want me to go ahead on the accounting for profits. I suppose that this will be contested as stubbornly as the rest of the litigation to date. No doubt the defendant will seek to charge against the book its proportionate share of travelling salesmen, income tax, rent and everything else they can think of, and what the result will be I do not profess to say. I sent you some time ago a letter with some excerpts, showing the uncertainty of the law, so that both the law and the facts are uncertain. I imagine the hearings before a master will consume from several to a good many days and that we shall have to have a public stenographer—with whose schedule of charges you are already familiar.

I am not setting out all of these things to throw any cold water but in order to give you as fair a picture of what is probably or possibly ahead of you as I can.

I fancy I see a rift developing between "the gallant leader of forlorn hopes" as you call him and his client.

I cannot understand Rollins altogether. Sometimes he writes quite cheerily and says I will "eventually see the end of the case etc." Then again he will send forth a note like this. It would almost sound as if he thought it wiser not to go ahead with the accounting. But what sense would there be in that after we have fought the case all this time and won. We might far better have dropped it years ago if we are not to have the accounting. Of course I don't expect to get any money out of it—never did. Profits are certainly there—a book does not sell 20,000 copies without some profits. But the Pages will continue some way to make it seem there are none. But I mean to *know*.

Rollins' reference to "the rift etc" arouses my curiosity. What can it mean? That Pages are dissatisfied with their lawyer? Very likely I shall never know more for it would be of no use to ask Rollins. He is too wary to commit his opinion to paper.

Play practice was to be here tonight. But for the first time in my life—as far as I can remember—I have flunked. I simply could not face the prospect of drilling and prompting from nine to twelve. So I have told Elsie to tell them to go ahead and practice in the parlor and I am going to bed.

Tuesday, Mar. 24, 1925
The Manse, Leaskdale

I went. I fell into a heavy sleep almost at once. I felt somewhat better this morning but unrest and morbidity returned at noon. I could not eat or work. Ewan seems very dull. He moans constantly in his sleep and lies around moodily in his waking hours.

I have a most terrible feeling of hopeless imprisonment. I have not felt like this since those miserable winters of 1909 and 1910. If I could get away by myself and have a good cry I think it would relieve me but that seems impossible. Elsie or the children or Ewan are round all the time. I have a horrible feeling that if it were not because I have to live for the children I would gladly die. I think the grave would be very sweet.

This has been one of the most dreadful days I've ever lived through.

Wednesday, Mar. 25, 1925

I slept well but my nerves are very sick still. Everything worries me. Trifles that ordinarily I would not give a second thought to harass me unbearably. I could cry bitterly over every little difficulty.

We took Dodgie out for the first today. This is the earliest we have ever used it. I shall be glad when we can go round freely with it again. Both of us will feel better then. Ewan continues very dull.

The Manse, Leaskdale, Ont.
Friday, March 27, 1925

I do not sleep. Some nights I fall asleep about three but waken at dawn and lie there in the grip of silly, senseless, gnat-like worries. We had a terrific thunder and lightning storm last night and heavy rain.

I forced myself to work all day but my nerves were sick. I feel as if there were no escape and never could be any escape from "the wheel of things." I never felt more unhappy and hopeless in my whole life than I did today. This is a real attack of neurasthenia and if I cannot soon recover from it I do not know what will become of me.

I would soon recover if only Ewan were well. It is the long-drawn out agony of the past six years and the biting dread of this winter that he would get as he did last March that has brought me to this. He was very miserable today. Lay around and chanted mournful hymns. His eyes stared into vacancy with a distraught look. Sometimes, watching that fixed, almost maniac glare, I could hardly keep myself from screaming aloud.

When, as now, I cannot work I realize how hideously lonely my life is. I have no friends here—no sympathy—no companionship. Nothing to divert my thoughts and give my nerves a chance to heal up. And I can't go away for a change. It would be impossible to leave Ewan as he is just now.

I suppose there is no use writing in this strain. But it helps a little. This journal seems like an understanding friend and to confess my worries in it is like talking them over with such a friend.

Saturday, March 28, 1925

I slept fairly well last night and felt fairly well all day. I was thankful for this as Elsie is laid up with grippe[483] and I had everything to do. I felt no nervous unrest until five when it returned and I was miserable all the evening.

Ewan came home from Uxbridge with the news that George Allan Smith will leave the Presbyterian church and this added to my depression.

We are feeling badly, too, over the way Mr. Macdonald of Wick is behaving to us. We feel we have not deserved it after our long friendship merely because we happen to think differently from him on the Union question.

Sunday, March 29, 1925

A perfectly hellish day in every way. It rained and snowed all day. Elsie is still laid up. Ewan has been very dull and repulsive all day. I went with him to Zephyr church and we made some sick calls afterwards. The roads were bad. I came home with a severe headache and the miserable forebodings of the neurasthenic. I can't see any chance of happiness or even of peace again. Nothing but worry and loneliness in the solitude of unshared thought. I can't help crying. Chester, too, had a bad headache today and this always worries me because Ewan's first attack of his malady came as recurrent headaches when he was Chester's age.

Monday, March 30, 1925

The most dreadful day yet. I could not sleep all night and today I literally could not do anything except a few necessary things which I painfully forced myself to do. Ewan was very dull and lay around.

I feel aghast over my condition. My hands tremble. I cannot eat. To add to the day's delight I had a wild letter from Stell worrying about Dan who has lost his job and is bitterly discontented and homesick. I feel as if I could not go on living. I am a soul in torture. I have lost all sense of proportion—trifles torment me as savagely as if they were great. The real cause of all this is my unceasing secret dread of Ewan getting like he was last winter.

My head aches violently tonight. I cannot shake off the tragedy of the Union mess not only around here but through the whole church. What a lack of statesmanship the "leaders" of the church have shown in thus wrecking it in their mad haste "drunk with sight of power."[484]

---

483   That is, influenza.

484   From Kipling's poem "Recessional" (1897); LMM also uses this expression on page 315.

Saturday, April 4, 1925
The Manse, Leaskdale

Last Tuesday I came down with flu and have been terribly bad with it. This is my first day up. I am as weak as a baby and of course the nervous depression that generally accompanies influenza has intensified my wretchedness. But I am thankful to be able to be up. To lie in bed, sick and helpless, and think of nothing but worries was very dreadful. Ewan has been canvassing Zephyr this week to try to find out who will leave and whom we can depend on. The results are not so hopeless. John Lowry will stay and something Mrs. Will Sellers said indicates they will, too, though she said they had not yet decided. It is well-known that Will himself does not want to go but she rules the roost there. Will Curls are going to leave. She was a Methodist. But they hardly ever came to church so it is only their small financial support that is lost.

The Legislature has awarded Knox College to the Presbyterian church.[485] This will be a bitter pill for the Unionists. Principal Gandier is, they say, frenzied about it. It serves him beautifully right. He thought he had a sort of divine right to Knox.

An item sent me today by a clipping bureau states that half a million copies of *Green Gables* have been sold, that the original plates are completely worn out and the publishers are having a new set made. This would please me if I could feel pleasure in anything.

Ewan has seemed a little better this week. Oh, for one *real* friend to come in and talk to me for a little while!

One thing I *am* thankful for is that Lily has not been here during these dreadful weeks. If I had to endure her tantrums, too!!!

Sunday, April 5, 1925

Last night Ewan came home with the upsetting news that Fred Walkers are going to leave. We had not expected this for they did not vote and her father is a strong opponent of Union. They are poor church goers but they pay a little and have two of the few children in Zephyr church. This upset me and I got no sleep. I felt so miserable I did not go out to church this morning. Couldn't eat and spent the day in an agony of nervousness. But Ewan came home from Zephyr with the better news that Julie Madill, though she voted for Union, has promised to stay with the church. This heartened me up a bit so that I was able to eat some supper. But I am very tired and weak.

---

485   Knox College was founded in 1844 as a theological college for the Presbyterian Church, originally located in downtown Toronto. In 1885 it became part of the University of Toronto. Alfred Gandier was Principal of the College from 1909 to 1925.

Monday, April 6, 1925

I had a good sleep last night and felt much better this morning. It was a nice bright sunny day, too. We motored down to Uxbridge in the afternoon and saw Marshall Pickering going into Grieg's law office. This significant conjunction of malign planets upset me again and I spent the rest of the day in agony. Not ameliorated by Miss Bowman, the teacher,[486] flying into Ewan publicly before several people about Chester's misbehavior in school. Miss B. has been a miserable failure as a teacher and cannot keep order at all. Chester, even according to her, has been guilty of nothing worse than talking in school when she had ordered him not to. Of course he should have obeyed. But it seems a small thing for her to make an insulting fuss about. She is the first teacher who had any trouble with Chester. He was one of Miss MacVicar's favorite pupils.

Ewan was in Zephyr tonight and came home with the good news that Maurice MacNelly will stay with us. Frank Walker said he would not decide till June 10. He is one of the people who hardly ever go to church and one of the kind who will stay if enough of the others stay and go if they don't. Their leaving will be no loss to the church except financially and at that they never gave much.

Tuesday, April 7, 1925
The Manse, Leaskdale

I took veronal last night and got some sleep but had a miserable morning of nervous unrest. I could shake myself for worrying so over these silly things but I cannot help it.

Ewan went to Zephyr. Saw Mrs. Jas. Lockie who raved insultingly about several things. I don't think that woman's mind is sound just at present. I believe she feels so mortified about her husband's behavior that she has to visit her humiliation on anybody who comes along.

Then he went to see Mrs. Warren who is the new treasurer of Zephyr. He asked her if any of the Pickerings had been trying to find out about the state of the salary. She said, no, so we feel a little easier. For it *is* behind now, of course, nearly $200 and if Pickering knew he could and would make trouble for us.

I am worried about Elsie, too. The child's appetite has been wretched since she had the flu. She is not strong, having been troubled for three years with what her doctor tells her is chronic appendicitis. There is certainly something wrong with her.

I certainly feel very lonely and dreary. But Ewan has been much better these last three days and that helps me. But there are so many nasty worrisome little things in life just now and *no* pleasant ones to offset them.

---

486   Miss Bowman was one of a series of one-year appointees to teach in the local school; she taught during the 1924–25 academic year.

Wednesday, April 8, 1925

I slept well and felt better all day. Finished reading proofs of *Emily Climbs*. Got one nasty little scare when a car stopped at the gate and a strange man came up the walk. I had a moment of sickening fear that it was some minion of Grieg's. But it was only a harmless agent.

We all went to an amateur play in Sandford tonight. It was very good and we laughed so much that it did us all good.

Thursday, April 9, 1925

Today seemed like an eternity and tomorrow will, I suppose, be just as bad. My mind goes around and around in a miserable circle and I get nowhere.

Early this morning before breakfast Mrs. Warren phoned over. I knew before she said a word that something was wrong or she would not be calling at that unearthly hour. She said she "wanted to see Mr. Macdonald about the matter they were discussing the other day"—i.e. the Pickering affair. I could eat no breakfast. Ewan, as soon as he swallowed his went right over. I shut myself in my room and walked the floor on tenterhooks till he returned.

It was as we feared. Pete Arnold, Pickering's son in law, had been asking Herb Warren about the salary and saying that if any was owing they would garnishee it. Herb said—or says he said—that it was all paid up as far as he knew.

We did not know what to do. We could not go to Will Sellars now to arrange matters. And could we trust anyone else. We had to. Ewan went to see Wm. Weldon and had a little talk with him. The result was that Weldon as manager agreed to *lend* the church the necessary sum to pay the salary up to the end of June. So that is that. But if Pickering does as Pete Arnold told Warren he would do—take both Ewan, the treasurers and the managers all into court—it may be a very nasty mess. Of course if Herb Warren really told him what he said he did Pickering can have no "good cause" for getting such an order. But did he? Warren is not a man on whose word you can rely.

I am sick of it all. I wish Ewan had let me pay that money long ago. Unjust as it was, it would have been better than this ever-recurrent worry & humiliation.

Wilmot Bain is going to stick to Zephyr church. And Ewan seems very well again. But as soon as one worry lifts another takes its place.

Friday, April 10, 1925
The Manse, Leaskdale

I felt a little better today and got to work. Ewan went to see Will Sellars tonight to see if he could get him to say definitely what he meant to do. I spent a mis-

erable evening of suspense but hoped it would be decided one way or another. But Sellers would say nothing except that he would not decide until June 10. This looks bad to me. I feel that they mean to leave but haven't the face to tell Ewan so plainly.

I *wish* it were June 10. We will *know* then what to expect. This constant suspense is eating the heart out of me.

Saturday, Apr. 11, 1925

Slept badly and had to force myself to work all day. Very restless, nervous and with a terrible cough, the legacy of the flu. But Ewan is certainly much better and if he keeps so I'll soon get back my grip on myself.

As it is, I am dreading the heavy spring work and worrying lest Grieg and Pickering are hatching up some devilment.

Ewan, in talking things over with Rob Shier tonight made a curious discovery. There are twenty five men in the tiny village of Zephyr who never darken a church door. Four of these are in our church, the remaining twenty one are nominal Methodists. So it would seem that Zephyr people are not devoted church goers to any church.

Sunday, April 12, 1925

This was another dreadful day. I have been horribly nervous. Couldn't keep from crying all day and between nine and ten this evening I had the worst hour I've had this winter. I walked the floor in agony and dreaded everything. Nothing seemed before me but endless repetition of these dreadful six years. I have no courage, no hope. Of course this is all a nervous breakdown consequent on worry and influenza. But the knowledge doesn't help me any.

Monday, April 13, 1925

Today I felt better. Was able to work and *forget*. Mr. Garvin of Toronto[487] called in the afternoon on some literary quest and the chat I had with him did me no end of good. Heartened me right up. After all, there *are* some people in the world besides the Lockies and the Armstrongs and Zephyr is not the hub of the Presbyterian church in Canada. My appetite is better. Ewan seems real well and if I were not all the time dreading that Grieg and Pickering are devising iniquity upon their beds I could soon pick up.

---

487   John William Garvin (1872–1934) had published several collections of poetry by Canadian poets. He was married to Katherine Hale, the pen name of novelist Amelia Beers Warnock.

Tuesday, April 14, 1925
The Manse, Leaskdale

No so well today. Nervous and restless. Hands tremble. Put in a miserable day. But Ewan came home from Toronto with good church news. Six hundred churches have already voted out and a strong Presbyterian church in Canada is assured. We will not belong to a mere sect. The general outlook is encouraging and I feel better and hope to get a good sleep tonight.

Wednesday, April 15, 1925

I had it. So felt real well all day until dusk when some nervous unrest returned, with that dread of something happening which makes these attacks so terrible. But we had a nice social guild this evening and I feel better again. Ewan is better these days than he has been for a year and a half. The *suddenness* of his recoveries is almost as uncanny as the suddenness of his attacks.

Sunday, April 19, 1925

I have got on fairly well since Wednesday. Though I have always got a little nervous and restless in the evening I have got through the days nicely. Have been busy housecleaning and getting on much better than I had feared. Ewan, too, has been very well this week—perfectly well to all seeming. He has tackled the job of clearing up the yard—something he has never done since 1919. The springs have hitherto been very bad times with him. I am very glad of this for I have been wondering how I would get the yard done. Other springs I had Lily to help me but Elsie is not strong enough for it. However, it has proved one of those bridges we never have to cross.

Snow scene this morning

Last night we had a most curious weather experience. All night it thundered, "lightninged" and *snowed*. Six inches of snow fell and this morning the manse was surrounded by bigger drifts than any we had all winter. This has had an evil effect on me and I have been nervous and restless and *imprisoned* all day.

Monday, April 20, 1925

I slept well last night and that always makes the following day bearable. It was fine but cold today and I went down to Uxbridge over the sloppy slushy roads

to give a talk on the Mammoth Cave to the Hypatia Club. I had a nice time. Companionable women—nice supper. I felt quite cheered up. And a letter from Stella was much more cheerful than her last. Dan has got a good job again. But Stell is having a lot of trouble with her eyes. Poor Stell has cried wolf about so many things in her life that one can't be sure when the wolf really appears. Sometimes I feel horribly afraid that she has some serious kidney trouble. I don't know what I'd do if anything happened to Stell. In spite of everything, she is the only one of the race of Joseph left to me and the ties between us are so old and strong and tender that they can't be easily broken. I wouldn't want to live in the same house with Stell. She is too domineering and quick tempered for that. But in different houses we are exceedingly fond of each other and are allies and comrades in everything. We always fight under the same flag. Stell was certainly rather awful the winter she was here with me. But I know now what I did not know then that it was during that winter that Irv first began to neglect her and act strangely.[488] The worry and dread engendered by this made her unhappy and irritable. I cannot wonder at it and I excuse her, though I would not be willing to repeat the experiences of that winter.

The worst of my condition just now is that I live in constant expectation of something nasty happening—and too often it *does* happen. This is not a wholesome state of mind or feeling. But I shall soon pick up if only Ewan keeps well.

Wednesday, Apr. 22, 1925
The Manse, Leaskdale, Ont.

Yesterday we heard the encouraging news that Sonya[489] had voted out.

Ewan was not quite so well today. His head bothered him again.

Yesterday I was busy housecleaning all day and went to play practice tonight. It seems to me that we will *never* get that play up. Most of the performers don't *try* to get it up. They never study their parts—they make the same mistakes over and over again and *over* again. Last practice night I made Bert Collins repeat six times a short, two-sentence speech where he always went wrong. Tonight he made the same mistake again!

I came home wretchedly tired. Found Ewan in bed and half-asleep, he having got home before me from a Zephyr meeting. He roused himself to tell me that Marshall Pickering was confined to his bed with a paralytic stroke.

---

488   Stella Campbell had been engaged to Irving Howatt for many years but in the end the engagement was broken off; LMM had given the pair several loans during this time.
489   A small hamlet 18 km/11 miles east of Leaskdale.

I admit candidly that I did not worry much over this. Instead, I went to bed with a distinct feeling of relief. If Pickering and Grieg have not already set some devilry in motion it is not likely they will do so now. Pickering will have something else to take up his attention.

Thursday, April 23, 1925

Busy housecleaning today. Ewan was away to a Presbyterian Congress in Lindsay and came home much encouraged but with the depressing news that Will Rynard's hired man and Will Sellar's "home girl" have been telling around that they are going to leave the Presbyterian church. If this is so I think they might have told us themselves and not have left us to hear it from their servants. We have not deserved such an insult and I feel blue over it.

We had another play practice tonight and I feel more discouraged than ever. It seems to me they know their parts *less* well than before. The only thing that keeps me up at all is the remembrance that the last play practices were almost as bad and yet it came out pretty well at the last.

Sunday, April 26, 1925

I went to Zephyr service today. As usual the atmosphere was depressing. Mrs. Will Lockie told Ewan that they were going to leave on June 10. We knew that before and if they were all that left the church would be far better off without them. But the trouble is their going will influence others to go. Armstrong has not been coming to church since February. I feel instinctively that that man is hatching some plot.

This evening we went to Uxbridge church and called on Minnie Gould afterwards. Of course the talk was of Union *ad nauseam*. But as we were all of one mind and one heart about it it was a relief to get some of our soreness and sense of injustice out of our systems by talking it out, none daring to make us afraid. Minnie Gould says George Allan Smith will never sleep or rest until he gets all his family into the Unionist church. So farewell Will Sellers.

We have been hoping Mt. Albert will take a vote as there is a strong party there who will are opposed to Union. Then they could come in with Zephyr and Leaskdale and make a self-supporting congregation. But the Session there are all Unionists and won't agree to have a vote and it seems as if there were not much hope of it now. So I feel down-hearted again.

Thursday, Apr. 30, 1925
The Manse, Leaskdale

A queer little incident happened today. It shows what Unionists will stoop to.

We are members of the local Ministers' Association. Mr. Watch, the

Methodist minister of Uxbridge, is President, Mr. Dyer of Greenbank is Secretary. Dyer has been very bitter against Ewan, I understand, because he would not go in for Union and blames him for Sonya and Uxbridge voting out. Ewan certainly did what in him lay to influence Sonya and Uxbridge. He did not have to ask Mr. Dyer's permission to do the work he was asked to do by the Presbyterian Association. But Dyer is bitter with the bitterness of defeat because in spite of his efforts Lindsay Presbytery has gone strongly for Union.

Dyer's own record in regard to Union is a curious one. When he first came to Mt. Albert, a weak congregation, he was for Union and tried to arrange a Union between his church and the local Methodist church. All went swimmingly until Mr. Dyer discovered that the Methodists would not have *him* as minister in the United Church. Then he turned his coat out of hand and became a bitter opponent of Union. Last year, however, he got a chance to become minister of Greenbank United Church. Presto, the coat was turned again and Mr. Dyer fairly foamed at the mouth in his efforts to aid the Unionist cause. I am wasting a lot of perfectly good space detailing all this unimportant stuff but it makes clear the reason for what happened today.

Last fall when the programme was being made up Dyer asked me to take the May meeting—a meeting that nobody wanted because it came right in housecleaning time and, as supper has to be served, means a lot of extra work. I didn't want it either but Dyer solicited so earnestly I agreed. And this past week in addition to housecleaning like mad to get at least upstairs finished I have been planning and arranging my menu, ordering the necessary supplies etc.

Today Mr. Watch called here on the 'phone. Ewan was away so he had to tell me the burden of his soul. He began by the rather extraordinary question, "Would it inconvenience you, Mrs. Macdonald, if we had the meeting in Uxbridge instead of Leaskdale next Monday?"

Why he though it might "inconvenience me" to have the burden of such an entertainment taken off my list only the mind of a Unionist could explain. But I "sensed" the situation at once. Dyer's fine Italian hand was very plainly in evidence. Poor old senile Watch was merely his tool.

"Not at all," I said promptly and crisply.

Watch maundered on, trying feebly to explain. It was the last meeting of the season—they wanted a good turn-out—and the ministers were "all so *busy*" that they couldn't "spare the time" to come to Leaskdale.

This was absolutely nauseating. With the sole exception of Dyer every rural minister in the Association is much nearer Leaskdale than Uxbridge. And as half of the Uxbridge ministers are retired Methodist ministers I didn't think *they* were so exceedingly busy. I cut Watch's puerilities short by a curt repetition of my statement that it would not matter to me at all and hung up the phone.

I am glad enough to be rid of the meeting but I resent the insult. I know quite well that Dyer and Watch have cooked this up between them, for with every other minister in the Association we were on good terms, despite the Union question, with the exception of Macdonald of Wick who might not want to come here but who hates Dyer, so is not very likely to have been a party to the plot.

This evening I walked up the hill in the owl's light to see Mrs. Alex Leask. Lucky went with me half way up and then, becoming frightened by a car, ran into the bushes by the side of the road. Three hours later I came down the hill, enjoying the cool, starry darkness of the spring night—one cannot be altogether hopeless in spring—and not thinking of Lucky at all, supposing that he had gone home long ago. But as I passed that very clump of bushes I heard a little meow and the next moment out popped a purring, delighted little cat who had been waiting patiently there all that time for my return. I gathered him up and snuggled him against my neck; and then—since it was so dark that the parish could not be scandalized—I carried him home, singing his song of triumph. The love of even a faithful little animal is very precious. What care I for old Granny Watch and conceited Dyer? I snap my fingers under their very noses. They simply do not exist in my world at all. They have never entered its magic gates—they never can.

May 1, 1925
Leaskdale Manse

Elsie and I worked hard all day cleaning the spare room. Then I went to play practice at night. It went fairly well but the date of the concert draws nigh and they are far from perfect. I am so tired that I begin to feel again that I *cannot* bear this life any longer. The Zephyr obsession always returns when I get overtired and tonight I can think of nothing else.

Luck

An item of news in a letter from Myrtle also saddened me. She said the Cavendish manse had been sold to Nelson MacCoubrey who meant to remove it to his own farm and the new manse would be built in New Glasgow. This marks another step in the decline of Cavendish—a thing I hate to see. Cavendish is the mother section of that congregation and the manse has always been there. It is a shame to move it—and I think in the long run it will prove an unwise step. But New Glasgow has been grasping after the manse for years and at last it has got its way.

Saturday, May 2, 1925

I woke at five and could not sleep again. Felt somewhat obsessed and restless all day. But I worked hard all day and in the cold gray evening we went over to Zephyr and called on two ignorant families whom we suspect will go over to the Union church though they have not yet committed themselves. The visit was not an exhilarating one and I am feeling very morose.

Sunday, May 3, 1925
The Manse, Leaskdale

There are two girls in my Sunday School class whom at times I feel tempted to take by the scruff of their necks, knock their silly giggling heads together and throw them out into the horse sheds—and think I did God service. Of course I never do. I smile and smile and am a villain still.[490] But I don't know how much longer my patience with them will hold out. They cannot be shamed or inspired to better behavior, it seems, and of course it would be of no use to scold or satirize them. Wow!

But I felt better today and had a nice quiet restful afternoon of reading—though Ewan came home from Zephyr discouraged as usual. That goes without saying.

Cavendish Manse

Monday, May 4, 1925

In Uxbridge today we met Mr. Baldwin, the Baptist minister, who is a member of the Association. He is boiling with indignation over the removal of the meeting from us. He had never been consulted about it but Mr. Taylor, the Anglican, who is Vice President, was. Watch told him first what he told us—that the members thought it "too far" to go to Leaskdale. Taylor said he did not want it changed—that he had been looking forward to going and wanted to go. Then Watch, seeing that Taylor was not coming to heel properly, told him the truth—or rather, the truth as far as he and Dyer were concerned. "That the ministers didn't want to go to Leaskdale because of Mr. Macdonald's *views on Union.*"

So it seems that the Rev. Mr. Watch, Methodist minister, told *me* a deliberate *lie*. Verily, Wisdom is justified of her children.

Taylor gave in then—which he should not have done—but was so

490　From *Hamlet*, I.5.107–108: "meet it is I set it down / That one may smile, and smile, and be a villain—."

disgruntled that he would not go to the meeting. Baldwin did not go, either, partly because of the affront to us, partly because of the way Watch and Dyer had used *him* in regard to something last winter. Rev. Mr. Edmonds, a retired Methodist minister who has sometimes supplied for Ewan, telephoned up this evening in great agitation to assure us that he had never been consulted and had nothing to do with it. Of course he hadn't. Nobody had but Watch and Dyer—who are worthy of each other.

I went to practice again this evening and am deadly tired.

Tuesday, May 5, 1925

Another devilish day. Worked hard at housecleaning all day. In the middle of the afternoon Mrs. Herb Warren phoned over a mysterious message. Could Mr. Macdonald come to Zephyr this evening? She wanted to see him about something, and "others wanted to see him, too." This alarmed us muchly. A bit of gossip we heard lately seemed to indicate that Pickering, despite his paralysis, was devising some devilry and this cryptic message fitted in with our secret fears. Had Grieg served a summons on Mrs. Warren as treasurer and were "the others" the managers who had also been summoned? If so, we were in for a dreadful time all round. I went to practice, sick with secret worry. We had to be there till midnight, fixing up the stage and having a dress rehearsal—at which they did miserably. The whole evening seemed like a nightmare to me. And a quite unnecessary nightmare. When I came home at midnight Ewan was calmly reading in bed. All Mrs. Warren had wanted was to consult him about Zephyr Sunday School and "the others" were the other teachers. Why the deuce couldn't she have said so? Why be so confoundedly mysterious?

Thursday, May 7, 1925
The Manse, Leaskdale

Our play came off last night. We had a capacity audience and made sixty dollars. The thing went off fairly well. Much better than I had dreaded, although they made plenty of mistakes and omissions.

Not one of the performers said a word of thanks to me for all my trouble. At the end of our last play George Kennedy thanked me. But there are none of his type in this lot. I own I felt it. They simply did not think of it. But one would like a slight show of appreciation. Of course "the minister's wife" has nothing whatever to do but work for other people!

Ewan came home from Zephyr tonight with an astonishing piece of gossip. Unpleasant? Of course. Could any other kind emanate from Zephyr?

It is said *Jim Lockie* is going Union.

This, in a way, seems almost incredible, if it were not so characteristic of the Lockies. Jas. Lockie is one of the elders and as cranky as all the Lockies are. He and all his family voted against Union. But of course they thought when Union was voted down that all would stick. When at the annual meeting last winter Will Lockie and Armstrong "acted up" it was found hard to get a new treasurer. Jas. Lockie was not there. Although an elder he never does go to an Annual Meeting. He always stays away and then growls at everything that is done. Someone moved that he be elected treasurer. His own wife said that it was no use to put him in as he would not act. In the disorganization caused by the Unionist stampede it was impossible to get a male treasurer so Mrs. Warren was put in as treasurer. Jim Lockie nearly went off his head about this. He raved to us that awful evening we spent there about "a woman treasurer." Anyone would imagine it was a terrible disgrace. Most people think he wanted to be treasurer himself. I believe it is simply because he did not want Mrs. Warren to find out how little he, an elder and "leader," gave.

Anyhow, he has never come to church since. An elder, the very man who should have stood by his pastor and backed him up and helped him out in this crisis. And he has simply done nothing but sulk. Now he is reported as going Union. Well, it's the best place for him but if we lose that family with all the rest the church will have to close. And I would be sorry to see that for Leaskdale's sake and also because Armstrong and Will Lockie would rejoice and triumph.

The whole petty squabble is nauseous. I despise myself that I cannot help suffering from it. If Ewan only keeps well I won't suffer long. But I live in daily dread of its effect on him.

I spent today bringing home all my stage "properties" from the church and carrying the books out of the library. And therefore I am so tired I am not quite sane.

Monday, May 11, 1925

Ewan's head troubled him somewhat again today and this worried me so much that my neurasthenia and hopelessness returned.

Tuesday, May 12, 1925

I had a miserable night. Couldn't sleep until nearly six when I fell into a brief doze and had a most delightful dream—a dream I have often had all my life but not a dream that ever turned out to have any special significance. In it I suddenly discovered a door never before seen in my house. I opened it and went in—found a most beautiful suite of rooms with open fireplace and electric light. I was so delighted; and so oddly disappointed when I woke.

Had a busy day. Housecleaned the parlor and went to the Missionary meeting at Mrs. Leask's. We had to disband and reorganize as an Auxiliary of the Continuing Presbyterian church. A disagreeable necessity. But it was very easy here compared to what it is in some societies. Here we are all of one mind. Nobody is leaving us. So all went smoothly. Nevertheless, something about it all hurt. It emphasized the passing of the old order and the beginning of the new.

Thursday, May 14, 1925
The Manse, Leaskdale

I am worried over Ewan again. He was dull, grumpy, contrary all day. This seesaw of persistent hope and dread is wearing my life out. Went to Guild tonight and conducted a programme of "Canadian Humor." Did not feel humorous.

Friday, May 15, 1925

An unsettled restless sort of day. Had a headache and touch of cystitis again. Cleaned all the dishes and silver in the dining room. A letter came from Rollins enclosing a big bill for over a thousand dollars, and with a disheartening forecast of the length of time and work yet to come on that interminable case. Stuart had toothache all day.

Anything more?

I have concluded, however, that Grieg is not going to do anything. If he had intended he would have shot his bolt before now. So I am easier on that score.

The papers carried the announcement of Rider Haggard's death today.[491] I heard it with a feeling of personal loss. When I was a girl his fine tales of adventure and magic were a great delight to me. Are yet, indeed, in certain moods when the humdrumness of a constantly worried life gets on my nerves. Of course, they weren't even reflections of "literature," but they were "darn good yarns." I didn't care for his later stories. The magic had gone out of them.

Tuesday, May 19, 1925

Ewan has seemed better the past few days. There was a good turn-out at Zephyr in both church and Sunday School and for once he did not come home blue.

But they had a terrible time in Presbytery today. It was worse than any political meeting. The Unionists seem actually to be beside themselves. Having lost the Presbytery they are determined to have revenge at least. Oh, I am so

---

491   English novelist Henry Rider Haggard's (1856–1925) adventure novels were often set in Africa; one of the best-known is *King Solomon's Mines*, published in 1885.

sick at heart over everything.

Thank heaven it is the last Presbytery meeting at which the Unionists will be present.

Wednesday, May 20, 1925

Cleaned the kitchen today and finished planting the garden. Ewan is only fair. His head troubles him much. And he is worried over Jim Lockie. He is really going to leave. Ewan called at his home today. He was away and Mrs. Lockie said he was going and "was making it very hard for the rest of them." Of course they'll all go if he does. In her heart I feel sure Mrs. Lockie wants an excuse for going. She does not want to be connected with a small struggling church. I know Mrs. Lockie pretty well by this time. Well, if they go good-bye to Zephyr Presbyterian church.

Had another rather gloomy letter from Rollins today. I don't know just what it means but I think he and French are both tired of the case and have put their heads together to end it. French tried, I know, to induce Page to quit but of course failed. So now they want subtly to discourage me. But what can I do? It would be absurd to drop the case now it is won, all but the accounting. What sense would there be in such a course after having fought it to victory? I don't really know what to do and am in no fit condition to mull over it.

Thursday, May 21, 1925
The Manse, Leaskdale

I had a sleepless night and a bad day. Finished cleaning the kitchen. I am extra glad that housecleaning is finally done. Elsie isn't strong. She is troubled much with a recurrent pain in side and I feel constantly worried lest she hurt herself lifting.

But tonight I felt better. We went for a drive through the beautiful spring evening and made some calls. The calls were boring but one led us to a lovely place where I never was before. The house has just been occupied by one of our young couples. It is far off the road on a hill. We reached it by a long, grassy maple shaded lane. I got out and while Ewan backed and filled about the yard getting the car turned before going in I stood there and found myself for a few marvellous moments "alone with God"—*my* God—the God of Beauty. It was the darkest moment of twilight just before it turns tonight. All round me were young cherry trees, white with bloom in the dusk. Such young, tiny cherry trees and all blooming their hardest. Away in the south the Uxbridge lights made a faint far glory in the sky. All that had once made magic for me suddenly made it again. I gasped and shivered and trembled with the old ec-

stasy. It is long—long—since I felt so. And somehow, in those few moments, my starved soul gulped down so much divine nutriment that I think it will not feel so hungry for a time.

Tuesday, May 26, 1925

Whether I am accursed by the God of the Unionists or whether I am just a plain fool who doesn't have sense enough to take care of herself I know not. But I suspect the latter. Because I know I have been foolish; and because I think it likely the Unionist God has his hands full just now keeping the Unionists in order and hasn't time to bother tormenting me.

Friday night we had such a thunderstorm all night that I couldn't sleep. Saturday was cloudy, damp and bitter cold. I worked hard all day, was tired at night, and *should* have gone straight to bed. Instead, I suggested to Ewan that we make a call we have overlong been promising to make. So we drove over to Vallentyne[492] to call on the young Methodist minister and his sister, who are friendish to us and rather nice folks. Mr. Newell is a Unionist but not an offensive one, so I hardly think he infected me with any germs of malice prepense. But at three o'clock Saturday night I woke with a dreadful cold. Such a kind of cold as I never had before. I could not get my breath at all—just lay there, gasping. Of course I should have stayed in bed and not got up at all. But I did get up and went to Sunday School and taught my class. Came home from church and went to bed, blue and discouraged. It was bitter cold and gray. Long icicles formed on the roof—and this the last week in May. I had a dreadful night and had to stay in bed all day Monday. It was Uxbridge fair day and Ewan, Stuart and Elsie went. I would have been very lonesome had it not been for Luck, who grows in beauty day by day, and who curled up on my bed the whole day and never left me for a moment. A blessing on all good gray cats, say I.

I managed to get up today and work but feel terribly shaky and have what old folks used to call a "graveyard cough."

Sunday night John Blanchard told Ewan that he had been talking to John Lockie who told him that he didn't think Will Sellers or Will Rynard would leave our church. As John Lockie is going himself he ought to have a pretty good idea who is or is not going. This has encouraged us greatly for we have been feeling woefully sure that both those families meant to go.

Yesterday I had a letter from Mary Beaton.[493] She thinks of coming up to Toronto to the Presbyterian Congress and coming out for a visit. I am glad and have written urging her to come. But I do wish it was any other time. My

---

492　A small hamlet some 9 km/6 miles north of Leaskdale.
493　Mary Campbell Beaton, a cousin, had also been LMM's roommate at Prince of Wales College.

enjoyment of her visit will be spoiled by the Union situation. It will co-incide with the worst time of all—the final scenes of the tragedy. And I would wish to be alone then to bear my suffering unseen of even the friendliest eye.

I am thankful I can breathe easily again. But Ewan has been dull and "heady" enough lately.

Today I finished reading Stoddard's Lectures[494]—a series I bought years ago. I have been at them off and on all winter and they have been a boon in that they have helped me over many a dismal day. While reading them I felt that I had escaped from the confines of Scott township and roamed through all the beauty of the world. Not that there is any literary charm about them. In fact they are rather smug and platitudinous. But the illustrations are wonderful and gave enchanting glimpses of loveliness that beckoned and allured my soul.

Wednesday, May 27, 1925
The Manse, Leaskdale

For the first of several nights I had a fair sleep but wakened early with coughing and couldn't sleep again. But I could eat a little today. Ewan was so dull and morose that I felt terribly disheartened and found myself crying over every trifle. Then at night I must go to another practice of the play. The Guild has been asked to give it at Udora and had to rehearse it again. They made an awful mess of it. Seem to have half forgotten it. I was so nervous I could hardly sit still and prompt them.

Thursday, May 28, 1925

I slept well but have had a miserable day. My cold is worse again and is very bad this evening. I cough hard and almost constantly. And I am so disheartened and worried. Ewan was so dull and lifeless all day. I tried to begin writing again—it is so long since I have got any done. I wrote a poem "On An Old Face" and think it was not so bad. But when I had finished it I felt *done*. I have *no* strength just now—physical or nervous. As for spiritual strength I haven't had any for months. Virtue has gone out of me.

Saturday, May 30, 1925

I had a wretched night Thursday night and felt so miserable all day yesterday that I stayed in bed till four. I should have gone on staying there but I got up,

---

494   American writer John Lawson Stoddard (1850–1931) composed a series of lectures based on his travels around the world.

dressed, and went to the play at Udora. The performers thought they couldn't get through with it if I wasn't there. It's hard to see how much worse they could have done if I hadn't been. They simply made a frightful mess of it. Of course, the unfamiliar stage and setting made them nervous. Then Bert Collins made a fool mistake and spoiled a whole scene. This rattled them all; they lost their grip and went to pieces. Moved and spoke like puppets—forgot their points—oh, it was a nightmare! It was hot and close—I was ill—mortified at seeing my performers do so badly in a strange community. Perhaps it seemed worse to me than it really was; but it *was* bad.

Anyhow, that is the end of the devilish thing!

I came home, went to bed and had a most miserable night until about three. I should have died then—or taken pneumonia. But instead, I took a sudden turn for the better. Nerves and cough suddenly ceased to plague me and I fell on sleep. But today has been miserable. Constant cough. No appetite. No interest in life. A horrible weariness. But I feel a little better tonight. Or, rather, I feel a *desire* to feel better. I haven't felt this desire since that night at Valentine parsonage. My old persistent thirst for life seemed quenched utterly. If innocuous Unionists have such an effect on me what would happen if I fell in with some virulent ones!!!

Sunday, May 31, 1925

A warm, showery, breathless day. Had a poor night. Poorer day. Cough very bad. Weak and depressed. Couldn't help crying all the afternoon when I was alone. Can't eat. Have a horrible taste in my mouth. Feel like a walking patent medicine ad. before taking.

Ewan is dull, too.

Well, May is ended. A most horrible May. It is a fact that since 1914 I have not known *one* happy spring. Every spring of the war was terrible because every spring brought some sudden successful drive of the enemy. Then, when the war ended the spring of 1919 brought Ewan's attack of melancholia and every spring since he has been more miserable than at any other time of year. But this spring has been the worst of all, I think. *Everything* has been so hard—so *many* pestiferous, gnawing, malignant little worries like a multiplied cancer of the soul.

But the worst of the agony will soon be over at least. The fatal tenth of June will soon be here. We shall *know* the worst then—know where we stand—know who will or will not leave. This hateful suspense will be over. We will know who are with us and those who are not with us will have gone out from among us. There will be a desolation called peace.

Monday, June 1, 1925
The Manse, Leaskdale

Today was very warm and smothery. We have never, that I remember, had such heat in June. I felt ghastly all day. Can't eat a mouthful and the slightest exertion plays me out. Of course I'm taking medicine but nothing seems to do me any good. If I could get away for a complete rest and change! But I cannot just now.

Ewan said moodily today that "he felt none too good." This means that he is feeling very badly indeed. This sent me into the depths. If he has another bad attack—and just now of all times—I shall go to pieces. I feel quite sure of that. I've reached the end of my nervous strength. Six years of almost unremitting worry and dread have left me a broken creature.

Wednesday, June 3, 1925

I slept poorly Monday night and another fearfully hot day yesterday almost undid me. I went to a W.M.S. at Mrs. Clark's today and then came home and spent an evening of miserable suspense because Ewan had gone to Zephyr. There was a terrific thunderstorm last night and he did not get home till it was over. His news was depressing. Jim Lockie's family are going to stay but Jim himself is going Union, so eventually they will go, too. And there is no doubt Will Sellars are going. Ewan was there last night. He could not get them to say what they were going to do and that very fact indicates that they are going because they must have decided by now. It seems that Ben Armstrong and Will Lockie started out the other day and visited every family in the congregation trying to induce everyone to go Union and making them put their names down. They had no manner of business to do this since the congregation has voted out. But they did it and moreover announced that they "were going to smash the Presbyterian church." What a beautiful Christian spirit. I would not have believed that even they could have said such a thing if Will Lockie's own son had not himself told our informant that they said it.

We don't know certainly yet who they got but we have a pretty good idea. When Ewan left Sellars' last night they knew it was the last time he would be in their house as their pastor. But they never said a kind parting word after all our close association and friendship. Ewan says they were ashamed to and I daresay that is the truth. But I feel it very keenly, especially in my present condition, and cried half the night about it. I don't care a rap about Ben Armstrong or Will Lockie. They have always been cranks and hindrances. But the Sellers have been good friends of ours and it hurts. They were always so opposed to Union. It was really for their sake we decided last fall to put up a fight to save the church for them. Verily, we have our reward.

I could not sleep all night and had terribly morbid thoughts. Today was stiflingly hot and Ewan was very dull. We went to Uxbridge and I went to see Dr. Shier. I haven't a very high opinion of any of the Uxbridge doctors—and my trouble is what no doctor can cure—ceaseless worry and dread. But something has to be done. Shier looked owl-grave, and said he must take my blood pressure. I followed him to the chair with an odd sensation. If worry, as they say, hardens the arteries, mine should be rock-bound. But I wondered what I would do if it turned out that I had high blood pressure. I know what *that* means. But as it happened—and I verily think a little to Shier's disappointment—my blood pressure turned out to be not high but slightly low for my age. So Shier gave me a bottle of tonic and I came home, restless, hopeless and imprisoned. "Who shall deliver me from this body of death?"[495]

The Manse, Leaskdale
Saturday, June 6, 1925

This whole week has been one of the most dreadful phenomenal heat. It makes Ewan so much worse and I, too, find it harder to endure when the thermometer climbs to such altitudes.

Last Thursday morning we motored into Toronto and I stayed till last night. The heat both days was terrible. Yesterday was the hottest June day on record in Ontario. But apart from the heat the two days' escape did me good. I was free from the miasma of Zephyr and its devilish emanations. I spent a quiet, peaceful evening in my room at the hotel, reading and enjoying it, without dread of Ewan coming in with some more bad or painful news.

I expected Mary on the Montreal train but she did not turn up. I felt much disappointed and came home by train very blue. But when I reached home there was a phone from Toronto that she had missed the first train but had come on the next and would be out to Uxbridge in the morning. So this morning we went down to meet her. I was shocked at my first sight of her. She was so thin—so haggard—her eyes looked as if they had wept unceasingly for a year.

And perhaps they have, poor soul. She told me all her troubles this afternoon. And they are no light ones. Her daughter Maud has been behaving the past year as if possessed of the devil. Up to then she was such a nice girl, devoted to her mother and liked by all. Engaged to a fine fellow, able to give her a nice home. All at once she changed utterly. Broke her engagement and began running around with all kinds of riff-raff. Deceived her mother, quarrelled with her brother. Wouldn't work. Would leave home and stay away for weeks—oh, space and time forbid me to tell of all her kididoes. Mary is

---

495   Romans 7:24: "O wretched man that I am! who shall deliver me from the body of this death?"

heartbroken and can't understand it at all. Neither can I—unless, as I strongly think, the girl is not in her right senses. Archie, it seems, was quite deranged in his mind for two years, a few years ago. I did not know this until Mary told me today. It was in the years when our correspondence had lapsed. So it is quite likely Maud is not quite sane. But she has all the cunning of such minds and contrives in a dozen ways to make Mary's life wretched.

I dread tomorrow more than I ever dreaded a Sunday before. It is the last Sunday before Union. And yet I welcome it. Better to know the worst.

Monday, June 8, 1925
The Manse, Leaskdale

Yesterday was a ghastly day. Intolerably warm. We went to Zephyr. Ewan spoke nicely to and about the Unionists from the pulpit, saying that he wished them well, etc. Of course Ben Armstrong and Will Lockie weren't there. They gave up going several Sundays ago. Will Sellers and Mrs. Will were there and gave no sign of any emotion of any kind, whatever they felt. But the thunderbolt came after the service. As I went down the steps Mrs. Jas. Lockie said to me, "Mrs. Jake Meyers voted Union and is going into the Union Church."

I was dumbfounded. Mrs. Meyers has always been one of our few intimate friends in Zephyr. She always talked against Union. Everyone supposed she voted against Union. When Ewan went to them they signed $25. to the new salary list and never said a word to lead him to suppose they would leave. And now!

"Mrs. Lockie, that is almost incredible," I gasped—quite conscious amid all my dismay that Mrs. Lockie had spoken almost triumphantly.

"She just told me so herself," said Mrs. Lockie. "And Maurice McNelly and Julia Madill are going too."

Two more that had promised to stay and signed E's paper! Is there any such thing as honor known to anyone in Zephyr? I turned and went to our car where Ewan was waiting. As I went I heard Mrs. Lockie say to someone, "Oh, I don't know whether I'll be back next Sunday either."

Before I could get into the car Mrs. Meyers came up to me and began to cry. All I could disentangle from her incoherent utterances was that she "would never have left if her husband had been a member of the church"—whatever that meant. I was so hurt that I permitted myself one bitter expression.

"I thought we could have depended on you, Mrs. Meyers."

She caught my hand and wept bountifully.

"Oh, you'll still come to see me as usual, won't you, Mrs. Macdonald?"

"No," I said. "You will belong to another congregation."

"Oh, that won't make any difference," she wailed.

"It will—to us," I said coldly. I got in. We drove away. It was a bitter drive home. After all our efforts. Well, that is the end of Zephyr Presbyterian church. It really deserves no better fate. But it is hard to be so humiliated before Ben Armstrong and Will Lockie who are our enemies simply because we have remained Presbyterian. They will exult in winning the victory. The strange part is that every one of those people who are leaving have been grumbling for years at Armstrong and Lockie and complaining that they were killing the church. Well, they have killed it. But perhaps God has yet something to say to Ben Armstrong and Will Lockie.

Not *one* of these people who are leaving are going because they sincerely believe that Union will "hasten the coming of the kingdom of God." Not one. We know the motives that have actuated everyone and in not one case is it a right motive.

I went all to pieces when I got home and cried bitterly. It is Leaskdale I am worried over. What will it do now? And we have built up such a good church here. It was a miserable congregation when we came—torn by feuds and cross-purposes. Now it is harmonious and flourishing, full pews, lots of young people coming into it every year—all a church should be. But it is not strong enough to stand alone.

Last night was sleepless. Nothing could medicine me to a few hours forgetfulness. Today Ewan and Mary left for Toronto to attend the Presbyterian congress. It has been a fearsomely hot day with a dreadful thunderstorm in the afternoon. I was very lonely all day, nervous and hag ridden. My whole soul seemed "wounds and bruises." But as yet, thank God, no "putrefying sores." No, my soul is healthy enough yet. I feel *that*, under all. And if fate would cease belaboring it with ceaseless blows the wounds and bruises would heal.

Tonight is cooler. What a blessed relief! I hope for a little sleep. But I seem to have such a horrible dread of the future. It is *indecent* to have to live so.

Tuesday, June 9, 1925
The Manse, Leaskdale.

I slept well and today was cool. But still it was for me one of misery and unrest. My nerves are in a dreadful state. I forced myself to work but wanted to cry all the time. I felt heartsick, lonely and despairing. I cannot see any path of escape from our present situation save to leave Leaskdale. And, in my present mood, that thought is terrible. It is home to me. And the thought of facing a new life in a new place among new people with Ewan as he has been for six years is intolerable. I cannot bear it.

In a letter in *The Globe* today Rev. George Ross[496] says that several of the Union leaders have admitted to him privately that Union has been "a tragic mistake." It is a terrible example of what "the lust of power" will do when it is let loose.

Wednesday, June 10, 1925

The fatal date. When our beautiful Presbyterian church is torn asunder by those who swore to protect and cherish her. It has been a terrible day for me. I cried myself to sleep last night. Slept fairly well but awakened at six heavy hearted. The whole day was filled with a terrible unrest. I forced myself to do what was necessary and walked the floor the rest of the time. I am literally obsessed with the Zephyr situation and all its galling humiliation. And the feeling of having been stabbed in the back by our friends. *That* is the thing I cannot—*cannot*—bear.

Thursday, June 11, 1925
The Manse, Leaskdale

Again a hard day after a poor night. The papers are full of flamboyant accounts of the "birth" of the Great United Church. Well, perhaps so. But in Nature the births of living things do not take place in this fashion and history does not show that great movements came into being with such clash of cymbals and clamour of trumpets.

No, tis no "birth." It is rather the wedding of two old churches, both of whom are too old to have offspring.

Davies and Taylor of Toronto called here this afternoon re the Torcas Co.[497] We had a hot debate on the Union question. Taylor is a rampant Union-Methodist, although he has completely discarded "the supernatural" in his religion. It was funny. He dared not say anything that would anger me, for fear I wouldn't buy his stock. So he had to take all my slams good-humoredly and smile as if he liked it. "Goodness, isn't mother trimming him?" whispered Chester to Elsie in the kitchen. But it did me heaps of good. I got something poisonous out of my soul that has been festering there ever since Sunday. Because of that and because it did me good to talk for awhile with some intelligent educated people I felt much better the rest of the day. Yes, one is all right when one *can* fight. But to lie in the dust and take kicks from people like

---

496   Rev. George Edward Ross (d. 1946) had graduated from the same seminary as Ewan Macdonald had attended, the Pine Hill Theological College (now the Atlantic School of Theology), in Halifax, in 1893. Ross was a leading opponent of Church union.

497   The Toronto Casualty, Fire and Marine Insurance Company; these two men were sales agents.

the Zephyrites requires more of the grace of God than I have ever had or ever will have.

Friday, June 12, 1925

Last night I slept better and got back a little of my sense of proportion. Tonight in Guild Mrs. James Cook told me how, when they used to live in Zephyr 30 years ago, they had such terrible times with the Lockies of that day—the father and uncles of Will and Jim. They would do and say the most dreadful things in the church and had to have their own way in everything. It does me a lot of good to hear someone abuse the Lockies!!!! And *say* just what I've always thought of them but dared not say.

Saturday, June 13, 1925

I felt better today with less nervous unrest but certainly not good for much. I found it hard to have the mission band and concentrate on sewing patches. But Ewan and Mary came home this afternoon in such good spirits over the splendid Presbyterian Congress and the assurance of a strong continuing Presbyterian church that it cheered me up by reflection. Ewan had to go to Sonya tonight so, though it was raining heavily, Mary and I went with him. In the car we did not mind the rain and we enjoyed the twelve mile drive through the cool, wet darkness. I love the sound and scent and freshness of rain in the dark.

And we found, too, that, given half a chance, we had not lost our olden power of making fun for ourselves.

Sunday, June 14, 1925

In spite of our pleasant drive I did not sleep well. This was a fine cool day and Leaskdale church was filled to the doors. I was glad to see Herb Pearson and his wife there. *So far as we know* not one person is leaving Leaskdale church. But there are a few we have been doubtful of and Herb was one of these. His wife was a Methodist and he has been mildly in favour of Union.

Then Ewan went to Zephyr. I spent the most miserable afternoon of suspense yet. I simply *dreaded* his return because of what news he might bring. But his news was much better than we had dared to hope. After all Mr. and Mrs. Jake Meyers have stayed with us. The reason why is funny. Jake is not a member of the church. He was brought up a Mennonite[498] and believes in

---

498   The Mennonites, a distinct cultural-religious group, came to Canada in the late eighteenth century, establishing a way of life involving a range of old-world traditions and religious practices.

Baptism by immersion. He came to our church with his wife, but would never join. Mrs. Meyers is evidently one of those women who believe that if a man is not a church member his chances of heaven are small but if he *is*, he is all right, no matter how or in what fashion he became so. It seems that she got into her head the extraordinary notion that if they went into the Union church he would automatically become a member. When she found out this was not so her chief reason for "going Union" disappeared. This explains her mysterious cry last Sunday. Besides, it seems her daughter did not want to leave our Sunday School. So back they are. All Jim Lockie's family were there except him—and after all his kididoes he has not gone to the Union church.

I felt better for a time but soon my depression returned and weighed on me heavily. However, the worst is over. And possibly since Lockies and Meyers have stayed the church may contrive to carry on.

Tues., June 16, 1925
The Manse, Leaskdale

Ewan went to Toronto yesterday morning, feeling and looking well. He has not been so well for eight months. Mary and I had a pleasant two days and I feel better but it will take me a long time to recover fully from the strain of these past 8 months.

Wednesday, June 17, 1925

Today we all went to a Presbyterian meeting at Woodville.[499] It was a large, enthusiastic gathering and on the *surface* I felt cheered and enjoyed the day. But *underneath* I was continually conscious of soul soreness. That exactly expresses my feeling.

Elsie's side is bothering her lately. She has often complained of pain in it but of late it has been almost continual. Her complaints do not irradiate life. I endured Lily's for years. They were unpleasant but did not worry me much because I knew the most of them were imaginary or pretended. But Elsie's *do* worry me because they are real. The girl is not well and I am afraid she will hurt herself in some way, lifting or reaching.

Oh, this talk about Union—Union. Everywhere we go—everyone we meet! It poisons the very air. No one can tell how sick I am of it. Sometimes I think, "Two minutes more of this and I shall throw up my head and howl."

It is almost as bad to be with those who are against it as those who are for it. They all rasp my sore spots. And I have such a terrible feeling of soreness continually—as if my soul were bruised to death.

499　A town some 220 km/137 miles to the southeast, on the south shore of Lake Ontario.

We heard today many more of the devilish things the Unionists have done to destroy the Presbyterian church. No, there will be no blessing on the United church.

Tuesday, June 23, 1925

Yesterday Ewan, Mary and I motored in to Toronto. We had a beautiful drive through a world of clover and for a time I felt much better. Mary and I had a pleasant time in Toronto and I saw her off on the Montreal train this morning with real regret. She has gone back to her problems, poor soul, and I have come home to mine. She told me last night of her hard life with Archie. He drank heavily for years and almost ruined them.

Ewan was in good spirits when I came home and *seems* perfectly well. As long as he keeps like this let the Unionists do their worst!

Wednesday, June 24, 1925
The Manse, Norval, Ont.

I feel very much better all day. I began writing again this morning and found I could carry on. This evening we were out calling and as we sped along the pleasant dark June roads, with the shadows and the stars I heard again the whisper eternal and found my way back to my dear world of fancy. I have been an exile from it for many moons and had oft times feared I should never be able to re-enter it. But I have found again, "the ivory gates and golden"[500] and so long as they keep open for me there is nothing I cannot bear. Freedom is a matter of the soul.

Friday, June 26, 1925

Things begin to have a little of their old flavor to me. Tonight I have been reading a volume of Landor's *Imaginary Conversations* and found much delight in it.[501] But I think he *just misses*. His dialogues are very clever but one always feels it is *Savage Landor* who is speaking, *not* Marcellus or Anne Boleyn. And he preaches too much. Some of the dialogues are much more like sermons than conversations. Nevertheless there are patches. I haven't read them for twelve years and I find them very tasty.

---

500   Lines from a song entitled "The Fairies" that had been popular from the mid-nineteenth century: "Some night, when the sun in darkness dips, we'll seek that dreamland olden, / And you shall touch with your fingertips the ivory gates and golden."

501   English writer Walter Savage Landor (1775–1864) published five volumes of imaginary conversations between 1824 and 1829, mainly between historical figures of classical Greece and Rome.

I am sleeping better but always waken too early—at three or four—and then cannot sleep again. I feel very dull and vapid most of the time. But that is better than active torture.

Elsie is very miserable. The doctor says it is chronic appendicitis and she must have an operation.

I have a nice thing to relate of our small black Dixie. It is the joy of that little dog's life to accompany anyone who goes down to the Post Office.

A June Road.

Yesterday I went down and Dixie bounded after me, every curve of his body quivering with delight. Luck also decided to follow and the two, who are excellent friends, trotted along behind me to the middle of the creek-bridge. Then a passing car alarmed Luck who bolted into the shrubbery and would not come out. What did Dixie? Did he come on with me and leave Luck to his fate? Not he, though his whole being yearned after me. That gentlemanly little dog sat right down by the trees into which Luck had disappeared and remained there until I had gone to the P. O. and returned. Then Luck took courage to emerge and he and Dixie trotted home with me. Loyalty and courtesy incarnate in a small black body with a tail like a sausage. Dixie, I salute thee. Thou art of the household of faith.

Sunday, July 5, 1925

Elsie went home today. She is to be operated on tomorrow. Myrtle Taylor is coming to help me until Elsie can return.

Elsie cried when she went away. "I have had six happy months here, Mrs. Macdonald," she sobbed. Poor child, I hope she will get on all right.

[Dixie]

Monday, July 6, 1925

Elsie was operated on this morning and got on very well.

Mr. Fraser was here today.[502] We have all outlived the coolness generated by the Brooklyn affair and are good friends again. I am glad because I always found J. R. an agreeable companion. He is very unhappy just at present. He has always been bitterly opposed to Union but he thought there would be no Presbyterian church worth while left and so went into Union and induced his

502   James R. Fraser (b. 1867), a widower with two children, had been minister at Chalmers Presbyterian Church in Uxbridge. In 1918, the friendship cooled when Fraser became minister at Brooklyn, a location that the Macdonalds had wanted.

church to go too. Now when he finds there is still a strong Presbyterian church he is homesick and regretful but cannot retrace his steps after influencing his congregation. Well, J.R. is a bit of a time server. He doesn't believe in the immortality of the soul, the Virgin birth, the deity of Jesus. Yet he preaches in a church which requires such belief. I do not blame him for not believing them. Very few thinking people do believe in miracles now—though most of us believe in some kind of immortality. But he should not be preaching them when he doesn't believe them. *That* is the canker at the heart of all the churches today. It will kill them. But equally of course preaching the falsity of belief in the supernatural will kill them, too. So either way the church, as it exists today, is doomed and will eventually die. Though something that has lived for 2000 years will take a long time in dying.

But suppose it does die. What matter? It has served its day as God's instrument. He is using another now—Science. Through Science the next great revelation will come. I may not live to see it in this incarnation but I am as certain of its coming as I am that the sun will rise tomorrow morning.

We heard in Zephyr today that only three of the Unionists who left our church were in Zephyr United church last Sunday evening though it was a lovely evening. It would seem that they are no better to go there than to their own of yore.

As for me I am slowly but surely recovering my wholesomeness. My secret spring of joy is bubbling up in my heart again. As long as Ewan keeps well I am the master of my soul. Selah.[503]

This evening about nine I went over to Mr. Leask's on an errand. The exquisite pale brilliance of the moonlight night made me suddenly and savagely homesick for the moonlight nights of old and the dear ones who shared them with me.

Thursday, July 9, 1925
The Manse, Leaskdale

This afternoon I went to a W.M.S. quilting in Zephyr church. There is something about the homely old art of quilting that I like. I could sit and quilt happily for hours. But the afternoon was spoiled for me by the presence of that devilish woman, Mrs. Jas. Lockie. She always seems to poison the atmosphere. Mrs. Ben Armstrong was there too, wife of the great and only Ben. What brought her I cannot imagine. Probably a desire to play the spy. At all events she made us all feel uncomfortable.

---

503   A Biblical word found at the end of some Psalm verses; the word's origin is unknown (one theory suggests it is a musical direction); LMM may be using it as a kind of ironically intoned "amen."

When it was over the rest of the day was pleasant. Ewan and I motored to the induction at Port Perry.[504] We had a delightful drive down through a green and purple evening and an enjoyable service. Ewan preached the sermon and did very well. It is always a dreadful strain on me when I know he is going to preach in a strange church. Sometimes, as tonight, he does well. But sometimes, when his black dog rides him, he does miserably and puerilely. And one can never be sure which it will be.

We had a pleasant social time afterwards. J.R. Fraser was there, looking more or less like a wistful dog out in the cold. I would not be at all surprised to see Fraser back in the Presbyterian church yet.

Will Lockie and Ben Armstrong have, I understand, reiterated their decision to "smash the Presbyterian church" and "give it two years in Zephyr." I am sadly afraid their prediction will come true. I really can't see any prospect ahead for Zephyr church, unless something very unforeseen comes to pass.

Wednesday, July 15, 1925
The Manse, Leaskdale, Ont.

Tonight was my first evening home since July 6th. Verily, 'tis a treat. I look forward nowadays to an evening home as I used to look forward in the leisurely old Cavendish days to an evening out.

Yesterday we motored to Kirkfield and spent the day with the Burkholders.[505] Very pleasant but of course, for me, marred by the ceaseless talk about Union and its results which made an otherwise excellent dinner a meal of bitter herbs.

Kirkfield is where father was married to his second wife.[506] The old MacKenzie house, where the reception was held, is still there, across the street from the manse. A beautiful place which has been shut up for years. The ceremony was performed in the old church which has been torn down. We went for a walk through a most beautiful long lane of lombardies on the MacKenzie estate. It was the part of the day I enjoyed the most. How I miss out of my life now the long intimate walks through woods and secluded fields, when I was a little sister to all the trees in the world and knew all the exquisite secrets of upland and hill spring.

Today I canned cherries and had splendid luck. I also wrote two hours at a series of short stories I am trying to get done for *The Delineator*.

---

504   A community 26 km/16 miles southeast of Leaskdale.

505   Kirkfield is 42 km/26 miles northeast of Leaskdale. Jenkins Burkholder was the minister.

506   LMM's father, Hugh John Montgomery (1841–1900), married Mary Ann McRae (his second wife) in April 1887. Kirkfield was the birthplace of McRae's uncle, Sir William Mackenzie, who (with Donald Mann) spearheaded the construction of the Canadian Northern Railway.

Thursday, July 16, 1925

Today I read an article in which the writer spoke of a book he had once hoped to write and never would. This set me thinking of the books *I* planned to write—but never did. There were several of them in my early teens, all carefully "thought out" and quite complete in my mental storehouse. Many a night I lay awake in that old farmhouse by the eastern sea—many an evening I walked alone in the afterglow of autumnal sunsets—composing them and a jolly good time I had of it.

One was to be called "How We Ran the Farm." This was an amusing story about two girls who, by some twist of circumstances, were left with a P.E. Island farm on their hands and determined to show all and sundry that they could run it. They had any number of adventures, especially when they daringly attempted to shingle the stable and build a "snake" fence. I really think it would not have been a dull little yarn.

Two other projected novels were very serious affairs. One centred around the fortunes and misfortunes of a young French Canadian—whose name was Louis—who was "only a hired man" but had endowments and aspirations beyond the rank and file of his race. He was to fall in love with his employer's daughter and she with him and the course of true love was to run deviously and turbulently and alas, to no happy haven. For in the end he was to go back to the forsaken sweetheart of his own race.

Another novel was to have been a chronicle of life in a country church. A minister well stricken in years was to be set aside in favour of a young man. A faction adhered to both and the story was to deal with the intrigues and counterintrigues of the said factions. At last, in a very dramatic scene—my eyes used to stream with tears as I pictured it—the two ministers became reconciled.

I think I could have written these books quite well. I shall never write them now but at times their "frustrate ghosts" loom reproachfully in the offing as if demanding why I called them into spiritual being yet refused to give them incarnation.

But I *did* write a book whereof no record remaineth. It was back I think in '99 or '00. I intended it for a "Sunday School Library book"—thinking that if I could get it accepted by one of the religious publishing houses I might make a few hundreds out of it. I modelled it after the fashion of the "Gypsy" and "Pansy" books of my childhood[507] and had no idea of attempting anything beyond a pot-boiler. It was called *A Golden Carol*—a title punned from the name

---

507   American author Isabella Macdonald Alden (1841–1930) wrote some 100 books under the pseudonym "Pansy." Most of her work is didactic fiction illustrating religious principles. American author Elizabeth Stuart Phelps (1844–1911) wrote a series of books for Sunday schools in 1866–67 featuring the character of tomboy Gypsy Breyton.

of the heroine, "Carol Golden," who was a girl at Halifax Ladies' College when the story opened. Summoned home suddenly by the death of her mother she had to stay there, rebelliously, to keep house for her father and young brother "Bobbles," who supplied the comedy relief to Carol's struggles and trials—said struggles of course culminating in a victory over self and a determination to live up to the college distortion of her name and make life "a golden Carol." It was all laid down on thoroughly conventional lines and would have passed any censor. Yet, *of its kind*, it wasn't a bad story. I thought then—and think still—that it was every whit as good as nine out of ten of the Sunday School stories that found publishers. I sent it away to the Presbyterian Board of Publications in Philadelphia and when they refused it I sent it to the Congregational Publishing Society of Boston.[508] Back it came. I never sent it out again.

Probably if I had kept on I might have found a publisher. I am exceedingly thankful I did not. To have had that book accepted would have been the greatest misfortune that ever happened to "my literary career." I could never have risen above it; and it would probably have committed me to a lifetime of writing "series" similar to it.

But I did not realize my lucky escape at the time. The cloud of disappointment seemed to have no silver lining and I cried myself to sleep for a week over the downfall of my humble little castle of dreams.

Eventually I boiled the book down to seven or eight chapters and sent it out to several Sunday School papers in the hope of having it taken as a serial. To condense it thus I had to cut out three quarters of it and as this included the "Bobbles" stunts all the salt and savour it had possessed utterly evaporated. Nobody would have it at any price and finally I burned it, vowing that never again would I try to create a Sunday School heroine. It was the re-action drove me to "Anne" and probably kept me from making a dummy of her.

I have several "unborn" books in my head yet. I hope they will some day come to birth. Perhaps they will; and perhaps not. It will all be according to predestination.

Monday, July 20, 1925
The Manse, Leaskdale

Last night Ewan left for the Island going down to make a third attempt to settle up Aunt Christie's tangled business affairs and get the store property sold. I shall have to do without a vacation this year. What with Elsie's illness and

---

508   The Congregational Sunday School and Publishing Society was active from 1841 to 1917.

preparations for Chester's going to St. Andrew's[509] I can't get away. But a certain kind of a vacation I mean to have while Ewan is away. I am excused from all "visiting" because I can't drive the car. *That* in itself constitutes a vacation. And though I shall have to work hard all the time I am going to work only at "jobs" I enjoy doing. And I'm going to rest and read as much as I can. I had a splendid day today full of steady pleasurable work.

Thursday, July 23, 1925

A lovely day. Fine and cool. And I was alone. Myrtle was away, Stuart went off to visit a chum. I found it very agreeable and restful for a change.

I went down to the Post Office in the forenoon and as I crossed the bridge I looked over to Mr. Leask's hayfield on my left. Wave after wave of sinuous, glistening, wind-shadows were going over it. I have not seen just that exact effect for years. A flood of ecstasy washed through my soul. The mystic curtain fluttered and I caught the glimpse of Eternal and Infinite beauty which "Emily" called her "flash." I fairly trembled with the wonder and loveliness of that supernal moment. Only a moment. But worth years of ordinary existence.

Then I went into the Post Office and bought two cans of peas and a packet of Cream of Barley. The body can't live on shadow-waves and flashes.

Sunday, July 26, 1925

A Mr. Noble came last night to preach today. Young, clever, a bit conceited. Eloquent but stentorian preacher. I think he could easily have been heard a quarter of a mile away. I went to Zephyr with him and after the church service we went up to the Decoration Service held in the cemetery. The Women's Institute arranges this and it is undenominational. Some of the ex-Presbyterian ladies came and spoke to me. Some did not. Mrs. W. Sellars, among the latter, though she smiled and bowed slightly across an open space. I think she is really shamefaced.

Lily Shier found a chance to whisper to me, "Have you heard about the fight in the Methodist church?" I said "No," and she said, "The ladies of the Institute are getting into sad messes." She had no chance to tell me more so I must suffer the pangs of deferred[510] but candidly confessed curiosity for a season.

Janet Myers, whom I had not seen since that dreadful Sunday in June,

---

509   St. Andrew's College was a private boys' school, founded in Toronto in 1899. From 1905 to 1926 it was located in Toronto's Rosedale neighbourhood. In 1926 the school relocated to Aurora, north of Toronto. At that time there were about 250 boys enrolled, mainly boarders.

510   LMM omits a word here, likely "pleasure" or "gratification."

came up to me in church, crying again. "I couldn't live without you, Mrs. Macdonald," she sobbed, "so I stayed."

Fudge! She stayed because her daughter made a fuss and because she found that her husband couldn't automatically become a church member and sure of heaven. I know my Janet. Though I think she likes me and did really feel badly when she purposed leaving.

I have a vaseful of Shirley poppies before me as I write. Exquisite things! Enough to compensate for Zephyr. Shirley Poppies always make me think of Myrtle Webb. The first Shirley poppies I ever saw were in a bouquet she brought over to me long ago, one evening in Cavendish when she was a newcomer to the place. I can see that lovely bouquet plainly yet. It is nearly a quarter of a century since that evening and those frilled things of rose and snow have been dust as long. But they bloom still in my garden of remembrance.

Monday, July 27, 1925
The Manse, Leaskdale

This evening I had a nasty return of nervous unrest—why I do not know, since the day has been peaceful and uneventful. And I was seized with a strange and sudden pang of homesickness for Park Corner as it was in the old days. Not Cavendish but Park Corner. To have it back for a little while—to be there with Aunty and Uncle John and Stell and Frede. To forget all the anguishes and worries and dreads of these recent years—to forget what a thing of shreds and tatters life has become—and laugh gaily through the old hall and down the winding road again where the wild blue irises bloomed in the hollow, and beyond the old iron gate a vision of jade-green waters with curling crests of ice-white foam. I ache for it.

Tuesday, July 28, 1925

A miserable day. I woke early and felt restless and unhappy all day. In these moods everything that has been bothering me these past years comes up and I feel all my chains—Ewan's melancholia—lawsuit nightmares—and loneliness eating like a cancer.

The winding road.

Sunday, Aug. 2, 1925

Haven't felt well all the week. Rev. R.J. Campbell and wife came today to take the services. I went to Zephyr with them. Only a few were out and I felt again all the old humiliation and depression Zephyr services have always inflicted

on me. But Mrs. Campbell is a very nice jolly little soul and we had such a pleasant evening of conversation that I ceased to feel lonely and nervous and became delightfully normal once more.

Had a letter from Mary Beaton today. She is still unhappy. Maud is behaving as queerly as ever and Rowland is determined to leave home and go west.

Wednesday, August 5, 1925

There has been a terrible tragedy in Zephyr. Mr. Barron, the night operator of the C.N.R.[511] there, was lighting a fire with coal oil. The stove exploded, house and contents were burned, and Mr. Barron so badly burned that he died this morning. The Barrons are Methodists so that it touches us only in so far as they are fellow creatures and human beings—which is far enough. The whole thing seems nightmarish and Zephyrian.

The house they lived in was right beside our church. The sheds caught fire and the church was only saved by the fire brigade from Mount Albert. I am sure the Unionists, especially Will Lockie and Ben Armstrong, must think that the prayers of the righteous did not avail for once, or the detestable building would have been removed by fervent heat from their midst.

Emily Climbs is out. My twelfth book.

I am sleeping splendidly now. I seem to be getting pretty well back to normal in this respect. For one thing, I suppose I am not disturbed by E's sighs and groans in his sleep. Even when he is pretty well in daytime he seems distressed in his sleep. He is having a nice time on the Island and I believe he is really going to get the store property sold at last. If so that will be one of our minor burdens removed.

A funny thing happened tonight. The phone rang and Myrtle came out. "Mount Albert is calling you." I had been expecting a call from Lily Shier in regard to a missionary meeting. So I was thunderstruck when I heard a voice saying, "This is *Ham Pickering* speaking."

For a moment a wave of sickening apprehension went over me. Ham is Marshall's brother and very bitter against us—although up to the time of the accident he hadn't been on speaking terms with Marshall for years. What deviltry was afoot? And in any case why should Ham phone *me*??

"Do you want any more of *them* raspberries?" demanded Ham. In considerable relief I realized that he had got the wrong number so I told him so, adding, "This is Mrs. Macdonald of Leaskdale," and hung up. I rather think the Mount Albert operator would get a calling down. Ham would feel a bit silly.

---

511   The Canadian National Railway. Since 1880 trains stopped in Zephyr on request .

Friday, August 7, 1925
The Manse, Leaskdale

A very warm day. I spent most of it helping Mrs. Leask get "the missionary quilts" together, ready for quilting. I was expecting Ewan home pleasurably and got a nice supper ready for him. When I heard the car I ran out to the gate to welcome him. Miss Dowswell had come up with him and I asked her to come in and have supper and said Ewan would take her to her destination. "Oh no, he must not," she said. "He has a bad headache and mustn't turn out again."

A headache! My heart seemed to turn to stone in my breast. I knew what that meant and all the light of life that had been flickering up not too dully in me a moment before died out again.

Sunday, Aug. 9, 1925

We are having our belated hot weather and it is very hard on Ewan who has been very dull and moody since coming home. Oh, how hard it all is! And I am so afraid his attack will develop into a bad one. Hitherto this has always happened after he has had a few weeks of being perfectly well. I wonder if the fact that while he was away he took no thyroid tablets had anything to do with it. I have begun giving them to him again. If the attack develops severely I will at least know they are no good. I long for cooler weather. The heat always aggravates his trouble.

Myrtle

Elsie came back tonight. I would rather she had not come back so soon but she seemed so anxious to come that I did not like to say a point-blank "no." But I am sure she cannot be fit for work yet and it worries me. Of course on Monday I will run the washing machine and bring in the pails of water and I will help her with all lifting but still there is a danger of her hurting herself.

To tell truth, Myrtle has spoiled me for Elsie. I never had anything like her—so quick, so neat, so efficient. A model little housekeeper. I never had to call *her* in the mornings. And everything would be done and well done by noon. She never "forgot"—never had to be told a thing twice. But her kind don't go out as regular servants so I must e'en get used to Elsie again and reconcile myself by reflecting how much better she is in all essential respects than Lily.

Monday, Aug. 10, 1925
The Manse, Leaskdale

Last night Ewan couldn't sleep so of course I couldn't. This seems like the beginning of a bad attack. His eyes were very wild all day. I am heartsick with worry. Oh, for cool weather!

We have heard all about the "row" in the Methodist church. The Pickering girls started it and made things pretty hot for Mrs. John Lockie and Mrs. Will Sellars. The whole thing is too sordid and petty to detail. I fancy Mrs. Sellars will realize that Ewan told her the truth when he told her the Zephyr Methodist church would be the same church for petty fights and squabbles for the next 20 years that it is today.

Tuesday, Aug. 11, 1925

It was cool today. Such a blessed relief! Ewan is still dull but slept fairly well last night. I spent the forenoon making sandwiches and putting quilts in the frames in the church. This afternoon we had the quilting and served tea. It was a rather hard day and it can't be said I enjoyed any part of it. But among all the forty women who were there there is not *one* with whom I feel ill at ease or who has the same effect on me that Mrs. Jimmy Lockie has. I felt that everyone there was my friend.

Thursday, Aug. 13, 1925

Had a bad night. Ewan was restless. We got up at five and motored into Toronto for a day's shopping. On our way home we stopped at Columbus manse and had tea with Mr. Fraser and Margaret.[512] I looked over the manse with a rather bitter curiosity. Had it not been for Fraser I would have been living in that manse for the past five years. We would have been spared the wretched Pickering affair and I think Ewan would not have been so melancholy. The manse is a very nice one with electric light and I felt a little of the old resentment surge up when I thought of the trick by which Fraser had got it. Well, I suppose it doesn't matter much now. These things are settled by fate.

The evening was a nightmare to me. When Ewan is normal his ordinary conversation in social intercourse while never brilliant or even cultured is a passable average. But when these spells come on him he talks like a child of twelve using a new language which he has learned very badly. I writhed in humiliation all the evening. Fraser must have thought him an ass. And his eyes looked so wild and hunted that I could hardly bear them. I had to clench my hands and grit my teeth in order to sit still while I talked to Fraser. On the way home I was tired out and only avoided tears by taking refuge in a new and vivid dream life which I have been living very splendidly all summer and which, by reason of the temporary escapes it has offered me, has been the only thing that has made it possible to endure. It is a curious thing that all through my life when some great strain or crisis came and all my old dream lives, lived so

---

512　　See note 30, page 9. Margaret was Mr Fraser's daughter.

often that they had at last grown stale and flavorless, failed to give these escapes, some new, vivid, and exhilarating dreamlife would come into being. For months I have been a member of a party seeking in the mountain deserts of South America the jewels hung on a stone god in a great underground cavern. I have gone through the most amazing adventures, risks, terrors, hardships, have found the jewels, outwitted foes and traitors and returned in triumph. How silly it all seems written down. Yet it has been a wonderful, breathless, exciting existence as lived, and seems now in retrospect as *real* as life I have actually lived. "The Hill of The Curse" is visible before my eyes. I know its geography by heart—every curve in the river at its foot beyond which on the one side were the deserts and on the other the mountains. I know every corner of that terrible underground cavern—every curve in "The Stairway of a Thousand Steps"—every mile of that dreadful, solitary journey back across rocky plains, subsisting on sun-cooked fish caught from the river, with the jewels of the plundered god twisted around my body under my ragged garments. All the others dead by the curse of the god—I, the sole survivor.

These dream lives are altogether different from the stories I "think out." When thinking out a story I am *outside* of it—merely recording what I see others do. But in a dream life I am *inside*—I am living it, not recording it. I do not know whether other people generally possess this power. All these various dream lives are just as real to me as if I *had* lived them and were looking back on them. And in these lives I am never hampered by facts and probabilities as I am in a story. Everything happens as it will whether it is possible or not. I don't know whether a river of bitter waters, containing edible fish, could really flow through a desert where no plant life is found. But it could and did in my dream journey. No difficulty at all about that or anything else! Oh, it has been fun.

Monday, Aug. 17, 1925
The Manse, Leaskdale

We had a poor night. Ewan very restless. Dull and morose all the morning but seemed a little better in the afternoon. It was very hot again. I have felt very lifeless and unhappy. This evening I have spent writing with Luck purring on the table beside me. It seems to me that he has been the only note of charm and beauty amid the horrible discords of life today.

Poor Elsie has whined all day about her side.[513] She *isn't* fit for work and it worries me. I am so afraid of her hurting herself. I can't get her to take a tonic which she certainly needs badly. Some people seem to have absolutely

---

513   Elsie came from a very poor rural family. In a later interview with Mary Rubio, she said that she loved working for the Macdonalds because she always had enough to eat with them. She returned to the Manse before she was recovered because she was afraid of losing the position.

no idea how to take care of themselves. I shall get her a bottle of iron pills and tell her she must take them or go home. Between Elsie, Ewan and the heat my nerves are raw.

[Lucky]

Wednesday, Aug. 19, 1925
The Manse, Leaskdale

Another dreadful day. Last night was intolerable. It was very hot. Ewan could not sleep and was so restless I finally got up and came down to the davenport in the library. But I could hear his groans in the room above all night so could not sleep there either. Today was excessively hot—the worst day this summer. Writing was out of the question but I worked all day at various jobs and made up a batch of pickles—by poor Frede's recipe. She haunted me all the time I was making them. I recalled the first fall I was here when we made them together.

Ewan was dull and morose all day and altogether, in the words of Carlyle, life seems to me "a haggard dream."[514]

Chester's *trunk*, too, came today and brought home with a pang the realization that he was going away from me.

This evening, feeling hunted by all the furies of worry, dread, grief, longing, I took a walk in along the sideroad—that pretty road I so seldom have time to walk on. It was a beautiful rose and purple twilight and my two gray pussies followed me along the shadowy wooded path. They were quaint and delightful. Pat has such a nice, prowly look when he is in the woods and Luck was adorable, trotting along with his tail up. Luck always walks with his tail up—Pat never does. I could not enjoy my walk but it soothed and helped me a little.

The old road.

Thursday, Aug. 20, 1925

Blessedly cool. And we had a lovely cool night. I slept fairly well and so have more courage today. E. is no worse today but seemed very dull and got away by himself in the garage two or three times. I had to hunt him out and induce him to return to the house. These efforts of his always terrify me. I can never be sure of what is in his mind when he wants to steal off like this.

Friday, Aug. 21, 1925

A fine clear day, almost cold. Courage always revives in me when a heat wave breaks. Ewan slept well last night but I could not sleep till late and woke early.

514   A term used by Scottish writer Thomas Carlyle (1795–1881) in *Sartor Resartus* (1836).

My nerves were in a wretched state but this morning I was able to lose myself in writing a short story and it helped me wonderfully. But Ewan was dull and staring all day and I feel very lonely and downhearted this evening.

Saturday, Aug. 22, 1925
The Manse, Leaskdale

Ewan seemed a little better today—a bit *cranky*, which is a good sign. This evening we took the boys down to Uxbridge to see a movie. This is an occasional treat we give them. And tonight it was a treat not only for them but for me. After a day packed full of many and, under present circumstances, carking routine duties, I was *thirsty* for something different—something that would take me for a little while into a different existence. The film was a good one and the "comic," detailing the adventures of a cross-words puzzle "fan" was the most excruciatingly funny thing I ever saw. I laughed until my cheeks ached and I felt young again. I am thankful I have never lost "the power to become a child again at will." We were just three kids together there tonight. Ewan didn't go. Never goes. Doesn't like movies. Spent the evening reading and brooding in the back room of Willis' drug store. If he had gone with us and had a good laugh over that irresistible comic it would have done him more good than many prayers.

Well, we had a good time, howling over it, and a lovely drive home, the three of us in the back seat, and had almost as much fun talking the movie all over again.

Monday, Aug. 24, 1925

Have been miserable since yesterday morning with another bad bronchial gasping cold. It was hot today, too, which made it harder to bear. I have had too many of these colds in the last four months.

I had a letter from Stell also which worried me—not because of what was in it but because of a letter from Ella which she enclosed. One of Ella's long, involved, whining letters. Boiled down it amounted to this. Ella finds she can't manage Amy. The latter, only fourteen; a big, handsome girl, maturing early like all the Campbell girls, is doing as she pleases and running around all hours of the night with all sorts of riff-raff. Ella, who, all her life, has tried to shoulder every responsibility on other people coolly asks Stell *to ask me* if I will take Amy up here and send her to school. Even Ella hadn't the face to ask this of me straight out, so she takes this roundabout way.

I shall, of course, do nothing of the sort. I have enough worries and responsibilities of my own without adding them to the care of Ella's spoiled and headstrong daughter. I am providing for Maud and that must do. Sometime

ago I also told Ella that when Amy was ready for P.W.C. I'd pay her way through to fit her for earning her own living. More I will not do. Besides, it would be of no use to bring Amy up here. Owing to the difference between the school systems of Ontario and P.E. Island she is far beyond Leaskdale school and would have to go to Uxbridge High. There she would be on her own, exempt from all control whatever, and I would never know an easy moment. Ella does exasperate me. Dan *has* some sense. He told Stell right off it would never do and he would write and tell his mother so. I hope he does and thereby saves me the ungracious task of refusing.

Saturday, Aug. 29, 1925

Tuesday I spent in bed with a cold. The rest of the week I was preparing for and entertaining "company to tea" twice. But Ewan has been much better and we had one glorious day on Friday. Bertie MacIntyre[515] was in Trenton on her way from England to Vancouver. She could not come here. Our one chance of meeting was to go to Trenton. We must go and come in one day as on Saturday I had people coming to supper. We left here at six in the morning and covered the hundred miles to Trenton by 10.20. We certainly smoked along. I admit there *is* a witchery in speed. We had a delightful drive and the effects of the early morning mists along the creek and river valleys were more exquisite than any I had ever seen before. We had a wonderful day at Trenton.

Bertie and I talked our souls out and dipped into all the affairs of the world once more. We had a merry, happy dinner party at eventide. Ewan so well, everybody smiling and jesting, laughter sparkling from lip to lip. We left at 8 and got home at one, after a pleasant and uneventful drive. But this morning—wow! It was the morning after the night before with a vengeance. We had the Baldwins to supper tonight and I'm dead—just about. I feel like the old man who said he must have all eternity to rest in.

But here's a joke:—

The carpenters who are working on Will Cook's new house under Jim Lockie have been complaining to Will of "the way Jim Lockie swears at them."

Yet James Lockie is, or was, an elder in the church, a self-appointed and intolerant censor of conduct and morals, a man who thinks no one but himself fit to fill any office in the church. Is it any wonder Zephyr church died under the rule of such men?

Since the Lockies and Ben Armstrong left the church we have been hearing so much about them that people never dared tell us before. We always *felt* that they were not what they professed to be, but we have never discussed our people to the others, so we did not *know* a great many things we are finding out now.

---

515   Bertie McIntyre was a daughter of Mary Montgomery McIntyre (LMM's father's sister).

Souvenirs of a Happy Day.

Monday, August 31, 1925
The Manse, Leaskdale

This day was full from dawn to bed time but there was only one thing worth recording. I went to the store on an errand at dusk. Coming back across the bridge I looked up from some rather depressed musings and saw a great harvest moon swing between two tall trees on the opposite bank of the creek—two lovely slender cedars of exactly the same height against the moonlit radiance like the twin spires of some Gothic cathedral. You never know how beautiful trees really are until you see them against a silvery moonlit sky. They were so exquisite that their beauty filled my starved soul as wine is poured into a dry cup and straightway every nerve thrilled to the stimulant of loveliness. I came in re-created.

Saturday, Sept. 5, 1925
The Manse, Leaskdale

On Wednesday we rose early, motored into Toronto and spent a long day on the Exhibition grounds.[516] Took in the Midway stunts, stayed for the grand stand and fireworks at night, left for home at eleven in a pouring rain, had a flat tire, took nearly an hour getting on our spare, and did not get home till two, dead tired. We go through all this for the boys' sake, repaid because they enjoy it so. But Chester is beginning to outgrow the midway. This year he did not care for many of his old delights. For Stuart however, it is still fairyland.

On Thursday we motored to the induction at Gamebridge.[517] On our way there we had the narrowest escape from death, or at least from serious injury to ourselves and destruction to our car that we ever had. It is too long and involved a story to tell here. It was nobody's fault—the trouble began with a pair of frightened horses bolting in a narrow road where the ditch was frightfully deep and steep. We escaped and finally rescued the car also, which a man

---

516   See note 92, page 50.
517   A small community some 40 km/25 miles north of Leaskdale.

had prevented from turning turtle[518] into the ditch by letting his horses go and grabbing the side of our car. But the incident took more out of me than a hard day's journey. I am not quite over the effects yet. The odd part is, that, just at the critical moment, when I felt sure that we were both going to be killed I was not in the least alarmed or apprehensive. When all was over and we were safe I sort of went to bits. Began to tremble, shiver, and want to cry. I didn't cry—but I think it would be better for me if I had.

Today we went down to see "the gardens" at Port Perry.[519] A wealthy Toronto man is making a hobby of his gardens there. It is a wonderful spot, especially the "Italian garden" and as I roamed about in it and drank my fill of beauty life seemed a different thing and childhood not so very far off. One felt safe from the hungry world in that garden. I came home with a fresh stock of courage and endurance.

Ewan has seemed fairly well, this week, too.

Sunday, September 6, 1925

This is Chester's last Sunday home. The last Sunday he will ever be here as a real member of an unbroken household. Henceforth he will come only as a guest on holidays. This bitter thought has been with me all day, like a dark cloud darkening still more gloomy hours of cloud and rain. This evening I took Chester into the parlor in the twilight and had a serious little talk with him, giving him some good advice and warnings, in such tone and language as I thought would win his co-operation instead of repelling him.

I have tried to teach and train Chester as wisely as possible in these past years—as wisely and well as a woman can who has no assistance or co-operation whatever from her husband. I know I have been too impatient at times—I know I have fallen far short in many ways. But I have done my best. And now he must fare forth into the world to sink or swim. I am glad he will be under masculine influence henceforth—and, as I hope and believe, good masculine influence. He has come to the age when he needs it. He cannot, alas, get it here. But at least I am thankful I can afford to send him where he can get it. My little little lad. He is so young to go so far away.

This evening I read an autobiography by Corra Harris,[520] a writer of some

---

518	That is, turning upside down.

519	Port Perry is 30 km/19 miles northeast of Leaskdale, on the shores of Lake Scugog.

520	American writer Corra Mae Harris (1869–1935) survived many difficult experiences, including a troubled marriage, the death of two infant sons, and financial destitution. She wrote extensively and was one of the first women war correspondents to go abroad in World War I. (She also held some controversial opinions, including views about race.) *A Circuit Rider's Wife* (1910) is an autobiographical account of the experience of a travelling minister's wife; Harris' Baptist husband suffered from bouts of alcoholism and depression, along with other problems; he committed suicide in 1910. LMM's quote here is from Harris' later autobiography, *As a Woman Thinks* (1925).

note in the U.S. In one striking respect her experience was very like my own. She was the wife of a minister who fell a prey to religious melancholia. She says:—

"I have written out in another place the life we lived during this period but not the terror and silence that fell upon me. That cannot be set down in words. The frantic efforts I made to save him from himself and to protect him from that terrible world in the church. I know where the spirit of all tragedies dwells—in the silence which you dare not break by even one call for help. I contracted the habit of holding my breath in those years of suspense. Even when my body slept it seemed to me that my heart was forever sitting up with Lundy in the dark hours of the night . . . . I used to wish I could find relief in a real battle, see the dreadful face of my enemy and feel his wounds rather than face the powers and principalities of Lundy's terrible darkness."

Oh, true, true! "The silence you dare not break by one call for help." It is as if my own heart had uttered that moan. And "holding my breath in those years of suspense." Yes, how often have I held mine since that ghastly spring of 1919.

Monday, Sept. 7, 1925

Ewan was very dull today. And this evening Miss Imrie came unexpectedly—an old maid of Zephyr who spent her youth in Leaskdale and occasionally comes over for her "vacation." Just why she chose to make this her headquarters I cannot say for I never asked her. But at any other time I would have been glad enough to see the poor soul and give her as decent a time as possible for I don't think her lot has ever been a very bright one. But she is one of those who feel, if they do not think, that no Christian woman should be beautiful—or interesting. And I did secretly resent her coming at this time and spoiling for me Chester's last days at home.

I didn't let the poor lady see this however. And she gave me lots of amusing gossip about Zephyr people as we sat in the parlor and crocheted. I found out several amusing bits. Ever since I knew Will Lockie and his wife I have *felt* that neither of them were normal. And now I find that my feeling was correct. Will Lockie's mother was quite out of her mind many of the earlier years of her life. This accounts for the odd streaks in both Will and Jim. And Mrs. Will Lockie herself has been quite "off" several times. I have always suspected this. Indeed, I don't think she is ever wholly "on." Then, too, I found from Miss Imrie that Ben Armstrong has always been considered an unbearable sort of a man by all the rest of the people. Nobody could ever get along with him. He domineered and dictated. Heaven help everybody concerned if they dared to differ from him. Miss Imrie expressed surprise that Ewan had been able to keep him in order for fifteen years.

Ewan has a knack that way. But perhaps if he had fought Armstrong out and put him in his place it might have been better for the church today. If Armstrong had left it years ago he could not have made the trouble he did in regard to Union.

The Manse, Leaskdale
Wednesday, Sept. 9

Today I packed Chester's trunk and valise. It does not seem very long since I used to be packing my own for school and college flittings. I am very very tired and sad tonight.

Friday, Sept. 11, 1925
The Manse, Leaskdale

On Wednesday night I went in as usual to see the boys before I went to sleep. Dear little fellows lying there. Never separated before. Always to be separated henceforth save for fleeting holidays. After I went to bed I lay awake for hours crying. Every time I had scolded Chester for some boyish peccadillo came up and reproached me. Hadn't I been too exacting with him? I felt as if I had—as if I had fallen terribly short of my ideal of motherhood.

We left at 6.30 yesterday morning and had a pleasant drive in. The world is always young again for just a little while at the dawn. The day was beautiful and "the flash" came so often that it made life worth while again. As if there were a great cistern of beauty in the universe from which we all may drink and be filled.

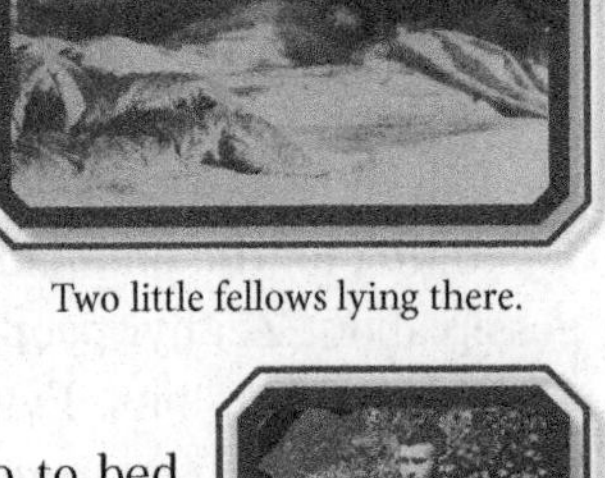
Two little fellows lying there.

We left Chester at St. Andrew's—all alone among a crowd of strange boys. He was plucky but I think he felt pretty blue at parting. "Thanksgiving will be Thanksgiving for the first time in my life this year, mother," he said.

We got home at 9.30. Poor Stuart would not go to bed until we got home—he was too lonesome. Then he went with his dog. When I went up he was asleep and Dixie was lying on Chester's pillow. Only one little boy where the night before there had been two!

[Chester]

I couldn't sleep for a long time. And when I did drop off a tremendous thunderstorm wakened me. All day I have missed Chester terribly. When we sat down to supper tonight and saw Stuart in Chester's place both Elsie and I broke down and cried. I miss Chester in so many ways. His kisses—he never passed me without

stopping for a kiss and asking his old baby question "Do you like me?" His music—he was always putting on Victrola records.[521] His "mother dearwums." His rosy healthy face! Oh, I suppose I'll "get used to it"—as I have got used to so many seemingly intolerable things. But just now it seems as if I couldn't.

Today has been warm and sultry and Ewan has been very dull.

Saturday, Sept. 12, 1925

It poured rain most of the day. It was the day of the Mission Band Tea—a yearly event and I was busy all the forenoon preparing for it. This evening Ewan said we would go in and see Chester two weeks from today. This has cheered me up and made it seem possible to carry on. I'm looking forward to it like a child.

Sunday, Sept. 13, 1925

A pouring rainy day. The long drought of August and early September has broken with a vengeance. I wrote Chester today. Henceforth this will be a weekly item. Of late years my personal correspondence has dwindled. Only very few regular correspondents remain out of the dozens with whom I used to exchange voluminous epistles thirty years ago. But now I shall have more letters to write again and receive.

Stuart wrote, too, and I laughed over two sentences in his letter. Speaking of a family that has had a great many operations he wrote, "Seemingly an operation is all in the day's work there" and in regard to the rain, "I guess the weather is sorry over your going away." Stuart has my gift of writing easy letters. Chester hasn't. His letters are stiff and stingy.

Monday, Sept. 14, 1925
The Manse, Leaskdale

Today I watched for the mail with the impatience of a maid waiting for a lover's epistle. The expected letter came. Not much news, of course—he wrote Saturday. I fear he is pretty lonesome though he does not complain. But he "can't sleep at nights." And he only "likes it fairly well."

I was amused tonight over something Mary Shier said. She knows the woman for whom Lily is working in Toronto now. Meeting her in Simpson's she asked her how she liked Lily. "Oh, fairly well," said the lady "but for a girl who had the responsibility she had she doesn't seem very capable of going ahead with things."

---

521   The Victor Talking Machine Company had introduced a turntable with the amplifying horn tucked away inside a wooden cabinet to resemble a piece of furniture, trademarked as the Victrola.

Responsibility! I could have howled. I suppose Lily has been telling her new mistress that she "kept" my house *in toto*. Poor Lily! Yet the thing annoys me—it is so untrue and grotesque. And false impressions travel as fast and last as long as lies.

Wednesday, Sept. 16, 1925
The Manse, Leaskdale

The School fair came off at Sandford today and of course we had to take Stuart and endure a day of boredom. Of course the children enjoy it so it is justified but for me the low descending sun of the school fair always counts for a day lost.

Today was also peppered with unpleasant moments when I met Zephyr Unionists who had left our church. I never know whether they would like me to speak to them or whether they would rather I'd take no notice of them. If I were in their shoes I'd certainly prefer the latter. But speak I must lest I give them welcome ground for criticism and my soul cringes in me at the meeting. In order to have some backing—I hate wandering around in such a crowd alone—I attached myself to Mrs. Jake Meyers, who is always a fairly agreeable companion, though she is very tasteless—a good egg without salt. Alas, Mrs. Jas. Lockie likewise attached herself to Mrs. M. and I was uncomfortably aware of her all day—though she seemed a little bit more like a human being and less like a demon incarnate than usual.

I had one comfort, though. A short distance across the fields behind the school was a bit of scenery that fed some hunger in me. One of those bits that you love at sight for no reason you can put into words. There was a spring—I knew there was, though I could not see it, the dimple in the little valley; and around that dimple was a cluster of trees. That is all the description I can give of it. The *soul* of it I cannot picture. But 'twas a darling place and all through the dreary, arid day my spirit pastured in it. If I could have but sat in it all day in the autumn sunshine and read or dreamed, enjoying the blessedness of not having to laugh unless I really wanted to, with a calm conviction that Mrs. Jas. Lockie had gone where good devils go, how happy a day it would have been!

But Stuart had a jolly time and got second prize for table bouquet. And Ewan picked up some amazing bits of gossip with which we regaled ourselves on the way home.

Item 1. William Lockie has been declaring publicly that "it is no harm for a Christian to swear!"

I wonder if he learned that in the Unionist church! It does not sound to me like Presbyterian doctrine.

Item 2. Will Lockie and Ben Armstrong never would stand in the Presbyterian church while the "Amen" was sung at the end of a hymn. They did not "approve" of "Amens" at the end of hymns, so as soon as the last word of the

hymn was sung down plumped the two gentlemen promptly on that part of their bodies the good Lord made for plumping. But in the United church they stand for the Amens without turning a hair.

Item 3. On the Sunday *following* Union Ewan spoke a few words in Zephyr church to the effect that now those who thought differently about Union had gone out those of us who remained were "of one heart and one soul etc." He spoke nicely and there was nothing in what he said to offend anyone. Mrs. Will Sellars is going about saying that if he hadn't said that she "might not have left the church." Now, the fact is that when he said it Mrs. Sellers had already left the church and at that very moment was over in the Methodist church joining it. So Mrs. Sellars seems to feel the need of justifying herself. It is a pity she has got a little mixed in her dates.

A letter from Christie bore the welcome news that the store property has been sold at last. So one of our worries is lifted from us and one that has been a very considerable one.

The reviews of *Emily Climbs* are coming in. They are mostly very good. Many reviews say it is "equal to my best." But I can't get excited over reviews as I once did.

Sunday, Sept. 20, 1925
The Manse, Leaskdale

There are certain times when I feel that I could take two giggling girls in my class by the scruff of the necks, knock their silly bobbed heads together, throw them out in the horse sheds and feel that I had done God service.

I had to get that out of my system before I went to bed.

Monday, Sept. 21, 1925

I have been miserable for three days with another bad cold. It seems to me that I have had nothing but bad colds ever since the first of the year. I could not breathe or sleep last night.

But we had a more cheerful letter from Chester today. He is getting acquainted and is tentatively on the "Junior Saints" football team, not without hope of making it permanently. There is a different tone to his letter from last week's and I feel more satisfied. But I am counting the days to Saturday.

Tuesday, Sept. 22, 1925
The Manse, Leaskdale

I had a really dreadful night last night. The difficulty of breathing caused by my cold prevented me from sleeping and I got badly depressed and Zephyr-obsessed. But I feel better today. And I had a little note from Miss Devigne, the St. Andrew's matron, saying that Chester was getting on nicely.

This evening I have finished reading *Charlotte Brontë and Her Circle* by Shorter.[522] Hitherto I have thought that the fascination Charlotte Brontë's life and personality held for me was largely due to the literary charm of Mrs. Gaskell's biography. But it is just as strong in this book so I have concluded that it is inherent in her.

Charlotte Brontë made only about seven thousand by her books—not a tenth of what one of the flimsy and ephemeral "best sellers" of today would bring in. It seems unfair and unjust.

What I admire most in Charlotte Brontë is her absolute clear-sightedness regarding shams and sentimentalities. Nothing of the sort could impose on her. And she always hewed straight to the line.

I have been asking myself "If I had known Charlotte Brontë in life how would we have reacted upon each other? Would I have liked her? Would she have liked me?" I answer "no." She was absolutely without a sense of humor. I could never find a kindred spirit in a woman without a sense of humor. And for the same reason she would not have approved of me at all. All the same, had she been compelled to live with me for awhile I could have done her whole heaps of good. A few jokes would have leavened the gloom and tragedy of that Haworth parsonage amazingly. Charlotte would have been thirty per cent better for it. But she would have written most scathing things about me to Miss Nussey and Mrs. Gaskell.

In one of her letters she speaks of "the canker of constant solitude." Ah, truly. If we could have had no soul contact in the House of Mirth we could have come together in the House of Lonely Years.

People have spoken of Charlotte Brontë's "creative genius." Charlotte Brontë had *no* creative genius. Her genius was one of amazing ability to describe and interpret the people and surroundings she *knew*. All the people in her books who impress us with such a wonderful sense of reality were drawn from life. She herself is "Jane Eyre" and "Lucy Snowe." Emily was "Shirley." "Rochester," whom she did "create" was unnatural and unreal. "Blanche Ingram" was unreal. "St. John" was unreal. Most of her men are unreal. She knew nothing of men except her father and brother and the Belgian professor of her intense and unhappy love. "Emmanuel" was drawn from him and therefore is one of the few men, if not the only man, in her books who is "real."

Thursday, Sept. 24, 1925

I finished today a series of four stories I have been working on since July, with an eye to the *The Delineator*—"What's In A Name?," "The Magic Door," "The

---

522   British journalist and literary critic Clement King Shorter (1857–1926) had published *Charlotte Brontë and Her Circle* in 1896, a discussion of the people around Brontë during her lifetime.

Bobbing of Marigold" and "Her Chrism of Womanhood." They centre around a new little heroine and I have been very happy in writing them. I think they are very good specimens of their *genre* and "Marigold" seems very real and enchanting to me. Perhaps I'll write a book about her sometime.

We were over to J. Meyers for supper this evening. I loathe visiting anywhere in Zephyr now. I always have the feeling that I am walking over a powder mine, even in the houses of our friends. And nearly always something is said that hurts our feelings or worries us, though it may not be so intended at all.

Friday, Sept. 25, 1925
The Manse, Leaskdale

I am tired tonight. Today seemed to be infested with a multiplicity of small duties. But—I am going to see Chester tomorrow—tomorrow—tomorrow. It has been singing itself in my heart all day.

Saturday, Sept. 26, 1925

We rose with the lark—only there was no lark—and had a lovely drive into Toronto under the coral of the morning sky, with faint violet or white plumes of smoke going up everywhere on the crystal air. When I ran up the steps of the Lower House there was Chester smiling down at me, looking the picture of health with his rosy face. He is getting on finely now. Has got acquainted and is quite happy. This is such a relief to me. When Ewan was a boy he had an attack of his malady whenever he went away from home—when he went to P.W.C. and again when he went to Dalhousie. No doubt this was brought on by the loneliness of change and strangers. I have always dreaded that it might be the same with Chester and that if the seeds of his father's melancholy lurked in his system it would make its appearance when he first went away from home. But now one dread has been removed from my life and I realize how oppressive it was by its sudden lifting.

We had lunch at Simpsons[523] and then I took Chester to a movie. Chester has been at St. Andrew's only two weeks but already it has put its stamp on him. He is a "public school" boy and talks the jargon of his guild as glibly as if he had been talking it for years. He got through his "initiation" in fine shape. One stunt was that he had to push the football over the gym floor with his nose. I had warned him before he went to take it all in good part. He did, with the happy result that the boys pronounced him "a good little kid."

He has scars on face, elbow and knee from football but displayed them

---

523   Now defunct, Canadian department store Simpsons was founded in 1858.

proudly as badges of honour. I am not without anxiety. They play Rugby at St. Andrew's and it is a rough game. But I do not voice my anxiety. Chester must take his chances. I am glad he is interested in sports. Ewan never went in for any kind of game or sport in his college life and realizes now what a mistake he made. On the other hand there is a danger that Chester may give more of his mind to sports than studies. However, it is on the knees of the gods. The older I grow the more convinced a fatalist do I become. I think we "fash" ourselves uselessly over things. It is all written. We cannot by any pleading or effort erase the future any more than the past.

On our way into Toronto we stopped for a moment at a shabby little house on a poor road because Elsie's grandmother lived there and she wanted to see her. Out came her uncle with her—a big, rough-looking man who proceeded to tell me that he had "read every one of my books he could get his hands on." He seemed from appearances the most unlikely person in the world to read anything much less books like mine. I can't decide whether it was a compliment or not.

Sunday, Sept. 27, 1925

I conducted the Sunday School review today—Mr. Gray shuffles it off on me whenever he can—and went to Zephyr in the afternoon with Mr. Atkins of Port Perry who exchanged with Ewan today. Will Sellars and wife were there. I spoke to them both. Got no impression of any kind from her but *felt* when Will shook hands that he was glad to be back in his old church, even as a visitor. They are too shamefaced to come when Ewan is there so sneak back when a stranger preaches. I wonder what they really felt like in their hearts.

Tuesday, Sept. 29, 1925
The Manse, Leaskdale

I had a real holiday today. It was the day of Scott fair and Ewan, Elsie and Stuart went. No fair for me an't please ye! But I treated myself to a holiday. I read and did fancy work alternately the whole day—nothing else—and thoroughly enjoyed myself.

Wednesday, Sept. 30, 1925

Ewan was to see Jim Lockies today and came home with the usual depressing gossip. I felt blue all the rest of the day. I'm foolish to mind it I suppose. But while it is easy to bear peas in someone else's shoes it is not so easy when they are in your own.

When Ewan told Mrs. Lockie the indisputable fact that there are just as many in Zephyr church on Sundays now as there were before the disruption she moaned that "they only came because they had to." Why they *have* to come or who is making them she did not explain. I detest that woman. I think, of course, that what is the matter with her is that she feels humiliated over the way her husband is acting. He won't go to church just because Mrs. Warren is treasurer and has made such an ass of himself that it is not likely he will ever go again in any event. And Mrs. Lockie wants to vent her discomfort over this on someone.

Thursday, October 1, 1925

Tonight we were at Tommy Marquis' to tea. When I was taking off my wraps in the little spare room off the dining room I happened to glance out of the window. Before me lay a long beautiful double row of spruce trees, with moonlight falling through them in enchanting shadows. Instantly I was swamped in a wave of homesickness for Park Corner, of which the scene reminded me—why I do not know, for there was nothing very like it at Park Corner. Perhaps because it linked up in some way with an old memory of a night when Frede and I were driving along a spruce bordered road back among the Irishtown hills and she remarked to me on the beauty of tree shadows in moonlight.

There was something else about the moment that had a strange sorrowful charm. I have been so long in Leaskdale that the events of the first years have begun to wear the hazy beauty of "long ago." I recalled an evening spent in that hill farmhouse the fall when Chester was a tiny baby. I recalled sitting there rocking him to sleep and looking out on those same spruces, with the happy eyes of the new mother cuddling a wee, white, dimpled son. And that was "long ago" and all kinds of changes had come there, too. Then Mrs. Marquis and her girls, Ada and Mabel, two nice "kindred spirits" were there. Now Ada and Mabel are married and gone. Mrs. Marquis was away, too. Tommy is married and he and his wife live there. Both Tommy and Mrs. Tommy are very nice young folks whom we like; but the pleasant old order of things has passed away there, too. It has to be; it is well that it is so; but growing pains are never pleasant.

I read a brief biographical sketch of myself in a paper today where it was stated that I "lived as a girl in Saskatchewan where my grandfather was the postmaster of Avonlea."

Truly, I have come to believe that "history is a narrative of things that never happened."

Friday, October 2, 1925

Ewan was not very well today. It poured rain all day and evening. Ergo, the preparatory service in Zephyr did not take place. Poor Zephyr. There has always seemed a doom on it.

But I have a dish of marigolds before me that are so lovely that I can't believe the world is wholly delivered to Satan.

Sunday, Oct. 4, 1925
The Manse, Leaskdale

Two new members joined Zephyr church today. So much for a start towards filling up the gaps.

Yesterday I had a letter from Bertie. I had asked her to inquire of the Perkins family in Vancouver of the whereabouts and welfare of Nora Lefurgey Campbell.[524] It is several years since I heard of her. Bertie did and was told among other things that Nora's only daughter Jessie, about twelve years old, died last spring of spinal meningitis. Poor poor Nora! She loved her children so intensely and was such a devoted mother. *What* is the meaning of these terrible rendings and tearings of our deepest ties and feelings?

Wednesday, Oct. 7, 1925

This is Stuart's birthday. He is ten years old. Soon I will have no child at all.

I wonder if Chester is warm enough in bed these cold nights.

Thursday, Oct. 8, 1925

I had two odd dreams last night. One was that I was in Cavendish, sitting down to supper with Grandma, Aunt Annie—and Mrs. George Harker! Of all women! The latter was a woman of no significance to me who died thirty years ago and of whom I don't believe I have thought since. But at that gruesome supper table three of the party were *dead*.

I wakened, slept, and dreamed again—an odd dream this time of Mr. James Mustard telling me "what a happy life he had had." When I came down I said to Elsie "If there is anything in the old saying, 'Dream of the dead and you'll hear of the living' I'm going to hear some special news today."

Sequel:—Presently the phone rang. It was a message to tell me of the sudden and dangerous illness of Mr. Jas. Mustard. The mail came. An envelope in Mary Beaton's hand. Containing an invitation to Maud's wedding—to the

---

524   Prince Edward Island native Nora Lefurgey (1880–1977), a young teacher, boarded at LMM's grandparents' house in Cavendish in 1902; during this time, she became good friends with LMM.

young man she was engaged to and threw over. This was what Mary worried so over in the summer. She liked Albert Middleton so well and wanted the match. I hope this indicates that Maud has come to her senses and that Mary's troubles are over as far as she is concerned. But Maud may have had a case too.

We were down to the induction at Uxbridge tonight. An interesting service. Mr. Robinson is the new minister. I hope he and his wife will be nice and companionable. He is the only near Presbyterian minister now. We couldn't fraternize with the Bennies at all and were relieved when they went away.

Friday, Oct. 9, 1925

A bitter cold day. High, snarling, quarrelsome wind blowing. Snowing. So far October has been a wretched month. We went to Sonya induction today. It has called a Mr. Douglas and is off Ewan's hands at last. But he has his hands full yet as Moderator of the Presbyterian minority at Wick. They have appealed their case to the Commission and Ewan has to get it into shape for them. However, he is always better when he has a task like this on hand. He has been pretty well this week.

Saturday, Oct. 10, 1925

A dreadful day of wind and cold—the coldest Oct. 10 for fifty years it is said. The leaves are frozen on the trees.

This evening I felt a bit blue. I had listened to eight sermons this week and I felt rather fed up. So I asked Ewan to take Stuart and me to Uxbridge to see a movie by way of counter irritant. I put it on the ground of Stuart's wish—he had been promised a movie for a birthday treat—but I really wanted a change of any kind. And they get very good movies in Uxbridge. The comic was so funny I laughed consumedly, felt ever so much better, and my theological indigestion vanished.

Ewan has got Lena Lockie into Normal, having moved heaven and earth to accomplish it. It is too long a story to go into here. But she owes it to him. *I* wouldn't have bothered myself about it had I been he, after the way Jim and Mrs. Jim have acted. They don't know the meaning of gratitude—but I think Lena *is* grateful.

Monday, Oct. 12, 1925
The Manse, Leaskdale

The Ministerial Association held its first meeting of the season at Rev. Taylor's, Uxbridge, today. And thereby hangs a tale—regarding that meeting that was to have been here last spring and was not.

We knew perfectly well that Dyer and Watch were at the bottom of it but we were not sure if they were the only ones. So, after leaving the matter fallow all summer we had decided that we would have it cleared up this fall. If Dyer and Watch were solely responsible for it, well and good. *They* did not matter an old shoe to us. But if any of the other members of the Association would not come here because of our Union views it was not well or good. We resolved to ferret out the truth. If Dyer, as we had very good reason to suspect, had contrived to make the Association shoulder the action of his own personal spite, he must be shown up.

Shown up he was. Oh, we cut the comb of that pompous young ornament of the United Church *be-yew-tifully*. In good old expressive Scotch he got his breeks warmed.[525]

The members of the Association turned out well. Dyer, who was secretary, came early, swelling like a little turkey cock, fraternizing markedly with a couple of Ex-Methodist ministers and discussing some of their own conference doings and plans as if on him and him alone depended their carrying out.

The election of officers proceeded. Mr. Robinson was nominated for secretary. The president said, "Any other nomination?" Dyer at once got up and said *he* didn't want to be re-elected. It was not necessary. Nobody wanted to re-elect him. He *felt* this and saved his face by declining a re-election before it was (*not*) offered him. The significant fact is that he had not declined it when nominations were first called for.

Robinson was elected secretary, Mr. Taylor president, Mr. Baldwin vice. So far, good. Here rose Ewan. He told simply of what had happened. Said Mr. Watch had told me that the members of the Association were too busy to come to Leaskdale. But that we had learned later from *reliable authority* (of course we couldn't drag Taylor's name into it as he had spoken to us in confidence) that the meeting was changed because of Ewan's views on Union. Ewan said he simply wished to know the truth. If, as Mr. Watch had said, the ministers were too busy to come that was all right. If on the other hand, the reason was Ewan's stand regarding Union, then we must know if the Association members were behind the Executive in this action. If they were, we, of course, could not continue in the Association.

During the progress of Ewan's remarks I had been watching Dyer. At first his expression was one of lofty indifference. Then, as the significance of Ewan's speech dawned on him, the most comical change came over his countenance. It was quite indescribable. And he did what a guilty person naturally would do—he looked at me. Then he was done for. I was gazing straight at him and I wickedly continued to gaze. Dyer was like a fascinated bird. He would look

---

525 "Breeks" is a Scots word for breeches, that is, pants.

away—then look back at me at once—to see, I suppose, if I were still looking at him. I never saw a mortal look more guilty or more exquisitely uncomfortable. If he were innocent he would not, of course, have found any special significance in the fact that I happened to be looking at him.

When Ewan finished Mr. Taylor said *he* had nothing to do with the change. In turn all the other ministers present got up and disclaimed any share in it. Dyer, seeing everyone was looking at him got up and stumbled through a jumble of confused remarks. He was utterly unprepared and made an ass of himself. He said all he knew of it was that Mr. Watch had rung him up and said, "What about the meeting at Leaskdale?" "And *I* said, 'Oh, I'll go anywhere'." (Who had suggested anything else to him?) And that was all *he* knew of it, dear innocent little man.

Down he sat. And if he had kept his head and said no more he would have won a kind of victory—for of course we could not *prove* anything, as we could not betray Taylor's confidence. Then one member moved that the Association express its regret that the Executive had seen fit to change the meeting etc. Dyer, realizing, I suppose, that this would go in the minutes and that if Watch ever heard he had thrown all the blame on him the fat would be in the fire, got up and blurted out the truth—the very opposite of what he had said before. He said the meeting had been changed because "Mr. Macdonald had been interfering in my pastoral work" and had "refused to shake hands" with him at a Presbytery meeting. That is to say, he himself had been the sole cause of changing the meeting on the ground of his own personal grievance but throwing the onus of it on the association—something which he had no business whatever to do and which most of them properly resented.

Now, in regard to the things Dyer had said:—

Ewan, of course, never had anything to do with Dyer's own congregation of Greenbank. But Dyer was interim moderator of Uxbridge up to the time of the "Union." He was determined that they should hear no speaker on the Presbyterian side but he himself propagandized on every hand. He could not, however, prevent Uxbridge from taking a vote but he got the session of Quaker Hill (which is part of Uxbridge congregation), three of whom were Unionists, to decide that they wouldn't have a vote. The Presbyterian Association wrote to Ewan and asked him to try to see what he could do towards getting a vote for Quaker Hill. Ewan went to see all the leading men of Quaker Hill church who were opposed to Union and got them to sign the necessary request for a vote. And Quaker Hill and Uxbridge both voted Presbyterian by large majorities. Poor Dyer was furious and at once resigned the moderatorship.

At the last meeting of Presbytery before "Union" Ewan did not exactly refuse to shake hands with Dyer but when Dyer came up to the group and began to shake hands with the other men Ewan turned and walked away.

This meeting was *three weeks after* the Association meeting and the reason why Ewan turned away was that he was not going to greet as a friend a man who had refused to come to our house.

And yet Dyer got up there and said that it was because of this that he had changed the meeting. Verily, the prophets are not all dead yet!

Now, if Ewan had just been quick enough to catch on to this, as I did, he could have exposed Dyer then and there for what he is—a cowardly little liar. But he did not. He thought at first that of course Dyer must be referring to the meeting of Presbytery *before* the May Association. And he knew he *had* shaken hands with Dyer then. I remembered him coming home and telling me that Dyer had not seemed to make any difference because of the Quaker Hill affair but had shook hands with seeming friendliness.

At this point Mr. Baldwin pressed the motion and it was carried unanimously. Dyer as secretary had to write it in the book himself and Ewan expressed himself as satisfied. The meeting ran its course and was closed. Dyer did not stay for the social part. He simply faded out of the picture. Nobody seemed to miss him. I am sure he could have eaten us all up alive.

Well, it had to be done and I do not regret that we did it. The thing had to be cleared up if we were to continue as members of the Association. But I hate such ructions. I fight well when I am at it, giving and asking no quarter, but when it is done I sicken over the necessity. In a sense this has spoiled the Association for us at least for a time. I have been sad and unhappy all the evening over it.

We are to have the next meeting. Dyer will certainly not be "among those present." In fact I fancy he will leave the Association. He must feel that the Association condemned his action and that, to one of his overweening conceit, must be a bitter pill.

It was a pretty severe lesson and the young cockerel deserved it. He had offered a pointed insult to me. Whatever Ewan had done on the battleground of Union *I* was guiltless of all offence towards him. I was the hostess, whom Dyer himself last fall entreated to take the May meeting. I do not choose to be made the butt of the petty spite of a creature like Dyer. But I regret the necessity of soiling my hands and vexing my spirit over him. It seems to leave more of a feeling of degradation than any exultation of victory. One certainly cannot feel proud of having stepped on the head of a venomous little snake.

Wednesday, Oct. 14, 1925
The Manse, Leaskdale

Ewan took a load of Wick men to Toronto today to see a lawyer re their appeal. He certainly has worked this fall to help those people out. Will he get any thanks for it. I have grown very cynical.

Friday, Oct. 16, 1925

Yesterday Mrs. Leask and I went to the W.M.S. at Wick. Mrs. Leask had to read a paper and I felt that I ought to help the Wick women a bit in their present uncomfortable chaotic condition. We had a pleasant time but I grudged the time.

Today there was in the papers some wonderful news—or what should prove wonderful news. France and Germany have sworn "perpetual peace" at Locarno.[526] Said peace being guaranteed by England and Italy. As far as man can dispose this ends at last the war begun eleven years ago in 1914. I certainly hope that it *does* end it and that henceforth distracted Europe will set its face to a new day.

This evening at 6.30, when I rose from the supper table I said to Ewan, "Let's run over and call on the Brydons this evening."

Mr. Brydon is the minister inducted some months ago in Woodville. To call on them is a duty that has been postponed too long. But the point I wish to bring out is this:—Woodville is 26 miles away. To "call" on the Brydons meant a run of 52 miles. Ewan said casually, "All right" and we went.

Suppose thirty years ago, I had got up from the supper table in Cavendish and said, "Grandpa, let's run in to Charlottetown tonight and see So-and-So." The good old gentleman would have thought I had gone crazy. And he would have been right.

The world moves faster now. But is it any happier a world?

We went but it was not the pleasant drive it sometimes is. We called at Cannington and took the Scotts along with us. I like Mrs. Scott but she is not entertaining. She talked during the whole drive of the doings at the last Presbyterial and kindred subjects. I get very tired of endless missionary diet. Then at Woodville it was Union—Union—Union. The subject of Union has more bite than that of missions but I am horribly fed up with it too. I don't deny that Brydon is a comfortable person to hear about Union. He is a man of first rate intellect and sees very clearly. His sizing up of the situation was masterly and his account of some of the doings of Unionist ministers very adequate. But it poured rain all the way home and we had a flat tire. So it was two when we got here and I was very tired. Mrs. Brydon did not consider it necessary to offer us even a cup of tea after—and before—our long drive. And so I think things were just as well thirty years ago!

526　In 1925, the Allied countries of World War I negotiated several agreements for improved relations with the new states of Central and Eastern Europe, as well as with Germany. The negotiations took place in Locarno, Switzerland, and were known as the "Locarno Treaties." These agreements eased political tensions in western Europe from 1924 to 1930; however, this comparative political calm would come to an end in 1936, when Hitler sent troops into the demilitarized Rhineland.

There is absolutely no autumn pomp this year—the first time I recall such a thing. This part of Ontario is usually very gorgeous in the fall. The bitter frost that came early in October actually *froze* the green leaves on the trees. I never saw such a bedraggled and melancholy landscape.

Ewan has not been so well again lately.

Thursday, Oct. 29, 1925
The Manse, Leaskdale

I have been in Toronto for a week. For a whole week I have been where I never heard the abominable word Zephyr and where nobody expected me to attend a missionary meeting. I had a very nice time and it has pepped me up for the two months that are before me—the hardest and *worriedest* months in the year.

We motored in last Wednesday. It was a lovely day with a crisp sunshiny air—a rare event this fall when it has rained or froze almost continually. The most abominable October since I came to Ontario—and indeed in my whole recollection.

My main occupation was shopping but I had some very pleasant teas and luncheons. Friday afternoon I went up to St. Andrew's to see the Junior saints play the Appleby boys and win. When I sat on the bench and tried to spot Chester in his team I couldn't do it. Not till he came up to me was I able to recognize him—due mostly to the fact that he had a helmet on—and it made him look absurdly as he looked when he was two years old, wearing that bear-cloth cap with the earlugs.

Mr. Tudball, the Lower School headmaster said Chester ought to make a good football player when he mastered the points of the game because he had just the build for it.

I felt sad as I sat there and watched them play in the cool gray autumn afternoon. I was thinking of Frede and how she had once said she would give anything to see Chester's first football game. When she said that it seemed such a far-off thing. Why, it would be years—long years—before that little white, dimpled baby would be playing football!

After the game the boys rushed into the tuckshop and entertained the defeated visitors. I came away and left Chester there, carousing with his mates and very happy I think.

One evening Mary and I went to see *Three Live Ghosts*.[527] It was the best comedy I ever saw and we laughed unceasingly all through it. How pleasant it would be to live where I could see a good play once a week—or even once a month.

---

527   A 1922 British comedy film, directed by George Fitzmaurice, based on a 1920 Broadway play of the same title by Frederic Isham.

Yet, in spite of my pleasant week and in spite of many rather delightful pomps and vanities and in spite of Zephyr and missionary meetings, I was glad enough to come back to my own orderly comfortable home. I got home last night through a wind pursuing tormented wreaths of snow over the hills. Today was bitter cold. Only 11 above zero! And this in October.

It was election day too. I voted for the conservative candidate. No Liberal ran in this riding and I would not vote for the U.F.O. man—an ignorant creature who is not fit to be in Parliament.[528]

I had a letter at last from Margaret Stirling. It is over a year since I wrote her. She and John are in the Union church. He was always a fanatic on the subject but Margaret used to be bitterly opposed to it. Of course she had to go with him—and now, I hear, she out-Unions the Unionist. Of which fact the psychology is tolerably clear.

I am sorry we are in different churches. There will always hereafter be a subject we cannot discuss. We have had many good laughs together over the various idiosyncrasies of the members of Presbytery and our mutual ministerial acquaintances. But never again! I *cannot* joke to Margaret of Unionist ministers and I *will* not of Presbyterian ministers. She will be in the same predicament and half our fun will be absent.

But our friendship has been too pleasant. The devil had to spoil it in some way. For some reason he could not kill Margaret as he did Frede so he just brewed up Church Union to spoil it.

I had another letter also but I have not opened it yet and will not till tomorrow. It is from Rollins—and I don't want to be worried until I get this house set to rights and all my belongings restored to order. I have been hard at work all day.

Ewan seems a bit dull and heady. But there is *one* encouraging bit of news in Zephyr. A certain Mr. Smith has bought one of the stores there and he is a Presbyterian. They are very nice people especially Mrs. Smith but have no family—at least none with them. Which is a pity. A few young people and children would be such an encouragement.

Last night when I came home I thought Dixie would go mad. He simply lay down before me and howled with joy. I could not get upstairs until Ewan dragged him away by the collar. The poor little dog seemed utterly out of his head. Luck was more dignified as became a cat, but he sat on the table and never took his eyes off me for a moment the whole evening. It seemed almost uncanny. Generally he sleeps all the evening beside me but last night it seemed as if he were afraid to shut or move his eyes lest I vanish again. Well,

---

528   The "U.F.O." party refers to the United Farmers of Ontario, the provincial branch of the United Farmers movement.

it is good to feel that my cat and dog won't rise up against me in judgment, at least. This evening after nine—I stop working at nine. No eight hour days in my scheme of things—I was re-reading *The South African farm*.[529] It made a tremendous sensation when it came out over thirty years ago. It would not make any now. But there is a charm about the book still. Whatever its faults, the people in it are *real*, so you are interested in them. I found myself disagreeing with a good many passages I had marked in agreement formerly. But in regard to many I could draw a second score of intensified agreement.

Dixie

Friday, Oct. 30, 1925
The Manse, Leaskdale

A day distractingly full of small things as well as the big one of getting the house into order for the Association meeting Monday—helping Stuart get his Hallowe'en Jacky Lantern ready—helping a young couple get dressed up as nuns for the masquerade at Sandford, writing a long letter re the con-

Luck

tracts for *The Blue Castle* and so on and so on. When things were pretty well done I went upstairs and opened Rollins' letter. It was short, enclosing one from Briesen and Schrenk as follows:—

"It gives us great pleasure to inform you that we have just been notified by the Clerk of the Appellate Division of the Supreme Court of the State of New York that the order of Judge McGoldrick dismissing the complaint in the case of L.C.Page Co. V. Macdonald has been affirmed unanimously and without opinion. This action, under normal conditions, brings the litigation to a definite end. There is still the possibility that counsel for the Page Co. may apply for re-argument or for leave to take the case to the Court of Appeals, which is the court of last resort in our state. As a rule, however, cases only go to the Court of Appeals where there is a certain lack of harmony among the judges constituting the Appellate division: in other words, in cases where there is a dissent on the part of some of the judges in the Appellate Division. For the time being we entertain the somewhat justifiable hope that the case will not be permitted to be taken to the higher court and that a petition for re-argument, if made, will result in its denial, and that Mrs. Macdonald before Christmas, will actually receive her money that has accumulated with the Stokes Co."

529   South African author Olive Schreiner's (1855–1920) first novel, *The Story of an African Farm* (1883), had met with immediate success. It is now considered to be an early feminist classic.

Well, so much further along. But I do not share B. and S.'s pious hope that Page will drop the case there if there is any possibility in the world of getting it before any other court.

Nevertheless, this heartened me up a bit for the day and a letter from *The Delineator* was another burst of sunshine. Mrs. Meloney wrote that she "loved Marigold" and would give $1600 for the four stories.

And the first year I wrote seriously I earned $75, writing ten times as much!

But I admit there was a difference in the quality.

This windfall set my mind at rest concerning a financial problem or two.

Today I read an account of Maud Beaton's wedding in the *Guardian*. It seems about three or four years since I read—having first written it—the account of her mother's wedding. In one way. In another way it seems a thousand years. There was really less vital change in the thousand years of from 800 to 1800 than there has been in the world during the last thirty years. (By the way, "the year 1" is now coming to mean 1901. In "my day" it meant 1801.)

It has been my misfortune to be a born conservative, hater of change, and to live my life in a period when everything has been, or is being turned topsy turvey, from the old religions down. My aunts and grandmothers lived practically their whole lives in an unchanged world. Changes came to them in the natural course of life but never were the foundations of their lives torn away from beneath their feet. For myself I have my own foundation and I stand firmly on it, unalarmed and unhurt by the crash of creeds and systems. But I cannot help being affected adversely by the changes in the world around me and the unrest and misery of an age that has thrown away everything because it has lost some things, and is itself lost and floundering now.

Reading *William Ashe*,[530] one of yesterday's forgotten sensations. Very interesting. But an incredible sort of ending.

Wednesday, Nov. 4, 1925
The Manse, Leaskdale

We had a meeting of the S.S. Executive here tonight. Mr. Gray, the Superintendent, shirked coming as usual and left the work to me—a trick he is expert at. Mrs. George Leask favored us with a silly outburst of fireworks because her *amour propre* has recently been much hurt by Mr. Gray. Of course it is he she is sore at, not us, but we had to do the there-there-baby business and soothe her plumage. I do not blame her for feeling nettled over Mr. Gray's odd remark but she might have a bit of decent dignity about it. Mrs. L. is a lady who takes

---

530   British writer Mary August Ward's (1851–1920) *The Marriage of William Ashe* (1905) depicts English life and manners; she published under her married name, Mrs Humphry Ward.

herself very seriously. If you pay her a compliment every day you can get along with her.

Thursday, Nov. 5, 1925

A day of rain and wind so dark we had to have the lamps lighted all day. Ewan talked, too, of resigning when and if Wick is joined to Leaskdale. Of course I realize that it is the proper thing to do but it disheartens me to think of it. I cannot bear the thought of leaving Leaskdale. And why? Leaskdale is a very average place. Life here has been growing intolerable for three or four years owing to the Church Union cleavage, the Zephyr situation, the Pickering misery and several other things over which we have no control. And yet how I love this old manse where my children were born and where I have tasted such rapturous happiness and endured so much hideous agony. I love its very faults. I love my garden and my trees and the pretty leafy corner of the side road and the sunsets over Mr. Leask's bush. I don't want to have to leave it all and go away to some strange new place among strange people. I shrink from the thought even while I know I must face it. I have long felt the coming change as one feels snow in the air before it comes. I went through all this years ago in Cavendish. I cannot bear to anticipate going through it again. Especially do I dread Ewan having to "candidate" again in his state of mind. If he found it hard to get a call what effect might it not have on his mental condition. Of course just now calls are easier to get. But not to the *desirable* places, for which everyone is striving.

Well, well, I really believe that everything is foreordained and that it doesn't matter what we do or don't do to bring it about. But when what is foreordained is quite as likely to be unpleasant as pleasant and moreso it is hard to say to Destiny "Thy Will be done." Of course my attitude is more or less the outcome of the past terrible seven years. I have become convinced in my subconscious mind that nothing good can come my way again—that all my life I must live just as I am living—or *worsely*—that any change must be for the worse. And I can't reason myself out of it try as I will.

We were at tea with a deadly dull family tonight. Mrs. Harrison, talking of the approaching Anniversary, said she thought a church ought to have an anniversary every year. "It killed the dead part."

Just what did the dear old lady mean?
And how can one kill a dead part?
Thank God, there's always a grin left in life.

Wednesday, November 11, 1925
The Manse, Leaskdale

Friday Ewan went to Toronto and brought Chester home for Thanksgiving. We had him till Tuesday morning. It seemed heavenly to have our big boy home again. Saturday it poured rain all day and all night. Nevertheless we all

Leaskdale Manse

went down to Uxbridge. We had promised Stuart and Chester that we would take them down to see a film that night and the promise must be kept though the heavens fall. We seemed to be motoring through a river there and back but in the little Jew theatre[531] itself we spent hours in another world. The film was *The Birth of a Nation*[532] and was very fine. We were three children together in our enjoyment of its thrills and laughter and agonies.

Tuesday morning we rose at 4.45 and got Chester back to his school at 8.30. Chester felt very blue over going back. Much worse than when he went first. "To come home for a couple of days like this is only a bite in the pie of aggravation," he said. But we had a splendid drive in through the clear frosty day, repeating yards of poetry together. Ewan was very well and like his old self.

I had a very nice note from one of the *Delineator* editors today saying that she loved my Marigold stories, especially the last one which "expressed the entire secret meaning of life and love."

I think I must write a book about Marigold some day.

But I've got to go to an Expense Fund tea[533] in Zephyr tomorrow. Wi-ow!

Monday, Nov. 16, 1925

Yesterday was Zephyr's anniversary and it poured from dawn till dark. Poor Zephyr! Whatever has ever been attempted there seems doomed. Ewan went to Cobourg to preach and Tom Goodwill came here. He is a good preacher and an agreeable guest. I hadn't seen him for over thirty years. Then he was kicking up a fearful and unreasonable quarrel in the Mock Trial at P.W.C. From all accounts he has been repeating that performance in most of his congregations.

I had a letter from Ella today, at last enclosing Maud's boot bill. Enclosing

531   There were relatively few Jewish people in the Uxbridge area at this time. I. Shulman had become manager of the Strand Theatre, on Main Street, in 1921.
532   This 1915 American silent film was set in the Civil War period (that is, 1861 to 1865; the Civil War was a conflict fought largely over the long-standing issue of slavery).
533   A fundraising event, possibly for the church itself or for the Women's Missionary Society.

also a somewhat cool request.

I told Ella when George died and again when Aunt Annie died that I would henceforth clothe Maud and give her at least enough education to earn her own living by. I really thought that was as much as I could or should be expected to do for this family, who, when all is said and done, have no claim whatever on me except that of common humanity. But here is what Ella coolly writes, evidently with no thought at all of the magnitude of the request she is making.

"I am feeling better as the days go by." (She had a bad rheumatic attack in the fall and Ella is one of those folks who imagine they are going to die if their little finger aches!) "But if I should ever be called away before you and you could see your way clear I would rather you than anyone in this world to take Georgie."

Now, I am quite willing to look after Maud, even to the extent of taking her into my own home if necessary; but I draw the line at Georgie. She is a wild little imp even now and has the makings of a handful in her. Besides, I have my own sons to educate and my purse is not unlimited as Ella seems fondly to imagine. Both Stella and Clara, with but one child apiece, told Ella they would gladly take and educate Georgie if ever need arose. Yet Ella will not be easy until she has put her off on me. Perhaps it is a compliment but it is one I could well spare.

Of course, just now, with a hundred pins pricking ceaselessly at me and with no escape in sight in these dull dark days of closing autumn I am inclined to be disgruntled over everything. But even making allowance for this mood I am a little tired of being looked to for all sorts of moral and financial help from people who have no claim on me or on my purse.

Yes, I think I am a very ill used creature!! I *will* pity myself.

Must start practising with the boys for the S.S. concert. I have three dialogues I am getting up and it means a lot of bother—which I would cheerfully and even with a certain enjoyment undergo if my mind were free from worries and pinpricks. But as it is the galled jade winces. From now on, too, the Saturday afternoon practices for the concert will be held and I must attend, to keep the youngsters from tearing down the church and reducing the girls of the committee to tears with impudence.

Monday Nov. 30, 1925
The Manse, Leaskdale, Ont.

We had a near-tragedy here last week. On Thursday evening our beautiful and beloved Good Luck went out about six o'clock for his usual evening prowl— and did not return. We went out for tea at five-thirty, leaving Luck sitting on a chair in the dining room, looking his beautiful*lest*. I bent over him and said jokingly, "Luck, you are *too* dear entirely. You will not escape the Jealous Power

which will not tolerate perfection. Anything as delightful as you will not long be permitted to exist in this world."

When we returned at 9.30 Luck had not come back, nor had he returned at 11. I went to bed, somewhat worried because Luck, in cold weather, had always come home early. I left the cellar window open but when I got up Friday morning Luck had not come home. I did begin to worry in right good earnest then, for I knew something had happened; but what? If I had been sure he was dead I would have paid my little pet the tribute of a real grief and some sincere tears. And then I would have said, "He is gone. His little life was perfectly happy while it lasted and I must not fret over his loss." But the uncertainty tortured me. Was he shut up somewhere cold and starving? Had he been poisoned and died alone in anguish? Was his little body lying stretched somewhere in the snow, stiff and stark, his bright, almost human eyes glazed and dull? Or—most hideous thought of all—had he been caught in some trap and held there in agony long drawn out, perhaps not even yet mercifully dead?

Luck.

If grouchy old Pat had disappeared we would not have minded so much. But our charming Luck with his adorable ways and graces!

I made a frenzied search in every barn and outhouse and stable in the village save one. No Luck. Everybody was concerned for everyone in Leaskdale is fond of Luck. I went to the door every ten minutes to call despairingly. I watched from every window in hope that I would see him coming. Elsie was as bad as I was.

I went to Social Guild that night and conducted the program very miserably. Hurried home after it, still hoping that when I came in Luck might run to meet me with his plumy tail waving, or that I might find him rolled up into an adorable ball in his favorite parlor rocker. No Luck.

I had a bad night with the miserable conviction that everything I loved, human or animal—but Luck *was* half human—must die. My love was doom to them.

Towards morning I slept and dreamed that I found Luck in a stable. I could not think of any stable I had not searched but I looked through several again. Then Stuart and I searched through the cedars along the brook, thinking we might find his body and *know* what had become of him.

After dinner I was in the library drearily concluding that it was time to go to that abominable practice, when I heard Elsie say "Mrs. Macdonald." I looked up. Elsie stood in the doorway with Luck in her arms.

We just made two fools of ourselves. I won't tell what we did or said. And I'm sure Luck never will.

We did not find out where he had been until last night when we discovered he had been shut up in John Lowrie's stable, the only one I hadn't searched because I had forgotten the Lowrie boys had a stable.

How he got there is a mystery. The Lowrie boys are two old bachelors who keep no horse and Jack says they hadn't been in it for weeks. He happened to go to it Saturday, looking for a tool. As he opened the door a gray streak shot past him and tore down through the back yards of the village.

I was so delighted I was perfectly happy for awhile, all worries, conscious or subconscious, ceasing to sting for a time. I went gaily to practice, and found it quite easy to keep my patience under all provocation. Came home and prepared for Rev. Mr. Anderson who was coming to preach our anniversary services. Yesterday we had them and as the day and roads were good they were considered to be "very successful." That is, the church was packed at both services—anniversaries being a species of religious dissipation very popular in Ontario—and they got a goodly collection.

Mrs. Albert Cook[534] called here this afternoon and said "You got your pussy back? I guess some prayers were answered." I said, "Well, I am not ashamed to say that *one* prayer was offered for his return." She looked at me shyly. "There was another," she said in a whisper.

Today was my birthday. I got more presents than I have had since I was ten years old! Stuart gave me a centrepiece he had embroidered himself. Elsie gave me an apron. Ewan a box of chocolates and Mrs. Mills a cushion. An *awful* cushion of log cabin silks in *purple* and *green*—the purplest purple and the greenest green—with a full, wide frill of glowing scarlet! The thing would put your eyes out. And yet the gratitude behind it made it of value and I was absolutely sincere in my expression of appreciation. But I shall stow it away in the same box with the autograph quilt Zephyr W.M.S. gave me and the other autograph quilt the Mission Band gave me. There are certain things one cannot have before their eyes all the time. I have endured considerable these past years. I may and fear I am fated to endure a good deal more. But I will *not* endure that green and purple and scarlet nightmare.

Saturday, Dec. 5, 1925
The Manse, Leaskdale

Another dark, busy, hurried week. Went to two Missionary meetings, "Annual business meetings" etc.—one in Leaskdale, one in Zephyr. They were encouraging, however, in that both had good financial reports. And Mrs. Jas. Lockie was *not* at the Zephyr meeting so it was not unpleasant. I shall breathe a sigh

---

534	The Cooks were a well-established family in Leaskdale. Albert (1858–1924) and his wife Sarah Elizabeth Town (1866–1944) lived beside the manse.

of relief when all these anniversaries, Thank-Offering meetings and "business meetings" are over. The last two months of the year are becoming a nightmare to me. It is just one mad rush and scramble from one thing to another.

Ewan has been terribly busy all week with the Wick business. It occupies his mind and that may be one reason why he is as well as he is this fall.

Today was a horrid day. It poured rain all day and was so dark we had to have dinner by lamplight. Half the children didn't get to practice and those who did seemed possessed by a legion of devils.

Sunday, Dec. 6, 1925

The weather was bad humored today—dull and dark, spitting snow and freezing. I have felt all day as if I could run round in circles.

Had an odd dream last night—the same dream of pregnancy I have had so often when a call was hoped for or attempted. But there is nothing of the sort in the wind just at present. Besides, in the dream the pregnancy was not false as it has always been before but real. It must mean something—it was one of the clear-cut dreams that always mean something. But what? I know not. But I feel it portends a change of some kind.

Later On.

A strange thing has happened. When Ewan came home from Zephyr he suggested that we go to Uxbridge to the evening anniversary service. Glad of a chance to get out of rather depressing surroundings I agreed. We had tea at the manse and then we met Rev. Mr. McKay, the Anniversary preacher. After supper he and I were talking in the parlor when he suddenly said, "Have you and Mr. Macdonald any idea of making a move some of these days?" I said it was possible we might, once the Wick affair was settled. He then said he was moderator of a very nice charge, Norval and Union, about thirty miles west of Toronto on the highway. There was a nice manse with electric light and bathroom and Norval was on a radial line etc.

I did not say much but I recalled my dream with a shock. Was this what it heralded?

On the way home Ewan said Mr. McKay had spoken to him about it and he had promised to preach on Dec. 20th.

I feel a strange and unhappy conviction that my life in Leaskdale is near its close. And I cannot bear the thought.

Monday, Dec. 7, 1925
The Manse, Leaskdale

I slept badly last night and am blue and lonely this evening. Also homesick. Today I got an invitation to Darnley Clark's golden wedding. If I could only go! I would see dozens of old friends—breathe once more my native air—see again the great white mystical gulf under the cold winter stars, the long fields stretching away into ebony and ivory, the woven moonlight in spruce valleys of shadow. I would drink some enchanted water of life again and my soul would be satisfied.

Sat. Dec. 12, 1925

On the whole, a depressing week. Peevish weather and such a multiplicity of small duties that I feel despairingly that I am a slave of time and must always be so. Then, too, three of the girls who were to take part in the S.S. concert have "got mad" and announced that they will not take part at all. I have no connection with the cause of their anger. They are furious because they are not in the "drill." Margaret Leask and Mary Stiver are getting that up and very properly concluded that it was no use to ask any High School girl to take part in it, as she could attend only one practice a week when three were absolutely needed to get it up in so short a time. Behold three badly disgruntled damsels! Now, these girls are in my S.S. class and for years I have tried to teach them high ideals of conduct and behavior. Two of them have seemed to respond, too. But now, at a purely imaginary slight they are acting like spoiled babies.

Ewan was at Jim Lockie's Friday to hear the usual disheartening gossip. Mrs. Lockie is certainly never happy except when she is putting tacks in somebody's tires.

Today with considerable regret I discarded my windowfuls of geraniums. Ever since I was twelve years old I have had geraniums and loved them. Lately I have decided that I cannot longer spare the time to care for them. I *must* cut out a few more non-essentials. Yet I disposed of them with a bitter feeling that the time spent on the beautiful things was better spent than the hours I am compelled to use training silly children or presiding at dismal guild meetings and mission bands.

Sunday, Dec. 13, 1925

A dull cheerless day. I have been very nervous and blue all day. Nothing new but just the same old worries having one of their spasms of being unendurable. We have got a superintendent for Zephyr S.S. at last—a splendid man, a Mr. Dunn, who with all his large family, has come over from the Unionist church. Nobody knows why but it is evident he did not find that church very congenial. He is a newcomer in Zephyr. Our little church there is picking up amazingly of late, now that the incubus of Will Lockie is gone. But I heard today of an

ill natured thing our Leaskdale superintendent, Mr. Gray, has recently said of my offering diplomas for attendance in Sunday School. It has brought the S.S. up to something worthwhile in the last two years, before which it was sagging badly. But Mr. Gray is bitterly opposed to anything new. He must go on in the same old ruts forever. I am foolish to mind his narrow-minded remarks—but I do.

Thurs., Dec. 17, 1925

On Tuesday night they sent down for me to go up to see Mrs. Jas. Blanchard who has been very ill all the fall and has lately quite gone out of her mind, poor thing. I stayed all night and had a rather terrible time. Sometimes she was very violent. At other times I had a little influence over her. She never stopped talking for a moment. She has turned against everyone, after the sad custom of the unsound in mind. It is a dreadful thing to look into the eyes of a friend where the light of reason is replaced by the glare of madness.

Yesterday I was agreeably surprised to get a letter from Stokes enclosing a check for all the long-withheld royalties. So that litigation is actually ended at last. Page had evidently been unable to find any loophole for a further appeal. I can hardly credit the good news. It has lighted up an otherwise dark and depressing week.

Last night I should have gone early to bed but instead must go to the school concert, else Stuart would have been heart-broken. It was a poor affair, compared to other years, and I was grievously tired. Also something Mrs. Alex Leask told me she had heard someone in Greenbank—evidently one of the Dyer Clique there—say about me,—a very nasty something—did not heighten my enjoyment at all. It was quite unnecessary for her to have told me. It did not atone for it that a few minutes later she told me that she had heard a gentleman who knew me say that I was "the most perfect woman he had ever known!" Mrs. Leask is a paw-and-claw friend. First a scratch, then a pat, I would prefer to dispense with both. But just now everything jars on me. I seem to have no resiliency of spirit. Ewan who has been pretty well all the fall, has been putting his hand to his head again this week—a gesture which always fills me with horror and foreboding.

Friday, December 18, 1925
The Manse, Leaskdale

Had a letter from Chester today in which he says he is "thrilled with anticipation" re the Xmas holidays. I wonder what it is like to be "thrilled with anticipation." It is so long since I had that experience that I have forgotten what it is like. My anticipations these past seven years have been anything but thrilling. However, I suppose that is the experience of anybody who is growing older.

And why regret it? Next time we are born we will be young and thrillable again. Life never stops. It only gets new garments for old and goes on.

Since I could not go to Darnley Clark's[535] golden wedding I sent my greetings in a little rhyme.

Here's to the bride of fifty years,
Of half a century's hopes and fears,
Of half a century's joys and tears!
May her well-known smile be just as bright
And her kind heart as merry and light
As fifty years ago tonight.
Fifty years—'tis a long, long time
But love does not chill with frost or rime
Or its music lose its tender chime.
Fifty years, to gray from gold,
But it's only heads not hearts that grow old
And love will last when life's tale is told.
So here's to the bridegroom and here's to the bride
Standing so faithfully side by side
In the golden light of their eventide.
All the good wishes our lips can say,
All the good prayers our hearts can pray—
And—ask us again for the diamond day!

It made me homesick to write it—homesick for the dear old Cavendish days—the only days of my life I look back to longingly—the only days I would wish to live over again, besides my P.W.C. and Bideford years.

I felt very dull and weary all day but better in the evening.

Monday December 21, 1925
The Manse, Leaskdale

Ewan went on Saturday to fulfil his Norval engagement. He did not return until tonight. He came in about eight in high spirits—a fact which told me all before he said a word. He had found Norval and Union a very nice charge and from what was said to him in both churches he feels it very probable that a call will ensue. I went over to the practice at the church with very mixed feelings. And I found, too, that all at once I felt *outside* that circle of young people. I knew something they did not—yet a something that concerned them. The knowledge gave me a queer, half-guilty feeling as if the secret were a barrier

535   Jane and Darnley Clark were neighbours in Cavendish.

between us. If we go I shall be sorry to leave these young people. I have worked among them so long—have seen them grow from children to young men and women.

After practice Ewan and I had a long talk—a veritable domestic council. He wishes to go if the call comes. I believe it *will* come—my dream foretold it. He says the manse is a fine large one and both church buildings very nice. The advantages seem to be many. No doubt there will be disadvantages also. One is apparent already. Both churches are very large—built in the day of big families, much too large for the families of today. Half the seats empty is not a nice thing to confront a minister every Sunday. And there is a United Church in Norval and great bitterness arising from the Union cleavage. Half of the Norval congregation left and went over to the Unionists. But half the Mount Pleasant people came in when their church went Union so that Norval is as strong as ever. Still, the situation will be a difficult one. Yet I suppose we will go. I could not dare urge Ewan to decline—though I feel no enthusiasm regarding it.

Tuesday, Dec. 22, 1925

This morning at 6 I was sent for to go up to Alec Leasks. Mrs. Leask, who has not been very well, had taken a weak turn. Mr. Leask was away and Margaret was terribly frightened. She thought her mother dying and rang for me. I hurried up through the shadowy gray-darkness of winter dawn. It is always an eerie thing to be out in winter dawn when no one is stirring and the world is, or seems, asleep. I felt as if I were the only living thing on a dead planet. And the chill subconsciousness of coming change lay heavy at my heart.

Mrs. Leask rallied after an hour or so, but I stayed with her until the afternoon. This evening we were summoned to see James Mustard who is dying; after weeks of illness. We are losing a good and loyal friend. Yes, it is time for us to go.

And yet I cannot feel that we *ought* to go. It seems to me that there is a work for us to do here yet. And ministers of our church are so scarce just now.

On the other hand the thing is decreed!

Wednesday, Dec. 23, 1925

I spent last night at Mrs. Leask's and this forenoon getting the Sunday School diplomas ready. When Ewan came up with the mail be beckoned me into the library and handed me a letter from Mr. McKay. It stated that Norval and Union wished to call him and that it would be unanimous.

So it is settled. I felt very strangely. I looked around my beautiful library. Already it seemed to me to wear a reproachful air. My home that I have loved.

And I must leave it.

We had our Xmas concert and tree tonight. I have taken part in fourteen such concerts since I came here. And this would be the last one. The knowledge haunted me all the evening and I moved among the gay folk and happy children like a ghost moving among revellers it has outgrown.

Thursday, Dec. 24, 1925
The Manse, Leaskdale

We celebrated Christmas today—as Elsie goes home tomorrow. We had our tree and our dinner. In reality it was a sorrowful day for me. Our last Christmas in Leaskdale manse!

My thoughts kept going back to our first one here. Frede and Stella were with me.

But Chester and Stuart were not.

In the evening came word that Mr. James Mustard had died. A sad ending to a day that was joyous outwardly.

After supper George Leask took the big, old-fashioned wood sleigh and carried a load of us—Ewan, myself, and half a dozen performing boys over to help the Zephyr Sunday School concert programme out. We had a good evening, too—church well filled and no thanks to Methodists or Unionists either. We have not had so many concerts in Zephyr as in Leaskdale—it is only within the past four or five years that the Zephyr folks dared defy Ben Armstrong to the extent of having a Sunday School concert. But the same feeling of sadness existed for me.

The boys and I sang old songs all the way home along the dim moonlit road, between the old gray fences in the softly falling snow. On the surface I enjoyed it but underneath—oh, how I hate the thought of leaving! And the thought of new places and people. I paused for a moment at the front gate as I came in. Will I have such a pretty view from my gate in Norval? The beautiful woods behind Mr. Leask's, the leaf-hung corner of the side-road, the lovely hill field beyond with the elms on its crest. I love these things and grieve to leave them. But what has my life been but a succession of leaving things I loved?

Ewan seems to have no feeling about the matter. He is more devoid than anyone I ever knew of any capacity for attachment to places or things. They mean nothing to him. I do not think it will mean more to him to leave Leaskdale after sixteen years than it would mean to leave it after so many weeks. Well, I suppose it is the best way to be. He does not have the agony of losing. But oh, neither does he ever have the exquisite pleasure the love of them can give. It is a question of price. Is it worth it? I say yes—after all—yes, verily.

I remember as if it were but yesterday the first time I suffered the anguish

of losing a *place* I loved. I was less than seven, for it was before Aunt Emily was married but how much less I do not know. Between our two hill fields was a narrow strip of grassland with a few little spruces in it where I often went to pick strawberries. It was full of ferns and red leaves and blue-eyed grasses and birds' nests and little winds and cloud-shadows—a most delectable place.

Grandfather decided to plough it up. To me that came as a calamity. I cried myself sick over it and pleaded wildly and vainly with Grandfather not to plough it up. I think still he might have granted my bitter prayer. The strip of grassland was very narrow and short—scarcely would it yield a bushel of grain or a bag of potatoes. It would have meant little to him—and it meant so much to me. What a kind and grateful remembrance I would have of him today if he had said gently, "Well, since you want it so badly, you can have it. I won't plough it up." But he refused—and refused harshly. The strip was ploughed up—and the hurt is in my heart today. The old scar aches when I touch it.

Sunday, December 27, 1925
The Manse, Leaskdale, Ont.

We are having a bitter cold spell. Today and yesterday it has been twenty five below zero. Yesterday was an unhappy day. We went through the icy world to J. Mustard's funeral.

Today was communion—our last one here.

We have got a superintendent at last for Zephyr Sunday School—a Mr. Dunn, a splendid man who has left the United Church with all his family and come over to ours. Why we don't know. But it is a good thing for Zephyr church. Mr. Dunn is a new-comer. Zephyr church has gone ahead amazingly this past two months. The people, with the exception of Mrs. Jas. Lockie, are all so united and harmonious now and bound to build up their church. It is *such* a different church from what it was when Will Lockie and Armstrong were there. I never thought I would be sorry to leave Zephyr church but I am. And somehow I feel that we ought not to desert it now—that we ought to stay and build it up; we *could* do that now. I cannot help a feeling that we are wrong to go.

But I dare not try to influence Ewan along these lines. If we did stay and then something went wrong he would always wish we had gone and I should blame myself.

Monday, Dec. 28, 1925

I slept better last night than for some nights but have felt depressed all day. Also much worried over Mrs. Will Cook who is ill with pneumonia. Yes, it may

be time we went. It is beginning to worry me too much when our friends here are ill or in trouble.

Tonight I happened to glance out of the kitchen window and noted how the frost-diamonds were glittering magnificently over the yard. Instantly I recalled—and saw—our old orchards in Cavendish where there used to be such a show of fairy jewels on frosty moonlit nights. And I saw the old dear trees and the firs beyond and the white hills I loved, lying in a great austere silence.

Ewan went to Wick today and stayed all night.

Tuesday, Dec. 29, 1925

Ewan came home today rather disheartened because Wick does not seem to want to come in with Leaskdale. This is foolish. They can't stand alone. And Leaskdale and Zephyr need them so. A good congregation could be worked up between the three if the people in all would be reasonable. But when are churches ever reasonable?

Chester's half-term report came today. He made a pretty good average—79 1/11.

Wednesday, Dec. 30, 1925
The Manse, Leaskdale

Today Mr. McKay wrote that he had moderated in the call. So the thing is a certainty. There is a certain resulting peace and comfort when a thing becomes irrevocable.

This being the case I decided that Elsie must be told. I had an idea that she would be much delighted at the thought of going to Norval. I knew she had secretly been frantic to get away from Leaskdale ever since Grant Widdifield jilted her. She was tremendously excited and quite overjoyed at the news.

I do not know if I am doing a wise thing in taking her. As a maid she does very well and is improving all the time. She knew almost nothing when she came here but she was willing and eager to learn and she has learned. And she admits freely that I have taught her all she knows. As far as her capability for service goes I am quite willing to take her.

The trouble is—she is *such* a ghastly fool in regard to boys. I have never seen anything like her and I have seen many foolish girls. She is an absolute idiot. Chases them openly. Seems content with *anything* that wears trousers. And is always being jilted and descending into the dumps for weeks until a new beau looms on the horizon. To take a girl like this away from home where her parents can keep some kind of tabs on her is a rather heavy responsibility.

However, it is highly likely she will be too homesick and lonesome to stay

long and it will mean much to have someone I know to help me move and get settled. So it is decided that she is to go with me.

Thursday, Dec. 31, 1925

We have decided that, as the Toronto road is still passable for cars, it would be better to take ours in at once and leave it in a garage there. Then we can take it out to Norval whenever we need it whereas, if we kept it here, we could not get it to Norval until late in the spring. So Ewan took Dodgie today. I watched him sadly. The last time of many that old Dodgie will be backed out of our lane and go off down the road. From now on the days will be full of "last things" each with its own little ache.

Ewan has been very well lately. Probably the excitement evoked by the Norval call has reacted favorably. But it is a whole year now since he has had a bad attack of melancholia. This is the longest time he has been free since the first one in that terrible spring of 1919. I wonder if it is possible that the change will cure him completely. I suppose it is too much to hope for.

Acknowledgements

With a complex writer like L.M. Montgomery, the expertise of many people is necessary for a project like this.

As always, I start with the first generation of LMM scholars: Gabriella Åhmansson, Father Francis W.P. Bolger, Elizabeth Rollins Epperly, Mary Henley Rubio, Elizabeth Hillman Waterston, and the late Christy Woster. The scrapbooks of Wilda Clark contain much useful information.

The research by Mary Beth Cavert for *The Shining Scroll* (among other sources) has been indispensable.

Bernadeta Milewski has an extraordinary store of knowledge, an amazing ability to dig up facts, and provided enormous help with proofreading. The same is true of David Stover. Others whose work has helped in a myriad of ways include Rita Bode, Kate Macdonald Butler, Geroge Campbell and his staff, Lesley D. Clement, Elaine Crawford, Lois Fraser, Kathy Gastle, Benjamin Lefebvre, Jennifer H. Litster, Jennie Macneill, Melanie Whitfield, and Emily Woster.

I am also grateful for the help of many scholars including the following: Alison Bailey, Lead Curator (Printed Heritage Collections 1901–2000, British Library); Beverly Lyon Clark, Department of English, Wheaton College, Massachusetts; Margaret R. Higonnet, Department of English and Comparative Literature, University of Connecticut; Porter White, Department of English, Harvard University; and Philip Williamson, Department of History, Durham University. Allan McGillivray is an exce;;ent historian of LMM's Leaskdale community in particular helped with many, many details, large and small.

I also am grateful to Presbyterian Church of Canada archivists, Kim Arnold and Bob Anger. And Philip L. Hartling, Reference Archivist at Nova Scotia Archives gave me a very nice tip on James A. Fraser!

The archivists at the University of Guelph's Montgomery Collection are always a huge help, particularly Melissa McAfee and Kathryn Harvey. I thank them for the care they take of these valuable handwritten manuscripts—such an important piece of Canadian history.

Jen Rubio, Hamilton, Ontario
May 2018

Index

Photo Index

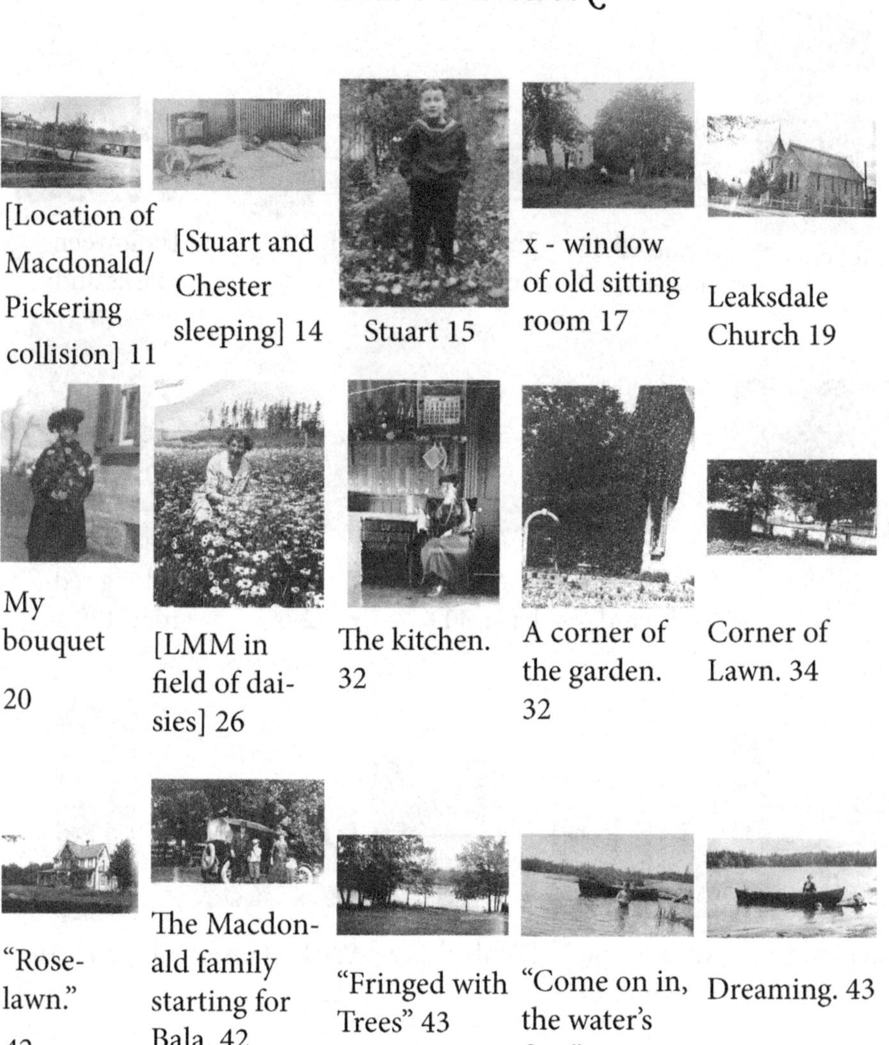

Kitchen. 53

Scene of Accident 58

The Blind Corner. 59

Lily 72

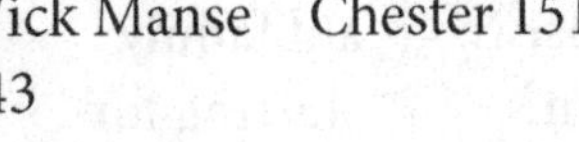

Hallowe'en masks and faces. 79

Paddy 89

Lottie Shatfords card 109

The new barn. 111

By the Birches 129

A long red road 129

Road to Uxbridge 140

My window at home. 141

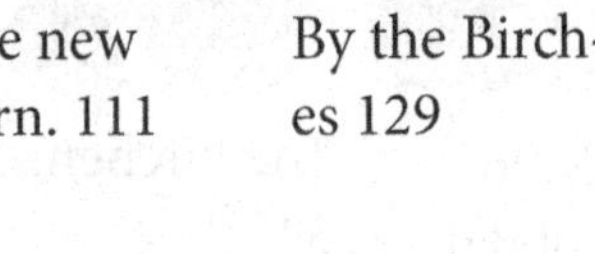

[Dodge] 143

Wick Manse 143

Chester 151

Heart's Desire 153

[Stuart and Chester] 155

[Moonlight, North River, Charlottetown] 155

[Stuart and kittens] 156

[LMM and Fannie Mutch] 157

Aunt Christie's 157

The Manse. 158

Entrance to Lover's Lane. 158

The field beyond the lane. 159

Stuart with Savonarola and Lorraine Webb 159

x Stuart and the Webb children 161

Alec's place. Gartmore Farm 163

Chester with Stuart in Lover's Lane 163

[Gartmore Farm] 166

Stuart and Mike 163

Hauling in hay. 164

The hill road. 165

[Gartmore Farm] 166

Children at Park Corner. 168

Aunty and her hens. 168

Jim and Chester 168

Maud and Georgie. 168

The birches behind the barn. 169

Birches down the lane 169

The old back yard. 171

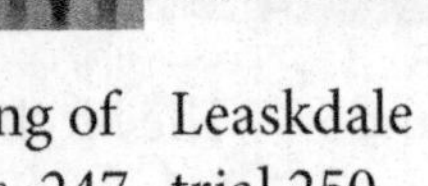

The old trees at the entrance. 173

[Breadalbane Manse] 174

Aylsworth Home. 177

[Macdonald family and Aylesworth children] 177

[Stuart] 180

The Lawn 184

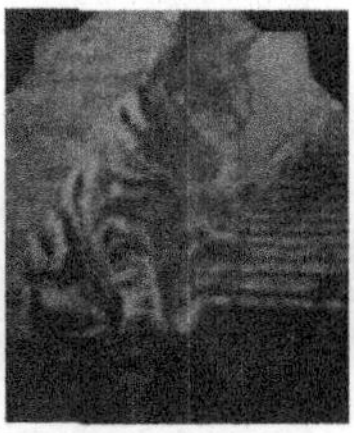

[Luck] 184

[Luck] 184

[Luck] 184

Chester and Stuart 197

Two pussy cats 197

The candlesticks 201

The spare room. 202

A corner of the parlor. 208

The Parlor 213

The "lookout" 215

"Airy voices" 247

Dreaming of Bubastis. 247

Leaskdale trial 250

"Let her went" 251

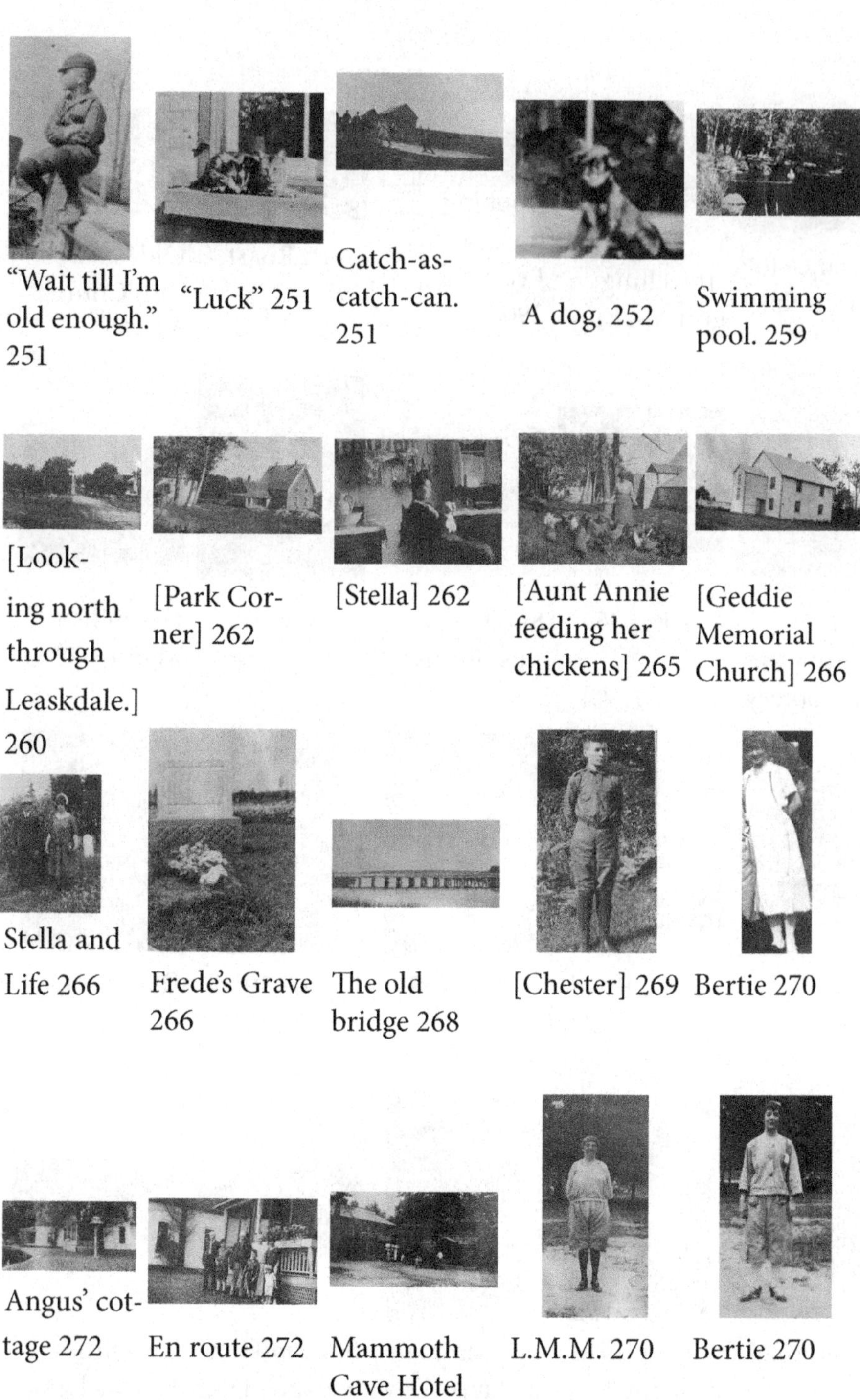

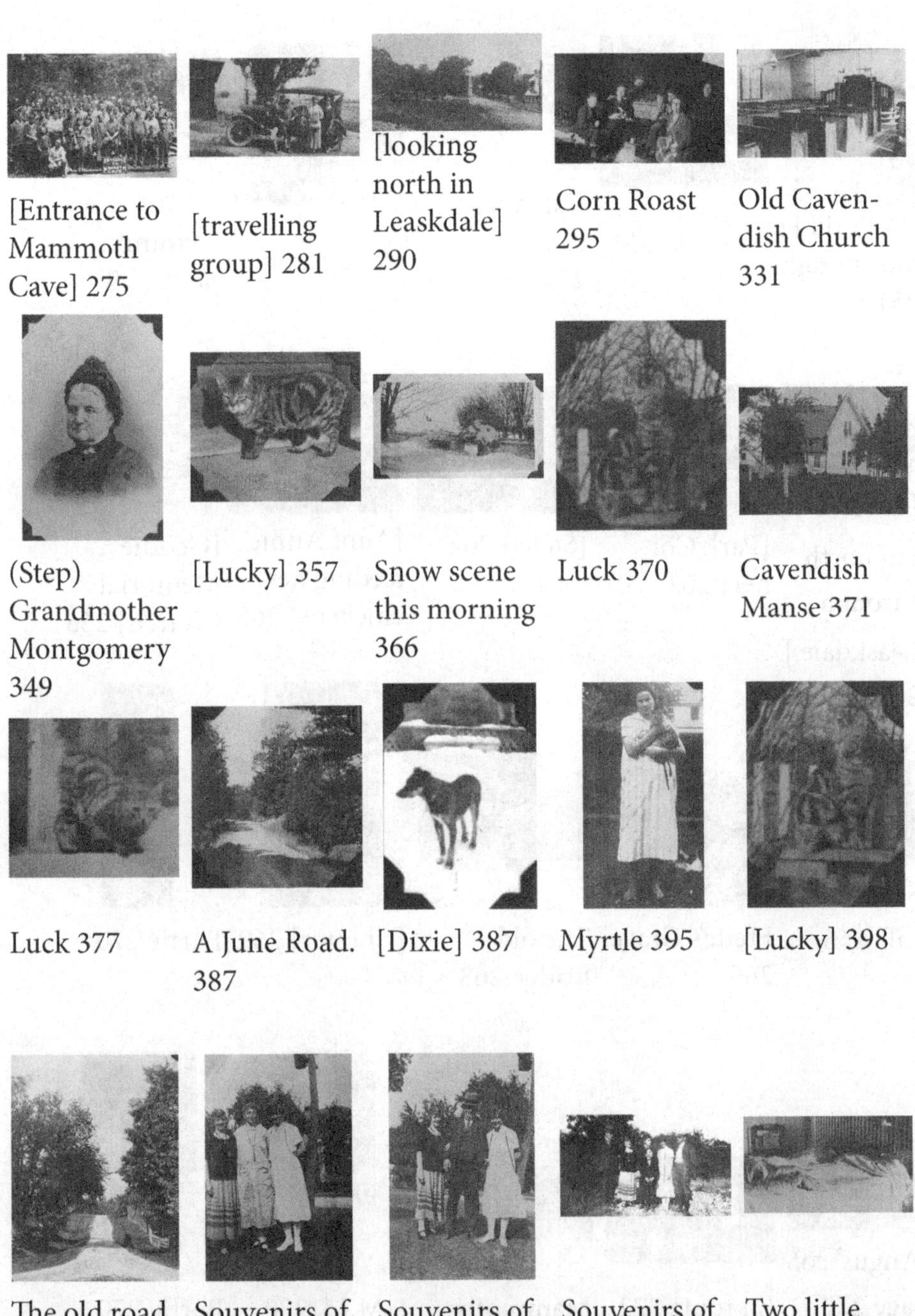

 [Chester] 404

 Dixie 420

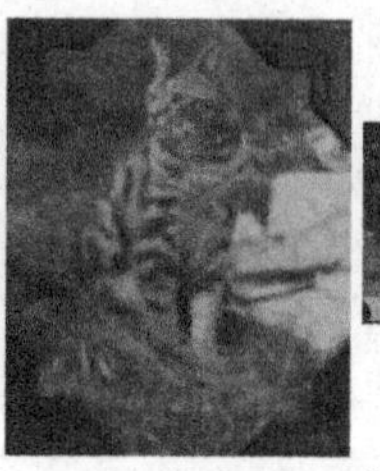 Luck 420

Leaskdale Manse 423

 Luck 425